COMPUTERS, ETHICS & SOCIAL VALUES

Edited by

Deborah G. Johnson
Rensselaer Polytechnic University

Helen Nissenbaum
Princeton University

Prentice Hall Upper Saddle River, NJ 07458

Library of Congress Cataloging-in-Publication Data

Computers, ethics & social values / [edited by] Deborah G. Johnson, Helen Nissenbaum.
    p. cm.
   ISBN 0–13–103110–4
   1. Computers and civilization. 2. Computer security.
I. Johnson, Deborah G., 1945– . II. Nissenbaum, Helen Fay. III. Title: Computers, ethics, and social values.
QA76.9.A25C6665   1995
174.9´0904—dc20

94–47307
CIP

Acquisitions Editor: Ted Bolen
Editorial Assistant: Meg McGuane
Production Editor: Tony VenGraitis
Buyer: Lynn Pearlman
Cover Design: Anthony Gemmellaro

© 1995 by Prentice-Hall, Inc.
A Simon & Schuster Company
Upper Saddle River, New Jersey 07458

Printed in the United States of America

10 9 8 7 6 5

ISBN 0-13-103110-4

Prentice-Hall International (UK) Limited, *London*
Prentice-Hall of Australia Pty. Limited, *Sydney*
Prentice-Hall Canada Inc., *Toronto*
Prentice-Hall Hispanoamericana, S.A., *Mexico*
Prentice-Hall of India Private Limited, *New Delhi*
Prentice-Hall of Japan, Inc., *Tokyo*
Simon & Schuster Asia Pte. Ltd., *Singapore*
Editora Prentice-Hall do Brasil, Ltda., *Rio de Janeiro*

CONTENTS

Chapter Five   The Risks of Computing   394

Chapter Six   Responsibility, Liability, and Professional Codes   470

Chapter Seven   The Networked World   606

PREFACE

The importance of computers is now well recognized. We are beginning to understand and document the many obvious as well as subtle ways they are changing the texture of our lives. In putting together this anthology of readings, our aim is to frame a discussion of the significance of computers in terms of the social values they affect and the ethical issues to which they give rise.

The introductory chapter addresses the nature of the subject area, examining the uniqueness and importance of computer ethical issues with readings that seek to understand how we might define and differentiate the field of computer ethics. Subsequent chapters are focused on particular social values (privacy, ownership) or on an area of controversy that challenges traditional ethical notions (crime, responsibility, risk). Our concluding chapter looks to the future, to the "networked world" where daily life will increasingly involve online communication and interaction in the growing information infrastructure.

We have seen how quickly computer technology evolves and develops. For example, just three years ago, who would have predicted the prominence and urgency of the issues related to interactions on the Internet? We have also seen how certain fundamental ethical and political values—privacy, justice, democracy, property—persist in being at the core of controversy and media attention. These values form the core of the anthology. We have also tried to provide a balanced picture.

Both of us teach undergraduate and graduate courses on the ethical issues surrounding computers. Our experiences in the classroom, at Rensselaer Polytechnic Institute, Stanford University, and Princeton University, have influenced the design of the book as well as the selection of readings. We anticipate that this book will be useful to those who teach college courses in computer ethics, though we hope it will also interest computer professionals and others who grasp the relevance of computing to society's values.

This book has been in the making for several years, and we are grateful to the many who helped us along the way. We want especially to thank Ted Bolen, our editor at Prentice Hall, for his encouragement and support. The comments of Leslie Burkholder of the University of British Columbia, the reviewer for Prentice Hall, were very helpful. We are particularly grateful to Jack Snapper for his willingness to work on the chapter on ownership and to write an original piece to be included in the book. There are many others, too numerous to identify, who encouraged us and pointed us to useful articles and books. Our thanks to each of you.

During the 1993–94 academic year, I received support from the National Science Foundation (NSF) to serve as a visiting professor in the School of Engineering and Applied Science of Princeton University. Spending the year in Princeton allowed Helen and me to meet regularly and design the book. Without this grant from the NSF Program of Visiting Professorships for Women in Science and Engineering, I suspect the book might never have been completed.

The Department of Science and Technology Studies (especially Shirley Gorenstein, the Chair of the department) at Rensselaer Polytechnic Institute continues to be a great source of intellectual stimulation and support that enriches all of my work.

I dedicate this book to Sam, Jesse, and Rose Johnson, who continue to keep me thinking and smiling!

Deborah G. Johnson
Troy, New York

This volume owes much to Terry Winograd with whom I co-taught computer ethics at Stanford University. This partnership gave me not only a broader vision of the subject area and exposure to issues and readings, but a deeper sense of its importance and excitement. I am deeply grateful to Terry Winograd for this, and for acquainting me with Computer Professionals for Social Responsibility, an organization for computer scientists and professionals concerned with the social, political, and ethical implications of their field.

The University Center for Human Values at Princeton University has provided an ideal setting for working, thinking, and teaching about ethics and human values in general, and in particular about the ethics of computer technology. Many individuals have contributed time and insight to the volume. Thanks especially to Batya Friedman for pointing to interesting articles and directions; to students of my computer ethics courses for enthusiasm and constructive views on readings; and to Valerie Kanka, Derek Dohn, Jennifer Pike, and Ruth Michaels, for valuable research and secretarial assistance. To my family, Peter, Dana, and Zoe, for fueling this project with joy and companionship, I offer my gratitude. I dedicate this book to Rose and Mike Nissenbaum.

Helen Nissenbaum
Princeton, New Jersey

Acknowledgments

Association for Computing Machinery, ACM code of ethics and professional conduct. *Communications of the ACM* 36, 2. Copyright 1991 by the Association for Computing Machinery. **John P. Barlow**, Coming into the country. *Communications of the ACM* 34, 3: 12–21. Copyright 1991 by the Association for Computing Machinery. Reprinted with permission; Private life in cyberspace. *Communications of the ACM* 34, 8: 23–25. Copyright 1991 by the Association for Computing Machinery. Reprinted with permission. **Jerry Berman and Janlori Goldman**, A federal right of information privacy: The need for reform. *Benton Foundation Project on Communications and Information Policy Options*. Paper no. 4, Washington, DC, 1989. Copyright 1989 by Benton Foundation. Reprinted with permission. **Alan Borning**, Computer system reliability and nuclear war. *Communications of the ACM* 30, 2: 112–31. Copyright 1987 by the Association for Computing Machinery. Reprinted with permission. **Anne W. Branscomb**, Rogue computer programs and computer rogues: Tailoring the punishment to fit the crime. From *Rutgers Computer and Technology Law Journal* 16 (1991): 1–61. Copyright 1990 by Anne W. Branscomb. **Brian Cantwell Smith**, The limits of correctness in computers. Center for the Study of Language and Information. Stanford University, CA. CSLI: 85–35. Copyright 1985 by CSLI. Reprinted with permission. **Gary Chapman and Marc Rotenberg**, The national information infrastructure: A public interest opportunity. *The CSPR Newsletter* 11, 2 (Summer 1993): 1–23. **David Chaum**, A new paradigm for individuals in the information age. © 1984 IEEE. Reprinted, with permission, from *Proceedings from IEEE 5th Symposium on Security and Privacy*. April 29–May 02, Oakland California: 99–103. **M. J. Culnan and H. J. Smith**, Lotus Marketplace: Households . . . managing information privacy concerns. *Georgetown University School of Business*, Case 192–123. Copyright 1991, 1992 by M. J. Culnan and H. J. Smith. Reprinted with permission. **Michael Davis**, Thinking like an engineer: The place of a code of ethics in the practice of a profession. From *Philosophy and Public Affairs* 20, 2: 150–67. Copyright © 1992 by Princeton University Press. Reprinted by permission of Princeton University Press. **Dorothy Denning**, A dialog on hacking and security. From *Computers Under Attack*, Peter J. Denning, ed. ACM Press/Addison Wesley, 1990. Reprinted with permission; The United States vs. Craig Neidorf. *Communications of the ACM* 34, 3: 23–32. Copyright 1991 by the Association for Computing Machinery. Reprinted with permission. **Ted Eisenberg, et al.**, The computer worm. *Cornell University* (February 6). Copyright 1989 by Cornell University. Reprinted with permission. **E. M. Forster**, "The Machine Stops" from *The Eternal Moment and Other Stories*. Copyright 1970 by Harcourt Brace. Reprinted with permission. **Ruth Gavison**, Privacy and the limits of law. Reprinted with permission of The Yale Law Journal Company and Fred B. Rothman & Company from *The Yale Law Journal*, Vol. 89, pages 421–71. (continued on page 714)

CHAPTER ONE

What Is Computer Ethics?

INTRODUCTION

Why Study Computer Ethics?

Computers are now so prevalent in our society that their importance hardly needs mentioning except that some may blindly assume that computerization only improves activities, not recognizing that it may change the character of an activity and have unexpected consequences. In fact, computers have subtly changed our lives and seem to be powerfully implicated in future change. They are likely to change the way we work, the way we communicate with one another, the way we are educated, and the way we are entertained.

We know from our experience with other technologies that adoption of a new technology often results in effects we didn't anticipate. We may get the benefits we sought (cheaper energy, greater mobility, better health care), but we also get effects that were not foreseen or effects that change our society in deep and irretrievable ways. Think, for example, of automobiles and how they have changed the character of our cities. Or think of how new medical technologies have forced us to confront life and death decisions of a kind we never before faced.

So it is with computers. They change the environments in which they are used, and in so doing give rise to questions of right and wrong, good and bad. The technological change alters (or calls attention to) the moral character of the environment, calling for ethical analysis and ethical decision making.

The study of computer ethics is the study of the ethical questions that arise as a consequence of the development and deployment of computers and computing technologies. It involves two activities. One is identifying and bringing into focus the issues and problems that fall within its scope, raising awareness of the ethical dimension of a particular situation. The second is providing an approach to these issues, a means of advancing our understanding of, and suggesting ways of reaching wise solutions to these problems. Of course, sometimes the computer's presence makes no moral difference. Suppose for example, that I formerly worked in an office with a desk and typewriter, and spent many hours sitting and typing at my desk. I now own a computer and spend roughly the same amount of time at my desk, only now I am word processing instead of typing. The presence of the computer in my office doesn't make an ethical difference. However, suppose that I hook up my computer to a dataline and begin to store files on the hard disk as well as on a mainframe. Now it is possible for individuals to violate my privacy, sabotage my files, or steal my ideas by new means, that is without entering my office. The fact that I am using a computer instead of a typewriter begins to make a moral difference. My responsibilities change—for example, my responsibility to protect confidential information calls for different sorts of actions than before. Instead of just locking my file cabinets and office, I must make sure that my files can only be accessed using my password. Perhaps now I should code the names of clients who are in my files so that even if someone does obtain unauthorized access, the intruder will not be able to identify the individuals associated with the information in my files. In addition, other people now have somewhat different obligations regarding respect for my rights. That is, they must refrain from different types of behavior, such as bypassing authorized access to my files, and ignoring what is on my computer screen when they are in my office talking to me.

In the first selection in this chapter, "What is Computer Ethics?" James Moor describes the ethical questions surrounding computers as coming about because computers create a vacuum. That is, when computers come to be used in certain environments, we find there is a vacuum of rules or policies regarding how one behaves in the new situation. We can imagine in the early days of computing that people didn't know whether it was appropriate to make a copy of a piece of software or to use someone else's account that they were able to access, not because they were ignorant of the policies and moral imperatives, but because the policies and moral imperatives were not yet there to be known. Filling this vacuum with laws and rules grounded in ethical principles is part of the work of computer ethics.

The vacuums we find surrounding computers are not always easy to fill because computers create conceptual puzzles. What is a computer program? Is sending e-mail comparable to sending a postcard or a letter or speaking to someone in a public place? When I design a piece of software for a client, am I providing a product or service? Computer activities do not always neatly fit the distinctions and ideas we ordinarily use to resolve ethical issues. Moor believes that because of these conceptual puzzles, much of the work of computer ethics is a matter of "proposing conceptual frameworks for understanding ethical problems involving computer technology."

Are the Issues Unique? Do We Need a New System of Ethics?

Some have argued that the ethical issues surrounding computers are unique in the sense that computers have unique characteristics which make traditional ethical concepts and theories inappropriate. In the second selection, "Coming into the Country," John P. Barlow depicts the world of computers as having fundamentally different characteristics than the physical world we live in. "It is," Barlow writes, "a place where trespassers leave no footprints, where goods can be stolen an infinite number of times and yet remain the possession of their original owners, where businesses you never heard of can own the history of your personal affairs." Others have argued that computers are unique because of the scale of activity they involve, or because computers can "think" or because computers are "inherently unreliable." Moor has a more complicated view because he emphasizes the malleability of computers and considers that this technology may be special because of its revolutionary potential. Others argue that the issues posed by computers are not new or unique. Rather they are the same old problems in a new guise or with a somewhat different twist. On this account the work of computer ethics is not to create a whole new system of ethics but rather to apply and, perhaps, extend our traditional concepts, values, and theories to the new technology.

This anthology of readings does not take a position on this question. However, we have found that the most salient controversies surrounding the use and development of computer technology can be framed in terms of traditional moral concepts, such as responsibility, and social values, such as privacy. Accordingly, we clustered readings around these traditional categories. Further, in several places we have included philosophical pieces that make no reference to computers because we found that they illuminated the moral notions affecting our thinking about situations involving computers.

In the third selection of this chapter, Donald Gotterbarn, claims that a lack of clarity about the realm of computer ethics has led to some dangerous misconceptions. He disagrees with those who think that an issue is one of computer ethics simply because a computer is present in the situation. Gotterbarn proposes a narrow focus for computer ethics. He argues that the only way to make sense of computer ethics "is to narrow its focus to those actions that are within the control of the individual *moral* computer professional." While we have not taken this narrow focus here, we have included issues of professional ethics as part of computer ethics. Indeed we hope that this set of readings will help students of computer science and engineering prepare for their professional lives. Though computer professionals often do not have much power, individually at least, it would seem that they are in a special position because of their expertise, to influence directions of development, use, and attitudes towards computer technology, collectively, if not individually.

At the same time, we should not delegate responsibility for the social and ethical implications of computing entirely to computer professionals. The importance of having a citizenry that understands computers and is aware of their social and ethical implications should not be underestimated. In this respect the study of computer ethics is important both for computer professionals and for individuals who will be decision makers in the future, even simply in virtue of their participation in the democratic process. Anyone living in the next decade will be affected. Many will help to manage the technology and shape personal and public policies that will determine whether or not this powerful technology is developed in socially beneficial ways.

The Organization of This Book

The field of computer ethics is new and still evolving. A variety of complementary approaches have been taken. One approach organizes the ethical issues according to particular sectors of society, or the particular contexts of use; for example the use by marketing firms, or the use of computers in criminal justice agencies, welfare agencies, in medicine, law, and the workplace. In these studies the emphasis is on how computers are affecting these sectors (for example, how they have changed the boundaries of the workplace); what problems are being encountered (for example, are workers rights violated); or what traditional values are being affected (for example, traditional work hierarchies or respect for individuals). A literature search will reveal that studies of this kind have been done on a wide variety of sectors and contexts.

A second approach—the one we have taken here—is to identify a set of basic issues and themes arising in a wide variety of contexts. These basic issues cut across sectors and roles. We have selected six such areas that have generated a great deal of interest, concern, and perplexity as well as a rich set of divergent views and commentaries. They are: disruptive or criminal behavior on-line; property rights in computer technology; privacy; risk and reliability; responsibility and professional responsibility; and finally, an issue which we call "the networked world," arising out of a massive digital network connecting people and computers across the nation and around the world. Each chapter in the book is dedicated to one of these topics.

Within each chapter, we have included a central case reading. This is meant to show the timeliness and importance of the topic, and to give it a "real world" orientation. Although real cases do not lend themselves to easy solutions because not all the information that is relevant to one's moral assessment is available, we think their presence in this volume serves two vitally important purposes: (1) To those who prefer the intellectual tidiness of theory and abstraction, they serve as reminders that the reach of ethical discussion must ultimately extend to problems in the real world no matter how messy with detail they be; and (2) To those who question the value of a systematic principled approach to value conflicts, we hope to demonstrate that by drawing on conceptual themes and basic principles we can achieve greater clarity and understanding, and move toward solutions of these real-world problems that respect fundamental social and moral values.

The case study at the beginning of each chapter is followed by a set of readings that will expose the reader to a variety of perspectives, and will provide conceptual tools for thinking about the issues. We have tried to bring together readings from diverse disciplinary traditions (including philosophy, law, sociology, and computing) that provide information on the present-state-of-affairs, analyze relevant concepts, and argue in favor of or against certain positions. We have tried to present a balanced picture and, where available, have included works that present views starkly divergent from our own. Our aim, then, is not to resolve the issues but to provide the foundation for intelligent and enlightened discussion.

The reader will soon become aware that the chapters are interconnected. For example, the issues raised about hackers in Chapter Two are inextricably tied to issues of privacy and property, for some would argue that hackers violate privacy when they "crack" passwords and access files which they are not authorized to access, and they violate property rights when they make copies of proprietary software. Issues of property and privacy overlap with each other when the concern for personal privacy has suggested to some authors that we should think about personal data as a form of private property. The chapter on risk raises all the questions of responsibility taken up in the chapter on responsibility. It is also tied to the chapter on hackers insofar as hackers create risks. Finally, broad concerns over privacy link the chapter on privacy and personal information with the chapter on the networked world with its concerns for the privacy of electronic communications. Because of the overlap of issues, it is possible to follow different paths through the book. The sequence of chapters that we finally decided on is based on a mixture of pedagogical and conceptual considerations.

Following this introductory chapter, we begin, in Chapter Two, with the topic of on-line crime and abuse. We choose this as the first topic because of the great interest it seems to hold for students, as well as its immediate relevance to them. Moreover, adventures in unauthorized access, unauthorized copying of software, viruses and worms, has captured the public imagination and attention—through the news media and works of science fiction—perhaps more than any of the other topics.

Chapter Three explores property rights surrounding computers. In a sense this broadens the perspective one might get from reading about hackers for it makes clear that who owns or should own computer software is more complicated than one might presume by reading about hackers as thieves. Many people other than hackers are critical of the system of property rights that has evolved around computers.

Chapter Four, dedicated to information privacy, is another issue of great public concern. A good deal of attention has been drawn to the ways in which computers affect privacy and already we have an abundance of legislation that attempts to deal with issues surrounding information. Having the chapter on privacy follow the chapter on property seemed appropriate because, as mentioned before, these two topics are tightly connected when one begins to think about information as property. In a sense, when the focus is on personal information, privacy is the proper label from the individual's point of view and property is the proper label from the information gatherer's point of view.

Chapter Five addresses the issues of risk and reliability that arise as we become more and more dependent on computers for the essential and fundamental undertakings in our society, for example, air travel, banking, and elections. Readings in this chapter explore the special risks involved in the use of computing to control such functions but especially those that are life-critical.

Chapter Six focuses on issues of responsibility. Here we raise questions both about what happens to lines of responsibility when computing becomes part of an environment and questions about the responsibility of computer professionals. This chapter could appropriately have begun the entire volume because all of the other topics are in a sense topics about an impact or implication of computers and who is responsible or should be responsible for it.

In Chapter Seven, we end with an assessment of the future of computing and the future of a networked world. We share the views expressed by observers of technology, social policy, and culture, that the massive digital networks connecting computers and people across the world will amplify the already diverse impacts computers have had. It is already clear that the decisions we make as a society (for example, whether to protect private communications over the networks) will determine what the networks are like, who will have access to them, and whose interests will primarily be served. Decisions along the way will determine whether electronic networks promote well-being and whether they provide a source of human fulfilment, or whether they will reintroduce all the problems we presently have and make them worse. We hope that this volume will stimulate thinking on these issues as well as a realization that these outcomes are not predetermined or inevitable; thus we also hope to ignite the passion to actively shape the future of computer networks for the good.

Ethical Theory and Analysis

We have selected readings that are accessible without a background in ethical theory. Nevertheless additional readings on ethical concepts and theories can complement and enhance the reader's understanding of the issues. We expect that this volume will be used in a variety of courses and, depending on the goals and orientation of the course and teacher, supplemental readings on general ethical theory can easily be added.

What we have opted to include, in Chapter One, (instead of traditional ethical theory) are two pieces on ethics by computer scientists. In one, Terry Winograd, who is a computer scientist not an ethicist, explores common sense notions about morality and provides a very insightful view of what is needed to think through the ethical issues surrounding computers. Even if one does not take up formal ethical theory, it seems important that those engaged in understanding ethical issues, reflect on the process of understanding ethics. In the other, W. Robert Collins and Keith W. Miller propose something like an algorithm for analysing cases or situations in computer ethics. They call their method a "paramedic" approach and they draw on traditional ethical theory, but what they outline is a procedure for uncovering the issues and consequences surrounding a particular case or situation.

WHAT IS COMPUTER ETHICS?

James H. Moor

A PROPOSED DEFINITION

Computers are special technology and they raise some special ethical issues. In this essay I will discuss what makes computers different from other technology and how this difference makes a difference in ethical considerations. In particular, I want to characterize computer ethics and show why this emerging field is both intellectually interesting and enormously important.

In my view, *computer ethics* is the analysis of the nature and social impact of computer technology and the corresponding formulation and justification of policies for the ethical use of such technology. I use the phrase "computer technology" because I take the subject matter of the field broadly to include computers and associated technology. For instance, I include concerns about software as well as hardware and concerns about networks connecting computers as well as computers themselves.

A typical problem is computer ethics arises because there is a policy vacuum about how computer technology should be used. Computers provide us with new capabilities and these in turn give us new choices for action. Often, either no policies for conduct in these situations exist or existing policies seem inadequate. A central task of computer ethics is to determine what we should do in such cases, that is, formulate policies to guide our actions. Of course, some ethical situations confront us as individuals and some as a society. Computer ethics includes consideration of both personal and social policies for the ethical use of computer technology.

Now it may seem that all that needs to be done is the mechanical application of an ethical theory to generate the appropriate policy. But this is usually not possible. One difficulty is that along with a policy vacuum there is often a conceptual vacuum. Although a problem in computer ethics may seem clear initially, a little reflection reveals a conceptual muddle. What is needed in such cases is an analysis that provides a coherent conceptual framework within which to formulate a policy for action. Indeed, much of the important work in computer ethics is devoted to proposing conceptual frameworks for understanding ethical problems involving computer technology.

An example may help to clarify the kind of conceptual work that is required. Let's suppose we are trying to formulate a policy for protecting computer programs. Initially, the idea may seem clear enough. We are looking for a policy for protecting a kind of intellectual property. But then a number of questions that do not have obvious answers emerge. What is a computer program? Is it really intellectual property that can be owned or is it more like an idea, an algorithm, which is not owned by anybody? If a computer program is intellectual property, is it an *expression* of an idea that is owned (traditionally protectable by copyright) or is it a *process* that is owned (traditionally protectable by patent)? Is a machine-readable program a copy of a human-readable program? Clearly, we need a conceptualization of the nature of a computer program in order to answer these kinds of questions. Moreover, these questions must be answered in order to formulate a useful policy for protecting computer programs. Notice that the conceptualization we pick will not only affect how a policy will be applied but to a certain extent what the facts are. For instance, in this case the conceptualization will determine when programs count as instances of the same program.

Even within a coherent conceptual framework, the formulation of a policy for using computer technology can be difficult. As we consider different policies we discover something about what we value and what we don't. Because computer technology provides us with new possibilities for acting, new values emerge. For example, creating software has value in our culture that it didn't have a few decades ago. And old values have to be reconsidered. For instance, assuming software is intellectual property, why should intellectual property be protected? In general, the consideration of alternative policies forces us to discover and make explicit what our value preferences are.

The mark of a basic problem in computer ethics is one in which computer technology is *essentially* involved and there is an uncertainty about what to do and even about how to understand the situation. Hence, not all ethical situations involving computers are central to computer ethics. If a burglar steals available office equipment including computers, then the burglar has done something legally and ethically wrong. But this is really an issue for general law and ethics. Computers are only *accidently* involved in this situation, and there is no policy or conceptual vacuum to fill. The situation and the applicable policy are clear.

In one sense I am arguing for the special status of computer ethics as a field of study. Applied ethics is not simply ethics applied. But, I also wish to stress the underlying importance of general ethics and science to computer ethics. Ethical theory provides categories and procedures for determining what is ethically relevant. For example, what kinds of things are good? What are our basic rights? What is an impartial point of view? These considerations are essential in comparing and justifying policies for ethical conduct. Similarly, scientific information is crucial in ethical evaluations. It is amazing how many times ethical disputes turn not on disagreements about values but on disagreements about facts.

In my view, computer ethics is a dynamic and complex field of study that considers the relationships among facts, conceptualizations, policies and values with regard to constantly changing computer technology. Computer ethics is not a fixed set of rules which one shellacs and hangs on the wall. Nor is the computer ethics the rote application of ethical principles to a value-free technology. Computer ethics requires us to think anew about the nature of computer technology and our values. Although computer ethics is a field between science and ethics and depends on them, it is also a discipline in its own right which provides both conceptualizations for understanding and policies for using computer technology.

Though I have indicated some of the intellectually interesting features of computer ethics, I have not said much about the problems of the field or about its practical importance. The only example I have used so far is the issue of protecting computer programs which may seem to be a very narrow concern. In fact, I believe the domain of computer ethics is quite large and extends to issues which affect all of us. Now I want to turn to a consideration of these issues and argue for the practical importance of computer ethics. I will proceed not by giving a list of problems but rather by analyzing the conditions and forces which generate ethical issues about computer technology. In particular, I want to analyze what is special about computers, what social impact computers will have, and what is operationally suspect about computing technology. I hope to show something of the nature of computer ethics by doing some computer ethics.

THE REVOLUTIONARY MACHINE

What is special about computers? It is often said that a Computer Revolution is taking place, but what is it about computers that makes them revolutionary? One difficulty in assessing the revolutionary nature of computers is that the word "revolutionary" has been devalued. Even minor technological improvements are heralded as revolutionary. A manufacturer of a new dripless pouring spout may well promote it as revolutionary. If minor technological improvements are revolutionary, then undoubtedly everchanging computer technology is revolutionary. The interesting issue, of course, is whether there is some nontrivial sense in which computers are revolutionary. What makes computer technology importantly different from other technology? Is there any real basis for comparing the Computer Revolution with the Industrial Revolution?

If we look around for features that make computers revolutionary, several features suggest themselves. For example, in our society computers are affordable and abundant. It is not much of an exaggeration to say that currently in our society every major business, factory, school, bank, and hospital is rushing to utilize computer technology. Millions of personal computers are being sold for home use. Moreover, computers are integral parts of products which don't look much like computers such as watches and automobiles. Computers are abundant and inexpensive, but so are pencils. Mere abundance and affordability don't seem sufficient to justify any claim to technological revolution.

One might claim the newness of computers makes them revolutionary. Such a thesis requires qualification. Electronic digital computers have been around for fifty years. In fact, if the abacus counts as a computer, then computer technology is among the oldest technologies. A better way to state this claim is that recent engineering advances in computers make them revolutionary. Obviously, computers have been immensely improved over the last forty years. Along with dramatic increases in computer speed and memory there have been dramatic decreases in computer size. Computer manufacturers are quick to point out that desk top computers today exceed the engineering specifications of computers which filled rooms only a few decades ago. There has been also a determined effort by companies to make computer hardware and computer software easier to use. Computers may not be completely user friendly but at least they are much less unfriendly. However, as important as these features are, they don't seem to get to the heart of the Computer Revolution. Small, fast, powerful and easy-to-use electric can openers are great improvements over earlier can openers, but they aren't in the relevant sense revolutionary.

Of course, it is important that computers are abundant, less expensive, smaller, faster, and more powerful and friendly. But, these features serve as enabling conditions for the spread of the Computer Revolution. The essence of the Computer Revolution is found in the nature of a computer itself. What is revolutionary about computers is *logical malleability*. Computers are logically malleable in that they can be shaped and molded to do any activity that can be characterized in terms of inputs, outputs, and connecting logical operations. Logical operations are the precisely defined steps which take a computer from one state to the next. The logic of computers can be massaged and shaped in endless ways through changes in hardware and software. Just as the power of a steam engine was a raw resource of the Industrial Revolution so the logic of a computer is a raw resource of the Computer Revolution. Because logic applies everywhere, the potential applications of computer technology appear limitless. The computer is the nearest thing we have to a universal tool. Indeed, the limits of computers are largely the limits of our own creativity. The driving question of the Computer Revolution is "How can we mold the logic of computers to better serve our purposes?"

I think logical malleability explains the already widespread application of computers and hints at the enormous impact computers are destined to have. Understanding the logical malleability of computers is essential to understanding the power of the developing technological revolution. Understanding logical malleability is also important in setting policies for the use of computers. Other ways of conceiving computers serve less well as a basis for formulating and justifying policies for action.

Consider an alternative and popular conception of computers in which computers are understood as number crunchers, that is, essentially as numerical devices. On this conception computers are nothing but big calculators. It might be maintained on this view that mathematical and scientific applications should take precedence over nonnumerical applications such as word processing. My position, on the contrary, is that computers are logically malleable. The arithmetic interpretation is certainly a correct one, but it is only one among many interpretations. Logical malleability has both a syntactic and a semantic dimension. Syntactically, the logic of computers is malleable in terms of the number and variety of possible states and operations. Semantically, the logic of computers is malleable in that the states of the computer can be taken to represent anything. Computers manipulate symbols but they don't care what the symbols represent. Thus, there is no ontological basis for giving preference to numerical applications over nonnumerical applications.

The fact that computers can be described in mathematical language, even at a very low level, doesn't make them essentially numerical. For example, machine language is conveniently and traditionally expressed in 0's and 1's. But the 0's and 1's simply designate different physical states. We could label these states as "on" and "off" or "yin" and "yang" and apply binary logic. Obviously, at some levels it is useful to use mathematical notation to describe computer operations, and it is reasonable to use it. The mistake is to reify the mathematical notation as the essence of a computer and then use this conception to make judgments about the appropriate use of computers.

In general, our conceptions of computer technology will affect our policies for using it. I believe the importance of properly conceiving the nature and impact of computer technology will increase as the Computer Revolution unfolds.

ANATOMY OF THE COMPUTER REVOLUTION

Because the Computer Revolution is in progress, it is difficult to get a perspective on its development. By looking at the Industrial Revolution I believe we can get some insight into the nature of a technological revolution. Roughly, the Industrial Revolution in England occurred in two major stages. The first stage was the technological introduction stage which took place during the last half of the eighteenth century. During this stage inventions and processes were introduced, tested, and improved. There was an industrialization of limited segments of the economy, particularly in agriculture and textiles. The second stage was the technological permeation stage which took place during the nineteenth century. As factory work increased and the populations of cities swelled, not only did well-known social evils emerge, but equally significantly corresponding changes in human activities and institutions, ranging from labor unions to health services, occurred. The forces of industrialization dramatically transformed the society.

My conjecture is that the Computer Revolution will follow a similar two stage development. The first stage, the introduction stage, has been occurring during the last forty years. Electronic computers have been created and refined. We are gradually entering the second stage, the permeation stage, in which computer technology will become an integral part of institutions throughout our society. I think that in the coming decades many human activities and social institutions will be transformed by computer technology and that this transforming effect of computerization will raise a wide range of issues for computer ethics.

What I mean by "transformed" is that the basic nature or purpose of an activity or institution is changed. This is marked by the kinds of questions that are asked. During the introduction stage computers are understood as tools for doing standard jobs. A typical question for this stage is "How well does a computer do such and such an activity?" Later, during the permeation stage, computers become an integral part of the activity. A typical question for this stage is "What is the nature and value of such and such an activity?" In our society there is already some evidence of the transforming effect of computerization as marked by the kind of questions being asked.

For example, for years computers have been used to count votes. Now the election process is becoming highly computerized. Computers can be used to count votes and to make projections about the outcome. Television networks use computers both to determine quickly who is winning and to display the results in a technologically impressive manner. During the last presidential election [1984] in the United States the television networks projected the results not only before the polls in California were closed but also before the polls in New York were closed. In fact, voting was still going on in over half the states when the winner was announced. The question is no longer "How efficiently do computers count votes in a fair election?" but "What is a fair election?" Is it appropriate that some people know the outcome before they vote? The problem is that computers not only tabulate the votes for each candidate but likely influence the number and distribution of these votes. For better or worse, our electoral process is being transformed.

As computers permeate more and more of our society, I think we will see more and more of the transforming effect of computers on our basic institutions and practices. Nobody can know for sure how our computerized society will look fifty years from now, but it is reasonable to think that various aspects of our daily work will be transformed. Computers have been used for years by businesses to expedite routine work, such as calculating payrolls; but as personal computers become widespread and allow executives to work at home, and as robots do more and more factory work, the emerging question will be not merely "How well do computers help us work?" but "What is the nature of this work?"

Traditional work may no longer be defined as something that normally happens at a specific time or a specific place. Work for us may become less doing a job than instructing a computer to do a job. As the concept of work begins to change, the values associated with the old concept will have to be reexamined. Executives who work at a computer terminal at home will lose some spontaneous interaction with colleagues. Factory workers who direct robots by pressing buttons may take less pride in a finished product. And similar effects can be expected in other types of work. Commercial pilots who watch computers fly their planes may find their jobs to be different from what they expected.

A further example of the transforming effect of computer technology is found in financial institutions. As the transfer and storage of funds becomes increasingly computerized the question will be not merely "How well do computers count money?" but "What is money?" For instance, in a cashless society in which debits are made to one's account electronically at the point of sale, has money disappeared in favor of computer records or have electronic impulses become money? What opportunities and values are lost or gained when money become intangible?

Still another likely area for the transforming effect of computers is education. Currently, educational packages for computers are rather limited. Now it is quite proper to ask "How well do computers educate?" But as teachers and students exchange more and more information indirectly via computer networks and as computers take over more routine instructional activities, the question will inevitably switch to "What is education?" The values associated with the traditional way of educating will be challenged. How much human contact is necessary or desirable for learning? What is education when computers do the teaching?

The point of this futuristic discussion is to suggest the likely impact of computer technology. Though I don't know what the details will be, I believe the kind of transformation I am suggesting is likely to occur. This is all I need to support my argument for the practical importance of computer ethics. In brief, the argument is as follows: The revolutionary feature of computers is their logical malleability. Logical malleability assures the enormous application of computer technology. This will bring about the Computer Revolution. During the Computer Revolution many of our human activities and social institutions will be transformed. These transformations will leave us with policy and conceptual vacuums about how to use computer technology. Such policy and conceptual vacuums are the marks of basic problems within computer ethics. Therefore, computer ethics is a field of substantial practical importance.

I find this argument for the practical value of computer ethics convincing. I think it shows that computer ethics is likely to have increasing application in our society. This argument does rest on a vision of the Computer Revolution which not everyone may share. Therefore, I will turn to another argument for the practical importance of computer ethics which doesn't depend upon any particular view of the Computer Revolution. This argument rests on the invisibility factor and suggests a number of ethical issues confronting computer ethics now.

THE INVISIBILITY FACTOR

There is an important fact about computers. Most of the time and under most conditions computer operations are invisible. One may be quite knowledgeable about the inputs and outputs of a computer and only dimly aware of the internal processing. This invisibility factor often generates policy vacuums about how to use computer technology. Here I will mention three kinds of invisibility that can have ethical significance.

The most obvious kind of invisibility which has ethical significance is invisible abuse. *Invisible abuse* is the intentional use of the invisible operations of a computer to engage in unethical conduct. A classic example of this is the case of a programmer who realized he could steal excess interest from a bank. When interest on a bank account is calculated, there is often a fraction of a cent left over after rounding off. This programmer instructed a computer to deposit these fractions of a cent to his own account. Although this is an ordinary case of stealing, it is relevant to computer ethics in that computer technology is essentialy involved and there is a question about what policy to institute in order to best detect and prevent such abuse. Without access to the program used for stealing the interest or to a sophisticated accounting program such an activity may easily go unnoticed.

Another possibility for invisible abuse is the invasion of the property and privacy of others. A computer can be programmed to contact another computer over phone lines and surreptitiously remove or alter confidential information. Sometimes an inexpensive computer and a telephone hookup is all it takes. A group of teenagers, who named themselves the "414s" after the Milwaukee telephone exchange, used their home computers to invade a New York hospital, a California bank, and a government nuclear weapons laboratory. These breakins were done as pranks, but obviously such invasions can be done with malice and be difficult or impossible to detect.

A particularly insidious example of invisible abuse is the use of computers for surveillance. For instance, a company's central computer can monitor the work done on computer terminals far better and more discreetly than the most dedicated sweatshop manager. Also, computers can be programmed to monitor phone calls and electronic mail without giving any evidence of tampering. A Texas oil company, for example, was baffled why it was always outbid on leasing rights for Alaskan territory until it discovered another bidder was tapping its data transmission lines near its Alaskan computer terminal.

A second variety of the invisibility factor, which is more subtle and conceptually interesting than the first, is the presence of invisible programming values. *Invisible programming values* are those values which are embedded in a computer program.

Writing a computer program is like building a house. No matter how detailed the specifications may be, a builder must make numerous decisions about matters not specified in order to construct the house. Different houses are compatible with a given set of specifications. Similarly, a request for a computer program is made at a level of abstraction usually far removed from the details of the actual programming language. In order to implement a program which satisfies the specifications a programmer makes some value judgments about what is important and what is not. These values become embedded in the final product and may be invisible to someone who runs the program.

Consider, for example, computerized airline reservations. Many different programs could be written to product a reservation service. American Airlines once promoted a service called "SABRE". This program had a bias for American Airline flights built in so that sometimes an American Airline flight was suggested by the computer even if it was not the best flight available. Indeed, Braniff Airlines, which went into bankruptcy for awhile, sued American Airlines on the grounds that this kind of bias in the reservation service contributed to its financial difficulties.

Although the general use of a biased reservation service is ethically suspicious, a programmer of such a service may or may not be engaged in invisible abuse. There may be a difference between how a programmer intends a program to be used and how it is actually used. Moreover, even if one sets out to create a program for a completely unbiased reservation service, some value judgments are latent in the program because some choices have to be made about how the program operates. Are airlines listed in alphabetical order? Is more than one listed at a time? Are flights just before the time requested listed? For what period after the time requested are flights listed? Some answers, at least implicitly, have to be given to these questions when the program is written. Whatever answers are chosen will build certain values into the program.

Sometimes invisible programming values are so invisible that even the programmers are unaware of them. Programs may have bugs or may be based on implicit assumptions which don't become obvious until there is a crisis. For example, the operators of the ill-fated Three Mile Island nuclear power plant were trained on a computer which was programmed to simulate possible malfunctions including malfunctions which were dependent on other malfunctions. But, as the Kemeny Commission which investigated the disaster discovered, the simulator was not programmed to generate simultaneous, independent malfunctions. In the actual failure at Three Mile Island the operators were faced with exactly this situation—simultaneous, independent malfunctions. The inadequacy of the computer simulation was the result of a programming decision, as unconscious or implicit as that decision may have been. Shortly after the disaster the computer was reprogrammed to simulate situations like the one that did occur at Three Mile Island.

A third variety of the invisibility factor, which is perhaps the most disturbing, is *invisible complex calculation*. Computers today are capable of enormous calculations beyond human comprehension. Even if a program is understood, it does not follow that the calculations based on that program are understood. Computers today perform and certainly supercomputers in the future will perform calculations which are too complex for human inspection and understanding.

An interesting example of such complex calculation occurred in 1976 when a computer worked on the four color conjecture. The four color problem, a puzzle mathematicians have worked on for over a century, is to show that a map can be colored with at most four colors so that no adjacent areas have the same color. Mathematicians at the University of Illinois broke the problem down into thousands of cases and programmed computers to consider them. After more than a thousand hours of computer time on various computers, the four color conjecture was proved correct. What is interesting about this mathematical proof, compared to traditional proofs, is that it is largely invisible. The general structure of the proof is known and found in the program and any particular part of the computer's activity can be examined, but practically speaking the calculations are too enormous for humans to examine them all.

The issue is how much we should trust a computer's invisible calculations. This becomes a significant ethical issue as the consequences grow in importance. For instance, computers are used by the military in making decisions about launching nuclear weapons. On the one hand, computers are fallible and there may not be time to confirm their assessment of the situation. On the other hand, making decisions about launching nuclear weapons without using computers may be even more fallible and more dangerous. What should be our policy about trusting invisible calculations?

A partial solution to the invisibility problem may lie with computers themselves. One of the strengths of computers is the ability to locate hidden information and display it. Computers can make the invisible visible. Information which is lost in a sea of data can be clearly revealed with the proper computer analysis. But that's the catch. We don't always know when, where, and how to direct the computer's attention.

The invisibility factor presents us with a dilemma. We are happy in one sense that the operations of a computer are invisible. We don't want to inspect every computerized transaction or program every step for ourselves or watch every computer calculation. In terms of efficiency the invisibility factor is a blessing. But it is just this invisibility that makes us vulnerable. We are open to invisible abuse or invisible programming of inappropriate values or invisible miscalculation. The challenge for computer ethics is to formulate policies which will help us deal with this dilemma. We must decide when to trust computers and when not to trust them. This is another reason why computer ethics is so important.

COMING INTO THE COUNTRY

John P. Barlow

Imagine discovering a continent so vast that it may have no end to its dimensions. Imagine a new world with more resources than all our future greed might exhaust, more opportunities than there will ever be entrepreneurs to exploit, and a peculiar kind of real estate that expands with development.

Imagine a place where trespassers leave no footprints, where goods can be stolen an infinite number of times and yet remain in the possession of their original owners, where businesses you never heard of can own the history of your personal affairs, where only children feel completely at home, where the physics is that of thought rather than things, and where everyone is as virtual as the shadows in Plato's cave.

Such a place actually exists, if *place* is the appropriate word. It consists of electron states, microwaves, magnetic fields, light pulses and thought itself—a wave in the web of our electronic processing and communication systems. I used to call it the Datasphere until I read William Gibson's Neuromancer and discovered he had already given it the evocative name of Cyberspace.

Of course, Gibson thought he was conjuring up some manifestation of a fanciful future. In fact, Cyberspace has been around, with rapidly increasing range and density, since that moment in March 1876 when a certain Mr. Watson encountered Alexander Graham Bell there.

While it is familiar to most people as the *location* of a long-distance telephone conversation, it is also the repository for all digital or electronically transferred information. As such, it is the venue for most of what is now commerce, industry, and broad-scale human interaction. Indeed, if you have any money besides what is crumpled in your pocket, it is probably in Cyberspace.

Few have even noticed this emergent domain, despite the fact that most of us use its resources daily. Every day millions of people use ATMs and credit cards, place telephone calls, make travel reservations, and access information of limitless variety without any clear perception of the digital machinations behind these transactions.

Our financial, legal, and even physical lives are increasingly dependent on realities of which we have only the dimmest awareness. We have entrusted the basic functions of modern existence to institutions we cannot name, using tools we have never heard of and could not operate if we had.

Thus, for all its importance to modern existence, Cyberspace remains a frontier region, across which roam the few aboriginal technologists and cyberpunks who can tolerate the austerity of its savage computer interfaces, incompatible communications protocols, proprietary barricades, cultural and legal ambiguities, and general lack of useful maps or metaphors.

Certainly, the old concepts of property, expression, identity, movement, and context, based as they are on physical manifestation, do not apply in a world where there can be none.

Sovereignty over this new world is not well defined. Large institutions own much of the hardware which supports it and therefore claim, with some justification, to hegemony over the whole thing.

Some of the locals—the Unix cultists, sysops, netheads and byte drovers—are like the mountain men of the fur trade. They may be somewhat uncivilized, but most of them have come here in the service of corporations. However grudgingly, they tend to accept the idea that institutions can own information.

Another group, the cyberpunks, are nomadic and tribal. They have an Indian sense of property and are about as agreeable to the notion of proprietary data as the Shoshones were to the idea that the Union Pacific owned the landscape of southern Wyoming. By asserting their freedom of both movement and access to the local resource—knowledge—they have developed a culture in which the violation of institutional boundaries is inevitable. This will lead to more adamant efforts at security. And they will be met with an ascending symmetry of cracker ingenuity until either security is perfect (at which time no system will be accessible) or the savages take on civilization.

As communications and data-processing technology continues to advance at a pace many times faster than society can assimilate it, additional conflicts have begun to occur on the border between Cyberspace and the physical world. Among the non-nerdly a kind of neo-Luddism is arising at the prospect of being dragged into a place they can not physically enter.

Every day it dawns on more ordinary corporate employees that they have become *knowledge workers*. They find themselves chained to a device which is maddeningly uncooperative and inflexible in its mysterious requirements, and with which they perform tasks of questionable necessity. Worse, each time they master one opaque interface, their MIS master imposes on them version 2.0 and they have to start all over again. They are stuck on the learning curve of Sisyphus. They are not happy there.

Nearly everyone now—office employee or not—has the nagging suspicion that somewhere out there are hard disks containing information about one's personal affairs—information which is either inaccurate or which he or she would prefer no one knew. Worse, one knows that little can be done to alter this condition.

Consequently, increasing numbers of people are coming to hate and fear not only the technology itself but the people who create it. In a very short time, the term "hacker" has gone from being an honorable appellation implying computer wizardry to a malign epithet of digital nihilism. There is a reason for this.

But Cyberspace is the homeland of the Information Age—the place where the citizens of the future are destined to dwell. We will all go there whether we want to or not and we would do better to approach the place with a settler's determination to civilize it as rapidly as possible.

What would it mean to civilize Cyberspace? To some, the answer to this question is simple and historically familiar: exterminate the natives, secure the resources into corporate possession, establish tariffs, and define culture strictly in terms of economy.

Such an approach, while highly advantageous to large institutions, might have serious consequences for the individuals of the future, whose privacy, freedom of expression, economic opportunity, and property rights could be foreclosed in a Cyberspace of this design. Indeed, it calls into question whether in the future the individual will count for very much at all.

Arising on the electronic frontier are questions which are subtle, profound, and of fundamental importance to the way tomorrow's society will function. With this column I hope to raise those questions and offer my own modest speculations about how we might begin the process of answering them.

This column will also address the development of a new social contract for the digital domain—sort of a Cyberspace equivalent to the Code of the West—and an attendant definition of the rights and responsibilities of the inhabitants. I also hope to help create an awareness of the cultural implications of electronic design. And, finally, I want to propose some fundamental revision of our notions of speech, property, and place.

Big undertaking, and easily ignored on that account. But a new world is being born. Uncorrected flaws in its design will scale up along with the rest of it. Today's minor misjudgements will become tomorrow's established horrors.

An example from the past might serve to illuminate this point. In the early days of broadcasting, the government decided that the airwaves (as well as the frequency resolution of crystal set receivers) had such limited bandwidth that it would be necessary for the government to license broadcasters. Well and good. However, someone also decided that if the government were going to regulate frequency allocation, it should regulate content as well.

Thus the most common medium for expression today exists under constraints of governmental censorship which the founding fathers would have found intolerable—all because of bureaucratic error which, at the time, seemed too insignificant to correct.

Similar errors are being made today around the subject of intellectual property and its interstate transport. In our zeal to protect this immaterial substance as though it were tangible as pig iron, we are enacting laws and regulations which will almost certainly limit free expression in the future unless we fix the system now.

Pretending that it ain't broke sure won't fix it, but, in the numerous discussions I have had with members of the computer community, there does not seem to be much willingness to tackle these issues at any depth. Most of you have your attentions so firmly fixed on the concrete business at hand—and important business it usually is—that it is hard to find time for shadow-boxing abstractions.

"Hey, I do bus architecture, I'm no social philosopher," is the sort of rejoinder I hear frequently. It is a hard one to argue with. Keep your head down, do what you know, and hope it is all headed someplace good.

The trouble is, the rest of society is so utterly perplexed by digital technology that most ordinary citizens are even less qualified than bus architects to engage in cybernetic social philosophy. As readers of this magazine, you are almost certainly more knowledgeable about the legal and cultural ambiguities surrounding digital communication and property than your computer-phobic fellow citizens. You are thus well suited to the task of civilizing Cyberspace. I hope you will join me on the electronic frontier, because I believe it is time for that process to consciously begin.

Consciously or unconsciously, we are presently shaping the future ethics and culture of Cyberspace. Only by bringing awareness to this task will we create the sort of place we would want our children to live in.

▷ COMPUTER ETHICS

Responsibility Regained

Donald Gotterbarn

In an address to the Computers and Quality of Life Conference in 1990, Gary Chapman, the director of Computer Professionals for Social Responsibility, described his perception of the state of work in computer ethics. He said that over the years he has attended many meetings where computer ethics and social issues were discussed and that he keeps hearing the same thing. In short, he has noticed no progress in the field. I think he is right.

The extensive discussion of computer ethics in the past few years has had little consequence. A look at the content of such discussion reveals a primary source of the problem, viz., the absence of a coherent concept of the subject. Starting from a clouded concept of computer ethics, one cannot derive clear ethical positions.

I will show the difficulties with the current concept and describe some of the problems created by this concept. Then I will offer an alternative approach to computer ethics that avoids the current difficulties and broadens the concept of computer ethics to include both proscriptive and prescriptive judgments.

The discussion of computer ethics includes such large social questions as:

- Should we sell computers to countries supporting terrorism?
- Is it right to replace unskilled workers with computer-guided robots?
- What are the health consequences of using video-display terminals?

The discussion also includes all sorts of individual abuses in the use of computers. There is a new species of "yellow journalism" about computing which consists of retelling stories of abuses committed with computers or of computer catastrophes. The problem is that these stories are presented as issues in computer ethics. They include stories of how someone committed fraud with the use of a computer, or of how someone used a computer to change grades or to design an effective drug-smuggling route. From these collections of tales one is supposed to abstract a coherent concept. If these are tales about computer ethics simply because they involve the use of a computer, then my use of a scalpel to rob someone is a problem of medical ethics and my hitting someone with a law book is a case of legal ethics. Both the physician and the lawyer would find it absurd if we used tales such as these as evidence of the moral failures of physicians and lawyers. In the same way, the fact that an unethical act was facilitated by the use of a computer does not entail that the act is an issue in computer ethics.

The computer is a device that has an impact on almost every aspect of our lives, and as such it can be used in a broad range of unethical activities. This involvement of a computer does not, however, transform every such activity into a problem of computer ethics, just as the use of a junkyard's car crusher to conceal a murder does not turn the murder into a problem of junkyard ethics.

The absence of a clear concept of computer ethics allows one to include all sorts of interesting moral dilemmas as issues. For example, the following has been used as a problem in computer ethics. Johnny's mother is suffering from a rare, but manageable, disease. If uncontrolled, it has an unalterable, painful, and fatal outcome. The medicine to manage the disease is so expensive that the only way Johnny can pay for it is to use his computer to commit fraud. What is the moral thing for Johnny to do? This problem includes such large social questions as the responsibility of society for health care and the obligations of children to their parents. It also includes issues about how one reasons ethically: does one base reasoning here on duty, or on consequences? This problem is so broad that it can not be considered an issue of any particular type of ethics. Nevertheless, because a computer is tangentially related to the story, it is portrayed as an issue in computer ethics. The fact that such a complex moral problem is exceedingly difficult to resolve is used as evidence that issues in computer ethics cannot be resolved.

The claim that such problems cannot be resolved is an extremely dangerous position. If there can be no resolution to problems in computer ethics, then clearly we should not waste our time worrying about them.

The "no-resolution view" has been reinforced by some recent works. For example, Donn Parker uses a voting methodology to decide what is ethical in computing. In his book *Ethical Conflicts in Computer Science and Technology* (1977) he gathered the opinions of people from several professions and ranges from accountants, attorneys, psychologists, and philosophy professors to computer professionals. They were asked to vote on the ethics of individuals described in scenarios. He says this work was not guided by a concept of computer ethics, nor was there an attempt to discover ethical principles. He called this approach "micro-ethics." Not only was there an absence of a concept of computer ethics, but the primary direction was an emphasis on proscribed activities. The only direction to the content given by Parker was that the scenarios were "written in such a way as to raise questions of unethicality rather than ethicality." He used the diversity of opinions expressed about these scenarios to argue that there was no such thing as computer ethics. And, *a fortiori*, if there is no such thing, then it could not be taught in a computer science curriculum.

Parker's conclusion is unjustified for two reasons. First, it does not follow from his own evidence. Second, the evidence examined has little to do with computer ethics. The presumption that there can be no agreement in ethics can be so strong that it corrupts one's view of the evidence. For example, at a conference, Parker described the results of his 1977 workshop. He began by saying that there was *agreement* on many scenarios. Then he went on to say, "We got a lot of very close votes. In other words, we were not able to obtain a consensus on what is unethical and what not unethical in the computer field." (See Donn Parker, "Ethical Dilemmas in Computer Technology," *Ethics and the Management of Computer Technology*, edited by W. Michael Hoffman, et al.) This conclusion requires that he ignore all the places where there was agreement. It does not follow from the existence of some gray areas in a domain that there are no clear areas in that domain. The existence of hard problems in math—like the discrete decimal value of 1/3—is not proof that there are no solutions in math. He handles the evidence in the same way in his *Ethical Conflicts in Information and Computer Science, Technology, and Business*, published in 1990, a revision of his 1977 book. The only cases he brings forward to the new book are those that generated the highest degree of diversity of opinion in the earlier book. He ignores those on which there has been a significant degree of unanimity.

More significant than the question of how the evidence is evaluated is the presumption that the scenarios are about issues in computer ethics. The discussion of the morality of a professor (who happens to be a computer science professor) who gave no acknowledgment of a student's contribution to the professor's research and the discussion of the engineer who used and marketed a computer device to calculate blackjack odds seem to have little relation to computer ethics.

I think the presumed breadth of the subject of computer ethics has contributed to development of other dangerous misconceptions. It is claimed that computer ethics is not like any other; it is described as both a new area of ethics and as a unique kind of it. Early attempts to define computer ethics, such as that of James Moor in "What is Computer Ethics?," (see p. 7) have argued for its uniqueness. The arguments for such are based on the speed of the technology, the logical flexibility of computers, or the computer's impact on society. The arguments for its newness, based on speed and social impact, have been addressed and rejected elsewhere. (See Richard H. Austing's and Lillian Cassel's *Computers in Focus*.) It is not unique because of its impact.

There are many devices that have had a significant impact on society—such as the printing press, for which we did not develop a new and unique ethics called printing-press ethics. The computer's ability logically to model an enormous number of events is the basis for the flexibility claim. This flexibility of the computer is due to the underlying strengths of the logical and mathematical capabilities implemented in the computer. The underlying flexibility of math and logic is greater than that of the computer, but we did not develop "logic ethics" and "mathematics ethics."

Why should we be concerned about these claims of newness and uniqueness? We generally think of newness and uniqueness as positive attributes. The newness claim leads people to think that computer ethics has not yet found its primary ethical standard (see Tom Forester's and Perry Morrison's recently released *ComputerEthics*); so the discussion of computer ethics is not yet directed by any guiding principles from which we can reason. This is different from our understanding of the older, more established professions. Medicine, for example, is viewed as having a primary ethical principle—prevent death—which physicians can use to guide their reasoning. The inference from the newness claim is that we cannot make ethical decisions in computer ethics because we have not yet found a primary ethical principle. The uniqueness claim is even more dangerous. It leads one to think that not only are the ethical standards undiscovered, but the model of ethical reasoning itself is yet to be discovered; that is, even if we find a primary principle, we will not know how to reason from it.

Why do people think that computer ethics is not like other ethics? Other forms of ethics seem to have fixed domains or methods for making decisions. Medical ethics defines patient–medical provider relationships. Legal ethics circumscribes the acceptable behavior of legal professionals. Because the concept of computer ethics has been stretched so far, there does not seem to be a clear domain for it. The scope of computer ethics has been made so broad that it includes numerous and conflicting values and methodologies. It is frequently characterized as encompassing *all* moral abuses committed with a computer. Austing and Cassell claim, "The moral values we place on computer use and misuse constitute the ethics of computer usage." Social scientists characterize computer ethics as including all discussions of social institutions transformed by computers. No wonder computer ethics seems like some confusing, amorphous area that is different from all other areas of ethics.

Under scrutiny, the notion that computer ethics includes all abuses committed with a computer leads to absurdity. This broad concept is dangerous. I maintain that computer ethics is not unique; the ethical issues of it as broadly defined above are either subsumable under the issues of general ethics or they are a type of professional ethics.

These confusions about computer ethics and the absence of a discussion about a concept of it have led to some significant confusions and dangerous conclusions. There is also a surprising lacuna in its literature.

In medical ethics, the discussion is about the actions of health professionals in their roles as health-care providers. In computer ethics as broadly construed, there is no discussion of the actions of the computing professionals in their role as computer professionals. Unlike the situation in medical ethics, most of the discussion in computer ethics is about things that are beyond the control of the individual professional. Most practicing computer professionals do not decide whether to sell computers to foreign countries, nor do they get to decide whether the federal government will use computer technology in its weaponry. Even when the described issues are within an individual's control, they have little to do specifically with the process of developing computing artifacts.

The only way to make sense of "Computer Ethics" is to narrow its focus to those actions that are within the control of the individual *moral* computer professional. Narrowing the domain of computer ethics in this way does not lessen the significance of those topics that have been mistakenly included as issues in computer ethics. I believe that such a correction will make the resolution of those broader issues easier. They will no longer suffer from the red herring that they cannot be solved because as issues in computer ethics they require some yet-to-be determined type of ethics and a new type of ethical reasoning.

Narrowing the focus in this way will also make computer ethics relevant for the typical computer professional who, I presume, is a moral individual. Computer ethics as broadly conceived is irrelevant to the typical computer professional, who does not want to commit fraud and who does not decide who will sell computers to another country. Furthermore, it also will draw attention to the positive side of computer ethics, to those acts that are prescribed as well as those which are proscribed.

Discussions of professional computer ethics are almost nonexistent in the general literature. There is little attention paid to the domain of professional ethics—the values that guide the day-to-day activities of computing professionals in their role as professionals. By computing professional I mean anyone involved in the design and development of computer artifacts. Computer artifacts include such things as program documentation, test plans and test cases, feasibility studies, source codes, user manuals, system maintenance manuals, and design documents, that is, all the products of the system development process. The ethical decisions made during the development of these artifacts have a direct relationship to many of the issues discussed under the broader concept of computer ethics. I believe many of those issues are the result of bad ethical decisions made during software development.

There are a variety of reasons for discussing the concept of a professional and whether particular groups are professionals. Employers do not like to consider their computing staff professionals, because then they would get a higher salary. Others deny the status of professional to some groups because they do not fit the definition of professional. I want to use the concept of professional to understand computer ethics as it relates to the builder of computer artifacts. Both Michael Bayles in his *Professional Ethics* and Deborah Johnson in her *Computer Ethics* point out several characteristics common to the concept of professionals. The occupation of a professional, which is primarily mental, generally requires advanced skill and training. Some organization generally certifies this skill and admits the person to the profession. The position of a professional generally involves some kind of service to society, such as practicing medicine or law.

Traditionally, it has also included the concept of autonomy. Training provides a variety of technical solutions to a problem, and then the professional picks among these, using his or her professional judgment to select the best solution. The existence of some form of autonomy is critical to ascribing moral responsibility to the professional, although some people have argued that the concept of autonomy no longer fits the concept of professional.

They point to the existence of professional organizations and maintain that there is no longer any autonomy of judgment. I think the notion of autonomy is critical to the concept of a professional, and it is just as evident in a physician's decision while practicing in a professional organization as it is for a computing professional working in a large corporation. When one enters a physician's office, even that of one who belongs to a professional organization, the physician has available a variety of cures for a particular ailment. The physician uses professional judgment in determining which cure would be the best in any particular case, or even whether a cure is needed. The same thing is true for the computing professional who, when presented with a particular problem, has several standard and effective methodologies of design from which to choose. There is still autonomy of judgment about how to achieve a particular end. There are, of course, some constraints on the options that can be chosen. There is a standard set of procedures that a physician goes through before recommending a particular solution. There is also a set of standards for use in determining whether professional physicians will exercise their skills in particular situations. If they did not exercise autonomous judgment, though, we would not consider them professional.

So far, we have focused on the technical skill and judgment of professionals in completing their tasks. But there is another significant element in professionalism that has not been articulated in these standard definitions. We have acted as if the standard of good professional judgment were purely technical. But there is something missing here. Consider the following example. What would you think of a physician who, when asked by a patient to cut off both of the patient's arms at the elbow, said "I will do it right now. I have been specially trained in surgery"? Even if the physician did this in a technically skilled fashion, we would not say he was acting professionally. Where was the exercise of the values for the well-being of the patient in this judgment? Technically, he chose the correct scalpel and anesthetic. What he failed to do was to condition his technical judgment on a set of moral values. Accepting a role of professional also carries with it a commitment to a set of ethical principles.

Insight into how these values are used will provide some insight into how ethics relates to the computing profession. One of the things that sets professional ethics apart is that ethical rules and judgments are made in a particular context, such as for medicine or law. The contexts in which these judgments are made alter the ordering of the application of moral rules. For example, in medical ethics the principle of "informed consent" is a primary ethical one, whereas in journalistic ethics this principle has a much weaker impact on ethical judgments. The "principle of confidentiality" has different weights in different contexts. The physician who learns of a patient's pregnancy in his or her role as a physician requires stronger reasons to divulge this pregnancy than does the patient's acquaintance who is asked by her own mother about the pregnancy. By analogy, ethics for the computing professional is not just another kind of ethics, but it is ethical rules and judgments applied in a computing context based on professional standards and a concern for the user of the computing product. The attitude of "let the buyer beware" is neither the attitude of the physician nor of the civil engineer, nor should it be the attitude of the computing professional.

I think the failure to see that computing products are used only to serve the needs of others and the failure of the professional to keep the welfare of the user in mind have led directly to several instances of unethical behavior. There are several causes for these failures. One is simple ignorance. We train computer scientists to solve problems, and the examples we use, such as finding the least common multiple (LCM) for a set of numbers, portray computing as merely a problem-solving exercise, analogous to doing a crossword puzzle. Solving the puzzle is an interesting exercise, but it lacks significant consequences.

The failure to realize that computing is a service profession for the user of the computing artifact has significant consequences. One of these is seen when we consider the case of a programmer who was asked to write a program that would raise and lower a large X-ray device. The programmer wrote and tested his solution to this problem. It successfully and accurately moved the device from the top of the support pole to the top of the table. The difficulty with this narrow problem-solving approach was shown when an X-ray technician told a patient to get off the table after an X-ray was taken, and then the technician set the height of the device to "table top height." The patient had not heard the technician and was crushed under the machine. The programmer solved a problem but did not consider the user.

Only in academe do students write programs that are designed to be thrown away or gather dust in the backs of their closets. In all other contexts, computing is a service industry. All computing artifacts are designed to be used. Computing has had a tendency, though, not to see itself as a service industry. Even the term "user" carries with it a derogatory connotation. We are one of only two occupations that I know of whose practitioners call their customers "users." There is a recent example of this attitude before the courts. A defense contractor was asked to develop a portable anti-aircraft system. The system which the contractor developed destroys aircraft effectively, but it also occasionally kills the person who launched the missile. The company has declared that this is not a problem because it "[is] in full compliance with the specifications given to [it] by the user." Being a professional involves using one's special skills to give careful and constant consideration to the impact of one's service on others. This consideration is guided by a set of ethical principles.

We have mistakenly understood computer ethics as different from other professional ethics. When we look at medical ethics, legal ethics, journalistic ethics, we have to distinguish the practitioners of those ethics from the ethical principles they affirm. The three professionals work in different contexts: medicine, law, and journalism. However, when we talk of their professional ethics we do not consider them three different kinds. The distinguishing characteristic among professional ethics is the context in which they are applied. Because there are three contexts, it does not follow that there are three distinct sets of ethical rules or three different kinds of moral reasoning. Nor does it follow that computer ethics is another unique set of ethical principles which is yet to be discovered.

By analogy with other "ethics," "computer ethics" can be divided into two spheres. The first embraces a set of ethical problems that can be reasoned about by analogy with most other traditional ethical abuses such as fraud, theft, and trespassing. But this should not even be called *computer* ethics. Ethics for computing professionals is not just another kind of ethics, but it is ethical values, rules, and judgments applied in a computing context based on professional standards and a concern for the user of the computing artifact. It is this sense of computer ethics that has received very little attention. Most of the attention has been directed at the results of the failures of professional ethics or abuses involving a computer. . . .

Computer ethics, as presented here, is modeled on other professional ethics. It can use moral-reasoning models that are similar to those in other professional ethics. The theory of computer ethics we have presented does not rule out the examination of such critical concerns as the impact of technology on the nature of work or computer fraud. The theory puts these concerns in other ethical categories. The former is a concern of sociology, and the latter is a concern of property rights.

Computer practitioners do not have a single representative organization that can control membership in the profession; there is no organization to impose sanctions for violations of professional behavior. But the absence of a single organization does not impede the development of professional ethical standards. The focus of this approach to computer ethics is on the individual professional's responsibility in the practice of his or her craft. As the standards of this craft are being developed, so are the standards of professional computer ethics. The judgments about these standards will be guided by the values of the professional.

Computer ethics as presented here attempts a clear description of the relation of values to the work of the computer professional and sets forth criteria for making ethical decisions in that process. Focusing on stories about the failures of the product has misdirected us. They may be interesting stories to listen to, but they convey little information about computer ethics. I maintain that a focus on the process will resolve many of the problems discussed at the beginning of this paper. This approach will lead to the development of better computing artifacts.

COMPUTERS, ETHICS, AND SOCIAL RESPONSIBILITY

Terry Winograd

INTRODUCTION

What Can a Computer Scientist Say?

Let me begin by admitting that it wasn't exactly clear to me just what the content should be for a "computer science keynote." The path seems clear for my colleagues who will present keynotes on philosophy and sociology, since those fields include ethics and values in their core subject matter. As a philosopher, one can develop theories of ethics. As a sociologist one can study the ways that people learn, change, and exhibit values. But as a computer scientist I don't study ethics and values; I study computers and computing. As we are all well aware, "ethics" and "values" aren't the kind of things to be addressed with the theories and techniques of computer science. For the computer scientist, they are not an object of study, but a domain in which we interpret and assess our actions as professionals.

My role, then, is not as an observer, but as a subject. As a computer professional and a teacher of future computer professionals, my concern is very personal. The questions aren't academic, but practical: not "What is done?" but "What should we do?"

So I will enjoy the liberty in this paper of not having to precisely define the difficult concepts we speak about or of having to argue the logical merits of a particular theory. Instead I will talk about how issues of computing and values show up in the work of our profession. You might think of it as being ichthyology from the point of view of the fish.

Also, in talking about these issues I will not try to draw a careful line between terms such as "ethics," "morals," "values," and "social responsibility." These distinctions can be important for some purposes, but I will interchange them freely here with more of a concern for the ring of the sentence than for the precise differentiation of the concepts.

The Personal Connection

When I speak of my own work, I include more than the narrow pursuit of research and development in computer science. For almost ten years I have been a participant in the work of Computer Professionals for Social Responsibility (CPSR), an organization that has brought together people from around the country (in fact, around the world) to share understandings and to act collectively in many of the areas that are being discussed in this text. That activity is not a diversion but a critical part of the work of a computer professional. One of the things I want to highlight is the way in which organizations like CPSR and the National Conference for Computing and Values (NCCV) play a central role in ethical conduct for computer professionals.

In addition, during the past three years, Helen Nissenbaum (now at Princeton) and I have developed and taught a course on "Computers, Ethics and Social Responsibility" for undergraduate computer science majors at Stanford University. As all of us in academia know well, there is no better way to expand your own understanding than to throw yourself into a room full of bright undergraduates who want to master a difficult topic and expect you to help. Much of my understanding has grown from the generative interaction that comes in teaching, and that too is a central part of my work as a computer scientist. It has forced me into some hard and productive thinking about the questions being raised at a conference on Computing and Values.

What I Will Say

In this paper I will present and contrast some common views of how ethics and values are related to computing and see what these views imply for the activities we can undertake to promote ethical behavior and social responsibility. My emphasis is on the fundamentally social nature of ethical concerns: with looking beyond the role of the individual to the larger context of discourse and action that generates the world in which individuals make choices and to act. Rather than focusing on the isolated individual faced with an ethical dilemma, I want to direct our gaze to the larger swirl of human discourse, which is the source of the interpretations, values, and possibilities that make ethical choice meaningful.

The announcement for the NCCV conference declared a vision:

> To integrate computer technology and human values in such a way that the technology advances and protects those values rather than doing damage to them.

This will require acts of individual moral courage, and it will be based on a lot more. We need to create an environment in which the consideration of human values in our technological work is not a brave act, but a professional norm. We need to produce a background of understanding in which it is simply taken for granted by all computer professionals that value considerations are foremost. We need to forge everyday practices and ways of teaching that reinforce that understanding.

In that spirit, I will argue that the kind of inquiry and discussion that motivate the conference, and that have been at the heart of CPSR's ten years of work, are a primary form of ethical behavior.

BEING A "GOOD" COMPUTER PROFESSIONAL

First, let us go back to the basic question of what values, ethics, and social responsibility have to do with computing. I said that ethics and values constitute "a domain in which we, and others, view and assess our actions as computer professionals." What do we mean by "assess our actions"?

Assessments and Competence

In every area of purposeful endeavor, there exist communities of assessment within which it is possible to meaningfully describe, compare, and evaluate action. As a computer scientist I am part of a scientific community with standards of practice, and practices of assessment. There may be no straightforward quantitative measure of whether I am a "good computer scientist," but there are ways in which all of us measure the achievements of others and of ourselves. In the academic world these include publication records, peer review, awards, election to various professional and honorary societies, and the like. They also include less tangible but still consensual domains of reputation, status, and in the longer run your "place in the history of the field." I identify myself as belonging to a scientific community and I participate in its consensual processes for assessment. For example, my kids may think I'm a fantastic computer scientist because I could get Tetris running on our Macintosh, but I don't value this in the same dimension as the judgment of colleagues whom I consider part of the community.

When we look to the computer science community in general we see a notable lack of concern for many of the values addressed at the NCCV conference. There is an implicit definition of "good computer scientist" that dismisses people like Joe Weizenbaum as bothersome troublemakers, and accepts without qualms people who are oblivious of the value consequences of their actions. One of my colleagues, in a note rejecting my questioning the sources of research funding said he feared I would describe him, as "Having the moral fiber of a styrofoam cup." In judging whether people are "good computer scientists" the professional norms are strongly attuned to particular concerns and kinds of action and not to others.

But in our common sense assignment of "good" and "bad," we take a broader view. A "good baseball player" isn't just one who hits home runs, but one who contributes to the efforts of the team as a whole. He may be a great source of spirit and enthusiasm, a kind mentor to younger players, and a contributor in many other ways to the success of the team.

But in talking of the success of the team we're back to assessments again: What constitutes "success" for the computer science team? Again there is a gap between what we see in many of our work settings and what we are striving for here. Our measure of success needs to be the one quoted above:

> To integrate computer technology and human values in such a way that the technology advances and protects those values rather than doing damage to them.

With this as our measure, we are ready to look for "good computer science."

What is the Domain of Ethical Action?

If our goal is to "advance and protect human values," then what kind of actions will further it? Ethics isn't an immediately obvious domain of actions. If you ask what competence is being developed in a cooking class, it is evidently "cooking." We can identify people at specific times as being engaged in cooking. But we are never "ethicking" in that simple sense. We may be performing an engineering job, making a living, doing scientific research, (or, for that matter, cooking) and find ourselves in situations where our actions raise some kind of ethical question. How do we identify those situations?

In some sense this is an "academic question." We all grow up with a tacit understanding that there can be things we do that are "right" and others that are "wrong," and that as autonomous individuals we have responsibility for choosing between them. We all have a sense that we *should* do what is right, even though that isn't always what we end up doing. We also grow up in today's global pluralistic society with an awareness that although everyone has a sense that there is a difference between right and wrong, there is no agreement on just what actions should fall under which category. There are tremendous disputes between different cultural, religious and political groups, which have led to arguments, wars, and disagreements at all levels of society throughout history. But, on the other hand, there seem to be commonalities. Nearly everyone would agree that it is wrong to simply walk up to someone on a whim and inflict pain, and that it is right to help others in need.

People have debated for thousands of years what moral and ethical standards should be. Is there a universal ethics that applies to all people in all ages? Or is ethics a purely relative matter in that what is considered a fundamental moral principle by one people at one time may be equally validly rejected in another culture?

Now if I were a philosopher I would feel compelled to try to make sense of all this: to come up with a coherent moral philosophy that could serve as a basis for understanding what we see in the historical discourse about morality and for making decisions about our own actions. But, as I said at the beginning, I am taking the easy way out. I will leave the philosophical analysis for our colleagues who are much more skilled and knowledgeable, and will appeal to a rather commonsensical basis of agreement. I think we can all accept that in at least some interesting range of cases it makes sense to talk about doing "good" and "bad," and furthermore that we all, to some degree, accept the value of "doing good."

Further, we seem to have some general understanding of what kind of "doing good" constitutes an ethical or moral act. If you take a course on programming languages, you may learn that it is "good" to have a grammar that can be parsed by an LR(1) parser, and "bad" to have ambiguous constructs. But this domain of assessment, which is proper to the computer professional, doesn't seem to have much to do with the kind of human values we are discussing here. Something is missing in the equation.

Taking the naive view again, it seems obvious that the missing element has to do with a regard for the interests of others. There is a popular refrain about acts that are "illegal, immoral or fattening." The distinction between law and morality is an important one we will not go into here. But it is clear that there is something different about "fattening." It may be stupid or unhealthy or unwise to fill myself up on chocolate bars and potato chips, but few of us would consider it unethical or immoral. In general we take moral questions to involve a potential for conflict of interests. In the case of religious morality, the "other" may be a deity. For secular ethics, it is among people (and perhaps other life forms or embodiments of intelligence).

To be fair, this is a very complicated issue, but again in the spirit of simplification, we can accept that for most of the issues that attract our interest, our actions have consequences of value to others. Consider, for example the four clusters of values that are the focus of this conference: Privacy, security, ownership and fair access. In each case it is easy to identify the different parties and potential conflicts of interest, and we do so as a matter of course in teaching about these topics.

Finally in completing this background discussion, I want to make a key point about the role of intentions. Putting it generally, the domain in which an action is assessed is not necessarily the same as the domain in which the actor interprets it. If I ask what some person is doing, you may say that she is busy "establishing an image of authority" even though she is not consciously acting in that realm. Someone can be assessed as a "great teacher" when what she sees herself doing is having an argument or commenting on a talk she is listening to.

Similarly, acts can be observed in the domain of ethics with respect to standard practices, independent of whether the person characterizes them that way. The fact that someone didn't think about the consequences of an act doesn't remove them from being subjected to moral judgment about it. In fact, we can take ethical obliviousness as a key sign of "bad" behavior.

But thinking a moment further, it also doesn't seem appropriate to assess an act as wrong if there was no background of understanding in which it could show up as such. If we now see harmful consequences of the farming practices of primitive tribes, it doesn't mean that they were acting unethically to do them.

Again, we must look to the social context. A person does not exist in a vacuum, but as part of one or more social collectivities, with their shared interpretations of actions, values and assessments. A person cannot be held responsible for considerations that lie completely outside the range of vision opened up within these backgrounds. There may often be cases where an individual rejects the current consensus of society and appeals to a larger context of human meanings and values. But in doing this he or she is responsible for participating in the social discourse and not simply ignoring the concerns of his or her co-denizens. This means that a key component of moral action is the development of understanding within a social background, which is what provides the relevant field of choice for individuals.

THREE CARTOONS FOR HOW TO "ETHIC" WELL

So far we have been taking the view of the observer: one who interprets and assesses the acts that have been done by someone (who may be him/herself) in the past. Let us shift to the view of the doer: the person who is engaged in action that can have consequences in areas of values and morals. Faced with a particular range of possibilities, how does one "ethic" well.

One of the things that becomes clear in teaching this material to students is that people come to this question with a variety of tacit pre-understandings of what we are trying to do. They draw on images that are deeply embedded in our culture, and I want to present some of them in the form of cartoons that exaggerate, but also point out some of the key features. For each of the images, we need to ask several questions:

What are the assumptions that lie behind its perspective?

What problems does it raise?

How from that perspective do we develop people's competence to act?

The Angel/Devil Debate

The cartoon shown in Figure 1 is the familiar angel/devil debate you've all seen on Saturday morning TV. A character is faced with an ethical choice and is obviously having trouble deciding what to do. Sitting on one of his shoulders is a little pointy-tailed demon whispering into his ear "C'mon, take it, he'll never know you did." And on the other shoulder a haloed cherub, sweetly whispering "You know you shouldn't

FIGURE 1: The angel/devil debate

steal." In the end one of them is brushed away with a flick of the fingers and the other dances gleefully in victory.

There are several assumptions implicit in this view of morality:

1. You know what is right or wrong in the particular case.
2. Some part of you wants to do the thing that is wrong.
3. You need to exert moral strength to overcome this impulse and do what is right.

If, in fact, this view were the whole story, then the teaching of computer ethics would be a very different matter from what we see here today. Education directed to this kind of ethical competence might include sermons, examples (stories of sinners sizzling in Hell), and practices such as self-denial. In fact much of the resistance to the teaching of computer ethics within computer science departments comes from the impression that this is what it will consist of, and a skepticism as to whether such moralizing has any positive effects.

The fallacy in the angel/devil view is obvious if we look at Bynum's characterization of the goals for teaching computer ethics. (Bynum, 1992)

1. To sensitize students to computer ethics issues
2. To provide tools and methods for analyzing cases
3. To provide practice in applying the tools and methods to actual or realistic cases
4. To develop in the student "good judgment" and "helpful intuitions" for spur-of-the-moment decision making as computer professionals and computer users

Faced with an ethically problematic situation we must first recognize it as such. It doesn't appear with angels and devils drawn in the corners, but must be seen through a background of interpretation in which ethical issues have been distinguished and made a part of our everyday discourse.

Of course I know I shouldn't kill other people. I walk around every day doing the right thing hundreds of times by not killing someone. But it isn't an ethical issue for me, it's part of the taken-for-granted background. But when I need to decide whether to build a worker-monitoring system or take research funding from a military agency, I am in the situation of debating what is in fact right and what the underlying issues are. It isn't a simple matter of steeling myself to be righteous. We must be able to recognize our specific situation as it fits into the context of issues and other cases that has shown up historically. These activities are skills to be learned and developed, not character traits like "moral will."

The Morality Computer

Having shifted the question from moral character to understanding and analysis, we find ourselves closer to the cartoon shown in Figure 2, the "morality computer."

Faced with a decision, you don't know which is the right action to take. Should you steal a horse to chase the bandit? Should you cut off life support to relieve suffering? Should you work on nuclear physics knowing the results may produce economic prosperity and also may lead to a weapon of mass destruction?

So you type the information into your morality computer, which has been programmed with the correct moral rules. It sifts the facts, weighs alternatives, makes judgments and pops out after a few microseconds with "Here's the right thing to do. . . ."

What are the assumptions lying behind this picture?

1. If you can figure out the right thing to do, then you will do it.

FIGURE 2: The morality computer

2. There is a basic set of moral rules from which to deduce the rightness of action in any given case.
3. You may know the rules but not know how to apply them in this case, and more data, knowledge, or computation is needed.

In the "morality computer" view, the problem is determining what is the ethical action. Competence consists in knowing the moral axioms and having deductive skill in applying them to cases where the question "What is the right thing to do?" comes up. This approach appeals strongly to people with a background in science and engineering. When they encounter ambivalence and ambiguity they see it as a symptom that the problem has not been well formulated, or that we do not have enough knowledge. The fix is the kind of fix that works in technical domains: get the rules right, find the correct methods of applying them, and the right answers will come out. It offers the possibility of a "technical fix to the ethics problem."

Education in this perspective, as in other forms of education in science and engineering, is a matter of giving students the right principles and giving them practice in applying them to cases. At times we hear frustration from some of the students who take our course because we are not providing them with this kind of structure: we aren't able to give them the precise rules and methods, so they can learn to plug in the data and come up with answers.

But, of course, it doesn't take sophisticated philosophical reading to recognize that despite millennia of debate, humankind doesn't seem close to reaching agreement as to the general grounding for moral reasoning at all, much less the specific rules. Within any moderately diverse group of people you will find a wide range of beliefs: Some will believe that morality is grounded in some form of divine intention, others that it is a feature of human psychology, and others that it is some kind of "optimization" principle concerned with the welfare of the species. Some will base their moral reasoning on a structure of absolute principles—do's and don'ts—while others see it as some kind of calculus of costs and benefits.

Regardless of which approach you take, no matter how certain you are about the basic principles and rules, you find yourself puzzled by individual cases. One of the things we have become painfully aware of in nearly a half century of work on artificial intelligence is that there is a huge distance from abstract rules to real situations. Before rules can be applied, there must be interpretation as to how the terms in them actually fit the situation, and in doing so there is a wide-open field of human judgment and implicit understanding that has not yielded to logical analysis.

This all may be painfully obvious to those who have been working in the field of computer ethics, but let me give an example to clarify what I am pointing at.

Assume that you accept some form of the rule "Thou shalt not steal." Then in order to apply it, you need to know when an act is "stealing." We may define it as something like "taking property that belongs to someone else, without their consent." That's a good start, but what is "property?" There are clear examples such as someone's wallet or car, but what about their "ideas." Are those the kind of things that can be property at all? Now we are in a complicated realm of definitions, which has occupied philosophers (and lawyers) for centuries. The apparently simple notion of "property" has different interpretations in different cultures, legal systems, and traditions. Further, what do we mean by someone's "consent." What kind of consent is implied by opening a box that has a label on it saying "By opening this box you hereby agree to. . . ."?

In reading the literature on computer ethics[1] we encounter many more such examples and become painfully aware of how difficult it is to come up with consistent principles and standards for applying them to cases we encounter. The point should be obvious: we are not able to provide the kind of rules and methods that work in normal science and engineering, to come up with answers to problems. The morality computer is an idealized fantasy, and can mislead us if it shifts attention to a quest for the "right answer," away from the questioning activity that is required of each of us and involves us in a never ending dialog with others.

A Troupe of Jugglers

And this leads us to the cartoon of Figure 3, a troupe of jugglers. It may seem that juggling is too frivolous an activity to be a relevant analogy, but let us look more closely at several key features of the situation.

1. Engaged Activity First we note that the jugglers are constantly engaged in action. The first two cartoons directed our attention to conscious moments of decision, and put the locus of ethical action in determining the outcome. This cartoon suggests that we are always "thrown" into acting and that the assessments of ethics apply to these actions, not just those where we stop to ponder. This is suggested by the fourth of Bynum's descriptions of what we are doing in teaching:

To develop in the student "good judgment" and "helpful intuitions" for spur-of-the-moment decision making as computer professionals and computer users.

This "spur of the moment decision making" is the basic condition of acting in the world. In fact, it often does not show up to the actor as decision making at all. We all remember the interviews with someone who has jumped into a river to save a drowning child, when the interviewer asks "What made you decide to do it?" and the hero or heroine says "Decide? I didn't decide, I just jumped in?" In order to be

FIGURE 3: A troupe of jugglers

skillful at "ethicking" we need to develop the kind of continuing judgment in action that a juggler exhibits, not just the kind of careful argument that a logician applies in constructing a proof.

2. Social Context Second, the focus is not on the isolated actions of an individual, but on the coordinated actions of the troupe as a whole. What I do makes sense—is "right" or "wrong"—in the context of what others are doing. When I look to alternatives, I need to consider not just what else I might do, but what we all might do through some kind of agreement and coordination. As I suggested earlier, this is a key feature of ethical action. If we wait until someone is put into a true moral dilemma, we may get exciting drama, but we will not further the overall pursuit of values as much as if we develop standard practices that make it natural rather than heroic to do the "right thing."

One of the most powerful ethical acts we can each do is to participate in creating a social context in which the future actions of ourselves and others are consistently in line with our values. This includes educating our colleagues and students, working to develop professional standards, exploring new technologies and identifying their consequences for values. Even though we may not face hard individual ethical decisions as part of that work, we are actively engaged in the juggling process.

3. Evolving Understandings, Practices, and Standards Finally, we recognize in a juggling troupe the eternal need to learn and change. There is no ultimate "right" way to juggle. Clearly, any form of juggling will have to conform to the laws of gravity and physical motion. Less obviously, but plausibly, there may be perceptions of what is "good" that are grounded in the nature of the human animal and will be true across cultures and times. But within this, the community evolves practices and standards in which its members are trained, and by which their actions are assessed. Part of the skill we recognize in a community of jugglers is their ability over time to recognize new possibilities, develop skills in areas that hadn't been previously explored, and be sensitive to the changing environment in which they perform.

In some cases, this may require focus on detail: evolving a new concept of just what constitutes property and ownership in a new domain such as software, interfaces and algorithms. At other times, we can make major leaps. When Gandhi proposed nonviolent civil disobedience as a way of furthering the human values he cared about, he created a new "clearing"—a new way of looking at possibilities and taking actions, which could have meaning and power in the world of the late 20th century.

Now it should be clear that I favor this third cartoon, and to be fair, we should apply the same questions as we did to the other two. First, what are the assumptions?

1. There is a social activity in which we are engaged, in which characterizations and assessments in an ethical domain can be made.

2. There is no formal system that determines what is right, but there is an ongoing structure of discourse within a community, in which rightness is the issue, and in which there are stable areas of agreement.

3. An individual is never fully aware of what is possible to do, what effects an act will have, or how it will be assessed, and nevertheless will continue to act.

In a way this is comforting and in a way it is challenging. It is comforting because it does not posit some unachievable ideal: either the ideal of always having the strength to do the right thing, or the ideal of being able to determine just what is the right thing. Instead it puts the emphasis on being committed to entering into discussion with others and to taking seriously their concerns and understandings.

At the same time, for the same reason, it is challenging. It says that we will never have the satisfaction of knowing exactly when to apply our social and ethical concerns, or being confident that "Now we have it figured out." We are always being thrown into activity which may, in unanticipated ways, have implications for values, and we are part of a community that is always responsible for evolving new understandings and ways of "juggling" to maintain those values. It's exciting, but at times can be a little shaky.

WHAT DOES IT MEAN TO *DO* ETHICS AND SOCIAL RESPONSIBILITY?

In the final section, I want to look at what all this implies for the kinds of activities engaged in by individuals and organizations committed to making connections between computing and values.

All along I have been emphasizing the "doing" side of ethics: the way in which our actions more than our deliberations speak to our values. There are three key components in "doing" ethics and social responsibility:

1. Identifying social/ethical issues
2. Entering into serious discourse about the possibilities, with yourself and with others
3. Taking actions

Each of these has both an individual and a social component. There are cases where one person alone is faced with recognizing a problem, considering what to do, and doing it. Many of the most powerful pieces of literature in our culture grip us because they let us feel what it is like to wrestle with this ultimate responsibility of the individual.

But in this paper I want to focus more on the ways in which each of these components is situated in the actions of larger groups, and in particular the kinds of organizations represented by NCCV and by CPSR.

The activities with which I am most familiar are the work over the last ten years of Computer Professionals for Social Responsibility. Initially we were motivated by what appeared to be a mad rush towards nuclear war on the part of our government. As with many groups that emerged in the early 1980s with the words "social responsibility" in their names, we felt that the only responsible thing to do in that climate was to work wherever we had the most possibility of influence, in order to avert catastrophe.

In fact, there were many clear connections between computing and nuclear war, and in particular we came to focus heavily on the proposed Strategic Defense Initiative, or Stars Wars system. As computer professionals, we were sensitized to the problems of reliability and complexity that made the plans unrealistic, and could lead both to tremendous wasted resources and to a false sense of security that could dangerously destabilize the nuclear situation.

We approached this problem in a number of ways. CPSR members, individually and together, wrote papers analyzing the problems and bringing them to the attention of policy makers, both directly and through publication in newspapers and magazines. A number of us were active in the movement to have scientists pledge not to take research money from the SDI office. It was clear that the promise of research funds was being used as a lure to get tacit approval from the scientific community for the project. One person in particular who recognized this was David Parnas, who resigned from the panel that was convened to develop an analysis of the computing requirements, and later made public his analysis of the problems and of the ways in which the Pentagon was trying to influence scientists' assessments.

I mention all this not just because it is an important piece of CPSR's history, but to illustrate the range of activities that constituted "ethicking" for people involved with the issue. Some of the actions, like Parnas' resignation, can be viewed as explicit and difficult ethical choices made by individuals, and are noteworthy as such. But the impact they had was magnified by the fact that they were part of a coordinated campaign, in the context of organizations that could bring them to public attention and connect them the basic issues being fought. If one scientist quietly decides not to do SDI research, the impact is on that person and his or her work. If a whole community is involved, not only is the political impact greater, but the thinking of the entire profession is moved. The ability to recognize the potential of issues with consequences for values and ethics is increased for all those who become party to the discussion, even if they don't take direct action at the moment.

As the imminent danger of nuclear war appeared to subside, CPSR was able to take into fuller consideration the recognition that "social responsibility" really does cover more than just preventing annihilation (even though that is certainly a good place to start). Our concerns have overlapped strongly with those that form the core of the NCCV conference: Privacy, security, ownership and fair access. For example, we recently took part in a successful nationwide campaign to block the sale of a product proposed by Lotus that would have made it possible to find out private information about millions of consumers. In that case computers played a helping role as well, with much of the education and awareness about the issue being transmitted by electronic mail.

There isn't sufficient space to go into detail here on all of the CPSR program areas, but I have recounted this history to serve as an example as we look back at the three components of "ethicking" previously mentioned:

1. Identify Social/Ethical Issues The first is to identify social and ethical issues to which computers and computing are relevant. Each of us needs to ask how our actions as a computer professional might have ethical and social consequences, and there are a variety of answers. In some cases, as with every profession, the consequences grow directly from specifics of conduct. If I am asked to write a piece of life-critical software then I must proceed in a way that is responsible: taking care as best I am able given current software practices, and being honest with the clients about the risks and limitations. If I do less, I am cheating.

In some cases, harmful consequences come not from the quality of the work itself, but from the uses to which it will be put. If I am asked to build a program that makes it possible for employers to invisibly monitor the details of a worker's activities, I need to be aware of the consequences such programs can have in the workplace. Often, there is no clear boundary between beneficial and harmful technologies. A data base system used by the FBI to track drug dealers may have a positive effect on reducing the drug traffic, but can also be used to keep track of people with unpopular political beliefs. Even then, if I see the danger as great enough (what if those beliefs are racist and violent?) it may be a net gain to society if I produce such a system. But where is the boundary?

To go a step farther, there will be cases where the work itself is positive, but there is a larger context in which it can play a harmful role. Much of the research sponsored by the Strategic Defense Initiative is of a general kind that most of us would assess as having positive applications. The developing of computer networking, although originally sponsored by military agencies, has had a tremendous affect on our ability to function as computer professionals, and is rapidly becoming available to the entire population.

But what about the larger context? When a General in the U.S. Army testifies before congress that the scientific community is in favor of the SDI plans, as evidenced by the number of them who are actively working on research for it, what consequences has our research had? When a tremendous proportion of the research in computing in general is directed by the military, what long-term effect does this have on the kind of problems that are posed, or on the role of military thinking on the direction of our national economy?[2]

There are rarely easy answers to such questions. In order to make responsible decisions about values, an individual needs a broad understanding of the consequences his or her actions might have in this overall situation. Such an understanding develops only through extended open discussion that brings in people from outside the computer profession as well as within it. It also extends beyond those who engage directly in it. The "styrofoam professor" I mentioned earlier has become conscious of issues of research funding through having interacted with me about my own rejection of military sponsorship. Even if he disagrees, the fact that the discussion exists (and has engaged his students as well) gives it a new standing in his "moral calculation."

2. Enter Into Serious Discourse about the Possibilities The second step in "ethicking" was to enter into serious discourse about the possibilities. I use the word "discourse" here instead of "thinking" to emphasize the social construction that is at the heart of decision-making even when a person does not directly enter into conversation with others. In a real, if extended sense, I am in discourse not only with the people I speak with but with those who have written the things that have influenced me, and those I have talked with, and in turn those in the future who will be influenced by what I say and write.

This includes people within the computer profession, and also in the larger society within which we work. The job of "public education" is a key part of creating the background of expectations that constitutes the fabric of ethical and social responsibility.

It should be obvious in looking at this conference, both at the participants and the materials that have been prepared and will be produced, that the weaving of the discourse is a function of groups of people who gather together (literally or through communications media) to think things through (or should we say "talk things through"?). This is a key role played by institutions and organizations devoted to issues of computers and ethics.

3. Take Actions Finally, the bottom line is the actions we take, both individually and collectively. It would be futile to try to catalog all of the different kinds of actions that have ethical implications. There are obvious individual acts such as whistle-blowing, in which a clear value statement is being made in spite of some potential damage or loss to the actor. There are many other acts, such as choosing whether or not to work on a particular project or to take a job with a company that pursues projects of social concern, in which the decision is more subtle and the ethical factor may be one of many, which cannot be untangled in looking back at why the decision was made.

As members of a profession and its professional organizations, we also take acts that are intended to affect the direction and activity of the profession as a whole. They often don't have the visceral quality of whistleblowing or rejection of funding, but they contribute to creating the atmosphere in which those acts can be given sense. These include teaching, public education, working with professional organizations, developing standards and many other forms of everyday "ethicking."

Some of these activities have an overt political objective, such as lobbying for legislation or providing expertise to lawmaking and judicial bodies. Others operate at a broader cultural level, helping people both in the profession and in the public learn to see the issues, understand their consequences and apply human values to technical decisions. Although it is easier to get an individual to consider "Is it ethical (or socially responsible) to work on a bomb project?" It is equally important and more frequently relevant to ask "Is it ethical NOT to contribute my part to being responsible for how the public and the profession guide the ways in which computers will be used?" At the CPSR annual meeting last year, the slogan on the posters was "Technology is driving the future. It's time to find out who's steering." In the end, we all have a hand on the wheel.

CONCLUSION

Looking back at the three cartoons we might come up with different views of what we are engaged in when we participate in a conference on Computing and Values. From the angel/devil perspective, we could see it as a "revival meeting" at which we encourage each other to act in accord with our values, and tell stories that will help us to be resolute and remain steadfast. From the morality computer perspective, the conference is a think tank: it is our job to come up with the right rules and descriptions that will form the knowledge base that computer professionals can use to figure out what they should do.

These both have some particle of truth, but I much prefer to see our activity as a working session in which we are engaged in juggling the issues, ideas and discussions that generate the world of possibilities in which we and our colleagues live and work. We are creating those possibilities, increasing our own understanding and commitment to their value, and building a community that can continue to create and learn in the future.

NOTES

1. For a wide variety of cases, see the papers in Ermann and Williams, Dunlop and Kling, 1991, Parker, Swope and Baker, 1990, and Johnson and Snapper, 1985. For a

list of syllabi covering a broad range of topics related to computing and ethics, see Friedman and Winograd, 1989.

2. For further discussion of the issues of military funding, see Winograd, 1989 and the papers in Mitcham and Siekevitz, 1989.

REFERENCES

1. Bynum, Terrell. 1992. "Human values and the computer science curriculum." In *Computing and Human Values*, T. Bynum, W. Maner and J. Fodor. New Haven/RCCS.

2. Bynum, Terrell W., Walter Maner, and John L. Fodor, eds. 1992. *Computing and Human Values: Proceedings of the 1991 Conference*. New Haven: Research Center on Computing and Society.

3. Dunlop, Charles and Rob Kling, eds. 1991. *Computerization and Controversy*. Boston: Academic Press.

4. Friedman, Batya and Terry Winograd, eds. 1989. *Computing and Social Responsibility: A Collection of Course Syllabi*. Palo Alto. Computer Professionals for Social Responsibility.

5. Johnson, Deborah G., and John W. Snapper. 1985. *Ethical Issues In the Use of Computers*. Belmont, CA: Wadsworth Publishing Company.

6. Mitcham, Carl, and Philip Siekevitz, eds. *Ethical Issues Associated with Scientific and Technological Research for the Military*. New York: New York Academy of Sciences.

7. Parker, Donn, Susan Swope, and Bruce Baker. 1990. *Ethical Conflicts in Information and Computer Science, Technology and Business*. Wellesley, MA: QED Information Sciences.

8. Winograd, Terry. 1989. Strategic computing research and the universities. In *Directions and Implications of Advanced Computing*, Vol. 1, ed. J. Jacky and D. Schuler, 18–32. Norwood, NJ: Ablex. Reprinted in Dunlop and Kling, 1991, 704–716.

PARAMEDIC ETHICS FOR COMPUTER PROFESSIONALS

W. Robert Collins and Keith W. Miller

Most computer professionals know that difficult ethical issues may arise in their work. We believe that these professionals want to "do the right thing." They accept their responsibilities as moral agents and they recognize that their special technical skills give them power and responsibilities. However, the will to act ethically is not sufficient; computer professionals also need skills to arrive at reasonable, ethical decisions. In this article we suggest a set of guidelines to help computer professionals consider the ethical dimensions of technical deci-sions and offer practical advice to individuals who need to make timely deci-sions in an ethical manner. We call our guidelines a paramedic method to sug-gest a medical analogy. We use our method on two realistic ethical dilemmas facing computer professionals. We gather and analyze the data and reach con-clusions much as the principals in our cases might. Our paramedic method is not a replacement for considered analysis by professional ethicists. It is a method by which computer professionals can quickly organize and view the facts of an ethical dilemma in a systematic and practical fashion.

INTRODUCTION

Most computer professionals know that difficult ethical issues may arise in their work. The following case illustrates the dilemmas which may plague the computer professional (indeed, this case may also plague the professionally trained ethicist).

Case Study Michael McFarland [1] of Boston College recently published an inter-esting ethical quandary in *IEEE Computer*:

> The past several months, George, an electrical engineer working for an aerospace con-tractor, has been the quality control manager on a project to develop a computerized con-trol system for a new military aircraft. Early simulations of the software for the control system showed that, under certain conditions, instabilities would arise that would cause the plane to crash. The software was subsequently patched to eliminate the specific prob-lems uncovered by the tests. After the repairs were made, the system passed all of the required simulation tests.
>
> George is convinced, however, that those problems were symptomatic of a funda-mental design flaw that could only be eliminated by an extensive redesign of the sys-tem. Yet, when he brought his concern to his superiors, they assured him that the prob-lems had been resolved, as shown by the tests. Anyway, to reevaluate and possibly redesign the system would introduce delays that would cause the company to miss the delivery date specified in the contract, and that would be very costly.
>
> Now, there's a great deal of pressure on George to sign off on the system and allow it to be flight tested. It has even been hinted that, if he persists in delaying release of the system, the responsibility will be taken away from him and given to someone who is more compliant. . . .
>
> What makes the situation so difficult for George is that he must choose between con-flicting duties: loyalty to self, family, employer, and superiors versus the obligation to tell the truth and to protect others from harm. . . .

We believe that most computer professionals want to "do the right thing." They accept their responsibilities as moral agents, and they recognize that their special technical skills give them power and responsibilities. However, the will to act ethi-cally is not sufficient; computer professionals also need skills to arrive at reasonable, ethical decisions. Many situations involving computing can be ethically as well as technically complex, as shown by the case presented here.

We believe that most important technical decisions have ethical implications [2], but we do not make that argument here. In this article, we suggest a method by which computer professionals can consider the ethical dimensions of technical decisions. There is a growing body of literature concerning computer ethics, but most of this literature concerns particular ethical issues, professional codes, and general exposition [3–7]. We focus instead on practical advice for individuals who need to make timely decisions, but wish to make them ethically.

Why Paramedic Ethics?

In a book on writing, Richard Lanham suggests a *paramedic method* for revising prose [8]. "I've called my basic procedure for revision a Paramedic Method because it provides emergency therapy, a first-aid kit, not the art of medicine." We think the notion of a paramedic method is also appropriate for computer ethics. In a medical emergency, we may be attended by paramedics, who are not physicians but who have been trained to administer necessary treatments. Paramedics either identify and treat relatively minor problems, or they stabilize the situation and deliver the patient to personnel and equipment better suited to the problem. Paramedic medicine is quick medicine; it should not be mistaken for shoddy medicine. Dealing with an ethical problem is in some ways similar to dealing with a medical problem. First, we must sense that something is wrong. Next we try to deal with the problem on our own. If necessary, we may seek help from knowledgeable friends.

Medicine and ethics have been studied for centuries. In both fields, traditions have evolved (some of them competing) that advise professionals and nonprofessionals how to deal with critical situations. In both fields, we often fend for ourselves unless we sense a need for professional help and are willing to invest time and money to obtain that help.

Although we do not anticipate ethical "emergencies" in which seconds are critical, we do expect that computer professionals will be faced with situations that demand timely decisions—decisions that have ethical content. A computer professional facing an ethical dilemma could use help from a consultant (or committee) with professional credentials in philosophy, computer science, economics, and business administration. It would be wonderful if this consultation could be immediately available at minimal cost. That rarely happens. Instead, by giving computer professionals practical advice on how to approach these designs, we hope that computer professionals will be better prepared to recognize ethical problems and make more ethical and more satisfying decisions on their own.

Themes in Our Paramedic Method

Our method is designed to be accessible and straightforward. The method draws upon our own views (as computer scientists) of themes in three theories of ethical analysis:

Theory	Themes
Social contract	Emphasizes negotiation and consensus agreement
Deontological	Duties, rights, obligations, and ethics of the act itself
Utilitarian	The greatest good for the greatest number ("utility")

We have used only those aspects of the theories (as we know them) that seem most appropriate for a limited analysis in a computer setting. There are several sources for readers trained in computer science, not ethics, but who are interested in further ethical study. For general introductions to ethics for professionals (not necessarily computer professionals) see references [6, 9–11]; for specific introductions to ethics and computers, see references [1, 6, 7, 12–15]. Readers interested in more analytic, philosophical treatments of ethics can start with historical sources such as [16] for social contract ethics, [17] for deontological ethics, and [18] for utilitarian ethics. For general technical references for deontological ethics see [19] and for utilitarian ethics see [20].

Our method reflects our belief that power relationships are central in many problems involving computers [6]. The method also encourages a decision maker to consider *all* the people who will be significantly affected by any potential decision, especially the most vulnerable.

We present our method in an algorithmic form. Computer professionals are familiar with algorithmic forms, but the issues considered within the forms are not nearly as familiar. We hope that the combination of a comfortable form and a novel content will invite computer professionals to view their own overly familiar ethical dilemmas in a new way. We recognize the danger of seeking a meticulously specified, quick-fix solution to complex ethical problems. However, our experience using our method with computer professionals and computer science students has convinced us that these people are well aware of the limitations of a paramedic method. Many are enthusiastic about finding a way to organize their thinking about computer ethics.

A PARAMEDIC METHOD FOR COMPUTER PROFESSIONALS

For the remainder of this article, we assume that the user of our method is a computer professional who faces one or more difficult ethical decisions involving some situation. There is a set of parties—people, corporations, and possibly society—also involved in this situation. The user is a special involved party since the user will have to decide on one of a number of alternatives concerning the situation. We use two terms, opportunity and vulnerability, to indicate what involved parties can gain or lose from alternatives. Generally, opportunities and vulnerabilities arise from human values such as enough pay to support one's family (i.e., security), pride in producing good work, making a profit, the joy of programming, a good reputation, and so on. The potential to make a larger salary is a security opportunity; the potential to lose one's job is a security vulnerability.

One value that occurs frequently in computer ethics cases is power. The computer has empowered individuals who control information more than they have been empowered in the past, due in part to the pervasive nature of computers and their logical malleability [7]. These individuals have power opportunities. A common vulnerability in computer cases, especially for the least privileged, is the potential loss of power. For example, data entry employees whose every keystroke is monitored by a computer program lose the power to manage their own rates and styles of work. Furthermore, this low-level intrusion into their workspaces causes undue stress and anxiety. In another example, consumers calling mass marketers may lose their ability to bargain fairly if the marketer employs technology such as caller ID and computerized data bases to gain informational advantage over the consumer.

An obligation is something to which we are bound or compelled and also the duty, promise, contract, etc., which binds us. Obligations arise from explicit or implicit contracts (for example, the obligations employees and employers have to each other), acceptable legal and moral standards (the obligation not to steal), and personal standards (the obligation to do a conscientious job).

A right is something we are entitled to have or receive. In some sense, rights are complements of obligations. If I have an obligation to you for something, then you have a right to receive that something from me. Some rights are granted globally, which means that they come from society in general, and society has an obligation to respect (empower, safeguard, guarantee) these rights.

Our method bears both a superficial and a deeper resemblance to the waterfall model for the software life cycle. On a superficial level, users of our method proceed sequentially through a series of phases. Each phase uses the previous one. However, as in software development, the process is dynamically reversible. Working through our method may trigger associated aspects not recognized initially. Users should iterate through the phases—expanding the number of people considered, expanding the aspects of the problem taken into consideration, and expanding the number of potential alternatives to examine—until the analysis stabilizes.

Phase 1: Gathering Data

In this phase, the user determines the alternatives, the parties, and the relations among the parties. The ethical dilemma is usually focussed on some decision the user must make. Therefore, a natural starting point is to list all the alternatives available to the user. From these, the user can ascertain the parties involved in the situation—the people or organizations directly affected by any alternative.

In the final step of this phase, the user determines (for the situation) the obligation and right relations between all possible pairs of parties by analyzing the relationship of each party with each of the parties. This requires a nested iteration through all of the parties for each party; that is, for each party, the user analyzes the obligations that party has to each of the other parties and the rights that party receives from each of the other parties.

Different analysts may generate different set of rights and obligations. Our individual values result in different perspectives when determining and weighing conflicting rights and obligations. For this reason, we have carefully refrained from defining ethical terms analytically. Our method is not intended to establish or define ethical norms; it is an aid for computer professionals in organizing their own moral values.

We have found it helpful to use pictorial representations and a blackboard when determining parties and their obligations. Each party corresponds to a vertex in a graph, and interrelations among the parties are edges between vertices. Adding a new party corresponds to adding a new vertex and the analogous set of new edges. An edge may connect a vertex to itself; this corresponds to a party's obligation to itself.

Tips and hints

- Another way of determining obligations and rights is to list, for each party, the rights and obligations of that party that are related to the situation, without regard to other parties. Then, for each party, determine to which party the obligation is due and from which party the right is owed. Recall that in general, one party's right is another party's obligation. Look at pairs of parties not yet related to each other and check whether either one has an obligation to the other. Lastly, be sure to check for obligations a party may have to itself. At this stage it may be necessary to add more parties to complete the obligation or right relation domain.

- Always keep in mind that the user is one of the parties.
- Try to restrict the obligations and rights to those germane to the situation.
- We have found that we typically underestimate the number of alternatives and overestimate the number of parties and the relevant relations between them. Alternatives are added in Phase 3; unnecessary parties and obligations become apparent in Phase 2.

Phase 2: Analyzing Data

In the second phase, the users assesses how the alternatives affect each of the parties. For each alternative, the user iterates through each of the parties. For each party, the user determines how the alternative can improve the party's lot, or make it worse. These are the opportunities and vulnerabilities for the party engendered by the alternative. Again, for each alternative, the user iterates through each of the parties to determine, for each party, how the alternative is related to that party's rights and obligations. Does the alternative violate or reinforce an obligation? A right? All parties, including the user, are analyzed in this fashion.

We find it helpful to use matrices whose columns correspond to alternatives, and whose rows correspond to parties. The entry for a column and a row corresponds to the impact the alternative has on the party. As before, while filling in entries the user may uncover new parties or create additional alternatives. If a new party is uncovered, then the user completes the first part of this phase and then adds a new row to the matrix. If an additional alternative is created, the user adds a new column to the matrix.

Tips and hints

- Another way of approaching the issue of opportunities and vulnerabilities is to ask if an alternative enhances, maintains, or diminishes a value of the party. Enhancing a value corresponds to an opportunity; diminishing a value corresponds to a vulnerability.
- Check to see if an alternative enhances or diminishes the power of the party.
- It can be the case that one party's opportunity comes at the expense of another party. In that case, the second party should have a vulnerability.

Phase 3: Negotiating an Agreement

In this phase we apply social contract ethics to create new alternatives. Sometimes the user can create new solutions to the situation by trying to negotiate an agreement from the perspectives of all the parties. These solutions seem to be hidden from the user since they usually require cooperation among the parties, and the user sees the quandary from an individual viewpoint.

The goal of applied social contract ethics is that all parties come to a consensus agreement. The user is the only party present in our method, so the user has to pretend to be all the other parties, playing the role of each of the parties, so to speak, in order to come to an agreement. For an agreement to be fair and acceptable to all the parties, the user must try to make the agreement assuming that the user could become any one of the affected parties. (Rawls [16] calls this fiction "situated behind a veil of ignorance.") For each party and for each potential agreement, the user asks, "If I were this party, could I live with this agreement? Would I choose this agreement?" If no agreement can be made acceptable to all, then the process fails. New consensus agreements are added to the existing list of alternatives already constructed and reanalyzed according to the data gathering phase.

Tips and hints

- People fear a bad situation more than they desire a good one; the one party whose concurrence is critical is the one made most vulnerable by the agreement. Special and careful consideration should be given to the least privileged party.
- In particular, pay attention to the party that loses the most power in an agreement.

Phase 4: Judging Data

In this phase, the user applies parts of deontological and utilitarian ethics to ethical issues in the computer profession. We give guidelines for judging the data with both of these ethical theories, simplifying and abridging the theories to fit our notion of a paramedic method.

Deontological Ethics Deontological ethics stresses the decision itself. Does it violate rights? Does it meet obligations? Does it allow parties to carry out their duties? Each alternative has some bearing on the rights and obligations of the parties; for some parties the effects of an alternative might be good, for other parties the effects of the same alternative might be bad. Moreover, even when two alternatives affect all parties in the same direction (the same rights violated; the same obligations missed), they may not affect all parties with the same intensity. What we suggest is that each alternative be compared with the other alternatives on how well the alternative meets obligations and preserves rights, on how little the alternative forfeits obligations and tramples rights, and on how closely the decisions leading to the alternative adhere to the user's personal moral standards. Then the user ranks the alternatives from best to worst—for this particular situation.

It may be difficult or impossible to come up with a linear ordering; a partial ordering will still have utility. Rankings may also differ among different analysts: differing users may weigh the effects of an alternative differently or place differing importance on the same obligations and rights. (Even such a clearly defined question as whether hackers should go to jail leads to diverse answers from people who may all consider themselves moral [15].) If there is considerable difficulty in comparing the moral values of alternatives, it may be that deontological analysis is not appropriate for the problem. Nonetheless partial information, like a clearly least ethical decision, may prove valuable in the end. In some cases, codes of professional conduct may provide some guidelines in ordering the values.

Utilitarian Ethics Utilitarian ethics stresses the results of the decision. The alternative that leads to the most opportunity and least vulnerability for the most parties is the best alternative. Therefore, for each alternative, the user analyzes the effect it has on opportunities and vulnerabilities. In some sense, the user is computing a "score" for each alternative by "adding" the opportunities and "subtracting" the vulnerabilities. Then the alternatives are ranked from highest to lowest score. The same comments that apply to the rankings in the deontological case also apply here: it may be just as difficult to compare opportunities and vulnerabilities for different parties under different alternatives as it is to compare obligations and rights.

Making a Final Decision In the best of all possible worlds, a single alternative stands out as viable and as most appropriate. Otherwise, the user exercises judgment to select an alternative that does well in the analyses. Sometimes the user can create a new alternative which shares features of the best existing alternatives. In the case when there is an unresolvable conflict, at least the user will be consciously and systematically working from a reasonable set of data.

The user may fall into some typical pitfalls when trying to deal with value-laden personal decisions. Our method encourages rational analysis, and so the user should avoid using nonethical reasoning based solely on

- emotion
- what the user's conscience says
- what the user intuits
- the law
- religious faith
- the majority position.

However, the user should not be afraid of a compelling conclusion suggested by emotion, conscience, intuition, the law, or religion. The conclusion may be valid, though the reasoning is not apparent. We suggest that the user analyze the conclusion dispassionately to find out why it seems so appealing.

GEORGE REVISITED

In this section and the next we apply our method to the case described in the Introduction. We do not mean to imply that our analysis is definitive. We draw on our own values to analyze George's quandary, and we expect users to draw on their own values. We present our personal analysis to show how our method works.

Phase 1: Gathering Data

Recall MacFarland's case of George, the quality control manager who hesitates to sign off on the computerized control system. George must decide between signing off or delaying approval. In either case he may decide to blow the whistle (Figure 1).

MacFarland created this case to encourage computer professionals to "act together to make sure the norms and structures that support ethical activity are in place" [1]. As a consequence, MacFarland concludes that George has no good decision available to him. While we agree that George's position is difficult, we use our method to explore the alternatives George can select among and the effects of these alternatives.

Relations Among the Parties The obligations among the parties are summarized in Figure 2. George, at the center of this dilemma, has obligations to all the other parties. George owes himself and his dependents financial and emotional support. He also must maintain his personal integrity. George has important obligations to the company; he should be a conscientious, loyal employee; generally, George is paid to do what his supervisor requests, and by accepting his pay he accepts an obligation to follow these requests. As a citizen in a position of some authority, George has obligations to society to be honest in his evaluations and to protect society from harm. George also has a direct and personal responsibility to the test pilot who will fly the plane in question: although the test pilot expects some risk, George's honest evaluation can help the test pilot give an accurately informed consent to the pending flight. Since a plane crash could injure people on the ground too, George has a responsibility to society to help prevent a crash.

Just as George has an obligation to be a good employee, the company has an obligation to be a good employer, to avoid making unreasonable demands on George, and to pay him for his work. The company is obliged to take reasonable precautions for the test pilot's safety. In turn, the pilot has an obligation to do his job. Finally, the contract between society (i.e., its governmental agency) and the company is driving the development of the airplane: the company is committed to produce the airplane on time, within budget, and without endangering the public. Society agrees to pay the company for this work. Like George, the company has an obligation to avoid harming people in a crash.

Phase 2: Analyzing Data

Opportunities and Vulnerabilities For the two decisions George will make, Table 1 shows the benefits each party may gain and Table 2 shows the risks. By signing off, George will continue the benefits of his job (at least in the short term), but we anticipate a loss of self respect and possible long-term liabilities if the test flight causes a disaster.

The company has important opportunities and vulnerabilities whether George signs off or not. If George signs off and the flight is a success, the company stands to gain. If George signs off and the flight is a disaster, the company could have sig-

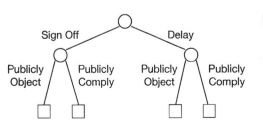

FIGURE 1: George's alternatives.

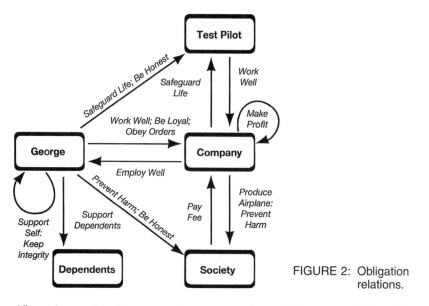

FIGURE 2: Obligation relations.

nificant losses. In either case, the company loses if George publicly objects to the company's actions.

Society may get a plane more quickly and cheaply if the company ignores George. On the other hand, society may also get a disaster or a substandard plane if George's criticisms are not taken into account. Of course, unless George publicly objects, society may never know of his suspicions about the plane.

Finally, George's dependents share George's vulnerabilities and opportunities. At this stage in the data gathering, listing the dependents as a separate entity seems superfluous; it might be just as valid to include George's dependents as part of George's node in our original graph. However, we suggest that the decision maker always be a separate, independent node.

Obligations Affected by George's Alternatives For each alternative, the user analyzes how the various obligations are affected. Table 3 summarizes our analysis. A plus (+) sign indicates that the alternative fulfills the obligation listed; a minus sign

TABLE 1.   Potential Opportunities Created by George's Two Decisions

	SIGN OFF	DELAY	PUBLICLY COMPLY	PUBLICLY OBJECT
George		Gain self-esteem		Gain self-esteem
Company	Project completion	Avoid disaster		
Society	Get airplane	Get better airplane eventually		Gain information about airplane
Test Pilot				Gain information about airplane
Dependents				

TABLE 2.   Potential Vulnerabilities Created by George's Two Decisions

	SIGN OFF	DELAY	PUBLICLY COMPLY	PUBLICLY OBJECT
George	Loss of self-esteem; personal liability to society, test pilot	Lose job	Loss of self-esteem	Lose job; bad reputation as whistle blower; personal liability to company
Company	Personal liability to society, test pilot	Loss of profit; liability for being late		Loss of profit; bad publicity
Society	Harm to people; bad product	Late product	Ignorance of problem	
Test Pilot	Lose life; injury		Ignorance of problem	
Dependents		Loss of support		Loss of support

(−) indicates that the alternative fails to fulfill the obligation. When an alternative fulfills some aspects of the obligation but not others, or when the obligation may be satisfied for a time but not always, we indicate this mixed result with the "±" symbol.

Some obligations interact with these alternatives in a complicated fashion. By refusing to sign off immediately on the plane, George may temporarily safeguard the pilot's life; however, if the company replaces George and the test goes on anyway (without any improvements), the test pilot is still in danger. In a personal sense, George has fulfilled the "letter of the law" with respect to this obligation; however, his delay may not safeguard the pilot.

George's obligations to the company are particularly interesting in the first decision. The company hired George to evaluate software; in doing this task to the best of his ability, George wants to delay the test flight. However, the company gives a conflicting order to George to abandon his responsibilities. This is the basis of the no-win situation MacFarland justly condemns.

Although none of the alternatives fulfills all of George's obligations, there is one alternative that stands out as particularly disadvantageous to George. If George signs off on the plane and later publicly objects, he loses his integrity initially and only regains part of it later by publicly objecting after his initial decision. By publicly objecting, he risks losing his job and he violates his loyalty obligation to the company; he cannot necessarily stop the test anyway. Thus, signing off and then publicly objecting seems to be the least useful alternative for George. The company's best interests are not so clear. If George is wrong, and the plane is ready for testing, then signing off is advantageous for the company. However, if George is right about the plane, his delay could save them from abrogating many obligations. On the other hand, the company fulfills its obligations to itself and society much more easily if George keeps his objections private.

Other obligations are clear from the table. Note that society does not admit any

TABLE 3. Obligations Affected by George's Two Decisions

	SIGN OFF	DELAY	PUBLICLY COMPLY	PUBLICLY OBJECT
George				
to George	Keep integrity − Support self +	Keep integrity + Support self −	Keep integrity − Support self +	Keep integrity + Support self −
to Company	Work well − Obey orders +	Work well + Obey orders −	Be loyal +	Be loyal −
to Society	Prevent harm −	Prevent harm ±	Be honest −	Be honest +
to Test Pilot	Safeguard life −	Safeguard life ±	Be honest −	Be honest −
to Dependents	Support family +	Support family −	Support family +	Support family −
Company				
to Company	Make profit +	Make profit −	Make profit +	Make profit +
to Society	Prevent harm − Produce plane +	Prevent harm ± Produce plane −	Produce plane +	Produce plane −
to Test Pilot	Safeguard life −	Safeguard life +		
Society				
to Company	Pay fee +	Pay fee ±	Pay fee +	Pay fee −

+, Alternative fulfills obligation.
−, Alternative fails to fulfill obligation.
±, Alternative fulfills some but not all aspects of obligation.

bligations to support George, no matter what he decides—the very point McFarland
nakes.

hase 3: Negotiating an Agreement

Ve imagine that all of the parties have gathered together in a negotiating session to
ecide what George should do. In these negotiations, the parties' own identities and
nterests are hidden from themselves behind a veil of ignorance. The negotiators have
eneral knowledge of the situation, but are not aware of which party is which. The
egotiators must try to reason to a fair conclusion, with the fear that any of them may
e the most vulnerable party. Our job is to make this negotiation plausible.

In this situation, we expect the parties to recognize that George and the test
nlot are the most vulnerable parties. The test pilot's danger is immediate and physi-
al: if the plane behaves badly enough, the test pilot could die. This vulnerability is
f a unique type, however: the test pilot's job is to take risks with unproven aircraft.
would seem that if the test pilot knew of George's objections, knew how the plane
ould be affected if George's worst scenario came true, and decided to fly anyway,
nen the pilot would agree that George was free to sign off on the plane.

While the test pilot may accept his vulnerabilities when his informed consent
obtained, society cannot protect itself so simply. Society is concerned with ensur-
ng that innocent people are not harmed by an airplane crash and also getting value
or its money—an airplane that performs satisfactorily. The second objective, while
nportant, is not so immediate as the first. An agreement by society to initiate air-
lane flights over desolate areas (as was done for the stealth bomber) may be suffi-
ient counterweight to George's objections. Meanwhile, to safeguard that George's
bjections are met, society could insist that George be allowed to prove or disprove
is assertion. Whether this could be accomplished with outside consultants or with
ne company assigning extra manpower to George are negotiable issues.

Under our veil of ignorance, no party would want to see George severely
njured, but the company's policies are making it inevitable that George will be
njured. The only way the social contract option could work is if George has differ-
nt choices, and this is entirely dependent on the company.

George wants to do the right thing. He does not want an unsafe plane harming
eople during a test flight; he does not want a bad product ultimately delivered to
ociety. He would like to keep his job. Refusing to sign off will not achieve any of
is goals. A public objection will almost certainly cost him his job. However, a pub-
c objection may not be necessary to protect the test pilot and society; they might be
atisfied with informed consent. According to the vulnerability table, the company
ill lose if George objects publicly and the company could be liable to serious con-
equences if the plane malfunctions. If the company could support George with
nformed consent, then it is possible that George could sign off, assuming that the test
nlot and society were satisfied with informed consent.

The social contract analysis affords George a fifth alternative: George signs off
n the airplane. In return, the company agrees to inform the test pilots about possi-
le airplane malfunctioning. The company holds George responsible for determining
rhat bad behavior there could be. The company will probably have to agree to extra
nticements for the test pilots. In addition, the company agrees to modify testing
olices to minimize incidental damage to people and property from a potential crash.
astly, the company agrees to inform the buying agency about George's objections

and tries to resolve the objections one way or another. We call this alternative "th social contract alternative" and analyze it like the other alternatives (Table 4).

Phase 4: Judging the Data

Deontological Analysis We've already discussed how various alternatives affec obligations. Of all alternatives, the social contract alternative comes closest to fulfill ing all obligations. However, this alternative requires the company's cooperation. I

TABLE 4.   Effects of George's Social Contract Alternative

	OPPORTUNITIES	VULNERABILITIES	OBLIGATIONS	
George	Some gain of self-esteem: some chance of keeping job	Reputation as trouble maker	To George	
			Keep integrity	+
			Support self	±
			To Company	
			Work well	+
			Be loyal	±
			Obey orders	±
			To Society	
			Be honest	+
			Prevent harm	+
			To Test Pilot	
			Safeguard life	±
			Be honest	+
			To Dependents	
			Support family	±
Company	Project completion	Some chance of late product; some chance of loss of profit	To George	
			Employ well	±
			To Company	
			Make profit	±
			To Test Pilot	
			Safeguard life	±
			To Society	
			Prevent harm	+
			Produce airplane	+
Society	Gain information about airplane; timely, good product	Chance of late product	To Company	+
			Pay fee	
Test Pilot	Gain information about airplane	Some chance of loss of life, injury		
Dependents		Some chance of loss of support		

+, Alternative fulfills obligation.
±, Alternative fulfills some but not all aspects of obligation.

the company refuses to compromise, it is impossible for George to fulfill all his obligations to the company, and he must look elsewhere to weigh the alternatives.

If George has some confidence that he can support himself and his family with a new job, his obligations to society and his own integrity would seem to dominate in this analysis. Assuming that he decides to delay the test flight and the company follows through on its threat to replace George, then George can either acquiesce or blow the whistle. Again, assuming he can support himself and his dependents, blowing the whistle fulfills important obligations to society and to George. After being fired, George would have little responsibility to be loyal to the company.

If George has serious doubts about his ability to support himself if he is fired, the decision to delay and blow the whistle becomes difficult indeed. George must weigh his need for personal integrity and his obligation to society and the test pilot against his chances of keeping his job after making the two decisions. The analysis suggests that signing off and then publicly objecting is the least desirable alternative. The delay/publicly object alternative is the most honest approach, but endangers his financial situation the most. The sign off/publicly comply alternative fulfills financial obligations, but sacrifices integrity. The delay/publicly comply alternative has advantages only if it reduces the possibility that George will be fired.

Depending on George's judgments about the possibilities of being fired and the probability of a disaster if his objections are not dealt with, he may be able to choose one of the alternatives. Nonetheless, if the company will not compromise, the deontological analysis does not reveal a clear winner among the alternatives.

Utilitarian Analysis Utilitarian analysis, like deontological analysis, requires George to make significant subjective judgments. How unsafe is the plane in its current state? Is it likely that his delay will result in any significant improvements in the plane? Will he recover financially from being fired? Will society force the company into responsible actions if George goes public with his objections? How likely is it that George's objections are valid? Each of these questions must be answered before George can make a utilitarian calculation to determine the greatest good.

For example, if George is convinced that the company will do exactly the same thing no matter what he does, the sign off/publicly comply option may be the best alternative. If the test results in disaster, society will recognize problems exist and force the company to make the kinds of changes George advocates. If the tests prove George wrong, then George will (presumably) still have his job. By staying in the company, George retains the opportunity to improve the plane in the future. Being disloyal, either within the company or by publicly blowing the whistle, may remove George from a position in which he can bring about positive change.

As with the deontological analysis, the utilitarian analysis identifies the social contract alternative as probably the best. However, if the company refuses to compromise, the utilitarian analysis suggests that staying in the company is a better idea than the deontological analysis indicated.

George's Final Decisions As mentioned above, the social contract analysis strongly suggests that George seek an alternative not originally given in the problem description and actively try to persuade the company to compromise. Failing this, George must decide which of his bad alternatives is the least objectionable.

George's first decision is to sign off on the plane or delay the test flight by refusing to sign off. Although the utilitarian argument seems the most immediately practical, we suspect that George should not sign off on the plane. The personal and professional obligation to tell the truth is of prime importance in this case. The utilitarian argument requires many assumptions, none of which George can guarantee in advance. On the other hand, the appeal to honesty is a strong argument regardless of the eventual outcomes (which are uncertain). Perhaps George can make some accommodation so that he can step aside gracefully without lying. But if the company insists that George sign his name to statement he does not believe, we think George should resist.

Once George declares his intention to not sign off, the company will have to respond. If the company does not fire George, the company could either bypass George or try to work with him on meeting his objections or convincing him that they are unfounded. As long as the company deals with George and society in good faith, we think George should honor his obligations to the company by doing his job conscientiously and not going public with his objections.

If the company fires George, or if the company ignores his objections and tries to conceal facts about the plane, then George is faced with a second dilemma: should he blow the whistle? Since George has not lied, he has essentially fulfilled his central personal and professional obligations. However, George may feel as a citizen and a human being that he should try to stop the test. If he feels this strongly enough, he may decide to publicly object to the company's behavior. In so doing, George puts himself, his dependents, and the company at risk.

We believe that such an action, though laudable, is not required of George by our analysis. If George blows the whistle publicly, we would label that action heroic. Essentially, George would have to trade his own well being and that of his dependents against the potential harm to society, and George would have to abandon his relationship with the company. Our analysis does not preclude that decision, but it also does not require George to make it.

We do not claim that our conclusion is the only one justified in George's situation. However, by using the paramedic method we can make our assumptions and reasoning explicit and well organized. Others can examine our judgments and adjust them according to their own values and insights. . . .

CONCLUSION

We are convinced that many technical decisions have ethical dimensions that should not be ignored. We hope this method, and subsequent ideas from others, will encourage computer professionals to make responsible, thorough inquiries into the ethical issues they encounter.

One way to think of our method is as a series of questions about an ethical decision:

- Who is involved?
- What are possible solutions to the problem at hand?
- What can everyone involved agree on?
- What is the best solution according to the information now available?

Table 5 summarizes the four steps that reflect these questions.

Several disclaimers apply to this (or any) effort to "popularize" the application of ethical principles. First, our method is not a substitute for extended study in ethics.

TABLE 5. Abbreviated Paramedic Method for Computer Professionals

Computer professional X faces a difficult ethical decision involving situation S.
Step 1. Gather data systematically about the parties.
- Determine the set of all possible alternatives.
- Determine the set of all involved parties.
- For each pair (p, q) of involved parties (including $X = p$ and $X = q$)
  - identify those obligations of p to q that are related to S;
  - identify those rights of p from q that are related to S.

Step 2. Analyze the data systematically for the alternatives.
For each alternative a and for each party p (including $X = p$)
  - determine the new opportunities for p that a introduces;
  - determine the new vulnerabilities for p that a introduces;
For each alternative a, for each party p, and for each of p's obligations and rights
  - determine how a affects p's obligation;
  - determine how a affects p's right.

Step 3. Try to negotiate a social contract agreement on a.
- Each party is represented at a negotiating session by X.
- X pulls the veil of ignorance over each of his or her identities.
- X tries to effect a consensus agreement a among all parties (X is careful about the party with greatest vulnerability).
- If X is successful and if the alternative a is new, then add a to the set of alternatives and redo Step 2 for a.

Step 4. Judge each of the alternatives, according to ethical theories.
- For each alternative a
  - select the best deontological alternative a.
    - Weigh the relative importance of the rights and obligations.
    - Compare a with X's standards.
- select the best utilitarian alternative a with maximum score [(sum of opportunities) − (sum of vulnerabilities)].
- select the best alternative.
- if no one alternative stands out, then create an alternative from the best features of existing alternatives.

We hope that people who use the method will become motivated to study ethics, although this study is not required to use the method.

Our method is not a code for professional conduct. As Deborah Johnson [6] has pointed out, professional codes serve many purposes other than ethical inquiry. Our method does not establish standards of behavior, nor does it list particular rights and obligations. Instead, the method helps computer professionals generate possible solutions and choose between those solutions.

Our method is not an automated system for ethical analysis. We designated our method "paramedic" because there are tradeoffs between brevity and universality, between accessibility and accuracy, and between immediate application and considered theory. This method tries to avoid the appearance of a technical "quick fix" to inherently subjective and difficult problems. Ethical problems have unquantifiable nuances and we do not wish to suggest otherwise [21]. We do not claim that ethical problems are amenable to unequivocal algebraic solutions; however, we do claim that ethical problems in computer science can be approached rationally and systematically. We hope this method helps to guide computer professionals in this difficult task.

NOTES

1. McFarland, M. C. 1990. Urgency of ethical standards intensifies in computer community. *IEEE Computer* 23: 77–81.

2. Miller, K. 1988. Integrating ethics into the computer science curriculum. *Comp. Sci. Educ.* 1: 37–52.

3. Horning, J., M. Moore, and D. Weiss. 1985. Computing in support of battle management. *Software Engineering Notes* 10: 24–29.

4. ACM code of professional conduct. 1980. *Commun. ACM* 23: 425.

5. Institute of Electrical and Electronics Engineers, IEEE code of ethics. 1975. *IEEE Spectrum* 12: 65.

6. Johnson, D. 1985. *Computer Ethics*. Englewood Cliffs, New Jersey: Prentice-Hall.

7. Moor, J. 1985. What is computer ethics? *Metaphilosophy* 16, 266–275.

8. Lanham, R. A. 1979. *Revising Prose*, p. viii. New York: Charles Scribner's Sons.

9. Lebacqz, K. 1986. *Six Theories of Justice*. Minneapolis: Augsburg Publishing House.

10. Beauchamp, T. L. and J. F. Childress. 1989. *Principles of Biomedical Ethics*. 3d ed. New York: Oxford University Press.

11. Baum, R. 1980. *Ethics and Engineering Curricula*. Hastings-on-Hudson, New York: The Hastings Center.

12. Shinn, R. 1986. Ethics in an age of computers. In *New Ethics for the Computer Age?*, ed. A. Parent et. al., 17–33. Washington, DC: The Brookings Institute.

13. Johnson, D. and J. Snapper. 1985. *Ethical Issues in the Use of Computers*, Belmont, California: Wadsworth Publishing Company.

14. Bynum, T., ed. 1985. Special issue on computer ethics, *Metaphilosophy* 16: 263–377.

15. Hitt, J. and P. Tough. 1990. Is computer hacking a crime? *Harper's* 80 (March): 45–57.

16. Rawls, J. 1971. *A Theory of Justice*. Cambridge, MA: Harvard University Press.

17. Kant, I. 1969. *Foundations of the Metaphysics of Morals*. Indianapolis: Bobbs-Merrill.

18. Mill, J. S. 1902. *Utilitarianism*. Chicago: University of Chicago Press.

19. Fried, C. 1978. *Right and Wrong*. Cambridge, MA: Harvard University Press.

20. Bayles, M. D., ed. 1968. *Contemporary Utilitarianism*. New York: Anchor Books.

21. Mahowald, M. B. and A. P. Mahowald. 1982. Should ethics be taught in a science course? *The Hastings Center Report* 12: 18.

CHAPTER TWO

Crime, Abuse, and Hacker Ethics

When people hear the phrase "computer ethics," they generally think of behavior such as making illegal copies of proprietary software or gaining unauthorized access to computer systems or planting viruses and worms. In this chapter we focus in particular on unauthorized access and disruptive behaviors such as virus launching. However, it should be noted that the territory that we are calling "crime, abuse, and hacker ethics" is not so well defined and the issues are not easily separated from topics we take up in other chapters.

Several scholars working in the field of computer ethics (including one of the editors of this volume) used to consider unauthorized access and illegal copying out of the purview of computer ethics. They thought there were no interesting ethical issues here because "crime is crime." What else is there to say but that illegal entry is wrong or that making a copy of something which the law prohibits one from copying is wrong. On closer examination, however, it turns out that there are a number of important issues here. In particular there are ethical questions that precede and follow from declaring some form of behavior illegal. What should the rules be? What forms of behavior should we criminalize? What role should intention to do harm play in either the determination of guilt or the assignment of punishment? Are the forms of behavior that we decide to prohibit wrong independent of being illegal or do they become immoral only because they are made illegal? What punishment is fair for breaking these laws? How far should criminal justice agencies be permitted to go to enforce these laws?

The reader will quickly become aware that the issues addressed in this chapter are closely tied to those in subsequent chapters, most notably the chapters on property and privacy. Moreover, since all of the behavior we are concerned about here involves navigating through datalines, the issues here are inextricably tied to the issues presented in Chapter 7, The Networked World. In this chapter we decided to take up issues having to do with disruptive behavior that is generally thought to be criminal. In Chapter 7, we take up a broader set of issues including access, civil liberties on-line, and the social implications of a national information infrastructure.

As already indicated, then, the focus in this chapter will be on behavior that is considered disruptive and undesirable. Often this behavior is called "hacking" and those who engage in such behavior are called "hackers." However, it should be noted that the term "hacking" used to have a much more neutral, if not positive, connotation, in referring to those who were very enthusiastic about computing, spent hours sitting at their keyboards, and were able to accomplish clever and creative feats with computers.

We begin this chapter with the case of Robert T. Morris which involved the release of a worm that disrupted a large number of computer systems across the country. The Robert T. Morris case is particularly noteworthy because of the scale of disruption it caused and because of the widespread public attention it received. The press caught onto the story and publicized it across the world, making it the first case to draw widespread public attention to the vulnerability of our computer systems to sabotage. The case is also noteworthy because it was the first to be successfully prosecuted under the Computer Fraud and Abuse Act of 1986. The account that is provided here is the Report to the Provost of Cornell University on an Investigation Conducted by The Commission of Preliminary Enquiry. Robert T. Morris was a graduate student in Cornell's Computer Science Program and the worm was fairly quickly traced back to Cornell. The Commission's Report provides an accurate account of what happened, identifies a number of important issues, and reveals the complexities of how a university must struggle with its responsibilities for computing on campus. (Note: Along with this reading you might also read the case reading in Chapter 7, the case of Craig Neidorf. Neidorf was accused of unauthorized access and copying proprietary information. He made this information available to others through an on-line "hacker" bulletin board.)

In the next reading, "Rogue Computer Programs and Computer Rogues: Tailoring the Punishment to Fit the Crime," Anne Branscomb fills in our picture of the problem by describing some of the recent outbreaks of, what she has labeled, "rogue behavior," and by identifying types of perpetrators and motives. She provides a thorough review of state and federal legislation addressing the problem, and points out the problems with and alternatives to this legislation.

In the early days of computing, before cases had been prosecuted and new state and federal statutes had been created, there was some ambiguity about what behavior was "illegal." (It was unclear whether copying of programs or use of someone else's computer account or files was "illegal" or even immoral.) Moreover, the popular press and other media expressed a significant degree of ambivalence about "hackers." They seemed often to be portrayed as heroes, because they were so clever and because they "beat the system" with their wits—for example, by breaking into the computer systems of big corporations or government agencies. In the last decade much, though not all, of that ambivalence seems to have disappeared, perhaps, because much of the behavior has been clearly defined as criminal (either by extension of old laws or creation of new ones).

In any case, it is important to remember that we can always ask why a certain type of behavior was declared illegal and whether the decision to make it so was the best decision. Is breaking into a computer system, for example, immoral in itself or only immoral because it is illegal. Would we be better off restructuring the way in which computing is done in our society? To keep such questions in mind, we have included several pieces that represent the perspective of those who do not like the rules as they have come to be established. The first is a letter by Richard Stallman which appeared in the *Communications of the ACM* in 1984. (Richard Stallman is well known for his zealous defense of free software and his project to develop GNU, an operating system that will be compatible with Unix but will not be copyrighted. Stallman is also the recipient of the prestigious MacArthur Foundation award.) While Stallman does not defend unauthorized access or virus launching, he argues that the nature of the computer technology is such that rules other than those that have developed might serve us just as well or better; that is, they might make better use of the technology.

The piece by Stallman is followed by an interview by Dorothy Denning of Frank Drake, a well-known computer hacker. We have included this interview to give the reader a sense of what the counterculture of computing is about. Drake gives us a very different view of one's aims and responsibilities in using computer systems.

One of the important tasks of the field of computer ethics is to critically examine activities surrounding computing, to look at the arguments for and against various rules, to consider the arguments defending hacking behavior, as well as the arguments against. Those who engage in disruptive behavior—gaining unauthorized access, launching worms—do not always have the opportunity to publicly defend their behavior, but the debate can, nevertheless, take place if we can formulate the arguments as we suppose hackers might make them or as we read them between the lines of what is in fact said. In "Are Computer Hacker Break-Ins Ethical?", Eugene Spafford has formulated a defense of "hacking" into a set of cogent arguments. After identifying the arguments, Spafford then lays out what is wrong with each. While you may not want to take his arguments as the final word on the topic, Spafford has raised the level of argument about hacking. His arguments will have to be addressed by those who claim their behavior is justified.

The last reading is testimony that Marc Rotenberg, Director of the Washington Office of the Computer Professionals for Social Responsibility (CPSR), made before the Subcommittee on Criminal Justice, Committee on the Judiciary of the U.S. House of Representatives in 1989. CPSR is an organization of computer professionals and Rotenberg reports, among other things, on the response of that community to the Robert T. Morris incident. Rotenberg's testimony makes clear that while CPSR recognizes the severity of the problem of security in our computer networks, it is concerned about an overreaction to the Morris incident. In setting out the concerns of his organization, Rotenberg emphasizes individual accountability as the cornerstone of computer ethics, underscores our society's growing dependence on complex computer networks, opposes efforts to restrict the exchange of information about computer viruses, and encourages public discussion of the vulnerabilities of computer networks. He also discusses alternative solutions and problems with proposed legislation.

CASE
▷ THE COMPUTER WORM:

A Report to the Provost of Cornell University on an Investigation Conducted by The Commission of Preliminary Enquiry

Ted Eisenberg *Law*
David Gries *Computer Science*
Juris Hartmanis *Computer Science*
Don Holcomb *Physics*
M. Stuart Lynn *Office of Information Technologies (Chair)*
Thomas Santoro *Office of the University Counsel*

INTRODUCTION

This is a report of the Commission of Preliminary Enquiry appointed in response to Provost Barker's letter of November 7, 1988, to Vice President for Information Technologies, M. Stuart Lynn. Provost Barker's letter requested an investigation of the apparent use of Cornell computers to construct and launch the "worm"[1] that disrupted computer networks and systems nationwide beginning November 2, 1988. Provost Barker's letter was prompted by widespread press reports alleging that a Cornell first-year computer science graduate student, Robert Tappan Morris, had created the worm and had unleashed it on the Internet, a collection of national computer networks linking research and instructional facilities in universities as well as government and industrial research establishments.

The worm reportedly disrupted the operations of over 6,000 computers nationwide[2] by exploiting certain security loopholes in applications closely associated with the operating system.[3] Computers affected were limited to those running a version of the UNIX operating system[4] known as 4.3 BSD, which was developed by the Computer Systems Research Group (CSRG) of the University of California, Berkeley, and distributed at no charge other than distribution costs to universities and research institutions around the country. It also affected versions of UNIX that were derived from the CSRG work, in particular versions of SUN, which ran on SUN Microsystems computers.

The Commission was charged to:

1. Accumulate all evidence concerning the potential involvement of Mr. Robert Tappan Morris in the computer worm attack, and to assess such evidence to determine whether or not Morris was the likely perpetrator.
2. Accumulate all evidence concerning the potential involvement of any other member of the Cornell community, and to assess such evidence to determine whether or not any other member of the Cornell community was involved in the worm attack or was aware of the potential worm attack.
3. Evaluate relevant computer policies and procedures to determine which, if any, were violated and to make preliminary recommendations as to whether any of such policies and procedures should be modified to inhibit potential future security violations of this general type.

SUMMARY OF FINDINGS AND COMMENTS

Findings

Based on the evidence presented to the Commission, the Commission finds[5] that:

Responsibility for the Acts:

- The worm attack occurred as described in Section 3.
- Robert Tappan Morris, a first year computer science graduate student at Cornell, created the worm and unleashed it on the Internet.
- In the process of creating and unleashing the worm, Morris violated Computer Science Department policy on the use of departmental research computing facilities.

Impact of the Worm:

- The performance of computers "infected" by the worm degraded substantially, unless remedial steps were taken. Eventually such infected computers would come to a halt. These symptoms were caused by uncontrollable replication of the worm clogging the computer's memory. The worm, however, did not modify or destroy any system or user files or data.
- Based on anecdotal and other information, several thousand computers were *in*fected[6] by the worm. The Commission has not systematically attempted to estimate the exact number infected. Many thousands more were *af*fected in the sense that they had to be tested for infection and preventive measures applied even if the computers were not infected. It appears that the operation of most infected and potentially affected computers and of the research done on those computers was brought to a halt in order to apply remedial or preventive measures, all of which required the diversion of considerable staff time from more productive efforts.

Mitigation Attempts:

- Morris made only minimal efforts to halt the worm once it had propagated, and did not inform any person in a position of responsibility as to the existence and content of the worm.

Violation of Computer Abuse Policies:

- The Cornell Computer Science Department "Policy for the Use of the Research Computing Facility" prohibits "use of its computer facilities for browsing through private computer files, decrypting encrypted material, or obtaining unauthorized user privileges." All three aspects of this Policy were violated by Morris.
- Morris was apparently given a copy of this Policy but it is not known whether he read it. Probably he did not attend the lecture during orientation when this Policy was discussed, even though he was present on campus.

Intent:

- Most probably Morris did not intend for the worm to destroy data or other files or to interfere with the normal functioning of any computers that were penetrated.
- Most probably Morris intended for the worm to spread widely through host computers attached to the network in such a manner as to remain undiscovered. Morris took steps in designing the worm to hide it from potential discovery, and yet for it to continue to exist in the event it actually was discovered. It is not known whether he intended to announce the existence of the worm at some future date had it propagated according to this plan.
- There is no direct evidence to suggest that Morris intended for the worm to replicate uncontrollably. However, given Morris' evident knowledge of systems and networks, he knew or clearly should have known that such a consequence was certain, given the design of the worm. As such, it appears that Morris failed to consider the most probable consequences of his actions. At the very least, such failure constitutes reckless disregard of those probable consequences.

Security Attitudes and Knowledge:

- This appears to have been an uncharacteristic act for Morris to have committed, according to those who knew him well. In the past, particularly while an undergraduate at Harvard University, Morris appears to have been more concerned about protecting against abuse of computers rather than in violating computer security.
- Harvard's policy on misuse of computer systems contained in the Harvard Student Handbook clearly prohibited actions of the type inherent to the creation and propagation of the worm. For this and other reasons, the Commission believes that Morris knew that the acts he committed were regarded as wrongful acts by the professional community.

- At least one of the security flaws exploited by the worm was previously known by a number of individuals, as was the methodology exploited by other flaws. Morris may have discovered the flaws independently.
- Many members of the UNIX community are ambivalent about reporting security flaws in UNIX out of concern that knowledge of such flaws could be exploited before the flaws are fixed in all affected versions of UNIX. There is no clear security policy among UNIX developers, including in the commercial sector. Morris explored UNIX security issues in such an ambivalent atmosphere and received no clear guidance about reporting security flaws from his peers or mentors at Harvard or elsewhere.

Technical Sophistication:

- Although the worm was technically sophisticated, its creation required dedication and perseverance rather than technical brilliance. The worm could have been created by many students, graduate or undergraduate, at Cornell or at other institutions, particularly if forearmed with knowledge of the security flaws exploited or of similar flaws.

Cornell Involvement:

- There is no evidence that anyone from the Cornell community aided Morris or otherwise knew of the worm prior to its launch. Morris did inform one student earlier that he had discovered certain security weaknesses in UNIX. The first that anyone at Cornell learned that any member of the Cornell community might have been involved came at approximately 9:30 P.M. on November 4 when the Cornell News Service was contacted by the *Washington Post*.

Ethical Considerations:

- Prevailing ethical beliefs of students towards acts of this kind vary considerably from admiration to tolerance to condemnation. The computer science profession as a whole seems far less tolerant, but the attitudes of the profession may not be well communicated to students.

Community Sentiment:

- Sentiment among the computer science professional community appears to favor strong disciplinary measures for perpetrators of acts of this kind. Such disciplinary measures, however, should not be so stern as to damage permanently the perpetrator's career.

University Policies on Computer Abuse:

- The policies and practices of the Cornell Computer Science Department regarding computer abuse and security are comparable with those of other computer science and many other academic departments around the nation.

- Cornell has policies on computer abuse and security that apply to its central facilities, but not to departmental facilities.
- In view of the pervasive use of computers throughout the campus, there is a need for *university-wide* policy on computer abuse. The Commission recommends that the Provost establish a committee to develop such policy, and that such policy appear in all legislative and policy manuals that govern conduct by members of the Cornell community.
- In view of the distributed nature of computing at Cornell, there is also a need for a university-wide committee to provide advice and appropriate standards on security matters to departmental computer and network facility managers. The Commission recommends that the Vice President for Information Technologies be asked to establish such a committee.

Comments

The Commission believes that the acts committed in obtaining unauthorized passwords and in disseminating the worm on the national network were wrong and contrary to the standards of the computer science profession. They have little if any redeeming technical, social or other value. The act of propagating the worm was fundamentally a juvenile act that ignored the clear potential consequences. The act was selfish and inconsiderate of the obvious effect it would have on countless individuals who had to devote substantial time to cleaning up the effects of the worm, as well as on those whose research and other works was interrupted or delayed.

Contrary to the impression given in many media reports, the Commission does not regard this act as an heroic event that pointed up the weaknesses of operating systems. The fact that UNIX, in particular BSD UNIX, has many security flaws has been generally well known, as indeed are the potential dangers of viruses and worms in general. Although such security flaws may not be known to the public at large, their existence is accepted by those who make use of UNIX. It is no act of genius or heroism to exploit such weaknesses.

A community of scholars should not have to build walls as high as the sky to protect a reasonable expectation of privacy, particularly when such walls will equally impede the free flow of information. Besides, attempting to build such walls is likely to be futile in a community of individuals possessed of all the knowledge and skills required to scale the highest barriers.

There is a reasonable trust between scholars in the pursuit of knowledge, a trust upon which the users of the Internet have relied for many years. This policy of trust has yielded significant benefits to the computer science community and, through the contributions of that community, to the world at large. Violations of such a trust cannot be condoned. Even if there are unintended side benefits, which is arguable, there is a greater loss to the community as a whole.

This was not a simple act of trespass analogous to wandering through someone's unlocked house without permission but with no intent to cause damage. A more apt analogy would be the driving of a golf cart on a rainy day through most houses in a neighborhood. The driver may have navigated carefully and broken no china, but it should have been obvious to the driver that the mud on the tires would soil the carpets and that the owners would later have to clean up the mess.

Experiments of this kind should be carried out under controlled conditions in an isolated environment. Cornell Computer Science Department faculty would certainly have cooperated in properly establishing such an experiment had they been consulted beforehand.

The Commission suggests that media exaggerations of the value and technical sophistication of this kind of activity obscures the far more accomplished work of those students who complete their graduate studies without public fanfare; who make constructive contributions to computer science and the advancement of knowledge through their patiently constructed dissertations; and who subject their work to the close scrutiny and evaluation of their peers, and not to the interpretations of the popular press.

BACKGROUND

The Chronology

This abridged chronology is intended only as background for understanding the balance of this Report.

Shortly after[7] 7:26 P.M. on Wednesday, November 2, 1988 (all times in this Report will be Eastern Standard Time unless otherwise indicated), a computer "worm" was unleashed on the Internet, the interconnected set of national research networks that provide for communications between computers located at research universities and governmental and industrial research establishments around the nation. The worm was initially thought to be a "virus", based on some preliminary technical findings before the program had been completely analyzed, and this term was popularly adopted by the media. However, technically it was indeed a "worm" insofar as it propagated itself and did not need to attach itself to a host program to facilitate propagation. Also, it was not strictly a *network* worm, but a *host computer* worm that was transmitted over networks. The networks themselves functioned correctly and securely throughout the incident.

The worm spread rapidly among computers across the nation. By the following morning, it appears that several thousand computers had been penetrated. The worm did not destroy any data or files but, for reasons described later in this report, it replicated wildly, causing contaminated computers to slow down from overload and, eventually, to crash.

The worm attacked the Massachusetts Institute of Technology (MIT) computer, PREP, around 8:00 P.M.[8]. This appears to have been the first penetration[9] by the worm, although this particular penetration was not discovered until later. PREP is known to be an insecure computer[10]. Morris had a guest account on PREP with userid[11] RSM and password RSM. It has been speculated that the worm was remotely launched from this account. This is certainly consistent with observed facts but cannot be verified from the records. Curiously, early on the morning of November 3, someone erased the PREP system file which recorded remote log-ins, making it difficult, if not impossible, to trace the history of the worm on that computer. Coincidentally, and unfortunately, the mail program which logged all system transactions was set to log those transactions to a remote disk server which had been down the entire previous week.

Perhaps because of the time difference, the worm was apparently first noticed at several installations on the West Coast. The first infection on the West Coast may have been at 6:24 P.M. PST at the Rand Corporation in Santa Monica. However, its first actual discovery may have occurred when several undergraduates[12] at the University of California, Berkeley returned from dinner at around 7:00 P.M. PST, logged on to one of the computers, and observed from the system status log that "someone" was repeatedly and rapidly trying to log onto the computer. . . . After contacting staff members and together analyzing the attack, the Berkeley team developed fixes to destroy the worm on infected computers and to prevent reinfection.

Suggestions for preventive measures were distributed nationwide over the networks at about 2:30 A.M. on November 3. The first patches to fix infected systems and prevent infections were distributed nationwide about 6:00 A.M. on November 3 (for the so-called SENDMAIL attack) but other fixes were not distributed until about 10:00 P.M. on November 3 (for the so-called Finger Daemon attack). By that time, staff members at Purdue University, the University of Utah, and at Project Athena at MIT had also become involved in helping to analyze the worm and provide cures.

With such assistance, most installations were able to detect infestations and repair damage by late evening, November 3, although there have been reports of several installations taking much longer, even several days. All of these detection, eradication and prevention activities took long hours of work at affected institutions.

From computer records it appears that the first known instance of the fully developed worm attacking Cornell computers occurred at 10:55 P.M. the evening of November 2. This was about the same time it was attacking other computers around the nation. Computer Science Department student users noticed strange behavior in the small hours of the morning of November 3 and informed staff members. However, it was not until early the following morning that staff members first positively identified the presence of the worm at Cornell.

The national press started to report the worm on November 3, with the coverage gaining in momentum. At that time, it was merely speculated that the worm had originated somewhere in the Northeast.

On Friday, November 4, at about 9:30 P.M., Dennis Meredith of the Cornell News Service received a call from the *Washington Post* reporting that the *New York Times* was to carry a story the following morning naming Robert Tappan Morris, a Cornell graduate student, as the author of the worm. Apparently, the Times had learned this information from unnamed friends of Morris. The report of Morris' alleged involvement was first announced to the nation on CNN television news later that night.

This was the start of a press crescendo that grew for the next week or more.

The Worm

The worm itself was a sophisticated program, in spite of its design flaws and programming errors. A brief overview is presented in this section. A full understanding of this Section is not essential to understanding the balance of the report. . . .

The worm consisted of two parts: a 99-line "probe" written in high-level language[13] and a much larger "corpus", which had been compiled into binary machine language[14]. The probe would attempt a limited penetration of a computer on the network and, if successful, would compile and execute itself on the penetrated host and then send for the corpus.

The worm had four main methods of attack and several methods of defense, the latter to avoid discovery and elimination. We shall refer to the methods of attack as

Method-F (for Finger Daemon), Method-S (for SENDMAIL), Method-P (for passwords), and Method-R (for rexec).

Method-F and Method-S exploited design or security flaws in the so-called SENDMAIL and Finger Daemon programs that were incorporated in some of the versions of UNIX distributed by the Computer Systems Research Group at the University of California, Berkeley, the so-called BSD versions of UNIX; or in derivatives of the BSD distribution, such as that distributed by SUN Microsystems. Actually, there were two versions of the corpus of the worm, one specifically designed for Digital Equipment Corporation VAX computers running BSD UNIX and the other for certain SUN Microsystems computers.

Method-F exploited a feature of BSD whereby it is possible for a user to obtain certain information about another user on a remote computer. This feature employs an old program that lacks an important check to determine that the request is limited in length. Method-F exploited this oversight by submitting long requests that overran the space allocated by the program and using the "twilight zone" overrun space for its own nefarious purposes.

Method-S exploited a debugging capability that was left by the designer[15] of the SENDMAIL program, a program that allows users to send electronic mail to each other. The capability allowed the designer to test SENDMAIL on remote hosts without having to require special privileges on that host. The designer argues that this type of capability is important for maintaining programs on a distributed network. The debug facility could be turned off or on by the systems manager when installing the UNIX system. The default in the BSD distribution was that it was turned on (some other versions of UNIX, even those based on the BSD distribution, reverse this default). The worm was able to combine this capability with another capability, namely the ability, if this debug capability was turned on, to use the name of a command process (program) instead of a person as the recipient of an electronic message. In these circumstances, the worm would send an electronic message containing the "probe" program as the message to a command process, which would indirectly compile the probe and then execute it. Such execution would in turn cause the probe to drag over the corpus and build a new, complete worm.

Method-P attempted to infect remote computer accounts by "guessing" at passwords using techniques well known in the literature that exploit users' predilections for selecting easily remembered passwords, such as permutations of their userids. Thus, a user with an account userid "msl" might use "lsm" as a password. Method-P also referenced a standard list of passwords, which we now know[16] to have been developed by Morris over a period of time by cracking various computer accounts using a variety of standard techniques.

Method-R exploited a design feature of BSD UNIX that is not necessarily a flaw. As a convenience, the feature allows for a user with an account on one computer to use the same password on an account with the same userid (account name) on another computer. One way this feature was exploited by the worm was that it was programmed to look for accounts on remote hosts with the same userid as the account that the worm had already successfully infected, and, if successful, to attempt to crack that account by using the same password. Method-R was also used in conjunction with Method-P. Method-R was the preferred method, insofar as it was attempted before the other methods.

The worm program contained code to propagate itself using these four methods in various ways. It contained code that attempted to prevent enormous replication, which in fact failed to perform as apparently intended (see discussion of Intent). It contained code that attempted to cover the tracks of the worm so that it was not easily discoverable (the failure of the antireplication code was what led to the worm's ultimate discovery). It contained code apparently directed at ensuring the worm's survival even if it was discovered. It contained code that was apparently intended to give the appearance that the worm was sending information to a computer at the University of California, Berkeley in order to direct suspicion to that computer.

METHODS OF INVESTIGATION

The Commission primarily relied for evidence upon interviews conducted by the Judicial Administrator of the University and by the Chairperson of the Commission, and upon analysis of the files contained on the backup tapes of Morris' accounts on Computer Science Department computers[17]. The Commission also reviewed various documents.

Interviews were conducted with the seven graduate students who shared an office with Morris; with the graduate student in charge of new graduate student orientation; with Professor Dexter Kozen who is the graduate advisor to new computer science students; with Professor John Hopcroft, Chairman of the Computer Science Department; with Dr. Dean Krafft, Computer Science Department computer facilities manager; with staff members of the Electrical Engineering and Computer Science Departments and of the Cornell Theory Center; with several present or former staff members and students of Harvard University who knew Morris as an undergraduate, including Mr. Andrew Sudduth who was contacted by Morris late at night on November 2; with Mr. Glen Adams of MIT; and with staff of the University of California, Berkeley, who had been involved in analyzing and developing antidotes to the worm on November 2 and 3. Several of the interviews were conducted by telephone.

In spite of repeated attempts, the Commission has been unable to reach Mr. Paul Graham, a Harvard graduate student and a staff member of the Aiken Computational Laboratory at Harvard who knew Morris well. This is unfortunate in view of the role he apparently played on the night of November 2 as described by Mr. Sudduth (see next section) and in view of other light he may have been able to shed on the matter. The Commission believes that Mr. Graham may possess helpful information.

The computer files, most of which had been encrypted by Morris, were obtained from "backup" tapes routinely maintained by the Computer Science Department. Backup tapes may be used, for example, to recover from subsequent system malfunctions that may occur. These tapes, made every two days, contain a snapshot of the status of all files and other records on the computer systems at the time. They cannot record ephemeral activity that may occur between backups. Thus, for example, it is possible for a user to create, modify, or erase a file between backups, in which case no trace of the activity would exist on the subsequent backup.

Dr. Krafft was ingeniously able to decrypt the computer files associated with Morris' accounts and thereby provide the Commission with key information. These files, dating back to Morris' arrival at Cornell, were examined for relevant information. Other computer records obtained from the backup tapes were also helpful, including system log-on and mailfile records. The staff of the University of California, Berkeley graciously provided a decompilation of the worm object[18] program as well as other helpful technical information, as did Dr. Donn Seeley of the University of Utah.

Documents examined include policy statements and orientation material provided by the Computer Science Department; various technical reports and papers relating to computer security in general and UNIX security in particular, as well as to the worm itself; telephone records pertaining to the use of the telephone in Morris' office; network bulletin board material containing comments by various individuals on the computer virus; editorial letters, articles and editorials reflecting on professional attitudes to activities of this type; and many press reports, the most comprehensive of which were articles in the *New York Times* and the *Wall Street Journal*.

Acting under the advice of his attorney, Morris has chosen not to be interviewed by the Commission. He has at no time affirmed or denied his responsibility. The Commission does not take this as evidence one way or the other, given Morris' potential problems with violations of federal and state law.

Although the interviews conducted and the material analyzed were not exhaustive, the Commission feels the evidence it obtained was sufficient to support the conclusions reached. Moreover, it is unlikely that further interviews or analysis conducted without the imperative of legal or other judicial powers would add sufficient new information to change or further refine our findings.

INTRODUCTION TO THE EVIDENCE

Most of the evidence is presented in the next section along with the Commission's Findings. This section is intended only as a brief introduction to that evidence to provide a foundation for the next section.

Computer Files

The richest lode of evidence came from Morris' computer files. Among other material was an early source code version of the worm dated October 15, 1988, containing remarks that suggest the intent of the worm; almost-complete (filed 12:13 P.M. on November 2) and complete (filed 8:26 P.M. on November 2[19]) source code versions of the worm that had been encrypted[20], the latter being structurally equivalent to the decompiled[21] version obtained by University of California, Berkeley staff; files containing userid/password combinations to other accounts at Cornell and elsewhere; a file containing a list of passwords substantially similar to the list of passwords contained in the worm itself and almost identical to the passwords contained in the userid/password list[22]; mail records indicating communications on November 2 and November 3 with Paul Graham, a student at Harvard University, and Andrew Sudduth, then a staff member at Harvard University[23], the significance of which will be described below; and certain log-on records that confirm the likelihood and timings of Morris' access to his accounts.

Sudduth Evidence

Mr. Andrew Sudduth, then[24] a staff member of the Aiken Computational Laboratory at Harvard University, had known Morris for two years when Morris was an undergraduate at Harvard. Morris had intermittently worked at the Aiken Laboratory during that time, often without compensation. Mr. Sudduth had remained in contact with Morris over the several months since Morris had graduated from Harvard.

Mr. Sudduth reported that he and Mr. Paul Graham, another staff member[25] were conversing about 11:00 P.M. on November 2 when Morris called and spoke with Mr. Graham. Subsequently, according to Sudduth, Graham told him that "something big was up." Upon being pressed by Sudduth, who was concerned about the potential effect on the Aiken computers, Graham related that Morris had told him that he had released a virus (sic) that was clogging the computers at Cornell and that it was probably all over the country. Sudduth sent Morris a mail message asking him to call.

Sudduth also stated that Morris called about 11:30 P.M. and told him that something was going on, but that it would not affect the Aiken computers since the exposure underlying Method-F[26] had been closed on those computers some years previously;[27] and that Morris suggested measures to protect against the other vulnerabilities. According to Sudduth, Morris did not say specifically during the conversation that he had launched the worm, but from their conversation such a conclusion was obvious to Sudduth. Sudduth stated that he had the clear impression that Morris had told Graham that Morris had indeed launched the worm. Sudduth also reported that he gave Morris advice on how to remain anonymous.

Later, about 2:30 A.M. on November 3, Morris called Sudduth back. Morris told Sudduth that he wanted to broadcast a message of apology across the network containing advice on how to prevent infection by the worm. They discussed ways on how to broadcast the message in such a way as to protect the anonymity of both Sudduth and Morris. Morris seemed preoccupied but appeared to believe that he had made a "colossal" mistake. No conclusions were reached on how to send the message, but Sudduth assured Morris that he would find a way. Sudduth did indeed broadcast an anonymous message of apology at about 3:30 A.M., but it went over an obscure route and there was at least a 24-hour delay before it reached the community, long after the Berkeley group and others had already broadcast other preventive measures. Much later, on November 5, after the media broke the story alleging Morris' complicity, Sudduth broadcast another message acknowledging that he was the author of the earlier message, but he still protected Morris' identity. Morris called Sudduth from an unknown location on Friday, November 4, to determine that Sudduth had indeed broadcast the original message of apology.

Sudduth also told the Commission that Morris repeatedly called Graham between November 2 and November 6. Graham reportedly told Sudduth that Morris had launched the worm through MIT's PREP computer. Graham had also given the same impression to Glen Adams of MIT[28].

Morris had visited Harvard between October 20 and 22. Curiously, it is known from versions of the worm derived from Morris' files in the backup tapes that the design of the worm changed significantly after that visit: Method-S was added. There had been no suggestion of Method-S in the remarks in the October 15 version concerning the proposed design of the worm. Harvard staff interviewed by the Commission, including Sudduth, deny any discussions with Morris during that visit on the subject of the worm. Mr. Graham might be able to shed some light on this matter. It would be interesting to know, for example, to what Graham was referring in an October 26 electronic mail message to Morris when he enquired as to whether there was "Any news on the brilliant project?".

Sudduth also gave information regarding Morris' possible prior knowledge of security flaws in UNIX and regarding Morris' attitudes towards security. The Commission also obtained such information from other former Harvard colleagues of Morris. This is discussed in the section entitled "Security Attitudes and Knowledge."

Evidence of Cornell Students

Other evidence came from interviews with Morris' officemates. One student, Dawson Dean, reported a conversation with Morris on October 28 at about 7:00 P.M. Morris reported that he had broken the UNIX password system and had obtained passwords from other accounts, and also that two years earlier he had figured out Method-F. Dean was initially skeptical, but became convinced when Morris gave him sufficient detail to substantiate the claim. He asked what Morris intended to do with the knowledge; Morris replied nothing, he was just doing it for fun. Dean also reported seeing Morris on the telephone while sitting before one of the office computer terminals on the night of November 2 around midnight. He overheard Morris referring to Harvard and MIT. These times are also consistent with Sudduth's evidence.

Michael Hopcroft, another officemate who was also friendly with Morris, reported conversations with Morris about UNIX security. Morris had spoken confidently of being able to crack UNIX security. Other student officemates had little of significance to report. Morris had apparently not made any close friends during his two months at Cornell. He seemed to prefer to work alone and, according to some reports, spent many hours programming at the computer.

Samir Khuller, the graduate student in charge of orientation of new graduate students reported that Morris was not present at the first day of orientation when certain talks were given by the faculty. He recalls Morris coming to his office on the second or third day of the orientation period, most probably the latter. He gave Morris a set of the orientation materials, including a copy of the Computer Science Department Policy for Use of the Research Computing Facility. The latter contained the following statement:

> Confidential material is maintained on the systems. Any attempts by unauthorized individuals to "browse" through private computer files, decrypt encrypted material, or obtain user privileges to which they are not entitled will be regarded as a very serious offense. Any of these actions will result in loss of all computer privileges, and may, for student users, result in expulsion from the graduate program.

Khuller did not discuss the Policy with Morris and cannot affirm whether Morris read the Policy. From log-on records, it appears that Morris lost no time. He immediately obtained his password from the department graduate secretary and directly logged onto the computer. Khuller did report that Morris was at lunch the next day following which, at a different location, Dean Krafft, Computer Science Department Facilities Manager, gave a talk on, among other matters, computer security, in which he pointed out that security violations are serious matters and referenced the Policy. It appears that Morris of his own volition skipped this talk, since he was apparently logged onto the computer at that time. The record of log-ins to Morris' account contains an entry starting at 1:57 P.M. and ending at 2:16 P.M. on August 23rd, which overlaps the key first 16 minutes of Krafft's 2:00 P.M. talk.

Other Evidence

In understanding and analyzing the structure of the worm, the Commission has relied on the evidence of Dr. Krafft; of various members of the CSRG at Berkeley; of analysis presented in various reports; and on its own reading of selected parts of the code.

INTERPRETATION AND FINDINGS

Responsibility for the Acts

Two separate but related acts need to be considered:

- The act of violating departmental policies, including the unauthorized possession of passwords and of unauthorized access to computer accounts; and
- The act of unleashing the worm on the Internet in such a manner as to penetrate other computers and computer accounts and to cause interruptions to the normal performance of those computers.

From the evidence, the Commission concludes[29] that Robert Tappan Morris committed the first act, and that such an act is contrary to the written policies of the Computer Science Department. The reasons behind the Commission's conclusions are discussed on page 74.

The Commission also finds Morris to be responsible for the second act. Copies of the worm were found in his computer account in various stages of development culminating in the final version, finishing touches to which were implemented on the afternoon of November 2. The October 15 version contains statements of early design intent, which were generally reflected in the final version. According to Dr. Krafft, the final version is structurally identical to the "decompiled" version[30] of the actual worm detected on various computers attached to the Internet. This decompiled version was developed by the CSRG group at Berkeley and others.

The evidence clearly indicates that it was Morris who was responsible for these versions of the virus found in his account. Morris was observed on numerous occasions using the computer. There was no other account to which he had legitimate access. He did not report any suspicious use of his account. Other legitimate material was found in his account (coursework and electronic mail, for example) indicating that he used his account repeatedly. The Commission found no evidence or suggestion of use of Morris' account by others.

The Commission, therefore, does not believe anyone else could have developed the worm program without Morris' knowledge and certainly not without his collusion and involvement. The Commission has found no evidence for the involvement of any other party.

Furthermore, the Commission has found no evidence to suggest that any other party unleashed the worm once it had been created. To the contrary, we have the evidence of Sudduth that it was Morris who not only reportedly had unleashed the worm, but who also subsequently made an inadequate attempt to distribute an antidote and an apology.

Impact of the Worm

The Commission has not attempted to determine systematically how far the worm spread. The press has reported that it penetrated over 6,000 computers. Apparently, this number was determined by extrapolating the experience of one institution[31] to the entire network and may therefore be suspect, although, based on anecdotal and other evidence, the order of magnitude is likely to be correct.[32]

In assessing the impact, it is helpful to distinguish between the number of computers *in*fected and the number *af*fected. Even if a computer was not infected, it may have been affected, since time had to be devoted to determine whether it was in fact infected; and even if it was not infected, preventive measures had to be installed. The press figure of 6,000 computers was an estimate of the number of infected computers. Furthermore, the worm was able to penetrate a number of computers other than SUN and DEC VAX computers, but the worm could only regenerate itself and replicate on SUN and DEC VAX computers running specific versions of UNIX.

Institutions contacted by the Commission had not tabulated precisely how many computers were infected at their location. Neither did Cornell, although Dr. Krafft estimates that 100–150 computers were infected throughout the campus, with the majority being in the College of Engineering. Berkeley estimated around 100 computers. Judging from these experiences and similar anecdotal information from comparable institutions, the total number of infected computers was surely in the thousands. The number of affected computers must have been considerably higher since all VAX and SUN computers on the network running the vulnerable versions of UNIX were potentially at risk.

Anecdotal evidence also suggests that slowdowns or shutdowns on infected and affected computers delayed research and other productive work, but no evidence of lasting damage has come to the Commission's attention. The main impact was on the time of hundreds of staff members around the nation, often working late into the night, diverting their efforts from productive work into cleanup work.

The time taken to purge the effects of the worm varied considerably from institution to institution. Berkeley estimated about twenty people days. Other institutions reported more or less, depending upon (1) how long the worm had spread before it was detected[33]; (2) how many computers were affected or potentially affected; and (3) local skills available. Fortunately, Berkeley and several other institutions reacted quickly, and remedial and preventive procedures were being broadcast across the networks during the night of November 2 to November 3. Cornell did not know it was affected until early on the morning of November 3. By late that morning, staff personnel in the Theory Center[34] had isolated Cornell from the national networks. Staff in various campus departments began to implement the remedial and preventive steps that had been recommended by Berkeley and others. Cornell was back on the air by the evening of November 3.

One industry association has estimated that the worm caused about $96 million of damage. This self-serving estimate appears to be grossly exaggerated. It depends upon assigning a most hypothetical hourly value to computer downtime. Since the association's estimate was based on the press' assumption of 6,000 affected computers, this averages $16,000 per affected computer, a highly unlikely and inflated number, considering no work or data were irretrievably lost.

It has been suggested that the worm also had certain benefits, namely that it demonstrated that UNIX is vulnerable and that it heightened public awareness of the vulnerability of computer networks, upon many of which society critically depends, such as air traffic control networks or banking networks.

As to the first of these, most people in the UNIX user community are well aware of its vulnerabilities. In fact, the paper by Ritchie that is distributed as part of the Unix Users' Manual clearly states[35]:

> The first fact to face is that UNIX was not developed with security, in any realistic sense, in mind; this fact alone guarantees a vast number of holes.

UNIX was originally developed as a small system to run on a departmental computer among friendly, cooperating users. Its use has grown faster than its ability to cope with security across a network of thousands of users, including potentially hostile users. This is well known. It is also well recognized that users in such an environment depend upon mutual trust to provide security. Morris violated that trust.

The public's awareness may have been heightened as a result of the worm, but this was an accidental byproduct of the event and the resulting display of media interest. Society does not condone burglary on the grounds that it heightens public concern about safety and security. Besides, it is quite likely that the public has been misled by this event into believing that *all* networks and computer systems are as vulnerable as the Internet and UNIX, which is simply not the case.

In any event, the Commission cannot condone wildly conducted experiments as a means to heighten public awareness. The potential consequences of such irresponsible experiments can be far greater than intended by the author. What would happen if some individual, who had access to the details of this worm and who was impressed by the attendant media hype, chose to launch a similar experiment on a more critical network, even a more secure network, to determine its vulnerability? The unintended consequences could have far-reaching effects.[36]

Mitigation Attempts

The Commission finds that Morris made only minimal efforts to limit the damage of the worm once it had been propagated. He contacted a friend, Mr. Sudduth, at Harvard, and asked him to distribute an anonymous apology and antidote on the network. This message only reached the community long after others had already developed antidotes to the worm, although it is not likely that Morris could have anticipated this delay. Through Sudduth, Morris relied on electronic mail for communication, which, even in the best of circumstances, would most likely not have been widely read until the following morning, long after the worm would have had considerable effect. Apart from Sudduth, Morris did not use the telephone to call anybody who could have caused rapid actions to occur. Sudduth clearly did not have the experience or stature necessary to act nationally on such matters. Morris did not call, for example, Dr. Krafft or Professor John Hopcroft, his department chairman, or Professor Dexter Kozen, the first-year graduate student advisor.

The Commission accepts that Morris' judgement was probably clouded by a degree of panic, but his behavior appears to underscore his avoidance of taking clear responsibility for his acts. His futile and limited attempts to mitigate the damage were confused by his apparently greater desire to remain anonymous.

Violation of Computer Abuse Policies

As stated earlier, the Commission finds that Morris violated departmental policy on use of departmental research computing facilities. The Commission finds Morris to have been in unauthorized possession of passwords to computer accounts and to have had unauthorized access to computer accounts.

Lists of userid/password combinations were found in his account, as were programs capable of obtaining such passwords and exploiting them once found. The userid/password combinations were to accounts on other computers at Cornell.[37] On behalf of the Commission, Dr. Krafft has spot checked four of these accounts that belong to Computer Science faculty members and determined that the owners did not grant permission to Morris to access their accounts and did not give him their passwords. Furthermore, there is the clear statement of intent contained in the October 15 version of the worm program, which openly describes the design intent, including such phrases as "methods of breaking into other systems" and "rsh from local host, maybe after breaking a local password ..." and "stealing the password file".

For the same reasons presented on page 72 the Commission does not find it believable that anyone else could have been responsible for the presence of these passwords and userid/password combinations in Morris' account.

The Computer Science Department Policy for the Use of the Research Computing Facility prohibits the "use of its computer facilities for browsing through private computer files, decrypting encrypted material, or obtaining unauthorized user privileges."

The work done to obtain passwords to other computer accounts and the probing used to test the worm or segments of the worm (see later discussion) prior to launch required "browsing" through private computer files and obtaining unauthorized user privileges. Furthermore, since UNIX password files are encrypted, obtaining passwords from those files requires the decryption of encrypted material. Thus the mere possession of passwords obtained in an unauthorized manner violates all three aspects of the Policy, regardless of the further use of the passwords. In addition, the post-launch work done by the worm required "browsing" through private computer files and obtaining unauthorized user privileges.

Thus the acts of obtaining, possessing and using the passwords were all contrary to departmental policy and therefore unauthorized.

Was Morris aware that such acts were contrary to policy or otherwise unauthorized? There is evidence that Morris received a copy of the Policy. As part of his orientation, Morris was also informed of and expected to be present at Dr. Krafft's lecture, which included observations on the importance of the Policy. Morris apparently chose not to attend this lecture even though he was present on campus at the time. In the Commission's view, his failure to attend the lecture does not provide a legitimate reason for any possible lack of awareness of the Policy.

Even if Morris had attended Dr. Krafft's lecture he may not have listened attentively. Of four students interviewed by the Commission who were at Dr. Krafft's lecture and had received the orientation material containing the Policy, only one recalled any mention of the Policy. One other student was aware of the Policy and even believed he had signed something to the effect that he had read it (he had not). The other two students were unaware of the Policy, although one of the two assumed some such policy probably existed. The implications of this evidence are touched on later (see "University Policies on Computer Abuse").

The Harvard University Handbook for Students contains a clear statement of policy on "Misuse of Computer Systems". Morris was surely familiar with this policy. The acts of developing and launching the worm were contrary to this policy. It would only be reasonable to assume that what is unlawful or unethical at Harvard was most likely to be unlawful or unethical elsewhere.

The fact that Morris chose to remain anonymous strongly suggests that he was quite aware that he had committed a wrongful act.

In any event, a policy should not be necessary to describe what is common sense, namely that actions that trespass on the property of others are simply not acceptable, whether or not damage is intended or caused. The acts of obtaining passwords to other accounts and exploiting such passwords to obtain unauthorized access is, at best, an unacceptable practice and possibly illegal. Given Morris' experience in the field[38], and given the attitudes of his father, which surely must have permeated their conversations[39], the Commission believes that Morris knew, or certainly should have known, that such acts are clearly not accepted as legitimate by the profession. This point is elaborated upon in the discussion of "Ethical Considerations" on page 83.

Intent

It is not possible to determine with certainty the intentions of the creator of the worm. There have been many speculations reported by the press and by friends of Morris, but the only convincing information is that which can be inferred from the structure of the worm itself, and such information only suggests probabilities, not certainties.

The evidence suggests that the author of the worm did not intend for it to do any damage to files and data. He did not intend for it to replicate as rapidly as it did and bring so many computers to a halt. Rather, the intent was for the worm to spread and remain undiscovered on a multitude of host computers attached to the network. One can only speculate as to whether, when, and in what manner the author intended to reveal the worm's existence.

The evidence that the author did not intend for it to damage files and data is that there is no provision in the program for such action, and that no files or data were damaged or destroyed. Furthermore, there is no such intent stated in his early design comments in the October 15 version. It would have been a simple matter for the author to add instructions to cause such damage had that been his intention, but he did not. Such actions, in any event, would have rapidly announced the existence of the worm and are therefore at cross-purposes with the perceived intent of a latent, undiscovered worm.

The evidence that the author did not intend for the worm to replicate rapidly is somewhat more complex, since there is contradictory evidence. On the one hand, the worm contained code to check whether a penetrated node was already infected. If the worm detected another copy of itself at a given node, one or the other of the two copies would normally be "killed" according to a mechanism similar to the roll of a dice.

If the author had intended for the worm to replicate unchecked, there would have been no point in including such code. An infected node could be reinfected many times until it choked on the infestations. Thus, it is reasonable to conclude that the author did not intend massive replication.

However, a certain level of replication was clearly intended. For example, the point at which a given node was checked for infection was after the new arriving worm had already done considerable work: in particular, after it had already attempted to penetrate other computer nodes attached to the node under attack. A degree of replication was therefore assured. In fact, it was attempting to send out so many copies of itself prior to the roll of the dice that the node under attack would literally choke on itself.

Furthermore, one out of every seven times, the roll of the dice did not take place, thus guaranteeing extensive replication. To add insult to injury, the arriving worm in such circumstances became "immortal" and would always survive future "mano a mano's". Since immortal worms could only cumulate and never die unless human intervention occurred, worm replication would be assured by this mechanism alone.

Even an arriving worm that lost the roll of the dice did not die immediately but would do considerable work first. It would not die until the body of the main loop of the program had been executed several times and done other work, during which time it would give birth to new copies of the worm. These new copies were unaware that their "parent" had been killed during childbirth and would proceed as if all was well. Under these conditions, a computer was bound to become massively and rapidly infected.

The worm also had built-in mechanisms that gave it a predilection for seeking out "gateway" machines on networks. It would be expected that such machines would be connected to many other machines, thus enhancing the spread of the worm.

There were other problems, too, not the least of which was one of several programming bugs: one in particular reportedly[40] resulted in the loser in the roll of the dice not actually being killed as apparently planned, but massive replication would have occurred even if this error had been corrected.

Regardless of programming errors, quiet, not massive, replication may have been the intent of all of the above. That goal is not inconsistent with the actual program. The author may have speculated that some measure of replication was necessary to defend the worm against extinction in the event of detection and any defense mechanisms that might then be imposed. That the author anticipated the possibility of detection and defense is evidenced by the extent to which mechanisms were provided to hide the existence of the worm and to cover its tracks.

However, any individual capable of creating a program of the sophistication of the worm should have been quite capable of realizing that massive replication was a foregone conclusion given the design of the worm. Such a conclusion required little analysis.

Analogies can be drawn with population dynamics. It would have been extraordinarily difficult to achieve ecological balance between the continued existence of the worm and a potentially hostile environment, particularly given the complex structure of the network and the lack of any simulation of the behavior of the worm on such a complex network. The program was clearly designed so that the worm population would not wither away in the absence of massive human intervention. Fluctuating population states were certainly possible, but given the design of the worm the most probable consequence was uncontrolled growth to the point of saturation as in fact occurred. In the absence of conclusive evidence that the population would fluctuate within defined limits (and the author clearly did not and could not possess such evidence) it would be most logical to assume uncontrolled growth as the basis for considering potential consequences of the act.

The Commission finds it difficult to reconcile the degree of intelligence shown in the detailed design of the worm with the obvious replication consequences. We can only conclude that either the author's intent was malicious or that the author showed no regard for such larger consequences—he was so completely absorbed in his activities that he simply did not consider the potential repercussions. We lean towards the latter conclusion only because greater damage could have been done had the author so chosen.

Another hypothesis that is consistent with the evidence is that the worm behaved exactly as planned, causing just enough damage to cripple thousands of computers but not enough to damage programs or data. This, however, seems farfetched.

It appears, therefore, that Morris did not pause to consider the potential consequences of his actions. He was so focused on the minutiae of tactical issues that he failed to contemplate the overall potential impact of his creation. His behavior, therefore, can only be described as constituting reckless disregard. It is the responsibility of any member of the computer science profession (as in society in general) to consider the consequences of one's acts, especially when those acts may affect thousands of individuals across the nation.

Morris displayed naive conceit in assuming that he could launch an untested, unsimulated, complex worm onto a complex network and have it work correctly the first time. Even undergraduate students are taught in introductory courses that untested programs contain errors, that such errors are often subtle, and that one should never assume that one's programs function as intended without the most careful of testing.

The Commission doubts that Morris intended either to demonstrate security flaws in UNIX or to heighten public awareness of the vulnerability of computers and networks, both of which were described as possible benefits of the worm in the previous Section. We cannot reconcile either intention with the design of the worm: either objective could have been achieved if the worm had been designed to replicate uncontrollably without any of the features to inhibit replication or to disguise the worm's existence.

As Professor John Hopcroft, Chairman of the Cornell Computer Science Department, has pointed out:[41]

> I do not believe that this was just a "clever experiment that got out of hand."[42] It was an experiment that never should have taken place. If someone plans to conduct an experiment with the potential to cause serious damage, it should be properly reviewed and organized so that it does not go astray.
>
> If we had known of this work beforehand, we would have arranged for the experiment to be conducted on an isolated network of work stations so that the consequences would have been minimal.

In the next section, it is suggested that this act of launching the worm was not consistent with Morris' previous attitudes towards violations of computer security. It was an uncharacteristic act. Uncharacteristic as it may have been, however, the creation of the virus was not a sudden impetuous act. It was created over a two week period and required sustained dedication, and the sustained commission of wrongful acts, namely the acts of obtaining passwords to other peoples' accounts. The actual launch itself may have been impetuous. Perhaps once having created the worm, Morris simply could not resist the grandiose act of testing the performance of his creation "in vivo".

We may never know Morris' true intentions. The Commission would not place much credulity even on any *post facto* explanations that Morris might give, since they may constitute rationalization rather than explanation. It is quite possible that even Morris does not and did not know his true intentions either now or at the time of creation. It may simply have been the unfocused intellectual meandering of a hacker completely absorbed with his creation and unharnessed by considerations of explicit purpose or potential effect.

Security Attitudes and Knowledge

Although the act was reckless and impetuous, it appears to have been an uncharacteristic act for Morris. According to several of his friends and former Harvard colleagues who knew him well, Morris was preoccupied in his undergraduate days with developing and implementing measures for improving computer security, not with violating it[43]. As an occasional staff member at two Harvard computational facilities[44], he would often alert management to security flaws, at times working only for professional curiosity and without pay. He exploited superuser privileges to obtain user passwords, but only for the purpose of informing management of the widespread use of English language passwords that were trivial to obtain illegally[45]. He always cared about not taking actions to alter or destroy files and data belonging to others, a concern that was manifest in the design of the worm. His preoccupation with computers and computer security may have led to the neglect of his academic studies, according to friends and former colleagues at Harvard, but not to malfeasance. Those who spoke with the Commission were uniformly surprised that he had launched the worm, but were not surprised that he had the technical ability to create it.

The attitudes of the UNIX community in general, and of Morris' former colleagues at Harvard in particular, towards UNIX security flaws may have shaped Morris' own beliefs. There is no clear consensus in the UNIX community as to whether new security flaws should be reported and, if so, to whom. Until about two years ago, the Berkeley Computer Systems Research Group (CSRG) who maintain BSD UNIX[46] did not take much if any responsibility[47] for fixing flaws, particularly between new releases of BSD UNIX, or for distributing patches. Publicly posting flaws on bulletin boards, say, only drew attention to the vulnerability for potential miscreants to exploit. These same flaws could also be present in commercial versions of UNIX, and commercial vendors are much slower to fix the problems because of the laborious procedures that are often followed. Security flaws in BSD UNIX are discovered frequently.

This situation has now changed, in that Berkeley is most responsive in this regard (see, for example, discussion of the FTP flaw below). Most people now report such flaws. CSRG reported that they were informed of seven separate flaws this past summer alone after a lull of several months. The practice of CSRG is to develop a fix for any flaw reported and to distribute the fix in the form of a patch to the operating system. It is the responsibility of system administrators to apply these patches. Periodically, a new release is issued by Berkeley with all patches applied. This has become standard practice.

However, some, but by no means all, members of the community are still concerned that fixing the problem in the BSD distribution may nevertheless highlight the possible vulnerability in commercial versions of UNIX. Thus, there is still ambivalence about reporting security flaws.

This ambivalence was certainly present among members of the Harvard community who spoke with the Commission. Scott Bradner[48], who supervised Morris during his freshman year, recalled several conversations with Morris about certain flaws that Morris had discovered and their mutual concerns about reporting them to Berkeley.[49] Andrew Sudduth stated that it would never occur to him to report flaws to Berkeley. Nicholas Horton, however, a former systems manager at the Aiken Computational Laboratory, seemed surprised that flaws were not reported as standard procedure.

As Clifford Stoll, a computer security expert at Harvard University, said: "An obvious worry is how to get the word out to people wearing white hats without letting the black hats know."

Mr. Sudduth, for example, reported to the Commission that on October 23 Morris informed him of a new (to Morris) flaw he had discovered in UNIX associated with the File Transfer Protocol (FTP)[50]. Sudduth in turn later mentioned the flaw to Glen Adams at MIT. Adams, not Sudduth, reported the vulnerability to a small list of people, including Keith Bostick at CSRG, who distributed an operating system patch two days later, closing the loophole on machines to which the patch was applied. The patch was distributed on October 29.[51]

Morris had spoken of this and other flaws to various people, including Mr. Sudduth and Mr. Dean (one of his Cornell officemates referenced earlier). Some have speculated that Morris was in haste to launch the worm because he was concerned that word of the remaining flaws might leak back to the CSRG, who presumably would close the loopholes. The Commission cannot confirm this. However, Sudduth reports that Morris sent him electronic mail early on the afternoon of November 2 asking whether he had discussed the FTP flaw with anyone. Sudduth replied that he had only mentioned it to members of the Harvard UNIX systems milieu so that they could take preventive action. Sudduth stated that he hoped he had "done nothing wrong" by so divulging the information. Morris did not reply.

This ambivalent attitude towards reporting UNIX security flaws is not unique to Harvard. The greatest concern behind this ambivalence is the lack of clearly stated policy by either Berkeley, or, more importantly, by commercial vendors. Commercial vendors bear even greater responsibility insofar as they market their software and have some obligation, legal or otherwise, for its security. Staff members of CSRG have expressed their own frustration with the lack of coordination with commercial vendors. In fact, only a few weeks after the worm incident, another security breach gained national attention when the FTP flaw was exploited in a network penetration through a computer at the MITRE corporation running an old release of ULTRIX, a version of UNIX marketed by Digital Equipment Corporation, a decisive example of the fears expressed by those who prefer not to report security flaws. There were also several other attempted network penetrations in the weeks following the release of the FTP patch by CRSG[52].

Morris explored UNIX security amid this atmosphere of uncertainty, where there were no clear ground rules and where his peers and mentors gave no clear guidance. It is hard to fault him for not reporting flaws that he discovered. From his viewpoint, that may have been the most responsible course of action, and one that was supported by his colleagues.

Some have speculated that Morris may have become so frustrated at the inability of the UNIX community to address these matters of security that he decided to develop and launch the worm as an intended silent demonstration of UNIX vulnerability. The Commission has no evidence of this. What is clear, however, is that there were other avenues he could have explored, such as running a controlled experiment in an isolated network with the knowledge and support of the Cornell Computer Science Department, as suggested by the remarks of Professor Hopcroft quoted earlier. Furthermore, Morris actions seemed to have spawned a rash of new break-ins.

It is one thing to discover flaws and not report them. It is another matter when such flaws are exploited in a harmful manner, such as was the case when Morris designed and launched the worm.

The Commission has not examined in depth the extent to which the particular flaws exploited by the worm were previously known to members of the community, or how widely, or when they were first discovered by or came to the attention of Morris. From various reports, it appears that the Method-S and Method-F flaws may have been known to several individuals for some time, and may have been independently rediscovered by several people. However, neither of these flaws had been reported to the Berkeley CSRG (see information regarding Method-F).

According to Harvard's Scott Bradner, the Method-F flaw was discovered several years ago by Dan Lanciani for one, who had succeeded Morris at the Harvard Psychology Department Computer Based Laboratory. The knowledge was widely circulated at Harvard and fixes applied to most Harvard computers[53] running UNIX. No one reported it to Berkeley for the reasons described above. Also, no one from Harvard who spoke with the Commission can recall any specific conversation with Morris on Method-F earlier than last spring, or can shed any light on whether Morris learned of it from others or independently discovered it. They all assumed he knew of it. Certainly the methodology underlying the Method-F flaw was quite widely known. Stories that have circulated that Morris was given the responsibility of reporting flaws to Berkeley appear to be quite apocryphal.

Ironically, last summer. the Berkeley CSRG did receive[54] a report of the Method-F flaw. However, it was incompletely reported as a problem with the Finger command itself, which exploits the Finger Daemon where the actual flaw existed. The CSRG checked the Finger command and determined there was no problem and no action was required.

It seems likely that Morris first heard of or discovered Method-S on his October 20–22 visit to Harvard.[55] The Commission has not been able to determine whether this particular flaw was already known, not having attempted to verify many rumors received by the Commission of fairly widespread knowledge of this flaw in the UNIX community. There have been several known flaws based around SENDMAIL, and it is possible that these flaws have been confused with the particular flaw underlying Method-S.

Technical Sophistication

Even though it failed to achieve its presumed objective, the worm was a sophisticated, albeit misguided, computer program.

Morris must have worked extremely hard at developing the worm between October 15 and November 2. It required perseverance and dedication, perhaps to the exclusion of concerns about his legitimate academic activities. According to Sudduth, who knew Morris during his student days at Harvard, Morris was the kind of student who was bright but bored by routine homework, and often devoted his main energies elsewhere. He apparently continued this pattern at Cornell.

The case for sophistication rests on the program's complexity: it exploited several security flaws using several means of attack. It was carefully designed to hide itself from detection, to masquerade as something else, and to spread insidiously and efficiently across the network. Morris had paid careful attention to designing, programming and testing the details of the program. Unfortunately, he apparently ignored and failed to test its potential overall impact.

However, the consensus of the UNIX community appears to be that many UNIX "hackers" (we do not use that word pejoratively) could have written this or a similar program, certainly given knowledge of the particular security flaws or similar flaws. The methodology underlying these flaws, if not the details of the flaws themselves, was quite widely known. Many students, graduate or undergraduate, at many institutions could have accomplished this act. The knowledge and skill required are possessed by most UNIX hackers.

Cornell Involvement

The Commission finds no evidence that anyone else at Cornell was involved or knew of the worm before it was launched. Although unusual behavior was observed on Electrical Engineering computers as early as October 29,[56] this could have been the result of actions to test and debug parts of the worm or to obtain passwords for use in Method-P. These probes did not cause the replication phenomenon that ultimately led to the worm's discovery. Although department staff were puzzled and concerned, there was no way of tracing the source of the probes. Had (applying hindsight) a change to all passwords been implemented at that time as a security measure, Morris, were he indeed responsible for these probes, could easily have switched his focus to testing on other computers.

Two people interviewed by the Commission reported that they had observed strange behavior on Computer Science Department computers on October 30 and 31. Unusual "Disk Full" errors were observed and subsequent repeated crashes occurred. However, Dr. Krafft has determined that this behavior had nothing to do with the worm but was due to other causes.

During the late afternoon of November 2, one of the Computer Science Department computers, CUARPA, was subjected to repeated attacks by a program exploiting Method-S. This was not realized at the time but only determined from later analysis of the computer records. It is likely that these attacks were last-minute testing by Morris (according to accounting records, it appears that Morris was logged on at the time), perhaps testing the code that had been added to utilize the password attacks between the penultimate version produced in the middle of the day and the final version, which was completed at 7:26 P.M.[57] Morris logged off at 8:45 P.M. and did not sign on again until 10:28 P.M. This testing, incidentally, was more in the nature of debugging the details of the program, not system testing of the type that would have revealed its overall effect on network computers and the massive replication that occurred.

As stated earlier, the first known occurrence of the worm was around 8:00 P.M. on the PREP computer at MIT. It has been speculated that Morris launched the worm through his guest account on this computer, operating remotely from Cornell. This cannot be confirmed from the computer records since, as stated earlier, the key system accounting record was suspiciously deleted by someone the following morning. It would not have required assistance from anyone at Cornell or elsewhere for Morris to have launched the worm remotely through MIT.

As stated earlier, the worm was first positively identified at Cornell early in the morning of November 3.

Morris informed his officemate, Dawson Dean, of his knowledge of UNIX security flaws several days before the worm had been launched, but not of his work in progress on the worm or of his plan to exploit these flaws. To the contrary, he told Dean that he did not intend to do anything with the knowledge. To Dean, this appeared to be idle chitchat between students about operating system security, with Morris showing off his knowledge. Dean cannot be faulted for not reporting the conversation. Someone more experienced might have asked Morris whether he had reported the flaws, perhaps to the CSRG group at Berkeley.

Other than Morris, the first knowledge at Cornell that a member of the Cornell community might be linked to the creation of the worm came at approximately 9:30 P.M. on the night of November 4, when the *Washington Post* contacted the Cornell Press Department to inform them that the *New York Times* was publishing a story alleging that Morris was the perpetrator.

Ethical Considerations

The opinions of the computer science community, particularly the student community, vary considerably from regarding the launching of the worm as an heroic act that heightened awareness of computer security; to regarding it as an immoral and possibly illegal act that caused millions of dollars of damage. The consensus, however, appears to be that the act was clearly wrong and under no circumstances should have been carried out. At the same time, the community appears to recognize that there are few clear guidelines or applicable laws in this regard.

Regardless of legal and policy considerations, the basis for considering the act to be wrong is that it presumed upon the time of countless individuals without their consent. As such, it was a selfish act.

It was also a juvenile act. In an adult community, one does not need policies or laws or procedures to know that acts have consequences and that one is largely responsible for the consequences of ones' acts; or that those consequences should be assessed before initiating the acts.

There is also the matter of whether it is wrong to intrude into other peoples' computer accounts without their consent. Since, in this case, there appears to have been no evidence of any intent to cause damage, this particular incident has been likened to the act of trespassing in someone's house, rather than breaking and entering. The former is regarded generally as a misdemeanor in law rather than a felony, as is the act of usurping someone's automobile without their consent, taking it for a joyride, and returning it undamaged.

A more appropriate analogy, however, would be to liken the intrusion to taking a golf cart and driving it around someone's house uninvited on a rainy day. Perhaps the driver navigated carefully and broke no china (intentionally or otherwise) but he should have clearly been aware that the mud on the tires would leave tracks throughout the house that someone else would have to clean up. In the case at hand, the driver proceeded to drive again and again through every house in the neighborhood.

There is also the matter of reasonable expectation of privacy. Passwords on computers are not used to guarantee security against determined intruders. They are there to serve notice to one and all that this is private space and entry is unwelcome without possession of a search warrant. People generally do not lock their houses with the fortitude of Fort Knox—the locks used are sufficient to deter all but determined intruders and exist to serve clear warning: Keep Out.

A community of scholars should not have to build walls as high as the sky to achieve a reasonable expectation of privacy, particularly when such walls will equally impede the free flow of information. Besides, attempting to build such walls is likely to be futile in a community of individuals possessed of all the knowledge and skills required to scale the highest barriers.

There is a reasonable trust between scholars in the pursuit of knowledge, a trust upon which the users of the Internet have relied for many years. This policy of trust has yielded significant benefits to the computer science community and, through the contributions of that community, to the world at large. Violations of such a trust cannot be condoned. Even if there are unintended side benefits, which is arguable, there is a greater loss to the community as a whole.

The somewhat informal policies governing the development and distribution of Berkeley UNIX have yielded important benefits, as have the practices of sharing informal code and debugging remotely across networks. Much has been learned and much has been developed that would have been most unlikely or impossible under more restrictive conditions. The computer science community will lose if restrictive measures are imposed that inhibit the kind of creative growth that has occurred.

As the Cornell Computer Science Department faculty stated in a resolution passed on November 9, 1988:

> Computer scientists are fully aware that computers are easily misused with potentially catastrophic consequences. As such, we have a special duty to exercise and promote the highest sense of responsibility and the most exacting sense of ethical behavior. We insist that all members of the department use all equipment with care and responsibility. We shall do everything possible to prevent a repetition of the deplorable events of last week.

By any reasonable standards, the acts involved in the creation and distribution of this worm were selfish and wrong and violated the trust that exists between members of the computer science community in the use of computer facilities and networks.

Community Sentiment

It is the responsibility of the various Cornell campus judicial bodies to consider potential disciplinary measures. It is not part of the charge of the Commission of Preliminary Enquiry to recommend specific disciplinary measures. Nevertheless, in view of the unusual nature of this case and the lack of campus and other precedent that exists, the Commission feels it might be useful to describe what it perceives to be the general community sentiment based on interviews conducted and materials read.

The Commission has spoken with a large number of individuals, mostly members of the computer science community, during the course of its investigations. It has also read many documents including press reports, reports of several computer scientists, papers and correspondence that have appeared in the computer science literature prior to this event, and electronic mail circulated on bulletin boards reflecting the opinions of many individuals. Based on this information, the Commission detects a general sentiment that the perpetrator of the computer worm incident should be subject to serious disciplinary measures for both the act of obtaining unauthorized access to other computers and computer accounts, including the unauthorized possession of passwords to such accounts, and for the act of unleashing the worm itself on the network. However, the general sentiment also seems to be prevalent that such disciplinary measures should allow for redemption and as such not be so harsh as to damage permanently the perpetrator's career.

The Commission emphasizes that this is not a conclusion reached from a systematic study, but a summary of impressions gained from the aforementioned sources. Even among those sources, there was a wide range of opinion.

University Policies on Computer Abuse

The same moral and ethical standards that apply to other areas within our society should also apply to the use of the computer. We do not condone entering an unlocked office and searching through a file cabinet; we should not condone browsing through the computer files of others. Theft of computing resources or information stored on a computer is the same as theft from a store or home. Any willful act that causes loss of money, materiel, time, or information should be subject to retribution, regardless of whether the act involved the use of the computer.

However, the pervasive use of computers, particularly on distributed networks, is still such a relatively new phenomenon, and has opened up so many new modes of operation, that society has not had time to adjust fully to it. Furthermore, the rapid changes in technology and its use imply that new questions about use and abuse are introduced faster than society can answer questions raised by earlier technologies. Who, for example, owns the contents of users' computer files at Cornell? Cornell? Who may, ethically or legally, browse through or change its contents? May a computer account be used for personal matters in off-hours, the way a typewriter may be used? May the local electronic mail systems, like the telephone, be used for personal messages?

Many more questions than answers arise from delving into these issues. The issues are often complex and change with technology. Society's laws often cannot keep pace, even if the ethical issues are clear.

Well aware of the problems of security, Cornell's Computer Science Department has for some time had a policy regarding the use of its research computing facilities, and has actively sought to communicate this policy to incoming graduate students. The policies and practices of the Computer Science Department in this regard are similar to those of other computer science departments around the nation. The Department's computer facilities are also comparable in security with those of most academic departments. Nevertheless, there was abuse, and it caused damage.

There are various ways the Computer Science department could enhance its computer security and make students, staff and faculty more aware of computer abuse and its consequences (for example, it could require the policy to be signed by all members of the Department indicating they have received and read it). However, the next abuse may not be in that Department, but in any Cornell unit that uses computers. It could possibly come at the hands of someone who does not even have a legitimate computer account. Computers have pervaded all of Cornell, expertise is growing everywhere, and some forms of computer abuse require little expertise.

Cornell's central computer facility managers have wrestled with many of the questions concerning computer abuse for many years, and have also promulgated several policies and security practices. However, these policies are only applied to those who use central facilities. The rapid pace of decentralization of computer facilities of recent years has not been accompanied by corresponding decentralization of such policies.

Given this situation, it behooves Cornell University to develop a university-wide policy on computer abuse, including a clear statement of moral and ethical standards regarding the use of computers that it expects every member of the Cornell community to follow, and to attempt to develop a clear statement of precisely what constitutes computer abuse and the range of applicable penalties for such abuse. It should be given to and should apply to every member of the community—faculty, students and staff. It should appear in all legislative and policy manuals that govern conduct by members of the community.

The Commission recommends that the Provost form a broadly based committee to develop such a university-wide policy.

The Commission also recommends that the Vice President for Information Technologies be asked to form a university-wide security committee as an advisory body to develop reasonable security standards and procedures governing the use of distributed computing facilities and networks, and to act as a consultative body to managers of departmental facilities. The Commission recognizes that this committee is separate from the Security Committee that coordinates the security of central facilities and systems, but recommends that there be cross-representation to ensure coordination.

The Commission nevertheless wishes to take it clear that even the most comprehensive policy or the most reasonable security measures might not have deterred Morris from this particular mission. The University can only encourage reasonable behavior. It cannot guarantee that University policies and procedures will be followed.

NOTES

1. The press popularly referred to the worm as a "virus", which was the early "diagnosis" of some technical experts before the program had been fully analyzed. However, technically the program was a "worm" since it did not attach itself to a host program in order to propagate itself across the networks.

2. This estimate by the press may not be accurate. See Section on 6, "Impact of the Worm".

3. The operating system of a computer is a complex piece of software that controls the operations of the computer, providing the environment in which applications software can function. Every computer requires an operating system.

4. UNIX is a registered trademark of AT&T, the original developers of the system.

5. The Commission has chosen not to adopt an express standard of proof for its findings. The findings are only qualified where the Commission cannot reach a definitive conclusion.

6. We use the term "infect" to signify that at least one copy of the worm was left on the penetrated computer.

7. See following note.

8. Glen Adams of MIT, who has nominal responsibility for PREP although PREP has in reality been loosely managed by a group of graduate students, made an entry in his notebook following discovery of the worm on PREP that the attack occurred at "approximately 8:00 P.M.". From independent evidence, the Commission can verify that the worm was not launched before 7:26 P.M. Unfortunately, Adams did not keep the original computer records.

9. PREP was first identified as the site of the earliest attack in the *New York Times* article of November 5. According to Glen Adams, the author of that article, John Markoff, told him that he had reliably received that information from Paul Graham, a Harvard graduate student, who had been contacted by Morris the night of November 4 (see page 70 of this report). Adams contacted Graham by electronic mail. Graham's later electronic mail response apparently gave Adams the clear impression that Morris had confirmed the PREP launch of the worm to Graham otherwise, according to the impression given in Graham's response, Graham would not have reported such to the *New York Times*. Unfortunately, Adams did not keep a copy of that message and cannot recall the exact wording.

10. For example, a later analysis by the PREP System Manager revealed that between 200 and 500 of the accounts of PREP used passwords (see following note) which could trivially be cracked, such as the supposedly secure password being the same as the userid. Apparently MIT intends to remove PREP from service shortly.

11. A "userid" is the name by which an individual identifies him/herself to a computer when signing (logging) on. It is usually not a confidential piece of information

Additionally, the user is most often required to provide a secure "password", which is usually known only to that user and to certain privileged staff members who maintain the computer's software.

12. Staff members at Berkeley may have noticed it at about the same time.

13. The "C Language".

14. From the original source version decrypted from Morris' files, we know that this comprised about 3,568 lines of source C code.

15. Eric Allman, now at the International Computer Science Institute of the University of California at Berkeley, was a Berkeley graduate student and later a CSRG staff member when he designed SENDMAIL.

16. See "Introduction to the Evidence."

17. Every computer science graduate student has access to at least two computer accounts, one on a networked cluster of SUN workstations and the other on a VAX computer, SVAX. Both systems run versions of UNIX that were vulnerable to the worm.

18. The original worm "source" program was written in the computer language "C" and then compiled into an "object" program of machine language instructions. "Decompilation" is a form of reverse engineering that converts the object program, which is not easily understandable by even the most skilled computer programmers, back into a more understandable "C" program, which closely resembles the original source program.

19. See note 57

20. The October 15 version, which contains some of the most telling remarks on Morris' intent, had been left unencrypted. This may not have been an oversight by Morris. The computer may have performed its backup (see Section 4) procedure that night while Morris was working on the worm program and thus taken a snapshot of Morris' files while the worm program was unencrypted.

21. See note 18.

22. The significance of this is that it is now clear that the list of passwords contained in the worm was generated from knowledge obtained from the userid/passwords combinations. In other words, the perpetrator knew that each password in the list was a password to at least one account on the Internet.

23. Mr. Sudduth has since left Harvard University.

24. See previous note.

25. See comments concerning Graham on page 68.

26. See description of the worm on page 66.

27. See discussion of the events behind this closure on page 80.

28. See note 9.

29. See note 5.

30. See note 18.

31. Apparently someone at MIT had roughly estimated that the worm infected 10% of the computers they have attached to the network. Glen Adams has confirmed that the worm infected 90 computers running UNIX in the MIT Artificial Intelligence Laboratory, out of 300 computers altogether in the Laboratory (the rest are LISP machines). However, this number includes 50 Hewlett-Packard computers which the worm was able to penetrate but not infect, since the worm contained no Hewlett-Packard specific code which enabled it to regenerate itself on that computer.

32. Other estimates, based upon applying population dynamics to simulations of the network, have placed the number of infested computers closer to 3,000.

33. Berkeley students and staff detected the worm almost immediately after it arrived on the campus and were therefore able to analyze it rapidly and take immediate preventive and remedial action.

34. Cornell's links to the Internet come through the TC-GOULD computer located in the Cornell Center for Theory and Simulation.

35. Dennis M. Ritchie, "On the Security of UNIX".

36. See page 80. Something like this, in fact, happened.

37. As well as to computers at other universities, including Stanford and Berkeley, the latter including accounts on ERNIE, the VAX computer that was intended to play a special role in the spread of the worm.

38. Morris had recurrently worked on computer security at the Aiken Laboratory and other computer installations at Harvard University. He had also worked on computer security for various companies including AT&T, the original developer of UNIX.

39. His father has devoted much of his professional career to the improvement of computer security, and has testified before the U.S. Congress about the need to deglamorize computer hackers.

40. There is some dispute as to whether this was indeed a bug.

41. Letter to the Editor, New York Times, November 29, 1988.

42. Quoted from Peter Wayner's Letter to the Editor, New York Times, November 15, 1988.

43. Besides Sudduth, others who have commented along these lines include Scott Bradner (Technical Associate of the Harvard Psychology Department Computer Based Laboratory and Senior Preceptor in Psychology); Nicholas Horton, now at the Oregon Research Institute but who was Systems Manager at the Aiken Computational Laboratory in 1984–85; and Eric Roberts of the DEC Systems Information Research Center where Morris worked one summer under Roberts' supervision.

44. The Aiken Computational Laboratory and the Harvard Psychology Department Computer Based Laboratory.

45. Superuser privileges on UNIX systems are privileges normally only available to the systems programmers responsible for managing the system that give such programmers access to all files stored on the computer. Ethical practices in the profession permit the use of such privileges only for the purposes of improving and maintaining the system and not for the purpose of "snooping" through user files.

46. We focus on BSD UNIX. However, similar remarks apply to the version of UNIX that runs on SUN Microsystems computers, which is closely related to BSD UNIX.

47. BSD UNIX is distributed on an "as is" basis for research purposes. Apart from nominal distribution fees, there are no charges to users.

48. See note 43.

49. For example, the so-called IOCTL flaw.

50. UNIX security flaws are often discovered independently by several people.

51. Dean Krafft reported receiving the patch for this flaw several days before the worm hit and applying it to the Computer Science Department computers.

52. Adams reported that there had been several attempted penetrations at MIT alone.

53. Which is one reason why most Harvard computers running UNIX were not penetrated by the worm.

54. From Jim Haynes of the University of California at Santa Cruz.

55. See page 70.

56. There had been repeated unsuccessful attempts as early as October 19 to connect to the Electrical Engineering Department computer, but it is unknown whether these

attempts had anything to do with the worm. It would not have been possible to trace the origin of these attempts.

57. Although the final version of the worm was compiled at 7:26 P.M., it was not encrypted until 8:26 P.M. Having launched the worm sometime after 7:26 P.M., it is possible that Morris was waiting to see whether it worked before encrypting the final version and signing off.

ROGUE COMPUTER PROGRAMS AND COMPUTER ROGUES: TAILORING THE PUNISHMENT TO FIT THE CRIME

Anne W. Branscomb

INTRODUCTION

As computer networks become more ubiquitous, desktop computers more commonplace, and society becomes more dependent upon them, the potential for harm grows accordingly. Ironically, the laws to cope with such deleterious behavior lag disturbingly even as network managers become more concerned, cautious, and critical.

Policy analysts have conflicting views over the nature of the harm which can be inflicted and how it can be curbed. Law enforcement officers have doubts about what sanctions should be imposed against perpetrators. Security specialists are not confident that technological barriers can be erected to guarantee protection. Computer professionals are devising nonlegal strategies for coping with what some of them characterize as "technopathic" behavior. Users are apprehensive that excessive barriers, either legal or technological, may inhibit the ease of communications which computer networks have facilitated. Thus, there is little agreement concerning the level of legal protection which is currently available, appropriately applied or optimally desirable.

A review of existing state and federal legislation reveals a wide divergence of strategies for protection, some serious gaps in coverage of the more recent outbreaks of "rogue programs" including "computer viruses", "worms", "Trojan horses", "time bombs", and a host of other ailments. Legislators are rushing to their drafting boards to devise new statutes, to plug loopholes in existing laws, to cast wider legal nets to catch the newer transgressors, and to tailor the punishment to fit the crime.

The purpose of this article is to review several of the most recent incidents involving rogue behavior in computer networks, to review existing state and federal statutes which might cover these sets of facts, and to summarize the bills pending in Congress and considered by several state legislatures in the spring of 1989.

RECENT OUTBREAKS OF ROGUE BEHAVIOR

The Internet Worm

A disease, not unlike the bubonic plague of medieval times, struck the computer world on the evening of Wednesday, November 2, 1988. Of a universe of about 60,000 computers which might have been infected by the strange malady, some 6,200 (or about 10%) were slowed down to a halt by what computer specialists call a "worm," and the uninitiated call a "virus," because it spreads rapidly from victim to victim. Injected into the ARPANET, the worm quickly replicated itself into MILNET, and Internet.

Within a few hours, the electronic highways were so congested with traffic that computer specialists around the country went scurrying to their consoles trying to contain it. Indeed, the rogue computer software multiplied so rapidly that efforts of its creator to impede its growth were not effective. Eventually major computer centers around the country were involved, including NASA Ames Laboratory, Lawrence Livermore National Laboratory, SRI International, Massachusetts Institute of Technology (MIT), the University of California at both the Berkeley and San Diego campuses, Stanford, the University of Maryland, and the Rand Corporation. It was some forty-eight hours before calm was restored and the computer networks were back to normal.

According to the Computer Virus Industry Association (CVIA), whose members sell "vaccines" to assist in the rehabilitation of such infestation of computer software, the siege caused an estimated $96 million in labor costs to contain by clearing out the memories of the computers and checking all the software for signs of recovery. Higher estimates run from $186 million to $1.1 billion. In the aftermath, more sober minds have calculated that probably fewer than 2000 computers were affected and the value of the "down time" was closer to $1 million.

According to the experts, no actual damage to the computer hardware or the computer software was inflicted. For example, no files were destroyed, no software was wrecked, no classified systems were compromised. As a consequence it is not clear that any crime was committed, although a team of investigators went to work immediately to determine whether to indict. It was expected that the Internet worm would become the first prosecution under the federal Computer Fraud and Abuse Act.

Most computer crime laws require an intent to inflict harm, which was allegedly lacking in this case. Friends of the worm creator, Robert T. Morris, Jr., or RTM, as he is known for his computer "log-on" ID, reported that his motives were to test the vulnerability of the system in order to learn how to make it more secure. Nevertheless, the methodology was clandestine. According to friends, RTM entered the worm remotely via a computer at MIT. The program code was encrypted and designed to assume the identity of other users and report back to a remote computer suggesting an audit trail that would lead to other points of entry as the source of the questionable code.

As the alleged perpetrator was a first year graduate student at Cornell University, there is unlikely any personal source of financial largesse for money damages to be paid under tort law, although his behavior can likely meet the tests of ordinary negligence as well as reckless disregard for the consequences. It is conceivable that some tort action law would lie against Berkeley, where the UNIX program was issued (without charge to other universities), for permitting the imperfections in the software which facilitated the intrusion to remain uncorrected. These imperfections known as 'trap doors" allow access to an otherwise secure operating system. They are deliberately designed to permit a programmer with knowledge of the trap door to re-enter and correct errors or improve performance. Many computer programmers find these trap doors a convenience which do not in any way harm ordinary users. Thus, it might be difficult to show that the trap door per se was either negligent or the proximate cause of the harm which occurred.

It is also possible that a suit in tort might lie against one of the universities for failure to exert due supervision over its authorized users, although Cornell has completed an extensive investigation purported to exonerate it from any actionable negligence. Furthermore, to date the National Center for Computer Crime Data has reported no damage suits filed against computer network or service providers.

Ironically, the alleged culprit (who reportedly danced on the desk top when he discovered the trap door in the Berkeley version of UNIX through which he could insert his computer program) is a bright young twenty-three year old graduate of Harvard University where he was so trusted that he was given "super user" status on the Aiken Computers in order to assist in their maintenance.

RTM is the son of Robert T. Morris, Sr., the chief scientist of the National Computer Security Center. Mr. Morris is a nationally recognized and highly respected expert on computer break-ins, a twenty-six year veteran of the Bell Telephone Laboratories, and (not entirely coincidentally) one of the three designers of the first known computer virus played as a high tech recreational game known as "Core War" by computer programmers after hours to hone their skills. In fact, Robert T. Morris, Sr., testified before Congress several years ago, in an inquiry into the effects of computer viruses, that it would be a good omen if young computer scientists were so skilled as to be able to write such sophisticated programs.

Thus, the nature of the incident and the identity of the initiator suggest a dilemma as to whether or not criminal punishment is appropriate under the circumstances. Many computer scientists have been reported to predict that the younger RTM will mature and "make important discoveries in the computer field." Indeed, among some of the young computer literati (often referred to as "hackers"), RTM is looked upon as a folk hero. Even among the more seasoned citizenry, many equate RTM's behavior with that of Matthias Rust, the young German who flew his small plane through the Soviet border controls and landed in Red Square. Some even laud the invasion of the Internet worm as precipitating a therapeutic look at the security of the systems, because the incident has sent multitudes of computer professionals to the drawing boards to design more impenetrable network environments.

Many computer scientists and government officials fear that the pranksters and computer professionals who manipulate the software "for fun" or "for fame" may instruct potential saboteurs and terrorists on how to achieve their more destructive purposes. Thus, there was substantial disagreement among computer scientists over the request by the National Computer Security Center (NSSC) for Purdue to keep secret the details of the Internet worm's source code, which they decompiled. Many managers of information systems are opposed to such secrecy because they want to know the internal structure of the offending code in order to better protect their computers from further attack of viral infections.

Federal officials were, according to published reports, at odds on the nature of the indictment, if any. The U.S. Attorney for the Northern District of New York (where the entry point to the network originated at Cornell) was reported to favor plea bargaining a misdemeanor conviction in exchange for further disclosure of the circumstances surrounding the incident. The Department of Justice lawyers and the Federal Bureau of Investigation reportedly favored felony charges as a deterrent to would-be computer hackers, telephone "phreakers" and other assorted pranksters. When the indictment was finally issued on July 26, 1989, by a federal grand jury in Syracuse, New York, RTM was accused of gaining access to federal interest computers, preventing authorized access by others, and causing damage in excess of $1,000.

The Aldus Peace Virus

On March 2, 1988, the anniversary of the advent of Apple Computer's MacIntosh II and SE models, the following message popped up on the monitors of thousands of MacIntosh personal computers in the United States and Canada:

> Richard Brandow, the publisher of MacMag, and its entire staff would like to take this opportunity to convey their universal message of peace to all MacIntosh users around the world.

Beneath the message appeared a picture of the globe. Brandow, publisher of a computer magazine based in Montreal, Canada, acknowledged in a telephone interview to an Associated Press writer that he had written the message. However, he only intended to show how widespread software piracy had become. Indeed, he proved his point beyond his own expectations as an estimated 350,000 MacIntosh computers displayed the peace message. The software had been conceived some year or so earlier and previously tested by its designers—a co-worker, Pierre M. Zovile', and Drew Davidson of Tucson. According to Brandow, it was imbedded in a popular game program called "Mr. Potato Head" and left on a MacIntosh in the offices of MacMag, a popular gathering place for MacIntosh users, for only two days during a Mac users conference.

The message later turned up in Freehand, a program distributed by the Aldus Corporation, a software company based in Seattle, Washington, precipitating the recall of some 5,000 copies of the program. This is the first known contamination of off-the-shelf (commercially marketed) software, since it had been assumed in the past that such viruses were distributed in freely exchanged disks or on electronic bulletin boards. The transfer to commercially marketed software was accomplished, without his knowledge, by Marc Canter, President of Macromind, Inc., of Chicago, Illinois, who reviewed the infected disk on a computer which was later used for copying of a self instructional program intended for distribution by the Aldus Corporation. Less than half of the duplicated disks were actually distributed to retailers, but the computer industry has become permeated by fear of viral contamination, as many of the major software companies are customers of Macromind, including Ashton-Tate, Lotus, and Microsoft.

Lotus, Microsoft, and Apple claim that none of their products have been contaminated, and Ashton-Tate has declined to comment. However, Apple hastened to design a vaccine which would remove hidden codes in tainted programs. Further, it distributed the vaccine free of charge on many electronic bulletin boards and networks.

According to the best available information, the program was "benign" in that it destroyed no files, interfered with no functions, and erased itself after popping up on the computer screens as triggered by its timing device on March 2, 1988. However, its very existence created consternation among leaders of the computer industry that users would perceive its products as unreliable.

The Pakistani Brain

In the late spring of 1988, Froma Joselow, a reporter for the *Journal-Bulletin*, of Providence, Rhode Island, booted a disk containing the last six months of her work product including the notes for the article she intended to write. Appearing each time she tried to call up a file was the warning "DISK ERROR." Upon further examination by a Systems Engineer at the *Journal-Bulletin*, the following message appeared on the computer monitor.

WELCOME TO THE DUNGEON

1986 Basit & Amjad (pvt) Ltd.

BRAIN COMPUTER SERVICES

[address and telephone in Lahore, Pakistan]

Beware of this Virus

Contact Us for Vaccination

This was a well designed and cleverly executed device by two Pakistani brothers, Amjad Farooq Alvi (age twenty-six) and Basit Farooq (age nineteen), who studied physics at Punjab University, taught themselves computer programming, and operated a small computer store in Lahore, Pakistan. According to an interview given to a reporter for *The Chronicle of Education*, Basit admitted introducing the message "for fun" which was well hidden within popular software such as Lotus 1-2-3 and Wordstar. He disavowed any knowledge of how it came to reside in the computers of the *Journal-Bulletin* or on the disks of hundreds of students at the Universities of Pittsburgh, Pennsylvania, Delaware, George Washington, and Georgetown.

Later Amjad admitted that their original intentions had been to protect their own computer software from local pirates who would have to contact them to decontaminate the disks which had been copied rather than purchased. As the program evolved, however, it was deliberately imbedded in commercially available and copyrighted software which the Farooq brothers sold to foreign tourists. "Because you are pirating, . . . [y]ou must be punished," Amjad was quoted as saying, thus admitting to be an accessory to a form of electronic lynching in order to punish foreigners who were contravening their copyright law and depriving their countrymen from potential sales. Computer software was not then covered by Pakistani copyright statutes, so it was quite legal, under Pakistani law, to import from abroad expensive issues of computer software and resell copies on the domestic Pakistani market for as little at one dollar and fifty cents.

According to Harold Highland, editor of *Computers and Security*, the Pakistani Brain virus was very sophisticated and cleverly designed. It never infected a hard disk and was quite media specific, imbedding itself only into DOS formatted disks. One admirer complimented Amjad, "This virus is elegant. He may be the best virus designer the world has ever seen."

However, this brotherly calling card was quite destructive, attacking the disks primarily of university students and journalists. It was less troublesome systemically, because it did not attack hard disks or main frames or enter any widely used computer networks. However, various versions continue to erupt in one part of the world or another. For example, a second infestation of the Pakistani Brain virus erupted in November 1988 in the School of Business at the University of Houston, this time in a slightly modified version but with the old copyright notice! It is difficult to ascertain how many users were affected, as the reports vary from a few hundred to an estimated 10,000 at George Washington University alone.

The Burleson Revenge

On September 21, 1985, an employee of the USPA & IRS, Inc., a brokerage house and insurance company in Fort Worth, Texas, discovered to his dismay that 168,000 of the firm's sales commission records had vanished without a trace. The only clue was an unusual entry into the computer at 3:00 A.M. earlier that morning, a time when no employee should have been operating the system. Working all weekend, the MIS crew restored the records from back-up tapes, thinking they had repaired the damage. On the contrary, when other employees reported for work on Monday morning and turned on their computer consoles, the entire system "crashed" and became inoperable.

Reconstructing the pathway to this crisis, the audit trail led to an instruction to "power down" (a command to disable the computer) which was invoked by a simple retrieval command. The computer professionals referred to the intricately designed software as "trip wires" and "time bombs" designed "to wipe out two sections of memory at random, then duplicate itself, change its own name, and execute automatically one month later unless the memory area was reset." No permanent damage was done to the system and the data processing staff was able to reconstruct the system from scratch including the installation of a new operating system from IBM.

The breach of security was eventually determined to be the work of an employee, with access to all of the passwords of the company, who had been dismissed three days earlier.

Donald Gene Burleson, who was variously described as arrogant, rebellious against authority, and a superbly skilled programmer, was ultimately indicted and convicted of computer abuse under the Texas Penal Code which permits a felony charge to be filed if the damage exceeds $2,500 from altering, damaging, destroying data, causing a computer to malfunction or interrupting normal operations. Moreover, under the applicable Texas statutes, using a computer or accessing data without the consent of the owner is a misdemeanor.

Burleson was likely guilty of all of the above. There was no question that there was malice aforethought. The software which contained an instruction to disable the company's computers was created, according to the computer records on September 3, almost three weeks before the execution. A jury of six males and six females convicted Burleson who was later fined $11,800 in damages and sentenced to seven years probation.

The Compulsive "Cyberpunk"

One of the first miscreants to be charged and convicted early in 1989 under the Computer Fraud and Abuse Act of 1986 was Kevin David Mitnick, a 25-year-old computer rogue whose psychological profile can be described as a typical compulsive "cyberpunk." According to his colleague and fellow rogue, Leonard DiCicco, who turned him into the authorities, Mitnick could not pass a day happily without invading some computer network or data base into which he was not authorized to enter.

Many of these computer excursions were not harmful, as they were merely invasions to prove his capability to bypass established security procedures. The defending lawyer described Mitnick's miscreant behavior as an effort to achieve self-esteem, "an intellectual exercise ... [to] see if he could get in. It's Mt. Everest—because it's there." Like RTM, Mitnick was a student whose computer skills were described as quite outstanding by the Director of the Computer Learning Center in Los Angeles.

However, the Mitnick intrusions were not always benign. Law enforcement officers around the country referred to him as "an electronic terrorist" afflicted by an addiction to breaking into secure computer systems. Mitnick reputedly mangled the credit records of a judge who sentenced him to a term in the reformatory, and he had a long record of juvenile offenses which were computer related. Ironically, or perhaps justifiably, his last caper (among many for which he was convicted) was purloining, electronically, a new program designed by Digital Equipment Corporation to apprehend such unwanted invaders as Mitnick himself.

Significantly, Mitnick never owned a computer, was financially insolvent, and was using a computer of the University of Southern California when apprehended. Thus, neither sequestering his equipment nor requiring restitution would have any efficacy whatsoever. Lauded by his teachers as a genius with computer programs, Mitnick was treated as a hardened criminal by his enforcement officers. Denied bail by the judge, and prohibited from making telephone calls, the handling of his pending trial was unusually severe. The prosecutors likened a computer in the hands of Mitnick as dangerous as a gun in the hands of a sharpshooting outlaw.

Sentenced to a year in jail, Mitnick's future prospects are clouded. However, he serves as an example of the commonly accepted characterization of a hacker described by his classmates as a fat slob who sat around eating junk food all the time staring at a computer terminal. Thus, his sense of achievement came from his ability to manipulate the computer environment in which he operated.

The aberrant behavior, described herein, is better characterized as that of a cyberpunk rather than a hacker, which, as originally conceived by the computer community, was not considered a pejorative term. Cyberpunks are motivated by a compulsive desire to exert controlling power over their environment. This is not dissimilar from the behavior of "ghetto gangs" or motorcycle clubs out on a "rumble" or rampage. Their behavior propels them to greater and more deleterious exploits in order to get a "fix" or "high" from the experience.

Other Well Known Rogue Programs

One of the earliest virus outbreaks, which was treated as a hacker's prank, was the program known as "The Cookie Monster." When serious students were busy at their consoles a message would pop up on the screen, "I want a cookie!" The message would not go away, thus disabling further work, until the weary student figured out that it was necessary to enter "COOKIE" on the keyboard. In a similar vein is the PAC MAN program, considered by some to be a "delightful hack," which devours the work in progress on the screen. There is also the PING PONG (or Italian) virus which bounces ping pong balls across the monitor. Other more deleterious programs devoured all memory, as well as work in progress, then gloated on the screen with a message which said "Arf, arf, Gotcha!"

Most of these early rogue programs were characterized as more or less harmless computer games. These replicated in the electronic environment the not always benign tricks or pranks which college students play on each other. A more devastating prank was a program listed as RCK.VIDEO with an animation featuring the popular singer Madonna which erased all files while she was performing and then announced to the bewildered viewer, "You're stupid to download a video about rock stars."

Not quite so benign in its consequences either was the IBM Christmas card which was innocently sent to a friend by a West German law student through the European Academic Research Network (EARN) in early December of 1987. The message, with a Christmas tree graphic, was sent through an electronic mail system designed to resend itself to all addresses on the addressees' mailing lists. So promptly did this message propagate itself that the entire internal IBM messaging system, which reaches 145 countries, was brought to a halt by the runaway Christmas spirit. IBM only acknowledged to its employees on December 14, 1987, that a "disruptive file" entitled "CHRISTMA.EXEC" had produced "an excessive volume of network traffic" and was an inappropriate use of IBM assets.

The various rogue programs requiring unauthorized entry into computer networks had no special capability to violate security except by discovering and copying names and addresses, passwords, or identification codes of users, many of whom were careless in their selection of words or numbers which could be easily guessed. Thus, it is asserted by responsible government officials that no high level secured computers have been compromised by destructive rogue programs.

However, much publicity has circulated concerning the antics of members of a computer club in Hamburg, West Germany, called CHAOS, whose presence has been perceived in numerous high level government computers in Europe and the United States. According to Herwart "Wau" Holland (age thirty-six), the club's founder, the entire purpose of the club is creative and benevolent—to increase the flow of public information which is tightly held and controlled by overly zealous public authorities. Indeed, the group was said to be quite instrumental in keeping the press well informed concerning the Chernobyl incident, contradicting official reports designed to calm the fears of the population.

Systems managers who have diligently observed the persevering and plodding efforts to crack open the closed computer networks are not so kind in their characterizations of these electronic "break-ins," since it is impossible to tell the difference between voyeurism and espionage. Also unimpressed are security officers of the systems who find that their protective protocols have been penetrated when they discover the "calling cards" left by CHAOS members. So far these have been benign and seem to fall in the category of the "Kilroy was Here" graffiti which adorned many edifices during World War II. The primary vice other than "unauthorized entry" would appear to be publicizing the methods used for "breaking and entering."

Not everyone condemns the activities of the CHAOS Computer Club. Some observers applaud the efforts of these electronic Robin Hoods to disseminate the riches of the information age to the information poor. As for CHAOS, its leaders disavow any purpose other than to expose excessive government secrecy to a little therapeutic sunlight.

Most of the highly sensitive national security and financial industry systems have either not been breached or those who have suffered viral maladies are not admitting to any harm. However, a number of intracorporate networks have been invaded, and recently the Databank System, Ltd., in Wellington, New Zealand, was the first electronic funds transfer system to admit publicly that it had been infected with a virus which read "Your PC is Now Stoned! LEGALIZE MARIJUANA!"

The Soviet Union has not escaped infection, as Sergei Abramov, a computer specialist at the USSR Academy of Sciences, revealed on Radio Moscow in December 1988. A group of Soviet and foreign school children attending a summer computer camp unleashed the "DOS-62" virus which affected 80 computers at the academy. Prior to August of 1988, there had been no evidence of such infestations, but since then two distinct viruses have turned up in at least five different locations.

Clearly, the epidemic of rogue behavior is a global problem which cannot be contained merely by state or even national laws but will likely require a considerable amount of coordination at the international level if the electronic highways are to be safe. However, the problem of containment cannot be any more challenging than controlling the highwaymen of medieval times or the pirates of the high seas.

MOTIVATIONS OF THE TRANSGRESSORS

An analysis of the purposes for which these rogue programs are written discloses the following:

A. *Prowess*—Much of the unauthorized entry would appear to be accomplished by young computer enthusiasts seeking thrills by exercising their computer skills. This appears to be by far the most prevalent motivation among the so called hackers such as RTM, many of whose young admirers thought he had achieved the "ultimate hack." Indeed, the original use of the word was to describe programmers who were capable of writing elegant code which was the envy of their colleagues. Thus the most numerous and most often benign instances of unauthorized entry of rogue programs into computer networks are merely for the fun of it.

B. *Protection*—In some cases, the motivation seems to have been an effort to penetrate systems in order to better understand how to protect them. Indeed, such penetration of security systems has demonstrated skills which have led some of the hackers into employment as security consultants.

C. *Punishment*—In a few cases the purpose can be likened to a self described posse. For example, the Farooq brothers imbedded their destructive programs in software sold to foreign customers purportedly to punish them for what they perceived to be unethical purchases of software which they should have purchased from their own countrymen at market prices on their domestic market.

D. *Peeping*—This would appear to constitute a sort of electronic voyeurism. Such unauthorized entries would not qualify as viruses unless the voyeur left a calling card which contained a self replicating message. There is evidence that some of the systems purported to be the most secure in design have been penetrated by voyeurs, not by viruses. The young accomplice of Mitnick who turned him in to the authorities was quoted as saying, "Our favorite was the National Security Agency computer because it was supposed to be so confidential. It was like a big playground once you got into it."

E. *Philosophy*—Many of the computer hackers look upon information as a public good which should not be hoarded, therefore, entry should not be prohibited. They can be characterized as "Information Socialists" who believe that all systems should have open access and their contexts be shared.

F. *Potential Sabotage*—There has, as yet, been revealed to the public little evidence of the work product of terrorists invading computer systems. However, there have been reports that both the Central Intelligence Agency (CIA) and the National Security Agency (NSA) are experimenting with the use of viruses as a strategic weapon. Some analysts predict that it is merely a matter of time before electronic terrorism becomes a more common occurrence.

PERPETRATORS

From a review of the above cases, it would appear that there are a variety of perpetrators, some of whom can easily be characterized as maliciously motivated but many of whom cannot. These include the following:

A. *Employees*—Most of the devastating incidents are caused by authorized employees acting outside the scope of their employment for their own benefit or to the detriment of the organization. Certainly this was the case with Donald Gene Burleson. The number of such incidents is unknown, since it is thought to be information tightly held by the companies afflicted. Indeed, in one known case the employee was dismissed quietly but given a lavish going away party to disguise the nature of his exodus from the company.

B. *Software Developers*—Developers of software initially turned to protected disks which performed poorly, if at all, when copied without authorization. These contained "bugs" or malfunctions deliberately written into the software code in order to prevent piracy, as in the case of the Pakistani Brain Virus. There is likely to be less of this type of situation as the major software firms have discovered that sales were inhibited by substantial user abhorrence of this technique.

However, it is well known that some software programs have imbedded within their code logic sequences designed to disable use of the programs at the termination of a lease. Thus laws designed to reach secret messages entered without notifying the user might overreach their intended purpose and catch in their net practices considered by the industry as both efficacious and desirable.

C. *Pranksters*—The word prankster is used more aptly than hackers to describe young computer users, mostly in their teens, attempting to develop their computer skills and deliberately, but usually not maliciously, entering systems purportedly closed to them. Damage, when it occurs, is usually caused by the prankster's ineptness rather than intention. The prankster's intent is merely to "beat the system" to prove his cleverness. This type of incident is characterized by the so-called "Milwaukee Microkids" who ran rampant through many of the major computer systems of the U.S. government and played havoc with the monitoring systems of cancer patients in a New York City hospital in 1983. The FBI took concerted and coordinated action against the "microkids," seizing the computers of a number of these youngsters in order to send a message of disapproval to all potential pranksters.

D. *Professionals*—Computer "professionals" fall into three categories—those with criminal intent, those who are apprentices attempting to improve their skills, and those who are deliberately attempting to break into closed systems in order to test their vulnerability and increase awareness of the defects. The latter case is much like the antic efforts of Nobel laureate physicist, Richard Feynman, at Los Alamos, who broke into the safes of his colleagues leaving only an amusing calling card to prove his successful entry thereby proving that they were quite vulnerable to spies.

In this category should be included the so-called hackers, a term which originally applied only to skilled computer programmers who genuinely felt that computer systems should be open. Such hackers believed the effort to improve computer software was an ongoing process in which all the "cognoscenti" should be able to participate, and they were committed to designing advanced computer hardware and software. The Cornell report carefully avoids using the word hacker pejoratively.

E. *Cyberpunks*—This term has come to be used in describing computer skilled but anti-social individuals who deliberately disrupt computer systems merely for the joy and personal satisfaction which comes from such achievement. The term is derived from a popular science fiction genre which describes such cyberpunks as engaged in sophisticated high technology games. They constitute a form of outlaw society akin to the gangs or teenagers who roam the poverty-stricken areas of inner cities, where young people have nothing better to do to satisfy their egos than take control of their areas of habitation. The primary motivation of cyberpunks is to take control over their electronic environment.

F. *Saboteurs or Terrorists*—So far there have been no incidents of entries which have been publicly disclosed of deliberate destruction or interruption of service attributed to terrorist groups, although there have been incidents of voyeurism and espionage. However, there is much apprehension among computer security officials that terrorists are capable of acquiring sophisticated computer programming skills and may apply them to the many networks upon which international commerce, finance, and industry have come to rely.

CRIMINAL LIABILITY UNDER EXISTING STATE STATUTES

Although every one of the fifty states except Vermont now has some kind of computer crime or computer abuse law, the Burleson case is the first conviction under a state law for inserting into a computerized environment what has been characterized by some (but not by others) as a computer virus. Thus its implications have created much interest among law enforcement officers and computer professionals concerning this new threat to computer integrity.

Unfortunately, the case does not offer much insight into the applicability of other state laws to computer virus cases. It was a rather clean cut fact situation in which the perpetrator was a disgruntled employee who had been dismissed but retained access to the security codes of the company. His retaliation was easily proved to be maliciously inspired. Moreover, the prosecution was conducted by a young prosecutor who was skilled and understood the nature of the behavior which was offered in evidence in the trial. The brightest spot in retrospect is that the jury disclaimed any difficulty in following the case or in reaching its conclusions.

The Internet worm case, on the other hand, suggests the difficulty in proving beyond a reasonable doubt that criminal behavior has occurred without an admission on the part of the perpetrator that such was his or her intent. In the worm case, the audit trail uncovered that the virus' point of entry into the system was an MIT source and that the program code required the virus to report back to a Berkeley node whenever it succeeded in invading another host. Without the software designer's error in the code which never reported back to the Berkeley computer and the surrounding circumstances of a telephone call to a friend in the Aiken Laboratory at Harvard University warning that "his virus had kind of gotten loose," an intended saboteur might easily have caused the disruption within the nation's academic networks without leaving a trace of the actual origin.

It can be concluded, from a review of state laws, that they cover a variety of circumstances and fall into several different categories. Since most of the state laws use the words "alter, damage, or destroy," the *Burleson* case might easily have been prosecuted under the majority of state laws since files were destroyed. However, it is not so clear that the Internet worm situation falls within the ambit of more than a few state statutes, since the problems which occurred were loss of memory and inability of the computer networks to accommodate their users in the manner to which they had become accustomed.

State statutes cover at least ten distinct categories of offenses as follows:

Definition of Property Expanded

A few states have merely modified existing criminal statutes to include within the definition of "property" information residing on a computer disk or within a computer network or mainframe. Montana defines "property" as including "electronic impulses, electronically processed or produced data or information, ... computer software or computer programs, in either machine- or human-readable form, computer services, any other tangible or intangible item of value relating to a computer, computer system, or computer network, and any copies thereof." The Massachusetts statute is even more succinct, defining "property" to include "electronically processed or stored data, either tangible or intangible, [and] data while in transit. ..."

Although such statutes define property as including computer mediated information, this does not necessarily resolve the problem of a conviction for larceny or theft. Usually the requirement for a conviction is a "taking" with the intent to deprive the owner of the possession or use thereof. Voyeurism with no intent to deprive or harm and/or viruses which have benign consequences (such as the Aldus Peace message) do not deprive the owner or user of access to or use of any computer files or computer services, except perhaps momentarily while an unwanted message appears on the screen. Nonetheless, costs are incurred to verify that no damage has been done, and recent legislative efforts, such as that in the state of Oklahoma, are beginning to address this problem.

Unlawful Destruction

Many state statutes seek to prohibit acts which "alter, damage, delete, or destroy" computer programs or files. Such statutory language appears commonly in computer abuse statutes and is sufficient to cover the most dangerous forms of activities. Presumably viral code requires some alteration of the sequences in the computer memory in order to function; however, a worm can be inserted by an authorized user without altering any existing files or the operating system.

The Illinois statute is written more broadly than many of the other states' statutes. It refers to the crime of "computer tampering" which would presumably cover even worms. However, the Illinois statute is aimed more particularly at the disruption of vital services of the state, as well as death or bodily harm resulting from the tampering. This would presumably include modification of medical records which were the proximate cause of death or resulted in the negligent treatment of patients.

Use to Commit, Aid, or Abet Commission of a Crime

Many of the state laws also cover use of a computer or its capacities to aid or abet the commission of a crime such as theft, embezzlement of fraud. One such statute is in place in Arizona, which penalizes the use of alteration of computer programs with the intent to "devise or execute any scheme or artifice to defraud or deceive, or control property or services. . . ."

Crimes Against Intellectual Property

Other state statutes treat these unwanted computer acts as offenses against intellectual property. The Mississippi statute specifies such offenses as the "[d]estruction, insertion or modification, without consent, of intellectual property; or [alternatively, as the d]isclosure, use, copying, taking or accessing, without consent, of intellectual property."

Although the Mississippi statute requires that such acts be intentional and not accidental, there is no requirement that they be malicious or harmful. Thus, the most innocent voyeurism, even though no actual damage occurred, could be "accessing" within the meaning of the act.

Knowing Unauthorized Use

Some states regard "knowingly unauthorized use" of a computer or computer service as unsanctioned behavior. A Nevada statute is typical of this group of states, which broadly define "unlawful use" to include that which "modifies, destroys, discloses, uses, takes, copies, enters." However, this does not specifically prevent the authorized use which was the problem in the case of the Internet worm. The Nebraska statute, on the other hand, contains the phrase "knowingly and intentionally exceeds the limits of authorization," which would likely cover the RTM behavior. Although RTM was an authorized user of the institutions through which he entered the computer networks, the Cornell report at least purports to establish that his use of his account went beyond the limits of his authorization.

The Ohio statute prohibits the unauthorized use of property which includes "computer data or software." The statute has what appears to be the broadest prohibition against any use "beyond the scope of the express or implied consent of, the owner. . . ." The New Hampshire statute prohibits an act which "causes to be made an unauthorized display, use or copy, in any form. . . ." These two statutes are surely broad enough to encompass the Aldus virus, which was benign, yet disturbing, because users were not assured that it was benign when it popped up on their screens.

Unauthorized Copying

A statute, such as New York has enacted, prohibits both unauthorized duplication or copying of computer files or software, as well as receipt of goods reproduced or duplicated in violation of the Act. Very few states have included provisions of this type.

Prevention of Authorized Use

Approximately one-fourth of the states refer to interfering with, or preventing normal use by, authorized parties. This presumably would cover the existence of a worm, such as the Internet worm, which allegedly did no actual damage to files, software, or equipment but occupied so much space in memory that it exhausted the computers' capacities and prevented normal functioning of the networks. Typical of this type of statute is the Wyoming statute which describes a "crime against computer users" as "knowingly and without authorization" accessing computer files, or denying services to an authorized user.

Unlawful Insertion

Several states have enacted statutes which are broad enough to cover even the benign Aldus virus. These statutes prohibit any unauthorized addition of material into a computerized environment. The Connecticut statute, which is probably the most comprehensive state law, prohibits an act which "intentionally makes or causes to be made an unauthorized display, use, disclosure or copy, in any form, of data. . . ." The Delaware statute also refers to "interrupt[ing] or add[ing] data" and the Mississippi statute includes "insertion" of material without authorization as a specifically prohibited act. It would appear that no harm need occur for these offenses to be committed. Such breadth in the statutes, however, may not be objectionable if they are rationally administered.

Voyeurism

A few of the statutes cover unauthorized entry with the purpose only of seeing what is there. The Missouri statute refers to "[i]ntentionally examin[ing] information about another person" as a misdemeanor, thus recognizing a right of electronic privacy. On the other hand, the Kentucky statute specifically excludes from criminal behavior accessing a computerized environment only "to obtain information and not to commit any other act proscribed by this section. . . ." Thus, the statute excludes mere voyeurism from prosecution. Other states are beginning to see the implications of excessive criminalization. For example, the Massachusetts legislature is presently considering a bill which would exempt employees who purloin time using computers or programs outside the scope of their employment if no injury occurs and the value of the time is less than $100.00. West Virginia has specifically excluded those who have reasonable ground to believe they had the authority or right to do what otherwise would be an offense.

"Taking Possession of"

A few of the existing statutes and several of the proposed bills refer to "taking possession of" the computer or software. This presumably means to exert control over a computer network or system.

The term is somewhat ambiguous and abstruse. It is not clear whether or not the phrase is intended to cover the kind of antisocial behavior described above as that of cyberpunks. Surely actual theft of the computer itself would be covered under the normal definition of theft of physical property. Thus, it must be assumed that some other meaning was intended by the drafters. The Wisconsin statute prohibits willfully, knowingly, and without authorization taking "possession of data, computer programs or supporting documentation." Perhaps the program known as "the cookie monster" is an apt example of this aberrant behavior. If prosecution is to proceed under such a statute, the aid of computer scientists will be required to describe what anti-social behavior should be proscribed more particularly.

NEWLY ENACTED AND PROPOSED STATE LEGISLATION

Several states have enacted new computer abuse legislation or are considering new computer abuse legislation. This spate of legislative initiatives suggests that existing statutes are not perceived to be entirely satisfactory for the prosecution of perpetrators of destructive rogue computer programs. Even in states where the statutes may be presently adequate, such as California, refinements are sought to make infringements which endanger the health of computer networks and systems easier to prosecute. A review of recently enacted and proposed state legislation follows.

Minnesota

The original Minnesota bill was the first piece of legislation proposed to cover specific computer rogue programs including statutory language which would define them. The proposed bill would have revised the existing computer abuse statute by adding a new section defining "destructive computer programs" to specifically include viruses, trojan horses, worms, and bacteria.

The proposed definition of a worm included the intention to disable or degrade performance. Whether the Internet worm would be covered by this definition is not clear, given the ambiguities surrounding the worm designer's intent. It was RTM's reported intention to inject a slowly self-replicating worm whose presence would not be obvious or easily detected, or damage other programs existing within the network. However, Minnesota's proposed statutory definition of destructive products would cover precisely this situation. The definition of destructive products included producing unauthorized data that makes computer memory space unavailable for authorized computer programs.

There was apprehension among lawyers representing computer software companies who reviewed the proposed bill that the attempt to enumerate types of rogue programs so specifically might create more problems than it solved. As a consequence, the legislation, as enacted, was written more broadly to describe the unacceptable consequences rather than the miscreant programs themselves:

"Destructive computer program" means a computer program that performs a destructive function or produces a destructive product. A program performs a destructive function if it degrades performance of the affected computer, associated peripherals or a computer program; disables the computer, associated peripherals or a computer program; or destroys or alters computer programs or data. A program produces a destructive product if it produces unauthorized data, including data that make computer memory space unavailable; results in the unauthorized alteration of data or computer programs; or produces a destructive computer program, including a self-replicating program.

Maryland

The Maryland amendment was signed into law by the governor on May 25, 1989. In referring to harmful access to computers, the bill adds two new sections prohibiting acts which: (1) "cause the malfunction or interrupt the operation of a computer" or (2) "alter, damage, or destroy data or a computer program." The latter phrase merely extends coverage to offenses which most of the other states already prohibit. The first term appears to be broader than the majority of the state statutes now include and seems to cast a wide enough net to capture the Internet worm and the Aldus virus, as well as the Pakistani Brain.

West Virginia

The West Virginia legislature has enacted in the 1989 legislative session its first computer abuse law. According to sponsors of the legislation, enactment of this bill puts West Virginia at the forefront of states most hospitable to the computer software industry. The overall effect of the bill has been described as broad enough to cover the introduction of a virus "that destroys the intellectual integrity of [a] program." The bill specifically addresses tampering, as well as invasions of privacy.

As initially proposed, the bill would have included other innovative provisions which were not adopted. One such proposal permitted equipment that is used in the commission of a crime to be confiscated and turned over to the West Virginia educational system. Another proposal would hold corporate officers accountable for illegal activities within their organizations. Both Georgia and Utah have adopted a similar provision imposing a duty to report knowledge of prohibited computer related activities.

Texas

In Texas, the Burleson case was successfully prosecuted under that state's computer crime legislation. A minor amendment was proposed to permit the confiscation of computer equipment. Such a sanction is considered appropriate in order to deter teenage hackers who cruise the computer networks looking for excitement. A similar provision is found in New Mexico's Computer Crimes Act. In addition, California legislation permits confiscated computer equipment to be assigned to a local government or public entity or nonprofit agency.

Furthermore, the Texas legislature passed a bill which was more comprehensive, both defining computer viruses and prohibiting their introduction into a "computer program, computer network, or computer system." The new Texas statute also liberalizes the venue requirements and authorizes a civil right of action for damages incurred.

Illinois

The Illinois General Assembly Legislative Research Unit has issued a report entitled "Computer Viruses and the Law." The report finds the substantive law adequate in its definitions, but suggests amending the Illinois statutes to reenact a now superseded civil right of action for miscreant computer behavior in a computerized environment. In addition, legislation was recently enacted which creates a new offense of inserting or attempting to insert a program while "knowing or having reason to believe" that it may damage or destroy.

Pennsylvania

The Pennsylvania Legislative Budget & Finance Committee issued a report entitled, "Computer 'Viruses' and their Potential for Infecting Commonwealth Computer Systems." The report recommends that the proscribed behavior should be better defined. However, the proposed statute broadly defines a computer virus as "a program or set of computer instructions with the ability to replicate all or part of itself. . . ." This is arguably overreaching in its thrust as it is intended to prohibit all insertions of computer viruses into computer memories, networks, or systems. Thus, it proscribes utilitarian as well as deleterious programs designed to replicate themselves.

New York

Two bills recently proposed in New York purport to increase the maximum fines and years of incarceration to more nearly approximate the magnitude of the damages inflicted. These bills would liberalize the criteria of intent necessary for a conviction to include a reasonable knowledge that damage would result. This provision would likely ease one of the problems encountered under the federal legislation where behavior considered in reckless disregard of the consequences is not considered.

Massachusetts

There were four bills introduced in Massachusetts in early 1989, only one of which was designed explicitly to cover computer viruses. This bill distinguishes between computer larceny and computer breaking and entering. Computer larceny is defined as "knowingly releas[ing] a computer virus that destroys or modifies data." Computer breaking and entering is defined as the release of "a computer virus that does not destroy or modify the data but does interfere with the user's ability to use the computer." There are three levels of fines and imprisonment imposed under the bill according to the degree of interference. For computer breaking and entering, the maximum fine is $500 and the maximum length of imprisonment is one year. For computer larceny limited to modification of data, the punishment is imprisonment for not more than one year and a maximum fine of $750. If data is completely destroyed, the maximum fine is $25,000 and the maximum imprisonment is ten years.

California

The California legislature received four bills between January and March 1989. Senate Bill No. 1012, which was approved by the Governor on September 29, 1989, increases the penalties "against persons who tamper, interfere, damage, and access without authorization into . . . computer systems."

Assembly Bill No. 1858 expanded the circumstances under which extradition could be requested as follows: "[T]he demand or surrender on demand may be made even if the person whose surrender on demand may be made even if the person whose surrender is demanded was not in the demanding state at the time of the commission of the crime and has not fled from the demanding state." This was clearly intended to cover situations involving computer networks where the perpetrator of the act which injured parties or equipment within the demanding state was in another jurisdiction at the time of the act.

Senate Bill No. 304 and Assembly Bill No. 1859, enacted September 30, 1989 and October 2, 1989, respectively, are companion bills designed to cover computer rogue programs which are generically referred to as "computer contaminants." The prohibited act is knowingly introducing a computer contaminant into a computer network or system without the specific approval of the proprietor. The operative language reads:

> "Computer contaminant" means any set of computer instructions designed to modify, damage, destroy, record, or transmit information within a computer, computer system, or computer network without the intent or permission of the owner of the information. They include, but are not limited to, a group of computer instructions commonly called viruses or worms, which are self-replicating or self-propagating and are designed to contaminate other computer programs or computer data, consume computer resources, modify, destroy, record, or transmit data, or in some other fashion usurp the normal operation of the computer, computer system, or computer network.

Other more questionable provisions provide for a five year exclusion from employment with computers upon conviction of any such computer abuse law, and the withholding of degrees by California colleges and universities. This sanction has also been proposed in New York. Additionally, there is a provision for forfeiture of equipment which can be turned over to a local government or nonprofit agency. Moreover, the amendment would impose a duty on those persons aware of acts of computer abuse within their purview to report such violations to law enforcement authorities. This would eliminate a major problem which is the failure of employers to bring incidents to the attention of the authorities.

New Mexico

In New Mexico, a greatly expanded Computer Crimes Act was recently enacted. In addition to a more comprehensive coverage of unauthorized computer use, the major thrust is toward forfeiture of equipment used to accomplish the prohibited acts. As effective as this may be in deterring miscreants who own their equipment, it would have no impact on hackers such as RTM or technopaths such as Mitnick who used computer resources belonging to third parties.

FEDERAL STATUTES

According to published reports, federal prosecutors considered at least four possible offenses under Title 18 of the U.S. Code for which the perpetrator of the Internet worm might have been indicted. These Title 18 offenses are included among other potentially available federal offenses listed below:

Section 1029	Fraud and Related Activity in Connection with Access Devices
Section 1030	The Computer Fraud and Abuse Act
Section 1343	Fraud by Wire, Radio, or Television
Section 1346	Scheme or Artifice to Defraud
Section 1362	Malicious Mischief—with Government Property
Section 2510	The Electronic Privacy Act of 1986
Section 2701(a)	Unlawful Access to Stored Communications

Under § 1029 the definition of an access device includes "other means of account access that can be used to obtain money, goods, services, or any other thing of value." However, its use must be done "knowingly and with intent to defraud."

The expectation had been that Section 1030 would be the appropriate statutory authority under which to indict RTM, the perpetrator of the Internet worm. The Computer Fraud and Abuse Act is directed primarily toward unauthorized and intentional access to classified government data, financial data, or interference with the use of federal agency computers. Section 1030(a)(4) requires an intent to defraud by unauthorized use of a federal interest computer which includes computers accessed from more than one state. Section 1030(a)(5) covers intentional acts which prevent authorized use of a federal interest computer, but couples that with a loss of $1,000 or more. Federal prosecutors indicted RTM only under Section 1030(a)(5) and a quick reading would suggest that they may be successful. However, a careful analysis suggests that it may be difficult to prove beyond a reasonable doubt either intent, direct damage or exceeding authorized use.

Many computer scientists and some lawyers now conclude that releasing a computer virus is per se malicious. Indeed, Congressman Herger, in announcing his sponsorship of H.R. 55, described a virus as "a malicious program that can destroy or alter the electronic commands of a computer." The media has contributed to this conception by defining a computer virus as "an agent of infection, insinuating itself into a program or disk and forcing its host to replicate the virus code."

On the other hand, others argue that a virus not only can be benign in its consequences—as for example, the Aldus peace virus, which merely appeared on the screen and then destroyed itself—but that one can produce a virus with both good intentions and good effects. For example, one could imagine a self-replicating program intended to update the FBI's ten most wanted list in all files existing for that purpose, while deleting outmoded material and not affecting any other files or applications. In this mode a virus becomes an automatic tool for broadcasting file updates to all members of a user set of unknown size, with user consent to this behavior. Hebrew University used a computer virus to identify and delete the Friday the Thirteenth virus which was detected there prior to the date on which it was to release its killer capabilities.

Furthermore, the Xerox Corporation at its Research Park in Palo Alto has been experimenting with benign uses of computer viruses for some years. Several types of worm programs were developed which could harness the capabilities of multiple computers linked by communications lines into extended networks, thereby coordinating the operations, maximizing the efficiency and increasing the output of the network. In effect, the sum of the whole could be greater than its parts, according to computer consultant John Clippinger. As described by John Shoch, who coordinated the research for Xerox, new programming techniques were developed which could organize complex computations by harnessing multiple machines. The various utilitarian applications included bulletin boards which distributed graphics, e.g., a cartoon a day to ALTOS computer users, alarm clock programs which scheduled wake up calls or reminders, multiple machine controllers, and diagnostic worms which would seek out available computers and load them with test programs. Thus, the placement of a rogue program into a computer network or operating system or program is not necessarily done with malicious intent.

Section 1346 was enacted to ensure that a scheme or artifice to defraud includes depriving "another of the intangible right of honest services" which would cover the behavior of the Internet worm. The scheme, however, must still have been devised with intent to defraud, which is not easily established by incontrovertible evidence.

Section 1362 is directed toward willful or malicious injury to or destruction of property including "other means of communication" controlled by the U.S. government. The operative prohibition is that which "obstructs, hinders, or delays the transmission over any such line."

Section 2510, the Electronic Privacy Act of 1986, defines electronic communication as "any transfer of signs, signals, writing, images, sounds, data, or intelligence of any nature . . ." and electronic communications service as "any service which provides to users thereof the ability to send or receive . . . electronic communications." Rogue programs, such as the Internet worm, if inserted either without authorization or in excess of authorized use, arguably could constitute a prohibited invasion of electronic privacy in an electronic mail system.

PROPOSED FEDERAL LEGISLATION

The Herger Bill, entitled The Computer Virus Eradication Act of 1989, is intended to plug the gap in existing legislation which clearly did not anticipate viruses as one of the maladies then being addressed. The bill contains the word virus in the title, but does not use the word within the operative clauses. The behavior prohibited is "knowingly insert[ing] into a program for a computer, or a computer itself, information or commands knowing or having reason to believe that such information or commands may cause loss, expense, or risk to health or welfare. . . ."

This is coupled with a clause which penalizes the perpetrator only if the program is inserted without the knowledge of the recipient. This second requirement is intended to relieve from liability persons who include a time bomb to self-destruct at the end of a license period, and the use of viruses for study or for benign purposes known to system users. Perhaps the two phrases should have been connected with "or" rather than "and". If they are coupled in this manner, a deleterious virus program could be inserted into a computer network with the collusion of a recipient person. However, the transfer of an infected disk to an innocent party would certainly fall within the ambit of the proposed legislation.

Furthermore, a statutory requirement of disclosure to the recipient of all potential harmful consequences would, in effect, impose strict liability upon software developers to completely "debug" their software before issue or force them to carry sufficient insurance to ward against all eventualities. Such a requirement might hamstring an industry which has been characterized by rapid innovation and close the door to small entrepreneurs who could not enter a market overburdened with high insurance costs.

The MacMillan Bill, entitled the Computer Protection Act of 1989, essentially addresses willful sabotage and authorizes appropriate compensatory damages. However, the proposed language does not specify what constitutes sabotage. Thus, the language may be too restrictive to include benignly intended program "pranks" such as the Aldus-virus, yet may be too vague to withstand constitutional challenge.

There is more legislation to come, as William Sessions, Director of the Federal Bureau of Investigation promised to submit recommendations to Senator Patrick Leahy at a Senate hearing held on May 15, 1989. According to Sessions, who said the agency has trained more than 500 agents for investigation of computer crimes, a team is being organized to concentrate on computer worms and viruses, for which there is no specifically applicable federal statute.

SUMMARY OF LEGISLATION COVERING ROGUE COMPUTER PROGRAMS AND COMPUTER ROGUES

In summary, state laws seem to be quite varied, perhaps too diverse, for an electronic environment in which computerized networks are interconnected both nationally and transnationally. Federal statutes, although extensive, have not yet been perfected to encompass the more recent aberrant behavior of computer rogues.

At a minimum, state legislation can be improved substantially to harmonize the behavior which is considered objectionable and to minimize the likelihood that harmful insertion of viruses will escape prosecution. Yet such legislation needs to be carefully drawn. Otherwise, it may sweep up in its net the legitimate experiments of the computer novices whose ambitions to improve their skills need to be encouraged and who would benefit from access to a legitimate electronic playground. Thus, one question for legislators and educators alike is how to better provide a challenging electronic playground in which young apprentice programmers can cut their teeth without wreaking havoc on the nation's privileged and/or proprietary strategic, financial, and commercial networks.

Overly restrictive legislation can also handicap the computer professionals who need a reasonably open environment in which to develop new software and to modify it for their own purposes. Such legislation may inhibit needlessly the efforts of computer software companies to provide technological protection. Most lamentable may be the suppression of the very openness and ease of communication which computer networking has made possible. Just as the telephone system becomes more valuable with larger numbers of telephones connected, so it is with computer networks that openness is a virtue to be sought rather than to be prevented.

Some computer scientists believe that more robust computer systems can be designed which will withstand the invasions of rogue computer programs without diminishing the user friendliness of the electronic environment. The challenge is whether or not adequate laws can be written to prohibit behavior which endangers the integrity of computer networks and systems without inhibiting the ease of use which is so desirable. Clearly what is greatly needed in the present circumstances is clear heads and innovative minds to sculpt statutes which prohibit excesses but do not deter user friendly computer networks.

PROBLEMS ENCOUNTERED AND CURRENT LEGISLATIVE TRENDS

There are a number of problems which will be encountered as legislators and lobbyists confront the amendment of existing statutes or try to fashion new ones applicable to the computer rogue programs.

Definitions

The most important new trend in legislative initiatives is in defining more precisely the activities to be prohibited, particularly how to include such rogue behavior as exemplified by the interjection of worms and viruses into computer networks. Specifically, legislators must decide whether to be generic or specific in the description of the transgressions to be prohibited. Phrases used in recent legislation and proposed bills include such terms as:

> "take possession of";
>
> "tampers with";
>
> "degrades," or "disables";
>
> "disrupts or causes the disruption of computer services or denies or causes the denial of computer services";
>
> "disrupts or degrades or causes the disruption or degradation of computer services";
>
> "interrupt[s] the operation [of]" or "causes the malfunction [of]";
>
> "self-replicating or self-propagating" and "designed to contaminate . . . consume computer resources . . . or . . . usurp the normal operation of the computer";
>
> "inserts a computer virus."

The legislative history of the new amendments to Minnesota's computer abuse statute reveals the apprehension with which computer professionals and their lawyers perceive statutory definitions specifically designed to describe precisely what aberrant behavior will not be tolerated. Even so, it is not easy either to draft legislation which purports to proscribe generic behavior without encompassing normal activities to which criminal liability should not attach.

Intent

The second most important trend is in establishing what level of intent is necessary to prove criminal liability. Proving express intent to do harm has proven elusive in many of the incidents involving rogue computer programs, which, though unintentional, do inflict economic costs even upon those who must verify that no harm has been done. Thus, the legislative tendency to substitute or add "knowingly" or "willfully exceeds the limits of authorization" within computer abuse statutes. However, it is not clear what the difference is between "knowingly" and "intentionally" since either can be interpreted to be with knowledge that harm may result. Furthermore, "reckless disregard for the consequences" may imply an intent to disregard the harm which may be caused by the act in question.

There is a growing realization that what have been considered to be harmless pranks cannot be tolerated on the dynamic electronic highways which sustain modern day banking, news media, health care, commerce, and industry. Thus higher standards of care are being forged both among computer professionals and within the legislative and judicial systems.

Making the Punishment Fit the Crime

Another troubling question is how to assess damages, especially in instances where the perpetrators are judgment-proof. Thus, an important new trend is tailoring sanctions to be imposed to the particular circumstances. In several instances we have seen an increase in the fines to be levied or the imprisonment to be imposed. New York has proposed the most stringent limits with a sliding scale which measures the punishment according to the amount of damage incurred. For example, computer tampering in the first degree from altering or destroying data or programs is subject to damages exceeding one million dollars, in which case the judge can order reparations up to one hundred thousand dollars. This may deter the professional employee hackers who cause the greatest harm. However, increasing the financial liability will not reach young impecunious students. Of course, a prosecutor may fail to prosecute if the penalty does not seem to fit the nature of the crime, and judges seem to be very imaginative in prescribing community service and other forms of alternative retribution.

Only a few statutes currently provide for either compensatory or punitive damages resulting from the prohibited offenses. Arkansas provides for recovery "for any damages sustained and the costs of the suit . . . [and] '[d]amages' shall include loss of profits." Presumably, restitution for damages incurred as a result of disks infected with the Aldus Peace Virus could be claimed under this statute.

Connecticut provides for a fine "not to exceed double the amount of the defendant's gain from the commission of such offense," and California permits a civil suit to be brought for "compensatory damages, including any expenditure reasonably and necessarily incurred by the owner or lessee to verify that a computer system, computer network, computer program, or data was or was not altered, damaged, or deleted by the access." This provision also would seem to cover the Aldus virus. Although the Aldus virus caused no direct harm which might be the subject of litigation, software developers whose products were suspected to be contaminated did incur substantial expenses in verifying that no harm had occurred. However, for those companies whose products, networks, or software were not "accessed," this avenue for relief might not be adequate.

Virginia authorizes restitution to the victim through compensatory as well as punitive damages. Damages are measured by loss of profits and by adding the costs of verification that no damage has occurred.

Greater freedom and discretion to authorize confiscation of equipment used to commit an offense would appear to be more appropriately designed to deter teenage offenders whose activities are primarily pranks or voyeurism. For such young pranksters codes of ethical behavior need to be inculcated which will prevent or contain rogue behavior and nip it in the bud.

Venue

Another troubling question is how best to handle litigation involving multiple jurisdictions. The jurisdiction within which a case may be tried is determined by the venue statutes which require a substantial relationship to the place where the prohibited behavior occurred. Although modifying the venue statutes to cover network behavior which has deleterious consequences within the jurisdiction does not solve the problem of gaining service upon an offender, it does facilitate forum shopping to determine where best to litigate an interstate infraction of the laws.

Approximately one-fourth of the states already have enacted liberal venue statutes to encompass computer networks. Georgia seems to have one of the most comprehensive clauses granting jurisdiction to "any county from which, to which, through which, any access to a computer or computer network was made."

The number of potentially harmful occurrences which straddle two or more jurisdictions is very likely to increase with greater computer connectivity. Thus, liberalized venue statutes and jurisdictional harmonization seem highly desirable. Of the cases used herein as examples, only the Burleson case neatly falls within the jurisdiction of only one state, and several involve multiple countries, e.g., the Pakistani Brain, the Aldus Peace Virus, the Computer Chaos Club, the IBM Christmas card. Thus an extension of liberal venue provisions to other states seems a likely trend for the future.

Reporting Computer Abuses

An especially troubling question arises in determining whether or not to impose strict accountability on employers to report their experiences with rogue programs and to identify perpetrators. One of the greatest deterrents to law enforcement appears to be the reluctance of employers to report the miscreant activities of their own employees, choosing instead to absorb any financial loss incurred and to cover up the facts surrounding the damaging circumstances. A few states have taken the step of requiring employers to make known circumstances which should lead to a prosecution. However, this is an especially troublesome area, as the facts are known only to those who experience the loss and, therefore, the policing of compliance would be especially difficult.

Overreaching Statutes and Overzealous Prosecution

At present the primary concern is that existing statutes may be inadequate and that prosecutors will be too busy, uninterested, or unskilled in collecting evidence to prosecute violations under existing statutes. However, as the rogues become more proficient and more deleterious in their activities, the question of how to avoid over-reaching prohibitions which may inhibit innovation may arise.

State legislators, especially in states where the computer industry constitutes a major contributor to the local economy, may be too quick to respond to the pleas of their constituents to plug loopholes in existing statutes or enact new ones to encompass newer rogue activities. Overreaching statutes may not be objectionable, if they are rationally administered. However, the risk is incurred that an overzealous prosecutor might jail a bunch of gifted pranksters, thus jeopardizing the development of a computer-skilled work force.

Authorization of such new and unusual punishments as prohibition against employment within the computer industry and/or the denial of degrees, such as that contained in the proposed California legislative initiatives, are quite controversial and may deter qualified candidates from entering the field of computer science. This would be unfortunate at a time when the country so critically needs more scientific talent than is being nurtured.

It would also be unfortunate if the imposition of stricter criminal statutes and more vigorous prosecution placed such stringent rules upon users that a "user-unfriendly" environment discouraged the use of computer systems and networks. The age of the computer may seem to have arrived. However, many users are still stumbling along trying to sort out how best to use these new networks to enhance their productivity. Thus, even a little discouragement goes a long way toward inhibiting incorporation of computer access into normal work habits.

ALTERNATIVES TO CRIMINAL STATUTES

On the other hand, if more and stricter criminal laws do not provide the optimum or only answer, other sanctions need to be considered to deal with reckless drivers on the electronic highways of the future.

There are, of course, many alternatives to the enactment of criminal statutes. One strategy is to impose strict legal liability upon the providers of computer systems, services, networks, and software providers requiring them to put into place adequate technological barriers to unauthorized invasions of their computer networks and products and/or to carry sufficient insurance to cover any losses which occur.

Compulsory insurance coverage, such as that required by operators of motor vehicles or pooled insurance provided by industry cooperatives may provide compensation for unanticipated losses. At some point policy makers will have to determine what level of insurance should be adequate to guard against unforeseen disasters and whether the federal government should assume some responsibility to offer support to the computer industry similar to the Federal Deposit Insurance Corporation (FDIC) for banks. However, it might be a rather unusual step to provide such support for an industry which has matured within a largely unregulated environment during a national trend toward deregulation.

Establishment of higher standards of ethical values within the user communities is clearly needed. At this point, there is no reliable standard of behavior which can be relied upon in tort litigation. Indeed, there is a certain amount of controversy over what the "rational computer programmer" would do under the circumstances. Lacking a viable code of ethics, it is difficult to draft criminal legislation and even more difficult to rely solely upon the common law to sort out what should be acceptable computer etiquette. The Cornell Report cites substantial rules in place to cover such errors in judgment as afflicted RTM. However, computer professionals must assume an even greater responsibility to define and make public what they consider to be viable rules of the road within the newly created computer network environment.

Thus, codes of ethics must be promulgated for the various types of computer networks establishing what standard of care should be exercised by operators or providers of computer equipment, networks, and services. Moreover, it it not yet apparent whether such standards will be established by private groups or public groups, or in their absence by state or federal law.

Better computer security—e.g., passwords, protocols, closing of trap doors— will continue to be stressed in the future as it has been in the past. The boundaries of technological protection through encryption, protected gateways, and viral detection mechanisms are not impenetrable. Indeed, a substantial army of computer security experts currently are hard at work. More often than in the past, their recommendations are being followed by their institutional leaders. Many more security experts are needed and more must be trained. However, they may have to survive without an influx of hackers who in the past have demonstrated their skills by penetrating the very systems that they must strive to protect.

In addition, more and better qualified investigators are needed to conduct audits of computer abuse and to track the footprints of computer criminals. The birddogs of the computer world must be human rather than canine. So far, few such skilled professionals exist, and many who have the skills do not have the incentive to perfect their talents. Thus, we need to encourage a new profession of computer auditors who can analyze the evidence necessary to guarantee conviction under the criminal statutes presently in place.

There is yet much room for improvement in determining what kinds of audit trails are necessary to track computer misuse and abuse, as well as what skills are needed to conduct the audits. In addition, pioneering prosecutors, such as Davis McCown in the Burleson case, are developing rules of evidence to prove a case in court assuming that an indictable offense or litigable event has taken place.

The recent outbreak of rogue programs has spawned a veritable covey of entrepreneurs designing antiviral software. There are at least twenty-five companies producing vaccines at the present time. Such technological solutions will continue to provide at least some efficacy. Although antiviral programs increase the cost of doing business, as indeed does encryption, more and more companies will need to inoculate their software and implant monitoring devices to detect the presence of damaging rogue programs. This may be a lamentable alternative to compliance with established codes of ethical behavior. However, even as airports have become crowded with lines of passengers waiting to go through detection devices before boarding airplanes, users of computer networks will have to turn to whatever technological tools are available to assure access to trouble-free electronic passageways on computer traffic lanes.

Licensing of computer professionals has been suggested as one way of addressing the problem of reckless driving on the electronic highways of the future. However, as the medium within which the programmers and users are operating is also intended for communications, this might risk a first amendment challenge in the same way that licensing of journalists raises questions of "chilling free speech." On the other hand, the time may have come to provide a judicial definition of what constitutes yelling "FIRE" in a crowded theater as applied to computer communities.

CONCLUSION

Computer viruses present new challenges to law enforcement officers and legislators, as well as computer executives, scientists, programmers, and network managers. Certainly tighter state and federal legislation offer some possible antidotes. There appears to be a need for legal enhancement through criminal and tort laws at both state and federal levels. More importantly, there is a great need for global cooperation, as computer networks do not honor the boundaries of sovereign nations very comfortably. Thus, electronic terrorists may find as many hospitable havens in which to hide as did the pirates of the high seas in past centuries.

In summary, it is difficult to determine whether the rogue programs are a transient problem which will go away as hackers develop a different ethical standard; whether they are a drop in the bucket of problems which may arise as the criminally motivated become more computer literate; or whether they are like the common cold afflictions which come with the use of computers with which we must learn to live. Very likely all three suppositions have equal validity. Strategies which are designed to address them will serve their proponents well and provide a sound foundation upon which to build a safer computer environment for the future.

ARE COMPUTER PROPERTY RIGHTS ABSOLUTE?

Richard Stallman

I am sad to see that *Newsweek's* misquote of my words has been propagated in the editorial "Moral Clarity in the Computer Age." Readers of *Newsweek*, and now readers of *Communications*, have been shown no sign that there exists a serious alternative to the moral position taken on the subject of computer security.

The alternative is that security breaking is not a grave problem, but is a response to an underlying problem which is grave: the trigger-happy hostility, suspicion, and general bad-neighborliness of the owners of computer installations. Computer security is the tool they use to implement policies of inhospitality. It causes frustration for both the computer system users and for outsiders who might be friends, and therefore it receives the brunt of their anger.

Newsweek's misquote is relevant here. I did not say, "We [hackers] do not believe in property rights." This would have been extreme, as well as speaking for others who do not in fact generally agree with me. My actual words to the *Newsweek* reporter were, "I do not believe in absolute property rights." What this means is that the property owner has the right to use the property but does not have the right to waste it deliberately. Supposed violations of property rights are only wrong according to the damages they do, and the good of all concerned must be considered, not just the owner's.

When applied to computers, this means that the owner has the right to use the computer without interference; but when the owner has no use for it (every night and weekend, for most computers) he ought to allow it to be used for other socially constructive purposes, such as, for a teenager to learn to program. (This is what most security crackers want, and why so many of them stop trying to break security when offered a chance to use a computer openly.) If the owner attempts to prevent it, he is being the dog in the manger (as well as stupid to miss a great recruiting technique).

Teenagers tend to play pranks, sometimes destructive, on any bad neighbor. These second wrongs do not make rights, but it is a mistake to concentrate on suppressing the pranks without correcting the grievances which inspired them. Even worse is trying to suppress the pranks by adding to the underlying problem (tightening security) because they will solidify the hostility and prevent reconciliation.

I am told that, in Canada, entering a house is not a crime. Unless there has been damage or theft, the person entering cannot be arrested.

It is also necessary to consider the harm that the security measures do to the "legitimate" computer users. Most users don't see this harm because they haven't imagined the possibility of it not being there. To see it, you must map it into a different perceptual field: imagine a country set up like the timesharing system you use. There are a few people who can control exactly what things you are allowed to do, and even at what times of day you can do them. They can spy on you at any moment, and censor your files; they don't allow you to look at their files. The job you are supposed to do requires actions that you aren't trusted or permitted to do, and which you must each time ask a member of the elite to do for you. As a result, you must remain on good terms with the elite, whatever they may demand. The system (ambiguity intentional) is designed to keep the elite in power, so only they are permitted to modify the system. The ordinary citizen user has no control over the system whose flaws can make his life frustrating.

Countries like this are called totalitarian police states, and are generaly considered undesirable.

For technical reasons, totalitarianism is the only way to maintain privacy on a shared computer. It is not so for offices or desks. You don't need to watch and handcuff people 24 hours a day to keep them out of a single desk. You must do so, however, to keep them away from even a single file in a computer. You cannot have privacy for some users and permit the rest in the same system, to work unfettered.

Privacy for computer users is a good thing, if all else were equal. But between privacy in a police state and freedom in public view, I choose the latter. I strongly resist attempts to impose the police state on me in the name of privacy. If there are a few files that need protection, such as the lab's personnel records, it is better to store them on a cheap micro inaccessible to the computers on which the real work is done.

It may say that this imposition is excusable because a person can always quit his job rather than accept it. But what happens when every job requires surrendering one's freedom as a condition of employment? What use is a guarantee of any sort of rights if commercial pressures force nearly everyone to waive those rights? That is why the founding fathers conceived the idea of inalienable rights: rights which one should not renounce for any consideration.

In my career I have seen numerous occasions on which generally useful programming work was obstructed by security measures. The work usually required an action which nobody would object to but which required access to parts of the system that would have enabled the users, had they been maliciously minded (which they were not), to cause harm. Sometimes there was a malfunction, and security prevented the users present from correcting it.

The few people I have encountered at MIT who were interested in breaking security have caused comparatively little harm. Our lab's ancient spirit of nearly nonexistent security and acceptance of guest users inspired strangers to take a friendly attitude in return. (We have not encountered any serious criminals, for example, trying to steal money by changing financial records. We have no reason to fear them, since computational research does not tempt them.)

For all of these reasons, I judge computer security a disease rather than a cure, except for banks and such. My duty is to oppose it as I would oppose bureaucracy or governmental corruption.

I have not been in a position to need to sneak through computer security to get access: as an operating system implementor, I am a natural candidate for the elite, but I won't accept as a special privilege for myself what everyone ought to have. I choose passwords that are obvious so that other people can guess them, and I get thank-you notes from grateful people who were able to get work done as a result. In fact, when passwords were first introduced on a computer at Project MAC, I urged all the users to adopt a single, well-publicized password. A considerable fraction of the users did so. In those days, I was one of a large community which held these views, and neither the first nor the foremost.

I and many others who have worked at the Artificial Intelligence Lab in its period of greatness know that the absence of security can benefit the productivity of eager, talented people, without incurring a serious risk of harm, and can also teach strangers the idea of cooperation based on mutual consideration rather than force and fear. As a result of unrelated commercial pressures, the Artificial Intelligence Lab no longer exists in healthy form to demonstrate the advantages of nonsecurity, but I hope we will not be the last to have tried it and enjoyed it.

Finally, I urge that security breakers be called "crackers" rather than "hackers." Cracker is more suggestive of their activity and hacking only tangentially relates to security or the breaking of it. It is a shame that the term "hacker," proudly chosen by the founders of the Artificial Intelligence Lab to describe themselves, is being made into a slur.

Incidentally, the picture in *Newsweek* was intended to depict man and computer joining in a line dance. I was holding hands with an old robot arm. It's a serious statement of not exactly serious emotions, and an example of a hack. Unfortunately, the robot arm turned out to be hard to recognize if you don't know what it is.

P.S. The following people wish to add their support to this letter:

Russell Brand, MIT-LCS
Jonathan Solomon, BBN Communications
Richard Mlynarik, MIT
Marc A. Elvy, Harvard
Chris Hanson, MIT AI Lab
Gill Pratt, MIT and Lisp Machines Inc.
Joel D. Isaacson, Southern Illinois University
Amy Hendrickson, MIT
Kim A. Barrett, MIT

Stallman's piece stimulated many responses to the ACM Forum. In March 1984, one critic said he agreed with Stallman that there ought not be absolute property rights but disagreed with him on the interpretation of such a principle. He said that he saw it in his own and in the public's interest to lock his car at night. He concluded that security is appropriate in the vast majority of multiuser systems, not the small minority Stallman implies. Stallman replied:

Borrowing cars and borrowing computer access are separate moral issues about which a person can reach different conclusions. Here are some factors that affect one's conclusions about cars: (1) Using a car involves moving it. It becomes inaccessible to its owner. He cannot say, "Guests, please log out," if he needs it. (2) If the borrower accidentally or deliberately fails to return the car, the owner may be lastingly or permanently, deprived of its use. (3) Cars are dangerous. A trained operator must concentrate to avoid damaging the car, other cars, or human beings. Good will is not sufficient.

Such problems do not exist with remote access to a well-designed computer system. In particular, experience at MIT shows that accidental damage is slight and infrequent, just as is malicious damage.

> In April 1984 a Canadian critic said Stallman was wrong in believing that entering someone's house in Canada is not an offense. He said Stallman would mind if someone entered Stallman's house and read his private letters and tax returns. He said that Stallman's view of property is common in Marxist countries but not in the United States. He said that security mechanisms are motivated not by totalitarian impulses but by a desire to maintain the privacy of information entrusted to us by others.
>
> In the same issue, another critic said that business and trade secrets cannot be left open to browsing hackers—their theft could deprive the business of its market position and put many people out of work. He also said that cheap personal computers make it possible for hackers to have training grounds that don't involve access to multiuser computers.
>
> Another writer worried about the push for federal laws to govern privacy and access to computers. He said these laws are too easily misused. For example, storing personal information in a computer file could become a federal crime, whereas writing the same information on a desk-top pad would not. He feared the "surveillance society" that may be arising because enforcement of the laws would require detailed recording of every action of every person. Even in mild forms, these laws would interfere with the sharing of knowledge, the fundamental reason for the preeminence of this country.
>
> In May 1984, a critic said that Stallman uses the "blame the victim tactic" by claiming that security is not protection but provocation. He also said that MIT Ph.D. students with whom Stallman shares offices wouldn't share unpublished files about their research because they'd lose their claims of originality. He responded to Stallman's statement that hackers can help fix systems by saying he's seen many cases where their supposed corrections were misguided or wrong.
>
> In July 1984, Stallman replied to these letters, focusing mainly on the May critic.

With regard to his letter in the May Forum (p. 412; 522) [my critic] might be interested to know that I recently served on the panel of ethics and social responsibility at the IEEE/ACM Conference on Software Engineering. If he could have his wish for an authority to "settle" this issue, he might be surprised to find me presented as one. But he need not fear this, because a moral issue cannot be settled by appeal to authority.

I note in his letter the implicit claim that security breaking is synonymous with destruction. The examples he gives of "security breaking"—smashing windows, erasing files—are all examples of destruction. The experience—at MIT, with the 414s, and in many other instances—shows that would-be guests or potential security breakers hardly ever want to destroy. The so-called victims have usually not really been harmed. All that is clear is that they are afraid they will be harmed, and based on these fears take actions which are indubitably hostile.

[My May critic] makes another implicit assumption which many other people share: that only the "owner" of a file or object has any say in deciding whether it should be locked up. People at the AI lab sometimes thought that way and caused great difficulties for the other lab members. Time after time I sneaked over ceilings or under floors to unlock a room at the AI lab which contained equipment useful for all lab members (and usually belonging to MIT, though this does not figure in my own ethical consideration), but which was locked because one professor considered the room to be "his" and wanted to store some other valuable there. He believed that the decision of whether the room should be locked was his to make for only his own benefit; I believed that it was to be decided for the good of all. If the equipment had to be accessible, the door should not have been locked, and if he did not like the other valuables to be accessible, he could put them elsewhere. Usually these conflicts were ultimately settled amicably by compromises whereby the objects that needed to be locked up were concentrated in rooms which did not contain anything generally useful.

On the same basis, I resist attempts to lock up computers containing generally useful files, and the solution I advocate—concentrating what needs to be locked in a place away from where most users are—is the same compromise.

The problem of plagiarism in Ph.D. research is serious if it really happens; I have not heard much suggestion that it has happened to anyone at the AI lab, where access to anyone's files is fairly easy, but I do not think that the solution to such a problem is more locks. That would be treating one relatively minor symptom of a deep problem.

The warning that users might make mistakes in attempting to fix bugs is amusing because anyone who changes a system does that. I, an operating system implementor, have made more incorrect bug fixes than all of [my critic's] users; should I be forbidden to change the systems I am developing? It is by trying, and sometimes making mistakes, that people become wizards who can occasionally fix something properly. Self-reliance and competence are more important to the prosperity of society than order. Let us encourage people to develop them.

But arguing about protecting system files is not really germane. Being forced, for the sake of security, to protect system files will not bother [my critic], but this does not reduce the unpleasantness for people who do not agree with him.

Some individuals, including me, may not even wish to protect our own files from others. If I am granted access to maintain any system program, then someone could place a trojan horse in my personal files which would install another trojan horse in the program I maintain which would access or change a file when run by the file's owner. There cannot be security for one user on a system on which I am doing my usual work unless I treat all strangers with suspicion on his behalf.

Therefore, his ostensibly unimposing wish for privacy on a shared file system is in fact a complex of demands that I and everyone else who shares it treat anyone he does not trust with complete suspicion. The request for privacy is unobjectionable in the abstract, but these demands are intolerable. If he should be able to have privacy at his option, I am just as entitled to be open and hospitable at my option; other parties should side with me because my hospitality helps others. It is important not to allow selfish organizations like corporations and universities to force all the users to use totalitarian computer systems based on the excuse that a user's request for privacy should be granted regardless of the harm this entails.

▷ A DIALOG ON HACKING AND SECURITY

Dorothy Denning
Frank Drake

INTRODUCTION BY DOROTHY DENNING

In the fall of 1989, Frank Drake (not his real name), editor of the now defunct cyberpunk magazine *W.O.R.M.*, invited me to be interviewed for the magazine. The interview was conducted electronically. We completed the interview after two rounds of questions, and the result was published in the Winter 1989 issue of *W.O.R.M.* I then invited him to switch sides so that I could learn more about the views of one person in the cyberpunk culture. What I learned is that he is much more concerned about the ethical and social issues centered around our information society than I had expected based on reading accounts of hackers in the press. . . .

INTERVIEW OF FRANK DRAKE
BY DOROTHY DENNING

DD: What led you to be the editor of *W.O.R.M.*, and what do you want to achieve with the magazine?

FD: I'm not sure what caused me to start *W.O.R.M.* To some degree it was that after reading *Neuromancer* I grew very excited about the possibilities of "cyberpunk," of coupling technology with punk, a subculture that I think has grown somewhat stale. I thought that I would be able to attract like-minded people and together we could find out new information and follow the shining path into the future. As you can see my grip on reality isn't always the greatest.

DD: How many subscribers do you have? What percentage of them are female?

FD: Each issue goes to about 50 paying subscribers and 30 nonpaying subscribers. Each issue gets shown to a lot of other people. The result is that quite a few people have seen a copy of *W.O.R.M.* but I have never heard of *them*.

I have only two female subscribers as far as I know. However, strangely enough they are both major contributors. One is a bio grad who has written two columns (cloning, DNA fingerprints) for *W.O.R.M.*, and one is a psych grad who has written lots of miscellaneous stuff.

DD: What is the social responsibility of a computer security professional?

FD: First, to not help make a system secure if the information contained in the system should not be kept secret. Second, to not help make a system secure if the information contained in the system violates an individual's privacy or has not been volunteered by the individual. Which is all very nice and all, but of course each of those rules requires a value judgment which is much harder to define.

DD: What criteria would you use for determining whether information violates an individual's privacy? As a hypothetical scenario, suppose I construct a file labeled *frank*, into which I put everything I know about you. Am I violating your privacy even if I got my information from other sources? Was Brian Reid's privacy invaded when his email message announcing a security flaw was intercepted and later published in *W.O.R.M.*?

FD: There is definitely a fine line. I would not consider your hypothetical file on me an invasion. What I would consider an invasion would be if you broke into my room and put a hidden tape recorder in. I think what differentiates these two is that in your scenario, all your information has been basically volunteered by me (e.g., I might not like that someone told you stuff about me, but I need to take the responsibility for giving them the information in the first place). However, if you bug my room, you are actively going after "new" information. I have a bad feeling that there are examples out there that would not divide so neatly into these two camps.

The Brian Reid situation is almost one of these. Here I could argue, lacking conviction perhaps, that since it had been intercepted by another hacker and then distributed, the information had become part of the public domain. But this is splitting hairs. I think the better argument would be based on what I said in reply to your first question, that this letter should have been public in the first place and hence "stealing" it was not an invasion of privacy. And you didn't ask the more interesting question: Why did I censor out the technical details from the letter?

DD: Why did you?

FD: I'm not sure; it seemed like the right thing to do. Partly because I didn't want some incompetent hacker to just follow the step by step directions and then do something stupid and also to partially cover my ass. So in some ways it's an example of "information elitism" on my part. Whoops.

DD: What is the social responsibility of a person with a PC and modem?

FD: First, not to erase or modify anyone else's data. Second, not to cause a legitimate user on a system any problems.

DD: Does "problems" include having your network shut down for a few hours while someone checks out the system for damage even when there is none? (It is definitely a problem for me.) Does "problems" include the time spent by the system manager to check out the system for damage?

FD: *Any* rule can be taken to the point of absurdity. Examples are "don't kill," which is of course impossible even for a Jannist if you want to consider microorganisms life; and does the war against drugs include the endorphin high from jogging? There is no "scientific" way to determine when a exception to a social rule is so minor as to be insignificant; instead it must be looked at on a case-by-case basis. In this case I think the problem is caused more by the network managers than by the hacker. I think I could show why this is so in a specific case, but basically I believe there are other solutions to this problem: channeling hackers into different directions, having public accounts, and of course security software without bugs. Still, it is a hard question, which like I said must be taken on a case-by-case basis to see if the network going down is due to improper actions by a hacker or an over-zealous network/system manager.

DD: Have you taken any courses in computers and society? Did your parents or teachers in high school discuss computer ethics? Have you read any articles or books on computer ethics?

FD: I have taken two years of computer science in college and one class in high school. None of my college classes have considered computer ethics (there are two upper division computer ethics courses offered here, although they are not mandatory); my high school class (Advanced Placement Pascal) mentioned ethics in the most basic way (e.g., piracy is bad). My parents, while not discussing computer ethics per se, certainly have discussed ethics which can be transferred to the computer domain. I have read lots of articles on computer ethics and many books which discussed computer ethics.

DD: Do you think that information should be free and that it is the "locking up" of computer resources that is the crime?

FD: I think information should be free in the sense of public; however, it can still be "owned" by someone. While perhaps not a crime, I do believe that computer resources should be better shared with the young and poor. I just read an article [1/31/90] in the *Los Angeles Times* concerning a U.S. government report on the growing "information gap" between the rich and poor.

DD: Earlier you suggested that there might be some information that should be kept secret. Could you say more about what criteria you would use for deciding whether information should be public or secret?

FD: Ok, I see the apparent contradiction in my statements that "information should be public" versus "some information should be secret." I run into this problem a lot because I am a utopian-anarchist, but I don't believe that we are ready for anarchy yet. Hence sometimes I'll answer questions in the framework of the current political structure and sometimes in terms of the way I think "it ought to be." This admittedly is a bad practice on my part. The second problem is that the word "information" covers such a huge amount of stuff, namely, *everything*. The result of this is that there aren't any hard-and-fast rules you can make about information, because you'll always be able to come up with a counterexample. However one useful way to divide "information" is information owned by an individual concerning themselves and then everything else. I believe that in the future-ideal-world any information of the second type should be public. Information of the first type can be public or private depending on the whim of the individual (of course the individual may have to pay the price of not surrendering information, as I discussed with you when we met). However, in our current political framework, it is more complicated. Some information which is not owned by individuals needs to be secret simply because complicated structures have been "built" on top of the assumption that certain information will be secret, and if it is suddenly made public, the system will fall apart. An example is of course military information. Since we have gotten ourselves involved with an asinine idea like M.A.D., we are stuck with keeping some military information secret.

DD: As for the growing information gap between the rich and poor, I agree this is unfortunate, but what does it have to do with making information public? I doubt that the reason people are poor has much to do with lack of access to information. There is tons of free information everywhere: in schools, libraries, etc. Many, maybe most, poor people are illiterate (both English-wise and computer-wise), so having computer access to information isn't going to help them much. What they need (among other things) are skills that have value to someone in the market, and the credentials (where necessary) to market their skills. In short, they need easy access to training and certification programs, not information.

FD: Whew, I thought for sure I was going to get the old fish story ("give a man a fish . . .") quoted at me. But in any case I think you make a false polarity between information and education. A person requires information to access more information. For example a person needs to know they can dial NPA-555-1212 to get out-of-state information (I've been shocked a number of times by people who don't know this) before they can get the phone number for out of state businesses. The great advantage that computers *should* give is access to information without requiring the user to know a great deal of information first. This is possible through user interfaces which use user models and all the other elements of good MMI/CHI. However, those who can't afford computers need to have access to them somehow first before a large enough demand for these types of programs is created. I think that there should be

Computer Resource Centers in lower-income areas. I have heard of a few private efforts for this in the late '70s but they didn't have the capital to pull it off. Also, I think you're badly exaggerating the case when you say "they need easy access to training and certification programs, not information." Information is what will provide them with easy access (they need to know where to go) and all training is in information.

DD: Do you differentiate between malicious hacking and hackers who look around computer systems for fun, or do you think hacking is always right or wrong in some moral sense?

FD: Yes, I think there is a huge difference between malicious hackers and browsing hackers. Malicious hackers are vandals and pests. Browsing hackers harm no one and bring excitement into the drab lives of people like Cliff Stoll.

DD: What is your general impression of hackers and phone phreaks?

FD: Like everything, 90% of them are bad. Bad both technically and ethically. However the remaining 10% are some of the most intellectually stimulating people I have ever met.

DD: What is your general impression of computer security professionals?

FD: I divide them into two camps: the high-profile media people and the real technical people. The high-profile people are normally pompous and close minded, and I don't have much affection for them. The technical members seem (from what I have read) intelligent and well meaning, although I would argue that they should sometimes think about what they're doing more.

DD: What, specifically, would you like them to think about? If you could run a workshop for computer security professionals, what issues would you have them address?

FD: Well I had this great plan a few years ago of taking a group of computer security professionals and a group of hackers and putting them into a locked room together after giving them the empathy raising drug MDMA (Ecstacy). But that's probably not what you're asking for. One of the main things I think security people should think more about is *nontechnical* (i.e., social/psychological) ways to keep computers secure. Another important area would of course be on the finer ethical points, things like: the importance of anonymity (e.g., the problem with "caller id"), appropriate use of security (e.g., don't hide things from people unnecessarily), and the morality of government cryptography. Oh, and by the way, don't think that I would want to be giving these lectures. I'd definitely be in the audience to learn with everyone else.

DD: How do you see computer "crime" changing in the future? Will hacking become more or less common? Will most hacking be profit motivated? What about hacking by terrorists?

FD: Sadly, computer crime will be more for profit in the future simply because that's "where the money is." I don't see hacking by terrorists as a particularly big problem but certainly possible. The hacking underground definitely seems to be shrinking, and I think that as the amount of information required to start hacking increases there will be a decrease in "casual" hackers.

DD: How do you see computer security changing in the future?

FD: Becoming more of a science, less of a gimmick. Better integrated into all software instead of a tack-on.

DD: Have you read *Shockwave Rider, Neuromancer*, or *1984*? If so, what did you think of them?

FD: Yes, I have read these books. I think *Shockwave Rider*, while somewhat poorly written, has important things to say about information and how it should be treated. I think *Neuromancer* is brilliant. As to why, as you point out, some computer professionals dislike *Neuromancer*, I think it has to do with background. If you haven't read William Burroughs, listened to the Velvet Underground, been in some sort of underground, a *lot* of allusions are just going to go over your head, and William Gibson's shorthand technique of writing will just sound like nonsense. As for being technically inaccurate, read any of the UCLA brain-computer interface papers, or pick up an issue of *SIGCHI* where they discuss "artificial realities." *1984* is, of course, great.

DD: Do you see DES as being a success or failure? What has it taught us about what the government's (especially NSA's) role in cryptography should be?

FD: I think DES was a disaster and an example of government ineptitude. While it was widely accepted as the standard, due to the slowness and cost of the earlier DES chips, it never was that well used. By the time the chips had become practical, the NSA was admitting that DES was no longer secure. DES will continue to be used and give people a false sense of security. If the NBS had listened to Hellman and Diffie instead of the NSA, this could have been delayed. In general the NSA's opinion on a cryptographic standard should be taken with a large grain of salt because of their code-breaking role.

DD: Given your views of DES as a disaster, how do you explain why BNR, the company that Diffie works for, markets DES-base products? How do you explain why many respected cryptographers produce and promote DES-based products and sit on standards communities that have adopted DES? These people are all keenly aware of the original criticism made by Diffie and Hellman, and they are not stupid.

FD: Well, yes; but just because I believe DES was a disaster doesn't mean I don't agree that it has a place in the market. I think that DES will fulfill most cryptographic users needs; it's just that a better DES would even better fulfill their needs. I think right now the only things DES has going for it is (1) inertia and (2) at least it's a standard, and who wants to start up yet another standards committee? And actually, I don't expect my opinions on cryptography matters to be taken too seriously; I just like having them.

DD: In your opinion, what's the computer security professional's role, especially when it comes to disseminating information?

FD: Most examples seem to bear out my opinion that it's better to let everyone know about a bug than to try to pretend it doesn't exist. Otherwise it's way more likely that the "bad guys" will find out before the system operators.

DD: Ok, but how do you let all the "good guys" know right away? What if they are on vacation for two weeks? What if it will take them several days to fix it? What if they are swamped with urgent requests from their bosses, which they must respond to first? One "bad guy" could do considerable damage while 100,000 good guys are trying to respond to the situation. I'm not necessarily disagreeing with you, but I am saying that it is easier said than done.

FD: Details, details. Actually I think nowadays the Computer Emergency Response Team is doing a very good job on immediately distributing information on bugs to the "appropriate" people. So I think your question is kind of moot, since it's been/being demonstrated to be workable.

DD: What's your opinion on how law enforcement agencies treat computer "crime?" For example, was Mitnick treated too harshly? How should Morris be treated?

FD: Because few in the police or SS are knowledgeable about computer "crime" they often exacerbate the problem. Mitnick was treated much too harshly by the press, though his sentence was basically reasonable. Morris, on the other hand, was treated much nicer by the press; and we'll just have to see what happens.

DD: Have your views on hacking or computer security changed since you went to college?

FD: I decided that hacking after age 18 was a *bad idea*.

DD: How do you like the computer science program at your university? Is there anything you'd like to see changed?

FD: Hmm, the computer science program has been pretty much as I would expect. So far the classes I have taken have been easy due to my prior experience. The majority of my teachers have been good. There exists an antiundergraduate attitude, but I'm sure this is true at all colleges.

DD: What would you like to do when you graduate?

FD: Geez, I wish I knew. I'm interested in user interface design, full-text information retrieval systems, and of course computer security. I think I want to be a project leader for large programs in one of these areas.

DD: Hobbies?

FD: Lots of reading (Burroughs, Kerouac, Gibson, Robert Wilson), music (punk and industrial), programming, and technology in general.

ARE COMPUTER HACKER
BREAK-INS ETHICAL?*

Eugene H. Spafford
Department of Computer Sciences, Purdue University, West Lafayette, Indiana

Recent incidents of unauthorized computer intrusion have brought about discussion of the ethics of breaking into computers. Some individuals have argued that as long as no significant damage results, break-ins may serve a useful purpose. Others counter that the break-ins are almost always harmful and wrong. This article lists and refutes many of the reasons given to justify computer intrusions. It is the author's contention that break-ins are ethical only in extreme situations, such as a life-critical emergency. The article also discusses why no break-in is "harmless."

INTRODUCTION

On November 2, 1988, a program was run on the Internet that replicated itself on thousands of machines, often loading them to the point where they were unable to process normal requests [2–4]. This Internet Worm program was stopped in a matter of hours, but the controversy engendered by its release has raged ever since. Other

*An earlier version of this paper appeared as [1].

incidents, such as the "wily hackers"* tracked by Cliff Stoll [5], the "Legion of Doom" members who are alleged to have stolen telephone company 911 software [6], and the growth of the computer virus problem [7–10] have added to the discussion. What constitutes improper access to computers? Are some break-ins ethical? Is there such a thing as a "moral hacker" [11]?

It is important that we discuss these issues. The continuing evolution of our technological base and our increasing reliance on computers for critical tasks suggest that future incidents may well have more serious consequences than those we have seen to date. With human nature as varied and extreme as it is, and with the technology as available as it is, we must expect to experience more of these incidents.

In this article, I will introduce a few of the major issues that these incidents have raised, and present some arguments related to them. For clarification, I have separated several issues that often have been combined when debated, it is possible that most people agree on some of these points once they are viewed as individual issues.

WHAT IS ETHICAL?

Webster's Collegiate Dictionary defines ethics as "the discipline dealing with what is good and bad and with moral duty and obligation." More simply, it is the study of what is right to do in a given situation—what we ought to do. Alternatively, it is sometimes described as the study of what is good and how to achieve that good. To suggest whether an act is right or wrong we need to agree on an ethical system that is easy to understand and apply as we consider the ethics of computer break-ins.

Philosophers have been trying for thousands of years to define right and wrong, and I will not make yet another attempt at such a definition. Instead, I will suggest that we make the simplifying assumption that we can judge the ethical nature of an act by applying a deontological assessment: regardless of the effect, is the act itself ethical? Would we view that act as sensible and proper if everyone were to engage in it? Although this may be too simplistic a model (and it can certainly be argued that other ethical philosophies may also be applied), it is a good first approximation for purposes of discussion. If you are unfamiliar with any other formal ethical evaluation method, try applying this assessment to the points I raise later in this article. If the results are obviously unpleasant or dangerous in the large, then they should be considered unethical as individual acts.

Note that this philosophy assumes that right is determined by actions, not results. Some ethical philosophies assume that the ends justify the means; our society does not operate by such a philosophy, although many individuals do. As a society, we profess to believe that "it isn't whether you win or lose, it's how you play the game." This is why we are concerned with issues of due process and civil rights, even for those espousing repugnant views and committing heinous acts. The process is important no matter the outcome, although the outcome may help to resolve a choice between two almost equal courses of action.

Philosophies that consider the results of an act as the ultimate measure of good are often impossible to apply because of the difficulty in understanding exactly what

---

*Many law-abiding individuals consider themselves *hackers*—a term formerly used as a compliment. The press and general public have co-opted the term, however, and it is now commonly viewed as pejorative. Here, I will use the word as the general public now uses it.

results from any arbitrary activity. Consider an extreme example: the government orders 100 cigarette smokers, chosen at random, to be beheaded on live nationwide television. The result might well be that many hundreds of thousands of other smokers would quit cold turkey, thus prolonging their lives. It might also prevent hundreds of thousands of people from ever starting to smoke, thus improving the health and longevity of the general populace. The health of millions of other people would improve because they would no longer be subjected to secondary smoke, and the overall impact on the environment would be favorable as tons of air and ground pollutants would no longer be released by smokers or tobacco companies.

Yet, despite the great good this might hold for society, everyone, except for a few extremists, would condemn such an act as immoral. We would likely object even if only one person were executed. It would not matter what the law might be on such an issue; we would not feel that the act was morally correct, nor would we view the ends as justifying the means.

Note that we would be unable to judge the morality of such an action by evaluating the results, because we would not know the full scope of those results. Such an act might have effects, favorable or otherwise, on issues of law, public health, tobacco use, and daytime TV shows for decades or centuries to follow. A system of ethics that considered primarily only the results of our actions could not allow us to evaluate our current activities at the time when we would need such guidance; if we are unable to discern the appropriate course of action prior to its commission, then our system of ethics is of little or no value to us. To obtain ethical guidance, we must base our actions primarily on evaluations of the actions and not on the possible results.

More to the point here, if we attempt to judge the morality of a computer break-in based on the sum total of all future effect, we would be unable to make such a judgment, either for a specific incident or for the general class of acts. In part, this is because it is so difficult to determine the long-term effects of various actions and to discern their causes. We cannot know, for instance, if increased security awareness and restrictions are better for society in the long term, or whether these additional restrictions will result in greater costs and annoyance when using computer systems. We also do not know how many of these changes are directly traceable to incidents of computer break-ins.

One other point should be made here: it is undoubtedly possible to imagine scenarios where a computer break-in would be considered to be the preferable course of action. For instance, if vital medical data were on a computer and necessary to save someone's life in an emergency, but the authorized users of the system could not be located, breaking into the system might well be considered the right thing to do. However, that action does not make the break-in ethical. Rather, such situations occur when a greater wrong would undoubtedly occur if the unethical act were not committed. Similar reasoning applies to situations such as killing in self defense. In the following discussion, I will assume that such conflicts are not the root cause of the break-ins; such situations should very rarely present themselves.

MOTIVATIONS

Individuals who break into computer systems or who write vandalware usually use one of several rationalizations for their actions. (See, for example, [12] and the discussion in [13].) Most of these individuals would never think to walk down a street, trying every door to find one unlocked, then search through the drawers of the furniture inside. Yet these same people seem to give no second thought to making repeated attempts at guessing passwords to accounts they do not own, and once into a system, browsing through the files on disk.

These computer burglars often give the same reasons for their actions in an attempt to rationalize their activities as morally justified. I present and refute some of the most commonly used ones; motives involving theft and revenge are not uncommon, and their moral nature is simple to discern, so I shall not include them here.

The Hacker Ethic

Many hackers argue that they follow an ethic that both guides their behavior and justifies their break-ins. This hacker ethic states, in part, that all information should be free [11]. This view holds that information belongs to everyone and there should be no boundaries or restraints to prevent anyone from examining information. Richard Stallman states much the same thing in his GNU Manifesto [14]. He and others have stated in various forums that if information is free, it logically follows that there should be no such thing as intellectual property, and no need for security.

What are the implications and consequences of such a philosophy? First and foremost, it raises some disturbing questions of privacy. If all information is (or should be) free, then privacy is no longer a possibility. For information to be free to everyone and for individuals to no longer be able to claim it as property means that anyone may access the information if they please. Furthermore, as it is no longer property of any individual, anyone can alter the information. Items such as bank balances, medical records, credit histories, employment records, and defense information all cease to be controlled. If someone controls information and controls who may access it, the information is obviously not free. But without that control, we would no longer be able to trust the accuracy of the information.

In a perfect world, this lack of privacy and control might not be cause for concern. However, if all information were to be freely available and modifiable, imagine how much damage and chaos would be caused in our real world! Our whole society is based on information whose accuracy must be assured. This includes information held by banks and other financial institutions, credit bureaus, medical agencies and professionals, government agencies such as the IRS, law enforcement agencies, and educational institutions. Clearly, treating all their information as "free" would be unethical in any world where there might be careless and unethical individuals.

Economic arguments can be made against this philosophy, too, in addition to the overwhelming need for privacy and control of information accuracy. Information is not universally free. It is held as property because of privacy concerns, and because it is often collected and developed at great expense. Development of a new algorithm or program or collection of a specialized data base may involve the expenditure of vast sums of time and effort. To claim that it is free or should be free is to express a naive and unrealistic view of the world. To use this to justify computer break-ins is clearly unethical. Although not all information currently treated as private or controlled as proprietary needs such protection, that does not justify unauthorized access to it or to any other data.

The Security Arguments

These arguments are the most common ones offered within the computer community. One argument is the same as that used most often to defend the author of the Internet Worm program in 1988: break-ins illustrate security problems to a community that will otherwise not note the problems.

In the Worm case, one of the first issues to be discussed widely in Internet mailing lists dealt with the intent of the perpetrator—exactly why the worm program had been written and released. Explanations put forth by members of the community ranged from simple accident to the actions of a sociopath. Many said that the Worm was designed to reveal security defects to a community that would not otherwise pay attention. This was not supported by the testimony of the author during his trial, nor is it supported by past experience of system administrators.

The Worm author, Robert T. Morris, appears to have been well known at some universities and major companies, and his talents were generally respected. Had he merely explained the problems or offered a demonstration to these people, he would have been listened to with considerable attention. The month before he released the Worm program on the Internet, he discovered and disclosed a bug in the file transfer program *ftp*; news of the flaw spread rapidly, and an official fix was announced and available within a matter of weeks. The argument that no one would listen to his report of security weaknesses is clearly fallacious.

In the more general case, this security argument is also without merit. Although some system administrators might have been complacent about the security of their systems before the Worm incident, most computer vendors, managers of government computer installations, and system administrators at major colleges and universities have been attentive to reports of security problems. People wishing to report a problem with the security of a system need not exploit it to report it. By way of analogy, one does not set fire to the neighborhood shopping center to bring attention to a fire hazard in one of the stores, and then try to justify the act by claiming that firemen would otherwise never listen to reports of hazards.

The most general argument that some people make is that the individuals who break into systems are performing a service by exposing security flaws, and thus should be encouraged or even rewarded. This argument is severely flawed in several ways. First, it assumes that there is some compelling need to force users to install security fixes on their systems, and thus computer burglars are justified in "breaking and entering" activities. Taken to extremes, it suggests that it would be perfectly acceptable to engage in such activities on a continuing basis, so long as they might expose security flaws. This completely loses sight of the purpose of the computers in the first place—to serve as tools and resources, not as exercises in security. The same reasoning would imply that vigilantes have the right to attempt to break into the homes in my neighborhood on a continuing basis to demonstrate that they are susceptible to burglars.

Another flaw with this argument is that it completely ignores the technical and economic factors that prevent many sites from upgrading or correcting their software. Not every site has the resources to install new system software or to correct existing software. At many sites, the systems are run as turnkey systems—employed as tools and maintained by the vendor. The owners and users of these machines simply do not have the ability to correct or maintain their systems independently, and they are unable to afford custom software support from their vendors. To break into such systems, with or without damage, is effectively to trespass into places of business; to do so in a vigilante effort to force the owners to upgrade their security structure is presumptuous and reprehensible. A burglary is not justified, morally or legally, by an argument that the victim has poor locks and was therefore "asking for it."

A related argument has been made that vendors are responsible for the maintenance of their software, and that such security breaches should immediately require vendors to issue corrections to their customers, past and present. The claim is made that without highly-visible break-ins, vendors will not produce or distribute necessary fixes to software. This attitude is naive, and is neither economically feasible nor technically workable. Certainly, vendors should bear some responsibility for the adequacy of their software [15], but they should not be responsible for fixing every possible flaw in every possible configuration.

Many sites customize their software or otherwise run systems incompatible with the latest vendor releases. For a vendor to be able to provide quick response to security problems, it would be necessary for each customer to run completely standardized software and hardware mixes to ensure the correctness of vendor-supplied updates. Not only would this be considerably less attractive for many customers and contrary to their usual practice, but the increased cost of such "instant" fix distribution would add to the price of such a system and greatly increase the cost borne by the customer. It is unreasonable to expect the user community to sacrifice flexibility and pay a much higher cost per unit simply for faster corrections to the occasional security breach, assuming it is possible for the manufacturer to find those customers and supply them with fixes in a timely manner—something unlikely in a market where machines and software are often repackaged, traded, and resold.

The case of the Internet Worm is a good example of the security argument and its flaws. It further stands as a good example of the conflict between ends and means valuation of ethics. Various people have argued that the Worm's author did us a favor by exposing security flaws. At Mr. Morris's trial on Federal charges stemming from the incident, the defense attorneys also argued that their client should not be punished because of the good the Worm did in exposing those flaws. Others, including the prosecuting attorneys, argued that the act itself was wrong no matter what the outcome. Their contention has been that the result does not justify the act itself, nor does the defense's argument encompass all the consequences of the incident.

This is certainly true; the complete results of the incident are still not known. There have been many other break-ins and network worms since November 1988, perhaps inspired by the media coverage of that incident. More attempts will possibly be made, in part inspired by Mr. Morris's act. Some sites on the Internet have restricted access to their machines, and others were removed from the network; other sites have decided not to pursue a connection, even though it will hinder research and operations. Combined with the many decades of person-hours devoted to cleaning up after the worm, this seems a high price to pay for a claimed "favor."

The legal consequences of this act are also not yet known. For instance, many bills have been introduced into Congress and state legislatures over the last three years in part because of these incidents. One piece of legislation introduced into the House of Representatives, HR-5061, entitled "The Computer Virus Eradication Act of 1988," was the first in a series of legislative actions that have the potential to affect significantly the computer profession. In particular, HR-5061 was notable because its wording would prevent it from being applied to true computer viruses.* The passage of similar well-intentioned but poorly defined legislation could have a major negative effect on the computing profession as a whole.

The Idle System Argument

Another argument put forth by system hackers is that they are simply making use of idle machines. They argue that because some systems are not used at a level near their capacity, the hacker is somehow entitled to use them.

This argument is also flawed. First of all, these systems are usually not in service to provide a general-purpose user environment. Instead, they are in use in commerce, medicine, public safety, research, and government functions. Unused capacity is present for future needs and sudden surges of activity, not for the support of outside individuals. Imagine if large numbers of people without a computer were to take advantage of a system with idle processor capacity: the system would quickly be overloaded and severely degraded or unavailable for the rightful owners. Once on the system, it would be difficult (or impossible) to oust these individuals if sudden extra capacity were needed by the rightful owners. Even the largest machines available today would not provide sufficient capacity to accommodate such activity on any large scale.

I am unable to think of any other item that someone may buy and maintain, only to have others claim a right to use it when it is idle. For instance, the thought of someone walking up to my expensive car and driving off in it simply because it is not currently being used is ludicrous. Likewise, because I am away at work, it is not proper to hold a party at my house because it is otherwise not being used. The related positions that unused computing capacity is a shared resource, and that my privately developed software belongs to everyone, are equally silly (and unethical) positions.

The Student Hacker Argument

Some trespassers claim that they are doing no harm and changing nothing—they are simply learning about how computer systems operate. They argue that computers are expensive, and that they are merely furthering their education in a cost-effective manner. Some authors of computer viruses claim that their creations are intended to be harmless, and that they are simply learning how to write complex programs.

There are many problems with these arguments. First, as an educator, I claim that writing vandalware or breaking into a computer and looking at the files has almost nothing to do with computer education. Proper education in computer science and engineering involves intensive exposure to fundamental aspects of theory, abstraction, and design techniques. Browsing through a system does not expose someone to the broad scope of theory and practice in computing, nor does it provide the

*It provided penalties only in cases where programs were introduced into computer systems; a computer virus is a segment of code attached to an existing program that modifies other programs to include a copy of itself [7].

critical feedback so important to a good education [16, 17]; neither does writing a virus or worm program and releasing it into an unsupervised environment provide any proper educational experience. By analogy, stealing cars and joyriding does not provide one with an education in mechanical engineering, nor does pouring sugar in the gas tank.

Furthermore, individuals "learning" about a system cannot know how everything operates and what results from their activities. Many systems have been damaged accidently by ignorant (or careless) intruders; most of the damage from computer viruses (and the Internet Worm) appear to be caused by unexpected interactions and program faults. Damage to medical systems, factory control, financial information, and other computer systems could have drastic and far-ranging effects that have nothing to do with education, and could certainly not be considered harmless.

A related refutation of the claim has to do with knowledge of the extent of the intrusion. If I am the person responsible for the security of a critical computer system, I cannot assume that *any* intrusion is motivated solely by curiosity and that nothing has been harmed. If I know that the system has been compromised, I must fear the worst and perform a complete system check for damages and changes. I cannot take the word of the intruder, for any intruder who actually caused damage would seek to hide it by claiming that he or she was "just looking." To regain confidence in the correct behavior of my system, I must expend considerable energy to examine and verify every aspect of it.

Apply our universal approach to this situation and imagine if this "educational" behavior was widespread and commonplace. The result would be that we would spend all our time verifying our systems and never be able to trust the results fully. Clearly, this is not good, and thus we must conclude that these "educational" motivations are also unethical.

The Social Protector Argument

One last argument, more often heard in Europe than the United States, is that hackers break into systems to watch for instances of data abuse and to help keep "Big Brother" at bay. In this sense, the hackers are protectors rather than criminals. Again, this assumes that the ends justify the means. It also assumes that the hackers are actually able to achieve some good end.

Undeniably, there is some misuse of personal data by corporations and by the government. The increasing use of computer-based record systems and networks may lead to further abuses. However, it is not clear that breaking into these systems will aid in righting the wrongs. If anything, it may cause those agencies to become even more secretive and use the break-ins as an excuse for more restricted access. Break-ins and vandalism have not resulted in new open-records laws, but they have resulted in the introduction and passage of new criminal statutes. Not only has such activity failed to deter "Big Brother," but it has also resulted in significant segments of the public urging more laws and more aggressive law enforcement—the direct opposite of the supposed goal.

It is also not clear that these hackers are the individuals we want "protecting" us. We need to have the designers and users of the systems—trained computer professionals—concerned about our rights and aware of the dangers involved with the inappropriate use of computer monitoring and record keeping. The threat is a relatively new one, as computers and networks have become widely used only in the last few decades. It will take some time for awareness of the dangers to spread throughout the profession. Clandestine efforts to breach the security of computer systems do nothing to raise the consciousness of the appropriate individuals. Worse, they associate that commendable goal (heightened concern) with criminal activity (computer break-ins), thus discouraging proactive behavior by the individuals in the best positions to act in our favor. Perhaps it is in this sense that computer break-ins and vandalism are most unethical and damaging.

CONCLUSION

I have argued here that computer break-ins, even when no obvious damage results, are unethical. This must be the considered conclusion even if the result is an improvement in security, because the activity itself is disruptive and immoral. The results of the act should be considered separately from the act itself, especially when we consider how difficult it is to understand all the effects resulting from such an act.

Of course, I have not discussed every possible reason for a break-in. There might well be an instance where a break-in might be necessary to save a life or to preserve national security. In such cases, to perform one wrong act to prevent a greater wrong may be the right thing to do. It is beyond the scope or intent of this paper to discuss such cases, especially as no known hacker break-ins have been motivated by such instances.

Historically, computer professionals as a group have not been overly concerned with questions of ethics and propriety as they relate to computers. Individuals and some organizations have tried to address these issues, but the whole computing community needs to be involved to address the problems in any comprehensive manner. Too often, we view computers simply as machines and algorithms, and we do not perceive the serious ethical questions inherent in their use.

However, when we consider that these machines influence the quality of life of millions of individuals, both directly and indirectly, we understand that there are broader issues. Computers are used to design, analyze, support, and control applications that protect and guide the lives and finances of people. Our use (and misuse) of computing systems may have effects beyond our wildest imagining. Thus, we must reconsider our attitudes about acts demonstrating a lack of respect for the rights and privacy of other people's computers and data.

We must also consider what our attitudes will be towards future security problems. In particular, we should consider the effect of widely publishing the source code for worms, viruses, and other threats to security. Although we need a process for rapidly disseminating corrections and security information as they become known, we should realize that widespread publication of details will imperil sites where users are unwilling or unable to install updates and fixes.* Publication should serve a useful purpose; endangering the security of other people's machines or attempting to force them into making changes they are unable to make or afford is not ethical.

---

*To anticipate the oft-used comment that the "bad guys" already have such information: not every computer burglar knows or will know *every* system weakness—unless we provide them with detailed analyses.

Finally, we must decide these issues of ethics as a community of profession-als and then present them to society as a whole. No matter what laws are passed, and no matter how good security measures might become, they will not be enough for us to have completely secure systems. We also need to develop and act accord-ing to some shared ethical values. The members of society need to be educated so that they understand the importance of respecting the privacy and ownership of data. If locks and laws were all that kept people from robbing houses, there would be many more burglars than there are now; the shared mores about the sanctity of per-sonal property are an important influence in the prevention of burglary. It is our duty as informed professionals to help extend those mores into the realm of com-puters.

REFERENCES

1. Spafford, E. H. Is a computer break-in ever ethical? *Info. Tech. Quart.* IX:9–14 (1990).

2. Seeley, D. A tour of the worm, In *Proceedings of the Winter 1989 Usenix Con-ference*, The Usenix Association, Berkeley, CA, 1989.

3. Spafford, E. H. The internet worm: crisis and aftermath. *Commun. ACM* 32, 678–698 (1989).

4. Spafford, E. H. An analysis of the internet work. In *Proceedings of the 2nd Euro-pean Software Engineering Conference* (C. Ghezzi and J. A. McDermid, eds.), Springer-Verlag, Berlin, Germany, 1989, pp. 446–468.

5. Stoll, C. *Cuckoo's Egg*, Doubleday, New York, 1989.

6. Schwartz, John. The hacker dragnet, *Newsweek* 65, (April, 1990).

7. Spafford, E. H., K. A. Heaphy, and D. J. Ferbrache. *Computer Viruses: Dealing with Electronic Vandalism and Programmed Threats.* Arlington, Virginia: ADAPSO, 1989.

8. Hoffman, L., ed., *Rogue Programs: Viruses, Worms, and Trojan Horses.* Van Nostrand Reinhold, 1990.

9. Stang, D. J., *Computer Viruses*, 2nd ed., National Computer Security Association, Washington, DC, 1990.

10. Denning, P. J., ed., *Computers Under Attack: Intruders, Worms, and Viruses.* Reading, MA: ACM Books/Addison-Wesley, 1991.

11. Baird, B. J., L. L. Baird, Jr., and R. P. Ranauro. 1987. The moral cracker? *Comp. Sec.* 6:471–478.

12. Landreth, W. *Out of the Inner Circle: a Hacker's Guide to Computer Security*, Microsoft Press, New York, 1984.

13. Adelaide, J. P. Barlow, R. J. Bluefire, R. Brand, C. Stoll, D. Hughes, F. Drake, E. J. Homeboy, E. Goldstein, H. Roberts, J. Gasperini (JIMG), J. Carroll (JRC), L. Felsenstein, T. Mandel, R. Horvitz (RH), R. Stallman (RMS), G. Tenney, Acid Phreak, and Phiber Optik, Is computer hacking a crime? *Harper's Magazine* 280, 45–57 (March 1990).

14. Stallman, R. The GNU manifesto. In *GNU EMacs Manual*. Free Software Foun-dation, Cambridge, MA: pp. 239–248 (1986).

15. McIlroy, M. D. Unsafe at any price, *Info. Techn. Quart.* IX, 21–23 (1990).

16. P. J. Denning, D. E. Comer, D. Gries, M. C. Mulder, A. Tucker, A. J. Turner, and P. R. Young, Computing as a discipline, *Commun. ACM* 32, 9–23 (1989).

17. Tucker, A. B., et al. *Computing Curricula 1991*, IEEE Society Press, Piscataway, NJ, 1991.

COMPUTER VIRUS LEGISLATION: PREPARED TESTIMONY AND STATEMENT FOR THE RECORD BEFORE THE SUBCOMMITTEE ON CRIMINAL JUSTICE, COMMITTEE ON THE JUDICIARY U.S. HOUSE OF REPRESENTATIVES NOVEMBER 8, 1989

Marc Rotenberg

Mr. Chairman, members of the Committee, thank you for the opportunity to testify today on legislation regarding computer viruses. My name is Marc Rotenberg and I am the director of the Washington Office of Computer Professionals for Social Responsibility (CPSR).

CPSR is a national membership organization of computer scientists and other specialists that seek to inform the public about the social impact of computer systems. Our membership includes a Nobel Laureate and five Turing Award winners, the highest honor in computer science. CPSR members have examined several national computing issues and prepared reports on funding priorities in computer science, the Strategic Defense Initiative, computer risk and reliability, and the proposed expansion of the FBI's records system.[1]

You have asked me to examine legislation that has been introduced in the House of Representatives related to computer viruses. I appreciate this opportunity and am glad that you have taken an interest in this subject.

It was just a year ago last week that the Cornell "virus" swept through the Internet.[2] For many people in this country it was the first that they had heard of computer viruses and similar programs that could bring a nationwide computer system to a halt. Even as system managers were clearing the code out of their computers, discussions about the vulnerabilities of computer systems and the rights and responsibilities of computer users were taking place all across the country.

CPSR MEMBERS ADDRESS THE COMPUTER VIRUS

In Palo Alto, California, CPSR members met shortly after the Internet virus to discuss the significance of the event. Over the course of several days our members discussed the wide ranging issues raised by the incident.[3] The discussion revealed many concerns about network security, ethical accountability, and computer reliability. It also revealed a division within our organization about the moral responsibility of the virus author. Some of our members believed that the person responsible for the virus had performed a great service for the computer community by drawing attention to the security flaws in the Internet, particularly the UNIX operating system. Others felt strongly that this person had violated a fundamental understanding within the computer community not to exploit known security flaws and had caused great damage to users of the Internet. The division within our organization reflected a division within the computer science community.[4]

In the end we issued a statement on the computer virus that has been widely circulated in the computer community and republished in computer journals.[5] I have attached the CPSR statement to my testimony and ask that it been entered into the hearing record.

On the issue of the culpability of the person responsible for the virus we said clearly that the act was irresponsible and should not be condoned. The author of the virus had treated the Internet as a laboratory for an untested experiment in computer security. We felt this was very risky, regardless of whether data was altered or destroyed.

But we did not view our task primarily as sitting in judgment over the author of the Internet virus. There had been other viruses in the past, and there would be more in the future. More important, we believed, was to set out the various concerns of our organization for the public, policy makers, and others within the profession who were examining the significance of the computer virus and considering various responses. We reached the following conclusions:

- First, we emphasized individual accountability as the cornerstone of computer ethics. We said that the openness of computer networks depends on the good will and good sense of computer users. Criminal penalties may be appropriate for the most pernicious acts of computer users. But for the vast majority of cases, far more would be accomplished by encouraging appropriate ethical guidelines.

- Second, we said that the incident underscored our society's growing dependence on complex computer networks. Although the press and the public tended to focus on the moral culpability of the virus writer, we believed that the incident also raised significant policy questions about our reliance on computer systems. Since its inception, CPSR has been particularly concerned about the development of complex computer systems, especially in the military, that are difficult to test and may produce misplaced trust. There is little that tougher criminal penalties can do to correct the problems of computer risk and reliability.

- Third, we opposed efforts to restrict the exchange of information about the computer virus. Shortly after the virus incident, officials at the National Security Agency (NSA) attempted to limit the spread of information about the computer virus and urged Purdue University to destroy copies of the virus code.[6] We thought this was short sighted. Since that time, several technical reports and the widespread exchange of information through the Internet have helped users in the computer community more fully understand how the virus operated and provided the necessary data to correct security flaws.[7] We continue to believe that the needs of network users will be better served through the open and unrestricted exchange of technical information.

The importance of open computer networks was also demonstrated recently during the earthquake in the San Francisco Bay area. Before the national networks were able to report on the unfolding events, computer users were dialing up networks to search for friends and to reassure relatives. According to one account, a user of the Prodigy service in the Bay Area sent a message out through the network to subscribers in central Kansas, asking that someone pass the word on to his son, a soldier based at Fort Riley, that everybody back home was OK. The soldier, who had been unable to reach home, received the message from a complete stranger.[8]

- Fourth, we encouraged a public discussion about the vulnerabilities of computer networks and the various technical, ethical, and legal questions raised by the incident. Since the meeting, CPSR members, along with others in the computer community, have been involved in a variety of activities, hosting panel discussions on the virus incident, drafting papers, and encouraging an examination of ethical standards. We believe that these efforts will help develop a broader understanding of the rights and responsibilities of network users.

COMPLEXITY OF THE VIRUS PROBLEM

I will, this morning, describe some of the concerns of the computer community and make several recommendations about what Congress might do to respond to the problem of computer viruses. I will also address some of the potential problems posed by proposed federal legislation. At the outset, I should make one fundamental point: The problems raised by computer viruses are far reaching and complex. There is no simple technical or legal solution. In many ways, we are confronting a whole new series of policy questions that raise fundamental issues about privacy and access, communications and accountability. Public policy must be brought up to date with new technologies, but in the effort to ensure that our laws are adequate Congress should not reach too far or go off in directions that are mistaken or may ultimately undermine the interests we seek to protect.

There are several issues that should be considered in the efforts to develop appropriate legislation to respond to malicious code. First is the increased interdependence of computer systems. The technological developments that makes possible the spread of computer viruses also makes possible the transfer of vast amounts of computer information. Through computer networks, we are now able to send electronic mail, research findings, and tips on security fixes far more rapidly than ever before. Efforts to restrict the exchange of computer viruses run the risk of limiting the flow of this valuable information.

Throughout the computer community, there is a deep concern that solutions to computer security problems not destroy the trust between computer users. Ken King, the President of EDUCOM has warned against short-sighted solutions.[9] Cliff Stoll, the Berkeley astronomer turned computer security expert, speaks of the need to preserve honesty and trust within the computer community and warned against measures that could restrict exchange of computer communications.[10]

As computer networks have developed, so has our concern about the reliability of computer systems. We must reexamine our growing dependence on complex computer networks, particularly in the military. Simply put there are too many computer systems in use today that are dangerously unstable.[11] A report produced recently by the staff of the Subcommittee on Investigations and Oversights of the House Science Committee highlights the enormous risk of the current software development process.[12] We are automating too many complex problems with the expectation that computer systems can solve problems that we ourselves don't fully understand. In areas that involve life-critical functions, the consequences of computer error could be great.[13]

I raise these issues because there is a need to be wary of quick legal or technical fixes that do little to address the underlying problems we must confront. There is a widely shared belief among computer security experts that there is no "silver bullet" that will solve the problem of computer viruses.[14] Though there is much that can be done to improve computer security and operations, it should be understood that no system will ever be 100 percent secure.

NEED FOR TEACHING COMPUTER ETHICS

A large part of the task that lies ahead is to develop a system of ethics that teaches computer users about the appropriate uses of computer systems. We need to discourage computer users from making use of shared resources in ways that make systems less useful to others. To suggest an approach to computer ethics that avoids some of the shortcomings of legislation based on rapidly changing technical terms or ambiguous legal phrases I would like to set out an elaborate analogy. The more I have tried to understand this issue, the more I have been struck by the similarity between our evolving computer networks and interconnected databases, and our public libraries.

A library provides a great wealth of information for its users, but not all information is equally accessible. In many libraries, I can freely roam the stacks and pull out what I need. But other libraries might require that I put my request on paper before the materials are delivered. Certain materials at a reference desk are only accessible after I have spoken with the appropriate person and obtained permission.

A computer system operates in much the same way. On many systems, I am allowed to look through large reams of data without harm to anyone. But for certain information, I need permission. If I were to reach over the reference librarian's desk to take an article I wanted or to look at circulation records, I would be violating a library rule. So too, does the computer user violate a computer rule when he or she enters a system's operating system, knowing that only system managers and other privileged users are authorized. We need to remind system users about the difference between space that is public and that which is private.[15]

There are also other users in the library. In some libraries, users might be asked to leave books in study carrels so that others can find them. But my right to look at a book in another person's carrel would not extend to a right to go through the person's book bag. Similarly, it may be perfectly appropriate to look at another person's computer files if it is clear that they are publicly accessible, as long as I do not go through the person's private files.

A library also relies on the trust and good will of its users. A person who steals a book, or tears a page out of a magazine has not just caused harm to the library, but has deprived other users of the library of a valuable resource. Computer users, like users of a library, must increasingly understand the consequences of their actions in terms of the needs and activities of others.

Of course it is worth noting that there are laws against theft of library materials and destruction of library resources. But neither these laws nor the threat of prosecution have much effect on the habits of library users, since the likelihood of prosecution is so remote. When sanctions are imposed, it is by the library and not the federal government.

PARTIAL SOLUTIONS

The complexity of the computer virus problem requires a multi-part approach. Computer users, system managers, vendors, professional organizations, educators, and the government all have a role to play.

In the federal government much is happening, though more could be done.[16] The National Institute of Standards and Technology (NIST) recently prepared a special publication on computer viruses intended for managers of federal computer systems that is useful and easy to read.[17] It should be made widely available for all of the federal agencies.

Another step that has been taken is the development of the Computer Emergency Response Team (CERT). The proposal was developed last December at a closed-door session with UNIX users and vendors at the National Computer Security Center.[18] While it is good to see the cooperative undertaking between the federal government and the user community, it is not an ideal arrangement. CERT operates through the National Security Agency and the Department of Defense. Military control of computer security is precisely what Congress tried to avoid with the passage of the Computer Security Act.[19] As CPSR has noted in the past, broad claims of national security should not provide carte blanche for the Department of Defense and intelligence agencies to extend their authority over computer security.[20]

Moreover, it is not even clear that CERT's advice is error free. A recent posting to the "Risks" computer bulletin board on the Internet noted that CERT had mistakenly sent out an advisory to network users recommending the use of potentially infected system utilities to correct known security flaws. As one computer user noted, this was not good advice.[21]

The General Accounting Office (GAO) produced a useful overview of virus issues in a report released in June [1989].[22] The GAO recommended that the White House Science Adviser assume responsibility for improving computer security. Although the GAO's concerns about lax security practices is well taken, I suspect that many users in the computer science community would object to centralizing authority for computer security for several reasons. Based on the experience with the Internet, it seems that the university and research community, Berkeley and MIT in particular, were more effective in responding to the virus than the federal agencies.[23]

One of the lessons of the Internet virus is that responses should be developed at the host level and not the network level. As Jeff Schiller, the manager of the MIT Network and Project Athena Operations Manager, has said "anybody can drive up to your house and probably break into your home, but that does not mean we should close down the road or put armed guards on exit ramps."[24]

The great value of the Internet for the user community is its decentralized structure. Like the phone network, it provides rapid access for users across the country.

System security requirements will vary from site to site, depending on whether the user is located at a university, in private industry, or a military agency. If the GAO recommendations are followed, it should only be to strengthen the flow of information about network security. Any steps to create a coercive authority in the White House for computer security on the Internet, such as the creation of a computer security czar, would be a serious mistake.

Universities and research institutions can also take steps to ensure that adequate policies are established to minimize the risk of computer viruses. Universities that fail to take reasonable steps to ensure that their systems are not used for the perpetration of a virus may find themselves civilly liable under tort law.[25] Many universities have already established policies that outline the responsibilities of users of computer facilities, which can serve as models for other schools.[26]

Research in computer ethics will also help reduce the likelihood of computer misuse. The National Science Foundation is planning a major conference to bring together leaders in the computer science community and philosophers to discuss how more might be done to incorporate ethics into computer education. This is a sensible undertaking and should build upon the work that has already been done to improve computer ethics.[27] At the same time, it is important to note that much of the discussion about computers and ethics focuses on the responsibilities of individual users of computer systems and not on the large organizations or institutions that maintain and operate these systems. A coherent system of ethics that binds a community of users, like a system of democratic government, must be based on an implied contract between the individual and the institution. The individual will uphold his or her responsibility if the institution does as well. Concerns about privacy, security, data quality and accountability should also be addressed as institutions move forword with their recommendations for computer ethics.

REVIEW OF LEGISLATION

The last five years has been a period of rapid development in computer security legislation. Congress has three times passed laws designed to extend criminal statutes to computer technology.[28] Virtually all of the states have adopted new statutes, and many are looking at possible changes and additions.[29] There are available to prosecutors today a wide range of theories to base criminal charges for computer related crime.[30]

Based on the views of CPSR members, the experience of the Internet virus, and our general concern about protecting open computer networks, I will describe the potential problems with the proposed federal legislation.

It is important to remember that a computer virus may also be a form of speech, as was the Aldus Peace Virus, and that to criminalize such activities may run afoul of First Amendment safeguards. Restrictions on speech should be carefully examined to ensure that free expression is not suppressed. Computer networks are giving rise to new forms of communication. The public debates in the town square of the eighteenth century are now occurring on the computer networks that will take us into the twenty-first century. These are fragile networks, and the customs and rules are still evolving. The heavy hand of the government could weaken the electronic democracy that is now emerging.[31]

Our legal system protects the fundamental right of free speech in a democratic society and gives special attention to laws that may unduly restrict the exchange of information. It would be wrong to criminalize a computer communication if the communication caused no damage, even if the communication did not follow traditional pathways. It is often those individuals and organizations without great resources who turn to these alternative methods of communication to convey a message.

I wonder also if in casting such a broad net, these statutes might not meet constitutional challenge on overbreadth grounds.[32] A criminal law should clearly distinguish between prohibited and permissible conduct. If it fails to do this, it grants too much discretion to law enforcement officials to choose which cases to prosecute. Where speech is involved, such a law might unnecessarily chill protected speech.

Some of the state statutes are poorly conceived. Those with the software trade association who have been pushing to extend the reach of computer security statutes might consider whether the products of their own members violate restrictions on "alteration of data" or "unauthorized use of resources."[33] To some extent, every computer program takes control of the user's systems. If the program acts as intended, then there are no problems. But if the program misfires, as it sometimes does, software developers may be criminally liable.

A further problem lies in the attempt to define the criminal act in terms of a technical phrase such as a "virus." A virus is not necessarily malicious. Some viruses may only display a Christmas greeting and then disappear without a trace.[34] Other viruses might alter or destroy data on a disk. To treat the two acts as similar because an identical technique is involved would be similar to punishing all users of cars because some cars might cause the death of a person. It is the "state of mind" of the actor and the harm that results which should be the two guiding principles for establishing criminal culpability.[35]

More interesting from a technical viewpoint is that computer viruses may be used both to enhance computer security and to facilitate the exchange of computer information.[36] Although computer security experts have said that such programs are potentially as dangerous as the disease they are designed to cure,[37] it is not clear that disseminating a benign virus should necessarily be a criminal act. Hebrew University used a computer virus to identify and delete a malicious virus that would have destroyed data files across Israel if it had remained undetected.[38]

I would recommend that the Congress wait until there is more case law under the 1986 Act and until more of the state statutes have been tested, before enacting new computer security legislation. Congress should also obtain information from the Justice Department about the effectiveness of the current laws, and see whether state courts can develop common law analogies to prosecute the computer equivalents of trespassing, breaking and entering, and stealing.[39] This is a process that happens gradually over time. The extension of common law crimes to their computer equivalents may provide a more durable and lasting structure than federal statutes that must be updated every couple of years.

FUNDING

It is difficult to talk about the role of Congress in improving computer security without noting the importance of funding to implement the Computer Security Act, the law passed by Congress designed to address the computer security needs of the federal agencies. I was very disturbed to learn two weeks ago that the conference committee cut the proposed appropriation for NIST from $6 million to $2.5 million, even after OMB had approved the funding for NIST and encouraged NIST's new role as the lead agency for civilian computer security.[40] According to one news account, the cut came at the urging of a member who had tried unsuccessfully to redirect part of NIST's 1989 appropriation to a special research testing facility in his home state. If this news account is accurate, then that member's short-sighted and parochial concerns may cost the federal agencies dearly in needed assistance with computer security.

CONCLUSION

I believe that Peter Neumann, a computer Security expert at SRI and a member of CPSR, described the problem best when he said:

> Better laws that circumscribe malevolent hacking and that protect civil and constitutional rights would be of some help, but they cannot compensate for poor systems and poor management. Above all, we must have a computer-literate populace—better educated, better motivated and more socially conscious.[41]

Tougher criminal penalties may help discourage malicious computer activities that threaten the security of computer networks, but they might also discourage creative computer use that our country needs for technological growth.[42] Though we have a great deal of criminal law that could potentially apply to the acts of computer users, it is still very early in the evolution of computer networks. In the rush to criminalize the malicious acts of the few we may discourage the beneficial acts of the many and saddle the new technology with more restrictions than it can withstand.[43]

NOTES

1. More information about CPSR is available from the CPSR National Office (P.O. Box 717, Palo Alto, CA 94302 (415) 322-3778) and the CPSR Washington Office (1025 Connecticut Ave., NW, Suite 1015, Washington, DC 20036 (202) 775-1588).
2. It should be noted that there is a debate within the computer community about the correct term to apply to the program that traveled across the Internet. Purists, following the established taxonomy of computer security, prefer the term "worm" because the Internet program did not attach itself to another program, as viruses technically do, but rather was a free-standing program that infiltrated the network. However, the broad scope and rapid rate of the program's impact suggested to many that the term "virus" was more descriptive than "worm." The press and many within the computer community followed this usage.
3. John Schmeridewaind, "The Virus Perpetrator: Criminal or Hero?" *The San Francisco Chronicle*, November 23, 1988, at C1.
4. Compare Aaron Haber, "Give No Quarter to Creator of Computer Virus," *PC Week*, December 5, 1988, editorial, "Faint Praise," *Computerworld*, November 14, 1988, at 24, Edwards A. Parrish, "Breaking Into Computers Is A Crime—Pure and Simple", *Los Angeles Times*, December 4, 1988 (Dr. Parrish is dean of the Vanderbilt University School of Engineering and President of the IEEE Computer Society) with Jon A. Rochlis and Mark W. Eichin, "With Microscope and Tweezers: The Worm from MIT's Perspective," 32 *Communications of the ACM* 689, 697 (June 1989).
5. "CPSR Statement on the Computer Virus," 7 *The CPSR Newsletter* 2–3 (Winter 1989), reprinted in 32 *Communications of the ACM* 699 (June 1989). The virus incident caused several other organizations to examine the need for ethical standards.

See, e.g., "NSF Poses [sic] Code of Networking Ethics," 32 *Communications of the ACM* 688 (June 1989) (National Science Foundation code), "Teaching Students About Responsible Use of Computers," 32 *Communications of the ACM* 704 (June 1989) (describing the statement of ethics for MIT's Project Athena), "Ethics and the Internet," 32 *Communications of the ACM* 710 (June 1989) (Internet Activities Board code).

Several national data processing, computer, and engineering organizations had well-established codes prior to the virus incident. See "DPMA Code of Ethics, Standards of Conduct and Enforcement Procedures," (Data Processing Management Association), "ACM Code of Professional Conduct: Procedures for the Enforcement of the ACM Code of Professional Conduct," (Association for Computing Machinery), "IEEE Code of Ethics," (Institute of Electrical and Electronics Engineers), reprinted in part in *Proceedings of the 12th National Computer Security Conference* 547–52 (1989).

6. John Markoff, "U.S. Moving to Restrict Access to Facts About Computer Virus," *The New York Times*, November 11, 1988.

7. See, e.g., Jon A. Rochlis and Mark W. Eichin, "With Microscope and Tweezers: The Worm from MIT's Perspective," 32 *Communications of the ACM* 689 (June 1989), Don Seeley, "A Tour of the Worm" (November 1988) (Department of Computer Science, University of Utah), Eugene H. Spafford, *The Internet Worm Program: An Analysis, Purdue Technical Report* CSD-TR-823 (Nov. 28, 1988), reprinted in 19 *Computer Communications Review* 1 (January 1989). See also Spafford, "Crisis and Aftermath," 32 *Communications of the ACM* 678 (June 1989), John Markoff, "The Computer Jam: How It Came About," The New York Times, November 9, 1988, at D10. See generally, *Proceedings: 1988 IEEE Symposium on Security and Privacy, Proceedings: 1989 IEEE Symposium on Security and Privacy.*

8. T.R. Reid, "Bulletin Board Systems: Gateway to Citizenship in the Network Nation," *The Washington Post*, November 6, 1989, at 27 (Washington Business section).

9. King, K.M. "Overreaction to External Attacks on Computer Systems could be More Harmful than the Viruses Themselves," *Chronicle of Higher Education*, November 23, 1988, at A36.

10. Cliff Stoll, *The Cuckoo's Egg* 302–03, 311 (1989). See also, Cliff Stoll, Testimony on Computer Viruses, The Subcommittee on Technology and the Law, Committee on the Judiciary, United States Senate, May 15, 1989.

11. See, e.g., "Proposed NORAD Computer System Called Flawed," *The Washington Post*, December 16, 1988, at A22.

12. "Bugs in the Program: Problems in Federal Government Computer Software Development and Regulation," Staff study by the Subcommittee on Investigations and Oversight, Committee on Science, Space, and Technology, U.S. House of Representatives, August 3, 1989. See also Evelyn Richards, "Study: Software Bugs Costing U.S. Billions: Document is Critical of Government's Role," *The Washington Post*, October 17, 1989, at D1.

CPSR has been engaged in an ongoing review of the problems of computer risk and reliability, particularly in defense-related systems. See, e.g., *Computers in Battle: Will They Work?* (1987) (edited by Gary Chapman and David Bellin), *Risk and Reliability: Computers and Nuclear War* (1986) (videotape available from CPSR), and *Losing Control?* (1989) (videotape available from CPSR).

13. Peter G. Neumann, "A Glitch in Our Computer Thinking: We Create Powerful Systems With Pervasive Vulnerabilities," *The Los Angeles Times*, August 2, 1988,

part II, at 7. See also Ken Thompson, "Reflections on Trusting Trust," 27 *Communications of the ACM* 761 (August 1984) (1983 ACM Turing Award Lecture).

14. John Markoff, "Virus Outbreaks Thwart Computer Experts," *The New York Times*, May 30, 1989, at C1.

15. Computer security experts take a slightly different approach to this problem. They speak of "least privilege" which means allowing users to have access to only those files of the system for which they are authorized. Following this approach, it is possible to develop elaborate security schemes, based on a hierarchy of privileges, that clearly describe the privileges of each user. This model is appropriate for many large systems, but may be too formal for other computer systems, such as community bulletin boards, where there is little difference in the status of various system users.

16. Even as new programs are being developed to respond to computer viruses, it is disappointing to see that some system managers have failed to correct known security flaws that were exposed by the Internet virus last year. A rogue program recently attacked the same security holes at NASA that had been exploited last fall. John Markoff, "Computer Network at NASA Attacked by Rogue Program," *The New York Times*, October 7, 1989.

17. John P. Wack and Lisa J. Carnahan, *Computer Viruses and Related Threats: A Management Guide* (August 1989) (NIST Special Publication 500–166). The report can be ordered from NIST at (202) 783-3228 or through the Superintendent of Documents, Washington, DC 20402-9325 (stock number 003-003-02955-6). See also Stanley A. Kurzban, "Viruses and Worms—What Can you Do?" 7 *ACMSIG Security Audit and Control Review* 16 (Spring 1989). For more general information about computer security policy, see Charles K. Wilk, *Defending Secrets Sharing Data: New Locks and Keys for Electronic Information* (October 1987) (Office of Technology Assessment), Louise G. Becker, *Computer Security: An Overview of National Concerns* (February 1983) (Congressional Research Service).

18. Martin Marshall, "Virus Control Center Proposed," *Infoworld*, December 12, 1989, at 8. See also General Accounting Office, *Computer Security: Virus Highlights Need for Improved Internet Management* 24–25 (June 1989) (GAO/IMTEC-89-57).

19. See Computer Security Act of 1987: Hearings on H.R. 145 Before a Subcommittee of the Committee on Government Operations, House of Representatives, 100th Cong., 1st Sess. 525–26, 456, 23 (statements of Congressman Brooks, Congressman Glickman, and Congressman English).

Prior to passage of the Computer Security Act, President Reagan attempted to establish primary computer security authority at the National Security Agency and to expand government classification authority under NSSD-145. Agents visited private information vendors and public libraries, and the free flow of information diminished. See Bob Davis, "Federal Agencies Press Data-Base Firms to Curb Access to 'Sensitive' Information," *The Wall Street Journal*, January 28, 1987, Judith Axler Turner, "Pentagon Planning to Restrict Access to Public Data Bases," *The Chronicle of Higher Education*, January 21, 1987; Connie Oswald Stofko, "Inquiry by FBI Causes Libraries to Assess Records," *SUNY Reporter*, February 12, 1987; Jerry J. Berman, "National Security vs. Access to Computer Databases: A New Threat to Freedom of Information," 2 *Software Law Journal* 1 (1987). The NSA also approached election officials and investigated computerized vote-counting software. Burnham, "US Examines if Computer Used in '84 Elections is Open to Fraud," *The New York Times*, September 24, 1985, at A17.

Library associations, public interest organizations, and experts on information policy described the risks of reduced access to information under NSDD-145. See American Library Association, *Less Access to Less Information by and about the U.S. Government* (1988); Steven L. Katz, "National Security Controls, Information, and Communications in the United States," 4 *Government Information Quarterly* 63 (1987); People For the American Way, *Government Secrecy: Decisions without Democracy* (1987); John Shattuck & Muriel Morisey Spence, *Government Information Controls: Implications for Scholarship, Science and Technology,* excerpted in "When Government Controls Information," 91 *Technology Review* 62 (April 1988).

The Computer Security Act followed widespread public opposition to NSDD-145. See House Committee on Science, Space, and Technology, H.R. Rep. No. 153, pt. 1, 100th Cong., 1st Sess. 18, 19, 19 (1987), reprinted in 1988 U.S. Code Congressional and Administrative News 3133, 3134, 3133 (Statement of Jack W. Simpson, President, Mead Data Central; statement of John M. Richardson, Chairman, Committee on Communications and Information Policy, Institute of Electrical and Electronic Engineering; statement of Cheryl W. Helsing, American Bankers Association). See generally Marc Rotenberg, Testimony on the Computer Security Act, Before the Subcommitte on Legislation and National Security, Committee on Government Operations, U.S. House of Representatives 2–5, May 4, 1989.

20 See Mary Karen Dahl, " 'Sensitive,' Not 'Secret': A Case Study," 5 *CPSR Newsletter* 1 (Fall 1987), Marc Rotenberg, Testimony on the Computer Security Act, Before the Subcommittee on Legislation and National Security, Committee on Government Operations, U.S. House of Representatives, May 4, 1989, Letter to Representative Dan Glickman from Marc Rotenberg regarding NSA effort's to suppress dissemination of encryption technology, August 18, 1989. See also "Computer Security Questioned," *The Baltimore Sun*, April 10, 1989, at A7.

21. Anonymous, "Warning About CERT Warnings," 9 *Forum on Risks to the Public in Computers and Related Systems* 36 (October 27, 1989) (Internet computer conference moderated by Peter Neumann).

22. General Accounting Office, *Computer Security: Virus Highlights Need for Improved Internet Management* (June 1989) (GAO/IMTEC-89-57). See also statement of Jack L. Brooks, Director, Government Information and Fiscal Management Issues, Information Management and Technology Division, Hearing Before the Subcommittee on Telecommunications and Finance, Committee on Energy and Commerce, House of Representatives, July 20, 1989.

23. Jon A. Rochlis and Mark W. Eichin, "With Microscope and Tweezers: The Worm from MIT's Perspective," 32 *Communications of the ACM* 689, 697 (June 1989).

24. Ibid.

25. See American Council on Education and United Educators Insurance, *A White Paper on Computer Viruses* (May 1989) (prepared by David R. Johnson, Thomas P. Olson, and David G. Post). See also "The Computer Worm: A Report to the Provost of Cornell University on an Investigation Conducted by the Commission of Preliminary Enquiry" (February 1989) (Cornell University).

26. See, e.g., *Handbook for Students, Harvard College 1987–1988* 85 ("Misuse of Computer Systems").

27. See, e.g., Donn B. Parker and Bruce N. Baker, "Ethical Conflicts in Information and Computer Science, Technology and Business" (August 1988), Deborah Johnson and John W. Snapper, *Ethical Issues In the Use of Computers* (1985), Glenda Eoyang, "Acquisition and Maintenance of Ethical Codes," and John Ladd, "Ethics and the Computer Revolution," *DIAC-88: Directions and Implications of Advanced*

Computing 102, 108 (Computer Professionals for Social Responsibility 1988) (edited by Nancy Leveson and Douglas Schuler).

28. In October 1984, the Computer Fraud and Abuse Act was signed into law. P.L. 99-473 and 99-474 codified at 18 U.S.C. 1030. In 1986 the law was amended and expanded to include "federal interest computers." A companion statute addresses fraud and related activity in connection with an access devices. 18 U.S.C. 1029. See also Electronic Communications Privacy Act of 1986, particularly 18 U.S.C. 2510 ("Wire and electronic communications and interception oral communications") and 18 U.S.C. 2701 ("Unlawful access to stored communication").

29. See Anne W. Branscomb, *Rogue Computer Programs—Viruses, Worms, Trojan Horses, and Time Bombs: Pranks, Prowess, Protection or Prosecution?* 20–28, 33–42 (September 1989) (Program on Information Resources Policy, Harvard Center for Information Policy Research). Another useful source is the Congressional Research Service report by Robert Helfant and Glenn J. McLoughlin, "Computer Viruses: Technical Overview and Policy Considerations" (August 15, 1988) (88-556 SPR).

30. See Branscomb at 28–31. See also Department of Justice, *Computer Crime: Legislative Resource Manual* (Bureau of Justice Statistics).

31. A compelling argument for the need to avoid restrictions on electronic communication can be found in Ithiel de Sola Pool, *Technologies of Freedom* (1983).

32. See Lawrence Tribe, *American Constitutional Law* 1022-39 (2d ed. 1988).

33. The president of an organization of programmers called the Software Development Council has stated, "release a virus, go to jail." "Invasion of the Data Snatchers!" *Time*, September 26, 1989, at 67.

34. The so-called Aldus Peace Virus is an example of a benign virus. See Anne W. Branscomb, *Rogue Computer Programs—Viruses, Worms, Trojan Horses, and Time Bombs: Pranks, Prowess, Protection or Prosecution?* 5–6 (September 1989) (Program on Information Resources Policy, Harvard Center for Information Policy Research).

35. See Wayne R. LaFave and Austin W. Scott, Jr., *Criminal Law* 5–6 (1972).

36. Indeed, someday a computer virus might be needed to free society from tyrannical rule. John Brunner, *The Schockwave Rider* (1975).

37. John Markoff, "Computer Virus Cure May Be Worse Than Disease," *The New York Times*, October 7, 1989, at A1.

38. Anne W. Branscomb, *Rogue Computer Programs—Viruses, Worms, Trojan Horses, and Time Bombs: Pranks, Prowess, Protection or Prosecution?* 41 (September 1989) (Program on Information Resources Policy, Harvard Center for Information Policy Research).

39. See Statement of Senator Patrick Leahy, Hearing on Computer Viruses, Senate Subcommittee on Technology and the Law, Committee on the Judiciary, United States Senate, May 15, 1989.

40. Vanessa Jo Grimm, "Hill Halves NIST Budget For Security," *Government Computer News*, October 30, 1989, at 1.

41. Peter G. Neumann, "A Glitch in Our Computer Thinking: We Create Powerful Systems With Pervasive Vulnerabilities," *The Los Angeles Times*, August 2, 1988, part II, at 7. A similar view was expressed by Professor Pamela Samuelson:

> Probably more important than new laws or criminal prosecutions in deterring hackers from virus-related conduct would be a stronger and more effective ethical code among computer professionals and better internal policies at private firms, universities, and government institutions to regulate usage of computing resources. If hack-

ers cannot win the admiration of their colleagues when they succeed at their clever stunts, they may be less likely to do them in the first place. And if owners of computer facilities make clear (and vigorously enforce) rules about what is acceptable and unacceptable conduct when using the system, this too may cut down on the incidence of virus experiments.

"Can Hackers Be Sued for Damages Caused by Computer Viruses?" 32 *Communications of the ACM* 666, 668–69 (June 1989).

42. The heads of many top U.S. computer companies could probably have been classified as "hackers" in their younger days. See generally Steven Levy, Hackers (1984). In fact, the chief scientist at the National Security Agency was one of the early pioneers of Core Wars, the precursor to today's computer "virus." There has already been discussion within the computer community about how to redirect the energies of hackers toward socially beneficial goals. See, e.g., John A.N. Lee, Gerald Segal, Rosalie Steier, "Positive Alternatives: A Report on an ACM Panel on Hacking," 29 *Communications of the ACM* 297 (April 1986).

43. Other countries are also confronting the question of whether to develop new laws for computer crime. In Great Britain at least one journal has questioned the wisdom of rushing forward with new legislation. "Halting Hackers," *The Economist*, October 28, 1989, at 18 ("Laws that try to make untenable distinctions between computer crime and ordinary crime are neither fair nor comprehensible").

CHAPTER THREE

Ownership of Computer Software

by John W. Snapper

INTRODUCTION: COMING TO NOTICE THE ETHICAL PROBLEM

Theft of software is common. Researchers secretly acquire software and decompile it to learn their competitor's algorithms. Programmers incorporate code copied from programs written by others. Distributors sell products without paying royalties or under false trademarks. The most common form of software theft is the unauthorized installation of applications software. You might, for instance, want to print a document with a prettier type face. If a friend has the software needed for the task, you borrow it, install it on your computers, and run it as needed. This is done casually by most people, with only a momentary pause to overcome a slight worry about the law. The fact is, of course, that this use of the software is often against the law. And that raises a number of ethical and social issues. Is the law appropriate? How seriously should we view the legal rules? Would there be a moral duty to respect the work of others, even if there were no legal protections?

We must decide, both as individuals and as a society, whether or not software theft is a serious breach of ethical duties or of legal rules. For many users, the use of pirated software on a personal computer is a minor offense, no worse than driving a few miles an hour over the posted speed limit. Is this how we are going to view the software piracy: as a minor step across a regulatory limit that only deserves enforcement for egregious violations? Or are we to take a more serious view of piracy? Is it more like shoplifting, which, although also common, is not condoned like speeding? Most Americans will punish a child caught shoplifting, even as we teach our children to push the speed limit when they drive. What is the better approach? Should we accept the fact that software piracy is common as a sign that we should simply accept it, or should we view this as a mark of moral laxity and promote programs that help us to live up to the ideals written into our law?

Our attitude towards software ownership matters a great deal to how we lead our lives. For instance, some businesses (including many universities) have recently established a policy of policing company computers—company representatives enter offices and look into the hard disks of computers on the desks of their employees, checking for proprietary files. Is such interference with worker's lives justified by the seriousness of the offense? Is any infringement of a software copyright a basis for dismissal, or should only repeated or major infringements be noted? An enquiry into these issue will soon involve us with serious philosophical questions about the nature of software ownership and the social justifications for setting up a legal system that recognizes software ownership.

DISTINGUISHING THE ETHICAL, THE SOCIAL, AND THE LEGAL ISSUES

Few ethical and social issues are more closely tied to legal studies than an enquiry into software ownership. The issues include what sorts of laws we want, why we want them, how they should be written, and whether they should be enforced. Our lead-off piece, for instance, the evolution of case law on the scope of copyright law, is reviewed. Everyone agrees that it is illegal to duplicate copyrighted code line by line into a "new" program. But, the duplication of look and feel is another matter. The debate draws attention to philosophical questions about what we want the copyright law to do for society and for the software industry. And it draws attention to economic theories about how to best achieve those ends. But it also demands a judicial decision that determines how a particular feature of the law will be enforced. When investigating software ownership, the ethicist and social theorist must remain constantly aware of our tradition of "intellectual property law," which includes the laws of copyrights, patents, and trade secrets. For this reason, we include articles in this chapter that provide a background into the general legal environment for the debate over software ownership. Readers who want a more inclusive introduction to the general law of intellectual property are well-advised to begin with the West Nutshell books on the subject, especially Arthur Miller on *Intellectual Property* and Charles McManis on *Unfair Trade Practices*. (These will be available at the bookstore of almost any American law school.)

That the debate over software ownership seems to focus on legal niceties does not, however, mean that it is removed from general ethical and social questions. The debate belongs to a broader philosophical inquiry into the definition and significance of the notion of "property." It is, for instance, not obvious that what we call "intellectual property" protections for software should really be called "property" in the first place. For instance, "trade secret" law (which forbids improper discovery of commercially valuable secrets) is generally said to recognize an inventor's claim to "own ideas." But some theorists argue that, on the contrary, the law is designed to punish industrial spying as an unfair trade practice, and that it is a mistake to discuss it in terms of "owned ideas." Arthur Kuflik provides us with a discussion of the problems entailed by the very notion of "owning ideas."

There are also debates over the basic philosophical justification for our legal recognition of software property. It is usually claimed that patent and copyright protection for software is ultimately justified by a societal interest in promoting the "practical sciences." As a philosophical basis for the law, however, this popular view is far from self-evident. Helen Nissenbaum, for instance, discusses and rejects the suggestion that the law is meant to protect an inventor's natural right to the products of his or her labor, regardless of whether society as a whole is better or worse off when we recognize that right. Even if we accept the usual view that patents and copyrights promote technological progress, it is far from clear how the law should be written to best achieve this end. There are at least three currently popular theories on the economic mechanism for the promotion of science by copyright. (a) The opportunity for profit from licensing software may be an incentive that entices good researchers to work on new software. (b) If the alternative to copyrights and patents is trade secrets, then the copyright and patent law provides a way for researchers to openly publish their results (which would encourage future research based on their discoveries) while still making a profit from their works. (c) By enriching those who have a good record in developing useful software, the patent and copyright laws place society's resources in the hands of those most likely to use it for making future technological contributions. This last theory, sometimes called the "prospect theory," is now very popular, in part because it explains why we grant so many important software copyrights to a few rich research corporations.

The theoretical discussions are inseparable from the legal issues. For instance, there is now a debate in the law over whether the owner of a software copyright may view the information encoded in unreadable machine code as a trade secret. The "exchange for secrecy theory" would apparently deny this form of double protection, while the "prospect theory" may justify it as a way to increase the transfer of wealth to research-oriented organizations. The papers reprinted in this chapter all blend ethics and social policy theory with a sense of the law. The issue is never simply what the law says, but also what the law should say.

AN OUTLINE OF SOME OF THE ISSUES

Although the most common form of software theft is unauthorized use of software on personal computers, most of the legal debate has focused on disputes between corporations over claims to certain features of their innovative software. The issues include how much protection and what form of protection should be claimed by software developers. The most extreme view is that we should simply do away with any proprietary protection for software. This minority position has been taken by a number of highly respected computer scientists and industry specialists. It is argued here in the paper by Richard Stallman (a computer scientist who is famous for both his programming accomplishments and for his work with the Free Software Foundation). Most people in the software industry, however, would like to see some sort of protection for their works, and the debate is over the details of how that protection is to be granted. There is disagreement, for instance, about the proper term for protections: Most copyrights last for 75 years, patents for 17 years, semiconductor chip registrations for 10 years, while trade secrets and trademarks can be held forever. Computer scientists will then argue about which term is appropriate for software, given the speed at which software innovations are introduced and the period for which software remains commercially valuable before it is modified and improved.

One of the most debated issues has to do with the status of software patents. Patents and copyrights are the main forms of traditional protection for innovations. Patents traditionally protect industrial processes (as well as machines and new sorts of materials) by giving inventors authority to say who may run the process in industrial contexts. Copyrights traditionally protect documents written on paper by giving authors the right to say who may make copies of the documents. Computer software can both be read as a document and used to run industrial processes, and it is not initially clear which form is appropriate. The courts, however, have generally been hostile to attempts to patent software, and the preferred form of software protection today is the copyright. Because you cannot use software to run a process without making a copy of it, copyright licenses are used by the software industry to determine who may run a process with the software. Although many theorists object to this confusion between the realms of patent and copyright protections, a few software patents have recently been granted, and this continues to create controversy.

There are advantages and disadvantages to the software industry in the preference for copyrights over patents. The copyright is easy to get for a few dollars at the copyright office. Patents, however, are only granted after a long and expensive process in which the patent holder demonstrates the innovativeness of the new invention. Both the inventors who seek protection and the government agencies that grant it prefer the cheap and easy copyright procedure. But there are also advantages to patent protection. The copyright only protects the manner in which an algorithm is written, and a competitor can (at least in theory) get around a programmer's copyright by independently rewriting the algorithm. One of the issues is whether the competing software is a copy or an independent reprogramming of the algorithms found in the original. A major advantage to patents is that they do indeed protect the very algorithm itself, regardless of how it is written down. The software patent would therefore be a much broader protection for the underlying algorithm. The issue is whether the software industry needs or deserves patent protection in addition to copyright protection. We include articles here by Brian Kahin and Richard Stern.

Another major issue for the industry is what can be protected by copyright. There has been much discussion, for instance, of "look and feel" copyrights as illustrated by our lead case. To appreciate this dispute, consider a publisher who produces a new edition of Shakespeare's plays. Although there can be no copyright on the text, the publisher might claim a copyright over how the plays are displayed on the page. Although the publisher has no claim against a copyist who retypes the words from the text, a photocopy that reproduces the "look" of the new edition infringes on the new copyright. The issue is how this notion of the copyrighted "look" applies to software. Can the producer of a word processing program, for instance, claim a copyright on the arrangement of icons on the screen or on the choice of special control keys for the performance of certain functions. These affect the look of the program and (in the case of keys) the feel of the program to a fast typist. This underlying social issue is whether the protections over look and feel will encourage or discourage the development of new and useful software. This is one of the issues that arises in Pamela Samuelson's analysis of the Lotus decision.

Finally, let us take special note of disputes over "fair use." In traditional copyright, some copying is permitted without permission. Within limits, authors quote each other in scholarly manuscripts. Inventors may do experiments on patented processes for the sake of making new discoveries. Uses for which no permission is required are "fair uses." With software, there have suddenly appeared a variety of uses for which it is not clear whether permission is needed. How much of a subroutine may I quote in my new programs? May I keep a copy of my word processor on both my home machine and my vacation home machine (on condition that both machines are never used at once)? May I make a copy for the sake of decompiling a program and discovering its underlying algorithms? Such issues appear and reappear throughout the articles included in this chapter.

WHY INTELLECTUAL PROPERTY IS A SPECIAL ETHICAL ISSUE WHEN APPLIED TO SOFTWARE

The history of intellectual property law is filled with interesting disputes. This is not surprising, since the law is meant to deal with innovations and innovations by their very nature tend to fit poorly into pre-established legal categories. Software does slip between the cracks of the traditional categories of "works of authorship" and "inventions." No one has ever been able to provide a distinction between a text file (of a story or a customer list) and an executable program (viewed as a list of ways to react to certain conditions) that is sufficiently precise for a legal distinction between copyrightable files and patentable programs. But this observation does not in itself explain the extent of the fierce debate over the appropriate level of protection for software. A full philosophical analysis must explain why the issues are distinctly part of computer ethics and why they do not arise for traditional invention or creative writing. As a starting point, we may observe a few features of software that are frequently highlighted in these discussions:

Computer software is easy to reproduce and distribute. Unlike traditionally copyrighted books that (before the photocopier) could only be reproduced with effort by competing publishers, software is pirated with ease by individuals.

Computer software is tied to computer hardware. The hardware is itself protected by separate patents, but remains useless without the software that it calls upon.

Computer software has made possible a huge acceleration in the rate of innovation. At one time, innovative modifications of machine processes had to be built into new machine prototypes and tested at great expense. But today, this can be a trivial exercise.

Computer software can be produced by groups of more or less independent authors working over extended networks. It is often impossible to identify the authors of a text that grows from the contributions of many residents in the "cyberspace" of lists and bulletin boards.

Computer software can be used by several people at one time. Unlike machines and books that could be passed on from person to person for use at different times, software can be accessed simultaneously by many interacting users in local networks.

This is just the start for a list. Ethicist, social commentators, and legalist must identify the special features of software that bear on their special concerns. We must continually ask why the issues discussed in the following papers are special ethical issues for computer users in particular.

CASE
▷ **EVOLUTION OF CASE LAW
ON COPYRIGHTS
AND COMPUTER SOFTWARE**

Office of Technology Assessment

Complete coverage of software copyright case law is beyond the scope of this report. However, protection of software via copyright has involved several key issues. Three of the most important are: (1) whether object as well as source code is protected; (2) whether a program's structure, sequence, and organization is protected (and what such protection implies); and (3) whether the user interface is protected. A summary of the evolution of cases addressing these three key issues follows.

Apple v. Franklin

The case of *Apple* v. *Franklin*[1] specifically addressed the question of whether a copyright can exist in a computer program expressed in object code as well as source code. The court described source code as usually written in a higher-level programming language and object code as the version of the program in which the source code language is converted into (binary or hexadecimal) machine language. The court determined that both the source code and the object code are copyrightable.

In its decision, the court traced the legislative history which, it stated, suggests that computer programs are considered copyrightable as literary works under section 102(a) of the Copyright Act.[2]

CONTU later recommended that the copyright law be amended "to make it explicit that computer programs, to the extent that they embody an author's original creation, are proper subject matter of copyright."[3] In accord with the CONTU report recommendations, the 1980 amendments to the Copyright Act included a definition of a computer program:

> A "computer program" is a set of statements or instructions to be used directly or indirectly in a computer in order to bring about a certain result. (17 U.S.C. 101.)

The court further noted that language of 17 U.S.C. 117 carves out an exception to normal proscriptions against copying of computer programs, thus indicating that programs are, in fact, copyrightable and are otherwise afforded copyright protection. Indeed, the Third Circuit Court of Appeals had, in the prior case of *Williams Electronics, Inc.* v. *Artic International Inc.*,[4] concluded that "the copyrightability of computer programs is firmly established after the 1980 amendment to the Copyright Act."

In arriving at its finding that object code as well as source code are copyrightable, the court in *Apple* v. *Franklin* also stated that, under the statute, copyright extends to works in any tangible means of expression "from which they can be perceived, reproduced, or otherwise communicated, either directly or with the aid of a machine or device."[5] As stated above, the definition of a "computer program" adopted by Congress in the 1980 amendment is a "set of statements or instructions to be used *directly* or *indirectly* in a computer in order to bring about a certain result."[6] Since source code instructions must be translated into object code before they can be utilized by the computer, only instructions expressed in object code can be used "directly" by the computer, and as such, object code falls under the definition in the statute. Further, the court emphasized that a computer program in object code could be classified as a literary work, since the category "literary work," one of the seven copyrightable categories in section 101, includes expression not only in words but also "numbers, or other . . . numerical symbols or indicia." Thus, the court held that a computer program, whether in object code or source code or whether an operating system or application program, is a "literary work" and is protected from unauthorized copying. The court cited *Midway Mfg. Co.* v. *Strohon*[7] and *GCA Corp.* v. *Chance*[8] as in accord with its holding.

Apple v. Franklin addressed the issue of copyrightability of operating and application systems. While Franklin conceded that application programs are an appropriate subject of copyright, it contended that operating systems are not the proper subject of copyright regardless of the language or medium in which they are fixed, and that operating system programs are per se excluded from copyright protection under the express copyright terms of section 102(b) of the Copyright Act and under the precedent and underlying principles of *Baker* v. *Selden*.[9] According to the court, "an application program usually performs a specific task for the computer user" (e.g., word processing, checkbook balance function) while "operating system programs generally manage the internal function of a computer or facilitate the use of an application program" (e.g., translates an application program from source code to object code.) Franklin based its argument on the grounds that an operating system program is either a "process," "system," or "method of operation" and hence uncopyrightable, since section 102(b) specifically precludes copyright protection for these.

In *Apple* v. *Franklin*, the court found that operating system programs are copyrightable. The court pointed to prior courts which rejected the distinction between application programs and operating system programs. The court also cited the CONTU majority and the Congress, neither of which distinguished between operating system and application programs. The court reasoned that, since both operating system programs and application programs instruct the computer to do something, it should make no difference under section 102(b) whether these instructions tell the computer to prepare an income tax return or translate high level language from source to binary object code. The court stated that, "Since it is only the instructions which are protected, a process is no more involved because the instructions in an operating system program may be used to activate the operation of the computer than it would be if instructions were written in ordinary English in a manual which described the necessary steps to activate an intricate complicated machine."[10] The court found no reason to afford any less copyright protection to the instructions in an operating system program than to the instructions in an application program.

Structure, Sequence and Organization[11]

The concept of "structure, sequence, and organization" is found outside the area of computer software in elements such as the plot, subplot, sequence of scenes, setting characterization and patterns of dialogue in works of fiction or drama; or in the detailed outline and organization and selection, coordination and arrangement of information in textbooks or other nonfiction works. In computer software, structure, sequence, and organization include the arrangement of computer program modules in relation to each other, as opposed to the literal text of the program.[12] The cases addressing the issue of the protectability of the structure, sequence, and organization of a program have found that courts must look beyond the literal text of the defendant's program to determine whether there is substantial similarity to the plaintiff's program.

Whelan Assocs., Inc. v. *Jaslow Dental Laboratory, Inc.*[13] presented the issue of whether there can be "substantial similarity" of computer programs when the similarity exists in the structure, sequence, and organization of the program and there is no line-for-line copying. The case involved a program designed by the plaintiff to run a dental laboratory business, written for the IBM Series 1 computer in Event Driven Language (EDL). The defendant's program was written in BASIC for the IBM PC computer. The evidence demonstrated the defendant's access to the plaintiff's source code.

The court found that computer programs were protected under copyright against "comprehensive nonliteral similarity," and held that "copyright protection of computer programs may extend beyond a program's literal code to its structure, sequence and organization." In the particular case of *Whelan*, copyright did protect the structure, sequence, and organization. The court defined the protectable expression in the structure, sequence, and organization to include everything about the program's construction and design except its basic purpose or function (i.e., "efficient operation of a dental laboratory").[14] Thus, it was possible to infringe the copyright of a computer program without verbatim copying of the computer code. In a significant footnote, the court stated that it did not intend to imply by this characterization of copyrightable expression that the idea or purpose behind every utilitarian or functional work will be exactly what it accomplishes, so that structure and organization would therefore always be part of the expression of those works. It drew the distinction between the situation in *Whelan*, and instances where the idea or purpose behind a utilitarian work is to accomplish a certain function in a *certain way*, such that the structure or function of a program is essential to that task.[15]

Other cases reflect the court's reasoning in *Whelan*.[16] In *SAS Institute, Inc.* v. *S&H Computer Systems, Inc.*[17] the court found that S&H infringed the copyright held in a program called SAS 79.5, which was written to run on IBM and IBM-compatible computers by converting it to run on Digital computers. The court cited instances of "literal, near literal and organizational copying," of structural detail and nearly exact duplication of the SAS structure and organization. The court also discussed the idea of merger of idea and expression, stating:

> . . . throughout the preparation of a complicated computer program such as SAS, the author is faced with a virtually endless series of decisions as to how to carry out the assigned task . . . At every level, the process is characterized by choice, often made arbitrarily, and only occasionally dictated by necessity. Even in the case of simple statistical calculations, there is room for variation, such as the order in which arithmetic operations are performed . . . As the sophistication of the calculation increases, so does the opportunity for variation of expression.

Finding that the processes of SAS could be expressed in a variety of ways, the Court stated that:

. . . to the extent that similarities between the SAS and the S&H product have existed, they represent unnecessary, intentional duplication of expression.

Q-Co. Industries, Inc. v. *Hoffman*[18] reflected the idea/expression merger concept. The defendants' program was written to run on an IBM PC in Pascal and IBM Assembler language. The court found that the defendants' program did not infringe plaintiff's program, written in Basic and Atari to run on an Atari 800-XL, in spite of similarities in the structure, sequence, and organization of the program, in addition to similarities in the program text between plaintiff's and defendants' programs. In making this finding, the court stated that the similarities between the two programs were similarities in ideas rather than in expression. The use of functionally similar modules in the same sequence in the two programs was an inherent part of any program of the type developed by the plaintiff.

In *Healthcare Affiliated Services, Inc.* v. *Lippany*[19] the court held that the result of very general creative decisions were not protectable structure, sequence, and organization. Basing its findings upon plaintiff's comparison of the first 50 lines of the two programs, the court stated:

> The evidence merely documents that certain choices were made among factors at a gross level, *e.g.*, the scope of the system, the number of variables to be used or the portions of the work force to be included in calculations of labor hours. The result of these choices, however, do [not] constitute the programs' structure, sequence and organization within the meaning of *Whelan*.

The Fifth Circuit Court of Appeals did not follow *Whelan* in *Plains Cotton Cooperative Ass'n* v. *Goodpasture Computer Serv., Inc.*[20] Relying on expert testimony, the court found no copying when an allegedly infringing program, designed to run on a personal computer rather than a mainframe computer, was found very similar to the plaintiff's program on the functional specification. Even though the court found the two programs very similar with respect to programming and documentation levels, and found that portions of the design appeared to be direct copies, the court looked to other evidence and found no copying. The court did not adopt the *Whelan* holding that the structure, sequence, and organization of a computer program is copyrightable. The court held that similarities in the two programs—each of which was designed to perform the same particular task within the agricultural cotton market—were dictated by the "externalities of the market." The record indicated that the market significantly affected the determination of the sequence and organization of cotton marketing software, since both programs attempted to provide the same information to the user. The court did not hold that such patterns could not constitute an idea in the context of computers. Thus, the decision in *Plains Cotton* narrowed *Whelan* such that the defendant can show that similarities in structure and organization may be dictated by market factors—externalities—so that the same information must be presented to the user.

NEC Corp. v. *Intel Corp.*[21] involved two parties whose microprocessors both utilized the Intel 8086/88 instruction set. NEC's V-series microprocessors contained similarities to the hardware of the 8086/88 microprocessor, but also had additional hardware. Intel claimed that NEC's microcode violated its 8086/88 microcode copyrights, but not that the hardware similarities or use of the macroinstruction set violated its copyright. The court found no infringement, basing its holding on the following findings:

1. no substantial similarity of the works "considered as a whole;"
2. insufficient evidence that NEC copied important parts of Intel's microcode;
3. programming "constraints" accounting for similarities between the two microcodes; and
4. the limited number of ways in which to express the ideas underlying some of Intel's more basic microroutines.

The findings of the court were particularly well supported through the evidence of "Clean Room" microcode presented to the court. NEC had contended that many of Intel's microsequences were not copyrightable because they were made up of only a few obvious steps and thus lacked the originality necessary for copyright protection. NEC focused on cases cited by Melville Nimmer, in which copyright protection was denied to fragmentary words or phrases, noncreative variations of musical compositions, and forms of expression dictated solely by functional considerations. The court looked to Clean Room microcode, developed by a third party, as compelling evidence that the similarities between the NEC microcode and the Intel microcode resulted from constraints. It found that the Clean Room microcode was governed by the same constraints of hardware, architecture, and specifications as applied to the NEC microcode, and that copying was not involved. The developer of the 8086 microcode for Intel acknowledged that the microarchitecture of the 8086 microprocessor affected the manner in which he created his microcode, and that he would expect that another independently created microcode for the 8086 would have some similarities to his. The court found that the similarities between the Clean Room microcode and the Intel microcode must be attributed in large part to these constraints.

With respect to the issues of copying and the limited number of ways in which to express ideas underlying basic microroutines, the court cited testimony that independently created microcode for the 8086 would have fewer similarities in the longer sequences than in the shorter sequences, because more opportunities exist for longer sequences to be expressed differently. The court found that this was borne out: the longer sequences in NEC's code and in Intel's microcode were not nearly so much alike as the shorter sequences.

The court in *Computer Associates International, Inc.* v. *Altai, Inc.*[22] rejects the Whelan test of "structure, sequence and organization" to determine similarities in computer programs. Instead, the court applied the "levels of abstractions test" articulated by Learned Hand in *Nichols* v. *Universal Pictures*,[23] which, they stated, was the law of the Second Circuit Court of Appeals. The "levels of abstractions test" of *Nichols* reads:

> Upon any work . . . a great number of patterns of increasing generality will fit equally well, as more and more of the incident is left out. The last may perhaps be no more than the most general statement of what the [work] is about and at times might consist only of its title; but there is a point in this series of abstractions where they are no longer protected, since otherwise the [author] could prevent the use of his "ideas" to which, apart from their expression, his property is never extended.[24]

Applying this test, the court found no infringement of Computer Associates' copyright.

User Interface (the Screen Display Cases)

Courts have also addressed copyright issues in disputes relating to computer program screen displays, distinguishing copyrightable expression from unprotected elements in the text, menu hierarchies, command structures, key sequences, and other aspects of a program's "interface" with the user.

The court in *Broderbund Software, Inc.* v. *Unison World, Inc.*[25] held that the structure, sequence and organization of screen displays in defendant's "Print Master" infringed the copyright on the audiovisual displays of the plaintiff's program, "The Print Shop." Citing *Whelan*, the court upheld protection for the "overall structure of a program, *including its audiovisual displays* [emphasis added]." According to the court, the *idea of creating printed materials* (which may vary infinitely in their combination of text and graphics) is the concept behind "The Print Shop" and "Print Master." The created printed materials may vary indefinitely in their combination of text and graphics, and thus the idea is separable from the expression in the screens.

Broderbund differs from the earlier case of *Synercom Technology, Inc.* v. *University Computing Co.*,[26] in which the court considered the issue of whether the sequence and ordering of plaintiff's input formats used in a structural analysis program was protected expression or an unprotected idea. Synercom supplied its customers with instructions describing the order in which data should be entered in the analysis program. University Computing, providing its users with similar printed input instructions, filed suit. The court held that the sequence and ordering of data was inseparable from the idea underlying the formats. These were not, therefore, copyrightable.

In the case of *Digital Communications Associates* v. *Softklone Distributing Corporation*[27] the court was confronted with the question of what elements in a single menu screen constituted an idea and what elements constituted expression. The court concluded that the copied elements of the defendant's program that were nonessential to program operation constituted expression and therefore were infringements. It rejected Softklone's arguments that: (1) the idea and expression of the Crosstalk screen merged because the screen was a "necessary expression of its idea," and (2) the status screen was nothing more than an unprotectable "blank form" designed to record the user's choices of parameter values.

This issue was most recently addressed in *Lotus Development Corporation* v. *Paperback Software International*.[28] The *Lotus* decision extended the copyrightability of the nonliteral elements of computer programs to menu command structures. The structure, sequence, and organization of the menu command system were all found copyrightable—including the overall structure, the choice of letters, words, or "symbolic tokens" used to represent each command, the structure and order of the command terms in each menu line, the presentation of the command terms on the screen, and the long prompts.

Lotus brought suit in 1987 against Paperback Software International for copyright infringement of Lotus 1-2-3 by Paperback's VP-Planner, which was advertised by Paperback to be a "workalike" of Lotus 1-2-3. The programs were similar in appearance, and knowledge of Lotus 1-2-3 could be transferred to VP Planner without retraining. Although Paperback had not copied the literal elements of Lotus 1-2-3 (the source code or object code), the court found Paperback had copied the copyrightable nonliteral elements of the program.

The Lotus court established a three-part test for determination of the copyrightability of a particular nonliteral element. Applying this test, the court held that the idea of an electronic spreadsheet was not copyrightable. The rotated "L" at the top of the screen used by Lotus to represent the headings and columns normally found on a paper spreadsheet the court found, was a format used by most other electronic spreadsheet computer programs. For these reasons, the court held that the rotated "L" was not copyrightable. The court also held that the use of the slash key to evade the menu, the "enter" key to invoke a command, and the arithmetic symbol keys were not copyrightable, because of the limited number of keys remaining on the computer keyboard which had not already been assigned some specific purpose (such as an alphabetical or numerical value).

The court in *Lotus* also concluded that the menu command structure is not essential to the idea of an electronic spreadsheet and that, as a result, Lotus 1-2-3's menu command structure was copyrightable expression and infringed by VP-Planner. The court emphasized that each nonliteral element of the user interface may or may not be protectable and that the computer program must be viewed as a whole. "The fact that some of these specific command terms are not quite obvious or merge with the idea of such a particular command term does not preclude copyrightability for the command structure taken as a whole." To determine if illegal copying had occurred, the court found that it need only identify copyrightable elements and decide if those elements considered as a whole had been copied.

In the recent case of *Engineering Dynamics, Inc.* v. *Structural Software, Inc. and S. Rao Guntur*,[29] the court, in spite of plaintiff's urgings, did not follow the reasoning of *Lotus*, looking instead to the Fifth Circuit for guidance. Citing *Plains Cotton*, the court held that formats are not copyrightable. Engineering Dynamics claimed defendants infringed several of its manuals in the development and marketing of defendant's product StruCAD. It also claimed that defendants infringed its copyright in the "user interface," comprised mainly of input and output reports. The court found that the scope of infringed materials included the text, pictures, diagrams, illustrative examples and flow charts depicted in the manuals, but not the input and output formats since the law of the Fifth Circuit provides that a user interface in the form of input and output reports is not copyrightable.

DATABASES

Databases are protected under copyright law as compilations. Under the copyright law, a compilation is:

> A work formed by the collection and assembling of preexisting materials or of data that are selected, coordinated, or arranged in such a way that the resulting work as a whole constitutes an original work of authorship (17 U.S.C. Section 101).

Copyright protection in a compilation does not provide protection for every element of the compilation. Section 103(b) of the Copyright Act provides that:

> The copyright in the compilation ... extends only to the material contributed by the author of such work, as distinguished from the preexisting material employed in the work, and does not imply any exclusive right in the preexisting material. The copyright

in such work is independent of, and does not affect or enlarge the scope, duration, ownership or subsistence of, any copyright protection in the preexisting material.

Circuit courts of appeal have been inconsistent in their treatment of compilations. The Ninth Circuit Court of Appeals has consistently held that the discovery of a fact, regardless of the necessary input of labor and expense, is not the work of an author, so that verbatim repetition of certain words in order to use the nonprotectible facts is also noninfringing. To hold otherwise, according to the Ninth Circuit, would extend copyright protection to facts.[30] It is well established that copyright law never protects the facts and ideas contained in published works.[31] Indeed, the Ninth Circuit in *Cooling Systems & Flexibles Inc.* v. *Stuart Radiator, Inc.*[32] stressed the narrow range of protectable expression in factual works, acknowledging that to whatever extent the arrangement and expression of facts is original, an author is protected against its copying.[33] Similarly, the Second Circuit requires that selection, coordination or arrangement is necessary to form a copyrightable compilation.[34]

The Eighth Circuit case of *West Publishing Co.* v. *Mead Data Central*[35] expands the scope of what is protectable as a compilation. West publishes texts of cases decided in State and Federal Courts and has developed a citation system in which cases can be found by reference to the volume number of the West volume and the page number on which that case appears. Mead Data publishes Lexis, a computer database of cases published by West as well as other Federal and State Court decisions. Mead Data uses the West citation system to locate cases, placing in its databases the first page on which a case appears and also the "jump pages" for each case. West claimed that the page numbering system of its reporters was copyrightable and the court agreed, holding that the compiling and arranging of the cases meets the originality requirement of the copyright law. Mead Data's infringement consisted of taking the arrangement of the cases, not the numbers themselves. However, by using the citation system Mead had infringed West's copyright in the arrangement and selection of cases.

The Seventh Circuit, on the other hand, took into consideration the author's industry, or "sweat of the brow" in producing a compilation. In *Schroeder* v. *William Morrow & Company*,[36] an action for infringement of a copyright on a gardening directory, the court stated that copyright protects not individual names and addresses but compilation, *the product of the compiler's industry* [emphasis added]. In making its finding of infringement, the court stated that:

[i]t is clear . . . that the bulk of compilations in plaintiff's directory were made with substantial independent effort and not by merely copying from other sources. The use of another copyrighted directory to obtain sources of information or for verification and checking, to the extent it occurred, was not wrongful and did not put plaintiff's compilation beyond the protection of the statute.[37]

The Supreme Court finally addressed this issue in *Feist Publications Inc.* v. *Rural Telephone Service Co., Inc.*[38] in which it rejected the "sweat of the brow" basis for copyrightability in fact-based works such as compilations. The court concluded instead that the Copyright Act of 1976 indicated that originality is the proper test in such cases. The *Feist* case involved the suit by Rural Telephone against Feist for copyright infringement, on grounds that Feist had illegally copied Rural Telephone's phone listings.

The Court noted that the case involved two propositions of law which are traditionally in tension: first, that facts are not copyrightable and second, that compilations of facts generally are. The court concluded that while Feist clearly appropriated a significant amount of factual information from Rural Telephone's directory, Rural Telephone's selection, coordination and arrangement of its white pages did not satisfy requirements for copyright protection. The Court, therefore, held that Feist's taking of the listing could not constitute an infringement

Two new cases flow from Feist and appear to establish an emerging line of authority regarding the treatment of spreadsheets. The Second Circuit, in *Kregos* v. *Associated Press*,[39] found baseball pitching forms to be sufficiently original in the selection for copyright protection of nine categories out of the universe of pitching statistics. In *Key Publications Inc.* v. *Chinatown Today Publishing Enterprises Inc.*,[40] the Second Circuit upheld the copyright in the yellow pages of a Chinese–American community directory. The copyright was based upon the compiler's original selection and arrangement of business listings. At the same time, the court found the copyrighted directory not infringed by a competing directory that used a different arrangement of categories and principles of selection for included listings. This finding of non-infringement suggests that thin protection exists in a compilation.[41]

Other Concerns About Copying

Software developers, especially packaged software developers, have also been concerned about two issues related to unauthorized copying: software rental and States' sovereign immunity from money damages for copyright infringement. These concerns have received congressional attention resulting in new legislation in the 101st Congress: Title VIII of Public Law 101-650 makes it an infringement of copyright to rent computer software without the copyright holder's permission; Public Law 101-553 allows Federal courts to hold the States and their agencies and employees liable for copyright infringement. Before the latter was enacted, Federal courts had refused to hold the States or their agencies (e.g., State universities) liable for money damages for copyright infringement, on the grounds that the copyright law does not clearly show the intent of Congress to abrogate the States' sovereign immunity under the 11th Amendment.[42]

The rental legislation was motivated by software industry concerns that most software rentals would be motivated by the desire to copy, rather than to "try before buying," and that software rental to potential copiers would displace sales. Similar concerns had previously resulted in the record-rental provisions of the current copyright law.

The Semiconductor Chip Act   The Semiconductor Chip Protection Act of 1984 was enacted to extend legal protection to a new form of statutory subject matter, semiconductor chip products and mask works.[43] According to the legislative history, the Semiconductor Chip Protection Act is intended to combat the problem of chip piracy,[44] as Congress perceived that the existing law failed to address that problem. In effecting this purpose, Congress attempted to incorporate the goals of the U.S. Constitution regarding copyrights and patents: to reward authors and inventors for their labors, to provide them with an incentive for future creativity, so as to ultimately benefit the public.

The Chip Act is a special or *sui generis* law, creating a statutory scheme to provide proprietary protection for chip products separate from and independent of the

Copyright Act.[45] Protection for domestic products attaches upon fixation and commercial exploitation.[46] Registration with the Copyright Office is a condition of mask work protection. Protection is forfeited if the mask work is not registered within 2 years after the date of first commercial exploitation. The Copyright Office makes provisions for registration. The act provides for a 10 year term. Owners of a protected mask work are granted the right to bar reproduction of the mask work by any means and the right to import or distribute a semiconductor chip product in which the mask work is embodied. The Act establishes reverse engineering as a defense to a claim of infringement. The reverse engineering provisions provide an exemption from infringement liability in spite of proof of unauthorized copying and striking similarity, as long as the resulting chip product was the result of study and analysis and contained technological improvement. The act also provides remedies similar to those associated with copyright protection. However, criminal penalties are not available, and the limit on statutory damages is higher than that provided for by the Copyright Act.[47]

Design Patent Protection Design patents provide protection for designs for an article of manufacture that are new, original, and ornamental. The design may be surface ornamentation, configuration or a combination of both. Courts have defined a patentable ornamental design as one that must "appeal to the eye as a thing of beauty."[48] As with other inventions granted patent protection, the subject of design patent protection must undergo an examination process in the Patent and Trademark Office and meet the standards of novelty and nonobviousness. The configuration of a useful object may constitute a patentable design, so that the elements of a design may be functional. However, a design dictated by considerations of function is not a proper subject for a design patent. A design is not patentable if the only points of novelty or nonobviousness over prior designs are dictated by functional improvement or alteration.[49] Once a patent is granted for a design, the term of protection is 14 years. For infringement of a design patent to exist, the accused article must be so similar to the protected one "as to deceive an observer, inducing him to purchase one supposing it to be the other . . ."[50]

Industrial Design Bills in the United States Industrial design protection is crafted to protect designs inadequately protected under patent, trade dress and copyright law. The history of proposals in the Congress of this method of protection is long.[51]

Several proposals to protect industrial designs were presented to the 100th Congress.[52] These proposals use a similar modified copyright approach. All three would have amended Title 17 to protect designs that are "original." The bills provided for copyrightlike registration process, rather than a patentlike examination process. Commonplace designs, those "dictated solely by utilitarian function" were excluded from protection. All provided for a term of protection of 10 years. Design rights, under the statute, would not affect any rights under patent, trademark, or copyright law. The bills required that notice of protection appear on the article. Copying an article without knowing that it was a protected design would not constitute an infringement.[53]

Opponents of the industrial design bills have argued that there is already sufficient incentive for production of articles of industrial design.[54] Other critics of the bills maintain that an industrial design bill might, by virtue of its characterization as "industrial," cover functional designs, such as automobile windshields, replacement parts, and product packaging, thus favoring original equipment manufacturers and brand name marketers over the makers of less-expensive after-market auto parts and store brand consumer products. Publishers are concerned about liability for publishing books that contain type face designs protected under the legislation.[55]

H.R. 1790, the Design Innovation and Technology Act of 1991, was introduced in the 102d Congress. This bill would amend the copyright law to provide for the protection of industrial designs of useful articles, including typefonts.[56] The bill sets the term of protection at 10 years and provides for requirements for marking, application, and fees. The bill specifies criteria for determination of infringement of a protected design and grants the owner of a protected design the exclusive right to make, import, or distribute for sale or use in trade any useful article embodying the design.

H.R. 1790 addresses concerns raised during hearings on design legislation held in 1990. As a result, it requires that protected designs meet a standard of "originality" if they are to be protected, such that the design must be the result of a designer's creative endeavor that provides a "distinguishable variation over prior work pertaining to similar articles." This variation must be more than trivial and must not have been copied from another source. The bill also expands an exemption for certain replacement parts for automotive and other products. The bill protects distributors and retailers who innocently trade in infringing products. Publishers are not subject to infringement actions under the legislation for reproducing, modifying or distributing printed materials even if these contain an infringing typeface. The aggrieved party must seek a remedy from the actual infringer. Finally, the legislation requires that the registrant for design protection forego simultaneous protection under the patent and copyright laws.

Design protection granting the designer or other owner of the design exclusive rights in the use of his creation has been enacted in foreign countries including Canada, France, the Federal Republic of Germany, India, Italy, Japan, the Netherlands, and the United Kingdom.[57] Such legislation in the United Kingdom and Canada has been recently enacted. Other laws, such as those of Germany and Italy, have been amended in recent years. The definition of industrial design may vary from country to country. However, it appears that generally design protection involves elements such as configuration, shape, pattern, and combinations of lines and colors which provide a product with a new or aesthetically improved appearance. Novelty and the industrial application of the design are generally required to obtain protection. In the countries listed above, the term of protection ranges from 8 to 15 years. The laws in these countries are enforced and provide for civil remedies in cases of infringement of exclusive rights. In some cases, the law provides for imposition of sanctions for criminal offenses.[58]

HYBRID DESIGN PROTECTION

One intellectual property scholar, Professor Jerome Reichman, has suggested that software is, like industrial design, an example of a "legal hybrid" falling between the patent and copyright systems.[59] Other examples are biotechnology and medical processes. These hybrids are characterized by the fact that considerable investment is required to achieve incremental innovation, and the "know-how" is vulnerable to rapid duplication by competitors who bear no part of the development expenditure. However, these products have fallen outside the copyright regime, and patent protection would not be available because the innovation is incremental, not "non-obvious."

Reichman believes that a *sui generis* know-how law built on modified copyright principles could provide adequate protection to this kind of legal hybrid without embracing the full copyright paradigm. He believes that this approach would eventually unify the treatment of innovations such as computer software and industrial design.

Reichman has written that:

> [t]he fundamental problem remains that of rewarding or simply recompensing large expenditure for incremental innovations that fall chronically short of the current legal threshold for patentable inventions.[60]

These technologies are not adequately protected because they deviate from the assumptions underlying the classical forms of intellectual property.[61] The solution, in Reichman's view, is a new intellectual property paradigm that provides this incremental innovation with artificial lead time in which investors can recoup their investment and turn a profit.[62]

Other commentators have also argued that the patent and copyright laws are not appropriate for computer software, and that a *sui generis* law based on a modified copyright approach would be better.[63] However, while Professor Reichman argues that software belongs to a larger class of "legal hybrids" requiring a new intellectual property regime, these commentators favor the creation of a law specifically directed at computer software. One of the arguments which has been advanced against a *sui generis* regime for software is that it risks being obsoleted by changing technology.

Other arguments have been advanced for continuing to work within the existing patent and copyright regimes. First, it is argued that the present regimes are working well, and their economic effects are appropriate.[64] The CONTU report concluded that copyright law was an appropriate mechanism for protecting computer programs and, they claim, the case law has been evolving properly.[65] Further arguments against *sui generis* protection are that a new regime would create uncertainty, and that international copyright agreements provide a framework for the protection of computer programs in other countries.[66] (See box 2-H for discussion of Analogous Copyright Law in Foreign Countries.)

NOTES

1. *Apple* v. *Franklin* 714 F.2d 1240 (3rd Cir. 1983).
2. See H.R. Rep. No. 1476, 94th Cong., 2d Sess. 54, reprinted in 1976 U.S. Code Cong. & Ad. News 5659, 5667 (" 'literary works' . . . include[s] . . . computer programs").
3. National Commission on New Technological Uses of Copyrighted Works, *Final Report*.
4. *Williams Electronics, Inc.* v. *Artic International Inc.*, 685 F.2d 870 (3rd Cir. 1983).
5. 17 U.S.C. Section 102(a).
6. 17 U.S.C. Section 101.
7. *Midway Mag. Co.* v. *Strohon* 564 F. Supp. at 750–751.
8. *GCA Corp.* v. *Chance* 217 U.S.P.Q. at 719–720.
9. *Baker* v. *Selden*, 101 U.S. 99, 25 L.Ed. 841 (1879).
10. *Apple* v. *Franklin*, 714 F.2d at 1251.

11. For a more extensive discussion of issues of structure, sequence, and organization, see Morton David Goldberg, "Copyright Protection for Computer Programs: Is the Sky Falling?" *American Intellectual Property Assn. Quarterly Journal*, vol. 17, pp. 294–322 (1989).

12. Ibid.

13. *Whelan Assocs., Inc. v. Jaslow Dental Laboratory, Inc.*, 609 F. Supp. 1307 (E.D.Pa. 1985), *aff'd*, 797 F.2d 1222 (3d Cir. 1986), *cert. denied*, 479 U.S. 1031 (1987).

14. This aspect of the *Whelan* decision has been the subject of heavy criticism.

15. *Whelan Assocs. v. Jaslow Dental Laboratory*, 807 F.2d 1256, 1260, footnote 34.

16. A number of cases uphold structure, sequence and organization protection as a legal principle and find substantial similarity on at least some of the facts in each case. See *Johnson Controls, Inc. v. Phoenix Control Systems, Inc.*, 886 F.2d 1173 (9th Cir. 1989); *Broderbund Software, Inc. v. Unison World, Inc.*, 648 F. Supp. 1127 (N.D. Ca. 1986); *Dynamic Solutions, Inc. v. Planning & Control, Inc.*, [1987] Copyright L. Dec. (CCH) Para. 26,062 (S.D.N.Y. 1987); *Pearl System, Inc. v. Competition Electronics, Inc.* 8 U.S.P.Q. 2d 1520 (S.D. Fla. 1988); *Soft Computer Consultants, Inc. v. Lalehzarzadeh*, [1989] Copyright L. Dec. (CCH Par. 26,403 (E.D.N.Y. 1988); *Manufacturers Technologies, Inc. v. CAMS, Inc.*, 706 F. Supp. 984 (D. Conn. 1989); *Lotus Development Corp. v. Paperback Software Int'l.* 740 F. Supp. 37 (D. Mass. 1990); Customs Service Decision 90-40 (Jan. 10, 1990) File: HQ 732291 CPR-3 CO:R:C:V 732291 SO. 24 Cust. B & Dec. No. 14, p. 28, [1990] Guide to Computer Law (CCH) Par 60,212 (Apr. 4, 1990).

17. *SAS Institute, Inc. v. S&H Computer Systems, Inc.*, 605 F. Supp. 816 (M.D. Tenn. 1985).

18. *Q-Co. Industries, Inc. v. Hoffman*, 625 F. Supp. 608 (S.N.D.Y. 1985).

19. *Healthcare Affiliated Services, Inc. v. Lippany*, 701 F. Supp. 1142 (W.D. Pa. 1988). Additional cases have upheld structure, sequence, and organization as a principle but found the evidence or pleading insufficient. See *Q-Co Industries, Inc. v. Hoffman*, 625 F. Supp. 608 (S.D.N.Y. 1985); *Digital Communications Associates, Inc. v. Softklone Distributing Corp.*, 659 F. Supp. 449 (N.D. Ga. 1987); *Telemarketing Resources v. Symantec Corp.*, 12 U.S.P.Q. 2d 1991 (N.D. Cal. 1989); *Bull HN Information Systems, Inc. v. American Express Bank Limited*, [1990] Copyright L. Dec. (CCH) Par. 26,555 (S.D.N.Y. 1990).

20. *Plains Cotton Cooperative Ass'n. v. Goodpasture Computer Serv., Inc.*, 807 F.2d 1256 (5th Cir.) *cert. denied*, 484 U.S. 821 (1987).

21. *NEC Corp. v. Intel Corp.*, 645 F. Supp. 590 (N.D. Cal. 1986), *vacated*, 835 F.2d 1546 (9th Cir. 1988), 10 U.S.P.Q. 2d 1177 (N.D. Cal. 1989).

22. *Computer Associates International, Inc. v. Altai, Inc.* No. CV 89-0811, U.S. District Court, E.D. New York, Aug. 9, 1991. This decision has been appealed; arguments were to be heard January 9, 1992.

23. *Nichols v. Universal Pictures* 45 F.2d 119, 121 (2d Cir. 1930), *cert. denied*, 282 U.S. 902 (1931).

24. *Nichols v. Universal Pictures*, 45 F.2d at 121.

25. *Broderbund Software, Inc. v. Unison World, Inc.*, 648 F. Supp. 1127 (N.D. Cal. 1986).

26. *Synercom Technology, Inc. v. University Computing Co.*, 462 F. Supp. 1003 (N.D. Tex. 1978).

27. *Digital Communications Associates v. Softklone Distributing Corporation*, 659 F. Supp. 449 (N.D. Ga. 1987).

28. *Lotus Development Corporation* v. *Paperback Software International*, 740 F. Supp. 37 (D. Mass. 1990).

29. *Engineering Dynamics, Inc.* v. *Structural Software, Inc. and S. Rao Guntur*, Civ. Act. No. 89-1655.

30. *Worth* v. *Selchow & Righter Co.*, 827 F.2d 569 (9th Cir. 1987).

31. *Harper & Row, Publishers, Inc.* v. *National Enterprises*, 471 U.S. 539, 105 Sup.Ct. 2218, 85 L.Ed. 588 (1985); *Mazer* v. *Stein*, 347 U.S. 201, 217, 74 Sup.Ct. 460, 470, 98 L.Ed. 630, *reh'g denied*, 347 U.S. 949, 74 Sup.Ct. 637, 98 L.Ed. 1096 (1954).

32. *Cooling Systems & Flexibles Inc.* v. *Stuart Radiator, Inc.*, 777 F.2d 485 (9th Cir. 1985).

33. Ibid., p. 492; See also *Landsberg* v. *Scrabble Crossword Game Players Inc.*, 736 F.2d 485 (9th Cir. 1984) *cert. denied* 469 U.S. 1037 (1984).

34. *Eckes* v. *Card Price's Update*, 736 F.2d 859 (2d Cir. 1984), *Financial Information, Inc.* v. *Moody's Investor Service, Inc.*, 751 F.2d 501 (2d Cir. 1984); 808 F.2d 204 (2d Cir. 1986).

35. *West Publishing Co.* v. *Mead Data Central*, 799 F.2d 1219 (8th Cir. 1987).

36. *Schroeder* v. *William Morrow & Company*, 566 F.2d 3 (7th Cir. 1977).

37. See also *Gelles-Widmer Co.* v. *Milton Bradley Co.*, 313 F.2d 143 (7th Cir. 1963).

38. *Feist Publications Inc.* v. *Rural Telephone Service Co., Inc.,*—U.S.—, 111 Sup. Ct. 1282 (1991).

39. *Kregos* v. *Associated Press* 937 F.2d 700, 19 U.S.P.Q. 2d 1161 (2d Cir. 1991).

40. *Key Publications Inc.* v. *Chinatown Today Publishing Enterprises Inc.*, 20 USPQ 1122 (2d Cir. 1991).

41. A number of other rulings have flowed from *Feist. Bellsouth Advertising & Pub. Corp.* v. *Donnelly Info. Pub.*, 933 F.2d 952 (11th Cir. 1991) held that copying the categories of a yellow page directory infringed that directory even though the copying was for unrelated use. *Victor Lalli Enterpr.* v. *Big Red Apple, Inc.*, 936 F.2d 671 (2d Cir. 1991) held that an particular format for reporting racing-related data was not copyrightable because it was a format used by many others and was dictated entirely by the intended use as a means to gamble on the numbers game.

42. See *BNA Patent, Trademark, and Copyright Journal*, vol. 41, January 1991, pp. 301–302.

43. Semiconductor chips are integrated circuits containing transistors, resistors, capacitors and their interconnection, fabricated into a very small single piece of semiconductor material. A mask work is a set of images fixed or encoded at a later stage of manufacturing, that produces the circuitry of the final chip product. Stanley M. Besen and Leo J. Raskind, "An Introduction to the Law and Economics of Intellectual Property," *The Journal of Economic Perspectives*, vol. 5, No. 1, pp. 3–27, at 19.

44. The legislative history indicates that incentives for piracy are great. There is a great disparity between the cost of developing a chip and the cost of copying it; the legislative reports indicate that initial development can cost as much as $100 million, while copying costs as little as $50,000.

45. See Robert W. Kastenmeier and Michael J. Remington, "The Semiconductor Chip Protection Act of 1984: A Swamp or Firm Ground?" *Minnesota Law Review*, vol. 70, No. 2, December 1985, pp. 417–470. According to Kastenmeier and Remington, while working in harmony with the copyright law, The Semiconductor Chip Protection Act avoids tailoring copyright principles to accommodate the singular character of the use of chip designs in the manufacturing process so as to distort the way in which copyright was applied to other categories of copyrightable works. At

the base of their theory is the proposition that dissimilar things should not be treated in a similar fashion. See especially pages 443–444.

46. Foreign products are granted protection by the president upon a finding that a foreign nation extends to U.S. nationals the same protection as the United States accords to the foreign nationals.

47. Ibid.

48. *Wabern Packaging Indus., Inc.* v. *Cut Rate Plastic Hangers, Inc.*, 652 F.2d 987, 210 U.S.P.Q. 777 (2d Cir. 1981) *Bliss* v. *Gotham Indus., Inc.*, 316 F.2d 848, 137 U.S.P.Q. 189 (9th Cir. 1963).

49. Chisum, *Patents*, Section 1.04[2][d].

50. *Gorham Mfg. Co.* v. *White*, 81 U.S. (14 Wall.) 511, 20 L.Ed. 731 (1872).

51. See, Jacques M. Dulin, "Design Protection: Walking the Pirate Plank?" *Bulletin, Copyright Society of the U.S.A.*, vol. 12, No. 6, August 1965; Note, "Protection of the Design of Useful Articles: Current Inadequacies and Proposed Solutions," *Hofstra Law Review*, vol. 11, spring 1983, p. 1043 at p. 1065.

52. See H.R. 902, H.R. 3017, H.R. 3499.

53. "Court Rescinds Ruling That dBase Copyright Is Invalid," *BNA Patent, Trademark & Copyright Journal*, vol. 4, p. 543.

54. For a discussion of some of the economic considerations associated with the protection of industrial design, see Robert C. Denicola, "Applied Art and Industrial Design: A Suggested Approach to Copyright in Useful Articles," *Minnesota Law Review*, vol. 67, pp. 707, 721–727.

55. Ibid.

56. The bill specifically excepts designs that are: 1) not original; 2) staple or commonplace; 3) different from comonplace or staple designs in insignificant ways; 4) determined solely by a utilitarian function; 5) embodied in a useful article that was made public by the designer or owner in the United States or in a foreign country more than one year before the date of application for registration; 6) composed of three dimensional features of shape and surface in wearing apparel; 7) a semiconductor chip product already protected under another provision; 8) embodying a process or idea or system; or 9) for motor vehicle glass.

57. See Giovanni Salvo, "Industrial Design Protection," document of the Law Library of Congress, European Law Division, March 1990, LL90-23, pp. 1–2.

58. Ibid.

59. J. H. Reichman, "Computer Programs as Applied Scientific Know-How: Implications of Copyright Protection for Commercialized University Research," *Vanderbilt Law Review*, vol. 42, No. 3, April 1989, p. 655.

60. Ibid., at p. 653.

61. Ibid., at p. 661.

62. J. H. Reichman, "Proprietary Rights in the New Landscape of Intellectual Property Law: An Anglo-American Perspective," study prepared for the International Literary and Artistic Association (ALAI), Congress of the Aegean Sea II, Athens, June 19–26, 1991.

63. See Pamela Samuelson, "Benson Revisited: The Case Against Patent Protection for Algorithms and Other Computer Program-Related Inventions," *Emory Law Journal*, vol. 39, No. 4, p. 1025, p. 1150; Richard H. Stern, "The Bundle of Rights Suited to New Technology," *University of Pittsburgh Law Review*, vol. 47, No. 4, p. 1229. Professor Paul Goldstein argues that copyright law runs the risk of providing too much protection to functional aspects of works belonging in the domain of patents.

He further perceives problems with patent protection for software (prior art problems, problems of patenting obvious subject matter, etc.) so that, he asserts, subject matter is being protected which is not appropriately covered by patent or copyright law. He believes that, if improperly applied, the law will result in consumers paying higher prices for software than warranted, among other dislocations. See generally, Paul Goldstein, "Infringement of Copyright in Computer Programs," *University of Pittsburgh Law Review*, vol. 47, No. 4, Summer 1986.
64. Ronald T. Reiling, Chairman, Proprietary Rights Committee, Computer and Business Equipment Manufacturers Association, Testimony at Hearings before the House Subcommittee on Courts, Intellectual Property and the Administration of Justice, Nov. 8, 1989, Serial No. 119, p. 167.
65. Morton David Goldberg, op. cit. at footnote 166.
66. Ronald T. Reiling, op. cit. at footnote 218.

MORAL FOUNDATIONS
OF INTELLECTUAL PROPERTY RIGHTS

Arthur Kuflik

Patents and copyrights are among the most conspicuous examples of what is authoritatively classified as *intellectual property*. With equal authority, however, it is also said that nobody can legitimately patent or copyright an *idea*.

There is something of a puzzle here. For if ideas cannot be patented or copyrighted, then in what sense do patents and copyrights secure or protect intellectual property? A moment's reflection on this puzzle only leads to other, morally more significant, perplexities: Would the practice of granting a person proprietary rights to an idea be morally defensible? If intellectual property law does *not* make a person the owner of an idea, then to what do patentees and copyright holders have proprietary claim? And on what basis?

If one listens to what some of the staunchest defenders of private property have had to say about intellectual property, the puzzlement is likely to be exacerbated, not alleviated. On the one side, one might hear that "patents are at the heart and core of property rights . . . once they are destroyed, the destruction of all other rights will follow automatically, as a brief postscript" (Rand 1967). On the other side, one might be told, "Patents . . . invade rather than defend property rights" (Rothbard 1977).

In what follows, I address two issues: First, do patents and copyrights create (or secure) property in ideas? And second, is the practice of assigning patents, copyrights, and other forms of intellectual property morally defensible? And I argue for two theses: First, the intellectual property system cannot be satisfactorily grounded in the principle that a person literally owns, as a matter of natural right, the ideas that he is the first to conceive. And second, underlying, and to some extent shaping, the practice of granting patents, copyrights, and other forms of intellectual property is the need to strike a suitable balance among three important considerations: freedom of thought and expression, incentive to authorship and to technological innovation, and fairness.

INTELLECTUAL PROPERTY LAW
AND THE OWNERSHIP OF IDEAS

What Is Owned, If Not Ideas?

Do patents and copyrights bestow ownership of ideas? And if they do not, to what do they give their holders title? Federal law makes it perfectly clear that what is copyrighted is not an idea, but the particular expression that it has been given. Thus, United States Code 17, section 102 reads:

> (a) Copyright protection subsists ... in original works of authorship fixed in any tangible medium of expression ... (b) In no case does copyright protection for an original work of authorship extend to any idea, procedure, process, system, method of operation, concept, principle, or discovery, regardless of the form in which it is described, explained, illustrated, or embodied in such work.

But what about patents? Do they secure property in ideas? To secure a patent one must be able to specify a new, useful, and nonobvious process, machine, manufacture, or composition of matter and to do so in such detail as would enable any person skilled in the relevant "art" or discipline "to make and use the same" (35 U.S.C. secs. 102, 103, 112).

Here the term *process* refers to a method for transforming or reducing a physical substance to a different state or thing; it does not refer either to a method of thinking or of solving intellectual problems or to a method of doing business. Indeed, abstract ideas, mental processes, methods of thinking or of solving intellectual problems—no matter how new and original they might be—are not proper subject matter for a patent application (*Gottschalk* v. *Benson*, 409 U.S. 63 [1972]).

In light of all this, it is tempting to suggest that what a person patents, and thereby comes to own, is not simply an idea, but a useful or practical idea. But this theory does not quite fit the phenomenon it is intended to explain. There are two objections to it. First, having a useful idea—even granted that it is not only new but also nonobvious—is not a sufficient basis for holding a patent. Second, patenting, even when one has a sufficient basis for it, does not literally give one ownership of an idea.

Being the First to Put Forward a Useful Idea Is Not a Sufficient Basis for Holding a Patent Consider the following dialogue:

> "I've just come up with a brilliant idea: I've noticed that snow melts at different rates on different kinds of surfaces. Now, imagine a substance you could spread over the sidewalks so that whenever it snows, the snow melts almost as soon as it falls!"
>
> "What is that substance?"
>
> "I don't know, but as the first person to think up this very clever idea, I'm going to patent it; then I can draw royalties from anybody who does manage to find a substance that does the job I have in mind."

Clearly, if the useful idea—brilliant and original though it may be—concerns the general function or purpose that some (as yet unspecified) device, substance, or process would serve, it does not provide a sufficient basis for holding a patent.

Granted that a person cannot get a patent merely by virtue of being the first to conceive a useful function, one might suppose that contributing new, nonobvious, and useful ideas about how the specified function is to be performed would qualify someone for a patent.

But then consider the following—someone discovers the special theory of relativity. Pondering $E = mc^2$, he realizes that it may be possible to derive significant amounts of energy from matter. He suggests that the heaviest, most unstable elements—uranium, for example—are likely to provide the most promising material basis for effecting such a conversion. Though he has practical insights indispensable to the development of an extremely important technology—insights for which others might be more than willing to pay a handsome price—this person does not have a sufficient basis for a patent.

Persons who put forward new and nonobvious ideas indispensable to the development of new and useful technologies are not rewarded by the patent system. Only those who go further and offer specific instructions about how to compound a useful chemical substance, engage in a productive process of manufacture, and so forth are entitled to the prerogatives of a patent holder. Moreover, these instructions must be sufficiently clear and precise to enable persons skilled in the relevant art or discipline to replicate, without further experimentation or invention, what has been specified.

Even When One Has a Sufficient Basis for a Patent, It Does Not Literally Give One Ownership of an Idea Imagine that someone has not only envisioned a function to be performed, but has also conceived, and in detail sufficient to enable others in the field to "make and use" the same, something that is capable of performing that function. And suppose he has obtained a patent. The fact remains that anybody has the right to think the thoughts that characterize whichever design, formula, or process he has conceived. Thus, anybody has the right to believe that if certain materials are put together in a certain way one will have something (whether it be a machine, or a manufactured product, or a chemical compound, or what have you) that is capable of performing the designated function. Nobody needs the permission of the inventor either to hold such beliefs or to discuss them with others. Thus someone who can specify a new, useful, and nonobvious machine, process of manufacture, or formula can obtain the right to exclude others from making, using, or selling anything that meets that specification. But he cannot prevent them from thinking about, discussing, and otherwise deriving inspiration from the practical insights that underlie his invention.

To sum up, what qualifies a person for a patent is not that he has an idea—even a useful idea—but that he has a useful idea of a highly specific and practicable sort. That is, it is the design for a machine or mechanism, the formula for a composition of matter, or the process for the transformation and reduction of a physical substance to a different state or thing. And what he comes to own, or indeed monopolize, is not the idea as such but, for a limited period of time, the right to "make, use, or sell" that which answers to it.

Freedom of Thought and Speech as a Constraint on Intellectual Property Rights

There is a parallel here between copyright and patent. Just as the person who holds a copyright does not have a proprietary right to an idea, but to a particular tangible expression of it, so it might be said that the patent holder does not have proprietary claim to the useful ideas behind his invention, but rather, to their actual practical application.

It would be a mistake to suppose that this observation holds only idle intellec tual interest. For underlying the fact that ideas as such can be neither patented nor copyrighted is a fundamental moral concern: the rules of the intellectual property system must not be formulated in ways that might jeopardize freedom of thought and speech.

Other important features of intellectual property law attest to this same concern Thus, patentability does not extend to scientific laws or to methods for solving mathematical problems. As the Supreme Court has ruled, these are the "basic tools" of scientific and technological research and cannot be preempted by anybody (*Gottschalk* v. *Benson* [1972]). Also relevant to the present point is the fact that the specification of a granted invention must be placed in the public record, in "full, clear, concise and exact terms" (35 U.S.C. sec. 112). In virtue of this, others have the opportunity to assimilate and draw inspiration from the inventor's insights.

Turning to the laws governing copyright, one finds that the rights of the copyright holder are delimited by the "fair use" doctrine under which a work may be reproduced "for such purposes as criticism, comment, news reporting, teaching (including multiple copies for classroom use), scholarship, or research" without infringing the copyright holder's proprietary rights (17 U.S.C. sec. 107). Nor is it an infringement of copyright "for a library or archives, or any of its employees acting within the scope of their employment, to reproduce no more than one copy or phonorecord" provided that (1) it is done "without any purpose of direct or indirect commercial advantage"; (2) the collections of the library or archive are open to the general public or to the body of scholars in the relevant field; and (3) a notice of copyright is included (17 U.S.C. sec. 108).

To make sense of such provisions and qualifications it is plausible to suggest that the intellectual property system has been so designed that, whatever the purpose to be served by granting authors and inventors copyrights and patents, the basic freedom to think about and to discuss the ideas and insights that underlie their writings and inventions needs to be protected.

JUSTIFICATIONS FOR INTELLECTUAL PROPERTY RIGHTS

As has been shown, the laws of patent and of copyright are generally formulated within a framework that is intended to preserve basic freedom of thought and expression. But why should intellectual property rights be assigned and protected in the first place? In what follows, I will first consider the question of whether the practice of granting patent rights is morally defensible, and if so, on what ground. Then, after noting an important contrast between the way in which the laws of copyright and of patent deal with the question of independently arrived at but significantly similar achievements, I will explore the question of whether the considerations that seem to provide the most significant support for the patent system support the copyright system as well.

A Libertarian Argument

One may begin by recalling the somewhat vague but provisionally appealing principle that people should be free to do as they choose so long as they do not interfere in other people's lives. Could the inventor's right to patent his invention be a simple exercise of this right to freedom? Whatever the merit of the principle, it is simply too weak to yield the desired conclusion.

Thus, consider the following: Someone invents the wheel and starts wheeling things around. Others get the idea and, after duly acknowledging and praising the person who is the source of their inspiration, make wheels of their own for their own personal use. To be sure, when the inventor makes wheels and starts wheeling things around, he does not interfere in the lives of others or limit their liberty in any way that could provide legitimate ground for complaint. But the same could be said of the others: when they make wheels for their own personal use, they are not interfering in his life or limiting his liberty to make and to use wheels.

It is tempting to object that their use of the idea does constitute an interference in his life. After all, they took the idea from him without his permission. But this objection is subject to the following line of criticism. When someone takes my car without my permission and drives it around, then all the while he is driving around, he deprives me of the personal use of it. But when someone takes my idea and—after acknowledging me as the source of his inspiration—makes use of it in his personal life, he does not thereby deprive me of the liberty to do the same, that is, to make use of the idea in my own personal life.

Indeed, there are at least three senses in which a person who gets an idea from me need not be taking it away from me: (1) I can still think it; (2) I can still enjoy whatever praise or admiration others might be disposed to give to me as the person who thought of it first; and (3) I can still use it, to all the same personal advantage, in my own personal life. Here it may be objected that if others are at liberty to use the idea without his permission, then the person who came up with the idea first will not make so much money as he would have made otherwise. So in putting it to one's personal use, one does take something away from the other person. One deprives him of something that is rightfully his.

But note that "so much money as he would have made otherwise" here signifies so much money as he would have made if he had had the authority to decide who shall use the idea and on what terms—in short, if he had enjoyed monopoly control.

Thus, to decide whether the use that other people make of an idea has deprived the person who first thought of it of something that is rightfully his, one has to decide whether the first to think of it is entitled to exclude anyone else from using the idea without his permission. Such an entitlement is not a mere liberty, but a power or prerogative: to have it is to have a measure of authority or control over the lives of others. It may be a perfectly legitimate authority, but appealing to personal freedom is not going to be sufficient to legitimatize it. One must appeal to other (presumably stronger) considerations.

The Appeal to a Natural, Inherent Property Right in the Products of One's Own Mind

Consider then the suggestion that the right to patent is not simply a matter of freedom, but an implication of the principle that a person owns the products of his own mind. On at least one reading, this principle is certainly very appealing. After all, an idea that is yours (that is, that you have thought up on your own) ought to be yours; you should have the right to think it and to put it to any use that does not violate anybody else's rights. (This last qualification applies to rights in general: my right to my knife does not give me the right to put it in your chest.) But those who argue for patent rights need a stronger argument to help them establish a stronger conclusion. They need to argue that a person not only owns (nonexclusively) the application of any useful idea that is the product of his own mind but also has, if he is the first to think up the idea and reduce it to practice, the right to exclude others from using it.

To establish this conclusion one might reason along the following lines: In giving a person exclusive right to the application of an idea that originated with him, no one else's position is worsened. Since the invention would not exist if not for him, it is and ought to be entirely his.

Perhaps the first thing to note is that if the patent system is really to be based on the principle that a person has a natural right to monopolize the application of a useful idea that he is the first to conceive, then it ought to be possible to obtain exclusive right to the application of more general ideas—for example, the idea of using electricity to provide indoor illumination, or the idea of converting unstable elements such as uranium into nuclear energy. As I have already noted, however, there are many important ideas of great practical significance whose application is not, at least under the present system, made the exclusive right of their first discoverers.

This observation leads to another, more damaging, one: If the right to patent is grounded in the principle that there is a natural right to the exclusive use of the original products of one's own mind, then there seems to be no reason that that right should not also extend (a) to theoretical as well as to practical ideas, and (b) to their public discussion as well as to their technological application. In short, the putative right, and the proposed line of argument based on it, are difficult to reconcile with freedom of thought and expression. What is needed is a coherent account of why, even though people have such a right, it applies only to certain products of their mental activity—specific inventions, particular works of authorship—rather than to all such mental products. But even if such an account could be constructed, the approach in question would still be highly questionable on at least two other counts.

First, it is implausible to suppose that someone who is the first to think up a useful idea has conceived something that would not have come into existence otherwise. Brilliant though it was, the idea of the wheel would have independently occurred to others. Proof of this is provided by the fact that the idea of the wheel did occur, at different times and in different places, to peoples who had no contact, whether direct or indirect, with one another. And of course, the same can be said, with better documentation, about more recent technological advances. But the patent system gives the first discoverer a right to exclude—for the duration of the patent term—even those who, operating independently, make the same discovery shortly afterward. Presumably, these independent inventors are equally entitled to the products of their own minds. Thus, the putative right to appropriate the product of one's own mind does not support, but actually tells against, the policy of giving exclusive rights to first inventors.

Of course, it is not always entirely clear just when a technological development would have occurred in the absence of its actual first discoverer. This might suggest something like the following line of argument: The policy of granting a seventeen-year patent term is an—admittedly often inaccurate—approximation to the period of time it would have taken others to come up with the invention on their own. Letting the patent pass into the public domain after that period of time is a way of recognizing the fact that sooner or later the continued enjoyment of exclusive rights would indeed constitute a wrongful worsening of the situation of at least some (not necessarily identifiable) individuals (compare Nozick 1974).

But if this reasoning were indeed appropriate, then it would hardly justify anything like the present system. This is because nearly contemporaneous, independent inventors could not be rightly excluded even for seventeen years. Furthermore, in cases in which the public disclosure of an invention occurs soon enough to put an end to further independent research, the policy of assigning the very same fixed term of exclusive rights, without regard to the particular invention or the general field in which it occurred, would be unjustly crude. Different areas of research and development will exhibit demonstrably different rates of overall progress. Even within a given field, progress on a particular technical problem will vary according to the stage of the field's development and the intensity of effort devoted to the problem. The principle that people have exclusive right to the product of their own mental activity, just so long as others are not made worse off than they would have been in the absence of that mental activity, would call upon society to make a scrupulous effort to obtain the best available evidence on such matters and to set up the rules of the patent system in a way that more adequately reflects these variations.

Second, whoever is the first to think up some important idea, whether practical or theoretical, he is almost certainly not drawing upon his own mental resources only. According to ancient legend, Athena sprang full grown from the head of Zeus. But human beings do not spring full grown from either a human or a divine parent. Certainly, they add to and enrich the life of the community in which they live, but their capacity to do so, as well as the more particular ways in which they do it, are made possible by a shared and historically transmitted heritage of language, culture, experience, and craft. When hailed as a great and original genius, Isaac Newton responded that he was, after all, only standing "on the shoulders of giants." Indeed, even in making this admirably humble remark, Newton was standing on the shoulders of others; the phrase was not original with him but had a long and illustrious history of its own (Merton 1967).

Thus, from a putative right to the products of one's own mental activity it does not follow that anybody can rightly claim exclusive control over a useful invention that he is the first to conceive. For nobody can rightly claim that a useful invention, or indeed any intellectual achievement, is fully and solely the product of his own mental activity.

Right to Privacy and Freedom of Contract as the Basis for Patent Rights

As I have already noted, an important feature of the patent system is that the applicant must make a disclosure of his innovation in such detail as would be sufficient to enable "any person skilled in the relevant art to make and use the same." This may suggest something like the following line of argument.

The right to privacy implies that an inventor has the right not to disclose his invention. Patent right—the right to exclusive control over the production and distribution of the invention—arises as part of a contractual agreement between the inventor and the government. The inventor discloses his invention in return for being granted a (limited) monopoly privilege. In virtue of this bargain between society and the inventor, the inventor comes to have the right to exclude others from making, using, and selling the invention in question. On this view, patent rights are not basic rights but they are the legitimate product of the exercise of two other rights: the right to privacy (which implies the right not to disclose any details about one's invention) and the right to make contracts.

A crucial objection to this line of argument begins with the observation that freedom of contract is not unlimited: a person has no right to make a "hit" contract for example. Thus, to decide whether the would-be patent holder can legitimately demand that nobody else—not even near-contemporaneous independent inventors—be allowed to make, use, or sell whatever is in question, one needs to know if he has the right to make such a demand. If what is demanded is illegitimate, then freedom of contract will not somehow bestow legitimacy upon the corresponding concession. Thus, to show that monopoly privilege is a legitimate demand, one cannot merely appeal to the right to privacy and the right to make a contract. The relatively strong proprietary right involved in holding a patent can only be justified by appeal to some other, presumably stronger, consideration.

Patent Right as a Matter of Just Desert

In order to provide the added justificatory strength, it is tempting to invoke the notion of just desert. On this approach, the power or prerogative that is afforded by a patent is legitimate insofar as it is deserved. Deserved in virtue of what? Possible candidates are effort and accomplishment. In either version, the principle that people ought to be rewarded according to what they deserve would prescribe more than it seems reasonable to do.

A principle of desert for effort would imply that unsuccessful researchers who nevertheless have expended a great deal of effort and money in an earnest attempt to come up with something useful to the public, and are therefore very deserving, ought to be rewarded. But the patent system does nothing of the kind. Nor does it seem plausible to suppose that it should. A principle of desert for successful accomplishment would imply that independently successful inventors also ought to be rewarded.

Whatever the basis for desert, there is the further problem of fixing the *size* of the deserved reward. How much of a reward does an innovator deserve (whether for his effort or accomplishment)? It is difficult to believe that, regardless of effort or accomplishment, the innovator's deserved reward is whatever income he can secure through holding and exercising a seventeen-year monopoly.

Finally, and more generally, it is far from clear that desert is an appropriate basis for the design of legal and political arrangements. What people deserve is often quite properly contrasted with the (institutional) entitlements that they (morally) ought to have. A baseball team may rightfully lay claim to a victory that was really deserved by the other team. Why the contrast? If both teams play fairly and in full observance of the rules, then the team that actually wins is the rightful victor. But if the other team both has the greater talent and has made the greater effort then it might be said to be more deserving of a victory. Why then did it lose? "Bad luck," one might say. Of course, who is to decide which team is more talented or has made the greater effort?

An institutional arrangement that superimposed upon its system of announced rules and regulations an authority with the discretion to determine who is really most deserving after all, and to award victory accordingly, would not seem morally defensible. The discretion in question would be too susceptible to arbitrary or discriminatory exercise. It is not that the notion of desert has no meaning. Rather, if one is to think of it as a principle of institutional design, it seems more appropriate for God or some other supposedly incorruptible and omniscient being than for ordinary mortals.

From these reflections, this point emerges: no plausible conception of what people deserve and why they deserve it would lead to anything like the present patent system. It is, in any event, questionable whether the notion of desert ought to play a significant role in the design of legal and political arrangements.

Progress in Technology: A Forward-Looking Defense of Patent Rights

Perhaps the most plausible argument for the special authority that is vested in patent holders turns on the long-term effects of the patent system upon research and development efforts. The suggestion is that, as an incentive to greater technological progress, the normal condition of free and open competition may need to be, from time to time and for a limited period of time, suspended.

In this spirit, the U.S. Constitution in article 1, section 8 does not call upon Congress to make laws protecting a person's natural proprietary right to the products of his own mind. Instead, as is well known, the Constitution authorizes Congress to enact laws whose purpose is "to promote the progress of science and useful arts, by securing for limited times to authors and inventors the exclusive right to their respective writings and discoveries." The basic philosophical point is elaborated by the Supreme Court:

> The patent monopoly was not designed to secure to the inventor his natural right in his discoveries. Rather, it was a reward, an inducement, to bring forth new knowledge. The grant of an exclusive right to an invention was the creation of society—at odds with the inherent free nature of disclosed ideas—and was not to be freely given. Only inventions and discoveries which furthered human knowledge, and were new and useful, justified the special inducement of a limited private monopoly. (*Graham* v. *John Deere Co.*, 383 U.S. 1, 9 [1966])

Thus the patent system emerges as a device for getting the best of both worlds. Monopoly privilege serves as an initial incentive to innovation; its limited duration eventually allows for the usual effect of free and open competition. Moreover, all this takes place within a framework that preserves the basic freedom of thought and speech so essential to the long-term progress of both science and technology.

There is a good deal of common sense in this line of argument. Those who engage in research and development often have to expend significant amounts of time, energy, and money without much assurance of success. Moreover, those who do succeed face the prospect of being undersold by competitors who are able to discern and duplicate what is usefully innovative without having to incur comparable research and development expenses.

In virtue of these two difficulties—the greater uncertainty of success and the relative ease of free riding—research and development efforts are likely to fall short of what the long-term health and well-being of society would seem to warrant. The patent system can be viewed as a device for correcting, at least to some extent, for these difficulties. Does it correct enough, or perhaps too much? Some would claim that the patent system overstimulates technological innovation and fosters wasteful duplication of research effort. Others would argue that the incentive it provides is not strong enough.

To evaluate such complaints one needs to be able to measure the impact of the patent system upon the rate of technological development. The state of affairs that would have obtained were patent rights not actually recognized has to be evaluated against the state of affairs that does obtain in virtue of them. It is not easy to verify or validate this rather complicated counterfactual comparison. Moreover, one needs to know more about what rate of technological development is supposed to be optimal and why. It is one thing to maintain that under the normal operation of market forces, research and development efforts would surely be inadequate, yet quite another to claim that one can specify with any precision an optimum level of such effort.

Now, there may well be cases in which—without knowing just what level of research would be optimal—one can nevertheless be reasonably confident that more research than is presently being undertaken would be desirable. This hardly constitutes a fatal criticism of the practice of recognizing patent rights as such. If greater incentive to research and development is needed, it can generally be achieved through modifications of the patent system itself (for example, extending the life of the patent, granting the patentee the right to make licensing agreements that bar challenges to the legal validity of the patent) or through additional mechanisms (government research grants, prizes) that can operate in conjunction with the patent system.

Of course, in evaluating an institutional design or public policy, one must look not only at the prospective benefits but at the costs as well. Competition in the marketplace is generally regarded as a spur to higher quality of production at lower prices. Monopoly is thought to be counterproductive of these good effects. Thus, whatever contribution the patent system makes to the progress of technology needs to be weighed against the reduction of quality and the increase in price that are the usual consequences of monopoly privilege.

In addition, it seems likely that the supposed benefit of having the patent system—namely, incentive to innovation—will vary considerably along with the nature of the technology. Securing a patent tends to be a prolonged, costly, and uncertain process; once a patent has been obtained, the effort to protect it through infringement suits can also be costly and prolonged. Thus, for fields in which there is rapid technological development, patent rights may bring too little too late to provide any real incentive. In these areas, simply getting there first may be its own, and the most significant, reward.

Even so, the rate of technological innovation has certainly been greatest in those social systems which do recognize intellectual property rights. It has yet to be demonstrated that other factors—cultural rather than legal—have played the more significant role. In the absence of such a demonstration, it seems highly unlikely that, even without a measure of intellectual property protection, technological progress would have been just as great.

Moreover, the alleged conflict between providing a healthy incentive to innovation and maintaining a vigorously competitive marketplace is not so clearcut as might appear. Once again, much depends on the particular field or industry. There are areas in which significant research and development can be meaningfully undertaken by relatively new and smaller firms. Failure to provide some measure of exclusivity to their accomplishments may only ensure that such firms have little chance of surviving, no matter how innovative they are. Without such protection, the Goliaths of the industry could readily assimilate any commercially viable innovations and bring them to market at prices that the smaller firms cannot match. In some fields, then, limited monopoly protection may not only spur innovation, but actually help the Davids to establish themselves against the Goliaths. The net result, of course, would be to widen and invigorate, rather than to weaken, the competitive field.

On the other hand, there are fields in which technological change comes mainly from very large firms that have invested heavily in research and development too costly and complicated for newer and smaller firms to handle. In these areas, there may be little chance for the field of competitors to widen—unless other firms do have the guaranteed opportunity to bring innovations to market, while paying reasonable royalties to the innovating firm. An obvious problem here is to determine a reasonable royalty rate. But if some policy of this sort could be put into practice, it might represent an appropriate balance between the need to encourage innovation and the need to keep markets in new technologies reasonably competitive.

The Appeal to Fairness

A useful invention can make a positive contribution to the good of others. To arrive at it, the inventor(s) may have to expend a considerable amount of time, energy, and money. Sometimes, other people come along and—being in a position to imitate, duplicate, or reverse engineer the invention without sustaining comparable research and development costs—produce the same, or an obviously similar, product at a lower price. By free riding on the efforts of the original discoverer, they achieve a superior competitive position. It seems unfair that the persons whose efforts have helped to make a technological benefit possible are, by very reason of those efforts, placed at a significant competitive disadvantage.

Of course, as has already been seen, free riding can be worrisome—not because it is inherently unfair, but (from a more purely forward-looking or consequentialist perspective) in virtue of how it weakens the incentive to engage in innovative research and development in the first place. An interesting question, then, is the extent to which free riding can be regarded as objectionable in its own right, quite apart from its impact upon the rate of technological development. Grant, for the sake of argument, that free riding of this sort is, in some sense, unfair; one may still well wonder what would be fair?

Fairness might seem to imply that, at the very least, the persons who have shouldered the burden of making a benefit to others possible ought to receive adequate compensation. This raises the obvious question, When is compensation adequate? Unfortunately, the obvious answer—When it is enough to cover the costs of research and development—is not without difficulties of its own. Thus, it is perfectly conceivable that the time, money, and effort actually expended were excessive and that a more efficiently managed research and development project would have yielded the same result at lower cost. Alternatively, it is possible that the benefit to others—though real—is not great enough to have warranted the heavy expense of (even the most efficiently undertaken) research and development. So from the mere fact that someone has managed to produce a technological result that is beneficial to others, it cannot be inferred that he or she ought to receive a monetary return that completely covers his original research and development costs.

It might be thought that what fairness requires is not that inventors be compensated for their efforts but rewarded in proportion to the value of the contribution those efforts have made to the well-being of others. But what is the value of a given contribution? And what would count as an appropriate reward? Providing a satisfactory account of such matters would seem to be an even harder task than working out a theory of adequate compensation.

Instead of trying to answer these questions with any precision, or even at all, a plausible route to take might be to protect the innovator against blatant free riding but then to let his financial return be determined by the forces of the marketplace. He would accept the outcome whether those forces accurately reflect the long-term value of his contribution to society and whether this original investment is recovered. Taking this route avoids the unpleasant and illiberal prospect of giving someone the power and discretion to sit in Washington and impose upon the community of innovators and upon society as a whole his own particular view of what has value.

, On this theory, the intellectual property system results from an attempt to achieve a measure of fairness within the limits of a safely decentralized economy. In essence, inventors are thought to be entitled—not to compensation or reward—but rather, to a fair chance to achieve a market determined return on their investment. . . .

CONCLUDING REMARKS

I began by asking whether the intellectual property system as we know it confers ownership of ideas. In arriving at a negative answer, I also came to the realization that an important constraint operating upon the design of the intellectual property system is the concern to preserve basic freedom of thought and expression. Patents and copyrights give people special rights, not to ideas as such, but to their practical application and to their particular expression. I then investigated possible justifications for instituting the rules of the patent system. Some arguments (from personal liberty, from the right to privacy together with the right to make contracts) proved too little. Other arguments (from an alleged right to the products of one's own mental activity, or from just desert) would, if they were to work, prove far too much. They also, as it happened, proved to be inherently confused and implausible. This left two reasonably plausible and relevant concerns: to promote technological progress and to prevent unfair free riding.

Acknowledgment

I received valuable criticism on earlier versions of this essay from the Cal Tech Philosophy Discussion Groups, the Society for Philosophy and Public Policy in New York, and in particular, Stefan Mengelberg, a member of the latter group.

REFERENCES

Merton, R. K. 1967. *On the Shoulders of Giants: A Shandean Postscript.* New York: Harcourt Brace Jovanovich.

Nozick, R. 1974. *Anarchy, State, and Utopia.* New York: Basic Books.

Rand, A. 1967. *Patents and Copyrights in Capitalism: The Unknown Ideal.* New York: New American Library, p. 133.

Rothbard, M. N. 1977. *Power and Market: Government and the Economy.* 2d ed. New York: New York University Press, p. 71.

INTELLECTUAL PROPERTY PROTECTIONS FOR COMPUTER SOFTWARE

John W. Snapper
Illinois Institute of Technology

Claims by computer scientists to own "their works" must be understood against the background of legal and social policies that define "intellectual property." Many of these policies are controversial, especially in the software industry. Consider, for example, the extent to which we should give credit to the individuals who work on a research team. It is a policy in the U.S. that a patent must be taken out in the name of the individual people who invent the patentable object (even if those people work under a contract which assigns the patent licensing rights to a corporation). On the other hand, a copyright may be held directly by the corporation that hires people to write a manuscript, and the copyright need not mention those people in any way. So the present preference for copyrighting (rather than patenting) software has the consequence that individual researchers are not recognized by name for their contributions to the software. The student of ethics and social policy must ask whether this is a fair policy. We cannot answer such questions unless we understand why the patent and copyright laws differ on these matters.

Let us begin by noting that the term "intellectual property" has no clear legal definition. The term is, in fact, very misleading. It suggests that we can own ideas or ways of thinking about things. But many of the policies at the core of U.S. intellectual property law explicitly deny that you can own "ideas" or "ways of thinking." Moreover, the term suggests that there is a coherent set of policies that make up the tradition of "intellectual property." On the contrary, it is a complex of policies that are based on many separate legal traditions, and that are as a consequence often confused and even self-contradictory. There is even disagreement over what areas of the law should be included under the notion of intellectual property. The student of intellectual property is immediately faced with the difficult task of making sense of a mass of tangled policies grouped under a misleading label.

AN OUTLINE OF THE LAW OF INTELLECTUAL PROPERTY

Keeping in mind that we should distrust any simple picture of the tangled mess known as "intellectual property law," we can all the same give a crude outline of the law in the U.S. The picture will change, of course, in other countries. The present outline is for U.S. policy, not because only the U.S. matters, but because we must choose one policy to present and this discussion appears in a book published in the United States.

I. Federal Law
   A. Based on U.S. Constitution I.8.viii.
      1. Patents

       2. Copyrights
       3. Semiconductor Masks
       4. Etc.
    B. Based on Other Federal Powers
       1. Trademarks
       2. Anti-Trust Policy
       3. Etc.
    C. Based on International Treaty
       1. Patents
       2. Copyrights
       3. Etc.
II. Not Based on Federal Law
    A. Trade Secrecy
       1. Contractual Agreements
       2. The Uniform Code
       3. Standards of Ethical Conduct
    B. And Lots More
       1. Shrink-wraps
       2. Pseudo-property
       3. Etc.

If taken too literally, the outline is as misleading as the term it attempts to explain. Patent policy, for instance, is placed here under *I.A*, since it is primarily defined by federal law. But one requirement of patent law is that incremental progress on an invention be kept as a trade secret until the invention is ready for patenting. Federal patent policy therefore relies on trade secrecy policy that is grouped under *II.A*, since it is primarily determined by the state laws. With this warning firmly in mind, let's go through the outline. [Readers unfamiliar with the United States should note that it consists of fifty separate states that independently write laws governing such basic matters as how you pay your taxes and where you can buy a bottle of wine. The federal government then imposes an additional layer of laws on top of the widely differing state laws. It is confusing, even to the experts.]

Most of the recent debate in the computer industry concerns part *I.A.* of the outline—policies established by the U.S. Congress under its power:

> to promote the Progress of Science and the useful Arts, by securing for limited Times to Authors and Inventors the exclusive Right to their respective Writings and Discoveries. (U.S. Constitution 1.8.viii)

This passage suggests a division between protection for functional inventions (patents) and protection for the written expression of ideas (copyrights). Sadly, this natural division has created problems for some computer industries whose products do not fit neatly into either category.

Traditionally there are three sorts of patentable subject matter: (a) machines (e.g., a hearing aid); (b) substances (e.g., a superconducting ceramic), (c) processes that transform materials (e.g., a way to cure rubber). The underlying theme is on the physical: physical machines, physical stuff, and physical alterations of the material world. Although the patent owner has a right to license use of his invention to perform a physical process, he may not prevent others from studying the ideas on which his invention is based nor from developing other inventions and technology based on those ideas. It is this emphasis on the physical that justifies the cliché that patents do not protect either "ideas" or "ways of thinking." This exclusion naturally creates problems for the software industry that wants patents on algorithms that may be viewed as ways to solve problems. Insofar as computer algorithms can be "walked through" with the aid of pencil and paper, they are apparently intellectual processes and not ownable in the central tradition of patent law. As we will see below, however, this central tradition has been modified to accommodate the computer industry.

The paradigm case of a copyrightable manuscript is an article that appears in a scientific journal. The copyright owner has (as the word "copyright" suggests) the right to say who may copy the words in the order in which they are published. He or she traditionally has no right to limit other uses: you may re-sell, or burn, or mark up and modify your copy without violating any copyright. The copyright covers the way the theory is expressed. It is not over the theory as such, and cannot be used to prevent other scientists from discussing the theory. Although to present someone else's theory as your own is condemned by academics as "plagiarism," this is not a copyright infringement unless the plagiarist uses the same words (or closely follows the same outline) as the original author. This emphasis on the form of expression is the copyright version of the cliché that you may not own "ideas" or "ways of thinking." As with patent law, it creates problems for software developers who wish to claim ownership over algorithms. Since copyrights are only on the form of expression, they may not restrict the performance of functions described in a copyrighted manuscript. A copyright on the rules of a card game does not give the copyright holder a right to control who may play the game (so long as the players make no copies of the rules). Insofar as the value of software lies in the performance of a computer function, it is not protectable by copyright on this central tradition.

If the story were to end with the above summary of patent and copyright law, it would seem that computer software would remain unprotected by federal law. Indeed, in the early 1980s some legal commentators drew the conclusion that software engineers should turn to other means of protecting their work (e.g., to trade secrecy). But this is not the end of the story for federal law, for at least two reasons.

First, Congress is not restricted to patents and copyrights. It can create "sui generis" protection for specific industries. The classic example is the Plant Varieties Protection Act that gave rights to seed companies that developed new strains of plants (e.g., a new type of corn). The Semiconductor Mask Protection Act is a form of sui generis protection for the computer industry. A mask is a template for the "circuitry" on a semiconductor chip. The Act gives the creators of masks the right to say who may directly copy the pattern in that mask. To many, this seems like a compromise between patent and copyright protection: the mask is functional like a patentable invention, but protected against copying like a copyrighted manuscript.

Second, Congress can extend copyright and patent protection beyond their traditional limits. This has been done in many areas. For instance, patents have been given to life-forms developed in a laboratory. And some patent protection has recently been given to certain forms of computer programs. And Congress has modified copyright law so that copyright is now the preferred form of protection for most software. There are many interesting philosophical, ethical, and social-policy questions concerning the consequences of this extension. For instance, an extension of the patent law will protect software for seventeen years and an extension of the copyright law protects it for about seventy-five years. When policy-makers consider extending these laws, they must consider which term of protection is appropriate. (Semiconductor mask protection was set at ten years.)

Although administered by the same bureaucracy that registers patents, copyrights, and masks, the law of trademarks is based on a different congressional power—the power to regulate commerce as specified in the Constitution, I.8.iii. For instance, the striped apple with a piece missing is a familiar computer trademark. The software used to prepare the present paper displays the "WordPerfect" trademark. The law of trademarks is designed to help businesses establish their identities and prevent competitors from misleading the public. We may note the difference between trademarks and copyrights by looking again at the term of protection. Since trademarks do not grant control over important industrial processes, Congress is less concerned about limiting the period of protection. In theory a trademark could be held by a company for all eternity. Trademarks are less problematic than patents and copyrights, but some issues do arise. If, for instance, we expect to perform a software function by pointing to a picture of a paintbrush on a computer screen, then a trademark on the icon of a paintbrush can become a controversial constraint on the competitive development of compatible software. (Again we should note that our outline oversimplifies when it includes trademarks under federal licensing policy. Much trademark policy is "common law." It is based on a long tradition of judge-made law that includes British legal disputes predating the creation of the U.S. Congress with its power to regulate commerce.)

There are other aspects of congressional regulation of trade that have a direct impact on intellectual property. We have in the U.S., for instance, "antitrust" policies that promote open markets over monopolies. Patents and copyrights, however, do just the opposite by granting limited monopolies over inventions or works of authorship. These opposing aims must be balanced. So antitrust policy limits how corporations may use their patent rights to gain control over a market. For instance, antitrust policy forbade IBM from "tieing" use of its patented central processors to use of IBM subsidiary equipment. That is, the patent monopoly on one piece of computer equipment cannot, according to antitrust policy, be used as a means to gain a further monopoly on associated equipment. We must never forget that the law of intellectual property is just one policy that governs business practice. As such, it cannot be separated from the rest of our policies on commerce.

It is rare that a computer company can restrict its market to one country. Indeed computer technology has been a major factor in the creation of global economies. Therefore the definition of intellectual property must take international law into account. It is, for instance, a big problem for the registration of semiconductor masks that this form of protection is only recognized in the United States. The fact that patents and copyrights are also recognized internationally is a strong argument for preferring them over sui generis protection for software. For the most part, when a U.S. company files for a U.S. patent, it also claims a patent in all foreign markets. When the American and international definitions of patent or copyright differ (as they often do), it can be a difficult question to determine which rules are to be followed.

It is tempting to restrict our discussion of U.S. intellectual property to the protections granted by federal law. Federal law is fairly well defined in statutes and policy statements. And we know how to change the policies that we think deserve change: we can ask Congress (or the Patent Office, or the Court) to act. The other forms of intellectual property are much more confusing. They change from state to state and are often based on nothing more than traditions of "fair practice" that are tacitly recognized by industry. But they cannot be ignored.

A trade secret is commercially valuable information that is kept secret. For instance, a method for producing a semiconducting material may be kept secret, even when the product is sold publicly. Of course, insofar as the company keeps its methods truly secret, there is no need for a legal policy on trade secrets—who would know o institute a legal proceeding? (One exception: sometimes companies are forbidden from keeping secrets on such things as food ingredients that might affect public health.) The legal problems generally occur when a secret is discovered by "improper means," such as when a competitor bribes an engineer working for your company. In that case, the courts can help the "owner" regain control over a lost secret, by forbidding the competitor to use it. Or the owner may ask for compensation for the loss.

It is often remarked that trade secrecy, in contrast to other forms of intellectual property, is ownership of knowledge itself. The point is that trade secrecy makes no distinction (such as is found in patent law) between an idea and the application of the idea, or (such as is found in copyright law) between an idea and its expression. Trade secrecy law recognizes a company's right to control the knowledge used in a new technology. It recognizes the right of a company to prevent competitors from doing research based on improperly discovered secrets. With trade secrets, the software developer may protect an algorithm for intellectually solving problems without confronting those limits that in patent and copyright law preserve "ways of thinking" as unprotectable. This makes trade secrecy appealing for software developers. There are, however, obvious limits to its use. A software developer, for instance, cannot easily preserve as secret the algorithms that go into a widely distributed applications program.

There are a number of legal bases for trade secrecy. In the most common case, the owner has a contract with those who have access to his information (typically either confidential employees or clients who lease software) which spells out what is secret and the consequences of disclosing a secret. But it would be a mistake to conclude that the notion of "trade secret" is defined by a private agreement between the signees of the contract. Since a contract is only valid if the courts are willing to enforce it, public policy determines what sorts of trade secrecy conditions may be included. The courts, for instance, do not like (and will not enforce) employment contracts that make it impossible for professionals to change jobs while continuing to make use of specialized skills learned on the first job. But the courts will recognize "reasonable" employment contracts that forbid employees from taking specific pieces of factual information to a new employer. We should note the wide variety of foundations for contract law: It is largely determined by a history of common law that varies from one area of the country to another. It is also largely determined by written state laws, which also change from state to state. And, of course, it is influenced by federal trade policies as well.

There are also many ways in which trade secrets may be misappropriated when there is no contract. The industrial spy who taps a telephone acts improperly without violating a contract. The notion of a "trade secret" therefore depends on the computer industry's standards for proper or improper means of discovery. These standards are part of a larger tradition of professional and ethical standards for doing business, which are rarely written down or defined in careful legal terms.

Although trade secrecy based on common law has a long history, modern discussions can look to the Uniform Trade Secrets Act, which has now been endorsed in some form by most states (starting about 1985). It defines a trade secret as "information, including a formula, pattern, compilation, program, device, method, technique, or process" that has "independent economic value" and is the "subject of efforts . . . to maintain its secrecy." The authors obviously had computers in mind when they emphasized formulas, patterns, compilations, and programs at the start of the definition. The act gives only a vague definition of improper means of discover. These include "theft, bribery, misrepresentation, . . . breach of a duty to maintain secrecy . . . or other means." In fact, to a large degree, the law is still determined by legal precedence and a general sense of professional ethics. For instance, most professional engineers consider it standard practice to "reverse engineer" a commercially available "object code," by decompiling it to discover its algorithms. If this is standard practice, it does not infringe on trade secrets. But what about a hacker who discovers secrets through unauthorized access to computer files? Whether or not that is theft may depend on the degree to which the files were guarded and the effort needed to break in. This is an area where industrial standards have yet to be firmly established.

Finally, so as not to give the impression that the above discussion is anywhere near complete, let us note a variety of additional social policies that seem to establish proprietary rights. For instance, there has been much debate in recent years over "shrink-wrap" licenses. Most software sold in stores comes in a plastic bag printed with a notice that tells the buyer that to open the bag is to agree to certain conditions on use of the software. Some of these conditions relate to the buyer's proprietary rights. For instance, some shrink-wraps forbid the buyer to modify or resell the software. But copyright law explicitly gives the buyer of a copyrighted work the right to modify the item for personal use. The shrink-wrap "contract" is an attempt by software developers to strengthen their ownership claims beyond what is generally granted under their copyrights. As always, there then is a debate over whether this "contract" will be enforced. (See *Vault Corp.* v. *Quaid Software Lmt* (1988) for a decision that throws considerable doubt on the enforceability of this sort of shrink wrap contract, especially when it conflicts with federal copyright policy.)

There are many more possible sources of ownership claims. Lawyers sometimes use the words "pseudo-property" or "quasi-property" to refer to ownership claims that do not fall under a traditional category of property law. We might include such things as attempts by movie stars to control their "look." (For instance, if the Charlie Chaplin estate owned the "Charlie Chaplin Look," then modern actors would not be permitted to do the Chaplin walk, with cane and turned out feet, while wearing the little mustache.) Of more interest to the computer professions, we may note that news services can prevent competing news services from "stealing" information off of their news broadcasts. And we should also note that some discussions of "personal privacy" are based on the claim that individuals "own" the facts about their private lives that are kept in computer data files. There is a great variety of such additional sorts of ownership.

A SHORT HISTORY OF INTELLECTUAL PROPERTY AND COMPUTERS

From the beginning, there have been disputes over how to grant protection to computer technology. If we define computer technology broadly as the electronic storage, manipulation, and transmission of information, then the first important modern piece of computer technology may have been the telegraph. And that was the first controversy. Samuel Morse's application for a broad patent covering all uses of electromagnetism to send messages was denied because it would have given him a monopoly over a whole technology, a whole field of intellectual study. He was later granted a patent on the telegraph key, a physical machine.

A simply amazing number of disputes over intellectual property have been created by the computer industry's attempt to claim ownership over pieces of software since 1960. The debates are particularly urgent and difficult, for they involve an industry of tremendous economic importance whose products do not fit nicely into the traditional categories assumed by the law. So without diminishing the importance of hardware innovations (including semiconducting materials, transistors, LED screens, switching technology, magnetic recording, etc.), let us focus on the history of conflicts between intellectual property policy and the software industry.

In the late 1960s, most of the discussion of protection for software focused on patents. But in a series of decisions, beginning with *Gotshalk* v. *Benson* (1972), the Patent Office and the courts established a strong opposition to software patents. The Benson algorithm is used to translate the representation of a number from base 10 to base 2. It is hard to imagine an invention with greater value. All computers are constantly translating back and forth between the base-10 human interface and base-2 machine representations. If granted a patent, Benson would have controlled almost every computer in use for 17 years! The patent, however, was denied on the basis of a policy that bars patents on mathematical formulas or on abstract processes (such as can be performed by a series of mental steps with the aid of pencil and paper). Given that a mental walk through the Benson algorithm is a popular exercise for beginning computer science students, the algorithm is clearly not patentable on traditional policy.

Since no software could ever be patentable on the so-called "mental-steps doctrine" which bars patents on calculations, that doctrine has been rejected as the courts struggled to reinterpret patent law in ways that can accommodate the software industry. All the same, the doctrine made sense as a traditional test of when a patent applicant sought to own an industrial process (patentable) as opposed to an idea (free to all). Whether we reject or maintain a mental steps doctrine, patent policy must somehow distinguish ownable industrial processes from open scientific theory. The recent history of patent law is largely a search for a new way to draw that distinction while satisfying the software industry's desire for patent protection.

The most quoted decision on software patents is *Diamond* v. *Diehr* (1981), in which the Supreme Court struggled with the problems of the above paragraph. Diehr computerized the production of rubber tires. On the one hand, it looked like Diehr had a new patentable process or machine: it physically transformed rubber into rubber tires. On the other hand, it looked like Diehr had only a new computer program, for all the components (molds, thermometers, computers) of Diehr's machine were traditional technology, except for how the computer was programmed. Since software patents were clearly out of the question in 1980, Diamond (the director of the Patent Office) denied Diehr's patent application. On appeal to the Supreme Court, Diehr got a patent on a narrow (5 to 4) decision. Although this is popularly seen as the first successful application for a software patent, the Court did not see it that way. Even the five judge majority repeats the principle that computer algorithms are not patentable. They said, however, that Diehr's invention was not just the computer program, but the rubber molding process as a whole. Sadly the majority failed to provide a good criterion for distinguishing patentable machines that incorporate programmed computers from unpatentable computer programs used in established technology. And for the most part, software related patents remained oddities in the patent law.

Frustrated in its attempts to get patents in the 1970s and 1980s, the software industry tried the traditional alternative: copyrights. There were, however, in the 1970s also obstacles to software copyrights. In a much quoted case (*Smith Music Company* v. *Apollo*, 1908), the courts had rejected a copyright on a roll for a player piano. (A piano roll is a scroll of heavy paper with a pattern of holes punched into it. This is passed over a sensor that plays a note for each hole.) A human readable score for the music would have been copyrightable, but a machine readable roll was a machine part and not patentable. The analogy to computer software is obvious: since you do not read machine code, it is not copyrightable subject matter.

The readability problem is only a surface feature of a core assumption of copyright policy reflected in the piano roll decision. Copyrights grant protection over the way processes are described in a manuscript, and do not grant control over either machine parts or "utilitarian" processes described in the manuscript. So long as we care more about performing processes (e.g., producing a graphic representation of some data) than about expressing ideas (e.g., describing the algorithms used to produce that graph), the patent is the intuitively correct form of protection. (Of course, if there is a trade-secrecy issue, software developers might also care about customers trying to "read" the code. But this is not the main concern of most software producers.) All the same, after the patent route to protection was denied, the copyright route was approved by the courts. Since a computer needs a copy of the software to run a process, an exclusive right to make copies effectively extends to ownership of the process too. Although many critics continue to view this as a perversion of the basic assumptions of copyright law, it has turned out in practice to be a useful means of protection for the software industry.

The path to software copyright was opened by congressional action. In 1979, the National Commission on New Technological Uses of Copyrighted Works (called CONTU) called for changes in law that would overcome the problems discussed above. In 1980, Congress responded by revising the law. The new law says that copyrights protect computer "programs," and defined programs as "instructions . . . to bring about a certain result." Congress also added a new section to clarify how copyrights limit use of protected programs. There is very good reason to see this congressional action as a response to the software industry's cries for some sort of protection after having been denied patents. The watershed legal decision is *Franklin* v. *Apple*. In 1981, Franklin sold computers that included copies of programs used to run the Apple personal computers. Franklin claimed that this was permissible because Apple's copyrights were invalid. Franklin challenged the copyright because (among other things) the code was an unreadable machine part. Although the case was never finally resolved in the courts, there is a famous decision (1982) in a hearing over whether Franklin could continue to use the copied software while the main case wound its way through the court system. The court, basing its decision on the CONTU revisions to the copyright law, was so hostile to Franklin, that Franklin simply gave up. The message was clear: under the revised copyright law, you could have a copyright on an unreadable, executable computer program. And the whole software industry jumped on the copyright bandwagon.

At about the same time as the CONTU report, Congress was working on the Semiconductor Chip Protection Act (enacted in 1984). Ten years later, this act now seems unlikely to be very important. We may view it as a symptom of the confused intellectual property picture of the 1970s and early 1980s. At that time software innovators were trying all sorts of ways to get their ownership claims recognized in a federal license. [A patent lawyer tells me when he failed to get his client a patent (in England) for a process performed with a programmed computer in the early 1980s, he simply hard-wired some circuitry to do the same task. This hard-wired box was then patented. He had no idea what would happen if this patent were to be infringed by a programmed computer.] Some commentators despaired of getting federal licenses for software, and proposed a heavy dependency on trade secrecy instead. Given the hostility of the patent and copyright office to software protection, it seemed entirely reasonable to create a new form of federal license for the new forms of inventions. But just as the Chip Act took effect, the problems with copyright protection were getting resolved. And, for most purposes, the copyright is preferable. There have been few cases concerning the Chip Act in the courts, and it seems likely that sui generis protection will now be ignored by most of the industry. The Chip Act made sense at the time, but its lesson now seems to be that the problems with sui generis protections (e.g., lack of international recognition) are so extreme that we do better to find a way to twist patent and copyright law to meet the needs of new technology than to create new forms of intellectual property.

By the mid 1980s the intellectual property picture began to clear up due to the greater acceptance of software copyrights. But this is far from the end of the story. As I write this paper (spring of 1994), there is a resurgence of interest in the software patent, partly brought on by recent decisions to limit the extent of protections afforded by copyrights. The mood of the courts seems to be that copyright protection are, for the most part, overly strong for software. For instance, some major "look and feel" claims are being denied. There are hints that developing copyright policy is to give less and less to the owners and to let software imitators do more and more. Already in May 1993, the "Legal Beat" article (by J.M. Moses) in the *Wall Street Journal* began with the comment that "Computer companies, rebuffed in a spate of recent copyright cases, are discovering that there is more than one way to protect their software." The article goes on to discuss the industry's return to trade secrets and patents as forms of protection that begin to look very appealing once again.

The fact is that the copyright is mostly useful for protecting lengthy pieces of code that require thousands of man-hours to write, as opposed to protecting ingenious algorithms for solving problems. Copyright law holds to the principle that it is permissible to rewrite copyrighted code to perform a given process, so long as the original code is not simply copied. And if the algorithm cannot be rewritten in a natural way, the copyright is invalid. In *Franklin* v. *Apple*, Franklin had claimed that the Apple copyrights were invalid since the code itself was so constrained by hardware considerations that there were few alternative ways to rewrite it. The court accepted this line of reasoning, but never got around to deciding whether in fact the Apple programs were rewritable. (The Benson algorithm, which opened the debate over computer patents, would have failed to be copyrightable on these grounds: if you give it to a class of beginning computer students, you will find that most students generate one of a small number of alternative codes.) Although many believe that copyrights provide too much protection for software, it is also commonly accepted that copyrights provide insufficient protection for those who have new and ingenious algorithms. We therefore must look again at patent law, where protection would be over the process or algorithm itself, and not simply over the way it is coded. (Note the difference: Patents only protect ingenious and novel items, while copyrights can protect any written work. This partly explains why patents, but not copyrights, are made in the name of the individual inventor.)

In *In re Iwahashi* (1989), a patent was granted over a computerized method of estimating solutions to a complicated mathematical formula. Since this is not a patent on a method to alter a physical substance, but a patent on a process that manipulates numbers in a computer, it is a radical departure from the patent principles put forth in *Diamond* v. *Diehr*. It is in fact the first example of a true software patent. It has led to a sudden spurt of activity in the field of software patents. But the Patent Office still needs a test for when a computer program is a patentable industrial process rather than an unpatentable piece of mathematical theory. In *Iwahashi* the court draws a distinction based on how the program is written into read-only-memory hardware, which the court views as a machine part. It is unlikely that this test is sufficiently precise to do what is needed, and we can expect much more debate over the issues. We live in interesting times.

▷ WHY SOFTWARE SHOULD BE FREE

Richard Stallman

INTRODUCTION

In the time that I've worked as a programmer, I've watched the field change from one of cooperation and sharing, where people could reuse previous work to advance the state of the art, to one in which cooperation is largely forbidden by trade secrecy and sharing is illegal.

These events led me to ask myself, as a software designer, what I should do with the software I develop in order to benefit humanity the most. In particular, I asked the question of whether it was ethical to make software proprietary.

Most people in the field do not ask this question. Usually they consider only whether it is profitable to do this, and compare the legal or other methods for doing so. In other words, they ask what developing software can do for them. But this selfishness is an unworthy goal for an ethical person. Following John F. Kennedy, we must ask what we, as programmers together, can do for the freedom of mankind. We must ask what we ought to do, not just what is profitable.

This question cannot be answered in terms of current law. The law should conform to ethics, not the other way around. Nor does current practice answer this question, although it is sometimes the start of an answer.

The only way to judge this question is to see who is helped and who is hurt by recognizing owners of software, why, and how much. In other words, we should perform a cost-benefit analysis on behalf of society as a whole, taking account of individual freedom as well as production of material goods.

In this essay, I will describe the effects of having owners, and show that this is bad for society. My conclusion is that I and other programmers have the duty to encourage others to share, redistribute, study and improve the software we write: in other words, to write *free* software. (The word "free" here refers to freedom, not to price.)

HOW OWNERS TRY TO JUSTIFY THEIR DEMANDS

Those who benefit from the current system where programs are property offer two arguments in support of their claims to own programs: the emotional argument and the economic argument.

The emotional argument goes like this: "I put my sweat, my heart, my soul into this program. It comes from *me*, it's *mine*!"

This argument does not require serious refutation. The feeling of attachment is one that people can cultivate when it suits them, but is not inevitable. Consider, for example, how willingly the same authors usually sign over all rights to a large corporation for a salary; the attachment mysteriously vanishes. By comparison, consider the great artists and artisans of medieval times, who didn't even sign their names to their work. To them, the name of the artist was not important. What mattered was that the work was done—and the purpose it would serve. This view prevailed for hundreds of years.

The economic argument goes like this: "I want to get rich (usually described inaccurately as 'making a living'), and if you don't allow me to get rich by programming, then I won't program. Everyone else is like me, so nobody will ever program. And then you'll be stuck with no programs at all!" This threat is usually veiled as friendly advice from the wise.

I'll explain later why this threat is a bluff. First I want to address an implicit assumption that is more visible in another formulation of the argument.

This form of the argument starts by comparing the social utility of a proprietary program with that of no program, and then concludes that proprietary software development is, on the whole, beneficial, and should be encouraged. The fallacy here is in comparing only two outcomes: proprietary software vs. no software. These are not the only alternatives.

In our current system, software development is usually linked with deliberate obstruction by an owner of its use. As long as this linkage exists, we are often faced with the choice of proprietary software or none. However, this linkage is not inherent or inevitable; it is a consequence of the specific social/legal policy decision that we are questioning: the decision to have owners. To formulate the choice as between proprietary software vs. no software is to presuppose this decision. That is begging the question.

THE ARGUMENT AGAINST HAVING OWNERS

The question at hand is, "Should development of software be linked with having owners to restrict the use of it?"

In order to decide this, we have to judge the effect on society of each of those two activities *independently*: the effect of developing the software (regardless of its terms of distribution), and the effect of restricting its use (assuming the software has been developed). If one of these activities is helpful and the other is harmful, we would be better off dropping the linkage and doing only the helpful one.

To put it another way, if restricting the use of a program already developed is harmful to society overall, then an ethical software developer will not do it except in extremity.

To determine the effect of restricting use, we need to compare the value to society of a restricted (i.e., proprietary) program with that of the same program, available to everyone.

To elucidate this argument, let's apply it in another area: road construction.

It would be possible to fund the construction of all roads with tolls. This would entail having toll booths at most street corners. Such a system would provide a great incentive to improve roads. It would also have the virtue of causing the users of any given road to pay for that road. However, a toll booth is an artificial obstruction to smooth driving—gratuitous, because it is not a consequence of how roads or cars work.

Comparing free roads and toll roads by their usefulness, we find that (all else being equal) roads without toll booths are cheaper to construct, cheaper to run, safer, and more satisfying and efficient to use. The conclusion is that toll booths (i.e., obstructions to use which are relaxed for a fee) are a bad way to raise funds for road construction. Use of roads, once built, should be free.

The advocates of toll booths would consider them simply a matter of how to raise funds for the road, but this is incorrect. They also degrade the road. The toll road is not as good as the free road; giving us more or technically superior roads may not be an improvement if this means substituting toll roads for free roads.

The issues of pollution and traffic congestion do not alter this conclusion. If we wish to make driving more expensive to discourage driving in general, it is disadvantageous to do this using toll booths, which contribute to both pollution and congestion. Likewise, a desire to enhance safety by limiting maximum speed is not relevant; a free access road enhances the average speed by avoiding stops and delays, for any given speed limit.

Of course, the construction of a free road does cost money, which the public must somehow pay. However, this does not imply the inevitability of toll booths. We who must pay in either case should at least get full value for our money: a free road instead of a toll road.

Note that this argument does not involve a claim that a toll road is worse than no road at all. That would be true if the toll is so great that hardly anyone uses the road—but this is unlikely. However, as long as the toll booths cause significant waste and inconvenience, it is better to raise the funds in a less obstructive fashion.

To apply the same argument to software development, I will now show that having "toll booths" for useful software programs costs society dearly: it makes the programs more expensive to construct, more expensive to distribute, and less satisfying and efficient to use. It will follow that program construction should be encouraged in some other way. In the following chapter I'll go on to explain other ways in which development can be encouraged and (to the extent actually necessary) funded.

The Harm Done by Obstructing Software

Consider for a moment that a program has been developed, and any necessary payments for its development have been made; now society must choose either to make it proprietary or allow free sharing and use.

Assuming that the program is one whose very existence is not harmful, and ignoring the consequences of linking this decision with software development, restrictions on the distribution and modification of the program cannot facilitate its use. They can only interfere. So the effect can only be negative. But how much? And what kind?

Three different levels of material harm come from such obstruction:

- Fewer people use the program.
- None of the users can adapt or fix the program.
- Other developers cannot learn from the program, or base new work on it.

Each level of material harm has a concomitant form of psychosocial harm. This refers to the effect that people's decisions have on their subsequent feelings, attitudes and predispositions. These changes in people's ways of thinking will then have a further effect on their relationships with their fellow citizens, and can have material consequences.

The first two levels of material harm waste part of the value that the program could contribute, but they cannot reduce it to zero. If they waste nearly all the value of the program, then writing the program harms society by at most the effort that went into writing the program. Arguably a program that is profitable to sell must provide some net direct material benefit.

However, taking account of the third level of material harm, and the various kinds of psychosocial harm, there is no limit to the harm that proprietary software development can do.

Obstruction of Use

The first level of harm impedes the simple use of a program. A copy of a program has nearly zero marginal cost (and you can pay this cost by doing the work yourself), so in a free market, it would have nearly zero price. A license fee is a significant disincentive to use the program. If a widely useful program is proprietary, far fewer people will use it.

But this does not reduce the amount of work it takes to *develop* the program. As a result, the efficiency of the whole process, in delivered user satisfaction per hour of work, is reduced.

Here is a crucial difference between copies of programs and cars, chairs, or sandwiches. There is no copying machine for material objects outside of science fiction. But programs are easy to copy; *anyone* can produce as many copies as are wanted, with very little effort. This isn't true for material objects because they are conserved: each new copy has to be built in the same way that the first copy was built.

With material objects, a disincentive to use them makes sense, because fewer objects bought means less raw materials and work needed to make them. It's true that there is usually also a startup cost, a development cost, which is spread over the production run. But as long as the marginal cost of production is significant, adding a share of the development cost does not make a qualitative difference. It does not require additional restrictions on the freedom of ordinary users.

However, imposing a price on something that would otherwise be free makes a large change. A centrally imposed fee for software distribution becomes a powerful disincentive.

What's more, central copying of software is simply more work than user copying. Central copying involves putting copies on transport media such as floppy disks or tapes, enclosing them in packaging, shipping large numbers of them around the world, and storing them for sale. This cost is presented as an expense of development; in truth, it is part of the waste caused by having owners.

Damaging Social Cohesion

If you want to use a program and your neighbor wants to use the program, then in ethical concern for your neighbor, you should want *both* of you to have it. You shouldn't be satisfied with a solution where you get it and the neighbor does not.

Signing a typical software license agreement means betraying your neighbors: "I promise to be unfriendly, I promise to tell my neighbors to get stuffed. To hell with everyone else—just give me a copy! Me, me, me!" People who think this way have become bad neighbors; public spirit suffers. This is psychosocial harm associated with the material harm of discouraging use of the program.

Many users unconsciously recognize this, so they decide to ignore the licenses and laws, and share programs anyway. But they feel guilty about doing so, because they haven't considered the matter clearly. They know that they must break the rules in order to be good neighbors, but they still consider the rules authoritative, and they conclude that being a good neighbor is naughty or shameful. That is also a kind of psychosocial harm, which one can escape by deciding that these licenses and laws have no moral force.

Programmers also suffer psychosocial harm knowing that many users will not be allowed to use their work. This leads to a general attitude of cynicism or denial. I have often heard a programmer describe enthusiastically the work that he finds technically exciting; then when I ask him, "Will I be permitted to use it?", his face falls, and he says, probably not. But he despairs of changing this, so he makes a joke about how the world is a jungle and one shouldn't expect otherwise, then distracts himself with what he hopes to buy with the proceeds of obstructionism.

Since the age of Reagan, our greatest scarcity is not technical innovation, but rather the willingness to cooperate for the public good. It makes no sense to encourage the former at the expense of the latter.

Obstruction of Custom Adaptation

The second level of material harm is the inability to adapt programs. The ease of modification of software is one of its great advantages over older technology. But most commercially available software isn't available for modification, even if you pay for it. It's available for you to take it or leave it, as a black box—that is all.

A program that you can run consists of a series of numbers whose meaning is obscure. No one, not even a good programmer, can easily change the numbers to make the program do something different.

Programmers normally work with the "source code" for a program, which is text written in a programming language. It contains names for the data being used and for the parts of the program, and it represents operations with symbols such as + for addition and − for subtraction. This is because programming languages are designed to help programmers read and change programs.

But you can't do this unless you have the source code. Usually the source code for a proprietary program is kept secret by the owner, lest anybody else learn something from it. This means that only the owner can change the program.

A friend once told me of working as a programmer in a bank for about six months, writing a program similar to something that was commercially available. She thought that if she could have gotten the source code for that commercially available program, it could easily have been adapted to their needs. The bank was willing to pay, but source code was not available—it was a secret. So she had to do six months of make-work, work that inflates the GNP but was actually wasted.

I have had a similar experience. In the MIT Artificial Intelligence lab, our first graphics printer was the XGP, given to us by Xerox around 1977. It was run by free software to which we added many convenient features. For example, it would send you a message when your document had actually been printed; if there was a paper jam, it would send a message to everyone who had a job in the queue, asking someone to fix the jam.

Later Xerox gave us a newer, faster printer, one of the first laser printers. It was driven by proprietary software that ran in a separate dedicated computer, so we couldn't add any of our favorite features. We could arrange to send you a notification that "Your document has been sent", but that just meant it was sent to the dedicated computer. There was no way to find out when the job was actually printed; you could only guess. And no one was informed when there was a paper jam, so the printer might sit for an hour without being fixed. People would send jobs to the printer, receive the "has been sent" message, and then wait for an hour before looking for the output. So nobody would notice the jam.

The system programmers at the AI lab were capable of fixing such problems, probably as capable as the original authors of the program. But it was profitable for Xerox to prevent us, so we could do nothing but suffer. The problems were never fixed.

Most good programmers I have met have experienced the frustration of using a program whose deficiencies they were forbidden to correct. The bank could afford to cover the expense of circumventing this obstacle, but a typical user would simply have to give up.

Giving up causes psychosocial harm—to the spirit of self-reliance, which used to be prized in America. It is demoralizing to live in a house that you cannot rearrange to suit your needs. You come to say, "Yes, this system isn't what we want, but we'll never be able to change it. We'll just have to suffer." People who feel this way do not do good work and do not have happy lives.

Imagine what it would be like if recipes were hoarded in the same fashion as software. You'd say, "How do I change this recipe to take out the salt?", and the great chef would say, "How dare you insult my recipe, the child of my brain and my palate, by trying to tamper with it? You don't have the judgement to change my recipe and make it work right!"

"But my doctor says I'm not supposed to eat salt! What can I do? Will you take out the salt for me?"

"I would be glad to do that; my fee is only $50,000." Since the owner has a monopoly on changes, the fee tends to be large. "However, right now I don't have time. I am busy with a commission to design a new form of ship's biscuit for the Navy Department. I might get around to you in about two years."

Obstruction of Further Advances

The third level of material harm affects software development. Software development used to be an evolutionary process, where a person would take a program and rewrite parts of it for one new feature, and then another person would rewrite parts to add another feature; this could continue over a period of twenty years. Meanwhile, parts of the program would be "cannibalized" to form the beginnings of other programs.

The existence of owners prevents this kind of evolution, making it necessary to start from scratch when developing a program. It also prevents new practitioners from studying existing programs to learn useful techniques or even how large programs can be structured.

Owners also obstruct education. I have met bright students in computer science who have never seen the source code of a large program. They may be good at writing small programs, but they can't begin to learn the different skills of writing large ones if they can't see how others have successfully done it.

In any kind of intellectual field, progress is built by standing on the shoulders of others. That's no longer generally allowed in the software field—you can only stand on the shoulders of the other people *in your own company*.

The associated psychosocial harm affects the spirit of scientific cooperation, which used to be so strong that scientists would cooperate even when their countries were at war. In this spirit, Japanese oceanographers abandoning their lab on an island in the Pacific carefully preserved their work for the invading American army, and left a note explaining its purpose.

Conflict among individuals has destroyed what international conflict spared. Nowadays, I am told, scientists in many fields don't publish enough in their papers to enable you to replicate the experiment. They publish only enough to enable you to marvel at how much they were able to do. This is certainly true in computer science, where the source code for the programs reported on is usually secret.

It Does Not Matter How Sharing Is Restricted

I have been discussing the effects of preventing people from copying, changing and building on a program. I have not specified how this restriction is carried out, because it doesn't affect the conclusion. Whether it is done by copy protection, or copyright, or licenses, or encryption, or ROM cards, or hardware serial numbers, if it *succeeds* in preventing use, it does harm.

Users do consider some of these methods more obnoxious than others. I suggest that the methods most hated are those that accomplish their objective.

Software Should Be Free

I have shown how ownership of a program—the power to restrict changing or copying it—is obstructive. Its negative effects are widespread and important. It follows that society shouldn't have owners for programs.

WHY PEOPLE WILL DEVELOP SOFTWARE

If we eliminate this method of encouraging people to develop software, at first less software will be developed, but that software will be more widely available. It is not clear whether the overall delivered user satisfaction will be less; but if it is, or if we wish to increase it anyway, there are other ways to encourage development, just as there are ways besides toll booths to raise money for streets. Before I talk about how that can be done, first I want to question how much artificial encouragement is truly necessary.

Programming Is Fun

There are some lines of work that no one will enter except for money; road construction, for example. There are other fields of study and art in which there is little chance to become rich, which people enter for their fascination or their perceived value to society. Examples include mathematical logic, classical music, and archaeology; and political organizing among working people. People compete, more sadly than bitterly, for the few funded positions available, none of which is funded very well. They may even pay for the chance to work in the field, if they can afford to.

Such a field can transform itself overnight if it begins to offer the possibility of getting rich. This has happened in the field of software, and also that of genetics. When one worker gets rich, others demand the same opportunity. Soon you will find that no one is willing to work in the field without a clear shot at getting rich. Another couple of years go by, and people will deride the very idea. They will advise social planners to assume that work can never be done in this field unless workers have the chance to get rich; and they will prescribe special privileges, powers and monopolies as necessary to ensure them this chance.

This change happened in the field of computer programming in the past decade. Fifteen years ago, there were articles on "computer addiction": users were "onlining" and had hundred-dollar-a-week habits. It was generally understood that people loved programming enough to break up their marriages. Today, it is generally understood that no one would program without an exorbitant rate of pay. People have forgotten what they knew fifteen years ago.

It may be true at one moment that people will work in a field only for high pay, but it need not remain true. The dynamic of change can run backward as effectively as forward. If we were to take away the possibility of great wealth, then after a while, when the people had readjusted their attitudes, they would once again be eager to work in the field for the joy of discovery.

Funding Free Software

The question, "How can we pay programmers?", becomes an easier question when we realize that it's not a matter of paying them a fortune. A mere living is easier to raise.

Institutions that pay programmers do not have to be software houses. Many other institutions already exist which can do this.

Hardware manufacturers must support software development even if they cannot restrict its use. In 1970, much of their software was free because they did not consider restricting it. Today, their increasing willingness to join consortiums shows that they are realizing that owning the software is not what is really important for them.

For example, universities conduct many programming projects. Today, they often sell the results, but in the 1970s, they did not. Is there any doubt that universities would develop free software if they were not allowed to sell software? These projects could be supported by the same government contracts and grants which now support proprietary software development.

It is common today for university researchers to get grants to develop a system, develop it nearly to the point of completion and call that "finished", and then start companies where they really finish the project and make it usable. Sometimes they declare the unfinished version "free"; if they are thoroughly corrupt, they instead get an exclusive license from the university. This is not a secret; it is openly admitted by everyone concerned. Yet if the researchers were not exposed to the temptation to do these things, they would still do their work.

Programmers can also make their living as I have for six years: by making custom improvements to free software. I have been hired to port the GNU C compiler to new hardware, and to make user-interface extensions to Emacs. (I offer these improvements to the public once they are done.) There is now a successful corporation which operates in this manner.

New institutions such as the Free Software Foundation can also fund programmers. Most of our funds come from people buying tapes through the mail. The software on the tapes is all free, which means that every user has the freedom to copy it and change it, but many people will still pay to get a copy. (Recall that "free software" refers to freedom, not to price.) Some people order tapes who already have a copy, as a way of making a contribution they feel we deserve. We are also getting increasing amounts of donations from computer manufacturers.

The Free Software Foundation is a charity, and its income is spent on hiring as many programmers as possible. If it had been set up as a business, offering the same products to the public, it would provide a very good living for its founder.

Because the Foundation is a charity, programmers often work for the Foundation for half of what they could make elsewhere. They do this because we are free of bureaucratic silliness, and because they feel better about themselves, knowing that their work will not be prevented from benefiting humanity to the fullest of its potential. Most of all, they do it because programming is fun. In addition, increasing numbers of volunteers write useful programs for us. (Recently even technical writers have begun to volunteer.)

This confirms that programming is among the most fascinating of all fields, along with music and art. We don't have to fear that no one will want to program.

What Do Users Owe To Developers?

There is a good reason for users of software to feel a moral obligation to contribute to its support. Developers of free software are contributing to the users' activities, and it is both fair and in the long-term interest of the users to give them funds to continue.

However, this does not apply to proprietary software, since obstructionism deserves a punishment rather than a reward.

We thus have a paradox: the developer of useful software is entitled to the support of the users, but any attempt to turn this moral obligation into a requirement destroys the basis for the obligation. A developer can either deserve a reward or demand it, but not both.

I believe that an ethical developer faced with this paradox must act so as to deserve the reward, but should also entreat the users for voluntary donations. Eventually the users will learn to support developers without coercion, just as they have learned to support public radio and television stations.

WHAT IS "SOFTWARE PRODUCTIVITY"?

If software were free, there would still be programmers, but perhaps fewer of them. Would this be bad for society?

Not necessarily. Today we have fewer farmers than in 1990, but we do not think this is bad for society, because the few deliver more food to the consumers than the many used to do. We call this improved productivity. Free software would require far fewer programmers to satisfy the demand, because of increased software productivity at all levels:

- Wider use of each program that is developed.
- The ability to adapt existing programs for customization instead of starting from scratch.
- Better education of programmers.
- The elimination of duplicate development effort.

When people object to cooperation because it would result in the employment of fewer programmers, they are actually objecting to increased productivity. Yet these people usually accept the widely held belief that the software industry needs increased productivity. How is this?

"Software productivity" can mean two different things: the overall productivity of all software development, or the productivity of individual projects. Overall productivity is what society would like to improve, and the most straightforward way to do this is to eliminate the artificial obstacles to cooperation which reduce it. But researchers who study the field of "software productivity" focus only on the second, limited, sense of the term, where improvement requires difficult technological advances.

IS COMPETITION INEVITABLE?

Is it inevitable that people will try to compete, to surpass their rivals in society? Perhaps it is. But competition itself is not harmful; the harmful thing is *combat*.

There are many ways to compete. Competition can consist of trying to achieve ever more, to outdo what others have done. For example, in the old days, there was competition among hackers—competition for who could make the computer do the most amazing or pretty thing, or for who could make the shortest or fastest program for a given task. This kind of competition can benefit everyone, *as long as* the spirit of good sportsmanship is maintained.

Constructive competition is enough competition to motivate people to great efforts. For example, a number of people are competing to be the first to have visited all the countries on Earth. They even spend fortunes trying to do this. But I have not heard that they bribe ship captains to strand their rivals on desert islands. They are content to let the best man win.

Competition becomes combat when the competitors begin trying to impede each other instead of advancing themselves—when "Let the best man win" gives way to "Let me win, best or not." Proprietary software is harmful, not because it is a form of competition, but because it is a form of combat among the citizens of our society.

Competition in business is not necessarily combat. For example, when two grocery stores compete, their entire effort is to improve their own operations, not to sabotage the rival. But this is not due to any ethical commitment; it simply happens that there is nothing much to be gained from combat in this line of business. Such is not true in all areas of business. Withholding information that could help everyone advance is a form of combat.

American business ideology does not prepare people to resist the temptation to combat the competition. Some forms of combat have been made illegal with anti-trust laws, truth in advertising laws, and so on, but rather than generalizing this to reject combat in general, executives invent other forms of combat which are not specifically prohibited. Our society's resources are being squandered on economic civil war.

"WHY DON'T YOU MOVE TO RUSSIA?"

Any advocate of other than the most extreme form of laissez-faire selfishness has often heard this question. The idea that citizens should have aims other than purely selfish ones is identified in America with communism. But how similar are they?

Communism as practiced in the Soviet Union is (or at least was until recently) a system of central control where all activity is regimented, supposedly for the common good. And where copying equipment was closely guarded to prevent illegal copying.

The American system of intellectual property exercises central control over distribution of a program, and guards copying equipment with automatic copying protection schemes to prevent illegal copying.

By contrast, I advocate a system where people are free to decide their own actions; in particular, free to help their neighbors, and free to alter and improve the objects which they use in their daily lives. A system based on voluntary cooperation, and decentralization.

Clearly it is the software owners, if anyone, who ought to move to Russia.

CONCLUSION

We like to think that helping your neighbor is as American as apple pie; but each time we reward someone for obstructionism, or admire them for the wealth they have gained in this way, we are sending the opposite message.

Software hoarding is one form of our general willingness to disregard the welfare of society for personal gain. We can trace this disregard through all of society, from Ronald Reagan to Ivan Boesky, from Jim Bakker to Exxon, from the Walker family to Neil Bush. This spirit feeds on itself, because the more we see that other people will not help us, the more it seems futile to help them. Thus society decays into a jungle.

If we don't want to live in a jungle, we must change our attitudes. We must start sending the message that a good citizen is one who cooperates when appropriate, not one that is successful at taking from others. I hope that the free software movement will contribute to this: at least in one area, we will replace the jungle with a more efficient system which encourages and runs on voluntary cooperation.

SHOULD I COPY MY NEIGHBOR'S SOFTWARE?[1]

Helen Nissenbaum

INTRODUCTION

Consider the following situation: Millie Smith is pleased with the way the home bookkeeping application, Quicken, organizes her financial records, even printing checks. Knowing how useful this would be to a good friend of hers, Max Jones, who lives precariously from one paycheck to the next, and yet knowing that the program's price tag puts it outside of Max's financial reach, Millie is tempted to help Max out by offering him a copy of hers. She has read the lease agreement on the outside package which prohibits making copies of the diskette for any purpose other than archival backup, so she suspects she might be breaking the law. However, Millie is not as concerned about breaking the law (nor about the second-order question of the morality of law breaking) as she is about violating moral principles. If she is to copy Quicken for Max would her doing so be justifiable "not so much in a court of law as in the court of conscience"?[2] For private consumers of commercial software Millie's situation is all too familiar.

Although the majority of these private end-users admit to frequently making and sharing unauthorized copies, they experience a nagging and unresolved sense of wrong-doing. Posing as the "conscience" of these wayward software copiers, a vocal group, whom I refer to as supporters of a "strong no-copy view," urges users like Millie Smith to refrain from unauthorized copying[3] saying that it is always wrong. Jon Barwise, for example, in promoting a strong no-copy position, concludes in a series of scenarios whose protagonists must decide whether or not to copy an $800 piece of software, that even in the case of a professor providing a copy of his diskette to a student who needs it to finish a dissertation, "we should answer all of the (above) questions no."[4] Green and Gilbert, in an article directed specifically to users in educational institutions, recommend that "campuses should view and treat illegal copying as a form of plagiarism or theft" and that they should pursue ways of reducing "illegal and unethical copying."[5]

In the following discussion I challenge the no-copy position, arguing that it emphasizes the moral claims and interests of software producers while failing to consider other morally relevant claims—most notably, those of the private end-user. Accordingly, Millie would not be violating moral principles if she were to share a copy with Max. I show that there are morally compelling factors that motivate many acts of software copying, not simply brazen self-interest, irrationality, or weakness of the will. Although I argue that in *some* cases copying is not a violation, I do not support the position on the other end of the ideological spectrum, which completely rejects the constraints of software copy protection. Rather, we need to judge distinct types of situations according to their individual merits. In some situations there will be an overriding case in favor of copying, in others not. In still others, agents confront a genuine dilemma, trying to respond to equally convincing sets of opposing claims.

To reach this conclusion I focused on the arguments, both consequentialist and rights based, that have been proffered in support of the strong no-copy position.

Upon analysis I find that, as a universal position, a strong no-copy position is not defensible.

Two Caveats

First, a word on how I set about recreating the justifications for a strong no-copy position. I've drawn from pieces written for computing trade publications, other non-philosophical journals, electronic-mail communications, as well as conversations. Although the arguments given in favor of a moral prohibition on copying are generally not presented here in a framework of traditional ethical theory, I find this framework useful in organizing and evaluating them. For example, I classify the arguments that predict undesirable consequences of unauthorized copying under the general heading "consequentialist arguments." In a second working category, I classify arguments that claim unauthorized copying to be violations of moral rights and respect for persons. Although this group is more of a grab bag, the label "deontological/ rights-based" captures its hybrid spirit. My first caveat, however, is that while the philosophical categories are enlightening, suggestive of potential strengths and weaknesses of the arguments, they should be viewed as rough guides only. Moreover, because few of the commentators offer explicit or complete treatments, I've taken liberties in filling in steps. While I fleshed out the arguments and filled in gaps, I tried to stay strictly within the parameters set by their originators.

Second, in order to simplify the discussion I assume throughout this discussion that programs are written and owned by a single programmer. In the real world of commercial software, teams of software developers rather than single programmers create software products. And for many products, the title usually goes to the software corporation, rather than directly to its employees, the program's authors. In other instances, it goes to intermediate agents such as marketing firms, or vendors. The assumption of a single programmer, should not affect the substantive moral thesis.

Consequentialist Arguments

According to the arguments in this category, it is morally wrong to make unauthorized copies because doing so would have negative consequences. Although copying might appear to offer a short-term gain for the copier, the longer term and broader ramifications will be a loss for both consumers and producers alike. Barwise, for example, charges, ". . . software copying is a very serious problem. It is discouraging the creation of courseware and other software, and is causing artificially high prices for what software that does appear."[6]

Barwise's remarks suggest that we can expect at least two types of negative consequences. The first is a probable decline in software production. Because copying reduces the volume of software sales it deprives programmers of income. With an erosion of potential revenues, fewer individuals will be attracted into software production. A smaller population of programmers and other software personnel will result in a reduction of available software. Furthermore, a slowing in software development would have a dampening effect on general welfare. The second negative impact of copying is a projected rise in software prices. Wishing to recoup anticipated losses caused by unauthorized copying, programmers will charge high prices for their software. Giving as an example Wolfram's *Mathematica*, which in 1989 was priced at $795, Barwise blames copying for the artificially high prices of software applications. How good are these arguments?

Embodied in the consequentialist line of arguments are a number of empirical assumptions and predictions which, I contend, are open to challenge. For consequentialist arguments to provide a moral as well as a prudential rationale, they must demonstrate links between copying and reduced income, between reduced income and decline in the software industry, and decline in production and an overall decline in society's welfare. If copying hurts the software industry but has no effect on general welfare a prohibition is not morally justifiable on consequentialist grounds. If copying is not directly related to income, nor income to a decline in the industry, then too, the argument breaks down. On close scrutiny these links don't stick. Furthermore, even if some damage could be attributed to unauthorized copying, I conclude that it's insufficient to warrant the all-out prohibition of the strong no-copy position.

Consider the claim that unauthorized copying leads to loss of sales. Although on the face of it, the argument is compelling, the implied link between copying and reduced sales is not always direct. Imagine a situation in which you are deciding whether to buy software application A or copy it from a friend. Although the consequentialists would have us think of all instances of copying as situations in which an agent must decide between the exclusive alternatives, buy A, or copy A, in many real-life situations this is not so. Computer users copy software that they would not buy for a number of reasons: because they could not afford it; are not yet sure that they want the product; or quite simply, have placed higher priority on other needs. For them, the choice is: copy A, or not have A.

Moreover, copying can actually lead to an increase in overall spending on computer software, at least for some individuals. Software sharing opens opportunities for trial and experimentation to otherwise timid users who thereby grow more comfortable with computers and software. As a result they become more active and diversified consumers of software than they would have been without those opportunities. We also find that users who are impressed by a particular piece of copied software, in order to own the manual and enjoy some of the additional benefits of "registered users," will go on to buy the application. In other words, much unauthorized copying would not result in loss of sales and some, in fact, would lead to increases.

The prediction that reduced income will discourage further creation of software belies a complicated story about motivation, action, and reward. Whereas wholesale fluctuations and extreme reductions probably would discourage would-be programmers, the effects of smaller fluctuations are not clear. Richard Stallman[7] ably makes the point that directly tying software production to monetary reward paints an overly simplistic picture of the rewards that motivate programmers. Well-known for his active support of an open environment for information technology, Stallman suggests that besides the satisfaction of contributing to a social good, the fascination with programming itself will keep many of the most talented programmers working. He also raises the question of how much is enough. Although we would not expect many good programmers to have a monk-like devotion to programming and can agree that people work better when rewarded, it's not clear that any increment in reward will make them work proportionately better. (Furthermore, as suggested earlier, we still do not have a realistic idea of the extent to which cases like Millie Smith's actually affects potential earnings.)

Turning the tables on the usual consequentialist chain of reasoning, Stallman counters that prohibitions on copying, and other restrictions on the free distribution of computer code, has the opposite effect on computer technology. It is slowing progress rather than encouraging it. He and others suggest that the free exchange of ideas and code characteristic of the early days of systems and software development was responsible for the remarkable pace of progress, whereas limiting free exchange would dampen innovation and progress, moreover, laws restricting access to software would favor large, powerful and generally more conservative software producers. With a greater capacity to exert legal clout, they could control the production, development, and distribution of software, gradually squeezing out of the commercial arena the independent-minded, creative software-engineer, or "hacker". Even if we see a proliferation of commercially available software, we may also see a slowing of the cutting edge. If Stallman's predictions are sound, they offer moral justification for promoting free copying of software, and not the reverse.

So far, I have questioned the empirical basis for the claims that link copying with loss of revenue; claims that link loss of revenue with a decrease in software production; and, more generally, claims that link copying with a loss to the software industry as a whole. What about effects on general welfare? At this level of generality it is probably impossible to draw a meaningful connection between software and welfare. To the extent that software is a social good, it is surely through high-quality, well-directed software and not sheer quantity.[8] To discourage a potential copier, an extreme no-copy position must show the clear social benefits of abstaining without which there is little to offset the immediate loss. This question deserves more thorough exploration than I'm able to give it here because the connection between software production and overall utility or welfare, is complex. It does suggest, however, that the effects on general welfare of a particular act of copying would vary according not only to the context of copying, but also to the type of software being copied. It would also need to be measured against the projected utility to the potential copier

Let us now consider the alleged connection between copying and cost and the claim that producers are forced to charge high prices in anticipation of losses through copying. An obvious rejoinder to software producers, like Wolfram, is that if software applications were more reasonably priced, consumers would be less tempted to copy. If products were appropriately priced, the marginal utility of buying over copying would increase. This pattern holds true in the case of recorded music which could provide a model for computer software.[9] Because the cost of a tape, for example, fits many budgets, it is more convenient to buy the tape than search for someone who might have it. Though both the claim and rejoinder appear to hold genuine insights, they leave us in an uncomfortable standoff. Looking at high prices, pointing at consumers, critics say: "It's your fault for copying." Whereas consumers point back claiming: "It's your fault for charging such high prices." The average user apparently cannot afford to buy software at the current rates, and the programmer cannot afford to drop his or her price. Though we may agree that this is not a desirable equilibrium, it's not easy to see who should take the first step out of this circle of accusations. Resolving the standoff requires asking difficult questions about burden. Upon whom do we place the burden of maintaining a healthy software industry—consumer or producer? This question brings me to my concluding comments.

I agree with defenders of a consequentialist line that a prolific software industry with a high-quality output, which provides genuine choices to a wide variety of consumers, is a goal worth striving for. I disagree, however, that prohibiting copying is the only, or best, way of ensuring this. First, I have tried to show that the empirical grounds upon which they support their claims are open to dispute. Moreover, if a consequentialist approach is to be at all useful in guiding decisions about unauthorized copying, then it must distinguish among different types of copying—for their consequences surely differ. For example, cases like Millie's sharing a copy with Max would have a vastly different effect than cases in which a user places a copy on the software on a public network. Consequentialist moral injunctions should recognize these differences.

Finally, the no-copy position unreasonably focuses on private end-users, placing on their shoulders the onus of maintaining the health of the software market. But consumer copying is but one variable, among many, that affect the software industry. Holding fixed the other variables might serve some interests, but it gives disproportionate weight to the effects of copying. Decisions by commercial hardware manufacturers and even government agencies can significantly impact software. For example, if a hardware manufacturer perceives that a particular software product is critical to the sale of its machines it may, quite rationally, decide to support the software.[10] In addition, software companies have the capability to influence the actions of potential users by offering not only a good product as code on a diskette, but by also including attractive services such as consulting, good documentation, and software updates. In this way they make it worthwhile for the user to buy software, rather than copy it. The many flourishing software companies stand as evidence that good products and marketing works, despite alleged copying. Because other players—namely, government, hardware producers, software companies—have the power to significantly affect the software industry, we should not ignore their responsibilities when we assess the burden of maintaining the strength of software production. It is wrong for the private consumer to be unfairly burdened with responsibility.

Deontological/Rights-Based Arguments

In urging individual consumers not to make unauthorized copies some supporters refer to the "rights of programmers" and "respect for their labor". Regardless of its effects on the general welfare, or on the software industry, copying software without permission is immoral because it constitutes a violation of a moral right, a neglect of moral obligations. Depriving a programmer of earnings is wrong not only because of its undesirable ramifications, but because it is unjust and unfair. And even if programmers' earnings are not appreciably affected by copying, we have an obligation to respect their desire that we not make unauthorized copies. The obligation is absolute, not broken merely at the discretion of the private end-user.[11] Millie ought not make a copy of Quicken for Max because doing so would be unfair, it would violate the programmers' rights. But what are the rights to which these commentators refer; and does all copying, in fact, violate them?

Rights-based justifications of no-copy require a satisfactory resolution to both questions. They not only must identify the rights of programmers relevant to the question of unauthorized copying, but must demonstrate that copying always violates these rights. Supporters usually cite property rights as relevant to the question of copying. A justification of the position should, accordingly, ask whether programmers do in fact qualify as owners of their programs so that they would have the appropriate rights of private property over them. But justification does not stop here. For even if we resolve that programmers do own their programs, it doesn't follow necessarily that all copying will violate their property rights. Or to put it another way, it is not obvious that property rights over programs include the right to restrict copying to the extent desired. A justification of the no-copy position needs a second step, to follow the finding that programmers own their programs. And that is, to show that copying violates these property rights. Many commentators fail to recognize the need for the second step, simply concluding that owning implies an unlimited right to restrict copying.

In the discussion that follows I will spell out the two steps in a rights-based position beginning with the question of private ownership, and then moving to the question of whether owning a program implies the right to place absolute limits on reproduction. I will conclude that the second step is the weak one. As before, in recreating the arguments I've worked from informal written pieces, electronic mail messages, and verbal communications. In some cases this has meant filling in missing steps; steps that I judge necessary to making the best possible case for a rights-based justification. Finally, though recognizing that some might object to the very fabric of rights-based justifications of moral injunctions, I offer my criticisms from within this framework, and will not challenge the very idea of a rights-based approach.

Programming and Private Property

First, let's examine the following claim: Because a programmer writes, or creates, software he or she owns it. For some, this claim is so obvious as to not even need justification. To them, a program is an extension of the person's self and so, obviously, belongs to that person. For others, labor theories of property such as John Locke's, which claims that when individuals invest labor in a previously unowned item they earn property rights over it, offer a more traditional moral grounding for private ownership over programs. Locke writes, "Thus Labour, in the beginning, gave a right of property, wherever any one was pleased to employ it upon what was common."[12] Because programmers invest labor in creating a program, they are entitled to the "fruits of their labor." Although Locke's theory addresses the somewhat different issue of private acquisition of physical property, such as parcels of land and harvests, and focuses on the taking of initial title over a previously unowned item (or one held in common), his theory adapts well to intellectual labor. In fact, the case of intellectual property is somewhat easier for a labor theory in that it avoids a common pitfall identified by Locke's critics who, in the context of physical items, worry about the morally "correct" mix of labor with the physical entity.[13] I will concede then, that a programmer, in producing a program, accrues property rights over it, accepting as justification for this claim—if it is even needed—basic ideas of a labor theory of property.

Some have questioned the justice of extensive property rights over programs claiming that software creation is an essentially cumulative activity. Most programs, draw heavily on work that has preceded them so that giving rights to the programmer who happened to write the line of code in question rests on the unwarranted assumption that we can tell accurately where one programmer's labor really begins and the other's ends. For example, most commercial software on today's market is the product of a long line of cumulative work most notably Lotus 1–2–3.[14] However, this objection does not challenge, rather it implicitly adopts, a form of the labor theory because it suggests that *all* those who contributed their effort toward creating a software product deserve proprietary rights over it, and not just those who happen to cross some arbitrary finishing line first. Just because they have made a bigger marketing effort, happen to be more worldly, belong to a large organization, or have good legal representation, does not vest in them a stronger moral claim. Although the question of just rewards for joint labor is an important one in light of the history of the development of computer software, for the remainder of my discussion, I will assume that we can talk meaningfully about *the* programmer who contributed most significantly to a program's creation. It is about this programmer that the discussion about property rights that follows applies.

As stated earlier, showing that programmers own their programs is not sufficient for a no-copy position. Its supporters must still demonstrate that owning a piece of software implies a moral right to restrict copying to the extent desired (and thus the duty in others to refrain from copying). How might I demonstrate this "second step," required of a rights-based justification of strong no-copy? In the next section I will examine whether a universal prohibition on copying software necessarily follows from general property rights over it.

Owning Software and Prohibiting Copying

In general, ownership implies a set of rights, rights defining the relationship between an owner and a piece of property. Typically the rights of an owner over private property fall into a number of set categories including: one that covers conditions on initial acquisition over a previously unowned object;[15] another that refers to the extent of use and enjoyment an owner may exercise over that property; a third that determines the extent to which an owner may restrict access to her property (or alienate others from her property), and a fourth that endows upon an owner the power to determine the terms of transfer of title. Thus abstractly conceived, the concept of private ownership yields a fairly well-defined set of rights. When instantiating these rights in actual cases of owning a specific given item, the specific rights an owner has over that item, can vary considerably according to a host of factors. First, at the most general level, certain social, economic, political, and cultural factors greatly affect our ideas about private property rights, their nature and extent, and what sorts of objects can be owned privately in the first place. To simplify matters, for purposes of this discussion, I will assume a common background of roughly Western, free-market, principles. A second variable that also significantly determines the specific rights an owner can have over an item[16] is its metaphysical character, or type. For example, the specific rights a child has over his peanut butter sandwich might include the rights to consume it, to chop it into twenty pieces and to decide whether to share it or not with a friend. But such rights make no sense in the case of landowners and plots of land, pet owners and their pets, car owners and their vehicles, and so forth. When we determine the appropriate set of rights instantiating the general rights of use and enjoyment, restricting access, terms of sale, on items of varying metaphysical character, we come up with distinct sets of specific rights. Whereas intellectual property stretches classical ideas of locking away or fencing ("restricting access"), consuming ("use and enjoyment"), and bartering ("transfer of title") deciding what it means to own software poses an even harder puzzle.

Computer software has raised a host of challenges to property theory, testing the traditional concepts and rationales in novel ways. Because even relatively simple programs have numerous components and moreover have various aspects, the first problem is to define, or identify, the "thing" that is *the* program, the thing that is the proper subject of private ownership. A program can be identified by its source code and object code, a formal specification defining what the program does, its underlying algorithm, and its user interface, or "look and feel." Each of the various components—or aspects—has a distinct metaphysical character and consequently suggests a distinct set of property rights. For example, because a program's source code is considered similar to a written work, it it considered by most to be covered by copyright laws. By contrast some judge a program's algorithm to be a process (and not a mathematical formula) and thus claim that it is patentable. Legal debates address the issue of whether one can abstract a program's so-called look and feel and claim to own that, in addition to, and independently of, the code, algorithm, and so on. And if so, they argue over whether legal protection ought to be through copyright, patent, or something else. There are many instructive works dedicated to the question of the optimal form of legal protection of all these aspects of software in a growing literature which is written from legal, philosophical, and technical perspective.[17]

Fortunately, we need not wait for a resolution to the entire range of puzzles that software ownership raises in order to gain a better understanding of Millie's dilemma. We acknowledge, in her case, that she explicitly duplicated object code, and thus we bypass many of the complexities. However, it is important to note the existing backdrop of uncertainty over how to categorize the metaphysics of software, and thus, how to fit it into our network of ideas on property rights. We are drawing conclusions about software ownership on the basis of imperfect analogies to other forms of private property. This leaves open the possibility of significant differences.

We are ready now to return to this section's central question of how one might derive a prohibition on copying from ownership. On the basis of earlier observations about private property we can conclude that a programmer, or owner, has rights over the program including rights to restrict access and rights of use and enjoyment. Presumably, the programmer's right to generate earnings from his program would instantiate the latter. The programmer could choose to give others limited access to her program by selling diskettes, upon which she has copied the program, at a price she determines. But because the programmer still owns the program itself, she may impose restrictions on its use—in particular she retains the right to prevent buyers of the diskettes from making copies of the program that she has not explicitly authorized. Thus, we derive the programmer's specific right to restrict unauthorized copying from the general right property owners have to restrict access by others to their property. To distinguish transactions of this type from other types of sales, commercial software vendors adopt the jargon "software license" rather than "software sale." Thus, the argument from rights would dictate that Millie not copy because doing so would violate a programmers' valid claim to both use and enjoy his or her property (by depriving them earnings) and restrict access by others to it (by making unauthorized copies).

But this picture leaves out an important component of property theory. Like other rights, property rights restrict the freedoms of others by imposing certain obligations on them. For example a promisee's rights imply an obligation on the part of the promiser to keep the promise; a landowner's rights implies an obligation on would-be trespassers not to cross his or her land. As I stated earlier, the precise nature of property restrictions will vary according to the metaphysical character of the property. But there is yet another factor that shapes the extent and nature of property—and in fact all—rights. Even theorists of a libertarian bent, who support extensive rights over private property, recognize that these rights are not absolute. For example, Locke argued that morality allowed the appropriation of previously unowned property only "where there is enough, and as good, left in common for others."[18] And Nozick, also recognizing limitations on property rights, illustrates one source of these restrictions with his colorful example: "My property rights in my knife allow me to leave it where I will, but not in your chest."[19] In other words, although owning a knife implies extensive rights of use and enjoyment, these rights are constrained by justified claims, or rights, of others—in this case, their right not to be harmed. While I wish to avoid either endorsing or criticizing the more far-reaching agendas of these two authors, I want to draw attention to an important insight they offer about private property rights: that property rights are subject to the limitations of countervailing claims of others.

Actual practice demonstrates that, as a rule rather than an exception, when we determine the nature and extent of property rights, we acknowledge the justified claims of others. For example, in determining the rights of the owner of a lethal weapon we're influenced not only by its general metaphysical features (when we determine the types of actions that constitute use and enjoyment), but are concerned about the well-being of others. And so we restrict the way people may carry lethal weapons—either concealed or unconcealed depending on the accepted wisdom of the city or state in which they happen to live. We regulate construction projects of urban property owners for far less concrete counterclaims than freedom from bodily harm, but in the interest of values like aesthetic integrity of a neighborhood, effects on the quality of life of immediate neighbors, and so forth. We restrict the rights of landowners over water traversing their land, preventing them, for example, from damming a flowing river. We also constrain the behavior of motor vehicle drivers. In all these cases where we perceive a threat to justified claims of other individuals, or of a social order, we limit the extent of owners' rights over their property. It makes sense to carry this principle over to the case of software asking not only about the claims of programmers, but the claims of end-users.

Does Millie Smith have a reasonable counter-claim that might limit the extent to which Quicken's owners can constrain her actions. She would like to duplicate her Quicken software for Max, an act of generosity, helping satisfy a friend's need. Despite the programmer's preferring that Millie not share a copy, Millie is motivated by other values. She views making a copy as a generous act which would help a friend in need. Copying software is a routine part of computer use. Millie's proposed action is limited; she has no intention of making multiple copies and going into competition with the programmer, she wouldn't dream of plagiarizing the software or passing it off as a product of her own creation. The entire transaction takes place within the private domain of friends and family. She would view offering a copy to Max as a simple act of kindness, neither heroic nor extraordinary. Interfering with the normal flow of behavior, especially as pursued in the private realm, would constitute unreasonable restriction of an agent's liberty. Thus, Millie's countervailing claim is the freedom to pursue the virtue of generosity within the private circle of friends and family.

The conclusion of this line of reasoning is *not* that, from a perspective of rights, *all* unauthorized duplication of software is morally permissible. I am suggesting merely that we decide the question whether to share or not to share in a case by case fashion. Although in some cases a programmer's desire that the user not copy software is a defensible instantiation of the right to restrict access to private property, in others the restriction will not be defensible because it conflicts with the valid claims of another agent. And even in the cases where making a copy would not be immoral it would not follow that the programmer has somehow lost all the property rights over his or her program. Commentators like Green and Gilbert are right to draw attention to programmers' claims over their software, and to encourage respect for intellectual labor; but they overlook the possibility of relevant, conflicting, counterclaims. When, at the beginning of the paper, I referred to the copier's dilemma, it was the dilemma created by conflicting obligations: on the one hand an obligation to respect a programmer's property rights, which in some cases includes the right to restrict copying; and on the other an obligation to help others, tempered by the belief that one ought not have one's behavior unduly restricted within the private domain.

Consider some objections. One objection is that no matter what Millie might think about helping Max, you just cannot get away from the fact that she's violating the programmer's property rights. And this is the reason that her copying—and all unauthorized copying—is immoral.

This objection fails to recognize that counterclaims can substantively affect what counts as a moral (property) right, in any given situation. Consider the rights of a landlord with respect to a leased apartment. When that apartment is vacant, the owner may come and go as he wishes; he may renovate it, choose to rent it, or to let it stand empty. However, once the apartment is leased, the landlord's rights of entry are limited by a tenant's competing right to privacy. Even if it would suit a landlord to stipulate in his lease the right to make surprise checks, this wish would be overridden by the justified claims of his tenants not to be disturbed, not to have their privacy violated. We would not say that the landlord's property rights are violated by the tenant; we would say that the landlord no longer has the right of free entry into his leased property. Consider another example. Let's say someone buys a word-processing package. On the outside of the customary sealed envelope containing the diskette, the buyer finds not only the usual terms of a lease agreement, but one further condition. The programmers stipulate that consumers are free to use the word processor any way they want, except to produce a document that promotes abortion. They reason that the abortion stipulation is merely an additional instantiation of their rights as owners to restrict access by others to their property. However, I think that the buyer could quite reasonably object that despite the programmer's intellectual property rights over the word processor, these rights do not include the right to control its use to the extent that it overrides valid, competing, claims to freedom of expression. Similarly, Millie, judging that in the private domain she should be largely unrestricted, could argue that the moral arm of the programmer does not extend into the private domain. We conclude, therefore, that in copying for Max she does not violate a moral right.

In a second objection, a critic could charge that if we judge Millie Smith's copying to be morally permissible, this would open the door to a total disregard for the rights of programmers. There would be no stopping agents from making multiple, unauthorized, copies and selling them in competition with the original programmer.

This objection doesn't hold because Millie's case, being significantly different from those other cases, would not lead us down a slippery slope. A potential copier must show a justifiable claim that conflicts with the programmer's. In the objector's example, and even in the case of a do-gooder who decides to place a piece of privately owned software on a public domain network,[20] copying takes place in a public domain lacking Millie's personal and private motivations. They lack the compelling counterclaim. Specifically for the public, commercial arena, we would expect to generate a network of laws and regulations to cover the many cases which moral principles alone could not decide.

Another objection asserts that Millie would be acting immorally in making a copy for Max because copying is stealing. But this objection begs the question because it *assumes* that copying is stealing. In this section we've been examining whether or not copying always violates property rights and therefore constitutes wrongful seizure of another's possession. In other words, whether copying is stealing. This objection assumes that we've satisfactorily established that copying is theft, and thus assumes the issue we're trying to establish.

Conclusion

There is a prevailing presumption—in my opinion a disturbing one—that were we to follow the dictates of moral conscience, we would cease completely to make unauthorized copies of software. Yet when we examine the arguments given in support of that presumption we find that they fall short of their universal scope. The soundness of a rights-based rationale depends on successfully showing that owning software entails a right to restrict copying. I have argued that this step is not obvious, and that at least in some well-defined cases the entailment fails—notably, cases in which there are strong counterclaims. In practice this means that we should give equal consideration to the rights of end-users as well as to those of programmers. To simply insist that property rights override end-user freedoms is to beg the issue at hand.

Consequentialist rationales are also equivocal in that they rest on a number of sweeping empirical assumptions—many of which exaggerate the effects of copying, some of which are open to doubt. Moreover, it places squarely on the shoulders of private end-users the onus of maintaining a flourishing industry when in fact there are other agents well placed to share the burden. Many software manufacturers who have been vocal in their complaints, despite current levels of copying, appear to be enjoying overwhelming successes. Perhaps because they offer incentives like good consulting services, free upgrades, and reasonable prices they raise the marginal utility of buying over copying.

Finding that there are insufficiently strong moral grounds for universally prohibiting copying, I conclude not that all unauthorized copying is morally acceptable, but that that some copying is acceptable. There is sufficient variability in the types of situations in which software users copy to suggest that we ought to evaluate them case-by-case. In cases like Millie's and Max's, the argument against copying is not a compelling one.

Finally, some critics insist that the best approach to solving this issue is a hardline economic one. Clearly, a rights-based approach, which unearths the usual set of conflicting rights is not helpful and leads us to a deadlock. Let the free market decide. We ought to allow software producers to place any conditions whatever on the sale of their software, and in particular, any limits on duplication. Consumers will soon make their preferences known. Defenders of no-copy say that current commercial software conditions are more or less in that position today, except that users are not keeping up their end of the bargain when they make copies of software. But even from this hard-line economic standpoint, a no-copy line is disturbing because it lets the robustness of a market depend on a mode of behavior to which most do not conform, and many find distasteful, that is, restricting the inclination to private acts of beneficence and generosity. Unless we alter human nature, experience suggests that this would be a shaky equilibrium.

On a final idealistic note, I echo strains of Richard Stallman in observing that if we can eradicate copying only when individuals ignore a natural tendency to respond to the needs of those close to them, we may not be maximizing expected utility after all.

NOTES

1. An earlier version of this paper was presented at the Fifth Annual Computers and Philosophy Conference, Stanford University, August 8–11, 1990. Several members of the audience, with their sharp criticisms and suggestions, helped clarify my thinking a great deal. I'd also like to thank members of Partha Dasgupta's Applied Ethics Seminar at Stanford (1989) for useful and creative comments.

2. David Lyons, "The New Indian Claims and Original Rights to Land" in *Reading Nozick: Essays on Anarchy, State and Utopia*, (Ed) Jeffrey Paul, Rowman and Littlefield, Totowa, New Jersey. 1981.

3. I will not be dealing with unlikely cases in which copy in software might save a life or avert a war. I assume that even those committed to a no-copy position would find rationale to permit those acts.

4. Jon Barwise, "Computers and Mathematics: Editorial Notes." in *Notices of the A.M.S.*

5. K. Green and S.W. Gilbert, "Software Piracy: Its Cost and Consequences" in *Change*, pp. 47–49. January/February 1987.

6. Jon Barwise, "Computers and Mathematics: Editorial Notes." in *Notices of the A.M.S.*, 1989.

7. R. Stallman, "The GNU Manifesto" in *GNU Emacs Manual*. Copyright 1987 Richard Stallman.

8. Joseph Weizenbaum in Chapter 1 of *Computer Power and Human Reason*, San Francisco, Freeman, 1976, makes suggestive comments arguing that consumerism needn't necessarily lead to greater choices among genuinely distinct products. A conservative market might remain unimaginatively "safe," coming up with only trivially diverse products.

9. Although some claim that the loss in sound-quality is a major reason for recorded music being less frequently copied, this doesn't tell the story for all (the average) listeners.

10. Both Stallman, *ibid.* and Barwise, *ibid.* (and probably others) have made similar points.

11. Though strictly speaking, a rule-based approach could ultimately be grounded in utilitarian terms, the ones I consider here merge the rights-based and deontological styles of moral reasoning. They cite programmers' rights, inferring from them absolute obligations on the parts of software users.

12. John Locke, Section 45 in *Second Treatise of Government*, originally published 1690, Hackett Publishing Company, Indianapolis, 1980.

13. Nozick's discusses this problem quite extensively in *Anarchy, State, and Utopia*, Basic Books, Inc. 1974.

14. For an interesting history of software inter-dependence see Bill Machrone's, "The Look-and-Feel Issue: The Evolution of Innovation" in *Computers, Ethics, & Society*, M.D. Ermann, M. B. Williams, C. Gutierrez, Oxford University Press, New York, 1990.

15. This was Locke's central preoccupation.

16. Metaphysical character can co-vary with cultural–social factors to make for an even more complex picture. Consider the potentially diverse views of descendents of European traditions and those of Native American traditions on property rights over land, sea, and air.

17. See, for example: M. Gemignani, "The Regulation of Software," *Abacus*, vol. 5, no. 1, Fall 1987, pp. 57–59; D.G. Johnson, "Should Computer Programs Be Owned?",

Metaphilosophy, vol. 16, no. 4, October 1985, pp. 276–288, P. Samuelson, "Why the Look and Feel of Software User Interfaces Should Not Be Protected by Copyright Law," *Communications of the ACM*, vol. 32, no. 5, May 1989. pp. 563–572.
18. Locke, *ibid*, Chapter 5 Section 27.
19. *Anarchy, State and Utopia* by Robert Nozick p. 171.
20. I confess to being stymied by cases such as that of a school teacher in a poor ghetto school deciding to make unauthorized copies of a software applications that be believes would help his students, who would not ordinarily be able to afford it.

THE SOFTWARE PATENT CRISIS

Brian Kahin

An explosion of patents on software processes may radically change the programming industry—and our concept of human expression in the computer age.

Last August, Refac International, Ltd., sued six major spreadsheet publishers, including Lotus, Microsoft, and Ashton-Tate, claiming they had infringed on U.S. Patent No. 4,398,249. The patent deals with a technique called "natural order recalc," a common feature of spreadsheet programs that allows a change in one calculation to reverberate throughout a document. Refac itself does not have a spreadsheet program and is not even in the software industry. Its business is acquiring, licensing, and litigating patents.

Within the last few years, software developers have been surprised to learn that hundreds, even thousands, of patents have been awarded for programming processes ranging from sequences of machine instructions to features of the user interface. Many of the patents cover processes that seem conventional or obvious, and developers now fear that any of the thousands of individual processes in their programs may be subject to patent-infringement claims.

The Refac suit demonstrates the vulnerability of the industry to such claims. Patent no. 4,398,249 was applied for in 1970, granted in 1983, and only recently acquired by Refac. In the meantime, software developers have been busily creating spreadsheets and other new products unmindful of patents. The industry accepted copyright and trade secret as adequate protection for its products, and most programmers assumed that patents were not generally available for software.

Never before has an industry in which copyright was widely established suddenly been subjected to patenting. As it is, only a few companies that create microcomputer software have the resources to try to defend against patent infringement claims. Most small firms will be forced to pay license fees rather than contest the claims, even though many software patents may not stand up in court.

In the long run, the costs of doing business in a patent environment will radically restructure the industry. Many small companies will fold under the costs of licensing, avoiding patent infringement, and pursuing patents defensively. The individual software entrepreneur and inventor may all but disappear. There will be fewer publishers and fewer products, and the price of software will rise to reflect the costs.

Especially disturbing is that the broad claims of many recent software patents appear to establish monopolies on the automation of such common functions as generating footnotes and comparing documents. Some claims even cover processes for presenting and communicating information, raising troubling questions about the effect of patents on the future of computer-mediated expression.

PATENT VS. COPYRIGHT

Software patents, like all patents, give an inventor the right to exclude all others from making, selling, or using an invention for 17 years. In return, the patentee discloses his or her "best method" of implementing the invention, thereby relinquishing trade secrets that might otherwise be enforced forever (like the formula for Coca-Cola).

To obtain a patent, an applicant must convince Patent Office examiners that the invention would not be obvious to a "person of ordinary skill in the art" who is familiar with all the "prior art," which includes previous patents and publications. In contrast, copyright inheres in books, poems, music, and other works of authorship, including computer programs, from the moment they are created. Registering one's work with the Copyright Office is a simple, inexpensive procedure that has important benefits (it is a precondition for filing suit, for example), but the copyright itself is automatic when the work is fixed on paper or on disk.

Copyright and patent protect different things. Copyright protects expression but not underlying ideas. Patents protect useful processes, machines, and compositions of matter. Traditionally "processes" have included methods of physically transforming materials but not business methods or mental steps. Thus, computer programs fall somewhere between the traditional territories of copyright and patent.

From the 1960s to the early 1980s, the Patent Office and the courts grappled with the question of whether algorithms—the elemental processes on which computer programs are built—are patentable as either processes or machines. Early on, the Patent Office granted some patents for processes built into computer hardware that today would be contained in software, but it was reluctant to grant patents for programs per se. As the 1966 Report of the President's Commission on the Patent System pointed out, the Patent Office had no system for classifying programs. The report also noted that even if this were remedied, the volume of programs being created was so enormous that reliable searches of "prior art" would not be feasible or economical.

However, the Court of Claims and Patent Appeals (CCPA) maintained that computer programs were patentable and overturned numerous Patent Office decisions denying patentability. The Supreme Court vindicated the Patent Office in two decisions, *Gottschalk* v. *Benson* (1972) and *Parker* v. *Flook* (1978), holding that mathematical algorithms were not patentable subject matter. Still, the CCPA continued to uphold patentability in other cases. Finally, in *Diamond* v. *Diehr* (1981), a sharply divided Supreme Court upheld the patentability of a process for curing rubber that included a computer program. The majority concluded that programs that did not preempt all uses of a computer algorithm could be patented—at least when used in a traditional process for physically transforming materials.

That case has been the Supreme Court's last word on the subject. But despite the narrowness of the ruling, the Patent Office underwent a radical change of heart. Until very recently, there were no reported appeals of adverse Patent Office decisions, leading observers to conclude that the office was eventually granting almost all applications for software patents. Although articles began appearing in legal periodicals a few years ago noting that patents were being routinely granted for many software processes, not until 1988 did the industry realize that the rules were changing, or had already changed, in the middle of the game. By the spring of 1989, the patents that entered the pipeline after *Diamond* v. *Diehr* were starting to flow out in significant numbers—by one count, nearly 200 in the first four months of that year.

PROCESSING PROBLEMS

Unfortunately, the Patent Office classification system remains unchanged, and the volume of software being created has grown exponentially. This makes searching for prior art—processes already in public use—time-consuming and expensive.

The search is extraordinarily difficult because the field's printed literature is thin and unorganized. Software documents its own design, in contrast to physical processes, which require written documentation. Also, software is usually distributed without source code under licenses that forbid reverse engineering. This may amount to suppressing or concealing the invention and therefore prevent the program from qualifying as prior art. The search for prior art may require securing oral testimony from people who developed software at universities many years ago, an expensive proposition.

Many programmers suspect that patent examiners lack knowledge of the field, especially since the Patent Office does not accept computer science as a qualifying degree for patent practice (it accepts degrees in electrical engineering). Moreover, attracting and holding individuals with expertise in a field like software, where industry demand is high, is not easy for a government agency. Less qualified examiners create problems because they naturally have a lower standard in determining the hypothetical "person having ordinary skill in the art," and are thus more apt to grant patents for obvious processes. Since the examination process is conducted ex parte (as a private matter between the Patent Office and the applicant), less qualified personnel are also more likely to be influenced by sophisticated patent attorneys and the apparent expertise of the applicant.

The quality of software patents being awarded has aroused concern even among patent lawyers and other advocates of the new regime. But it will be left to firms being sued for infringement to prove that a process should not have been patented because it was obvious in view of the prior art. Meanwhile, software patents stand as intimidating weapons for those who hold them.

RESTRUCTURING THE INDUSTRY

Perhaps because of some of these problems, applications for software patents take an average of 32 months to be approved and published. That's significantly longer than the overall average of 20 months, and a very long time given the short product cycles of the software business.

Unlike copyright, independent creation is irrelevant to patent infringement. Every developer is charged with knowledge of all patents. Even if someone is not aware of a patent, he or she can still infringe against it. Furthermore, patent applications and the examination process are confidential, so there are ordinarily several years of patents in the pipeline that no search will reveal. Although no infringement occurs until the patent issues, an inventor may find that a newly awarded patent covers a feature he or she has already incorporated and marketed in a finished product. While this is a problem for the patent system as a whole, it is intolerable for software developers because of the industry's rapid pace of innovation and long patent-processing period.

The problem is compounded by the fact that a modern software package may contain thousands of separately patentable processes, each of which adds to the risk of infringing patents that are already in the pipeline. Since software functions are interdependent and must be carefully integrated, developers can find it difficult to excise a process built into the original program.

The patent system exacts a high penalty in an industry as decentralized as software. Programming requires no special materials, facilities, or tools: to design software is to build it. Because barriers to entry are low, the industry attracts many small players, including hundreds of thousands of individuals who work as consultants or short-term employees. Rather than a handful of competitors working on the same problem, there are likely to be dozens, hundreds, even thousands. Since under the patent system one winner takes all, many others—including developers without lawyers—are deprived of the fruits of their independent labor and investments.

Patent proponents argue that this uninhibited duplication of effort wastes resources. But the "waste" could be cut only by reducing the number of players and slowing the pace of development to fit the cycles of the patent system. The result would be a handful of giants competing on a global scale, bidding for the ideas and loyalty of inventive individuals.

However, many programmers believe that there are diseconomies of scale in software development—that the best programs are authored rather than assembled. The success of Visicalc, Lotus 1-2-3, WordPerfect, and other classic programs testifies to the genius of individuals and small teams. Certainly there has been no evidence that they need more incentives. Quite the contrary, the freewheeling U.S. software industry has been a model of creative enterprise.

A COSTLY SYSTEM

Even software developers and publishers who do not wish to patent their products must bear the costs of operating under a patent system. While these costs may initially come out of the software industry's operating margins, in the long run, they will be borne by users.

At the first level is the expense of analyzing prior art to avoid patent infringement. A precautionary search and report by outside patent counsel can run about $2,000—that's per process, not per program.

Next are the direct costs of the patent monopoly—the license fees that must be paid to patent holders. If the patent holder refuses to license at a reasonable fee, developers must design around the patent, if that is possible. Otherwise, they must reconceive or even abandon the product.

The third set of costs are those incurred in filing for patents. Searching for prior art, plus preparing, filing, negotiating, and maintaining a patent, can total $10,000 to $25,000, not including internal staff time. Seeking foreign patents can make the bill substantially higher.

The notoriously high costs of patent litigation must be borne by both sides. Just the discovery phase of a lawsuit is likely to cost each side a minimum of $150,000, and a full trial can cost each from $250,000 to millions. Again, these figures do not include internal staff time, which could easily double the real cost. While a small patent holder may be able to secure a law firm on a contingency basis or sell an interest in the patent to speculators, the defendant has no such options.

Litigation also involves the possibility and further expense of an appeal. All appealed patent cases now go directly to the Court of Appeals for the Federal Circuit CAFC, successor to the CCPA), where panels in patent cases are usually led by patent lawyers turned judges. Whereas patents once fared poorly on appeal, the CAFC has found patents to be both valid and infringed in over 60 percent of the cases that have come before it. The CAFC has greatly strengthened the presumption of patent validity and upheld royalties ranging from 5 to 33 percent.

While a large software company may be able to absorb these costs, they will disproportionately burden smaller companies. The first to suffer will be independent developers who cannot afford to market their own products. These developers typically receive royalties of 10 to 15 percent from publishers who serve as their distributors. Such modest margins, out of which developers must recoup their own costs, would be wiped out by the need to pay royalties to a few patent holders.

The high costs of a patent environment give patentees considerable leverage over small firms who will, as a practical necessity, pay a license fee rather than contest a dubious claim. To establish credibility, the patentee will settle for small fees from the initial licensees. The patent holder can then move on to confront other small firms, pointing to such licensings as acknowledgments of the patent's validity and power. This tactic has a snowballing effect that can give the patent holder the momentum and resources to take on larger companies.

Cross-licensing—where firms secure patents to trade for the right to other patents—seems to work reasonably well in many industries and has been touted as the answer to these problems. However, cross-licensing is of little value to smaller companies, which have little to bring to the table. And cross-licensing may prove of limited value even to large companies, since it does not protect against companies like Refac that have no interest in producing software and therefore no need to cross-license.

Of course, the power that software patents afford may induce some venture capitalists to invest in them. But investing in software patents is one thing; investing in robust, complex products for a mass market is another.

In fact, software publishers hold very few patents. The vast majority are held by large hardware companies, computer manufacturers that have in-house patent counsel and considerable experience in patenting and cross-licensing. Nearly 40 percent of the software patents that the U.S. Patent and Trademark Office now issues go to Japanese hardware companies. It is quite possible that the separate software publishing industry may cease to exist as companies find that they need the patent portfolios and legal resources that the hardware giants can provide. The result will be a loss of diversity in software products, reduced competition, and, many believe, a less productive software industry.

PROTECTING IDEAS AND INFORMATION

A deeper, more disturbing problem in patenting programs was barely evident before computers became ubiquitous personal tools and software became infinitely versatile. More than a "universal machine," the computer has developed into a medium for human expression and a mediator of human experience. Software is designed to satisfy specific needs for shaping and delivering information. Thus, what is increasingly at stake in software patents is the generation and flow of information. This becomes more threatening when the claims in a patent extend far beyond the disclosed means of implementation to cover general ideas.

Broad patent claims covering abstract processes are not limited to software, or even to computer hardware. Consider patent no. 4,170,832, granted in 1979 for an "interactive teaching machine." The patent discloses a clumsy-looking combined videotape deck and television with a set of push buttons.

The patent includes a process claim for a procedure commonly used in interactive video: showing an introductory video segment, presenting the viewer with a limited number of choices, registering the viewer's decision, and then revealing the likely outcome of that decision. The disclosed machine, which was never marketed, contributes nothing to the public domain: it simply reveals one person's way of implementing a basic instructional technique.

In a notorious 1983 case, a federal district court upheld the patentability of Merrill Lynch's Cash Management Account system, a procedure for moving investment funds among different types of accounts. Acknowledging that the system—essentially a method of doing business—would not be patentable if executed with pencil and paper, the court nevertheless upheld the patent because it made use of a computer.

The Patent Office has taken this principle one step further. Besides granting monopolies on new procedures such as the Cash Management Account system, the office is also awarding patents merely for automating familiar processes such as generating footnotes (patent no. 4,648,067) and comparing documents (patent no. 4,807,182). But software developers have been routinely automating such common office functions, bookkeeping procedures, learning strategies, and modes of human interaction for years. The principle that patents are granted to induce inventors to disclose trade secrets has no relevance here. These processes are part of everyday life, and can and should be computerized in a number of ways.

What's more, information per se is traditionally the substance and territory of copyright. The intelligent ordering of information is the very heart of grammar, rhetoric, and graphic design. Why should information be subject to the pervasive restraints of patent simply because it is interactive rather than linear? Should human expression that is assembled, communicated, or assimilated with the aid of a computer be restrained by patents? If the computer is seen as an extension of the human mind rather than vice versa, the answer is no.

CHANGING PATENT POLICY

Software developers who understand the impact of patents are demoralized. Lawyers assure them that patents are here to stay, and that programmers must seek new patents to protect against other patents. These lawyers point to the growing torrent of software patents, the presumption of patent validity, and the fervidly propatent record of the Court of Appeals for the Federal Circuit. Smaller companies that cannot afford this advice can only hope that companies with deeper pockets will afford more visible and attractive targets for patent holders bringing suit.

But the narrowness of the Supreme Court decision in *Diamond* v. *Diehr* remains. The Court never explicitly rejected the traditional doctrines against the patentability of mental steps and business methods, doctrines that may yet defeat many of the patents that have issued. If the hue and cry grows, Congress could amend the Patent Act to make it clear that the scope of patenting is still limited to physical processes.

The software industry was not broke, but it is in the process of being "fixed." The question is whether the fixing will be done by the gush of awards from private proceedings in the Patent Office—or by a public decision about whether software patents serve "to promote the Progress of Science and useful Arts," as the Constitution requires.

TALES FROM THE ALGORITHM WAR

Richard H. Stern

INTRODUCTION

Algorithms have not been respected under our intellectual property laws. Copyright law has always rejected protection for algorithms on the ground that they are unprotectable ideas. The received doctrine under patent law is that algorithms cannot be protected, as such. But they have been admitted through the patent system's back door, on and off over the last 25 years. In its latest decision on algorithms, *In re Iwahashi*,[1] the Federal Circuit (CAFC) has effectively thrown the patent system's doors wide open to algorithms—if the correct formalities are observed. This article examines how this came to be, questions how sensible the result is, and considers whether there may be some better way to arrange matters.

DEFINING ALGORITHMS

Algorithms are of several sorts and are variously defined. At one extreme of generality, an algorithm may be defined as any procedure for accomplishing a specified function or task.[2] At an opposite extreme of specificity, an algorithm may be defined as a finite series of steps (or sequence of actions) for making a numerical or other mathematical calculation, terminating with provision of the result of the calculation. A definition of somewhat different scope, appropriate here, is a clearly defined set of steps describing a procedure for accomplishing a specified data-manipulation task to be performed by means of a general-purpose digital computer.

For example, this is an algorithm for multiplying a multiplicand by a three-digit multiplier to get their product (base 10):

Set Register A to zero. Send multiplicand to Register A.

Set Register B to zero. Send multiplier to Register B.

Add the number in Register A to the number in Register B as many times as the units digit of the multiplier.

Put a zero at the end of the number in Register A.

Add the number in Register A to the number in Register B as many times as the tens digit of the multiplier.

Put another zero at the end of the number in Register A.

Add the number in Register A to the number in Register B as many times as the hundreds digit of the multiplier.

Read as the answer the number in Register B.[3]

SOME ALGORITHM HISTORY

In the 1960's there was great concern that granting patents on algorithms would have an adverse affect on the progress of software technology. The same concern exists in the software industry today, fueled by the Patent and Trademark Office's lately having issued many patents that seem so broad as to cover any uses of certain algorithms, and further fueled by the *Iwahashi* decision's check to the Office's attempt to halt that tide of algorithm patents. In the 1960s the President appointed a commission to study the patent system and recommended necessary changes to overhaul it. One of the commission's recommendations in its report was that patents on computer programs should expressly be prohibited.[4] The Johnson Administration then drafted a patent reform bill embodying the commission's recommendations. Among other things, the bill would have outlawed patents on any "plan of action" in the form of a computer program. Congress did not enact the proposal, but the Executive Branch continued to oppose software patents, throughout the next several Administrations.

Benson

At about this time came the first of four algorithm cases that went to the Supreme Court. Bell Laboratories applied for a patent on a method of converting binary-coded decimal (BCD) numbers into pure-binary numbers.[5] The method was intended principally for use in telephone switching systems, but the claims presented were not so limited. The claimed algorithm essentially called for multiplying the tens-place BCD digit by ten in binary (1010) and adding the result to the units-place digit, all according to the rules of binary arithmetic. The Patent Office refused to allow the patent, the Court of Customs and Patent Appeals (CCPA) reversed, and the case went to the Supreme Court.

The Supreme Court sided with the Patent Office in *Gottschalk* v. *Benson*.[6] The Court ruled that patents cannot be granted on abstract ideas, but only on concrete methods or apparatus for using ideas. To allow patents that wholly preempted the use of algorithms, as this one did, the Court held, would more hinder than promote technological progress, because such patents would deprive workers in the software field of the use of the necessary tools of technological advancement. Benson's patent claims had no apparatus or other limitations that prevented their total preemption of the use of the algorithm. Accordingly, the claims could not be allowed.

The CCPA, convinced that the Supreme Court did not understand the situation, then ruled that the *Benson* decision was limited to method claims. It also reemphasized its earlier-enunciated legal fiction that a general-purpose digital computer, into which a new computer program was inserted, became a new machine.[7] The CCPA therefore continued to reverse the Patent Office when applicants claimed algorithms in the form of a newly programmed machine.

Johnston

Again, an algorithm case was taken to the Supreme Court. This time, the Office had refused a patent on a "machine system" for sorting different payee-types of bank check from one another (e.g., rent, food, fuel, repairs) by tagging each of them with an appropriate numerical indicator. In *Dann* v. *Johnston*,[8] the Supreme Court once again reversed the CCPA and reinstated the Office's decision to refuse a patent. In an excess of zeal, however, government counsel argued not only that the programmed machine/new machine theory was nonsense (akin to claiming that putting a new piano roll into a player piano turned the machine into a different player piano), but also that the claimed system was obvious. The Supreme Court bypassed the question of the patentability of algorithms as programmed machines, and held that the algorithm was obvious.

Flook

In the next round, an algorithm was claimed for a method for monitoring petro-chemical processing plants by comparing a current parameter reading (e.g., observed temperature) with a weighted, moving-time average of past readings of the parameter. If the difference exceeded a predetermined amount, that signified a possible run-away condition, and an alarm was sounded. The Office denied the patent, the CCPA reversed, and the government took the case to the Supreme Court. The Court reversed, reinstating the Office's refusal to patent the system, in *Parker* v. *Flook*.[9]

The CCPA had considered it important that the method was limited to use in petrochemical plants (more specifically, to use in a process for catalytic chemical conversion of hydrocarbons, or "hydrocracking"). Thus, the use of the algorithm was not wholly preempted, because use outside the petrochemical field would presumably not infringe the claim. But the Supreme Court dismissed the significance of this limitation, holding that "a claim for an improved method of calculation, even when tied to a specific end use, is unpatentable subject matter."[10]

The Court said that, in assessing algorithm-related patents, one must disregard any novelty and unobviousness of the algorithm, itself. One must regard the algorithm as if it were old and part of the prior art, however new it might be. It was therefore unnecessary to attempt to determine the novelty or obviousness of the algorithm (a difficult task for which the Office concededly was ill-equipped). The patentable invention, if any, would have to be in the remainder of the claimed subject matter, or in the entire subject matter considered as a whole (without focusing on any merit of the algorithm as such). The Supreme Court's ruling suggested that an algorithm-related patent could be sustained only if the implementation of the algorithm in apparatus was itself novel and unobvious.[11]

Diehr

The CCPA did not give up.[12] In *Diamond* v. *Diehr*,[13] its ruling that an algorithm-related patent should be granted was finally upheld in the Supreme Court, 5–4. The claimed invention was a method of operating a rubber-curing mold equipped with internal thermocouple sensors for continuously monitoring temperature inside the mold. The temperature data was fed to a computer, which calculated a total cure time based on the temperature readings. When the elapsed time reached the calculated value, the process was terminated and the cured rubber article was removed from the mold. While the formula (the so-called Arrehenius Equation) was known, the prior art allegedly did not disclose any system in which internal temperature was continuously monitored with thermocouples for purposes of determining cure time.

The Court ruled that involvement of an algorithm in a claim to a machine system did not preclude patentability of the claimed system or of an industrial process using the system, where the system as a whole was novel and unobvious. The Supreme Court's ruling in *Diehr* suggested that an algorithm-related patent could be sustained if the implementation of the algorithm in apparatus was novel and the system as a whole was unobvious.[14] *Diehr*, decided a decade ago, was the last algorithm or computer program patent case that the Supreme Court has reviewed.

Since then, the federal appellate court for patent cases, now designated the Court of Appeals for the Federal Circuit, has increasingly supported patentability of algorithm-related claims. It has reinstituted the CCPA's process-machine distinction, and has sustained machine-format claims if they had any colorable apparatus limitations in them. In doing so, the court has gone far beyond *Diehr's* approval of patents on machine systems to which algorithms were incidental.

IWAHASHI

The latest decision of the Federal Circuit, *Iwahashi*, for all practical purposes goes back to the CCPA's immediately pre-*Benson* standard. In the words of Yogi Berra, *It's deja vu all over again.* After *Iwahashi*, virtually any algorithm can be patented if the claims draftsman will use the proper format. The facts of *Iwahashi* demonstrate that conclusion.

Iwahashi invented an improvement in an aspect of a system for voice pattern recognition. Such systems utilize signal-autocorrelation coefficients, which ordinarily are calculated by multiplication, a tedious and computer-intensive procedure. Iwahashi eliminated the multiplication steps by substituting addition and use of squares. This provided a less expensive system. The Patent and Trademark Office denied the claim because it was directed to an algorithm, and an appeal followed.

The sole claim presented was in "means-for" format, which Section 112 of the patent act expressly authorizes. The process format and means-for format for drafting claims are isomorphic. Any skilled claims draftsman can convert a claim from one format to the other. The isomorphism is illustrated in the following claims, showing the two formats for claiming the same thing—as applied to making a peanut butter sandwich. One claim shown is directed to a method for making a sandwich. The other claim is directed to a machine system (or what I prefer to call a "pseudomachine") for making the sandwich.[15]

The following claims illustrate method and machine-system formats for a method and system for making a peanut butter sandwich:

A. *A method of making a peanut butter sandwich, comprising:*

1. placing on a substantially horizontal support a first slice of bread having upper major and lower major substantially planar surfaces, said lower major surface of said slice of bread being adjacent to and above said support;

2. dispensing a predetermined quantity of peanut butter onto said upper major surface of said slice of bread;

3. spreading said predetermined quantity of peanut butter over and thereby substantially covering said upper major surface with a layer of said peanut butter; and

4. placing on top of said layer of peanut butter and generally contiguous therewith a major surface of a second slice of bread generally similar in size and shape to said first slice of bread.

B. *A peanut-butter-sandwich-making system comprising:*

support means for supporting bread slices;

means for transporting an initial bread slice to said support means whereby said initial bread slice is moved onto and is supported by said support means;

means for dispensing a predetermined quantity of peanut butter onto said initial bread slice supported by said support means;

means for spreading said peanut butter over said initial bread slice, thereby forming a layer of said peanut butter thereon;

means for transporting a further bread slice to the vicinity of said support means; and

means for placing said further bread slice on top of said initial bread slice and generally contiguous therewith.

Iwahashi's claim recited a series of interconnected means for doing the various steps of the algorithmic calculation, such as means for calculating a sum. The only element of the entire claim that was not in means-for format was a read-only memory in which was stored a list of squares of numbers (a so-called "look-up ROM").[16] The Office considered Iwahashi's use of pseudomachine format immaterial. It regarded the claim as indistinguishable from a method claim wholly preempting "any and every means for performing the functions" to which the claim was directed. The Federal Circuit disagreed and reversed, because of the ROM, which the court said was "a specific piece of apparatus." The claim did not wholly preempt the use of the algorithm, because any use without a ROM or its equivalent would not infringe the claim. Accordingly, the court held that the claim was directed to statutorily permissible subject matter.[17]

THE AFTERMATH OF *IWAHASHI*

How widely the *Iwahashi* court opened the door to algorithm patents may be shown by way of an example. The example is a simplified form of Iwahashi's algorithm claim. Those who remember the binomial theorem will recognize the following equations:

$$(a + b)^2 = a^2 + 2ab + b^2.$$
$$(a - b)^2 = a^2 - 2ab + b^2.$$
$$(a + b)^2 - (a - b)^2 = 4ab.$$
$$0.25\,(a + b)^2 - 0.25\,(a - b)^2 = ab.$$

The illustrative algorithm to which these equations relate is Area $= A = LW =$ $0.25 (L + W)^2 - 0.25 (L - W)^2$. Steps for carrying out the area calculation algorithm are:

1. sum length and width, and square the sum;
2. subtract width from length, and square the difference, and
3. subtract a quarter of the result of the second step from a quarter of the result of the first step, to get the answer.

As in the case of Iwahashi's algorithm, computer time and expense can be saved by looking up the squares instead of doing multiplication.

Finally, I have attempted to imitate closely the *Iwahashi* claim language, in the following claim directed to a pseudomachine for carrying out the foregoing algorithm:[18]

> The subject matter claimed is an area calculation unit for providing area coefficients for use as parameters in calculating an amount of substance to be supplied to an applicator for applying substance to rectangular surfaces having length L and width W, said unit comprising:
>
> a ROM in which has been stored at each address thereof a numerical value representative of 0.25 the square of said address;
>
> said ROM having means for fetching and outputting said numerical values when said ROM is addressed;
>
> summing means for summing a signal representative of L and a signal representative of W, providing a sum-input signal representative of a sum $(L + W)$;
>
> first infeed means for feeding said sum-input signal from said summing means to said ROM as an address-input thereto;
>
> first outfeed means for feeding from said ROM a sum-output signal representative of $0.25(L + W)^2$;
>
> first subtracting means for subtracting from a signal representative of L a signal representative of W, providing a difference-input signal representative of a difference $(L - W)$;
>
> second infeed means for feeding said difference-input signal from said first subtracting means to said ROM as an address-input thereto;
>
> second outfeed means for feeding from said ROM a difference-output signal representative of $0.25(L - W)^2$;
>
> second subtracting means for receiving from said first outfeed means said sum-output signal, and for receiving from second outfeed means said difference-output signal, and for subtracting said difference-output signal from said sum-output signal, whereby a signal representative of LW is provided for use as a said area coefficient.

I have used this claim to illustrate what *Iwahashi* holds, because the quarter-square algorithm and $A = LW$ are easier to follow than the mathematics of *Iwahashi* (where the algorithm of the claim uses Sigmas, subscripts, variables, and other complexities). But in all material respects, this claim tracks that of the *Iwahashi* case.

The question may now be asked whether the claim will be denied because it wholly preempts the use of the algorithm. The answer, according to the *Iwahashi* decision, should be that the claim is directed to permissible subject matter. First, the claim is directed to a machine rather than a process, for whatever difference that makes.[19] The claim does not claim the algorithm, but instead claims a machine (pseudomachine) that uses the algorithm. Second, the claim has an element that is not in means-for format, viz., a ROM as in *Iwahashi*. Hence the claim covers only those machines using the ROM or its equivalent. To paraphrase the decision of the court in *Iwahashi*, others are free to use the algorithm and to calculate area as the product of length and width, so long as they do not use a ROM or its equivalent to do so.

One may then ask what is the significance of the ROM limitation. That is, what does the ROM limitation exclude from the reach of the claim? As a practical matter, nothing. The ROM limitation excludes from the claim any way of carrying out the algorithm that does not use a look-up table. Ordinarily, that would mean carrying out the algorithm by computing squares each time, by multiplying by itself the quantity to be squared. But the whole point of the algorithm is to look up the squares instead of carrying out a tedious multiplication operation. The only convenient way not to multiply L by L to get L^2 is to look up the answer.[20] If you are going to look something up, you will need to use a look-up means. It is difficult to imagine any such computer-related means that is not a ROM or its equivalent.[21] Accordingly, the answer to the question posed is that the ROM limitation does not exclude anything of significance from the reach of the claim.

The ROM of the claim is what may be characterized as "nominal hardware." That is to say that the presence of the hardware limitation in the claim does not, as a practical matter, cause the claim to cover any less ground than it would if the hardware language were omitted from the claim. Other examples of nominal hardware could be:

- limiting a claim to an algorithm for voice-recognition or voice-actuation applications to use in systems in which a signal is transmitted to the system from a microphone or other sound-actuated transducer;[22]
- limiting a claim to a visual-display algorithm to use in which the output signal modifies the display shown on a display device;[23]
- limiting a claim to an algorithm for converting barcode data to binary format to use with data input from, or use in a system including, an optical wand or scanner (i.e., a barcode reading device);
- limiting a claim to an algorithm for shape-pattern recognition to use with robotic or assembly-line equipment.

The ultimate in nominal hardware limitations would be using an algorithm only in a system including a digital computer, which would carry things beyond the end.[24] Inserting a nominal hardware limitation into a computer-algorithm claim written otherwise in means-for format would appear to make the claim satisfy the *Iwahashi* test for patentable subject matter. By the same token, the way is now paved for patenting computer-related algorithms in almost all cases. The ROM limitation alone, if insinuated into the middle of the claim, will suffice in a great many cases. For the others, the ingenuity of patent draftsmen should be adequate to find an innocuous or nominal hardware limitation.

After *Iwahashi*, therefore, the Office will probably be unable to reject any algorithm-related patent claim as being directed to nonstatutory subject matter. If the claim has a ROM in its middle—for example, if the claim is similar to that set out earlier in text—the Office will be reversed in the Federal Circuit if it rejects the claim as nonstatutory. Instead of a ROM, a claim may have a different nominal piece of hardware, such as one of the earlier-mentioned examples, assuming that the claims draftsman knows the technology well enough to devise an appropriate nominal hardware limitation. If a "specific piece of apparatus" limits the scope of the claim, the Federal Circuit should conclude that there is no difference in principle from *Iwahashi*. If the Office seeks to reject the claim, therefore, it will have to show prior art that anticipates the invention or makes it obvious, rather than simply refusing to consider the claim on the ground that the subject matter is outside the statute. The poor documentation and indexing of computer art, of course, make rejection on the basis of prior art difficult or even infeasible. That is why the Office has long sought to hold the subject matter nonstatutory.[25]

PTO Reaction The Office has realized that the *Iwahashi* decision, literally interpreted, would require that virtually any computer algorithm be patented. The Office has therefore published a notice in which it interprets the decision to rest on the court's finding that *Iwahashi's* claim was "truly drawn to specific apparatus," and that a ROM was not the same thing as a means for storing data.[26] The Office states that its policy will be to treat apparatus limitations in other patent applications on a case-by-case basis. If apparatus limitations appear to the Office not to stop the claim from "encompass[ing] any and every means for performing" the functions involved, the Office will deny a patent unless the applicant proves that the claim is actually narrower than that in scope. "The issue of claim scope should be treated as a matter of burden of proof," the Office said, and it will be the applicant's "burden to show that the functionally-defined disclosed means do not encompass any and every means for performing the recited function."

This language is, perhaps deliberately, susceptible to various interpretations. A likely interpretation is that the Office will deny an algorithm-related patent claim having what appears to the Office to be a nominal hardware limitation, unless the applicant proves that its hardware limitation is meaningful.[27] But that approach will be difficult to sustain in court. Generally, it is considered that the Office must issue a patent to an applicant unless the Office has a basis in the statute for refusing to do so.[28] The onus is on the Office to show, prima facie, that the claimed subject matter is unpatentable. In some instances that can be done by taking notice of generally accepted scientific principles—for example, that perpetual motion machines are inoperable and thus unpatentable, because of the thermodynamic "law" about conservation of energy. But the present case is not in that category. An examiner may deny an application on the basis of facts known to him, but to do so he must first file his affidavit stating those facts.[29] The present case is probably one invoking that principle.

Consider the earlier-proposed example of the microphone-using, voice-actuated system based on an algorithm—the idea being that you need a microphone or its equivalent to get a signal into a voice-actuated system.[30] An examiner could, but probably would be unwilling to, file an affidavit stating that he is an expert in that technology and he knows that no apparatus exists for performing the kind of procedure claimed by the applicant other than the microphone mentioned in the claim as a hardware limitation, or its equivalent. Indeed, in *Iwahashi* the examiner might well (*should*, it seems to me) have filed an affidavit stating that in his expert opinion one cannot carry out the invention without using a look-up ROM *or its equivalent*, and therefore the algorithm must entirely preempt the presently known use of the algorithm in the field claimed.

The Office's notice seeks to avoid this onus and shift to the applicant the onus of negating a critical fact (i.e., whether the hardware limitation is merely nominal). Therefore, the Federal Circuit will probably reverse any requirement by the Office that an applicant must prove that other devices exist that would fall outside the patent. The court might point out, for example, that any applicant who did know of another device that would work would claim its use in the same or a different patent application. Perhaps, failure to make an explicit such claim suggests that the applicant and his patent attorney cannot think of any alternatives. But that would hardly be an excuse for the Office to disregard its ordinary burden of proof to show nonentitlement to a patent, and the Federal Circuit is unlikely to approve an Office rule requiring applicants to prove entitlement.[31]

After *Iwahashi*, therefore, unless the Federal Circuit does an about face, or the Supreme Court plays *deus ex machina* after a decade of abstinence or benign neglect, many or most algorithms will be patentable. There are some caveats. Adroit draftsmanship is required. Moreover, the insertion of nominal hardware will frequently result in a field-of-use limitation on the claim. For example, claims on algorithms relating to voice-actuation may be limited to voice-actuation applications, because of the hardware selected. No doubt some algorithm implementations will resist the ingenuity of claims draftsmen to insinuate nominal hardware limitations into them. It is possible, too, that the examining staff will overcome its historical allergy to, or excessive diffidence about, filing affidavits. More likely than not, however, we are in for a period of stasis; no clarifying litigation appears in sight. *Iwahashi* is likely to be the last word for a while.

AFTER THE AFTERMATH

After more than 20 years of advancing not at all in our method of dealing with algorithms, perhaps the time has come to consider whether we may have been proceeding on the wrong track. Although one of the draftsmen of the Johnson Administration's legislation described earlier, and one of the government's counsel in the *Benson*-to-*Flook* anti-algorithm cases of the 1970s, I now wonder whether that effort was misguided, indeed ill-conceived as a matter of policy. First of all, it has turned out to be a King-Canute-and-the-tide process. Second, we have ended up with the courts often treating computer program copyrights as if they were patents, which makes even less sense than issuing patents via the patent office and after examination for novelty and technical merit. Third, I still believe that our side read the precedents correctly and the CCPA and Federal Circuit read them wrongly, but I have come to question whether the precedents properly extrapolate to computer-program algorithms.

What is wrong with algorithm patents? What is the reason for the often-stated concern about wholly preempting the use of the tools of scientific progress? In what circumstances would algorithm patents more hinder than promote the progress of science and useful arts?

We may begin with the antithesis of the last question: When are algorithm patents not so bad? Consider first the patent, as yet untested in court, on Narenda Karkarmar's linear programming algorithm for optimizing path selections or equipment allocations.[32] That advance is said to be the veritable $E = mc^2$ of linear programming. Considerable benefits should flow to society from its exploitation, and it should stimulate the creation of further improvements by others in the field. It is possible that Karmarkar did not wish to work without pay; it is possible that his employer, Bell Labs, did not wish to operate as a nonprofit institution for the general better-ment of mankind.[33] That is to say, might not the same reasons that justify intellectual property protection of computer programs and hardware apply to algorithms? It may be that the incentives of the patent or copyright system would induce algorithm cre-ation in the same way as they induce other industrial property creativity.

There would hardly be any ground for complaint if Bell licensed all applicants at a very modest royalty rate. Suppose that every diskette sold that contained a com-puter program utilizing the Karmarkar algorithm bore a 25-cent royalty. Would that substantially retard the rate of advance of software or other technological progress? And if it would, which I greatly doubt, then what about a penny?

That is the positive side of the matter. What is the negative side of the social bal-ance sheet? Suppose that Bell Labs as the owner of the Karmarkar patent decided to enjoin all competitive use of the algorithm. Or that it insisted on a very, very high roy-alty rate until the year 2005. Then multiply that by all of the other algorithm patents.[34] The problem about algorithms as intellectual property is thus seen more to concern remedies than rights, and the question is one of degree. A penny a diskette clearly can-not hinder technological progress (and probably will not generate enough revenue to encourage innovation significantly, either). A thousand dollars per diskette plus injunc-tions plus threats of jail most surely would lock up the algorithm, even against those who independently rediscovered it, and would likely more hinder than promote tech-nological progress. That is why the question is one of degree, not principle.

To be sure, one can recount anecdotes that purport to show that any solecism in the law, however small, must not be tolerated. There is the G.B. Shaw story about getting to the point of determining the price of the services contemplated rather than determining the character of the person furnishing them. There is the story about the Victorian-period, unwed maidservant's baby being so small that it should not be com-plained about. Those are not sensible anecdotes, or at least they are uninstructive in this context. Small solecisms in the law are often preferable to large dichotomies between extreme solutions neither of which make sense.[35]

At least three dichotomous solutions of the algorithm problem have been attempted so far, each very unsatisfactory. The first solution was to allow full patent rights on any algorithm—more or less the CCPA's pre-*Benson* approach. The result was to make excessive, "wholly preemptive" remedies available to proprietors of algorithms, which frightened the industry and in turn the Executive Branch.

The second solution, in support of which I labored for many years, overreact-ed to a perceived danger of wholly preempting algorithms and thereby depriving soft-ware artisans of needed tools. That solution, endorsed during the 1970s by the Supreme Court, was to slam shut the door to any industrial property protection and thus to deny any patent incentives to algorithm creators and proprietors.

A third such solution is to allow full patent remedies to proprietors of algo-rithms who pass the judicial tests endorsed by the Federal Circuit. At the moment that court's test in actual operation closely parallels the CCPA's first solution, *deja vu*. But the Federal Circuit test purports to be a compromise between the first and second solutions and purports to protect the public and software industry from any complete preemption of algorithms. In point of fact, however, after *Iwahashi* if you can figure out how to insinuate a ROM into the middle of the claim you can wholly preempt the algorithm for all practical purposes. As a result, this regime self-deludedly pur-ports to be saving the world from the perceived danger of preemption, but in actual-ity it delivers the keys of the city gates to algorithm claimers.

A PROPOSED LEGISLATIVE COMPROMISE

A better solution than any of these would be to recognize—of necessity by legislation—that there is nothing inherently wrong with providing intellectual property incentives to the creation of algorithms, provided that the remedies are kept sufficiently within bounds and the administrative and transactional costs do not become excessive. Perhaps, the same principle applies to any other ideas, and, indeed, to discoveries of mathematical formulas or phenomena of nature. The maidservant's baby is not objectionable, if it is small enough and keeps quiet enough not to be a bother. It makes no sense to complain about it as a matter of principle, when it is so difficult to find decent help these days. That applies to algorithms too.

This solution would require legislation, but that would be preferable to further attempts at judicial legislation, which is what we have been getting in this field for at least a decade. Indeed, in *Benson* and *Flook*, the Supreme Court said that Congress, rather than the courts, should decide how best to promote the technological progress in the field of algorithms.[36] It is time to take that advice. The Algorithm War has gone on for too long, and both sides have gone too far.

A compromise solution to the problem of what to do about algorithms is almost certainly preferable to any of the dichotomous regimes that have been tried so far. One element of a compromise would be to stop straining at the gnat, to stop making legal distinctions that are unworkable, and to allow algorithms to be protected under a different part of the patent system or under an industrial property system like that for utility models or for chip layouts. This dispensation would deal with the spector of "complete preemption of the algorithm" by adjusting permissible relief. A regime, for example, in which the relief were only damages not to exceed a reasonable royalty would not be unduly preemptive.[37]

Patent or Utility Model?

The proposed compromise could be effected within the present patent system, if one adopts one set of rules, but must be done under a new, utility-model-like system, if one adopts another set of rules. If the only difference between algorithm protection and that of the remainder of the subject matter of patents is the relief, that could be accomplished by a single section, similar to present 28 U.S.C. § 1498, plus a definitional section.[38]

In addition however, it might be considered appropriate to have one or more of the following differences between algorithm and patent protection:

- Registration with rather cursory first-instance examination (and thus low front-end costs) instead of true, patentlike examination of degree of technical advance, thus deferring more searching inquiry until litigation, if any, occurred.
- Modest term of protection, perhaps ten years.
- Different standard of technical merit or advance, which might be lower (or higher) than inventive step or unobviousness.

These changes, especially the last, could require creation of a separate industrial property system distinct from patent law. Probably, there is little to choose between here, and either approach would be equally satisfactory. Legislation is required in any event. Questions of political expediency would seem to dominate any choice. Thus, if expanding the concept of section 1498 to nongovernment patent troubled some persons, as modifying some copyright principles for the purposes of chip protection troubled some copyright owners, the utility model approach might seem preferable. Otherwise, staying within the patent system (along with design patents and plant patents) may seem preferable.

Drawing the Line Around Algorithms

A major problem of implementation still remains, and it would represent the second major element of the proposed compromise. It is necessary to draw the line between two categories of subject matter over which patents may be claimed. One category is machines (and industrial processes) that incidentally utilize algorithms, which would remain patentable under the regular patent system. The other is algorithms, which would be placed into another part of the patent system or even into another industrial property law. The line-drawing problem does not go away because of the proposed compromise; the compromise can only make it easier to resolve the problem in a rational and reasonable manner.

We know that there is a continuum at one end of which are located algorithms; at the other end is the conventional subject matter of the patent system, since machines and processes typically operate in accordance with or take advantage of what may be considered algorithms. What is needed, and has been lacking so far, is a very clear way to draw the line between patentable machine systems and unpatentable algorithms—creation of a "bright-line" distinction. That is needed to effectuate the compromise, promote business certainty, and minimize the cost to industry of administering the applicable legal system.

But it is not enough that the line be bright. It must also be located sensibly. The result must not be to undermine the compromise or create a worse problem. Thus, to protect algorithms separately, and at the same time issue regular patents on them wherever they are claimed with nominal hardware, would undermine the idea of the compromise. At the other extreme, to take machines out of the patent system merely because the principle of their operation is based on a known or unknown algorithm or equation, such as $E = mc^2$, $F = ma$, $A = LW$, or $d^2s/dt^2 = a = 32$ ft/sec^2, would not be accepted, either, if made an element of the compromise.

The task is to find a clearly recognizable distinction between algorithms and algorithm-using machines. A boundary must be drawn somewhere along the continuum described above. (A necessary predicate to success is finding an appropriate discontinuity along that continuum.)

The author then proposes a substitute for present law which is summarized in the following.

In a nutshell, the focus of this test is whether selecting and adapting the particular algorithm would be obvious to one who knew about the algorithm. Would a knowledgeable person in this field, knowing this algorithm and wanting computer assistance for this task, select and implement this algorithm to accomplish the task? If so, there is no patent for the implementation, unless the implementation is patentable in itself (the *Flook* test). If not, the implementation is patentable even if the apparatus is old or straightforward, because then the subject matter as a whole *will* be unobvious.

To make this more concrete, consider two earlier examples:

- Would a person of ordinary skill in the telephone line routing art or in the art of deploying trucks at supply depots, who knew of the Karmarkar linear programming algorithm and wanted to computerize the task, use that algorithm to computerize the task? If so, the application is obvious (assuming use of conventional, unpatentable equipment).
- Would a person who knew about measuring the area of rectangles (or whatever the pertinent art is), who also knew the binomial theorem, and who did not want to do a tedious and computer-intensive multiplication process, find it obvious to obtain the product of L and W by taking one-fourth of the difference between the square of the sum of L and W and the square of their difference?

To be sure, that one knows an algorithm does not necessarily mean that it is obvious to use it for a particular task,[39] especially when the application is subtle. But if selecting the algorithm for the task is what one would readily decide to do, it should not be a patentable invention to make that selection. That would be like selecting a conventional herbicidal composition, once somebody else has discovered the herbicidal utility of the active chemical.[40]

I submit that the proposed test would be a reasonable compromise. The scope of the patent monopoly granted under this test is limited to applying the algorithm to the defined task in the defined field of use, so that the amount of algorithm-preemption is correspondingly limited. The rule is administratively practical: It is clear that the proposed rule is at least as easy to administer as the rules presently in effect, from which it differs only by eliminating one consideration about where to attribute unobviousness.

NOTES

1. 888 F.2d 1370 (Fed. Cir. 1989).
2. The court in *Iwahashi* pointed out that this definition would include any step-by-step process, even those not computer-related. *Id.* at 1374. *See also* Diamond v. Diehr, 450 U.S. 175, 219 (1981) (dissenting opinion of Stevens, J.); *In re* Walter, 618 F.2d 758, 765 n.4 (CCPA 1980).
3. This may not seem to be much of an algorithm, but the first algorithm case to go to the U.S. Supreme Court involved an algorithm very similar to it. In any event, it illustrates the type of algorithm with which this article is concerned, and the possible tediousness of a long computerized multiplication operation, with which the invention in the *Iwahashi* case was concerned.
4. *"To promote the Progress of . . . Useful Arts," Report of the President's Commission on the Patent System* 13 (1966).
5. In BCD notation, a decimal number such as *35* is written as a sequence of binary numbers, here the binary number for *3* and the binary number for *5*. Decimal *35* is 0011 0101 in BCD. In pure binary that number would be expressed as 100101.
6. 409 U.S. 63 (1972).

7. *See, e.g., In re* Noll, 545 F.2d 141, 148 (CCPA 1976), *cert. denied*, 434 U.S. 875 (1977); *In re* Bernhart, 417 F.2d 1395, 1400 (CCPA 1969); *In re* Prater, 415 F.2d 1393, 139_n.29 (CCPA 1969).

8. 425 U.S. 219 (1976).

9. 437 U.S. 584 (1978).

10. *Id.* at 595, n.18. The Court compared the end-use limitation to limiting a claim to the use of the formula $C = 2\pi r$ to determining the circumference of wheels. *Id.*

11. The Court said that the discovery of a phenomenon of nature or mathematical formula "cannot support a patent unless there is some other inventive concept in its application." *Id.* at 594. It also said that, conversely, "an inventive application of the principle may be patented." *Id.*

12. The CCPA said in post-*Flook* decisions that the *Flook* Court had confused different parts of the patent act with one another. The court attributed this to "subversive nonsense" that government counsel had argued "with a seeming sense of purpose" to befuddle the Court. *In re* Bergy, 596 F.2d 952, 962–63 (CCPA 1979).

13. 450 U.S. 175 (1981).

14. Compare text preceding *supra* note 11 (*Flook* test).

15. This type of "machine" has also been termed "illusory apparatus." *In re* Walter, 618 F.2d 758, 769 (CCPA 1980).

16. A read-only memory (ROM) is a device for storing information that is ordinarily read from time to time, but once programmed with the information is ordinarily not rewritten, at least not frequently. A ROM is commonly a semiconductor chip, often an ultraviolet-erasable programmable ROM chip (EPROM). A floppy diskette or hard disk would ordinarily be considered a ROM or its equivalent. In some circumstances, volatile memory such as RAM may be equivalent to ROM.

In a look-up ROM, data is stored in the various locations or addresses of the ROM. When a signal representative of an address is input to the ROM, the data stored at that address is output.

17. The Federal Circuit made a second point about claim scope, but it seems to be a mere quibble. The court said that the means-plus-function elements of the claim were limited to the equivalents of the structures disclosed for claim elements. The means-plus-function elements of this claim were such things as means for adding and means for feeding signals. It is doubtful that any conceivable means for adding or feeding signals would not be equivalents here, because the mode of accomplishing those functions is immaterial to the invention. The court, consistent with the Supreme Court's decision in *Flook*, placed no stress on the factor that the claim was limited to a specific end use (voice pattern recognition systems).

18. The claim should be understood as following a specification describing the desirability of correctly and automatically metering the amount of substance to be applied to a rectangular surface, a predicate to which is determining (calculating) the needed amount of substance as the area (L × W) times the required per-unit-area amount of substance. The specification gives examples of use of the system, such as painting a wall using a paint sprayer and applying fertilizer to a field with a spreader.

19. In my opinion, the result would be the same in the Federal Circuit (but perhaps not the PTO) if the claim were rewritten as a method claim. *See In re* Meyer, 688 F.2d 789, 795–96 (CCPA 1980). While the shoe is ordinarily placed on the foot that an all means-for claim is as preemptive as a broad method claim, the same shoe should fit the foot that a method claim tied to a specific apparatus is no more preemptive than a claim to specific apparatus. Thus, *Diehr* involved such a method claim.

20. Another possible but less convenient way to avoid multiplication is to look up the logarithm in a look-up device, add the logarithm to itself, and find out what num-

ber has the sum as its logarithm. The doubling can be done in binary by just shifting the logarithm one place to the left in a shift register, an easy operation, but the rest of the procedure is inconvenient. If this method made any sense, the applicant would want to add a second claim to the case, covering it, or more likely file a second patent application. This would not be the same algorithm.

21. An applicant could address this point by placing a statement in the specification to the effect that a preferred form of storage is an EPROM in which the quarter squares have been stored, but the same function can be accomplished in the same way to use the teaching or gist of the invention by utilizing alternative storage-media expedients. These would include floppy diskettes, hard disks, tapes, cores, and punched cards, or even better a RAM appropriately loaded from another medium before using the algorithm. Presumably, a court in an infringement action would interpret the term "ROM" in the claim to cover all of the alternative expedients that were expressly listed in the specification as structures or materials equivalent to a ROM.

22. This system is suggested by the court's reasoning in *In re* Abele, 684 F.2d 902 (CCPA 1982). In that case, independent method claim 5 was held nonstatutory because it was directed to an algorithm. Method claim 6, dependent on claim 5, was held statutory. The difference between the claims was that claim 6 stated that the input data used in the method was X-ray attenuation data, which the court interpreted to mean the result of producing an X-ray beam with a CAT scanner apparatus, passing the beam through an object, and detecting the exiting rays.

It would probably be better for an applicant to draft such a claim in terms of the input signal having been transmitted to the system from a microphone, and also to mention some surrounding background apparatus still farther upstream from the microphone, if possible. The Office may argue that apparatus limitations in data-gathering steps are to be ignored. *See Patentable Subject Matter*, 1106 O.G. 5, 9 (Sept. 5, 1989); *cf. In re* Grams, 888 F.2d 835 (Fed. Cir. 1989) (data-gathering step without specific apparatus insufficient to make algorithm patentable). The *Abele* decision seems to contradict the position that apparatus limitations to the data-gathering part of a method claim are immaterial, however, since the *Abele* court deemed the limitation to a CAT scanner X-ray beam source important. *Accord, Grams, id.* at 840.

It has been suggested that *Grams*, decided by a different CAFC panel a few days before *Iwahashi*, may be inconsistent in rationale with *Iwahashi* and more supportive of the PTO's position. However, the very general diagnostic method claimed in *Grams* was not limited by even nominal hardware, by the claims or (for what it is worth) in the descriptive part of the specification.

23. Just as apparatus at the far upstream end of the claimed subject matter may be ignored, so, too, may apparatus at the far downstream end. So-called "insignificant post-solution activity" is ignored. *See Flook*, 437 U.S. at 590 (altering number, presumably in memory); *In re* Walter, 618 F.2d 758, 770 (CCPA 1980) (recordation of result in magnetic medium). In *Abele* the court ignored a post-solution visual display aspect of the claim.

24. In *Benson* the Court said that the "mathematical formula involved here has no substantial practical application except in connection with a digital computer, which means that . . . the patent would . . . in practical effect be a patent on the algorithm itself." 409 U.S. at 71–72. Presumably, a nominal limitation of this type is still beyond the pale. Benson's claim 8 specifically mentioned that the process was to be carried out in "a reentrant shift register," *see id.* at 73, which is at least as much "a specific piece" of computer hardware as is a ROM.

25. *See Benson*, 409 U.S. at 72. The government's main brief in *Benson* said that "it is highly questionable whether an effective system for the examination of computer

programs can be developed." It gave as reasons "the problems of enormous volume and the economic and personnel constraints faced by the Patent Office" and also pointed to the "difficulties of developing an adequate examination system [that] are inherent in the classification of broad abstract mental processes." Br. for Pet. 32.

The government still appears to perceive this difficulty. A recent study concluded that the published literature does not completely embody software and computer science prior art, much prior art exists only in product form without publication in journals, and "it is virtually impossible to find, let alone count or profile, all software-related or algorithmic patents" because they are not classified and indexed in a way that permits effective search and study. U.S. Cong., Office of Technology Assessment, *Computer Software and Intellectual Property—Background Paper* 9 (1990).

26. *Notice Interpreting In re Iwahashi (Fed. Cir. 1989)*, 1112 Off. Gaz. 16 (Mar. 13, 1990).

27. The language is based on a passage from Application of Walter, 618 F.2d 758, 768 (CCPA 1980):

> If the functionally-defined disclosed means and their equivalents are so broad that they encompass any and every means for performing the recited functions, the apparatus claim is an attempt to exalt form over substance since the claim is really to the method or series of functions itself. . . . In such cases the burden must be placed on the applicant to demonstrate that the claims are truly drawn to specific apparatus distinct from other apparatus capable of performing the identical functions.

But *Walter* does not direct a general shifting of the *onus probandi* to the applicant in algorithm-related cases. It merely states that, *if* the recited means are so broad that they include every way to perform the algorithm-related function, *then* the burden should shift to the applicant to demonstrate that he claims less than all apparatus capable of performing the algorithm-related function. There must be an *if*-clause predicate to invoke the *then*-clause. Where is that predicate here?

28. That appears to be the underlying structure of the present statute. Thus, 35 U.S.C. § 102 begins, "A person shall be entitled to a patent *unless*" specified circumstances exist. The CCPA has observed that "any process [or] machine . . . constitutes statutory subject matter *unless* it falls within a judicially determined exception." *In re* Pardo, 684 F.2d 912, 916 (CCPA 1982).

29. *See* Rule 107(b), 37 C.F.R. § 1.107(b). For example, in this context, the examiner might swear that on the basis of his expert knowledge of the relevant technology he knows that no alternative hardware exists and therefore the entire possible use of the algorithm has been preemptively claimed. The applicant may then controvert the examiner's affidavit. *Id.* My experience and that of many colleagues is that most examiners are rarely (or perhaps never) willing to file Rule 107(b) affidavits.

30. This is based on the same principle that applied in the *Abele* case. You need a CAT scanner to generate a signal for processing in accordance with a CAT scanning algorithm.

31. In a wide variety of contexts, the CCPA and Federal Circuit have held that the burden is on the Office to establish that an applicant is not entitled to a patent, rather than on the applicant to establish entitlement. That is, before the Office can shift any burden of proof to an applicant, the Office must have a prima facie case against patentability. The prima facie case can be made out by actual evidence, authoritative literature, or reasoning from accepted scientific principles.

For example, the burden of proof is on the Office to establish a prima facie case of obviousness. *In re* Carleton, 599 F.2d 1021, 1024 (CCPA 1979); *In re* Warner, 379

P2d 1011, 1017 (CCPA 1967), *cert. denied*, 389 U.S. 1057 (1968) (Office must not resort to speculation or unfounded assumption); *In re* Soli, 317 F.2d 931 (CCPA 1963) (must have some basis in logic or scientific principle; cannot merely allege obviousness and hereby force applicant to prove conclusively that Office is wrong). (How to apply this principle in the case of a chemical having a molecular structure similar to a known chemical has been the subject of a vast amount of litigation. The most recent decision is *In re* Dillion, 919 F.2d 688 (Fed. Cir. 1990).) In the absence of citation of prior art, it must be assumed that the applicant's subject matter is novel. *In re* Boller, 332 F.2d 382, 386 (CCPA 1964).

The Office must establish that the specification is not an enabling disclosure to support a rejection on that ground. *In re* Budnick, 537 F.2d 535, 537 (CCPA 1976); *In re* Mazocchi, 439 F.2d 220, 223–24 (CCPA 1971) (incumbent on Office to explain why it doubts truth or accuracy of specification and to back up assertions with evidence or reasoning). The same is true as to an applicant's allegation of what is the best contemplated mode. *In re* Sichert, 566 F.2d 1154, 1164 (CCPA 1977).

32. U.S. Pat. 4,744,028, on "Methods and apparatus for efficient resource allocation," issued May 1988 to Bell Labs. See *New York Times*, May 12, 1989, p. 1. col. 5 ("Software Industry in Uproar Over Recent Rush of Patients").

33. Bell Labs was the assignee of the patent application in the *Benson* case, as well. It is understood that Bell is deriving revenue from third-party use of the invention.

34. One response to this has been, "Don't worry, it won't happen." *See* Chisum, *The Patentability of Algorithms*, 47 U. Pitt. L. Rev. 959, 1016–17 (1986) ("There is every reason to believe that algorithm patents will be extensively licensed at reasonable royalty rates."). Others may view such statements as on a par with the proverbial, "The check is already in the mail." *See* Newell, *Response: The Models Are Broken! The Models Are Broken!* 47 U. Pitt. L. Rev. 1023, 1033–34 (1986). Perhaps that is what the Supreme Court thought in *Benson* and *Flook*.

Another response, proposed below, might be more noncommittal about whether this will in fact occur. Without predicting what will occur, one may simply take appropriate steps to insure that it does not occur and to calm the apprehensions of those who fear that it will occur.

35. *Contra, Cheney Bros.* v. *Doris Silk Corp.*, 35 F.2d 279 (2d Cir. 1929) (L. Hand, J.), *cert. denied*, 281 U.S. 728 (1930).

36. *Flook*, 437 U.S. at 595–96; *Benson*, 409 U.S. at 73.

37. *See* 28 U.S.C. § 1498 (when Government infringes patent or copyright, no injunction may be granted, but intellectual property owner is entitled to "reasonable and entire compensation.") In the present situation, it might be appropriate to add a proviso so limiting relief only where the party accused of infringement did not unreasonably refuse to pay anything upon demand.

38. For example, see text following *supra* note 2.

39. *Cf. Dillion, supra* note 42, which holds it only prima facie, or rebuttably, obvious to make a chemical whose structure is similar to that of a known chemical with a known utility. If the later-discovered chemical has a valuable property not possessed by the known chemical, or possesses the same utility to an unexpectedly greater degree, the presumption of obviousness to make the later-discovered chemical is rebutted.

40. *See In re* Merck, 800 F.2d 1091 (Fed. Cir. 1986).

▷ **LOTUS DEVELOPMENT CORPORATION
V. PAPERBACK SOFTWARE
INTERNATIONAL AND STEPHENSON
SOFTWARE, LIMITED**

Civ. A. No. 87-76-K.
United States District Court, D. Massachusetts.
June 28, 1990.

Action was brought for infringement of copyright for computer spreadsheet program. The District Court, Keeton, J., held that: (1) menu command structure of the computer program, including choice of command terms, the structure and order of those terms, their presentation on the screen, and the long prompts, was copyrightable; (2) infringement liability was established; and (3) copyright holder was not barred from relief under the doctrines of laches and equitable estoppel.

So ordered.

KEETON, District Judge.

The expression of an idea is copyrightable. The idea itself is not. When applying these two settled rules of law, how can a decisionmaker distinguish between an idea and its expression?

Answering this riddle is the first step—but only the first—toward disposition of this case in which the court must decide, among other issues, (1) whether and to what extent plaintiff's computer spreadsheet program, Lotus 1-2-3, is copyrightable, (2) whether defendants' VP–Planner was, on undisputable facts, an infringing work containing elements substantially similar to copyrightable elements of 1-2-3, and (3) whether defendants' proffered jurisdictional and equitable defenses are meritorious.

The outcome of this case depends on how this court, and higher courts on appeal, should answer a central question about the scope of copyrightability of computer programs. For the reasons explained in this Opinion, I conclude that this question must be resolved in favor of the plaintiff, Lotus.

A BACKGROUND STATEMENT
ABOUT COMPUTERS, COMPUTER PROGRAMS,
AND COPYRIGHTABILITY

Though their influence in our society is already pervasive, digital computers—along with computer "programs" and "user interfaces"—are relatively new to the market, and newer still to litigation over "works" protected by intellectual property law.

This case concerns two competing application programs—Lotus 1-2-3 and VP–Planner—which are primarily spreadsheet programs, but which also support other tasks such as limited database management and graphics creation. Programs such as these, because they can perform several different kinds of tasks, are called "integrated" application programs.

Congress has defined "computer program" as follows:

> A "computer program" is a set of statements or instructions to be used directly or indirectly in a computer in order to bring about a certain result.

> 17 U.S.C. § 101 (1988).

This "set of statements or instructions," in its literal or written manifestation, may be in the form of object code or source code. It may also be represented, in a partially literal manifestation, by a flowchart. A copyrightable work designed for use on a computer may include, as well, text that appears, for example, in a problem manual or a manual of instructions. These elements of text, however, ordinarily are not referred to in the industry as part of a "computer program" unless they appear on the computer screen and serve a purpose like that of the components of a "help screen" available to a user whenever needed. Elements of this textual type are not at issue in this phase of this case.

During the early period of computing, "programmers" ordinarily wrote programs exclusively in machine language. Today, object code is rarely written directly by computer programmers. Rather, modern programmers typically write computer programs in a "higher"-level programming language. These programs are called source programs, or source code. Although "source code" has been defined far more broadly in some of the literature in the field, and in some of the expert testimony in this case, more commonly the term "source code" refers to a computer program written in some programming language—such as FORTRAN (*FOR*mula *TRAN*slation), COBOL (*CO*mmon *B*usiness *O*riented *L*anguage), Pascal, BASIC, or C—that uses complex symbolic names, along with complex rules of syntax.

Unlike machine language, which is unique to each kind of CPU and which is executed directly by the computer, source code programming languages are universal to almost all computers. As a consequence, source code is executed indirectly. Thus, a program written in source code must be translated into the appropriate object code for execution in one type of computer, and into a different object code for execution in another type of computer. A distinctive "interpreter" or "compiler" program is available for each type of source code programming language and each type of CPU.

A partly literal and partly pictorial manifestation of a computer program, still farther removed from direct use with the computer, is the flowchart. A flowchart is a graphic representation of a computer program that is written in symbols, rather than in bits or symbolic names, and with a syntax that is graphic rather than grammatical.

The parties agree, as a general proposition, that literal manifestations of a computer program—including both source code and object code—if original, are copyrightable. Also, it appears that flowcharts, if sufficiently detailed and original, are entitled to copyright protection:

> Flowcharts ... are works of authorship in which copyright subsists, provided they are the product of sufficient intellectual labor to surpass the "insufficient intellectual labor hurdle". . . .

> National Commission on New Technological Uses of Copyrighted Works, *Final Report and Recommendations* 43 (1978) (hereinafter "*Final Report*").

Defendants vigorously dispute, however, the copyrightability of any nonliteral elements of computer programs. That is, defendants assert that only literal manifestations of computer programs are copyrightable. Plaintiff, on the other hand, maintains that copyright protection extends to all elements of computer programs that embody original expression, whether literal or nonliteral, including any original expression embodied in a program's "user interface."

One difficulty with plaintiff's argument is the amorphous nature of "nonliteral" elements of computer programs. Unlike the written code of a program or a flowchart that can be printed on paper, nonliteral elements—including such elements as the overall organization of a program, the structure of a program's command system, and the presentation of information on the screen—may be less tangibly represented. Whether these elements are copyrightable, and if so, how the nonliteral elements that are copyrightable may be identified, are central to deciding this case.

CONSTITUTIONAL CONSTRAINTS

In considering the legal issues relevant to whether nonliteral elements of Lotus 1-2-3 are copyrightable, and if so, to what extent, one may appropriately begin with a provision of the Constitution of the United States:

> The Congress shall have Power . . . To promote the Progress of Science . . . by securing for limited Time to Authors . . . the exclusive Right to their . . . Writings. . . .

> U.S. Const., Art. I, § 8, cl. 8. The copyright law, codified in Title 17 of the United States Code, rests upon this explicit grant of legislative authority.

Under this constitutional mandate, Congress has broad though not unlimited authority to grant copyright monopolies as needed to promote progress. If Congress were to determine, for example, that copyright protection is unnecessary to "promote the Progress of" computer programming—because, for example, in Congress' view the financial incentives alone of developing new computer programs (without the added benefit of copyright) are enough to encourage innovation, or because incremental innovation might be stifled by expansive copyright protection—then Congress could, without offending the Constitution, provide no copyright protection for computer programs. At the other extreme, were Congress to find that strong copyright protection is necessary to promote the progress of computer programming, Congress could provide for expansive copyright protection for all aspects of computer programs, again without having strayed beyond the bounds of the constitutionally permissible.

Because the constitutional grant of power authorizes Congress to take either path—or to chart some middle course—this case does not raise constitutional issues. Rather, the issues at stake here are issues of statutory meaning. The central question is not whether Congress could render nonliteral elements such as those of 1-2-3 copyrightable, but whether it has done so. *Banks* v. *Manchester, Ohio*, 128 U.S. 244, 252, 9 S.Ct. 36, 39, 32 L.Ed. 425 (1888) ("No authority exists for obtaining a copyright beyond the extent to which Congress has authorized it. A copyright cannot be sustained as a right existing at common law; but, as it exists in the United States, it depends wholly on the legislation of Congress.").

THE LEGAL TEST FOR COPYRIGHTABILITY APPLICABLE TO THIS CASE

Functionality, Useful Articles, and the Useful–Expressive Distinction

Defendants suggest that the user interface of Lotus 1-2-3 is a useful, "function[al]" object like the functional layout of gears in an "H" pattern on a standard transmission, the functional assignment of letters to keys on a standard QWERTY keyboard, and the functional configuration of controls on a musical instrument (*e.g.*, keys of a piano). Lewis Affdvt. ¶¶ 52–54. These "functional" "useful articles," defendants contend, are not entitled to copyright protection.

A similar analogy was made in *Synercom* where the court concluded that a sequence of data inputs for a statistical analysis program was like the "figure-H" pattern of a standard transmission. 462 F.Supp. at 1013. *Synercom*, though, was published less than a month after the publication of the CONTU report (which it never cites) and well before the 1980 amendments. Since then, congressional and judicial development of the law of copyrightability of computer programs has advanced considerably, and *Synercom's* central proposition—that the expression of nonliteral sequence and order is inseparable from the idea and accordingly is not copyrightable—has been explicitly rejected by several courts. E.g., *Whelan*, 797 F.2d at 1240, 1248 ("copyright protection of computer programs may extend beyond the programs' literal code to their structure, sequence, and organization"); *Broderbund Software, Inc.* v. *Unison World, Inc.*, 648 F.Supp. 1127, 1133 (N.D.Cal.1986) ("copyright protection is not limited to the literal aspects of a computer program, but rather . . . it extends to the overall structure of a program, including its audiovisual displays"). Moreover, even those courts that have not gone as far as *Whelan* and *Broderbund* have still gone much farther in protecting computer programs than *Synercom*. E.g., *SAS Institute, Inc.* v. *S&H Computer Systems, Inc.*, 605 F.Supp. 816, 830 (M.D.Tenn.1985) ("copying of the organization and structural details" can form basis for infringement); *Manufacturers Technologies, Inc.* v. *CAMS, Inc.*, 706 F.Supp. 984, 993 (D.Conn.1989) ("screen displays or user interface" copyrightable); *Johnson Controls, Inc.* v. *Phoenix Control Systems, Inc.*, 886 F.2d 1173, 1175 (9th Cir.1989) (nonliteral aspects such as "structure, sequence and/or organization of the program, the user interface, and the function, or purpose, of the program," are copyrightable to the extent that they embody expression rather than idea); *Telemarketing Resources* v. *Symantec Corp.*, 12 U.S. P.Q.2d 1991, 1993, 1989 WL 200350 (N.D.Cal.1989) (holding that "[c]opyright protection applies to the user interface, or overall structure and organization of a computer program, including its audiovisual displays, or screen 'look and feel,' " but finding no infringement in this case); *Q–Co. Industries* v. *Hoffman*, 625 F.Supp. 608, 615–16 (S.D.N.Y.1985) (similarity of "structure and arrangement" can form basis of infringement suit, but here, structural similarities were dictated by functional considerations and hence were non-copyrightable ideas rather than copyrightable expression); *Pearl Systems, Inc.* v. *Competition Electronics, Inc.*, 8 U.S.P.Q.2d 1520, 1524, 1988 WL 146047 (S.D.Fla.1988) ("Copyright protection of computer software is not limited to the text of the source or object code"). *But see Softklone*, 659 F.Supp. at 455, 465 (rejecting *Broderbund's* conclusion that audiovisual screen displays are copyrightable, although holding that separate copyright on status screen display was infringed where "total concept and feel" was copied); *Plains*

Cotton Cooperative Association v. *Goodpasture Computer Service, Inc.*, 807 F.2d 1256, 1262 (rejecting *Whelan's* protection for structure, sequence, and organization, court instead held that sequence and organization, where dictated by market forces, is non-copyrightable idea rather than copyrightable expression), *reh'g denied*, 813 F.2d 407 (5th Cir.), *cert. denied*, 484 U.S. 821, 108 S.Ct. 80, 98 L.Ed.2d 42 (1987). In any event, *Synercom's* input formats are quite different from, and distinguishable from, the nonliteral aspects of 1-2-3 at issue in this case.

Defendant's proposed analogy is also similar to the analogy drawn by Commissioner Hersey between a computer program and an object that is designated to do work—for example, the cam of a drill. CONTU, *Final Report* at 58–60 (Hersey, C., dissenting). His view, however, was in dissent, and not a view advanced by CONTU. Because Congress adopted CONTU's recommendations practically verbatim, it is reasonable to infer that Congress did not adopt Commissioner Hersey's view.

Moreover, I conclude that defendants' contentions, to the extent they are similar to *Synercom's* central proposition and to Commissioner Hersey's views in dissent, are inconsistent with the legislative history and statutory mandates explained above. If, in a context such as that of *Synercom* or of this case, an idea and its expression were taken to be inseparable and the expression therefore not copyrightable, copyright law never would, as a practical matter, provide computer programs with protection as substantial as Congress has mandated—protection designed to extend to original elements of expression however embodied. I credit the testimony of expert witnesses that the bulk of the creative work is in the conceptualization of a computer program and its user interface, rather than in its encoding, and that creating a suitable user interface is a more difficult intellectual task, requiring greater creativity, originality, and insight, than converting the user interface design into instructions to the machine. Defendants' contentions would attribute to the statute a purpose to protect only a narrowly defined segment of the creative development of computer programs, and to preclude from protection even more significant creative elements of the process. Such a result is fundamentally inconsistent with the statutory mandates.

Also, defendants' contention would have the additional consequence that computer programmers would have little, if any, more protection for nonliteral elements of expression embodied in their original works of authorship than is already provided by trade secret law. If the intellectual effort and creativity embodied in a user interface were protectable only by trade secret law, the length of protection for computer programs would be very short—merely the time it takes to examine a program and then duplicate the nonliteral elements in a newly written computer program. This short period of protection is fundamentally inconsistent with the mandates of the copyright law.

It may be quite true, with respect to "useful articles"—indeed I believe it to be so—that their utilitarian aspects are not copyrightable, and that things that *merely* utter work, such as the cam of a drill, are not copyrightable. It is not true, however, that every aspect of a user interface that is "useful" is therefore not copyrightable. For example, Lotus 1-2-3 is surely "useful." It does not follow that when an intellectual work achieves the feat of being useful as well as expressive and original, the moment of creative triumph is also a moment of devastating financial loss—because the triumph destroys copyrightability of all expressive elements that would have been protected if only they had not contributed so much to the public interest by helping to make some article useful.

Defendants' contention misses this point by proceeding on an erroneous assumption about the role of "functionality" in copyright law. It is true that "function-ality" of an article does not itself support copyrightability. Thus, it never strengthens a claim for copyright to show that the "work" for which copyright protection is claimed is useful. A congressional mandate that "proof that an intellectual work is a 'useful article' does not support the author's claim for copyright" is not, however, a mandate that "if one who copied the author's work proves that the work was 'useful' or 'functional,' the author loses *all* copyright protection." Transforming a mandate that "proof of usefulness *does not strengthen* a copyright claim" to a mandate that "proof of usefulness *destroys* a copyright claim" is, to say the least, a remarkable intellectual leap. Defendants have not advanced such a proposition explicitly. But this is in fact an implicit premise of their contention—or a consequence of it, if one takes a hindsight view of having applied their proposed rule in decisionmaking. In effect, their proposed rule would work this way: Anything that is useful is a "useful article"; nothing about a "useful article" is ever copyrightable; because 1-2-3 is useful, and is an article, it is not copyrightable.

A more sensible interpretation of the statutory mandate is that the mere fact that an intellectual work is useful or functional—be it a dictionary, directory, map, book of meaningless code words, or computer program—does not mean that none of the elements of the work can be copyrightable. Also, the statute does not bar copy-rightability merely because the originality of the expression becomes associated, in the marketplace, with usefulness of the work to a degree and in dimensions not pre-viously achieved by other products on the market. *Brandir International, Inc. v. Cas-cade Pacific Lumber Co.*, 834 F.2d 1142, 1147 (2d Cir.1987) ("[A] copyrighted work ... does not lose its protected status merely because it subsequently is put to func-tional use."); *NEC Corp. v. Intel Corp.*, 645 F.Supp. 590, 595 (N.D.Cal. 1986) ("func-tion performed by defendant's microprograms ... does not affect their status as copy-rightable subject matter), *vacated on grounds of judge's recusal, see* 835 F.2d 1546 (9th Cir.1988). To hold otherwise would be to deny copyright protection to the most original and least obvious products of the creative mind merely because the market-place accepts them as distinctively "functional." Such a rule would grant copyright protection for only those products that fall far short of being the best available. Rather than promoting and encouraging both the development and disclosure of the best, such a rule would offer incentives to market only the second, or third, or tenth best, and hold back the best for fear that it is too good for copyrightability. Copyrighta-bility is not a synonym for imperfection.

Accordingly, I conclude that a court, in determining whether a particular ele-ment is copyrightable, must not allow one statutory mandate—that functionality or usefulness is not itself a basis for copyrightability—to absorb and destroy another statutory mandate—that elements of expression are copyrightable. Elements of expression, even if embodied in useful articles, are copyrightable if capable of iden-tification and recognition independently of the functional ideas that make the article useful. This mandate may be viewed as a corollary of the central distinction of copy-right law between idea and expression, which is explored further immediately below.

The Idea–Expression Riddle: Four Additional Concepts

It is by now plain that an idea is not copyrightable and an expression may be. It does not follow, though, that every expression of an idea is copyrightable. To begin to get an understanding of the legally significant contrasts among an idea, noncopyrightable expressions of the idea, and a copyrightable expression, we must take account of four more concepts.

Earlier parts of this Opinion refer to two of these four—"originality" and "functionality." The expression of an idea is copyrightable only if it is original—that is, if the expression originated with the author. 17 U.S.C. § 102(a); *see* Part III(A)(2)(b), *supra*. Even then the expression of the idea is not copyrightable if the expression does no more than embody elements of the idea that are functional in the utilitarian sense. 17 U.S.C. § 102(b); *see* Part IV(A) *supra*.

The third concept is "obviousness." When a particular expression goes no farther than the obvious, it is inseparable from the idea itself. Protecting an expression of this limited kind would effectively amount to protection of the idea, a result inconsistent with the plain meaning of the statute. *E.H. Tate Co.* v. *Jiffy Enterprises, Inc.*, 16 F.R.D. 571, 573 (E.D.Pa.1954) (small sketch and accompanying instruction "Apply hook to wall" so obvious that it is not entitled to copyright protection).

It is only a slight extension of the idea of "obviousness"—and one supported by precedent—to reach the fourth concept: "merger." If a particular expression is one of a quite limited number of the possible ways of expressing an idea, then, under this fourth concept, the expression is not copyrightable:

> When the uncopyrightable subject matter is very narrow, so that "the topic necessarily requires," if not only one form of expression, at best only a limited number, to permit copyrighting would mean that a party or parties, by copyrighting a mere handful of forms, could exhaust all possibility of future use of the substance. In such circumstances it does not seem accurate to say that any particular form of expression comes from the subject matter. However, it is necessary to say that the subject matter would be appropriated by permitting the copyrighting of its expression. We cannot recognize copyright as a game of chess in which the public can be checkmated.
>
> *Morrissey* v. *Procter & Gamble Co.*, 379 F.2d 675, 678–79 (1st Cir.1967)
> (citations omitted).

See also Concrete Machinery Co. v. *Classic Lawn Ornaments, Inc.*, 843 F.2d 600, 606 (1st Cir.1988) ("When there is essentially only one way to express an idea, the idea and its expression are inseparable and copyright is no bar to copying that expression."); *Herbert Rosenthal Jewelry Corp.* v. *Kalpakian*, 446 F.2d 738, 742 (9th Cir.1971) (idea of a jewel-encrusted life-like bee pin inseparable from expression; thus expression not copyrightable because "protecting the 'expression' in such circumstances would confer a monopoly of the 'idea' upon the copyright owner"). *Cf. Atari, Inc.* v. *North American Philips Consumer Electronics Corp.*, 672 F.2d 607, 616 (7th Cir.), *cert. denied*, 459 U.S. 880, 103 S.Ct. 176, 74 L.Ed.2d 145 (1982) (*scènes à faire* of literary works—"stock literary devices" such as "incidents, characters or settings which are as a practical matter indispensable, or at least standard, in the treatment of a given topic"—"are not protectible [sic] by copyright"); *Landsberg* v. *Scrabble Crossword Game Players, Inc.*, 736 F.2d 485, 489 (9th Cir.) (*scènes à faire* not copyrightable because granting a copyright "would give the first author a monopoly on the commonplace ideas behind the *scènes à faire*"), *cert. denied*, 469 U.S. 1037, 105 S.Ct. 513, 83 L.Ed.2d 403 (1984).

If, however, the expression of an idea has elements that go beyond all functional elements of the idea itself, and beyond the obvious, and if there are numerous other ways of expressing the non-copyrightable idea, then those elements of expression, if original and substantial, are copyrightable.

Elements of the Legal Test for Copyrightability

A "legal test," as I use the phrase here, is a statement of the elements of fact, or law, or both fact and law, that must be addressed by a decisionmaker to decide a question potentially decisive of some claim or defense. "Copyrightability" of nonliteral elements of Lotus 1-2-3 is essential to the claim of the plaintiff in this case.

As already noted, the legal test for deciding copyrightability, in a factual context such as is presented here, has not been precisely defined either in the copyright statute or in precedents interpreting and applying it. Nevertheless, the statute and the precedents contain many mandates—"markers" of the borderline between copyrightability and non-copyrightability—that narrow the scope of the questions remaining to be answered to determine what test to apply.

Drawing into one statement the fundamental truths about ideas and their expression that were sketched above, one may accurately say that the issue of copyrightability of a "work" turns not on whether the work expresses ideas but instead on whether, in addition to expressing one or more ideas, in some material respect it does more, and in an original way. One need not totally disentangle the idea from its expression in order to conclude that a particular aspect is expression. Indeed, to speak as if it were ever possible completely to disentangle an idea from an expression of that idea is to speak abstract fiction rather than real-life fact. Disentanglement, then, is not an "either-or," "0–1," "negative-positive," or "binary" matter. It is, instead, a matter of degree.

Still, even if the "idea" cannot be completely disentangled from its expression, to determine what is copyrightable a decisionmaker must understand the meaning of "idea" within the idea-expression distinction. To do so one must take note also of another distinction—one between generality and specificity of conceptualizing the idea. Thus, a statement of the most significant elements of the legal test for copyrightability, consistent with precedents, begins:

> FIRST, in making the determination of "copyrightability," the decisionmaker must focus upon alternatives that counsel may suggest, or the court may conceive, *along the scale from the most generalized conception to the most particularized*, and choose some formulation—some conception or definition of the "idea"—for the purpose of distinguishing between the idea and its expression.

As Learned Hand recognized in a 1930 case concerning the alleged infringement of the copyright of a play:

> Upon any work, and especially upon a play, a great number of patterns of increasing generality will fit equally well, as more and more of the incident is left out. The last may perhaps be no more than the most general statement of what the play is about, and at times might consist only of its title; but there is a point in this series of abstractions where they are no longer protected, since otherwise the playwright could prevent the use of his "ideas," to which, apart from their expression, his property is never extended. Nobody has ever been able to fix that boundary, and nobody ever can.
>
> *Nichols*, 45 F.2d at 121 (citations omitted). *See also Shipman* v. *R.K.O. Radio Pictures*, 100 F.2d 533, 538 (2d Cir. 1938) (L. Hand, J., concurring) ("*Nichols* . . . held that there is a point where the similarities are so little concrete (and therefore so abstract) that they become only 'theme', 'idea', or skeleton of the plot, and that these are always in the public domain; no copyright can protect them. The test is necessarily vague and nothing more definite can be said about it.")

Thirty more years of experience in judging did not change Learned Hand's view: "Obviously, no principle can be stated as to when an imitator has gone beyond copying the 'idea,' and has borrowed its 'expression.' Decisions must therefore inevitably be ad hoc." *Peter Pan Fabrics, Inc.* v. *Martin Weiner Corp.*, 274 F.2d 487, 489 (2d Cir. 1960) (L. Hand, J.). In another context, Hand described such "ad hoc" decisionmaking as "fiat." *Sinram* v. *Pennsylvania Railroad Co.*, 61 F.2d 767, 771 (2d Cir. 1932) (L. Hand, J.). In whatever way this kind of decisionmaking may be described, Hand offered us no formula for distinguishing between idea and expression like that he devised for the calculus of reasonable care in *United States* v. *Carroll Touring Co.*, 159 F.2d 169, 173 (L. Hand, J.) (articulating the "BPL" formula), *reh'g denied*, 160 F.2d 482 (2d Cir. 1947). It seems the better part of wisdom, if not valor, not to press the search for a suitable brightline test of copyrightability where Learned Hand, even after decades of experience in judging, found none.

For all these reasons, as a practical necessity, whether explicitly or only implicitly, courts apply an abstractions scale in determining copyrightability. In doing so they make a decision involving choice and judgment of a type that human minds make regularly in daily affairs, but computers of the current state of the art cannot make.[1] Still, though "judgment" is required and the answer to be given is not precisely "calculable," analogies to arithmetic calculations and to "scales of justice" may aid the human mind in choosing and "weighing" factors that properly go into the metaphoric calculus.

In summary, one among the principal elements to be weighed in determining copyrightability when the idea-expression distinction applies is to conceive and define the idea in a way that places it somewhere along the scale of abstraction (somewhere between the most abstract and the most specific of all possible conceptions). Illustrations from the evidence in this case will help to explain in a more concrete way this element of the legal test for copyrightability. *See* Part V(C), *infra*. Before turning to those illustrations, however, I state in a similarly abstract way, to be explained later by illustrations, two more elements that I conclude a decisionmaker must consider to determine copyrightability of a computer program like that at issue in this case.

In addition to taking account of the distinction between generality and specificity, to make use of Hand's abstraction scale for applying the idea-expression distinction we need to identify and distinguish between essential and nonessential details of expressing the idea. Some, but of course not all, details, are so essential that their omission would result in a failure to express *that* idea, or in the expression of only a different and *more general* idea. Accordingly, two more elements in the legal test for copyrightability are:

> **Second**, the decisionmaker must focus upon whether an alleged expression of the idea is limited to elements essential to expression of *that* idea (or is one of only a few ways of expressing the idea) or instead includes identifiable elements of expression not essential to every expression of that idea.
>
> **Third**, having identified elements of expression not essential to every expression of the idea, the decisionmaker must focus on whether those elements are a substantial part of the allegedly copyrightable "work."

In addressing this third element of the test for copyrightability, the decisionmaker is measuring "substantiality" not merely on a quantum scale but by a test that is qualitative as well. *SAS Institute*, 605 F.Supp. at 829–30 ("the piracy of even a quantitatively small fragment ('a rose by any other name would smell as sweet') may be qualitatively substantial").

By its nature, a legal test that requires weighing of factors or elements such as these is not a bright-line or an either-or test. It requires of the decisionmaker, instead, an evaluative or "judgmental" weighing of all relevant characteristics of the work in which a copyright is claimed, all relevant characteristics of the allegedly infringing work, and all of the relevant circumstances of their development and use. It requires, also, not a step-by-step decisionmaking process, but a simultaneous weighing of all the factors or elements that the legal test identifies as relevant. I do not suggest that the three elements identified here are an all-inclusive list. They do appear, however, to be the principal factors relevant to decision of copyrightability of a computer program such as Lotus 1-2-3.

If the decisionmaker, weighing the relevant factors, determines that the legal test applying the idea-expression distinction is satisfied, copyrightability is established. Issues may remain, of course, as to whether a copyright was perfected and whether the alleged infringing work, measured by the "substantial similarity" test, did contain elements that infringed upon the copyrightable elements that infringed upon the copyrightable elements of the copyrighted "work." Also, issues may remain as to whether damages have been proved, or whether the controversy over infringement is instead " 'a trivial pother,' a mere point of honor, of scarcely more than irritation, involving no substantial interest," *Fred Fisher, Inc.* v. *Dillingham*, 298 F. 145, 152 (S.D.N.Y.1924) (L. Hand, J.) (citations omitted), for which only statutory damages should be awarded. 17 U.S.C. § 504(c) (1988).

APPLICATION OF THE LEGAL TEST TO LOTUS 1-2-3

"Look and Feel"

In musical, dramatic, and motion picture works, and works of literature, nonliteral elements that are copyrightable have sometimes been described as the "total concept and feel" of a work, "the fundamental essence or structure" of a work, or "the 'pattern' of the work". In the context of computer programs, nonliteral elements have often been referred to as the "look and feel" of a program. Initially, plaintiff too referred to these elements as "look and feel," though plaintiff—in trial, at least—has not rested its contentions primarily on this terminology.

Despite its widespread use in public discourse on the copyrightability of nonliteral elements of computer programs, I have not found the "look and feel" concept, standing alone, to be significantly helpful in distinguishing between nonliteral elements of a computer program that are copyrightable and those that are not.

One may argue that the phrase "look and feel" is analogous to the "total concept and feel" test developed in *Roth Greeting Cards*, 429 F.2d at 1110, and used in *Krofft Television*, 562 F.2d at 1167. In these cases, however, the "total concept and feel" test, was not invoked—at least, not explicitly—as an aid to the court in determining which nonliteral elements were copyrightable and why. Rather, these courts used the concept, not in determining copyrightability, but, apparently assuming copyrightability, in applying the substantial similarity test to determine whether forbidden copying had occurred. For example, in *Roth Greeting Cards*, the court considered whether the "text, arrangement of text, art work, and association between art work and text" of defendant's greeting cards were substantially similar to (e.g., copied the "total concept and feel" of) those elements of plaintiff's greeting cards. 429 F.2d at

1109. And in *Krofft Television*, the inquiry focused on whether defendant McDonald's, with its television commercials, copied the "total concept and feel" of plaintiff's H.R. Pufnstuf children's television series by copying its locale (both occurred in imaginary world with similar trees, caves, a pond, a road and a castle), fictional characters (both were inhabited by talking trees, mayors with disproportionately large round heads and long wide mouths, "Keystone cops" characters, crazy scientists, and a multi-armed evil creature), costumes and sets (created for defendant by former employees of plaintiff), voices (executed for defendant by same voice expert who did the voices for plaintiff's television series), and plot.

It may be true that the issues of copyrightability and substantial similarity are so interrelated that these precedents are relevant. The fact remains that they are not directly in point for determining copyrightability in this case. Moreover, "look and feel" is a conclusion, and the usefulness and applicability of a precedent depends on the *reasons* the conclusion was reached in a particular context, not on the *conclusion* itself. Thus, in trying to understand the relevance of "concept and feel" precedents, we need to look to details of those cases that appear to have been relied upon in reaching the conclusion, rather than merely embracing the conclusion without regard for underlying reasons. As we probe the circumstances of these precedents that closely, we are likely to do something akin to applying the three-element test described above.

Elements of the User Interface as Expression

Applying to 1-2-3 the legal test stated in Part IV(C), *supra*, I consider first where along the scale of abstraction to conceive the "idea" for the purpose of distinguishing between the idea and its expression.

At the most general level of Hand's abstractions scale, *Nichols*, 45 F.2d at 121—the computer programs at issue in this case, and other computer programs that have been considered during the course of trial, are expressions of the idea of a computer program for an electronic spreadsheet. Defendants are quite correct, then, in asserting that the idea of developing an electronic spreadsheet is not copyrightable—that the core idea of such a spreadsheet is both functional and obvious, even to computer users who claim no technical competence. Thus, even though programs like VisiCalc, 1-2-3, Multiplan, SuperCalc4, and Excel are very different in their structure, appearance, and method of operation, each is, at the most basic level, just a different way of expressing the same idea: the electronic spreadsheet. It does not follow, however, that every possible method of designing a metaphorical spreadsheet is obvious, or that no form of expressing the idea of the spreadsheet metaphor can possibly have such originality in pressing beyond the obvious as is required for copyrightability, or that no special form of metaphorical spreadsheet can possibly be a distinctive expression of a particular method of preparing financial information.

The idea for a two-line moving cursor menu is also functional and obvious, and, indeed, is used in a wide variety of computer programs including spreadsheet programs. Nevertheless, it does not follow that every possible method of designing a menu system that includes a two-line moving cursor is non-copyrightable.

Of course, if a particular expression of the idea of an electronic spreadsheet communicates no details beyond those essential to stating the idea itself, then that expression would not be copyrightable. The issue here is whether Lotus 1-2-3 does go beyond those details essential to any expression of the idea, and includes substantial elements of expression, distinctive and original, which are thus copyrightable.

The idea for an electronic spreadsheet was first rendered into commercial practice by Daniel Bricklin. As a student at Harvard Business School in the late 1970s, Bricklin envisioned a "magic blackboard" that would recalculate numbers automatically as changes were made in other parts of the spreadsheet. Eventually, aided by others, he transformed this idea into VisiCalc, the first commercial electronic spreadsheet. *See* Bricklin Affdvt. ¶¶ 48–96 (Docket No. 217). Bricklin's idea for VisiCalc was a revolutionary advance in the field of computer programming. Dauphinais Affdvt. ¶ 98 (Docket No. 280).

Although VisiCalc was a commercial success, implementational characteristics limited the scope and duration of its marketability as a spreadsheet product. Most notably, VisiCalc was originally programmed for use on the Apple II computer, which had limited memory (32K of RAM), limited screen display capabilities (only 40 characters per line), and limited keys available on the keyboard (no function keys and no up and down cursor keys). When VisiCalc was later rewritten for use on the IBM PC (which was introduced in August 1981), it was transferred with minimal changes and without taking advantage of many of the PC's more extensive capabilities.

Mitchell Kapor and Jonathan Sachs, the original authors of 1-2-3, exploited this opportunity. Building on Bricklin's revolutionary idea for an electronic spreadsheet, Kapor and Sachs expressed that idea in a different, more powerful way. 1-2-3 took advantage of the IBM PC's more expansive memory and more versatile screen display capabilities and keyboard. 1-2-3, like many electronic spreadsheet programs since, could thus be thought of as an evolutionary product that was built upon the shoulders of VisiCalc.

Just as 1-2-3 expressed the idea of an electronic spreadsheet differently from VisiCalc, so did Microsoft's Excel. Originally written for the Apple Macintosh computer, it exploits the enhanced graphics capabilities of the Macintosh, as well as the mouse input device that is standard with the Macintosh. Excel has pull-down bar menus rather than a two-line moving-cursor menu, and a very different menu-command hierarchy. Tr. Ex. 79.

As already noted, these three products—VisiCalc, 1-2-3, and Excel—share the general idea of an electronic spreadsheet but have expressed the idea in substantially different ways. These products also share some elements, however, at a somewhat more detailed or specific point along the abstractions scale. One element shared by these and many other programs is the basic spreadsheet screen display that resembles a rotated "L." Although Excel uses a different basic spreadsheet screen display that more closely resembles a paper spreadsheet, there is a rather low limit, as a factual matter, on the number of ways of making a computer screen resemble a spreadsheet. Accordingly, this aspect of electronic spreadsheet computer programs, if not present in every expression of such a program, is present in most expressions. Thus the second element of the legal test weighs heavily against treating the rotated "L" screen display as a copyrightable element of a computer program. *Morrissey*, 379 F.2d at 678–79.

Another expressive element that merges with the idea of an electronic spreadsheet—that is, that is an essential detail present in most if not all expressions of an electronic spreadsheet—is the designation of a particular key that, when pressed, will invoke the menu command system. The number of keys available for this designation is limited for two reasons. First, because most of the keys on the keyboard relate either to values (*e.g.*, the number keys and mathematical operation keys) or labels (*e.g.*, the letter keys), only a few keys are left that can be used, as a practical matter, to invoke the menu command system. Without something more, the programmed computer would interpret the activation of one of these keys as an attempt by the user to enter a value or label into a cell. Second, because users need to invoke the command system frequently, the key designated for this purpose must be easily accessible. For example, the user should not be required to press two keys at the same time (such as "Shift," "Alt," or "Ctrl" along with another key).

As just noted, when all the letter, number, and arithmetic keys are eliminated from consideration, the number of keys remaining that could be used to invoke the menu command system is quite limited. They include the slash key ("/") and the semi-colon key (";"). The choice of the creators of VisiCalc to designate the slash ("/") key to invoke the menu command system is not surprising. It is one of very few practical options. Thus the second element of the legal test weighs heavily against copyrightability of this aspect of VisiCalc—and of 1-2-3. This expression merges with the idea of having a readily available method of invoking the menu command system.

Other elements of expression a decisionmaker may regard as either essential to every expression of an electronic spreadsheet, or at least "obvious" if not essential, include the use of the "+" key to indicate addition, the "−" key to indicate subtraction, the "*" key to indicate multiplication, the "/" key within formulas to indicate division, and the "enter" key to place keystroke entries into the cells. *See* Dauphinais Affidavit, ¶ 78.

Each of the elements just described is present in, if not all, at least most expressions of an electronic spreadsheet computer program. Other aspects of these programs, however, need not be present in every expression of an electronic spreadsheet. An example of distinctive details of expression is the precise "structure, sequence, and organization," *Whelan*, 797 F.2d at 1248, of the menu command system.

Consider first the menu command system of VisiCalc. The main menu command line reads: "Command: BCDEFGIMPRSTVW−". *See* Appendix 1. Each of these letters (or, to use defendants' experts' preferred terminology, "symbolic tokens") stands for a different command—in this case: Blank, Clear, Delete, Edit, Format, Global, Insert, Move, Print, Replicate, Storage, Titles, Version Number, Window, and "−" for "Label Repeating." Many of these commands invoke submenus which also contain a series of letters, each of which represents a submenu command choice. *See* VisiCalc Command Structure Chart (Tr. Ex. 140, pp. 3–3 and 3–4).

This particular expression of a menu structure is not essential to the electronic spreadsheet idea, nor does it merge with the somewhat less abstract idea of a menu structure for an electronic spreadsheet. The idea of a menu structure—including the overall structure, the order of commands in each menu line, the choice of letters, words, or "symbolic tokens" to represent each command, the presentation of these symbolic tokens on the screen (*i.e.*, first letter only, abbreviations, full words, full words with one or more letters capitalized or underlined), the type of menu system used (*i.e.*, one-, two-, or three-line moving-cursor menus, pull-down menus, or command-driven interfaces), and the long prompts—could be expressed in a great many if not literally unlimited number of ways.

The fact that some of these specific command terms are quite obvious or merge with the idea of such a particular command term does not preclude copyrightability for the command structure taken as a whole. If particular characteristics not distinctive individually have been brought together in a way that makes the "whole" a distinctive expression of an idea—one of many possible ways of expressing it—then the 'whole" may be copyrightable. The statutory provisions regarding "compilation," 17 U.S.C. §§ 101, 103, are not essential to this conclusion, but do reinforce it. A different total structure may be developed even from individual components that are quite similar and limited in number. To determine copyrightability, a court need not—and, indeed, should not—dissect every element of the allegedly protected work. Rather, the court need only identify those elements that are copyrightable, and then determine whether those elements, *considered as a whole*, have been impermissibly copied. *Atari Games Corp. v. Oman*, 888 F.2d 878, 882–83 (D.C.Cir.1989) (rejecting "component-by-component analysis," and ruling instead that focus must ultimately be on 'work as a whole").

It is plain that plaintiff did not impermissibly copy copyrighted elements of VisiCalc. Lotus 1-2-3 uses a very different menu structure. In contrast with VisiCalc's one-line main menu that reads "Command: BCDEFGIMPRSTVW–", the main menu of Lotus 1-2-3, which uses a two-line moving-cursor menu system, reads: "Worksheet Range Copy Move File Graph Data Quit". Most of the submenus similarly present a list of up to about ten full-word menu choices, presented in order of predicted frequency of use rather than alphabetically. Other spreadsheet programs have also expressed their command structures in completely different ways.

I conclude that a menu command structure is capable of being expressed in many if not an unlimited number of ways, and that the command structure of 1-2-3 is an original and nonobvious way of expressing a command structure. Emery Decl. ¶ 15. Accordingly, the menu structure, taken as a whole—including the choice of command terms, the structure and order of those terms, their presentation on the screen, and the long prompts—is an aspect of 1-2-3 that is not present in every expression of an electronic spreadsheet. It meets the requirements of the second element of the legal test for copyrightability.

Finally, I consider the third element of the legal test—whether the structure, sequence, and organization of the menu command system is a substantial part of the alleged copyrighted work—here Lotus 1-2-3. That the answer to this question is "yes" is incontrovertible. The user interface of 1-2-3 is its most unique element, and is the aspect that has made 1-2-3 so popular. That defendants went to such trouble to copy that element is a testament to its substantiality. Accordingly, evaluation of the third element of the legal test weighs heavily in favor of Lotus.

Taking account of all three elements of the legal test, I determine that copyrightability of the user interface of 1-2-3 is established.

COPYING OF LOTUS 1-2-3

As noted at the beginning of this Opinion, the parties' stipulation regulating this first phase of trial reserved for a later, jury phase, any issues of fact requiring jury determination with respect to any alleged copying of Lotus 1-2-3. If in this first phase the court had rejected Lotus' claim of copyrightability of nonliteral elements of the user interface, a jury phase would plainly have been required under that stipulation to determine whether any copying of source code or object code had occurred. Because, however, the court has decided instead that Lotus prevails on this issue, the court must next consider whether any issue remains that must be submitted to a jury before the court considers whether defendants are liable for infringement of Lotus' copyright in 1-2-3.

For the reasons stated below, the answer to that inquiry must be "no." Not only is the copying in this case so "overwhelming and pervasive" as to preclude, as a matter of law, any assertion of independent creation, *see Midway Manufacturing Co.* v. *Bandai–America, Inc.*, 546 F.Supp. 125, 141 n. 11, 149 (D.N.J.1982) ("overwhelming and pervasive" copying can preclude, as a matter of law, finding of independent creation, and can support grant of summary judgment for plaintiff, but such virtual identity not shown in this case), but also, defendants in this case have *admitted* that they copied these elements of protected expression.

Dr. James Stephenson, founder of defendant Stephenson Software, is the original developer of the program that was eventually released as VP–Planner. Like Kapor and Sacks, Stephenson recognized that VisiCalc, although a "pioneering spreadsheet approach," Stephenson Affdvt. ¶ 19 (Docket No. 287), was not sufficient to meet the financial planning needs of some companies and did not take advantage of technological advances in computer hardware. Accordingly, in January 1982, Stephenson began to develop his own electronic spreadsheet that he referred to as FIPS ("Financial Information and Planning System"). *See id.* at ¶¶ 13–59.

By January 1983, Stephenson had developed much of the user interface for his spreadsheet program including the menu command hierarchy. *See* Tr. Ex. 1014. By April 1983, Stephenson installed at his client's business an operational version of his spreadsheet program, which had substantially the same menu hierarchy as the January 1983 version. That hierarchy is differently expressed from the hierarchy of both VisiCalc and 1-2-3. *See* Tr. Ex. 1019; Stephenson Affdvt. ¶¶ 56–60.

Stephenson first saw 1-2-3 in operation in February 1983, after he had developed the menu hierarchy for FIPS. Throughout the rest of that year, he continued to improve FIPS, changed its name to VP–Planner, and began to consider marketing his program. By December 1983, Stephenson entered into a letter of intent with Adam Osborne regarding publication of VP–Planner. Osborne thereafter organized defendant Paperback Software. Stephenson Affdvt. ¶¶ 66–82.

Throughout 1984, defendants continued to improve VP–Planner. In the autumn, they recognized the success of 1-2-3 and reached the conclusion that spawned this litigation: VP–Planner, in order to be a commercial success, would have to be "compatible" with 1-2-3. "The only way to accomplish this result," defendants believed, "was to ensure that *the arrangement and names of commands and menus in VP–Planner conformed to that of Lotus 1-2-3.*" *Id.* at ¶ 117 (emphasis added). *See generally id.* at ¶¶ 99–130. Such compatibility would allow users to transfer spreadsheets created in 1-2-3 to VP–Planner without loss of functionality for any macros in the spreadsheet. Also, such compatibility would allow users to switch from 1-2-3 to VP–Planner without requiring retraining in the operation of VP–Planner.

To some degree at least, defendants' premises have proved incorrect in hindsight. That is, first, as Excel has proved, a spreadsheet program did not have to be exactly compatible with 1-2-3 in order to be a commercial success. Second, copying the menu structure was not the *only* way to achieve aspects of this desired compatibility. For example, defendants could have instead added a macro conversion capability as the creators of Excel have successfully done (the Microsoft Excel Macro Translation Assistant), and could have provided an on-line help function that would show users the VP–Planner equivalent for 1-2-3 commands. *See Excel Reference Guide* at 491, 425–26 (Tr. Ex. 79). *See also* Morgan Decl. ¶¶ 3–7 (Docket No. 308) (Lotus itself created a "macro conversion utility" to translate macros among different-language editions of 1-2-3 (*e.g.*, North American, international English, French, German, Italian, Spanish, and Swedish)); Turner Decl. ¶ 10 (Docket No. 309). These points do not weigh significantly in the present decision, however, because even if

VP–Planner otherwise would have been a commercial failure, and even if no other technological ways of achieving macro and menu compatibility existed, the desire to achieve "compatibility" or "standardization" cannot override the rights of authors to a limited monopoly in the expression embodied in their intellectual "work."

Defendants admit that, once these fateful decisions were made by Stephenson and Osborne, defendants converted VP–Planner into a program more like 1-2-3— indeed, a program that they have publicly advertised as a "workalike for 1-2-3." *VP Planner* Manual 1.11 (1985) (Tr. Ex. 9). It is incontrovertible that, in the process, they copied the expressive elements of 1-2-3 that the court has concluded are copyrightable:

> [M]aking the changes required for macro compatibility meant that we had to revise existing elements of the [VP–Planner] spreadsheet interface, including the hierarchical menu structure; ensure that keystroke sequences would bring about the same operational result in both programs; add certain functional elements found in Lotus 1-2-3 which VP–Planner did not yet support; and discard certain features which, although beneficial, were inconsistent with the macro compatibility requirement. . . .
>
> Several types of changes were required in the VP–Planner program to achieve keystroke macro compatibility. First, the menu structure had to be altered so that all menu commands would have the same first letter and be in the same location in the menu hierarchy as in Lotus 1-2-3.

Stephenson Affdvt. ¶¶ 144, 146. See generally id. at ¶¶ 142–157.

After these changes were made, the VP–Planner manual could truthfully declare:

> VP–Planner is designed to work like Lotus, 1-2-3, keystroke for keystroke. . . . VP–Planner's worksheet is a feature-for-feature workalike for 1-2-3. It does macros. It has the same command tree. It allows the same kind of calculations, the same kind of numerical information. Everything 1-2-3 does, VP–Planner does.

VP–Planner Manual at xi, 1.11.

The court's comparison of the 1-2-3 menu command hierarchy and the VP–Planner menu hierarchy confirms that VP–Planner "has the same command tree" as 1-2-3—that is, that defendants copied the expression embodied in the 1-2-3 menu hierarchy. It is true that there are some differences between 1-2-3's menu structure and VP–Planner's menu structure. For example, most VP–Planner menu lines begin with a help ("?") command, and some additional commands are included at the end of some menu lines (*i.e.*, "DBase, Multidimensional" on the "/File Erase" menu line; and "Page #, No Page #, Row/Col. #, Stop Row/Col. #, Background" on the "/Print Printer Options Other" menu line). Other differences between the two programs appear in the start-up screens, the placement on the screen of the menu lines, the exact wording of the long prompts, the organization of the help screens, the increased width of the VP–Planner screen, and the ability of VP–Planner to hide certain columns. *See* Stephenson Affdvt. ¶¶ 161–176. The works are, nevertheless, substantially, indeed, strikingly, similar. As Judge Learned Hand held in a copyright case involving a pattern on a bolt of cloth that was used to make dresses, infringement may be found despite some differences between two works:

> the ordinary observer, unless he set out to detect the disparities, would be disposed to overlook them, and regard their aesthetic appeal as the same. That is enough; and

indeed, it is all that can be said, unless protection against infringement is to be denied because of variants irrelevant to the purpose for which the design is intended.

> *See also Atari* v. *Philips*, 672 F.2d at 618 ("[A] laundry list of specific differences . . . will not preclude a finding of infringement where the works are substantially similar in other respects. . . . When analyzing two works to determine whether they are substantially similar, courts should be careful not to lose sight of the forest for the trees.").

From the perspective of both an expert and an ordinary viewer, the similarities overwhelm differences. Thus, as in *Peter Pan Fabrics*, the two works at issue are substantially similar. Indeed, by using the option in VP–Planner that allows a user to move the menu from the bottom of the screen to the top of the screen, a user could easily think 1-2-3 rather than VP–Planner was the program in use. Certainly purchasers of a book designed to teach users how to master *1-2-3*, which is distributed with demonstration copies of *VP–Planner*, would be likely to overlook the disparities between 1-2-3 and VP–Planner. *See* L. Ingalsbe, *Lotus 1-2-3 with Version 2.0 for the IBM PC* (1987) (Tr. Ex. 215).

Moreover, even if some elements of VP–Planner were very different, it would not give defendants a license to copy other substantial elements of 1-2-3 verbatim. If one publishes a 1,000–page book of which only a 10–page segment is an unauthorized reproduction of copyrighted material, and if the 10–page segment is a qualitatively substantial part of the copyrighted work, it is not a defense to a claim of infringement that the book is 99 percent different from the copyrighted material. *Sheldon*, 81 F.2d at 56 ("no plagiarist can excuse the wrong by showing how much of his work he did not pirate"); *SAS Institute*, 605 F.Supp. at 829–30. Thus, defendants' proof that VP–Planner has many features that are different from Lotus 1-2-3 is off point. The more relevant question is: does it have significant features that are substantially similar? I conclude, on the record before me, that there is no genuine dispute of material fact on this question. The answer to this question must be "yes."

Accordingly, I conclude that it is indisputable that defendants have copied substantial copyrightable elements of plaintiff's copyrighted work. I therefore conclude that, subject to consideration of other contentions advanced by defendants, liability has been established.

NOTE

1. Despite *Time* magazine's decision to honor "the computer" as its 1982 "Man of the Year," and despite advances in the field of artificial intelligence, I take it as a premise of decisionmaking in this case that computers, for better or worse, do not yet have the human feelings, strengths, and failings that lie beyond those we describe as logical, or cognitive, or intellectual in the broadest sense.

HOW TO INTERPRET THE LOTUS DECISION (AND HOW NOT TO)

Pamela Samuelson

On June 28, 1990, a federal court judge in Boston made public his decision in favor of Lotus Development Corporation in its software copyright lawsuit against Paperback Software. People in the software industry had been waiting for this decision since the lawsuit was first filed in January 1987, certain that it would be a landmark case and would resolve many vexing questions about copyright protection for user interfaces.

The trade press has abounded with varying interpretations of Judge Keeton's opinion in the Lotus case: Some have said the decision is a narrow one, making illegal only the direct copying of another firm's interface [9]; Some have seen it as a much broader ruling—one that will have a chilling effect on development of competitive software products [5]; Others have asserted the case draws a reasonable line, and will have a positive effect overall [4]; Several have argued the ruling will be harmful because it ignores the interests of users of software, and will make standardization of user interfaces impossible to achieve. [3] Still others perceive the opinion as only setting the stage for a new confrontation over the issues in the appellate courts. [1] Lotus has given some indication of how broadly it interprets the Paperback decision by filing a new round of user interface copyright lawsuits against two of its other spreadsheet competitors.

This column, rather than just adding one more interpretation of the Lotus decision to the bin of those already expressed, will give the reader a glimpse of the nature of the legal process and of judicial opinions so he or she can see why people can interpret the Lotus opinion differently. The following three factors make it difficult to know what the Lotus decision means: (1) The legal process is not yet over, and the meaning of the case will depend in part on the outcome of this further process. (2) While Judge Keeton makes some statements that seem to suggest his ruling is a narrow one, some of his other statements could be interpreted much more broadly. (3) Even from unambiguous statements Judge Keeton makes, different people can draw reasonable but nonetheless differing inferences about what the judge would do in similar (though somewhat different) cases. For these reasons, it is impossible to know with any certainty what the law concerning copyright protection for user interfaces is in the aftermath of the Lotus decision.

IT'S NOT OVER TILL IT'S OVER

Let us begin with something of which we can be certain. Paperback Software has been held liable for copyright infringement because it copied the entire menu structure of the Lotus 1-2-3 program, which Judge Keeton decided was protectable "expression" of the Lotus program. (It is a basic principle of copyright law that a copyright protects against unauthorized copying of an author's "expression," but not copying of the "ideas" in the work.) The fact that Paperback lost at the trial court level does not, of course, mean that it has necessarily lost the case forever, for Paperback can and will appeal Judge Keeton's ruling to a federal appellate court. (Paperback cannot just appeal the court's ruling because it does not like the outcome. An appeal has to be based on a claim that the judge made some errors of law—that is, misinterpreted the law in some way. Paperback will, therefore, have to identify the specific legal errors it thinks Judge Keeton made in his analysis of copyright law as applied to the facts of this case to make its appeal.)

If the appellate court (which usually consists of a panel of three judges) agrees with Paperback that Judge Keeton made some errors of law, it can reverse his ruling. Or if it agrees with Lotus that Judge Keeton made no legal error, it will affirm his ruling. The appellate court can also send a case back to the trial judge for additional proceedings if it decides the trial judge did not make some determination he or she should have made. (For example, the appellate court in the Lotus case could decide that Judge Keeton should have made detailed findings about Paperback's claim that the Lotus commands constitute an unprotectable language or that Lotus' interface had become a *de facto* standard, and could send the case back for specific findings on these issues.)

If Paperback loses in the appellate court, it will probably try to persuade the U.S. Supreme Court to review the appellate court's ruling, again arguing that errors of law were made by the judges who had previously ruled on the case. (Lotus, of course, would be the one to seek Supreme Court review if Paperback won in the appellate court.) However, the Supreme Court takes only about 150 cases of the many thousands that seek its attention each year, which means that the appellate court decision in the Lotus case will probably be the final resolution of the copyright dispute between Lotus and Paperback (unless that court sends it back to the trial court for further proceedings).

The appellate process will take some time to happen. It may be another year before the appellate court decides on Paperback's appeal, and perhaps another year after that before the Supreme Court decides whether it will review the case. Should the Supreme Court decide to hear an appeal in the *Lotus* v. *Paperback* case, final resolution of the case will obviously take even longer. The Supreme Court can also send the case back to the lower courts for further proceedings, which, of course, would further delay final resolution and would probably set off a new round of appeals after the trial judge made the new findings for which the case was sent back.

Whatever the federal appellate court eventually does with the Paperback appeal will become "the law" within the First Circuit (which includes Massachusetts, Maine, New Hampshire, Rhode Island, and Puerto Rico) unless the Supreme Court takes the case and makes a ruling which would then be the law throughout the United States Elsewhere, the opinion of the First Circuit Court of Appeals would most likely be taken into account (that is, given some deference) in similar cases, but the *Lotus* v. *Paperback* decision will not be binding in these other jurisdictions unless judges in other cases decide to follow what the First Circuit has done—which they need not do.

The primary reason for the recent filing by Borland of a lawsuit in California asking the court to rule that the interface of its Quattro program does not infringe Lotus' copyright was to get its legal dispute with Lotus started in a jurisdiction where the *Lotus* v. *Paperback* opinion is not a binding precedent. Judges in other circuits can sometimes be persuaded to disagree with the ruling from a particular circuit, and can adopt a conflicting rule which will then become the law within that circuit. The judge for Ashton Tate's lawsuit against Fox Software, for example, could reject Judge Keeton's ruling. (It is when different circuits have different rules on the same issue, that the Supreme Court is most likely to take an appeal to resolve whatever conflict exists between or among circuits. But sometimes conflicting rules exist for many years before the Supreme Court takes a case to resolve the conflict.)

WHAT THE APPEALS COURT SAYS

We need to await the First Circuit's ruling in the *Lotus* v. *Paperback* case—not only to know whether the trial judge's ruling will be affirmed, reversed, or sent back for further proceedings—but also because the First Circuit's opinion is likely to give us a clearer view about the correct interpretation of that case. In general, appellate court opinions, unless they are very short and explicitly endorse the trial judge's reasoning, are more influential (that is, they are given more weight as precedent) than trial court decisions. Often, after an appellate court issues a decision in a case, the earlier trial court opinion ceases to be used as a source of understanding the meaning of the case.

Certainly, to the extent there is a difference of opinion between what the appellate court and the trial court say about the case, the appellate court opinion is the one that lawyers understand should be followed. If, for example, the appellate court agrees with a trial judge's ruling, but has a completely different set of reasons for doing so, the appellate court's reasons are the ones that will matter (until and unless they are modified or abandoned in subsequent cases). An appellate court can decide to state the ruling in the case more narrowly or more broadly than did the trial court. If it criticizes what a trial court has said on an issue, or even says it is unnecessary to reach an issue which the trial court decided, the appellate court opinion will change the meaning that can be ascribed to the case.

We should hope the appellate opinion in the *Lotus* v. *Paperback* case will clarify and not obscure its meaning. But in the meantime, all we have is the trial judge's opinion, and it is a fair question to ask what interpretation should be given to it.

INTERPRETING THE LOTUS OPINION: HOLDINGS V. DICTA

One of the first (and most frustrating) lessons law students must learn is how to separate the true "holding" of a judicial opinion from all the other statements a judge might make in the course of an opinion (which lawyers call *dicta* after its Latin expression) about issues connected to the case. One reason the *Lotus* v. *Paperback* opinion is difficult to interpret is that Judge Keeton wrote a 110-page opinion to explain his decision in favor of Lotus. (Its length alone is an indication that this opinion has a higher than average dicta-to-holding ratio.) More importantly, interpretation is difficult because there are some sections of the opinion in which the judge seems to take a very broad view of what Lotus' copyright protects about the 1-2-3 interface, and other sections where he seems to be deciding the case on a much narrower basis. One cannot really know until the issues are tested in subsequent litigation whether the broader or narrower interpretation is the correct one, and what, therefore, the true "holding" of the Lotus case is.

Let us consider a very clear example of *dicta* from the Lotus decision, after which we will work our way into some more subtle problems of sorting the *dicta* from the holding in the case. One of the main reasons the judge in the Lotus case decided against Paperback was the following: the commercial success of other spreadsheet programs with user interfaces different from 1-2-3 demonstrated that it was not necessary, as Paperback had contended, to have the same menu structure as Lotus 1-2-3 in order to have a commercially viable spreadsheet program. The judge pointed to Excel's macro conversion facility for Lotus commands as one alternative to copying the 1-2-3 menu structure; he pointed out the possibility of using a help screen to show which Paperback commands were equivalent to the Lotus 1-2-3 commands as another alternative to copying Lotus' menu structure.

Yet after taking some trouble to explain all of this, the judge went on to say: "even if VP-Planner otherwise would have been a commercial failure, and even if no other technical ways of achieving macro and menu compatibility existed, the desire to achieve 'compatibility' or 'standardization' cannot override the rights of authors to a limited monopoly in the expression embodied in their intellectual work."

This last statement is *dicta*, plain and simple. The facts of the Paperback case, at least as perceived by this judge, did not present for resolution the issue of how copyright law should be applied if commercial failure was sure to result unless Paperback used the same command structure as Lotus and there were no technical alternatives but copying the menu structure to achieve compatibility. The judge got carried away with discussing the issues, and made some statements not necessary for the resolution of the case before him. While no lawyer would be pleased at the prospect of arguing a case presenting the *dicta* issue to that particular judge, lawyers know that one cannot really predict how a case presenting a different configuration of facts would be resolved.

THE NARROW STATEMENTS

Now we will move to an examination of statements from the Lotus opinion upon which broad and narrow interpretations of the Lotus decision might be based. First, the narrow one: At several points in the Lotus decision, the judge, in explaining why he found copyright infringement, stressed that Paperback had copied the *whole* of Lotus' menu structure. Paperback had used the same command terms as Lotus, had ordered and grouped them in the same way, and presented them on menu screens in the same way as Lotus had. It is reasonable to infer from language of this sort that the holding of the case was that copying the whole of another firm's menu command structure is copyright infringement.

If the holding in the Lotus case is only that copying the whole menu structure is infringement, that would suggest that Paperback might only have to arrange the commands differently from Lotus to avoid infringement. A different arrangement would present a different menu structure, would it not? In a similar software user interface case decided a few years ago in Georgia (*Digital Communications Associates* v. *Softklone Distributing Corp.*), a federal judge ruled that it was not an infringement for a competitor to have the same set of commands as another copyrighted program, but only to order the commands in the same way when there were lots of other arrangements that could have been made of that set of commands. The Lotus opinion does not say whether Judge Keeton agreed or disagreed with this aspect of the Softklone decision. (Even if Judge Keeton disagreed, however, the Softklone case is still the law in Georgia.)

If the holding in the Lotus case is this narrow one, the Lotus decision may not have much relevance for how the *Apple* v. *Microsoft* case will be resolved. The license between Microsoft and Apple—which the judge in that case has already ruled covers a considerable amount of what Microsoft is said to have taken from Apple—

is one important difference between the two cases. There are also more differences between the Apple and Microsoft interfaces than between the Lotus and Paperback interfaces.

The judge's discussion of ways to achieve compatibility with Lotus 1-2-3 other than by directly copying the whole menu structure is another bit of evidence that the holding in the Lotus case is a narrow one. The judge's use of Excel's macro conversion facility as an example of an alternative Paperback had besides copying Lotus' menu structure, suggests (although the judge does not directly say so) that the judge does not think it would infringe Lotus' copyright to adopt such an alternative. Similarly, by giving the example of a help screen to display Paperback's equivalents to Lotus' commands, the judge suggests that this too would not infringe (although he does not specifically say so). Nor does the judge indicate how he would rule if Paperback simply allowed users to input Lotus commands but did not display them on the screen, or allowed users to create their own menu structure. But to the extent that the holding in the Lotus case is a narrow one, making only the copying of the whole of a menu structure an infringement, this conduct too would seem to be noninfringing.

Lotus, however, might take quite a different view of the interpretation that should be given to Judge Keeton's opinion. Lotus might argue that even if Paperback (or someone else) arranged the commands differently, converted them in some way, or accepted the Lotus commands without displaying them on the screen, copyright infringement should still be found because these competitive interfaces would still be based on and copied from Lotus' interface. They would still take a free ride on the intellectual work done by Lotus and the value created by Lotus. Since it is possible to design a different interface for a spreadsheet program, Lotus would argue its competitors should be required to do so. Lotus could look to some broad statements in Judge Keeton's opinion to support its arguments on these points.

THE BROAD STATEMENTS

Judge Keeton's opinion, for example, refers to Lotus' interface as its "most unique and valuable" aspect, seeming to say this was why the interface must be protected by copyright law. He also indicates that Lotus' copyright covers its "user interface," not just the "screen displays" that the Lotus program might generate. Judge Keeton emphasizes that "nonliteral" elements of the Lotus interface can be protected by copyright law. (No, the judge does not clearly define what he means by "nonliteral," or indicate which nonliteral features of an interface are protectable and which are not, although he does say it is acceptable for others to use the " \ " key as Lotus does.) He also cites an article written by an IBM lawyer to the effect that user interfaces need "strong" copyright protection.

But perhaps the broadest statement from the judge is this: "The bulk of the creative work is in the conceptualization of a computer program and its user interface, rather than its encoding, and . . . creating a suitable user interface is a more difficult intellectual task, requiring greater creativity, originality, and insight than converting the user interface design into instructions to the machine." This and some similar statements in Judge Keeton's opinion would seem to suggest that *anything* about the Lotus 1-2-3 interface that Lotus thinks is valuable enough to sue about could be the basis for a successful copyright infringement lawsuit against its competitors.

(Here, it may be worth noting that the copyright statute makes clear that however brilliant a concept may be and however many alternative concepts might exist, concepts are not protected by copyright; nor are systems, procedures, processes, or methods of operation.)

Lotus, Apple, and plaintiffs in other software copyright lawsuits will look to statements of this sort to persuade judges in other cases that the holding in the Lotus case was a broad one, or even if *dicta*, the broad statements are nonetheless proper interpretations of the law.

THE REJECTION OF PAPERBACK'S PUBLIC POLICY ARGUMENTS

Another reason Judge Keeton's opinion in the Lotus case may have broad implications for other user interface copyright lawsuits is because of its strong rejection of several public policy arguments made by Paperback. Often, if one judge has rejected a public policy argument, judges in later cases will reject a similar argument because of its rejection in the earlier case, saving themselves the trouble of reconsidering what one judge has presumably thought through quite carefully. We will now discuss Judge Keeton's reaction to three of Paperback's public policy arguments: (1) that the Lotus interface is a language which is unprotectable by copyright law, (2) that the public interest in standardization overrides Lotus' private interest in protecting its command structure, and (3) that it would be inappropriate to grant broad copyright protection for user interfaces because of the harmful effects such a rule would have on progress in the software field.

Paperback argued that the Lotus command terms, because they were the method by which users could communicate with the program and because they could be used to construct macros, were a kind of language. Languages themselves, Paperback argued, cannot be protected by copyright law, although particular expressions of them may be. The creator of Esperanto, for example, could copyright a dictionary defining the words in the language, or a book explaining how to use it. But a copyright in such books, Paperback argued, would not mean that others would infringe by speaking Esperanto or writing their own books in or about Esperanto. Languages are, in their nature, a shared resource of a community, and unprotectable by copyright law. Paperback submitted a sworn statement from a computer scientist detailing how and why the Lotus commands should be considered a language. The judge's response to this argument was to castigate Paperback's defense lawyer for engaging in "word games." He was not persuaded that the Lotus commands constituted a language, but went on to say that Paperback had cited no precedent to show that a language could not be protected by copyright law. (This may have been a legal error [2].)

Paperback's standardization argument had two strands. The company first argued that its interface, like Lotus' before it, built upon a common base of innovations from previous spreadsheet programs. Paperback pointed to respects in which the Lotus command structure was similar to the command structure of Visicalc which was the first commercial electronic spreadsheet program, and ways in which its interface differed from Lotus'. From this, Paperback argued that it had copied only standard features of spreadsheet interfaces, and argued that its addition of new interface elements demonstrated that Paperback had continued the pattern of incremental advances that had been characteristic of evolution of the software field. But Paperback also argued that to the extent that Lotus' interface was distinctive from previous spreadsheet interfaces, Lotus' interface had become a *de facto* standard, much like the QWERTY keyboard has become for typewriters, and consequently, public policy considerations favoring standardization should override Lotus' private interest in the protection of the Lotus 1-2-3 interface.

Judge Keeton rejected both strands of the standardization argument. He did not see the same degree of similarity between the Visicalc and Lotus interfaces as Paperback did—but more significantly, was not persuaded by the incremental improvement argument. Paperback, he said, was not just selling whatever incremental improvement on the spreadsheet program concept it had developed; it was selling copies of Lotus' expression as well. That, the court ruled was impermissible as long as other interfaces could be created for spreadsheet programs.

The *de facto* standard argument was even more forcefully rejected by the judge. He seemed, in fact, to be outraged at the very idea underlying the argument: "The more innovative the expression of an idea is, the more important is copyright protection for that expression. By arguing that Lotus 1-2-3 was so innovative that it occupied the field and set a *de facto* industry standard, and that therefore the defendants were free to copy the plaintiff's expression, defendants have flipped copyright on its head. Copyright would be perverse if it only protected mundane increments while leaving unprotected as part of the public domain those advancements that are more strikingly innovative." The judge made no findings as to whether the Lotus interface had, in fact, become a *de facto* standard because he perceived no basis in copyright law for the standardization argument. Judge Keeton did not even discuss possible interests of the user community in standardization. (Because there is some case law permitting standardization map symbol systems and permitting user interests in standardized computer program input formats to be considered in the assessment of what copyright protects, Judge Keeton may have committed legal error on this issue as well.)

The judge allowed Paperback considerable latitude to submit opinion evidence about the likely effects of the Lotus case on progress in the software industry. Dan Bricklin, the codeveloper of Visicalc, was one of a number of computer science and software industry people who submitted lengthy sworn statements expressing the opinion that copyright protection for user interface command structures would have negative consequences for progress in the software field. The judge was also given a copy of an article reporting the results of the survey by Samuelson and Glushko [7, 8] at CHI '89 on the user interface field's view of the look and feel lawsuits. [7, 8] That survey showed that while people in the field thought copyright should protect source and object code, they overwhelmingly opposed copyright protection for look and feel, commands, and most other aspects of user interfaces. The survey also showed that people in the field opposed the kind of "strong" copyright protection for user interfaces being sought in the Lotus and Apple cases because of the harmful consequences they thought such decisions would have for the field. (Lotus, of course, also submitted sworn statements from experts predicting positive consequences from recognizing copyright protection for its interface.)

Judge Keeton's opinion discusses the Bricklin statement and twice cites the CHI '89 survey report, but he ultimately disregarded all of the opinion evidence submitted in the case as irrelevant to resolution of the case before him. The judge thought that even if Paperback was right in asserting that progress in the software industry would be impaired by protecting Lotus' interface, its arguments were nonetheless misdirected. Public policy arguments of this sort should be made, said the judge, to the Congress; they should not be made to a judge who has a responsibility to follow the mandates of Congress which in this case meant applying copyright law to computer programs.

CONCLUSION

I am a lawyer. I interpret cases for a living. I have read Judge Keeton's opinion carefully and I have worked very hard to figure out what it means. I would tell you what it means if I could understand it, but I cannot. And neither can anyone else. So anyone who says he or she is sure the Lotus decision is a very narrow one and only makes copying the whole of someone else's interface illegal is giving his opinion and making a prediction; but only time and further litigation will tell if that person is right or wrong. (Because I believe it should be a narrow opinion, I am tempted to tell you it is one, but I cannot honestly do that.) Similarly, anyone who is sure that the Lotus opinion means that Ashton Tate will win its lawsuit against Fox, or that Apple will win its lawsuit against Microsoft is also offering a prediction which may or may not turn out to be true.

People who tell you they cannot tell exactly what Judge Keeton's opinion means (except for cases involving the copying of the whole of another's interface) are being honest, but who wants to pay a lawyer $200 an hour to be told "your guess is as good as mine"? A cautious lawyer might well say to a client who is about to design a user interface for a program that will compete with others already in the marketplace: "The only completely safe thing to do is to make your interface as different as possible from other interfaces in the marketplace, or if you decide to make it similar, be prepared to defend your decision and to document it, for it will be an uphill battle once evidence is presented that it can be done differently."

I have always thought *Lotus* v. *Paperback* was a close case. I thought it was close because copyright law has long protected compilations (whether of words, facts, statistics, pictorial images, or some combination of these things). It is very difficult for a copyright lawyer to look at a set of screen displays like those that present Lotus' commands in a particular arrangement, and not see a protectable compilation of words. What made the Paperback case so strong for Lotus was that, notwithstanding all the talk in Judge Keeton's opinion about the "nonliteral" similarities in the two interfaces, Paperback's interface was *literally* very similar to Lotus': It used the same commands, ordered them in the same way, and displayed them in very much the same way. (As the terms are usually used in copyright cases, two works are "literally similar" when they are identical or nearly so, e.g., word for word copying. "Nonliteral similarities" have a more abstract character, as when detailed sequences of the plot of a drama are copied, but all the words of the dialogue are different. As best I can make it out, Judge Keeton used the term "literal similarities" to mean source or object code copying, and regarded all other similarities as "nonliteral.") I could have written an opinion for Judge Keeton that would have concluded Paperback infringed Lotus' copyright. (I think I could have written an even better opinion in Paperback's favor, but that is because I take the language, standardization, and functionality arguments Paperback made more seriously than Judge Keeton did.)

One thing readers should realize is that Judge Keeton worked very hard on this case (evidenced, in part, by the 110 page opinion). He tried very hard to do the right thing and to apply copyright law as best he could to the complex problems thrown at him by the lawyers. He knew everybody would be looking at what he did (and why) in applying copyright law to user interfaces. While his opinion is, at times, somewhat idiosyncratic in its analysis of copyright law, Judge Keeton's opinion was consistent with some—though not with all—user interface cases.

I have for some years argued that copyright law is far from an optimal form of intellectual property protection for computer programs because of the functional character of programs. [6] Copyright law is a very distinct body of rules and principles that has a long tradition of protecting written texts and pictorial works—where the greater the diversity of expression, the more enriched is the culture. Over the years, the copyright distinction between *idea* and *expression* has been worked out reasonably well for these kinds of works. But computer programs are different. Programs are functional in the same way that machines, machine processes, and human-machine interfaces are. Copyright law has never before protected functional works of those sorts. That is why there is so little precedent in copyright law to give guidance on how to resolve cases like *Lotus* v. *Paperback* which involve an interface between human users and a machine. Paperback raised a functionality defense but Judge Keeton rejected it, saying that Lotus' interface wasn't functional (which would have made it unprotectable by copyright law) because there was more than one way to build an interface for a program that performed spreadsheet functions.

If people in the software industry do not think that the outcome in the *Lotus* v. *Paperback* case was the right outcome, or are worried about the broader implications of what Judge Keeton said in his opinion, or want a fast rather than litigation's tediously slow method of resolution of the issues about what copyright law should protect about program interfaces, they might want to think about supporting legislative initiatives. For now, all we can do is hope that the First Circuit Court of Appeals will clarify what interpretation should be given to the Lotus case.

REFERENCES

1. Ferranti, M. Judge rules in Lotus' favor in copyright suit. *PC Week* 7, 26 (July 2, 1990), 6.
2. Lowry, E. Copyright protection for computer languages: Creative incentive or technological threat? *Emory Law J.*, To be published.
3. Margolis, N. Users biggest losers in spreadsheet wars. *Computerworld* 24, 29 (July 16, 1990), 8.
4. The Paperback opinion draws a reasonable line, *PC Week* 7, 27 (July 16, 1990), 34.
5. Parker, R. Lotus' copyright protection is turning into a feeding frenzy. *Infoworld*, 12, 28 (July 9, 1990), 42.
6. Samuelson, P. CONTU revisited: The case against copyright protection for computer programs in machine-readable form. *Duke Law J.*, (1984).
7. Samuelson, P. and Glushko, R. Comparing the views of lawyers and user interface designers on the software copyright look and feel lawsuits. *Jurimetrics J.* 30 (1989), 121.
8. Samuelson, P. and Glushko, R. Survey on the look and feel lawsuits, *Commun. ACM 33* (May 1990), 483.
9. Zachman, W. Lotus-Paperback precedent need not harm the industry. *PC Week* 7, 27 (July 9, 1990), 10.

CHAPTER FOUR

Privacy and Databases

INTRODUCTION

Information Privacy and Communications Privacy

Concern over personal privacy has grown in response to two areas of development in computing and related technologies. First, databases used as a surveillance tool for amassing, storing, and disseminating personal information have provoked fears that privacy, and along with it autonomy and freedom, are being eroded. We refer to concerns for privacy generated by personal databases, as concerns over "information privacy." Second, our vastly expanded communications capabilities, including electronic mail and the much-touted potential of fiber optic "data-highways" (popularly now referred to as the National Information Infrastructure), and wireless communications networks, raise questions about the appropriate degree of privacy that should be assured for these new forms of communications. We will refer to these as issues of "communications privacy." Although the two issues have much in common, we have chosen, in this chapter, to focus on information privacy and the challenge of maintaining privacy in the face of personal databases.[1] We will return to issues of communications privacy in Chapter Seven, where we examine a range of social issues having to do with computing and networks. For these later discussions, readers will find some of the articles in this chapter useful—especially those dealing with foundations of privacy.

The literature on information privacy is very extensive. In this chapter we have offered a sampling of writings on a variety of issues, perspectives, and disciplinary approaches. These writings are about government and corporate databases; privacy in conflict with other social goods; ethical foundations; and legal and policy issues.

Although computers did not create the practice of collecting, recording, and storing personal information, they vastly expanded the capacity to do so. An expanded capacity to collect and work with personal information has sparked ideas for further uses of it, which in turn creates a need for even *more* information, spiraling upward in ever expanding cycle of need and capacity. To introduce readers to the range of databases and their impacts on society we have included Larry Hunter's

---

[1]The terms "personal databases" and "databases of personal information" refer broadly to databases that contain information about persons. The information can range from impersonal, such as name, phone number, address, to more sensitive information such as medical, arrest, or financial records.

engaging and prescient article. Hunter's paper captures one of the important differences between other prying technologies and computers. "Our revolution," he observes, "will not be in gathering data—don't look for TV cameras in your bedroom—but in analyzing the information that is already willingly shared." Experience with databases over the past twenty years has not completely borne out Hunter's prediction, because we know that databases hold information that is not necessarily *willingly* shared by their subjects. Yet Hunter's observation that computers are not providing better "cameras in bedrooms"—metaphorically speaking—and yet are powerful tools for invading the private lives of individuals captures the essence of why computing poses not only a practical challenge for privacy, but a conceptual puzzle as well. The puzzle is this: If computers are not generating new information about people but simply working with information already known, how do we explain the commonly held belief, that databases threaten to undermine privacy? How do we provide principled means to guide policies for protecting privacy? Even when computers are not delving into confidential information they continue to undermine privacy—why? Articles in this chapter attempt, at least in part, to address these questions.

Government versus the Private Sector

For two reasons government first emerged as the dominant client for computerized personal databases. First, to manage and provide social services and maintain security within large impersonal bureaucracies, readily accessible information is a key to successful functioning. A variety of government functions, including taxation, social welfare, crime prevention, national security, and immigration are critically dependent on information about their clientele. To the agencies and bureaucracies managing these functions, the capacity to communicate and exchange information via networked computers is an added boon. Second, because computing power was at first very expensive and required expert management, the ability to purchase and run computerized databases was limited to government agencies and other relatively large, wealthy institutions.

Although the growing infrastructure of databases was welcomed by many as a means of making government more effective and more efficient in areas such as administration of services, welfare, and especially law enforcement, it caused great unease in others. For them, the growing infrastructure of databases signified a challenge to the well-defined but limited government role in the lives of individual citizens—a political tradition that is highly valued in the United States. Comprehensive, linked databases promised to strengthen the power of centralized government over individuals raising the specter of a kind of totalitarian governance illustrated starkly by George Orwell's Big Brother in his novel *1984*. In response to this fear, the landmark Privacy Act, passed in 1974, placed restrictions on the extent and use of government held databases.

But changes in the world of computing—most importantly dramatic drops in the cost and size of computer equipment, and increases in the amount of mass-produced consumer software, including powerful database programs—ushered in a new demand for personal databases from a different sector of society. The value of personal information was not limited to governments in managing their bureaucracies and controlling behavior, but extended into the private sector. As a marketing tool and as a guide to insurance companies, banks, and potential employees, personal information is a valuable commodity. The uses also can be very specialized, as for example, databases that allows doctors to learn whether certain individuals has filed a medical malpractice suit.[2] Personal information is so valuable that companies like Thomison, Ramos, and Woodridge (TRW), whose primary trade is personal information itself, are able to flourish by selling this information to other corporate entities. George Orwell's "Big Brother" metaphor, and the power relationship between individual and government, will not explain the consternation over private sector holdings of personal information. Nevertheless, even these privately held databases challenge the array of interests captured under the conceptual umbrella of a right to privacy, which covers a right to anonymity, control over information about oneself, and the right to be "let alone."

Case Studies

We have included two case studies in this chapter. Lotus Marketplace is a case from the private sector. The other, featuring the FBI's National Crime Information Center (NCIC), is a case from government. The article by M. J. Culnan and H. J. Smith describes Lotus Marketplace, a database that was to have been jointly produced by Lotus Development Corporation a software development company and Equifax, a national list vendor. Lotus Marketplace would have contained information about a targeted population including such things as name, address, age, gender, and purchasing propensity as measured by actual buying habits across 100 product categories. The database, which would have been recorded on CD-ROM disks, was primarily intended for use by mail-order companies and other direct marketers. Vociferous public objection to Lotus Marketplace, and a grassroots opposition facilitated by electronic networks, led officials of the companies to cancel the project.

The excerpt from Kenneth Laudon's book, *Dossier Society*, describes databases devised by the FBI for use by law enforcement agencies

---

[2]Lewin, Tamar, "Philadelphia Doctors to Be Offered Data on Patients Who Have Sued," in *The New York Times*, Friday, August 27, 1993.

throughout the country. Although many recognize the value of these systems in preventing crime and catching criminals, they worry about law enforcement excesses, about abuse of the personal data held in these systems, and about the appropriateness of some of the information required for these databases. Both cases are instructive because supporters and critics of both systems under contention have offered interesting and often compelling arguments for and against. Readers are encouraged to identify these arguments and attempt their own assessment of the cases.

Privacy in Conflict with Other Social Goods

The two case studies raise an issue that is common to much of contemporary discussion about personal databases and their threat to privacy. On the face of it one might think that because privacy is a good, more of it is better; any invasion of it is to be opposed. On reflection, however, one can see that although personal databases diminish the degree of privacy we have, at the same time they may serve other interests. For example, the NCIC serves as an important tool for fighting crime and apprehending criminals; IRS databases ensure fair taxation; databases about welfare applicants ensure that only those eligible for it receive government welfare. Corporations in the private sector, whose business relies on personal information, face a similar conflict. They would operate more efficiently if allowed free access to personal information, but tread on privacy if not restrained in any way. For example, direct marketers could serve their clients better if they knew more about them and their needs; banks could better serve their clients if they could accurately distinguish good loans from bad; employees would function better if they could freely delve into a potential employee's life in order to predict future performance.

Several of the articles we include in this chapter focus on this question of trade-offs—of balancing privacy against other values. In general because personal databases provide a tool for efficiently and justly providing important social services, their supporters argue that abridging the use and extent of databases, might lead to an abridgment of the power to protect other interests. The articles by R. P. Kusserow and J. Shattuck, which discuss computer matching by government agencies, present opposing views on how to balance the conflicting values. Kusserow argues that the use of matching procedures helps identify fraudulent welfare claims and is therefore justified; Shattuck counters that such procedures fly in the face of privacy and related rights and interests. J. P. Barlow, reflecting on the furor over Lotus Marketplace, expresses regret at strident opposition to it. His regret, it seems, is over the anachronistic ideal of a small town where citizens know each others' business, but care enough about one another so as not to react to this knowledge in a harmful or vindictive way. Barlow and others also favor greater freedom for the private sector, arguing that restraints on private industry's attempts to profit from personal information constitutes unjustifiable interference in a free-market economy, and might even amount to unjustified curtailment of freedom of speech. Their opponents rebut that in spite of the restrictions this might place on business practice, personal privacy ought to be protected to the extent we would protect other important rights and values.

The article by James Rule, Douglas McAdam, Linda Stearns, and David Uglow clearly etches out the counterpoint between privacy and other values of contemporary Western society. They suggest that personal privacy is at risk not so much from a malevolent third party who seeks to interfere and control, but from our own desire for efficiency and fairness within a society driven by large anonymous organizations. They suggest that we will protect privacy only by making dramatic changes to the contemporary social fabric.

Philosophical and Ethical Foundations

Although privacy activists regard the Lotus Marketplace incident as a victory for privacy, and critics of the NCIC cite specific abuses as evidence of its problematic nature, we believe that meaningful resolution of many of these concrete cases will require a better understanding of general principles that ground the various positions. While it may be true that the ground swell of public opposition was directly responsible for reversing the course for Lotus Marketplace, unless we can articulate the principles underlying opposition the resolution may remain superficial and short lived. Consider that even in announcing that Lotus Marketplace was being struck down, corporate officials claimed that it was for public relations reasons only and not for reasons of principle or law. In the absence of a principled grounding, it is not clear how the case of Marketplace could serve as a precedent for similar proposals in the future. To uncover some of the principled arguments found in privacy debates we have included in this chapter several readings dedicated to the philosophical, ethical, and legal foundations of privacy as they apply, particularly, to questions about information privacy.

Objections to various proposals to create, expand, or use personal databases frequently refer to a legal, or at least a moral, right to privacy. To evaluate these objections, we must reflect on the foundations of privacy, so that we can reach a better understanding of what privacy is. A better grasp on what privacy is, will provide a sounder basis for evaluating whether a given proposal violates it. Furthermore, a better grasp of the value of privacy gives a sounder basis for making decisions that involve trade-offs between privacy rights and other values. As an illustration, consider the example of an airline passenger who is asked to submit to a search of body and personal belongings. First, we ask whether this constitutes a violation of privacy? If yes, we may further want to ask whether the violation of privacy is justifiable on grounds that other more important interests—such as the safety of the airplane and its passengers—are thereby protected. A third reason to refer to the ethical and legal foundations of privacy is that they yield general principles that can help clarify baffling practical conundra.

We have included two articles that address philosophical and ethical foundations of privacy. Ruth Gavison's article offers an excellent conceptual framework within which to articulate some of the central controversies surrounding privacy, including a discussion of the notion of a "neutral concept of privacy." The article by James Rachels takes up similar questions from a philosophical perspective. Rachels draws a useful and important distinction (not clearly articulated by many who write about privacy) between the value of privacy as a means and the value of privacy as an end in itself. Many contemporary writers defend strong protection of privacy on the grounds that an invasion of privacy can lead to various harms. For example, someone might suffer social ostracism if her neighbors in a conservative town probe confidential medical records and discover she has had an abortion. Thus the harm is not directly from the loss of privacy, but the reaction of townsfolk to the information. Although Rachels acknowledges that privacy is of value as a means, the central focus of his article is its *intrinsic* value. He finds that privacy is essential in enabling individuals to control the type of relationship as well as the degree of closeness of their relationships to others. The two articles share a common recognition that while absolute privacy is not necessarily a good thing, a certain degree of privacy is essential to a good life and healthy society. The degree of privacy the law ought to protect (as a legal right) is the degree of privacy that is necessary for a satisfactory personal and social life, protection of democratic institutions, and individual liberty and autonomy.

Richard Posner's approach differs from the others. Instead of considering the value of privacy to the individual, he recommends an "economic" perspective on the value of privacy, performing a type of cost–benefit analysis to infer the optimal degree of protection for personal privacy. He argues that social welfare is not well served by strong protections of personal privacy because it is those with "something to hide" who benefit most from strong privacy protections. Those with nothing to hide need not fear publicity and can be harmed by those who are intent on withholding personal information.

Privacy, Law, and Policy

If we can agree that privacy is an important social value, the challenge that remains is to find a just and effective course to protect it in our society. This can be through law, voluntary compliance with recommendations, or through the use of special technologies. Although several of the articles in this chapter include suggestions on how to protect privacy, the articles by Jerry Berman and Janlori Goldman, and David Chaum make it their central focus. Berman and Goldman, who focus on legal mechanisms for protecting privacy, explore the relationship between a perceived "right to privacy" and a national tradition of limiting government interference in the private domain. They evaluate the policy and legal standing of privacy in the post-Privacy Act era, suggesting that there are several significant legal gaps that need to be filled. David Chaum proposes an interesting technical scheme that protects personal privacy while it enables individuals to participate in the many convenient transactions of contemporary living that typically demand intensive exchanges of personal information. Thus, he may disagree with Rule, *et al*, arguing that a technical solution could go a long way to protecting personal privacy.

In addition to the proposals discussed in the articles in this chapter, several others have found support among the community of people actively engaged in privacy policy and analysis. Some would establish in the United States a privacy commission to oversee its protection at the state and federal levels. Others support the idea of investing individuals with property rights over personal information. These proposals offer ways to shift the burden of proof. Presently, it is the individual about whom the information concerns who must bear the burden of proving why he or she considers the use of the information undesirable. Shifting the burden would mean that the collectors and disseminators of information would need to prove that their actions neither harm, nor violate the privacy of the individual in question. We encourage readers, as they progress through this chapter, to bear in mind the values at stake and who the stake-holders are. They should consider who would benefit, and who would be harmed by different approaches. For example, if Posner is right, then investing individuals with strong privacy rights will be detrimental to society, while benefiting those who are out to trick, deceive, or harm. On the other hand, if governments and corporations are allowed to collect and use personal information freely, individuals may become vulnerable to harassment and harm, and face an end to a valued way of life.

CASE
LOTUS MARKETPLACE:
HOUSEHOLDS . . . MANAGING
INFORMATION PRIVACY CONCERNS (A)

M. J. Culnan and H. J. Smith

By mid-January 1991, it was apparent both to privacy advocates and executives at Lotus and Equifax that the uproar surrounding the upcoming introduction of the *Lotus Marketplace: Households* (hereafter, "Marketplace: Households") product was coming to a head. Lotus announced the new desktop product for Macintosh computers on April 10, 1990. According to the product announcement, *Marketplace: Households* was a CD-ROM (compact-disc, read-only memory) database containing actual and inferred information (name, address, age, gender, marital status, household income, lifestyle, and purchasing propensities) for 120 million individuals in 80 million U.S. households. The product also included software which would enable users to generate mailing lists for targeting prospective customers by identifying records within the database that met specific marketing requirements. The product was a joint venture between Lotus Development Corporation, which developed the analytic software and was responsible for pressing the discs and for physically distributing the product, and Equifax Inc., which provided the consumer data. It was targeted for sale to owners of small businesses, who would not ordinarily have access to such forms of information.

On the same day in April 1990, Lotus also announced *Lotus Marketplace: Business* a comprehensive database of 7.5 million business establishments. The data were supplied by Trinet, Inc., and included business name, address, telephone number, SIC codes, annual sales, number of employees, names and titles of executives, and key contacts. At a list price of $695, both the business and households versions of *Lotus Marketplace* were scheduled to be available for purchase from authorized Lotus retail outlets by third quarter 1990. (See *Exhibit 1* for product background information.)

During the months following the April 1990 announcement, the *Marketplace: Households* product had come under intense public scrutiny. Privacy concerns about the product were raised during two hearings held before the U.S. House of Representatives. Articles in the local and national press detailed the potential privacy threats from the product. Heated discussions began on several public computer conferencing networks, and an informal electronic grass-roots campaign urged people to protest to Lotus and Equifax, to refuse to be listed in the product, and to complain to their legislators.

Executives from Lotus and Equifax spent much time defending *Marketplace: Households*, arguing that it provided adequate privacy safeguards. Lotus released a statement on a public computer conference arguing that (1) much of the information contained in *Marketplace: Households* could be accessed elsewhere, (2) the product would only be sold to legitimate businesses, (3) individuals could have their names removed from *Marketplace: Households* by writing to Lotus, and (4) the product did not contain telephone numbers.[1] Both Lotus and Equifax argued that the product would benefit small businesses by making it feasible for them to use target marketing to offer goods and services of potential interest to consumers. The net result to consumers, they asserted, might be "an extra bit of mail."[2]

Although the *Lotus Marketplace: Business* product shipped on schedule in October 1990, the release date for *Marketplace: Households* was slipped to Spring 1991. As January 1991 dawned, the Lotus/Equifax executives' arguments seemed to be falling on deaf ears. With a targeted shipment date just two months away and consumer protests received by Lotus and Equifax numbering over 30,000 and growing, it was clear that some additional steps to address the privacy concerns were required.

THE COMPANIES[3]

Marketplace: Households was a joint venture between Lotus Development Corporation and Equifax Inc.

Lotus Development Corporation

Founded in 1982 in Cambridge, Massachusetts, Lotus Development Corporation developed, marketed, and supported business software. Its first product, Lotus 1-2-3 (a spreadsheet), was the most popular personal computer (PC) software program in the world, with more than 14 million users. Over time, Lotus had developed and marketed other software products, including Agenda (a personalized information retrieval system) and Symphony (an integrated package that included spreadsheet, word processing, database, and communications applications). Lotus marketed its products in more than 65 countries. Its 1990 net income was $23 million on sales of $685 million.

In 1986, with several software product successes already under its belt, Lotus announced that it would enter the financial information market. It would begin to sell several databases containing data about stocks and bonds on CD-ROM. With weekly updates to subscribers, the new product would provide access to 20 years of price information about stocks as well as to other services for investment advice and financial statistics.[4] Most industry observers saw this as a new and important business direction for Lotus.

Equifax Inc.

Equifax was a leading provider of information for consumer financial transactions. Founded in Atlanta in 1899 as a credit bureau, Equifax served customers in the United States, Canada and the Caribbean through more than 1,000 locations. Equifax's operations were divided along two major lines of business:

- Equifax Credit & Marketing Services provided consumer credit reports, fraud-detection services, account management, market research, statistical modeling, credit marketing and target marketing information. Equifax was one of the "Big Three" consumer credit bureaus. Its credit data base contained credit histories on more than 150 million Americans.

- Equifax Insurance and Special Services provided a growing group of automated information services and systems to major U.S. insurance companies, mortgage lenders, real estate brokers, and all types of employers.

In addition, Equifax Canada provided Equifax's Canadian customers with most of the services available in the United States. In 1989, *The Wall Street Journal* named Equifax as one of its 56 "Corporate Stars of the Future."

Equifax made a number of acquisitions throughout the late 1980s. Many of these were local credit bureaus acquired as a basis for solidifying its position as a national credit reporting agency. In July 1988, Equifax acquired National Decision Systems (NDS), which specialized in building databases to support geo-demographic analysis and other market segmentation decisions. At the time of the acquisition, C. B. (Jack) Rogers, Jr., president and chief executive officer of Equifax stated, "The critical issue for businesses is long-range profitability. As decision-making becomes more and more complex . . . all of our activities, including the combining of Equifax's consumer data with NDS' analytical and technical expertise, will enable us to address both marketing and risk decisions, and deliver solutions based on the problem at hand."[5] After its 1990 acquisition of Telecredit, a firm specializing in third-party check authorization, Equifax's revenues topped the $1 billion mark, and it joined the ranks of the Fortune Service 500.

THE TARGET MARKETING INDUSTRY[6]

Target marketing (or direct marketing) involved the use of targeting to deliver a message directly to a selected, identifiable group of customers or prospects; direct or targeted mail was one communication medium used to deliver the message. One goal of target marketing was to generate a measurable response and/or transaction from an identifiable individual. Within the multi-billion dollar target marketing industry, three sources of information were normally used to generate mailing lists. First, lists were compiled from printed sources such as public records (motor vehicle records, property records, voter registration lists, telephone directories), directories or membership lists. Second, lists were generated from customer or donor lists, or when individuals returned a rebate form or a warranty card. Typically, these lists were managed by a "list broker" on behalf of the list owner. Finally, lists were sometimes the result of original research, such as a survey. One industry directory, the Standard Rate and Data Service *Direct Mail List Rate and Data*, contained descriptions of more than 50,000 mailing lists available for rental.

Organizations typically used mailing lists in two ways. First, an organization could use their own data to profile their existing customers. The firm used these profiles to identify the demographic and psychographic characteristics of *prospective* customers it wished to target; it then rented mailing lists reflecting these characteristics. Second, to enable better targeting of their *existing* customers, a firm might have asked a list compiler or a list broker to match the firm's customer database against a third-party marketing database. When a match occurred between the two files, new information from the marketing database was added to the customer database for that individual. For example, a firm could have sought to overlay its customer database with the customer's telephone number, estimated income, type of motor vehicle owned, psychographic characteristics, or additional demographic information such as age or family size.

THE PRODUCT[7]

Marketplace: Households resulted from discussions between Lotus and Equifax that took place during the second half of 1988. Initially, the two firms had discussed a marketing analysis tool which would have been made available to small businesses. The tool would have allowed users to segment populations by a number of geographic/demographic factors. As the discussions progressed, it became apparent that an even stronger product could be developed for small businesses: a CD-ROM database product which would also allow the creation of specific mailing lists for target marketing. Early in these discussions, a well-known privacy expert, Dr. Alan Westin of Columbia University, was asked to join the internal task force to examine the privacy implications of the product and to develop privacy safeguards.

The product concept became better refined during 1989 and 1990, as the two companies continued work on the technical aspects of implementation. The names and addresses in the database were to be derived from Equifax's credit report database. The remaining fields were to be taken from the Equifax Consumer Marketing Database (ECMD). Equifax had been selling mailing lists from the ECMD to its large corporate customers since 1988.[8] These mailing lists were often segmented by credit card, level of available spending, and psychographics.

Compared to the mailing lists being sold to large corporate customers, the *Marketplace: Households* database contained a relatively spartan amount of actual information with regard to specific individuals. In addition to name and address, the *Marketplace: Households* disk included the following:

- *Geographic information* (zip, Standard Metropolitan Statistical Area, and dwelling type), derived from U.S. Postal Service tapes which were readily available. Dwelling type was identified by the Postal Service as either single-family, multi-family, or business.

- *Gender* was inferred from an Equifax-developed "name table" which categorized over 4500 common first names as male, female or "unknown."

- *Age* was to be reported in ranges. Age data were taken from publicly available sources such as voter registration records and, in roughly half the states, drivers license records. Additionally, Equifax purchased age data from vendors who extracted the data from these sources.

- *Marital status* reflected what credit grantors reported to Equifax. For example, an individual whose credit report showed only individual accounts would be listed as "single" on the *Marketplace: Households* disk.

- *Income* was modeled by computer, based on self-reported incomes from a survey of consumers, extrapolated across the population within the same zip+4 area. The income range was assumed to be the same for each household within the area. Equifax did not maintain records on actual incomes of individuals.

- *"Neighborhood lifestyle"* consisted of one of 50 categories developed in a proprietary Equifax modeling product, MicroVision. Based on Census Bureau information, every address in the country was assigned to one of the 50 categories such as "Lap of Luxury," "Movers and Shakers," or "White Picket Fence."

PRIVACY CONCERNS

As the product definition and development progressed, Westin performed a "privacy audit" of the prototype product and proposed a number of controls to address privacy concerns regarding data security and access. In addition, Equifax conducted eight focus groups in various U.S. cities with a representative sample of consumers, who provided input on privacy concerns for incorporation into the product design. Armed with this additional information, the Lotus/Equifax executives developed a set of privacy principles and protection mechanisms which were widely distributed.

During Fall 1990, the prototype product was demonstrated or explained to privacy groups, the media, and consumer groups. Lotus and Equifax contracted with a third party to test the security of the data encryption scheme. Within the two firms, agreement was reached to build into the contract with business users of *Marketplace: Households* a serious warning that the firms would aggressively seek penalties and sue users for damages to their respective corporate reputations resulting from any misuse of the product. Internal discussions focused on the need for greater public awareness of the "opt-out" provisions, which allowed consumers to request that they not be included on the disks.

General Privacy Concerns: Media and Legislative

During this same time period, information privacy issues began to receive extensive coverage in the media and scrutiny from Congress. *Business Week* ran a cover story on privacy on September 4, 1989. Subsequently, many newspapers throughout the country followed suit. Privacy issues also received coverage on a number of television programs. Two Congressional hearings on the Fair Credit Reporting Act (FCRA)[9] were held in October 1989 and June 1990. While the FCRA included a provision that allowed the use of credit report data for any legitimate business provision involving the consumer, some members of Congress questioned the legitimacy of the use of credit report data for transactions which were not initiated by the consumer, such as the use of credit report data for prescreening consumers for offers of credit, or for target marketing.

In early 1990, as media and legislative attention to privacy increased, Equifax commissioned Westin and Louis Harris & Associates to conduct a national public opinion survey regarding information privacy. Some of the results of the Equifax Survey are highlighted in *Exhibit 1*. In June 1990, Westin presented the survey results to the public in Washington, D.C. at a major conference on consumer privacy co-sponsored by the National Consumers League and the White House Office of Consumer Affairs.

The Product Under Attack

Specific privacy concerns about *Marketplace: Households* were first raised in May 1990, one month after the product's announcement. Computer Professionals for Social Responsibility (CPSR), a public interest organization, voiced objections to *Marketplace: Households* before a House of Representatives Government Operations

Subcommittee hearing "Data Protection, Computers, and Changing Information Practices."[10] An article published in the *Privacy Times*, a newsletter covering privacy issues, reported that Lotus/Equifax had no plans to notify individuals or inform the public that the service would be marketing data about them, nor was there any way individuals could gain access to data about them and correct any inaccuracies.[11] Equifax went on to state, "this information [in Marketplace] generally consists of aggregate data that places individuals in a marketing category. It is not confidential information . . . information on individuals is neither reviewable nor retrievable by the individual's name." However, consumers could "opt out" of the system by contacting either Equifax or the Direct Marketing Association (DMA).[12]

A few months later, the general public became more widely aware of *Marketplace: Households* after *The Wall Street Journal* ran a story in November 1990.[13] Marc Rotenberg, Director of CPSR's Washington office and a privacy advocate, was quoted as saying, "They've crossed the line . . . it simply shouldn't be allowed on the market." A Lotus executive argued that the product "lowered the bar" for owners of small businesses who wanted to use targeted direct mail but could not afford to rent conventional lists. "What's the harm in that? Lots of people like to get mail," he continued. This article was noted or posted in its entirety on a number of public computer conferences. In at least one instance, the article was forwarded to a public conference from a computer conferencing system within a large corporation in the computer industry. The electronic mail address for Jim Manzi, the chief executive officer (CEO) of Lotus, was disseminated across the network with a call for people seeing the message to write to Manzi and express their concerns. In December, one message circulated on at least three public computer conferences included an open letter to Lotus which said in part:

> In conclusion, if you market this product, it is my sincere hope that you are sued by every person for whom your data is [sic] false, with the eventual result that your company goes bankrupt. That would be a pity, since you make many fine products. . . . It would be better if your chief officers went to jail, but that will apparently require new laws to be passed. If you persist in your plans to market this product, a lot of people will be pushing to make that happen. I suggest that you abandon this project while there is time to do so.

REACHING A CRITICAL JUNCTURE

With the rescheduled release date for *Marketplace: Households* rapidly approaching, public concerns regarding the product were reaching epic proportions. With consumer "defections" from the database mounting daily, it was no longer clear that the initial concept for the product was still viable. The privacy debates assumed a rancorous tone. CPSR released a press release formally opposing *Marketplace: Households*[14]. By mid-January 1991, it was reported that Lotus had been "barraged by some 30,000 callers and letter-writers who believe[d] the product [was] a clear invasion of their privacy and [didn't] want their names included in its databases."[15]

International discussions continued between Lotus and Equifax. Each firm had made their own initial projections of investment and return. What became clear was that the additional investments required to address the growing privacy concerns and the heightening of consumer concerns were making return-on-investment (ROI) calculations more and more speculative. Observers could only wonder what steps, if any, could be taken to stem the tide of privacy concerns.

EXHIBIT 1*
SUMMARY OF FINDINGS
FROM PRIVACY SURVEY

Equifax distributed the following summary of the results of the national privacy survey conducted by Louis Harris and Associates and Professor Alan F. Westin. The survey questions covered a wide range of issues. The results related to information privacy are summarized here:

The American public expresses widespread concern with threats to personal privacy in America today. Nearly four Americans in five (79%) express general concern about threats to personal privacy. . . . Most business executives share this public concern.

Americans express growing concern over having to reveal personal information. Three in ten Americans today have decided not to apply for a job, credit, or insurance because they did not want to provide certain kinds of information about themselves.

The American people regard privacy as a fundamental right and are not satisfied with the way some organizations currently collect and use information about individuals. By a 71–27% margin, Americans agree that consumers have lost all control over how personal information about them is circulated and used by companies.

Despite the concern expressed over having to reveal personal information, Americans admit they would be upset if they were denied the opportunities which are only made possible through the collection and use of personal information. More than three out of four Americans (78%) say they would be upset if they could not obtain credit based upon their record of paying bills. When looking at people's responses by age, sex, race, and level of education, at least 70% in every demographic grouping say they would be upset.

Consumer attitudes about direct marketers' use of information about individual consumers depend on how Americans perceive their relationship with direct marketers. When consumers are made aware of various protective measures that are currently used or could be applied by list-making companies, and of the benefits consumers enjoy, very large majorities of the public approve direct marketers' use of information about individual consumers. When the relationship between direct marketers and consumers is presented in a way that stresses only the advantage to the direct marketers, a 69–28% majority of Americans oppose direct marketers being able to buy from list-making companies information about their own consumer characteristics. However, when the relationship between direct marketers and consumers is presented in a way that stresses the benefits to both, a 67–31% majority of Americans find it acceptable for direct marketers to buy names and addresses of people in certain age groups, income groups and residential areas.

*Source: Executive Summary, *The Equifax Report on Consumers in the Information Age*, 1990, available from Equifax Inc., Atlanta, Georgia.

LOTUS MARKETPLACE:
HOUSEHOLDS . . . MANAGING
INFORMATION PRIVACY CONCERNS (B)

On January 23, 1991, Lotus Development Corporation and Equifax Inc. announced the cancellation of *Marketplace: Households*. The press release issued jointly by the two firms said the decision to cancel the product "came after an assessment of the public concerns and misunderstanding of the product, and the substantial, unexpected additional costs required to fully address consumer privacy issues."

Jim Manzi, chief executive officer of Lotus stated, "The market for tools like Marketplace is a viable one. At the same time, the product is not part of our core business, and Lotus would be ill-served by a prolonged battle over consumer privacy."

C. B. (Jack) Rogers, Jr., president and chief executive officer of Equifax added, "Equifax is a technology leader and, equally important, a pioneer in the area of consumer privacy protection in the information industry. While we remain committed to using the most sophisticated technology available, we are equally committed to maintaining the delicate balance between legitimate information needs of business and consumers' privacy concerns."

The same day, Lotus announced that it would also discontinue sale of *Marketplace: Business*, a CD-ROM database of information on seven million U.S. businesses that began shipping in October 1990. Trinet, the data supplier for *Marketplace: Business* had just been acquired by American Business Information (ABI). After lengthy negotiations, ABI declined to extend the existing contract between Trinet and Lotus.[16]

On July 11, 1991, Marketplace Information Corporation announced that it would begin marketing *Marketplace: Business* under a licensing agreement with Lotus. MarketPlace Information was a start-up company formed by five former Lotus employees who had worked on the Lotus Marketplace products. The data for *Marketplace: Business* were provided by Dun & Bradstreet's Marketing Service. Marketplace Information said that it would not sell the consumer version of the database, and did not expect any controversy to surround the introduction of *Marketplace: Business*. Doug Borchard, president of Marketplace Information said, "the controversy was focused completely on Households, the consumer version of the product. We have no intention of selling that."[17]

In early August 1991, Equifax announced that it would discontinue sales of direct marketing lists derived from the consumer credit file. The company would continue to sell FTC-approved prescreening services for credit offers and marketing services not based on the credit file. John A. Baker, senior vice president of Equifax indicated that Equifax's mailing list business did over $10 million in business in 1990, with a profit margin of roughly 10 to 15 percent.[18]

The decision was hailed by some in the direct marketing industry. One trade newspaper published an editorial which stated:

> Finally. A major database supplier has exhibited the common decency—and common sense—to forgo profits in favor of a principle. The principle is that consumers should have a say on how their names are used on lists. If they can't easily opt out, their names shouldn't be used at all.[19]

While TRW and Trans Union, Equifax's two major competitors in the credit-reporting business sold similar lists, both firms said they had no plans to follow Equifax's lead and abandon their mailing list businesses.[20]

NOTES

1. Message from Doug Borchard of Lotus posted on the Computers & Society public computer conference, January 3, 1991.

2. Prof. Alan Westin quoted in "Peering into Private Lives," *Washington Post*, January 20, 1991. p. H6.

3. Much of the information in this section is based on the companies' annual reports.

4. William M. Bulkeley, "Lotus Pioneering Step in Marketing Financial Information on Compact Disks," *Wall Street Journal*, September 23, 1986, p. A8.

5. "Equifax Acquires National Decision Systems," press release, July 1, 1988.

6. Much of the information in this section is based on the following sources: (1) Ed Burnett, *The Complete Direct Mail List Handbook*, Prentice-Hall, 1988; (2) Ed Burnett, "How Consumer List Overlay Files Have Grown," *DM News*, October 15, 1988, p. 70; (3) Edward L. Nash, Editor, *The Direct Marketing Handbook*, Second Edition, McGraw-Hill, 1992; (4) Nat G. Bodian, *NTC's Directory of Direct Mail and Mailing List Terminology and Techniques*, NTC Business Books, 1990.

7. Some of the information in this section is based on testimony by John A. Baker, senior vice president of Equifax Inc., during a hearing on public and corporate attitudes on privacy, Subcommittee on Information, Justice & Agriculture, Government Operations Committee, U.S. House of Representatives, April 10, 1991.

8. "New Equifax Database Fuels Privacy Debate," *DM News*, August 15, 1988, p. 1.

9. See the Harvard Business School publication, "Note on the Credit Bureau Industry and the Fair Credit Reporting Act (FCRA)," 190-044 for additional background information.

10. Testimony and Statement of Computer Professionals for Social Responsibility, Subcommittee on Government Information, Justice and Agriculture, Government Operations Committee, U.S. House of Representatives, May 16, 1990.

11. "New Equifax/Lotus Database Covers 80 Million Homes, 7 Million Firms," *Privacy Times*, Vol. 10, No. 9, May 9, 1990.

12. The DMA was an industry association for direct marketers. It had developed its own set of ethical principles.

13. John R. Wilke, "Lotus Product Spurs Fears About Privacy," *The Wall Street Journal*, November 13, 1990, B1.

14. "CPSR Opposes Lotus Marketplace," Press Release of Computer Professionals for Social Responsibility, January 15, 1991.

15. Daniel Mendel-Black and Evelyn Richards, "Peering into Private Lives," *Washington Post*, January 20, 1991, pp. H1, H6.

16. "Lotus Cancels CD-ROM Project Among Privacy Concerns," *Direct Marketing*, March 1991, 8.

17. Glenn Rifkin, "Lotus Business Data Base Is Now Being Sold by Licensee," *New York Times*, July 11, 1991, D5.

18. "Equifax Is Pulling Its Credit Lists from Market; Cites Privacy Fear," *DM News*, August 12, 1991, 1.

19. Ray Schultz, "Equifax Bites the Bullet," *DM News*, August 12, 1991, 38.

20. Michael W. Miller, "Equifax to Stop Selling Its Data to Junk Mailers," *Wall Street Journal*, August 9, 1991, B1.

CASE
▷ **INFORMATION SYSTEMS
IN A DEMOCRACY**

Kenneth Laudon

The idea of America in the beginning was to free people from the unlimited surveillance and control of the state, guilds, churches, and other groups in the Old World who claimed such powers in the interest of social order, security, efficiency, and convenience. The genius of American politics was to realize this idea by fracturing power into small bits and pieces across a vast political and physical landscape, creating regional, functional, and jurisdictional cleavages in order to prevent tyranny by a single government or authority. Perhaps this was the only sensible way to govern such a vast country, given the available administrative technologies of the eighteenth and nineteenth centuries. Despite the pleas of Hamilton and Jay in the *Federalist Papers* for a strong central government, America has struck the balance more in favor of individual freedom and diversity than organizational demands for control and efficiency.

Contemporary technology can radically alter the organization of power in the United States and with it our traditional conceptions and experience of individual freedom, security, privacy, due process, and, in general, the relationship between individuals and organizations. Fourth generation hardware—microprocessors and computers on a microchip—combined with powerful new concepts in software provide politicians, bureaucrats, and legislators with new tools of governance.

I call this new world a "dossier society"—the other side of the information economy. From the individual's point of view, the most significant characteristic of the dossier society is that decisions made about us as citizens, employees, consumers, debtors, and supplicants rely less and less on personal face-to-face contact, on what we say, or even on what we do. Instead, decisions are based on information that is held in national systems, and interpreted by bureaucrats and clerical workers in distant locations. The decisions made about us are based on a comprehensive "data image" drawn from diverse files.

From a technical and structural view, the central characteristic of the dossier society is the integration of distinct files serving unique programs and policies into more or less permanent national databases. These centralized databases serve regional and local users in distributed locations through powerful telecommunications networks, and the end users themselves increasingly possess local machine intelligence (microcomputers) for further local processing of information.

From a political and sociological view, the key feature of the dossier society is an aggregation of power in the federal government without precedent in peacetime

America. From a cultural view, the dossier society is one which exposes thousands of officially selected moments in your past to confront you with the threads of an intricate web, revealing your "official life," the one you must live with and explain to whatever authority chooses to demand an explanation.

The technical means are now available and cheap enough to centralize and integrate the bits and pieces of American government and society into single, large, national constellations of power. As a result, these new technologies are increasingly important in determining how much and what kind of freedom, security, privacy, due process, and efficiency we will have.

The fully capable dossier society is perhaps a decade away, at most. The pillars of this new order are the emerging national information systems in both the public and private sectors. By observing these systems we can see and understand the dossier society yet to come.

This is a study of national information systems, the emerging constellations of governmental power at the center of which are fourth generation computer technology and information systems. My focus is not on the technology but on the value choices made by key actors in the conception, design, and operation of national systems. Not everything about these systems is predetermined, outside of the fact that they will be built and operated. Important features of national information systems and the dossier society they make possible are yet to be designed. At critical moments in their conception and design, choices are available which will determine the impact of these systems on important American values. The persons who make these value choices and how they are made are the principal themes of my story. Whenever bureaucrats in Washington meet to design national information systems, in reality a small constitutional convention is in progress.

A LOST CHOICE OPPORTUNITY

In November 1974, the American public lost an important opportunity to shape the broad outlines of the dossier society. Both the Senate and the House had approved the Privacy Act, the first effort by Congress to legislate structural limitations on executive branch use of information and to define individual rights vis-a-vis this information. Proposed by Sam Ervin of the Senate Judiciary Committee, the Privacy Act forbade the executive branch from using information gathered in one program area in an entirely different and unrelated area. The Act wisely permitted the executive branch to create whatever advanced information systems were necessary in order to administer specific programs authorized by Congress but forbade, without express congressional approval, the sharing of information among programs. The IRS, Social Security, the FBI, Defense—each could develop contemporary systems limited to authorized programs. They could not share this information among themselves by claiming some "generalized governmental interest" in the information. In the 1960s and early 1970s, Congress repeatedly denied authorization for a National Data Center and a network of federal computer systems (FEDNET). The Privacy Act simply expressed a long held congressional fear of executive information systems expanding beyond the boundaries of existing congressional review and appropriations. To enforce the will of Congress, the Privacy Act created a Privacy Protection Commission, a permanent small agency appointed jointly by the Congress and the President.

In December 1974, President Ford sent word to Ervin that he would veto the

Privacy Act unless Congress agreed to downgrade the Privacy Commission from an agency to a study group, a Privacy Protection Study Commission. In addition, Ford wanted the legislation to be enforced by the Office of Management and Budget, an executive branch agency controlled by the President (Burnham 1983d:204).

With a congressional Christmas recess imminent, the possibility that the reaction to Watergate, so important for creating fear of the executive and enthusiasm for limits on executive uses of information, was weakening, Ervin had little choice but to agree to the compromise and save that part of the Privacy Act which defined individual rights. The Privacy Act was intended to forbid the executive from sharing information collected in distinct program areas, thereby creating integrated national information systems (U.S. Senate 1976).

As I describe in later chapters, the OMB in subsequent administrations has unfortunately refused to enforce the principles outlined in the Privacy Act. As a result, the development of integrated, general purpose, national information systems is proceeding unabated.

How will you know who received information from your file? Who will control, manage, audit, and oversee these systems? How can you change, seal, remove, and purge information from these systems? How accurate and complete will the information be? Are there any limits on the use of information about your past? The answers to these and other questions are still incomplete or not yet determined. There still is time for choice.

1984 AND THE RETREAT FROM PRIVACY

In 1984 Congress signaled a virtual retreat from the Privacy Act by passing the Deficit Reduction Act of 1984 which contained provisions establishing a de facto National Data Center capability. Without any debate (most of the debate focused on the national deficit), Congress required all states to participate in file merging, matching, and linking programs to verify the eligibility of beneficiaries in Food Stamp, Medicare, Aid to Families with Dependent Children (AFDC), and a host of other "needs" and insurance based programs. Involved here is the systematic merging and linking of Social Security, medical, and personal data with Internal Revenue, and private employer data.

While most of these "matching" and "linking" programs are currently limited to less popular groups such as federal employees, benefit recipients (some 50 million Americans), and draft dodgers, there is no reason they cannot be extended to IBM, Bank of America, or General Motors. As defense contractors and federally chartered institutions, these organizations, and thousands of other private corporations, could easily be asked to submit digital records of their employees to the federal government to discover, for insurance, how many IBM employees receive welfare, how many have failed to repay student loans, how many have criminal records, how many have failed to pay alimony, and so forth.

NATIONAL INFORMATION SYSTEMS: DE FACTO NATIONAL DATA CENTERS

At last count there were 50 million Social Security beneficiaries, 95 million individual and 75 million business taxpayers, 21.2 million recipients of food stamps, 10.6

million recipients of Aid to Families with Dependent Children (AFDC), 24 million criminals and 60 million civilians with fingerprints at the FBI, 3.9 million elderly receiving Supplemental Security Income (SSI), 21.4 million recipients of Medicaid, 61.8 million people covered by private health plans, more than 500,000 doctors and dentists who generated 1.1 million office visits, 49.8 million public school students, 9.5 million arrests, 294,000 people in jail, 5.8 million defense industry workers, 2 million members of the armed forces, 36 million living veterans of all wars, 51 million credit card holders, 62 million credit records held in private credit data systems, 154 million registered motor vehicles, and 140 million licensed drivers (U.S. Bureau of the Census 1980).

Lacking a precise definition, one could point to any of these programs or populations and find a national information system which either administers the program, delivers the service, or keeps track of individual transactions. We can think of these systems as truly *national* in scope (as opposed to local or regional), linked to the administration of one or several national programs or private services, inherently *large*, e.g., involving millions of individuals and a large number of data elements on each individual, and *complex*, i.e., data is entered and accessed at several levels, from local to national. The systems also maintain files requiring frequent, sometimes *sophisticated, updating and change*. These systems are centralized insofar as they serve centrally defined programs and decision criteria, the systems generally involve a central repository of data and technical managerial staff.

Many of these systems originated in the 1930s as necessary adjuncts to the daily administration of specific programs. They have since grown into extremely large repositories of data which are linked with other systems and hence perform more general purpose functions. For instance, as I describe in later chapters, information on tax files can be used to locate absent parents, and information on selective service files can be used to allocate federal college loans or other program benefits. Increasingly, programs intersect with each other. Increasingly, executives, legislators, and citizens are coming to the realization that the most efficient way to administer these intersecting programs is to create linkages—sometimes permanent—among the separate information systems.

Describing the evolution of these systems requires detailed knowledge of specific program areas, the nature of decision making in those areas, a microlevel understanding of how information is used, and an appreciation of the macrolevel policy context within which programs and systems evolve. Rather than superficially study all or many national information systems, this study focuses on a single, national information—a national computerized criminal history system—intended to make us all feel more secure from crime by identifying to police, prosecutors, and criminal court magistrates, and thereby singling out for special treatment, those criminals who are serious, repetitive offenders. This seems like a supportable cause around which most Americans would gladly rally. But there is a cost even if the benefits promised are actually delivered.

As an unintended result of pursuing domestic security, this system may actually increase the incidence of crime by denying employment and promotion to millions of ex-convicts as well as persons guilty of nothing more than an arrest record.

With advances in fingerprint search technology taken into account, and though unintended by designers, legislators, and managers, this system containing the fingerprints of more than half the adult population may turn out to be at the center of a national identity center useful for conducting widespread social surveillance of both individuals and businesses.

A central issue in this research is how security from crime and freedom from harassment and surveillance can be reconciled with the planning, design, and implementation of a large national information system. Who will determine whether the promised benefits of crime reduction are worth the social costs? How can we measure the benefits and costs?

Beyond Ideology

Neither liberal nor conservative ideology provides much guidance on the issue of national information systems, privacy, and due process. Liberals, ironically, created the very state apparatus in the 1930s which is now reaching out with a data dragnet to ensnare large parts of the population. Many liberals, feeling the heat of attacks by conservatives on social security, and fraud and waste in welfare programs, gladly espouse the new computerized surveillance techniques as the only hope of saving their cherished programs. Other liberals believe national information systems are unfairly directed towards welfare recipients as opposed to defense contractors and small business loan recipients. They call for more data surveillance of large corporations—but do not disagree with the principle of such surveillance.

Conservatives, ironically, opposed the growth of the welfare state and all forms of big government, but find irresistable the temptation to use the instruments of federal government computers to expose welfare fraud and other crimes. Instead of getting big government off our backs, these policies are putting big government in our kitchens and living rooms.

WHY STUDY THE FBI'S NATIONAL COMPUTERIZED CRIMINAL HISTORY (CCH) SYSTEM?

There are four reasons why the FBI's plans for a national computerized criminal history (CCH) system provide an ideal perspective from which to observe the interaction between computer systems technology and American culture and politics. The FBI's national CCH is, in fact, many systems in one, each posing unique value choices.

First, this system directly affects decisions about freedom versus incarceration for the 9.5 million persons arrested each year. The perception and reality of domestic security will be affected indirectly by how well this system operates. Few decisions in a democracy based on due process are more crucial. Second, the CCH directly affects the employment and promotion possibilities for the estimated 36 million individuals (30 million of whom are active in the labor force) who have a record of criminal arrest. Third, unlike systems at IRS and Social Security which operate within a single national jurisdiction, the FBI's CCH system illustrates the way in which local and state functions are integrated and coordinated through national information systems. Fourth, considered as a potential national identity center based on nearly universal fingerprinting, the FBI's national CCH and elated civilian systems raise unique questions about the adequacy of privacy and other legislation designed to limit national authorities and to hold national systems accountable to Congress.

A Criminal Justice System

In 1968 the FBI proposed the development of a national computerized criminal history system in response to what was seen then as America's major domestic problem, crime. Responding to recommendations of scientists and engineers on its own staff and elsewhere, and recommendations of the President's Commission on Law Enforcement and the Administration of Justice, the FBI sought to develop a National Crime Information Center (NCIC) which would computerize and centralize in Washington, D.C., criminal information such as warrants for arrest and records of stolen property, firearms, and criminal history. The focus of my study is on criminal history records because these records, generated primarily by states and localities, directly affect the freedom and security of citizens and raise the most significant political and social issues.

Most Americans do not know what a criminal history record is, nor are they aware of the size and importance of these records in the United States. They are even less aware of the significant changes that have taken place in this record system over the last ten years through extensive centralization and computerization.

There are 195 million criminal history records in the United States. Thirty-five million of these are maintained by the states, 25 million by the federal government, and the remaining 135 million in local police agencies, often in shoe boxes and file drawers, as Figure 1.1 shows (SEARCH Group 1976). Criminal history records provide a list of a person's arrests and sometimes include information on the actual court decision ("disposition") and sentence (see Table 1.1). Traditionally, these records have remained in the localities where they originated. However, 34 states have developed a computerized state criminal history systems; the FBI operates a huge manual system called the Identification Division which stores about 24 million criminal records and about 70 million fingerprint records of civilians, who are, for the most part, current and former members of the armed forces or government employees. The FBI also operates the National Crime Information Center which indexes over 9 million computerized criminal histories and contains several hundred thousand warrants for arrest (the Wanted Persons System).

Criminal history records are created routinely by the police whenever an arrested person is fingerprinted. Regardless of the merits of the arrest, the criminal history record tends to remain a permanent part of an individual's dossier. Following an arrest, criminal history records are used by district attorneys in the arraignment process to establish bail and initial charges. They are also used by criminal court magistrates to establish length of sentence, and by probation/parole personnel as a part of background character studies (presentence investigation reports). Finally, the record is used by correctional agencies for placement purposes in a correctional institution.

The principal actors in the creation and use of criminal history records are the police (who submit names), courts (which are requested to submit court disposition information to criminal history record systems), and correctional agencies (which submit location and dates of sentence execution). As I discuss below, once created, the criminal history record has a large and expanding audience.

The FBI and other groups now propose to greatly expand, automate, and integrate existing manual and state computerized systems into a single national entity. A national system promises to distribute criminal history records more widely throughout the society and thereby alter a number of strictly criminal justice decisions. Whether or not you are under special police surveillance, are treated harshly or

TABLE 1.1   Ideal Version of a Criminal History Record

CONTRIBUTOR OF FINGERPRINTS	NAME AND NUMBER	ARRESTED OR RECEIVED	CHARGE	DISPOSITION

PD
  Peoria, Ill.
	John Lee Doe
	  34653
		8/12/74	OMVWI	charge
				  dismissed
				  12/18/74

PD
Daytona Beach, Fla.
	John Doe
	ID-104200
	SID FL4261893
		4/21/75	shoplifting	4/29/75
				sentence
				  suspended
				  30 days

SO
Oregon, Ill.
	John L Doe	5/2/76	burglary
			  2 counts
				6/10/76
				1 yr Ill.
				Dept. of
				  Corrections

Rec & Class Ctr. Joliet, Ill.	John Lee Doe C61778	7/1/76	burglary	1 yr

PD
Peoria, Ill.
	John L Doe
	34653
		8/3/78	theft	9/1/78
				1 yr/6 mos
				  to 4 yr/6 mos
				  guilty Ill.
				Dept. of
				  Corrections

Rec & Class Ctr. Joliet, Ill.	John Doe C61778	9/29/78	theft	1 yr 6 mos to 4 yr 6 mos

Source: Identification Division, Federal Bureau of Investigation, July 1979.

leniently by prosecutors and judges, where you serve time, and how long—each of these decisions will be affected by this new system. For the 30 million Americans in the labor force who have a criminal record, this system will affect basic decisions about freedom and incarceration. For all Americans the proposed system promises to affect our real and perceived security from crime.

Seen strictly as a criminal justice system, the FBI's CCH system offers citizens, politicians, and bureaucrats a number of value choices. Should police have street access to this system and relate to citizens on the basis of past criminal behavior or current behavior? In order to protect the President, should persons with lengthy criminal records be placed under surveillance or perhaps detained when the President visits a city? Should such persons be fitted with a tiny radio transmitter to track their movements through a city as a part of their parole conditions? (The feasibility of this was demonstrated recently by an LEAA-funded experiment in a Tucson court). If a person were arrested five years ago for armed robbery but no conviction was obtained, should a prosecutor seek to deny bail in a current arrest for armed robbery? What if the prior arrest led to a conviction? What if the prior arrest occurred in another state and city? Should the state legislature mandate that judges give determinate and severe sentences to felons with two prior felony convictions anywhere in the United States, or should this be left to the discretion of judges? After how many years should a conviction for a crime be ignored? How should a misdemeanor be treated? What level of accuracy and currency of information is acceptable in these kinds of decisions?

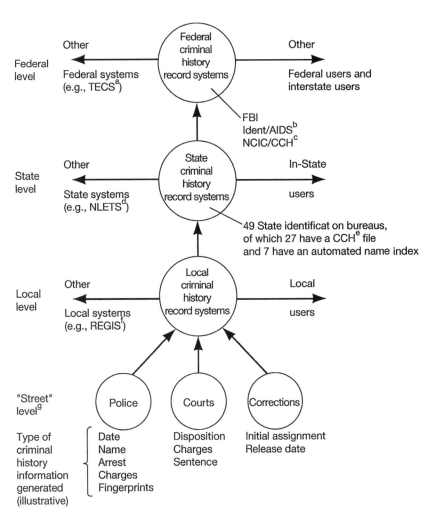

NOTES:

[a]TECS = Treasury Enforcement Communication System.

[b]Ident/AIDS = Manual and Automated Identification Division System records (including fingerprints) maintained by the FBI's Identification Division.

[c]NCIC/CCH = FBI's National Crime Information Center computerized criminal history records.

[d]NLETS = National Law Enforcement Telecommunications Systems.

[e]CCH = Computerized Criminal History.

[f]REGIS = Regional governmental information systems which frequently transmit criminal history information (as in St. Louis, Missouri region).

[g]May also include prosecution files and records maintained by pretrial diversion and probation/parole agencies.

FIGURE 1.1: Overview of Criminal History Records System *Source: Office of Technology Assessment, adapted from Sarwar A. Kashmeri, "REJIS—A New Concept for Regional Criminal Justice Agencies," in LEAA, Proceedings of the Second International Symposium on Criminal Justice Information and Statistics Systems, Washington, D.C., 1974, p. 380.*

In all of these value choices the crucial issue is how to judge a person's current behavior using the past as a guide when information, which we will see later, is of uncertain quality. A national CCH exposes a limited part of a person's past and makes it available to decision makers. Often there are neither resources nor time to develop a complete understanding of the person, and judgment must be made summarily on the basis of the available criminal history record. A national CCH provides this limited information about a person, but it does not tell us how to evaluate that information. Here we have to rely on our own sense of decency, fear, hopes, suspicions, and beliefs about the person we are judging and the information system which delivers the information.

The incompleteness of available information raises a host of empirical questions. Will prosecutors actually use criminal history records to deny bail and raise charges? (In how many cases and by how much?) Will judges treat felons with lengthy records more harshly than first offenders? (How many cases are involved and how many additional months of prison?) Will probation officers and rehabilitation workers be able to use criminal history records to assign offenders to correctional facilities more rationally? And if all this happens, what difference will it make for the incidence of crime?

The new information technology offers us new decision possibilities. It also acts as a mirror, reflecting our own values. How police, prosecutors, criminal court judges, public defenders and others will actually use the new technical capability of a national CCH forms a large part of our story.

A National Employment Screening System

If the FBI's national CCH were simply a criminal justice system, my story would be less complex and this book a good deal shorter. Less well known than its immediate criminal justice uses, the FBI's national CCH is equally important as an employment screening tool. The existing criminal files held in the Identification Division contain the fingerprints and criminal records of 24 million individuals. Of the total cases in which this file is used, more than half are for employment screening, making the existing system the largest employment screening tool in the nation.

To some, the existing system is the largest "blacklist" in history. This system is used to screen public and private sector employees from school teachers and janitors to go-go girls and peanut vendors, to security vendors in federally insured financial institutions. When more fully computerized and centralized, the FBI's CCH system will encompass most, if not all, of the 30 million workers—one-third of the labor force—who have criminal records. Certainly, many of our relatives both near and distant must be in that group. If history is any guide at all, employers of all sorts and administrators of many government programs will surely seek access. Who could resist a centralized database of youthful misdemeanors and even crimes?

Here the value choices are more difficult, because the connection between employment opportunity and past criminal behavior, or even the accusation of such behavior, is so confused in public rhetoric and policy. As one wag noted, when a really difficult policy decision is needed in America, the response is a number of contradictory programs to appease various interest groups and perspectives, half of which exacerbate the problem.

Should a convicted nineteen-year-old car thief be employed as a school janitor when he is twenty-five? Should an ex-convict trained in prison as a barber be denied a state license to work as a barber? Should a partner in a Wall Street brokerage firm be fired when it is discovered that at age twenty he was convicted of petty theft? Should all meter readers working for public utilities and routinely entering private homes be screened for prior criminal arrests and/or convictions? Should sex offenders be permitted employment in any setting? If so, which ones? Should criminal statutes be amended to prescribe not just criminal penalties but also lifelong civil penalties, such as exclusion from labor markets? Should a family, one member of which has a criminal record, be permitted to live in public housing? What is the meaning of rehabilitation if ex-convicts will not be allowed to work? While millions of dollars are spent on prison training programs and parole "job creation," should additional millions be spent to assure ex-convicts cannot work?

The central element in these value choices is the treatment of prior misdemeanors, crimes, and the allegation of crime in evaluating a person's employment and promotion. Now that we have a technology capable of cataloging prior, official deviance, what kinds of policy controls are appropriate?

A National Information and Identity Center

The significance of a national CCH extends beyond the treatment of persons with a prior criminal record. Creating a single system is a multijurisdictional, multiorganizational effort which requires linking more than 60,000 criminal justice agencies with more than 500,000 workers, thousands of other government agencies, and private employers, from the local school district to the Bank of America, who will use the system for employment screening. A national CCH represents a nationalization of what was previously a primarily local and state function.

In addition to the 36 million individuals with criminal records likely to find themselves in a national CCH, the FBI maintains a civilian file with another 70 million individual fingerprint records. These are current and former members of the armed forces, defense contractors and workers, nuclear plant workers, federal employees, and others who by choice or by dint of employment circumstances submitted their prints to the FBI. The technology now exists to automate the searching of fingerprint files, something that until recently was a lengthy manual procedure. Moreover, the political climate is now one in which there is growing pressure for government agencies to reduce fraud by sharing information from one program, for example, Social Security, with other programs, such as Selective Service, parent locator systems, and welfare. With these so-called "matching" programs, the federal government has carried out, since the Carter administration in the late 1970s, an aggressive expansion of its data matching and processing capabilities.

Although politically popular, these programs are barely cost effective because they rely on Social Security numbers and other personal identifiers of great uncertainty in order to identify potential fraudulent persons. How much better and more efficient it would be if positive identification were made a requirement for participation in government programs and, in the case of aliens, employment.

It takes little imagination to see a national computerized fingerprint system operated by the FBI at the center of a web of other federal and federal/private systems (e.g., medical insurance underwriters). Indeed, universal fingerprinting ... was a primary goal of the FBI's Identification Division when it began operations in 1927. Neither the technology nor the political circumstances were supportive at that time. The complexity of government programs in the 1980s, their relationships with each other and private sector activities, may make positive identification based on a national fingerprint file a necessity.

Here the value choices are particularly difficult because such fundamental and opposing values are involved. Both the tradition and ideology of America have extolled the fragmentation of power as a bulwark of democracy although European democracies have far more centralized traditions. Congress has repeatedly denied authorization for the creation of a National Data Center or anything like it, whenever it was given the opportunity to vote on a coherent proposal for one. Congress went on record in the Privacy Act of 1974 as prohibiting federal agencies from using information gathered in one program in an entirely different program, with the express intent of preventing the accretion of executive power.

On the other hand, the strength of contemporary computer and software technology lies in its ability to move data efficiently across organizational boundaries and combine it with data from entirely different programs and files. Efficiency, with its promise of national and individual wealth, is also a popular American value. In the belief that the government has a generalized interest in any and all information it gathers, regardless of how or where and often without explicit authorization of Congress, the executive branch has begun to share information among government programs and with the private sector on an ad hoc basis. Efficiency and effective program administration are always the stated goals. The targets vary with the times and the whims of public opinion, beginning with absconding fathers in 1974 who refused to pay alimony and child support to, most recently, the pursuit of draft dodgers, welfare cheats, and debtors. The list of potential targets for these so-called matching programs is large and growing rapidly.

Do we have the policy mechanisms and institutions in place to control, monitor, audit, and manage this sharing of information to ensure it can be held accountable to democratic practices and values? How can executive abuse of these new capabilities be prevented? Is the FBI an appropriate agency to operate the national identity center? If created, what new kinds of oversight mechanisms are needed?

TWO VISIONS OF A NATIONAL CCH

From its inception in President Johnson's Commission on Law Enforcement and the Administration of Justice in 1968, the idea of a national CCH has been informed by two visions of what, ideally, such a system would do to American society.

The first can be called the "professional record keeper" vision. It foresees a more rational world in which instantly available and accurate information would be used to spare the innocent and punish the guilty. It is held primarily by persons recruited from the ranks of police, district attorneys, and criminal courts, who operate the existing record systems of criminal justice agencies, as well as the systems analysts, programmers, and system managers at federal, state, and local levels. For these persons, the "criminal history record is the fundamental information thread which weaves together the components" of the criminal justice system (Cooper 1984).

In the professional record keeper's vision, criminal offenders with multistate records constitute a significant part of the workload of criminal justice decision makers. With a national CCH, no matter how far criminal offenders move from the locality and state in which they committed a crime, their records would be potentially retrievable by law enforcement officials. Police officers on the beat will have instantaneous access to prior criminal history information. They will use this information to make decisions about whom to investigate, whom to place under surveillance, and whom to arrest. It is a world in which district attorneys at bail hearings and at the point of sentencing will be able to bring to the judiciary a complete criminal history of all the prior arrests and convictions of a defendant.

In this vision, the district attorney will be able to prevent violent, serious, repeat felons from obtaining light or no bail. It is a world in which judges, once presented with a complete background of a person, will judge more severely those with such a record and will judge less severely those without a record. Briefly, it is a world in which apprehension, prosecution, and judicial decision making will be adjusted to the nature of the current crime and the nature of the criminal's past behavior. Probation, which has responsibilities for pretrial diversion and presentence investigation reports, will now for the first time be able to obtain complete and comprehensive criminal history information, to assess more rationally its recommendations for pretrial release, and to judge more rationally and uniformly the underlying character of the offender. And, within correctional facilities, correctional officers will be able to discriminate among the various types and kinds of offenders, assuring that each receives the appropriate treatment merited by his criminal history record.

In this vision, there are few problems with accuracy, ambiguity, and completeness of criminal history records. Perfect information is assumed. Here, criminal justice decision makers would be able to rapidly interpret and make decisions based upon this new information.

A national CCH would also make, in this view, a significant contribution to our understanding and knowledge about the origins of crime and the appropriate treatment for convicted offenders. A national CCH system would permit the development of a comprehensive statistical database, allowing society for the first time to judge the merits of anticrime programs, variations in sentencing length and severity, and the overall effectiveness of the criminal justice system. This is a world in which information is the key driving force directly affecting organizational decision making.

A second vision can be called the "dossier society vision," widely held by liberal groups, the American Civil Liberties Union, many district attorneys, criminal court magistrates, state and federal legislative research staff, and defense attorneys. In this view, a national CCH system would be a gargantuan "runaway" file not limited to criminal justice uses and composed largely of minor, misdemeanor offenders. This system would pose significant difficulties for the preservation of due process and inhibit the ability for criminals (as well as those merely arrested but not found guilty of anything) to rehabilitate themselves and find gainful employment. It is a vision of a system composed of a great deal of information on minor criminal offenders, on accused persons not found guilty of anything, which, once removed from its local context, can no longer be interpreted unambiguously.

Ultimately, the system would have little impact on the efficiency and effectiveness of criminal apprehension, prosecution, or correction. This vision assumes imperfect information and incomplete knowledge. Criminal justice decision makers at the local level will tend to discount this information from a national system and rely on local information systems whose meaning can be easily interpreted.

In this vision a national CCH system will come to play a leading non-criminal justice role as a national information system operated by the federal government and linked to other national systems, such as those operated by the Social Security Administration, the Department of Defense, and the Internal Revenue Service. Its use as a device to screen from public and private jobs persons who have arrest records will encourage the creation of a caste of unemployable people, largely composed of minorities and poor persons, who will no longer be able to rehabilitate themselves or find gainful employment in even the most remote communities.

A national CCH system in this view presents unsurmountable problems of federal and state legislative oversight and would be subject to significant abuse by political executives. It would be virtually impossible to control the dissemination of information from such a system involving more than 60,000 agencies and 500,000 employees. Given the size and complexity of the system, it would be virtually impossible to audit or to conduct congressional oversight. Briefly, a national CCH system would be one system whose social impact will be mostly negative and whose impact upon criminal justice decision making will be minuscule and potentially harmful to the rights of individual citizens. Such systems will ultimately be used by police as a weapon to stigmatize individuals in a community.

The goal of my research is to empirically examine these two visions—one intensely positive and hopeful for a more rational society, the other intensely negative and threatening, a less humane and even repressive society—in light of the organizational, social, and political realities of American society and the criminal justice system in particular.

Perspectives

Given the immensity of national information systems like CCH and the complexity of issues ranging from the efficiency of law enforcement and the origins of crime to federalism, constitutional questions of due process, and political questions about the organization of federal executive power, no single perspective or academic discipline is adequate to fully explain the importance of a national CCH system or its likely social impact. Three perspectives are employed in this research. A national CCH is, first, considered as an effort by a single federal agency to develop a new information system to control crime. Second, development of a national CCH can be seen as an effort by the federal government to create a new national information system with potential linkages to other national information systems in other functional areas. Third, the development of a national CCH can be seen in the context of a political democracy attempting to reconcile the strengths of contemporary computer technology with the requisites of democracy, privacy, and due process.

Bureaucratic Juggernaut

Considered as an effort by a single, large, bureaucratic entity to develop a new information system to control crime, several questions come to the fore. From this limited perspective, the most important question is, would it work? Would a national CCH reduce the incidence of crime, or in some measurable fashion affect the decision making of criminal justice officials?

Proponents of a national CCH cite the need for this system due to the increased mobility of criminals from one jurisdiction to the next. The image conveyed is one of a criminal who hops a plane in New York to commit a morning burglary in San Francisco and returns in the evening to New York. Once in New York, the criminal takes a train to Connecticut to cause further mayhem. But is this a realistic vision? Crime is still predominantly a local phenomenon in the United States, especially the violent and interpersonal crime which concerns most Americans. Perhaps state and local systems are the appropriate levels on which to attack this problem of crime. Police, prosecutors, and judges are all local officials who, by constitutional design, are required to respond to local political realities, not federal anti-crime initiatives.

Citing rapidly growing crime rates, the proponents of a national CCH claim it is one solution. But will this system lead to a greater probability of apprehension, higher charges at arraignment, longer sentences, better correction and rehabilitation? From 1960 to 1980, the number of persons arrested in the United States roughly doubled, from 4.8 to 9 million arrests in 1980. The number of federal and state prisoners in this same period increased by 100 percent to nearly 600,000 prisoners in all federal, state, and local jails by 1982. The U.S. incarceration rate now trails only those of the Soviet Union and South Africa; two-thirds of the jails are under court order to improve living conditions. And in this same period, the length of time served by prisoners in federal and state institutions increased nearly one-third, from 32 to 44 months, making the United States the harshest sentencer of convicted criminals in the Western world (Bureau of Justice Statistics 1982). Given these accomplishments of the criminal justice system, still higher levels of arrest and more and longer prison sentences may have little or nothing to do with the incidence of crime.

Citing the administrative chaos of courts and local district attorneys working under archaic nineteenth-century conditions, where courts have often released felons on bail even though they were wanted elsewhere for other crimes, the proponents cite the need for a national CCH as an important tool for managing the greater workloads imposed on the criminal justice system in the last twenty years. Do district attorneys and courts pay much attention to criminal records of persons if the crimes occurred elsewhere in other jurisdictions? Moreover, is it proper or appropriate to punish criminals not simply for the crime they committed, but for previous crimes for which they may have already been punished?

To some extent, these are traditional questions of both criminal justice and systems analysis: to what problem is the proposed system a solution, what is the nature of the problem, are there alternative solutions, what costs are involved, and how feasible is the system given the organizational realities?

National Information System

A single agency perspective alone is insufficient to capture the reality of a national CCH system since it is not simply a single agency system. It is an attempt to develop a system that ranges far beyond the functional boundaries of any one organization and beyond the scope of any single function such as criminal justice. Given the scope of the FBI's proposal to develop a national CCH system which could be used by 50 states, 60,000 criminal justice agencies, and countless thousands of other agencies for employment screening, the perspective of a single agency is too limiting for analysis. A second level of analysis is required which I will call a "national information system" perspective. Here, a national CCH system is seen in light of other bureaucratic and political forces that shape national information policy. One must consider the information policy of the President, the efforts of a number of executive agencies to develop their own, related national systems, and finally, the efforts of Congress to spur or discourage these developments.

Given the diversity of users, from local sheriffs in Iowa to cops on the beat in New York, is there any possibility that a single-record system can be standardized at the national level, be given universal significance and meaning beyond its local origins, and be interpreted fairly and uniformly across the spectrum of American society? Put another way, given the peculiarities of the Los Angeles Police Department, is a black person's arrest for resisting arrest in Los Angeles easily understood and interpreted by a court in, for example, Minneapolis? Should he be hired or fired from his job?

A national information system perspective permits my research to consider the other bureaucratic and political forces at work in the development of a national CCH system. Since the early 1970s, the states and localities have been developing the vital building blocks of national systems, namely, state computerized repositories of criminal history records. Crime control is a popular political stance, especially if you can get the federal government to pay for it. What technological and social forces have led the states to develop these systems?

While the perspective of a national information system introduces other bureaucratic and political forces that are shaping the development of a national CCH system, this perspective does not capture some of the broader social impacts of a national CCH in a political democracy.

Systems in a Political Democracy

Most Americans want a society where serious felons are effectively brought to justice. Most Americans want a society where government programs are effectively and efficiently administered using, where necessary, advanced information technology. On the other hand, most Americans want a society where they are not exposed to routine social surveillance and screening, where the actions of government can be held accountable to elected representatives in Congress, and where government administrators do not act capriciously, maliciously, or arbitrarily. With every new generation of computer and telecommunications technology, new questions arise about the power and size of the federal government and the protection of individual liberties.

From the perspective of a political democracy, the question raised here is quite simple: can a national CCH system be built which will help to achieve effective criminal justice without, at the same time, destroying the experience of freedom and the constitutional guarantees of privacy, due process, and equality before the law?

The strength of contemporary computing and telecommunications technology is their ability to efficiently combine information from several functionally and physically distinct files and make it available to decision makers. The virtues of modern telecommunications and database management technology are also the principal threats which information technology poses for democratic forms of government which seek to limit the power of the executive by making it difficult to amass either the information or the power to make decisions unilaterally. Power is limited by segmenting authority, segregating information flows, creating multiple checkpoints, and encouraging lengthy and slow deliberation. These practical principles of political democracy are very much at odds with the virtues of contemporary information technology.

Congress sought in 1974, and in more than twenty major pieces of legislation which followed, to reconcile, not balance, the opposing virtues of information technology and political democracy. Aside from clearly stating for the first time the rights of individual citizens vis-à-vis government record keepers and establishing principles of management which federal record keepers must follow, the most important contribution of the Privacy Act was to proscribe the development of general purpose national information systems.

Yet, advances in the capabilities of contemporary technology, coupled with changes in political sentiment and power groups in Washington, have led to the development of matching, computer profile, and screening programs that permit the effective integration of information collected by diverse and sundry agencies (U.S. Senate 1982). These developments suggest that the first generation of privacy legislation may no longer be capable of controlling and shaping the uses of computer technology by the federal government. More to the point, the Privacy Act of 1974, as well as other first generation privacy act statements, appears incapable of preventing what Congress most feared, namely, the development of general purpose national systems.

Given these developments in national information systems, what role will a national CCH system play? Does the creation of a national CCH, for instance, make it more likely that applicants for college loans will be required to undergo a criminal history background check? Currently, applicants for federally funded college loans and grants must submit clearances from the Selective Service Administration to demonstrate that they have registered for the draft. With a little stretch of the imagination, it is conceivable that one day, with a national CCH in existence, students will be required to verify their criminal history background. A national CCH may also have implications for the private sector: in order to protect their clients, customers, and themselves from lawsuits, private employers may begin to routinely inquire of a national CCH system for all new job applicants and promotions.

These questions go considerably beyond the efforts of a single agency such as the FBI to develop a national CCH. Questions are raised here concerning the appropriate role of national information systems in a political democracy and the public policy tools which ensure that systems designed to make government more efficient do not lead to the demise of democracy.

PUBLIC IMAGE

Larry Hunter

Headed for a PhD in computer science, Larry Hunter has been playing with computers since he was ten. He uses a powerful, state-of-the-art workstation at Yale and telecommunicates to it from home on an itsy-bitsy lap computer. The encompassing reach of computers which he describes in this article has made two differences in his own life. It has granted him computer expertise to assist his favored local politicians in their campaign strategies, and it has frightened him into the habit of keeping his paper-life to a minimum and withholding his ID and Social Security numbers from anyone who does not legally require them.—Kevin Kelly

I live in your future. As a graduate student in Artificial Intelligence at Yale University, I am now using computer equipment that will be commonplace five years from now. I have a powerful workstation on my desk, connected in a high-speed network to more than one hundred other such machines, and, through other networks, to thousands of other computers and their users. I use these machines not only for research, but to keep my schedule, to write letters and articles, to read nationwide electronic "bulletin boards," to send electronic mail, and sometimes just to play games. I make constant use of fancy graphics, text formatters, laser printers—you name it. My gadgets are both my desk and my window on the world. I'm quite lucky to have access to all these machines.

But with this privilege comes a certain sobriety: I've begun to contemplate some of the effects the computer will have on society. It is impossible to predict what our interconnected, information-oriented society will look like in detail, but some of the outlines are becoming clearer. The ubiquity and power of the computer blur the distinction between public and private information. Our revolution will not be in gathering data—don't look for TV cameras in your bedroom—but in analyzing the information that is already willingly shared. Without any conspiratorial snooping or Big Brother antics, we may find our actions, our lifestyles, and even our beliefs under increasing public scrutiny as we move into the information age.

Profile of a Buyer

Shoppers who think they are only vague entries on some company's list might lose that anonymity if they hold Mastercard or Visa credit cards. A new service by Citicorp Credit Services, a Citicorp subsidiary, will provide businesses that accept Mastercard and Visa credit cards with a detailed profile of their customers. The data will come close to pinpointing the bank card shoppers' income, education, family, housing type and value, age, vocation, even "lifestyle."

Alan Newman, vice president and marketing director for Citicorp Credit Services, said that until now, businesses that subscribed to bank cards have only been able to get generalized demographic profiles of those who use the cards. But an arrangement with Donnelley Marketing Information Services, a Dun & Bradstreet subsidiary, will allow Citicorp to combine Donnelley demographic data with Citicorp's own cardholder data, he says, "even to the very block of a community."

——*New York Times*, 18 March 1984

How does Citicorp know what your lifestyle is? How can they sell such information without your permission? The answer is simple: You've been giving out clues about yourself for years. Buying, working, socializing, and travelling are acts you do in public. Your lifestyle, income, education, home, and family are all deducible from existing records. The information that can be extracted from mundane records like your VISA or MasterCard receipts, phone bill, and credit record is all that's needed to put together a remarkably complete picture of who you are, what you do, and even what you think.

BLOC MODELLING

A powerful technique used by managers of large amounts of data is called *bloc modelling*. The goal of bloc modelling is to evaluate how people fit into an organization or group, based on their relations with other members of the group. The primary use of this practice, which was developed more than a decade ago, has been to examine how employees fit into the firm where they work. Bell Labs, ABC, the Wharton School, and even the Institute for Social Management in Bulgaria are among those who have used the technique.

The mathematics and computations behind the process are complicated, but the underlying idea is simple: While the relationship between two people in an organization is rarely very informative by itself, when many pairs of relationships are connected, patterns can be detected. The people being modelled are broken up into groups, or *blocs*. The assumption made by modellers is that people in similar positions behave similarly. Blocs aren't tightly knit groups. You may never have heard of someone in your bloc, but because you both share a similar relationship with some third party you are lumped together. Your membership in a bloc might become the basis of a wide variety of judgements, from who gets job perks to who gets investigated by the FBI.

Where does the initial data come from? In the office, it may be who you talk to on the intercom, whose phone calls you return (or don't return), who you eat lunch with, who you send your memos to, even who you play softball with. Fancy telephone systems, electronic mail, and bulletin boards make gathering this relational data even easier. When personal computers are on every desk, routine information about who says what to whom is automatically generated and easily collected. Employers and others can keep track of that mundane information, and save it in a database that can be bloc modelled later.

Bloc modelling is used to separate people, cliques, and whole organizations into categories which determine the way the modeller may ultimately treat the groups. While conceptually similar to the more familiar "redlining," it is unlike other kinds of discrimination, since the blocs found are generally inconspicuous, and the members may easily fail to recognize their common fate. Furthermore, the existing laws protecting privacy, such as those that guarantee individuals access to their own files, do not address bloc modelling. It is difficult to imagine what remedies might be devised for this new form of guilt by association.

WHEN IS PRIVATE INFORMATION PUBLIC?

We live in a world of private and public acts. We consider what we do in our own bedrooms to be our own business; what we do on the street or in the supermarket is open for everyone to see. In the information age, our public acts disclose our private dispositions, even more than a camera in the bedroom would. This doesn't necessarily mean we should bring a veil of secrecy over public acts. The vast amount of public information both serves and endangers us.

To make this idea clear, I'd like to use an example invented by Jerry Samet, Professor of Philosophy at Bentley College. He suggests that, although we consider it a violation of privacy to look in somebody's window and notice what they are doing, we have no problem with the reverse: someone sitting in his living room looking *out* his window. If I'm looking out my window and I notice you walking down my street, I may notice that you are wearing a red sweater, holding hands with someone else, or heading towards the local bar. If I wanted to, I might write down what I saw out my window. Consider what happens if I write down everything I see out my window, and all my neighbors do, too. Suppose we shared notes and compiled the data we got just by looking out our own windows. When we sorted it all out, we would have detailed personal profiles of everyone we saw. If every move anyone made in public were recorded, correlated, and analyzed, the veil of anonymity protecting us from constant scrutiny would be torn away. Even if that record were never *used*, its very existence would certainly change the way we act in public. The idea that someone is always watching is no less threatening when the watching goes on in the supermarket, in the department store, and in the workplace than when it goes on in our homes.

The harmful consequences of just keeping personal profiles pale in comparison with the problems associated with their use. We don't have to look far into the future to imagine how such files could be used. There is a pressing example already apparent in two proposed additions to the National Crime Information Computer. The computer, or NCIC as it is commonly called, was set up to track wanted criminals and stolen property across state lines. When a policeman makes a routine traffic stop or otherwise confronts a stranger, the first thing he does is check the name through NCIC. If his name is in NCIC, the officer can search or arrest him, or take other discretionary action. The FBI now wants to add people to the database who have been accused of nothing, but are *suspected*, of organized crime connections, terrorism, or narcotics possession, or are "known associates" of drug traffickers. Their avowed goal is to keep track of the whereabouts of such people. The FBI claims that this represents a "logical progression" of the crime center's efforts. The idea that associating with someone who gets arrested could get your name into the national crime database is scary enough. Worse yet, the Secret Service wants to get into the act. They want to sidestep the judicial process by directly entering the names of people they consider to be dangerous to the President or other high officials into NCIC without obtaining warrants. If the FBI and the Secret Service get their way, having the wrong friends or being on the wrong side of the Executive Branch could get your name into the computer, subjecting you to police harassment, surveillance, even detention. Since just adding a name to NCIC doesn't legally deprive anyone of liberty or property, constitutional due process constraints do not apply.

Why not make gathering this information against the law? Think of Samet's metaphor: do we really want to ban looking out the window? The information about groups and individuals that *is* public is public for a reason. Being able to write down what I see is fundamental to freedom of expression and belief, the freedoms we are trying to protect. Furthermore, public records serve us in very specific, important ways. We can have and use credit because credit records are kept. We can prevent the sale of handguns to convicted felons because criminal records are kept. Supermarkets must keep track of their inventories, and since their customers prefer that they accept checks, they keep information on the financial status of people who shop in their stores. In short, keeping and using the kind of data that can be turned into personal profiles is fundamental to our way of life—we cannot stop *gathering* this information.

What we have to do is find a way to control its *use*. We need to make it possible to draw distinctions between the kinds of information processing, dissemination, and use we want to allow and the kinds we want to prohibit. Some uses of personal information are quite reasonable. Using conviction records to avoid selling guns to criminals is a legitimate use of personal data. Keeping track of who I call on the telephone and for how long is legitimate if the purpose is to bill me for those calls. Writing down what books I buy is fine, so long as the intent is to maintain the inventory at my local bookstore. There are a variety of traditional, necessary, and non-threatening uses of personal information. Ideally, any use of information outside the scope of these traditional ones should require the knowledge and consent of the person the information is about. Marketing and direct advertising are not traditional uses of personal information, and should not be thought of as such. I should be able

:o choose whether or not I want my local bookstore to keep a list of the books I buy, even if they just want to mail me ads for new books they think I'd like. I should be able to prevent a company from selling my name and address to someone else without my permission. I don't want the FBI to be able to look at my consumer records and decide that my lifestyle fits their model of a subversive or a drug user. I certainly do not want employers to use bloc modelling to fire people on the basis of who they associate with, or politicians to use it to identify their "enemies."

INFORMATION AS PROPERTY

People under scrutiny ought to be able to exert some control over what other people do with that personal information. Our society grants individuals control over the activities of others primarily through the idea of property. A reasonable way to give individuals control over information about them is to vest them with a *property interest* in that information. Information about me is, in part, my property. Other people may, of course, also have an interest in that information. Citibank has some legitimate interests in the information about me that it has gathered. When my neighbor writes down that I was wearing a red sweater, both of us should share in the ownership of that information.

What does it mean to own information? To share in such ownership? How can existing laws about property be interpreted to make judgements about the use and control of information? These questions must ultimately be answered by the legislators who draft laws giving information property status, and the courts who interpret those laws. We can begin to imagine some of the implications of such an approach. What makes information different from other kinds of property is that it is intangible: it cannot be touched, held, or seen directly. The same information can be in two places at once. Other than that, information is like other kinds of property: it can have monetary value, it can be produced, improved, or degraded, and one can share, withhold, or transfer it to others.

Is information enough like property to be successfully integrated into property law? The process has already begun in many legislatures. Across the country laws are being passed that make unauthorized access, duplication, or tampering with information stored in computers a crime. These laws are deemed necessary because existing burglary statutes don't apply to copying information, or looking at it, especially if the access was by remote computer. When computer data is copied by an unauthorized outsider that action resembles burglary, and it is treated as such in these new laws. If it is like burglary, then something is being stolen. In this context, information is already being implicitly treated as if it were property.

If we are to treat information as property *explicitly*, some of our ideas about property will have to be changed. Information can be stolen by copying it, leaving the original behind. If information is merely what is known, how can it be taken away? How can vesting the individual with the rights associated with property, particularly the right of excluding others from that property, be specifically translated into control over analysis of data? How can we define information so that knowledge in a computer is property that can be controlled, but knowledge inside someone's head is not? Enforcement presents another problem: how can we tell if someone is using personal information illicitly? The example of copyright law suggests that, while finding small abuses of intangible property is difficult, finding major violations is no harder than other law enforcement tasks.

SEARCH AND SEIZURE OF INFORMATION

Treating information as property has an additional benefit. As the law currently stands, information isn't property, but computers are. The owner of the computer has been held to control everything "inside" his computer. That means that if I write a personal note on my office workstation, my employer has the right to read it. By contrast, he has no right to read a note I write on company stationery with a company pen and put in my (company owned) desk. More importantly, my employer can give permission to law enforcement agencies to go on a fishing expedition through my files in his computer, which, metaphorically, gives the police the right to rummage at random through any employee's "desk." This is not hypothetical; a case of just such abuse was reported by Larry Layton, a government employee.

Layton worked in a Defense Department office (DARCOM) which was fully electronic. Most employees had computers and all used electronic mail to communicate with each other. There were over 3000 users with access to the system, and 500 in-house users of internal workplace computers. All writing and interoffice communication, as well as other office support, was done on a computer. At least three times, the Army Criminal Investigation Division, in conjunction with the FBI, obtained complete dumps of all the workplace automation computers without any type of court order or specification of what they were looking for, other than "wrongful use of government property." A "complete dump" means that every bit of information was printed out and examined. Using the analogy to desks, it is as if the FBI went through every employee's desk looking at every piece of paper, through every address book, reading every memo and every piece of mail. After finding one person who had a recipe in an electronic mail message, and another who had a baby sitter's phone number in a telephone number file, the FBI read each his rights and threatened retribution. The legal staff of the operation advised the managers that the searches were legal since computer files don't fall under any of the same protections that, say, telephone usage does. The searches have resulted in the employees refraining from using the system for communication, electronic mail, filing, and many other applications.

This sort of witch-hunt is only the beginning. Electronic mail typically goes through several computers before reaching its final destination. The owner of each of those computers apparently has the full legal right to read, copy, and disseminate anything contained in his computer, including that mail. Since the U.S. Postal Service, MCI, and a host of other similar entities are operating electronic mail services, one might think that electronic mail had the same protection and privacy as a paper letter or a phone call. It does not. It is, for the time being, completely open to anyone through whose computer it passes. We must extend the special status of the letter and the phone call to all forms of electronic communication. The idea of *information as property* will protect that information with the rules of search and seizure that apply to other kinds of property. It will provide the connection between sending a letter and sending electronic mail necessary to protect the content of our communication.

PUBLIC IMAGES, LIMITED

It is time our legal technicians turned their attention to framing answers in the language of the law. We will need to define many gray areas, and insure that we tread carefully in these sensitive areas of personal information. I think we can specify the uses we consider traditional, and separate those we consider new or threatening.

Lawyers, computer scientists, businessmen, and an informed public must work together to bring to our legal system a carefully crafted new framework for thinking about information.

Computers and electronic communication are ushering in a new age. We will be able to talk to more people in more ways than ever before. The dramatic increase in our ability to communicate may be the glue that we need to hold our fragile world together. Computers also help us analyze all the information we can gather and exchange, helping us to understand the world around us. It is precisely those abilities which make computers threatening, too. Soon celebrities and politicians will not be the only ones who have public images but no private lives—it will be all of us. We must take control of the information about ourselves. We should own our personal profiles, not be bought and sold by them.

THE GOVERNMENT NEEDS COMPUTER MATCHING TO ROOT OUT WASTE AND FRAUD

Richard P. Kusserow

More information will be collected, stored, and retrieved in our lifetime than in all other generations combined. This information explosion, however, is creating new problems for the government manager.

Crucial issues revolve around the use of computer technology to insure that tax-payers' money is being safeguarded and to manage personal data without sacrificing individuals' rights to privacy. Predictions about the dehumanizing effects of technology heat the issues.

Unfortunately, *computer matching*, charged with myth and misconception, has become fuel for this emotional debate. Critics depict mere man against massive computers and evoke the specter of the Orwellian *1984* and "Big Brother."

In reality, computer matching covers many processes used to detect payment errors, increase debt collection, and identify abusive grant or procurement practices. The Department of Education, for instance, uses computer matches to identify federal workers who default on student loans. The National Science Foundation screens research fund applicants against its employee and consultant lists to prevent any conflict of interest in grant awards.

My office in the federal Department of Health and Human Services (HHS) uses matches to unearth doctors who are double-billing Medicare and Medicaid for the same service. Over 230 problem health providers were removed from participation in the Medicare program in the last fiscal year—a 253 percent increase over the previous year. We have also matched the Social Security benefit rolls against Medicare's record of deceased patients and discovered thousands of cases of administrative error and fraud. This project alone resulted in savings of over $25 million.

Without the computer, government could not fulfill many mandated missions. Forty million Social Security checks are issued each month—an impossible feat without automated data processing.

Computers are here to stay and will become even more pervasive. We are witnessing the virtual disappearance of hardcopy, a development of special importance to the government manager, auditor, and investigator. Without a paper trail, government workers must use innovative techniques to meet this new challenge.

Computer matching is an efficient and effective technique for coping with today's expensive, complex, and error-prone government programs. For instance, computer matching and other innovative techniques helped my office identify $1.4 billion in savings—about a 300 percent increase over the previous year.

THE HIGH COST OF ERRORS AND FRAUD

Over $350 billion is paid out every year through government entitlement programs to millions of recipients. Ineligibility and payment errors cost the taxpayers billions of dollars annually. Add to this the dollars lost through loan delinquencies, excessive procurement costs, and other abuses, and the losses become even more staggering. Perceptions of waste and cheating in government programs erode public support for the programs and respect for government itself.

Government managers cannot simply rely on chance discovery, voluntary compliance, or outdated manual procedures to detect errors. They have a responsibility to use innovative techniques to monitor the expenditures of program dollars, to detect fraud, to determine who is ineligible or being paid incorrectly, etc.

COMPUTER MATCHING: NOT A NEW TECHNIQUE

Computer matching is not a new technique. The basic approach of matching one set of records to another has been used by both public and private sectors for years. Although matching predates the computer, the computer has made it quick and cost effective.

In 1977, Congress, recognizing the effectiveness of computer matching, passed Public Law 95-216. This law mandated that state welfare agencies use state wage information in determining eligibility for Aid to Families with Dependent Children (AFDC). Subsequent legislation also required similar wage matching for the Food Stamp program.

Computer matching can serve many objectives:

- assuring that ineligible applicants are not given costly program benefits;
- reducing or terminating benefits for recipients who are being paid erroneously;
- detecting fraudulent claims and deterring others from defrauding the program;
- collecting overpayments or defaulted loans more effectively;
- monitoring grant and contract award processes;
- improving program policy, procedures, and controls.

Simply defined, computer matching is a technique whereby information within two or more records or files is compared to identify situations that *could* indicate program ineligibility or payment errors.

The process, however, should not and does not stop there. The computer does *not* decide who is getting erroneous payments and does *not* automatically decide who should be terminated from the payment rolls. The computer merely provides a list of items that *could* indicate an erroneous or aberrant situation. The matched items must be investigated by program staff. Only then can an agency determine whether a payment should be adjusted or stopped, or the file record corrected.

Early computer matching efforts, which acted upon "raw hits" without proper follow-up, were justifiably criticized. Today, computer matching is far more effective, efficient, and less intrusive. A manual examiner had to search through *all* records in a file. A computer, however, picks out only those records that match and ignores all the others: it only scans for aberrations. In this sense, computer matching is far less of an invasion than 100 percent manual review.

PRESIDENT'S COUNCIL ON INTEGRITY AND EFFICIENCY

In 1981, President Reagan formed the President's Council on Integrity and Efficiency (PCIE) to coordinate efforts to attack fraud and waste in expensive, government programs. One of its major activities is the Long-Term Computer Matching Project, which I cochair with the Inspector General of the Department of Labor.

Our overall objective is to expand the cost-effective use of computer matching techniques that prevent and detect fraud, abuse, and erroneous payments and, at the same time, to protect the rights and privacy of individuals. The Project does not run computer matches. Rather, through its membership of federal and state program administrators, the Project

- gathers and shares information about federal and state matching activities,
- analyzes and removes technical and administrative obstacles to computer matching, and
- fosters increased federal and state cooperation in computer-matching activities.

So far, the Project has inventoried federal and state matches, established a clearinghouse and a newsletter, and launched an effort with eight states to test standardized data extraction formats for computer matching. The standardized formats will make matching "hits" more reliable, thereby reducing the need for manual review of client files.

One of the Project's first tasks was to revise the Office of Management and Budget's (OMB's) "Guidelines for Conducting Computer Matching Programs." The Guidelines were originally set forth in 1979 to implement the Privacy Act of 1974, in the context of federal computer matching efforts. The 1982 revision streamlined paper-work requirements and reiterated requirements for privacy and security of records.

The Guidelines call for public notice of proposed matches and strict safeguards concerning use, storage, and disclosure of information from matches. In his December 1982 testimony before Senator William S. Cohen's Subcommittee on Oversight of Government Management, David F. Linowes, former chairman of the Privacy Protection Study Commission, stated that the 1982 Guidelines make "sound provisions for protecting the privacy of the individual."

FEARS OF A NATIONAL DATABASE ON INDIVIDUALS UNGROUNDED

A major concern is that computer matching will ultimately result in the creation of a national database of computerized information on every individual. OMB Guidelines insure that such would be impossible. Once a match is completed, Guidelines require that the files be returned to the custodian agency or destroyed.

To be effective, computer matching must be built into the administration of a government program—not just run as an ad hoc investigation. Also, matching should be performed *before* payments are made, as well as used in an ongoing monitoring effort. In this way, matching stops payment errors before they occur.

Prepayment screens using computer matching techniques not only detect errors, they also deter fraud and abuse in government programs. California, for instance, routinely checks public assistance claims against wage records, saving an estimated $1 million per month in overpayments.

Computer matching is racially, sexually, and ethnically blind. No person or group is targeted.

SOME EXISTING PRIVACY SAFEGUARDS

A number of privacy safeguards have already been institutionalized. "The Computer Matching Reference Paper," published by the PCIE, sets forth "purpose" standards. An agency considering a match must first conduct a study to determine the match's scope and purpose, identify agencies and records involved, and ascertain the information and follow-up actions needed. A key aspect is the assessment of the estimated costs and benefits of a match.

Another safeguard is OMB's "Model Control System." This document suggests that government officials carefully analyze the hits from a computer match to verify the data with the source agency and determine whether the hit is the result of error or abuse. For large matches, officials would have to analyze only a sample of the hits to verify the matching process. After doing this, officials should take corrective measures, proceeding cautiously against any individual where doubt exists.

A third privacy safeguard is provided by a memorandum sent by the deputy director of OMB, Joseph A. Wright, Jr., to the heads of all government agencies on December 29, 1983.

That memorandum provides instructions for preparing a Computer Match Checklist, to be completed by each government agency involved in matching federal data records. This checklist and the Model Control System help agencies to comply with the Privacy Act of 1974 and the OMB Computer Matching Guidelines of May 11, 1982.

Relevant government agencies must complete this checklist immediately following their announced intent (as indicated by publication in the *Federal Register*) to conduct a computer match. This checklist must be on file for review by OMB, Government Accounting Office (GAO), and others interested in insuring that safeguards are being followed to protect personal data.

Still another privacy safeguard, the PCIE reference paper, calls upon government managers to do a cost-benefit analysis both before and after a computer-matching project. In some cases it will make sense to do a pilot match based on a sample. The results of this pilot study would provide a better idea of what could be achieved from a full-scale matching project. In any event, pilot matches are subject to Privacy Act safeguards.

Finally, the OMB Matching Guidelines require government managers to prepare a matching report at least 30 days prior to the start of the match project. It would be published in the *Federal Register* to give relevant parties an opportunity to comment.

CONCLUSION

Any computer match that does not consider privacy, fairness, and due process as among its major goals is not a good project. Well-designed computer matches are cost effective.

The government's need to insure a program's integrity need not be incompatible with the individual's right to privacy and freedom from government intrusion. The point is to *balance* these competing interests. Government managers have a responsibility to insure that program funds are spent as intended by Congress. At the same time, these managers must carry out those responsibilities within the requirements and spirit of the Privacy Act. Such a balance is both possible and essential.

Additional Comments

In addressing the concerns raised by John Shattuck (see article on page 305), I must first put federal computer-matching projects into perspective. A common misconception is that computer matching is primarily an investigative tool. In reality, matches are used primarily to assist in government audits to identify inappropriate data (e.g., mistakes or errors) in the records under review. Most of our computer-assisted audits use computer screens rather than tape-to-tape matches, which are usually performed on a one-time basis.

The goals of these matches are twofold: (1) to purify the databases, and (2) to build in routine front-end prevention procedures. ("Front-end matches" match data to an existing database before payments are made.) Shattuck's premise seems to be that computer-matching programs have enlarged the number of individuals subjected to government inquiry. This is not true. The criteria for identifying a "hit" are no different than the criteria for evaluating the need for further information received by other means. Computer matches have not created new areas of audit or investigation, but they have allowed agencies to improve their methods.

I fail to see the merit of requiring agencies to limit themselves to less effective audit activities. That argument is based on the unfounded belief that sophisticated proactive audit techniques are per se violative of individual rights.

Shattuck's comments demonstrate a lack of understanding of the procedures followed in federal computer matchings. The individuals whose records are included in a match are not really under investigation. The only records that can result in an inquiry are those that produce a hit. Such indicates a mistake, error, or possible fraud or abuse. In an Aid to Families with Dependent Children (AFDC) state-to-state match, for instance, records indicating a recipient receives AFDC benefits in several jurisdictions would be identified for further review. Since this clearly raises a question of eligibility, an eligibility review can hardly be characterized as a "fishing expedition."

The only real change from computer matches is the increased number of cases identified. Much of the alleged impact on individual rights discussed by Shattuck are issues separate and distinct from computer matching. Once hits are identified for further review, the reviews should be evaluated as any other reviews based on information from any source.

Examples cited by Shattuck of actions taken as a result of matches reflect his disagreement with the evidentiary criteria used by some agencies in pursuing an adverse action. They are in no way an indictment of computer matching for identifying cases for review. The two issues are separate.

The information produced by a matching program is no different from that produced by any other audit or law enforcement inquiry. Once that is recognized, the constitutional concerns raised by Shattuck can be put into perspective. I am unaware of any court decision even remotely indicating that computer-assisted audits of government records run afoul of the fourth amendment protections against unlawful search and seizure.

I also fail to see how a law enforcement inquiry based on a computer-matching hit has any impact on the presumption of innocence in a criminal proceeding. This presumption places the burden on the government to prove guilt in a criminal case. None of the examples cited by Shattuck have any bearing on this principle.

It is equally misleading to imply that computer matching has resulted in any weakening of due process. The right to confront an accuser has never applied to the purely investigative stages of a law enforcement inquiry. Shattuck apparently believes that individuals identified in a computer match should be afforded rights never afforded any investigative subject. Law enforcement inquiries can often be closed without a subject interview. This is equally true for inquiries triggered by a computer match. This in no way violates any legally recognized due process standards.

Criticisms made against computer matching are generally unfounded. I strongly oppose Shattuck's recommendations as being unnecessary and inappropriate. His intent is to greatly restrict, if not totally eliminate, the use of computer-matching projects by the federal government.

Requiring congressional authorization for each match and affording persons whose records are being matched rights far in excess of those available to the actual subjects of a law enforcement inquiry would not improve—but end—the use of matching. This is far too vital an audit technique to lose—especially in view of the fact that Shattuck has failed to provide even a *single* example of a federal computer match that violated an individual's legal rights.

The rights of individuals in federal criminal, civil, or administrative proceeding are already protected by constitutional and other legal constraints. I agree with Shattuck that matches should not be conducted prior to an analysis of their cost effectiveness. In fact, no federal agency has the resources to conduct such matches without careful consideration of costs versus benefits. Further restrictions are, therefore, unnecessary.

COMPUTER MATCHING IS A SERIOUS THREAT TO INDIVIDUAL RIGHTS

John Shattuck

More and more frequently, government agencies have been employing a new investigative technique: the matching of unrelated computerized files of individuals to identify suspected law violators. This technique—*computer matching*—provides a revolutionary method of conducting investigations of fraud, abuse, and waste of government funds. It permits the government to screen the records of whole categories of people, such as federal employees, to determine who among them also falls into separate, supposedly incompatible categories, such as welfare recipients.

Computer matching raises profound issues concerning individual privacy, due process of law, and the presumption of innocence. It also poses serious questions about cost effectiveness and the internal management of government programs.

COMPUTER MATCHING VERSUS INDIVIDUAL RIGHTS

To understand the impact of computer matching on individual rights, it is first necessary to grasp the difference between a computer-matching investigation and a traditional law enforcement investigation.

A traditional investigation is triggered by some evidence that a person is engaged in wrongdoing. This is true for cases of tax evasion, welfare fraud, bank robbery, or traffic speeding. The limited resources of law enforcement usually make it impracticable to conduct dragnet investigations. More importantly, our constitutional system bars the government from investigating persons it does not suspect of wrongdoing.

A computer match is not bound by these limitations. It is directed not at an individual, but at an entire category of persons. A computer match is initiated not because any person is suspected of misconduct, but because his or her category is of interest to the government. What makes computer matching fundamentally different from a traditional investigation is that its very purpose is to generate the evidence of wrongdoing required before an investigation can begin. That evidence is produced by "matching" two sets of personal records compiled for unrelated purposes.

There are four ways in which a computer match differs from a conventional law enforcement investigation in its impact on individual rights:

Fourth Amendment

The Fourth Amendment protects against unreasonable searches and seizures, the most blatant of which have been "fishing expeditions" directed against large numbers of people. From the "writs of assistance" used in the eighteenth century by royal revenue agents, to door-to-door searches for violations of the British tariff laws in the American Colonies, to the municipal code inspections of the twentieth century to enforce health and safety standards, the principle that generalized fishing expeditions violate the right to be free from unreasonable searches has held firm in American law.

That principle is violated by computer matching. The technique of matching unrelated computer tapes is designed as a general search. It is not based on any preexisting evidence to direct suspicion of wrongdoing to any particular person. Although systematic searches of personal records are not as intrusive as door-to-door searches, the result is the same: a massive dragnet into the private affairs of many people.

Presumption of Innocence

People in our society are not forced to bear a continuous burden of demonstrating to the government that they are innocent of wrongdoing. Although citizens are obliged to obey the law—and violate it at their peril—presumption of innocence is intended to protect people against having to prove that they are free from guilt whenever the government investigates them.

Computer matching can turn the presumption of innocence into a presumption of guilt. For instance, Massachusetts welfare recipients have been summarily removed from welfare rolls as the result of a computer match. These people fought for reinstatement based on information the state neglected to consider after their names appeared as "hits" in the match.

Another example of this "presumption of guilt" occurred three years ago in Florida. The state's attorney for a three-county area around Jacksonville obtained case files for all food stamp recipients in the area. He then launched fraud investigations against those receiving allotments of more than $125 a month. A federal court of appeals invalidated the file search and enjoined the investigation on the ground that the targeted food stamp recipients were put in the position of having to prove the allotment they had received was *not* based on fraud. Construing the Food Stamp Act, the Court held that "it did not allow the [state food stamp] agency to turn over files . . . for criminal investigation *without regard to whether a particular household has engaged in questionable behavior.*"

Once a computer match has taken place, any person whose name appears as a "raw hit" is presumed to be guilty. In part, this is because the technology of computer matching is so compelling and in part because its purpose—the detection of fraud and waste—is so commendable. The worst abuses of computer matching, such as summary termination of welfare benefits, have occurred when authorities have casually transformed this "presumption" into a conclusive proof of guilt.

Privacy Act

The most important principle governing collection and use of personal information by the government is that the individual has a right to control information about himself and to prevent its use without his consent for purposes wholly unrelated to those for which it was collected. This principle is imperfectly embodied in the Privacy Act of 1974.

The Privacy Act restricts disclosure by federal agencies of personally identifiable information—*unless* the subject consents. There are two major exceptions. The first involves a "routine use," defined as "the use of (a) record for a purpose which is compatible with the purpose for which it was collected." The second involves a "law enforcement" disclosure, which enables an agency to be responsive to a request by another agency for information relevant to the investigation of a specific violation of law.

When computer matching was in its infancy, the Privacy Act was correctly perceived by several federal agencies to be a major stumbling block. The Civil Service Commission initially balked in 1977 at the plans of Health, Education and Welfare (HEW) Secretary Joseph Califano to institute a match of federal employee records and state welfare rolls, on the ground that the use of employee records for such a purpose would violate the Privacy Act. The Commission's General Counsel, Carl F. Goodman, stated that the proposed match could not be considered a "routine use" of employee records, since the Commission's "information on employees was not collected with a view toward detecting welfare abuses." Similarly, it could not be considered a "law enforcement" use, continued Goodman, since "at the 'matching' stage there is no indication whatsoever that a violation or potential violation of law has occurred."

This reasonable interpretation of the Privacy Act soon gave way to a succession of strained readings. Since enforcement of the Privacy Act is left entirely to the agencies it regulates, it is hardly surprising that the agencies have bent the Act to their own purposes. They have now miraculously established that computer matching is a "routine use" of personal records. All that is required, they say, is to publish each new computer matching "routine use" in the *Federal Register*.

The Privacy Act has now been so thoroughly circumvented by executive action that it can no longer be seen as an effective safeguard. Nevertheless, the principle underlying the Act—that individuals should be able to exercise control over information about themselves that they provide to the government—is a bedrock principle of individual privacy. That principle is at war with the practice of computer matching.

Due Process of Law

Once a computer match has taken place, it will result in a series of hits. All those identified are in jeopardy of being found guilty of wrongdoing. To the extent that they are not given notice of their situation and an adequate opportunity to contest the results of the match, they are denied due process of law.

This is precisely what has happened in several matching programs. For example, the results of Secretary Califano's Operation Match were kept secret from federal employees whose records were matched with welfare rolls, because the Justice Department viewed the investigation "as a law enforcement program designed to detect suspected violations of various criminal statutes." The Justice Department ordered the Civil Service Commission not to notify any of the federal employees whose names showed up as hits, since "[t]he premature discussion of a specific criminal matter with a tentative defendant is in our view inimical to the building of a solid prosecutorial case." In Massachusetts, welfare authorities have terminated benefits of persons showing up as hits without even conducting an *internal* investigation.

This approach makes a mockery of due process. Due process is the right to confront one's accuser and introduce evidence to show that the accuser is wrong. When the accuser is a computer tape, the possibility of error is substantial. Keeping the subject of a raw hit in the dark increases the likelihood of an error's going undetected.

SOME COMMENTS ON THE OFFICE OF MANAGEMENT AND BUDGET'S (OMB'S) GUIDELINES

Since 1979 computer matching at the federal level has been regulated by guidelines issued by the OMB. These guidelines, which were considerably looser in May 1982, are intended to "help agencies relate the procedural requirements of the Privacy Act to the operational requirements of computerized matching." Although Kusserow cites the guidelines as evidence of the federal government's concern about privacy protection, in fact, they constitute an effort to paper over the profound conflict between (1) the Privacy Act principle that personal records are to be used by federal agencies only for purposes compatible with those for which they were compiled and (2) the computer matching practice of joining personal records compiled for wholly unrelated purposes.

OMB's matching guidelines have rendered meaningless the central principle of the Privacy Act. In 1980, for instance, the Office of Personnel Management (OPM) published a notice in the *Federal Register* concerning its proposed use of personnel records for a matching program to help the Veterans' Administration (VA) verify the credentials of its hospital employees. The notice dutifully stated that the proposed match of OPM and VA records was a "routine use," which it explained as follows:

> "An integral part of the reason that these records are maintained is *to protect the legitimate interests of the government* and, therefore, such a disclosure is compatible with the purposes for maintaining these records."

Under that broad justification any disclosure or matching of personal records would be permissible, since all federal records are purportedly maintained for the "legitimate interests of the government."

The guidelines, on which Kusserow so heavily relies, contain no requirements or limitations on the conduct of computer matching in these critical areas:

1. **The nature of the record systems to be matched**—There are no personal records, no matter how sensitive (e.g., medical files, security clearance records, intelligence records), that are beyond the reach of computer matching for any investigative purpose.
2. **The procedures to be followed in determining the validity of hits**—No particular procedures are required to insure that the subjects of hits are afforded due process of law.
3. **The standards and procedures to be followed for securing OMB approval of a proposed match**—Since the first guidelines were promulgated in 1979, OMB has not disapproved a single computer match.
4. **The projected costs and benefits of a proposed match**—The 1982 guidelines have deleted all reference to cost–benefit analyses or reports on computer matches. It is entirely at an agency's discretion whether to undertake a proposed match or to report the costs and benefits of the match.

It is impossible not to conclude that computer matching at the federal level is a huge unregulated business, the only clear effect of which to date has been the undermining of individual privacy.

SOME EXAMPLES OF COMPUTER MATCHING

In the seven years since the technique was first used, over 200 computer matches have been carried out. At the federal level there have been matches for a wide variety of investigative purposes, using a broad range of personal record systems of varying degrees of sensitivity.

These include matches of federal employee records maintained by the Civil Service Commission with files of persons receiving federal Aid to Families with Dependent Children, to investigate "fraud"; federal personnel records maintained by OPM with the files of VA hospital employees, to check "accreditation"; federal personnel records of Agriculture Department employees in Illinois with Illinois state files on licensed real estate brokers, to "ascertain potential conflicts of interest"; Internal Revenue Service (IRS) records of taxpayer addresses with lists of individuals born in 1963 supplied by the Selective Service System, to locate suspected violators of the draft registration law; and Labor Department files of persons entitled to receive Black Lung benefits with Health and Human Services (HHS) records of Medicare billings, to investigate double-billing medical fraud.

These matches are only a handful of the total conducted. Even with these, very little hard data are available, thanks to the extraordinarily weak oversight and reporting requirements of the OMB guidelines and to the lack of attention to this subject by Congress.

CONCLUSION

Computer matching is an attractive investigative technique. It appears to permit law enforcement officials to instantaneously root out all instances of a particular kind of wrongdoing in a particular segment of the population. It constitutes a general surveillance system that supposedly can detect and deter misconduct wherever it is used. It appeals to the view that "if you haven't done anything wrong, you don't have anything to worry about."

But there are heavy costs associated with computer matching, both in terms of individual rights and in terms of law enforcement expenditure. It is not at all clear that the benefits of the technique outweigh the costs.

The comparison of unrelated record systems is fraught with difficulty. Data on the computer tapes may be inaccurate or inaccurately recorded. It may present an incomplete picture. It is unlikely to be sufficient to "answer" difficult questions, such as whether a person is entitled to receive welfare or is engaged in a conflict of interest.

On the other hand, computer matching erodes individual rights: the Fourth Amendment right to be free from unreasonable search, the right to the presumption of innocence, the right to due process of law, and the right to limit the government's use of personal information to the purposes for which it was collected.

Moreover, the rapid and unchecked growth of computer matching leads inexorably to the creation of a de facto National Data System in which personal data are widely and routinely shared at all levels of government and in the private sector.

RECOMMENDATIONS

As a general framework for safeguarding individual rights, I propose the following.

1. The Privacy Act should be amended to clarify that computer matches are not ipso facto "routine uses" of personal record systems.

2. No further federal computer matches should be permitted without express congressional authorization.

3. Congress should not authorize computer matches of sensitive personal records systems (the confidentiality of which is otherwise protected by statute) such as taxpayer records maintained by the IRS, census records maintained by the Census Bureau, or bank records maintained by federally insured banking institutions.

4. No computer match should be authorized unless and until an analysis has been made of its projected costs and projected savings in the recoupment of funds owed to the government. The match should not be authorized unless the public benefit will far outweigh the cost—and unless individual rights will be protected. The results and full costs of any match should be published.

5. Procedural due process protections for the persons whose records are to be matched should be specified by statute, including the right to counsel, the right to a full hearing, and the right to confidentiality of the results of a match.

The thrust of my comments has been to raise some basic questions about computer matching. I recommend a moratorium on all further matching so Congress and the public can study the results of all computer-matching programs conducted to date and assess the long-term consequences.

In closing, I second the view of Justice William O. Douglas, when he said, "I am not ready to agree that America is so possessed with evil that we must level all constitutional barriers to give our civil authorities the tools to catch criminals."

▷ PRIVATE LIFE IN CYBERSPACE

John P. Barlow

I have lived most of my life in a small Wyoming town, where there is little of the privacy which both insulates and isolates suburbanites. Anyone in Pinedale who is interested in me or my doings can get most of that information in the Wrangler Café. Between them, any five customers could probably produce all that is known locally about me—including a number of items that are well known but not true.

For most people who have never lived in these conditions, the idea that one's private life might be public knowledge—and, worse, that one's neighbors might fabricate tales about him or her when the truth would do—is a terrifying thought. Whether they have anything to hide or not (and we all harbor something we are not too proud of), people often assume others would certainly employ their private peccadillos against them. But what makes the fishbowl community tolerable is a general willingness of small towns to forgive in their own way all that should be forgiven. The individual is protected from the malice of his fellows, not by their lack of dangerous information about him, but by their disinclination to use it.

I found myself thinking a lot about this during the recent San Francisco Conference on Computers, Privacy, and Freedom. Like most of the attendees, I had arrived there bearing the assumption that there is some necessary connection between privacy and freedom and that among the challenges computers may present to our future liberties is their ability to store, transfer, and duplicate the skeletons from our closets.

With support from the Electronic Frontier Foundation (EFF), Apple Computer, the WELL, and a number of other organizations, the conference was sponsored by Computer Professionals for Social Responsibility, a group that has done much to protect Americans' privacy. Their Man in Washington, Marc Rotenberg, hit the hot key which resulted in Lotus getting 30,000 letters, phone calls, and e-mail messages protesting the release of Lotus Marketplace: Households.

In case you haven't left your terminal in awhile, this was a CD-ROM-based product of addresses and demographic information that would have ushered in the era of Desktop Junkmail. Suddenly anyone with 600 bucks and a CD-ROM drive could have been stuffing your mailbox with urgent appeals.

Marketplace withered under the heat, and I didn't hear a soul mourn its passage. Most people seemed happy to leave the massive marketing databases in institutional hands, thinking perhaps that junkmail might be one province where democracy was better left unspread.

I wasn't so sure. For example, it occurred to me that Lotus could make a strong legal, if not commercial, case that Marketplace was a publication protected by the First Amendment. It also seemed that a better approach to the scourge of junkmail might be political action directed toward getting the Postal Service to raise its rates on bulk mailing. (Or perhaps even eliminating the Postal Service, which seems to have little function these days beyond the delivery of instant landfills.) Finally, I wondered if we were not once again blaming the tool rather than the workman—as though the problem were information and not its misuse. I felt myself gravitating toward the politically incorrect side of the issue, and kept quiet about it.

At the conference, no one was keeping quiet. Speaker after speaker painted a picture of gathering informational fascism in which Big Brother was entering our homes dressed in the restrained Italian suit of the Marketroid. Our every commercial quiver was being recorded, collated, and widely redistributed. One began to imagine a Cyberspace smeared with his or her electronic fingerprints, each growing into a full-blown virtual image of himself as Potential Customer.

There was discussion of opting out of the databases, getting through modern American life without ever giving out one's National Identity Number (as the Social Security Number has indisputably become by default), endeavoring to restrict one's existence to the physical world. The poor fellow from Equifax mouthed smooth corporatisms about voluntary restraints on the secondary use of information—such practices as selling the fact of one's purchase from one catalog to 15 other aspirants—but no one believed him. Everyone seemed to realize that personal information was as much a commodity as pork bellies, fuel oil, or crack and that the market would be served.

They were right. In the week following the conference, I got a solicitation from CACI Marketing Systems that began: "Now Available! Actual 1990 Census Data." This despite Department of Commerce assurances that Census Data would not be put to commercial use. Marketplace is dead. Long live Marketplace.

When it came to solutions, however, a canonical approach that was all too familiar seemed to be developing: let's write some laws. The European Community's privacy standards, scheduled to be implemented by the member nations in 1992, were praised. Similar U.S. legislation was proposed.

Quite apart from the impracticality of entrusting to government another tough problem (given its fairly undistinguished record in addressing the environmental, social, or educational responsibilities it already has), there is a good reason to avoid this strategy. Legally ensuring the privacy of one's personal data involves nothing less than endowing the federal government with the right to restrict information.

It may be that there is a profound incompatibility between the requirements of privacy (at least as achieved by this method) and the requirements of liberty. It doesn't take a paranoid to believe that restrictions placed on one form of information will expand to include others. Nor does it take a libertarian to believe that the imposition of contraband on a commodity probably will not eliminate its availability. I submit, as Exhibit A, the War on Some Drugs.

I began to envision an even more dystopian future in which the data cops patrol Cyberspace in search of illicit personal info, finding other items of legal interest along the way. Meanwhile, institutions that could afford the elevated price of illegal goods would continue to buy them from thuggish Data Cartels in places like the Turks and Caicos Islands, as sf-writer Bruce Sterling predicted in *Islands in the Net.*

I returned to Wyoming in a funk. My ghostly electronic selves increased their number on my way home, as I bought airline tickets, charged to my credit card, made long distance phone calls, and earned another speeding ticket. The more I thought about it, the more I became convinced that nothing short of a fugitive cash-based existence would prevent their continued duplication.

Back in Pinedale, where I am also on record, my head started to clear. Barring government regulation of information, for which I have no enthusiasm, it seemed inevitable that the Global Village would resemble a real village, at least in the sense of eliminating the hermetic sealing of one's suburban privacy. Everyone would start to lead as public a life as I do at home.

And in that lies at least a philosophical vector toward long-term social solution. As I say, I am protected in Pinedale, not by the restriction of information, but by a tolerant social contract which prohibits its use against me (unless, of course, it's of such a damning nature that it ought to be used against me). What may be properly restricted by government is not the tool, but the work that is done with it. If we do not like junkmail, we should make it too expensive to send. If we do not trust others not to hang us by our errors, we must work to build a more tolerant society.

But this approach has a fundamental limit on its effectiveness. While it may, over the long run, reduce the suffering of marketing targets, it does little to protect one from the excesses of a more authoritarian government than the one we have today. This Republic was born in the anonymous broadsides of citizens who published them under Latinate pseudonyms like *Publius Civitatus*. How would the oppressed citizens of the electronic future project the source of rebellion?

Furthermore, much of the tolerance I experience in Pinedale has to do with the fact that we experience one another here. We are not abstracted into information, which, no matter how dense it becomes, does not produce a human being. And it will be a long time before we exist in Cyberspace as anything but information.

While I generally resist technical solutions to social problems, it seems the best approach to this digital dilemma is also machine-based: encryption. At the conference, EFF co-founder John Gilmore called on the computer industry to include as part of its products, tools that would enhance the privacy of their communications. These might include hardware-based public-key encryption schemes, though these are probably too narrow in scale to cover the whole problem.

He also noted it is possible to have an electronic identity that is not directly connected to one's physical self. I agree with him that it is not only possible, but advisable. From the standpoint of credit assurance, there is no difference between the information that John Perry Barlow always pays his bills on time or that account #345 8849 23433 (to whomever that may belong) is equally punctilious.

There are a number of problems with encrypted identity, not the least of which is the development of a long-term credit record attached to a disembodied number. And keeping that number disembodied over the same long term is not a trivial enterprise. Finally, there is the old political question: "What are you trying to hide?" in which the effort to conceal is taken to be a statement of guilt. This might limit a willingness on the part of information carriers to engage in the compliance necessary to make this system work.

Of course, neither machine-based encryption systems nor encrypted identities will become reality unless the computer, communications, and information industries perceive there to be technically feasible methods of providing these services and people willing to pay for them. ACM members are well situated to provide both the technology and the initial market for it.

And, as usual, we would be well advised to keep abreast of political developments. As I write this, there are before Congress a couple of bills which would render encryption meaningless. Sen. Joseph Biden has introduced Senate Bill 266 which declares:

> It is the sense of Congress that providers of electronic communications systems permit the government to obtain the plain text contents of voice, data, and other communications when appropriately authorized by law.

It appears the FBI's requesting this language was a consequence of the difficulty of tapping multiplexed phone lines, but the bill nevertheless says, "turn over your encryption keys." These words probably will not become law, but even if they don't, it seems certain that we haven't seen the last of them, inasmuch as similar language is also to be found in S. 618, The Violent Crime Control Act of 1991. Both bills address a legitimate law-enforcement concern: how to build a case when all the evidence is encrypted, but as in other areas of information vs. action, they should place their focus on the dirty deed—and not the planning of it.

Legislative efforts to amend the Electronic Communications Privacy Act to more adequately address cellular and other wireless technologies is an area to watch. This is especially relevant since, as Nicholas Negroponte has predicted, information which has traditionally flowed through cables, (ex. telephone conversations) is taking to the air while broadcast information is moving underground. Entirely different assumptions prevail between broadcast and one-to-one communications which will now be questioned legally and technically.

EFF believes legal constraints on intercepting private wireless communications will not be sufficient to address the problem. Cellular manufacturers and service providers must be urged to provide their customers with the cheap encryption methods that are already available. At the same time, they should be legally required to inform their customers of the easy interception of nonencrypted communications. Finally, in our zeal to protect the privacy of cellular conversation, we should be careful not to criminalize simple scanning of the airwaves, most of which has no specific target or intent, lest we pass laws which inhibit access to information.

All in all, we are looking at some tough challenges, both technologically and politically. Computer technology has created not just a new medium, but a new place. The society we erect there will probably be quite different from the one we now inhabit, given the fact that this one depends heavily on the physical properties of things while the next one has no physical properties at all. Certain qualities should survive the transfer, however, and these include tolerance, respect for the privacy of others, and a willingness to treat one's fellows as something other than potential customers.

But until we have developed the social contract of Cyberspace, we must create, through encryption and related means, the virtual envelopes and rooms within which we can continue to lead private lives as we enter this new and very public place.

$\triangleright$

PRESERVING INDIVIDUAL AUTONOMY IN AN INFORMATION-ORIENTED SOCIETY

James B. Rule
Douglas McAdam
Linda Stearns
David Uglow

To locate our viewpoint among the variety of approaches to these issues, let us say that our emphasis has been less strictly technological and less optimistic. That is, we tend to see the most profound changes in relations between personal information and individual autonomy as effects of changes in social relationships, rather than as those of technological change. Furthermore, we see the social changes as so far-reaching as to defy easy resolution through the reform of personal data management. Thus stated, we realize, these characterizations amount to little more than a confession of bias. The implications of such biases for concrete analysis, however, should be amply apparent in what follows.

SOME SOCIOLOGICAL BACKGROUND

Modern Americans inhabit a social environment virtually composed of formal organizations. The main source of the privacy controversies of the 1960s and 1970s has been the demands of formal organizations for information on the people with whom these organizations must deal. Each major life juncture seems to entail involvement of some formal organization. Birth, immunization, education, military service, marriage and divorce, the use of credit and insurance, homeownership, medical care, and, ultimately, death—these and countless other key life events require the participation of formal organizations. Such participation almost always seems to require intake of information on the persons concerned. Sometimes these intakes serve the purposes of certification of a key life transition such as a birth, immunization or treatment for a disease, or educational attainments. Elsewhere information helps the organization concerned to distinguish what treatment is to be accorded the individual concerned. In any event, the flow of personal information between organizations and individuals clearly affects the interests of the people concerned. The privacy issues of the 1960s and 1970s have amounted to conflicts over uses made by formal organizations of documentary information on the people with whom these organizations must deal.

Simply to characterize this new reality as reflecting the "appetite" of organizations for personal information would be accurate, but would miss much of the significance of these changes.[1] The growth of modern, bureaucratic personal data systems attests to the formation of new *relationships* between ordinary Americans and formal organizations. The organizations concerned hardly developed their present appetite for personal data as an end in itself. Rather, they did so in order to satisfy demands for authoritative action concerning the people depicted in the records. People expect certain organizations to deal intelligently with a heterogeneous array of people. These dealings are as multifarious in content as are the organizations themselves. In every case the organization is expected to render to each person his or her "due," that is, the "correct" form of bureaucratic action, in light of all relevant information on that person's past history and current statuses. (see Rule, 1974, especially pp. 320–326). Clearly, such discriminating decision making can only take place by reliance on detailed recorded information on the persons concerned.

Income taxation, for example, entails assessment of precise liability for each taxpayer reckoned in terms of income, dependency status, assets and losses during the tax year, and a host of other circumstances. Given that the payment of taxes is a distasteful obligation, and that most persons strive to avoid paying any more than necessary, no system of enforcement could avoid collecting and using voluminous data on the persons concerned. Such data not only enable the organization concerned (the IRS, in this case) to assess the obligation to pay, but they also provide the basis on which to adjudicate disputes with taxpayers over their obligation and to locate those taxpayers judged delinquent or suspect.

The same observations could be offered for most other bureaucratic personal data systems that have sprung up since the last century. Consumer-credit data files, for example, enable credit-granting organizations to assess precisely how much credit it should be extended to the person concerned. Insurance reporting systems afford insurance companies sophisticated bases for discriminating judgments about whether to insure people, and if so, at what rates. Law-enforcement records enable these organizations to distinguish their treatment of the literally millions of persons with whom they deal every year, according to the kinds of action which such people deserve.

Although one may not normally think of it this way, this organizational monitoring of persons is of a piece with broad ranges of other bureaucratic activity. Sociologists have often characterized formal organizations as systems for coping with uncertainty in their environments (Perrow, 1972; Thompson, 1967). All organizations must keep track of more or less unpredictable aspects of their environments—making plans, adjustments, rearrangements, and the like, so as to achieve their desired results. If the critical goal is selling automobiles at a profit, then the organization must attend to variations in supplies of raw materials, costs of power, fluctuations in demand, availability of labor, and a host of other things in order to remain viable. If the goal is the administration of a church diocese, central management must monitor the attitudes of the clergy, the faithfulness of the communicants, the costs of maintaining the physical plant, the attitudes of the larger community toward the church, and many other potential sources of uncertainty. Formal organizations are not the only social forms that facilitate human action in the face of otherwise uncertain conditions. However, only formal organizations in the modern sense devote themselves so systematically and self-consciously to searching for unpredictable or disruptive elements in the environment and attempting to master them so as to achieve desired results.

For the organizational activities of interest here, the environment is people; the uncertainties to be mastered are ambiguities as to which people deserve what organizational responses. Modern income taxation systems are charged with enforcing an obligation according to complex principles, in the light of circumstances that differ in every case. Not only must such systems apply these principles to heterogeneous cases; they must also reckon with people's often strenuous efforts to withhold information. To confront this "blooming, buzzing confusion" of people's financial affairs and to enforce a modicum of compliance entails real mastery of uncertainty. The same holds true for other organizations that systematically demand and use personal information in dealing with very large publics. They can no more do without authoritative information on the people with whom they deal than can General Motors meet its goals without data about the costs of raw materials, the demand for finished automobiles, costs of transportation, and the thousands of uncertain circumstances that make formal organizations necessary in the first place.

Systems of detailed personal records do not appear *whenever* organizations deal with large numbers of people. Instead, they develop under conditions of complex obligations and extended mutual dependency between organizations and their publics. In *Private Lives and Public Surveillance*, Rule (1974) characterized these conditions as most propitious:

1. When an agency must regularly deal with a clientele too large and anonymous to be kept track of on a basis of face-to-face acquaintance;
2. When these dealings entail the enforcement of rules advantageous to the agency and potentially burdensome of the clientele;
3. When these enforcement activities involve decision-making about how to act towards the clientele . . . ;
4. When the decisions must be made discriminatingly, according to precise details to each person's past history or present situation;
5. When the agency must associate every client with what it considers the full details of his past history, especially so as to forestall people's evading the consequences of their past behavior [p. 29].

Thus, Yankee Stadium will require no detailed documentation on ticket purchasers, despite variation in ticket prices and seat assignment. When organizations enter into relationships enduring over time, whose outcomes must be geared to details of people's lives, the recourse to personal data systems as bases for action is very likely.

Thus the growth of vast, bureaucratic personal data systems, both computerized and conventional, often marks the development of characteristically modern forms of *social control*. By this we mean direct patterns of influence by organizations over the behaviors of individuals. Such influence may be benign, as in systems for administering medical care, or coercive, as in the development of dossiers on political enemies. The systematic collection and monitoring of personal information for purposes of social control we term *surveillance*—again, whether the purposes are friendly or not. The development of efficient systems of mass surveillance and control is one of the distinctive sociological features of advanced societies. Never before our own era have large organizations been able to remain in direct interaction with literally millions of persons, both keeping abreast of their affairs and reaching out with authoritative bureaucratic action in response to such monitoring.

THE EXTENSION OF SURVEILLANCE

We believe that these rather abstract concepts earn their keep by helping us to formulate a question of fundamental interest: How far can we expect the development of modern surveillance and control to go? What forms of previously private information are most likely to come into demand as grist for the mills of bureaucratic surveillance? What forms of behavior are most likely to be subjected to centralized organizational control through the use of such information?

Much organizational interest in the details of people's private lives relates to the effort to curtail one or another form of deviant behavior. Credit systems serve largely to counteract disruptive effects from those unwilling or unable to pay; police record systems serve to aid in the control of crime and criminals. Thus, new forms of surveillance are especially likely when they promise to enable organizations to root out some troublesome form of misbehavior. Innovations in surveillance that promise to identify potential shoplifters to department stores, or terrorists to airlines, or illegal aliens to immigration authorities, then, are bound to attract intense interest from the organizations involved.

The nature of deviant activity, however, may be only indirectly related to the personal data sought for its control. This makes it especially difficult to foretell what forms of personal information are most likely to come into demand. When organizations take the record of past deviant behavior to predict future propensities for such behavior, the link is clear enough. No one is surprised that the police use criminal records from the past to anticipate and act against future criminality. But organizations also seek to predict the future behavior of those with whom they deal by studying nonintuitive statistical correlates of such behavior. Thus, if the IRS came to suspect that tax evasion was highly associated with venereal disease, that agency would probably seek the same sweeping power to delve through people's medial records that it now enjoys relative to their bank accounts. One ought not to smile too quickly at this seemingly far-fetched example. Social science research has turned up associations no less improbable than this one. Furthermore when a given form of deviant behavior offends particularly powerful interests, the efforts to seek out information on its possible correlate may become intense.

But the interest in understanding and thereby controlling deviant behavior is not the only occasion for the extension of bureaucratic surveillance. Many efforts to document details of persons' private lives arise in an attempt to document and define what one might term "fine-grained" bureaucratic obligations. The enormous amounts of personal documentation required for medical insurance and social security, for example, serve largely to establish eligibility for those services. The growing importance of these bureaucratically determined benefits is hardly less important in fueling the spread of surveillance than the effort to suppress deviance in the ordinary sense. The point is, both bureaucracies and the publics to which they respond expect exact distinctions to be drawn between the guilty and the innocent, between those likely to prove guilty and those not so likely, between the eligible and the ineligible, and among different forms and degrees of eligibility among the same people over time. When distinctions can be drawn in the treatments owing to different members of the public, one can expect efforts to document the bases for these distinctions and hence to render them grist for the mills of bureaucratic action.

In virtually all innovations in mass surveillance, the pressure of public demand plays an important part. One can point to few systems of collection and use of detailed personal information in America which were foisted on a wholly unwilling public simply for narrow bureaucratic purposes. On the contrary, people often want and even demand the fine-grained decision making afforded by personal data systems. Criminal record systems could not exist without the demands of the great majority of the public for keeping vigorous track of criminals. Credit systems would be impossible without the considerable public enthusiasm for the comforts of easy, convenient credit. People may feel that their privacy is threatened by the demands for personal information characteristic of the modern world; but they often seem willing enough to yield personal data in specific instances where desired services are at stake.

Indeed, available evidence suggests that people's desire to "justice" done, in one way or another, accounts for much of the popular demand for extension of surveillance. People seek their own just deserts, in terms of the credit privileges, insurance rates, tax liability, passport use, or whatever, to which they feel themselves entitled. At the same time, the public also demands effective discriminations *against* welfare cheaters, poor credit risks, dangerous drivers, tax evaders, criminals, and the like. These discriminations in the treatment of persons by organizations can only be achieved by recourse to personal data keeping. The instinct of demanding justice in the allocation of scarce resources is of course as old as social life itself. However, the capabilities of modern organizations have made it possible for organizations to apply such principles in decision-making relations with literally millions of persons.

Often, it is difficult to say whether popular demands represent the cause or the effect of the growing sophistication of organization in surveillance and control. The result, in either event, is a secular trend toward increasingly effective bureaucratic attention to and demand for such information. Thus we confess real doubt about observations such as the following by Alan Westin (1967):

> A close survey of the positions adopted by leading ideological and civic groups toward issues of surveillance and privacy since 1945 indicates that there is now a general identification of privacy and liberty, and that concern over unlimited governmental or private surveillance runs the ideological spectrum from the Daughters of the American Revolution to the New Student Left, and from the *National Review* to the *Nation.* . . . The cry that "Big Brother Is Watching" is now raised by any person or group protesting against what he or it considers unfair surveillance. . . . Anxious articles and editorials about restoring norms of privacy have appeared in business, labor, legal, and academic journals, and many civic groups have adopted policy resolutions deploring erosions of privacy [p. 378].

It all sounds good. No one, after all, is likely to come out *against* privacy. But a close look at the clamor for more of it suggests that its proponents do not all have the same thing in mind. The Daughters of the American Revolution may well deplore, let us say, government snooping into the tax-exempt status of conservative educational organizations but they are likely to be the first to demand more vigorous invasion of the privacy of groups like the New Student Left. *The Nation* may well deplore invasions of the privacy, for example, of welfare mothers; but it would be quick to support FBI investigation of right-wring militant groups.

People do indeed protest what they consider "unfair surveillance," often in the same breath with which they demand more vigorous surveillance for purposes that they support. Nearly everyone can point to some form of surveillance with which they are unhappy, either because it strikes them as ineffective or because the form of control at which it aims seems undesirable in itself. The more fundamental public reflex, however, seems to be to insist that discrimination based on detailed personal data be made whenever the ends of such discrimination seems desirable. Public and private bureaucracies are usually only too willing to accommodate these demands, where indeed they have not encouraged them to begin with. The long-term effect can only be further pressure against individual privacy and autonomy, in the sense in which most people use these terms.

Given the forces fostering the growth of surveillance, we can identify no "natural limit" to the incorporation of personal information into the attentions of personal data systems. That is, we can conceive of no form of personal information that might not, under certain conditions, comes to serve the purposes of bureaucracies aiming at some form of social control. Such forms of control may be brutal or humane; they may be instituted autocratically or with the widest popular participation. But so long as what we term the "efficiency criterion" continues to guide bureaucratic innovation in these respects, the potential for extension of surveillance to more and more areas of life is endless. The theoretical endpoint of such trends is a world in which every thought and action of everyone registers at once with a centralized monitoring agency. To note this extreme is scarcely to announce its imminent attainment; but the implications of this theoretical endpoint for present developments bear reflection nonetheless.

Certainly no area of human life is inherently too private to attract the application of bureaucratic surveillance. Indeed, the most sensitive and personal aspects of life are often most associated with the social uncertainties that make systematic monitoring and control attractive. People yield all sorts of embarrassing or otherwise sensitive information to medical personnel as one of the costs of modern medical care. Similarly, they provide documentary accounting of the disorders and treatments involved to insurance bureaucracies as a requirement for reimbursement for such treatment. As connections arise between forms of personal information and possibilities for urgently desired social control, demands for the data in question are sure to follow.

Thus, a fundamental trend in modern, highly developed societies is the progressive centralization of social control in large bureaucracies and the incorporation of more and more personal information in these bureaucratic systems to guide the workings of control. Other trends mitigate these effects to some extent. As the demands of centralized bureaucracies grow in these respects, those of local forms of surveillance and control—the family, the community, or the kinship system, for example—may subside (see Rule, 1974, pp. 331–332, 342–343). But no one can doubt that the growth of bureaucratic surveillance and control constrain individual autonomy and privacy in the sense in which most people use these terms. The value issues raised by the workings of a relative handful of mammoth systems of surveillance and control are bound to be weightier than those associated with the independent workings of many dispersed, local systems.

THE PROTECTION OF PRIVACY
AND ITS LIMITATIONS

In due course, the growing papers concentrated in bureaucratic systems of personal data management began to arouse considerable public anxiety. Who sets the purposes of bureaucratic surveillance? Can the systems be trusted?

The privacy issue, as it took shape in the late 1960s, represented a minefield for America's political and administrative elites. Dissatisfaction over organizational handling of personal data threatened to place important prerogatives up for grabs. On the one hand, ability to collect, store, and use personal information had become a major resource for key American bureaucracies, both public and private. On the other hand, some of the early objections to these practices sounded serious indeed. Given rising public mistrust of the official exercise of power, culminating, ultimately, in the Watergate affair, the nascent privacy protection movement of the late 1960s might have led to fundamental attacks upon established power positions. Whether this would occur depended on the meaning attributed to the protection of privacy in the emergent public understanding of that notion.

In fact, no frontal collision has occurred between an aroused public opinion and organizations engaged in what we term surveillance. The emergent official interpretation of privacy protection has forestalled any such confrontation. In this view, the noxious or dangerous feature of bureaucratic surveillance systems appear not as things inherent in their nature, but as failures to work "correctly"; and "correct," in this context, means consistent with the longer-term bureaucratic ends governing the systems. This convenient accommodation, from the standpoint of established forces, has made it possible to pursue the "reform" of these systems in ways that enhance, rather than threaten, their key interests. It would be difficult to overestimate the significance of this interpretation.

The domestication of the privacy issue has many parallels in the history of attempted regulation of noxious practices by powerful institutions in America.[2] In these instances, lost opportunities for thorough reshaping of the practices involved pass so subtly and quietly as to be virtually unnoticed. In the case of privacy, as with many other issues, the fateful turning points came out in the heat of public debate but at that subtle point where key assumptions are taken for granted.

Of enormous importance in these developments was the early penchant to focus on notorious abuses of personal data management. Congressional hearings, journalistic and popular writings, and scholarly treatments of the emergent issue all tended to dramatize certain categories of particularly ugly misuses of personal information. They publicized cases of credit bureaus causing damage by maintaining and reporting erroneous information, or they focused on instances of erroneous or misleading arrest data unjustly affecting a person's access, let us say, to employment, or they centered attention on cases of an early education record unfairly stigmatizing a child throughout his or her school career.

The more resourceful representatives of organizations engaged in surveillance basically accepted critics' objections to such abuses and the legitimacy of efforts to correct these. In so doing, however, they helped to shift the debate over privacy protection to one over elimination of particular sets of abusive practices. This was construed to mean making surveillance systems work *better*, on the assumption that both organizations and the individuals depicted in the systems shared an interest in achieving the ends for which the systems were created. By concentrating attention on abuses of personal record-keeping so extreme that they served neither individuals nor organizations, participants in this debate shut out examination of the larger desirability of the growing power of surveillance systems *in general.*

Perhaps even more important, by fostering an interpretation of privacy protection in these terms, both the critics and the defenders of surveillance practices could avoid the really difficult and painful questions: How much surveillance is a desirable thing? How far should the development or bureaucratic monitoring of otherwise private affairs be extended? Instead of engaging these enormously difficult and contentious questions, the privacy planners eventually evolved what we term the efficiency criterion. By this criterion, privacy is deemed protected if three conditions are met in managing personal data: (1) that the data be kept accurate, complete, up-to-date, and subject to review and correction by the persons concerned; (2) that the uses of filed data proceed according to rules of due process that data subjects can know and, if necessary, invoke; and (3) that the organizations collecting and using personal data do so only insofar as necessary to attain their appropriate organizational goals. Under these principles, organizations can claim to protect the privacy of the persons with whom they deal, even as they accumulate more and more data·on those persons and greater and greater power over their lives. It would be difficult to imagine a more advantageous interpretation of privacy protection from the standpoint of surveillance organizations.

However, the terms of this emergent compromise neglect something very important. The growth of modern bureaucratic surveillance, we have argued, represents a social trend of enormous significance in itself. That significance extends far beyond the issues surrounding abuse of particular systems in their present form. It demands consideration of the directions of social change implicit in present practices and of the alternatives to increasing reliance on surveillance.

A hard look at these matters reveals many reasons for seeking limits to the extension of bureaucratic surveillance—not simply as a source of unfairness or inefficiency, but as a bad thing in itself. The simplest of these reasons is what we have termed "aesthetic" reactions against intensive surveillance. No one really wants to live in a world where every previously private moment becomes a subject of bureaucratic scrutiny. There is something inherently desirable, at least for most people, about maintaining realms where experiences are shared only by the parties to them (see Fried, 1968). Even when the ends of surveillance are impeccable and even when the agencies concerned carry out their monitoring with full rectitude and discretion, the monitoring of every moment would strike most people as unacceptable.

To be sure, present surveillance systems have hardly brought us to the point of total monitoring. But again, the logic of change in these systems suggests no natural limit to their further extension. So long as the efficiency criterion continues to guide the development of these systems, their attentions will continue to spread over larger and larger areas of what has been private experience. At some point, nearly everyone would acknowledge, such extension passes the point of moral or aesthetic acceptability. Where that point lies is not an objective matter. It can only be identified through earnest debate and thoughtful reflection on the values of privacy and autonomy versus those of efficiency. There are no grounds for assuming that such debate and reflection would yield consensus among all thoughtful parties, but this hardly justifies ignoring the incontestable fact that modern surveillance systems promise eventually to reach the limits of acceptability by everyone's standards. Where that point occurs is a matter that ought to be explored in any thoughtful treatment of the privacy issue. Yet the official response to these matters evades these difficult issues, rather than encouraging us to confront them.

Another reason for limiting the unrestricted growth of bureaucratic surveillance lies in the value of preserving what one might term a desirable "looseness" in social relations. Other differences notwithstanding, many, if not most, surveillance systems work to make people responsible for their pasts. Criminal records ensure that people to do not escape the repercussions of their criminal acts; insurance reporting works to link disreputable people to their community reputations; credit reporting helps credit grantors to hold people responsible for their past credit-using behavior.

Most Americans probably feel that these processes are legitimate and desirable, at least in some measure. However, most people probably also feel that there ought to be limits to the extent to which people's records are held against them. Statements like the following (House Committee on Government Operations, 1968) from a spokesman for the country's largest insurance and employment reporting firm do leave one a little uneasy:

> It is a fact that the interchange of business information and the availability of record information imposes a discipline on the American citizen. He becomes more responsible for his performance whether as a driver of his car, as an employee in his job performance, or as a payor to his creditors. But this discipline is a necessary one if we are to enjoy the fruits of our economy and the present freedom of our private enterprise.

Is a system of soliciting and reporting accounts of people's lives from friends, neighbors, co-workers really essential to the enjoyment of freedom? More generally, is it desirable that people always be held fully responsible for all of what prospective employers, creditors, or insurors would consider their past shortcomings? (See Greenawalt, 1975.) It is true that the conventional wisdom in America endorses the notion that people must "reap as they sow," but popular sentiment also endorses the worth of "a fresh start" or "a clean slate." Systematic forgetting of a person's pasts, even when troublesome from the standpoint of bureaucratic efficiency, may reflect a social value of considerable importance. Whether the values of efficiency or those of "wiping the slate clean" ought to prevail in any particular setting is bound to be a contentious issue.

We hardly insist on any particular resolution of the issue; indeed, the nature of the choices seems to us to preclude any programmatic solution, apart from piecemeal compromises on a case-by-case basis. We do, however, insist that the issue be confronted directly, and that the interests of efficiency alone not serve as a satisfactory basis for such confrontation. Again, the official response to the privacy issue has most often obscured these agonizing choices precisely when they need to be dramatized.

A third compelling reason for limiting the growth of bureaucratic surveillance has to do with the effects of these systems on social power relations. The growth of modern surveillance inevitably brings about cumulative change in relations between what Shils (1975) would term "centers" of social power and the "peripheries." Surveillance makes it possible for those at the centers to monitor the activities of large populations and "teach out" with forceful actions to shape and control those behaviors. Often, of course, the purposes for which surveillance capacities are originally developed may be strictly mundane or indeed purely humanitarian. That is, the social control that the systems afford may entail nothing more humanitarian. That is, the social control that the systems afford may entail nothing more objectionable than enforcing tax obligations or providing health care. However, once these surveillance capabilities are in place, these is always some risk of their appropriation for purposes of repression by centralized powers. Under these conditions, it may matter rather little what were the original intentions of those who created the system, or even whether the system is governmental or private. Changes in political climates, for example, may leave bank or credit card files more open to government snooping than even some government records. The results of increasing the power of centralized institutions over those who make up the peripheries cannot always be foreseen.

These powers need not always be exercised in order to have their undesirable effects. We must recall the chilling effect that stems from people's knowledge of the data-monitoring capabilities of centralized institutions (see Wessel, 1974). Events of the 1970s have certainly altered many American's views of what centralized institutions, especially government ones, are capable of in these respects. Now it is much more difficult than it once was to dismiss the possibility that one's phone is being tapped, or that one's tax returns may be used for unfriendly political purposes, or that one's life has become the subject of a CIA file. The realization that these activities *might* take place, whether they really do or not in any particular instance, has potentially destructive effects on the openness of social systems to innovation and dissent. Clearly, the best way to avoid these effects is to cut back the instrumentalities that convey such threats.

Virtually everyone would acknowledge some point at which surveillance by bureaucracies simply becomes too thoroughgoing, even when carried out with total discretion for seemingly unimpeachable purposes. What if, instead of electronic funds transfer (EFT) systems, someone were to propose a "wireless funds transfer" system, in which people were equipped with miniature radios, to be carried or worn at all times, capable of authorizing debits from their accounts. Such a system would obviously offer even greater convenience than EFT, since one would always have total access to one's resources. Most people, however, would begin to feel uneasy, we suspect, about any system that provided such intimate and potentially unerring contact between private persons and centralized powers. At some point, a measure of insulation between what Shils terms center and periphery becomes a highly desirable thing in itself.

Consider a medical surveillance system designed to provide timely intelligence on threats to people's physical or mental health. Suppose that a tiny radio transmitter could be implanted under one's skin, to send continuous signals to a central computer for recording and monitoring. The cumulative record of such things as heartbeat, blood sugar, electroencephalogram, and the like could provide a database for predicting all sorts of dangerous conditions, ranging from heart attacks to psychopathic outbursts. Indeed, if participation in the monitoring were required of everyone, the expanded database would afford insights to benefit the sick and the well alike. Furthermore, if the system embodied a way of pinpointing the location of each user, heart attack victims and others involved in emergencies could count on prompt help. Continuous monitoring and analysis of data, under a system like this, could make it possible to transmit timely warnings, perhaps through the radio transmitter itself, to people who, in light of their record, were in danger of ill health or antisocial behavior. From one point of view, a system like this would represent the ultimate in preventive health care.

No one, we imagine, would find fault with the ultimate ends of such an undertaking—improving the quality of health care, and providing such care in the widest and most timely way. Nor would most people deny that public institutions have an authentic interest in establishing control over the uncertainties of public health. After all, the burdens of ill-health invariably fall in one way or another on society as a whole. There would be no insuperable difficulty in ensuring privacy in the conventional sense in a system like this. Procedural guarantees could well ensure such things as confidentiality, access rights, and due process in the user of data.

We suspect, however, that none of these redeeming possibilities would suffice to make such an arrangement acceptable to most people. Even if administered with the most scrupulous guarantees on behalf of impeccable ends, a system like this would strike most of us as excessive. Such examples cause us to smile, or, if we take them seriously, to shudder, because these arrangements simply go too far in breaking down barriers that insulate individuals from larger institutions. Aesthetically, such arrangements revolt us because they would destroy the sense of aloneness and autonomy that most people count essential ingredients of life. Strategically, the powers that such systems would confer on an overbearing regime are so sweeping that the risks implicit in their existence are simply better not taken. Even without repressive intent, the administration of such a system could hardly remain indefinitely free of pressures to share its capabilities for surveillance and control with other systems. The accretion of extraneous social control functions in the case of Social Security would be trivial compared to the demands made on systems like the ones imagined here.

Spokesmen for programs of privacy protection through due process in personal data management have generally characterized their intent as that of "restoring the balance" between individuals and data-keeping institutions (for further discussion see Westin, 1967; Miller, 1971; PPSC, 1977). Although the details are never very clearly specified, the idea seems to be that procedural guarantees like those discussed above eliminate dangers potentially arising from misuse of personal data systems. But in the light of larger patterns of social change, the notion of "balancing" the prerogatives of data-keeping organizations and those of individuals, or of weighing the demands of privacy against the need for information, seems superficial. Procedural reforms may indeed provide an arena where individuals can assert their interests in the uses of their personal documentation; but these safeguards are matters of social convention. They endure only as long as the political and social climate in which they arise. In a more profound sense, the balance between individuals and centralized organizations is permanently altered once such systems are in place. Certainly one would always prefer procedural safeguards to their absence wherever personal data systems exist. However, it is misleading to argue that such safeguards somehow return the balance of social power to its status before the establishment of centralized institutions.

Let us remember that bureaucratic structures have no *purposes* of their own. Formal organizations develop capabilities to do certain kinds of things and of mastering given forms of uncertainty, but the ends that these skills serve are not dictated by the tools. A list of names and addresses, an array of pertinent information, or a bureaucratic mechanism for collecting and ordering such data, once in place, exists for the benefit of whoever controls them at any given time. The purposes leading to the founding of such a system need not necessarily shape their continued working. Creating pluralistic rules of the game by which individuals are accorded some influence over treatment of their data is desirable in itself, but it has no effect beyond the point where participants stop playing by the rules.

Again, there need be no question of the sincerity of the intentions of the founders of these systems, or of the seriousness with which procedural safeguards are originally instated. The point is simply that political and social climates change and that the inherent capabilities of organizational forms typically outlive the frame of mind of those who bring them into existence. David J. Seipp (1978) has found a remarkable quote from a spokesman for the FBI back in 1931. Asked whether the Bureau would consider resorting to wiretapping, he replied,

> No sir. We have a very definite rule in the bureau that any employee engaging in wire-tapping will be dismissed from the service of the bureau. . . . While it may not be illegal, I think it is unethical, and it is not permitted under the regulations by the Attorney General [p. 108].

The speaker was a young J. Edgar Hoover, replying to a query in a Congressional committee on Expenditures hearing.

What constitutes "acceptable practice" does change, then, and the tempting availability of sophisticated personal-data-monitoring techniques may bring about recourse to practices previously foresworn. This makes it risky to place too much confidence in the self-restraint of any institution. Consider the following quote (Westin, 1967) from the middle 1960s:

> The history of police-force use of eavesdropping is sufficiently stained with misconduct throughout the nation that use of physical surveillance devices at the state level should be strictly limited to district attorney's offices and state attorney generals' offices, and at the federal level to the FBI and military agencies [p. 376].

Obviously, any attempt to safeguard individual privacy and autonomy while leaving the powers of personal-data collection intact must identify some institution as a trustworthy repository of such powers. In light of events since the 1960s, however, the choice of the FBI and the military for this role can only be described as quaint.

The Alternative: A Looser, More Private World

We suspect that most people, confronted with the foregoing concerns, would hardly remain indifferent. No one really likes the idea of endless growth of bureaucratic surveillance, but what alternative can there be?

The fact that it may be difficult to conceive of realistic alternatives reflects the important gaps in most discussions of the privacy issue. A key assumption in these interpretations is that of organizations' needs for personal data. The underlying logic in this approach seems to go something like this:

1. The needs of organizations for personal data are relentlessly rising.
2. The continued satisfaction of these needs is a condition for a more bountiful, more efficient, more "advanced" social world.
3. The only policy is to satisfy such needs while making organizational demands for data as fair and as palatable to the public as possible.

Obviously, we share the view that modern formal organizations have characteristic reasons for relying on personal documentation, but the lock-step argument noted above caricatures the thoughtful analysis of this reliance which the issue requires. The message seems to be that we can choose only between increasing loss of personal information to bureaucratic surveillance and a return to some sort of organizational "Stone Age." Yet a searching look at the needs of organizations for personal information suggests that they hardly represent a *sine qua non* of organizational life. In fact, one can identify a range of alternatives to increasingly intense use of personal data in organizational decision-making; these alternatives have not received the attention that they deserve.

Organizations collect personal information largely in order to sustain discriminating decision-making processes concerning the persons depicted by the data. In an effort to produce just the proper treatment of each individual, and hence to forestall squandering resources on improper treatments, organizations seek more and more pertinent data to afford closer and closer discrimination among cases. However, what represents an improper application of resources is not eternally given; it is a social convention that might well be reconsidered in the interests of protecting privacy and autonomy. If organizations were not expected to make such fine discriminations in their treatments of persons, the need for rigorous data-collection would be greatly eased. The alternative to endless erosion of personal privacy and autonomy through increased surveillance lies in lessening discriminations among people in the application of organizational resources.

Today organizations, both governmental and private, invest enormous resources in pursuing what has been termed fine-grained discrimination. What we are proposing is a reallocation of resources to develop and underwrite less discriminatory, and hence less information-intensive, ways of dealing with people. What we face here is not simply a choice between meeting the information needs of organizations and seeing these organizations grind to a halt. Instead, the choice lies between meeting the costs of discriminating and paying the costs of relaxing such discrimination. For every degree of intimacy of surveillance relinquished by organizations, benefits accrue in privacy and autonomy.

Pursuit of less information-intensive alternatives would entail a fundamental change in expectations about the treatments that organizations owe to their publics. It would mean minimizing differences in how people are treated in light of their records, and hence minimizing the necessity for developing such records. Instead of sharpening their discriminations, organizations would be expected to provide a baseline of adequate resources for all, with minimal differences according to cases.

Again, the alternatives here are not binary choices, but choices among many possible degrees of discrimination and the commensurately rising demands on privacy. Such tradeoffs are easily noted, for example, in income taxation. From its relatively simple beginnings, the U.S. income tax system has become a giant consumer of personal data. The rise in the range and frequency of data intake, of course, corresponds directly to the growing multiplicity of personal circumstances which tax laws take into account in assessing liability. A major impetus for such growth, one supposes, is public demand for "just consideration" of various extenuating circumstances. Simpler tax laws might well aim at limiting the range of circumstances bearing on tax obligations. If discrimination were made less complicated, then demands for personal information would drop commensurately. Planners for tax reform could make an enormous contribution to privacy protection by cutting back the range of personal data that bears on tax liability.

A relatively easy avenue for seeking less information-intensive forms of bureaucratic action lies in those areas where the use of personal information is least cost-effective. One of the most intrusive bureaucratic demands now widespread in America is that associated with security clearances. Millions of people must routinely undergo such investigations as conditions of their employment. Yet to our knowledge, compelling statistical associations between the results of these investigations and, let us say, unauthorized leaks of security-related information have never been

demonstrated. We suspect that the information needs attributed to our security apparatus in these respects simply would not withstand close examination. Such an examination would more likely show that whatever benefits such procedures yield do not
nearly warrant the costs in loss of privacy and the chilling effects of dissent and
diversity in American life.

Attacking demands on personal privacy that do not really pay off in terms of
organization gain, however, is easy. Indeed, nearly all writers on the subject have
exploited this argument. The difficult cases concern organizational use of personal
information that is both useful by the standards presently prevailing in organizations
and destructive of privacy and autonomy.

Here we feel that serious consideration of the arguments put forward above
demands foreswearing bureautically attractive uses of personal data. This would mean
setting policies in which organizations would relax or abandon the single-minded pursuit of efficient discrimination among persons in favor of other considerations.

No doubt the easiest settings in which to begin applying this thinking are in the
planning for bureaucratic systems that do not yet exist. The prospect of national
health insurance, for example, is receiving increasingly serious discussion at the time
of this writing. The degree of discrimination built into a system of this kind is obviously full of implications for personal privacy. Systems that embody complicated eligibility requirements and other forms of discrimination governing access to treatment
are driven to make very intensive demands on personal data. The most appealing
alternative is a system that offers its services to all, as in Britain's National Health
Service. Since every Briton is eligible, the system need not develop the detailed
inquiries into the backgrounds of its clients which would otherwise be the case. Thus,
the system actually entails relatively loose central record-keeping. What there is
serves mainly to keep track of the numbers of patients for whom individual physicians are responsible. Case histories and other personal background information are
stored locally, much as they are in countries where medicine is private.

One can also envisage ways to enhance privacy by restricting surveillance
where it is already well established, although resistance would be greater here. Consider the case of consumer credit. The first consumer-credit reporting operations were
basically simple listings of bad debts held in common among several firms, to enable
each to avoid giving credit to persons who had defaulted elsewhere. Today, by contrast, credit surveillance entails use of a very wide variety of information pooled
among many different sources. The sophistication of modern credit systems depends
on the use of these rich informational resources to predict which credit applicants
should be trusted and to what extent. The interests of privacy would be well served
by deliberately blunting some of these discriminations.

This possibility has not gone altogether unnoticed among writers on privacy.
Kent Greenawalt (1975), in his thoughtful study of the status of privacy in American
law, has commented,

> If information about credit standing is easily available on a national basis, it is virtually
> impossible to avoid one's low credit rating. This information allows credit-granting agen-
> cies to make more intelligent decisions about risk, but is it socially desirable that per-
> sons who admittedly pose a high risk be unable to get credit? Perhaps it would be social-
> ly preferable in credit were more freely available, even if good credit risks ended up
> paying the tab (e.g., in increased prices) so that poor credit risks could get credit [p. 92].

Nonetheless, Greenawalt's remarks here are exceptional; most writers have taken
the sacredness of organizational efficiency for granted in these matters. We share

Greenawalt's view. The effectiveness of discriminations between good and poor credit risks is hardly the only social value that ought to be considered in this important relationship. Competing values here are those of a looser social world, one with less potential for serving the needs of oppressive centralized powers and more capacity for extending opportunities to those who, in light of "all the facts," may appear to be poor risks. We favor a commitment of resources to pursuit of these latter values over and against those of pure efficiency in discriminating as to who will be the most profitable credit customers.

Any number of concrete measures, more or less sweeping, might serve to put this principle into effect. One might restrict the retention of derogatory credit information to, let us say, 2 years. This would have the effect of wiping the slate clean after a relatively short period for those who have been unwilling or unable to pay in the past. Or one might do away with centralized credit reporting altogether, so that every firm extending credit would have to develop its own bases for deciding whether to open an account with a given applicant.[3] This would surely countervail against the thoroughgoing and intrusive character of modern credit investigations. Our point is not to argue for any particular measure, but rather to emphasize alternatives to the single-minded pursuit of efficient discrimination that characterizes current credit policy. Whether the resulting policies are sweeping or cautious matters less than recognizing that protection of privacy requires compromises in bureaucratic efficiency.

Similar less information-intensive alternatives can be envisaged for many other social settings now marked by growing reliance on surveillance. In all of these cases, gains for privacy and autonomy can be purchased at incremental costs in the relinquishment of fine discriminations among persons in the application of bureaucratic resources. Whether such costs are warranted in any particular instance is not a question to be answered *a priori* for all settings at all times. Indeed, it is misleading to suggest that such questions have objective solutions, independent of the values of any particular thinker. We scarcely mean to insist, then, on anything so heavy-handed as curtailment of surveillance in all cases as a matter of principle; but we do insist that values of bureaucratic efficiency are not the only ones that ought to inform policy in personal data systems.

CONCLUSION

One might view very modern, "advanced" societies as characterized by reliance on especially powerful technologies. These include not only technologies in the usual sense, but also what one might term social technologies—techniques for mobilizing the actions of large numbers of people. These techniques afford relative handfuls of decision makers the means, for example, to activate party faithful in politics; or to direct the movement of investment capital; or to orchestrate the movement of armies in military campaigns; or to determine what people will read or hear or see via mass communications. Surveillance systems, of course, represent simply another refinement in social technologies. They enable elites to monitor the individual behavior of very many people at a time and to use the data so acquired to shape people's behavior in return.

The growth of such powerful technologies—surveillance very much included here—raises the *stakes* of social planning. When the technologies of small-scale, simple social systems go wrong, the numbers of persons to be affected will at least not be too great. But when the powerful technologies of large-scale modern societies meet with destructive uses, the results may take the form of nuclear warfare or total-itarianism. Individually, there may not be a great deal to choose between victimiza-tion in a witch hunt in a small seventeenth-century New England town and persecu-tion in a modern totalitarian regime. Collectively, the scope of human tragedy in the second case must surely be counted far greater.

The dawning realization of the potential evils of powerful technologies gone wrong has injected into contemporary culture a remarkable ambivalence about sci-ence and its status in society. Throughout most of the nineteenth century, the idea grew that enhanced scientific understanding of both the natural and social worlds would lead to a richer, more materially bountiful and less socially conflict-ridden existence for everyone. "Know, in order to foretell; foretell, in order to control," thus one might translate Comte's optimistic dictum on the spirit of science. Certainly the growth both of scientific understanding and of the resulting scope of human control have, if anything, overfulfilled Comte's predictions. The expanding sphere of human control has not been an unmixed blessing, however. For members of advanced, afflu-ent societies, life has become more comfortable in countless ways. Yet the unintend-ed effects of the technologies that afford such affluence give rise to the possibility of all sorts of man-made disasters on a scale never before possible. The use in warfare of sophisticated technologies for mobilizing energy for the first time raises the pos-sibility of the extinction of the species. The applications of other sophisticated natur-al science technologies raises serious possibilities of environmental disaster. And the growth of social technologies, including but by no means limited to surveillance, rais-es the possibility of totalitarianism. The growth of human control, it would seem, offers the drawbacks of its successes.

These realizations cast an ironic light on the original, almost unbounded opti-mism concerning the social effects of science, an optimism that social science has until very recently helped to promote.[4] In many of the earlier evolutionary interpre-tations of social development, the enhancement of human control was seen as a vir-tually unambiguous gain in the *security* of social life. After all, the growth of more powerful technologies promised to preserve human life from the uncertainties of dis-ease, scarcity, superstition and the like. These uncertainty-reducing features of social organization thus seemed to offer a more secure role of humankind on the planet. A number of social scientists have contended, even very recently, that growing under-standing of social processes will make social systems more rational. Now we must face the fact that modern natural technologies have created highly *un*steady states (Granovetter, 1979). Though we may live in many ways a more bountiful material life, say, than the indigenous North American peoples, we know that present patterns of technology and energy use, drawing as they do on zero-sum resources and push-ing against limited environments, cannot continue indefinitely. Thus our relations with our natural environments are *less* stable over the longer run than those of less-developed peoples. Similarly, the development of surveillance and the countless other sophisticated social arrangements of bureaucratic civilization offer all sorts of enrich-ing comforts and conveniences. No one, however, can be certain when we may come to regret the longer-term effects of the application of such powerful systems.

In 1969, we suspect, these arguments would have struck nearly everyone as hopelessly utopian. Today, perhaps, this is slightly less the case. We have lately been witnessing, in American and other highly developed societies, a remarkable disen-chantment with powerful technologies, at least as they relate to the nonhuman world. These attitudes are perhaps most evident with regard to environmental and energy policy. As everyone knows who has been attentive to public debates on these matters, antagonism toward powerful, centralized approaches to these issues goes very deep among many people. These are of course the same people who prefer soft energy technologies such as wind and water power, technologies that disperse both social and natural power into as many relatively autonomous elements as possible.

In our view, some elements of radical environmentalism have their own irrational tinge, but many of the concerns of the technological skeptics, as we have called them, seem to us to embody certain unassailably valid principles. Very powerful technologies, both social and natural, entail the risks of putting all of one's eggs in a single basket; any disaster is apt to be a very large-scale disaster indeed. By contrast, the failures of soft, dispersed technologies at least limit the scope of the resulting damage. No one who thinks carefully about it can really like the idea of a world in which man-made concentrations of power grow larger endlessly. Yet only self-conscious efforts to enlarge the array of alternatives considered in planning for these things can reverse the trend in this direction.

If we are right, the current erosion in the once seemingly boundless faith in the prospects of growing human control represents a trend of major significance. At a gut level, people are growing skeptical of more and more powerful technologies as solutions to the problems of highly developed societies. These changes in public attitudes cry out for a redefinition of rationality in these respects. Thoughtful, scientifically reputable people must be prepared to affirm that preference for smaller, more modest forms of control need not be superstitious or irrational. On the contrary, people need to hear it said that limitations on the scope of human intervention need not be antiscientific, but may simply reflect the humility due to planning for situations where the stakes may grow very great indeed. Such humility, it seems to us, is particularly fitting where the damage inflicted by misapplied human powers affects far more people than the planners themselves. In short, we need a program for rational limits to the extension of rational human control.

Happily, a number of thoughtful commentators have begun to play this role. Regarding the risks of nuclear power production, for example, Amitai Etzioni (1974) has written,

> To say that reactors have a 1 out of 10,000 chance to blow each year (or 1 out of 1,000,000 per community), which makes them about as safe as flying, does not take into account the number of persons to be killed in a nuclear disaster. . . . Most persons who would accept a $10.00 bet at odds of 99 to 1 in their favor, would hesitate if the bet was $1000 at the *same* odds, and refuse a $100,000 bet at *identical* odds. Why? Only because the disutility changed.

Moreover, as Etzioni would undoubtedly also emphasize, calculations regarding nuclear power must be calculations of *cumulative* probability. That is, one's concern must be with the probability of such systems' *ever* going seriously wrong; these probabilities of course rise steadily over the time span under consideration. And we hold that planning for powerful technologies in general, either natural or social, must rely on this form of thinking. One wishes to be as certain as possible that a surveillance system *never* becomes a vehicle for repressive control. Given the uncertainty that seems to make the changing political and social climates in which such systems exist, such assurances are difficult to come by.

In another context, Kenneth Boulding (1977) has written,

> One of the major principles of the universe as a general system is that over a long enough period of time very improbable events will have happened. It is easy to show

that an event with a probability of $1/n$ in a year has a probability of happening equal to 0.9995 at sometime in a period of $10n$ years. Thus, a 100-year floor is virtually certain to happen sometime within 1000 years. Within the ten-billion-year-history of the universe it is virtually certain that some event with a probability of one billionth per annum will have come off [p. 301].

Of course, it is comforting to assume that events that we regard as unlikely are really such remote possibilities as to be discountable. However, Boulding's observation should remind us of the cumulative increase of unwanted risks over time. In developing social and technological powers that have the potential to shape both our world and that of succeeding generations, prudence in dealing with risks of very serious occurrences is surely warranted.

NOTES

1. For discussion of a number of these issues, see Edward Shils' (1975) remarks on the "cognitive passion" of government and related demands on privacy in "Privacy and Power" in his book of collected essays.
2. For those familiar with the work of Theodore Lowi, the similarity between this interpretation and his ideas will quickly be apparent. (See Lowi, 1971, especially the Prologue and Chapter 1.)
3. To the consternation of the credit-reporting industry, certain large credit grantors, mostly petroleum companies, are developing systems to evaluate applicant credit worthiness without recourse to centralized credit files. Moreover, they are refusing to disclose information about existing accounts to credit bureaus.
4. The durability of such reflexive optimism in the face of all sorts of danger signs is truly remarkable. See, for example, Pool *et al.* (1971).

REFERENCES

Boulding, K. (1977). The universe as a general system. Fourth annual Ludwig von Bertalanffy Memorial Lecture, *Behavioral Science*, 22.

Etzioni, A. (1974). Letter to the editor, *New York Times Magazine*, (March 24).

Fred, C. (1968). Privacy, *Yale Law Journal*, 77.

Granovetter, M. (1979). The idea of "advancement" in theories of social evolution and development, *American Journal of Sociol.*, 85.

Greenawalt, K. (1975). *Legal protections of privacy*. Washington, D.C.: Office of Telecommunications Policy.

House Committee on Government Operations. 90th Congress, 2nd Session. Testimony of May 16 1968. Washington, D.C.: U.S. Government Printing Office, 1968.

Lowi, TG. (1971). *The politics of disorder*. New York: Basic Books.

Miller, A. (1971). *Assault on privacy*. Ann Arbor: University of Michigan Press.

Perrow, C. (1972). *Complex organizations: A critical essay*. Glenview, Ill.: Scott Foresman and Co.

Pool, I., S. McIntosh, and D. Griffel, (1971). Information systems and social knowledge. In A Westin (Ed.), *Information technology in a democracy*. Cambridge, Mass.: Harvard University Press.

Privacy Protection Study Committee. *Personal privacy in an information society.* Washington, D.C.: U.S. Government Printing Office, 1977.

Rule J. (1974). *Private lives and public surveillance.* New York: Schocken Books.

Rule, J., D. McAdam, L. Stearns, and D. Uglow, (1980). *The politics of privacy: Planning for persona data systems as powerful technologies.* New York: Elsevier.

Seipp, D. J. (1978). *The right to privacy in American history.* Cambridge, Mass.: Harvard University Program on Information Resources Policy.

Shils, E. (1975). Privacy and power. In E. Shils (Ed.), *Center and periphery: Essays in macrosociology.* Chicago: University of Chicago Press.

Thompson, J. (1967). *Organizations in action.* New York: McGraw-Hill.

Wessel, M. (1974). *Freedom's edge: The computer threat to society.* Reading, Mass.: Addison-Wesley.

Westin, A. (1967). *Privacy and freedom.* New York: Atheneum.

▷ PRIVACY AND THE LIMITS OF LAW

Ruth Gavison[†]

Anyone who studies the law of privacy today may well feel a sense of uneasiness. On one hand, there are popular demands for increased protection of privacy, discussions of new threats to privacy, and an intensified interest in the relationship between privacy and other values, such as liberty, autonomy, and mental health.[1] These demands have generated a variety of legal responses. Most states recognize a cause of action for invasions of privacy.[2] The Supreme Court has declared a constitutional right to privacy, a right broad enough to protect abortion and the use of contraceptives.[3] Congress enacted the Privacy Act of 1974 after long hearings and debate. These activities seem to imply a wide consensus concerning the distinctness and importance of privacy.

On the other hand, much of the scholarly literature on privacy is written in quite a different spirit. Commentators have argued that privacy rhetoric is misleading: when we study the cases in which the law (or our moral intuitions) suggest that a "right to privacy" has been violated, we always find that some other interest has been involved.[4] Consequently, they argue, our understanding of privacy will be improved if we disregard the rhetoric, look behind the decisions, and identify the real interests protected. When we do so, they continue, we can readily see why privacy itself is never protected: to the extent that there is something distinct about claims for privacy, they are either indications of hypersensitivity[5] or an unjustified wish to manipulate and defraud.[6] Although these commentators disagree on many points, they are

[†]This Article develops some of the themes of my doctoral thesis, Privacy and Its Legal Protection, written under the supervision of Professor H.L.A. Hart. Much of the inspiration of this piece is still his. I am grateful to Bruce Ackerman, Bob Cover, Owen Fiss, George Fletcher, Harry Frankfurt, Jack Getman, Tony Kronman, Arthur Leff, Michael Moore, and Barbara Underwood, who read previous drafts and made many useful comments.

united in denying the utility of thinking and talking about privacy as a legal right, and suggest some form of reductionism.[7]

This Article is an attempt to vindicate the way most of us think and talk about privacy issues: unlike the reductionists, most of us consider privacy to be a useful concept. To be useful, however, the concept must denote something that is distinct and coherent. Only then can it help us in thinking about problems. Moreover, privacy must have a coherence in three different contexts. First, we must have a neutral concept of privacy that will enable us to identify when a loss of privacy has occurred so that discussions of privacy and claims of privacy can be intelligible. Second, privacy must have coherence as a value, for claims of legal protection of privacy are compelling only if losses of privacy are sometimes undesirable and if those losses are undesirable for similar reasons. Third, privacy must be a concept useful in legal contexts, a concept that enables us to identify those occasions calling for legal protection, because the law does not interfere to protect against every undesirable event.

Our everyday speech suggests that we believe the concept of privacy is indeed coherent and useful in the three contexts, and that losses of privacy (identified by the first), invasions of privacy (identified by the second), and actionable violations of privacy (identified by the third) are related in that each is a subset of the previous category. Using the same word in all three contexts reinforces the belief that they are linked. Reductionist analyses of privacy—that is, analyses denying the utility of privacy as a separate concept—sever these conceptual and linguistic links. This Article is an invitation to maintain those links, because an awareness of the relationships and the larger picture suggested by them may contribute to our understanding both of legal claims for protection, and of the extent to which those claims have been met.

I begin by suggesting that privacy is indeed a distinct and coherent concept in all these contexts. Our interest in privacy, I argue, is related to our concern over our accessibility to others: the extent to which we are known to others, the extent to which others have physical access to us, and the extent to which we are the subject of others' attention. This concept of privacy as a concern for limited accessibility enables us to identify when losses of privacy occur. Furthermore, the reasons for which we claim privacy in different situations are similar. They are related to the functions privacy has in our lives: the promotion of liberty, autonomy, selfhood, and human relations, and furthering the existence of a free society. The coherence of privacy as a concept and the similarity of the reasons for regarding losses of privacy as undesirable support the notion that the legal system should make an explicit commitment to privacy as a value that should be considered in reaching legal results. This analysis does not require that privacy be protected in all cases; that result would require consideration of many factors not discussed here. I argue only that privacy refers to a unique concern that should be given weight in balancing values.

My analysis of privacy yields a better description of the law and a deeper understanding of both the appeal of the reductionist approach and its peril. The appeal lies in the fact that it highlights an important fact about the state of the law—privacy is seldom protected in the absence of some other interest. The danger is that we might conclude from this fact that privacy is not an important value and that losses of it should not feature as considerations for legal protection. In view of the prevalence of the reductionist view, the case for an affirmative and explicit commitment to privacy—vindicating the antireductionist perspective—becomes compelling.

THE MEANING AND FUNCTIONS OF PRIVACY

"Privacy" is a term used with many meanings. For my purposes, two types of questions about privacy are important. The first relates to the *status* of the term: is privacy a situation, a right, a claim, a form of control, a value? The second relates to the *characteristics* of privacy: is it related to information, to autonomy, to personal identity, to physical access? Support for all of these possible answers, in almost any combination, can be found in the literature.

The two types of question involve different choices. Before resolving these issues, however, a general distinction must be drawn between the concept and the value of privacy. The concept of privacy identifies losses of privacy. As such, it should be neutral and descriptive only, so as not to preempt questions we might want to ask about such losses. Is the loser aware of the loss? Has he consented to it? Is the loss desirable? Should the law do something to prevent or punish such losses?

This is not to imply that the neutral concept of privacy is the most important, or that it is only legitimate to use "privacy" in this sense. Indeed, in the context of legal protection, privacy should also indicate a value. The coherence and usefulness of privacy as a value is due to a similarity one finds in the reasons advanced for its protection, a similarity that enables us to draw principles of liability for invasions. These reasons identify those aspects of privacy that are considered desirable. When we claim legal protection for privacy, we mean that only those aspects should be protected, and we no longer refer to the "neutral" concept of privacy. In order to see which aspects of privacy are desirable and thus merit protection as a value, however, we must begin our inquiry in a nonpreemptive way by starting with a concept that does not make desirability, or any of the elements that may preempt the question of desirability, part of the notion of privacy. The value of privacy can be determined only at the conclusion of discussion about what privacy is, and when—and why—losses of privacy are undesirable.

In this section I argue that it is possible to advanced a neutral concept of privacy, and that it can be shown to serve important functions that entitle it to prima facie legal protection. The coherence of privacy in the third context—as a legal concept—relies on our understanding of the functions and value of privacy; discussion of the way in which the legal system should consider privacy is therefore deferred until later sections.

The Neutral Concept of Privacy

The Status of Privacy The desire not to preempt our inquiry about the value of privacy by adopting a value-laden concept at the outset is sufficient to justify viewing privacy as a situation of an individual vis-à-vis others, or as a condition of life. It also requires that we reject attempts to describe privacy as a claim,[8] a psychological state,[9] or an area that should not be invaded. For the same reasons, another description that should be rejected is that of privacy as a form of control.

This last point requires some elaboration, because it may appear that describing privacy as a form of control does not preempt important questions. Were privacy described in terms of control, for example, we could still ask whether X has lost control, and whether such loss is desirable. The appearance of a nonpreemptive concept is misleading, however, and is due to an ambiguity in the notion of control. Hyman Gross, for example, defines privacy as "control over acquaintance with one's personal affairs.[10] According to one sense of this definition, a voluntary, knowing disclosure does not involve loss of privacy because it is an exercise of control, not a loss of it. In another, stronger sense of control, however, voluntary disclosure is a loss of control because the person who discloses loses the power to prevent others from further disseminating the information.

There are two problems here. The weak sense of control is not sufficient as a description of privacy, for X can have control over whether to disclose information about himself, yet others may have information and access to him through other means. The strong sense of control, on the other hand, may indicate loss of privacy when there is only a threat of such loss.[11] More important, "control" suggests that the important aspect of privacy is the ability to choose it and see that the choice is respected. All possible choices are consistent with enjoyment of control, however, so that defining privacy in terms of control relates it to the power to make certain choices rather than to the way in which we choose to exercise this power. But individuals may choose to have privacy or to give it up.[12] To be nonpreemptive, privacy must not depend on choice. We need a framework within which privacy may be the result of a specific exercise of control, as when X decides not to disclose certain information about himself, or the result of something imposed on an individual against his wish, as when the law prohibits the performance of sexual intercourse in a public place. Furthermore, the reasons we value privacy may have nothing to do with whether an individual has in fact chosen it. Sometimes we may be inclined to criticize an individual for not choosing privacy, and other times for choosing it. This criticism cannot be made if privacy is defined as a form of control.

Insisting that we start with a neutral concept of privacy does not mean that wishes, exercises of choice, or claims are not important elements in the determination of the aspects of privacy that are to be deemed desirable or of value. This insistence does mean, however, that we are saying something meaningful, and not merely repeating the implications of our concept, if we conclude that only choices of privacy should be protected by law.

Resolving the status of privacy is easier than resolving questions concerning the characteristics of privacy. Is privacy related to secrecy, freedom of action, sense of self, anonymity, or any specific combination of these elements? The answers here are not constrained by methodological concerns. The crucial test is the utility of the proposed concept in capturing the tenor of most privacy claims, and in presenting coherent reasons for legal protection that will justify grouping these claims together. My conception of privacy as related to secrecy, anonymity, and solitude is defended in these terms.

The Characteristics of Privacy In its most suggestive sense, privacy is a limitation of others' access to an individual. As a methodological starting point, I suggest that an individual enjoys *perfect* privacy when he is completely inaccessible to others.[13] This may be broken into three independent components: in perfect privacy no one has any information about X, no one pays any attention to X, and no one has physical access to X. Perfect privacy is, of course, impossible in any society. The possession or enjoyment of privacy is not an all or nothing concept, however, and the total loss of privacy is as impossible as perfect privacy. A more important concept, then, is *loss* of privacy. A loss of privacy occurs as others obtain information about an individual, pay attention to him, or gain access to him. These three elements of secrecy, anonymity, and solitude are distinct and independent, but interrelated, and the complex concept of privacy is richer than any definition centered around only one of them. The complex concept better explains our intuitions as to when privacy is lost, and captures more of the suggestive meaning of privacy. At the same time, it remains sufficiently distinctive to exclude situations that are sometimes labeled "privacy," but that are more related to notions of accountability and interference than to accessibility.

Information Known About an Individual

It is not novel to claim that privacy is related to the amount of information known about an individual. Indeed, many scholars have defined privacy exclusively in these terms, and the most lively privacy issue now discussed is that related to information-gathering. Nevertheless, at least two scholars have argued that there is no inherent loss of privacy as information about an individual becomes known. I believe these critics are wrong. If secrecy is not treated as an independent element of privacy, then the following are only some of the situations that will not be considered losses of privacy: (a) an estranged wife who publishes her husband's love letters to her, without his consent; (b) a single data-bank containing all census information and government files that is used by all government officials;[14] and (c) an employer who asks every conceivable question of his employees and yet has no obligation to keep the answers confidential. In none of these cases is there any intrusion, trespass, falsification, appropriation, or exposure of the individual to direct observation. Thus, unless the amount of information others have about an individual is considered at least partly determinative of the degree of privacy he has, these cases cannot be described as involving losses of privacy.

To talk of the "amount of information" known about an individual is to imply that it is possible to individuate items or pieces of information, to determine the number of people who know each item of information about X, and thus to quantify the information known about X. In fact, this is impossible, and the notion requires greater theoretical elaboration than it has received until now. It is nevertheless used here because in most cases its application is relatively clear. Only a few of the many problems involved need to be mentioned.

The first problem is whether we should distinguish between different kinds of knowledge about an individual, such as verbal as opposed to sensory knowledge, or among different types of sensory knowledge. For example, assume Y learns that X is bald because he reads a verbal description of X. At a later time, Y sees X and, naturally, observes that X is bald. Has Y acquired any further information about X, and if so, what is it? It might be argued that even a rereading of a verbal description may reveal to Y further information about X, even though Y has no additional source of information.

A related set of problems arises when we attempt to compare different "amounts" of knowledge about the same individual. Who has more information about X, his wife after fifteen years of marriage, his psychiatrist after seven years of analysis, or the biographer who spends four years doing research and unearths details about X that are not known either to the wife or to the analyst?[15]

A third set of problems is suggested by the requirement that for a loss of privacy to occur, the information must be "about" the individual. First, how specific must this relationship be? We know that most people have sexual fantasies and sexual relationships with others. Thus, we almost certainly "know" that our new acquaintances have sexual fantasies, yet they do not thereby suffer a loss of privacy. On the other hand, if we have detailed information about the sexual lives of a small number of people, and we are then introduced to one of them, does the translation of the general information into personal information about this person involve a loss of privacy? Consider the famous anecdote about the priest who was asked, at a party, whether he had heard any exceptional stories during confessionals. "In fact," the priest replied, "my first confessor is a good example, since he confessed to a murder." A few minutes later, an elegant man joined the group, saw the priest, and greeted him warmly. When asked how he knew the priest, the man replied: "Why, I had the honor of being his first confessor."

The priest gave an "anonymous" piece of information, which became information "about" someone through the combination of the anonymous statement with the "innocent" one made by the confessor. Only the later statement was "about" a specific individual, but it turned what was previously an anonymous piece of information into further information "about" the individual. The translation here from anonymous information to information about X is immediate and unmistakable, but the process is similar to the combination of general knowledge about a group of people and the realization that a certain individual is a member of that group.

Problems of the relationship between an individual and pieces of information exist on another level as well. Is information about X's wife, car, house, parents, or dog information about X? Clearly, this is information about the other people, animals, or things involved, but can X claim that disclosure of such information is a loss of his privacy? Such claims have often been made. Their plausibility in at least some of the cases suggests that people's notions of themselves may extend beyond their physical limits.

A final set of problems concerns the importance of the truth of the information that becomes known about an individual. Does dissemination of false information about X mean that he has lost privacy? The usual understanding of "knowledge" presupposes that the information is true, but is this sense of "knowledge" relevant here? In one sense, X has indeed lost privacy. People now believe they know more about him. If the information is sufficiently spectacular, X may lose his anonymity and become the subject of other people's attention. In another sense, however, X is not actually "known" any better. In fact, he may even be known less, because the false information may lead people to disregard some correct information about X that they already had.[16] Another difficulty is revealed when we consider statements whose truth is not easily determinable, such as "X is beautiful" or "X is dumb and irresponsible." Publication of such statements clearly leads to some loss of privacy: listeners now know what the speaker thinks about X, and this itself is information about X (as well as about the speaker). But does the listener also know that X is indeed beautiful? This is hard to tell.

Attention Paid to an Individual

An individual always loses privacy when he becomes the subject of attention. This will be true whether the attention is conscious and purposeful, or inadvertent. Attention is a primary way of acquiring information, and sometimes is essential to such acquisition, but attention alone will cause a loss of privacy even if no new information becomes known. This becomes clear when we consider the effect of calling, "Here is the President," should he attempt to walk the streets incognito. No further information is given, but none is necessary. The President loses whatever privacy his temporary anonymity could give him. He loses it because attention has focused on him.

Here too, however, some elaboration is needed. X may be the subject of Y's attention in two typical ways. First, Y may follow X, stare at him, listen to him, or observe him in any other way. Alternatively, *Y* may concentrate his thoughts on *X*. Only the first way of paying attention is directly related to loss of privacy. Discussing, imagining, or thinking about another person is related to privacy in a more indirect way, if at all. Discussions may involve losses of privacy by communicating information about a person or by creating an interest in the person under discussion that may itself lead to more attention. Thinking about a person may also produce an intensified effort to recall or obtain information about him. This mental activity may in turn produce a loss of privacy if new information is obtained. For the most part, however, thinking about another person, even in the most intense way, will involve no loss of privacy to the subject of this mental activity. The favorite subject of one's sexual fantasies may have causes for complaint, but it is unlikely that these will be related to loss of privacy.

Physical Access to an Individual

Individuals lose privacy when others gain physical access to them. Physical access here means physical proximity—that *Y* is close enough to touch or observe *X* through normal use of his senses. The ability to watch and listen, however, is not in itself an indication of physical access, because *Y* can watch *X* from a distance or wiretap *X*'s telephone. This explains why it is much easier for *X* to know when *Y* has physical access to him than when *Y* observes him.

The following situations involving loss of privacy can best be understood in terms of physical access: (a) a stranger who gains entrance to a woman's home on false pretenses in order to watch her giving birth;[17] (b) Peeping Toms; (c) a stranger who chooses to sit on "our" bench, even though the park is full of empty benches; and (d) a move from a single-person office to a much larger one that must be shared with a colleague. In each of these cases, the essence of the complaint is not that more information about us has been acquired, nor that more attention has been drawn to us, but that our spatial aloneness has been diminished.

What Privacy Is Not

The neutral concept of privacy presented here covers such "typical" invasions of privacy as the collection, storage, and computerization of information; the dissemination of information about individuals; peeping, following, watching, and photographing individuals; intruding or entering "private" places; eavesdropping, wiretapping, reading of letters; drawing attention to individuals; required testing of individuals; and forced disclosure of information. At the same time, a number of situations sometimes said to constitute invasions of privacy will be seen not to involve losses of privacy per se under this concept. These include exposure to unpleasant noises, smells, and sights; prohibitions of such conduct as abortions, use of contraceptives, and "unnatural" sexual intercourse; insulting, harassing, or persecuting behavior; presenting individuals in a "false light"; unsolicited mail and unwanted phone calls; regulation of the way familial obligations should be discharged; and commercial exploitation. These situations are all described as "invasions of privacy" in the literature, presumably indicating some felt usefulness in grouping them under the label of "privacy," and thus an explanation of the reasons for excluding these cases from my argument seems appropriate. Such an explanation may also clarify the proposed analysis and its methodological presuppositions.

The initial intuition is that privacy has to do with accessibility to an individual, as expressed by the three elements of information-gathering, attention, and physical access, and that this concept is distinct. It is part of this initial intuition that we want and deem desirable many things, and that we lose more than we gain by treating all of them as the same thing. If the concepts we use give the appearance of differentiating concerns without in fact isolating something distinct, we are likely to fall victims to this false appearance and our chosen language will be a hindrance rather than a help. The reason for excluding the situations mentioned above, as well as those not positively identified by the proposed analysis, is that they present precisely such a danger.

There is one obvious way to include all the so-called invasions of privacy under the term. Privacy can be defined as "being let alone," using the phrase often attributed—incorrectly—to Samuel Warren and Louis Brandeis. The great simplicity of this definition gives it rhetorical force and attractiveness, but also denies it the distinctiveness that is necessary for the phrase to be useful in more than a conclusory sense. This description gives an appearance of differentiation while covering almost any conceivable complaint anyone could ever make. A great many instances of "not letting people alone" cannot readily be described as invasions of privacy. Requiring that people pay their taxes or go into the army, or punishing them for murder, are just a few of the obvious examples.

For similar reasons, we must reject Edward Bloustein's suggestion that the coherence of privacy lies in the fact that all invasions are violations of human dignity. We may well be concerned with invasions of privacy, at least in part, because they are violations of dignity. But there are ways to offend dignity and personality that have nothing to do with privacy. Having to beg or sell one's body in order to survive are serious affronts to dignity, but do not appear to involve loss of privacy.

To speak in privacy terms about claims for noninterference by the state in personal decisions is similar to identifying privacy with "being let alone." There are two problems with this tendency. The first is that the typical privacy claim is not a claim for noninterference by the state at all. It is a claim *for* state interference in the form of legal protection against other individuals, and this is obscured when privacy is discussed in terms of noninterference with personal decisions. The second problem is that this conception excludes from the realm of privacy all claims that have nothing to do with highly personal decisions, such as an individual's unwillingness to have a file in a central data-bank. Moreover, identifying privacy as noninterference with private action, often in order to avoid an explicit return to "substantive due process," may obscure the nature of the legal decision and draw attention away from important considerations. The limit of state interference with individual action is an important question that has been with us for centuries. The usual terminology for dealing with this question is that of "liberty of action." It may well be that some cases pose a stronger claim for noninterference than others, and that the intimate nature of certain decisions affects these limits. This does not justify naming this set of concerns "privacy," however. A better way to deal with these issues may be to treat them as involving questions of liberty, in which enforcement may raise difficult privacy issues.[18]

Noxious smells and other nuisances are described as problems of privacy because of an analogy with intrusion. Outside forces that enter private zones seem similar to invasions of privacy. There are no good reasons, however, to expect any similarity between intrusive smells or noises and modes of acquiring information about or access to an individual.

Finally, some types of commercial exploitation are grouped under privacy primarily because of legal history: the first cases giving a remedy for unauthorized use of a name or picture, sometimes described as invasions of privacy, usually involved commercial exploitation. The essence of privacy is not freedom from commercial exploitation, however. Privacy can be invaded in ways that have nothing to do with such exploitation, and there are many forms of exploitation that do not involve privacy even under the broadest conception. The use of privacy as a label for protection against some forms of commercial exploitation is another unfortunate illustration of the confusions that will inevitably arise if care is not taken to follow an orderly conceptual scheme.

The Functions of Privacy

In any attempt to define the scope of desirable legal protection of privacy, we move beyond the neutral concept of "loss of privacy," and seek to describe the positive concept that identifies those aspects of privacy that are of value. Identifying the positive functions of privacy is not an easy task. We start from the obvious fact that both perfect privacy and total loss of privacy are undesirable. Individuals must be in some intermediate state—a balance between privacy and interaction—in order to maintain human relations, develop their capacities and sensibilities, create and grow, and even to survive. Privacy thus cannot be said to be a value in the sense that the more people have of it, the better. In fact, the opposite may be true.[19] In any event, my purpose here is not to determine the proper balance between privacy and interaction; I want only to identify the positive functions that privacy has in our lives. From them we can derive the limits of the value of privacy, and then this value can be balanced against others.

The best way in which to understand the value of privacy is to examine its functions. This approach is fraught with difficulties, however. These justifications for privacy are instrumental, in the sense that they point out how privacy relates to other goals. The strength of instrumental justifications depends on the extent to which other goals promoted by privacy are considered important, and on the extent to which the relationship between the two is established. In most cases, the link between the enjoyment of privacy and other goals is at least partly empirical, and thus this approach raises all the familiar problems of social science methodology.

Two possible ways to avoid these difficulties should be discussed before I proceed further. One approach tests the desirability of privacy on a want-satisfaction basis, and the other argues that privacy is an ultimate value. The want-satisfaction argument posits the desirability of satisfying wishes and thus provides a reason to protect all wishes to have privacy. It does not require empirical links between privacy and other goals. Moreover, the notion that choice should be respected is almost universally accepted as a starting point for practical reasoning. The want-satisfaction argument cannot carry us very far, however. It does not explain why we should prefer X's wish to maintain his privacy against Y's wish to pry or acquire information. Without explaining why wishes for privacy are more important than wishes to invade it, the want-satisfaction principle alone cannot support the desirability of privacy. Indeed, some wishes to have privacy do not enjoy even prima facie validity. The criminal needs privacy to complete his offense undetected, the con artist needs it to manipulate his victim; we would not find the mere fact that they wish to have privacy a good reason for protecting it. The want-satisfaction principle needs a supplement that will identify legitimate reasons for which people want and need privacy. This is the task undertaken by an instrumental inquiry. These reasons will identify the cases in which wishes to have privacy should override wishes to invade it. They will also explain why in some cases we say that people need privacy even though they have not chosen it.[20] Thus, these instrumentalist reasons will explain the distinctiveness of privacy.

The attractiveness of the argument that privacy is an ultimate value lies in the intuitive feeling that only ultimate values are truly important, and in the fact that claims that a value is ultimate are not vulnerable to the empirical challenges that can be made to functional analyses. But these claims also obscure the specific functions of privacy. They prevent any discussion with people who do not share the intuitive belief in the importance of privacy. Given the current amount of skeptical commentary, such claims are bound to raise more doubts than convictions about the importance and distinctiveness of privacy.

Thus it appears that we cannot avoid a functional analysis. Such an analysis presents an enormous task, for the values served by privacy are many and diverse. They include a healthy, liberal, democratic, and pluralistic society; individual autonomy; mental health; creativity; and the capacity to form and maintain meaningful relations with others. These goals suffer from the same conceptual ambiguities that we have described for privacy, which makes it difficult to formulate questions for empirical research and very easy to miss the relevant questions. More important, the empirical data is not only scant, it is often double-edged. The evaluation of links between privacy and other values must therefore be extremely tentative. Nevertheless, much can be gained by identifying and examining instrumental arguments for privacy; this is the indispensable starting point for any attempt to make sense of our concern with privacy, and to expose this concern to critical examination and evaluation.

It is helpful to start by seeking to identify those features of human life that would be impossible—or highly unlikely—without some privacy. Total lack of privacy is full and immediate access, full and immediate knowledge, and constant observation of an individual. In such a state, there would be no private thoughts, no private places, no private parts. Everything an individual did and thought would immediately become known to others.

There is something comforting and efficient about total absence of privacy for all. A person could identify his enemies, anticipate dangers stemming from other people, and make sure he was not cheated or manipulated. Criminality would cease, for detection would be certain, frustration probable, and punishment sure. The world would be safer, and as a result, the time and resources now spent on trying to protect ourselves against human dangers and misrepresentations could be directed to other things.

This comfort is fundamentally misleading, however. Some human activities only make sense if there is some privacy. Plots and intrigues may disappear, but with them would go our private diaries, intimate confessions, and surprises. We would probably try hard to suppress our daydreams and fantasies once others had access to them. We would try to erase from our minds everything we would not be willing to publish, and we would try not to do anything that would make us likely to be feared, ridiculed, or harmed. There is a terrible flatness in the person who could succeed in these attempts. We do not choose against total lack of privacy only because we cannot attain it, but because its price seems much too high.[21]

In any event, total lack of privacy is unrealistic. Current levels of privacy are better in some ways, because we all have some privacy that cannot easily be taken from us.[22] The current state is also worse in some ways, because enjoyment of privacy is not equally distributed and some people have more security and power as a result. The need to protect privacy thus stems from two kinds of concern. First, in some areas we all tend to have insufficient amounts of privacy. Second, unequal distribution of privacy may lead to manipulation, deception, and threats to autonomy and democracy.

Two clusters of concerns are relevant here. The first relates to our notion of the individual, and the kinds of actions we think people should be allowed to take in order to become fully realized. To this cluster belongs the arguments linking privacy to mental health, autonomy, growth, creativity, and the capacity to form and create meaningful human relations. The second cluster relates to the type of society we want. First, we want a society that will not hinder individual attainment of the goals mentioned above. For this, society has to be liberal and pluralistic. In addition, we link a concern for privacy to our concept of democracy.

Inevitably, the discussion of functions that follows is sketchy and schematic. My purpose is to point out the many contexts in which privacy may operate, not to present full and conclusive arguments.

Privacy and the Individual Functional arguments depend on a showing that privacy is linked to the promotion of something else that is accepted as desirable. In order to speak about individual goals, we must have a sense of what individuals are, and what they can and should strive to become. We do not have any one such picture, of course, and certainly none that is universally accepted. Nonetheless, privacy may be linked to goals such as creativity, growth, autonomy, and mental health that are accepted as desirable by almost all such theories, yet in ways that are not dictated by any single theory. This may give functional arguments for privacy an eclectic appearance, but it may also indicate the strength of these arguments. It appears that privacy is central to the attainment of individual goals under every theory of the individual that has ever captured man's imagination. It also seems that concern about privacy is evidenced in all societies, even those with few opportunities for physical privacy. Because we have no single theory about the nature of the individual and the way in which individuals relate to others, however, it should be recognized that the way in which we perceive privacy contributing to individual goals will itself depend on the theory of the individual that we select.

In the following discussion, I will note where a difference in perspective may dictate different approaches or conclusions. These different perspectives relate to theories of human growth, development, and personality. It is easy to see that different answers to questions such as the following may yield different arguments for privacy: Is there a "real self" that can be known? If there is, is it coherent and always consistent? If not, can we identify one that is better, and that we should strive to realize? Are human relations something essential, or a mere luxury? Should they ideally be based on full disclosure and total frankness? Or is this a misguided ideal, not only a practical impossibility?

Contextual Arguments

Some arguments for privacy do not link it empirically with other goals. These arguments contend that privacy, by limiting access, creates the necessary context for other activities that we deem essential. Typical of these contextual arguments is the one advanced by Jeffrey Reiman that privacy is what enables development of individuality by allowing individuals to distinguish between their own thoughts and feelings and those of others.[23] Similarly, Charles Fried advanced a contextual argument that privacy is necessary for the development of trust, love, and friendship. Contextual arguments are instrumental, in that they relate privacy to another goal. They are strengthened by the fact that the link between privacy and the other goal is also conceptual.

A similar argument can be made about the relationship between privacy and intimacy. Here too, it is not simply the case that intimacy is more likely with increasing amounts of privacy. Being intimate in public is almost a contradiction in terms. Such contextual arguments highlight an important goal for privacy, similar to that indicated by examining the possible consequences of a total loss of privacy. We can now move to a detailed examination of more specific functions of privacy.

Freedom from Physical Access

By restricting physical access to an individual, privacy insulates that individual from distraction and from the inhibitive effects that arise from close physical proximity with another individual. Freedom from distraction is essential for all human activities that require concentration, such as learning, writing, and all forms of creativity. Although writing and creativity may be considered luxuries, learning—which includes not only acquiring information and basic skills but also the development of mental capacities and moral judgment—is something that we all must do. Learning, in turn, affects human growth, autonomy, and mental health.

Restricting physical access also permits an individual to relax. Even casual observation has an inhibitive effect on most individuals that makes them more formal and uneasy. Is relaxation important? The answer depends partially upon one's theory of the individual. If we believe in one coherent "core" personality, we may feel that people should reflect that personality at all times. It could be argued that relaxation is unimportant—or undesirable—because it signals a discrepancy between the person in public and in private. The importance that all of us place on relaxation suggests that this theory is wrong, however, or at least overstated. Whatever the theory, people seem to need opportunities to relax, and this may link privacy to the ability of individuals to maintain their mental health. Furthermore, freedom from access contributes to the individual by permitting intimacy. Not all relationships are intimate, but those that are tend to be the most valued. Relaxation and intimacy together are essential for many kinds of human relations, including sexual ones. Privacy in the sense of freedom from physical access is thus not only important for individuals by themselves, but also as a necessary shield for intimate relations.[24]

Because physical access is a major way to acquire information, the power to limit it is also the power to limit such knowledge. Knowledge and access are not necessarily related, however. Knowledge is only one of the possible consequences of access, a subject to which we now turn.

Promoting Liberty of Action

An important cluster of arguments for privacy builds on the way in which it severs the individual's conduct from knowledge of that conduct by others. Privacy thus prevents interference, pressures to conform, ridicule, punishment, unfavorable decisions, and other forms of hostile reaction. To the extent that privacy does this, it functions to promote liberty of action, removing the unpleasant consequences of certain actions and thus increasing the liberty to perform them.

This promotion of liberty of action links privacy to a variety of individual goals. It also raises a number of serious problems, both as to the causal link between privacy and other goals, and as to the desirability of this function.

Freedom from censure and ridicule. In addition to providing freedom from distractions and opportunities to concentrate, privacy also contributes to learning, creativity, and autonomy by insulating the individual against ridicule and censure at early stages of groping and experimentation. No one likes to fail, and learning requires trial and error, some practice of skills, some abortive first attempts before we are sufficiently pleased with our creation to subject it to public scrutiny. In the absence of privacy we would dare less, because all our early failures would be on record. We would only do what we thought we could do well. Public failures make us unlikely to try again.[25]

Promoting mental health. One argument linking privacy and mental health, made by Sidney Jourard,[26] suggests that individuals may become victims of mental illness because of pressures to conform to society's expectations. Strict obedience to all social standards is said inevitably to lead to inhibition, repression, alienation, symptoms of disease, and possible mental breakdown. On the other hand, disobedience may lead to sanctions. Ironically, the sanction for at least some deviations is a social declaration of insanity. By providing a refuge, privacy enables individuals to disobey in private and thus acquire the strength to obey in public.

Mental health is one of the least well-defined concepts in the literature. It appears that Professor Jourard's argument for privacy uses the term in a minimalistic sense: avoiding mental breakdown. Whether mental breakdown is always undesirable is questionable. More serious problems are raised when we examine the link between mental health and privacy. Must chronic obedience always lead to mental breakdown? This is plausible if individuals obey social norms only because of social pressures and fear of sanctions, but this is not the case. Professor Jourard identifies a need for privacy that applies only to those who do not accept the social norms. The strength of his argument thus depends on the likelihood that people reject some norms of their society, and may be adequate only for extremely totalitarian societies. It will probably also depend on the nature of the norms and expectations that are not accepted. Moreover, even if pressures to conform to social norms contribute to mental breakdown, the opposite may also be true. It could be argued that too much permissiveness is at least as dangerous to mental health as too much conformity. One of the important functions of social norms is to give people the sense of belonging to a group defined by shared values. People are likely to lose their sanity in the absence of such norms and the sense of security they provide. Nevertheless, some individuals in institutions do complain that the absence of privacy affects their mental state, and these complaints support Jourard's argument.

Promoting autonomy. Autonomy is another value that is linked to the function of privacy in promoting liberty. Moral autonomy is the reflective and critical acceptance of social norms, with obedience based on an independent moral evaluation of their worth. Autonomy requires the capacity to make an independent moral judgment, the willingness to exercise it, and the courage to act on the results of this exercise even when the judgment is not a popular one.

We do not know what makes individuals autonomous, but it is probably easier to be autonomous in an open society committed to pluralism, toleration, and encouragement of independent judgment rather than blind submissiveness. No matter how open a society may be, however, there is a danger that behavior that deviates from norms will result in harsh sanctions. The prospect of this hostile reaction has an inhibitive effect. Privacy is needed to enable the individual to deliberate and establish his opinions. If public reaction seems likely to be unfavorable, privacy may permit an individual to express his judgments to a group of like-minded people. After a period of germination, such individuals may be more willing to declare their unpopular views in public.

It might be argued that history belies this argument for privacy in terms of autonomy: societies much more totalitarian than ours have always had some autonomous individuals, so that the lack of privacy does not mean the end of autonomy. Even if we grant that privacy may not be a necessary condition for autonomy for all, however, it is enough to justify it as a value that most people may require it. We are not all giants, and societies should enable all, not only the exceptional, to seek moral autonomy.

Promoting human relations. Privacy also functions to promote liberty in ways that enhance the capacity of individuals to create and maintain human relations of different intensities. Privacy enables individuals to establish a plurality of roles and presentations to the world. This control over "editing" one's self is crucial, for it is through the images of others that human relations are created and maintained.

Privacy is also helpful in enabling individuals to continue relationships, especially those highest in one's emotional hierarchy, without denying one's inner thoughts, doubts, or wishes that the other partner cannot accept. This argument for privacy is true irrespective of whether we deem total disclosure to be an ideal in such relations. It is built on the belief that individuals, for reasons that they themselves do not justify, cannot emotionally accept conditions that seem threatening to them. Privacy enables partners to such a relationship to continue it, while feeling free to endorse those feelings in private.

Each of these arguments based on privacy's promotion of liberty shares a common ground: privacy permits individuals to do what they would not do without it for fear of an unpleasant or hostile reaction from others. This reaction may be anything from legal punishment or compulsory commitment to threats to dissolve an important relationship. The question arises, then, whether it is appropriate for privacy to permit individuals to escape responsibility for their actions, wishes, and opinions.

It may be argued that we have rules because we believe that breaches of them are undesirable, and we impose social sanctions to discourage undesirable conduct. People are entitled to a truthful presentation and a reasonable consideration of their expectations by those with whom they interact. Privacy frustrates these mechanisms for regulation and education; to let it do so calls for some justification. In general, privacy will only be desirable when the liberty of action that it promotes is itself desirable, or at least permissible. It is illuminating to see when we seek to promote liberty directly, by changing social norms, and when we are willing to let privacy do the task.

Privacy is derived from liberty in the sense that we tend to allow privacy to the extent that its promotion of liberty is considered desirable. Learning, practicing, and creating require privacy, and this function is not problematic. Similarly, because we usually believe that it is good for individuals to relax and to enjoy intimacy, we have no difficulty allowing the privacy necessary for these goals.

The liberty promoted by privacy also is not problematic in contexts in which we believe we should have few or no norms; privacy will be needed in such cases because some individuals will not share this belief, will lack the strength of their convictions, or be emotionally unable to accept what they would like to do. Good examples of such cases are ones involving freedom of expression, racial tolerance, and the functioning of close and intimate relations. The existence of official rules granting immunity from regulation, or even imposing duties of nondiscrimination, does not guarantee the absence of social forces calling for conformity or prejudice. A spouse may understand and even support a partner's need to fantasize or to have other close relations, but may still find knowing about them difficult to accept. In such situations, respect for privacy is a way to force ourselves to be as tolerant as we know we should be. We accept the need for privacy as an indication of the limits of human nature.

A related but distinct situation in which privacy is permitted is that in which we doubt the desirability of norms or expectations, or in which there is an obvious absence of consensus as to such desirability. Treatment of homosexual conduct between consenting adults in private seems to be a typical case of this sort. Another context in which we sometimes allow privacy to function in this way is when privacy would promote the liberty of individuals not to disclose some parts of their past, in the interest of rehabilitation or as a necessary protection against prejudice and irrationality.

Privacy works in all these cases to ameliorate tensions between personal preferences and social norms by leading to nonenforcement of some standard.[27] But is this function desirable? When the liberty promoted is desirable, why not attack the norms directly? When it is not, why allow individuals to do in private what we would have good reasons for not wanting them to do at all?

Conceptually, this is a strong argument against privacy, especially because privacy perpetuates the very problems it helps to ease. With mental health, autonomy, and human relations, the mitigation of surface tensions may reduce incentives to face the difficulty and deal with it directly. When privacy lets people act privately in ways that would have unpleasant consequences if done in public, this may obscure the urgency of the need to question the public regulation itself. If homosexuals are not prosecuted, there is no need to decide whether such conduct between consenting adults in private can constitutionally be prohibited. If people can keep their independent judgments known only to a group of like-minded individuals, there is no need to deal with the problem of regulating hostile reactions by others. It is easier, at least in the shortrun and certainly for the person making the decision, to conceal actions and thoughts that may threaten an important relationship. Thus, privacy reduces our incentive to deal with our problems.

The situation is usually much more complex, however, and then the use of privacy is justified. First, there are important limits on our capacity to change positive morality,[28] and thus to affect social pressures to conform. This may even cause an inability to change institutional norms. When this is the case, the absence of privacy may mean total destruction of the lives of individuals condemned by norms with only questionable benefit to society. If the chance to achieve change in a particular case is small, it seems heartless and naive to argue against the use of privacy. Although legal and social changes are unlikely until individuals are willing to put themselves on the line, this course of action should not be forced on anyone. If an individual decides that the only way he can maintain his sanity is to choose private deviance rather than public disobedience, that should be his decision. Similarly, if an individual prefers to present a public conformity rather than unconventional autonomy, that is his choice. The least society can do in such cases is respect such a choice.

Ultimately, our willingness to allow privacy to operate in this way must be the outcome of our judgment as to the proper scope of liberty individuals should have, and our assessment of the need to help ourselves and others against the limited altruism and rationality of individuals. Assume that an individual has a feature he knows others may find objectionable—that he is a homosexual, for instance, or a communist, or committed a long-past criminal offense—but that feature is irrelevant in the context of a particular situation. Should we support his wish to conceal these facts? Richard Posner and Richard Epstein argue that we should not. This is an understandable argument, but an extremely harsh one. Ideally, it would be preferable if we could all disregard prejudices and irrelevancies. It is clear, however, that we cannot. Given this fact, it may be best to let one's ignorance mitigate one's prejudice. There is even more to it than this. Posner and Epstein imply that what is behind the wish to have privacy in such situations is the wish to manipulate and cheat, and to deprive another of the opportunity to make an informed decision. But we always give only partial descriptions of ourselves, and no one expects anything else. The question is not whether we should edit, but how and by whom the editing should be done.[29] Here, I assert, there should be a presumption in favor of the individual concerned.

It is here that we return to contextual arguments and to the specter of a total lack of privacy. To have different individuals we must have a commitment to some liberty—the liberty to be different. But differences are known to be threatening, to cause hate and fear and prejudice. These aspects of social life should not be overlooked, and oversimplified claims of manipulation should not be allowed to obscure them.

The only case in which this is less true is that of human relationships, where the equality between the parties is stronger and the essence of the relationship is voluntary and intimate. A unilateral decision by one of the parties not to disclose in order to maintain the relationship is of questionable merit. The individual is likely to choose what is easier for him, rather than for both. His decision denies the other party an understanding of the true relationship and the opportunity to decide whether to forgive, accommodate, or leave. Although we cannot rely on the altruism and willingness to forgive of employers or casual acquaintances, to deny a life partner the opportunity to make informed decisions may undermine the value of the relationship. This is another point at which our theories about human relations become relevant. The extent to which paternalistic protection should be a part of relationships between adults, and the forms such concern may appropriately take, are relevant in deciding this issue.

Limiting exposure. A further and distinct function of privacy is to enhance an individual's dignity, at least to the extent that dignity requires nonexposure. There is something undignified in exposure beyond the fact that the individual's choice of privacy has been frustrated. A choice of privacy is in this sense distinct from a choice to interact. Rejection of the latter frustrates X's wish, but there is no additional necessary loss of dignity and selfhood. In exposure, there is. It is hard to know what kind of exposures are undignified, and the effect such unwanted exposures have on individuals. The answer probably depends on the culture and the individual concerned, but this is nonetheless an important function of privacy.

Privacy and Society We desire a society in which individuals can grow, maintain their mental health and autonomy, create and maintain human relations, and lead meaningful lives. The analysis above suggests that some privacy is necessary to enable the individual to do these things, and privacy may therefore both indicate the existence of and contribute to a more pluralistic, tolerant society. In the absence of consensus concerning many limitations of liberty, and in view of the limits on our capacity to encourage tolerance and acceptance and to overcome prejudice, privacy must be part of our commitment to individual freedom and to a society that is committed to the protection of such freedom.

Privacy is also essential to democratic government because it fosters and encourages the moral autonomy of the citizen, a central requirement of a democracy. Part of the justification for majority rule and the right to vote is the assumption that individuals should participate in political decisions by forming judgments and expressing preferences. Thus, to the extent that privacy is important for autonomy, it is important for democracy as well.

This is true even though democracies are not necessarily liberal. A country might restrict certain activities, but it must allow some liberty of political action if it is to remain a democracy. This liberty requires privacy, for individuals must have the right to keep private their votes, their political discussions, and their associations if they are to be able to exercise their liberty to the fullest extent. Privacy is crucial to democracy in providing the opportunity for parties to work out their political positions, and to compromise with opposing factions, before subjecting their position to public scrutiny. Denying the privacy necessary for these interactions would undermine the democratic process.

Finally, it can be argued that respect for privacy will help a society attract talented individuals to public life. Persons interested in government service must consider the loss of virtually all claims and expectations of privacy in calculating the costs of running for public office. Respect for privacy might reduce those costs.

NOTES

1. The best general treatment of privacy is still A. WESTIN, PRIVACY AND FREEDOM (1967). For treatment of a variety of privacy aspects, see NOMOS XIII, PRIVACY (R. Pennock & J. Chapman eds. 1971) (Yearbook of the American Society for Political and Legal Philosophy) [hereinafter cited as NOMOS].

2. W. PROSSER, THE LAW OF TORTS 804 (4th ed. 1971).

3. *Roe* v. *Wade*, 410 U.S. 113, 152-55 (1973) (right to privacy cited to strike down abortion statute); *Eisenstadt* v. *Baird*, 405 U.S. 438, 453 (1972) (right to privacy includes right of unmarried individual to use contraceptives); *Griswold* v. *Connecticut*, 381 U.S. 479, 484-86 (1965) (right to privacy includes right of married couple to use contraceptives). *See generally* Richards, *Unnatural Acts and the Constitutional Right to Privacy: A Moral Theory*, 45 FORDHAM, L. REV. 1281 (1977); Comment, *A Taxonomy of Privacy: Repose, Sanctuary, and Intimate Decision*, 64 CALIF. L. REV. 1447 (1976) (developing constitutional right to privacy).

4. For studies of legal protection in this vein, see *e.g.*, Davis, *What Do We Mean by "Right to Privacy"?* 4 S.D. L. REV. 1 (1959); Dickler, *The Right of Privacy*, 70 U.S. L. REV. 435 (1936); Kalven, *Privacy in Tort Law—Were Warren and Brandeis Wrong?* 31 LAW & CONTEMP. PROB. 326 (1966); Prosser, *Privacy*, 48 CALIF. L. REV. 383 (1960). For a similar study of moral intuitions, see Thomson, *The Right to Privacy*, 4 PHILOSOPHY & PUB. AFF. 295 (1975).

5. *See, e.g.*, Kalven, *supra* note 6, at 329 & n.22.

6. This aspect of privacy has been emphasized by Richard Posner. *See, e.g.*, Posner, *Privacy, Secrecy, and Reputation*, 28 BUFFALO L. REV. 1 (1979) [hereinafter cited as *Secrecy*]; Posner, *The Right to Privacy*, 12 GA. L. REV. 393 (1978) [hereinafter cited as *Privacy*]. Other commentators have followed his lead. *See, e.g.*, Epstein, *Privacy, Property Rights, and Misrepresentations*, 12 GA. L. REV. 455 (1978).

7. All reductionists claim that the concept of privacy does not illuminate thoughts about legal protection. Professor Posner's version is the most extreme: he denies the

utility of all "intermediate" values, and advocates assessing acts and rules by the single, ultimate principle of wealth maximization. *E.g., Secrecy, supra* note 8, at 7-9; *Privacy, supra* note 8, at 394.

8. Alan Westin has defined privacy as the "claim of individuals, groups, or institutions to determine for themselves when, how, and to what extent information about them is communicated to others." A. WESTIN, *supra* note 1, at 7. For a discussion of the influence of this definition on the study of privacy, see Lusky, *Invasion of Privacy: A Clarification of Concepts*, 72 COLUM. L. REV. 693, 693-95 (1972). It is interesting to note that Professor Westin also gives a second and quite different description of privacy: "Viewed in terms of the relation of the individual to social participation, privacy is the voluntary and temporary withdrawal of a person from the general society through physical or psychological means. . . ." A. WESTIN, *supra* note 1, at 7.

9. If we define privacy as a state of mind, we shall not be able to discuss losses of privacy that are unknown to the individual or whether such awareness is relevant to the desirability of such losses.

10. Gross, *Privacy and Autonomy*, in NOMOS *supra* note 1, at 169, 169 [hereinafter cited as *Autonomy*]. *But see* Gross, *The Concept of Privacy*, 42 N.Y.U. L. REV. 34, 35-36 (1967) (defining privacy as "the condition of human life in which acquaintance with a person or with affairs of his life which are personal to him is limited") [hereinafter cited as *Concept*]. Gross does not even refer to his earlier contribution in his 1971 article in NOMOS].

11. People may simply be uninterested in an individual, and thus not care to acquire information about him. Such an individual will have "privacy" even if he resents it. To say that an individual controls the flow of information about himself is thus not enough to tell us whether he is known in fact. We also must know whether there are restrictive norms, whether these are obeyed, how the individual has chosen to exercise his control, and whether others have acquired information about him in other ways or at all. The view of privacy presented by Alan Westin is not vulnerable to this difficulty. *See* A. WESTIN, *supra* note 1.

12. For example, an individual may voluntarily choose to disclose everything about himself to the public. This disclosure obviously leads to a loss of privacy despite the fact that it involved an exercise of control.

13. I use "enjoys" although individuals would doubtless suffer if exposed to "perfect privacy," and may resent privacy that is imposed on them against their will. "Perfect" privacy is used here only as a methodological starting point. There is no implication that such situations exist or that they are desirable.

14. *See* Benn, *Privacy, Freedom, and Respect for Persons*, in NOMOS, at 1, 11-12 (data banks as paradigmatic privacy issue). Unused data banks do not cause a loss of privacy, of course, because the mere existence of information on file does not make it known to anyone. Access to such data banks does create a threat that losses of privacy may occur. *See generally* Farhi, *Computers, Data Banks and the Individual: Is the Problem Privacy?* 5 ISRAEL L. REV. 542 (1970).

15. The "amount" of information may not be as important as the quality and extent of the information. There is a difference between knowing a person, and knowing about him.

16. *See* Roberts & Gregor, *Privacy: A Cultural View*, in NOMOS, *supra* note 1, at 199, 214 (promotion of privacy through systematic denial of truth).

17. *See De May v. Roberts*, 46 Mich. 160, 9 N.W. 146 (1881) (finding for plaintiff on these facts). Note that *De May* preceded what is considered the seminal article on

privacy, Warren & Brandeis, *The Right to Privacy* 4 Harv. L. Rev. 193 (1890), by almost a decade.

18. *See, e.g., Griswold* v. *Connecticut,* 381 U.S. 479, 484-85 (1965); P. Devlin, The Enforcement of Morals 1-25 (1968).

19. Some critics of contemporary society frequently complain that we suffer from too much privacy, that we exalt the "private realm" and neglect the public aspects of life, and that as a result individuals are alienated, lonely, and scared. *See, e.g.,* H. Arendt, The Human Condition 23-73 (1958); Arndt, *The Cult of Privacy,* 21 Austl. Q., Sept. 1979, at 68, 70-71 (1949). Other social critics emphasize the threat to privacy posed by modern society. *See, e.g.,* V. Packard, The Naked Society (1964). Indeed, much of the privacy literature seems to share the assumption that additional legal protection is needed. Taken together, these two sets of complaints suggest that something is wrong with the contemporary balance between privacy and interaction. Contributions remain to be made to this critical literature.

20. This is true because we can judge some of the effects of loss of privacy as bad, even if the individual has chosen that loss. An obvious example is the cheapening effect of life in the limelight. Public life, especially in a publication-oriented culture, involves a serious risk that individuals will receive almost constant publicity. Even though a person is insensitive to his own need for privacy, he may nonetheless need it.

21. *See, e.g.,* Bloustein:

> The man who is compelled to live every minute of his life among others and whose every need, thought, desire, fancy or gratification is subject to public scrutiny, has been deprived of his individuality and human dignity. Such an individual merges with the mass. His opinions, being public, tend never to be different; his aspirations, being known, tend always to be conventionally accepted ones; his feelings, being openly exhibited, tend to lose their quality of unique personal warmth and to become the feelings of every man. Such a being, although sentient, is fungible; he is not an individual.

For a similar analysis, see Bazelon, *Probing Privacy,* 12 Gonz. L. Rev. 587, 592 (1977).

22. The contents of our thoughts and consciousness, now relatively immune from observation and forced disclosure, may not always be free from discovery. Lie detectors are only one kind of technological development that could threaten this privacy. *See, e.g.,* Note, *People* v. *Barbara: The Admissibility of Polygraph Test Results in Support of a Motion for New Trial,* 1978 Det. C. L. Rev. 347; Note, *The Polygraph and Pre-Employment Screening,* 13 Hous. L. Rev. 551 (1976). It is this sense of privacy that George Fletcher uses when he argues that the rule that people cannot be punished for thoughts alone serves to protect privacy. Fletcher, *Legality as Privacy,* in Liberty and the Rule of Law 182-207 (R. Cunningham ed. 1979).

23. Reiman, *Privacy, Intimacy, and Personhood,* 6 Philosophy & Pub. Aff 26, 31-36 (1977).

24. *See, e.g.,* Bloustein, *Group Privacy: The Right to Huddle,* 8 Rut.-Cam. L.J. 219, 224-46 (1977).

25. For example, many pianists refuse to practice in the presence of others, and not simply to avoid distraction, inhibition, or self-consciousness. They practice alone so that they are the ones to decide when they are ready for an audience. It could be argued that privacy thus has its costs in terms of what the world learns about human achievement; some perfectionists are never sufficiently pleased with their creations, yet their work may be superior to much that is made public by others. Even if this

were true, it does not prove that the lost masterpieces would have been created in the absence of privacy. Perfectionists are just as vulnerable to criticism as anybody else, perhaps even more so.

26. Jourard, *Some Psychological Aspects of Privacy*, 31 LAW & CONTEMP. PROB. 307, 309-11 (1966).

27. Alan Westin sees this as one of the major functions of privacy. A. WESTIN, *supra* note 1, at 23-51. It is important to note that this function would not be as strong in cases in which the level of legal enforcement was high. *See* note 98 *infra*.

28. *See* H.L.A. HART, THE CONCEPT OF LAW 171-73 (1961) (distinction between law and morality is that law may be deliberately and consciously changed, whereas morality can not).

29. For example, we would have less sympathy for an employer who demanded a "yes or no" answer from his employee to the question of whether the employee had a criminal record or was a member of the Communist Party. Such an employer may draw unwarranted inferences if the employee has no opportunity to explain his answer. Professor Posner has suggested that any such "irrational" conduct by prejudiced employers will ultimately be corrected by the market, because the victimized employees will command below-average wages, and the unprejudiced employers who hire them will obtain a competitive advantage. *Secrecy, supra* note 8, at 12 (example of ex-convicts). This is beside the point, however, because in the interim the employee suffers from high emotional and economic costs (in the form of irrational stigma and lower wage rates).

WHY PRIVACY IS IMPORTANT

James Rachels

According to Thomas Scanlon, the first element of a theory of privacy should be "a characterization of the special interest we have in being able to be free from certain kinds of intrusions." Since I agree that is the right place to begin, I shall begin there. Then I shall comment briefly on Judith Jarvis Thomson's proposals.

Why, exactly, is privacy important to us? There is no one simple answer to this question, since people have a number of interests that may be harmed by invasions of their privacy.

(a) Privacy is sometimes necessary to protect people's interests in competitive situations. For example, it obviously would be a disadvantage to Bobby Fischer if he could not analyze the adjourned position in a chess game in private, without his opponent learning his results.

(b) In other cases someone may want to keep some aspect of his life or behavior private simply because it would be embarrassing for other people to know about it. There is a splendid example of this in John Barth's novel *End of the Road*. The narrator of the story, Jake Horner, is with Joe Morgan's wife, Rennie, and they are approaching the Morgan house where Joe is at home alone.

"Want to eavesdrop?" I whispered impulsively to Rennie. "Come on, it's great! See the animals in their natural habitat."

Rennie looked shocked. "What for?"

"You mean you never spy on people when they're alone? It's wonderful! Come on, be a sneak! It's the most unfair thing you can do to a person."

"You disgust me, Jake!" Rennie hissed. "He's just reading. You don't know Joe at all, do you?"

"What does that mean?"

"*Real* people aren't any different when they're alone. No masks. What you see of them is authentic."

... Quite reluctantly, she came over to the window and peeped in beside me.

It is indeed the grossest of injustices to observe a person who believes himself to be alone. Joe Morgan, back from his Boy Scout meeting, had evidently intended to do some reading, for there were books lying open on the writing table and on the floor beside the bookcase. But Joe wasn't reading. He was standing in the exact center of the bare room, fully dressed, smartly executing military commands. About *face*! Right *dress*! 'Ten-*shun*! Parade *rest*! He saluted briskly, his cheeks blown out and his tongue extended, and then proceeded to cavort about the room—spinning, pirouetting, bowing, leaping, kicking. I watched entranced by his performance, for I cannot say that in my strangest moments (and a bachelor has strange ones) I have surpassed him. Rennie trembled from head to foot.[1]

The scene continues even more embarrassingly.

(c) There are several reasons why medical records should be kept private, having to do with the consequences to individuals of facts about them becoming public knowledge. "The average patient doesn't realize the importance of the confidentiality of medical records. Passing out information on venereal disease can wreck a marriage. Revealing a pattern of alcoholism or drug abuse can result in a man's losing his job or make it impossible for him to obtain insurance protection."[2]

(d) When people apply for credit (or for large amounts of insurance or for jobs of certain types) they are often investigated, and the result is a fat file of information about them. Now there is something to be said in favor of such investigations, for business people surely do have the right to know whether credit-applicants are financially reliable. The trouble is that all sorts of other information goes into such files, for example, information about the applicant's sex-life, his political views, and so forth. Clearly it is unfair for one's application for credit to be influenced by such irrelevant matters.

These examples illustrate the variety of interests that may be protected by guaranteeing people's privacy, and it would be easy to give further examples of the same general sort. However, I do not think that examining such cases will provide a complete understanding of the importance of privacy, for two reasons.

First, these cases all involve relatively unusual sorts of situations, in which someone has something to hide or in which information about a person might provide someone with a reason for mistreating him in some way. Thus, reflection on these cases gives us little help in understanding the value which privacy has in *normal* or *ordinary* situations. By this I mean situations in which there is nothing embarrassing or shameful or unpopular in what we are doing, and nothing ominous or threatening connected with its possible disclosure. For example, even married couples whose sex lives are normal (whatever that is), and so who have nothing to be ashamed of, by even the most conventional standards, and certainly nothing to be blackmailed about, do not want their bedrooms bugged. We need an account of the value which privacy has for us, not only in the few special cases but in the many common and unremarkable cases as well.

Second, even those invasions of privacy that *do* result in embarrassment or in some specific harm to our other interests are objectionable on other grounds. A woman may rightly be upset if her credit-rating is adversely affected by a report about her sexual behavior because the use of such information is unfair; however, she may also object to the report simply because she feels—as most of us do—that her sex-life is *nobody else's business*. This, I think, is an extremely important point. We have a "sense of privacy" which is violated in such affairs, and this sense of privacy cannot adequately be explained merely in terms of our fear of being embarrassed or disadvantaged in one of these obvious ways. An adequate account of privacy should help us to understand what makes something "someone's business" and why intrusions into things that are "none of your business" are, as such, offensive.

These considerations lead me to suspect that there is something important about privacy which we shall miss if we confine our attention to examples such as (a), (b), (c), and (d). In what follows I will try to bring out what this something is.

I want now to give an account of the value of privacy based on the idea that there is a close connection between our ability to control who has access to us and to information about us, and our ability to create and maintain different sorts of social relationships with different people. According to this account, privacy is necessary if we are to maintain the variety of social relationships with other people that we want to have, and that is why it is important to us. By a "social relationship" I do not mean anything especially unusual or technical; I mean the sort of thing which we usually have in mind when we say of two people that they are friends or that they are husband and wife or that one is the other's employer.

The first point I want to make about these relationships is that, often, there are fairly definite patterns of behavior associated with them. Our relationships with other people determine, in large part, how we act toward them and how they behave toward us. Moreover, there are *different* patterns of behavior associated with different relationships. Thus a man may be playful and affectionate with his children (although sometimes firm), businesslike with his employees, and respectful and polite with his mother-in-law. And to his close friends he may show a side of his personality that others never see—perhaps he is secretly a poet, and rather shy about it, and shows his verse only to his best friends.

It is sometimes suggested that there is something deceitful or hypocritical about such differences in behavior. It is suggested that underneath all the role-playing there is the "real" person, and that the various "masks" that we wear in dealing with some people are some sort of phony disguise that we use to conceal our "true" selves from them. I take it that this is what is behind Rennie's remark, in the passage from Barth, that, "*Real* people aren't any different when they're alone. No masks. What you see of them is authentic." According to this way of looking at things, the fact that we observe different standards of conduct with different people is merely a sign of dishonesty. Thus the cold-hearted businessman who reads poetry to his friends is "really" a gentle poetic soul whose businesslike demeanor in front of his employees is only a false front; and the man who curses and swears when talking to his friends, but who would never use such language around his mother-in-law, is just putting on an act for her.

This, I think, is quite wrong. Of course the man who does not swear in front of his mother-in-law may be just putting on an act so that, for example, she will not disinherit him, when otherwise he would curse freely in front of her without caring what she thinks. But it may be that his conception of how he ought to behave with his mother-in-law is very different from his conception of how he may behave with his friends. Or it may not be appropriate for him to swear around *her* because "she is not that sort of person." Similarly, the businessman may be putting up a false front for his employees, perhaps because he dislikes his work and has to make a continual, disagreeable effort to maintain the role. But on the other hand he may be, quite comfortably and naturally, a businessman with a certain conception of how it is appropriate for a businessman to behave; and this conception is compatible with his also being a husband, a father, and a friend, with different conceptions of how it is appropriate to behave with his wife, his children, and his friends. There need be nothing dishonest or hypocritical in any of this, and neither side of his personality need to be the "real" him, any more than any of the others.

It is not merely accidental that we vary our behavior with different people according to the different social relationships that we have with them. Rather, the different patterns of behavior are (partly) what define the different relationships; they are an important part of what makes the different relationships what they are. The relation of friendship, for example, involves bonds of affection and special obligations, such as the duty of loyalty, which friends owe to one another; but it is also an important part of what it means to have a friend that we welcome his company, that we confide in him, that we tell him things about ourselves, and that we show him sides of our personalities which we would not tell or show to just anyone.[3] Suppose I believe that someone is my close friend, and then I discover that he is worried about his job and is afraid of being fired. But, while he has discussed this situation with several other people, he has not mentioned it at all to me. And then I learn that he writes poetry, and that this is an important part of his life; but while he has shown his poems to many other people, he has not shown them to me. Moreover, I learn that he behaves with his other friends in a much more informal way than he behaves with me, that he makes a point of seeing them socially much more than he sees me, and so on. In the absence of some special explanation of his behavior, I would have to conclude that we are not as close as I had thought.

The same general point can be made about other sorts of human relationships: businessman to employee, minister to congregant, doctor to patient, husband to wife, parent to child, and so on. In each case, the sort of relationship that people have to one another involves a conception of how it is appropriate for them to behave with each other, and what is more, a conception of the kind and degree of knowledge concerning one another which it is appropriate for them to have. (I will say more about this later.) I do not mean to imply that such relationships are, or ought to be, structured in exactly the same way for everyone. Some parents are casual and easy-going with their children, while others are more formal and reserved. Some doctors want to be friends with at least some of their patients; others are businesslike with all. Moreover, the requirements of social roles may vary from community to community—for example, the role of wife may not require exactly the same sort of behavior in rural Alabama as it does in New York or New Guinea. And, the requirements of social roles may change: the women's liberation movement is making an attempt to redefine the husband–wife relationship. The examples that I have been giving are drawn, loosely speaking, from contemporary American society; but this is mainly a matter of convenience. The only point that I want to insist on is that *however* one conceives one's relations with other people, there is inseparable from that conception an idea of how it is appropriate to behave with and around them, and what information about oneself it is appropriate for them to have.

The point may be underscored by observing that new types of social institutions and practices sometimes make possible new sorts of human relationships, which in turn make it appropriate to behave around people, and to say things in their presence, that would have been inappropriate before. "Group therapy" is a case in point. Many psychological patients find the prospect of group therapy unsettling, because they will have to speak openly to the group about intimate matters. They sense that there is something inappropriate about this: one simply does not reveal one's deepest feelings to strangers. Our aspirations, our problems, our frustrations and disappointments are things that we may confide to our husbands and wives, our friends, and perhaps to some others—but it is out of the question to speak of such matters to people that we do not even know. Resistance to this aspect of group therapy is overcome when the patients begin to think of each other not as strangers but as *fellow members of the group*. The definition of a kind of relation between them makes possible frank and intimate conversation which would have been totally out of place when they were merely strangers.

All of this has to do with the way that a crucial part of our lives—our relations with other people—is organized, and as such its importance to us can hardly be exaggerated. Thus we have good reason to object to anything that interferes with these relationships and makes it difficult or impossible for us to maintain them in the way that we want to. Conversely, because our ability to control who has access to us, and who knows what about us, allows us to maintain the variety of relationships with other people that we want to have, it is, I think, one of the most important reasons why we value privacy.

First, consider what happens when two close friends are joined by a casual acquaintance. The character of the group changes; and one of the changes is that conversation about intimate matters is now out of order. Then suppose these friends could *never* be alone; suppose there were always third parties (let us say casual acquaintances or strangers) intruding. Then they could do either of two things. They could carry on as close friends do, sharing confidences, freely expressing their feelings about things, and so on. But this would mean violating their sense of how it is appropriate to behave around casual acquaintances or strangers. Or they could avoid doing or saying anything which they think inappropriate to do or say around a third party. But this would mean that they could no longer behave with one another in the way that friends do and further that, eventually, they would no longer *be* close friends.

Again, consider the differences between the way that a husband and wife behave when they are alone and the way they behave in the company of third parties. Alone, they may be affectionate, sexually intimate, have their fights and quarrels, and so on; but with others, a more "public" face is in order. If they could never be alone together, they would either have to abandon the relationship that they would otherwise have as husband and wife or else behave in front of others in ways they now deem inappropriate.[4]

These considerations suggest that we need to separate our associations, at least to some extent, if we are to maintain a system of different relationships with different people. Separation allows us to behave with certain people in the way that is appropriate to the sort of relationship we have with them, without at the same time violating our sense of how it is appropriate to behave with, and in the presence of, others with whom we have a different kind of relationship. Thus, if we are to be able to control the relationships that we have with other people, we must have control over who has access to us.

We now have an explanation of the value of privacy in ordinary situations in which we have nothing to hide. The explanation is that, even in the most common and unremarkable circumstances, we regulate our behavior according to the kinds of relationships we have with the people around us. If we cannot control who has access to us, sometimes including and sometimes excluding various people, then we cannot control the patterns of behavior we need to adopt (this is one reason why privacy is an aspect of liberty) or the kinds of relations with other people that we will have. But what about our feeling that certain facts about us are "simply nobody else's business"? Here, too, I think the answer requires reference to our relationships with people. If someone is our doctor, then it literally is his business to keep track of our health; if someone is our employer, then it literally is his business to know what salary we are paid; our financial dealings literally are the business of the people who extend us credit; and so on. In general, a fact about ourselves is someone's business if there is a specific social relationship between us which entitles them to know. We are often free to choose whether or not to enter into such relationships, and those who want to maintain as much privacy as possible will enter them only reluctantly. What we cannot do is accept such a role with respect to another person and then expect to retain the same degree of privacy relative to him that we had before. Thus, if we are asked how much money we have in the bank, we cannot say, "It's none of your business," to our banker, to prospective creditors, or to our spouses, because their relationships with us do entitle them to know. But, at the risk of being boorish, we could say that to others with whom we have no such relationship.

Thomson suggests, "as a simplifying hypothesis, that the right to privacy is itself a cluster of rights, and that it is not a distinct cluster of rights but itself intersects with the cluster of rights which the right over the person consists of, and also with the cluster of rights which owning property consists of." This hypothesis is "simplifying" because it eliminates the right to privacy as anything distinctive.

"The right over the person" consists of such "un-grand" rights as the right not to have various parts of one's body looked at, the right not to have one's elbow painted green, and so on. Thomson understands these rights as analogous to property rights. The idea is that our bodies are *ours* and so we have the same rights with respect to them that we have with respect to our other possessions.

But now consider the right not to have various parts of one's body looked at. Insofar as this is a matter of *privacy*, it is not simply analogous to property rights; for the kind of interest we have in controlling who looks at what parts of our bodies is very different from the interest we have in our cars or fountain pens. For most of us, physical intimacy is a part of very special sorts of personal relationships. Exposing one's knee or one's face to someone may not count for us as physical intimacy, but exposing a breast, and allowing it to be seen and touched, does. Of course the details are to some extent a matter of social convention; that is why it is easy for us to imagine, say, a Victorian woman for whom an exposed knee would be a sign of intimacy. She would be right to be distressed at learning that she had absent-mindedly left a knee uncovered and that someone was looking at it—if the observer was not her spouse or her lover. By dissociating the body from ideas of physical intimacy, and the complex of personal relationships of which such intimacies are a part, we can make this "right over the body" seem to be nothing more than an un-grand kind of property right; but that dissociation separates this right from the matters that make *privacy* important.

Thomson asks whether it violates your right to privacy for acquaintances to indulge in "very personal gossip" about you, when they got the information without violating your rights, and they are not violating any confidences in telling what they tell. She thinks they do not violate your right to privacy, but that if they do "there is trouble for the simplifying hypothesis."

This is, as she says, a debatable case, but if my account of why privacy is important is correct, we have at least some reason to think that your right to privacy can be violated in such a case. Let us fill in some details. Suppose you are recently divorced, and the reason your marriage failed is that you became impotent shortly after the wedding. You have shared your troubles with your closest friend, but this is not the sort of thing you want everyone to know. Not only would it be humiliating for everyone to know, it is none of their business. It is the sort of intimate fact about you that is not appropriate for strangers or casual acquaintances to know. But now the gossips have obtained the information (perhaps one of them innocently overheard your discussion with your friend; it was not his fault, so he did not violate your privacy in the hearing, but then you did not know he was within earshot) and now they are spreading it around to everyone who knows you and to some who do not. Are they violating your right to privacy? I think they are. If so, it is not surprising, for the interest involved in this case is just the sort of interest which the right to privacy typically protects. Since the right that is violated in this case is not also a property right, or a right over the person, the simplifying hypothesis fails. But this should not be surprising, either, for if the right to privacy has a different *point* than these other rights, we should not expect it always to overlap with them. And even if it did always overlap, we could still regard the right to privacy as a distinctive sort of right in virtue of the special kind of interest it protects.

NOTES

1. John Barth, *End of the Road* (New York, 1960), pp. 57–58.
2. Dr. Malcolm Todd, President of the A.M.A., quoted in the *Miami Herald*, 26 October 1973, p. 18-A.
3. My view about friendship and its relation to privacy is similar to Charles Fried's view in his book *An Anatomy of Values* (Cambridge, Mass., 1970).
4. I found this in a television program-guide in the *Miami Herald* 21 October 1973, p. 17.

> "I think it was one of the most awkward scenes I've ever done," said actress Brenda Benet after doing a romantic scene with her husband, Bill Bixby, in his new NBC-TV series, "The Magician."
>
> "It was even hard to kiss him," she continued. "It's the same old mouth, but it was terrible. I was so abnormally shy; I guess because I don't think it's anybody's business. The scene would have been easier had I done it with a total stranger because that would be real acting. With Bill, it was like being on exhibition."

I should stress that, on the view that I am defending, it is *not* "abnormal shyness" or shyness of any type that is behind such feelings. Rather, it is a sense of what is appropriate with and around people with whom one has various sorts of personal relationships. Kissing *another actor* in front of the camera crew, the director, and so on, is one thing; but kissing *one's husband* in front of all these people is quite another thing. What made Ms. Benet's position confusing was that her husband *was* another actor, and the behavior that was permitted by the one relationship was discouraged by the other.

▷ AN ECONOMIC THEORY OF PRIVACY

Richard A. Posner

Much ink has been spilled in trying to clarify the elusive and ill-defined concept of "privacy." I will sidestep the definitional problem by simply noting that one aspect of privacy is the withholding or concealment of information. This aspect is of particular interest to the economist now that the study of information has become an important field of economics. It is also of interest to the regulator, and those affected by him, because both the right to privacy and the "right to know" are becoming more and more the subject of regulation.

Heretofore the economics of information has been limited to topics relating to the dissemination and, to a lesser extent, the concealment of information in explicit (mainly labor and consumer-good) markets—that is, to such topics as advertising, fraud, price dispersion, and job search. But it is possible to use economic analysis to explore the dissemination and withholding of information in personal as well as business contexts, and thus to deal with such matters as prying, eavesdropping, "self-advertising," and gossip. Moreover, the same analysis may illuminate questions of privacy within organizations, both commercial and noncommercial.

I shall first attempt to develop a simple economic theory of privacy. I shall then argue from this theory that, while personal privacy seems today to be valued more highly than organizational privacy (if one may judge by current legislative trends), a reverse ordering would be more consistent with the economics of the problem.

Theory

People invariably possess information, including the contents of communications and facts about themselves, that they will incur costs to conceal. Sometimes such information is of value to other people—that is, other people will incur costs to discover it. Thus we have two economic goods, "privacy" and "prying." We could regard them as pure consumption goods, the way turnips or beer are normally regarded in economic analysis, and we would then speak of a "taste" for privacy or for prying. But this would bring the economic analysis to a grinding halt because tastes are unanalyzable from an economic standpoint. An alternative is to regard privacy and prying as intermediate rather than final goods—instrumental rather than final values. Under this approach, people are assumed not to desire or value privacy or prying in themselves but to use these goods as inputs into the production of income or some other broad measure of utility or welfare. This is the approach that I take here; the reader will have to decide whether it captures enough of the relevant reality to be enlightening.

Not So Idle Curiosity Now the demand for private information (viewed, as it is here, as an intermediate good) is readily understandable where the existence of an actual or potential relationship, business or personal, creates opportunities for gain by the demander. These opportunities obviously exist in the case of information sought by the tax collector, fiancé, partner, creditor, competitor, and so on. Less obviously, much of the casual prying (a term not used here with any pejorative connotation) into the private lives of friends and colleagues that is so common a feature of social life is, I believe, motivated—to a greater extent than we usually think—by rational considerations of self-interest. Prying enables one to form a more accurate picture of a friend or colleague, and the knowledge gained is useful in one's social or professional dealings with that friend or colleague. For example, one wants to know in choosing a friend whether he will be discreet or indiscreet, selfish or generous. These qualities are not necessarily apparent on initial acquaintance. Even a pure altruist needs to know the (approximate) wealth of any prospective beneficiary of his altruism in order to be able to gauge the value of a gift or transfer to him.

The other side of the coin is that social dealings, like business dealings, present opportunities for exploitation through misrepresentation. Psychologists and sociologists have pointed out that even in everyday life people try to manipulate other people's opinion of them, using misrepresentation. The strongest defenders of privacy usually define the individual's right to privacy as the right to control the flow of information about him. A seldom-remarked corollary to a right to misrepresent one's character is that others have a legitimate interest in unmasking the misrepresentation.

Yet some of the demand for private information about other people seems mysteriously disinterested—for example, that of the readers of newspaper gossip columns, whose "idle curiosity" has been deplored, groundlessly in my opinion. Gossip columns recount the personal lives of wealthy and successful people whose tastes and habits offer models—that is, yield information—to the ordinary person in making consumption, career, and other decisions. The models are not always positive. The story of Howard Hughes, for example, is usually told as a morality play, warning of the pitfalls of success. That does not make it any less educational. The fascination with the notorious and the criminal—with John Profumo and with Nathan Leopold— has a similar basis. Gossip columns open people's eyes to opportunities and dangers; they are genuinely informative.

Moreover, the expression "idle curiosity" is misleading. People are not given to random undifferentiated curiosity. Why is there less curiosity about the lives of the poor (as measured, for example, by the infrequency with which poor people figure as central characters in popular novels) than about those of the rich? One reason is that the lives of the poor do not provide as much useful information for the patterning of our own lives. What interest there is in the poor is focused on people who were like us but who became poor, rather than on those who were always poor; again, the cautionary function of such information should be evident.

Samuel Warren and Louis Brandeis once attributed the rise of curiosity about people's lives to the excesses of the press (in an article in the *Harvard Law Review*, 1890). The economist does not believe, however, that supply creates demand. A more persuasive explanation for the rise of the gossip column is the increase in personal income over time. There is apparently very little privacy in poor societies, where, consequently, people can readily observe at first hand the intimate lives of others. Personal surveillance is costlier in wealthier societies, both because people live in conditions that give them greater privacy and because the value (and hence opportunity cost) of time is greater—too great, in fact, to make the expenditure of a lot of it in watching the neighbors a worthwhile pursuit. An alternative method of informing oneself about how others live was sought by the people and provided by the press. A legitimate and important function of the press is to provide specialization in prying in societies where the costs of obtaining information have become too great for the Nosy Parker.

Who Owns Secrets? The fact that disclosure of personal information is resisted by (is costly to) the person to whom the information pertains, yet is valuable to others, may seem to argue for giving people property rights in information about themselves and letting them sell those rights freely. The process of voluntary exchange would then ensure that the information was put to its most valuable use. The attractiveness of this solution depends, however, on (1) the nature and source of the information and (2) transaction costs.

The strongest case for property rights in secrets is presented where such rights are necessary in order to encourage investment in the production of socially valuable information. This is the rationale for giving legal protection to the variety of commercial ideas, plans, and information encompassed by the term "trade secret." It also explains why the "shrewd bargainer" is not required to tell the other party to the bargain his true opinion of the values involved. A shrewd bargainer is, in part, one who invests resources in obtaining information about the true values of things. Were he forced to share this information with potential sellers, he would get no return on his investment and the process—basic to a market economy—by which goods are transferred through voluntary exchange into successively more valuable uses would be impaired. This is true even though the lack of candor in the bargaining process deprives it of some of its "voluntary" character.

At some point nondisclosure becomes fraud. One consideration relevant to deciding whether the line has been crossed is whether the information sought to be concealed by one of the transacting parties is a product of significant investment. If not, the social costs of nondisclosure are reduced. This may be decisive, for example, on the question whether the owner of a house should be required to disclose latent (nonobvious) defects to a purchaser. The ownership and maintenance of a house are costly and productive activities. But since knowledge of the house's defects is acquired by the owner costlessly (or nearly so), forcing him to disclose these defects will not reduce his incentive to invest in discovering them.

As examples of cases where transaction-cost considerations argue against assigning a property right to the possessor of a secret, consider (1) whether the Bureau of the Census should be required to *buy* information from the firms or households that it interviews and (2) whether a magazine should be allowed to sell its subscriber list to another magazine without obtaining the subscribers' consent. Requiring the Bureau of the Census to pay (that is, assigning the property right in the information sought to the interviewee) would yield a skewed sample: the poor would be over-represented, unless the bureau used a differentiated price schedule based on the different costs of disclosure (and hence prices for cooperating) to the people sampled. In the magazine case, the costs of obtaining subscriber approval would be high relative to the value of the list. If, therefore, we are confident that these lists are generally worth more to the purchasers than being shielded from possible unwanted solicitations is worth to the subscribers, we should assign the property right to the magazine, and this is what the law does.

The decision to assign the property right away from the individual is further supported, in both the census and subscription-list cases, by the fact that the costs of disclosure to the individual are low. They are low in the census case because the government takes precautions against disclosure of the information collected to creditors, tax collectors, or others who might have transactions with the individual in which they could use the information to gain an advantage over him. They are low in the subscription-list case because the information about the subscribers that is disclosed to the list purchaser is trivial and cannot be used to impose substantial costs on them.

Even though the type of private information discussed thus far is not in general discreditable to the individual to whom it pertains, we have seen that there may still be strong reasons for assigning the property right away from that individual. Much of the demand for privacy, however, concerns discreditable information—often information concerning past or present criminal activity or moral conduct at variance with a person's professed moral standards—and often the motive for concealment is, as suggested earlier, to mislead others. People also wish to conceal private information that, while not strictly discreditable, would if revealed correct misapprehensions that the individual is trying to exploit—as when a worker conceals a serious health problem from his employer or a prospective husband conceals his sterility from his fiancée. It is not clear why society in these cases should assign the property right in information to the individual to whom it pertains; and under the common law, generally it does not. A separate question, taken up a little later, is whether the decision to assign the property right away from the possessor of guilty secrets implies that any and all methods of uncovering those secrets should be permitted.

An analogy to the world of commerce may clarify why people should not—on economic grounds in any event—have a right to conceal material facts about themselves. We think it wrong (and inefficient) that a seller in hawking his wares should be permitted to make false or incomplete representations as to their quality. But people "sell" themselves as well as their goods. A person professes high standards of behavior in order to induce others to engage in social or business dealings with him from which he derives an advantage, but at the same time conceals some of the facts that the people with whom he deals need in order to form an accurate picture of his character. There are practical reasons for not imposing a general legal duty of full and frank disclosure of one's material personal shortcomings—a duty not to be a hypocrite. But each of us should be allowed to protect ourselves from disadvantageous transactions by ferreting out concealed facts about other individuals that are material to their implicit or explicit self-representations.

It is no answer that, in Brandeis's phrase, people have "the right to be let alone." Few people want to be let alone. They want to manipulate the world around them by selective disclosure of facts about themselves. Why should others be asked to take their self-serving claims at face value and prevented from obtaining the information necessary to verify or disprove these claims?

Some private information that people desire to conceal is not discreditable. In our culture, for example, most people do not like to be seen naked, quite apart from any discreditable fact that such observation might reveal. Since this reticence, unlike concealment of discreditable information, is not a source of social costs and since transaction costs are low, there is an economic case for assigning the property right in this area of private information to the individual; and this is what the common law does. I do not think, however, that many people have a *general* reticence that makes them wish to conceal nondiscrediting personal information. Anyone who has sat next to a stranger on an airplane or a ski lift knows the delight that some people take in talking about themselves to complete strangers. Reticence appears when one is speaking to people—friends, family, acquaintances, business associates—who might use information about him to gain an advantage in business or social transactions with him. Reticence is generally a means rather than an end.

The reluctance of many people to reveal their income is sometimes offered as an example of a desire for privacy that cannot be explained in purely instrumental terms. But I suggest that people conceal an unexpectedly low income because being thought to have a high income has value in credit markets and elsewhere, and they conceal an unexpectedly high income in order to (1) avoid the attention of tax collectors, kidnappers, and thieves, (2) fend off solicitations from charities and family members, and (3) preserve a reputation for generosity that would be shattered if the precise fraction of their income that was being given away were known. Points (1) and (2) may explain anonymous gifts to charity.

Prying, Eavesdropping, and Formality To the extent that personal information is concealed in order to mislead, the case for giving it legal protection is, I have argued, weak. Protection would simply increase transaction costs, much as if we permitted fraud in the sale of goods. However, it is also necessary to consider the *means* by which personal information is obtained. Prying by means of casual interrogation of acquaintances of the object of the prying must be distinguished from eavesdropping (electronically or otherwise) on a person's conversations. A in conversation with B disparages C. If C has a right to hear this conversation, A, in choosing the words he uses to B, will have to consider the possible reactions of C. Conversation will be more costly because of the external effects and this will result in less—and less effective—communication. After people adjust to this new world of public conversation, even the C's of the world will cease to derive much benefit in the way of greater information from conversational publicity: people will be more guarded in their speech. The principal effect of publicity will be to make conversation more formal and communcation less effective rather than to increase the knowledge of interested third parties.

Stated differently, the costs of defamatory utterances and hence the cost-justified level of expenditures on avoiding defamation are greater the more publicity given the utterance. If every conversation were public, the time and other resources devoted to ensuring that one's speech was free from false or unintended slanders would rise. The additional costs are avoided by the simple and inexpensive expedient of permitting conversations to be private.

It is relevant to observe that language becomes less formal as society evolves. The languages of primitive peoples are more elaborate, more ceremonious, and more courteous than that of twentieth-century Americans. One reason may be that primitive people have little privacy. There are relatively few private conversations because third parties are normally present and the effects of the conversation on them must be taken into account. Even today, one observes that people speak more formally the greater the number of people present. The rise of privacy has facilitated private conversation and thereby enabled us to economize on communication—to speak with a brevity and informality apparently rare among primitive peoples. This valuable economy of communication would be undermined by allowing eavesdropping.

In some cases, to be sure, communication is not related to socially productive activity. Communication among criminal conspirators is an example. In these cases—where limited eavesdropping is indeed permitted—the effect of eavesdropping in reducing communication is not an objection to, but an advantage of, the eavesdropping.

The analysis here can readily be extended to efforts to obtain people's notes, letters, and other private papers; communication would be inhibited by such efforts. A more complex question is presented by photographic surveillance—for example, of the interior of a person's home. Privacy enables a person to dress and otherwise disport himself in his home without regard to the effect on third parties. This economizing property would be lost if the interior of the home were in the public domain. People dress not merely because of the effect on others but also because of the reticence, noted earlier, concerning nudity and other sensitive states. This is another reason for giving people a privacy right with regard to the places in which these sensitive states occur.

Ends and Means The two main strands of my argument—relating to personal facts and to communications, respectively—can be joined by remarking the difference in this context between ends and means. With regard to ends, there is a prima facie case for assigning the property right in a secret that is a by-product of socially productive activity to the individual if its compelled disclosure would impair the incentives to engage in that activity; but there is a prima facie case for assigning the property right away from the individual if secrecy would reduce the social product by misleading others. However, the fact that under this analysis most facts about people belong in the public domain does not imply that intrusion on private communications should generally be permitted, given the effects of such intrusions on the costs of legitimate communications.

Admittedly, the suggested dichotomy between facts and communications is too stark. If you are allowed to interrogate my acquaintances about my income, I may take steps to conceal it that are analogous to the increased formality of conversation that would ensue from abolition of the right to conversational privacy, and the costs of these steps are a social loss. The difference is one of degree. Because eavesdropping and related modes of intrusive surveillance are such effective ways of eliciting private information and are at the same time relatively easy to thwart, we can expect that evasive maneuvers, costly in the aggregate, would be undertaken if conversational privacy were compromised. It is more difficult to imagine people taking effective measures against casual prying. An individual is unlikely to alter his income or style of living drastically in order to better conceal his income or private information from casual or journalistic inquiry. (Howard Hughes was a notable exception to this generalization.)

We have now sketched the essential elements of an economically based legal right of privacy: (1) Trade and business secrets by which businessmen exploit their superior knowledge or skills would be protected. (The same principle would be applied to the personal level and would thus, for example, entitle the social host or hostess to conceal the recipe of a successful dinner.) (2) Facts about people would generally not be protected. My ill health, evil temper, even my income would not be facts over which I had property rights, though I might be able to prevent their discovery by methods unduly intrusive under the third category. (3) Eavesdropping and other forms of intrusive surveillance would be limited (so far as possible) to the discovery of illegal activities.

Application

To what extent is the economic theory developed above reflected in public policy? To answer this question, it is necessary to distinguish sharply between common law and statutory responses to the privacy question.

The Common Law The term common law refers to the body of legal principles evolved by English and American appellate judges in the decision of private suits over a period of hundreds of years. I believe, and have argued in greater detail elsewhere, that the common law of privacy is strongly stamped by the economic principles (though nowhere explicitly recognized by the judges) developed in this article.

That law contains the precise elements that an economically based right of privacy would include. Trade secrets and commercial privacy generally are well protected. It has been said by one court: "almost any knowledge or information used in the conduct of one's business may be held by its possessor secret." In another well-known case, aerial photography of a competitor's plant under construction was held to be unlawful, and the court used the term "commercial privacy" to describe the interest it was protecting.

An analogy in the personal area is the common law principle that a person's name or photograph may not be used in advertising without his consent. The effect is to create a property right which ensures that a person's name or likeness (O. J. Simpson's, for example) will be allocated to the advertising use in which it is most valuable. Yet, consistent with the economics of the problem, individuals have in general no right in common law to conceal discrediting information about themselves. But, again consistent with the economics of the problem, they do have a right to prevent eavesdropping, photographic surveillance of the interior of a home, the ransacking of private records to discover information about an individual, and similarly intrusive methods of penetrating the wall of privacy that people build about themselves. The distinction is illustrated by Ralph Nader's famous suit against General Motors. The court affirmed General Motors' right to have Nader followed about, to question his acquaintances, and, in short, to ferret out personal information about Nader that the company might have used to undermine his public credibility. Yet I would expect a court to enjoin any attempt through such methods to find out what Nader was about to say on some subject in order to be able to plagiarize his ideas.

When, however, we compare the implications of the economic analysis not with the common law relating to privacy but with recent legislation in the privacy area, we are conscious not of broad concordance but of jarring incongruity. As noted, from the economic standpoint, private business information should in general be accorded greater legal protection than personal information. Secrecy is an important method of appropriating social benefits to the entrepreneur who creates them, while in private life it is more likely simply to conceal legitimately discrediting or deceiving facts. Communications within organizations, whether public or private, should receive the same protection as communications among individuals, for in either case the effect of publicity would be to encumber and retard communication.

The Trend in Legislation But in fact the legislative trend is toward giving individuals more and more privacy protection with respect to facts and communications, and business firms and other organizations (including government agencies, universities, and hospitals) less and less. The Freedom of Information Act, sunshine laws opening the deliberations of administrative agencies to the public, and the erosion of effective sanctions against breach of government confidences have greatly reduced the privacy of communications within the government. Similar forces are at work in private institutions such as business firms and private universities (note, for example, the Buckley Amendment and the opening of faculty meetings to student observers). Increasingly, moreover, the facts about an individual—arrest record, health, credit-worthiness, marital status, sexual proclivities—are secured from involuntary disclosure, while the facts about business corporations are thrust into public view by the expansive disclosure requirements of the federal securities laws (to the point where some firms are "going private" in order to secure greater confidentiality for their plans and operations), the civil rights laws, "line of business" reporting, and other regulations. A related trend is the erosion of the privacy of government officials through increasingly stringent ethical standards requiring disclosure of income.

The trend toward elevating personal and downgrading organizational privacy is mysterious to the economist (as are other recent trends in public regulation). To repeat, the economic case for privacy of *communications* seems unrelated to the nature of the communicator, whether a private individual or the employee of a university, corporation, or government agency, while so far as *facts* about people or organizations are concerned, the case for protecting business privacy is stronger, in general, than that for protecting individual privacy.

Some of the differences in the protection accorded governmental and personal privacy may, to be sure, simply reflect a desire to reduce the power of government. Viewed in this light, the Freedom of Information Act is perhaps supported by the same sorts of considerations that are believed by some to justify wire-tapping in national security or organized crime cases. But only a small part of the recent legislation output in the privacy area can be explained in such terms.

A good example of legislative refusal to respect the economics of the privacy problem is the Buckley Amendment, which gives students (and their parents) access to their school records. The amendment permits students to waive, in writing, their right to see letters of recommendation, and most students do so. They do so because they know that letters of recommendation to which they have access convey no worthwhile information to the recipient. The effect on the candor and value of communication is the same as would be that of a rule that allowed C to hear A and B's conversations about him. Throwing open faculty meetings or congressional conferences to the public has the identical effect of reducing the value of communication without benefiting the public, for the presence of the public deters the very communication they want to hear.

As another example of an economically perverse legislative response to privacy issues, consider the different treatment of disclosures of corporate and of personal crime. The corporation that bribes foreign officials must make public disclosure of the fact, even though the crime may benefit the corporation, its shareholders, the United States as a whole, and even the citizens of the foreign country in question. Yet the convicted rapist, the recidivist con artist, and even the murderer "acquitted" by reason of insanity are not only under no duty to reveal to new acquaintances their criminal activities but are often assisted by law in concealing these activities.

Through the Fair Credit Reporting Act, credit bureaus are forbidden to report to their customers a range of information concerning applicants for credit—for instance, bankruptcies more than fourteen years old and all other adverse information (including criminal convictions and civil judgments) more than seven years old. These restrictions represent an extraordinary intervention in the credit process that could be justified only if credit bureaus systematically collected and reported information that, because of its staleness, had negligible value to its customers in deciding whether credit should be extended. No such assumption of economic irrationality is plausible.

These examples could be multiplied, but the main point should be clear enough. Legislatures are increasingly creating rights to conceal information that is material to prospective creditors and employers, and at the same time forcing corporations and other organizations to publicize information whose confidentiality is necessary to their legitimate operation.

A Contrary View I know of only one principled effort to show that individual privacy claims are stronger than those of businesses and other organizations. Professors Kent Greenawalt and Eli Noam of Columbia, in an unpublished paper, offer two distinctions between a business's (or other organization's) interest in privacy and an individual's interest. First, they say that the latter is a matter of rights and that the former is based merely on instrumental, utilitarian considerations. The reasons they offer for recognizing a right of personal privacy are, however, utilitarian—that people need an opportunity to "make a new start" (that is, to conceal embarrassing or discreditable facts about their past), that people cannot preserve their sanity without privacy, and so on. Yet Greenawalt and Noam disregard the utilitarian justification for secrecy as an incentive to investment in productive activity—the strongest justification for secrecy and one mainly relevant, as I have argued, in business contexts.

The second distinction they suggest between the business and personal claims to privacy is a strangely distorted mirror of my argument for entrepreneurial or productive secrecy. They argue that it is difficult to establish property rights in information and even remark that secrecy is one way of doing so. But they do not draw the obvious conclusion that secrecy can promote productive activity by creating property rights in valuable information. Instead they use the existence of imperfections in the market for information as a justification for government regulation designed to extract private information from business firms. They do not explain, however, how the government could, let alone demonstrate that it would, use this information more productively than firms, and they do not consider the impact of this form of public prying on the incentive to produce the information in the first place.

Conclusion

Discussions of the privacy question have contained a high degree of cant, sloganeering, emotion, and loose thinking. A fresh perspective on the question is offered by economic analysis, and by a close examination of the common law principles that have evolved under the influence (perhaps unconsciously) of economic perceptions. In the perspective offered by economics and by the common law, the recent legislative emphasis on favoring individual and denigrating corporate and organizational privacy stands revealed as still another example of perverse government regulation of social and economic life.

▷ A NEW PARADIGM FOR INDIVIDUALS IN THE INFORMATION AGE

David Chaum
Computer Science Department, University of California,

Today, individuals provide substantially the same identifying information to each organization with which they have a relationship. In a new paradigm, individuals provide different "pseudonyms" or alternate names to each organi-

zation. A critical advantage of systems based on such pseudonyms is that the information associated with each pseudonym can be insufficient to allow data on an individual to be linked and collected together, and thus they can prevent the formation of a dossier society reminiscent of Orwell's 1984.

A system is proposed in which an individual's pseudonyms are created and stored in a computer held and trusted only by the individual. New cryptographic techniques allow an organization to securely exchange messages or payments with an individual known under a pseudonym—without the communication or payments systems providers being able to trace messages or payments. Other new techniques allow a digitally signed credential to be transformed by the individual, from the individual's pseudonym with the issuing organization, to the individual's pseudonym with a recipient organization. Credentials can be transformed only between pseudonyms of a single individual, and an individual can obtain at most one pseudonym with a particular organization, but even a conspiracy of all organizations can gain no information from the pseudonyms about their correspondence. The combination of these systems can prevent abuses by individuals, while averting the potential for a dossier society.

INTRODUCTION

As the use of computers becomes more pervasive, they are bound to have substantial influence on our relationships with organizations. Currency and paper checks as a way to pay for goods and services will largely be replaced by electronic means. Electronic mail will be the main way we send and receive messages. Our personal credentials will often be presented in electronic form. Below, two different paradigms for automation of the informational relationships between individuals and organizations will each be illustrated by an example scenario.

Current Paradigm

The current paradigm is characterized by "identification" of the individual during every transaction. In an example scenario based on the logical extension of this paradigm, credit card sized computers held by individuals would provide an identifying account number to an organization receiving payment from the individual card holder. In a similar way, the card might provide the name and mailing address of its holder to an organization with a need to send messages to the individual, routinely (e.g., monthly statements) or only under exceptional circumstances (e.g., manufacturers recall or request for return of rented or borrowed things). An organization may require credentials (e.g., credit, professional license, citizenship, good tenant, education, or past employment) of the individual for establishing or maintaining a relationship with the individual. When credentials are required by an organization, the card would provide detailed identification and references to that organization which would allow the credentials to be checked with other organizations. Notice that in this paradigm identification is required presumably to allow detection and remedies against abuses and frauds perpetrated by individuals, such as default of payment, situations requiring legal notice, or the use of false credentials.

These identifying numbers, addresses, and references allow the various records and transaction details relating to a particular individual to be linked and collected together into a "dossier" or comprehensive file on the individual. While limited dossiers can be and are assembled today, the amount and nature of data which could automatically be captured in the scenario above would radically increase the significance of the dossier. For example, if all payments transactions are captured, a great deal about a person's habits, entertainment, travel, organizational affiliations, information consumption, etc. would be included in the dossier. Similarly, in an electronic mail environment, a comprehensive history of the identity of all correspondents as well as the timing and length of correspondences could be very revealing. Finally, links to previous activities and details of past associations might be of great significance. If it is possible for dossiers to be compiled, but their compilation is officially denied, there may be concern that compilation is taking place secretly. Even if compilation does not occur, there should still be concern that dossiers could be constructed at a later time based on current records; it is very difficult to be convinced that all copies of some obsolete information are destroyed. It is worth noting that advances in some areas of computer science, such as pattern recognition, make automated analysis of dossiers a possibility.

New Paradigm

In a new paradigm, instead of identifying information, individuals provide each organization with a different "pseudonym" or alternate name. Pseudonyms would be created and stored in the credit card sized computer held by the individual. The critical advantage of systems based on such pseudonyms is that the information they contain is insufficient to allow data on an individual to be linked together, and thus they can prevent the formation of a dossier society, reminiscent of Orwell's *1984*.

There are three fundamental kinds of interactions required in the new paradigm:

1. individuals need to communicate with organizations,
2. individuals need to pay or be paid by organizations, and
3. organizations need to exchange information about individuals.

Sometimes the communication or payments can be anonymous, such as with a simple purchase at a shop or an inquiry about an organization's policy or services. In other cases, authorizing messages must come from the holder of a particular pseudonym, or confidential messages must be sent by an organization in such a way that they can only be received by the holder of a particular pseudonym. Organizations also need to communicate amongst themselves about an individual; the term credentials will be used for this kind of communication. Sometimes credentials are positive, such as a diploma or certificate of good health issued to an individual. The individual can then supply the credential to organizations other than the issuer. In other cases, a credential may be negative in the sense that it is in the individual's interest not to provide the credential information, such as reporting income from an organization to the IRS or informing a credit agency about an additional debt incurred.

The following introduces and highlights some of the desired properties and considerations in the design of each of these three components of the new paradigm.

Communication

A communication system in which messages are routed through a number of nodes, any one of which is able to obscure the correspondence between messages in its input and those in its output, was described by the author [1981]. This system was based on public key cryptography. From the perspective of the new paradigm, its important properties might be described as follows:

Individual Protected from System Provider Even the system provider can not trace a message under normal conditions.

Organization Protected from Individual The individual can use a digital pseudonym to provide "third party authentication" (see section on cryptographic techniques) of a message sent to the organization under the pseudonym.

Society Protected from Individual Threats or other illegal messages are traceable to the point of origin, but consensus of a large number of parties who may not be mutually sympathetic is required for each message traced, and thus a trace is unlikely to be carried out covertly.

Individual Protected from Organization An individual may send messages to an organization, without the organization being able to determine the origin of the message. An individual may receive messages from an organization without the organization knowing the location of the recipient. Such messages are sent with an "untraceable return address," which the individual supplies to the organization. An individual can create as many untraceable return addresses as desired, but none of these addresses can be linked together or to the individual. Untraceable return addresses can each be used only to send a single message, and thus the individual can control to a large extent the quantity and origin of messages received. Messages sent with an untraceable return address can be read only by the individual who created the address.

Payments

A new kind of payments systems was proposed by the author [1982]. The basis of the scheme is a new kind of cryptographic system called a "blind signature" cryptographic system (also discussed in the next section), which allows a signer to make a digital signature without knowing what is being signed. The way this is used in a payments system is that an individual forms a bank note and the bank signs it—only after taking from the individual's account the amount of money corresponding to the kind of signature made. Then the individual transforms the signed note so that the bank can not recognize it but still maintaining the digital signature property that allows anyone to determine that the note was actually signed by the bank. When the individual pays an organization with the transformed note, the organization sends it to the bank. The bank checks the signature on the note, and that the note has not already been deposited, and credits the organization's account for the value of the signature on the note. From this point of view of the new paradigm, this payments system has the following properties.

Individual Protected from System Provider The provider of the payments system, such as a bank, is unable to determine the correspondence between notes withdrawn and notes deposited. Of course the payments system provider knows the balance of each account, and also when each account balance is changed. But because funds are withdrawn and held in a bearer form, something like unmarked bills, before being deposited to another account, knowledge of timing of changes in account balance does not necessarily reveal the correspondence between a particular withdrawal and the ultimate deposit of the same funds. Also because transfers are accomplished using amounts represented as units of standard denomination, much like coins and banknotes, the amount deposited does not necessarily reveal the account the funds were withdrawn from.

Organization Protected from Individual An organization is able to clear a payment received from the individual and know with certainty that it will be honored.

Society Protected from Individual Stolen media use can be stopped once reported, and use before a stop payment is in place is traceable, at least to the recipient. Any payer (e.g., a customer of a black market, a person making a payoff or bribe) can reveal the payee.

Individual Protected from Organization When an organization receives payment from an individual, the organization is not able to trace the payment to the account from which it originated. If an individual makes payment, but the organization later denies receipt of the funds, then the individual can demonstrate to the system provider that payment was received by the organization.

Credentials

Credential schemes allow the individual to control the transfer of information about the individual between organizations. The essential idea of these schemes is that each organization knows an individual by a different pseudonym, and the individual can transform a digitally signed credential received from an organization in a way that preserves the digital signature but changes the pseudonym within the credential. Credential schemes do not require a separate system provider. From the point of view of the new paradigm, credential schemes may have the following properties.

Individual Protected from Organizations Even a conspiracy of all the organizations can not derive any information from the pseudonyms about which pseudonyms correspond to a particular individual, or even which correspond to the same individual. If pseudonyms are changed periodically, and records from old periods are passed forward only through credentials, then it is possible for individuals to be assured that certain information from previous periods can not be linked to current pseudonyms.

Organizations/Society Protected from Individual Individuals can not create or alter credentials; they may only transform them from one pseudonym to another. Credentials can not be transformed between pseudonyms of different individuals, even if many individuals conspire before the credential system is established. An organization can ensure that it receives at most one pseudonym from any individual. An individual can provide substantiation, which is capable of third party authentication, that some negative credential information was transmitted to an organization responsive to a particular request made by a second organization. The expectation of a positive or negative credential can be established for all clients of an organization, or on an individual basis, such that if no credential is supplied then the negative one is assumed.

BACKGROUND

Two major literatures are related to the present work: one largely to its impact on society, and the other to the predecessors of the fundamental cryptographic techniques which are the precursors of the mechanisms discussed above.

The Policy Debate

The computers and privacy debate is the subject government reports of many countries, tens of books, hundreds of scholarly articles in a variety of disciplines, and thousands of articles addressed at a broader audience. It is far beyond the scope of the present work to survey this vast literature (but see, e.g., the bibliographies of Harrison [1969] Latin [1976] and Stone & Stone [1979]). It is clear from this literature, however, that there is substantial public concern about the continuing emergence of an unprecedented collection of information by organizations about individuals.

There have been five major studies of actual systems and practices in English [DCDJC 1972; PPSC 1977; Rule 1973; Westin 1972; Younger 1972]. These have suggested three major policy alternatives: (1) freeze or dismantle the record collection systems planned or in place; (2) provide individuals with a right to inspect and challenge the accuracy of records about themselves, expect that only pertinent data will be collected, and expect that personal data will only be used for the purposes intended; (3) restructure the major systems using detailed personal information, such as taxation, credit, welfare, and employment, in such a way that they require less detailed information. The first alternative is of course not a credible option. The second alternative, in various forms, has been recommended by many, and has found its way into law. Proponents of the third approach maintain that the second does not actually address the privacy problem or the danger of a massive surveillance capability, and that a real solution requires some restructuring of the rules of major institutions.

Mention of the subtleties of the interrelation between policy and mechanism appears conspicuously absent from these studies. Theorists, most notably Mumford [1934], have argued extensively that societal forces, such as policy, significantly influence development and adoption of new technologies. (Also see Kuhn [1962] for discussion of the power of societal forces within a scientific community.) In the other direction, the policy alternative(s) raised by the present work have not been considered in the policy literature, and thus they are an example of new mechanisms providing unanticipated policy alternatives. It appears from the literature that those scholars involved in the computer privacy debate and those scientists concerned with the mechanisms of information technology have drifted apart after only brief initial inquiries and a few defections from one camp to the other. It is hoped that the present work will re-open interaction between the two camps and spawn new contributions from each.

Cryptographic Techniques

The literature on cryptology is also rather broad, but much of it is concerned with classical cryptologic techniques, and is of little relevance here. In the last several years, there have been several major open meetings devoted to modern cryptology, and several new textbooks on the topic have appeared. Efforts in the field seem to be dividing up into a number of separate areas, such as protocols; verification of protocols; cryptanalysis of modern systems; development of new algorithms which implement standard types of modern systems; complexity analysis aimed at formalizing and ultimately proving cryptographic strength; and the whole spectrum of more applied concerns, from actual engineering, to applications of standard types of systems. The present work, however, is primarily concerned with development and application of new types of cryptographic techniques, and so only a summary of the various fundamental types of cryptographic systems proposed in the literature will be presented.

One-way functions (i.e., functions that are publically known, but whose inverse is supposed to be difficult for anyone to compute) were proposed first in the literature by Purdy [1974]. Lamport suggested a technique for providing "third party authentication," (a technique mentioned elsewhere in the present work, sometimes called a "digital signature" technique, in which, after an initial agreed on set-up, anyone can check a signed message and know that it could have only been formed by the holder of a particular secret key) based on one way functions [Diffie and Hellman 1976b]. Diffie and Hellman proposed the existence of commutative one way functions, offered an example algorithm, and showed how they could be used to build a "public key distribution system" (i.e., a way for two parties to develop the same secret key while only using a channel that provides authentication but no secrecy). So called "conventional" cryptographic techniques (a cryptosystem in which a function and its inverse can be derived from a secret key) appear to have been in use for thousands of years [Kahn 1967]. The possibility of commutative conventional cryptosystems was suggested and illustrated by an actual algorithm by Shamir, Rivest and Adleman [1981] in a solution to Floyd's mental poker problem. The existence of true public key schemes (cryptosystems in which the creator of a public one way function retains the exclusive ability to compute its inverse) was first proposed by Diffie and Hellman [1976a], and a potentially viable algorithm was first suggested by Rivest, Shamir and Adleman [1978]. The possibility of publically generated invertible functions which commute with the functions of a public key system was suggested by Chaum [1984], and forms the basis of the blind signature payments system discussed in the present work. Actual algorithms have been developed which appear to meet the requirements for a blind signature system [Chaum 1984a]. Parameterized blind signatures have also been suggested and actual algorithms proposed [Chaum 1984b], that allow a greater flexibility in the payments and credentials mechanisms described.

SUMMARY

A new paradigm, in which identification of individuals is replaced by use of cryptographic pseudonyms, can provide secure informational relationships while averting the potential for a dossier society.

NOTES

1. Chaum, D., "Untraceable Electronic Mail, Return Addresses, and Digital Pseudonyms," *Communications of the ACM*, February 1981.

2. Chaum, D., "Blind Signatures for Untraceable Payments," *Proceedings of CRYPTO 82* Plenum Press, 1983.

3. Chaum, D., "New Secret Codes Can Prevent a Computerized Big Brother," *Communications of the ACM* to appear.

4. Chaum, D., "Parameterized Signatures," in preparation.

5. Department of Communications/Department of Justice, Canada, *Privacy and Computers*, Information Canada, Ottawa, 1972.

6. Diffie, W. and Hellman, M. E., "Multiuser Cryptographic Techniques," *NCC 1976a*, pp. 109–112.

7. Diffie, W. and Hellman, M. E., "New Directions in Cryptography," *IEEE Trans. Info. Theory*, vol IT-22, pp. 644–654, November 1976b.

8. Harrison, A. *The Problem of Privacy in the Computer Age: Ann Annotated Bibliography*, (2 volumes) Rand Report: RM-5495/1-PR/RC, Rand Corporation, Santa Monica CA, December 1969.

9. Stone, E., and Stone, D., *Information Privacy: A Bibliography With Key Word and Author Indices*, Information Privacy Research Center Working Paper No. 6, Purdue University, Laffeyete IN, May 1979.

10. Kahn, D., *The Codebreakers: The Story of Secret Writing*, Macmillan Co., N.Y., 1967.

11. Kuhn, T. S. *The Structure of Scientific Revolutions*, University of Chicago Press, Chicago, 1962.

12. Latin, H. A., *Privacy: A Selected Bibliography and Topical Index of Social Science Materials*, Fred B. Rothman & Co., South Hackensack, NJ, 1976.

13. Mumford, L. *Technics and Civilization*, Harcourt, Brace and Co., N.Y., 1934.

14. Privacy Protection Study Commission, *Personal Privacy in an Information Society*, U.S. Government Printing Office, Washington D.C., July 1977.

15. Purdy, G. B., "A High Security Log-in Procedure," *Communications of the ACM,* vol. 17, no. 8, August 1974, p. 442.

16. Rivest, R., Shamir, A. and Adleman, L., "A Method for Obtaining Digital Signatures and Public-Key Cryptosystems," *Communications of the ACM*, vol. 21, no. 2, February 1978.

17. Rule, James, *Private Lives and Public Surveillance*, Allen Lane, London 1973.

18. Shamir, A., Rivest, R., Adleman, L., "Mental Poker," in *The Mathematical Gardner*, Klarner, D. (Ed.), Prindle, Weber & Schmidt, Boston, 1981, pp. 37–43.

19. Westin, A. and Baker, M., *Databanks in a Free Society: Computers, Record-Keeping, and Privacy*, Quadrangle Books, N.Y., 1972.

20. Younger, K., *Report of the Committee on Privacy*, Cmnd. 5012, Her Majesty's Stationery Office, London 1972.

▷ **A FEDERAL RIGHT OF INFORMATION PRIVACY: THE NEED FOR REFORM**

Jerry Berman and Janlori Goldman

INTRODUCTION

The constitutional right to privacy is, as Justice Brandeis first stated, "the right to be left alone—the most comprehensive of rights and the right most valued by civilized men."[1] Brandeis' formulation has long been the starting point for any discussion of the meaning of privacy. But what value does privacy hold for us? What does privacy look like in the late 1980s? Are we truly able, or even entitled, to live certain areas of our lives outside of the public eye? Is privacy still the most valued and comprehensive of rights?

"Who cares about privacy?"[2] National polls document a growing public demand for privacy protection. In a 1983 analysis of their survey results, Louis Harris and Associates concluded:

> Particularly striking is the pervasiveness of support for tough new ground rules governing computers and other information technology. Americans are not willing to endure abuse or misuse of information, and they overwhelmingly support action to do something about it. This support permeates all subgroups in society and represents a mandate for initiatives in public policy.[3]

Most people cherish their right to be able to live certain areas of their lives outside of the public eye.[4] Yet today, these same people are overwhelmed by institutional demands for information. Crucial to one's sense of "self" is the right to maintain some decision-making power over what information to divulge, to whom, and for what purpose. Although there is broad public support for privacy, individual voices are often scattered and powerless, forcing a reliance on organized constituencies.

The confirmation hearings of Judge Robert Bork to the United States Supreme Court brought home the degree to which an individual's sense of freedom and identity depends on governmental respect for privacy. Voicing this belief, the majority of Senators who voted against Judge Bork's confirmation expressed concern over Bork's hostile view of the constitutional right to privacy.

Citizens are losing control of personal, sensitive information as government agencies and private institutions escalate the collection and exchange of personal information. In 1988, a number of federal agencies proposed massive expansions of their information systems by linking their records with the separately maintained record systems of other agencies. The FBI, for example, proposed enhancing its law enforcement efforts by connecting its National Crime Information Center (NCIC) to the computerized record systems of the Department of Health and Human Services (HHS), the Internal Revenue Service (IRS), the Social Security Administration (SSA), and the Immigration and Naturalization Service (INS). The Bureau's plan was ultimately defeated, in part due to the efforts of privacy advocates and computer security experts who submitted a report to the agency recommending that the linkage proposal be abandoned.[5] However, other proposals may soon be implemented. HHS recently announced its plan to link electronically thousands of computers containing the prescription records of Medicare beneficiaries in pharmacies nationwide. HHS claims this new system will streamline the Medicare bureaucracy.[6]

Many have long feared that such coordinated information collection would eventually lead to the creation of a national database containing lifetime dossiers on all citizens, held in one centrally controlled mainframe computer. However, advanced information technology now allows information maintained in completely separate databases to be linked. In a recent study, the Office of Technology Assessment (OTA) concluded that a *de facto* national database already exists on U.S. citizens.[7] Privacy legislation is necessary to respond to the present reality that advanced information technology now gives institutions, both public and private, the power to nearly instantly exchange, compare, verify, profile, and most importantly, link information.

Technology has overtaken current law, leaving society without a new set of social mores to limit and define the extent to which advanced technology can be used to know all we can about each other. The danger is that a watched society is a conformist society, one in which people are afraid to act or believe in ways that call attention to themselves or arouse suspicions. As one commentator observed:

> [A person] who is compelled to live every minute of . . . life among others and whose every need, thought, desire, fancy or gratification is subject to public scrutiny, has been deprived of . . . individuality and human dignity. Such an individual merges with the mass. [That person's] opinions, being public, tend never to be different; . . . aspirations, being known, tend always to be conventionally accepted ones; . . . feelings, being openly exhibited, tend to lose their quality of unique personal warmth and to become the feelings of every [person]. Such a being, although sentient, is fungible, [and] is not an individual.[8]

This paper addresses a number of different information privacy[9] issues and examines the reasons why information privacy is an enduring and cherished value in this country, resonating at the heart of individual freedom, autonomy, and individuality. The right of individuals to control information about themselves once they have given it over to a governmental entity is examined. The Privacy Act of 1974—the federal law regulating the government's collection, dissemination, maintenance, and use of personal information—is discussed in depth, including an analysis of its legislative history, implementation, and shortcomings. The right of individuals to control information about themselves once they have given it over to a private institution is also examined. In this context, the paper considers whether there is a constitutional basis for information privacy. In conclusion, the paper recommends a proposed rewrite of the Privacy Act and a policy blueprint for future information privacy initiatives to protect records held by the private sector.

IS THERE A CONSTITUTIONAL BASIS FOR A RIGHT OF INFORMATION PRIVACY?

Although the right to privacy is not explicitly granted by the U.S. Constitution, the United States Supreme Court has interpreted the Constitution to grant individuals a right of privacy, based on the First Amendment freedom of association and expression,[10] the Fifth Amendment privilege against self-incrimination,[11] penumbras of the

Bill of Rights and the Ninth Amendment,[12] the Fourteenth Amendment's guarantee of "ordered liberty",[13] but principally rooted in the Fourth Amendment protection of persons, places, papers, and effects against unreasonable searches and seizures.[14] The primary concern of this section is whether there is a constitutional right to privacy in personal information held by others and whether restrictions may be placed on personal information held by the government.

The Fourth Amendment was drafted two hundred years ago to curtail the "writs of assistance" used by officials to search door-to-door for British tariff law violations. The Framers could not imagine today's widespread collection and use of personal information by businesses and other institutions or the massive and easily accessed body of personal information held by the government. In the 1700s, "personal information was difficult to collect, and files were handwritten, rarely reproduced, and easily lost."[15] However, despite major changes in the way individuals handle their papers, the Court has been reluctant to extend the reach of the Fourth Amendment to protect records from intrusion once they are held by someone else.

The application of the Fourth Amendment had traditionally hinged on property-based notions of liberty that ground peoples' rights in their relationships to particular places, such as the "home-as-castle." However, in an early case, *Boyd* v. *United States*, the Supreme Court brought the Fourth Amendment into the late nineteenth century, reasoning that the founding principle of the Amendment were broadly worded to:

> apply to all invasions on the part of the government and its employees of the sanctity of a man's home and the privacies of his life. It is not the breaking of his doors or the rummaging of his drawers that constitute the essence of the offense; but it is the invasion of his indefensible right of personal security, personal liberty and private property.[16]

The Fourth Amendment, the *Boyd* Court noted, reflects the colonists' struggle with the arbitrary power of government. Thus, they cautioned, "constitutional provisions for the security of property and person should be liberally construed. A close and literal construction deprives them of half of their efficacy, and leads to a gradual depreciation of the right, as if it consisted more in sound than in substance."[17] The Justices recognized that the Fourth Amendment protection of property extends to government intrusions outside one's home.

The Constitution also has been interpreted to extend protection to information that implicates both First Amendment and privacy values. In *NAACP* v. *Alabama*,[18] the Court recognized the severe chilling effect on First Amendment freedoms that can result from the unauthorized disclosure of an organization's membership, finding damage in the mere revelation of one's personal, political beliefs.

In 1967, the Supreme Court, in ruling that warrantless wiretapping is unconstitutional, held that the Fourth Amendment protects people, not places. (*Katz* v. *United States*.[19]) In *Katz*, the Court set forth a standard for determining constitutionally protected "zones of privacy"—whether the expectation of privacy in the area to be searched outweighs the government's interest in searching that area, factoring into this analysis the degree of intrusion involved. With *Katz* and preceding cases, the Court developed an interpretation of the Fourth Amendment, and the Bill of Rights as a whole, as protections not only of tangible property, but also of an individual's communications, personality, politics, and thoughts.

The problem with the *Katz* formulation is that its relative standard—a "reasonable expectation of privacy"—can only reflect, not prevent, deterioration in societal respect for privacy. Applying this "reasonable expectation" standard, the Court in later cases often determined that an individual's privacy had not been violated by certain intrusions because society's "expectation of privacy" had been persistently lowered by the circumstances of modern existence. Many people can no longer claim to reasonably expect privacy even in the most intimate activities of their lives.[20]

In a recent case, for example, the Court ruled that the Fourth Amendment protection against unreasonable searches and seizures does not extend to one's garbage once it is removed from the home. The Court rationalized that the garbage is placed on the curb "for the express purpose of conveying it to a third person." (*California v. Greenwood.*[21]) The Court did not place great emphasis on the fact that the garbage owner intended to convey the garbage to the trash collector and not to the police. In this context, it is nearly impossible for one to reasonably tie one's intentions to one's expectations. As one commentator has argued, the flaw in the Court's reasoning in *Greenwood*:

> is that constitutionally protected security is not lost merely because *some* invasion may be expected from *some* invader. The Fourth Amendment protects a car parked overnight on a city street although the owner knows that thieves frequently break into parked cars to steal radios. . . . So it cannot be, as the majority would have it, that a citizen's security is totally lost by the reasonable anticipation that someone—illegally, officially or casually—is likely to penetrate an otherwise protected space. We commonly relinquish interest and control to limited classes of people and for limited and specific purposes.[22]

One's constitutional rights should not depend on the extent to which institutions wear down societal expectations of privacy. Nowhere is the fallibility of the *Katz* "reasonable expectation of privacy" standard more evident than in the Court's holding in *United States* v. *Miller*.[23] The Court in *Miller* ruled that one does not have a constitutionally protected privacy interest in personal records held by a bank. The Court found that a person's bank records do not fall within the "zone of privacy" and are not therefore within the scope of the Fourth Amendment. Bank records may thus be made available to law enforcement without a showing of probable cause to believe that a crime has been committed. The *Miller* decision ultimately turned on the fact that the bank customer could not assert ownership of his documents. The Court held that because Miller's documents were the bank's business records, the expectation of privacy he asserted was not reasonable.[24] The Court reached this conclusion even though most bank customers probably do have an expectation of privacy in these records.

The Court in *Miller* applied a flawed principle. Banks maintain customer records both as a service to customers and for the banks' own recordkeeping purposes. The customer may voluntarily relinquish physical possession of his or her records (or maintain duplicates) but clearly does not intend to lose all control over those records.[25] Customers continue to maintain an interest in the records of a transaction because those records directly represent the transaction. As Justice Brennan dissented in the 5–4 opinion in the *Miller* case:

> A bank customer's reasonable expectation is that, absent a compulsion by legal process, the matters he reveals to the bank will be utilized by the bank only for internal banking purposes. . . . [A] depositor reveals many aspects of his personal affairs, opinions, habits, associations. Indeed, the totality of bank records provides a virtual current biography. . . . Development of photocopying machines, electronic computers and other sophisticated instruments have accelerated the ability of government to intrude into areas which a person normally chooses to exclude from prying eyes and inquisitive minds. Conse-

quently, judicial interpretations of the constitutional protection of individual privacy must keep pace with the perils created by these new devices.[26]

People *do* expect that they are entitled to privacy in their financial affairs. Such a right is essential in a modern society. Financial records, and other records that reflect what we buy, where we travel, what we read, who we communicate with, are extensions of our selves, regardless of where they are stored. They are the "papers" explicitly and separately named as protected by the Fourth Amendment. Nowhere in the Amendment does it say that one's papers must be kept in the home in order to be safe from unwarranted government intrusion.

The *Miller* decision demonstrates the Court's unwillingness to bring the Fourth Amendment into the information age. The fundamental principle of the Fourth Amendment—that individuals have the right to be secure against unreasonable searches and seizures by the government—requires the government to justify the privacy intrusions that result from these searches. However, the Court in *Miller* refused to make the conceptual leap to apply this constitutional standard to personal information held by others.

If there is a constitutional basis for privacy in records stored in the home, the Bill of Rights must also recognize information as private when stored or maintained outside the home. Refusing, however, to move beyond the era in which people stored their personal papers and records in the home, the Supreme Court has stopped short of extending constitutional protection to personal information held by others from whom we receive services and with whom we do business. Although modern society may change the form in which information is stored, the conflict between the government's interest in expanding its power through access to personal information and the individual's interest in retaining a sphere of autonomy against that power, remains the same.

If, as the Supreme Court stated in *Katz*, the Fourth Amendment protects people and not places, it follows that the price of engaging in often unavoidable transactions should not be that we are forced to relinquish any expectation that transactions outside the home are private, particularly given the highly sensitive and intimate nature of many records. Financial, and most other, records generated in the course of one's life, reveal an enormous amount about an individual. More importantly, the combination of separately maintained personal records enables both the prosecutor and the merely curious to create a lifetime dossier and an individual biography.

The Court has only rarely dealt with the issue of whether there are constitutional limits to the government's ability to use personal information that it lawfully possesses. Shortly after the *Miller* decision in 1977, the Supreme Court ruled in another information privacy case on whether the government's mere collection and maintenance of personal information in centralized, computerized files rises to the level of constitutional invasion into an individual's privacy. In *Whalen* v. *Roe*[27] the Court held that a state may maintain files containing the names and addresses of all people who lawfully obtain prescription drugs. The Court found that although one may assert a constitutional privacy right to not disclose personal matters, the state's centralized file did not pose a "sufficient grievous threat to disclosure." In one sense, *Whalen* may be viewed as a positive decision because the Court upheld the statute in question on the grounds that it incorporated "due process safeguards," such as confidentiality and security provisions, to protect against unwarranted disclosures.

The *Whalen* Court asked whether the government's collection of personal information posed a threat to privacy, and decided that it did:

We are not unaware of the threat to privacy implicit in the accumulation of vast amounts of personal information in computerized data banks or other massive government files. The collection of taxes, the distribution of welfare and social security benefits, the supervision of public health, the direction of our Armed Forces, and the enforcement of the criminal laws, all require the orderly preservation of great quantities of information, much of which is personal in character and potentially embarrassing or harmful if disclosed. The right to collect and use such data for public purposes is typically accompanied by a concomitant statutory or regulatory duty to avoid unwarranted disclosures. [We] recognize that in some instances that duty arguably has its roots in the Constitution. ... Broad dissemination of such information, however, would clearly implicate constitutionally protected rights. ... [T]he central computer storage of the data thus collected ... vastly increases the potential for abuse of that information.[28]

The Fourth Amendment is elastic enough to apply to privacy intrusions created by advances in information technology and policy. Because the Court has rigidly refused to expand the scope of the Fourth Amendment to explicitly recognize the right to be secure in one's personal papers held by others, privacy advocates have turned to Congress to address the issue in legislation. Congress has responded by creating zones of privacy around certain information, and enacting a number of information privacy statutes in direct response to Supreme Court decisions.[29]

THE CONGRESSIONAL RESPONSE

The Privacy Act of 1974

Congress has struggled with the problems posed by increasing information collection and use, and the development of new information technologies that transform the way institutions handle information. In the 1960s and early 1970s, Congress held a series of hearings on computers, privacy, and the protection of personal information.[30] Throughout most of the 1960s, Congress considered a proposal to create a centralized national data center on all U.S. citizens containing information such as Social Security numbers, and income and census data. Backers of the proposal argued that the center was necessary to serve the needs of the "welfare state." After years of hearings, studies, and debates, the national data center was overwhelmingly condemned as "Big Brother" government, and a threat to individual autonomy, dignity, and liberty.

At a 1966 hearing, one Representative expressed fear that a centralized federal facility, into which would be "poured information collected from various government agencies and from which computers could draw selected facts, ... could lead to the creation of ... the 'Computerized Man' ... stripped of his individuality and privacy."[31] At the same hearing, Representative Frank Horton (R-NY) extolled the virtues of inefficiency and bureaucracy: "One of the most practical of our present safeguards of privacy is the fragmented nature of present information. It is scattered in little bits and pieces across the geography and years of our life. Retrieval is impractical and often impossible. A central data bank removes completely this safeguard."[32] The plan was abandoned.[33]

It should be noted that one witness at the 1966 hearing on "The Computer and the Invasion of Privacy" warned privacy advocates of the dangers of focusing attention on the central data bank issues.

The problems of the invasion of privacy are, in my view, significant, and they will exist whether or not the central computer bank is created by the Government. Individual data systems, both public and private, now being developed, can be tied together eventually into a network that will present essentially the same problems. . . . Today we are already building the bits and pieces of separate automated information systems in both the private and government sectors that so closely follow the pattern of development to the present integrated communications structure that a de facto version of the system you are now pondering is already in the construction phase. It is in many ways more dangerous than the single data bank now being considered.[34]

By 1973, the Watergate scandal contributed to what had become a national crisis of faith in government institutions and a heightened sensitivity to the unfettered ability of the government to intrude into the personal affairs of its citizens. In this environment, the public became increasingly concerned about the unhampered collection and use of personal records by the government.

Accelerated data sharing of such personally identifiable information among increasing numbers of federal agencies through sophisticated automated systems, coupled with the recent disclosures of serious abuses of governmental authority represented by the collection of personal dossiers, illegal wiretapping, surveillance of innocent citizens, misuse of tax data, and similar types of abuses, have helped to create a growing distrust or even fear of their government in the minds of millions of Americans.[35]

In 1973, an advisory committee within the Department of Health, Education, and Welfare (HEW) published a report entitled *Records, Computers and the Rights of Citizens,*[36] proposing a Code of Fair Information Practices to be used by federal agencies. The basic principles of the Code, which was incorporated into the Privacy Act of 1974 and become legally binding on agencies, are: (1) there must be no personal data record-keeping systems whose very existence is secret; (2) there must be a way for an individual to find out what information is in his or her file and how the information is being used; (3) there must be a way for an individual to correct information in his or her records; (4) any organization creating, maintaining, using, or disseminating records of personally identifiable information must assure the reliability of the data for its intended use and must take precautions to prevent misuse; and (5) there must be a way for an individual to prevent personal information obtained for one purpose from being used for another purpose without consent. This last principle became the heart of the Privacy Act and the information privacy legislation that followed. In passing the Privacy Act of 1974, Congress explicitly recognized that:

1. The privacy of an individual is directly affected by the collection, maintenance, use, and dissemination of personal information by Federal agencies;
2. The increasing use of computers and sophisticated information technology, while essential to the efficient operations of the government, has greatly magnified the harm to individual privacy that can occur from any collection, maintenance, use, or dissemination of personal information;
3. The opportunities for an individual to secure employment, insurance, and credit, and his right to due process, and other legal protections are endangered by the misuse of certain information systems;
4. The right to privacy is a personal and fundamental right protected by the Constitution of the United States; and

> 5. In order to protect the privacy of individuals identified in information systems maintained by Federal agencies, it is necessary and proper for the Congress to regulate the collection, maintenance, use, and dissemination of information by such agencies.[37]

In introducing the Senate version of the Bill, Senator Sam Ervin (D-NC) said: "[T]he appetite of government and private organizations for information about individuals threatens to usurp the right to privacy which I have long felt to be among the most basic of our civil liberties as a free people. . . . [T]here must be limits upon what the government can know about each of its citizens."[38] In drafting the Privacy Act, Congress sought to block the creation of a national data center containing personal information, and curtail the use of the Social Security number (SSN) as a uniform national identifier. Further, Congress found that "[i]f the use of the SSN as an identifier continues to expand, the incentives to link records and broaden access to them are likely to increase."[39]

The purpose of the Act was to "promote accountability, responsibility, legislative oversight and open government with respect to the use of computer technology in the personal information systems and databanks of the federal government."[40] The Act was to serve as an "Information Bill of Rights" for citizens and a "Code of Fair Information Practices" for federal agencies.

To accomplish these goals, the Act establishes a right of privacy in personal information held by federal agencies. With certain exceptions, the Act prohibits government agencies from disclosing information collected for one purpose for a different purpose without the individual's consent. Under the Act, citizens have a right of access to their records and the opportunity to amend their records upon showing that they are not accurate, relevant, timely, or complete. The Act also limits the use of the Social Security number for identification purposes, unless otherwise authorized by law, and prohibits the government from collecting information on the political activities of citizens. Individuals may sue for injunctive relief to enforce some of the Act's provisions, and damages may be awarded by proving that harm occurred as the result of a willful or intentional agency violation of privacy.

The Privacy Act reflects a compromise between very different House and Senate passed bills. The Senate bill created a Privacy Board with oversight powers. The House bill, supported by the Ford Administration, emphasized access to and correction of records. In the final negotiations, many of the stronger Senate provisions were dropped.

Despite the good intentions and clear objectives of its drafters, the Privacy Act has fallen far short of achieving many of its original goals, at best serving as a procedural hoop-jump for federal agencies. A number of factors have severely undermined the Act's effectiveness, including flaws in the Act itself, administrative interpretation, and lack of enforcement. The basic principles of the Privacy Act have failed to limit significantly the government's use of personal information. In fact, agencies have escalated the collection and dissemination of personal information.[41]

For instance, Congress' original intent in enacting the Privacy Act was thwarted by the government's interpretation of the "routine use" exemption, which allows agencies to disclose personal information if the disclosure is *compatible* with the purpose for which it was collected.[42] Government officials have interpreted the exemption to allow the computerized matching of separate agency record systems, arguing that detecting waste, fraud, and abuse in government programs is a legitimate government interest, and is thus compatible with *any* original purpose for which records were collected.[43]

The legislative history of the Act, though, makes it clear that the routine use exemption was intended to facilitate the exchange of information for "*housekeeping measures*," such as completing payroll checks. The purpose of the exemption was to "discourage the unnecessary exchange of information to another person or to agencies who may not be as sensitive to the collecting agency's reasons for using and interpreting the material."[44] A witness at a recent congressional hearing on computer matching testified that the "routine use provision is so big an exemption that you could drive a truck through it."[45]

The government's sweeping interpretation of the exemption contradicts the Act's core provision—that, as a general matter, information collected for one purpose may not be used for a different purpose without the individual's consent.

Debate over the Act's routine use exemption began in 1977 when the Carter Administration instituted "Project Match," a scheme to use computers to compare the Department of Health, Education, and Welfare's (HEW) list of welfare recipients with the Civil Service Commission and the Defense Department federal payroll files in eighteen states. This proposed matching of computerized lists sparked a heated feud between those who viewed matching as an important investigative and auditing tool, and those who believed that the matching of records violated the Privacy Act and intruded on individual liberties.

Many agency officials cited the Act's routine use exemption to justify extensive, inter-agency matching. However, a literal reading of the exemption does not appear to permit matching. In a 1977 letter to HEW, the Civil Service Commission's General Counsel opposed "Project Match" on the grounds that the matching of disparate records violated the Privacy Act. He argued: "Although the literal terms of [the exemption] obviously can not be followed with precision in practical application to agency operations, it is evident that this information on employees was not collected with a view toward detecting welfare abuses."[46] The Commission's counsel went further:

> At the matching stage there is no indication whatsoever that a violation or potential violation of law has occurred . . . It cannot fairly be said . . . that disclosure of information about a particular individual at this preliminary stage is justified by any degree of probability that a violation or potential violation of law has occurred.[47]

The computer matching proponents prevailed. "Project Match" went forward and touched off widespread computer matching within the federal government.[48] The outcome of this debate marked the political swing away from privacy and towards bureaucratic efficiency and revealed the Privacy Act's structural and conceptual weaknesses.

The Privacy Act also prohibits a local, state, or federal agency from requiring an individual's Social Security number as a condition of receiving services or benefits, unless this is authorized by law.[49] The drafters were concerned that the Social Security number was on its way to becoming a national identifier, and would be used as the uniform identifier in linking separate records systems. Yet, Congress has since not only authorized the use of the number, but mandated it. The most striking example is the 1986 Tax Reform Act provision requiring all children over the age of five claimed as dependents on tax returns to have a Social Security number.[50]

To make matters worse, it is extremely difficult for individuals harmed by violations of the Act to bring suit under the Act. The Act's lack of both a broad injunctive relief and liquidated damages provision prevent meaningful litigation of the Act's intent and application. Privacy violations often result in intangible harm to individuals, making it very difficult to prove actual damages as required by the Act.[51]

In 1977, at the height of the initial controversy over the legality of computer matching, the Privacy Protection Study Commission, charged with studying the issues raised by the Privacy Act and recommending future legislation, issued its report, *Personal Privacy in an Information Age*.[52] The Commission was created by the Privacy Act in a provision adopted during final negotiations and accepted as less controversial than creating an Executive branch oversight agency.

The Commission's report recommended that the Privacy Act be more vigorously enforced, and suggested a number of ways to make the Act more effective. The Act, the Commission found, "has not resulted in the general benefits to the public that either its legislative history or the prevailing opinion as to its accomplishments would lead one to expect."[53] The report included a proposed revision of the Act that clarified ambiguities, provided individuals with broader remedies, and tightened the "routine use" exemption. The Commission found that the exemption had "unintended effects," and had been "applied loosely and exclusively from the agency's point of view."[54] It is important to note that these recommendations were published *prior to* the entrenched institutionalization of computer matching. The Commission also recommended that Congress pass additional information privacy legislation to protect information held in private sector databases.

Some privacy advocates blame the Act's failure on Congress' failure to create a federal privacy oversight agency to implement the law. The drafters of the Act did delegate oversight and guidance responsibilities to the Office of Management and Budget (OMB). However, the Privacy Commission, in its report, found that "neither OMB nor any of the other agencies . . . have played an aggressive role in making sure that the agencies are equipped to comply with the Act and are, in fact, doing so. . . . [M]uch of the early momentum appears to have been lost."[55] By 1983, the general consensus among privacy advocates was that OMB had "virtually abdicated responsibility"[56] for enforcing and overseeing the Act.

The Privacy Act is now viewed as a law that requires agencies merely to *notify* individuals before using personal records for a purpose different from that for which they were collected. Notice has become synonymous with consent. Under the Act, individual control over personal information is illusory. As Representative Glenn English (D-OK) remarked during 1983 Privacy Act oversight hearings:

> One of my chief concerns is that the bureaucracy, with the approval of OMB, has drained much of the substance out of the Act. As a result, the Privacy Act tends to be viewed as strictly a procedural statute. For example, agencies feel free to disclose personal information to anyone as long as the proper notices have been published in the Federal Register. No one seems to consider any more whether the Privacy Act prohibits a particular use of information.[57]

The Act's core principles gave way under pressure from the "rise of the computer state,"[58] which provided the government with a hard-to-resist temptation to shift its emphasis away from giving individuals some control over personal information to fostering a system of nearly unrestrained collection and use. The political pendulum swung away from protecting privacy and fostering government accountability and towards improving bureaucratic efficiency. Today, the official presumption appears to be: the more the government knows about you, the better.

A recent development in government efficiency is the use of a technique called "front-end verification." This technique allows government officials to verify information electronically by matching records on a case-by-case basis *at the time* an individual applies for benefits; i.e., at the "front end." For bureaucrats, the appeal of front-end verification is that it reduces benefit payment errors; noneligibility is detected before, rather than after, an individual has received any benefits. Some argue that this process is less of a privacy intrusion than traditional matching because it involves a search through a particular person's files rather than a massive search or "fishing expedition." However, the unchecked growth of verification systems linking various databases of personal information on every citizen poses a serious danger to individual autonomy and privacy.

The success of front-end verification depends on systems that provide rapid access to complete and accurate information. The threat is thus the same as in computer matching—concern for efficiency presses for the aggregation and linkage of multiple agency databases to create a *de facto* national database on all citizens. In fact, an FBI Advisory Policy Board recently proposed providing the Bureau access to the record systems of the Department of Health and Human Services, the Internal Revenue Service, the Social Security Administration, and the Immigration and Naturalization Service. For now, the Bureau's attempt to create a federal agency clearinghouse of information for use by the law enforcement community has been defeated.[59]

Despite the long-standing concerns of Congress and privacy advocates about the government's attempt to establish a national data center, it appears that a *de facto* national database already exists, sustained by on-line linkages that allow information to be stored in decentralized form, but instantly assembled at the press of a button. A crucial element in this database linkage is the use of one form of identification, most often the Social Security number.

Congress has encouraged this development by enacting legislation that undermines the Privacy Act's original principles, allowing greater information collection and exchange through the mandated linkage and comparison of personal information held in separate databases, and requiring the use of the Social Security number to facilitate this process. For instance, in establishing the Income Eligibility Verification System (IEVS) in the Deficit Reduction Act of 1984, Congress authorized the use of the Social Security number for all needs-based programs to make possible the accurate identification of applicants and to permit the computerized retrieval of information on applicants in discrete databases containing information on wage, pension, unemployment insurance, and other income data, including unearned income from Internal Revenue Service (IRS) files.[60]

In addition, the Tax Reform Act of 1986 includes a provision requiring all children over the age of five who are claimed as dependents on a tax return to have a Social Security number.[61] The stated reason for this sweeping requirement is to catch non-custodial parents who claim their children as dependents. Although tax fraud is a legitimate government problem, this provision reflects Congress' current unwillingness to address the threat posed by a national identification system that numbers all individuals for government record-keeping purposes.[62]

Front-end verification—and the systems needed to sustain it—pose the grave problem of greater collection of an access to personal information, resulting in the ultimate loss of individual control, autonomy, and dignity. It is not only the danger of being "just a number" that is of concern here, but also providing the government and private institutions the ability to track and profile us from birth to death, creating what Arthur Miller termed a "womb-to-tomb dossier."[63]

Despite its apparent abandonment of privacy as a primary goal of federal policy, in 1988 Congress enacted the first significant amendment to the Privacy Act. The Computer Matching and Privacy Protection Act of 1988[64] brings the computerized matching of records under the wing of the Act. Under the new law, matching is no longer treated as a "routine use" of personal records held by federal agencies. The Act prohibits agencies from taking any adverse action against an individual based on a match until the results have been independently verified. Before conducting a match, agencies must now enter into written agreements specifying the purpose of the match, the records to be matched, and a cost/benefit analysis of the match. The legislation does not limit in any way the content or types of records that can be matched, but does create an important procedural framework of more adequate notice to individuals, the right to a hearing before benefits are cut off or denied, and mandatory reporting requirements for agencies that match records.

Protecting Personal Records
Held By Private Institutions

In the last eighteen years, Congress has made substantial progress in legislation regulating government and private access to privately held personal information.

—In 1970, Congress passed the Fair Credit Reporting Act,[65] prohibiting credit and investigation reporting agencies that collect, store, and sell information on consumers' credit worthiness from disclosing records to anyone other than authorized customers. The Act requires the agencies to allow consumers to review their own records and correct inaccurate information. The legislation created a legal framework in which the reporting companies could operate, and was passed in response to the public's growing awareness and concern about personal information maintained by credit reporting bureaus.

—Four years later, the Family Educational Rights and Privacy Act[66] was passed, limiting disclosure of educational records to third parties. The law requires schools and colleges to let students see their records and challenge and correct inaccurate information in their records.

—In 1978, Congress passed the Right to Financial Privacy Act,[67] in response to the Supreme Court's decision on the privacy of bank records in the *Miller* case and in direct response to the Privacy Protection Study Commission's recommendation that *Miller* be superceded by remedial legislation. Congress strengthened the Privacy Act's "consent" principle by creating a statutory Fourth Amendment protection for bank records. The Right to Financial Privacy Act includes a minimum due process standard, and a court order provision that requires law enforcement to meet a standard of relevance before records can be released. The Act is the result of a hard-won compromise between the civil liberties community, bankers, the Department of Justice, and Congress.

—In 1980, Congress passed the Privacy Protection Act[68] to prohibit the government from searching press offices without a warrant if no one in the office is suspected of committing a crime.

—In 1982, Congress passed the Debt Collection Act[69] requiring federal agencies to provide individuals with due process protections before an individual's federal debt information may be referred to a private credit bureau.

—In 1984, Congress enacted the Cable Communications Policy Act to safeguard the confidentiality of interactive cable television subscriber records. The Act includes the highest court order standard ever enacted that must be met by law enforcement before subscriber records can be disclosed. The Act requires that cable subscription records may only be disclosed pursuant to a court order that shows by "clear and convincing evidence that the subject of the information is reasonably suspected of engaging in criminal activity and that the information sought would be material evidence in the case." Further, the individual must have the opportunity to challenge the court order before the records are disclosed.[70]

—In 1986, the Electronic Communications Privacy Act (ECPA) was passed, amending the Wiretap Law to cover the interception of *non*-aural communications. Under the Act, law enforcement officials may not obtain information held by a data communications company, such as MCI, without a warrant that meets the probable cause standard. ECPA also overturns the Supreme Court's ruling in *Smith v. Maryland* that telephone toll records are not private. Under ECPA, law enforcement officials must show there is "reason to believe the contents of a wire or electronic communication, or the records or other information sought, are relevant to a legitimate law enforcement inquiry," before obtaining access to transactional data such as telephone toll records. ECPA represents a recognition of the need to protect information regardless of the technological advances that have shaped its use.

—The Video Privacy Protection Act of 1988, passed at the end of the 100th Congress, includes a strong court order standard modeled on the Cable Act. Videocassette rental records, like cable subscriber records, can reveal information about individual preferences and political beliefs. Congress has been quick to create strong protections in such areas where First and Fourth Amendment concerns intersect.[71]

These recent laws reflect Congress' willingness to fashion strict disclosure standards for sensitive information held by private institutions. Implicit in these new laws is a legislative recognition that expectations of privacy can be created and enforced—a particularly crucial recognition in an age in which information practices continue to erode our constitutionally protected "reasonable" expectations.

PROPOSALS FOR THE FUTURE

The Rewrite of the Privacy Act

There is a general consensus that the Privacy Act of 1974 is ineffective, obsolete, and needs to be rewritten.[72] Neither the absence of a vigorous privacy protection commission nor scattered, weak implementation by OMB can be blamed exclusively for the law's failure. At this stage, the emphasis should be on rewriting the Privacy Act. A privacy oversight agency, without strong, clear provisions to enforce, would continue to be a political tool in the hands of changing administrations.[73]

Only enforceable limits on what personal information can be collected and how it can be used can give individuals meaningful control over the information they divulge in exchange for receiving benefits and services from the government. The Act currently lacks such substantive limits.

In addition, much of the Act has been rendered obsolete by advances in information technology and the drive to adopt new technological capacities for data collection and consolidation. Recent statutes take into account more modern techniques of intrusion, but, on the whole, privacy legislation has not effectively erected barriers around information. Instead, the Privacy Act and the bulk of information privacy statutes aimed at information held by private institutions, require only that a series of procedural maneuvers be completed before an agency or institution can divulge records.

Due process safeguards are more than just good "data use manners," and may be genuinely protective in some instances, but more is needed to protect individuals. Notice and consent procedures are not strong enough protection for personal information in the control of the government; *the government's collection and use of certain types of information, such as for tax, census, and public benefit purposes, should be limited, and even, in some cases, prohibited.* Such limits are necessary to give individuals meaningful control over information about themselves; to grant people the right to control what the government (and others) may know about their lives.

The law should be redrafted to strengthen the Act's fundamental principles, giving individuals tangible control over information they disclose to government agencies either by law (i.e., for census and tax purposes) or as a condition of receiving government benefits or services. Government agencies should be authorized to collect only information that is necessary and relevant to their particular purpose. Agencies must inform individuals of the reasons why personal information is being collected and for what purposes it will be used. An individual must have the right to challenge a particular collection or use either through administrative or court action. The Privacy Act already includes an adequate procedure for agencies to follow before disclosing records pursuant to a law enforcement investigation.

In addition, the Act's "routine use" exemption must be revamped so that the law will work as intended. A clear and restrictive definition of routine use must be added to the statute clarifying that disclosure for a routine use must be *consistent* with the original purpose for which the information was initially collected. Individuals must have the right to challenge a proposed routine use on the grounds that it is not consistent with the purpose for which the information was originally collected. Routine use disclosures under this definition must be benign and not for the purpose of taking adverse action against an individual.

The Privacy Act needs a new remedy section that provides both liquidated damages and injunctive relief for any aggrieved individual. Currently, an individual may not sue under the Act unless he or she can prove willful and intentional misconduct by an agency official. Individuals must be able to collect damages for intangible harms caused by violations of the Act.

Information Privacy Policy Initiatives

For the future, privacy advocates must push for policy initiatives to protect medical, insurance, personnel, and retail records as well as personal information held by the government. The policy goal is the creation of federal statutory rights of information privacy, tailoring standards that incorporate a balance between the sensitivity of the information at stake and the institutional justification or need for the information—the more sensitive the information, the more compelling the need must be for its collection and the higher the standard must be for its disclosure to others.

The guiding principles in drafting legislation should be:

1. Information Collected for One Purpose Should Not Be Used for a Different Purpose Without the Individual's Consent Any unauthorized use of the information must give rise to an enforcement action by the harmed individual. The goal is to create legislatively mandated expectations of privacy in information.

2. Policy Should Be Developed with an Eye Towards New Advances in Information Technology and Telecommunications It may not be possible to anticipate every advance, but the law should be elastic enough to apply to information regardless of whether it is in electronic or manual form. In this way, the numbing cliché that technology is constantly outpacing the law may be overcome.

3. Legal Limits Should Be Placed on the Collection and Use of Sensitive Information—The More Sensitive the Information, the More Rigorous the Disclosure Standard Personal information, such as census data and certain medical records, should never be disclosed for any purpose, whereas less sensitive records might be available for legal proceedings. For sensitive information, law enforcement officials must demonstrate probable cause or reasonable suspicion to believe a crime has been committed and that the information they seek relates to that crime. Individuals must receive notice before a court-ordered disclosure, and have an opportunity to challenge the disclosure.

4. Individuals Must Be Provided with Easy Access to Their Records, Including Access to Computerized Records, for the Purpose of Copying, Correcting, or Completing Information in the Records Computer technology should allow individuals on-line access to their records.[74] Legislation should mandate an access procedure, and require that information be kept accurate, complete, and up-to-date. Records that are no longer relevant for the purpose for which they were collected should be destroyed.

5. Exemptions for Non-Disclosure Should Be Clearly Justified and Narrowly Tailored to Suit the Requestor's Need Exemptions should explicitly define the intended scope of the allowable disclosure to avoid expansion or misinterpretation of the provision.

6. Legislation Should Include Enforcement Mechanisms, Such as Injunctive Relief, Civil Damages, Criminal Penalties, and Reimbursement of Attorney's Fees and Costs By putting teeth into information privacy legislation, individuals will be able to enforce the law and seek redress for violation of their privacy rights. Injunctive relief can prevent damage before it occurs, damages can compensate aggrieved individuals, and criminal penalties can punish those who violate the law. In addition, these individual enforcement mechanisms can be buttressed by institutional enforcement and oversight, such as by the promulgation of implementation guidelines, giving Privacy Act officers in each agency greater enforcement powers, and strengthening congressional oversight. Each of these enforcement mechanisms will deter unauthorized information gathering and exchange.

Momentum exists for building on recent successes to press for new information privacy initiatives. Work should continue towards the passage of laws that incorporate standards tailored to the sensitivity of the information involved.

CONCLUSION

Our right to privacy dwindles each year, giving way under the tremendous institutional pressure to collect and use information. The push for strong laws to protect information privacy is not a partisan issue. As stated in the 1980 Republican Party Platform:

> Government in recent years, particularly at the Federal level, has overwhelmed citizens with demands for personal information and has accumulated vast amounts of such data through the IRS, the Social Security Administration, the Bureau of the Census, and other agencies. Under certain limited circumstances, such information can serve legitimate societal interests, but there must be protection against abuse. ... We are alarmed by Washington's growing collection and dissemination of such data. There must be protection against its misuse and disclosure.

The momentum to protect personal information held by federal agencies, sparked by years of hearings, privacy abuses and culminating in the Watergate scandal, was maintained long enough for Congress to pass the Privacy Act of 1974. In addition, Congress has responded to the pressing need to protect personal information maintained by private institutions. Privacy advocates must continue to seize upon such targets of opportunity to heighten public awareness about the need for privacy legislation. Advances in information technology create legislative opportunities. Again, the Department of Health and Human Services is moving forward with a plan to link computers in 52,000 pharmacies nationwide to centralize, exchange, and audit information on Medicare beneficiaries. The FBI is proposing a massive expansion of its central computer system. These proposals all pose serious threats to individual privacy. Privacy advocates must inject their voices into the planning process to create a forum for debate on information and individual privacy.

NOTES

1. *Olmstead v. United States*, 277 U.S. 438, 478 (1928) (J. Brandeis dissenting).
2. House Comm. on Government Operations, *Who Cares About Privacy? Oversight of the Privacy Act of 1974 by the Office of Management and Budget and the Congress*, H.R. Rep. 455, 98th Cong., 1st Sess. (1983).
3. L. Harris, *The Road After 1984: A Nationwide Survey of the Public and Its Leaders in the New Technology and Its Consequences for American Life* (1983) (hereinafter Harris Survey). This Harris Survey documented that in 1983 forty-eight percent of the public described themselves as "very concerned" about technology and threats to personal privacy, double those in 1978. Sixty percent of the public believe the use of computers must be severely limited to safeguard privacy. A majority of the public takes the position that the release of personal information by government agencies to other agencies seriously invades personal privacy.
4. Harris Survey.

5. In 1987, Congressman Don Edwards (D-CA) convened a panel of privacy, criminal justice, and computer security experts to evaluate a set of FBI-developed changes to its information systems. The panel's report, submitted for consideration to the FBI's Advisory Policy Board (APB), appears to have had an impact on the decisionmaking process. Of the 246 proposals originally contemplated by the APB, only 81 were ultimately recommended for implementation. The panel is continuing to critique an FBI proposal to use the NCIC to track and surveil individuals suspected of certain crimes.

6. The proposed system involves the participation of 52,000 pharmacies across the nation in a computer network designed to process electronically the prescription drug bills of 32 million Medicare beneficiaries. The Health Care Financing Administration branch of HHS is currently seeking input on the implementation of the system, with a proposal for funding to be submitted in the fall of 1989. Privacy advocates plan to press for the incorporation of substantive privacy protections before the funding proposal is submitted.

7. Office of Technology Assessment, *Federal Government Information Technology: Electronic Record Systems and Individual Privacy* at 1 (1986) (hereinafter OTA Report).

8. Bloustein, *Privacy as an Aspect of Human Dignity: An Answer to Prosser*, 39 N.Y.U. L. Rev. 962 (1964).

9. For purposes of this paper, the ability to control information about one's self is termed "information privacy," traditionally defined as "the claim of individuals, groups or institutions to determine for themselves when, how, and to what extent information about them is communicated to others." A. Westin, *Privacy and Freedom*, at 39 (1967).

10. *NAACP* v. *Alabama* 357 U.S. 449 (1958); *Stanley* v. *Georgia* 394 U.S. 557 (1969).

11. *Mapp* v. *Ohio* 367 U.S. 643 (1961).

12. *Griswold* v. *Connecticut* 381 U.S. 479 (1965).

13. *Meyer* v. *Nebraska*, 262 U.S. 390 (1923).

14. *Boyd* v. *United States*, 116 U.S. 616 (1886); *Katz* v. *United States*, 389 U.S. 347 (1967).

15. Shattuck, *In the Shadow of 1984: National Identification Systems, Computer Matching, and Privacy in the United States*, 35 Hastings L.J. 991 (1984).

16. *Boyd* v. *United States*, 116 U.S. 616, 630 (1886).

17. Shortly after *Boyd*, came the publication of Warren and Brandeis, *The right to Privacy* 4 Harv. L. Rev. 193 (1890).

18. *NAACP* v. *Alabama* 357 U.S. 449 (1958).

19. *Katz* v. *United States*, 389 U.S. 347, 353 (1967).

20. In 1986 the Supreme Court in *Bowers* v. *Hardwick* 478 U.S. 186 (1986), *rehearing denied* 478 U.S. 1039 (1986), upheld Georgia's sodomy statute, finding that one does not have a constitutional right to privately engage in consensual sexual conduct. In that case, Georgia charged a man with violating the state's criminal sodomy statute after "catching" him in the act in his own bedroom. The police entered the home to execute a warrant for a traffic violation.

21. 56 U.S.L.W. 4409 (U.S. May 16, 1988) (No. 86-684).

22. Uviller, "The Fourth Amendment: Does It Protect Your Garbage?", *The Nation, October 10, 1988, at 303.*

23. 425 U.S. 345 (1976).

24. A similar analysis was used to find that one does not have a reasonable expectation of privacy in telephone toll records, *Smith* v. *Maryland*, 442 U.S. 735 (1979).

25. Banks, in essence, perform a fiduciary/trustee function with regard to customer records. Thus, a customer may relinquish physical possession of his or her records, while still maintaining some element of control or ownership of the records.

26. *United States* v. *Miller* at 449–452, quoting *Burrows* v. *Superior Court* 529 P.2d 590 (1974).

27. 429 U.S. 589 (1977).

28. *Id.* at 605. In a recent case involving whether the FOIA applies to the release of criminal history records maintained by the FBI, Judge Starr of the District Court of Appeals noted in his dissent that if the FBI is required to release records from its name-indexed, computerized files, "the federal government is thereby transformed in one fell swoop into *the* clearinghouse for highly personal information, releasing records on any person, to any requester, for any purpose. ... [T]his new-fangled regime will have a pernicious effect on personal privacy interests in conflict with Congress' express will." The Supreme Court agreed to hear the case, and briefs were submitted in June, 1988. *Reporter's Committee for Freedom of the Press* v. *Department of Justice* 831 F.2d 1124 (D.C. Cir. 1987), *cert. granted*, 56 U.S.L.W. 3718 (U.S. April 18, 1988) (No. 87-1379)

29. *See* text at 385–386 *infra*.

30. *The Computer and Invasion of Privacy: Hearing Before the Special Subcomm. on Invasion of Privacy of the House Comm. on Government Operations* 89th Cong., 2d Sess. (1966) (hereinafter 1966 House Privacy Hearings); *Federal Data Banks, Computers and the Bill of Rights: Hearings Before the Subcomm. on Constitutional Rights of the Senate Comm. on the Judiciary*, 92nd Cong., 1st Sess. (1971) (hereinafter 1971 Senate Privacy Hearings; and *Privacy: The Collection, Use and Computerization of Personal Data: Joint Hearings Before the Subcomm. on Privacy and Information Systems of the Senate Comm. on Government Operations and the Subcomm. on Constitutional Rights of the Senate Comm. on the Judiciary*, 93rd Cong., 2d Sess. (1974).

31. 1966 House Privacy Hearings, at 2 (statement of Rep. Cornelius Gallagher (D-NJ)).

32. *Id.* at 6 (statement of Rep. Horton).

33. The House Special Committee on Invasion of Privacy released a report in 1968 "Privacy and the National Data Concept," recommending that plans for a data center be postponed until the confidentiality and security of centralized information could be assured.

34. 1966 House Privacy Hearings, at 120–122 (testimony of Paul Baran, Rand Corp.)

35. H.R. Rep. No. 1416, 93rd Cong., 2d Sess. 3 (1974), *reprinted in* Source Book, at 296. Also during this period, a number of books were published that signaled the decline of freedom in the new age of computerized data banks. See Miller, *The Assault on Privacy* (1971) and Westin and Baker, *Databanks in a Free Society: Computers, Recordkeeping, and Privacy* (1972).

36. U.S. Department of Health, Education, and Welfare, *Records, Computers and the Rights of Citizens: Report of the Secretary's Advisory Committee on Automated Personal Data Systems* (1973).

37. Privacy Act of 1974, 5 U.S.C. §552a(2)(a)(1974).

38. Cong. Rec. S. 6741 (May 1, 1974) (Introductory Remarks of Sen. Ervin on S.3418) *reprinted in* Senate Comm. on Government Operations and Subcomm. on Government Information and Individual Rights of the House Comm. on Government Operations, 94th Cong., 2d Sess., *Legislative History of the Privacy Act of 1974 S.3418 (Public Law 93-579): Source Book on Privacy*, 5 (Joint Comm. Print 1976) (hereinafter Source Book).

39. *Id.* at 30, *reprinted in* Source Book, at 183. The Senate Committee report on the Privacy Act described the burgeoning use of the Social Security number as "one of the most serious manifestations of privacy concerns in the nation," clearing the way for a national data bank. *Id.* at 28, *reprinted in* Source Book, at 181.

40. S. Rep. No. 1183, 93rd Cong., 2d Sess. 1 (1974), *reprinted in* Source Book, at 154.

41. In a 1986 report, the congressional Office of Technology Assessment (OTA) found that federal agencies and departments held 3.5 billion records in the record systems as defined by the Privacy Act. Nearly half of those systems were computerized, with agencies reporting an increase in microcomputers from a few thousand in 1980 to 100,000 in 1985. OTA Report, at 12.

42. 5 U.S.C. § 552a(b)(3)(1974).

42. A 1980 notice of a proposed match published in the *Federal Register* stated that a match between the records of Office of Personnel Management (OPM) and the Veterans' Administration was for a "routine use": "An integral part of the reason these records are maintained is to protect the legitimate interests of the government, and therefore, such a disclosure is compatible with the purposes for maintaining these records."

44. Source Book, at 859–860.

45. *Computer Matching and Privacy Protection Act of 1986: Hearings on S.2756 Before the Subcomm. on Oversight of Government Management of the Senate Comm. on Governmental Affairs* 99th Cong., 2d Sess. at 29 (Comm. Print 1986) (Ronald Plesser testifying on behalf of the American Bar Association).

46. Letter from Carl F. Goodman, General Counsel, Civil Service Commission, to Charles Ruff, Deputy Inspector General, Department of Health, Education and Welfare, (July 27, 1977), *reprinted in, Oversight of Computer Matching to Detect Fraud and Mismanagement in Government Programs: Hearings Before the Subcomm. on Oversight of Government Management of the Senate Comm. on Governmental Affairs* 97th Cong., 2d Sess. at 122–25 (Comm. Print 1982).

47. *Id.*

48. A 1986 Office of Technology Assessment (OTA) report found that matching has become an integral part of the operation of many government agencies. In 1984, agencies conducted 110 separate matching programs, totalling nearly 700 matches and involving 2 billion separate records. OTA Report.

49. 5 U.S.C. §552a (1974).

50. Tax Reform Act of 1986, 26 U.S.C. § 6109(e) (1986).

51. In contrast, all of the federal wiretap statutes provide for liquidated damages. *See* e.g., the Electronic Communications Privacy Act of 1986, 18 U.S.C. § 2703 (1986).

52. The Privacy Protection Study Commission, *The Privacy Act of 1974: An Assessment*, (1977) (hereinafter Privacy Protection Commission Report).

53. Privacy Protection Commission Report, app. 4, at 113.

54. *Id.* at 120.

55. *Id.* at 21.

56. *Oversight of the Privacy Act of 1974: Hearings before a Subcomm. of the House Comm. on Government Operations* 98th Cong., 1st Sess. 259 (1983) (statement of John Shattuck, ACLU) (hereinafter 1983 House Privacy Act Oversight Hearings). *See also*, House Comm. on Government Operations, *Who Cares About Privacy? Oversight of the Privacy Act of 1974 by the Office of Management and Budget and the Congress* H.R. Rep. No. 455, 98th Cong., 1st Sess. (1983).

57. 1983 House Privacy Act Oversight Hearings, at 5 (opening Statement of Rep. English (D-OK)).

58. David Burnham, *The Rise of the Computer State* (1985).

59. *See* note 4 *supra*.

60. Deficit Reduction Act of 1984, 98-369, 98 Stat. 494 (1984).

61. 26 U.S.C. § 6109(e) (1986).

62. The legislative history of the Privacy Act reveals Congress' previously deep concern about the expanded use of the Social Security number: "[O]nce the Social Security number is set as a universal identifier, each person would leave a trail of personal data behind him for all his life which could be immediately reassembled to confront him. ... [W]e can be pinpointed wherever we are, we can be more easily manipulated, we can be more easily conditioned and we can be more easily coerced." Cong. Rec. (September 19, 1974) (statement of Sen. Goldwater), *reprinted in* Source Book, at 760. In addition, government agencies are considering proposals for a national identification card to enforce the Immigration Reform Act, to distribute food stamps, and to process welfare applications.

63. 1971 Senate Privacy Hearings, pt. 1, at 9.

64. The Computer Matching and Privacy Protection Act of 1988, 5 U.S.C. 552a (1988).

65. § 15 U.S.C. § 1681 (1970).

66. 20 U.S.C. § 1232g (1974).

67. 12 U.S.C. § 3401 (1978).

68. 42 U.S.C. § 2000aa (1980).

69. 31 U.S.C. § 952 (1982).

70. Cable Communications Policy Act, 47 U.S.C. § 551 (1984).

71. The initiative for the Video Privacy Protection Act grew out of the unauthorized disclosure of the Bork family's video rental list to a reporter during Judge Robert Bork's confirmation hearings for the United States Supreme Court. At that time, many Senators expressed outrage at this intrusion into the Bork family's privacy, characterizing the disclosure as an "issue that goes to the deepest yearning of all Americans that we ... cherish our freedom ... [and] we want to be left alone." *Nomination of Robert H. Bork to be Associate Justice of the Supreme Court of the United States: Hearings before the Senate Committee on the Judiciary* 100th Cong., 1st Sess., 1374 (1987) (remarks of Sen. Patrick Leahy, D-VT).

72. In its 1986 report, OTA concluded that "federal use of new electronic technologies in processing personal information has eroded the protections" of the Privacy Act. OTA found that many information practices are not covered by the Act, and that there is scant oversight and inadequate remedies to ensure agency compliance. OTA Report at 4.

73. In 1977, the Privacy Protection Study Commission recommended that a privacy protection agency be established, but in conjunction with the passage of strong, enforceable information privacy laws. At that point, the Privacy Act should have been strengthened by legislative amendment, agency regulations, and strict congressional oversight.

74. Computer technology should be used to enhance privacy. For instance, computer audit trails can be used to inform citizens about how information about them is used, and may act as a deterrent to unauthorized access and unnecessary uses of personal information.

CHAPTER FIVE

The Risks of Computing

INTRODUCTION

Computer systems are present in virtually all spheres of public and private life, holding the key to the quality of life and, at times, to life itself. They control the functioning of life-critical equipment such as spacecraft, aircraft, medical treatment machines, power plants, vast communications networks, and military equipment. They support the infrastructures of governments, corporations, and financial institutions. And even in the mundane and basic machinery of day-to-day life we rely on computers—on automated teller machines, microwaves, telephones, libraries, stereo systems, and of course, personal computers. An increasing dependence on computers and digital technology implies an increasing vulnerability to malfunction. In this chapter we focus on the implications for society of faulty computers and computer-controlled systems, the harms they cause, and the harms they threaten. The readings in this chapter describe and explain cases of computer malfunctions providing insight into the sources of failure, and what can be done about them. Their purpose is to illustrate the practical risks of computing and at the same time stimulate thinking about how we may balance these risks against the advantages that computerization offers to society.

When Things Go Wrong: Cases and Examples

Anyone who has worked with computers or with computer-controlled systems, will almost certainly have had experience with computer "downtime", with systems "out of order", and with bugs. What is the extent of these malfunctions, and how do computer malfunctions affect the various systems they control? Actual cases provide sound beginnings for more general discussions of system reliability and the risks inherent in computing. Through readings that describe specific cases of computer system failures readers will gain practical insight into the nature and scope of computer system malfunctions and their associated risks. The articles by Alan Borning, and Bev Littlewood and Lorenzo Strigini are rich in case materials, and provide insight into failures, and near-failures, of systems in a variety of arenas including, for example, mass transportation, communications networks, and the military.

Studying examples from real-life experience with a technology serves a dual purpose. On the one hand, it can provide valuable technical lessons to those engaged in developing and applying a technology on the nature and scope of risks. Computer professionals can learn from past mistakes how to improve their practice and their products. On the other, because actual cases inevitably involve more than merely technical conundra, they are fruitful subjects of discussion from an ethical and social perspective. In many cases, it is not merely the failure of a technology that causes a problem, but in addition, a failure in social, or organizational decision making.

Sources of Failure and Risk—Comparison with Other Technologies

Someone might question whether it is necessary to separate the study of the risks of computing from the study of the risks of technologies in general. There are a number of common themes that emerge from the general study of technological failures and malfunctions, such as reckless disregard for warning signals, insufficient attention to safety, and shortsightedness, that emerge also in notable cases in computing. Cases like the ones described by Littlewood and Strigini, and Borning share many of these elements with other well-known historical cases, like the explosion of the space shuttle *Challenger*, the sinking of the *Titanic*, and the fatally flawed Ford Pinto gas tank. However, some authors have argued that computing is different enough from other technologies to warrant special attention. In other words, while there is much that we can learn from the experiences of other technologies, there are some lessons that need to come from the study of computing failures themselves.

Fernando J. Corbato's article identifies similarities and differences between computers and other products of technology as it focuses on the challenge of creating large, yet reliable, complex computer systems. He uses the notion of an "ambitious system" to describe systems that are elaborate, extensive, and complex, and that stretch the limits of organizational and individual capacities beyond current state-of-the-art. While ambitious systems can be found in all spheres of technology, computing has more than its fair share because of the fast pace of change and progress that has characterized the field over the past few decades. Greater numbers of computer systems exist at the "cutting edge" of the field. On the positive side, ambitious systems contribute toward scientific and technological progress; on the negative side, they tend to be risky and unreliable. Corbato writes, "ambitious systems never quite work as expected. Things usually go wrong—sometimes in dramatic ways." The very features that entitle a system to be called "ambitious" are the features that increase their proneness to error.

Other authors have contended that in computing the demands of building reliable and safe systems are different from those of other technologies not only quantitatively—because of a faster pace of progress—but qualitatively—because of the nature of the technology. The articles by Bev Littlewood and Lorenzo Strigini, Brian Smith, and David Parnas, John van Schouwen, and Shu Po Kwan, highlight distinctive aspects of computer systems. These authors agree that it is virtually impossible to locate and eradicate all the errors (bugs) in complex computer systems and that furthermore, their impacts are highly unpredictable. Parnas explains that because a "small" fault can lead to a massive failure, one cannot ensure the safety of a system by means of traditional methods of "over-engineering." Smith points out that computer system correctness depends on correctness on at least two levels. Even if a program is formally correct—that is, is internally consistent, has no grammatical errors, and performs according to specification—the specifications themselves may be incorrect. Several of the articles in this section describe cases in which incorrect models of the world caused systems to fail. A dramatic example, which is discussed both by Smith and Borning, is the case of an early warning radar system that indicated an all-out attack by the Russians. It turned out that the warning was triggered by the moon's rising, which had not been taken into consideration by the system's model.

The paper by Henry Petroski offers yet another perspective on the source of the risks of computing. He focuses not on the failure of computer systems, as such, but failure in the way people use and perceive these systems. Petroski describes the collapse of a large public building, the Hartford Civic Center, which he attributes to overconfidence on the part of the engineers who designed the structure on the calculations of their computer-aided design systems. Had the engineers thought to confirm these calculations against the trained intuitions of traditional engineering know-how, they immediately would have seen that the design they proposed was unsound. Thus public well-being is at risk not only when systems actually fail, but when the users of these systems misunderstand their limitations.

Reducing Risks and Value Implications

Understanding the source of computer system failure and their risks to society is a first step toward achieving safer, more reliable, and more trustworthy systems. If perfection is not achievable, what should the intermediate goals be and how can we achieve them? The article by Parnas, van Shouwen and Kwan, suggests that many problems are caused by bad systems building practices. They prescribe various ways to significantly improve the degree of system safety and reliability, including a more systematic approach to systems engineering, better and more thorough testing practices designed to target the specific pitfalls associated with computer systems, a professional education that emphasizes issues of reliability and safety, and a more active role for professional organizations in promoting standards of excellence and promulgating a greater sense of professional responsibility.

Once we grasp that there are steps we could take toward building safer and more reliable systems, one may well wonder why the systems we have and use are not in fact safer and more reliable. Is it that software producers are willfully ignoring these recommendations, are merely sloppy, or insufficiently skilled? Although this may explain some of the inadequacies, several other considerations are relevant to the question of why software is not perfect, or at least, not as good as it could be. One is that despite the development of techniques in software engineering that offer the means to create better software than we created in the past, these techniques are not fail safe. Thus, software remains prone to the range of problems raised in the articles in this chapter—though their occurrence will be less frequent. Furthermore, because many of the proposed techniques are relatively new to the field, they take time to filter from development into production. Finally, the quest for safety and reliability is costly in a variety of ways and this too acts as a barrier to the achievement of less risky systems.

What are some of the costs of producing more reliable software, and safer systems? First, the producers of software will need to spend more money on a product to cover the extra time and effort it would take to develop and test it. Second, they are likely to see explicit guidelines for creating and testing software as a constraint on their business freedom— a cost they are likely to spurn. Finally, a better education for software engineers, which teaches more rigorous, safety-oriented engineering and testing procedures, is, at least in the short run, likely to be more expensive.

Because the benefits of less risky computing are likely to be accompanied by these costs, we will need to face questions about competing values. The pursuit of less risky software becomes, therefore, not merely a technical one, but an ethical one as well. Questions we will want to consider include: How safe *should* a system be? At what cost should we insist upon safer systems? If too costly, should we forgo safety, or forgo the system? To what extent are we willing to sacrifice the sheer quantity of software being produced by insisting on a certain degree of safety? And finally, in whose hands should we place these decisions: corporate producers, politicians, engineering professionals, or end-users?

When reading the articles in this chapter, readers should bear in mind these questions about values. In the chapter that follows, we continue to focus on the quality of computing, shifting perspective from risk to responsibility.

CASE
▷ **COMPUTER SYSTEM RELIABILITY AND NUCLEAR WAR**

Alan Borning

Given the devastating consequences of nuclear war, it is appropriate to look at current and planned uses of computers in nuclear weapons command and control systems, and to examine whether these systems can fulfill their intended roles.

How dependent should society be on computer systems and computer decision making? What are the cost-benefit trade-offs between the advantages of computerization (greater efficiency, speed, precision, and so forth), and the jeopardy we are in when critical computer systems break down or otherwise fail to meet our intentions? These questions arise most compellingly in the use of computers in command and control systems for nuclear weapons, and it is on such uses that this article will concentrate. In this context the problem of defining "reliability" is clearly at issue. Obviously the concept extends beyond merely keeping a system running and invades the realm of system intention or even of *what we should have intended—had we only known.* To what extent are we able to state and codify our intentions in computer systems so that *all* circumstances are covered? Such questions have profound implications for the entire field of computer science; they also have important practical implications about how and where it is appropriate for us to use computers in critical systems.

Computers are used extensively in military applications: for managing data on friendly and enemy forces, simulating possible battles, and aiding in the design of weapons systems, as well as for such mundane tasks as keeping track of personnel, inventories, and payrolls. Nuclear forces in particular depend heavily on computer systems to guide missiles, analyze sensor data and warn of possible attack, and control communications systems. In fact, it would be quite impossible at present to do without computers in these systems. The short warning times required by current nuclear strategies, for example, necessitate the use of computers for data analysis and control of communications systems. Computers also play an essential role in the monitoring systems used to verify arms control agreements and could play an important role in a future crisis control center. Several aspects of nuclear weapons systems and strategy that interact in significant ways with computer system reliability are discussed here.

FALSE ALERTS

On several occasions, the North American Aerospace Defense Command Center (NORAD) early warning system has mistakenly indicated that Soviet missiles were headed for the United States. These incidents raise certain questions: Could a computer failure, in either the U.S. or the Soviet warning systems, start an accidental nuclear war? What risks are associated with placing the nuclear forces of one or both powers on alert? Would it be responsible for a country to adopt a policy of launch-on-warning, in which missiles would be fired based on warnings that an attack was imminent? Only the nuclear forces of the United States and the USSR are examined here, but the warning systems and nuclear forces of other countries clearly add to the problems described.

Missile Attack Warning Systems

Both the United States and the Soviet Union maintain elaborate systems for the detection of attack by enemy missiles presumed to be carrying nuclear weapons. The primary sensors include satellites that can detect the infrared signature of a burning missile engine seconds after launch, and a variety of radar systems that can detect missiles in flight. Raw sensor data from the satellites must be processed by computer; processed data are available within minutes. Intercontinental ballistic missiles (ICBMs) have a flight time of about 30 minutes from the USSR to the United States; the U.S. ballistic missile early warning radars in Alaska, Greenland, and Britain can detect such missiles within 15 minutes, about halfway into their flight. Similar times apply to missiles launched from the United States toward the Soviet Union. There are shorter flight times for missiles launched from submarines off the coast of the enemy country, or for missiles launched from Western Europe toward the Soviet Union or vice versa [51, 83].

In the United States, the command post for the missile attack warning system is at NORAD, located 1200 feet under the solid granite of Cheyenne Mountain, Colorado. Other ground stations are located elsewhere in the United States and abroad. In the Soviet Union, the Air Defense Forces are responsible for early warning of nuclear attack and for attack assessment. A central underground Air Defense command center, similar to NORAD, is reportedly located about 50 kilometers from Moscow; there is also an extensive network of satellites, missile early warning radars, and communications facilities. (See [7] for more detailed descriptions of these systems.)

June 1980

On Tuesday, June 3, 1980, at 1:26 A.M., the display system at the command post of the Strategic Air Command (SAC) at Offutt Air Force Base near Omaha, Nebraska, indicated that two submarine-launched ballistic missiles (SLBMs) were headed toward the United States. Eighteen seconds later, the system showed an increased number of SLBM launches. SAC personnel called NORAD, who stated that they had no indication of SLBM launches. After a brief period, the SAC screens cleared. Shortly thereafter, the warning display at SAC indicated that Soviet ICBMs had been launched toward the United States. Then the display at the National Military Command Center (NMCC) in the Pentagon indicated that SLBMs had been launched. The SAC duty controller directed all alert crews to move to their B-52 bombers and to start their engines, so that the planes could take off quickly and not be destroyed on the ground by a nuclear attack. Land-based missile crews were put on a higher state of alert, and battle-control aircraft prepared for flight. In Hawaii, the airborne command post of the Pacific Command took off, ready to pass messages to U.S. warships if necessary. In the meantime, a Threat Assessment Conference was convened among the top duty officers at NORAD, SAC, and NMCC.[1] For the next three minutes, there was discussion among the three officers. There were a number of factors that made them doubt that an actual attack was under way: NORAD itself had no indications of an attack, the indications on the displays at SAC and NMCC did not follow any logical pattern, and the different command posts were receiving different information. Three minutes and 12 seconds into the alert, it was canceled. It was a false alert.

NORAD left the system in the same configuration in hopes that the error would repeat itself. The mistake recurred three days later, on June 6 at 3:38 P.M., with SAC again receiving indications of an ICBM attack. Again, SAC crews were sent to their aircraft and ordered to start their engines.

The cause of these incidents was eventually traced to the failure of a 74175 integrated circuit chip in a Data General computer used as a communications multiplexer. This machine took the results of analysis of sensor data and was part of the system that transmitted it from NORAD to SAC, NMCC, and Canadian Headquarters in Ottawa. The communications links were constantly tested by means of sending filler messages. At the time of the false alerts, these filler messages had the same form as attack messages, but with a zero filled in for the number of missiles detected. The system did not use any of the standard error correction or detection schemes for these messages. When the chip failed, the system started filling in the "missiles detected" field with random digits.

These false alerts received considerable press attention at the time [3, 22, 45, 48]. As a result of the publicity, on June 20, Senators Gary Hart and Barry Goldwater were asked to investigate the incidents by Senator John Stennis, chairman of the Senate Committee on Armed Services. They prepared both classified and unclassified versions of a report; the unclassified report [47] was the principal source of information for the above account of the incident. Other relevant U.S. government documents include [20], [26], and [93].

Other Incidents

The incidents of June 3 and 6, 1980, illustrate one sort of error—a hardware failure coupled with bad design—that can cause a false alert. Another incident illustrates a different realm of error: human operator error. On November 9, 1979, a test tape containing simulated attack data, used to test the missile warning system, was fed into a NORAD computer, which through human error was connected to the operational missile alert system. During the course of the ensuing six-minute alert, 10 tactical fighter aircraft were launched from bases in the northern United States and Canada, and as in the June 3 incident, a Threat Assessment Conference was convened [44, 47, 62]. (For information on other Threat Assessment Conferences during the period January 1977–May 1983 see [47] and the letter written by Col. J. H. Rix, director of administration at NORAD, to David C. Morrison, Center for Defense Information, Washington, D.C., November 4, 1983.)

Unsettling as the false alerts in November 1979 and June 1980 were, in the opinion of most reviewers of the incidents, including myself, the United States was nowhere near to launching its missiles and starting World War III. Most importantly, human judgment played an essential role in the procedures followed in the event of an alert, and these procedures provided enough time for the people involved to notice that a computer system was operating incorrectly. Also, NORAD procedures call for confirmation of the attack by an independent system—radar systems that observe the attacking missiles in flight, for example—and the chance of simultaneous false alerts from both systems under normal circumstances is very small.

What about similar failures in the Soviet warning systems? I have been unable to ascertain whether or not such failures have occurred, and it is unlikely that the Soviet government would choose to reveal them if they existed. For example, a recent paper on accidental nuclear war [35] by a member of the Soviet Academy of Sciences and former chairman of the State Committee for Atomic Energy of the USSR discusses U.S. warning system failures, without mentioning whether corresponding failures have occurred in the USSR. (Hints of the U.S. warning system failures were leaked to the press; the Pentagon stated that they would otherwise not have been made public [45].) At a news conference shortly after the June 1980 incident, Assistant Secretary of Defense Thomas Ross would not say whether the United States knew about similar false alerts in the USSR [45]. However, the Korean Airlines Flight 007 incident, in which a civilian aircraft was shot down by the USSR over two hours after it had entered Soviet airspace and just before it was back over international waters, would seem to indicate that the Soviet command and control system has problems. We do know that the state of the art in Soviet computer science lags several years behind that in the United States [28, 42, 87]. However, the NORAD computers are very old by computing-industry standards,[2] whereas Soviet military computers are on the leading edge of their technology [90, p. 75].

TIGHTLY COUPLED NUCLEAR FORCES

In looking at the false alert of June 3, 1980, one is struck by the widespread effects of the failure of a single integrated circuit chip: Some 100 B-52 bomber crews were directed to start their engines, a battle-control aircraft took off in Hawaii, land-based missile crews were put on a higher state of alert, and submarines were notified. It is quite possible that some of these preparations were observed by the Soviet Union. After the incident, it was feared that such Soviet observations could in turn lead them to move their forces to a higher state of readiness, causing an escalating series of alerts and moving the two powers dangerously close to war.

Pentagon officials stated that in the case of the June 3 incident there was no discernible rise in the level of Soviet readiness in response to the U.S. alert. At a news conference shortly afterwards, however, when Assistant Secretary of Defense Ross was asked about this danger of escalating responses, his reply was, "I'm going to duck that question" [45]. Similarly, at a subsequent press conference, neither Assistant Secretary of Defense Gerald Dinneen nor other officials could assure that such a chain reaction would not be caused by another false alert [63]. The start of World War I following the assassination of the archduke in Sarajevo, in which the alerts and mobilizations of the European powers interacted in just this way, is a historical precedent for this possibility [100, 65, 96].

In response to the very short time in which a nuclear war could begin, the command and control systems of both the United States and the USSR have become highly reactive; given the possibilities of interacting alerts, we can view the nuclear weapons and control systems of both countries as a *single* interacting system. (This point is discussed at length in [100] and from a more mathematical viewpoint in [12].)

During times of relative international calm, the combined U.S.–Soviet system probably has enough human checks—more abstractly, enough stability or hysteresis—to cope with a single mechanical or operator error, or perhaps even a few such errors. The situation would be different during a time of great tension or conventional war. Under such circumstances, the officers monitoring the systems would be less ready to dismiss a warning as being the result of a computer error, and the danger of escalating alerts on each side would be much greater. Again taking the single-system view, in times of tension and higher states of alert, the nuclear forces of the opposing sides become more tightly coupled.

A further danger comes from the possibility of compound stimuli to the system, perhaps from ambiguous or incomplete intelligence information. Bracken [100, pp. 65–66] describes one such example that occurred in 1956, at the time of the Suez Crisis and Hungarian uprising. On the night of November 5, the following four coincidental events occurred: First, U.S. military command headquarters in Europe received an urgent message that unidentified jet aircraft were flying over Turkey. Second, there were additional reports of 100 Soviet MiG-15 fighters over Syria. Third, there was a report that a British bomber had been shot down over Syria (presumably by the MiGs). Fourth, were reports that a Russian naval fleet was moving through the Dardanelles, perhaps to leave the Black Sea in preparation for hostilities. General Andrew Goodpaster was reportedly afraid that the events "might trigger off all the NATO operations plan," which at the time called for a single massive nuclear attack on the Soviet Union.

As it turned out, all four reports were incorrect or misinterpretations of more innocent activities: The jets over Turkey turned out to be a flock of swans, the MiGs over Syria were part of an official escort for the Syrian president, the British bomber was downed by mechanical difficulties, and the Russian fleet was on a scheduled exercise. In Bracken's words, "The detection and misinterpretation of these events, against the context of world tensions from Hungary and Suez, was the first major example of how the size and complexity of worldwide electronic warning systems could, at certain critical times, create a crisis momentum of its own."

The worldwide electronic warning and communications systems of today are immensely more complex and reactive than those of 1956. As in the 1956 incident, events that are in actuality unrelated may seem to be part of a larger pattern. Once the nuclear forces are placed on alert, further human or mechanical errors may occur. After the June 3, 1980, incident, the Hart–Goldwater report notes that, "Even though the command post controller prevented any undue reaction to the false and erroneous data, there seemed to be an air of confusion following the determination that the data were erroneous." It is likely that the "air of confusion" would be much worse if it were suspected that the indications of attack might be real.

An additional complication is the growing use of computer systems for "data fusion." One defense industry manager writes, "The most challenging information problem in modern command, control, communications and intelligence (C^3I) systems is the merging of diverse data into a single, coherent representation of the tactical, operational, or strategic situation. As C^3I systems have increased in complexity and scope, manual methods of merging data are no longer adequate, resulting in the need for fully automated methods, variously referred to as data fusion, multisource correlation or multisensor integration" [97, p. 217]. The motivation for this computerization is clear. The dangers are clear as well. As the amount of data increases and the time requirements become more stringent, less and less time is available for humans to check the outputs of the computer systems. Computer systems (including current artificial intelligence systems) are notoriously lacking in common sense: The system itself will typically not indicate that something has gone amiss and that the limits of its capabilities have been exceeded. This is an important aspect of automatic systems and one to which we will return.

To be at all confident about the reliability of complex systems, there must be a period of testing under conditions of actual use. As far as is publicly known, the command and control systems of the United States and the USSR have never been "tested" under conditions of simultaneous high alert; in fact, the highest level of conference in the U.S. missile warning system, the Missile Attack Conference, has never been called [47, p. 5]. Further, in a crisis situation, the very short times available for military personnel and national leaders to react and make decisions will undoubtedly lead to poorer judgment than under more usual circumstances, increasing the chances of misinterpretation of data and of error in operation of systems [14, 38]. The combination of the untestability of the warning and control systems under highly stressed conditions and the short times available for making decisions is grounds for considerable concern.

LAUNCH-ON-WARNING

Launch-on-warning is a strategy for retaliation to a nuclear attack, under which retaliatory missiles are launched in response to sensor indication that enemy missiles are on the way, before the warheads on the attacking missiles have detonated [40, 66, 75]. This strategy stands in contrast to "riding out the attack," a strategy in which a nation would absorb a nuclear strike and would retaliate only after positive verification had been obtained that an attack has taken place.[3]

Launch-on-warning makes stringent demands on a nation's nuclear weapons command and control systems. Warning data from sensors must be processed quickly, and it must be possible to relay launch orders through the command system quickly enough that missiles can be launched before the enemy missiles strike. Most importantly, the warning system must be exceedingly reliable, lest a retaliatory strike be triggered not by an enemy attack, but by computer or other error. (In recognition of this, if launch-on-warning were adopted as a strategy, it almost certainly would be activated only in times of crisis, rather than continuously [100, pp. 43–44]. Note that a policy of activation on this basis is an admission of distrust in the complete reliability of the warning systems and would result in a questionable system being activated at precisely the moment when the greatest caution was required.)

Given this danger of unintentional nuclear war, why would we consider adopting launch-on-warning? The reason is that the land-based missiles of both the United States and the Soviet Union have been growing more accurate over the years.[4] This increased missile accuracy puts at risk all fixed targets, such as land-based missile silos and command centers, even highly hardened ones. Although it is not at all certain that this vulnerability of fixed targets implies that a first strike could be successfully launched [21], strategic planners in both the United States and the USSR have nevertheless been concerned for decades with the problem. One way of dealing with it is launch-on-warning: If one side believes that an enemy attack is coming, retaliatory missiles can be launched and on their way, leaving the attacking warheads to explode on empty missile silos.

Although weapons based on submarines at sea and on aircraft are not threatened by this increasing accuracy, the present U.S. doctrine calls for all three "legs of the strategic triad" to be capable of inflicting retaliation. The risks to deterrence are more acute for the Soviet Union, which has a higher proportion of its strategic nuclear weapons on land-based missiles.

Launch-on-Warning Proposals in the United States

In April 1983, the President's Commission on Strategic Forces (often referred to as the Scowcroft Commission, after its chairman, retired Air Force Lt. Gen. Brent Scowcroft) issued its report on basing alternatives for the MX missile [75]. Acting on the committee's recommendation, the Reagan administration abandoned the goal of alternate basing modes and instead proposed that MX missiles be placed in existing Minuteman silos. This of course would leave them as vulnerable to Soviet attack as the Minuteman missiles.

In May 1983, in testimony before the Senate Appropriations Committee, Secretary of Defense Caspar Weinberger and the chairman of the Joint Chiefs of Staff, Gen. John Vessey, Jr., repeatedly told the committee that MX missiles deployed in existing silos would be vulnerable to a Soviet first strike "only if we ride out the attack" without launching a retaliatory strike. Vessey also said at one point, "The Soviets have no assurance that we will ride out the attack" [46]. However, on further questioning by senators, Weinberger and Vessey refused to say whether or not the United States was moving toward a launch-under-attack strategy.

Dr. Richard Garwin, a distinguished physicist and well-known defense consultant, has advocated the implementation of a system that can reliably support a launch-under-attack capability. The system would be enabled if it were determined that the U.S. submarine force had become vulnerable. In [40] Garwin advocates a system in which a limited number (50 or so) of Minutemen III missiles would be launched if an attack were detected. These missiles could be launched unarmed, subject to an encrypted command to arm them in flight. The decision process would be entirely predetermined, with the role of the U.S. National Command Authority (NCA) limited to assessing that a massive attack was indeed under way. Garwin also discusses alternatives, such as missiles launched armed but subject to a disarm command, or missiles launched irrevocably armed. In Garwin's proposal, an attack would be determined to be under way based on information from redundant infrared satellite sensors, not from reports of impacts or even radar data.

Launch-on-Warning Proposals in the Soviet Union

The Soviet Union has considered launch-on-warning as well, in particular as a threatened response to the Pershing II missile deployment by the NATO countries in Europe [30, 31, 99]. However, in a March 1983 statement, former Soviet Defense Minister Dmitri Ustinov categorically denied that the Soviets were adopting launch-on-warning [41]. While the political motivation behind these statements is clear, there appear to be real military issues as well. The Soviets would have 12 minutes or less from the time Pershing II missiles were launched until they hit [86, p. 46]. (Whether the current Pershing IIs could reach the command and control centers around Moscow is a matter of debate [85, p. 8].) The problem of short missile flight times is not new—missiles from Polaris submarines in the Arctic Ocean have been able to strike the Soviet Union since the 1960s—but the coupling of such short flight times with great accuracy is new.

More recently, Ustinov stated that the Soviet Union had increased the number of its nuclear-armed submarines off the U.S. coasts, to threaten the United States with more missiles with short flight times [76]. Although not the threatened response of launch-on-warning, in light of the previous discussion of tightly coupled forces, this action clearly has its dangers as well.

Discussion of Launch-on-Warning

Because of public perception of the risk of disaster due to computer or other error, the formal adoption of a launch-on-warning policy has always been controversial. Those authors who do advocate it do not appear to pay a great deal of attention to these dangers, particularly to the problems of very complex systems, short reaction times, and unanticipated events. For example, consider Garwin's discussion of accidental launch [40, pp. 124–125]:

> Launch under attack seems to present no more hazard of unauthorized or accidental launch than does the present system. . . .
> [The problem of an unauthorized launch] may be addressed by the use of PAL (permissive action links) in the silo and in the warhead. There are cryptographic safeguards which could be borrowed from modern message-security systems, which are adequate for the transmission of millions of characters per day with assurance against being "read" (deciphered) even if all the message traffic is intercepted by an enemy. These same systems could be used to encipher a short (20-digit) "go-code," receipt of which would cause the warhead to arm, while receipt of another go-code of similar length would fire the missile, having opened the silo door, and so on. The probability of accidental launch can be calculated as the number of candidate signals per year, times the likelihood that any one will be interpreted as a real go-code. Presumably very few putative go-codes would be received per year (the expected number is less than one per year, caused by lightning, electrical noise, or the like). If 1000 per minute were received, the pure-chance firing of the missiles would shorten the average human life by less than 0.1 seconds, even if only a single 20-digit code sufficed (and not 2, as assumed). For some cosmic-scale troublemaker to steal the actual go-code and so mimic the NCA launch order to the ICBM force, or bypass the wiring in the missile silos, is little different from what could be done now without a launch-under-attack system.
> . . . Only a limited number (say, 50) of Minutemen need or should be launched—unarmed, subject to command-arm in flight. One hopes that launch under attack will never occur inappropriately, in response to false indication of sensors, or other cause. Should such an unwarranted launch occur, however, we would prefer not to have armed the missiles, nor would we want to disarm ourselves by having launched the entire ICBM force, which would thus be lost to our future capability.

Some would argue that there are a number of important omissions in Garwin's analysis. The calculation of the probability of a randomly generated valid go-code, while correct in a narrow sense, is most misleading, as it ignores the host of other things that might go wrong. In Garwin's proposal, for example, the doctrine of dual phenomenology would be abandoned, so that a retaliatory strike would be launched based only on data from one kind of sensor, rather than two as at present. The discussion of launching missiles unarmed, subject to a command to arm them in flight, does not treat the real danger that the Soviet Union would observe the 50 missiles headed toward their territory and launch a retaliatory strike.

As mentioned previously, the formal adoption of a launch-on-warning policy— a declaration that launch-on-warning is the preferred response in a crisis—has always been controversial. Nevertheless, it appears that it is and has been regarded as an option by both the United States and the USSR. According to testimony by General Ellis of the U.S. Strategic Air Command [95, p. 3834],

> launch on warning is an option we have and must maintain. It remains a useful option because the enemy cannot be certain it will not be used or know the conditions under which it would be used . . . and therefore, he must always make it a part of his planning deliberations.

This is corroborated by recent testimony by General Herres, commander in chief, NORAD [94, p. 72]. A recent book on the U.S. Single Integrated Operating Plan (SIOP) for waging nuclear war states that launch-on-warning has *always* been an option in the SIOP [71, pp. 187–188]. More alarmingly, Bruce Blair, a former launch control officer and DoD official, has testified [94, pp. 32–34]

> declaratory doctrine is a poor guide to actual employment doctrine. At present, we are operationally geared for launch on warning, a reflection of the low confidence we have in our ability to absorb the brunt of an attack before retaliating. . . . I restress the fact that the United States relies heavily on launch on warning for positive control, for force coordination and for retaliation. Fortunately, our tactical warning system on which launch on warning depends is fairly fault tolerant. But again, it is not as tolerant as it should be to justify U.S. reliance on it.

Launch-on-warning is the subject of a current lawsuit,[5] in which the plaintiff complains that the secretary of defense is presently operating a launch-on-warning capability. This operation, according to the suit, unconstitutionally usurps the power of Congress to declare war, and unlawfully delegates presidential powers to subordinates, since the very short times involved would not allow time for a decision by the president.

Regarding the Soviet Union, a DoD publication [101, p. 20] states

> launch-under-attack circumstances would place the greatest stress on attack warning systems and launch coordination. To meet this demand, the Soviets have established a satellite-based ICBM launch detection system, built an over-the-horizon radar missile launch detection system to back up the satellites and have large phased-array radars ringing the U.S.S.R. These warning devices could give the Soviet leadership time to launch their forces after an enemy strike had been launched. To prepare for this possibility, the Soviets practice launching weapons under stringent time constraints.

Because of the very short times involved, there is doubt that launch-on-warning is a practical policy [83], since it would be difficult to maintain an acceptable level of control on the nuclear forces of the country that adopted it. From a broader viewpoint, launch-on-warning can be seen as one point on a spectrum of policies for retaliation, the dimension of the spectrum being how long a country waits to respond when it believes that an attack is imminent or under way. Taking this broader view, pressures toward launch-on-warning are actually a symptom of underlying problems. Among these problems are (1) the strategic doctrine that holds that military assets at known, fixed locations (land-based ICBMs and command posts) are an essential part of a nation's nuclear forces, (2) the perception that the vulnerability of these fixed targets is a pressing problem, (3) new weapons systems that make them more vulnerable, and (4) the consequent decrease in time available to make decisions in nuclear crises. (See [83] for a longer treatment of this viewpoint.)

THE RELIABILITY OF COMPLEX SYSTEMS

Would it be responsible for either the USSR or the United States to adopt weapons systems and policies that assume that computer systems, such as missile warning systems, can function without failure? I argue that it is not. I will not attempt to prove that failures will occur in complex military systems, but rather I will attempt to show that there is considerable doubt that adequate reliability can be achieved. The standard of reliability required of a military system that can potentially help precipitate a thermonuclear war if it fails must be higher than that of *any* other computer system, since the magnitude of disaster is so great.

Techniques for Building Reliable Systems

Much research and development effort has been devoted to the construction of reliable computer systems, and some impressive results have been achieved. As a comprehensive treatment of this topic is well beyond the scope of this article, an outline of some well-known techniques for achieving reliability is presented, along with references to the literature, with particular emphasis on military computer systems.

Hardware At the hardware level, one obvious technique is to use very reliable components. Here the large body of knowledge about quality control for other kinds of manufacturing can be applied, including quality control of raw materials, testing and tracking each component produced, destructively testing a certain percentage of the devices, and keeping records of the reliability of components produced by a particular line to spot variations in reliability. The MIL-SPEC program codifies standards for many kinds of devices that the military procures. In addition, the DoD has funded much work on building models of component reliability, such as the widely used MIL-HDBK-217C reliability model for estimating the failure rate for various kinds of integrated circuit chips [88]. Above the chip level, techniques for building reliable devices include component burn-in, careful signal routing, shielding, cabinet grounding, environmental controls, power supply regulation, and other conservative, well-established design practices.

Regardless of the methods used, in a very large system it is unreasonable to expect that every component will be totally reliable. For this reason, a body of techniques has been accumulated that allow a system to continue functioning even when individual components fail. These techniques all involve redundancy, and include *n*-modular redundancy with voting, error-correcting codes, and dynamically reconfigurable systems.

Complementing this work on the construction of reliable hardware has been development of modeling techniques; useful measures include mean time to failure, mean time to detection, mean time to repair, and availability. More information on hardware reliability, along with an extensive bibliography, may be found in [77]; [23] is a review of techniques for achieving hardware fault tolerance.

Software For large computer systems, the cost and complexity of the software typically dominate that of the hardware. To construct a very complex system at all, let alone to make it reliable, a disciplined approach is necessary. An extensive set of sources discussing the software development process is available. Texts on software engineering include [15], [36], [52], and [81]; these have references to many other sources, including seminal papers on software engineering in the literature.

It is generally accepted that reliability cannot be "tested into" a software system; it is necessary to plan for reliability at all points in the development process. As with hardware, the DoD has codified standards for how its software is to be specified, designed, written, and tested. One such standard is *DOD-STD-2167: Military Standard Defense System Software Development* [92], for the development of mission-critical software. It specifies such things as software requirements analysis standards, coding standards, and the information that must be gathered on software trouble reports. In addition, other administrative requirements may be imposed, such as formal requirements for a contractor's Quality Assurance Program (MIL-STD-1535 and requirements for configuration control (DOD-STD-480). Formal reviews of the software development process are required at each stage by DoD directives. As enumerated in [2, p. 186], these are

- a *Systems Requirements Review,*
- a *System Design Review,*
- a *Preliminary Design Review,*
- a *Critical Design Review,*
- a *Functional Configuration Audit,*
- a *Physical Configuration Audit,* and
- a *Formal Qualification Review.*

The DoD will typically contract with a company (other than the software contractor) to assist it with some of these reviews.

Testing is not simply performed at the end of coding, but rather must be planned and developed in parallel with the software system itself. A typical contractual requirement would be that, for every item in the system specification, a corresponding test be performed to check that the software meets each specification. Even after the system is installed, the set of tests should be kept and updated as well, so that, as the system is modified during maintenance, previous tests can be rerun to check that the system still meets them (regression testing). More information on software reliability, safety, quality assurance, testing, and validation may be found in [2] [4], [29], [49], [54], [56], and [57].

Quantifying Software Reliability Two kinds of software quality measures are in general use: estimates of the number of errors remaining in a program, and estimates of the mean time to failure (MTTF) of a system. Angus [5] describes the application of six models of the first sort to a major C^3I system, with poor results. Regarding estimates of MTTF, Currit, Dyer, and Mills [27] describe a procedure for producing a certified estimate of the MTTF of a system, using statistical testing.

Any estimate of the errors remaining in a program requires a complete specification against which the program can be compared. The testing regimes assume either that the testers know what kinds of inputs the system will be subjected to, or that the system can be extensively tested under conditions of actual use. (Even then, a problem with statistical testing is that it takes prohibitively long to obtain high confidence that the errors found are manifested only rarely.) The importance of these limitations will be discussed later in the article.

Sources of System Failure

The sources of computer system failure include incorrect or incomplete system specifications, hardware failure, hardware design errors, software coding errors, software design errors, and human error (such as incorrect equipment operation or maintenance). Particularly with complex, normally highly reliable systems, a failure may be caused by some unusual *combination* of problems from several of these categories.

Hardware failures are perhaps the most familiar cause of system failures, as in the NORAD failures of June 1980. As noted previously, individual components can be made very reliable by strict quality control and testing, but in a large system it is unreasonable to expect that no component will ever fail, and other techniques that allow for individual component failures must be used. However, when one builds very complex systems—and a command and control system in its entirety is certainly an example of a complex system—one becomes less certain that one has anticipated all the possible failure modes, that all the assumptions about independence are correct. A serious complicating factor is that the redundancy techniques that allow for individual component failures themselves add additional complexity and possible sources of error to the system.

Another potential cause of failure is a hardware design error. Again, the main source of problems is not the operation of the system under the usual, expected set of events, but its operation when *unexpected* events occur. For example, timing problems due to an unanticipated set of asynchronous parallel events that seldom occurs are particularly hard to find.

It is in the nature of computer systems that much of the system design is embodied in the computer's software. Errors may be introduced at any of the steps in its production: requirements specification, design, implementation, testing and debugging, or maintenance.

Errors in the system requirements specification are perhaps the most pernicious. It is at this level that the system's connection with the outside world is expressed; we must therefore anticipate *all* the circumstances under which the system might be used and describe in the requirements specification what action it should take under those circumstances. For a very complex system, it is unrealistic to imagine that one can foresee all of these circumstances. We can have confidence in such systems only after they have been tested for a considerable time under conditions of actual use.

Errors may also be introduced when the requirements are translated into a system design, as well as when the design is translated into an actual computer program. Again, the sheer complexity of the system is itself a basic cause of problems. Anyone who has worked on a large computer system knows how difficult it is to manage the development process; usually, there is *nobody* who understands the entire system completely. Given a complete requirements document, however, many of the errors at these levels can be prevented by using strategies such as modular design, information hiding, and the like; also, a wider range of automated tools is available to help us detect which parts of the program affect which other parts. Nevertheless, it is widely acknowledged that the process is not completely satisfactory.

The cost of maintenance usually dominates the other costs of military software development. Program maintenance, either to fix bugs or to satisfy new system requirements, is itself a frequent source of errors. Meyers [56, p. 252], for instance, states that "experience has shown that fixes have a high probability (usually from 20 to 50 percent) of introducing a *new* error into the program."

Another source of failure is human operator error. People do make mistakes despite elaborate training and precautions, especially in time of stress and crisis Dumas [33] cites some worrying statistics about alcohol, drug abuse, and aberran behavior among military personnel with access to nuclear weapons. Alcoholism is a major health problem in the Soviet Union and may be a problem among such personnel in the Soviet military as well [24].

Some Instructive Failures

There have been some impressive failures of computer (and other) systems designed to be reliable, and it is instructive to look at a few of these. I have attempted to cat egorize these failures using the sources of failure listed in the previous section; however, as will be seen, these failures often arise from a combination of errors.

Examples of failures due to hardware errors include the NORAD false alert described earlier. (However, it could also be said that these false alerts are illustra tions of hardware design errors instead, in that it is a grave oversight that such criti cal data should have been sent without using parity, cyclic redundancy, or other checks.) From a technical point of view, a more interesting and complex failure was the total collapse of a U.S. computer communications network (the ARPANET) in October 1980 due to an unusual hardware malfunction that caused a high-priority process to run wild and devour resources needed by other processes [74]. The ARPANET was designed to be highly available—the intent of the software design was that it should prevent a single hardware malfunction from being able to bring down the whole network. It was only after several years of operation that this prob lem manifested itself.

The launch of the first space shuttle was delayed at the last minute by a soft ware problem. For reliability, the shuttle used four redundant primary avionics com puters, each running the same software, along with a fifth backup computer running a different system. In the incident, a patch to correct a previous timing bug opened a 1 in 67 probability window that, when the system was turned on, the computers would not be properly synchronized. There are a number of noteworthy features of this incident: First, despite great attention to reliability in the shuttle avionics, there was still a software failure; second, this particular problem arose from the additiona complexity introduced by the redundant systems designed to achieve reliability; and third, the bug was introduced during maintenance to fix a previous problem. Garman [39] gives a detailed account of the incident, along with some pithy observations on the problems of complex software systems in the real world.

There are many examples of errors arising from incorrect or incomplete speci fications. One such example is a false alert in the early days of the nuclear age [13 50, 61], when on October 5, 1960, the warning system at NORAD indicated that the United States was under massive attack by Soviet missiles with a certainty of 99.9 percent. It turned out that the Ballistic Missile Early Warning System (BMEWS radar in Thule, Greenland, had spotted the *rising moon*. Nobody had thought abou the moon when specifying how the system should act.

Gemini V splashed down 100 miles from its intended landing point because a programmer had implicitly ignored the motion of the earth around the sun—in other words, had used an incorrect model [37, pp. 187–188]. In 1979 five nuclear reactors were shut down after the discovery of an error in the program used to predict how well the reactors would survive in earthquakes [59]. One subroutine, instead of tak ing the sum of the absolute values of a set of numbers, took their arithmetic sum instead.[6] In 1983 severe flooding along the lower Colorado River killed six persons and caused millions of dollars in damage. The governor of Nevada stated that this was caused by a "monumental mistake" in federal computer projections of snow melt-off flow, so that too much water was kept dammed prior to spring thaws [64].

ACM SIGSOFT Software Engineering Notes is a good place to find descriptions of real-world computer problems, catastrophic and otherwise (e.g., see [60]). See also [71] for a listing of some other incidents.

In hindsight, the blame for each of the above incidents can be assigned to individual component failures, faulty design, or specific human errors, as is almost always the case with such incidents. In designing automatic systems, we must anticipate all possible eventualities and specify what should happen in all cases. The real culprit is simply the complexity of the systems, and our inability to anticipate and plan for all of the things that can go wrong.

Outside of the realm of computer systems, incidents such as the tragic explosion of the space shuttle *Challenger* in 1986, the accidents at the nuclear power plants at Chernobyl in 1986 and Three Mile Island (TMI) in 1979, and the 1965 northeast power blackout are sobering reminders of the limitations of technology.

At Chernobyl, operators deliberately disabled warning and safety mechanisms so that they could conduct an experiment, with the catastrophic result of two explosions at the plant and the release of enormous amounts of radioactive material. The TMI accident began with an equipment failure (of a pressurizer relief valve), but its severity was compounded by subsequent operator error [73].[7] In another nuclear reactor accident, at Browns Ferry in Alabama in 1975, a single failure—a fire in an electrical cable tray—disabled a large number of redundant systems designed to ensure safety at the plant. This incident demonstrates that one should look with a skeptical eye at calculations indicating extremely low probabilities for failure due to independent systems.

Prospects for Military Computer System Reliability

What are the prospects for the reliability of military computer systems in the future?

Clearly, substantial improvements in the reliability of systems like NORAD are possible simply by using state-of-the-art hardware and software engineering techniques: A system that uses 1960s vintage computers or that as recently as 1980 transmitted critical data with no parity checks is not state of the art. Nor are these isolated incidents. The World-Wide Military Command and Control System (WWMCCS) has been plagued with problems of inadequate performance, cost overruns, and poor management [17]. In the 1977 PRIME TARGET exercises, for example, only 38 percent of the attempts to use the system were successful [25, p. 51]. There are also problems with personnel training and preparation. A recent book by Daniel Ford describes an incident in which Ford asked Gen. Paul Wagoner, at the time in charge of NORAD combat operations, to demonstrate the special black telephone that provides a direct link to the NMCC. This telephone would be used, for instance, for a Missile Attack Conference. Wagoner picked up the phone—and nothing happened. His subsequent explanation was that, "I didn't know that I had to dial '0' to get the operator." (See [100] for further discussion of the deficiencies of the current U.S. command and control system. Kling [53] discusses WWMCCS as an example of a socially complex computer system, points out the inadequacies of describing such systems in isolation, and advocates the use of "web models" as an appropriate tool for describing such systems.)

This is not to say that there have been *no* improvements in these systems—a good example of a positive step has been the installation of Permissive Action Links (PALs) on all U.S. nuclear weapons except SLBMs [58, p. 52]. The PAL system requires that a code be received from a higher authority before a nuclear weapon can be armed, thus reducing the probability of unauthorized use.

Nevertheless, substantial improvements are possible using existing state-of-the-art technology. What are the practical and theoretical limits of reliability, now and in the next decade?

In regard to the practical limits of reliability, most professional programmers today do not use such software engineering techniques as structured programming, modularity and information hiding, cooperating sequential processes, or formal program semantics [67]. The DoD is engaged in several efforts to develop new technology for software production and to make it widely available to military contractors [55]. The STARS (Software Technology for Adaptable, Reliable Systems) program [32, 91] and the Software Engineering Institute at Carnegie-Mellon University are examples. Large organizations move slowly, and it will be some years (at least) before these newer software engineering techniques are generally adopted. Use of these techniques should decrease, but not eliminate, errors in moving from the specification to the program.

Program maintenance, as noted previously, is itself a frequent source of errors. This problem is further aggravated by the fact that program maintenance is presently regarded as one of the least desirable programming jobs and is often assigned to junior or less-skilled employees. Programming support environments that keep track of versions, note the effects of changes, and the like are becoming available [9, 48]. Eventually, the use of these tools should help decrease the number of errors introduced during maintenance.

In the long term, formal techniques such as proofs of program correctness (program verification), automatic programming, and proofs of design consistency have been advocated as tools for improving computer system reliability. In a proof of program correctness, either a human or a computer proves mathematically that a program meets a formal specification of what it should do. In automatic programming, the program is written automatically from the specification. In a proof of design consistency, the proof must show that a formal specification satisfies a set of requirements, for example, for security or fault tolerance. (The difference between requirements and specifications in this case is generally that the former tend to be simply stated global properties, whereas the latter tend to be detailed sets of constraints defined functionally on state transitions or algebraically on inputs and outputs.)

In theory, these techniques could produce programs or designs guaranteed to meet their specifications. Some practical use is being made of design proof techniques, primarily in proving security properties of system designs, although such proofs are still nontrivial. Thus, one might prove that, within the computer, information cannot flow in the wrong direction in a multilevel security system.[8] Proofs about program correctness, however, are very much in the research stage. For example, simple compilers have been proved correct, but programs of the complexity of the real-time satellite data analysis programs are well beyond the state of the art. Automatic programming is even less advanced. A useful reference discussing program verification is [16]; for an up-to-date collection of papers on verification, see [6]. The current state of automatic programming is discussed in [68]; discussions of future applications of automatic programming to software engineering may be found in [8] and [10]. In [102] Parnas critiques the possible roles that automatic programming and program verification could play in the production of software for ballistic missile defense.

The hardest and most intractable problem in the construction of software for complex tasks, such as command and control systems, is specifying what the system should do. *How does one know that the specification itself is correct, that is, that it describes what one intends?* Are there events that may occur that were simply not anticipated when the specification was written? Program verification and automatic programming techniques can offer no help here. A proof of correctness, for example, simply shows that one formal description (the specification) is equivalent to another formal description (the program). It does not say that the specification meets the perhaps unarticulated desires of the user, nor does it say anything about how well the system will perform in situations never imagined when the specification was written. For example, in the 1960 false alert, proving that the system met its specifications would not help if nobody thought about the rising moon when writing the specifications. (The term *proof of correctness* is thus a misnomer—a better term might be *proof of relative consistency*. This point is discussed at length in [74].)

Both the practical and theoretical limits of reliability bump up against this problem of specification. It constitutes the major long-term practical barrier to constructing reliable complex systems. From a theoretical point of view, depending on the language used to express the specification, it may be possible to prove that it has certain properties, for example, that it is self-consistent or that, given a set of possible inputs, the action to be taken for each of these inputs is specified. However, the answers to such critical questions as, "Will the system do what we reasonably expect it to do?" or "Are there external events that we just didn't think of?" lie inherently outside the realm of formal systems.

On Testing

To be at all confident of the reliability of complex systems, there must be a period of testing under conditions of actual use. Simulations, analyses of possible modes of failure, and the like can each expose some problems, but all such tests are limited by the fact that the designers test for exactly those circumstances that they anticipate may occur.[9] It is the *unexpected* circumstances and interactions that cause the most severe problems.

Some problems, like spotting the rising moon, will be uncovered quickly when the system is in routine operation. However, the conditions under which command and control systems for nuclear forces are expected to function include not just peacetime, but also times of international tension and high alert. It is these latter situations that are of the most concern. Short of having many periods of great tension and high alert—clearly an unacceptably dangerous proposition—the nuclear weapons command and control systems simply cannot be tested completely. The most extreme situation in which, under current doctrine, these systems are expected to function is that of limited or protracted nuclear war; this topic is discussed in the next section.

A final issue is that systems in flux are more prone to problems than those that have remained stable for some time. As noted above, program maintenance is a frequent source of errors. Better programming environments will help eliminate some of these errors, but such errors also arise from changing specifications, in which some loophole or problem in the specification is introduced by other changes. If the arms race continues unabated, due to the changing nature of the weapons and their deployment, the specifications for the command and control systems for nuclear forces will necessarily be changing as well. . . .

CONCLUSIONS

How much reliance is it safe to place on life-critical computer systems, in particular, on nuclear weapons command and control systems? At present, a nuclear war caused by an isolated computer or operator error is probably not a primary risk, at least in comparison with other dangers. The most significant risk of nuclear war at present seems to come from the possibility of a *combination* of such events as international crises, mutually reinforcing alerts, computer system misdesign, computer failure, or human error.

A continuing trend in the arms race has been the deployment of missiles with greater and greater accuracies. This trend is creating increasing pressure to consider a launch-on-warning strategy. Such a strategy would, however, leave very little time to evaluate the warning and determine whether it were real or due to a computer or human error—we would be forced to put still greater reliance on the correct operation of the warning and command systems of the United States and the USSR. Deployment of very accurate missiles close to enemy territory exacerbates the problem.

C^3 systems should be such that leaders in both the United States and the USSR will not be forced into a "use it or lose it" situation, in which they feel they must launch a strike quickly lest their ability to retaliate is destroyed. Current war plans are more elaborate and include an array of options for flexible, limited nuclear responses. However, if a nuclear war should start, it is not at all clear that it would unfold according to these plans. We should always bear in mind that untested systems in a strange and hostile environment are not likely to perform reliably and as expected. In particular, it is impossible to determine exactly which components of a strategic command and control system would still work correctly after hostilities have commenced. This rules out strategies that depend on finely graded or complexly coordinated activities after the initial attack.

The construction of a ballistic missile defense system has been proposed. However, there could be no confidence that it would work as expected; in addition, its accidental activation during a crisis might trigger other hostilities. In the longer term, weapons systems equipped with extremely fast computers and using artificial intelligence techniques may result in battles (including nuclear ones) that must be largely controlled by computer.

Where then does that leave us? There is clearly room for technical improvements in nuclear weapons computer systems. I have argued, however, that adding more and more such improvements cannot ensure that they will always function correctly. The fundamental problems are due to untestability, limits of human decision making during high tension and crisis, and our inability to think through all the things that might happen in a complex and unfamiliar situation. We must recognize the limits of technology. The threat of nuclear war is a political problem, and it is in the political, human realm that solutions must be sought.

ACKNOWLEDGMENTS

Many people have helped me in gathering information and in developing the ideas described here. Some of the original research was done in connection with a graduate seminar on Computer Reliability and Nuclear War held in the University of Washington Computer Science Department in Autumn 1982, and I thank the other participants in the seminar. Subsequently, a number of members of Computer Professionals for Social Responsibility have been generous with their help; I would particularly like to thank Guy Almes, Andrew Black, Gary Chapman, Calvin Gotlieb, Laura Gould, William Havens, Robert Henry, Jonathan Jacky, Cliff Johnson, Ira Kalet, Ed Lazowska, Peter Neumann, Severo Ornstein, David Parnas, Scott Rose, and Philip Wadler. Thanks also to Milton Leitenberg and Herbert Lin for expert advice on arms and arms control, and to Rob Kling for useful recommendations and suggestions in his role as area editor for this article.

NOTES

1. This is a formal step in the alert process. The successive levels of formal conferences are the Missile Display Conference, a relatively routine event; the Threat Assessment Conference, which is more serious; and the Missile Attack Conference, in which the president and all other senior personnel are brought in.
2. One 1982 congressional report termed the NORAD computers "dangerously obsolete" [20]. There have been upgrades since that report; nevertheless, the five largest on-line computers at NORAD are currently Honeywell 6080s (personal communication by D. W. Kindschi, chief of the Media Relations Division of NORAD, August 23, 1984). The machines in the Honeywell 6000 series were designed in the mid 1960s primarily for batch processing [89, p. 1]. Current plans call for replacing the Honeywell machines with IBM 3083 computers in 1988 [43, pp. 86–87].
3. There are of course other strategies as well. In a launch-on-impact strategy, missiles are launched after indications have been received that at least one detonation has occurred. Launch-under-attack is defined differently by different authors: Sometimes it is used interchangeably with launch-on-warning, and sometimes to refer to a strategy that requires a higher confidence confirmation that an attack is under way. This higher confidence could be based either on reports of actual detonations (see [46]), making it the same as launch-on-impact, or on information from redundant sensors (as in [40]).
4. For example, the U.S. Minuteman III Mk 12 missile has a reported accuracy of 280 m circular error probable, whereas the older Titan II missile has an accuracy of 1300 m. Similarly, the Soviet SS-18 Mod 3 missile has an accuracy of 350 m; the older SS-11 Mod 1 an accuracy of 1400 m [51, pp. 118–119]. The Pershing II missile is even more accurate. It uses a new guidance technology in which live radar images of the landscape surrounding the target area are compared during its descent with internally stored map information, so that course corrections can be made before impact. Its accuracy is reportedly 30 m [51, p. 118]. Missiles with similarly high accuracies are scheduled for deployment on nuclear submarines as well, for example, the D-5 missile due to be deployed on the U.S. Trident II submarines starting in 1989 [85, p. 54].
5. *Johnson* v. *Secretary of Defense*, U.S. District Court, San Francisco, Calif., case C86 3334.

6. It is not clear whether this should be classified as an error in the specification or in the program—probably there *was* no separate formal specification or model, so that the program itself became the model.

7. See also [69] and [70] for a discussion of the TMI incident as a "normal accident"—an unanticipated accident in a complex, tightly coupled system. This "normal accident" viewpoint is also applicable to other complex systems such as nuclear weapons command and control systems.

8. Design proofs have been done successfully in the SCOMP kernel [78], while other relevant properties have been proved about the trusted code that runs on top of the kernel [11].

9. See [84] for an interesting although dated discussion of how the NORAD system was tested, including simulated battle exercises.

REFERENCES

1. Adams, J. A., and Fischetti, M. A. *STAR WARS*—SDI: The grand experiment. *IEEE Spectrum 22*, 9 (Sept. 1985), 34–64.

2. Adrion, W. R., Branstad, M. A., and Cherniavsky, J. C. Validation, verification, and testing of computer software. *ACM Comput. Surv. 14*, 2 (June 1982), 159–192.

3. Albright, J. False missile alert required 3 minutes to cancel. *San Jose Mercury* (June 15, 1980), 1 H.

4. Anderson T., and Randell, B., Eds. *Computing Systems Reliability: An Advanced Course*. Cambridge University Press, Cambridge, Mass., 1979.

5. Angus, J. E. The application of software reliability models to a major C³I system. In *Proceedings of the Annual Reliability and Maintainability Symposium* (San Francisco, Calif., Jan. 24–26). IEEE Press, New York, 1984, pp. 268–274.

6. Association for Computing Machinery. Proceedings of VERkshop III—A formal verification workshop. *Softw. Eng. Notes 10*, 4 (1985).

7. Ball, D. The Soviet strategic C³I system. In *C³I Handbook*. EW Communications, Palo Alto, Calif., 1986, pp. 206–216.

8. Balzer, R., Cheatham, T. E., and Green, C. Software technology in the 1990's: Using a new paradigm. *Computer 16*, 11 (Nov. 1983), 39–45.

9. Barstow, D. R., Shrobe, H. E., and Sandewall, E., Eds. *Interactive Programming Environments*. McGraw-Hill, New York, 1984.

10. Barstow, D. R. Domain-specific automatic programming. *IEEE Trans. Softw. Eng. SE-11*, 11 (Nov. 1985), 1321–1336.

11. Benzel, T. C. V., and Tavilla, D. A. Trusted software verification: A case study. In *Proceedings of the 1985 Symposium on Security and Privacy* (Oakland, Calif., Apr. 22–24). IEEE Press, New York, 1985, pp. 14–31.

12. Bereanu, B. Self-activation of the world nuclear weapons system. *J. Peace Res. 20*, 1 (1983), 49–57.

13. Berkeley, E. C. *The Computer Revolution*. Doubleday, New York, 1962.

14. Bloomfield, L. P. Nuclear crisis and human frailty. *Bull. At. Sci. 41*, 9 (Oct. 1985), 26–30.

15. Boehm, B. W. *Software Engineering Economics*. Prentice-Hall, Englewood Cliffs, N.J., 1981.

16. Boyer, R. S., and Moore, J. S., Eds. *The Correctness Problem in Computer Science*. Academic Press, New York, 1981.

17. Broad, W. J. Computers and the U.S. military don't mix. *Science 207*, 4436 (Mar. 14, 1980), 1183–1187.

18. Broad, W. J. Nuclear pulse (II): Ensuring delivery of the doomsday signal. *Science 212*, 4499 (June 5, 1981), 1116–1120.

19. Broad, W. J. Nuclear pulse (III): Playing a wild card. *Science 212*, 4500 (June 12, 1981), 1248–1251.

20. Brooks, J. NORAD computer systems are dangerously obsolete. House Rep. 97-449, Committee on Government Operations, United States House of Representatives, Washington, D.C., Mar. 8, 1982.

21. Bunn, M., and Tsipis, K. The uncertainties of a preemptive nuclear attack. *Sci. Am. 249*, 5 (Nov. 1983), 38–47.

22. Burt, R. False nuclear alarms spur urgent effort to find faults. *New York Times* (June 13, 1980), A16.

23. Carter, W. C. Hardware fault tolerance. In *Computing Systems Reliability: An Advanced Course*, T. Anderson and B. Randell, Eds. Cambridge University Press, Cambridge, Mass., 1979, Chap. 6, pp. 211–263.

24. Cockburn, A. *The Threat: Inside the Soviet Military Machine*. Random House, New York, 1983.

25. Comptroller General of the United States. The world wide military command and control system—Major changes needed in its automated data processing management and direction. Rep. LCD-80-22, Comptroller General of the United States, Washington, D.C., Dec. 14, 1979.

26. Comptroller General of the United States. *NORAD's Missile Warning System: What Went Wrong?* United States General Accounting Office, Washington, D.C., May 15, 1981.

27. Currit, P. A., Dyer, M., and Mills, H. D. Certifying the reliability of software. *IEEE Trans. Softw. Eng. SE-12*, 1 (Jan. 1986), 3–11.

28. Davis, N. C., and Goodman, S. E. The Soviet bloc's unified system of computers. *ACM Comput. Surv. 10*, 2 (June 1978), 93–122.

29. Deutsch, M. S. *Software Verification and Validation: Realistic Project Approaches*. Prentice-Hall, Englewood Cliffs, N.J., 1982.

30. Doder, D. Soviets said to consider faster nuclear missile launch in crisis. *Washington Post* (Apr. 11, 1982), A5.

31. Doder, D. Kremlin defense official warns of policy shift to quicken nuclear response. *Washington Post* (July 13, 1982), A1a.

32. Druffel, L. E., Redwine, S. T., and Riddle, W. E. The STARS program: Overview and rationale. *Computer 16*, 11 (Nov. 1983), 21–29.

33. Dumas, L. J. Human fallibility and weapons. *Bull. At. Sci. 36*, 9 (Nov. 1980), 15–20.

34. Eastport Study Group. *Summer Study 1985: A Report to the Director, Strategic Defense Initiative Organization*. Strategic Defense Initiative Organization, Dec. 1985.

35. Emelyanov, V. S. The possibility of an accidental nuclear war. In *The Arms Race at a Time of Decision*, J. Rotblat and A. Pascolini, Eds. Macmillan, New York, 1984, Chap. 9, pp. 73–79.

36. Fairley, R. E. *Software Engineering Concepts*. McGraw-Hill, New York, 1985.

37. Fox, R. *Software and Its Development*. Prentice-Hall, Englewood Cliffs, N.J., 1982.

38. Frei, D. *Risks of Unintentional Nuclear War*. Allanheld, Osmun and Co., Totowa, N.J., 1983.

39. Garman, J. R. The "bug" heard 'round the world. *Softw. Eng. Notes 6*, 5 (Oct. 1981), 3–10.

40. Garwin, R. Launch under attack to redress minuteman vulnerability? *Int. Secur. 4*, 3 (Winter 1979), 117–139.

41. Gelb, L. H. Soviet marshal warns the U.S. on its missiles. *New York Times* (Mar. 17, 1983), A1.

42. Goodman, S. E. Computing and the development of the Soviet economy. A Compendium of Papers Submitted to the Joint Economic Committee of the Congress of the United States, Washington, D.C., Oct. 10, 1979.

43. Gumble, B. Air Force upgrading defenses at NORAD. *Def. Electron. 17*, 8 (Aug. 1985), 86–108.

44. Halloran, R. U.S. aides recount moments of false missile alert. *New York Times* (Dec. 16, 1979), 25.

45. Halloran, R. Computer error falsely indicates a Soviet attack. *New York Times* (June 6, 1980), 14.

46. Halloran, R. Shift of strategy on missile attack hinted by Weinberger and Vessey. *New York Times* (May 6, 1983), 1:1.

47. Hart, G., and Goldwater, B. *Recent False Alerts from the Nation's Missile Attack Warning System*. United States Senate, Committee on Armed Services, Washington, D.C., 1980.

48. Henderson, P., Ed. *Proceedings of the ACM SIGSOFT/SIGPLAN Software Engineering Symposium on Practical Software Development Environments*. ACM, New York, 1984.

49. Howden, W. E. Validation of scientific programs. *ACM Comput. Surv. 14*, 2 (June 1982), 193–227.

50. Hubbell, J. C. You are under attack! The strange incident of October 5. *Reader's Dig. 78*, 468 (Apr. 1961), 37–41.

51. International Institute for Strategic Studies. *The Military Balance 1983–1984*. International Institute for Strategic Studies, London, 1983.

52. Jensen, R. W., and Tonies, C. C. *Software Engineering*. Prentice-Hall, Englewood Cliffs, N.J., 1979.

53. Kling, R. Defining the boundaries of computing across complex organizations. In *Critical Issues in Information Systems Research*, R. Boland and R. Hirschheim, Eds. Wiley, New York, 1987.

54. Leveson, N. G. Software safety: Why, what, and how. Rep. 86–04, Dept. of Information and Computer Science, Univ. of California, Irvine, Feb. 1986.

55. Lieblein, E. The Department of Defense Software Initiative—A status report. *Commun. ACM 29*, 8 (Aug. 1986), 734–744.

56. Meyers, G. J. *Software Reliability: Principles and Practices.* Wiley, New York, 1976.

57. Meyers, G. J. *The Art of Software Testing.* Wiley, New York, 1979.

58. Miller, G. E. Existing systems of command and control. In *The Dangers of Nuclear War,* Griffiths, Franklyn, and Polanyi, Eds. University of Toronto Press, Toronto, Ontario, 1979, pp. 50–66.

59. Neumann, P. G. An editorial on software correctness and the social process. *Softw. Eng. Notes 4,* 2 (Apr. 1979), 3–4.

60. Neumann, P. G. Letter from the editor. *Softw. Eng. Notes 10,* 1 (Jan. 1985), 3–11.

61. *New York Times.* Moon stirs scare of missile attack. *New York Times* (Dec. 8, 1960), 71:2.

62. *New York Times.* False alarm on attack sends fighters into sky. *New York Times* (Nov. 10, 1979), 21.

63. *New York Times.* Missile alerts traced to 46 cent item. *New York Times* (June 18, 1980), 16.

64. *New York Times.* Nevada governor says errors led to flooding. *New York Times* (July 4, 1983), I-10.

65. Nye, J. S., Allison, G. T., and Carnesale, A. Analytic conclusions: Hawks, doves, and owls. In *Hawks, Doves, and Owls,* G. T. Allison, A Carnesale, and J. S. Nye, Eds. Norton, New York, 1985. Chap. 8, pp. 206–222.

66. Office of Technology Assessment. MX missile basing—Launch under attack. Office of Technology Assessment, Washington, D.C., 1981.

67. Parnas, D. L., Clements, P. C., and Weiss, D. M. The modular structure of complex systems. In *Proceedings of the 7th International Conference on Software Engineering* (Orlando, Fla., Mar. 26–29). IEEE Press, New York, 1984, pp. 408–417.

68. Partsch, H., and Steinbruggen, R. Program transformation systems. *ACM Comput. Surv. 15,* 3 (Sept. 1983), 199–236.

69. Perrow, C. Normal accident at Three Mile Island. *Society 18,* 5 (July–Aug. 1981), 17–26.

70. Perrow, C. *Normal Accidents: Living with High-Risk Technologies.* Basic Books, New York, 1984.

71. Pollack, A. Trust in computers raising risk of errors and sabotage. *New York Times* (Aug. 22, 1983), 1.

72. Pringle, P., and Arkin, W. *S.I.O.P.: The Secret U.S. Plan for Nuclear War.* Norton, New York, 1983.

73. Rogovin, M., and Frampton, G. T. *Three Mile Island: A Report to the Commissioners and to the Public.* Nuclear Regulatory Commission Special Inquiry Group, U.S. Nuclear Regulatory Commission, Washington, D.C., 1980.

74. Rosen, E. Vulnerabilities of network control protocols: An example. *Softw. Eng. Notes 6,* 1 (Jan. 1981), 6–8.

75. Scowcroft, B. *Report of the President's Commission on Strategic Forces.* U.S. Department of Defense, Washington, D.C., Apr. 1983.

76. *Seattle Post-Intelligencer.* Russia puts more N-arms off U.S. Coast. *Seattle Post-Intelligencer* (May 21, 1984), A2.

77. Siewiorek, D. P., and Swarz, R. S. *The Theory and Practice of Reliable System Design*. Digital Press, Bedford, Mass., 1982.

78. Silverman, J. M. Reflections on the verification of the security of an operating system. In *Proceedings of the 9th ACM Symposium on Operating Systems Principles* (Oct.). ACM, New York, 1983, pp. 143–154

79. Smith, B. C. The limits of correctness. *ACM SIGCAS Newsl. 14, 4 and 15,* 1–3 (Winter–Fall 1985), 18–26.

80. Sokolovskiy, V. D. *Soviet Military Strategy*. Edited, with an analysis and commentary, by H. Fast Scott. Crane, Russak and Co., New York, 1975.

81. Sommerville, I. *Software Engineering*. Addison-Wesley, Reading, Mass., 1982.

82. Stein, D. L. Electromagnetic pulse—The uncertain certainty. *Bull. At. Sci. 39,* 3 (Mar. 1983), 52–56.

83. Steinbruner, J. D. Launch under attack. *Sci. Am. 250,* 1 (Jan. 1984), 37–47.

84. Stevens, R. T. Testing the NORAD command and control system. *IEEE Trans. Syst. Sci. Cybern. SSC-4,* 1 (Mar. 1968), 47–51.

85. Stockholm International Peace Research Institute. *World Armament and Disarmament: SIPRI Yearbook 1983*. Taylor and Francis, London 1983.

86. Stockholm International Peace Research Institute. *World Armament and Disarmament: SIPRI Yearbook 1984*. Taylor and Francis, London 1984.

87. Tasky, K. Soviet technology gap and dependence on the west: The case of computers. A Compendium of Papers Submitted to the Joint Economic Committee of the Congress of the United States, Washington, D.C., Oct. 10, 1979.

88. U.S. Department of Defense. *Military Standardization Handbook: Reliability Prediction of Electronic Equipment. MIL-STD-HDBK-217C* Notice 1 ed. U.S. Department of Defense, Washington, D.C., 1980.

89. U.S. Department of Defense. *Modernization of the WWMCCS Information System (WIS)*. The Assistant Secretary of Defense (CCCI) with the assistance of the WWMCCS System Engineer (DCA). U.S. Department of Defense, Washington, D.C., July 31, 1982.

90. U.S. Department of Defense. *Soviet Military Power*. 2nd ed. U.S. Government Printing Office, Washington, D.C., 1983.

91. U.S. Department of Defense. Software technology for adaptable, reliable systems. *Softw. Eng. Notes 8,* 2 (Apr. 1983), 55–84.

92. U.S. Department of Defense. *DOD-STD-2167: Military Standard Defense System Software Development*. U.S. Department of Defense, Washington, D.C., 1985.

93. U.S. House of Representatives. *Failures of the North American Aerospace Defense Command's (NORAD) Attack Warning System*. Hearings before a Subcommittee of the Committee on Government Operations, U.S. House of Representatives, 97th Congress, 1st session, May 19 and 20, 1981.

94. U.S. House of Representatives. *Our Nation's Nuclear Warning System: Will It Work If We Need It?* Hearings before a Subcommittee of the Committee on Government Operations, U.S. House of Representatives, 99th Congress, 1st session, Sept. 26, 1985.

95. U.S. Senate Committee on Armed Services. *Hearings, Department of Defense Authorization for Appropriations for FY 1982, Part 7*. U.S. Government Printing Office, Washington, D.C., 1981.

96. Van Evera, S. The cult of the offensive and the origins of the First World War. *Int. Secur. 9*, 1 (Summer 1984), 58–107.

97. Waltz, E. L. Data fusion for C³I systems. In *C³I Handbook*. EW Communications, Palo Alto, Calif., 1986, pp. 217–226.

98. *Washington Post*. Computer again gives signal of false Soviet attack. *Washington Post* (June 8, 1980), A7.

99. *Washington Post*. Soviet warns of automatic retaliation against new U.S. missiles. *Washington Post* (May 18, 1983), A12.

100. Bracken, P. *The Command and Control of Nuclear Forces*. Yale University Press, New Haven, Conn., 1983.

101. U.S. Department of Defense. *Soviet Military Power*. 3rd ed. U.S. Government Printing Office, Washington D.C., 1984.

102. Parnas, D. L. Software aspects of strategic defense systems. *Am. Sci. 73*, 5 (Sept.–Oct. 1985), 432–440.

ON BUILDING SYSTEMS THAT WILL FAIL

Fernando J. Corbató

It is an honor and a pleasure to accept the Alan Turing Award. My own work has been on computer systems, and that will be my theme. The essence of systems is that they are integrating efforts, requiring broad knowledge of the problem area to be addressed, and the detailed knowledge required is rarely held by one person. Thus the work of systems is usually done by teams. Hence I am accepting this award on behalf of the many with whom I have worked as much as for myself. It is not practical to name all the individuals who contributed. Nevertheless, I would like to give special mention to Marjorie Daggett and Bob Daley for their parts in the birth of CTSS and to Bob Fano and the late Ted Glaser for their critical contributions to the development of the Multics System.

Let me turn now to the title of this talk: "On Building Systems That Will Fail." Of course the title I chose was a teaser. I considered and discarded some alternate titles: "On Building Messy Systems," but it seemed too frivolous and suggests there is no systematic approach. "On Mastering System Complexity" sounded like I have all the answers. The title that came closest, "On Building Systems That Are Likely to Have Failures" did not have the nuance of inevitability that I wanted to suggest.

What I am really trying to address is the class of systems that for want of a better phrase, I will call "ambitious systems." It almost goes without saying that ambitious systems never quite work as expected. Things usually go wrong—sometimes in dramatic ways. And this leads me to my main thesis, namely, that the question to ask when designing such systems is not: "*if* something will go wrong, but *when* will it go wrong?"

SOME EXAMPLES

Now, ambitious systems that fail are really much more common than we may realize. In fact in some circumstances we strive for them, revelling in the excitement of the unexpected. For example, let me remind you of our national sport of football. The whole object of the game is for each team to play at the limit of its abilities. Besides the sheer physical skill required, one has the strategic intricacies, the ability to audibilize, and the quickness to react to the unexpected—all a deep part of the game. Of course, occasionally one team approaches perfection, all the plays work, and the game becomes dull.

Another example of a system that is too ambitious for perfection is military warfare. The same elements are there with opposing sides having to constantly improvise and deal with the unexpected. In fact we get from the military that wonderful acronym, SNAFU, which is politely translated as "situation normal, all fouled up." And if any of you are still doubtful, consider how rapidly the phrases "precision bombing" and "surgical strikes" are replaced by "the fog of war" and "casualties from friendly fire" as soon as hostilities begin.

On a somewhat more whimsical note, let me offer driving in Boston as an example of systems that *will* fail. Automobile traffic is an excellent case of distributed control with a common set of protocols called traffic regulations. The Boston area is notorious for the free interpretations drivers make of these pesky regulations, and perhaps the epitome of it occurs in the arena of the traffic rotary. A case can be made for rotaries. They are efficient. There is no need to wait for sluggish traffic signals. They are direct. And they offer great opportunities for creative improvisation, thereby adding zest to the sport of driving.

One of the most effective strategies is for a driver approaching a rotary to rigidly fix his or her head, staring forward, of course, secretly using peripheral vision to the limit. It is even more effective if the driver on entering the rotary, speeds up, and some drivers embellish this last step by adopting a look of maniacal glee. The effect is, of course, one of intimidation, and a pecking order quickly develops.

The only reason there are not more accidents is that most drivers have a second component to the strategy, namely, they assume everyone else may be crazy—they are often correct—and every driver is really prepared to stop with inches to spare. Again we see an example of a system where ambitious tactics and prudent caution lead to an effective solution.

So far, the examples I have given may suggest that failures of ambitious systems come from the human element and that at least the technical parts of the system can be built correctly. In particular, turning to computer systems, it is only a matter of getting the code debugged. Some assume rigorous testing will do the job. Some put their hopes in proving program correctness. But unfortunately, there are many cases for which none of these techniques will always work [1]. Let me offer a modest example.

Consider the case of an elaborate numerical calculation with a variable, f, representing some physical value, being calculated for a set of points over a range of a parameter, t. Now the property of physical variables is that they normally do not exhibit abrupt changes or discontinuities.

So what has happened here? If we look at the expression for f, we see it is the result of a constant, k, added to the product of two other functions, g and h. Looking further, we see that the function g has a behavior that is exponentially increasing with t. The function h, on the other hand, is exponentially decreasing with t. The resultant product of g and h is almost constant with increasing t until an abrupt jump occurs and the curve for f goes flat.

What has gone wrong? The answer is that there has been floating-point under-flow at the critical point in the curve, i.e., the representation of the negative exponent has exceeded the field size in the floating-point representation for this particular com-puter, and the hardware has automatically set the value for the function h to zero. Often this is reasonable since small numbers are correctly approximated by zero—but not in this case, where our results are grossly wrong. Worse yet, since the com-putation of f might be internal, it is easy to imagine that the failure shown here would not be noticed.

Because correctly handling the pathology that this example represents is an extra engineering bother, it should not be surprising that the problem of underflow is frequently ignored. But the larger lesson to be learned from this example is that sub-tle mistakes are very difficult to avoid and to some extent are inevitable.

I encountered my next example when I was a graduate student programming on the pioneering Whirlwind computer. One night while awaiting my turn to use it, the graduate student before me began complaining of how "tough" some of his cal-culations were. He said he was computing the vibrational frequencies of a particular wing structure for a series of cases. In fact, his equations were cubics, and he was using the iterative Newton-Raphson method. For reasons he did not understand, his method was finding one of the roots, but not "converging" for the others. He was try-ing to fix this situation by changing his program so that when he encountered one of these tough roots, the program would abandon the iteration after a fixed number of tries.

Now there were several things wrong: First, the coefficients to his cubic equa-tions were based on experimental data and some of his points were simply bad. Therefore, he only had one real root and a pair of imaginaries. Thus his iterative method could never converge for the second and third roots and the value of his first root was pure garbage. Second, cubic equations have an exact analytic closed form solution so that it was entirely unnecessary to use an iterative method. And third, based on his incomplete model and understanding of what was happening, he exer-cised very poor judgment in patching his program to ignore values that were seem-ingly difficult to compute.

AMBITIOUS SYSTEM PROPERTIES

Let me turn next to some of the general properties of ambitious systems. First, they are often vast and have significant organizational structures going beyond that of sim-ple replication. Second, they are frequently complicated or elaborate and are too much for even a small group to develop. Third, if they really are ambitious, they are pushing the envelope of what people know how to do, and as a result there is always a level of uncertainty about when completion is possible. Because one has to be an optimist to begin an ambitious project, it is not surprising that underestimation of completion time is the norm. Fourth, ambitious systems when they work, often break new ground, offer new services and soon become indispensable. Finally, it is often the case that ambitious systems by virtue of having opened up a new domain of usage, invite a flood of improvements and changes.

Now one could argue that ambitious systems are really only difficult the first time or two. It is really only a matter of learning how to do it. Once one has, then one simply draws up the appropriate PERT charts, hires good managers, ensures an adequate budget and gets on with it. Perhaps there are some instances where this works, but at least in the area of computer systems, there is a fundamental reason it does not.

A key reason we cannot seem to get ambitious systems right is change. The computer field is intoxicated with change. We have seen galloping growth over a period of four decades and it still does not seem to be slowing down. The field is not mature yet and already it accounts for a significant percentage of the Gross National Product both directly and indirectly. More importantly the computer revolution—this second industrial revolution—has changed our life-styles and allowed the growth of countless new application areas. And all this change and growth not only has changed the world we live in, but has raised our expectations, spurring on increasingly ambitious systems in such diverse areas as airline reservations, banking, credit cards, and air traffic control to name only a few.

Behind the incredible growth of the computer industry is, of course, the equally mind-boggling change that has occurred in the raw performance of digital logic.

Complicating matters too is that parallelism is not a solution for every problem. Certain calculations that are intrinsically serial, such as rocket trajectories, derive very limited benefit from parallel computers. And one of course is reminded of the old joke about the Army way of speeding up pregnancy by having nine women spend one month at the task.

It is not just performance that has fueled growth but rather cost/performance, or simply put, favorable economics. Again the ordinate is logarithmic, going from 10 million dollars in 1950 down to one thousand dollars in 1990. As we approach the present, corresponding to a personal computer, the graph really should become more complicated since one consequence of computers becoming super-cheap is that increasingly, they are being embedded in other equipment. The modern automobile is but one example. And it remains to be seen how general-purpose the current wave of palm-sized computers will be with their stylus inputs.

Further, when we look at a photograph taken around 1960 of a "machine room" staffed with one lone operator, we are reminded of the fantastic changes that have occurred in computer technology. The boxes are huge, shower-stall-sized, and the overall impression is of some small factory. You were supposed to be impressed and the operator was expected to maintain decorum by wearing a necktie. And if he did not, at least you could be sure an IBM maintenance engineer would.

Another reminder of the immense technological change which has occurred is in the physical dimensions of the main memories of computers. For example, if one looks at old photographs taken in the mid-1950s of core memory systems, one typically sees a core memory plane roughly the size of a tennis racquet head which could hold about 1,000 bits of information. Contrast that with today's 4megabit memory chips that are smaller than one's thumb.

The basis of the Award today is largely for my work on two pioneering time-sharing systems, CTSS [5, 6] and Multics [7, 9]. Indeed, it is from my involvement with those two systems that I gained the system-building perspective I am offering. It therefore seems appropriate to take a brief retrospective look at these two systems as examples of ambitious systems and to explore the reasons why the complexity of the tasks involved made it almost impossible to build the systems correctly the first time [2].

CTSS, THE COMPATIBLE TIME-SHARING SYSTEM

Looking first at CTSS, let us remember the dark ages that existed then. This was the early 1960s. The computers of the day were big and expensive, and the administrators of computing centers felt obliged to husband the precious resource. Users, i.e., programmers, were expected to submit a computing job as a deck of punched cards. These were then combined into a batch with other jobs onto a magnetic tape and the tape was processed by the computer operating system. It had all the glamour and excitement of dropping one's clothes off at a laundromat.

The problem was that even for a trivial input typing mistake, the job would be aborted. Time-sharing, as most of you know, was the solution to the problem of not being able to interact with computers. The general vision of modern time-sharing was primarily spelled out by John McCarthy, who I am pleased to note is a featured speaker at this conference. In England, Christopher Strachey independently came up with a limited kind of interactive computing, but it was aimed mostly at debugging. Soon there were many groups around the country developing various forms of interactive computing, but in almost all cases, the resulting systems had significant limitations.

It was in this context that my own group developed our version of the time-sharing vision. We called it The Compatible Time-Sharing System, or CTSS for short. Our initial aspirations were modest. First, the system was meant to be a demonstration prototype before more ambitious designs being attempted by others could be implemented. Second, it was intended to handle general-purpose programming. And third, it was meant to make it possible to run most of the large body of software that had been developed over the years in the batch-processing environment. Hence the name.

The basic scheme used to run CTSS was simple. The supervisor program, which was always in main memory, would commutate among the user programs, running each in turn for a brief interval with the help of an interval timer. User programs could do input/output with the typewriter-like terminals and with the disk storage unit as well.

But the diagram is oversimplified. The key difficulty was that main memory was in short supply and not all the programs of the active users could remain in memory at once. Thus the supervisor program not only had to move programs to and from the disk storage unit, but it also had to act as an intermediary for all I/O initiated by user programs. Thus all the I/O lines should only point to the supervisor program.

As a further complication, the supervisor program had to prevent user programs from trampling over one another. To do this required special hardware modifications to the processor such that there were memory bound registers that could only be set by the supervisor. Nevertheless, despite all the complications, the simplicity of the initial supervisor program allowed it to occupy about 22 Kbytes of storage—less storage than required for the text of this talk!

Most of the battles of creating CTSS involved solving problems which at the time did not have standard solutions. For example: There were no standard terminals. There were no simple modems. I/O to the computer was by word and not by character, and worse yet, did not accommodate lower case letters. The computers of the day had neither interrupt timers nor calendar clocks. There was no way to prevent user programs from issuing raw I/O instructions at random. There was no memory protection scheme. And, there was no easy way to store large amounts of data with relatively rapid random access.

The overall result of building CTSS was to change the style of computing, but there were several effects that seem worth noting. One of the most important was that we discovered that writing interactive software was quite different from software for batch operation and even today, in this era of personal computers, the evolution of interactive interfaces continues.

In retrospect, several design decisions contributed to the success of CTSS, but two were key. First, we could do general-purpose programming and, in particular, develop new supervisor software using the system itself. Second, by making the system able to accommodate older batch code, we inherited a wealth of older software ready-to-go.

One important consequence of developing CTSS was that for the first time, users had persistent on-line storage of programs and data. Suddenly the issues of privacy, protection and backup of information had to be faced. Another byproduct of the development was that because we operated terminals via modems, remote operation became the norm. Also, the new-found freedom of keeping information on-line in the central file system suddenly made it especially convenient for users to share and exchange information among themselves.

And there were surprises too. To our dismay, users who had been enduring several-hour waits between jobs run under batch processing were suddenly restless when response times were more than a second. Moreover, many of the simplifying assumptions that had allowed CTSS to be built so simply, such as a one-level file system, suddenly began to chafe. It seemed like the more we did, the more users wanted.

There are two other observations that can be made about the CTSS system. First, it lasted far longer than we expected. Although CTSS had been demonstrated in primitive form in November 1961, it was not until 1963 that it came into wide use as the vehicle of a Project MAC Summer Study. For a time there were two copies of the system hardware, but by 1973 the last copy was turned off and scrapped primarily because the maintenance costs of the IBM 7094 hardware had become prohibitively expensive, and up to the bitter end, there were users desperately trying to get in a few last hours of use.

Second, the then-new transistors and large random-access disk files were absolutely critical to the success of time-sharing. The previous generation of vacuum tubes was simply too unreliable for sustained real-time operation and, of course, large disk files were crucial for the central storage of user programs and data.

A MISHAP

My central theme is to try to convince you that when you have a multitude of novel issues to contend with while building a system, mistakes are inevitable. And indeed, we had a beauty while using CTSS. Let me describe it:

What happened was that one afternoon at Project MAC, where CTSS was being used as the main time-sharing workhorse, any user who logged in, found that instead of the usual message-of-the-day typing out on his or her terminal, he had the entire file of user passwords. This went on for 15 or 20 minutes, until one particularly conscientious user called the system administrator and began the conversation with "Did you know that . . . ?" Needless to say, there was general consternation with this colossal breach of security, the system was hastily shut down and the next twelve hours were spent heroically changing everyone's password. The question was how could this have happened? Let me explain.

To simplify the organization of the initial CTSS system, a design decision had been made to have each user at a terminal associated with his or her own directory of files. Moreover, the system itself was organized as a kind of quasi-user with its own directory that included a large number of supporting applications and files, including the message-of-the day and the password file. So far, so good. Normally a single-system programmer could login to the system directory and make any necessary changes. But the number of system programmers had grown to about a dozen in number, and, further, the system by then was being operated almost continuously so that the need to do live maintenance of the system files became essential. Not surprisingly, the system programmers saw the one-user-to-a-directory restriction as a big bottleneck for themselves. They thereupon proceeded to cajole me into letting the system directory be an exception so that more than one person at a time could be logged into it. They assured me that they would be careful to not make mistakes.

But of course a mistake was made. A software design decision in the standard system text editor was overlooked. It was assumed that the editor would only be used by one user at a time working in one directory so that a temporary file could have the same name for all instantiations of the editor. But with two system programmers editing at the same time in the system directory, the editor temporary files became swapped and the disaster occurred.

One can draw two lessons from this: First, design bugs are often subtle and occur by evolution with early assumptions being forgotten as new features or uses are added to systems. Second, even skilled programmers make mistakes.

MULTICS

Let me turn now to the development of Multics [12]. I will be brief since the system has been documented well and there have already been two retrospective papers written [3, 4]. The Multics system was meant to do time-sharing "right" and replace the previous ad hoc systems such as CTSS. It started as a cooperative effort among Project MAC of MIT, the Bell Telephone Laboratories, and the Computer Department of General Electric, later acquired by Honeywell. In our expansiveness of purpose we took on a long list of innovations.

Among the most important ones were the following: First, we introduced into the processor hardware the mechanisms for paging and segmentation along with a careful scheme for access control. Second, we introduced an idea for rings of protection around the supervisor software. Third, we planned from the start that the system would be composed of interchangeable multiple processors, memory modules, and so forth. And fourth, we made the decision to implement nearly all of the system in the newly defined compiler language, PL/I.

Let me share a few of my observations about the Multics experience. The novel hardware we had commissioned meant that the system had to be built from the ground up so that we had an immense task on our hands.

The decision to use a compiler to implement the system software was a good one, but what we did not appreciate was that new language PL/I presented us with two big difficulties: First, the language had constructs in it which were intrinsically complicated, and it required a learning period on the part of system programmers to learn to avoid them. Second, no one knew how to do a good job of implementing the compiler. Eventually we overcame these difficulties but it took precious time.

That Multics succeeded is remarkable, for it was the results of a cooperative effort of three highly independent organizations and had no administrative head. This meant decisions were made by persuasion and consensus. Consequently, it was difficult to reject weak ideas until considerable time and effort had been spent on them.

The Multics system did turn into a commercial product. Some of its major strengths were the virtual memory system, the file system, the attention to security, the ability to do online reconfiguration, and the information backup system for the file system.

And, as was also true with CTSS, many of the alumni of the Multics development have gone on to play important roles in the computing field [11].

A few more observations can be made about the ambitious Multics experience. In particular, we were misled by our earlier successes with previous systems such as CTSS, where we were able to build them "brick-by-brick," incrementally adding ideas to a large base of already working software.

We also were embarrassed by our inability to set and meet accurate schedules for completion of the different phases of the project. In retrospect, we should not have been, for we had never done anything like it before. However in many cases, our estimations should have been called guesses.

The Unix system [15] was a reaction to Multics. Even the name was a joke. Ken Thompson was part of the Bell Laboratories' Multics effort, and, frustrated with the attempts to bring a large system development under control, decided to start over. His strategy was clear—Start small and build up the ideas one by one as he saw how to implement them well. As we all know, Unix has evolved and become immensely successful as the system of choice for workstations. Still there are aspects of Multics that have never been replicated in Unix.

As a commercial product of Honeywell and Bull, Multics developed a loyal following. At the peak there were about 77 sites worldwide and even today many of the sites tenaciously continue for want of an alternative.

SOURCES OF COMPLEXITY

The general problem with ambitious systems is complexity. Let me next try to abstract some of the major causes. The most obvious complexity problems arise from scale. In particular, the larger the personnel required, the more levels of management there will be. We can see the problem even if we use simplistic calculations. Thus if we assume a fixed supervision ratio, for example six, the levels of management will grow as the logarithm of the personnel. The difficulty is that with more layers of management, the top-most layers become out of touch with the relevant bottom issues and the likelihood of random serendipitous communication decreases.

Another problem of organizations is that subordinates hate to report bad news, sometimes for fear of "being shot as the messenger" and at other times because they may have a different set of goals than the upper management.

And finally, large projects encourage specialization so that few team members understand all of the project. Misunderstandings and miscommunication begin, and soon a significant part of the project resources are spent fighting internal confusion. And, of course, mistakes occur.

My next category of complexity arises because of new design domains. The most vivid examples come from the world of physical systems, but software too is subject to the same problems, albeit often in more subtle ways.

Consider the destruction of the Tacoma Narrows Bridge, in Washington State, on November 7, 1940. The bridge had been proudly opened about four months earlier. Many of you have probably seen the amateur movie that was fortunately made of the collapse. What happened is that a strong but not unusual crosswind blew that day. Soon the roadbed, suspended by cables from the main span, began to vibrate like a reed, and the more it flexed, the better cross section it presented to the wind. The result was that the bridge tore itself apart as the oscillations became large and violent. What we had was a case of a new design domain where the classic bridge builder, concerned with gravity-loaded structures, had entered into the realm of aeronautics. The result was a major mistake.

Next, let us look at the complexities that arise from human usage of computer systems. In using online systems that allow the sharing or exchanging of information—and here networked workstations clearly fall in this class—one is faced with a dilemma: If one places total trust in all other users, one is vulnerable to the antisocial behavior of any malicious user—consider the case of viruses. But if one tries to be totally reclusive and isolated, one is not only bored, but one's information universe will cease to grow and be enhanced by interaction with others. The result is that most of us operate in a complicated trade-off zone with various arrangements of trust and security mechanisms. Even such simple ideas as passwords are often a problem. They are a nuisance to remember, they can easily be compromised inadvertently, and they cannot be selectively revoked if shared. Privacy and security issues are particularly difficult to deal with since responsibilities are often split among users, managers, and vendors. Worse yet, there is no way to simply "look" at a system and determine what the privacy and security implications are. It is no wonder mistakes occur all the time in this area.

One of the consequences of using computer systems is that increasingly information is being kept on-line in central storage devices. Computer storage devices have become remarkably reliable—except when they break—and that is the rub. Even the most experienced computer user can find him- or herself lulled into a false sense of security by the almost perfect operation of today's devices. The problem is compounded by the attitude of vendors, not unlike the initial attitude of the automobile industry toward safety, where inevitable disk failure is treated as a negative issue that dampens sales.

What is needed is constant vigilance against a long list of "what ifs": hardware failure, human slips, vandalism, theft, fire, earthquakes, long-term media failure, and even the loss of institutional memories concerning recovery procedures. And as long as some individuals have to "learn the hard way," mistakes will continue to be made.

A further complication in discussing risk or reliability is that there is not a good language with which to carry on a dialog. Statistics are as often misapplied as they are misunderstood. We also get absurd absolutes such as "the Strategic Defense Initiative will produce a perfect unsaturatable shield against nuclear attack" [14] or "it is impossible for the reactor to overheat." The problem is that we always have had risks in our lives, we never have been very good at discussing them, and with computers we now have a lot of new sources.

Another source of complexity arises with rapid change, change which is often driven by technology improvements. A result is that changes in procedures or usage occur and new vulnerabilities can arise. For example, in the area of telephone networks, the economies and efficiencies of fiber optic cables compared to copper wire are rapidly causing major upgrades and replacements in the national telephone plant. Because one fiber cable can carry at a reasonable cost the equivalent traffic of thousands of copper wires, fiber is quickly replacing copper. As a result, a transformation is likely to occur where network links become sparser over a given area and multiply interconnected nodes become less connected.

The difficulty is that there is reduced redundancy and a much higher vulnerability to isolated accidents. In the Chicago area not long ago there was a fire at a fiber optics switching center that caused a loss of service to a huge number of customers for several weeks. More recently, in New York City there was a shutdown of the financial exchanges for several hours because of a single mishap with a backhoe in New Jersey. Obviously in both instances, efficiency had gotten ahead of robustness.

The last source of complexity that I will single out arises from the frailty of human users when forced to deal with the multiplicity of technologies in modern life. In a little more than a century, there has been an awesome progression of technological changes from telephones and electricity, through automobiles, movies and radio—I will not even try to complete the list since we all know it well. The overall consequence has been to produce vast changes in our life-styles, and we see these changes even happening today. Consider the changes in the television editing styles that have occurred over a few decades, the impact of viewgraph overhead projectors on college classrooms, and the way we now do our banking with automatic teller machines. And the progression of life-style changes continues at a seemingly more rapid pace with word processing, answering machines, facsimile machines, and electronic mail.

One consequence of the many life-style changes is that some individuals feel stressed and overstimulated by the plethora of inputs. The natural defense is to increasingly depend on others to act as information filters. But the combination of stressful life-styles and insulation from original data will inevitably lead to more confusion and mistakes.

CONCLUSIONS

Most of this talk has been directed toward trying to persuade you that failures in complex, ambitious systems are inevitable. However, I would be remiss if I did not address ways to resolve the problem. Unfortunately, the list I can offer is rather short but worthy of brief review.

First, it is important to emphasize the value of simplicity and elegance, for complexity has a way of compounding difficulties and as we have seen, creating mistakes. My definition of elegance is the achievement of a given functionality with a minimum of mechanism and a maximum of clarity.

Second, the value of metaphors should not be underestimated. Metaphors have the virtue of an expected behavior that is understood by all. Unnecessary communication and misunderstandings are reduced. Learning and education are quicker. In effect, metaphors are a way of internalizing and abstracting concepts allowing one's thinking to be on a higher plane and low-level mistakes to be avoided.

Third, use of constrained languages for design or synthesis is a powerful methodology. By not allowing a programmer or designer to express irrelevant ideas, the domain of possible errors becomes far more limited.

Fourth, one must try to anticipate both errors of human usage and of hardware failure and properly develop the necessary contingency paths. This process of playing "what if " is not as easy as it may sound, since the need to attach likelihoods of occurrence to events and to address issues of the independence of failures is implicit.

Fifth, it should be assumed in the design of a system, that it will have to be repaired or modified. The overall effect will be a much more robust system, where there is a high degree of functional modularity and structure, and repairs can be made easily.

Sixth, and last, on a large project, one of the best investments that can be made is the cross education of the team so that nearly everyone knows more than he or she needs to know. Clearly, with educational redundancy, the team is more resilient to unexpected tragedies or departures. But in addition, the increased awareness of team members can help catch global or systemic mistakes early. It really is a case of "more heads are better than one."

Finally, I have touched on many different themes in this talk but I will single out three: First, the evolution of technology supports a rich future for ambitious visions and dreams that will inevitably involve complex systems. Second, one must always try to learn from past mistakes, but at the same time be alert to the possibility that new circumstances require new solutions. And third, one must remember that ambitious systems demand a defensive philosophy of design and implementation. In other words, "Don't wonder *if* some mishap may happen, but rather ask *what* one will do about it when it does occur."

REFERENCES

1. Brooks, F. P., Jr. No silver bullet. *IEEE Comput.* (Apr. 1987), 10–19.

2. Corbató, F. J. Sensitive issues in the design of multi-use systems. Unpublished lecture transcription of Feb. 1968, Project MAC Memo M-383.

3. Corbató, F. J., and Clingen, C. T. A managerial view of the Multics system development. In *Research Directions in Software Technology*, P. Wegner, Ed., M.I.T. Press, 1979. (Also published in *Tutorial: Software Management*, D. J. Reifer, Ed., IEEE Computer Society Press, 1979; Second Ed., 1981; Third Ed., 1986.)

4. Corbató, F. J., Clingen, C. T., and Saltzer, J. H. Multics: The first seven years. In *Proceedings of the SJCC* (May 1972), pp. 571–583.

5. Corbató, F. J., Daggett, M. M., and Daley, R. C. An experimental time-sharing system. In *Proceedings of the Spring Joint Computer Conference* (May 1962).

6. Corbató, F. J., Daggett, M. M., Daley, R. C., Creasy, R. J., Hellwig, J. D., Orenstein, R. H., and Horn, L. K. *The Compatible Time-Sharing System: A Programmer's Guide*. M.I.T. Press, June 1963.

7. Corbató, F. J., and Vyssotsky, V. A. Introduction and overview of the Multics system. In *Proceedings FJCC* (1965).

8. Daley, R. C. and Neumann, P. G. A general-purpose file system for secondary storage. In *Proceedings FJCC* (1965).

9. David, E. E., Jr. and Fano, R. M. Some thoughts about the social implications of accessible computing. In *Proceedings FJCC* (1965).

10. Glaser, E. L., Couleur, J. F. and Oliver, G. A. System design of a computer for time-sharing applications. In *Proceedings FJCC* (1965).

11. Neumann, P. G., a Multics veteran, has become a major contributor to the literature of computer-related risks. He is the editor of the widely-read network mag-

azine "Risks-Forum," writes the "Inside Risks" column for the CACM, and periodically creates digests in the ACM Software Engineering Notes.

12. Organick, E. I. *The Multics System: An Examination of its Structure*. MIT Press, 1972.

13. Ossanna, J. F., Mikus, L. and Dunten, S. D. Communications and input-output switching in a Multiplex computing system. In *Proceedings FJCC* (1965).

14. Parnas, D. L. Software aspects of strategic defense systems. *Am. Sci.* (Nov. 1985). An excellent critique on the difficulties of producing software for large-scale systems.

15. Ritchie, D. M. and Thompson, K. The UNIX time-sharing system. *Commun. ACM 17*, 7 (July 1974), 365–375.

16. Vyssotsky, V. A., and Corbató, F. J. Structure of the Multics Supervisor. In *Proceedings FJCC*, 1965.

▷ THE RISKS OF SOFTWARE

Bev Littlewood
Lorenzo Strigini

Programming bugs have disrupted telephone service and delayed shuttle launches. An inherent uncertainty in reliability may mean limiting a computer's role, especially in systems where software is critical for safety.

Most of us have experienced some kind of problem related to computer failure: a bill mailed in error or a day's work destroyed by some mysterious glitch in a desktop computer. Such nuisances, often caused by software faults, or "bugs," are merely inconvenient when compared with the consequences of computer failures in critical systems. Software bugs caused the series of large-scale outages of telephone service in the U.S. A software problem may have prevented the Patriot missile system from tracking the Iraqi Scud missile that killed 28 American soldiers during the Gulf War. Indeed, software faults are generally more insidious and much more difficult to handle than are physical defects.

The problems essentially arise from complexity, which increases the possibility that design faults will persist and emerge in the final product. Conventional engineering has made great strides in the understanding and control of physical problems. Although design faults are sometimes present in material products that do not contain computers, the relative simplicity of such machines has made design reliability less serious than it has become for software. The concerns expressed here, incidentally, go far beyond exotic military and aerospace products. Complex software is finding critical roles in more mundane areas, such as four-wheel steering and antilock braking in automobiles.

In this article we examine some major reasons for the uncertainty concerning software reliability and argue that our ability to measure it falls far short of the levels that are sometimes required. In critical systems, such as the safety systems of a dangerous chemical plant, it may be that the appropriate level of safety will be guaranteed only if the role of software is limited.

In theory at least, software can be made that is free of defects. Unlike materials and machinery, software does not wear out. All design defects are present from the time the software is loaded into the computer. In principle, these faults could be removed once and for all. Furthermore, mathematical proof should enable programmers to guarantee correctness.

Yet the goal of perfect software remains elusive. Despite rigorous and systematic testing, most large programs contain some residual bugs when delivered. The reason for this is the complexity of the source code. A program of only a few hundred lines may contain tens of decisions, allowing for thousands of alternative paths of execution (programs for fairly critical applications vary between tens and millions of lines of code). A program can make the wrong decision because the particular inputs that triggered the problem had not been used during the test phase, when defects could be corrected. The situation responsible for such inputs may even have been misunderstood or unanticipated: the designer either "correctly" programmed the wrong reaction or failed to take the situation into account altogether. This type of bug is the most difficult to eradicate.

In addition, specifications often change during system development, as the intended purpose of the system is modified or becomes better understood. Such changes may have implications that ripple through all parts of a system, making the previous design inadequate. Furthermore, real use may still differ from intended purpose. Failures of Patriot missiles to intercept Scud missiles have been attributed to an accumulation of inaccuracies in the internal time-keeping of a computer. Yet the computer was performing according to specifications: the system was meant to be turned off and restarted often enough for the accumulated error never to become dangerous. Because the system was used in an unintended way, a minor inaccuracy became a serious problem.

The intrinsic behavior of digital systems also hinders the creation of completely reliable software. Many physical systems are fundamentally continuous in that they are described by "well-behaved" functions—that is, very small changes in stimuli produce very small differences in responses. In contrast, the smallest possible perturbation to the state of a digital computer (changing a bit from 0 to 1, for instance) may produce a radical response. A single incorrect character in the specification of a control program for an Atlas rocket, carrying the first U.S. interplanetary spacecraft, *Mariner 1*, ultimately caused the vehicle to veer off course. Both rocket and spacecraft had to be destroyed shortly after launch.

In all other branches of engineering, simplicity and gradual change constitute the main elements of trustworthy design. But in software engineering the unprecedented degrees of novelty and flexibility that programming affords tempt workers to ignore these principles. Entirely new applications can be designed with apparent ease, giving a false sense of security to developers and clients who are not familiar with problems specific to software. Even the addition of novel features to a program may produce unexpected changes in existing features.

The problems of embedding complex decision rules in a design and forecasting the behavior of complex discontinuous systems are not limited to software. Designers of highly complex digital integrated circuits encounter similar problems. Software, however, is still the predominant medium for embodying extremely complex, specialized decision rules.

In addition to unintentional design bugs, flaws deliberately introduced to compromise a system can cause unacceptable system behavior. The issue of computer security, privacy and encryption requires special consideration that lies beyond the scope of this article.

Given that perfect software is a practical impossibility, how can we decide whether a program is as reliable as it is supposed to be? First, safety requirements must be chosen carefully to reflect the nature of the application. These requirements can vary dramatically from one application to another. For example, the U.S. requires that its new air-traffic control system cannot be unavailable for more than three seconds a year. In civilian airliners, the probability of certain catastrophic failures must be no worse than 10^{-9} per hour.

In setting reliability requirements for computers, we must also take into account any extra benefits that a computer may produce, because not using a particular system may itself incur harm. For example, military aircraft are by necessity much more dangerous to fly than are civilian ones. Survival in combat depends on high performance, which forbids conservative design, and a new computer system may improve the airplane's chances even if it is less safe than computers used in commercial airplanes. Similarly, in the design of a fly-by-wire civilian aircraft, such as the Airbus A320 or the Boeing 777, the possibility that software may cause accidents has to be weighed against the likelihood that it may avoid some mishaps that would otherwise be caused by pilot error or equipment failure.

We believe that there are severe restrictions on the levels of confidence that one can justifiably place in the reliability of software. To explain this point of view, we need to consider the different sources of evidence that support confidence in software. The most obvious is testing: running the program, directly observing its behavior and removing bugs whenever they show up. In this process the reliability of the software will grow, and the data collected can now generally be used, via sophisticated statistical extrapolation techniques, to obtain accurate measures of how reliable the program has become.

Unfortunately, this approach works only when the reliability requirements are fairly modest (say, in the range of one failure every few years) when compared with the requirements often set for critical applications. To have confidence at a level such as 10^{-9} failure per hour, we would need to execute the program for very many multiples of 10^9 hours, or 100,000 years. Clearly, this task is not possible. In the time spans for which it is feasible to test, assurance of the safety would fall many orders of magnitude short of what is needed.

The problem here is a law of diminishing returns. When we continue debugging a program for a very long time, eventually the bugs found are so "small" that fixing them has virtually no effect on the overall reliability or safety. Edward N. Adams of the IBM Thomas J. Watson Research Center empirically analyzed "bug sizes" over a worldwide data base that involved the equivalent use of thousands of years of a particular software system.

The most extraordinary discovery was that about a third of all bugs found were "5,000-year" bugs: each of them produced a failure only about once in 5,000 years of execution (the rates from other bugs varied by several orders of magnitude). These rare bugs made up a sizable portion of all faults because bugs that caused higher failure rates were encountered, and so removed, earlier. Eventually, only the 5,000-year bugs will make the system unreliable, and removal of one of these will bring negligible improvement in reliability.

Extrapolating from testing and debugging also implies an unsubstantiated assumption—namely, that a bug, once encountered, is simply corrected. In reality, an attempt to fix a bug sometimes fails. It may even introduce an entirely novel fault. Because nothing would be known about the new bug, its effect on the reliability of the system would be unbounded. In particular, the system might not even be as reliable as it was before the bug was found.

Therefore, a prudent course would be to discount completely the history prior to the last failure. This precaution, critically important in situations that involve safety, would require an evaluator to treat the software after the last fix as if it were a completely new program. Only the most recent period of error-free working would influence judgment about the safety of the program. But even this conservative course of action cannot provide much confidence. Our research has shown that under quite plausible mathematical assumptions, there is only about a 50–50 chance that the program will function without failure for the same length of time as it had before.

The problem of estimating safety is actually even more serious. To have any confidence in the numerical results, we must subject the program to situations it might encounter in reality. This approach ensures that inputs causing failures are encountered with the same frequency with which they would in fact arise. In addition, the tester should always be able to decide whether the program's output is actually correct. The problems here are similar to those of designing and implementing the software itself. To construct an accurate test environment, we need to be sure that we have thought of all circumstances that the software will meet. Just as the unexpected often defeats us in system design, so it is in test design. It would be wise to retain an element of skepticism about the representativeness of the testing and thus about the accuracy of the figures.

The problem in demonstrating extreme reliability or safety for any individual piece of software is simply lack of the necessary knowledge. For complex software, the unpalatable truth seems to be that there are severe limitations to the confidence one can place in a program. Merely observing a program's behavior is not the way to be sure that it will function properly for 100,000 years. How else might we acquire such confidence?

An obvious prerequisite for high reliability is that software be built with methods that are likely to achieve reliability. One method uses "formal" techniques, which rely on mathematical proofs to guarantee that a program will function according to specification. Indeed, formal techniques have become a topic of wide interest. Such methods, though currently limited by practical problems in their scope of application, can effectively avoid programming errors arising in the translation from the specification to the actual program.

Unfortunately, specifications must also be formal statements. In other words, the user's needs would have to be expressed in a mathematical language. That task is not simple: it requires a careful choice of those aspects of the real world to be described in the formal language and an understanding of both the detailed practical problems of the application and of the formal language. Errors would likely be introduced during this process, and we could not reasonably claim the program would never fail.

Another method now widely used (in avionic and railroad control applications, for instance) to achieve high reliability is fault tolerance, or protective redundancy. A typical way of applying redundancy is to have different design teams develop several versions of the program. The hope is that if the teams make mistakes, the errors will be different. Each version of the program provides its "opinion" of the correct output. The outputs pass to an adjudication phase, which produces a single output that would be correct if the majority of versions gave the correct result.

Some evidence exists that such design diversity delivers high reliability in a cost-effective manner. Different design teams, however, may make the same mistakes (perhaps because of commonalities in cultural background) or conceptually different mistakes that happen to make the versions fail on the same fault. The adjudicator would therefore produce incorrect output.

To measure the reliability of fault-tolerant software, it is necessary to gauge the statistical correlation between failures of the different versions. Unfortunately, the task turns out to be as hard as trying to measure the reliability by treating the whole system as a single entity—and we have seen the difficulty of doing that.

So if formal proofs do not enable one to claim that a program will never fail and if fault tolerance cannot guarantee reliability, there seems no choice but to evaluate reliability directly, using methods that are acknowledged to be of limited adequacy. How do the regulatory authorities and software users deal with this uncertainty?

There are three approaches. The first classifies design-caused failures as "nonquantifiable" errors and avoids specifying requirements for the software. This method is now in fairly wide use. For instance, in civil aviation, the U.S. Federal Aviation Administration Advisory Circular 25.1309-1A describes "acceptable" means for showing compliance with some federal aviation regulations. It states that catastrophic failure conditions (the worst category) must be "so unlikely that they are not anticipated to occur during the entire operational life of all airplanes of one type." The suggested quantitative expression is the probability of failure of not more than 10^{-9} per hour of flight. Software, however, is explicitly excluded from this circular, "because it is not feasible to assess the number or kinds of software errors, if any, that may remain after the completion of system design, development, and test."

The widely used document of the Radio Technical Commission for Aeronautics, RTCA/DO-178A, similarly avoids software measures. The document, which gives guidelines for manufacturers who must seek certification by aviation authorities, explicitly refuses to mandate quantitative terms or methods for evaluating software reliability or safety. Instead the commission regards a correct engineering approach—tight management, thorough reviews and tests, and analysis of previous errors—as more critical than quantitative methods. The basic message of RTCA/DO-178A "is that designers must take a disciplined approach to software: requirements definition, design, development, testing, configuration management and documentation." That is, the best assurance of reliability is to verify that utmost care was used in the design.

How good is such assurance? Arguably, not very good: there is no evidence that superior design and production methods consistently yield superior products. We cannot even be certain whether the best current methods ever produce sufficient reliability for the more demanding applications.

Eschewing the quantification of software safety poses a serious limitation for many potentially dangerous systems, especially those that require an overall probabilistic risk assessment before operation. Probabilities can be predicted with reasonable accuracy for physical failures caused by stress and wear. But this accuracy cannot be used in efforts to assess the risk that the entire system (that is, hardware and software) will fail if nothing more precise can be said other than that the best effort was made to avoid mistakes. Simply mandating the use of "best practice" does not solve the problem. We hasten to add that it would be foolish to abandon techniques known to improve reliability and safety just because we do not know exactly how much they help. Standards that encourage their use are certainly beneficial, but they do not solve the problem of knowing that the software has the required safety.

The second—and we think, better—approach would require that the system be designed so the role of software in it is not too critical. "Not too critical" here means that the required software reliability is sufficiently modest so the reliability can be demonstrated before the system is deployed. This approach has been taken for the new Sizewell B nuclear reactor in the U.K., where only a 10^{-4} probability of failure on demand is needed from the software-based protection system.

There are well-established methods for limiting the criticality of any one component. For example, an industrial plant whose operations are controlled primarily by computers may be equipped with safety systems that do not depend on any software or other complex design. A safety or backup system usually performs simpler functions than does the main control system, so it can be built more reliably. Safety is possible if the backup systems are completely separated from the main systems. They could be built with different technology or use alternative sensors, actuators and power sources. Then the probability that both primary and backup (or safety) systems will fail simultaneously may be justifiably considered low.

The third approach is simply to accept the current limitations of software and live with a more modest overall system safety. After all, society sometimes demands extremely high safety for what may be irrational reasons. Medical systems are a good example. Surgeons are known to have fairly high failure rates, and it would seem natural to accept a computerized alternative if the device is shown to be as good as or only slightly better than the human physician. Indeed, in the near future robotic surgeons will probably perform operations that are beyond the capabilities of humans.

The three approaches to regulating software safety may seem rather disappointing. Each sets limits on either the degree of safety in the system or the amount of complexity in the program. Perhaps the only way to learn more about the necessary compromises between safety and complexity is to study the failures (or lack thereof) of software in operation.

Unfortunately, there is a paucity of data from which to fashion statistical predictions. Information on software failure is seldom made public. Companies fear that sharing such knowledge would harm their competitive stance. They worry even more that publishing it would antagonize public opinion. People might see the detection of a software fault as an indication of low production standards, even though it may actually attest to a very thorough procedure applied to very high quality software. But secrecy can only allow expectations of safety to climb to increasingly unrealistic levels. Some investigators have suggested that the government make mandatory the logging and disclosing of failure data in critical software systems. Such regulations would remove the fear that companies volunteering the information would be hurt.

However it is obtained, an extensive collection of data would in time help to quantify the efficacy of different production and validation techniques. The information would help establish more realistic rules for gauging the trustworthiness of software systems. Thus, for software that is not fully tested statistically, the acceptable claims of safety could be tied to explicit upper bounds that would depend on the complexity of the program. Such an approach might allow us to justify claims for the reliability and safety of software beyond what is now believable.

In the meantime, we should remain wary of any dramatic claims of reliability. Considering the levels of complexity that software has made possible, we believe being skeptical is the safest course of action.

▷ EVALUATION OF SAFETY-CRITICAL SOFTWARE

David L. Parnas
A. John van Schouwen
Shu Po Kwan

Methods and approaches for testing the reliability and trustworthiness of software remain among the most controversial issues facing this age of high technology. The authors present some of the crucial questions faced by software programmers and eventual users.

It is increasingly common to use programmable computers in applications where their failure could be life-threatening and could result in extensive damage. For example, computers now have safety-critical functions in both military and civilian aircraft, in nuclear plants, and in medical devices. It is incumbent upon those responsible for programming, purchasing, installing, and licensing these systems to determine whether or not the software is ready to be used. This article addresses questions that are simple to pose but hard to answer. What standards must a software product satisfy if it is to be used in safety-critical applications such as those mentioned? What documentation should be required? How much testing is needed? How should the software be structured?

This article differs from others concerned with software in safety-critical applications, in that it does not attempt to identify *safety* as a property separate from reliability and trustworthiness. In other words, we do not attempt to separate safety-critical code from other code in a product used in a safety-critical application. In our experience, software exhibits *weak-link* behavior, that is failures in even the unimportant parts of the code can have unexpected repercussions elsewhere. For a discussion of another viewpoint, we suggest the work of N. G. Leveson [6, 7, 8].

We favor keeping safety-critical software as small and simple as possible by moving any functions that are not safety critical to other computers. This further justifies our assumption that all parts of a safety-critical software product must be considered safety critical.

WHY IS SOFTWARE A SPECIAL CONCERN?

Within the engineering community software systems have a reputation for being undependable, especially in the first years of their use. The public is aware of a few spectacular stories such as the Space Shuttle flight that was delayed by a software timing problem, or the Venus probe that was lost because of a punctuation error. In the software community, the problem is known to be much more widespread.

A few years ago, David Benson, professor of Computer Science at Washington State University, issued a challenge by way of several electronic bulletin board systems. He asked for an example of a real-time system that functioned adequately when used for the first time by people other than its developers for a purpose other than testing. Only one candidate for this honor was proposed, but even that candidate was controversial. It consisted of approximately 18,000 instructions, most of which had been used for several years before the "first use." The only code that had not been used before that first use was a simple sequence of 200 instructions that simulated a simple analogue servomechanism. That instruction sequence had been tested extensively against an analogue model. All who have looked at this program regard it as exceptional. If we choose to regard this small program as one that worked in its first real application, it is the proverbial "exception that proves the rule."

As a rule software systems do not work well until they have been used, and have failed repeatedly, in real applications. Generally, many uses and many failures are required before a product is considered reliable. Software products, including those that have become relatively reliable, behave like other products of evolution-like processes; they often fail, even years after they were built, when the operating conditions change.

While there are errors in many engineering products, experience has shown that errors are more common, more pervasive, and more troublesome, in software than in other technologies. This information must be understood in light of the fact it is now standard practice among software professionals to have their product go through an extensive series of carefully planned tests before real use. The products fail in their first real use because the situations that were not anticipated by the programmers were also overlooked by the test planners. Most major computer-using organizations, both military and civilian, are investing heavily in searching for ways to improve the state of the art in software. The problem remains serious and there is no sign of a "silver bullet." The most promising development is the work of Harlan Mills and his colleagues at IBM on a software development process known as "clean room" [3, 9, 12]. Mills uses randomly selected tests, carried out by an independent testing group. The use of randomly generated test data reduces the likelihood of shared oversights. We will discuss this approach in more detail later in this article.

WHY IS SOFTWARE USED?

If software is so untrustworthy, one might ask why engineers do not avoid it by continuing to use hard-wired digital and analogue hardware. Here, we list the three main advantages of replacing hardware with software:

1. Software technology makes it practical to build more *logic* into the system. Software-controlled computer systems can distinguish a large number of situations and provide output appropriate to each of them. Hard-wired systems could not obtain such behavior without prohibitive amounts of hardware. Programmable hardware is less expensive than the equivalent hard-wired logic because it is regular in structure and it is mass produced. The economic aspects of the situation also allow software-controlled systems to perform more checking; reliability can be increased by periodic execution of programs that check the hardware.

2. Logic implemented in software is, in theory, easier to change than logic implemented in hardware. Many changes can be made without adding new components. When a system is replicated or located in a physical position that is hard to reach, it is far easier to make changes in software than in hardware.

3. Computer technology and software flexibility make it possible to provide more information to operators and to provide that information in a more useful form. The operator of a modern software-controlled system can be provided with information that would be unthinkable in a pure hardware system. All of this can be achieved using less space and power than was used by noncomputerized systems.

These factors explain the replacement of hard-wired systems with software-controlled systems in spite of software's reputation as an unreliable technology.

HOW ARE SOFTWARE CONTROLLERS LIKE OTHER CONTROLLERS?

In the next section we will argue that software technology requires some refinements in policies and standards because of differences between software and hardware technology. However, it is important to recognize some common properties of software and hardware control systems.

In the design and specification of control systems, engineers have long known how to use a black box mathematical model of the controller. In such models, (1) the inputs to the controller are described as mathematical functions of certain observable environmental state variables, (2) the outputs of the controller are described as mathematical functions of the inputs, (3) the values of the controlled environmental variables are described as mathematical functions of the controller's outputs, and (4) the required relation between the controlled variables and observed variables is described. It is then possible to confirm that the behavior of the controller meets its requirements.

It is important to recognize that, in theory, software-implemented controllers can be described in exactly the same way as black box mathematical models. They can also be viewed as black boxes whose output is a mathematical function of the input. In practice, they are not viewed this way. One reason for the distinction is that their functions are more complex (i.e. harder to describe) than the functions that describe the behavior of conventional controllers. However, [4] and [17] provide ample evidence that requirements for real systems can be documented in this way. We return to this theme later.

HOW IS SOFTWARE DIFFERENT FROM OTHER CONTROLLER TECHNOLOGIES?

Software problems are often considered growing pains and ascribed to the adolescent nature of the field. Unfortunately there are fundamental differences between software and other approaches that suggest these problems are here to stay.

Complexity: The most immediately obvious difference between software and hardware technologies is their complexity. This can be observed by considering the size of the most compact descriptions of the software. Precise documentation, in a reasonably general notation, for small software systems can fill a bookcase. Another measure of complexity is the time it takes for a programmer to become closely familiar with a system. Even with small software systems, it is common to find that a programmer requires a year of working with the program before he/she can be trusted to make improvements on his/her own.

Error Sensitivity: Another notable property of software is its sensitivity to small errors. In conventional engineering, every design and manufacturing dimension can be characterized by a tolerance. One is not required to get things exactly right; being within the specified *tolerance* of the right value is good enough. The use of a tolerance is justified by the assumption that small errors have small consequences. It is well known that in software, trivial clerical errors can have major consequences. No useful interpretation of tolerance is known for software. A single punctuation error can be disastrous, even though fundamental oversights sometimes have negligible effects.

Hard to Test: Software is notoriously difficult to test adequately. It is common to find a piece of software that has been subjected to a thorough and disciplined testing regime has serious flaws. Testing of analogue devices is based on interpolation. One assumes that devices that function well at two close points will function well at points in-between. In software that assumption is not valid. The number of cases that must be tested in order to engender confidence in a piece of software is usually extremely large. Moreover, as Harlan Mills has pointed out, "testing carried out by selected test cases, no matter how carefully and well-planned, can provide nothing but anecdotes" [3, 9, 12].

These properties are fundamental consequences of the fact that the mathematical functions implemented by software are not continuous functions, but functions with an arbitrary number of discontinuities. The lack of continuity constraints on the functions describing program effects makes it difficult to find compact descriptions of the software. The lack of such constraints gives software its flexibility, but it also allows the complexity. Similarly, the sensitivity to small errors, and the testing difficulties, can be traced to fundamental mathematical properties; we are unlikely to discover a miracle cure. Great discipline and careful scrutiny will always be required for safety-critical software systems.

Correlated Failures: Many of the assumptions normally made in the design of high-reliability hardware are invalid for software. Designers of high-reliability hardware are concerned with manufacturing failures and wear-out phenomena. They can perform their analysis on the assumption that failures are not strongly correlated and simultaneous failures are unlikely. Those who evaluate the reliability of hardware systems should be, and often are, concerned about design errors and correlated failures; however in many situations the effects of other types of errors are dominant.

In software there are few errors introduced in the manufacturing (compiling) phase; when there are such errors they are systematic, not random. Software does not wear out. The errors with which software reliability experts must be concerned are design errors. These errors cannot be considered statistically independent. There is ample evidence that, even when programs for a given task are written by people who do not know of each other, they have closely related errors [6, 7, 8].

In contrast to the situation with hardware systems, one cannot obtain higher reliability by duplication of software components. One simply duplicates the errors. Even when programs are written independently, the oversights made by one programmer are often shared by others. As a result, one cannot count on increasing the reliability of software systems simply by having three computers where one would be sufficient [6, 7, 8].

Lack of Professional Standards: A severe problem in the software field is that, strictly speaking, there are no software engineers. In contrast to older engineering fields, there is no accrediting agency for professional software engineers. Those in software engineering have not agreed on a set of skills and knowledge that should be possessed by every software engineer. Anyone with a modicum of programming knowledge can be called a software engineer. Often, critical programming systems are built by people with no postsecondary training about software. Although they may have useful knowledge of the field in which the software will be applied, such knowledge is not a substitute for understanding the foundations of software technology.

SOFTWARE TESTING CONCERNS

Some engineers believe one can design black box tests without knowledge of what is inside the box. This is, unfortunately, not completely true. If we know that the contents of a black box exhibit linear behavior, the number of tests needed to make sure it would function as specified could be quite small. If we know that the function can be described by a polynomial of order "N," we can use that information to determine how many tests are needed. If the function can have a large number of discontinuities, far more tests are needed. That is why a shift from analogue technology to software brings with it a need for much more testing.

Built-in test circuitry is often included in hardware to perform testing while the product is in use. Predetermined values are substituted for inputs, and the outputs are compared to normative values. Sometimes this approach is imitated in software designs and the claim is made that built-in online testing can substitute for black box testing. In hardware, built-in testing tests for decay or damage. Software does not decay and physical damage is not our concern. Software can be used to test the hardware, but its value for testing itself is quite doubtful. Software self-testing does increase the complexity of the product and, consequently, the likelihood of error. Moreover, such testing does not constitute adequate testing because it usually does not resemble the conditions of actual use.

The fundamental limitations on testing mentioned earlier have some very practical implications.

We Cannot Test Software for Correctness: Because of the large number of states (and the lack of regularity in its structure), the number of states that would have to be tested to assure that software is correct is preposterous. Testing can show the presence of bugs, but, except for toy problems, it is not practical to use testing to show that software is free of design errors.

It Is Difficult to Make Accurate Predictions of Software Reliability and Availability: Mathematical models show that it is practical to predict the reliability of software, provided that one has good statistical models of the actual operating conditions. Unfortunately, one usually gains that information only after the system is installed. Even when a new system replaces an existing one, differences in features may cause changes in the input distribution. Nonetheless, in safety-critical situations, one must attempt to get and use the necessary statistical data. The use of this data is discussed later in this article.

Predictions of availability are even more difficult: estimates of availability depend on predictions of the time it will take to correct a bug in the software. We never know what that amount of time will be in advance: data from earlier bugs is not a good predictor of the time it will take to find the next bug.

It Is Not Practical to Measure the Trustworthiness of Software: We consider a product to be trustworthy if we believe that the probability of it having a potentially catastrophic flaw is acceptably low. Whereas reliability is a measure of the probability of a problem occurring while the system is in service, trustworthiness is a measure of the probability of a serious flaw remaining after testing and review. In fact, inspection and testing can increase the trustworthiness of a product without affecting its reliability.

Software does not need to be correct in order to be trustworthy. We will trust imperfect software if we believe its probability of having a serious flaw is very low. Unfortunately, as we will show, the amount of testing necessary to establish high confidence levels for most software products is impractically large. The number of states and possible input sequences is so large that the probability of an error having escaped our attention will remain high even after years of testing. Methods other than testing must be used to increase our trust in software.

There Is a Role for Testing: A number of computer scientists, aware of the limitations on software testing, would argue that one should not test software. They would argue that the effort normally put into testing should, instead, be put into a form of review known as mathematical verification. A program is a mathematical object and can be proven correct. Unfortunately, such mathematical inspections are based on mathematical models that may not be accurate. No amount of mathematical analysis will reveal discrepancies between the model being used and the real situation; only testing can do that. Moreover, errors are often made in proofs. In mature engineering fields, mathematical methods and testing are viewed as complementary and mutually supportive.

There Is a Need for an Independent Validation Agency: It is impossible to test software completely and difficult to test one's own design in an unbiased way. A growing number of software development projects involve independent verification and validation (V&V). The V&V contractor is entirely independent of the development contractor. Sometimes a competitor of the development contractor is given the V&V contract. The testers work from the specification for the software and attempt to develop tests that will show the software to be faulty. One particularly interesting variation of this approach has been used within the IBM Federal Systems Division. In IBM's *clean room* development approach the authors of the software are not allowed to execute their programs. All testing is done by an independent tester and test reports are sent to the developer's supervisors. The test cases are chosen using random number generators and are intended to yield statistically valid data. It was hypothesized that the software would be written far more carefully under these conditions and would be more reliable. Early reports support the hypothesis [3, 9, 12].

It is important that these validation tests not be made available to the developers before the software is submitted for testing. If the developers know what tests will be performed, they will use those tests in their debugging. The result is likely to be a program that will pass the tests but is not reliable in actual use.

SOFTWARE REVIEWABILITY CONCERNS

Why Is Reviewability a Particular Concern for Software?

Traditionally, engineers have approached software as if it were an art form. Each programmer has been allowed to have his own style. Criticisms of software structure, clarity, and documentation were dismissed as "matters of taste."

In the past, engineers were rarely asked to examine a software product and certify that it would be trustworthy. Even in systems that were required to be trustworthy and reliable, software was often regarded as an unimportant component, not requiring special examination.

In recent years, however, manufacturers of a wide variety of equipment have been substituting computers controlled by software for a wide variety of more conventional products. We can no longer treat software as if it were trivial and unimportant.

In the older areas of engineering, safety-critical components are inspected and reviewed to assure the design is consistent with the safety requirements. To make this review possible, the designers are required to conform to industry standards for the documentation, and even the structure, of the product. The documentation must be sufficiently clear and well organized that a reviewer can determine whether or not the design meets safety standards. The design itself must allow components to be inspected so the reviewer can verify they are consistent with the documentation. In construction, inspections take place during the process—while it is still possible to inspect and correct work that will later be hidden.

When software is a safety-critical component, analogous standards should be applied. In software, there is no problem of physical visibility but there is a problem of clarity. Both practical experience and planned experiments have shown that it is common for programs with major flaws to be accepted by reviewers. In one particularly shocking experiment, small programs were deliberately flawed and given to a skilled reviewer team. The reviewers were unable to find the flaws in spite of the fact they were certain such flaws were present. In theory, nothing is invisible in a program—it is all in the listing; in practice, poorly structured programs hide a plethora of problems.

In safety-critical applications we must reject the "software-as-art-form" approach. Programs and documentation must conform to standards that allow reviewers to feel confident they understand the software and can predict how it will function in situations where safety depends on it. However, we must, equally strongly, reject standards that require a mountain of paper that nobody can read. The standards must insure clear, precise, and concise documentation.

It is symptomatic of the immaturity of the software profession that there are no widely accepted software standards assuring the reviewability essential to licensing of software products that must be seen as trustworthy. The documentation standards name and outline certain documents, but they only vaguely define the contents of those documents. Recent U.S. military procurement regulations include safety requirements; while they require that safety checks be done, they neither describe how to do them nor impose standards that make those checks practicable. Most standards for code documentation are so vague and syntactic in nature that a program can meet those standards in spite of being incomprehensible. . . .

RELIABILITY ASSESSMENT FOR SAFETY-CRITICAL SOFTWARE

Should We Discuss the Reliability of Software at All?

Manufacturers, users, and regulatory agencies are often concerned about the reliability of systems that include software. Over many decades, reliability engineers have developed sophisticated methods of estimating the reliability of hardware systems based upon estimates of the reliability of their components. Software is often viewed as one of those components and an estimate of the reliability of that component is deemed essential to estimating the reliability of the overall system.

Reliability engineers are often misled by their experience with hardware. They are usually concerned with the reliability of devices that work correctly when new, but wear out and fail as they age. In other cases, they are concerned with mass-produced components where manufacturing techniques introduce defects that affect only a small fraction of the devices. Neither of these situations applies to software. Software does not wear out, and the errors introduced when software is copied have not been found to be significant.

As a result of these differences, it is not uncommon to see reliability assessments for large systems based on an estimated software reliability of 1.0. Reliability engineers argue that the correctness of a software product is not a probabilistic phenomenon. The software is either correct (reliability 1.0) or incorrect (reliability 0). If they assume a reliability of 0, they cannot get a useful reliability estimate for the system containing the software. Consequently, they assume correctness. Many consider it nonsense to talk about "reliability of software."

Nonetheless, our practical experience is that software appears to exhibit stochastic properties. It is quite useful to associate reliability figures such as MTBF (Mean Time Between Failures) with an operating system or other software product. Some software experts attribute the apparently random behavior to our ignorance. They believe that all software failures would be predictable if we fully understood the software, but our failure to understand our own creations justifies the treatment of software failures as random. However, we know that if we studied the software long enough, we could obtain a complete description of its response to inputs. Even then, it would be useful to talk about the MTBF of the product. Hence, ignorance should not satisfy us as a philosophical justification.

When a program first fails to function properly, it is because of an input sequence that had not occurred before. The reason that software appears to exhibit random behavior, and the reason that it is useful to talk about the MTBF of software, is because the input sequences are unpredictable. When we talk about the failure rate of a software product, we are predicting the probability of encountering an input sequence that will cause the product to fail.

Strictly speaking, we should not consider software as a component in systems at all. The software is simply the initial data in the computer and it is the initialized computer that is the component in question. However, in practice, the reliability of the hardware is high and failures caused by software errors dominate those caused by hardware problems.

What Should We Be Measuring?

What we intuitively call "software reliability" is the probability of not encountering a sequence of inputs that leads to failure. If we could accurately characterize the sequences that lead to failure we would simply measure the distribution of input histories directly. Because of our ignorance of the actual properties of the software, we must use the software itself to measure the frequency with which failure-inducing sequences occur as inputs.

In safety-critical applications, particularly those for which a failure would be considered catastrophic, we may wish to take the position that design errors that would lead to failure are always unacceptable. In other technologies we would not put a system with a known design error in service. The complexity of software, and its consequent poor track record, means we seldom have confidence that software is free of serious design errors. Under those circumstances, we may wish to evaluate the probability that serious errors have been missed by our tests. This gives rise to our second probabilistic measure of software quality, *trustworthiness*.

In the sequel we shall refer to the probability that an input will not cause a failure as the reliability of the software. We shall refer to the probability that no serious design error remains after the software passes a set of randomly chosen tests as the trustworthiness of the software. We will discuss how to obtain estimates of both of these quantities.

Some discussions about software systems use the terms *availability* and *reliability* as if they were interchangeable. Availability usually refers to the fraction of time that the system is running and assumed to be ready to function. Availability can depend strongly on the time it takes to return a system to service once it has failed. If a system is truly safety-critical (e.g., a shutdown system in a nuclear power station), we would not depend on it during the time it was unavailable. The nuclear reactor would be taken out of service while its shutdown system was being repaired. Consequently, reliability and availability can be quite different.

For systems that function correctly only in rare emergencies, we wish to measure the reliability in those situations where the system must take corrective action, and not include data from situations in which the system is not needed. The input sequence distributions used in reliability assessment should be those that one would encounter in emergency situations, and not those that characterize normal operation.

Much of the literature on software reliability is concerned with estimation and prediction of error-rates, the number of errors per line of code. For safety purposes, such rates are both meaningless and unimportant. Error counts are meaningless because we cannot find an objective way to count errors. We can count the number of lines in the code that are changed to eliminate a problem, but there usually are many ways to alleviate that problem. If each approach to repairing the problem involves a different number of lines (which is usually the case), the number of errors in the code is a subjective, often arbitrary, judgment. Error counts are unimportant because a program with a high error count is not necessarily less reliable than one with a low error count. In other words, even if we could count the number of errors, reliability is not a function of the error count. If asked to evaluate a safety-critical software product, there is no point in attempting to estimate or predict the number of errors remaining in a program.

Other portions of the literature are concerned with reliability growth models. These attempt to predict the reliability of the next (corrected) version on the basis of reliability data collected from previous versions. Most assume the failure rate is reduced whenever an error is corrected. They also assume the reductions in failure rates resulting from each correction are predictable. These assumptions are not justified by either theoretical or empirical studies of programs. Reliability growth models may be useful for management and scheduling purposes, but for safety-critical applications one must treat each modification of the program as a new program. Because even small changes can have major effects, we should consider data obtained from previous versions of the program to be irrelevant. . . .

CONCLUSIONS

There is no inherent reason that software cannot be used in certain safety-critical applications, but extreme discipline in design, documentation, testing, and review is needed. It is essential that the operating conditions and requirements be well understood, and fully documented. If these conditions are not met, adequate review and testing are impossible.

The system must be structured in accordance with information hiding to make it easier to understand, review, and repair. The documentation must be complete and precise, making use of mathematical notation rather than natural language. Each stage of the design must be reviewed by independent reviewers with the specialized knowledge needed at that stage. Mathematical verification techniques must be used to make the review systematic and rigorous.

An independent agency must perform statistically valid random testing to provide estimates of the reliability of the system in critical situations. Deep knowledge and experience with the application area will be needed to determine the distribution from which the test cases should be drawn.

The vast literature on random testing is, for the most part, not relevant for safety evaluations. Because we are not interested in estimating the error rates or conducting reliability growth studies, a very simple model suffices. Hypothesis testing will allow us to evaluate the probability that the system meets our requirements. Testing to estimate reliability is only practical if a real-time system has limited long-term memory.

Testing to estimate trustworthiness is rarely practical because the number of tests required is usually quite large. Trustworthiness must be assured by the use of rigorous mathematical techniques in the review process.

The safety and trustworthiness of the system will rest on a tripod made up of testing, mathematical review, and certification of personnel and process. In this article, we have focused on two of those legs, testing and review based on mathematical documentation. The third leg will be the most difficult to implement. While there are authorities that certify professional engineers in other areas, there is no corresponding authority in software engineering. We have found that both classical engineers and computer science graduates are ill-prepared for this type of work. In the long term, those who are concerned about the use of software in safety-critical applications will have to develop appropriate educational programs [15].

ACKNOWLEDGMENTS

Conversations with many people have helped to develop these observations. Among them are William Howden, Harlan Mills, Jim Kendall, Nancy Leveson, B. Natvik, and Kurt Asmis. In addition, we are thankful to the anonymous *Communications* referees and the editor for their constructive suggestions.

REFERENCES

1. Britton, K., and Parnas, D. A-7E software module guide. NRL Memo. Rep. 4702, December 1981.

2. Clements, P., Faulk, S., and Parnas, D. Interface specifications for the SCR (A-7E) application data types module. NRL Rep. 8734. August 23, 1983.

3. Currit, P. A., Dyer, M., and Mills, H. D. Certifying the reliability of software. *IEEE Trans. Softw. Eng. SE-12.* 1 (Jan. 1986).

4. Heninger, K. Specifying software requirements for complex systems: New techniques and their applications. *IEEE Trans. Softw. Eng. SE-6.* (Jan. 1980), 2–13.

5. Hester, S. D., Parnas, D. L., and Utter, D. F. Using documentation as a software design medium. *Bell Syst. Tech. J. 60*, 8 (Oct. 1981), 1941–1977.

6. Knight, J. C., and Leveson, N. G. An experimental evaluation of the assumption of independence in multi-version programming. *IEEE Trans. Softw. Eng. SE-12.* 1 (Jan. 1986), 96–109.

7. Knight, J. C., and Leveson, N. G. An empirical study of failure probabilities in multi-version software. Rep.

8. Leveson, N. Software safety: Why, what and how. *ACM Comp. Surveys 18*, 2 (June 1986), 125–163.

9. Mills, H. D. Engineering discipline for software procurement. COMPASS '87—Computer Assurance, June 29–July 3, 1987. Georgetown University, Washington, D.C.

10. Mills, H. D. The new math of computer programming. *Commun ACM 18.* 1 (Jan. 1975), 43–48.

11. Mills, H. D., Basili, V. R., Gannon, J. D., and Hamlet, R. G. *Principles of Computer Programming—A Mathematical Approach.* Allyn and Bacon, Inc., 1987.

12. Mills, H. D., and Dyer, M. A formal approach to software error removal. *J. Syst. Softw.* (1987).

13. Mills, H. D., Linger, R. C., and Witt, B. I. *Structured Programming: Theory and Practice.* Addison-Wesley, Reading, Mass., 1979.

14. Parker, A., Heninger, K., Parnas, D. and Shore, J. Abstract interface specifications for the A-7E device interface module NRL Memo Rep. 4385. November 20, 1980.

15. Parnas, D. L. Education for computing professionals. *IEEE Comp 23* (Jan. 1990), 17–22.

16. Parnas, D. L., and Clements, P. C. A rational design process: How and why to fake it. *IEEE Trans. Softw. Eng. SE-12.* 2 (Feb 1986), 251–257.

17. Parnas, D. L., Heninger, K., Kallander J., and Shore, J. Software requirements for the A-7E aircraft NRL Rep. 3876. November 1978.

18. Parnas, D. L., and Wang, Y. The Trace assertion method of module-interface specification. Tech. Rep. 89–261. Queen's University. TRIO (Telecommunications Research Institute of Ontario) October 1989.

19. Parnas, D. L., and Weiss, D. M. Active design reviews Principles and Practices. In *Proceedings of the 8th International Conference on Software Engineering* (London, August 1985).

FROM SLIDE RULE TO COMPUTER: FORGETTING HOW IT USED TO BE DONE

Henry Petroski

Twenty-five years ago, the undisputed symbol of engineering was the slide rule. Engineering students, who at the time were almost all males, carried the "slip sticks" in scabbard-like cases hanging from their belts, and older engineers wore small working models as tie clips that in a pinch could be used for calculations. When I became an engineering student myself, one of my most important decisions was which slide rule to purchase. Not only was $20 a big investment in 1959, but also I was choosing an instrument that I was told I would use for the rest of my professional life; I was advised along with all the other freshmen to get right at the start a good slide rule with all the scales I would ever need. After much comparative shopping, I chose a popular Keuffel & Esser model known as the Log Log Duplex Decitrig, and for a long time it was my most prized possession. Many of my fellow students also chose K & E rules, and the company was selling them at the rate of twenty thousand per month in the 1950s.

A slide rule was indispensible for doing homework and taking tests, for all our teachers assumed that every engineering student had a slide rule and knew how to use it. If we had not learned in high school, then we quickly studied the manual folded into the box. What our engineering instructors were interested in teaching us was not all the grand things that our various models of rules could do, but their common limitations. They told us about significant digits, for most engineering instruments then had analog dials and scales from which one had to estimate numbers between the finest divisions in much the same way we have to estimate sixteenths of an inch on a yard stick or tenths of a millimeter on a meter stick. The scales on the slide rule have the same limitations, and we were expected to know that we could only report answers accurate to three significant digits from our rules, unless we were on the extreme left of the scale where finer subdivisions existed.

We often had these things inculcated in us by trial and error. If the answer to a test question required us to multiply, say, 0.346 by 0.16892 and we reported the result as 0.05844632 we would be marked for an error in significant digits, for the result of a calculation could not have a greater accuracy than the least accurately known input number. (When older engineers write 0.346, it is implied to be known only to three digits after the decimal point, otherwise it would have been written as 0.3460 or 0.34600 or to whatever decimal place the number is known.) Since no one could ever read as many digits as those in 0.05844632 from his slide rule, the closest he would be expected to get would be 0.0585. (The extra digits were a dead giveaway that the student had forgotten his slide rule and had done the multiplication longhand on some scrap of paper and, worse yet, had forgotten the significance of significant digits.) We also learned how to estimate the order of magnitude of our answers, for the slide rule could not supply the decimal point to the product of 0.346 and 0.16892, and we had to develop a feel for the fact that the answer was about 0.06 rather than 0.6 or 0.006. These requirements on our judgment made us realize two important things about engineering: first, answers are approximations and should only be reported as accurately as the input is known, and, second, magnitudes come from a feel for the problem and do not come automatically from machines or calculating contrivances.

As I progressed through engineering school with my slide rule in the early 1960s, electronic technology was being developed that was to change engineering teaching and practice. But it was not then widely known, and as late as 1967 Keuffel & Esser commissioned a study of the future that resulted in predictions of domed cities and three-dimensional television in the year 2067—but that did not predict the demise of the slide rule within five years.

In 1968, an article entitled "An Electronic Digital Slide Rule" appeared in *The Electronic Engineer*. It could dare to prophesy, "If this hand-size calculator ever becomes commercial, the conventional slide rule will become a museum piece." In the article the authors, two General Electric engineers, described a prototype that they had built with some off-the-shelf digital integrated circuits. Their "feasibility model" looked like an electric blanket control and, at 1 1/2 × 5 × 7 inches, it resembled a novel in size. Yet their marvel could give four-digit answers to any four-digit multiplicands, and it could also divide and calculate square roots, exponentials, and logarithms. It had, however, one shortcoming, and the engineers made the concession that, "Since it has no decimal points, you must figure out your decimals as with a regular slide rule." As far as cost was concerned, that of course would depend upon the cost of the components, but there remained one big obstacle in 1968: "Only the digital readout still poses a problem, since at present there are no low-cost miniature devices available. But there is no question that this last barrier will soon be overcome."

They were right, of course, and within a few years Texas Instruments had developed the first truly compact, handheld, pocketsized calculator using an electronic chip. Texas Instruments started manufacturing pocket calculators in 1972, but they were still expensive in 1973, costing about ten times as much as a top-of-the-line slide rule. However, price breakthroughs came the next year, and Commodore was advertising its model SR-1400, a "37-key advanced math, true scientific calculator" that could do everything my Log Log Duplex Decitrig could do—and more. If one knew input to ten significant digits, then this calculator could handle it.

I was teaching at the University of Texas at Austin at the time of this great calculator revolution, and there were some engineering students whose daddies did not have to wait for the pocket calculator to become competitive in price with the slide rule. We faculty were thus faced with the question of whether students with electronic slide rules had an unfair advantage on quizzes and examinations over those with the traditional slip sticks, for the modern electronic device was a lot quicker and could add and subtract—something a slide rule could only do with logarithms. The faculty members generally were unfamiliar with all the features of the calculators that were still priced out of their reach, and there seemed to be many pros and cons and endless discussions over the issue of whether an electronic slide rule was equivalent to a wooden one. The question soon became moot, however, as prices plunged and just about anyone who could afford a conventional slide rule could afford an electronic model. By 1976 Keuffel & Esser was selling calculators made by Texas Instruments faster than traditional slide rules, which by then made up only five percent of K & E's sales, and the company consigned to the Smithsonian Institution the machine it once used to carve the scales into its wooden slide rules.

By the mid-1970s calculator manufacturers were making fifty million units a year, and soon just about everyone, including engineers who went through school in the old days, had a calculator. But no older engineer that I know discarded or consigned his slide rule to any museum. At most the old slip stick was put in the desk drawer, ready for use during power failures or other emergencies. A study conducted by the Futures Group in the early 1980s found that most engineers in senior management positions continued to keep slide rules close at hand and still used them "because they are more comfortable." But the always-growing younger generations naturally feel just the opposite. In 1981 I asked a class of sophomore engineering students how many used a slide rule, and I got the expected answer—none. (Some did own slide rules, perhaps because their engineer fathers bought one for the freshman to take away to engineering school. And K & E was selling out its remaining stock of 2,300 at the rate of only two hundred per month in 1981.) I did not ask my class how many used a calculator, for that would be like asking how many use a telephone. And I did not ask how many used a computer, for that was by then a requirement in the engineering curriculum. The trend is clearly that eventually no engineer will own or use a traditional slide rule, but that practicing engineers of all generations will use—and misuse—computers.

Engineering faculty members, like just about everyone else, got so distracted by the new electronic technology during the 1970s that more substantial issues than price, convenience, and speed of computation did not come to the fore. The vast majority of faculty members did not ask where all those digits the calculators could display were going to come from or go to; they did not ask if the students were going to continue to appreciate the approximate nature of engineering answers, and they did not ask whether students would lose their feel for the decimal point if the calculator handled it all the time. Now, a decade after the calculator displaced the slide rule, we are beginning to ask these questions, but we are asking them not about the calculator but about the personal computer. And the reason these questions are being asked is that the assimilation of the calculator and the computer is virtually complete with the newer generations of engineers now leaving school, and the bad effects are beginning to surface. Some structural failures have been attributed to the use and misuse of the computer, and not only by recent graduates, and there is a real concern that its growing power and use will lead to other failures.

The computer enables engineers to make more calculations more quickly than was conceivable with either the slide rule or the calculator, hence the computer can be programmed to attack problems in structural analysis that would never have been attempted in the pre-computer days. If one wished to design a complicated structure of many parts, for example, one might first have made educated guesses about the sizes of the various members and then calculated the stresses in them. If these stresses were too high, then the design had to be beefed up where it was overstressed; if some calculated stresses were too low, then those understressed parts of the structure could be made smaller, thus saving weight and money. However, each revision of one part of the structure could affect the stresses in every other part. If that were the case, the entire stress analysis would have to be repeated. Clearly, in the days of manual calculation with a slide rule—wooden or electronic—such a process would be limited by the sheer time it would consume, and structures would be generally overdesigned from the start and built that way. Furthermore, excessively complex structures were eschewed by designers because the original sizing of members might be too difficult to even guess at, and calculations required to assure the safety of the structure were simply not reasonable to perform. Hence engineers generally stuck with designing structures that they understood well enough from the very start of the design process.

Now, the computer not only can perform millions of simple, repetitive calculations automatically in reasonable amounts of time but also can be used to analyze structures that engineers of the slide rule era found too complex. The computer can be used to analyze these structures through special software packages, claimed to be quite versatile by their developers, and the computer can be instructed to calculate the sizes of the various components of the structure so that it has minimum weight since the maximum stresses are acting in every part of it. That is called optimization. But should there be an oversimplification or an outright error in translating the designer's structural concept to the numerical model that will be analyzed through the automatic and unthinking calculations of the computer, then the results of the computer analysis might have very little relation to reality. And since the engineer himself presumably has no feel for the structure he is designing, he is not likely to notice anything suspicious about any numbers the computer produces for the design.

The electronic brain is sometimes promoted from computer or clerk at least to assistant engineer in the design office. Computer-aided design (known by its curiously uncomplimentary acronym CAD) is touted by many a computer manufacturer and many a computer scientist-engineer as the way of the future. But thus far the computer has been as much an agent of unsafe design as it has been a super brain that can tackle problems heretofore too complicated for the pencil-and-paper calculations of a human engineer. The illusion of its power over complexity has led to more and more of a dependence on the computer to solve problems eschewed by engineers with a more realistic sense of their own limitations than the computer can have of its own.

What is commonly overlooked in using the computer is the fact that the central goal of design is still to obviate failure, and thus it is critical to identify exactly *how* a structure may fail. The computer cannot do this by itself, although there are attempts to incorporate artificial intelligence into the machine to make it an "expert system," and one might dream that the ultimate in CAD is to have the computer learn from the experience contained in files of failures (stored in computers). However, until such a farfetched notion becomes reality, the engineer who employs the computer in design must still ask the crucial questions: Will this improperly welded pipe break if an earthquake hits the nuclear reactor plant? Will this automobile body crumple in this manner when it strikes a wall at ten miles per hour? Will any one of the tens of thousands of metal rods supporting this roof break under heavy snow and cause it to fall into the crowded arena?

One *can* ask of the computer model questions such as these. Whether or not they *are* asked can depend on the same human judgment that dismissed the question of fatigue in the Comets and that apparently did not check the effects of the design change on the Hyatt Regency walkways. Even if one thinks of the critical questions and can phrase them so that the computer model is capable of producing answers to them, there may have to be a human decision made as to how exhaustive one can be in one's interrogation of the computer. While the computer works very quickly as a file clerk, it cannot work very quickly when it is asked to analyze certain engineering problems. One of the most important problems in design is the behavior of metal under loads that deform structural components permanently. While it takes only seconds to put a bar of ductile steel in a testing machine and pull the bar until it stretches out and breaks like a piece of taffy, simulating such an elementary physical test on the largest computer can take hours.

There can be miles of pipes in a typical nuclear reactor plant, and it could take some of the largest and fastest computers a full day of nonstop calculation to determine how wide and how long a crack in one ten-foot segment of the piping would grow under the force of escaping water and steam. The results of such a calculation are important not only to establish how large a leak might develop in the pipe but also to determine whether or not the pipe might break completely under the conditions postulated (by the human engineer). Since it could take years of nonstop computing and millions of dollars to examine every conceivable location, size, and type of crack in every conceivable piece of pipe, the human engineer must make a judgment just as in the old days as to which is the most likely situation to occur and which is the most likely way in which the pipe can fail. The computer does not work with ideas but with numbers, and it can only solve a single problem at a time. The pipe it looks at must have a specified diameter, a specified crack, a specified strength, and a specified load applied to it. Furthermore, the computer model of the cracked pipe must have a specified idea as to how a crack grows as the postulated accident progresses. All these specifications are made by human beings, and thus the results of the computer are only as conclusive about the safety of the system as the questions asked are the critical ones.

The computer is both blessing and curse for it makes possible calculations once beyond the reach of human endurance while at the same time also making them virtually beyond the hope of human verification. Contemporaneous explanations of what was going on during the accident at Three Mile Island were as changeable as weather forecasts, and even as the accident was in progress, computer models of the plant were being examined to try to figure it out.

Unfortunately, nuclear plants and other complex structures cannot be designed without the aid of computers and the complex programs that work the problems assigned them. This leads to not a little confusion when an error is discovered, usually by serendipity, in a program that had long since been used to establish the safety of a plant operating at full power. The analysis of the many piping systems in nuclear plants seems to be especially prone to gremlins, and one computer program used for calculating the stresses in pipes was reportedly using the wrong value for pi, the ratio of the circumference to the diameter of a circle that even a high school geometry student like my daughter will proudly recite to more decimal places than the computer stores. Another incident with a piping program occurred several years ago when an incorrect sign was discovered in one of the instructions to the computer. Stresses that should have been added were subtracted by the computer, thus leading it to report values that were lower than they would have been during an earthquake. Since the computer results had been employed to declare several nuclear plants earthquake-proof, all those plants had to be rechecked with the corrected computer program. This took months to do and several of the plants were threatened with being shut down by the Nuclear Regulatory Commission if they could not demonstrate their safety within a reasonable amount of time.

Even if a computer program is not in error, it can be improperly employed. The two and a half acres of roof covering the Hartford Civic Center collapsed under snow and ice in January 1978, only hours after several thousand fans had filed out following a basketball game. The roof was of a space-frame design, which means that it was supported by a three-dimensional arrangement of metal rods interconnected into a regular pattern of triangles and squares. Most of the rods were thirty feet long, and as many as eight rods had to be connected together at their ends. The lengthy calculations required to ensure that no single rod would have to carry more load than it could handle might have kept earlier engineers from attempting such a structure or, if they were to have designed it, they might have beefed it up to the point where it was overly safe or to where its own weight made it prohibitively expensive to build. The computer can be used to calculate virtually all the possibilities, which, so long as calculations are not made for rods that stretch or bend permanently, is not nearly so time consuming as the calculation for a cracked pipe, and engineers can gain an unwarranted confidence in the validity of the resulting numbers. But the numbers actually represent the solution to the problem of the space-frame model in the computer and not that of the actual one under ice and snow. In particular, the computer model could have understated the weight on the roof or oversimplified the means by which the rods are interconnected. The means of connection is a detail of the design that is much more difficult to incorporate into a computer model than the lengths and strengths of the rods, yet it is precisely the detail that can transmit critical forces to the physical rods and cause them to bend out of shape.

In reanalyzing the Hartford Civic Center's structure after the collapse, investigators found that the principal cause of failure was inadequate bracing in the thirty-foot-long bars comprising the top of the space truss. These bars were being bent, and the one most severely bent relative to its strength folded under the exceptional load of snow and ice. When one bar bent, it could no longer function as it was designed to, and its share of the roof load was shifted to adjacent bars. Thus a chain reaction was set up and the entire frame quickly collapsed. The computer provided the answer to the question of how the accident happened because it was asked the right question explicitly and was provided with a model that could answer that question. Apparently, the original designers were so confident of their own oversimplified computer model (and that they had asked of it the proper questions) that when workmen questioned the large sag noticed in the new roof they were assured that it was behaving as it was supposed to.

Because the computer can make so many calculations so quickly, there is a tendency now to use it to design structures in which *every* part is of minimum weight and strength, thereby producing the most economical structure. This degree of optimization was not practical to expect when hand calculations were the norm, and designers generally settled for an admittedly overdesigned and thus a somewhat extravagant, if probably extra-safe, structure. However, by making every part as light and as highly stressed as possible, within applicable building code and factor of safety requirements, there is little room for error—in the computer's calculations, in the parts manufacturers' products, or in the construction workers' execution of the design. Thus computer-optimized structures may be marginally or least-safe designs, as the Hartford Civic Center roof proved to be.

The Electric Power Research Institute has been sponsoring a program to test the ability of structural analysis computer software to predict the behavior of large transmission towers, whose design poses problems not unlike a three-dimensional space-frame roof. A full-size giant tower has been constructed at the Transmission Line Mechanical Research Facility in Haslet, Texas, and the actual structure can be subjected to carefully controlled loads as the reaction of its various members is recorded. The results of such real-world tests were compared with computer predictions of the tower's behavior, and the computer software did not fare too well. Computer predictions of structural behavior were within only sixty percent of the actual measured values only ninety-five percent of the time, while designers using the software generally expect an accuracy of at least twenty percent ninety-five percent of the time. Clearly, a tower designed with such uncertain software could be as unpredictable as the Hartford Civic Center roof. It is only the factor of safety that is applied to transmission towers that appears to have prevented any number of them from collapsing across the countryside.

In the absence of these disturbing tests, the success of towers designed by computer might have been used to argue that the factor of safety should be lowered. Conservative opposition to lowering a factor of safety would be hard to maintain for structures that had been experiencing no failures, and time, if nothing else, would wear down the opponents. But a lower factor of safety would invariably lead to a failure, which in turn would lead to the realization that the computer software was not analyzing the structure as accurately as was thought. But it would have been learning a lesson the hard way.

Thus, while the computer can be an almost indispensable partner in the design process, it can also be a source of overconfidence on the part of its human bosses. When used to crunch numbers for large but not especially innovative designs, the computer is not likely to mislead the experienced designer because he knows, from his and others' experience with similar structures, what questions to ask. If such structures have failed he will be particularly alert to the possibility of similar modes of failure in his structure. However, when the computer is relied upon for the design of innovative structures for which there is little experience of success, let alone failure, then it is as likely, perhaps more likely, for the computer to be mistaken as it was for a human engineer in the days of the slide rule. And as more complex structures are designed *because* it is believed that the computer can do what man cannot, then there is indeed an increased likelihood that structures will fail, for the further we stray from experience the less likely we are to think of all the right questions.

It is not only large computers that are cause for concern, and some critics have expressed the fear that a greater danger lies in the growing use of microcomputers. Since these machines and a plethora of software for them are so readily available and so inexpensive, there is concern that engineers will take on jobs that are at best on the fringes of their expertise. And being inexperienced in an area, they are less likely to be critical of a computer-generated design that would make no sense to an older engineer who would have developed a feel for the structure through the many calculations he had performed on his slide rule.

In his keynote address on the structural design process before the Twelfth Congress of the International Association for Bridge and Structural Engineering held in Vancouver in 1984, James G. MacGregor, chairman of the Canadian Concrete Code Committee, expressed concern about the role of computers in structural design practice because "changes have occurred so rapidly that the profession has yet to assess and allow for the implications of these changes." He went on to discuss the creation of the software that will be used for design:

> Because structural analysis and detailing programs are complex, the profession as a whole will use programs written by a few. These few will come from the ranks of the structural "analysts" . . . and not from the structural "designers." Generally speaking, their design and construction-site experience and background will tend to be limited. It is difficult to envision a mechanism for ensuring that the products of such a person will display the experience and intuition of a competent designer.
>
> In the design office the reduction in computation time will free the engineer to spend more time in creative thought—*or* it will allow him to complete more work with less

creative thought than today. Because the computer analysis is available it will be used. Because the answers are so precise there is a tendency to believe them implicitly. The increased volume of numerical work can become a substitute for assessing the true structural action of the building as a whole. Thus, the use of computers in design must be policed by knowledgeable and experienced designers who can rapidly evaluate the value of an answer and the practicality of a detail. More than ever before, the challenge to the profession and to educators is to develop designers who will be able to stand up to and reject or modify the results of a computer aided analysis and design.

The American Society of Civil Engineers considered the problem of "computer-extended expertise" such an important issue that it made it the subject of its 1984 Mead Prize competition for the best paper on the topic "Should the Computer Be Registered?" The title is an allusion to the requirement that engineers be registered by state boards before they can be in charge of the design of structures whose failure could endanger life. Professional engineering licenses come only after a minimum period of engineering work with lesser responsibility and after passing a comprehensive examination in the area of one's expertise. Computers, while really no more than elaborate electronic slide rules and computation pads, enable anyone, professional engineer or not, to come up with a design for anything from a building to a sewer system that looks mighty impressive to the untrained eye. The announcement for the Mead Prize summarized the issue succinctly:

> Civil engineers have turned to the computer for increased speed, accuracy and productivity. However, do engineers run the risk of compromising the safety and welfare of the public? Many have predicted that the engineering failures of the future will be attributed to the use or misuse of computers. Is it becoming easy to take on design work outside of the engineer's area of expertise simply because a software package is available? How can civil engineers guarantee the accuracy of the computer program and that the engineer is qualified to use it properly?

By throwing such questions out to its Associate Members, those generally young in experience if not in age and the only ones eligible to compete for the Mead Prize, the ASCE at the same time acknowledged and called to the attention of future professional engineers one of the most significant developments in the history of structural engineering.

▷ LIMITS OF CORRECTNESS
IN COMPUTERS

Brian Cantwell Smith

INTRODUCTION

On October 5, 1960, the American Ballistic Missile Early-Warning System station at Thule, Greenland, indicated a large contingent of Soviet missiles headed towards the United States.[1] Fortunately, common sense prevailed at the informal threat-assessment conference that was immediately convened: international tensions weren't particularly high at the time, the system had only recently been installed, Kruschev was in New York, and all in all a massive Soviet attack seemed very unlikely. As a result no devastating counter-attack was launched. What was the problem? The moon had risen, and was reflecting radar signals back to earth. Needless to say, this lunar reflection hadn't been predicted by the system's designers.

Over the last ten years, the Defense Department has spent many millions of dollars on a new computer technology called "program verification"—a branch of computer science whose business, in its own terms, is to "prove programs correct." Program verification has been studied in theoretical computer science departments since a few seminal papers in the 1960s,[2] but it has only recently started to gain in public visibility, and to be applied to real world problems. General Electric, to consider just one example, has initiated verification projects in their own laboratories: they would like to prove that the programs used in their latest computer-controlled washing machines won't have any "bugs" (even one serious one can destroy their profit margin).[3] Although it used to be that only the simplest programs could be "proven correct"—programs to put simple lists into order, to compute simple arithmetic functions—slow but steady progress has been made in extending the range of verification techniques. Recent papers have reported correctness proofs for somewhat more complex programs, including small operating systems, compilers, and other material of modern system design.[4]

What, we do well to ask, does this new technology mean? How good are we at it? For example, if the 1960 warning system had been proven correct (which it was not), could we have avoided the problem with the moon? If it were possible to prove that the programs being written to control automatic launch-on-warning systems were correct, would that mean there could not be a catastrophic accident? In systems now being proposed computers will make launching decisions in a matter of seconds, with no time for any human intervention (let alone for musings about Kruschev's being in New York). Do the techniques of program verification hold enough promise so that, if these new systems could all be proven correct, we could all sleep more easily at night? These are the questions I want to look at in this paper. And my answer, to give away the punch-line, is no. For fundamental reasons—reasons that anyone can understand—there are inherent limitations to what can be proven about computers and computer programs. Although program verification is an important new technology, useful, like so many other things, in its particular time and place, it should definitely not be called verification. Just because a program is "proven correct," in other words, you cannot be sure that it will do what you intend.

First some background.

GENERAL ISSUES IN PROGRAM VERIFICATION

Computation is by now the most important enabling technology of nuclear weapons systems: it underlies virtually every aspect of the defense system, from the early warning systems, battle management and simulation systems, and systems for communication and control, to the intricate guidance systems that direct the missiles to their targets. It is difficult, in assessing the chances of an accidental nuclear war, to imagine a more important question to ask than whether these pervasive computer systems will or do work correctly.

Because the subject is so large, however, I want to focus on just one aspect of computers relevant to their correctness: the use of *models* in the construction, use, and analysis of computer systems. I have chosen to look at modelling because I think it exerts the most profound and, in the end, most important influence on the systems we build. But it is only one of an enormous number of important questions. First, therefore—in order to unsettle you a little—let me just hint at some of the equally important issues I will not address:

1. Complexity: At the current state of the art, only very simple programs can be proven correct. Although it is terribly misleading to assume that either the complexity or power of a computer program is a linear function of length, some rough numbers are illustrative. The simplest possible arithmetic programs are measured in tens of lines; the current state of the verification art extends only to programs of up to several hundred. It is estimated that the systems proposed in the Strategic Defense Initiative (Stars Wars), in contrast, will require at least 10,000,000 lines of code.[5] By analogy, compare the difference between resolving a two-person dispute and settling the political problems of the Middle East. There's no a priori reason to believe that strategies successful at one level will scale to the other.

2. Human Interaction: Not much can be "proven," let alone specified formally, about actual human behavior. The sorts of programs that have so far been proven correct, therefore, do not include much substantial human interaction. On the other hand, as the moon-rise example indicates, it is often crucial to allow enough human intervention to enable people to over-ride system mistakes. System designers, therefore, are faced with a very real dilemma: should they rule out substantive human intervention, in order to develop more confidence in how their systems will perform, or should they include it, so that costly errors can be avoided or at least repaired? The Three-Mile Island incident is a trenchant example of just how serious this trade-off can get: the system design provided for considerable human intervention, but then the operators failed to act "appropriately." Which strategy leads to the more important kind of correctness?

A standard way out of this dilemma is to specify the behavior of the system *relative to the actions of its operators.* But this, as we will see below, pressures the designers to specify the system totally in terms of internal actions, not external effects. So you end up proving only that the system will *behave in the way that it will behave* (i.e., it will raise this line level 3 volts), not *do what you want it to do* (i.e., launch a missile only if the attack is real). Unfortunately, the latter is clearly what is important. Systems comprising computers and people must function properly as integrated systems; nothing is gained by showing that one cog in a misshapen wheel is a very nice cog indeed.

Furthermore, large computer systems are dynamic, constantly changing, embedded in complex social settings. Another famous "mistake" in the American defense system happened when a human operator mistakenly mounted a training tape, containing a simulation of a full-scale Soviet attack, onto a computer that, just by chance, was automatically pulled into service when the primary machine ran into a problem. For some tense moments the simulation data were taken to be the real thing.[6] What does it mean to install a "correct" module into a complex social flux?

3. Levels of Failure: Complex computer systems must work at many different levels. It follows that they can fail at many different levels too. By analogy, consider the many different ways a hospital could fail. First, the beams used to frame it might collapse. Or they might perform flawlessly, but the operating room door might be too small to let in a hospital bed (in which case you would blame the architects, not the lumber or steel company). Or the operating room might be fine, but the hospital might be located in the middle of the woods, where no one could get to it (in which case you would blame the planners). Or, to take a different example, consider how a letter could fail. It might be so torn or soiled that it could not be read. Or it might look beautiful, but be full of spelling mistakes. Or it might have perfect grammar, but disastrous contents.

Computer systems are the same: they can be "correct" at one level—say, in terms of hardware—but fail at another (i.e., the systems built on top of the hardware can do the wrong thing even if the chips are fine). Sometimes, when people talk about computers failing, they seem to think only the hardware needs to work. And hardware does from time to time fail, causing the machine to come to a halt, or yielding errant behaviour (as for example when a faulty chip in another American early warning system sputtered random digits into a signal of how many Soviet missiles had been sighted, again causing a false alert[7]). And the connections between the computers and the world can break: when the moon-rise problem was first recognized, an attempt to override it failed because an iceberg had accidentally cut an undersea telephone cable.[8] But the more important point is that, in order to be reliable, a system has to be correct at *every relevant level*: the hardware is just the starting place (and by far the easiest, at that). Unfortunately, however, we don't even know what all the relevant levels are. So-called "fault-tolerant" computers, for example, are particularly good at coping with hardware failures, but the software that runs on them is not thereby improved.[9]

4. Correctness and Intention: What does *correct* mean, anyway? Suppose the people want peace, and the President thinks that means having a strong defense, and the Defense department thinks that means having nuclear weapons systems, and the weapons designers request control systems to monitor radar signals, and the computer companies are asked to respond to six particular kinds of radar pattern, and the engineers are told to build signal amplifiers with certain circuit characteristics, and the technician is told to write a program to respond to the difference between a two-volt and a four-volt signal on a particular incoming wire. If being correct means *doing what was intended*, whose intent matters? The technician's? Or what, with twenty years of historical detachment, we would say *should have been intended*?

With a little thought any of you could extend this list yourself. And none of these issues even touch on the intricate technical problems that arise in actually building the mathematical models of software and systems used in the so-called "correctness" proofs. But, as I said, I want to focus on what I take to be the most important issue underlying all of these concerns: the pervasive use of models. Models are ubiquitous not only in computer science but also in human thinking and language; their very familiarity makes them hard to appreciate. So we'll start simply, looking at modelling on its own, and come back to correctness in a moment.

THE PERMEATING USE OF MODELS

When you design and build a computer system, you first formulate a model of the problem you want it to solve, and then construct the computer program in its terms. For example, if you were to design a medical system to administer drug therapy, you would need to model a variety of things: the patient, the drug, the absorption rate, the desired balance between therapy and toxicity, and so on and so forth. The absorption rate might be modelled as a number proportional to the patient's weight, or proportional to body surface area, or as some more complex function of weight, age, and sex.

Similarly, computers that control traffic lights are based on some model of traffic—of how long it takes to drive across the intersection, of how much metal cars contain (the signal change mechanisms are triggered by metal-detectors buried under each street). Bicyclists, as it happens, often have problems with automatic traffic lights, because bicycles don't exactly fit the model: they don't contain enough iron to trigger the metal-detectors. I also once saw a tractor get into trouble because it couldn't move as fast as the system "thought" it would: the cross-light went green when the tractor was only half-way through the intersection.

To build a model is to conceive of the world in a certain delimited way. To some extent you must build models before building any artifact at all, including televisions and toasters, but computers have a special dependence on these models: *you write an explicit description of the model down inside the computer*, in the form of a set of rules or what are called *representations*—essentially linguistic formulae encoding, in the terms of the model, the facts and data thought to be relevant to the system's behavior. It is with respect to these representations that computer systems work. In fact that's really what computers are (and how they differ from other machines): they run by manipulating representations, and representations are always formulated in terms of models. This can all be summarized in a slogan: no computation without representation.

The models, on which the representations are based, come in all shapes and sizes. Balsa models of cars and airplanes, for example, are used to study air friction and lift. Blueprints can be viewed as models of buildings; musical scores as models of a symphony. But models can also be abstract. Mathematical models, in particular, are so widely used that it is hard to think of anything that they haven't been used for: from whole social and economic systems, to personality traits in teenagers, to genetic structures, to the mass and charge of subatomic particles. These models, furthermore, permeate all discussion and communication. Every expression of language can be viewed as resting implicitly on some model of the world.

What is important, for our purposes, is that every model deals with its subject matter *at some particular level of abstraction*, paying attention to certain details, throwing away others, grouping together similar aspects into common categories, and so forth. So the drug model mentioned above would probably pay attention to the patients' weights, but ignore their tastes in music. Mathematical models of traffic typically ignore the temperaments of taxi drivers. Sometimes what is ignored is at too "low" a level; sometimes too "high": it depends on the purposes for which the model is being used. So a hospital blueprint would pay attention to the structure and connection of its beams, but not to the arrangements of proteins in the wood the beams are made of, nor to the efficacy of the resulting operating room.

Models *have* to ignore things exactly because they view the world at a level of abstraction ("abstraction" is from the Latin *abstrahere*, "to pull or draw away"). And it is good that they do: otherwise they would drown in the infinite richness of the embedding world. Though this isn't the place for metaphysics, it would not be too much to say that every act of conceptualization, analysis, categorization, does a certain amount of violence to its subject matter, in order to get at the underlying regularities that group things together. If you don't commit that act of violence—don't ignore some of what's going on—you would become so hypersensitive and so overcome with complexity that you would be unable to act.

To capture all this in a word, we will say that models are inherently *partial*. All thinking, and all computation, are similarly partial. Furthermore—and this is the important point—thinking and computation *have* to be partial: that's how they are able to work.

FULL-BLOODED ACTION

Something that is not partial, however, is action. When you reach out your hand and grasp a plow, it is the real field you are digging up, not your model of it. Models, in other words, may be abstract, and thinking may be abstract, and some aspects of computation may be abstract, but action is not. To actually build a hospital, to clench the steering wheel and drive through the intersection, or to inject a drug into a person's body, is to act in the full-blooded world, not in a partial or distilled model of it.

This difference between action and modelling is extraordinarily important. Even if your every thought is formulated in the terms of some model, to act is to take leave of the model and participate in the whole, rich, infinitely variegated world. For this reason, among others, action plays a crucial role, especially in the human case, in grounding the more abstract processes of modelling or conceptualization. One form that grounding can take, which computer systems can already take advantage of, is to provide feedback on how well the modelling is going. For example, if an industrial robot develops an internal three-dimensional representation of a wheel assembly passing by on a conveyor belt, and then guides its arm towards that object and tries to pick it up, it can use video systems or force sensors to see how well the model corresponded to what was actually the case. The world doesn't care about the model: the claws will settle on the wheel just in case the actualities mesh.

Feedback is a special case of a very general phenomenon: you often learn, when you do act, just how good or bad your conceptual model was. You learn, that is, if you have adequate sensory apparatus, the capacity to assess the sensed experience, the inner resources to revise and reconceptualize, and the luxury of recovering from minor mistakes and failures.

COMPUTERS AND MODELS

What does all this have to do with computers, and with correctness? The point is that computers, like us, participate in the real world: they take real actions. One of the most important facts about computers, to put this another way, is that we plug them in. They are not, as some theoreticians seem to suppose, pure mathematical abstractions, living in a pure detached heaven. They land real planes at real airports; administer real drugs; and—as you know all too well—control real radars, missiles, and command systems. Like us, in other words, although they base their actions on models, they have consequence in a world that inevitably transcends the partiality of those enabling models. Like us, in other words, and unlike the objects of mathematics, they are challenged by the inexorable conflict between the partial but tractable model, and the actual but infinite world.

And, to make the only too obvious point: we in general have no guarantee that the models are right—indeed we have no *guarantee* about much of anything about the relationship between model and world. As we will see, current notions of "correctness" don't even address this fundamental question.

In philosophy and logic, as it happens, there is a very precise mathematical theory called "model theory." You might think that it would be a theory about what models are, what they are good for, how they correspond to the worlds they are models of, and so forth. You might even hope this was true, for the following reason: a great deal of theoretical computer science, and all of the work in program verification and correctness, historically derives from this model-theoretic tradition, and depends on its techniques. Unfortunately, however, model theory doesn't address the model–world relationship at all. Rather, what model theory does is to tell you how your descriptions, representations, and programs *correspond to your model.*

The situation, in other words, is roughly as depicted in Figure 1. . . . You are to imagine a description, program, computer system (or even a thought—they are all similar in this regard) in the left hand box, and the very real world in the right. Mediating between the two is the inevitable model, serving as an idealized or preconceptualized simulacrum of the world, in terms of which the description or program or whatever can be understood. One way to understand the model is as the glasses through which the program or computer looks at the world: it is the world, that is, as the system sees it (though not, of course, as it necessarily is).

The technical subject of "model theory," as I have already said, is a study of the relationship on the left. What about the relationship on the right? The answer, and one of the main points I hope you will take away from this discussion, is that, at this point in intellectual history, we have no theory of this right-hand side relationship.

There are lots of reasons for this, some very complex. For one thing, most of our currently accepted formal techniques were developed, during the first half of this century, to deal with mathematics and physics. Mathematics is unique, with respect to models, because (at least to a first level of approximation) its subject matter *is* the world of models and abstract structures, and therefore the model–world relationship is relatively unproblematic. The situation in physics is more complex, of course, as is the relationship between mathematics and physics. How apparently pure mathematical structures could be used to model the material substrate of the universe is a question that has exercised physical scientists for centuries. But the point is that,

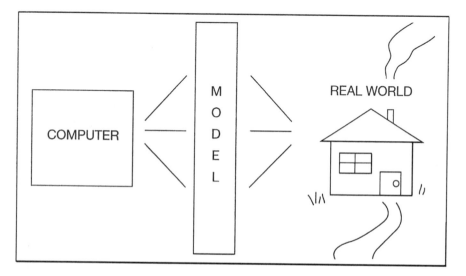

FIGURE 1: Computers, Models, and the Embedding World

whether or not one believes that the best physical models do more justice and there-fore less violence to the world than do models in so-called "higher-level" disciplines like sociology or economics, formal techniques don't themselves address the question of adequacy.

Another reason we don't have a theory of the right-hand side is that there is very little agreement on what such a theory would look like. In fact all kinds of ques-tions arise, when one studies the model–world relationship explicitly, about whether it can be treated formally at all, about whether it can be treated rigorously, even if not formally (and what the relationship is between those two), about whether any the-ory will be more than usually infected with prejudices and preconceptions of the the-orist, and so forth. The investigation quickly leads to foundational questions in math-ematics, philosophy, and language, as well as computer science. But none of what one learns in any way lessens its ultimate importance. In the end, any adequate the-ory of action, and, consequently, any adequate theory of correctness, will have to take the model–world relationship into account.

CORRECTNESS AND RELATIVE CONSISTENCY

Let's get back, then, to computers, and to correctness. As I mentioned earlier, the word "correct" is already problematic, especially as it relates to underlying intention. Is a program correct when it does what we have instructed it to do? or what we want-ed it to do? or what history would dispassionately say it should have done? Analyz-ing what correctness *should* mean is too complex a topic to take up directly. What I want to do, in the time remaining, is to describe what sorts of correctness we are presently capable of analyzing.

In order to understand this, we need to understand one more thing about build-ing computer systems. I have already said, when you design a computer system, that you first develop a model of the world, as indicated in the diagram. But you don't, in general, ever get to hold the model in your hand: computer systems, in general, are based on models that are purely abstract. Rather, if you are interested in proving your program "correct," you develop two concrete things, structured in terms of the abstract underlying model (although these are listed here in logical order, the program is very often written first):

1. A *specification*: a formal description in some standard formal language, specified in terms of the model, in which the desired behavior is described; and
2. The *program*: a set of instructions and representations, also formulated in the terms of the model, which the computer uses as the basis for its actions.

How do these two differ? In various ways, of which one is particularly important. The program has to say *how the behavior is to be achieved*, typically in a step by step fashion (and often in excruciating detail). The specification, however, is less con-strained: all it has to do is to specify *what proper behavior would be*, independent of how it is accomplished. For example, a specification for a milk-delivery system might simply be: "Make one milk delivery at each store, driving the shortest possible dis-tance in total." That's just a description of what has to happen. The program, on the other hand, would have the much more difficult job of saying how this was to be accomplished. It might be phrased as follows: "drive four blocks north, turn right, stop at Gregory's Grocery Store on the corner, drop off the milk, then drive 17 blocks north-east . . ." Specifications, to use some of the jargon of the field, are essentially *declarative*; they are like indicative sentences or claims. Programs, on the other hand, are *procedural*: they must contain instructions that lead to a determinate sequence of actions.

What, then, is a proof of correctness? It is a proof that any system that *obeys the program* will *satisfy the specification*.

There are, as is probably quite evident, two kinds of problems here. The first, often acknowledged, is that the correctness proof is in reality only a proof that two characterizations of something are compatible. When the two differ—i.e., when you try to prove correctness and fail—there is no more reason to believe that the first (the specification) is any more correct than the second (the program). As a matter of technical practice, specifications tend to be extraordinarily complex formal descriptions, just as subject to bugs and design errors and so forth as programs. In fact they are very much like programs, as this introduction should suggest. So what almost always happens, when you write a specification and a program, and try to show that they are compatible, is that you have to adjust both of them in order to get them to converge.

For example, suppose you write a program to factor a number C, producing two answers A and B. Your specification might be:

> *Given a number C, produce numbers A and B such that*
> $A \times B = C$.

This is a specification, not a program, because it doesn't tell you *how* to come up with A and B. All it tells you is what properties A and B should have. In particular, suppose I say: ok, C is 5,332,114; what are A and B? Staring at the specification just given won't help you to come up with an answer. Suppose, on the other hand, given this specification, that you then write a program—say, by successively trying pairs of numbers until you find two that work. Suppose further that you then set out to prove that your program meets your specification. And, finally, suppose that this proof can be constructed (I won't go into details here; I hope you can imagine that such a proof could be constructed). With all three things in hand—program, specification, and proof—you might think you were done.

In fact, however, things are rarely that simple, as even this simple example can show. In particular, suppose, after doing all this work, that you try your program out, confident that it must work because you have a proof of its correctness. You randomly give it 14 as an input, expecting 2 and 7. But in fact it gives you the answers A = 1 and B = 14. In fact, you realize upon further examination, it will *always* give back A = 1 and B = C. It does this, *even though you have a proof of its being correct*, because you didn't make your specification meet your intentions. You wanted both A and B to be *different* from C (and also different from 1), but you forgot to say that. In this case you have to modify both the program and the specification. A plausible new version of the latter would be:

> *Given a number C, produce numbers A and B such that*
> $A \neq 1$ and $B \neq 1$ and $A \times B = C$.

And so on and so forth: the point, I take it, is obvious. If the next version of the program, given 14, produces A = −1 and B = −14, you would similarly have met your new specification, but still failed to meet your intention. Writing "good" specifications—which is to say, writing specifications that capture your intention—is hard.

It should be apparent, nonetheless, that developing even straightforward proofs of "correctness" is nonetheless very useful. It typically forces you to delineate, very explicitly and completely, the model on which both program and specification are based. A great many of the simple bugs that occur in programs, of which the problem of producing 1 and 14 was an example, arise from sloppiness and unclarity about the model. Such bugs are not identified by the proof, but they are often unearthed in the attempt to prove. And of course there is nothing wrong with this practice; anything that helps to erradicate errors and increase confidence is to be applauded. The point, rather, is to show exactly what these proofs consist in.

In particular, as the discussion has shown, when you show that a program meets its specifications, all you have done is to show that two formal descriptions, slightly different in character, are compatible. This is why I think it is somewhere between misleading and immoral for computer scientists to call this "correctness." What is called a proof of correctness is really a proof of the compatibility or consistency between two formal objects of an extremely similar sort: program and specification. As a community, we computer scientists should call this *relative consistency*, and drop the word *"correctness"* completely.

What proofs of relative consistency ignore is the second problem intimated earlier. Nothing in the so-called program verification process per se deals with the right-hand side relationship: the relationship between the model and the world. But, as is clear, it is over inadequacies on the right hand side—inadequacies, that is, in the models in terms of which the programs and specifications are written—that systems so commonly fail.

The problem with the moon-rise, for example, was a problem of this second sort. The difficulty was not that the program failed, in terms of the model. The problem, rather, was that the model was overly simplistic; *it didn't correspond to what was the case in the world.* Or, to put it more carefully, since all models fail to correspond to the world in indefinitely many ways, as we have already said, it didn't correspond to what was the case *in a crucial and relevant way.* In other words, to answer one of our original questions, even if a formal specification had been written for the 1960 warning system, and a proof of correctness generated, there is no reason to believe that potential difficulties with the moon would have emerged.

You might think that the designers were sloppy; that they would have thought of the moon if they had been more careful. But it turns out to be extremely difficult to develop realistic models of any but the most artificial situations, and to assess how adequate these models are. To see just how hard it can be, think back on the case of General Electric, and imagine writing appliance specifications, this time for a refrigerator. To give the example some force, imagine that you are contracting the refrigerator out to be built by an independent supplier, and that you want to put a specification into the contract that is sufficiently precise to guarantee that you will be happy with anything that the supplier delivers that meets the contract.

Your first version might be quite simple—say, that it should maintain an internal temperature of between 3 and 6 degrees Centigrade; not use more than 200 Watts of electricity; cost less than $100 to manufacture; have an internal volume of half a cubic meter; and so on and so forth. But of course there are hundreds of other properties that you implicitly rely on: it should, presumably, be structurally sound: you wouldn't be happy with a deliciously cool plastic bag. It shouldn't weigh more than a ton, or emit loud noises. And it shouldn't fling projectiles out at high speed when the door is opened. In general, it is impossible, when writing specifications, to include *everything* that you want: legal contracts, and other humanly interpretable specifications, are always stated within a background of common sense, to cover the myriad unstated and unstatable assumptions assumed to hold in force. (Current computer programs, alas, have no common sense, as the cartoonists know so well.)

So it is hard to make sure that everything that meets your specification will really be a refrigerator; it is also hard to make sure that your requirements don't rule out perfectly good refrigerators. Suppose for example a customer plugs a toaster in, puts it inside the refrigerator, and complains that the object he received doesn't meet the temperature specification and must therefore not be a refrigerator. Or suppose he tries to run it upside down. Or complains that it doesn't work in outer space, even though you didn't explicitly specify that it would only work within the earth's atmosphere. Or spins it at 10,000 rpm. Or even just unplugs it. In each case you would say that the problem lies not with the refrigerator but with the use. But how is *use* to be specified? The point is that, as well as modelling the artifact itself, you have to model the relevant part of the world in which it will be embedded. It follows that the model of a refrigerator as a device that *always* maintains an internal temperature of between 3 and 6 degrees is too strict to cover all possible situations. One could try to model what appropriate use would be, though specifications don't, ordinarily, even try to identify all the relevant circumstantial factors. As well as there being a background set of constraints with respect to which a model is formulated, in other words, there is also a background set of assumptions on which a specification is allowed at any point to rely.

THE LIMITS OF CORRECTNESS

It's time to summarize what we've said so far. The first challenge to developing a perfectly "correct" computer system stems from the sheer complexity of real-world tasks. We mentioned at the outset various factors that contribute to this complexity: human interaction, unpredictable factors of setting, hardware problems, difficulties in identifying salient levels of abstraction, etc. Nor is this complexity of only theoretical concern. A December 1984 report of the American Defense Science Board Task Force on "Military Applications of New-Generation Computing Technologies" identifies the following gap between current laboratory demonstrations and what will be required for successful military applications—applications they call "Real World; Life or Death." In their estimation the military now needs (and, so far as one can tell, expects to produce) an increase in the power of computer systems of nine orders of magnitude, accounting for both speed and amount of information to be processed. That is a 1,000,000,000-fold increase over current research systems, equivalent to the difference between a full century of the entire New York metropolitan area, compared to one day in the life of a hamlet of one hundred people. And remember that even current systems are already several orders of magnitude more complex that those for which we can currently develop proofs of relative consistency.

But sheer complexity has not been our primary subject matter. The second challenge to computational correctness, more serious, comes from the problem of formulating or specifying an appropriate model. Except in the most highly artificial or constrained domains, modelling the embedding situation is an approximate, not a complete, endeavor. It has the best hopes of even partial success in what Winograd has called "systematic domains": areas where the relevant stock of objects, properties, and relationships are most clearly and regularly pre-defined. Thus bacteremia, or warehouse inventories, or even flight paths of airplanes coming into airports, are relatively systematic domains, at least compared to conflict negotiations, any situations involving intentional human agency, learning and instruction, and so forth. The systems that land airplanes are hybrids—combinations of computers and people—exactly because the unforeseeable happens, and because what happens is in part the result of human action, requiring human interpretation. Although it is impressive how well the phone companies can model telephone connections, lines, and even develop statistical models of telephone use, at a certain level of abstraction, it would nevertheless be impossible to model the content of the telephone conversations themselves.

Third, and finally, is the question of what one does about these first two facts. It is because of the answer to this last question that I have talked, so far, somewhat interchangeably about people and computers. With respect to the ultimate limits of models and conceptualization, both people and computers are restrained by the same truths. If the world is infinitely rich and variegated, no prior conceptualization of it, nor any abstraction, will ever do it full justice. That's ok—or at least we might as well say that it's ok, since that's the world we've got. What matters is that we not forget about that richness—that we not think, with misplaced optimism, that machines might magically have access to a kind of "correctness" to which people cannot even aspire.

It is time, to put this another way, that we change the traditional terms of the debate. The question is not whether machines can do things, as if, in the background, lies the implicit assumption that the object of comparison is people. Plans to build automated systems capable of making a "decision," in a matter of seconds, to annihilate Europe, say, should make you uneasy; requiring a person to make the same decision in a matter of the same few seconds should make you uneasy too, and for very similar reasons. The problem is that there is simply no way that reasoning of any sort can do justice to the inevitable complexity of the situation, because of what reasoning is. Reasoning is based on partial models. Which means it cannot be guaranteed to be correct. Which means, to suggest just one possible strategy for action, that we might try, in our treaty negotiations, to find mechanisms to slow our weapons systems down.

It is striking to realize, once the comparison between machines and people is raised explicitly, that we don't typically expect "correctness" for people in anything like the form that we presume it for computers. In fact quite the opposite, and in a revealing way. Imagine, in some by-gone era, sending a soldier off to war, and giving him (it would surely have been a "him") final instructions. "Obey your commander, help your fellow-soldier," you might say, "and above all do your country honor." What is striking about this is that it is considered not just a weakness, but a punishable weakness—a breach of morality—to obey instructions *blindly* (in fact, and for relevant reasons, you generally *can't* follow instructions blindly; they have to be interpreted to the situation at hand). You are subject to court-martial, for example, if you violate fundamental moral principles, such as murdering women and children, even if following strict orders.

In the human case, in other words, our social and moral systems seem to have built in an acceptance of the uncertainties and limitations inherent in the model–world relationship. We *know* that the assumptions and preconceptions built into instructions will sometimes fail, and we know that instructions are always incomplete; we exactly rely on judgment, responsibility, consciousness, and so forth, to carry someone through those situations—all situations, in fact—where model and world part company. In fact we never talk about people, in terms of their overall personality, being *correct*; we talk about people being *reliable*, a much more substantive term. It is individual actions, fully situated in a particular setting, that are correct or incorrect, not people in general, or systems. What leads to the highest number of correct human actions is a person's being reliable, experienced, capable of good judgment, etc.

There are two possible morals here, for computers. The first has to do with the notion of experience. In point of fact, program verification is not the only, or even the most common, method of obtaining assurance that a computer system will do the right thing. Programs are usually judged acceptable, and are typically accepted into use, not because we prove them "correct," but because they have shown themselves relatively reliable in their destined situations for some substantial period of time. And, as part of this experience, we expect them to fail: there always has to be room for failure. Certainly no one would ever accept a program without this *in situ* testing: a proof of correctness is at best added insurance, not a replacement, for real life experience. Unfortunately, for the ten million lines of code that is supposed to control and coordinate the Star Wars Defense System, there will never, God willing, be an *in situ* test.

One answer, of course, if genuine testing is impossible, is to run a *simulation* of the real situation. But simulation, as our diagram should make clear, *tests only the left-hand side relationship*. Simulations are defined in terms of models; they don't test the relationship between the model and the world. That is exactly why simulations and tests can never replace embedding a program in the real world. All the war-games we hear about, and hypothetical military scenarios, and electronic battlefield simulators, and so forth, are all based on exactly the kinds of models we have been talking about all along. In fact the subject of simulation, worthy of a whole analysis on its own, is really just our whole subject welling up all over again.

I said earlier that there were two morals to be drawn, for the computer, from the fact that we ask people to be reliable, not correct. The second moral is for those who, when confronted with the fact that genuine or adequate experience cannot be had, would say "oh, well, let's build responsibility and morality into the computers— if people can have it, there's no reason why machines can't have it too." Now I will not argue that this is inherently impossible, in a metaphysical or ultimate philosophical sense, but a few short comments are in order. First, from the fact that humans sometimes *are* responsible, it does not follow that we know what responsibility is: from tacit skills no explicit model is necessarily forthcoming. We simply do not know what aspects of the human condition underlie the modest levels of responsibility to which we sometimes rise. And second, with respect to the goal of building computers with even human levels of full reliability and responsibility, I can state with surety that the present state of artificial intelligence is about as far from this as mosquitos are from flying to the moon.

But there are deeper morals even than these. The point is that even if we could make computers reliable, they still wouldn't necessarily always do the correct thing. *People* aren't provably "correct," either: that's why we hope they are responsible, and it is surely one of the major ethical facts is that correctness and responsibility don't coincide. Even if, in another 1,000 years, someone were to devise a genuinely responsible computer system, there is no reason to suppose that it would achieve "perfect correctness" either, in the sense of never doing anything wrong. This isn't a failure, in the sense of a performance limitation; it stems from the deeper fact that models must abstract, in order to be useful. The lesson to be learned from the violence inherent in the model–world relationship, in other words, is that there is an *inherent* conflict between the power of analysis and conceptualization, on the one hand, and sensitivity to the infinite richness, on the other.

But perhaps this is an overly abstract way to put it. Perhaps, instead, we should just remember that there will always be another moon-rise.

REFERENCES

1. Edmund Berkeley, *The Computer Revolution*, Doubleday, 1962, pp. 175–177, citing newspaper stories in the *Manchester Guardian Weekly* of Dec. 1, 1960, a UPI dispatch published in the *Boston Traveller* of Dec. 13, 1960, and an AP dispatch published in the *New York Times* on Dec. 23, 1960.

2. McCarthy, John, "A Basis for a Mathematical Theory of Computation", 1963, in P. Braffort and D. Hirschberg, eds., *Computer Programming and Formal Systems*, Amsterdam: North-Holland, 1967, pp. 33–70. Floyd, Robert, "Assigning Meaning to Programs", Proceedings of Symposia in Applied Mathematics 19, 1967 (also in F. T. Schwartz, ed, *Mathematical Aspects of Computer Science*, Providence: American Mathematical Society, 1967). Naur, P, "Proof of Algorithms by General Snapshots", *BIT* Vol. 6 No. 4, pp. 310–316, 1966.

3. Al Stevens, BBN Inc., personal communication.

4. See for example R. S. Boyer, and Moore, J S., eds., *The Correctness Problem in Computer Science*, London: Academic Press, 1981.

5. Fletcher, James, study chairman, and McMillan, Brockway, panel chairman, *Report of the Study on Eliminating the Threat Posed by Nuclear Ballistic Missiles (U)*, Vol. 5, *Battle Management, Communications, and Data Processing (U)*, U.S. Department of Defense, February 1984.

6. See, for example, the Hart-Goldwater report to the Committee on Armed Services of the U.S. Senate: "Recent False Alerts from the Nation's Missile Attack Warning System" (Washington, D.C.: U.S. Government Printing Office, Oct. 9, 1980); Physicians for Social Responsibility, *Newsletter*, "Accidental Nuclear War", (Winter 1982), p. 1.

7. Ibid.

8. Berkeley, op. cit. See also Daniel Ford's two-part article "The Button", *New Yorker*, April 1, 1985, p. 43, and April 8, 1985, p. 49, excerpted from Ford, Daniel, *The Button*, New York: Simon and Schuster, 1985.

9. Developing software for fault-tolerant systems is in fact an extremely tricky business.

CHAPTER SIX

Responsibility, Liability, and Professional Codes

INTRODUCTION

The readings in the previous chapter discussed the harms and risks posed by malfunctioning and poorly designed computer systems, and sought to understand the sources of these problems and ways to prevent them in the future. In this chapter we turn to a related set of issues, having to do with *responsibility* for the harms and risks of computing, and more generally, responsibility for the quality and impacts of computing. Where the underlying ideals touted in the articles in the preceding chapter were perfectly bug-free and reliable computer systems—and if not perfectly reliable, at least perfectly safe, in this chapter the ideals include 1) answerability for harms caused by computer systems, 2) just compensation for victims and just punishment for wrong-doers, and 3) within the community of individuals involved in the production of computer systems and computerized systems, an understanding of their professional responsibilities combined with a deep commitment to them. Several of the articles of this chapter fill out these ideals by carefully examining what we mean by responsibility, what it means to be answerable, and what it means to justly compensate. Some of the articles consider the ways in which the real world of computing falls short of these ideals.

The readings in this chapter are drawn from discussions of responsibility in the philosophical, legal, and professional literatures. They fall into two groups. The first group focuses on questions of "backward-looking" responsibility. By this we mean the questions about responsibility that are asked in the wake of an event—more particularly, an event that has given rise to harm. One may ask who should answer for the harm, who is to blame for the harm, who should be punished for the harm, or simply, who is responsible for the harm. The second group of readings focuses on questions of "forward-looking" responsibility, in particular, the special responsibilities of the computer community with respect to the systems they create. As the case study for both these sets, we selected Nancy Leveson and Clark Turner's in-depth analysis of the malfunctioning Therac-25, a computer-controlled radiation treatment machine whose failure caused deaths and serious injuries. Although Leveson and Turner's explicit focus is with what went wrong and how the malfunction might have been avoided, their article provides rich material for the discussion of responsibility from both the backward-looking and the forward-looking perspectives. The Therac-25 incident, not only raises questions about who was to blame for the injuries, but also about what was the nature of the professional responsibilities of the various parties involved.

RESPONSIBILITY, BLAME, ACCOUNTABILITY, AND LIABILITY

Responsibility is a complex concept with many shades of meaning. In some cases it can be used simply to identify the cause of an event. For example, we may say that the power surge was responsible for the loss of files and mean simply that the power surge caused the loss of files. In some cases it can identify who is answerable for an event, such as when we say that Janet Reno is responsible for the actions of law enforcement agents in storming the Branch Davidian compound in Waco, Texas. In some cases, it identifies who is to blame for an event, such as when we hold Robert Morris responsible for harm to Internet users. And in some cases, it identifies who is liable to be punished or to compensate a victim. In the article by H. L. A. Hart, a legal philosopher whose influential work on responsibility and legal liability continues to guide philosophers and legal theorists, he spells out several senses of responsibility. Among them, the three that are most relevant to the study of computer ethics are blame, liability, and role-responsibility. Applying these to the context of computing we may need to identify whom to blame when things go wrong, and whom to hold liable for the wrongs. Finally, we might want to identify a coherent and realistic set of responsibilities that reasonably attach to the roles of members of the computer community. In special cases, we would recognize role responsibilities as professional responsibilities.

Helen Nissenbaum's article on accountability, an article that addresses the gap between the ideals of responsibility and the real world, cautions readers on the possibility of an erosion of accountability that can arise from the contexts in which computer systems are typically produced, and commonly held assumptions about the capabilities and limitations of computing systematically. These contexts and assumptions create barriers to accountability by providing those who would prefer to avoid responsibility with a range of "excuses." With diminished accountability we would regularly encounter harms caused by failed or malfunctioning computer systems for which no one takes responsibility, no one is blamed, and no one is held liable to compensate victims.

Questions of legal liability follow closely on the heels of questions about blame because in most instances where we seek to find the individual who is to blame for a harm, we may naturally want to assess whether the individual is liable for punishment, or liable to compensate any victims. It is common for the law of a country or state to explicate as exhaustively as necessary the conditions and extent of liability in the event that the actions of an individual or group are responsible for harm. The article by Pamela Samuelson examines this legal perspective, considering liability under current United States law for harms wrought by various defective computerized information. Samuelson's article includes a brief but useful overview of liability law. One also learns from this article the limitation of current laws with respect to computer software. The cases that Samuelson discusses are examples of how the presence of computers in our lives has required an extension, and in some cases a re-evaluation, of ethical and legal principles. For the law, which tends to be rooted in past experiences (case law), application to computing contexts frequently requires clarification and novel interpretation.

The paper by Joseph Weizenbaum takes a broad societal perspective on the implications of computing and the responsibilities for it. Weizenbaum, a researcher in artificial intelligence, was one of the earliest scholars to bring to public attention social and ethical concerns about computing. For example, in the paper we have included in this chapter, he cautions all of society about the dangers of giving over critical functions to the control of computers, he appeals especially to computer scientists to fulfill their responsibilities to society; namely, to build the best systems they can, at the same time that they publicize to the rest of society the limits of their profession.

PROFESSIONAL RESPONSIBILITY AND CODES

If we begin with the premise that computing (especially software of various kinds) involves risks—both risks of physical harm as well as risks of various social effects—then computer professionals come quickly into focus as a group that can be targeted for responsibility, as well as for blame and liability. Computer professionals are the experts. They have a knowledge of computing that allows them to understand the risks better than the computer illiterate. Moreover, computer professionals use their expertise to produce software and other computer products upon which users come to depend. Still, it is not so easy to conceptualize the connection between computer professionals and computer technology. For one thing, the connection is complicated. Computer professionals typically work in large and complex companies and they work in teams. Many factors shape the work they do. There are legal constraints, economic pressures, management hierarchies, and so on. Just what the social responsibilities of professionals are is a highly contested issue. In a sense the question, "What are the social responsibilities of computer professionals?" is a question about the connection between a person and the projects to which the person contributes as part of their professional role.

Because the question is a question about someone acting in a professional role, it has at least two parts. We can ask about the individual and we can ask about the profession—as a collective unit. They are, of course, related, but from the point of view of an individual acting in a professional role we are led to further questions about the individual's responsibilities to various parties—an employer or client—and about the various expectations and constraints present in a particular job. On the other hand, from the point of view of the profession, we are led to questions about how the collective organizes itself, how it controls admission to its membership, what standards it promulgates, and so on.

In this section of Chapter 6, we have gathered readings about the responsibilities of computer professionals from both perspectives. The readings begin with a chapter from Deborah G. Johnson's book, *Computer Ethics*. Johnson's excerpt covers quite a bit of territory in discussing what is special about professional ethics, asking whether computer professionals should be considered professionals at all, and then taking up the relationships into which computer professionals enter in their worklife (to employers, clients, society, and other professionals). Johnson is particularly concerned about the ways in which responsibilities to these parties may come into conflict.

Continuing with the perspective of the individual, Collins and Miller are concerned about the impact that poor quality and unsafe software will have on the public's view of computing and computer professionals. Collins and Miller argue for programmers taking more responsibility for good quality software. In particular, they argue for more realistic expectations for computers. "If we builders of programs," they warn, "do not encourage realism about our computer bridges, the public will rightly condemn us when some of our bridges crumble."

One of the most powerful steps any group of individuals can take—to accept responsibility for their worklife—is to organize themselves and act collectively. This is a step that computer professionals have taken in forming the Association for Computer Machinery (ACM), becoming members of International Electrical and Electronic Engineers (IEEE), joining the American Society of Information Scientists, and other organizations. Another key component of taking responsibility that goes with organizing is to formulate and promulgate a code of ethics or a code of professional conduct. Again, a number of computer professional organizations have taken this step. The final set of readings in this chapter focuses on professional codes of ethics, what they can and cannot do, what functions they serve, and what their limits are. The piece by Michael Martin and Roland Schinzinger is from their book, *Ethics in Engineering*, and is therefore aimed primarily at engineers, but even their discussion of codes in relation to their view of engineering as social experimentation seems directly relevant to computer professionals. Counterbalancing Martin and Schinzinger is a very popular piece by John Ladd in which he gives a series of very radical arguments against codes of ethics. Ladd argues that codes of ethics make moral issues into legal issues and have negative side effects. Still, while Ladd makes a good case against codes of ethics, Michael Davis provides a counter to Ladd in "Thinking Like an Engineer: The Place of a Code of Ethics in the Practice of a Profession." Using the shuttle disaster to focus his argument and understanding a code of ethics to be a convention between professionals, Davis shows why engineers should create and adhere to codes of ethics. Though his analysis focuses on engineers there is little, if anything, in his analysis that does not apply to computer professionals. We end this section with the ACM Code of Conduct.

CASE
▷ **AN INVESTIGATION OF THE THERAC-25 ACCIDENTS**

Nancy G. Leveson
Clark S. Turner

A thorough account of the Therac-25 medical electron accelerator accidents reveals previously unknown details and suggests ways to reduce risk in the future.

Computers are increasingly being introduced into safety-critical systems and, as a consequence, have been involved in accidents. Some of the most widely cited software-related accidents in safety-critical systems involved a computerized radiation therapy machine called the Therac-25. Between June 1985 and January 1987, six known accidents involved massive overdoses by the Therac-25—with resultant deaths and serious injuries. They have been described as the worst series of radiation accidents in the 35-year history of medical accelerators.[1]

With information for this article taken from publicly available documents, we present a detailed accident investigation of the factors involved in the overdoses and the attempts by the users, manufacturers, and the US and Canadian governments to deal with them. Our goal is to help others learn from this experience, not to criticize the equipment's manufacturer or anyone else. The mistakes that were made are not unique to this manufacturer but are, unfortunately, fairly common in other safety-critical systems. As Frank Houston of the US Food and Drug Administration (FDA) said, "A significant amount of software for life-critical systems comes from small firms, especially in the medical device industry; firms that fit the profile of those resistant to or uninformed of the principles of either system safety or software engineering."[2]

Furthermore, these problems are not limited to the medical industry. It is still a common belief that any good engineer can build software, regardless of whether he or she is trained in state-of-the-art software-engineering procedures. Many companies building safety-critical software are not using proper procedures from a software-engineering and safety-engineering perspective.

Most accidents are system accidents; that is, they stem from complex interactions between various components and activities. To attribute a single cause to an accident is usually a serious mistake. In this article, we hope to demonstrate the complex nature of accidents and the need to investigate all aspects of system development and operation to understand what has happened and to prevent future accidents.

Despite what can be learned from such investigations, fears of potential liability or loss of business make it difficult to find out the details behind serious engineering mistakes. When the equipment is regulated by government agencies, some information may be available. Occasionally, major accidents draw the attention of the US Congress or President and result in formal accident investigations (for instance, the Rogers commission investigation of the Challenger accident and the Kemeny commission investigation of the Three Mile Island incident).

The Therac-25 accidents are the most serious computer-related accidents to date (at least nonmilitary and admitted) and have even drawn the attention of the popular press. (Stories about the Therac-25 have appeared in trade journals, newspapers, *People Magazine*, and on television's *20/20* and *McNeil/Lehrer News Hour*.) Unfortunately, the previous accounts of the Therac-25 problems have been oversimplified, with misleading omissions.

In an effort to remedy this, we have obtained information from a wide variety of sources, including lawsuits and the US and Canadian government agencies responsible for regulating such equipment. We have tried to be very careful to present only what we could document from original sources, but there is no guarantee that the documentation itself is correct. When possible, we looked for multiple confirming sources for the more important facts.

We have tried not to bias our description of the accidents, but it is difficult not to filter unintentionally what is described. Also, we were unable to investigate firsthand or get information about some aspects of the accidents that may be very relevant. For example, detailed information about the manufacturer's software development, management, and quality control was unavailable. We had to infer most information about these from statements in correspondence or other sources.

As a result, our analysis of the accidents may omit some factors. But the facts available support previous hypotheses about the proper development and use of software to control dangerous processes and suggest hypotheses that need further evaluation. Following our account of the accidents and the responses of the manufacturer, government agencies, and users, we present what we believe are the most compelling lessons to be learned in the context of software engineering, safety engineering, and government and user standards and oversight.

GENESIS OF THE THERAC-25

Medical linear accelerators (linacs) accelerate electrons to create high-energy beams that can destroy tumors with minimal impact on the surrounding healthy tissue. Relatively shallow tissue is treated with the accelerated electrons; to reach deeper tissue, the electron beam is converted into X-ray photons.

In the early 1970s, Atomic Energy of Canada Limited (AECL) and a French company called CGR collaborated to build linear accelerators. (AECL is an arms-length entity, called a crown corporation, of the Canadian government. Since the time of the incidents related in this article, AECL Medical, a division of AECL, is in the process of being privatized and is now called Theratronics International Limited. Currently, AECL's primary business is the design and installation of nuclear reactors.) The products of AECL and CGR's cooperation were (1) the Therac-6, a 6 million electron volt (MeV) accelerator capable of producing X rays only and, later, (2) the Therac-20, a 20-MeV dual-mode (X rays or electrons) accelerator. Both were versions of older CGR machines, the Neptune and Sagittaire, respectively, which were augmented with computer control using a DEC PDP 11 minicomputer.

Software functionality was limited in both machines: The computer merely added convenience to the existing hardware, which was capable of standing alone. Industry-standard hardware safety features and interlocks in the underlying machines were retained. We know that some old Therac-6 software routines were used in the Therac-20 and that CGR developed the initial software.

The business relationship between AECL and CGR faltered after the Therac-20 effort. Citing competitive pressures, the two companies did not renew their cooperative agreement when scheduled in 1981. In the mid-1970s, AECL developed a radical new "double-pass" concept for electron acceleration. A double-pass accelerator needs much less space to develop comparable energy levels because it folds the long physical mechanism required to accelerate the electrons, and it is more economic to produce (since it uses a magnetron rather than a klystron as the energy source).

Using this double-pass concept, AECL designed the Therac-25, a dual-mode linear accelerator that can deliver either photons at 25 MeV or electrons at various energy levels. Compared with the Therac-20, the Therac-25 is notably more compact, more versatile, and arguably easier to use. The higher energy takes advantage of the phenomenon of "depth dose": As the energy increases, the depth in the body at which maximum dose buildup occurs also increases, sparing the tissue above the target area. Economic advantages also come into play for the customer, since only one machine is required for both treatment modalities (electrons and photons).

Several features of the Therac-25 are important in understanding the accidents. First, like the Therac-6 and the Therac-20, the Therac-25 is controlled by a PDP 11. However, AECL designed the Therac-25 to take advantage of computer control from the outset; AECL did not build on a stand-alone machine. The Therac-6 and Therac-20 had been designed around machines that already had histories of clinical use without computer control.

In addition, the Therac-25 software has more responsibility for maintaining safety than the software in the previous machines. The Therac-20 has independent protective circuits for monitoring electron-beam scanning, plus mechanical interlocks for policing the machine and ensuring safe operation. The Therac-25 relies more on software for these functions. AECL took advantage of the computer's abilities to control and monitor the hardware and decided not to duplicate all the existing hardware safety mechanisms and interlocks. This approach is becoming more common as companies decide that hardware interlocks and backups are not worth the expense, or they put more faith (perhaps misplaced) on software than on hardware reliability.

Finally, some software for the machines was interrelated or reused. In a letter to a Therac-25 user, the AECL quality assurance manager said, "The same Therac-6 package was used by the AECL software people when they started the Therac-25 software. The Therac-20 and Therac-25 software programs were done independently, starting from a common base." Reuse of Therac-6 design features or modules may explain some of the problematic aspects of the Therac-25 software (see page 507, "Therac-25 Software Development and Design"). The quality assurance manager was apparently unaware that some Therac-20 routines were also used in the Therac-25;

this was discovered after a bug related to one of the Therac-25 accidents was found in the Therac-20 software.

AECL produced the first hardwired prototype of the Therac-25 in 1976, and the completely computerized commercial version was available in late 1982. (Pages 507–509 provide details about the machine's design and controlling software, important in understanding the accidents.)

In March 1983, AECL performed a safety analysis on the Therac-25. This analysis was in the form of a fault tree and apparently excluded the software. According to the final report, the analysis made several assumptions:

1. Programming errors have been reduced by extensive testing on a hardware simulator and under field conditions on teletherapy units. Any residual software errors are not included in the analysis.
2. Program software does not degrade due to wear, fatigue, or reproduction process.
3. Computer execution errors are caused by faulty hardware components and by "soft" (random) errors induced by alpha particles and electromagnetic noise.

The fault tree resulting from this analysis does appear to include computer failure, although apparently, judging from these assumptions, it considers only hardware failures. For example, in one OR gate leading to the event of getting the wrong energy, a box contains "Computer selects wrong energy" and a probability of 10^{-11} is assigned to this event. For "Computer selects wrong mode," a probability of 4×10^{-9} is given. The report provides no justification of either number.

ACCIDENT HISTORY

Eleven Therac-25s were installed: five in the US and six in Canada. Six accidents involving massive overdoses to patients occurred between 1985 and 1987. The machine was recalled in 1987 for extensive design changes, including hardware safeguards against software errors.

Related problems were found in the Therac-20 software. These were not recognized until after the Therac-25 accidents because the Therac-20 included hardware safety interlocks and thus no injuries resulted.

In this section, we present a chronological account of the accidents and the responses from the manufacturer, government regulatory agencies, and users.

Kennestone Regional Oncology Center, 1985

Details of this accident in Marietta, Georgia, are sketchy since it was never carefully investigated. There was no admission that the injury was caused by the Therac-25 until long after the occurrence, despite claims by the patient that she had been injured during treatment, the obvious and severe radiation burns the patient suffered, and the suspicions of the radiation physicist involved.

After undergoing a lumpectomy to remove a malignant breast tumor, a 61-year-old woman was receiving follow-up radiation treatment to nearby lymph nodes on a

Major event time line

1985

JUN — 3rd: Marietta, Georgia, overdose.
Later in the month, Tim Still calls AECL and asks if overdose by Therac-25 is possible.

JUL — 26th: Hamilton, Ontario, Canada, overdose; AECL notified and determines microswitch failure was the cause.

SEP — AECL makes changes to microswitch and notifies users of increased safety.
Independent consultant (for Hamilton Clinic) recommends potentiometer on turntable.

OCT — Georgia patient files suit against AECL and hospital.

NOV — 8th: Letter from CRPB to AECL asking for additional hardware interlocks and software changes.

DEC — Yakima, Washington, clinic overdose.

1986

JAN — Attorney for Hamilton clinic requests that potentiometer be installed on turntable.
31st: Letter to AECL from Yakima reporting overdose possibility.

FEB — 24th: Letter from AECL to Yakima saying overdose was impossible and no other incidents had occurred.

MAR — 21st: Tyler, Texas, overdose. AECL notified; claims overdose impossible and no other accidents had occurred previously. AECL suggests hospital might have an electrical problem.

APR — 7th: Tyler machine put back in service after no electrical problem could be found.
11th: Second Tyler overdose. AECL again notified. Software problem found.
15th: AECL files accident report with FDA.

MAY — 2nd: FDA declares Therac-25 defective. Asks for CAP and proper renotification of Therac-25 users.

JUN — 13th: First version of CAP sent to FDA.

JUL — 23rd: FDA responds and asks for more information.

AUG — First user group meeting.

SEP — 26th: AECL sends FDA additional information.

OCT — 30th: FDA requests more information.

NOV — 12th: AECL submits revision of CAP.

DEC — Therac-20 users notified of a software bug.
11th: FDA requests further changes to CAP.
22nd: AECL submits second revision of CAP.

1987

JAN — 17th: Second overdose at Yakima.
26th: AECL sends FDA its revised test plan.

FEB — Hamilton clinic investigates first accident and concludes there was an overdose.
3rd: AECL announces changes to Therac-25.
10th: FDA sends notice of adverse findings to AECL declaring Therac-25 defective under US law and asking AECL to notify customers that it should not be used for routine therapy. Health Protection Branch of Canada does the same thing. This lasts until August 1987.

MAR — Second user group meeting.
5th: AECL sends third revision of CAP to FDA.

APR — 9th: FDA responds to CAP and asks for additional information.

MAY — 1st: AECL sends fourth revision of CAP to FDA.
26th: FDA approves CAP subject to final testing and safety analysis.

JUN — 5th: AECL sends final test plan and draft safety analysis to FDA.

JUL — Third user group meeting.
21st: Fifth (and final) revision of CAP sent to FDA.

1988

JAN — 29th: Interim safety analysis report issued.

NOV — 3rd: Final safety analysis report issued.

Therac-25 at the Kennestone facility in Marietta. The Therac-25 had been operating at Kennestone for about six months; other Therac-25s had been operating, apparently without incident, since 1983.

On June 3, 1985, the patient was set up for a 10-MeV electron treatment to the clavicle area. When the machine turned on, she felt a "tremendous force of heat ... this red-hot sensation." When the technician came in, the patient said, "You burned me." The technician replied that that was not possible. Although there were no marks on the patient at the time, the treatment area felt "warm to the touch."

It is unclear exactly when AECL learned about this incident. Tim Still, the Kennestone physicist, said that he contacted AECL to ask if the Therac-25 could operate in electron mode without scanning to spread the beam. Three days later, the engineers at AECL called the physicist back to explain that improper scanning was not possible.

In an August 19, 1986, letter from AECL to the FDA, the AECL quality assurance manager said, "In March of 1986, AECL received a lawsuit from the patient involved... This incident was never reported to AECL prior to this date, although some rather odd questions had been posed by Tim Still, the hospital physicist." The physicist at a hospital in Tyler, Texas, where a later accident occurred, reported, "According to Tim Still, the patient filed suit in October 1985 listing the hospital, manufacturer, and service organization responsible for the machine. AECL was notified informally about the suit by the hospital, and AECL received official notification of a lawsuit in November 1985."

Because of the lawsuit (filed on November 13, 1985), some AECL administrators must have known about the Marietta accident—although no investigation occurred at this time. Further comments by FDA investigators point to the lack of a mechanism in AECL to follow up reports of suspected accidents. The lack of follow-up in this case appears to be evidence of such a problem in the organization.

The patient went home, but shortly afterward she developed a reddening and swelling in the center of the treatment area. Her pain had increased to the point that her shoulder "froze" and she experienced spasms. She was admitted to West Paces Ferry Hospital in Atlanta, but her oncologists continued to send her to Kennestone for Therac-25 treatments. Clinical explanation was sought for the reddening of the skin, which at first her oncologist attributed to her disease or to normal treatment reaction.

About two weeks later, the physicist at Kennestone noticed that the patient had a matching reddening on her back as though a burn had gone through her body, and the swollen area had begun to slough off layers of skin. Her shoulder was immobile, and she was apparently in great pain. It was obvious that she had a radiation burn, but the hospital and her doctors could provide no satisfactory explanation. Shortly afterward, she initiated a lawsuit against the hospital and AECL regarding her injury.

The Kennestone physicist later estimated that she received one or two doses of radiation in the 15,000- to 20,000-rad (radiation absorbed dose) range. He does not believe her injury could have been caused by less than 8,000 rads. Typical single therapeutic doses are in the 200-rad range. Doses of 1,000 rads can be fatal if delivered to the whole body; in fact, the accepted figure for whole-body radiation that will cause death in 50 percent of the cases is 500 rads. The consequences of an overdose to a smaller part of the body depend on the tissue's radiosensitivity. The director of radiation oncology at the Kennestone facility explained their confusion about the accident as due to the fact that they had never seen an overtreatment of that magnitude before.

Eventually, the patient's breast had to be removed because of the radiation burns. She completely lost the use of her shoulder and her arm, and was in constant pain. She had suffered a serious radiation burn, but the manufacturer and operators of the machine refused to believe that it could have been caused by the Therac-25. The treatment prescription printout feature was disabled at the time of the accident, so there was no hard copy of the treatment data. The lawsuit was eventually settled out of court.

From what we can determine, the accident was not reported to the FDA until *after* the later Tyler accidents in 1986 (described in later sections). The reporting regulations for medical device incidents at that time applied only to equipment manufacturers and importers, not users. The regulations required that manufacturers and importers report deaths, serious injuries, or malfunctions that could result in those consequences. Health-care professionals and institutions were not required to report incidents to manufacturers. (The law was amended in 1990 to require health-care facilities to report incidents to the manufacturer and the FDA.) The comptroller general of the US Government Accounting Office, in testimony before Congress on November 6, 1989, expressed great concern about the viability of the incident-reporting regulations in preventing or spotting medical-device problems. According to a GAO study, the FDA knows of less than 1 percent of deaths, serious injuries, or equipment malfunctions that occur in hospitals.[3]

At this point, the other Therac-25 users were unaware that anything untoward had occurred and did not learn about any problems with the machine until after subsequent accidents. Even then, most of their information came through personal communication among themselves.

Ontario Cancer Foundation, 1985

The second in this series of accidents occurred at this Hamilton, Ontario, Canada, clinic about seven weeks after the Kennestone patient was overdosed. At that time, the Therac-25 at the Hamilton clinic had been in use for more than six months. On July 26, 1985, a 40-year-old patient came to the clinic for her 24th Therac-25 treatment for carcinoma of the cervix. The operator activated the machine, but the Therac shut down after five seconds with an "H-tilt" error message. The Therac's dosimetry system display read "no dose" and indicated a "treatment pause."

Since the machine did not suspend and the control display indicated no dose was delivered to the patient, the operator went ahead with a second attempt at treatment by pressing the "P" key (the proceed command), expecting the machine to deliver the proper dose this time. This was standard operating procedure and, as described in "The Operator Interface" on p. 509, Therac-25 operators had become accustomed to frequent malfunctions that had no untoward consequences for the patient. Again, the machine shut down in the same manner. The operator repeated this process four times after the original attempt—the display showing "no dose" delivered to the patient each time. After the fifth pause, the machine went into treatment suspend, and a hospital service technician was called. The technician found nothing wrong with the machine. This also was not an unusual scenario, according to a Therac-25 operator.

After the treatment, the patient complained of a burning sensation, described as an "electric tingling shock" to the treatment area in her hip. Six other patients were treated later that day without incident. The patient came back for further treatment on July 29 and complained of burning, hip pain, and excessive swelling in the region of treatment. The machine was taken out of service, as radiation overexposure was suspected. The patient was hospitalized for the condition on July 30. AECL was informed of the apparent radiation injury and sent a service engineer to investigate. The FDA, the then-Canadian Radiation Protection Bureau (CRPB), and the users were informed that there was a problem, although the users claim that they were never informed that a patient injury had occurred. (On April 1, 1986, the CRPB and the Bureau of Medical Devices were merged to form the Bureau of Radiation and Medical Devices or BRMD.) Users were told that they should visually confirm the turntable alignment until further notice (which occurred three months later).

The patient died on November 3, 1985, of an extremely virulent cancer. An autopsy revealed the cause of death as the cancer, but it was noted that had she not died, a total hip replacement would have been necessary as a result of the radiation overexposure. An AECL technician later estimated the patient had received between 13,000 and 17,000 rads.

Manufacturer Response. AECL could not reproduce the malfunction that had occurred, but suspected a transient failure in the microswitch used to determine turntable position. During the investigation of the accident, AECL hardwired the error conditions they assumed were necessary for the malfunction and, as a result, found some design weaknesses and potential mechanical problems involving the turntable positioning.

The computer senses and controls turntable position by reading a 3-bit signal about the status of three microswitches in the turntable switch assembly. Essentially, AECL determined that a 1-bit error in the microswitch codes (which could be caused by a single open-circuit fault on the switch lines) could produce an ambiguous position message for the computer. The problem was exacerbated by the design of the mechanism that extends a plunger to lock the turntable when it is in one of the three cardinal positions: The plunger could be extended when the turntable was way out of position, thus giving a second false position indication. AECL devised a method to indicate turntable position that tolerated a 1-bit error: The code would still unambiguously reveal correct position with any one microswitch failure.

In addition, AECL altered the software so that the computer checked for "in transit" status of the switches to keep further track of the switch operation and the turntable position, and to give additional assurance that the switches were working and the turntable was moving.

As a result of these improvements, AECL claimed in its report and correspondence with hospitals that "analysis of the hazard rate of the new solution indicates an improvement over the old system by at least five orders of magnitude." A claim that safety had been improved by five orders of magnitude seems exaggerated, especially given that in its final incident report to the FDA, AECL concluded that it "cannot be firm on the exact cause of the accident but can only suspect. . ." This underscores the company's inability to determine the cause of the accident with any certainty. The AECL quality assurance manager testified that AECL could not reproduce the switch malfunction and that testing of the microswitch was "inconclusive." The similarity of the errant behavior and the injuries to patients in this accident and a later one in Yakima, Washington, (attributed to software error) provide good reason to believe that the Hamilton overdose was probably related to software error rather than to a microswitch failure.

Government and User Response. The Hamilton accident resulted in a voluntary recall by AECL, and the FDA termed it a Class II recall. Class II means "a situation in which the use of, or exposure to, a violative product may cause temporary or medically reversible adverse health consequences or where the probability of serious adverse health consequences is remote." Four users in the US were advised by a letter from AECL on August 1, 1985, to visually check the ionization chamber to make sure it was in its correct position in the collimator opening before any treatment and to discontinue treatment if they got an H-tilt message with an incorrect dose indicated. The letter did not mention that a patient injury was involved. The FDA audited AECL's subsequent modifications. After the modifications, the users were told that they could return to normal operating procedures.

As a result of the Hamilton accident, the head of advanced X-ray systems in the CRPB, Gordon Symonds, wrote a report that analyzed the design and performance characteristics of the Therac-25 with respect to radiation safety. Besides citing the flawed microswitch, the report faulted both hardware and software components of the Therac's design. It concluded with a list of four modifications to the Therac-25 necessary for minimum compliance with Canada's Radiation Emitting Devices (RED) Act. The RED law, enacted in 1971, gives government officials power to ensure the safety of radiation-emitting devices.

The modifications recommended in the Symonds report included redesigning the microswitch and changing the way the computer handled malfunction conditions. In particular, treatment was to be terminated in the event of a dose-rate malfunction, giving a treatment "suspend." This would have removed the option to proceed simply by pressing the "P" key. The report also made recommendations regarding collimator test procedures and message and command formats. A November 8, 1985 letter signed by Ernest Létourneau, M.D., director of the CRPB, asked that AECL make changes to the Therac-25 based on the Symonds report "to be in compliance with the RED Act."

Although, as noted above, AECL did make the microswitch changes, it did not comply with the directive to change the malfunction pause behavior into treatment suspends, instead reducing the maximum number of retries from five to three. According to Symonds, the deficiencies outlined in the CRPB letter of November 8 were still pending when subsequent accidents five months later changed the priorities. If these later accidents had not occurred, AECL would have been compelled to comply with the requirements in the letter.

Immediately after the Hamilton accident, the Ontario Cancer Foundation hired an independent consultant to investigate. He concluded in a September 1985 report that an independent system (beside the computer) was needed to verify turntable position and suggested the use of a potentiometer. The CRPB wrote a letter to AECL in November 1985 requesting that AECL install such an independent upper collimator positioning interlock on the Therac-25. Also, in January 1986, AECL received a letter from the attorney representing the Hamilton clinic. The letter said there had been continuing problems with the turntable, including four incidents at Hamilton, and requested the installation of an independent system (potentiometer) to verify turntable position. AECL did not comply: No independent interlock was installed on the Therac-25s at this time.

Yakima Valley Memorial Hospital, 1985

As with the Kennestone overdose, machine malfunction in this accident in Yakima, Washington, was not acknowledged until after later accidents were understood.

The Therac-25 at Yakima had been modified in September 1985 in response to the overdose at Hamilton. During December 1985, a woman came in for treatment with the Therac-25. She developed erythema (excessive reddening of the skin) in a parallel striped pattern at one port site (her right hip) after one of the treatments. Despite this, she continued to be treated by the Therac-25 because the cause of her reaction was not determined to be abnormal until January or February of 1986. On January 6, 1986, her treatments were completed.

The staff monitored the skin reaction closely and attempted to find possible causes. The open slots in the blocking trays in the Therac-25 could have produced such a striped pattern, but by the time the skin reaction had been determined to be abnormal, the blocking trays had been discarded. The blocking arrangement and tray striping orientation could not be reproduced. A reaction to chemotherapy was ruled out because that should have produced reactions at the other ports and would not have produced stripes. When it was discovered that the woman slept with a heating pad, a possible explanation was offered on the basis of the parallel wires that deliver the heat in such pads. The staff X-rayed the heating pad and discovered that the wire pattern did not correspond to the erythema pattern on the patient's hip.

The hospital staff sent a letter to AECL on January 31, and they also spoke on the phone with the AECL technical support supervisor. On February 24, 1986, the AECL technical support supervisor sent a written response to the director of radiation therapy at Yakima saying, "After careful consideration, we are of the opinion that this damage could not have been produced by any malfunction of the Therac-25 or by any operator error." The letter goes on to support this opinion by listing two pages of technical reasons why an overdose by the Therac-25 was impossible, along with the additional argument that there have "apparently been no other instances of similar damage to this or other patients." The letter ends, "In closing, I wish to advise that this matter has been brought to the attention of our Hazards Committee, as is normal practice."

The hospital staff eventually ascribed the skin/tissue problem to "cause unknown." In a report written on this first Yakima incident after another Yakima overdose a year later (described in a later section), the medical physicist involved wrote

> At that time, we did not believe that [the patient] was overdosed because the manufacturer had installed additional hardware and software safety devices to the accelerator.
>
> In a letter from the manufacturer dated 16-Sep-85, it is stated that "Analysis of the hazard rate resulting from these modifications indicates an improvement of at least five orders of magnitude"! With such an improvement in safety (10,000,000 percent) we did not believe that there could have been any accelerator malfunction. These modifications to the accelerator were completed on 5,6-Sep-85.

Even with fairly sophisticated physics support, the hospital staff, as users, did not have the ability to investigate the possibility of machine malfunction further. They were not aware of any other incidents, and, in fact, were told that there had been none, so there was no reason for them to pursue the matter. However, it seems that the fact that three similar incidents had occurred with this equipment should have triggered some suspicion and investigation by the manufacturer and the appropriate government agencies. This assumes, of course, that these incidents were all reported and known by AECL and by the government regulators. If they were not, then it is appropriate to ask why they were not and how this could be remedied in the future.

About a year later (in February 1987), after the second Yakima overdose led the hospital staff to suspect that the first injury had been due to a Therac-25 fault, the staff investigated and found that this patient had a chronic skin ulcer, tissue necrosis (death) under the skin, and was in constant pain. This was surgically repaired, skin grafts were made, and the symptoms relieved. The patient is alive today, with minor disability and some scarring related to the overdose. The hospital staff concluded that the dose accidentally delivered to this patient must have been much lower than in the second accident, as the reaction was significantly less intense and necrosis did not develop until six to eight months after exposure. Some other factors related to the place on the body where the overdose occurred also kept her from having more significant problems as a result of the exposure.

East Texas Cancer Center, March 1986

More is known about the Tyler, Texas, accidents than the others because of the diligence of the Tyler hospital physicist, Fritz Hager, without whose efforts the understanding of the software problems might have been delayed even further.

The Therac-25 was at the East Texas Cancer Center (ETCC) for two years before the first serious accident occurred; during that time, more than 500 patients had been treated. On March 21, 1986, a male patient came into ETCC for his ninth treatment on the Therac-25, one of a series prescribed as follow-up to the removal of a tumor from his back.

The patient's treatment was to be a 22-MeV electron-beam treatment of 180 rads over a 10×17-cm field on the upper back and a little to the left of his spine, or a total of 6,000 rads over a period of 6 1/2 weeks. He was taken into the treatment room and placed face down on the treatment table. The operator then left the treatment room, closed the door, and sat at the control terminal.

The operator had held this job for some time, and her typing efficiency had increased with experience. She could quickly enter prescription data and change it conveniently with the Therac's editing features. She entered the patient's prescription data quickly, then noticed that for mode she had typed "x" (for X ray) when she had intended "e" (for electron). This was a common mistake since most treatments involved X rays, and she had become accustomed to typing this. The mistake was easy to fix; she merely used the cursor up key to edit the mode entry.

Since the other parameters she had entered were correct, she hit the return key several times and left their values unchanged. She reached the bottom of the screen where a message indicated that the parameters had been "verified" and the terminal displayed "beam ready," as expected. She hit the one-key command "B" (for "beam on") to begin the treatment. After a moment, the machine shut down and the console displayed the message "Malfunction 54." The machine also displayed a "treatment pause," indicating a problem of low priority (see the operator interface sidebar). The sheet on the side of the machine explained that this malfunction was a "dose input 2" error. The ETCC did not have any other information available in its instruction manual or other Therac-25 documentation to explain the meaning of Malfunction 54. An AECL technician later testified that "dose input 2" meant that a dose had been delivered that was either too high or too low.

The machine showed a substantial underdose on its dose monitor display: 6 monitor units delivered, whereas the operator had requested 202 monitor units. The operator was accustomed to the quirks of the machine, which would frequently stop or delay treatment. In the past, the only consequences had been inconvenience. She immediately took the normal action when the machine merely paused, which was to hit the "P" key to proceed with the treatment. The machine promptly shut down with the same "Malfunction 54" error and the same underdose shown by the display terminal.

The operator was isolated from the patient, since the machine apparatus was inside a shielded room of its own. The only way the operator could be alerted to patient difficulty was through audio and video monitors. On this day, the video display was unplugged and the audio monitor was broken.

After the first attempt to treat him, the patient said that he felt like he had received an electric shock or that someone had poured hot coffee on his back: He felt a thump and heat and heard a buzzing sound from the equipment. Since this was his ninth treatment, he knew that this was not normal. He began to get up from the treatment table to go for help. It was at this moment that the operator hit the "P" key to proceed with the treatment. The patient said that he felt like his arm was being shocked by electricity and that his hand was leaving his body. He went to the treatment room door and pounded on it. The operator was shocked and immediately opened the door for him. He appeared shaken and upset.

The patient was immediately examined by a physician, who observed intense erythema over the treatment area, but suspected nothing more serious than electric shock. The patient was discharged with instructions to return if he suffered any further reactions. The hospital physicist was called in, and he found the machine calibration within specifications. The meaning of the malfunction message was not understood. The machine was then used to treat patients for the rest of the day.

In actuality, but unknown to anyone at that time, the patient had received a massive overdose, concentrated in the center of the treatment area. After-the-fact simulations of the accident revealed possible doses of 16,500 to 25,000 rads in less than 1 second over an area of about 1 cm.

During the weeks following the accident, the patient continued to have pain in his neck and shoulder. He lost the function of his left arm and had periodic bouts of nausea and vomiting. He was eventually hospitalized for radiation-induced myelitis of the cervical cord causing paralysis of his left arm and both legs, left vocal cord paralysis (which left him unable to speak), neurogenic bowel and bladder, and paralysis of the left diaphragm. He also had a lesion on his left lung and recurrent herpes simplex skin infections. He died from complications of the overdose five months after the accident.

User and Manufacturer Response. The Therac-25 was shut down for testing the day after this accident. One local AECL engineer and one from the home office in Canada came to ETCC to investigate. They spent a day running the machine through tests but could not reproduce a Malfunction 54. The AECL home office engineer reportedly explained that it was not possible for the Therac-25 to overdose a patient. The ETCC physicist claims that he asked AECL at this time if there were any other reports of radiation overexposure and that the AECL personnel (including the quality assurance manager) told him that AECL knew of no accidents involving radiation overexposure by the Therac-25. This seems odd since AECL was surely at least aware of the Hamilton accident that had occurred seven months before and the Yakima accident, and, even by its own account, AECL learned of the Georgia lawsuit about this time (the suit had been filed four months earlier). The AECL engineers then suggested that an electrical problem might have caused this accident.

The electric shock theory was checked out thoroughly by an independent engineering firm. The final report indicated that there was no electrical grounding problem in the machine, and it did not appear capable of giving a patient an electrical shock. The ETCC physicist checked the calibration of the Therac-25 and found it to be satisfactory. The center put the machine back into service on April 7, 1986, convinced that it was performing properly.

East Texas Cancer Center, April 1986

Three weeks after the first ETCC accident, on Friday, April 11, 1986, another male patient was scheduled to receive an electron treatment at ETCC for a skin cancer on the side of his face. The prescription was for 10 MeV to an area of approximately 7 × 10 cm. The same technician who had treated the first Tyler accident victim prepared this patient for treatment. Much of what follows is from the deposition of the Tyler Therac-25 operator.

As with her former patient, she entered the prescription data and then noticed an error in the mode. Again she used the cursor up key to change the mode from X ray to electron. After she finished editing, she pressed the return key several times to place the cursor on the bottom of the screen. She saw the "beam ready" message displayed and turned the beam on.

Within a few seconds the machine shut down, making a loud noise audible via the (now working) intercom. The display showed Malfunction 54 again. The operator rushed into the treatment room, hearing her patient moaning for help. The patient began to remove the tape that had held his head in position and said something was wrong. She asked him what he felt, and he replied "fire" on the side of his face. She immediately went to the hospital physicist and told him that another patient appeared to have been burned. Asked by the physicist to describe what he had experienced, the patient explained that something had hit him on the side of the face, he saw a flash of light, and he heard a sizzling sound reminiscent of frying eggs. He was very agitated and asked, "What happened to me, what happened to me?"

This patient died from the overdose on May 1, 1986, three weeks after the accident. He had disorientation that progressed to coma, fever to 104 degrees Fahrenheit, and neurological damage. Autopsy showed an acute high-dose radiation injury to the right temporal lobe of the brain and the brain stem.

User and Manufacturer Response. After this second Tyler accident, the ETCC physicist immediately took the machine out of service and called AECL to alert the company to this second apparent overexposure. The Tyler physicist then began his own careful investigation. He worked with the operator, who remembered exactly what she had done on this occasion. After a great deal of effort, they were eventually able to elicit the Malfunction 54 message. They determined that data-entry speed during editing was the key factor in producing the error condition: If the prescription data was edited at a fast pace (as is natural for someone who has repeated the procedure a large number of times), the overdose occurred.

It took some practice before the physicist could repeat the procedure rapidly enough to elicit the Malfunction 54 message at will. Once he could do this, he set about measuring the actual dose delivered under the error condition. He took a measurement of about 804 rads but realized that the ion chamber had become saturated. After making adjustments to extend his measurement ability, he determined that the dose was somewhere over 4,000 rads.

The next day, an engineer from AECL called and said that he could not reproduce the error. After the ETCC physicist explained that the procedure had to be performed quite rapidly, AECL could finally produce a similar malfunction on its own machine. AECL then set up its own set of measurements to test the dosage delivered. Two days after the accident, AECL said they had measured the dosage (at the center of the field) to be 25,000 rads. An AECL engineer explained that the frying sound heard by the patient was the ion chambers being saturated.

In fact, it is not possible to determine the exact dose each of the accident victims received; the total dose delivered during the malfunction conditions was found to vary enormously when different clinics simulated the faults. The number of pulses delivered in the 0.3 second that elapsed before interlock shutoff varied because the software adjusted the start-up pulse-repetition frequency to very different values on different machines. Therefore, there is still some uncertainty as to the doses actually received in the accidents.[1]

In one lawsuit that resulted from the Tyler accidents, the AECL quality control manager testified that a "cursor up" problem had been found in the service mode at the Kennestone clinic and one other clinic in February or March 1985 and also in the summer of 1985. Both times, AECL thought that the software problems had been fixed. There is no way to determine whether there is any relationship between these problems and the Tyler accidents.

Related Therac-20 Problems. After the Tyler accidents, Therac-20 users (who had heard informally about the Tyler accidents from Therac-25 users) conducted informal investigations to determine whether the same problem could occur with their machines. As noted earlier, the software for the Therac-25 and Therac-20 both "evolved" from the Therac-6 software. Additional functions had to be added because the Therac-20 (and Therac-25) operates in both X-ray and electron mode, while the Therac-6 has only X-ray mode. The CGR employees modified the software for the Therac-20 to handle the dual modes.

When the Therac-25 development began, AECL engineers adapted the software from the Therac-6, but they also borrowed software routines from the Therac-20 to handle electron mode. The agreements between AECL and CGR gave both companies the right to tap technology used in joint products for their other products.

After the second Tyler accident, a physicist at the University of Chicago Joint Center for Radiation Therapy heard about the Therac-25 software problem and decided to find out whether the same thing could happen with the Therac-20. At first, the physicist was unable to reproduce the error on his machine, but two months later he found the link.

The Therac-20 at the University of Chicago is used to teach students in a radiation therapy school conducted by the center. The center's physicist, Frank Borger, noticed that whenever a new class of students started using the Therac-20, fuses and breakers on the machine tripped, shutting down the unit. These failures, which had been occurring ever since the center had acquired the machine, might appear three times a week while new students operated the machine and then disappear for months. Borger determined that new students make lots of different types of mistakes and use "creative methods of editing" parameters on the console. Through experimentation, he found that certain editing sequences correlated with blown fuses and determined that the same computer bug (as in the Therac-25 software) was responsible. The physicist notified the FDA, which notified Therac-20 users.[4]

The software error is just a nuisance on the Therac-20 because this machine has independent hardware protective circuits for monitoring the electron-beam scanning.

The protective circuits do not allow the beam to turn on, so there is no danger of radiation exposure to a patient. While the Therac-20 relies on mechanical interlocks for monitoring the machine, the Therac-25 relies largely on software.

The Software Problem. A lesson to be learned from the Therac-25 story is that focusing on particular software bugs is not the way to make a safe system. Virtually all complex software can be made to behave in an unexpected fashion under certain conditions. The basic mistakes here involved poor software-engineering practices and building a machine that relies on the software for safe operation. Furthermore, the particular coding error is not as important as the general unsafe design of the software overall. Examining the part of the code blamed for the Tyler accidents is instructive, however, in showing the overall software design flaws. The following explanation of the problem is from the description AECL provided for the FDA, although we have tried to clarify it somewhat. The description leaves some unanswered questions, but it is the best we can do with the information we have.

As described in the sidebar on Therac-25 software development and design, the treatment monitor task (Treat) controls the various phases of treatment by executing its eight subroutines. The treatment phase indicator variable (Tphase) is used to determine which subroutine should be executed. Following the execution of a particular subroutine, Treat reschedules itself.

One of Treat's subroutines, called Datent (data entry), communicates with the keyboard handler task (a task that runs concurrently with Treat) via a shared variable (Data-entry completion flag) to determine whether the prescription data has been entered. The keyboard handler recognizes the completion of data entry and changes the Data-entry completion variable to denote this. Once the Data-entry completion variable is set, the Datent subroutine detects the variable's change in status and changes the value of Tphase from 1 (Data Entry) to 3 (Set-Up Test). In this case, the Datent subroutine exits back to the Treat subroutine, which will reschedule itself and begin execution of the Set-Up Test subroutine. If the Data-entry completion variable has not been set, Datent leaves the value of Tphase unchanged and exits back to Treat's main line. Treat will then reschedule itself, essentially rescheduling the Datent subroutine.

The command line at the lower right corner of the screen is the cursor's normal position when the operator has completed all necessary changes to the prescription. Prescription editing is signified by cursor movement off the command line. As the program was originally designed, the Data-entry completion variable by itself is not sufficient since it does not ensure that the cursor is located on the command line. Under the right circumstances, the data-entry phase can be exited before all edit changes are made on the screen.

The keyboard handler parses the mode and energy level specified by the operator and places an encoded result in another shared variable, the 2-byte mode/energy offset (MEOS) variable. The low-order byte of this variable is used by another task (Hand) to set the collimator/turntable to the proper position for the selected mode/energy. The high-order byte of the MEOS variable is used by Datent to set several operating parameters.

Initially, the data-entry process forces the operator to enter the mode and energy, except when the operator selects the photon mode, in which case the energy defaults to 25 MeV. The operator can later edit the mode and energy separately. If the keyboard handler sets the data-entry completion variable before the operator changes the data in MEOS, Datent will not detect the changes in MEOS since it has already exited and will not be reentered again. The upper collimator, on the other hand, is set to the position dictated by the low-order byte of MEOS by another concurrently running task (Hand) and can therefore be inconsistent with the parameters set in accordance with the information in the high-order byte of MEOS. The software appears to include no checks to detect such an incompatibility.

The first thing that Datent does when it is entered is to check whether the mode/energy has been set in MEOS. If so, it uses the high-order byte to index into a table of preset operating parameters and places them in the digital-to-analog output table. The contents of this output table are transferred to the digital-analog converter during the next clock cycle. Once the parameters are all set, Datent calls the subroutine Magnet, which sets the bending magnets.

Setting the bending magnets takes about 8 seconds. Magnet calls a subroutine called Ptime to introduce a time delay. Since several magnets need to be set, Ptime is entered and exited several times. A flag to indicate that bending magnets are being set is initialized upon entry to the Magnet subroutine and cleared at the end of Ptime. Furthermore, Ptime checks a shared variable, set by the keyboard handler, that indicates the presence of any editing requests. If there are edits, then Ptime clears the bending magnet variable and exits to Magnet, which then exits to Datent. But the edit change variable is checked by Ptime only if the bending magnet flag is set. Since Ptime clears it during its first execution, any edits performed during each succeeding pass through Ptime will not be recognized. Thus, an edit change of the mode or energy, although reflected on the operator's screen and the mode/energy offset variable, will not be sensed by Datent so it can index the appropriate calibration tables for the machine parameters.

Recall that the Tyler error occurred when the operator made an entry indicating the mode/energy, went to the command line, then moved the cursor up to change the mode/energy, and returned to the command line all within 8 seconds. Since the magnet setting takes about 8 seconds and Magnet does not recognize edits after the first execution of Ptime, the editing had been completed by the return to Datent, which never detected that it had occurred. Part of the problem was fixed after the accident by clearing the bending-magnet variable at the end of Magnet (after *all* the magnets have been set) instead of at the end of Ptime.

But this was not the only problem. Upon exit from the Magnet subroutine, the data-entry subroutine (Datent) checks the data-entry completion variable. If it indicates that data entry is complete, Datent sets Tphase to 3 and Datent is not entered again. If it is not set, Datent leaves Tphase unchanged, which means it will eventually be rescheduled. But the data-entry completion variable only indicates that the cursor has been down to the command line, not that it is still there. A potential race condition is set up. To fix this, AECL introduced another shared variable controlled by the keyboard handler task that indicates the cursor is not positioned on the command line. If this variable is set, then prescription entry is still in progress and the value of Tphase is left unchanged.

Government and User Response. The FDA does not approve each new medical device on the market: All medical devices go through a classification process that determines the level of FDA approval necessary. Medical accelerators follow a procedure called pre-market notification before commercial distribution. In this process, the firm must establish that the product is substantially equivalent in safety and effectiveness to a product already on the market. If that cannot be done to the FDA's satisfaction, a pre-market approval is required. For the Therac-25, the FDA required only a pre-market notification.

The agency is basically reactive to problems and requires manufacturers to report serious ones. Once a problem is identified in a radiation-emitting product, the FDA must approve the manufacturer's corrective action plan (CAP).

The first reports of the Tyler accidents came to the FDA from the state of Texas health department, and this triggered FDA action. The FDA investigation was well under way when AECL produced a medical device report to discuss the details of the radiation overexposures at Tyler. The FDA declared the Therac-25 defective under the Radiation Control for Health and Safety Act and ordered the firm to notify all purchasers, investigate the problem, determine a solution, and submit a corrective action plan for FDA approval.

The final CAP consisted of more than 20 changes to the system hardware and software, plus modifications to the system documentation and manuals. Some of these changes were unrelated to the specific accidents, but were improvements to the general machine safety. The full implementation of the CAP, including an extensive safety analysis, was not complete until more than two years after the Tyler accidents.

AECL made its accident report to the FDA on April 15, 1986. On that same date, AECL sent a letter to each Therac user recommending a temporary "fix" to the machine that would allow continued clinical use. The letter (shown in its complete form) read as follows:

Subject: Change in Operating Procedures for the Therac 25 Linear Accelerator

Effective immediately, and until further notice, the key used for moving the cursor back through the prescription sequence (i.e., cursor "UP" inscribed with an upward pointing arrow) must not be used for editing or any other purpose.

To avoid accidental use of this key, the key cap must be removed and the switch contacts fixed in the open position with electrical tape or other insulating material. For assistance with the latter you should contact your local AECL service representative.

Disabling this key means that if any prescription data entered is incorrect then [an] "R" reset command must be used and the whole prescription reentered.

For those users of the Multiport option, it also means that editing of dose rate, dose, and time will not be possible between ports.

On May 2, 1986, the FDA declared the Therac defective, demanded a CAP, and required renotification of all the Therac customers. In the letter from the FDA to AECL, the director of compliance, Center for Devices and Radiological Health, wrote

We have reviewed Mr. Downs' April 15 letter to purchasers and have concluded that it does not satisfy the requirements for notification to purchasers of a defect in an electronic product. Specifically, it does not describe the defect nor the hazards associated with it. The letter does not provide any reason for disabling the cursor key and the tone is not commensurate with the urgency for doing so. In fact, the letter implies the inconvenience to operators outweighs the need to disable the key. We request that you immediately renotify purchasers.

AECL promptly made a new notice to users and also requested an extension to produce a CAP. The FDA granted this request.

About this time, the Therac-25 users created a user group and held their first meeting at the annual conference of the American Association of Physicists in Medicine. At the meeting, users discussed the Tyler accident and heard an AECL representative present the company's plans for responding to it. AECL promised to send a letter to all users detailing the CAP.

Several users described additional hardware safety features that they had added to their own machines to provide additional protection. An interlock (that checked gun current values), which the Vancouver clinic had previously added to its Therac-25, was labeled as redundant by AECL. The users disagreed. There were further discussions of poor design and other problems that caused 10- to 30-percent underdosing in both modes.

The meeting notes said

> ... there was a general complaint by all users present about the lack of information propagation. The users were not happy about receiving incomplete information. The AECL representative countered by stating that AECL does not wish to spread rumors and that AECL has no policy to "keep things quiet." The consensus among the users was that an improvement was necessary.

After the first user group meeting, there were two user group newsletters. The first, dated fall 1986, contained letters from Still, the Kennestone physicist, who complained about what he considered to be eight major problems he had experienced with the Therac-25. These problems included poor screen-refresh subroutines that left trash and erroneous information on the operator console, and some tape-loading problems upon start-up, which he discovered involved the use of "phantom tables" to trigger the interlock system in the event of a load failure instead of using a check sum. He asked the question, "Is programming safety relying too much on the software interlock routines?" The second user group newsletter, in December 1986, further discussed the implications of the "phantom table" parameterization.

AECL produced the first CAP on June 13, 1986. It contained six items:

1. Fix the software to eliminate the specific behavior leading to the Tyler problem.
2. Modify the software sample-and-hold circuits to detect one pulse above a nonadjustable threshold. The software sample-and-hold circuit monitors the magnitude of each pulse from the ion chambers in the beam. Previously, three consecutive high readings were required to shut off the high-voltage circuits, which resulted in a shutdown time of 300 ms. The software modification results in a reading after each pulse, and a shutdown after a single high reading.
3. Make Malfunctions 1 through 64 result in treatment *suspend* rather than *pause*.
4. Add a new circuit, which only administrative staff can reset, to shut down the modulator if the sample-and-hold circuits detect a high pulse. This is functionally equivalent to the circuit described in item 2. However, a new circuit board is added that monitors the five sample-and-hold circuits. The new circuit detects ion-chamber signals above a fixed threshold and inhibits the trigger to the modulator after detecting a high pulse. This shuts down the beam independently of the software.
5. Modify the software to limit editing keys to cursor up, backspace, and return.
6. Modify the manuals to reflect the changes.

FDA internal memos describe their immediate concerns regarding the CAP. One memo suggests adding an independent circuit that "detects and shuts down the system when inappropriate outputs are detected," warnings about when ion chambers are saturated, and understandable system error messages. Another memo questions "whether all possible hardware options have been investigated by the manufacturer to prevent any future inadvertent high exposure."

On July 23 the FDA officially responded to AECL's CAP submission. They conceptually agreed with the plan's direction but complained about the lack of specific information necessary to evaluate the plan, especially with regard to the software. The FDA requested a detailed description of the software-development procedures and documentation, along with a revised CAP to include revised requirements documents, a detailed description of corrective changes, analysis of the interactions of the modified software with the system, and detailed descriptions of the revised edit modes, the changes made to the software setup table, and the software interlock interactions. The FDA also made a very detailed request for a documented test plan.

AECL responded on September 26 with several documents describing the software and its modifications but no test plan. They explained how the Therac-25 software evolved from the Therac-6 software and stated that "no single test plan and report exists for the software since both hardware and software were tested and exercised separately and together over many years." AECL concluded that the current CAP improved "machine safety by many orders of magnitude and virtually eliminates the possibility of lethal doses as delivered in the Tyler incident."

An FDA internal memo dated October 20 commented on these AECL submissions, raising several concerns:

> Unfortunately, the AECL response also seems to point out an apparent lack of documentation on software specifications and a software test plan.
>
> . . . concerns include the question of previous knowledge of problems by AECL, the apparent paucity of software QA [quality assurance] at the manufacturing facility, and possible warnings and information dissemination to others of the generic type problems.
>
> . . . As mentioned in my first review, there is some confusion on whether the manufacturer should have been aware of the software problems prior to the [accidental radiation overdoses] in Texas. AECL had received official notification of a lawsuit in November 1985 from a patient claiming accidental over-exposure from a Therac-25 in Marietta, Georgia. . . If knowledge of these software deficiencies were known beforehand, what would be the FDA's posture in this case?
>
> . . . The materials submitted by the manufacturer have not been in sufficient detail and clarity to ensure an adequate software QA program currently exists. For example, a response has not been provided with respect to the software part of the CAP to the CDRH [FDA Center for Devices and Radiological Health] request for documentation on the revised requirements and specifications for the new software. In addition, an analysis has not been provided, as requested, on the interaction with other portions of the software to demonstrate the corrected software does not adversely affect other software functions.
>
> The July 23 letter from the CDRH requested a documented test plan including several specific pieces of information identified in the letter. This request has been ignored up to this point by the manufacturer. Considering the ramifications of the current software problem, changes in software QA attitudes are needed at AECL.

On October 30, the FDA responded to AECL's additional submissions, complaining about the lack of a detailed description of the accident and of sufficient detail in flow diagrams. Many specific questions addressed the vagueness of the AECL response and made it clear that additional CAP work must precede approval.

AECL, in response, created CAP Revision 1 on November 12. This CAP contained 12 new items under "software modifications," all (except for one cosmetic change) designed to eliminate potentially unsafe behavior. The submission also contained other relevant documents including a test plan.

The FDA responded to CAP Revision 1 on December 11. The FDA explained that the software modifications appeared to correct the specific deficiencies discovered as a result of the Tyler accidents. They agreed that the major items listed in CAP Revision 1 would improve the Therac's operation. However, the FDA required AECL to attend to several further system problems before CAP approval. AECL had proposed to retain treatment pause for some dose-rate and beam-tilt malfunctions. Since these are dosimetry system problems, the FDA considered them safety interlocks and believed treatment must be suspended for these malfunctions.

AECL also planned to retain the malfunction codes, but the FDA required better warnings for the operators. Furthermore, AECL had not planned on any quality assurance testing to ensure exact copying of software, but the FDA insisted on it. The FDA further requested assurances that rigorous testing would become a standard part of AECL's software-modification procedures:

> We also expressed our concern that you did not intend to perform the protocol to future modifications to software. We believe that the rigorous testing must be performed each time a modification is made in order to ensure the modification does not adversely affect the safety of the system.

AECL was also asked to draw up an installation test plan to ensure both hardware and software changes perform as designed when installed.

AECL submitted CAP Revision 2 and supporting documentation on December 22, 1986. They changed the CAP to have dose malfunctions suspend treatment and included a plan for meaningful error messages and highlighted dose error messages. They also expanded diagrams of software modifications and expanded the test plan to cover hardware and software.

On January 26, 1987, AECL sent the FDA their "Component and Installation Test Plan" and explained that their delays were due to the investigation of a new accident on January 17 at Yakima.

Yakima Valley Memorial Hospital, 1987

On Saturday, January 17, 1987, the second patient of the day was to be treated at the Yakima Valley Memorial Hospital for a carcinoma. This patient was to receive two film-verification exposures of 4 and 3 rads, plus a 79-rad photon treatment (for a total exposure of 86 rads).

Film was placed under the patient and 4 rads was administered with the collimator jaws opened to 22 × 18 cm. After the machine paused, the collimator jaws opened to 35 × 35 cm automatically, and the second exposure of 3 rads was administered. The machine paused again.

The operator entered the treatment room to remove the film and verify the patient's precise position. He used the hand control in the treatment room to rotate the turntable to the field-light position, a feature that let him check the machine's alignment with respect to the patient's body to verify proper beam position. The operator then either pressed the set button on the hand control or left the room and typed a set command at the console to return the turntable to the proper position for treatment; there is some confusion as to exactly what transpired. When he left the room, he forgot to remove the film from underneath the patient. The console displayed "beam ready," and the operator hit the "B" key to turn the beam on.

The beam came on but the console displayed no dose or dose rate. After 5 or 6 seconds, the unit shut down with a pause and displayed a message. The message "may have disappeared quickly"; the operator was unclear on this point. However, since the machine merely paused, he was able to push the "P" key to proceed with treatment.

The machine paused again, this time displaying "flatness" on the reason line. The operator heard the patient say something over the intercom, but couldn't understand him. He went into the room to speak with the patient, who reported "feeling a burning sensation" in the chest. The console displayed only the total dose of the two film exposures (7 rads) and nothing more.

Later in the day, the patient developed a skin burn over the entire treatment area. Four days later, the redness took on the striped pattern matching the slots in the blocking tray. The striped pattern was similar to the burn a year earlier at this hospital that had been attributed to "cause unknown."

AECL began an investigation, and users were told to confirm the turntable position visually before turning on the beam. All tests run by the AECL engineers indicated that the machine was working perfectly. From the information gathered to that point, it was suspected that the electron beam had come on when the turntable was in the field-light position. But the investigators could not reproduce the fault condition that produced the overdose.

On the following Thursday, AECL sent an engineer from Ottawa to investigate. The hospital physicist had, in the meantime, run some tests with film. He placed a film in the Therac's beam and ran two exposures of X-ray parameters with the turntable in field-light position. The film appeared to match the film that was left (by mistake) under the patient during the accident.

After a week of checking the hardware, AECL determined that the "incorrect machine operation was probably not caused by hardware alone." After checking the software, AECL discovered a flaw (described in the next section) that could explain the erroneous behavior. The coding problems explaining this accident differ from those associated with the Tyler accidents.

AECL's preliminary dose measurements indicated that the dose delivered under these conditions—that is, when the turntable was in the field-light position—was on the order of 4,000 to 5,000 rads. After two attempts, the patient could have received 8,000 to 10,000 instead of the 86 rads prescribed. AECL again called users on January 26 (nine days after the accident) and gave them detailed instructions on how to avoid this problem. In an FDA internal report on the accident, an AECL quality assurance manager investigating the problem is quoted as saying that the software and hardware changes to be retrofitted following the Tyler accident nine months earlier (but which had not yet been installed) would have prevented the Yakima accident.

The patient died in April from complications related to the overdose. He had been suffering from a terminal form of cancer prior to the radiation overdose, but survivors initiated lawsuits alleging that he died sooner than he would have and endured unnecessary pain and suffering due to the overdose. The suit was settled out of court.

The Yakima Software Problem. The software problem for the second Yakima accident is fairly well established and different from that implicated in the Tyler accidents. There is no way to determine what particular software design errors were related to the Kennestone, Hamilton, and first Yakima accidents. Given the unsafe programming practices exhibited in the code, it is possible that unknown race conditions or errors could have been responsible. There is speculation, however, that the Hamilton accident was the same as this second Yakima overdose. In a report of a conference call on January 26, 1987, between the AECL quality assurance manager and Ed Miller of the FDA discussing the Yakima accident, Miller notes

> This situation probably occurred in the Hamilton, Ontario, accident a couple of years ago. It was not discovered at that time and the cause was attributed to intermittent interlock failure. The subsequent recall of the multiple microswitch logic network did not really solve the problem.

The second Yakima accident was again attributed to a type of race condition in the software—this one allowed the device to be activated in an error setting (a "failure" of a software interlock). The Tyler accidents were related to problems in the data-entry routines that allowed the code to proceed to Set-Up Test before the full prescription had been entered and acted upon. The Yakima accident involves problems encountered later in the logic after the treatment monitor Treat reaches Set-Up Test.

The Therac-25's field-light feature permits very precise positioning of the patient for treatment. The operator can control the Therac-25 right at the treatment site using a small hand control offering certain limited functions for patient setup, including setting gantry, collimator, and table motions.

Normally, the operator enters all the prescription data at the console (outside the treatment room) before the final setup of all machine parameters is completed in the treatment room. This gives rise to an "unverified" condition at the console. The operator then completes the patient setup in the treatment room, and all relevant parameters now "verify." The console displays the message "Press set button" while the turntable is in the field-light position. The operator now presses the set button on the hand control or types "set" at the console. That should set the collimator to the proper position for treatment.

In the software, after the prescription is entered and verified by the Datent routine, the control variable Tphase is changed so that the Set-Up Test routine is entered. Every pass through the Set-Up Test routine increments the upper collimator position check, a shared variable called Class3. If Class3 is nonzero, there is an inconsistency and treatment should not proceed. A zero value for Class3 indicates that the relevant parameters are consistent with treatment, and the beam is not inhibited.

After setting the Class3 variable, Set-Up Test next checks for any malfunctions in the system by checking another shared variable (set by a routine that actually handles the interlock checking) called F$mal to see if it has a nonzero value. A nonzero value in F$mal indicates that the machine is not ready for treatment, and the Set-Up Test subroutine is rescheduled. When F$mal is zero (indicating that everything is ready for treatment), the Set-Up Test subroutine sets the Tphase variable equal to 2, which results in next scheduling the Set-Up Done subroutine, and the treatment is allowed to continue.

The actual interlock checking is performed by a concurrent Housekeeper task (Hkeper). The upper collimator position check is performed by a subroutine of

Hkeper called Lmtchk (analog/digital limit checking). Lmtchk first checks the Class3 variable. If Class3 contains a nonzero value, Lmtchk calls the Check Collimator (Chkcol) subroutine. If Class3 contains zero, Chkcol is bypassed and the upper collimator position check is not performed. The Chkcol subroutine sets or resets bit 9 of the F$mal shared variable, depending on the position of the upper collimator (which in turn is checked by the Set-Up Test subroutine of Datent so it can decide whether to reschedule itself or proceed to Set-Up Done).

During machine setup, Set-Up Test will be executed several hundred times since it reschedules itself waiting for other events to occur. In the code, the Class3 variable is incremented by one in each pass through Set-Up Test. Since the Class3 variable is 1 byte, it can only contain a maximum value of 255 decimal. Thus, on every 256th pass through the Set-Up Test code, the variable overflows and has a zero value. That means that on every 256th pass through Set-Up Test, the upper collimator will not be checked and an upper collimator fault will not be detected.

The overexposure occurred when the operator hit the "set" button at the precise moment that Class3 rolled over to zero. Thus Chkcol was not executed, and F$mal was not set to indicate the upper collimator was still in field-light position. The software turned on the full 25 MeV without the target in place and without scanning. A highly concentrated electron beam resulted, which was scattered and deflected by the stainless steel mirror that was in the path.

AECL described the technical "fix" implemented for this software flaw as simple: The program is changed so that the Class3 variable is set to some fixed nonzero value each time through Set-Up Test instead of being incremented.

Manufacturer, Government, and User Response. On February 3, 1987, after interaction with the FDA and others, including the user group, AECL announced to its customers

- a new software release to correct both the Tyler and Yakima software problems,
- a hardware single-pulse shutdown circuit,
- a turntable potentiometer to independently monitor turntable position, and
- a hardware turntable interlock circuit.

The second item, a hardware single-pulse shutdown circuit, essentially acts as a hardware interlock to prevent overdosing by detecting an unsafe level of radiation and halting beam output after one pulse of high energy and current. This provides an independent safety mechanism to protect against a wide range of potential hardware failures and software errors. The turntable potentiometer was the safety device recommended by several groups, including the CRPB, after the Hamilton accident.

After the second Yakima accident, the FDA became concerned that the use of the Therac-25 during the CAP process, even with AECL's interim operating instructions, involved too much risk to patients. The FDA concluded that the accidents had demonstrated that the software alone cannot be relied upon to assure safe operation of the machine. In a February 18, 1987 internal FDA memorandum, the director of the Division of Radiological Products wrote the following:

> It is impossible for CDRH to find all potential failure modes and conditions of the software. AECL has indicated the "simple software fix" will correct the turntable position problem displayed at Yakima. We have not yet had the opportunity to evaluate that mod-

ification. Even if it does, based upon past history, I am not convinced that there are not other software glitches that could result in serious injury.

For example, we are aware that AECL issued a user's bulletin January 21 reminding users of the proper procedure to follow if editing of prescription parameter is desired after entering the "B" (beam on) code but before the CR [carriage return] is pressed. It seems that the normal edit keys (down arrow, right arrow, or line feed) will be interpreted as a CR and initiate exposure. One must use either the backspace or left arrow key to edit.

We are also aware that if the dose entered into the prescription tables is below some preset value, the system will default to a phantom table value unbeknownst to the operator. This problem is supposedly being addressed in proposed interim revision 7A, although we are unaware of the details.

We are in the position of saying that the proposed CAP can reasonably be expected to correct the deficiencies for which they were developed (Tyler). We cannot say that we are [reasonably] confident about the safety of the entire *system* to prevent or minimize exposure from other fault conditions.

On February 6, 1987, Miller of the FDA called Pavel Dvorak of Canada's Health and Welfare to advise him that the FDA would recommend all Therac-25s be shut down until permanent modifications could be made. According to Miller's notes on the phone call, Dvorak agreed and indicated that they would coordinate their actions with the FDA.

On February 10, 1987, the FDA gave a Notice of Adverse Findings to AECL declaring the Therac-25 to be defective under US law. In part, the letter to AECL reads:

In January 1987, CDRH was advised of another accidental radiation occurrence in Yakima, which was attributed to a second software defect related to the "Set" command. In addition, the CDRH has become aware of at least two other software features that provide potential for unnecessary or inadvertent patient exposure. One of these is related to the method of editing the prescription after the "B" command is entered and the other is the calling of phantom tables when low doses are prescribed.

Further review of the circumstances surrounding the accidental radiation occurrences and the potential for other such incidents has led us to conclude that in addition to the items in your proposed corrective action plan, hardware interlocking of the turntable to insure its proper position prior to beam activation appears to be necessary to enhance system safety and to correct the Therac-25 defect. Therefore, the corrective action plan as currently proposed is insufficient and must be amended to include turntable interlocking and corrections for the three software problems mentioned above.

Without these corrections, CDRH has concluded that the consequences of the defects represents a significant potential risk of serious injury even if the Therac-25 is operated in accordance with your interim operating instructions. CDRH, therefore, requests that AECL immediately notify all purchasers and recommend that use of the device on patients for routine therapy be discontinued until such time that an amended corrective action plan approved by CDRH is fully completed. You may also advise purchasers that if the need for an individual patient treatment outweighs the potential risk, then extreme caution and strict adherence to operating safety procedures must be exercised.

At the same time, the Health Protection Branch of the Canadian government instructed AECL to recommend to all users in Canada that they discontinue the operation of the Therac-25 until "the company can complete an exhaustive analysis of the design and operation of the safety systems employed for patient and operator protection." AECL was told that the letter to the users should include information on how the users can operate the equipment safely in the event that they must continue with patient treatment. If AECL could not provide information that would guarantee safe operation of the equipment, AECL was requested to inform the users that they cannot operate the equipment safely. AECL complied by letters dated February 20, 1987, to Therac-25 purchasers. This recommendation to discontinue use of the Therac-25 was to last until August 1987.

On March 5, 1987, AECL issued CAP Revision 3, which was a CAP for both the Tyler and Yakima accidents. It contained a few additions to the Revision 2 modifications, notably

- changes to the software to eliminate the behavior leading to the latest Yakima accident,
- four additional software functional modifications to improve safety, and
- a turntable position interlock in the software.

In their response on April 9, the FDA noted that in the appendix under "turntable position interlock circuit" the descriptions were wrong. AECL had indicated "high" signals where "low" signals were called for and vice versa. The FDA also questioned the reliability of the turntable potentiometer design and asked whether the backspace key could still act as a carriage return in the edit mode. They requested a detailed description of the software portion of the single-pulse shutdown and a block diagram to demonstrate the PRF (pulse repetition frequency) generator, modulator, and associated interlocks.

AECL responded on April 13 with an update on the Therac CAP status and a schedule of the nine action items pressed by the users at a user group meeting in March. This unique and highly productive meeting provided an unusual opportunity to involve the users in the CAP evaluation process. It brought together all concerned parties in one place so that they could decide on and approve a course of action as quickly as possible. The attendees included representatives from the manufacturer (AECL); all users, including their technical and legal staffs; the US FDA; the Canadian BRMD; the Canadian Atomic Energy Control Board; the Province of Ontario; and the Radiation Regulations Committee of the Canadian Association of Physicists.

According to Symonds of the BRMD, this meeting was very important to the resolution of the problems since the regulators, users, and the manufacturer arrived at a consensus in one day.

At this second users meeting, the participants carefully reviewed all the six known major Therac-25 accidents and discussed the elements of the CAP along with possible additional modifications. They came up with a prioritized list of modifications that they wanted included in the CAP and expressed concerns about the lack of independent software evaluation and the lack of a hard-copy audit trail to assist in diagnosing faults.

The AECL representative, who was the quality assurance manager, responded that tests had been done on the CAP changes, but that the tests were not documented, and independent evaluation of the software "might not be possible." He claimed that two outside experts had reviewed the software, but he could not provide their names. In response to user requests for a hard-copy audit trail and access to source code, he explained that memory limitations would not permit including an audit option, and source code would not be made available to users.

On May 1, AECL issued CAP Revision 4 as a result of the FDA comments and users meeting input. The FDA response on May 26 approved the CAP subject to sub-mission of the final test plan results and an independent safety analysis, distribution of the draft revised manual to customers, and completion of the CAP by June 30, 1987. The FDA concluded by rating this a Class I recall: a recall in which there is a reasonable probability that the use of or exposure to a violative product will cause serious adverse health consequences or death.[5]

AECL sent more supporting documentation to the FDA on June 5, 1987, includ-ing the CAP test plan, a draft operator's manual, and the draft of the new safety analysis (described in the sidebar "Safety analysis of the Therac-25"). The safety analysis revealed four potentially hazardous subsystems that were not covered by CAP Revision 4:

1. electron-beam scanning,
2. electron-energy selection,
3. beam shutoff, and
4. calibration and/or steering.

AECL planned a fifth revision of the CAP to include the testing and safety analysis results.

Referring to the test plan at this, the final stage of the CAP process, an FDA reviewer said

> Amazingly, the test data presented to show that the software changes to handle the edit problems in the Therac-25 are appropriate prove the exact opposite result. A review of the data table in the test results indicates that the final beam type and energy (edit change) [have] no effect on the initial beam type and energy. I can only assume that either the fix is not right or the data was entered incorrectly. The manufacturer should be admonished for this error. Where is the QC [quality control] review for the test pro-gram? AECL must: (1) clarify this situation, (2) change the test protocol to prevent this type of error from occurring, and (3) set up appropriate QC control on data review.

A further FDA memo said the AECL quality assurance manager

> . . . could not give an explanation and will check into the circumstances. He subse-quently called back and verified that the technician completed the form incorrectly. Cor-rect operation was witnessed by himself and others. They will repeat and send us the correct data sheet.

At the American Association of Physicists in Medicine meeting in July 1987, a third user group meeting was held. The AECL representative gave the status of CAP Revision 5. He explained that the FDA had given verbal approval and he expected full implementation by the end of August 1987. He reviewed and commented on the prioritized concerns of the last meeting. AECL had included in the CAP three of the user-requested hardware changes. Changes to tape-load error messages and check sums on the load data would wait until after the CAP was done.

Two user-requested hardware modifications had not been included in the CAP. One of these, a push-button energy and selection mode switch, AECL would work on after completing the CAP, the quality assurance manager said. The other, a fixed ion chamber with dose/pulse monitoring, was being installed at Yakima, had already been installed by Halifax on their own, and would be an option for other clinics. Software documentation was described as a lower priority task that needed definition and would not be available to the FDA in any form for more than a year.

On July 6, 1987, AECL sent a letter to all users to inform them of the FDA's verbal approval of the CAP and delineated how AECL would proceed. On July 21, 1987, AECL issued the fifth and final CAP revision. The major features of the final CAP are as follows:

- All interruptions related to the dosimetry system will go to a treatment suspend, not a treatment pause. Operators will not be allowed to restart the machine without reentering all parameters.
- A software single-pulse shutdown will be added.
- An independent hardware single-pulse shutdown will be added.
- Monitoring logic for turntable position will be improved to ensure that the turntable is in one of the three legal positions.
- A potentiometer will be added to the turntable. It will provide a visible signal of position that operators will use to monitor exact turntable location.
- Interlocking with the 270-degree bending magnet will be added to ensure that the target and beam flattener are in position if the X-ray mode is selected.
- Beam on will be prevented if the turntable is in the field-light or an intermediate position.
- Cryptic malfunction messages will be replaced with meaningful messages and highlighted dose-rate messages.
- Editing keys will be limited to cursor up, backspace, and return. All other keys will be inoperative.
- A motion-enable foot switch will be added, which the operator must hold closed during movement of certain parts of the machine to prevent unwanted motions when the operator is not in control (a type of "dead man's switch").
- Twenty-three other changes to the software to improve its operation and reliability, including disabling of unused keys, changing the operation of the set and reset commands, preventing copying of the control program on site, changing the way various detected hardware faults are handled, eliminating errors in the software that were detected during the review process, adding several additional software interlocks, disallowing changing to the service mode while a treatment is in progress, and adding meaningful error messages.
- The known software problems associated with the Tyler and Yakima accidents will be fixed.
- The manuals will be fixed to reflect the changes.

In a 1987 paper, Miller, director of the Division of Standards Enforcement, CDRH, wrote about the lessons learned from the Therac-25 experiences.[6] The first was the importance of safe versus "user-friendly" operator interfaces—in other words, making the machine as easy as possible to use may conflict with safety goals. The second is the importance of providing fail-safe designs:

> The second lesson is that for complex interrupt-driven software, timing is of critical importance. In both of these situations, operator action within very narrow time-frame windows was necessary for the accidents to occur. It is unlikely that software testing will

discover all possible errors that involve operator intervention at precise time frames during software operation. These machines, for example, have been exercised for thousands of hours in the factory and in the hospitals without accident. Therefore, one must provide for prevention of catastrophic results of failures when they do occur.

I, for one, will not be surprised if other software errors appear with this or other equipment in the future.

Miller concluded the paper with

FDA has performed extensive review of the Therac-25 software and hardware safety systems. We cannot say with absolute certainty that all software problems that might result in improper dose have been found and eliminated. However, we are confident that the hardware and software safety features recently added will prevent future catastrophic consequences of failure.

LESSONS LEARNED

Often, it takes an accident to alert people to the dangers involved in technology. A medical physicist wrote about the Therac-25 accidents:

In the past decade or two, the medical accelerator "industry" has become perhaps a little complacent about safety. We have assumed that the manufacturers have all kinds of safety design experience since they've been in the business a long time. We know that there are many safety codes, guides, and regulations to guide them and we have been reassured by the hitherto excellent record of these machines. Except for a few incidents in the 1960s (e.g., at Hammersmith, Hamburg) the use of medical accelerators has been remarkably free of serious radiation accidents until now. Perhaps, though, we have been spoiled by this success.[1]

Accidents are seldom simple—they usually involve a complex web of interacting events with multiple contributing technical, human, and organizational factors. One of the serious mistakes that led to the multiple Therac-25 accidents was the tendency to believe that the cause of an accident had been determined (for example, a microswitch failure in the Hamilton accident) without adequate evidence to come to this conclusion and without looking at all possible contributing factors. Another mistake was the assumption that fixing a particular error (eliminating the current software bug) would prevent future accidents. There is always another software bug.

Accidents are often blamed on a single cause like human error. But virtually all factors involved in accidents can be labeled human error, except perhaps for hardware wear-out failures. Even such hardware failures could be attributed to human error (for example, the designer's failure to provide adequate redundancy or the failure of operational personnel to properly maintain or replace parts): Concluding that an accident was the result of human error is not very helpful or meaningful.

It is nearly as useless to ascribe the cause of an accident to a computer error or a software error. Certainly software was involved in the Therac-25 accidents, but it was only one contributing factor. If we assign software error as *the* cause of the Therac-25 accidents, we are forced to conclude that the only way to prevent such accidents in the future is to build perfect software that will never behave in an unexpected or undesired way under any circumstances (which is clearly impossible) or not to use software at all in these types of systems. Both conclusions are overly pessimistic.

We must approach the problem of accidents in complex systems from a system-engineering point of view and consider all possible contributing factors. For the Therac-25 accidents, contributing factors included

- management inadequacies and lack of procedures for following through on all reported incidents,
- overconfidence in the software and removal of hardware interlocks (making the software into a single point of failure that could lead to an accident),
- presumably less-than-acceptable software-engineering practices, and
- unrealistic risk assessments along with overconfidence in the results of these assessments.

The exact same accident may not happen a second time, but if we examine and try to ameliorate the contributing factors to the accidents we have had, we may be able to prevent different accidents in the future. In the following sections, we present what we feel are important lessons learned from the Therac-25. You may draw different or additional conclusions.

System Engineering

A common mistake in engineering, in this case and many others, is to put too much confidence in software. Nonsoftware professionals seem to feel that software will not or cannot fail; this attitude leads to complacency and overreliance on computerized functions. Although software is not subject to random wear-out failures like hardware, software design errors are much harder to find and eliminate. Furthermore, hardware failure modes are generally much more limited, so building protection against them is usually easier. A lesson to be learned from the Therac-25 accidents is not to remove standard hardware interlocks when adding computer control.

Hardware backups, interlocks, and other safety devices are currently being replaced by software in many different types of systems, including commercial aircraft, nuclear power plants, and weapon systems. Where the hardware interlocks are still used, they are often controlled by software. Designing any dangerous system in such a way that one failure can lead to an accident violates basic system-engineering principles. In this respect, software needs to be treated as a single component. Software should not be assigned sole responsibility for safety, and systems should not be designed such that a single software error or software-engineering error can be catastrophic.

A related tendency among engineers is to ignore software. The first safety analysis on the Therac-25 did not include software (although nearly full responsibility for safety rested on the software). When problems started occurring, investigators assumed that hardware was the cause and focused only on the hardware. Investigation of software's possible contribution to an accident should not be the last avenue explored after all other possible explanations are eliminated.

In fact, a software error can always be attributed to a transient hardware failure, since software (in these types of process-control systems) reads and issues commands to actuators. Without a thorough investigation (and without on-line monitoring or audit trails that save internal state information), it is not possible to determine whether the sensor provided the wrong information, the software provided an incorrect command, or the actuator had a transient failure and did the wrong thing on its own. In the Hamilton accident, a transient microswitch failure was assumed to be the cause, even though the engineers were unable to reproduce the failure or find anything wrong with the microswitch.

Patient reactions were the only real indications of the seriousness of the problems with the Therac-25. There were no independent checks that the software was operating correctly (including software checks). Such verification cannot be assigned to operators without providing them with some means of detecting errors. The Therac-25 software "lied" to the operators, and the machine itself could not detect that a massive overdose had occurred. The Therac-25 ion chambers could not handle the high density of ionization from the unscanned electron beam at high-beam current; they thus became saturated and gave an indication of a low dosage. Engineers need to design for the worst case.

Every company building safety-critical systems should have audit trails and incident-analysis procedures that they apply whenever they find any hint of a problem that might lead to an accident. The first phone call by Still should have led to an extensive investigation of the events at Kennestone. Certainly, learning about the first lawsuit should have triggered an immediate response. Although hazard logging and tracking is required in the standards for safety-critical military projects, it is less common in nonmilitary projects. Every company building hazardous equipment should have hazard logging and tracking as well as incident reporting and analysis as parts of its quality control procedures. Such follow-up and tracking will not only help prevent accidents, but will easily pay for themselves in reduced insurance rates and reasonable settlement of lawsuits when they do occur.

Finally, overreliance on the numerical output of safety analyses is unwise. The arguments over whether very low probabilities are meaningful with respect to safety are too extensive to summarize here. But, at the least, a healthy skepticism is in order. The claim that safety had been increased five orders of magnitude as a result of the microswitch fix after the Hamilton accident seems hard to justify. Perhaps it was based on the probability of failure of the microswitch (typically 10^{-5}) ANDed with the other interlocks. The problem with all such analyses is that they exclude aspects of the problem (in this case, software) that are difficult to quantify but which may have a larger impact on safety than the quantifiable factors that are included.

Although management and regulatory agencies often press engineers to obtain such numbers, engineers should insist that any risk assessment numbers used are in fact meaningful and that statistics of this sort are treated with caution. In our enthusiasm to provide measurements, we should not attempt to measure the unmeasurable. William Ruckelshaus, two-time head of the US Environmental Protection Agency, cautioned that "risk assessment data can be like the captured spy; if you torture it long enough, it will tell you anything you want to know."[7] E.A. Ryder of the British Health and Safety Executive has written that the numbers game in risk assessment "should only be played in private between consenting adults, as it is too easy to be misinterpreted."[8]

Software Engineering

The Therac-25 accidents were fairly unique in having software coding errors involved—most computer-related accidents have not involved coding errors but rather errors in the software requirements such as omissions and mishandled environmental conditions and system states. Although using good basic software-engineering practices will not prevent all software errors, it is certainly required as a minimum. Some companies introducing software into their systems for the first time do not take software engineering as seriously as they should. Basic software-engineering principles that apparently were violated with the Therac-25 include:

- Documentation should not be an afterthought.
- Software quality assurance practices and standards should be established.
- Designs should be kept simple.
- Ways to get information about errors—for example, software audit trails—should be designed into the software from the beginning.
- The software should be subjected to extensive testing and formal analysis at the module and software level; system testing alone is not adequate.

In addition, special safety-analysis and design procedures must be incorporated into safety-critical software projects. Safety must be built into software, and, in addition, safety must be assured at the system level despite software errors.[9,10] The Therac-20 contained the same software error implicated in the Tyler deaths, but the machine included hardware interlocks that mitigated its consequences. Protection against software errors can also be built into the software itself.

Furthermore, important lessons about software reuse can be found here. A naive assumption is often made that reusing software or using commercial off-the-shelf software increases safety because the software has been exercised extensively. Reusing software modules does not guarantee safety in the new system to which they are transferred and sometimes leads to awkward and dangerous designs. Safety is a quality of the system in which the software is used; it is not a quality of the software itself. Rewriting the entire software to get a clean and simple design may be safer in many cases.

Taking a couple of programming courses or programming a home computer does not qualify anyone to produce safety-critical software. Although certification of software engineers is not yet required, more events like those associated with the Therac-25 will make such certification inevitable. There is activity in Britain to specify required courses for those working on critical software. Any engineer is not automatically qualified to be a software engineer—an extensive program of study and experience is required. Safety-critical software engineering requires training and experience in addition to that required for noncritical software.

Although the user interface of the Therac-25 has attracted a lot of attention, it was really a side issue in the accidents. Certainly, it could have been improved, like many other aspects of this software. Either software engineers need better training in interface design, or more input is needed from human factors engineers. There also needs to be greater recognition of potential conflicts between user-friendly interfaces and safety. One goal of interface design is to make the interface as easy as possible for the operator to use. But in the Therac-25, some design features (for example, not requiring the operator to reenter patient prescriptions after mistakes) and later changes (allowing a carriage return to indicate that information has been entered correctly) enhanced usability at the expense of safety.

Finally, not only must safety be considered in the initial design of the software and its operator interface, but the reasons for design decisions should be recorded so that decisions are not inadvertently undone in future modifications.

User and Government Oversight and Standards

Once the FDA got involved in the Therac-25, their response was impressive, especially considering how little experience they had with similar problems in computerized medical devices. Since the Therac-25 events, the FDA has moved to improve the reporting system and to augment their procedures and guidelines to include software. The problem of deciding when to forbid the use of medical devices that are also saving lives has no simple answer and involves ethical and political issues that cannot be answered by science or engineering alone. However, at the least, better procedures are certainly required for reporting problems to the FDA and to users.

The issues involved in regulation of risky technology are complex. Overly strict standards can inhibit progress, require techniques behind the state of the art, and transfer responsibility from the manufacturer to the government. The fixing of responsibility requires a delicate balance. Someone must represent the public's needs, which may be subsumed by a company's desire for profits. On the other hand, standards can have the undesirable effect of limiting the safety efforts and investment of companies that feel their legal and moral responsibilities are fulfilled if they follow the standards.

Some of the most effective standards and efforts for safety come from users. Manufacturers have more incentive to satisfy customers than to satisfy government agencies. The American Association of Physicists in Medicine established a task group to work on problems associated with computers in radiation therapy in 1979, long before the Therac-25 problems began. The accidents intensified these efforts, and the association is developing user-written standards. A report by J.A. Rawlinson of the Ontario Cancer Institute attempted to define the physicist's role in assuring adequate safety in medical accelerators:

> We could continue our traditional role, which has been to provide input to the manufacturer on safety issues but to leave the major safety design decisions to the manufacturer. We can provide this input through a number of mechanisms. . . These include participation in standards organizations such as the IEC [International Electrotechnical Commission], in professional association groups . . . and in accelerator user groups such as the Therac-25 user group. It includes also making use of the Problem Reporting Program for Radiation Therapy Devices . . . and it includes consultation in the drafting of the government safety regulations. Each of these if pursued vigorously will go a long way to improving safety. It is debatable however whether these actions would be sufficient to prevent a future series of accidents.
>
> Perhaps what is needed in addition is a mechanism by which the safety of any new model of accelerator is assessed independently of the manufacturer. This task could be done by the individual physicist at the time of acceptance of a new machine. Indeed many users already test at least the *operation* of safety interlocks during commissioning. Few however have the time or resources to conduct a comprehensive assessment of safety *design*.
>
> A more effective approach might be to require that prior to the use of a new type of accelerator in a particular jurisdiction, an independent safety analysis is made by a panel (including but not limited to medical physicists). Such a panel could be established within or without a regulatory framework.[1]

It is clear that users need to be involved. It was users who found the problems with the Therac-25 and forced AECL to respond. The process of fixing the Therac-25 was user driven—the manufacturer was slow to respond. The Therac-25 user group meetings were, according to participants, important to the resolution of the problems. But if users are to be involved, then they must be provided with information and the ability to perform this function. Manufacturers need to understand that the adversarial approach and the attempt to keep government agencies and users in the dark about problems will not be to their benefit in the long run.

The US Air Force has one of the most extensive programs to inform users. Contractors who build space systems for the Air Force must provide an Accident Risk Assessment Report (AFAR) to system users and operators that describes the hazardous subsystems and operations associated with that system and its interfaces. The AFAR also comprehensively identifies and evaluates the system's accident risks; provides a means of substantiating compliance with safety requirements; summarizes all system-safety analyses and testing performed on each system and subsystem; and identifies design and operating limits to be imposed on system components to preclude or minimize accidents that could cause injury or damage.

An interesting requirement in the Air Force AFAR is a record of all safety-related failures or accidents associated with system acceptance, test, and checkout, along with an assessment of the impact on flight and ground safety and action taken to prevent recurrence. The AFAR also must address failures, accidents, or incidents from previous missions of this system or other systems using similar hardware. All corrective action taken to prevent recurrence must be documented. The accident and correction history must be updated throughout the life of the system. If any design or operating parameters change after government approval, the AFAR must be updated to include all changes affecting safety.

Unfortunately, the Air Force program is not practical for commercial systems. However, government agencies might require manufacturers to provide similar information to users. If required for everyone, competitive pressures to withhold information might be lessened. Manufacturers might find that providing such information actually increases customer loyalty and confidence. An emphasis on safety can be turned into a competitive advantage.

Most previous accounts of the Therac-25 accidents blamed them on a software error and stopped there. This is not very useful and, in fact, can be misleading and dangerous: If we are to prevent such accidents in the future, we must dig deeper. Most accidents involving complex technology are caused by a combination of organizational, managerial, technical, and, sometimes, sociological or political factors. Preventing accidents requires paying attention to *all* the root causes, not just the precipitating event in a particular circumstance.

Accidents are unlikely to occur in exactly the same way again. If we patch only the symptoms and ignore the deeper underlying causes or we fix only the specific cause of one accident, we are unlikely to prevent or mitigate future accidents. The series of accidents involving the Therac-25 is a good example of exactly this problem: Fixing each individual software flaw as it was found did not solve the device's safety problems. Virtually all complex software will behave in an unexpected or undesired fashion under some conditions—there will always be another bug. Instead, accidents must be understood with respect to the complex factors involved. In addition, changes need to be made to eliminate or reduce the underlying causes and contributing factors that increase the likelihood of accidents or loss resulting from them.

Although these accidents occurred in software controlling medical devices, the lessons apply to all types of systems where computers control dangerous devices. In our experience, the same types of mistakes are being made in nonmedical systems. We must learn from our mistakes so we do not repeat them.

THERAC-25 SOFTWARE DEVELOPMENT AND DESIGN

We know that the software for the Therac-25 was developed by a single person, using PDP 11 assembly language, over a period of several years. The software "evolved" from the Therac-6 software, which was started in 1972. According to a letter from AECL to the FDA, the "program structure and certain subroutines were carried over to the Therac 25 around 1976."

Apparently, very little software documentation was produced during development. In a 1986 internal FDA memo, a reviewer lamented, "Unfortunately, the AECL response also seems to point out an apparent lack of documentation on software specifications and a software test plan."

The manufacturer said that the hardware and software were "tested and exercised separately or together over many years." In his deposition for one of the lawsuits, the quality assurance manager explained that testing was done in two parts. A "small amount" of software testing was done on a simulator, but most testing was done as a system. It appears that unit and software testing was minimal, with most effort directed at the integrated system test. At a Therac-25 user group meeting, the same quality assurance manager said that the Therac-25 software was tested for 2,700 hours. Under questioning by the users, he clarified this as meaning "2,700 hours of use."

The programmer left AECL in 1986. In a lawsuit connected with one of the accidents, the lawyers were unable to obtain information about the programmer from AECL. In the depositions connected with that case, none of the AECL employees questioned could provide any information about his educational background or experience. Although an attempt was made to obtain a deposition from the programmer, the lawsuit was settled before this was accomplished. We have been unable to learn anything about his background.

AECL claims proprietary rights to its software design. However, from voluminous documentation regarding the accidents, the repairs, and the eventual design changes, we can build a rough picture of it.

The software is responsible for monitoring the machine status, accepting input about the treatment desired, and setting the machine up for this treatment. It turns the beam on in response to an operator command (assuming that certain operational checks on the status of the physical machine are satisfied) and also turns the beam off when treatment is completed, when an operator commands it, or when a malfunction is detected. The operator can print out hardcopy versions of the CRT display or machine setup parameters.

The treatment unit has an interlock system designed to remove power to the unit when there is a hardware malfunction. The computer monitors this interlock system and provides diagnostic messages. Depending on the fault, the computer either prevents a treatment from being started or, if the treatment is in progress, creates a pause or a suspension of the treatment.

The manufacturer describes the Therac-25 software as having a standalone, real-time treatment operating system. The system is not built using a standard operating system or executive. Rather, the real-time executive was written especially for the Therac-25 and runs on a 32K PDP 11/23. A preemptive scheduler allocates cycles to the critical and noncritical tasks.

The software, written in PDP 11 assembly language, has four major components: stored data, a scheduler, a set of critical and noncritical tasks, and interrupt services. The stored data includes calibration parameters for the accelerator setup as well as patient-treatment data. The interrupt routines include

- a clock interrupt service routine,
- a scanning interrupt service routine,
- traps (for software overflow and computer-hardware-generated interrupts),
- power up (initiated at power up to initialize the system and pass control to the scheduler),
- treatment console screen interrupt handler,
- treatment console keyboard interrupt handler,
- service printer interrupt handler, and
- service keyboard interrupt handler.

The scheduler controls the sequences of all noninterrupt events and coordinates all concurrent processes. Tasks are initiated every 0.1 second, with the critical tasks executed first and the noncritical tasks executed in any remaining cycle time. Critical tasks include the following:

- The treatment monitor (Treat) directs and monitors patient setup and treatment via eight operating phases. These are called as subroutines, depending on the value of the Tphase control variable. Following the execution of a particular subroutine, Treat reschedules itself. Treat interacts with the keyboard processing task, which handles operator console communication. The prescription data is cross-checked and verified by other tasks (for example, the keyboard processor and the parameter setup sensor) that inform the treatment task of the verification status via shared variables.
- The servo task controls gun emission, dose rate (pulse-repetition frequency), symmetry (beam steering), and machine motions. The servo task also sets up the machine parameters and monitors the beam-tilt-error and the flatness-error interlocks.
- The housekeeper task takes care of system-status interlocks and limit checks, and puts appropriate messages on the CRT display. It decodes some information and checks the setup verification.

Noncritical tasks include

- Check sum processor (scheduled to run periodically).
- Treatment console keyboard processor (scheduled to run only if it is called by other tasks or by keyboard interrupts). This task acts as the interface between the software and the operator.
- Treatment console screen processor (run periodically). This task lays out appropriate record formats for either displays or hard copies.

- Service keyboard processor (run on demand). This task arbitrates non-treatment-related communication between the therapy system and the operator.
- Snapshot (run periodically by the scheduler). Snapshot captures pre-selected parameter values and is called by the treatment task at the end of a treatment.
- Hand-control processor (run periodically).
- Calibration processor. This task is responsible for a package of tasks that let the operator examine and change system setup parameters and interlock limits.

It is clear from the AECL documentation on the modifications that the software allows concurrent access to shared memory, that there is no real synchronization aside from data stored in shared variables, and that the "test" and "set" for such variables are not indivisible operations. Race conditions resulting from this implementation of multitasking played an important part in the accidents.

THE OPERATOR INTERFACE

In the main text, we describe changes made as a result of an FDA recall, and here we describe the operator interface of the software version used during the accidents.

The Therac-25 operator controls the machine with a DEC VT100 terminal. In the general case, the operator positions the patient on the treatment table, manually sets the treatment field sizes and gantry rotation, and attaches accessories to the machine. Leaving the treatment room, the operator returns to the VT100 console to enter the patient identification, treatment prescription (including mode, energy level, dose, dose rate, and time), field sizing, gantry rotation, and accessory data. The system then compares the manually set values with those entered at the console. If they match, a "verified" message is displayed and treatment is permitted. If they do not match, treatment is not allowed to proceed until the mismatch is corrected. Figure A shows the screen layout.

When the system was first built, operators complained that it took too long to enter the treatment plan. In response, the manufacturer modified the software before the first unit was installed so that, instead of reentering the data at the keyboard, operators could use a carriage return to merely copy the treatment site data.[1] A quick series of carriage returns would thus complete data entry. This interface modification was to figure in several accidents.

The Therac-25 could shut down in two ways after it detected an error condition. One was a *treatment suspend*, which required a complete machine reset to restart. The other, not so serious, was a *treatment pause*, which required only a single-key command to restart the machine. If a treatment pause occurred, the operator could press the "P" key to "proceed" and resume treatment quickly and conveniently. The previous treatment parameters remained in effect, and no reset was required. This convenient and simple feature could be invoked a maximum of five times before the machine automatically suspended treatment and required the operator to perform a system reset.

Error messages provided to the operator were cryptic, and some merely consisted of the word "malfunction" followed by a number from 1 to 64 denoting an analog/digital channel number. According to an FDA memorandum written after one accident

> The operator's manual supplied with the machine does not explain nor even address the malfunction codes. The [Maintenance] Manual lists the various malfunction numbers but gives no explanation. The materials provided give *no* indication that these malfunctions could place a patient at risk.
>
> The program does not advise the operator if a situation exists wherein the ion chambers used to monitor the patient are saturated, thus are beyond the measurement limits of the instrument. This software package does not appear to contain a safety system to prevent parameters being entered and intermixed that would result in excessive radiation being delivered to the patient under treatment.

An operator involved in an overdose accident testified that she had become insensitive to machine malfunctions. Malfunction messages were commonplace—most did not involve patient safety. Service technicians would fix

PATIENT NAME: TEST			A	1
TREATMENT MODE: FIX	BEAM TYPE: X ENERGY (KeV):		25	
	ACTUAL	PRESCRIBED		
UNIT RATE/MINUTE	0	200		
MONITOR UNITS	50 50	200		
TIME(MIN)	0.27	1.00		
GANTRY ROTATION (DEG)	0.0	0	VERIFIED	
COLLIMATOR ROTATION (DEG)	359.2	359	VERIFIED	
COLLIMATOR X (CM)	14.2	14.3	VERIFIED	
COLLIMATOR Y (CM)	27.2	27.3	VERIFIED	
WEDGE NUMBER	1	1	VERIFIED	
ACCESSORY NUMBER	0	0	VERIFIED	

DATE: 84-OCT-26	SYSTEM: BEAM READY	OP. MODE: TREAT	AUTO
TIME: 12:55.8	TREAT: TREAT PAUSE	X-RAY	173777
OPR ID: T25VO2-RO3	REASON: OPERATOR	COMMAND:	

FIGURE A: Operator interface screen layout.

the problems or the hospital physicist would realign the machine and make it operable again. She said, "It was not out of the ordinary for something to stop the machine. . . It would often give a low dose rate in which you would turn the machine back on. . . They would give messages of low dose rate, V-tilt, H-tilt, and other things; I can't remember all the reasons it would stop, but there [were] a lot of them." The operator further testified that during instruction she had been taught that there were "so many safety mechanisms" that she understood it was virtually impossible to overdose a patient.

A radiation therapist at another clinic reported an average of 40 dose-rate malfunctions, attributed to underdoses, occurred on some days.

Reference

1. E. Miller, "The Therac-25 Experience," *Proc. Conf. State Radiation Control Program Directors*, 1987.

SAFETY ANALYSIS OF THE THERAC-25

The Therac-25 safety analysis included (1) failure mode and effect analysis, (2) fault-tree analysis, and (3) software examination.

Failure Mode and Effect Analysis An FMEA describes the associated system response to all failure modes of the individual system components, considered one by one. When software was involved, AECL made no assessment of the "how and why" of software faults and took any combination of software faults as a single event. The latter means that if the software was the initiating event, then no credit was given for the software mitigating the effects. This seems like a reasonable and conservative approach to handling software faults.

Fault-tree Analysis An FMEA identifies single failures leading to Class I hazards. To identify multiple failures and quantify the results, AECL used fault-tree analysis. An FTA starts with a postulated hazard—for example, two of the top events for the Therac-25 are high dose per pulse and illegal gantry motion. The immediate causes for the event are then generated in an AND/OR tree format, using a basic understanding of the machine operation to determine the causes. The tree generation continues until all branches end in "basic events." Operationally, a basic event is sometimes defined as an event that can be quantified (for example, a resistor fails open).

AECL used a "generic failure rate" of 10^{-4} per hour for software events. The company justified this number as based on the historical performance of the Therac-25 software. The final report on the safety analysis said that many fault trees for the Therac-25 have a computer malfunction as a causative event, and the outcome of quantification is therefore dependent on the failure rate chosen for software.

Leaving aside the general question of whether such failure rates are meaningful or measurable for software in general, it seems rather difficult to justify a single figure of this sort for every type of software error or software behavior. It would be equivalent to assigning the same failure rate to every type of failure of a car, no matter what particular failure is considered.

The authors of the safety study did note that despite the uncertainty that software introduces into quantification, fault-tree analysis provides valuable information in showing single and multiple failure paths and the relative importance of different failure mechanisms. This is certainly true.

Software Examination Because of the difficulty of quantifying software behavior, AECL contracted for a detailed code inspection to "obtain more information on which to base decisions." The software functions selected for examination were those related to the Class I software hazards identified in the FMEA: electron-beam scanning, energy selection, beam shutoff, and dose calibration.

The outside consultant who performed the inspection included a detailed examination of each function's implementation, a search for coding errors, and a qualitative assessment of its reliability. The consultant recommended program changes to correct shortcomings, improve reliability, or improve the software package in a general sense. The final safety report gives no information about whether any particular methodology or tools were used in the software inspection or whether someone just read the code looking for errors.

Conclusions of the Safety Analysis The final report summarizes the conclusions of the safety analysis:

> The conclusions of the analysis call for 10 changes to Therac-25 hardware; the most significant of these are interlocks to back up software control of both electron scanning and beam energy selection.
>
> Although it is not considered necessary or advisable to rewrite the entire Therac-25 software package, considerable effort is being expended to update it. The changes recommended have several distinct objectives: improve the protection it provides against hardware failures; provide additional reliability via cross-checking; and provide a more maintainable source package. Two or three software releases are anticipated before these changes are completed.
>
> The implementation of these improvements including design and testing for both hardware and software is well under way. All hardware modifications should be completed and installed by mid 1989, with final software updates extending into late 1989 or early 1990.

The recommended hardware changes appear to add protection against software errors, to add extra protection against hardware failures, or to increase safety margins. The software conclusions included the following:

> The software code for Beam Shut-Off, Symmetry Control, and Dose Calibration was found to be straight-forward and no execution path could be found which would cause them to perform incorrectly. A few improvements are being incorporated, but no additional hardware interlocks are required.
>
> Inspection of the Scanning and Energy Selection functions, which are under software control, showed no improper execution paths; however,

software inspection was unable to provide a high level of confidence in their reliability. This was due to the complex nature of the code, the extensive use of variables, and the time limitations of the inspection process. Due to these factors and the possible clinical consequences of a malfunction, computer-independent interlocks are being retrofitted for these two cases.

Given the complex nature of this software design and the basic multi-tasking design, it is difficult to understand how any part of the code could be labeled "straightforward" or how confidence could be achieved that "no execution paths" exist for particular types of software behavior. However, it does appear that a conservative approach—including computer-independent interlocks—was taken in most cases. Furthermore, few examples of such safety analyses of software exist in the literature. One such software analysis was performed in 1989 on the shutdown software of a nuclear power plant, which was written by a different division of AECL.[1] Much still needs to be learned about how to perform a software-safety analysis.

Reference

1. W. C. Bowman et al., "An Application of Fault Tree Analysis to Safety-Critical Software at Ontario Hydro," *Conf. Probabilistic Safety Assessment and Management*, 1991.

ACKNOWLEDGMENTS

Ed Miller of the FDA was especially helpful, both in providing information to be included in this article and in reviewing and commenting on the final version. Gordon Symonds of the Canadian Government Health Protection Branch also reviewed and commented on a draft of the article. Finally, the referees, several of whom were apparently intimately involved in some of the accidents, were also very helpful in providing additional information about the accidents.

REFERENCES

The information in this article was gathered from official FDA documents and internal memos, lawsuit depositions, letters, and various other sources that are not publicly available. *Computer* does not provide references to documents that are unavailable to the public.

1. J. A. Rawlinson, "Report on the Therac-25," OCTRF/OCI Physicists Meeting, Kingston, Ont., Canada, May 7, 1987.
2. F. Houston, "What Do the Simple Folk Do?: Software Safety in the Cottage Industry," *IEEE Computers in Medicine Conf.*, 1985.
3. C. A. Bowsher, "Medical Devices: The Public Health at Risk," US Gov't Accounting Office Report GAO/T-PEMD-90-2, 046987/139922, 1990.
4. M. Kivel, ed., *Radiological Health Bulletin*, Vol. XX, No. 8, US Federal Food and Drug Administration, Dec. 1986.

5. *Medical Device Recalls, Examination of Selected Cases*, GAO/PEMD-90-6, 1989.

6. E. Miller, "The Therac-25 Experience," *Proc. Conf. State Radiation Control Program Directors*, 1987.

7. W. D. Ruckelshaus, "Risk in a Free Society," *Risk Analysis*, Vol. 4, No. 3, 1984, pp. 157–162.

8. E. A. Ryder, "The Control of Major Hazards: The Advisory Committee's Third and Final Report," *Transcript of Conf. European Major Hazards*, Oyez Scientific and Technical Services and Authors, London, 1984.

9. N. G. Leveson, "Software Safety: Why, What, and How," *ACM Computing Surveys*, Vol. 18, No. 2, June 1986, pp. 25–69.

10. N. G. Leveson, "Software Safety in Embedded Computer Systems," *Comm. ACM*, Feb. 1991, pp. 34–46.

▷ RESPONSIBILITY AND RETRIBUTION

H. L. A. Hart

RESPONSIBILITY

A wide range of different, though connected, ideas is covered by the expressions "responsibility," "responsible," and "responsible for," as these are standardly used in and out of the law. Though connexions exist between these different ideas, they are often very indirect, and it seems appropriate to speak of different *senses* of these expressions. The following simple story of a drunken sea captain who lost his ship at sea can be told in the terminology of responsibility to illustrate, with stylistically horrible clarity, these differences of sense.

> As captain of the ship, X was responsible for the safety of his passengers and crew. But on his last voyage he got drunk every night and was responsible for the loss of the ship with all aboard. It was rumored that he was insane, but the doctors considered that he was responsible for his actions. Throughout the voyage he behaved quite irresponsibly, and various incidents in his career showed that he was not a responsible person. He always maintained that the exceptional winter storms were responsible for the loss of the ship, but in the legal proceedings brought against him he was found criminally responsible for his negligent conduct, and in separate civil proceedings he was held legally responsible for the loss of life and property. He is still alive and he is morally responsible for the deaths of many women and children.

This welter of distinguishable senses of the word "responsibility" and its grammatical cognates can, I think, be profitably reduced by division and classification. I shall distinguish four heads of classification to which I shall assign the following names:

(*a*) Role-Responsibility
(*b*) Causal-Responsibility
(*c*) Liability-Responsibility
(*d*) Capacity-Responsibility.

I hope that in drawing these dividing lines, and in the exposition which follows, I have avoided the arbitrary pedantries of classificatory systematics, and that my divisions pick out and clarify the main, though not all, varieties of responsibility to which reference is constantly made, explicitly or implicitly, by moralists, lawyers, historians, and ordinary men. I relegate to the notes[1] discussion of what unifies these varieties and explains the extension of the terminology of responsibility.

Role-Responsibility

A sea captain is responsible for the safety of his ship, and that is his responsibility, or one of his responsibilities. A husband is responsible for the maintenance of his wife; parents for the upbringing of their children; a sentry for alerting the guard at the enemy's approach; a clerk for keeping the accounts of his firm. These examples of a person's responsibilities suggest the generalization that, whenever a person occupies a distinctive place or office in a social organization, to which specific duties are attached to provide for the welfare of others or to advance in some specific way the aims or purposes of the organization, he is properly said to be responsible for the performance of these duties, or for doing what is necessary to fulfil them. Such duties are a person's responsibilities. As a guide to this sense of responsibility this generalization is, I think, adequate, but the idea of a distinct role or place or office is, of course, a vague one, and I cannot undertake to make it very precise. Doubts about its extension to marginal cases will always arise. If two friends, out on a mountaineering expedition, agree that the one shall look after the food and the other the maps, then the one is correctly said to be responsible for the food, and the other for the maps, and I would classify this as a case of role-responsibility. Yet such fugitive or temporary assignments with specific duties would not usually be considered by sociologists, who mainly use the word, as an example of a "role." So "role" in my classification is extended to include a task assigned to any person by agreement or otherwise. But it is also important to notice that not all the duties which a man has in virtue of occupying what in a quite strict sense of role is a distinct role, are thought or spoken of as "responsibilities." A private soldier has a duty to obey his superior officer and, if commanded by him to form fours or present arms on a given occasion, has a duty to do so. But to form fours or present arms would scarcely be said to be the private's responsibility; nor would he be said to be responsible for doing it. If on the other hand a soldier was ordered to deliver a message to H.Q. or to conduct prisoners to a base camp, he might well be said to be responsible for doing these things, and these things to be his responsibility. I think, though I confess to not being sure, that what distinguishes those duties of a role which are singled out as responsibilities is that they are duties of a relatively complex or extensive kind, defining a "sphere of responsibility" requiring care and attention over a protracted period of time, while short-lived duties of a very simple kind, to do or not do some specific act on a particular occasion, are not termed responsibilities. Thus a soldier detailed off to keep the camp clean and tidy for the general's visit of inspection has this as his sphere of responsibility and is responsible for it. But if merely told to remove a piece of paper from the approaching general's path, this would be at most his duty.

A "responsible person", "behaving responsibly" (not "irresponsibly"), require for their elucidation a reference to role-responsibility. A responsible person is one who is disposed to take his duties seriously; to think about them, and to make serious efforts to fulfil them. To behave responsibly is to behave as a man would who took his duties in this serious way. Responsibilities in this sense may be either legal or moral, or fall outside this dichotomy. Thus a man may be morally as well as legally responsible for the maintenance of his wife and children, but a host's responsibility for the comfort of his guests, and a referee's responsibility for the control of the players is neither legal nor moral, unless the word "moral" is unilluminatingly used simply to exclude legal responsibility.

Causal Responsibility

"The long drought was responsible for the famine in India." In many contexts, as in this one, it is possible to substitute for the expression "was responsible for" the words "caused" or "produced" or some other causal expression in referring to consequences, results, or outcomes. The converse, however, is not always true. Examples of this causal sense of responsibility are legion. "His neglect was responsible for her distress." "The Prime Minister's speech was responsible for the panic." "Disraeli was responsible for the defeat of the Government." "The icy condition of the road was responsible for the accident." The past tense of the verb used in this causal sense of the expression "responsible for" should be noticed. If it is said of a living person, who has in fact caused some disaster, that he *is* responsible for it, this is not, or not merely, an example of causal responsibility, but of what I term "liability-responsibility;" it asserts his liability on account of the disaster, even though it is also true that he is responsible in that sense *because* he caused the disaster, and that he caused the disaster may be expressed by saying that he was responsible for it. On the other hand, if it is said of a person no longer living that he was responsible for some disaster, this may be either a simple causal statement or a statement of liability-responsibility, or both.

From the above examples it is clear that in this causal sense not only human beings but also their actions or omissions, and things, conditions, and events, may be said to be responsible for outcomes. It is perhaps true that only where an outcome is thought unfortunate or felicitous is its cause commonly spoken of as responsible for it. But this may not reflect any aspect of the meaning of the expression "responsible for;" it may only reflect the fact that, except in such cases, it may be pointless and hence rare to pick out the causes of events. It is sometimes suggested that, though we may speak of a human being's action as responsible for some outcome in a purely causal sense, we do not speak of a person, as distinct from his actions, as responsible for an outcome, unless he is felt to deserve censure or praise. This is, I think, a mistake. History books are full of examples to the contrary. "Disraeli was responsible for the defeat of the Government" need not carry even an implication that he was deserving of censure or praise; it may be purely a statement concerned with the contribution made by one human being to an outcome of importance, and be entirely neutral as to its moral or other merits. The contrary view depends, I think, on the failure to appreciate sufficiently the ambiguity of statements of the form "X *was* responsible for Y" as distinct from "X *is* responsible for Y" to which I have drawn attention above. The former expression in the case of a person no longer living may be (though it *need* not be) a statement of liability-responsibility.

Legal Liability-Responsibility

Though it was noted that role-responsibility might take either legal or moral form, it was not found necessary to treat these separately. But in the case of the present topic of liability-responsibility, separate treatment seems advisable. For responsibility seems to have a wider extension in relation to the law than it does in relation to morals, and it is a question to be considered whether this is due merely to the general differences between law and morality, or to some differences in the sense of responsibility involved.

When legal rules require men to act or abstain from action, one who breaks the law is usually liable, according to other legal rules, to punishment for his misdeeds, or to make compensation to persons injured thereby, and very often he is liable to both punishment and enforced compensation. He is thus liable to be "made to pay" for what he has done in either or both of the senses which the expression "He'll pay for it" may bear in ordinary usage. But most legal systems go much further than this. A man may be legally punished on account of what his servant has done, even if he in no way caused or instigated or even knew of the servant's action, or knew of the likelihood of his servant so acting. Liability in such circumstances is rare in modern systems of criminal law; but it is common in all systems of civil law for men to be made to pay compensation for injuries caused by others, generally their servants or employees. The law of most countries goes further still. A man may be liable to pay compensation for harm suffered by others, though neither he nor his servants have caused it. This is so, for example, in Anglo-American law when the harm is caused by dangerous things which escape from a man's possession, even if their escape is not due to any act or omission of his or his servants, or if harm is caused to a man's employees by defective machinery whose defective condition he could not have discovered.

It will be observed that the facts referred to in the last paragraph are expressed in terms of "liability" and not "responsibility." In the preceding essay in this volume I ventured the general statement that to say that someone is legally responsible for something often means that under legal rules he is liable to be made either to suffer or to pay compensation in certain eventualities. But I now think that this simple account of liability-responsibility is in need of some considerable modification. Undoubtedly, expressions of the form "he is legally responsible for Y" (where Y is some action or harm) and "he is legally liable to be punished or to be made to pay compensation for Y" are very closely connected, and sometimes they are used as if they were identical in meaning. Thus, where one legal writer speaks of "strict responsibility" and "vicarious responsibility," another speaks of "strict liability" and "vicarious liability;" and even in the work of a single writer the expressions "vicarious responsibility" and "vicarious liability" are to be found used without any apparent difference in meaning, implication, or emphasis. Hence, in arguing that it was for the law to determine the mental conditions of responsibility, Fitzjames Stephen claimed that this must be so because "the meaning of responsibility is liability to punishment."[2]

But though the abstract expressions "responsibility" and "liability" are virtually equivalent in many contexts, the statement that a man is responsible for his actions, or for some act or some harm, is usually not identical in meaning with the statement that he is liable to be punished or to be made to pay compensation for the act or the harm, but is directed to a narrower and more specific issue. It is in this respect that my previous account of liability-responsibility needs qualification.

The question whether a man is or is not legally liable to be punished for some action that he has done opens up the quite general issue whether all of the various requirements for criminal liability have been satisfied, and so will include the question whether the kind of action done, whatever mental element accompanied it, was ever punishable by law. But the question whether he is or is not legally responsible for some action or some harm is usually not concerned with this general issue, but with the narrower issue whether any of a certain range of conditions (mainly, but not exclusively, psychological) are satisfied, it being assumed that all other conditions are satisfied. Because of this difference in scope between questions of liability to punishment and questions of responsibility, it would be somewhat misleading, though not unintelligible, to say of a man who had refused to rescue a baby drowning in a foot of water, that he was not, according to English law, legally responsible for leaving the baby to drown or for the baby's death, if all that is meant is that he was not liable to punishment because refusing aid to those in danger is not generally a crime in English law. Similarly, a book or article entitled "Criminal Responsibility" would not be expected to contain the whole of the substantive criminal law determining the conditions of liability, but only to be concerned with a specialized range of topics such as mental abnormality, immaturity, *mens rea*, strict and vicarious liability, proximate cause, or other general forms of connexion between acts and harm sufficient for liability. These are the specialized topics which are, in general, thought and spoken of as "criteria" of responsibility. They may be divided into three classes: (i) mental or psychological conditions; (ii) causal or other forms of connexion between act and harm; (iii) personal relationships rendering one man liable to be punished or to pay for the acts of another. Each of these three classes requires some separate discussion.

Mental or Psychological Criteria of Responsibility. In the criminal law the most frequent issue raised by questions of responsibility, as distinct from the wider question of liability, is whether or not an accused person satisfied some mental or psychological condition required for liability, or whether liability was strict or absolute, so that the usual mental or psychological conditions were not required. It is, however, important to notice that these psychological conditions are of two sorts, of which the first is far more closely associated with the use of the word responsibility than the second. On the one hand, the law of most countries requires that the person liable to be punished should at the time of his crime have had the capacity to understand what he is required by law to do or not to do, to deliberate and to decide what to do, and to control his conduct in the light of such decisions. Normal adults are generally assumed to have these capacities, but they may be lacking where there is mental disorder or immaturity, and the possession of these normal capacities is very often signified by the expression "responsible for his actions." This is the fourth sense of responsibility which I discuss below under the heading of "Capacity-Responsibility." On the other hand, except where responsibility is strict, the law may excuse from punishment persons of normal capacity if, on particular occasions where their outward conduct fits the definition of the crime, some element of intention or knowledge, or some other of the familiar constituents of *mens rea*, was absent, so that the particular action done was defective, though the agent had the normal capacity of understanding and control. Continental codes usually make a firm distinction between these two main types of psychological conditions: questions concerning general capacity are described as matters of responsibility or "imputability," whereas questions concerning the presence or absence of knowledge or intention on particular occasions are not described as matters of "imputability," but are referred to the topic of "fault" (*schuld, faute, dolo,* &c.).

English law and English legal writers do not mark quite so firmly this contrast between general capacity and the knowledge or intention accompanying a particular action; for the expression *mens rea* is now often used to cover all the variety of psychological conditions required for liability by the law, so that both the person who is excused from punishment because of lack of intention or some ordinary accident or mistake on a particular occasion and the person held not to be criminally responsible on account of immaturity or insanity are said not to have the requisite *mens rea.* Yet the distinction thus blurred by the extensive use of the expression *mens rea* between a persistent incapacity and a particular defective action is indirectly marked in terms of responsibility in most Anglo-American legal writing, in the following way. When a person is said to be not responsible for a particular act or crime, or when (as in the formulation of the M'Naghten Rules and s. 2 of the Homicide Act, 1957) he is said not to be responsible for his "acts and omissions in doing" some action on a particular occasion, the reason for saying this is usually some mental abnormality or disorder. I have not succeeded in finding cases where a normal person, merely lacking some ordinary element of knowledge or intention on a particular occasion, is said for that reason not to be responsible for that particular action, even though he is for that reason not liable to punishment. But though there is this tendency in statements of liability-responsibility to confine the use of the expression "responsible" and "not responsible" to questions of mental abnormality or general incapacity, yet all the psychological conditions of liability are to be found discussed by legal writers under such headings as "Criminal Responsibility" or "Principles of Criminal Responsibility." Accordingly I classify them here as criteria of responsibility. I do so with a clear conscience, since little is to be gained in clarity by a rigid division which the contemporary use of the expression *mens rea* often ignores.

The situation is, however, complicated by a further feature of English legal and non-legal usage. The phrase "responsible for his actions" is, as I have observed, frequently used to refer to the capacity-responsibility of the normal person, and, so used, refers to one of the major criteria of liability-responsibility. It is so used in s. 2 of the Homicide Act 1957, which speaks of a person's mental "responsibility" for his actions being *impaired,* and in the rubric to the section, which speaks of persons "suffering from diminished responsibility." In this sense the expression is the name or description of a psychological condition. But the expression is also used to signify liability-responsibility itself, that is, liability to punishment so far as such liability depends on psychological conditions, and is so used when the law is said to "relieve insane persons of responsibility for their actions." It was probably also so used in the form of verdict returned in cases of successful pleas of insanity under English law until this was altered by the Insanity Act 1964: the verdict was "guilty but insane so as not to be responsible according to law for his actions."

Causal or Other Forms of Connexion with Harm. Questions of legal liability-responsibility are not limited in their scope to psychological conditions of either of the two sorts distinguished above. Such questions are also (though more frequently in the law of tort than in the criminal law) concerned with the issue whether some form of connexion between a person's act and some harmful outcome is sufficient according to law to make him liable; so if a person is accused of murder the question whether he was or was not legally responsible for the death may be intended to raise the issue whether the death was too remote a consequence of his acts for them to count as its cause. If the law, as frequently in tort, is not that the defendant's action should have caused the harm, but that there be some other form of connexion or relationship between the defendant and the harm, e.g. that it should have been caused by some dangerous thing escaping from the defendant's land, this connexion or relationship is a condition of civil responsibility for harm, and, where it holds, the defendant is said to be legally responsible for the harm. No doubt such questions of connexion with harm are also frequently phrased in terms of liability.

Relationship with the Agent. Normally in criminal law the minimum condition required for liability for punishment is that the person to be punished should himself have done what the law forbids, at least so far as outward conduct is concerned; even if liability is "strict;" it is not enough to render him liable for punishment that someone else should have done it. This is often expressed in the terminology of responsibility (though here, too, "liability" is frequently used instead of "responsibility") by saying that, generally, vicarious responsibility is not known to the criminal law. But there are exceptional cases; an innkeeper is liable to punishment if his servants, without his knowledge and against his orders, sell liquor on his premises after hours. In this case he is vicariously responsible for the sale, and of course, in the civil law of tort there are many situations in which a master or employer is liable to pay compensation for the torts of his servant or employee, and is said to be vicariously responsible.

It appears, therefore, that there are diverse types of criteria of legal liability-responsibility: the most prominent consist of certain mental elements, but there are also causal or other connexions between a person and harm, or the presence of some relationship, such as that of master and servant, between different persons. It is natural to ask why these very diverse conditions are singled out as criteria of responsibility, and so are within the scope of questions about responsibility, as distinct from the wider question concerning liability for punishment. I think that the following somewhat Cartesian figure may explain this fact. If we conceive of a person as an embodied mind and will, we may draw a distinction between two questions concerning the conditions of liability and punishment. The first question is what general types of outer conduct (*actus reus*) or what sorts of harm are required for liability? The second question is how closely connected with such conduct or such harm must the embodied mind or will of an individual person be to render him liable to punishment? Or, as some would put it, to what extent must the embodied mind or will be the author of the conduct or the harm in order to render him liable? Is it enough that the person made the appropriate bodily movements? Or is it required that he did so when possessed of a certain capacity of control and with a certain knowledge or intention? Or that he caused the harm or stood in some other relationship to it, or to the actual doer of the deed? The legal rules, or parts of legal rules, that answer these various questions define the various forms of connexion which are adequate for liability, and these constitute conditions of legal responsibility which form only a part of the total conditions of liability for punishment, which also include the definitions of the *actus reus* of the various crimes.

We may therefore summarize this long discussion of legal liability-responsibility by saying that, though in certain general contexts legal responsibility and legal liability have the same meaning, to say that a man is legally responsible for some act or harm is to state that his connexion with the act or harm is sufficient according to law for liability. Because responsibility and liability are distinguishable in this way, it will make sense to say that because a person is legally responsible for some action he is liable to be punished for it.

Legal Liability Responsibility and Moral Blame

My previous account of legal liability-responsibility, in which I claimed that in one important sense to say that a person is legally responsible meant that he was legally liable for punishment or could be made to pay compensation, has been criticized on two scores. Since these criticisms apply equally to the above amended version of my original account, in which I distinguish the general issue of liability from the narrower issue of responsibility, I shall consider these criticisms here. The first criticism, made by Mr. A. W. B. Simpson,[3] insists on the strong connexion between statements of legal responsibility and moral judgment, and claims that even lawyers tend to confine statements that a person is legally responsible for something to cases where he is considered morally blameworthy, and, where this is not so, tend to use the expression "liability" rather than "responsibility." But, though moral blame and legal responsibility may be connected in some ways, it is surely not in this simple way. Against any such view not only is there the frequent use already mentioned of the expressions "strict responsibility" and "vicarious responsibility," which are obviously independent of moral blameworthiness, but there is the more important fact that we can, and frequently do, intelligibly debate the question whether a mentally disordered or very young person who has been held legally responsible for a crime is morally blameworthy. The coincidence of legal responsibility with moral blameworthiness may be a laudable ideal, but it is not a necessary truth nor even an accomplished fact.

The suggestion that the statement that a man is responsible generally means that he is blameworthy and not that he is liable to punishment is said to be supported by the fact that it is possible to cite, without redundancy, the fact that a person is responsible as a ground or reason for saying that he is liable to punishment. But, if the various kinds or senses of responsibility are distinguished, it is plain that there are many explanations of this last mentioned fact, which are quite independent of any essential connexion between legal responsibility and moral blameworthiness. Thus cases where the statement that the man is responsible constitutes a reason for saying that he is liable to punishment may be cases of role-responsibility (the master is legally responsible for the safety of his ship, therefore he is liable to punishment if he loses it) or capacity-responsibility (he was responsible for his actions therefore he is liable to punishment for his crimes); or they may even be statements of liability-responsibility, since such statements refer to part only of the conditions of liability and may therefore be given, without redundancy, as a reason for liability to punishment. In any case this criticism may be turned against the suggestion that responsibility is to be equated with moral blameworthiness; for plainly the statement that someone is responsible may be given as part of the reason for saying that he is morally blameworthy.

Liability Responsibility for Particular Actions

An independent objection is the following, made by Mr. George Pitcher.[4] The wide extension I have claimed for the notion of liability-responsibility permits us to say not only that a man is legally responsible in this sense for the consequences of his action, but also for his action or actions. According to Mr. Pitcher "this is an improper way of talking," though common amongst philosophers. Mr. Pitcher is concerned primarily with moral, not legal, responsibility, but even in a moral context it is plain that there is a very well established use of the expression "responsible for his actions" to refer to capacity-responsibility for which Mr. Pitcher makes no allowance. As far as the law is concerned, many examples may be cited from both sides of the Atlantic where a person may be said to be responsible for his actions, or for his act, or for his crime, or for his conduct. Mr. Pitcher gives, as a reason for saying that it is improper to speak of a man being responsible for his own actions, the fact that a man does not produce or cause his own actions. But this argument would prove far too much. It would rule out as improper not only the expression "responsible for his actions," but also our saying that a man was responsible vicariously or otherwise for harmful outcomes which he had not caused, which is a perfectly well established legal usage.

None the less, there are elements of truth in Mr Pitcher's objection. First, it seems to be the case that even where a man is said to be legally responsible for what he has done, it is rare to find this expressed by a phrase conjoining the verb of action with the expression "responsible for." Hence, "he is legally responsible for killing her" is not usually found, whereas "he is legally responsible for her death" is common, as are the expressions "legally responsible for his act (in killing her);" "legally responsible for his crime;" or, as in the official formulation of the M'Naghten Rules, "responsible for his actions or omissions in doing or being a party to the killing." These common expressions in which a noun, not a verb, follows the phrase "responsible for" are grammatically similar to statements of causal responsibility, and the tendency to use the same form no doubt shows how strongly the overtones of causal responsibility influence the terminology ordinarily used to make statements of liability-responsibility. There is, however, also in support of Mr. Pitcher's view, the point already cited that, even in legal writing, where a person is said to be responsible for his act or his conduct, the relevant mental element is usually the question of insanity or immaturity, so that the ground in such cases for the assertion that the person is responsible or is not responsible for his act is the presence or absence of "responsibility for actions" in the sense of capacity-responsibility, and not merely the presence or absence of knowledge or intention in relation to the particular act.

Moral Liability-Responsibility

How far can the account given above of legal liability-responsibility be applied *mutatis mutandis* to moral responsibility? The *mutanda* seem to be the following: "deserving blame" or "blameworthy" will have to be substituted for "liable to punishment," and "morally bound to make amends or pay compensation" for "liable to be made to pay compensation." Then the moral counterpart to the account given of legal liability-responsibility would be the following: to say that a person is morally responsible for something he has done or for some harmful outcome of his own or others' conduct, is to say that he is morally blameworthy, or morally obliged to make amends for the harm, so far as this depends on certain conditions: these conditions relate to the character or extent of a man's control over his own conduct, or to the causal or other connexion between his action and harmful occurrences, or to his relationship with the person who actually did the harm.

In general, such an account of the meaning of "morally responsible" seems correct, and the striking differences between legal and moral responsibility are due to substantive differences between the content of legal and moral rules and principles rather than to any variation in meaning of responsibility when conjoined with the word "moral" rather than "legal." Thus, both in the legal and the moral case, the criteria of responsibility seem to be restricted to the psychological elements involved in the control of conduct, to causal or other connexions between acts and harm, and to the relationships with the actual doer of misdeeds. The interesting differences between legal and moral responsibility arise from the differences in the particular criteria falling under these general heads. Thus a system of criminal law may make responsibility strict, or even absolute, not even exempting very young children or the grossly insane from punishment; or it may vicariously punish one man for what another has done, even though the former had no control of the latter; or it may punish an individual or make him compensate another for harm which he neither intended nor could have foreseen as likely to arise from his conduct. We may condemn such a legal system which extends strict or vicarious responsibility in these ways as barbarous or unjust, but there are no conceptual barriers to be overcome in speaking of such a system as a legal system, though it is certainly arguable that we should not speak of "punishment" where liability is vicarious or strict. In the moral case, however, greater conceptual barriers exist: the hypothesis that we might hold individuals morally blameworthy for doing things which they could not have avoided doing, or for things done by others over whom they had no control, conflicts with too many of the central features of the idea of morality to be treated merely as speculation about a rare or inferior kind of moral system. It may be an exaggeration to say that there could not logically be such a morality or that blame administered according to principles of strict or vicarious responsibility, even in a minority of cases, could not logically be moral blame; none the less, admission of such a system as a morality would require a profound modification in our present concept of morality, and there is no similar requirement in the case of law.

Some of the most familiar contexts in which the expression "responsibility" appears confirm these general parallels between legal and moral liability-responsibility. Thus in the famous question "Is moral responsibility compatible with determinism?" the expression "moral responsibility" is apt just because the bogey raised by determinism specifically relates to the usual criteria of responsibility; for it opens the question whether, if "determinism" were true, the capacities of human beings to control their conduct would still exist or could be regarded as adequate to justify moral blame.

In less abstract or philosophical contexts, where there is a present question of blaming someone for some particular act, the assertion or denial that a person is morally responsible for his actions is common. But this expression is as ambiguous in the moral as in the legal case: it is most frequently used to refer to what I have termed "capacity-responsibility," which is the most important criterion of moral liability-responsibility; but in some contexts it may also refer to moral liability-responsibility itself. Perhaps the most frequent use in moral contexts of the expression "responsible for" is in cases where persons are said to be morally responsible for the outcomes or results of morally wrong conduct, although Mr. Pitcher's claim that men are never said in ordinary usage to be responsible for their actions is, as I have attempted to demonstrate above with counter-examples, an exaggerated claim.

Capacity-Responsibility

In most contexts, as I have already stressed, the expression "he is responsible for his actions" is used to assert that a person has certain normal capacities. These constitute the most important criteria of moral liability-responsibility, though it is characteristic of most legal systems that they have given only a partial or tardy recognition to all these capacities as general criteria of legal responsibility. The capacities in question are those of understanding, reasoning, and control of conduct: the ability to understand what conduct legal rules or morality require, to deliberate and reach decisions concerning these requirements, and to conform to decisions when made. Because "responsible for his actions" in this sense refers not to a legal status but to certain complex psychological characteristics of persons, a person's responsibility for his actions may intelligibly be said to be "diminished" or "impaired" as well as altogether absent, and persons may be said to be 'suffering from diminished responsibility' much as a wounded man may be said to be suffering from a diminished capacity to control the movements of his limbs.

No doubt the most frequent occasions for asserting or denying that a person is "responsible for his actions" are cases where questions of blame or punishment for particular actions are in issue. But, as with other expressions used to denote criteria of responsibility, this one also may be used where no particular question of blame or punishment is in issue, and it is then used simply to describe a person's psychological condition. Hence it may be said purely by way of description of some harmless inmate of a mental institution, even though there is no present question of his misconduct, that he is a person who is not responsible for his actions. No doubt if there were no social practice of blaming and punishing people for their misdeeds, and excusing them from punishment because they lack the normal capacities of understanding and control, we should lack this shorthand description for describing their condition which we now derive from these social practices. In that case we should have to describe the condition of the inmate directly, by saying that he could not understand what people told him to do, or could not reason about it, or come to, or adhere to any decisions about his conduct.

Legal systems left to themselves may be very niggardly in their admission of the relevance of liability to legal punishment of the several capacities, possession of which are necessary to render a man morally responsible for his actions. So much is evident from the history sketched in the preceding chapter of the painfully slow emancipation of English criminal law from the narrow, cognitive criteria of responsibility formulated in the M'Naghten Rules. Though some continental legal systems have been willing to confront squarely the question whether the accused "lacked the ability to recognize the wrongness of his conduct and to act in accordance with that recognition,"[5] such an issue, if taken seriously, raises formidable difficulties of proof, especially before juries. For this reason I think that, instead of a close determination of such questions of capacity, the apparently coarser-grained technique of exempting persons from liability to punishment if they fall into certain recognized categories of mental disorder is likely to be increasingly used. Such exemption by general category is a technique long known to English law; for in the case of very young children it has made no attempt to determine, as a condition of liability, the question whether on account of their immaturity they could have understood what the law required and could have conformed to its requirements, or whether their responsibility on account of their immaturity was "substantially impaired," but exempts them from liability for punishment if under a specified age. It seems likely that exemption by medical category rather than by individualized findings of absent or diminished capacity will be found more likely to lead in practice to satisfactory results, in spite of the difficulties pointed out in the last essay in the discussion of s. 60 of the Mental Health Act, 1959.

Though a legal system may fail to incorporate in its rules any psychological criteria of responsibility, and so may apply its sanction to those who are not morally blameworthy, it is none the less dependent for its efficacy on the possession by a sufficient number of those whose conduct it seeks to control of the capacities of understanding and control of conduct which constitute capacity-responsibility. For if a large proportion of those concerned could not understand what the law required them to do or could not form and keep a decision to obey, no legal system could come into existence or continue to exist. The general possession of such capacities is therefore a condition of the *efficacy* of law, even though it is not made a condition of liability to legal sanctions. The same condition of efficacy attaches to all attempts to regulate or control human conduct by forms of *communication*: such as orders, commands, the invocation of moral or other rules or principles, argument, and advice.

"The notion of prevention through the medium of the mind assumes mental ability adequate to restraint." This was clearly seen by Bentham and by Austin, who perhaps influenced the seventh report of the Criminal Law Commissioners of 1833 containing this sentence. But they overstressed the point; for they wrongly assumed that this condition of efficacy must also be incorporated in legal rules as a condition of liability. This mistaken assumption is to be found not only in the explanation of the doctrine of *mens rea* given in Bentham's and Austin's works, but is explicit in the Commissioners' statement preceding the sentence quoted above that "the object of penal law being the prevention of wrong, the principle does not extend to mere involuntary acts or even to harmful consequences the result of inevitable accident." The case of morality is however different in precisely this respect: the possession by those to whom its injunctions are addressed of "mental ability adequate to restraint" (capacity-responsibility) has there a double status and importance. It is not only a condition of the efficacy of morality; but a system or practice which did not regard the possession of these capacities as a necessary condition of liability, and so treated blame as appropriate even in the case of those who lacked them, would not, as morality is at present understood, be a morality. . . .

NOTES

1. H. L. A. Hart, *Punishment and Responsibility* (Clarendon Press, Oxford) 1968, pp. 264–5.
2. *A History of The Criminal Law*, Vol. II, p. 183.
3. In a review of "Changing Conceptions & Responsibility," Chap. VIII, *supra*, in *Crim. L. R.* (1966) 124.
4. In "Hart on Action and Responsibility," *The Philosophical Review* (1960), p. 266.
5. German Criminal Code, Art. 51.

▷ COMPUTING AND ACCOUNTABILITY

Helen Nissenbaum

A teacher stands before her sixth-grade class demanding to know who shot the spitball in her ear. She threatens punishment for the whole class if someone does not step forward. Eyes are cast downward and nervous giggles are suppressed as a boy in the back row slowly raises his hand.

The boy in the back row has answered for his actions. We do not know whether he shot at the teacher intentionally or merely missed his true target, whether he acted alone or under goading from classmates, or even whether the spitball was in protest for an unreasonable action taken by the teacher. While all of these factors are relevant to determining a just response to the boy's action, the boy, in accepting responsibility for his action, has fulfilled the valuable social obligation of accountability.

In an increasingly computerized society, where computing, and its broad application, brings dramatic changes to our way of life, and exposes us to harms and risks, accountability is very important. A community (a society or professional community) that insists on accountability, in which agents are expected to answer for their work, signals esteem for high-quality work, and encourages diligent, responsible practices. Furthermore, where lines of accountability are maintained, they provide the foundations for just punishment as well as compensation for victims. By contrast, the absence of accountability means that no one answers for harms and risks. Insofar as they are regretted, they are seen as unfortunate accidents—consequences of a brave new technology. As with accidents due to natural disasters such as hurricanes and earthquakes, we sympathize with the victims' losses, but do not demand accountability.

This article maintains that accountability is systematically undermined in our computerized society—which, given the value of accountability to society, is a disturbing loss. While this systematic erosion of accountability is not an inevitable consequence of computerization, it is the inevitable consequence of several factors working in unison—an overly narrow conceptual understanding of accountability, a set of assumptions about the capabilities and shortcomings of computer systems, and a willingness to accept that the producers of computer systems are not, in general, fully answerable for the impacts of their products. If not addressed, this erosion of accountability will mean that computers are "out of control" in an important and disturbing way. This article attempts to explain why there is a tendency toward diminished accountability for the impacts, harms, and risks of computing, and it offers recommendations for reversing it.

My concern over accountability has grown alongside the active discussion within and about the computer profession[1] regarding the harms and risks to society posed by computers and computerized systems. These discussions appeal to computer professionals, to the corporate producers of computer systems, and to government regulators, to pay more heed to system safety and reliability in order to reduce harms and risks [1, 12–14, 17, 19, 23, 29]. Lives and well-being are increasingly dependent on computerized systems. Greater numbers of life-critical systems such as aircraft, spacecraft, other transportation vehicles, medical treatment machines, military equipment, and communications systems are controlled by computers. Increasing numbers of "quality-of-life-critical" systems, from the vast information systems (IS) supporting infrastructures of governments, corporations, and high finance, to community networks [22] and workplace systems [2], down to personal conveniences such as telephones, microwaves and toys, are controlled by computers. Consequently, lives, well-being, and quality-of-life, are vulnerable to poor system design and failure.

While this vulnerability gives compelling grounds for directing greater attention to system safety, reliability, and sound design, and for the technical strategies for overcoming shortcomings, it also indicates the need for greater accountability for failures, safety, risk, and harm. Why? Because those who are answerable for harms or risks are the most driven to prevent them. In this way, accountability serves as a powerful tool for bringing about better practices, and consequently more reliable and trustworthy systems. Accountability means there will be someone, or several people, to answer not only for the malfunctions in life-critical systems that cause or risk grave injuries and cause infrastructure and large monetary losses, but even for the malfunctions that cause individual losses of time, convenience, and contentment. Yet because of barriers generated by the contexts in which computer systems are produced, and assumptions about computing and its limitations, accountability for the harms and risks mediated by computing is becoming elusive. How does this occur? To understand how the barriers to accountability arise, some clarification of key concepts is needed.

ACCOUNTABILITY, BLAME, AND RESPONSIBILITY

For centuries, philosophers and legal scholars have sought to understand accountability and the related concepts of responsibility, blame, and liability, through definitions, prototypical cases, and sets of conditions that would capture their meanings and provide clear grounds for legal principles.[2] Take the concept of responsibility: A common denominator in most analyses of responsibility are two conditions that determine whether someone is responsible for a harm: (1) a causal condition, and (2) a mental condition. According to the causal condition a person's actions (or omissions) must have *caused* the harm; according to the mental condition, the person must have *intended* (decided), or *willed* the harm.[3] For example, a person who intentionally installs the Explode virus on her employer's computer is responsible for extensive damage to files because her *intentional* actions were *causally* responsible for the damage.

The concepts of accountability, liability, and blame, extend somewhat farther than the scope of the two preceding conditions. Take for example, the mental condition. Blame for harm is not limited to cases in which an individual willed, or intended it. Recall the case of Robert Morris's Internet Worm. Although the widespread harm it caused was a result of an unintended bug in Morris's code, few were willing to exonerate Robert Morris on the grounds that he had not directly intended the harm he, in fact, wrought. This case illustrates how the mental condition can be weakened to include even unintended harm, if the harm is brought about through negligence, carelessness, or recklessness. In general, if a person fails to take precautions of which he is capable, and that any reasonable person with normal capacities would have taken in those circumstances, then he is not excused from blame merely because he did not intend the outcome. We refer to this generalized version of the mental condition, which includes intent to harm, as well as negligence and recklessness, as "the fault condition" [5].

The causal condition, too, can be weakened to cover cases in which an agent's actions were not *the* cause, but merely one significant causal factor among a number of others. For example, we may blame a person whose actions, in conjunction with those of another, causes harm. We may even blame a person who causes injury while acting under someone else's orders. These variations on the two conditions, though truer to realistic notions of blame and responsibility, make drawing lines difficult. In an actual case, a judgment over whether an individual is blameworthy can depend on numerous factors particular to that case.

Responsibility and blameworthiness are only a part of what is covered when we apply the robust and intuitive notion of accountability—the notion exemplified by the boy in the back row "stepping forward." When we say someone is accountable for a harm, we may also mean that he or she is liable to punishment (e.g., must pay a fine, be censured by a professional organization, go to jail), or is liable to compensate a victim (usually by paying damages). In most actual cases these different strands of responsibility, censure, and compensation converge because those who are to blame for harms are usually those who must "pay" in some way or other for them. There are some important exceptions, including for example, the case of parents who must answer for injuries caused by their children's reckless behavior, or insurance companies who must cover damages caused by their clients. Strict liability is another. In its bearing on the goal of maintaining accountability in a computerized society, strict liability is of great importance.

To be strictly liable for a harm is to be liable to compensate for it even though one did not bring it about through faulty action. (In other words, one "pays for" the harm even though the fault condition is not satisfied.) This form of liability, which is found in the legal codes of most countries, typically applies to the producers of mass-produced consumer goods, to the producers of potentially harmful goods, and to owners of "ultrahazardous" property. For example, even if they have taken a normal degree of care, milk producers are strictly liable for illness caused by spoiled milk; owners of dangerous animals (for example, tigers in a circus) are strictly liable for injuries caused by escaped animals even if they have taken precautions to restrain them. Although critics of strict liability argue that it is unjust—because people are made to pay for harms that were not their fault—supporters respond that strict liability is nevertheless justified because it contributes significantly to the good of society. It serves a paramount public interest in protecting society from potentially harmful or hazardous goods and property, and provides incentive to sellers of consumer products and owners of potentially hazardous property to take *extraordinary* care. It assures compensation for victims by placing the risk on those best able to pay, and those best able to guard against the harm. And it reduces the cost of litigation by eliminating the onerous task of proving fault.

FOUR BARRIERS TO ACCOUNTABILITY

Accountability is obscured when we apply these conceptual understandings to the types of contexts in which computer systems are produced, combined with commonly held views about the nature of computing—both its capabilities and limitations. The barriers I will discuss are: 1) The problem of "many hands"—because computer systems are created predominantly in organizational settings, 2) Bugs—because bugs not only cause problems but commonly are conceived of as a fact of programming life, 3) The computer as scapegoat—because it can be convenient to blame a computer for harms or injuries, and 4) Ownership without liability—because in the clamor to assert rights of ownership over software, the responsibilities of ownership are neglected. These barriers to accountability can lead to harms and risks for which no one is answerable and about which nothing is done.

1. The Problem of Many Hands. Most computer systems in use today are the products not of single programmers working in isolation, but of groups, collectives, or corporations. They are produced by teams of diverse individuals, that might include designers, engineers, programmers, writers, psychologists, graphic artists, managers, and salespeople. Consequently, when a system gives rise to harm, the task of assigning responsibility, the problem of identifying who is accountable, is exacerbated and obscured because responsibility, characteristically understood in terms of a single individual, does not easily generalize to collective action. In other words, while our conceptual understanding of accountability directs us in search of "the one" who must step forward (for example, the boy in the back row answering for the spitball), collective action presents a challenge.

Where a mishap is the work of "many hands," it can be difficult to identify who is accountable because the locus of decision making (the "mental condition") is frequently different from the mishap's most direct causal antecedent; that is, cause and intent do not converge. Take for example, a bad course of action taken by a political leader, which was based on the word of a trusted adviser. Although the action is taken by the leader, the adviser's word has been a decisive factor. How do we figure the adviser's role into the question of accountability? Further, with the collective actions characteristic of corporate and government hierarchies, decisions and causes themselves are fractured. Boards of directors, task forces, or committees, make decisions jointly, sometimes according to a majority vote. It is the collective efforts of a team that give rise to a product. When high-level decisions work their way down from boards of directors to managers, from managers to employees, ultimately translating into actions and consequences, it is difficult to trace precisely the source of a given problem. As a result, the connection between outcome and the one who is accountable is difficult to make. The problem of many hands is not unique to computing but plagues other technologies, big business, government, and the military [4, 5, 11, 26, 28].

Computing is vulnerable to the obstacles of many hands because, first, as noted earlier, most software systems in use are produced in institutional settings, whether in small and middle-sized software development companies, or large corporations, government agencies and contractors, or educational institutions. (Some cynics argue that institutional structures are designed precisely to avoid accountability.) Second, computer systems themselves—usually not monolithic—are constructed out of segments, or modules. Some systems include code from earlier versions, while others borrow code from different systems entirely. When systems grow in this way, sometimes reaching huge and complex proportions, there may be no single individual who grasps the whole system, or keeps track of all the individuals who have contributed to its various components (See [10, 29]). Third, performance in a wide array of mundane and specialized computer-controlled machines—from rocket ships to refrigerators—depends on the symbiotic relationship of machine with computer system. When things go wrong, it can be difficult to discern whether the call goes to the manufacturers of the machine or to the producers of the computer software.

To see the problem of many hands in action, recall the case of the Therac-25, a striking example of the way many hands can obscure accountability, and at the same time a stark reminder of the practical importance of accountability. In a series of mishaps, now quite familiar to the computer community, the Therac-25, a computer-controlled radiation treatment machine, massively overdosed patients in six known incidents. (The primary sources for my discussion are Leveson and Turner's excellent and detailed account [13] and an earlier paper by Jacky [9].) These overdoses, which occurred over a two-year period from 1985 to 1987, caused severe radiation burns which in turn caused death in three cases, and irreversible injuries (one minor, two very serious) in the other three. Built by Atomic Energy of Canada Limited (AECL), the Therac-25 was the further development in a line of medical linear accelerators which destroy cancerous tumors by irradiating them with accelerated electrons and X-ray photons. Computer controls were far more prominent in the Therac-25, both because the machine had been designed from the ground up with computer controls in mind, and because the safety of the machine was largely left to software. Whereas earlier models had included hardware safety mechanisms and interlocks, designers of the Therac-25 did not duplicate software safety mechanisms with hardware equivalents.

The origin of the malfunction was traced not to a single source, but to numerous faults, including (among others) at least two significant software coding errors ("bugs"), and a faulty microswitch. The impact of these faults was exacerbated by the absence of hardware interlocks, obscure error messages, inadequate testing and quality assurance, exaggerated claims about the reliability of the system in AECL's safety analysis, and, in at least two cases, negligence on the parts of the hospitals where treatment was administered. In one instance monitors enabling technicians to observe patients receiving treatment were not operating at the time of malfunction; in another, the clinic kept poor treatment records. Aside from the important lessons in safety engineering that the case of Therac-25 provides, it offers a lesson in accountability—or rather the breakdown of accountability due to "many hands."

If we apply standard conceptions of accountability to identify who should step forward and answer for the injuries, we see an intricate web of causes and decisions. Since we can safely rule out intentional wrongdoing, we must try to identify causal agents who were also negligent or reckless. If none can be identified, we conclude that the mishaps were truly accidental, that no one is responsible, no one is to blame. First, consider the causal antecedents: AECL designers, safety engineers, programmers, machinists, corporate executives, hospital administrators, physicians, physicists, and technicians. Since each group bore a significant causal relationship to the existence and character of the machine, it is reasonable to examine their relationship to the malfunction, the massive overdoses, deaths and injuries. The machine technicians, who entered the doses and push buttons, are the most direct causal antecedents. The others are more distant. In one of the most chilling anecdotes, a machine technician is supposed to have responded to the agonized cries from a patient by flatly denying that it was possible he had been burned.

Although the machine technicians are most closely causally linked to the outcomes, they are not necessarily accountable. The second condition on responsibility directs the search to faulty action (the fault condition). According to Leveson and Turner's account, which spotlights the work of software engineers and quality assurance personnel, there is evidence of inadequate software engineering and testing practices, as well as a failure in the extent of corporate response to signs of a problem. The safety analysis was faulty in that it systematically overestimated the system's reliability, and evidently did not consider the role software failure could play in derailing the system as a whole. Computer code from earlier Therac models was used on the Therac-25 system and assumed unproblematic because no similar injuries had resulted. Further investigation showed that although the problems had always been present, because earlier models had included mechanical interlocks, they simply had not surfaced.

The practical implications of diminished accountability are tragically clear in the deaths and injuries at six different locations where Therac-25 accelerators were used. Until the physicist Fritz Hager, at Tyler Hospital, Tyler, East Texas took it upon himself to trace the source of one of the more serious problems, and many months later, the FDA stepped in, insisting on a regimen of upgrades and improvements, early responses to reports of problems were lackluster. AECL was slow to react to requests to check the machine, understand the problem, or to remediate (for example by installing an independent hardware safety system). Even after a patient filed a lawsuit in 1985 citing hospital, manufacturer, and service organization as responsible for her injuries, AECL's follow up was negligible. For example, no special effort was made to inform other clinics operating Therac-25 machines about the mishaps. (Because the lawsuit was settled out of court, we do not learn how the law would have attributed liability.)

In sum, the Therac-25, a complex computer-controlled system, whose malfunction caused severe injury, provides an example of the way many hands can lead to an obscuring of accountability. Because no individual was both an obvious causal antecedent and decision maker, it was difficult, at least on the face of it, to identify who should have stepped forward and assumed responsibility. Collective action of this type provides excuses at all levels, from those low down in the hierarchy who are "only following orders," to top-ranking decision makers who are only distantly linked to the outcomes.

We should not, however, confuse the *obscuring* of accountability due to collective action, with the *absence* of blameworthiness. Even Leveson and Turner, whose detailed analysis of the Therac-25 mishaps sheds light on both the technical aspects as well as the procedural elements of the case, appear unwilling to probe the question of accountability. They refer to the malfunctions and injuries as "accidents" and say they do not wish "to criticize the manufacturer of the equipment or anyone else." [13] Contrary to Leveson and Turner's own assessment of what they were doing, in identifying inadequate software engineering practices and corporate response, I think their analysis produces at the very least an excellent starting place for attributing accountability. If we consistently respond to complex cases by not pursuing blame and responsibility, we are effectively accepting agentless mishaps and a general erosion of accountability.

2. Bugs. To say that bugs in software make software unreliable and can cause systems to fail and be unsafe is to state the obvious. However, it is not quite as obvious how the way we think about bugs affects considerations of accountability. (I use the term "bug" to cover a variety of types of software errors including modelling, design, and coding errors.) The inevitability of bugs escapes very few computer users and programmers and their pervasiveness is stressed by most software, and especially safety, engineers. The dictum, "There is always another software bug," [13] especially in the long and complex systems controlling life-critical and quality-of-life-critical technologies, captures this fact of programming life. Errors in complex functional computer systems are an inevitable presence in ambitious systems [3]. Many agree with the claim that "errors are more common, more pervasive, and more troublesome, in software than in other technologies," and that even skilled program reviewers are apt to miss flaws in programs [19]. Even when we factor out sheer incompetence, bugs in significant number are endemic to programming. They are the natural hazards of any substantial system.

While this way of thinking about bugs exposes the vulnerability of complex systems, it also creates a problematic mind-set for accountability. On the one hand the standard conception of responsibility directs us to the person who either intentionally or by not taking reasonable care causes harm. On the other, the view of bugs as inevitable hazards of programming implies that while harms and inconveniences caused by bugs are regrettable, they cannot—except in cases of obvious sloppiness—be helped. In turn, this implies that it is unreasonable to hold programmers, systems engineers and designers, accountable for imperfections in their systems.

Parallels from other areas of technology can perhaps clarify the contrast that I am trying to draw between cases of failures for which one holds the protagonists accountable, and frequently blameworthy, and cases where—despite the failures—one tends not to hold anyone accountable. As an example of the former, consider the case of the space shuttle *Challenger*. Following an inquiry into the *Challenger's* explosion, critics found fault with NASA and Morton-Thiokol because several engineers, aware of the limitations of the O-rings, had conveyed to management the strong possibility of failure under cold-weather launch-conditions. We held NASA executives accountable, and judged their actions as reckless, because despite this knowledge, and the presence of cold-weather conditions, they went ahead with the space shuttle launch.

In contrast, consider an experience that was common during construction of several of the great suspension bridges of the late 19th century, such as the St. Louis and Brooklyn Bridges. During construction, hundreds of bridge workers succumbed to a mysterious disease, then referred to as "the bends," or "caisson disease."[4] Although the working conditions and inadequate response from medical staff were responsible for the disease, we cannot assign blame for the harm suffered by the workers or find any individual or distinct group accountable, such as the bridge companies, their chief engineers, or even their medical staff, because the causes and treatments were beyond the scope of medical science of their day.

For these suspension bridges, it was necessary to sink caissons deep underwater in order to set firm foundations—preferably in bedrock—for their enormous towers. Upon emerging from the caissons, workers would erratically develop an array of symptoms which might include dizziness, double vision, severe pain in torso and limbs, profuse perspiration, internal bleeding, convulsions, repeated vomiting, and swollen and painful joints. For some, the symptoms would pass after a matter of hours or days, while for others symptoms persisted and they were left permanently crippled. Others died. While doctors who treated these workers understood that these symptoms were related to exposure to the highly pressured air, they could not accurately pinpoint the causes of "the bends." They offered a variety of explanations; newness to the job, poor nutrition, overindulgence in alcohol. They tried assigning caisson work only to those whom they judged to be in "prime" physical shape, reducing the time spent in the caissons, and even outfitting workers with bands of zinc and silver about their wrists, arms, and ankles, all to no avail.

We have since learned that this "decompression sickness" is a condition brought on by moving too rapidly from an atmosphere of compressed air to normal atmospheric conditions. It is easily prevented by greatly slowing the rate of decompression. Ironically, a steam elevator that had been installed in both the Brooklyn Bridge and St. Louis Bridge caissons, as a means of alleviating discomfort for bridge workers so they would not have to make the long and arduous climb up spiral staircases, made things all the more dangerous. Nowadays, for a project in the same scope as the Brooklyn Bridge, a decompression chamber would surely be provided as a means of controlling the rate of decompression. Bridge companies not following the recommended procedures today would certainly be held blameworthy for any harms and risks.

What is the relation of these two examples to the way we conceive of bugs? Conceiving of bugs as an inevitable byproduct of programming would encourage a judgment of bug-related failures similar to the harms discussed in "the bends" example—inevitable, albeit unfortunate, consequences of a glorious new technology for which we hold no one accountable. The problem with this conception of bugs, is that it creates a barrier to recognizing the cases of bug-related failure that more closely parallels the *Challenger*, in which we recognize wrongdoing and therefore expect someone to "step forward" and be answerable. An explicitly more discerning approach to bugs would better enable us to discriminate the "natural hazards," the ones that are present despite great efforts and adherence to the highest standards of contemporary practice, from those that, with effort and good practice, could have been avoided. Finally, if this distinction cannot be drawn, then someone might reasonably suggest that, given the potential hazard and inevitability of bugs, the field of computing may not yet be ready for the various uses to which it is being put. This is an issue that computer professionals along with policy makers ought to seriously address.

3. "It's the Computer's Fault": The Computer as Scapegoat. It is likely that most of us have experienced the bank clerk explaining an error, the ticket agent excusing lost bookings, the students justifying a late paper, by blaming the computer. But while the practice of blaming a computer, on the face of it, appears reasonable and even felicitous, it is a barrier to accountability because, having found one explanation for an error or injury, the further role and responsibility of human agents may be underestimated.

Let us try to understand why, in the first place, blaming a computer appears plausible by applying the conceptual analysis of blame discussed earlier: cause and fault. Consider first the causal condition: Computer systems frequently function as mediators of interactions between machines and humans, and between one human and another. This means, first, that human actions are distanced from their causal impacts, including harms and injuries, and second, the computer's action is the more direct causal antecedent. Thus the first condition on blameworthiness is satisfied by the computer. But causal proximity is not sufficient. We do not, for example, excuse a murderer on grounds that it was the bullet entering the victim's head and not he who was directly responsible for the victim's death.

The mental condition must be satisfied too. Here, computers present a curious challenge and temptation. As distinct from many other inanimate objects, computers perform tasks previously performed by humans in positions of responsibility. They calculate, decide, control, and remember. For this reason, and perhaps even more deeply rooted psychological reasons [27], people attribute to computers and not to other inanimate objects (like bullets) the array of mental properties, such as intentions, desires, thought, preferences, that make humans responsible for their actions. Where a loan adviser approves a loan to an applicant who subsequently defaults on the loan, or a doctor prescribes the wrong antibiotic and a patient dies, or an intensive care attendant incorrectly assesses the prognosis for an accident victim and denies the patient a respirator, we hold accountable the loan adviser, the doctors, and the attendant. Now replace these human agents with the computerized loan adviser, the expert systems (ES) MYCIN and APACHE (a computer system that predicts a patient's chance of survival [6]). While on the face of it, it may seem reasonable to associate the blame with the *functions* even though they are now performed by computer systems and not humans, the result of not working out alternative lines of accountability means ultimately a loss of accountability for that function. (For other discussions and proposed solutions see [11, 16, 24].)

We can fairly easily explain some of the cases in which people blame computers. In the first place there are cases in which an agent, by blaming a computer, is obviously shirking responsibility. In the second place, there are cases in which an agent cites a computer because he is genuinely perplexed about who is responsible. For example, when an airline reservation system apparently malfunctions, it may be that accountability is already so obscured that the computer is indeed the most salient agent. In these cases, the computer serves as a stopgap for something elusive, the one who is, or should be, accountable. In the remaining cases, in which computers perform functions previously performed by humans who were held accountable for their actions, we need to rescue accountability. It is important that the ethical issue of who is accountable not hang in the balance on an answer to the metaphysical question of whether computers really decide, calculate, intend, and think. We need to adjust the lines of accountability to identify other humans who will be accountable for the impacts of these systems.

4. Ownership without Liability. The issue of property rights over computer software has sparked active and vociferous public debate. Should program code, algorithms, user interface ("look-and-feel"), or any other aspects of software be privately ownable? If yes, what is the appropriate form and degree of ownership—trade secrets, patents, copyright, or a new (*sui generis*) form of ownership devised specifically for software? Should software be held in private ownership at all? Some have clamored for software patents, arguing that protecting a strong right of ownership in software, permitting owners and authors to "reap rewards," is the most just course. Others urge social policies that would place software in the public domain, while still others have sought explicitly to balance owners' rights with broader and longer-term social interests and the advancement of computer science [18, 20, 25]. Significantly absent in these debates is any reference to owners' responsibilities.[5]

While ownership implies a bundle of rights, it also implies responsibilities. Along with the privileges of ownership comes responsibility. If a tree branch on private property falls and injures a person under it, if a pet Doberman escapes and bites a passerby, its owners are accountable. Holding owners responsible makes sense from a perspective of social welfare because owners are typically in the best position to directly control their property. In the case of software, its owners (usually the producers) are in the best position to directly affect the quality of the software they release to the public. Yet the trend in the software industry is to demand maximal property protection while denying, to the extent possible, accountability.

This is expressed in, for example, the license agreements that accompany almost all mass-produced consumer software which usually includes a section detailing the producers' rights, and another negating accountability. Accordingly, the consumer merely licenses a copy of the software application and is subject to various limitations on use and access to it. The disclaimers of liability are equally explicit: "In no event will Danz Development Corporation, or its officers, employees, or affiliates be liable to you for any consequential, incidental, or indirect damages . . .";

"Apple makes no warranty or representation, either expressed or implied, with respect to software, its quality, performance, merchantability, or fitness for a particular purpose. As a result, this software is sold 'as is,' and you, the purchaser are assuming the entire risk as to its quality and performance." The Apple disclaimer goes on to say, "In no event will Apple be liable for direct, indirect, special, incidental, or consequential damages resulting from any defect in the software or its documentation, even if advised of the possibility of such damages."

MAINTAINING ACCOUNTABILITY IN A COMPUTERIZED SOCIETY— RECOMMENDATIONS

An underlying premise of this article—and one I hope is shared with readers—is that accountability, and the responsible practice of computing, are social values worth sustaining and when necessary, rehabilitating. We have seen how features of the organizational contexts in which computer systems and computerized systems are created, and broadly held views about the power and limitations of computing can erode accountability for risks and injuries; namely, many hands, bugs, computers-as-scapegoat, and ownership without liability. Rehabilitating accountability in a computerized society does not, however, imply an obsession with pinning the blame on someone, or an insistence that someone be punished no matter what. Rather, it recommends an approach to harms, injuries, and risks, that is cognizant of the contexts and assumptions that are apt to obscure accountability. We should hold on to the assumption that someone is accountable, unless after careful investigation, we conclude that the malfunction in question is, indeed, no one's fault.

Beyond this general approach to rehabilitating accountability, I propose three specific lines of approach to promote accountability—one conceptual, the other two practical. The recommendations are addressed to the professional community—those actively engaged in the computing profession, their professional organizations, and the institutions that educate them. They are addressed also to policy makers, and to all of us living in this increasingly computerized society. With lines of accountability recovered, responsibility for the impacts of computing will, we hope, become as clear to the computing profession and the rest of society, as to the boy in the back row taking the first step forward toward accountability.

1. Keep Accountability Distinct from Liability to Compensate. The problem of many hands is profound and unlikely to yield easily to any general, or slick, solution. Greater success, at least for the present, is likely to come from careful case-by-case analysis, in which accountability is determined according to the details of a specific situation. A good system of liability offers a *partial* solution because, while we wrestle with the conceptual puzzles of blame and accountability, at least the needs of victims are being addressed.

Liability, however, is not the same as accountability. It ought not be accepted as a substitute for it because this would further obscure accountability. Liability is grounded in the plight of a victim. Its extent, usually calculated in terms of a sum of money, is determined by the degree of injury and damage suffered by the victim. For example, when harm is the result of collective action, because the weight of compensation can be shared, its burden on each agent is considerably eased. Furthermore, since compensation is victim-centered, identifying one satisfactory source of compensation lets others "off the hook." By contrast, accountability is grounded in the nature of the action, and the relationship of the agent to an outcome. (Recall the causal and fault conditions.) If several individuals are collectively responsible, we hold each fully accountable because many hands ought not make the burden of accountability light. Further, holding one individual accountable does not let others off the hook because several individuals may all be fully accountable for a harm.[6] From the general annals of engineering ethics, the fatal calculation of Ford executives in which they offset the value of life and injury against the cost of improving the Pinto's design, we see an example in which considerations of liability were primary. Had they been thinking about accountability to society and not merely liability, they would surely have reached a different conclusion.

2. Clarify and Vigorously Promote a Substantive Standard of Care. A growing literature, including several of the articles cited earlier (for example, [13, 19]) discusses guidelines for producing safer and more reliable computer systems. Among these guidelines is a call for simpler design, a modular approach to system building, formal analysis of modules as well as the whole, meaningful quality assurance, independent auditing, built-in redundancy, and excellent documentation. If such guidelines were to evolve into a standard of care, taken seriously by the computing profession, promulgated through educational institutions, urged by professional organizations, and even enforced through licensing or accreditation (a controversial issue), better and safer systems would be the direct result. Another result of a standard of care would be a nonarbitrary means of determining accountability. The standard of care provides a tool to distinguish between malfunctions (bugs) due to inadequate practices and those that occur in spite of a programmer or designer's best efforts. A standard of care offers a tool for distinguishing analogs of the failure to alleviate the bends in nineteenth century bridge workers from analogs of the *Challenger* space shuttle. For example, had the guidelines discussed by Leveson and Turner been known at the time the Therac-25 was created, we would have been able to conclude that the developers of the system were accountable for the injuries. In not meeting these standards they were negligent.

A standard of care could also be of benefit to systems engineers working within large organizations. It would provide an explicit measure of excellence that functions independently of pressures imposed by the organizational hierarchy.

3. Impose Strict Liability for Defective Consumer-Oriented Software, as Well as for Software Whose Impact on Society and Individuals Is Great. Strict liability would shift the burden-of-accountability to the producers of defective software and thereby would address an anomaly (perhaps even a paradox) in our current system of liability. We have seen, on the one hand, that strict liability is a way of assuring that the public is protected against the potential harms of risky artifacts and property. On the other hand, while the prevailing lore portrays computer systems as prone to error in a degree surpassing most other technologies, most producers of software explicitly deny accountability for harmful impacts of their products, even when they malfunction. Software seems, therefore, to be *precisely* the type of artifact for which strict liability is necessary—assuring compensation for victims, and sending an emphatic message to producers of software to take *extra*ordinary care to produce safe and reliable systems.

CONCLUSION

In the twentieth century B.C. the Code of Hammurabi declared that if a house collapsed and killed its owner, the builder of the house was to be put to death. In the twentieth century A.D. many builders of computer software would deny responsibility and pass the "entire risk" to the user. While the centuries have placed a distance between the harsh punishments meted out by Hammurabi's Code and contemporary legal codes, the call for accountability remains a standard worth restoring, and one whose achievement would be a source of professional pride.

NOTES

1. Here and elsewhere, I use the term "computer profession" very broadly to refer to the loose community of people who dedicate a significant proportion of their time and energy to building computer and computerized systems, and to those engaged in the science, engineering, design, and documentation of computing.
2. For excellent, and more thorough, contemporary discussions, see for example [5, 7, 8].
3. A precondition for blameworthiness, especially relevant to the legal domain, is that a person be in possession of certain mental capacities, including the capacities to distinguish right from wrong, and to control his or her actions. Since the issue of mental capacity has no bearing on computing and accountability, I will take it no further.
4. This case is drawn from David McCullough's book about the building of the Brooklyn Bridge [15].
5. For an exception see Samuelson's recent discussion of liability for defective information [21].
6. Compare this to the judge's finding in the "Red Hook Murder." Even though it was almost certainly known which one of the three accused pulled the trigger, the court viewed all three as equal and "deadly conspirators" in the death of Patrick Daley.

REFERENCES

1. Borning, A. Computer system reliability and nuclear war. *Commun. ACM 30*, 2 (1987), 112–131.
2. Clement, A. Computing at work: Empowering action by 'low-level users.' *Commun. ACM 37*, 1 (Jan. 1994).
3. Corbato, F. J. On building systems that will fail. *Commun. ACM 34*, 9 (1991), 73–81.
4. De George, R. Ethical responsibilities of engineers in large organizations: The Pinto case. In *Collective Responsibility*, L. May and S. Hoffman, Eds., 1991, Rowman and Littlefield, pp. 151–166.
5. Feinberg, J. Collective responsibility. In *Doing and Deserving*, J. Feinberg, Ed., 1970, Princeton University Press, Princeton, N.J.
6. Fitzgerald, S. *Hospital Computer Predicts Patients' Chances of Survival*. The *Miami Herald*, 1992, Miami, p. 6J.
7. Hart, H. L. A. *Punishment and Responsibility*. Clarendon Press, Oxford, 1968.

8. Hart, H. L. A. and Honore, T. *Causation and the Law*. Second ed., Clarendon Press, Oxford, 1985.

9. Jacky, J. Safety-critical computing: Hazards, practices, standards and regulations. Unpublished manuscript. University of Washington, 1989.

10. Johnson, D. G. and Mulvey, J. M. *Computer Decisions: Ethical Issues of Responsibility and Bias*. Statistics and Operations Research Series, Princeton University, 1993.

11. Ladd, J. Computers and moral responsibility: A framework for an ethical analysis. In *The Information Web: Ethical and Social Implications of Computer Networking*, C. C. Gould, Ed. Westview Press, Boulder, Colo. 1989.

12. Leveson, N. Software safety: Why, what, and how. *Comput. Surv. 18*, 2 (1986), 125–163.

13. Leveson, N. and Turner, C. An investigation of the Therac-25 accidents. *Computer 26*, 7 (1993), 18–41.

14. Littlewood, B. and Strigini, L. The risks of software. *Sci. Am.* (1992), 62–75.

15. McCullough, D. *The Great Bridge*. New York: Simon and Schuster, 1972.

16. Moor, J. What is computer ethics? *Metaphilosophy 16*, 4 (1985), 266–275.

17. Neuman, P. G. Inside RISKS. *Commun. ACM*.

18. Nissenbaum, H. Should I copy my neighbor's software? *Comput. Philos.* To be published.

19. Parnas, D., Schouwen, J. and Kwan, S. P. Evaluation of safety-critical software. *Commun. ACM 33*, 6, (1990), 636–648.

20. Samuelson, P. *Adapting Intellectual Property Law to New Technologies: A Case Study on Computer Programs*. National Research Council, 1992.

21. Samuelson, P. Liability for defective information. *Commun. ACM 36*, 1 (1993), 21–26.

22. Schuler, D. Community networks: Building a new participatory medium *Commun. ACM 37*, 1 (Jan. 1994).

23. Smith, B. The limits of correctness. Center for the study of language and information, Rep. CSLI-85-35, Stanford, 1985.

24. Snapper, J. W. Responsibility for computer-based errors. *Metaphilosophy 16* (1985), 289–295.

25. Stallman, R. M. The GNU manifesto. *GNU Emacs Manual*, 1987, 175–84.

26. Thompson, D. The moral responsibility of many hands. In *Political Ethics and Public Office*. Harvard University Press, Cambridge, Mass. 1987, pp. 40–65.

27. Turkle, S. *The Second Self*. Simon & Schuster, Inc., New York, 1984.

28. Velasquez, M. Why corporations are not morally responsible for anything they do. In *Collective Responsibility*, L. May and S. Hoffman, Eds. Rowman and Littlefield, 1991, pp. 111–131.

29. Weizenbaum, J. On the impact of the computer on society. *Science 176*, 12 (1972), 609–614.

LIABILITY FOR DEFECTIVE
ELECTRONIC INFORMATION

Pamela Samuelson

"Sticks and stones may break my bones, but words can never hurt me." This children's refrain may never have been completely true, but it has been definitively disproven now that computer program instructions control the operation of so many machines and devices in our society. Those who develop computer programs know programs often contain defects or bugs, some of which can cause economic or physical harms. Many people in the computing field are rightly concerned about what liability they or their firms might incur if a defect in software they developed injures a user.

The general public seems largely unaware of the risks of defective software. Even the popular press generally subscribes to the myth that if something is computerized, it must be better. Only certain freak software accidents ("Robot Kills Assembly Line Worker") seem to capture the mass media's attention. Within the computing field, Peter Neumann deserves much credit for heightening the field's awareness of the risks of computing through publication of the "RISKS Forum Digest." But even this focuses more on technical risks than legal risks.

It is fair to say that there have been far more injuries from defective software than litigations about defective software. Some lawsuits have been brought, of course, but they have largely been settled out of court, often on condition that the injured person keep silent about the accident, the lawsuit, and the settlement. No software developer seems to want to be the first to set the precedent by which liability rules will definitively be established for the industry.

The topic of what liability may exist when software is defective is too large to be given a full treatment in one column. But I can summarize in a sentence what the law's likely response would be to a lawsuit involving defective software embedded in machines such as airplanes, X-ray equipment, and the like: The developer is likely to be held liable if defects in the software have caused injury to a consumer's person or property; under some circumstances, the developer may also be held liable for economic losses (such as lost profits). That is, when an electronic information product behaves like a machine, the law will treat it with the same strict rules it has adopted for dealing with defective machines.

Less clear, however, is what rules will apply when software behaves more like a book than a machine. Courts have treated books differently for liability purposes than they have treated machines. They have been reluctant to impose liability on authors, publishers, and booksellers for defective information in books out of concern about the effect such liability would have on the free exchange of ideas and information. Only if erroneous statements defraud or defame a person or are negligently made by someone who claims to have superior knowledge (such as a professional) has the law imposed liability on authors, publishers, or booksellers. Whether the "no liability" rule applicable to print information providers will be extended to electronic information providers remains to be seen. There are some differences between the print world and the electronic world that may put electronic information providers at a greater risk of liability than print information providers.

AN EXAMPLE OF SOFTWARE BEHAVING
LIKE A BOOK

To explore the liability questions that may arise when software behaves like a book, I want you to imagine that a fellow named Harry wrote a computer program which he calls "Harry's Medical Home Companion." Harry works as a computer programmer for a manufacturer of medical equipment, but his avocation and deepest interest has been for many years the study of medical treatments for human diseases. He has read all the major medical textbooks used by practitioners today, as well as many books about herbal and other organic treatments used in traditional societies before the modern era.

Harry's goal is to sell his program to ordinary folk so they can readily compare what today's medical professionals and traditional societies would recommend for treatment of specific diseases. Harry believes people should be empowered to engage in more self-treatment for illnesses and that his program will aid this process by giving ordinary people knowledge about this subject. To make the program more user friendly and interesting, Harry has added some multimedia features to it, such as sound effects and computer animations to illustrate the effects of certain treatments on the human body.

Harry cannot, of course, practice medicine because he does not have a license to be a medical doctor. But that does not mean he cannot write a book or a computer program discussing treatments for various diseases, for in our society no one needs a license to be a writer or a programmer. Harry arranges for the program to be published by Lightweight Software. Lightweight intends to focus its distribution of this product initially to health food stores throughout the country.

If there is a defect in the information contained in "Harry's Medical Home Companion" on which a user relies to his or her detriment, what responsibility will Harry, Lightweight Software, or the health food store at which the user bought the program have if the injured consumer sues? (It is easy for computing professionals to imagine what kinds of errors might creep into an electronic text like Harry's program. A "0.1" might have been accidently transposed as a "1.0" or a fleck of dust on a printed page might, when processed by an optical character recognition program, cause a "1" to be recognized as a "7" which would cause the quantity of a herb or drug for use to treat a specific disease to be incorrect. Or Harry may have included some illustrations in the program, one of which turned out to be a deadly poisonous mushroom which his artist friend didn't know because she was not a trained botanist.) Interestingly, under the present state of the law, neither Harry nor the publisher nor the health food store may have much to worry about from a liability standpoint.

NO IMPLIED WARRANTY FOR INFORMATION
IN BOOKS: *CARDOZO V. TRUE*

Injured consumers have been largely unsuccessful when they have sued publishers or booksellers for breach of warranty involving defective information contained in books. Even though judges have regarded books as "goods" to which implied warranties of merchantability apply (see p. 545), they have not treated the information contained in the book as covered by these warranties. Information has instead been treated as an unwarranted part of the goods. The intangible information is treated as though it was a "service" embodied in the goods. The strong warranty rules that apply to goods do not apply to services which, of course, often include the delivery of information to the customer. (See p. 545 for a discussion on breach of warranty claims and the "goods" vs. "services" distinction.) Typical of the case law rejecting warranty liability for defective information is the *Cardozo* v. *True* case decided in Florida in 1977.

Cardozo got violently ill after she ate a piece of rare plant while preparing to cook it in accordance with a recipe in a cookbook written by True. To recover the cost of her medical expenses, she sued True and the bookstore where she bought the book. Against the bookstore, Cardozo claimed the bookseller had breached an implied warranty of merchantability (that the product was fit for the ordinary purpose for which it might be used) by failing to warn her the plant was poisonous if eaten raw.

Although finding the bookseller was a "merchant" whose books were "goods" subject to the Uniform Commercial Code's (UCC) implied warranty of merchantability rules, the court decided the implied warranty for the book only applied to its physical characteristics, such as the quality of the binding. The court regarded it as "unthinkable that standards imposed on the quality of goods sold by a merchant would require that merchant, who is a bookseller, to evaluate the thought processes of the many authors and publishers of the hundreds and often thousands of books which the merchant offers for sale." Consequently, the court affirmed dismissal of Cardozo's complaint against the bookseller.

(The issue before the court was only whether the bookseller could be liable for breach of warranty, not whether the author could be. But here is the problem with suing authors for breach of warranty when information in books is defective: The UCC only imposes implied warranty responsibilities on "merchants" of "goods" of the sort the case involves. Publishers and booksellers are "merchants" of books, and books are "goods" within the meaning of the UCC. Authors, however, are not merchants of "goods." They are at most sellers of intangible information that may later be embodied in goods when printed and bound by publishers.)

The *Cardozo* opinion is one of many in which judges have stated that publishers and booksellers cannot reasonably investigate all the information in the books they sell and should therefore not be subject to warranty liability when information in the work is defective. Judges worry that imposing a responsibility on publishers and bookstores to verify the accuracy of all information contained in the products they sell would unduly restrict the free flow of information and chill expression of ideas. It would thus be unwise as a matter of public policy. In addition, courts have feared a torrent of socially unproductive litigation if readers were able to sue publishers and bookstores whenever their expectations were disappointed after acting on information contained in books.

If the same rule is applied to "Harry's Medical Home Companion" as has been applied to purveyors of printed information, neither Harry, nor Lightweight Software, nor the health food stores that sell the program would have to worry about a lawsuit by a user of the program to recover damages for injuries resulting from defective information in the program on a breach of warranty theory.

NO STRICT LIABILITY IN TORT FOR BOOKS:
WINTER V. *PUTNAM*

There have been a number of cases in which injured consumers have asserted that publishers of books containing defective information should be held strictly liable in tort for having sold a defective product (see p. 547 on strict liability in tort). In general, these cases have not been successful.

Typical of the case law in which courts have rejected strict liability in tort claims made against publishers is *Winter* v. *G. P. Putnam's Sons* decided by a federal appellate court in California in 1991. Winter sued Putnam to recover the cost of the liver transplant he had after eating a mushroom erroneously depicted as safe for human ingestion in the Encyclopedia of Mushrooms published by Putnam. He claimed the publisher should be held strictly liable in tort or should be found negligent for publishing a book in which a poisonous mushroom was depicted as safe. The court upheld dismissal of both claims.

On the negligence claim, the court ruled the publisher had no duty to investigate the accuracy of information it published. Without a duty of care owed by the publisher to readers of the books it published, no negligence could be found. Even though authors of books may be more vulnerable to negligence claims than publishers, authors may successfully defend against such a lawsuit by showing they exercised reasonable care (e.g., hiring someone to check all the data for correctness) under the circumstances. Also, unless an author claims to be an expert on the subject, the law may not impose a higher duty on the author than it would impose on the reader (who, after all, must use his or her own judgment before taking an author's advice).

The judges in the *Winter* case decided that the strict liability in tort doctrine should only apply to the manufacture of tangible "products," such as tires and insecticides, for which the doctrine had been created. Expansion of the doctrine to make publishers strictly liable for intangible information contained in books would unduly interfere with the free exchange of ideas and information:

> We place a high priority on the unfettered exchange of ideas. We accept the risk that words and ideas have wings that we cannot clip and which carry them we know not where. The threat of liability without fault (financial responsibility for our words and ideas in the absence of fault or special undertaking of responsibility) could seriously inhibit those who wish to share thoughts and theories.

It was not that the judges thought no one should ever be held liable for delivering erroneous information injuring consumers. Professionals, for example, should be held responsible for injuries caused by their delivery of defective information, but not even they should be held strictly liable in tort:

> Professional services do not ordinarily lend themselves to "strict liability" because they lack the elements which gave rise to the doctrine. There is no mass production of goods or a large body of distant consumers whom it would be unfair to require to trace the article they used along the channels of trade to the original manufacturer and there to pinpoint an act of negligence remote from their knowledge. . . . Those who hire "professionals" are not justified in expecting infallibility, but can expect only reasonable care and competence.

If the same rule was applied to "Harry's Medical Home Companion" as was applied in *Winter*, Lightweight Software and the health food store would have nothing to worry about from a liability suit against them by an injured consumer. Under the *Winter* ruling, Harry would not have to worry about a strict liability suit. And he would have a reasonable chance of defending against a negligence lawsuit by showing he had exercised reasonable care in preparing the program. He might also point out that he was not holding himself out as a professional in the medical field so he should not be held to the same standard of care as would be imposed on a licensed doctor.

STRICT LIABILITY IN TORT FOR AERONAUTICAL CHARTS: *AETNA* V. *JEPPSEN*

There is, however, at least one circumstance in which an information product has been held to be a "product" for strict liability purposes. Ten years before the *Winter vs. Putnam* decision, the same court ruled that aeronautical charts were "products" for strict liability purposes. The case was *Aetna Casualty & Surety Co.* v. *Jeppsen & Co.* Aetna persuaded the trial judge that a defect in the design of an aeronautical chart manufactured by Jeppsen had caused an airplane insured by Aetna to crash at the Las Vegas airport. Interestingly, Aetna's claim was not that the chart contained inaccurate information, but that it failed in its design goal of graphically representing this information in a readily understandable way.

Jeppsen's principal argument on appeal was that the chart was not the sort of "product" to which strict liability rules should be applied. In explaining why it disagreed with Jeppsen on this point, the appellate court emphasized the chart was mass-produced for commercial purposes and those who used the chart relied on Jeppsen's expertise as much as consumers might rely on any other manufacturers' expertise. Aeronautical charts were, said the court, "highly technical tools" resembling compasses which would be treated as products for strict liability purposes. The court contrasted the charts with "how to do X" books which were "pure thought and expression."

If the same rule was applied to "Harry's Medical Home Companion" as was applied in *Jeppsen*, Lightweight Software and the health food store might well be held strictly liable in tort for physical injuries to a user resulting from a defect in the program. Because Harry does not himself sell the program to the public, he might not be held strictly liable in tort even if the publisher and health food store were. The strict liability in tort rules only apply to "sellers" of "products" of the kind that injured the consumer.

MORE LIABILITY RISKS FOR ELECTRONIC INFORMATION

The law proceeds by analogy. Judges faced with deciding a case brought by an injured consumer against a seller of a multimedia program containing defective information on medical treatments will decide what liability rule to apply by asking him- or herself whether to treat the case like *Winter* or like *Jeppsen*. I can think of a number of reasons why electronic information providers may be more at risk from liability suits than print information providers.

For one thing, electronic information products have a more technological character than books. Even when these products behave mainly like books, they also behave like machines. And there may be no simple way to separate their book-like and machine-like characteristics. In addition, electronic information products are often "engineered" similar to other manufactured products. They are certainly more engineered than books.

Given the emphasis the field places on the technological character of electronic information products, the field should not be surprised if the law takes it seriously by treating its products the way it treats other technological products. One of these days, for example, an electronic information provider's assertion that its product is "user friendly" may be treated not as mere marketing puffery, but as creating an express warranty, leading reasonable consumers to expect that "usability engineering" or "hypertext engineering" techniques or user interface standards or guidelines were used to develop it.

As the electronic information industry moves from handcrafted demonstration projects to mass-marketed products distributed to distant and anonymous customers, the argument for extending liability when defects in these information products cause injury to consumers grows stronger. Consumers of electronic information products and services provided by a distant vendor will probably rely heavily on the expertise of the electronic information provider. The more naive among these customers may well think (however erroneously) that because the information has been computerized, it is more trustworthy than if delivered orally or found in print. In addition, electronic information providers are likely to be in a better position than consumers to control the quality of the information delivered and to insure against liability. This is especially true when firms (and not just individual programmers like Harry) begin to develop electronic information products for the mass market.

Another reason providers of electronic information may in time have greater responsibilities than book publishers is that electronic information products are less readily inspectable by ordinary consumers than books. With books, a consumer can go to a bookstore and browse through the whole thing before buying it. The consumer can, not only examine the binding, but also skim the contents to see if it meets his or her needs. With electronic information products, nothing about the product (except advertising hype) can generally be seen before the purchasing decision is made. One cannot even examine the disk to see if it is scratched or warped. Once out of the box, the disk, of course, reveals nothing about its contents which can only be comprehended through extensive use of the software. With on-line services for which the consumer is charged by connect-time, the contents are similarly invisible until a charge is incurred for usage.

When so little of value in an electronic information product lies in its physical characteristics (such as the disk on which software may be borne), it is difficult to believe courts will not in time extend liability to the contents of such products.

In addition, it is worth noting books merely instruct a reader how to perform a task whereas software does the task. By making the reader an intermediary between the instructions and their execution, a book keeps the reader in the judgment loop which means he or she bears some responsibility for how well or poorly the task is done. The reader also has to exercise judgment about whether it is really a good idea to follow a particular author's advice. By contrast, electronic information products only leave the user in the judgment loop when they have been explicitly designed to do so. Thus, more of the control over and responsibility for proper execution of the task will lie with the electronic publisher. This too may contribute to an extension of liability to providers of electronic information. Moreover, some have argued the liability rules for print publishers should be changed [1], and if they are, electronic publishers would be affected as well.

One unexplored bulwark against liability for electronic information providers is the First Amendment. What has protected print publishers from liability for dissemination of defective information has largely been concerns about the effect liability rules would have on the free exchange of ideas and information. At the moment, many commercial electronic information providers may think the work of groups like the Electronic Frontier Foundation which seek to define civil rights in Cyberspace are somewhat remote from their core concerns. But when they realize First Amendment concerns may provide the best chance electronic information providers have to protect against liability for defective information, they may find more reason to support the work of such organizations.

Electronic information providers should, of course, be thinking not only about what kinds of First Amendment rights they may have, but also about what kinds of First Amendment responsibilities they may have. In law, rights and responsibilities tend to be intertwined. One generally does not get rights without some responsibilities as well. As broadcasters and cable TV firms have discovered to their dismay, print publishers often have greater First Amendment rights than other media types do, in part because of the greater historical role of print publishers in promoting free speech interests. Electronic information providers may want to begin thinking more about First Amendment issues and where they stand (or want to stand) in relation to print publishers and other media types.

Another set of questions people in the computing field should ask themselves is what liability standards they think ought to apply to their field. Should injured consumers be able to recover damages for defective delivery of electronic information or not, and why or why not? In addition, the field should be asking what steps can be taken to self-regulate to promote development of high-quality software production to forestall or at least limit the degree to which regulation will come about through lawsuits about defective electronic information products. Liability will be with the field for a long time. It is time to stop worrying about the problem and start addressing it.

LIABILITY CATEGORIES

There are three distinct categories the law employs when dealing with claims that defective products have caused physical or economic injury to someone other than their producer: breach of contractual warranties, negligence, and strict liability in tort.

Warranty

A warranty is a promise made by a manufacturer or seller of goods which is considered to be a part of the contract under which the product is sold. Warranties are of two sorts: express and implied.

Express warranties are created by a seller's statements about the product, its characteristics, or its performance which affect the consumer's decision to buy the product. Express warranties may arise from statements made in advertising, on the package in which the product is shipped, or by the salesperson who persuaded the consumer to buy it. Merely recommending purchase of the product or making statements about it that a reasonable consumer would understand to be mere "sales talk" or puffery will not create an express warranty. However, a seller need not intend to expressly warrant a product to do so.

When the seller is a merchant, the law will regard the act of selling the product in the marketplace as giving rise to an implied representation the product is of fair and average quality for goods of that kind and fit for ordinary consumer purposes. This is known as the implied warranty of merchantability. It attaches automatically by law to all sales transactions in jurisdictions that have adopted Article 2 of the Uniform Commercial Code (UCC). (In the U.S., this includes every state but Louisiana.) Implied warranties of fitness for a particular purpose will also automatically arise when a seller knows the purpose for which a customer is acquiring the goods and the customer relies on the seller's judgment that a particular product will fulfill that purpose.

Implied warranties can be disclaimed by a seller. However, the disclaimer must be explicit, unambiguous, conspicuous, and often must be in writing before the disclaimer will be effective (as are the bright orange stickers saying "as is" or "with all faults" appearing on the windows of automobiles in used car lots).

These warranty rules do not apply to all sales transactions, but only to sales of "goods." Sales of "services" are not subject to these rules. The law for services contracts more closely resembles the nineteenth century when "caveat emptor" (let the buyer beware) was the rule across the board.

The question of whether computer software should be treated as "goods" or "services" has been much discussed in the legal literature and in some case law. Insofar as software is an embedded component of a hardware device, such as an X-ray machine, it will almost certainly be treated as "goods" within the meaning of the UCC. It is somewhat less clear how software will be treated when it merely automates an information process previously done manually (which would then have been described as a "service"). The more customized the software or the more it resembles a book or a pure information service, the less likely it is to be treated as "goods" under the UCC. Even when an electronic information product is treated as "goods" under the UCC, there is some case law suggesting that warranties will not attach to the information in the work if it behaves like a book. (See article's discussion of the *Cardozo* v. *True* case.)

Negligence

When a person (or a firm) acts in a manner a reasonable person in the same circumstances would have recognized does not live up to a duty of care owed towards others and thereby causes harm to another, that person can be found liable for negligence. Negligence is generally harder to prove than breach of warranty because negligence requires a showing of fault on the part of the person being sued, whereas warranty liability can exist when a product simply fails to perform as stated or expected. There are also some occasions in which negligence claims fall because the law has not imposed a duty of care on the person being sued.

There is a long history of successful negligence lawsuits against manufacturers of defective products. Sometimes manufacturers have been found to have failed in the duty of care owed to consumers in not having taken sufficient care in the design of the product. Sometimes they have been found not to have provided adequate information about how the product should be used or what dangers might exist if the product is used in a particular way.

There have been far fewer successful lawsuits when claims of negligence are made after someone has provided inadequate or inaccurate information to a customer. It is fairly rare for the law to impose a stringent duty of care on information providers unless the information provider holds himself or herself out in the marketplace as having substantially superior knowledge, skill, or expertise. Professional information providers, such as doctors or lawyers, can be held liable for malpractice, for example, when they have conveyed inaccurate information (or otherwise provided a negligent service) and a less knowledgeable consumer relied on it to his or her detriment. It is generally quite difficult to win a malpractice action against a professional for delivering defective information, for one will need to show the provider was acting incompetently in delivering the defective information. There is often a difference of opinion among professionals in a field about what is or is not appropriate information to convey in particular circumstances. In addition, professionals generally do not like to call someone in their field an incompetent practitioner in a public forum such as a court and usually one will need an expert in the field to testify to a professional's incompetence.

I am aware that many people who develop software have ambivalent attitudes about whether they should be considered "professionals" in the sense in which this term is used in other fields. While I will not reignite the tired debate over whether software developers should be "licensed," as most other professionals are, it is an issue which may need to be revisited as greater responsibilities (i.e., duties of care) are imposed by law on publishers of electronic information.

Strict Liability in Tort

Manufacturers and sellers of defective products are held strictly liable, (that is, liable without fault) in tort (that is, independent of duties imposed by contract) for physical harm to person or property caused by the defect. This liability arises notwithstanding that "the seller has exercised all possible care in the preparation and sale of the product." These strict liability rules do not apply to all commercial transactions. Along similar lines to UCC warranty law, strict liability in tort exists only for "products" and not for "services."

When computer programs are embedded components of airplanes, X-ray equipment, and the like, they will almost certainly be treated as "products" for strict liability purposes. (The *Winter* case discussed in this article is such an example.) While some tricky causation questions may arise in product liability cases involving software, strict liability will be imposed on a software developer if there is a defect resulting in an injury to the consumer (and a defect will generally be easy to show if a consumer or user has been injured), almost as surely as night follows day.

But there are some computer programs which may not be treated as "products" for strict liability purposes. When programs behave more like a book than a machine or when they otherwise resemble an information service, strict liability rules may not be imposed on them. As this article explains, courts have decided that books should not be treated as "products" for strict liability purposes and that publishers of books should not be held strictly liable in tort when their products contain defective information.

Remedies

When a seller has breached implied or express warranties in connection with the sale of goods, the buyer can sue the seller to recover money damages for certain kinds of injuries arising from the breach. If, for example, a consumer is physically injured by a defective lawnmower and has to pay $10,000 in medical expenses, that $10,000 may be recovered from the manufacturer or the firm from which the consumer bought the lawnmower. If the lawnmower must be repaired or replaced, the consumer can generally recover in contract for these damages as well.

Contract damages, however, tend to be more limited than tort damages. Monetary damages to compensate an injured person for pain and suffering, for example, are recoverable in tort actions (such as negligence and strict liability) but may not be in contract actions. Some economic losses are also not recoverable in contract cases. Unless, for example, the manufacturer (or other seller) of a lawnmower had reason to know at the time of the sale that a particular buyer of the lawnmower needed it to operate a lawn-mowing service, the buyer would not be able to recover lost profits on his lawn-mowing business during the time the business was out of operation after the defect in it evidenced itself.

In negligence actions, successful plaintiffs can generally recover damages for a broad range of injuries flowing from the negligent act, including pain and suffering and some economic losses. In strict liability actions, only damages arising from physical harms to persons or property are generally recoverable.

One other respect in which tort and contract actions tend to differ is in the kinds of persons who can bring claims for what kinds of damages. Contract law tends (except where physical injury to persons or property is involved) to limit the class of possible plaintiffs to those who bought the goods and are thus the beneficiaries of the warranty promises that are part of the contract. Tort law is more generous about who can bring a lawsuit (e.g., if the buyer of the product gives it to another person as a gift and that person is harmed, he or she can sue in tort whereas that person might not be able to sue in contract).

Multiple volumes of thick treatises have been written to explain all the nuances of contract and tort liability arising from defective products. This brief synopsis is necessarily incomplete but will, I hope, give those in the computing field some grounding in the basics of these legal categories.

REFERENCE

1. Arnold, R. The persistence of caveat emptor: Publisher immunity from liability for inaccurate factual information. *U. Pitt. Law Rev. 53* (Spring 1992), 777.

ON THE IMPACT OF THE COMPUTER ON SOCIETY

How Does One Insult a Machine?

Joseph Weizenbaum

The structure of the typical essay on "The impact of computers on society" is as follows: First there is an "on the one hand" statement. It tells all the good things computers have already done for society and often even attempts to argue that the social order would already have collapsed were it not for the "computer revolution." This is usually followed by an "on the other hand" caution which tells of certain problems the introduction of computers brings in its wake. The threat posed to individual privacy by large data banks and the danger of large-scale unemployment induced by industrial automation are usually mentioned. Finally, the glorious present and prospective achievements of the computer are applauded, while the dangers alluded to in the second part are shown to be capable of being alleviated by sophisticated technological fixes. The closing paragraph consists of a plea for generous societal support for more, and more large-scale, computer research and development. This is usually coupled to the more or less subtle assertion that only computer science, hence only the computer scientist, can guard the world against the admittedly hazardous fallout of applied computer technology.

In fact, the computer has had very considerably less societal impact than the mass media would lead us to believe. Certainly, there are enterprises like space travel that could not have been undertaken without computers. Certainly the computer industry, and with it the computer education industry, has grown to enormous proportions. But much of the industry is self-serving. It is rather like an island economy in which the natives make a living by taking in each other's laundry. The part that is not self-serving is largely supported by government agencies and other gigantic enterprises that know the value of everything but the price of nothing, that is, that know the short-range utility of computer systems but have no idea of their ultimate social cost. In any case, airline reservation systems and computerized hospitals serve only a tiny, largely the most affluent, fraction of society. Such things cannot be said to have an impact on society generally.

SIDE EFFECTS OF TECHNOLOGY

The more important reason that I dismiss the argument which I have caricatured is that the direct societal effects of any pervasive new technology are as nothing compared to its much more subtle and ultimately much more important side effects. In that sense, the societal impact of the computer has not yet been felt.

To help firmly fix the idea of the importance of subtle indirect effects of technology, consider the impact on society of the invention of the microscope. When it was invented in the middle of the seventeenth century, the dominant commonsense theory of disease was fundamentally that disease was a punishment visited upon an individual by God. The sinner's body was thought to be inhabited by various so-called humors brought into disequilibrium in accordance with divine justice. The cure for disease was therefore to be found first in penance and second in the balancing of humors as, for example, by bleeding. Bleeding was, after all, both painful, hence punishment and penance, and potentially balancing in that it actually removed substance from the body. The microscope enabled man to see microorganisms and thus paved the way for the germ theory of disease. The enormously surprising discovery of extremely small living organisms also induced the idea of a continuous chain of life which, in turn, was a necessary intellectual precondition for the emergence of Darwinism. Both the germ theory of disease and the theory of evolution profoundly altered man's conception of his contract with God and consequently his self-image. Politically these ideas served to help diminish the power of the Church and, more generally, to legitimize the questioning of the basis of hitherto unchallenged authority. I do not say that the microscope alone was responsible for the enormous social changes that followed its invention. Only that it made possible the kind of paradigm shift, even on the commonsense level, without which these changes might have been impossible.

Is it reasonable to ask whether the computer will induce similar changes in man's image of himself and whether that influence will prove to be its most important effect on society? I think so, although I hasten to add that I don't believe the computer has yet told us much about man and his nature. To come to grips with the question, we must first ask in what way the computer is different from man's many other machines. Man has built two fundamentally different kinds of machines, nonautonomous and autonomous. An autonomous machine is one that operates for long periods of time, not on the basis of inputs from the real world, for example from sensors or from human drivers, but on the basis of internalized models of some aspect of the real world. Clocks are examples of autonomous machines in that they operate on the basis of an internalized model of the planetary system. The computer is, of course, the example par excellence. It is able to internalize models of essentially unlimited complexity and of a fidelity limited only by the genius of man.

It is the autonomy of the computer we value. When, for example, we speak of the power of computers as increasing with each new hardware and software development, we mean that, because of their increasing speed and storage capacity, and possibly thanks to new programming tricks, the new computers can internalize ever more complex and ever more faithful models of ever larger slices of reality. It seems strange then that, just when we exhibit virtually an idolatry of autonomy with respect to machines, serious thinkers in respected academies (I have in mind B. F. Skinner of Harvard University [1]) can rise to question autonomy as a fact for man. I do not think that the appearance of this paradox at this time is accidental. To understand it, we must realize that man's commitment to science has always had a masochistic component.

Time after time science has led us to insights that, at least when seen superficially, diminish man. Thus Galileo removed man from the center of the universe, Darwin removed him from his place separate from the animals, and Freud showed his rationality to be an illusion. Yet man pushes his inquiries further and deeper. I cannot help but think that there is an analogy between man's pursuit of scientific knowledge and an individual's commitment to psychoanalytic therapy. Both are undertaken in the full realization that what the inquirer may find may well damage his self-esteem. Both may reflect his determination to find meaning in his existence through struggle in truth, however painful that may be, rather than to live without meaning in a world of ill-disguised illusion. However, I am also aware that sometimes people enter psychoanalysis unwilling to put their illusions at risk, not searching for a deeper reality but in order to convert the insights they hope to gain to personal power. The analogy to man's pursuit of science does not break down with that observation.

Each time a scientific discovery shatters a hitherto fundamental cornerstone of the edifice on which man's self-esteem is built, there is an enormous reaction, just as is the case under similar circumstances in psychoanalytic therapy. Powerful defense mechanisms, beginning with denial and usually terminating in rationalization, are brought to bear. Indeed, the psychoanalyst suspects that, when a patient appears to accept a soul-shattering insight without resistance, his very casualness may well mask his refusal to allow that insight truly operational status in his self-image. But what is the psychoanalyst to think about the patient who positively embraces tentatively proffered, profoundly humiliating self-knowledge, when he embraces it and instantly converts it to a new foundation of his life? Surely such an event is symptomatic of a major crisis in the mental life of the patient.

I believe we are now at the beginning of just such a crisis in the mental life of our civilization. The microscope, I have argued, brought in its train a revision of man's image of himself. But no one in the mid-seventeenth century could have foreseen that. The possibility that the computer will, one way or another, demonstrate that, in the inimitable phrase of one of my esteemed colleagues, "the brain is merely a meat machine" is one that engages academicians, industrialists, and journalists in the here and now. How has the computer contributed to bringing about this very sad state of affairs? It must be said right away that the computer alone is not the chief causative agent. It is merely an extreme extrapolation of technology. When seen as an inducer of philosophical dogma, it is merely the reductio ad absurdum of a technological ideology. But how does it come to be regarded as a source of philosophic dogma?

THEORY VERSUS PERFORMANCE

We must be clear about the fact that a computer is nothing without a program. A program is fundamentally a transformation of one computer into another that has autonomy and that, in a very real sense, behaves. Programming languages describe dynamic processes. And, most importantly, the processes they describe can be actually carried out. Thus we can build models of any aspect of the real world that interests us and that we understand. And we can make our models work. But we must be careful to remember that a computer model is a description that works. Ordinarily, when we speak of A being a model of B, we mean that a theory about some aspects of the behavior of B is also a theory of the same aspects of the behavior of A. It follows that when, for example, we consider a computer model of paranoia, like that published by Colby et al. [2], we must not be persuaded that it tells us anything about paranoia on the grounds that it, in some sense, mirrors the behavior of a paranoiac. After all, a plain typewriter in some sense mirrors the behavior of an autistic child (one types a question and gets no response whatever), but it does not help us to understand autism. A model must be made to stand or fall on the basis of its theory. Thus, while programming languages may have put a new power in the hands of social scientists in that this new notation may have freed them from the vagueness of discursive descriptions, their obligation to build defensible theories is in no way diminished. Even errors can be pronounced with utmost formality and eloquence. But they are not thereby transmuted to truth.

The failure to make distinctions between descriptions, even those that "work," and theories accounts in large part for the fact that those who refuse to accept the view of man as machine have been put on the defensive. Recent advances in computer understanding of natural language offer an excellent case in point. Halle and Chomsky, to mention only the two with whom I am most familiar, have long labored on a theory of language which any model of language behavior must satisfy [3]. Their aim is like that of the physicist who writes a set of differential equations that anyone riding a bicycle must satisfy. No physicist claims that a person need know, let alone be able to solve, such differential equations in order to become a competent cyclist. Neither do Halle and Chomsky claim that humans know or knowingly obey the rules they believe to govern language behavior. Halle and Chomsky also strive, as do physical theorists, to identify the constants and parameters of their theories with components of reality. They hypothesize that their rules constitute a kind of projective description of certain aspects of the structure of the human mind. Their problem is thus not merely to discover economical rules to account for language behavior, but also to infer economic mechanisms which determine that precisely those rules are to be preferred over all others. Since they are in this way forced to attend to the human mind, not only that of speakers of English, they must necessarily be concerned with all human language behavior—not just that related to the understanding of English.

The enormous scope of their task is illustrated by their observation that in all human languages declarative sentences are often transformed into questions by a permutation of two of their words. (John is here → Is John here?) It is one thing to describe rules that transform declarative sentences into questions—a simple permutation rule is clearly insufficient—but another thing to describe a "machine" that necessitates those rules when others would, all else being equal, be simpler. Why, for example, is it not so that declarative sentences read backward transform those sentences into questions? The answer must be that other constraints on the "machine" combine against this local simplicity in favor of a more nearly global economy. Such examples illustrate the depth of the level of explanation that Halle and Chomsky are trying to achieve. No wonder that they stand in awe of their subject matter.

Workers in computer comprehension of natural language operate in what is usually called performance mode. It is as if they are building machines that can ride bicycles by following heuristics like "if you feel a displacement to the left, move your weight to the left." There can be, and often is, a strong interaction between the development of theory and the empirical task of engineering systems whose theory is not yet thoroughly understood. Witness the synergistic cooperation between aerodynamics and aircraft design in the first quarter of the present century. Still, what counts in performance mode is not the elaboration of theory but the performance of systems. And the systems being hammered together by the new crop of computer semanticists are beginning (just beginning) to perform.

Since computer scientists have recognized the importance of the interplay of syntax, semantics, and pragmatics, and with it the importance of computer-manipulable knowledge, they have made progress. Perhaps by the end of the present decade, computer systems will exist with which specialists, such as physicians and chemists and mathematicians, will converse in natural language. And surely some part of such achievements will have been based on other successes in, for example, computer simulation of cognitive processes. It is understandable that any success in this area, even if won empirically and without accompanying enrichments of theory, can easily lead to certain delusions being planted. Is it, after all, not terribly tempting to believe that a computer that understands natural language at all, however narrow the context, has captured something of the essence of man? Descartes himself might have believed it.

Indeed, by way of this very understandable seduction, the computer comes to be a source of philosophical dogma.

I am tempted to recite how performance programs are composed and how things that don't work quite correctly are made to work via all sorts of stratagems which do not even pretend to have any theoretical foundation. But the very asking of the question, "Has the computer captured the essence of man?" is a diversion and, in that sense, a trap. For the real question "Does man understand the essence of man?" cannot be answered by technology and hence certainly not by any technological instrument.

THE TECHNOLOGICAL METAPHOR

I asked earlier what the psychoanalyst is to think when a patient grasps a tentatively proffered deeply humiliating interpretation and attempts to convert it immediately to a new foundation of his life. I now think I phrased that question too weakly. What if the psychoanalyst merely coughed and the cough entrained the consequences of which I speak? That is our situation today. Computer science, particularly its artificial intelligence branch, has coughed. Perhaps the press has unduly amplified that cough—but it is only a cough nevertheless. I cannot help but think that the eagerness to believe that man's whole nature has suddenly been exposed by that cough, and that it has been shown to be a clockwork, is a symptom of something terribly wrong.

What is wrong, I think, is that we have permitted technological metaphors, what Mumford [4] calls the "Myth of the Machine," and technique itself to so thoroughly pervade our thought processes that we have finally abdicated to technology the very duty to formulate questions. Thus sensible men correctly perceive that large data banks and enormous networks of computers threaten man. But they leave it to technology to formulate the corresponding question. Where a simple man might ask: "Do we need these things?", technology asks "what electronic wizardry will make them safe?" Where a simple man will ask "is it good?", technology asks "will it work?" Thus science, even wisdom, becomes what technology and most of all computers can handle. Lest this be thought to be an exaggeration, I quote from the work of H. A. Simon, one of the most senior of American computer scientists [5]:

> As we succeed in broadening and deepening our knowledge—theoretical and empirical—about computers, we shall discover that in large part their behavior is governed by simple general laws, that what appeared as complexity in the computer program was, to a considerable extent, complexity of the environment to which the program was seeking to adapt its behavior.
>
> To the extent that this prospect can be realized, it opens up an exceedingly important role for computer simulation as a tool for achieving a deeper understanding of human behavior. For if it is the organization of components, and not their physical properties, that largely determines behavior, and if computers are organized somewhat in the image of man, then the computer becomes an obvious device for exploring the consequences of alternative organizational assumptions for human behavior.

and

> A man, viewed as a behaving system, is quite simple. The apparent complexity of his behavior over time is largely a reflection of the complexity of the environment in which he finds himself.
> ... I believe that this hypothesis holds even for the whole man.

We already know that those aspects of the behavior of computers which cannot be attributed to the complexity of their programs is governed by simple general laws—ultimately by the laws of Boolean algebra. And of course the physical properties of the computer's components are nearly irrelevant to its behavior. Mechanical relays are logically equivalent to tubes and to transistors and to artificial neurons. And of course the complexity of computer programs is due to the complexity of the environments, including the computing environments themselves, with which they were designed to deal. To what else could it possibly be due? So, what Simon sees as prospective is already realized. But does this collection of obvious and simple facts lead to the conclusion that man is as simple as are computers? When Simon leaps to that conclusion and then formulates the issue as he has done here, that is, when he suggests that the behavior of *the whole man* may be understood in terms of the behavior of computers as governed by simple general laws, then the very possibility of understanding man as an autonomous being, as an individual with deeply internalized values, that very possibility is excluded. How does one insult a machine?

The question "Is the brain merely a meat machine?", which Simon puts in a so much more sophisticated form, is typical of the kind of question formulated by, indeed formulatable only by, a technological mentality. Once it is accepted as legitimate, arguments as to what a computer can or cannot do "in principle" begin to rage and themselves become legitimate. But the legitimacy of the technological question—for example, is human behavior to be understood either in terms of the organization or of the physical properties of "components"—need not be admitted in the first instance. A human question can be asked instead. Indeed, we might begin by asking what has already become of "the whole man" when he can conceive of computers organized in his own image.

The success of technique and of some technological explanations has, as I've suggested, tricked us into permitting technology to formulate important questions for us—questions whose very forms severely diminish the number of degrees of freedom in our range of decision-making. Whoever dictates the questions in large part determines the answers. In that sense, technology, and especially computer technology, has become a self-fulfilling nightmare reminiscent of that of the lady who dreams of being raped and begs her attacker to be kind to her. He answers "it's your dream, lady." We must come to see that technology is our dream and that we must ultimately decide how it is to end.

I have suggested that the computer revolution need not and ought not to call man's dignity and autonomy into question, that it is a kind of pathology that moves men to wring from it unwarranted, enormously damaging interpretations. Is then the computer less threatening that we might have thought? Once we realize that our visions, possibly nightmarish visions, determine the effect of our own creations on us and on our society, their threat to us is surely diminished. But that is not to say that this realization alone will wipe out all danger. For example, apart from the erosive effect of a technological mentality on man's self-image, there are practical attacks on the freedom and dignity of man in which computer technology plays a critical role.

I mentioned earlier that computer science has come to recognize the importance of building knowledge into machines. We already have a machine—Dendral—[6] that commands more chemistry than do many Ph.D. chemists, and another—Mathlab—[7] that commands more applied mathematics than do many applied mathematicians. Both Dendral and Mathlab contain knowledge that can be evaluated in terms of the explicit theories from which it was derived. If the user believes that a result Mathlab delivers is wrong, then, apart from possible program errors, he must be in disagreement, not with the machine or its programmer, but with a specific mathematical theory. But what about the many programs on which management, most particularly the government and the military, rely, programs which can in no sense be said to rest on explicable theories but are instead enormous patchworks of programming techniques strung together to make them work?

INCOMPREHENSIBLE SYSTEMS

In our eagerness to exploit every advance in technique we quickly incorporate the lessons learned from machine manipulation of knowledge in theory-based systems into such patchworks. They then "work" better. I have in mind systems like target selection systems used in Vietnam and war games used in the Pentagon, and so on. These often gigantic systems are put together by teams of programmers, often working over a time span of many years. But by the time the systems come into use, most of the original programmers have left or turned their attention to other pursuits. It is precisely when gigantic systems begin to be used that their inner workings can no longer be understood by any single person or by a small team of individuals. Norbert Wiener, the father of cybernetics, foretold this phenomenon in a remarkably prescient article [8] published more than a decade ago. He said there:

> It may well be that in principle we cannot make any machine the elements of whose behavior we cannot comprehend sooner or later. This does not mean in any way that we shall be able to comprehend these elements in substantially less time than the time required for operation of the machine, or even within any given number of years or generations.
>
> An intelligent understanding of [machines'] mode of performance may be delayed until long after the task which they have been set has been completed. This means that though machines are theoretically subject to human criticism, such criticism may be ineffective until long after it is relevant.

This situation, which is now upon us, has two consequences: first that decisions are made on the basis of rules and criteria no one knows explicitly, and second that the system of rules and criteria becomes immune to change. This is so because, in the absence of detailed understanding of the inner workings of a system, any substantial modification is very likely to render the system altogether inoperable. The threshold of complexity beyond which this phenomenon occurs has already been crossed by many existing systems, including some compiling and computer operating systems. For example, no one likes the operating systems for certain large computers, but they cannot be substantially changed nor can they be done away with. Too many people have become dependent on them.

An awkward operating system is inconvenient. That is not too bad. But the growing reliance on supersystems that were perhaps designed to help people make analyses and decisions, but which have since surpassed the understanding of their users while at the same time becoming indispensable to them, is another matter. In modern war it is common for the soldier, say the bomber pilot, to operate at an enormous psychological distance from his victims. He is not responsible for burned children because he never sees their village, his bombs, and certainly not the flaming children themselves. Modern technological rationalizations of war, diplomacy, politics, and commerce such as computer games have an even more insidious effect on the making of policy. Not only have policy makers abdicated their decision-making responsibility to a technology they don't understand, all the while maintaining the illusion that they, the policy makers, are formulating policy questions and answering them, but responsibility has altogether evaporated. No human is any longer responsible for "what the machine says." Thus there can be neither right nor wrong, no question of justice, no theory with which one can agree or disagree, and finally no basis on which one can challenge "what the machine says." My father used to invoke the ultimate authority by saying to me, "it is written." But then I could read what was written, imagine a human author, infer his values, and finally agree or disagree. The systems in the Pentagon, and their counterparts elsewhere in our culture, have in a very real sense no authors. They therefore do not admit of exercises of imagination that may ultimately lead to human judgment. No wonder that men who live day in and out with such machines and become dependent on them begin to believe that men are merely machines. They are reflecting what they themselves have become.

The potentially tragic impact on society that may ensue from the use of systems such as I have just discussed is greater than might at first be imagined. Again it is side effects, not direct effects, that matter most. First, of course, there is the psychological impact on individuals living in a society in which anonymous, hence irresponsible, forces formulate the large questions of the day and circumscribe the range of possible answers. It cannot be surprising that large numbers of perceptive individuals living in such a society experience a kind of impotence and fall victim to the mindless rage that often accompanies such experiences. But even worse, since computer-based knowledge systems become essentially unmodifiable except in that they can grow, and since they induce dependence and cannot, after a certain threshold is crossed, be abandoned, there is an enormous risk that they will be passed from one generation to another, always growing. Man too passes knowledge from one generation to another. But because man is mortal, his transmission of knowledge over the generations is at once a process of filtering and accrual. Man doesn't merely pass knowledge, he rather regenerates it continuously. Much as we may mourn the crumbling of ancient civilizations, we know nevertheless that the glory of man resides as much in the evolution of his cultures as in that of his brain. The unwise use of ever larger and ever more complex computer systems may well bring this process to a halt. It could well replace the ebb and flow of culture with a world without values, a world in which what counts for a fact has long ago been determined and forever fixed.

POSITIVE EFFECTS

I've spoken of some potentially dangerous effects of present computing trends. Is there nothing positive to be said? Yes, but it must be said with caution. Again, side effects are more important than direct effects. In particular, the idea of computation and of programming languages is beginning to become an important metaphor which, in the long run, may well prove to be responsible for paradigm shifts in many fields. Most of the common-sense paradigms in terms of which much of mankind interprets the phenomena of the everyday world, both physical and social, are still deeply rooted in fundamentally mechanistic metaphors. Marx's dynamics as well as those of Freud are, for example, basically equilibrium systems. Any hydrodynamicist could come to understand them without leaving the jargon of his field. Languages capable of describing ongoing processes, particularly in terms of modular subprocesses, have already had an enormous effect on the way computer people think of every aspect of their worlds, not merely those directly related to their work. The information-processing view of the world so engendered qualifies as a genuine metaphor. This is attested to by the fact that it (i) constitutes an intellectual framework that permits new questions to be asked about a wide-ranging set of phenomena, and (ii) that it itself provides criteria for the adequacy of proffered answers. A new metaphor is important not in that it may be better than existing ones, but rather in that it may enlarge man's vision by giving him yet another perspective on his world. Indeed, the very effectiveness of a new metaphor may seduce lazy minds to adopt it as a basis for universal explanations and as a source of panaceas. Computer simulation of social processes has already been advanced by single-minded generalists as leading to general solutions of all of mankind's problems.

The metaphors given us by religion, the poets, and by thinkers like Darwin, Newton, Freud, and Einstein have rather quickly penetrated to the language of ordinary people. These metaphors have thus been instrumental in shaping our entire civilization's imaginative reconstruction of our world. The computing metaphor is as yet available to only an extremely small set of people. Its acquisition and internalization, hopefully as only one of many ways to see the world, seems to require experience in program composition, a kind of computing literacy. Perhaps such literacy will become very widespread in the advanced societal sectors of the advanced countries. But, should it become a dominant mode of thinking and be restricted to certain social classes, it will prove not merely repressive in the ordinary sense, but an enormously divisive societal force. For then classes which do and do not have access to the metaphor will, in an important sense, lose their ability to communicate with one another. We know already how difficult it is for the poor and the oppressed to communicate with the rest of the society in which they are embedded. We know how difficult it is for the world of science to communicate with that of the arts and of the humanities. In both instances the communication difficulties, which have grave consequences, are very largely due to the fact that the respective communities have unsharable experiences out of which unsharable metaphors have grown.

RESPONSIBILITY

Given these dismal possibilities, what is the responsibility of the computer scientist? First I should say that most of the harm computers can potentially entrain is much more a function of properties people attribute to computers than of what a computer can or cannot actually be made to do. The nonprofessional has little choice but to make his attributions of properties to computers on the basis of the propaganda emanating from the computer community and amplified by the press. The computer professional therefore has an enormously important responsibility to be modest in his claims. This advice would not even have to be voiced if computer science had a tradition of scholarship and of self-criticism such as that which characterizes the established sciences. The mature scientist stands in awe before the depth of his subject matter. His very humility is the wellspring of his strength. I regard the instilling of just this kind of humility, chiefly by the example set by teachers, to be one of the most important missions of every university department of computer science.

The computer scientist must be aware constantly that his instruments are capable of having gigantic direct and indirect amplifying effects. An error in a program, for example, could have grievous direct results, including most certainly the loss of much human life. On 11 September 1971, to cite just one example, a computer programming error caused the simultaneous destruction of 117 high-altitude weather balloons whose instruments were being monitored by an earth satellite [9]. A similar error in a military command and control system could launch a fleet of nuclear tipped missiles. Only censorship prevents us from knowing how many such events involving non-nuclear weapons have already occurred. Clearly then, the computer scientist has a heavy responsibility to make the fallibility and limitations of the systems he is capable of designing brilliantly clear. The very power of his systems should serve to inhibit the advice he is ready to give and to constrain the range of work he is willing to undertake.

Of course, the computer scientist, like everyone else, is responsible for his actions and their consequences. Sometimes that responsibility is hard to accept because the corresponding authority to decide what is and what is not to be done appears to rest with distant and anonymous forces. That technology itself determines what is to be done by a process of extrapolation and that individuals are powerless to intervene in that determination is precisely the kind of self-fulfilling dream from which we must awaken.

Consider gigantic computer systems. They are, of course, natural extrapolations of the large systems we already have. Computer networks are another point on the same curve extrapolated once more. One may ask whether such systems can be used by anybody except by governments and very large corporations and whether such organizations will not use them mainly for antihuman purposes. Or consider speech recognition systems. Will they not be used primarily to spy on private communications? To answer such questions by saying that big computer systems, computer networks, and speech recognition systems are inevitable is to surrender one's humanity. For such an answer must be based either on one's profound conviction that society has already lost control over its technology or on the thoroughly immoral position that "if I don't do it, someone else will."

I don't say that systems such as I have mentioned are necessarily evil—only that they may be and, what is most important, that their inevitability cannot be accepted by individuals claiming autonomy, freedom, and dignity. The individual computer scientist can and must decide. The determination of what the impact of computers on society is to be is, at least in part, in his hands.

Finally, the fundamental question the computer scientist must ask himself is the one that every scientist, indeed every human, must ask. It is not "what shall I do?" but rather "what shall I be?" I cannot answer that for anyone save myself. But I will say again that if technology is a nightmare that appears to have its own inevitable logic, it is our nightmare. It is possible, given courage and insight, for man to deny technology the prerogative to formulate man's questions. It is possible to ask human questions and to find humane answers.

NOTES

1. B. F. Skinner, *Beyond Freedom and Dignity* (Knopf, New York, 1971).
2. K. M. Colby, S. Weber, F. D. Hilf, *Artif. Intell.* 1, 1 (1971).
3. N. Chomsky, *Aspects of the Theory of Syntax* (M.I.T. Press, Cambridge, Mass., 1965); _____ and M. Halle, *The Sound Pattern of English* (Harper & Row, New York, 1968).

4. L. Mumford, *The Pentagon of Power* (Harcourt, Brace, Jovanovich, New York, 1970).
5. H. A. Simon, *The Sciences of the Artificial* (M.I.T. Press, Cambridge, Mass., 1969), pp. 22–25.
6. B. Buchanan, G. Sutherland, and E. A. Feigenbaum, in *Machine Intelligence*, B. Meltzer, Ed. (American Elsevier, New York, 1969).
7. W. A. Martin and R. J. Fateman, "The Macsyma system," in *Proceedings of the 2nd Symposium on Symbolic and Algebraic Manipulation* (Association for Computer Machinery, New York, 1971); J. Moses, *Commun. Assoc. Computer Mach.* 14 (No. 8), 548 (1971).
8. N. Wiener, *Science* 131, 1355 (1960).
9. R. Gillette, *ibid.* 174, 477 (1971).

PROFESSIONAL ETHICS

Deborah G. Johnson

SCENARIO ONE: CONFLICTING LOYALTIES

Carl Babbage is an experienced systems designer. He has been working for the Acme Software Company for over three years. Acme develops and sells computer hardware and software. It does this both by designing and marketing general purpose systems and by contracting with companies and government agencies to design systems for their exclusive use.

During the first two years that Carl worked for Acme, he worked on software that Acme was developing for general marketing. A year ago, however, he was reassigned to work on a project under contract with the U.S. Defense Department. The project involves designing a system that will monitor radar signals and launch nuclear missiles in response to these signals.

Carl initially had some reluctance about working on a military project, but he put this out of his mind because the project seemed challenging and he knew that if he did not work on it, someone else would. Now, however, the project is approaching completion and Carl has some grave reservations about the adequacy of the system. He is doubtful about the system's capacity for making fine distinctions (for example, distinguishing between a small aircraft and a missile) and the security of the mechanism that can launch missiles (for example, it may be possible for unauthorized individuals to get access to the controls under certain circumstances). Carl expressed his concern to the project director but she dismissed these concerns quickly, mentioning that Acme is already behind schedule on the project and has already exceeded the budget that they had agreed to with the Defense Department.

Carl feels that he has a moral responsibility to do something, but he doesn't know what to do. Should he ask for reassignment to another project? Should he go to executives in Acme and tell them of his concerns? It is difficult to imagine how they will respond. Should he talk to someone in the Defense Department? Should he go to newspaper or TV reporters and "blow the whistle"? If he does any of these things, he is likely to jeopardize his job. Should he do nothing?

SCENARIO TWO: SYSTEM SECURITY

After getting an undergraduate degree in computer science, Diane Jones was hired by a large computer company. She initially worked as a programmer, but over the years she was promoted to technical positions with increasing responsibility. Three years ago she quit her job and started her own consulting business. She has been so successful that she now has several people working for her.

At the moment, Diane is designing a database management system for the personnel office of a medium-sized company that manufactures toys. Diane has involved the client in the design process, informing the CEO, the director of computing, and the director of personnel about the progress of the system and giving them many opportunities to make decisions about features of the system. It is now time to make decisions about the kind and degree of security to build into the system.

Diane has described several options to the client, and the client has decided to opt for the least secure system because the system is going to cost more than they planned. She believes that the information they will be storing is extremely sensitive, because it will include performance evaluations, medical records for filing insurance claims, and salaries. With weak security, it may be possible for enterprising employees to figure out how to get access to these data, not to mention the possibilities for on-line access from hackers. Diane feels strongly that the system should be much more secure.

She has tried to explain the risks to her client, but the CEO, director of computing, and director of personnel are all willing to accept a system with little security. What should she do? For example, should she refuse to build the system as they request?

SCENARIO THREE: CONFLICT OF INTEREST

Marvin Miller makes a living as a private consultant. Small businesses hire him to advise them about their computer needs. Typically, a company asks him to come in, examine the company's operations, evaluate its automation needs, and make recommendations about the kind of hardware and software that it should purchase.

Recently, Marvin was hired by a small, private hospital, which was particularly interested in upgrading the software used for patient records and accounting. The hospital asked Marvin to evaluate proposals they had received from three software companies, each of which offered a system that could be modified for the hospital's use. Marvin examined the offers carefully. He considered which system would best meet the hospital's needs, which company offered the best services in terms of training of staff and future updates, which offered the best price, and so on. He concluded that Tri-Star Systems was the best alternative for the hospital, and he recommended this in his report, explaining his reasons for drawing this conclusion.

What Marvin failed to mention (at any time in his dealings with the hospital) was that he is a silent partner (a co-owner) in Tri-Star Systems. Was this unethical?

Should Marvin have disclosed the fact that he has ties to one of the software companies?

WHY PROFESSIONAL ETHICS?

. . . Why do we need to talk about "professional ethics" at all? If I find myself with an ethical problem, I should think it through using ethical theory, try to understand what rules or principles are at stake, and then act accordingly. That I act as a computer professional, or any other kind of professional, seems irrelevant.

There is some truth to this, for when one acts as a professional, one does not cease to be a moral agent. Nevertheless, the domain of professional ethics is special in several respects. For one thing, professional roles often carry special rights and responsibilities. Doctors, for example, are allowed to prescribe drugs and keep information confidential, and they are expected to respond when individuals are hurt in emergencies. Others (laypersons) are not allowed to do what doctors may do, nor are they expected to behave in the way doctors are expected to.

To be sure, some professional roles are more "strongly differentiated" than others.[1] Strongly differentiated roles are those that involve powers and privileges that are exceptions to ordinary morality. Think, for example, of the lawyer's obligation not to reveal confidential information given to her by a client, even when the information would affect the outcome of a trial; or think of the physical harm that police officers may inflict in the course of their work. These are behaviors that are prohibited by ordinary morality but allowed when performed by certain professionals acting in their professional roles. Other occupational roles are not strongly differentiated in that they do not allow or call upon one to act outside ordinary morality. For example, sales personnel, construction workers, and bus drivers have no special powers or privileges.

Even when an occupational or professional role carries no special powers or privileges, professional ethics can be thought of as a special domain in at least two respects. First, as mentioned at the onset, professionals function in a special context, a context that typically includes relationships with employers, clients, co-professionals, and the public. The context also involves legal, political, and economic constraints. Computer professionals, for example, are often employed by private corporations seeking a profit, constrained by law in a variety of ways, operating in a highly competitive environment, and so on. This context is usually very rich in complexity, and this cannot be ignored in analyzing ethical decision making.

Professional ethics can also be thought of as a special domain because of the "efficacy" of professionals. "Efficacy" refers to the power that professionals have to affect the world. Professionals generally have some skill or knowledge that they use to produce a product or provide a service. Sometimes they do this on their own, for example, when a doctor examines a patient and prescribes a method of treatment. More often professionals contribute their abilities and their activity to a larger enterprise wherein their contribution, together with that of others, leads to a product or service. Thus, for example, an engineer may use her skill to design one component of an airplane or a skyscraper; or a research scientist may work with a team of other scientists to develop the cure for a disease.

Skill and knowledge are an important part of the efficacy of a professional, but not the only part. Simply having skill and knowledge is not enough to produce an effect—one must exercise the skill and use the knowledge, and in most professions this cannot be done in isolation. One needs a business, clients, consumers, equipment, legal protection, and so on. Thus professionals, especially computer professionals, create their own businesses or obtain employment in companies or government agencies. The positions they fill give them the opportunity to exercise their professional skills and in so doing to affect the world in some way, for example, by creating software for missile detection systems, selling a computer that allows others to maintain records, developing software that assists individuals in financial planning, and so on.

So professionals have the capacity to affect the world because their skill and knowledge give them the ability and their jobs give them the opportunity. When they use their abilities and act in their jobs, their actions can directly or indirectly have powerful effects—on individuals and on the social and physical world we live in. Indeed, these effects are sometimes good and sometimes bad, sometimes foreseen and sometimes unforeseen.

Because professionals have this power to affect the world, we think of them as bearing special responsibility. That is, they acquire duties to behave in ways that do not harm individuals or public goods precisely because they have the capacity to do so.

ARE COMPUTER PROFESSIONALS "PROFESSIONALS"?

So far I have used the term "professional" rather loosely, to refer to individuals who make a living in a particular line of work, but the term has a variety of meanings. In the loose way in which I have been using the term, "professionals" might be thought of as members of an occupational group. Carpenters, truck drivers, and doctors alike would, then, be professionals. However, "profession" and "professional" are also often used in a narrower sense, to refer to a special set of occupations, which have, among other things, higher status.

Although there is no hard and fast definition, sociologists and ethicists often use doctors and lawyers as the paradigms of these special professions, and other occupations are seen as closer or farther from these on a continuum of profession–nonprofession. The following is a list of characteristics often associated with professions in this special sense of the term.

1. Professions require mastery of an esoteric body of knowledge, usually acquired through higher education. Only members of the profession possess this knowledge and it is this that justifies the next characteristic.

2. Members of professions typically have a good deal of autonomy in their work (as compared to other occupations in which one simply takes orders).

3. Professions usually have a professional organization (recognized by state government) that controls admission to the profession and sets standards for practice.

4. Professions fulfill an important social function or are committed to a social good (such as health, in the case of medicine).

Other characteristics sometimes associated with professions include that the profession has a division between those who are practitioners and those who do research (continually improving on the esoteric body of knowledge), members of professions are bound by a code of professional conduct or ethics, and members are seen as making a life commitment to the field of their profession. These characteristics are thought to justify the higher salaries usually associated with these special professions.

Now, are computer professionals "professionals" in this special sense of the term? Certainly computer professionals possess some of the appropriate characteristics. Most of them have, for example, mastered an esoteric body of knowledge and have done so through higher education. Computer professionals have varying degrees of autonomy. Those who own their own consulting firms and those who have worked their way up the ladder in corporate or government agencies may have a good deal of decision-making authority. As well, academic computer scientists and those who manage projects have a good deal of say about which projects are undertaken and how. On the other hand, many computer professionals have little autonomy. Programmers, for example, may simply implement the designs of others. There are professional organizations for computer specialists, but there is no single organization recognized by federal or state government as "the" legal body in charge of admission (by licensing, for example) or standards in the field of computing. As for fulfilling a social function, it seems clear that computing is now a crucial part of our society, but computing is not a good in itself in the way health and justice are. Computing is an activity that supports social institutions and professions, which in turn are aimed at fulfilling a variety of social functions.

Hence, it seems reasonable to conclude that computing does not fit the classic paradigm. That is, it is not a profession in the same way that law and medicine are. On the other hand, computer professionals are much closer to the paradigm of special professionals than, say, stockbrokers or carpenters or mail carriers.

In any case, whether or not the special meaning of the term "professional" applies to computer professionals is probably not so important as is identifying characteristics of the profession and of practice. An understanding of these is essential to understanding issues of professional ethics. Let us now focus on the relationships that computer professionals enter into at work.

PROFESSIONAL RELATIONSHIPS

When they take jobs, computer professionals typically enter into relationships with one or several of the following: (1) employers, (2) clients, (3) co-professionals (or the profession as a whole), and (4) the public.

Employer–Employee

When a person accepts a job in an organization, he or she enters into a relationship with an employer. Although many conditions of this relationship will be made explicit when the employee is hired (job title and associated responsibilities, salary, hours of work), many conditions will not be mentioned. Some are not mentioned since they are specified by law (for example, an employee may not be required to do anything illegal); they are assumed by both parties. Some aspects of the relationship may be negotiated through a union (for example, that employees with more seniority cannot be laid off before employees with less seniority). Yet many other conditions of the relationship will not be mentioned because neither party has an interest in them at the moment, because no one can anticipate all the situations that may arise, and probably because it is better not to press the uncertainties of some aspects of employer–

employee relations. For example, when you accept a job, do you, thereby, agree to work overtime whenever your supervisor requests it? If you work for a local government and it gets into financial trouble, will you accept your salary in script? Do you agree never to speak out publicly on political issues that may affect your employer? Do you agree to a dress code?

When one examines the moral foundation of the employer–employee relationship, it appears to be a contractual relationship. Each party agrees to do certain things in exchange for certain things. Generally, the employee agrees to perform certain tasks and the employer agrees to pay compensation and provide the work environment. Since the relationship is contractual in character, we may think of it as fulfilling the requirements of the categorical imperative. Each party exercises his or her autonomy in consenting to the terms of the contract, since each party is free to refuse to enter into the contract.

According to the categorical imperative, each individual should be treated with respect and never used merely as a means; thus it is wrong for either the employer or the employee to exploit the other. This means, among other things, that each party must be honest. An employee must be honest with her employer about her qualifications for the job and must do the work promised. Otherwise, she is simply using the employer to get what she wants without respecting the employer's interests. Likewise, the employer must pay a decent wage and must be honest with the employee about what she will be expected to do at work.

Workplace hazards illustrate the potential for exploitation here. If your employer says nothing about the dangers involved in a job and simply offers you a big salary and good benefits, making the job so attractive that it is hard to turn down, then the employer has not treated you with respect. He or she has not recognized you as an end in yourself, with interests of your own and the capacity to decide what risks you will or will not take. Your employer has kept important information from you in order to ensure that you will do what he or she wants. You are used merely as a means to what your employer wants. On the other hand, if your employer explains that you will be exposed to toxic substances at work and explains that this will increase the likelihood of your developing cancer, then if you agree to take the job, your employer has not exploited you.

For professional ethics, one of the most difficult areas of the employer–employee relationship has to do with what one rightfully owes an employer in the name of loyalty (or what an employer can rightfully expect or demand of an employee). Although loyalty is generally thought to be a good thing, closer examination reveals that it has both a good side and a bad. In her analysis of loyalty, Marcia Baron describes several negative effects of loyalty.[2] Loyalty is bad because (1) it invites unfairness, (2) it eschews reliance on good reasons, and (3) it invites irresponsibility. For example, if I am responsible for hiring a new employee and I, out of loyalty, choose my friend without considering the qualifications and experience of all other applicants, I have not treated the other applicants fairly. I have not used good reasons in making the decision; hence, I have acted irresponsibly in my position.

On the other hand, Baron points out that loyalty is a good thing because it allows us to have special relationships that are extremely valuable. Parenting and friendship are two powerful examples. Being a parent means treating certain people in special ways. If I were obligated to use my time and resources to help all children equally (that is, if "my" children had no special claims to my care and attention), then the idea that I was someone's parent would be without meaning. It is the same with friendship. If I treated my friends exactly as I treat all other persons, it would be hard to understand what it means to have a friend.

Both the good and bad implications of loyalty come into play in employer–employee relationships. Organizations could probably not function unless individuals recognize that they owe something special to their employers. Having individuals that will take orders and make efforts to coordinate their activities with others allows organizations to accomplish things that could not be accomplished otherwise. Hence, a certain degree of loyalty to an employer seems necessary and even worthy.

Nevertheless, we should not jump to the conclusion that employees owe their employers whatever they demand in the name of loyalty. There are limits. The hard part, of course, is to figure out where to draw the line. Clearly employers cannot demand every form of behavior that will serve the interests of the company. For example, companies have been known to pressure employees to vote in public elections for candidates who the company believes will further the company's interests. Such pressure threatens an employee's right as a citizen to vote as he or she sees fit. Indeed, it threatens democracy. Companies have also been known to expect their employees to buy only company products, that is, nothing made by a competitor. This expectation, especially when coupled with sanctions against those who do not comply, seems to overstep the bounds of legitimate employer expectations.

Trade secrecy is one area where the line is particularly difficult to draw. While employers have a legal right to expect their employees to keep trade secrets, it is unclear to what extent they should be allowed to go to protect their legitimate secrets. Trade secrets often involve information about the design of a new product, a formula, or a computer algorithm. Employers fear that employees may reveal these secrets to competitors, especially when they leave the company. Typically, employers have employees sign agreements promising not to reveal secrets.

Sometimes employees are even expected to agree not to work in the same industry for a certain period of time after they leave the company. Needless to say, employees often want to move on to another job and their best opportunities are likely to be, if not in the same industry, at least doing the same kind of work. Employees learn a great deal of what might be called "generic" knowledge while working at a company. It is not considered wrong for employees to take this knowledge with them to their next job. It is this knowledge and experience, in fact, that makes an employee attractive to another company. Still, employers have been known to try to prevent employees from moving on for fear that the employee will inadvertently, even if not intentionally, reveal valuable information to competitors. So the employer's legitimate concern about a trade secret has to be balanced against the right of an employee to work where he or she wants. Employers can abuse their rights by trying to stop their competitors from hiring a good employee.

The employer–employee relationship is more complicated and less well defined than you might expect. Employees do incur special responsibilities to their employers, but there are limits to this. The Carl Babbage scenario at the beginning of this article illustrates the point clearly enough. We cannot say that Babbage has no responsibilities to Acme. If he were to blow the whistle, a great deal of damage could be done to the company, and the damage would be done even if his concerns turned out to be wrong. On the other hand, it is hard to say that out of loyalty to the company he should do nothing. What he owes the company and when he should "break ranks" is not easy to figure out.

Client–Professional

The Carl Babbage scenario can also be understood to involve a conflict between an employee's responsibility to his employer and his responsibility to a client. The client in this case is the Defense Department, and technically it is Acme's client, only indirectly Babbage's. The Defense Department has entrusted its project to Acme, and it would seem that to be true to this trust, Acme should inform its client of the unanticipated problems. The problem here, of course, is that Acme does not appear to be behaving well, which creates the problem for Babbage. Babbage is expected by Acme to use the channels of authority in the organization. One can think of Acme's organizational structure as a mechanism for managing its responsibilities. Babbage has tried to work through this structure but it has not worked.

In both the Diane Jones scenario and the Marvin Miller scenario, the layers of bureaucracy are removed so that there is a more direct client–professional relationship. These are, perhaps, the better cases to use when first thinking through the character of client–professional relationships.

As with the employer–employee relationship, the client–professional relationship can be thought of as essentially contractual. Each party provides something the other wants, and both parties agree to the terms of the relationship: what will be done, how long it will take, how much the client will pay, where the work will be done, and so on. The important thing to keep in mind about client–professional relationships is the disparity in knowledge or expertise of the parties.

The client seeks the professional's special knowledge and expertise, but because the client does not himself possess that knowledge, he must depend on the professional. "Trust" is the operative term here. The client needs the professional to make or help make decisions that may be crucial to the client's business, and he must trust that the professional will use his or her knowledge competently, effectively, and efficiently. This is true of doctor–patient, lawyer–client, architect–client, and teacher–student relationships, as well as in relationships between computer professionals and clients.

Different models have been proposed for understanding how this disparity in professional–client relationships should be handled. Perhaps the most important are (1) agency, (2) paternalism, and (3) fiduciary.[3]

Briefly, on the *agency* model, the professional is to act as the agent of the professional and simply implement what the client requests. Here the implication is that the client retains all decision-making authority. The professional may make decisions but they are minor, that is, they are simply implications of the client's choice. I call a stockbroker, tell her what stocks I want to buy, how many, and at what price and she executes the transaction. She is my agent.

Some client–professional relationships are like this, but the problem with this model is that it does not come to grips with the special knowledge or expertise of the professional. Often the professional has knowledge that reflects back on what the client ought to be deciding. Professional advice is needed not just to implement decisions but to help make the decisions.

At the opposite extreme is the *paternalistic* model. Here the client transfers all decision-making authority to the professional, who acts in the interests of the client, making decisions that he believes will benefit the client. This model clearly recognizes the special expertise of the professional, so much so that the client has little "say." We used to think of the doctor–patient relationship on this model. I would go to a doctor, report my symptoms, and the rest was up to the doctor, who would decide what I needed and prescribe the treatment. I would simply be expected to accept what the doctor prescribed. How could I question the doctor's authority when I didn't have the expert knowledge? The problem, however, with this model of client–professional relationships is that it expects the client to turn over all autonomy to the professional and cease to be a decision maker. The client must place himself at the complete mercy of the professional.

The third model attempts to understand client–professional relationships as those in which both parties have a role and are working together. Clients retain decision-making authority but make decisions on the basis of information provided by the professional. This is called the *fiduciary* model, fiduciary implies trust. On this model both parties must trust one another. The client must trust the professional to use his or her expert knowledge and to think in terms of the interest of the client, but the professional must also trust that the client will give the professional relevant information, will listen to what the professional says, and so on. Decision making is shared.

On the fiduciary model, computer professionals serving clients will have the responsibility to be honest with clients about what they can and can't do, to inform them about what is possible, to give them realistic estimates of time and costs for their services, and much more. They will also have the responsibility to give clients the opportunity to make decisions about the parameters of the software or hardware they will get. Diane Jones seems to be working on the assumption of this sort of relationship in that she has informed her client of the possibilities and has made a recommendation. The problem now is that she doesn't think they are making the right decision. The fiduciary model would seem to call upon her to go back to her client and try to explain. It is hard to say what she should do if she is unsuccessful at convincing them. What is clear is that she owes her clients the benefits of her judgment.

In the Marvin Miller scenario, we see a computer professional doing something that threatens to undermine the trust that is so important to client–professional relationships. Miller has allowed himself to enter into a conflict-of-interest situation. His client—the hospital—expects him to exercise professional judgment on behalf of (in the interest of) the hospital. Although Miller may think he will be able to evaluate the offers made by each software company objectively, he has an interest in one of those companies that could affect his judgment. If representatives of the hospital find out about this, they might well conclude that Miller has not acted in the hospital's best interest. Even if Miller recommends that the hospital buy software from another company (not Tri-Star), there is the possibility that Miller's judgment has been distorted by his "bending over backward" to treat the other companies fairly. In that case, the hospital would not have gotten the best system either.

Imperative 1.3 of the 1992 Association for Computer Machinery (ACM) Code of Ethics specifies that an ACM member will "be honest and trustworthy." Included in the discussion of this imperative in the Guidelines to the Code is the statement: "A computer professional has a duty to be honest about his or her own qualifications, and about any circumstances that might lead to conflicts of interest." Rules of this kind recognize that clients (and the public) will lose confidence in a profession if they observe members abusing their roles. Indeed, in some professions, it is considered wrong for members to enter into any relationship that has even the appearance of a conflict of interest.

Society–Professional

When professionals exercise their skill and act in their professional roles, their activities may affect others who are neither employers nor clients. For example, you may design a computer system that will be used in a dangerous manufacturing process. Use of the system may put workers at risk or it may put residents in the neighborhood of the plant at risk. Or you might simply design a database for an insurance company, where the security of the system has implications for those who are insured. Because the work of computer professionals has these potential effects, computer professionals have a relationship with those others who may be affected.

This relationship is to a certain extent governed by law. That is, regulatory laws setting safety standards for products and construction are made in order to protect the public interest. But the law does not and cannot possibly anticipate all the effects that the work of professionals may have. At the same time professionals, including computer professionals, are often in the best position to see what effects their work will have or to evaluate the risks involved. Carl Babbage, for example, because of his expertise and familiarity with the system being designed, is in a better position than anyone outside of Acme to know whether or not the missile detecting system needs further evaluation.

The relationship between professionals and the individuals indirectly affected by their work can also be understood as contractual in nature, at least if we think of those affected as "society." Some of the sociological and philosophical literature on professions suggests that we understand each profession as having a social contract with society.[4] According to these accounts, we should think of society as granting the members of a profession (or the profession as a whole) the right to practice their profession (sometimes with special privileges) in exchange for their promise to practice the profession in ways that serve society, or, at least, in ways that do not harm society. This means maintaining professional standards and looking out for the public good. On this model, both parties give something and receive something in the exchange. Society gives professionals the right to practice and other forms of support and receives the benefits of having such professionals. Professionals receive the right to practice and other forms of societal support (protection of law, access to educational systems, and so on) and in exchange take on the burden of responsibility for managing themselves so as to serve the public interest. If a profession were not committed to public good, it would be foolish for society to allow members to practice.

The social contract account provides a useful framework for thinking about the ways in which computer professionals might organize themselves in the future, but it seems somewhat ill suited for understanding the field of computing as it is now constituted. That is, there is presently no single, formal organization of computer professionals that is recognized by government as having the right to issue licenses or set standards in the field of practice, and these are the most salient (and potent) aspects of a social contract.

We might better account for the responsibility of computer professionals to society by returning to the idea of their possessing special knowledge and skills, and the power of positions. What distinguishes computer professionals from others is their knowledge of how computers work, what computers can and cannot do, and how to get computers to do things. This knowledge, one might insist, carries with it some responsibility. When one has knowledge, special knowledge, one has a responsibility to use it for the benefit of humanity or, at least, not to the detriment of humanity. Special knowledge coupled with the power of position means that computer professionals can do things in the world that others cannot. Thus, they have greater responsibility than others.

The only problem with this account is that it simply asserts a correlation between knowledge and responsibility. The correlation is left as a primitive with no explanation. Thus, we cannot help but ask, why does responsibility come with knowledge? Why does it have to be so?

One way to establish this correlation between knowledge and responsibility is to base it on a principle of ordinary morality. Kenneth Alpern argues that the edict "Do no harm" is a fundamental principle of ordinary morality that no one will question.[5] He has to qualify the principle somewhat so that it reads, "Other things being equal, one should exercise due care to avoid contributing to significantly harming others." He then adds a corollary, which he calls the corollary of proportionate care: "Whenever one is in a position to contribute to greater harm or when one is in a position to play a more critical part in producing harm than is another person, one must exercise greater care to avoid so doing."

Focusing on engineers, Alpern then argues that while engineers are no different from anybody else in having the responsibility to avoid contributing to significant harm, they are different in that they are in positions (because of their work) in which they can do more harm than others. Thus, they have a responsibility to do more, to take greater care.

All of this seems to apply to computer professionals—at least, to many of them. Computer professionals are often in positions to use their expertise to contribute to projects that have the potential to harm others, as in the case of Carl Babbage. Since they act in ways that have the potential to do more harm, they have greater responsibility.

So Alpern's account does apply to computer professionals. The only problem is that if he is right, then it is not just computer professionals that bear responsibility but all those who contribute to projects with the potential to harm. Employed computer professionals can argue that they do not have nearly as much power as corporate managers, CEOs, or anyone above them in an organizational hierarchy. Alpern's proportionality thesis implies that the greater one's power, the greater one's responsibility. Of course, this need not be an either/or matter. Everyone, on Alpern's account, bears some responsibility, and so computer professionals bear their share of the responsibility along with managers and executives.[6]

Alpern's account is not exactly, then, an account of professional ethics but simply an account of the social responsibility of persons. Persons are responsible in proportion to their contribution to harm. Computer professionals are more powerful than some—in virtue of their knowledge and positions—and less powerful than others. They may not bear all the responsibility for a project, but they bear responsibility in proportion to their contribution.

Of course, to say that computer professionals have responsibility as persons and not as professionals is not to say that this is how it should be or has to be. Computer professionals might organize themselves in ways that create a stronger social responsibility and make the profession more of a "profession." They might take on a greater burden of responsibility in exchange for greater autonomy, which they might seek both as an organized professional group and as individual practitioners.

Throughout this article there have been hints about the kinds of things that computer professionals might do to bring this about. For example, creation of a professional organization with a code of conduct and a set of standards both for admission to the profession and for practice would be enormously helpful. Such an organization might have the power to grant licenses and to expel (or at least censure) individuals who engage in substandard behavior. The code of conduct would have to make clear the profession's commitment to public safety and welfare, and individuals might be required to take an oath to abide by the code before they are admitted to the profession. These actions would define the parameters of the social contract between society and computer professionals and make computing a distinctive, self-regulating field of endeavor.

Professional–Professional

Many professionals believe that they have obligations to other members of their profession. For example, professionals are often reluctant to criticize one another publicly, and they often help one another in getting jobs or in testifying at hearings when one of them is being sued. However, whether or not such behavior can be justified as a moral obligation is controversial.

It seems that the special treatment one professional gives to another may at times be good and at other times not. The earlier discussion of loyalty is relevant here. If one of your co-professionals is an alcoholic and, as a result, not doing a competent job, it is good that you try to help the person. On the other hand, if you keep his problem a secret, not wanting to jeopardize his career, this may result in injury to his employer or client. Similarly, when professionals get together to fix prices, this may be good for the professionals in that they can demand higher and higher prices, but it is not good for consumers who might benefit from a free market system.

One can take the cynical view that professionals only unite with one another to serve their self-interest, but even this line of thinking, when extended to long-term interests, leads to some constraints on what professionals should do. Every professional has an interest in the status and reputation of the profession as a whole for this affects how individual members are perceived and treated. Hence, each member of a profession may further her self-interest by forming alliances with other co-professionals and agreeing to constrain their behavior. For example, even though some might benefit from lying about their qualifications, or taking bribes, or fudging test results, in the long run such practices hurt the profession and, in turn, individual practitioners. The trust that clients and society must place in professionals is undermined and eroded when members of a profession behave in this way, so that all members of the profession are hurt. Clients become more reluctant to use computer systems and to rely on computer experts.

One way to think about what professionals owe one another is to think of what they owe each other in the way of adherence to certain standards of conduct, rather than simply to think of what they might do to help and protect one another in the short term. Rules about being honest, avoiding conflicts of interest, giving credit where credit is due, and so on can be understood to be obligations of one member of a profession to other members (in addition to their justification in moral theory).

CONFLICTING RESPONSIBILITIES

Managing one's responsibilities in the relationships just discussed is no small task, and the workplace is not structured to ensure that they will be in harmony. Issues of professional ethics often arise from conflicts between responsibilities to different parties.

Possibly the most common—at least, the most publicized—conflict is that between responsibilities to an employer and responsibility to society. The Carl Babbage case illustrates the typical situation. The employed professional is working on a project and has serious reservations about the safety or reliability of the product. For the good of those who will be affected by the project, the professional believes the project should not go forward yet. On the other hand, the employer (or supervisor) believes that it is in the interest of the company that the project go forward. The professional has to decide whether to keep quiet or do something that will "rock the boat."

To see why this conflict arises, we can return to our discussion of the characteristics of the work life of professionals and compare the situation of a typical employed computer professional with that of a stereotypical doctor. Perhaps the most striking difference is that the typical computer professional employed in a large private corporation has much less autonomy than a doctor in private practice. Computer professionals often work as employees of very large corporations or government agencies and have little autonomy.

Another characteristic of the work of computer professionals in contrast with that of doctors is its relatively fragmented nature. Computer professionals often work on small parts of much larger, highly complex projects. Their authority is limited to the small segment, with someone else having the designated responsibility for the whole project.

In addition, computer professionals are often quite distant from the ultimate effects of their activities. They may work on a project at certain stages of its development and then never see the product until it appears in the marketplace, having no involvement in how it is used, distributed, or advertised. Doctors, on the other hand, see in their patients the direct results of their decisions.[7]

Because of these characteristics of the work of computer professionals, they find themselves in a tension between their need for autonomy and the demands for organizational loyalty made by their employers.[8] On the one hand, they need autonomy because they have special knowledge. If they are to use that knowledge in a responsible manner and for the good of society, they must have the power to do so. However, insofar as they work for corporations with complex, highly bureaucratized organizational structures, and insofar as such large organizations need coordination of their various parts, there must be a division of labor, and they must often simply do what they are told. Carl Babbage's dilemma arises from this tension.

Acts of whistle-blowing arise out of precisely this sort of situation. Whistle-blowers opt against loyalty to their employer in favor of protecting society.[9] Whistle-blowing is, perhaps, the most dramatic form of the problem. Other issues that come up for computer professionals are more subtle aspects of this same tension—between loyalty to employer and social responsibility or professional responsibility. Should I work on military projects or other projects that I believe are likely to have bad effects? What am I to do when I know that a certain kind of system can never be built safely or securely enough, but I need the money or my company needs the contract? What do I do when a client is willing to settle for much less safety or security than I know is possible?

In the case of computer professionals, because the profession is relatively new and not well organized, the commitment to public safety and welfare is neither well entrenched in everyday practice nor well articulated in professional codes or literature. Nevertheless, the tension between protecting public good or adhering to professional standards and staying loyal to a higher organizational authority is there. It comes into clear focus now and then when cases involving public safety come to public attention. One of the first cases of whistle-blowing to be written about extensively involved three computer specialists working on the Bay Area Rapid Transit (BART) system.[10] The computer professionals in this case were concerned about the safety of the system controlling train speeds. They feared that under certain circumstances trains might be speeded up when they should be slowed. When their concerns were dismissed by their supervisors and then by the board monitoring the project, they went to newspaper reporters. In the same type of situation, more recently, David Parnas, a computer scientist, spoke out against funding for the Strategic Defense Initiative.[11] . . .

NOTES

1. Alan Goldman, *The Moral Foundations of Professional Ethics* (Totowa, N.J.: Rowan and Littlefield, 1980).

2. Marcia Baron, *The Moral Status of Loyalty* (Dubuque, Iowa: Kendall/Hunt, 1984).

3. See Michael Bayles, *Professional Ethics* (Belmont, Calif.: Wadsworth, 1981) for these and other models of the client–professional relationship.

4. Robert F. Ladenson, "The Social Responsibilities of Engineers and Scientists: A Philosophical Approach," in *Ethical Problems in Engineering*, Volume 1, 2nd ed., Albert Flores (Troy, N.Y.: Human Dimensions Center, 1980).

5. Kenneth Alpern, "Moral Responsibility for Engineers," *Business & Professional Ethics Journal*, 2, no. 2 (1983), 39–56.

6. For a fuller analysis of Alpern, see Deborah G. Johnson, "Do Engineers Have Social Responsibilities?" *Journal of Applied Philosophy*, 9, no. 1 (1992), 21–34.

7. I have identified these same characteristics of the work of engineers in "Do Engineers Have Social Responsibilities?" pp. 22–23.

8. Edwin Layton, *The Revolt of the Engineers: Social Responsibility and the American Engineering Profession* (Baltimore, Md.: Johns Hopkins University Press, 1971, 1986).

9. A good deal has been written about whistle-blowing. See, for example, Gene G. James, "In Defense of Whistleblowing," *Business Ethics: Readings and Cases in Corporate Morality*, ed. Hoffman and Mills (New York: McGraw-Hill, 1983); and James C. Petersen and Dan Farrell, *Whistleblowing: Ethical and Legal Issues in Expressing Dissent* (Dubuque, Iowa: Kendall/Hunt, 1986).

10. Robert M. Anderson et al., Divided Loyalties: Whistle-Blowing at BART (West Lafayette, Ind.: Purdue University, 1980).

11. David Parnas, "Professional Responsibility to Blow the Whistle on SDI," Abacus, 4, no. 2 (1987), 46–52.

PROGRAMMING AND THE PUBLIC TRUST

W. Robert Collins and Keith W. Miller

People do not like to trust computers, but increasingly they must. As computers become ubiquitous, so do complaints about the mistakes they make. Up to now, computer programmers have largely escaped widespread public animosity. The public's generosity toward programmers and animosity toward machines are both misplaced: computers do exactly what they are told to do with great reliability. Computers "misbehave" only when they are told to do the wrong thing. It is only a matter of time until the public's perception catches up to the reality.

Programmers have benefited from general ignorance about machines. If the public thinks that computers have a will of their own, then programmers are to be congratulated for controlling these obstinate machines as well as they do. However, computers do *not* have any will and, in fact, loyally do what programmers tell them to do. Therefore, programmers must take responsibility for how their programs behave. The situation is clarified if you think about lumberjacks and their chain saws. It takes a certain amount of skill and judgment to use a chain saw correctly, and we respect an expert woodcutter.

However, if the lumberjack endangers passersby or uses the chain saw on a job for which it is inappropriate, we do not blame the chain saw; we blame the lumberjack.

The analogy is not perfect; the complications of a computer program are orders of magnitude more difficult than the intricacies of a chain saw. We do not imply that the programmer's job is easy; it is not. A computer program of only moderate complexity includes a staggering amount of possible behavior.

Before the programmer can ascertain whether a program is "correct," someone must be able to express precisely what it should do in every situation in which it will be used. This type of expression, for both practical and theoretical reasons, is almost never possible.

Even if a complete and unambiguous description of the desired behavior were available, practical limitations make it impossible to guarantee correct behavior via testing. A program that transforms three 64 bit numbers (its input) into another number (its output) must theoretically contend with $2\text{-}2^{192}$ different input combinations. If all five billion people on earth could run and check a million, million test cases a second (far faster than the fastest supercomputer), it would take more than a billion, billion times the estimated age of the universe to exhaustively test this small program.

In the absence of exhaustive testing, programmers (and other computer professionals) must try more focused testing, formal analysis techniques, and other indirect methods to catch as many problems as possible before a program is released. For small programs used in well-known applications, these techniques are often (though not always) reasonably successful. For large, complicated programs, programmers do not expect to remove all the errors and strive only to remove as many as possible before schedules and budgets require the programmers to say that it is good enough.

Finally, even if we *could* express behavior unambiguously and if we *could* guarantee that behavior, we *still* could wind up with useless or dangerous software. Computer programs, once installed in a computer, are rigid, formal systems. However, the reality in which programs function is neither formal nor static. As the world and our perceptions of the world change, we biological creatures can adapt; computer programs do not. Furthermore, the number of people involved with software make it inevitable that a program will never please everyone. A computer program embodies hundreds of decisions, many of them hidden from most of the people who use the program. Any one of these decisions, though technically "correct" according to the people who designed and wrote the program, could be confusing, annoying, or even life-threatening to people using the program after it is installed.

When a United States Navy ship shot down an Iranian civilian airliner, the captain and crew apparently misinterpreted data shown on a computer screen. The numerical data reflected the motion of the airliner, but these data were either ignored or misread in the few moments before the Navy ship fired its missile. Was the computer program at least partly to blame? Probably. Even though it displayed the required information, the form of that information did not prevent the crew members from making a tragic mistake. Was the computer program "wrong"? Not in a technical sense. But the program was not as helpful as it could have been in this critical situation.

Computer programmers are well aware of these difficulties, and both researchers and practitioners are making progress in improving programming techniques. Many successful programming methods are adaptations of methods that were first used in other engineering fields. For example, interchangeable, standardized parts have dramatically raised the quality and lowered the price of computer hardware, and reusable software "parts" have gained importance in programming. However, the flexibility of software and the wide range of programming applications have made it more difficult than was anticipated to standardize software parts. So far, the gains in quality and affordability of computer software have lagged far behind the gains in hardware.

Engineering of any sort can never guarantee perfection. But good engineering knows its limits well. We reasonably expect bridges not to fall down suddenly, and when they do we expect someone will be held accountable. Bridge building has a long history, and the public trusts bridges. Computer programming is a younger branch of engineering, and the public is being asked to trust programs. The differences between bridges and programs make it easier for the public to trust programs when they should not.

A bridge built without a good plan and without a solid foundation will look bad and will shake visibly under a load. A bridge is a tangible object that obeys laws of physics, like the law of gravity. Although we may not intellectually understand gravity, we live with its effects and we feel as well as think about its reality. A computer obeys laws of physics in its circuitry, but a computer program, built on top of these circuits, creates its own reality using instructions to the computer. A program is a model of reality, not reality itself. The imperfections of the model and incorrect manipulations of it make computer programs fail. And the nature of computers makes these imperfections invisible to the public until the effects are manifest. If the program's faults are subtle, the problem can go undetected for years, only to become important in an instant.

Bridge builders can also hedge their bets by "over-engineering": using materials and techniques that give strength and durability exceeding requirements by factors of five or ten. As long as the builders' estimates are close, this over-engineering gives an extra measure of safety for the bridge. However, over-engineering is difficult for programmers: extra code does not necessarily mean a "stronger" program. In fact, the longer a program becomes, the more errors it tends to have. Over-engineering for programmers *should* mean using other sorts of backup for the software in case their programs fail.

This can mean physical backups (manual control of computer-controlled automobile brakes), physical fail-safe features (physical impossibility of all green lights in computer-controlled traffic lights), computer backups (two separate computers in fly-by-wire F16 aircraft), human monitoring (by nurses of computer-generated pharmaceutical instructions), and so on. Over-engineering for programmers may be more expensive than costs saved by using computers in the first place.

In the recent past, many mechanical devices were *removed* from machines and replaced by computer programs. Sad experiences with programming errors is leading to their reintroduction. The Malfunction 54 [Jonathan Jackie, "Programmed for Disaster," *The Sciences*, (Sept–Oct 1989), pp. 24–27.] disaster dramatizes the importance of total *system reliability*.

The Therac-25 radiation machine was used in medicine to help reduce tumors. Its complex electromechanical control systems were replaced by computers. What was physically impossible in the past because of interlocking circuitry, to engage a high-powered electron beam without a shield for the patient, become possible because of an error in the control software. As a result of this programming error, and as a consequence of a poorly conceived operator interface, several patients were severely injured and two were killed.

As programmers and other engineers are becoming more concerned with safety, they are beginning to design computer-controlled systems with mechanical interlocks and backups. This reintroduction is a hopeful sign; it reflects an understanding of the current limitations on computer programs and a realistic attitude toward coping with those limitations.

Is the situation hopeless? Hardly. Programs do work in many situations. The programming profession is making important progress in improving the quality of programs and techniques for verifying that quality. However, computer professionals are building enormous suspension-bridge programs to travel over great, dangerous chasms. These bridges are not pretty, and they are not strong enough. Malfunctioning X-ray machines, long-distance telephone disruptions, space-shuttle delays, and multi-million-dollar bank errors all illustrate the dangerous nature of our computer bridges.

If programmers are to gain the public's trust, they must insist on more realistic expectations for computers. We computer professionals must be cautious about computer automation until programming is better understood and better practiced. The public should demand better quality software where automation is appropriate and should resist automation in riskier applications. And programmers must not fight this go-slow approach but must in good conscience be leaders in demanding it. If we builders of programs do not encourage realism about our computer bridges, the public will rightly condemn us when some of our bridges crumble.

▷ CODES OF ETHICS

Michael Martin and Roland Schinzinger

ROLES OF CODES

Inspiration and Guidance Codes provide a positive stimulus for ethical conduct and helpful guidance and advice concerning the main obligations of engineers. Often they succeed in inspiring by using language with positive overtones. This can introduce a large element of vagueness, as in phrases like "safeguard the public safety, health, and welfare," a vagueness which may lessen their ability to give concrete guidance. Sometimes lofty ideals and exhortative phrases are gathered into separate documents, such as *Faith of the Engineer*, published by the Accreditation Board for Engineering and Technology (ABET), which succeeded the Engineering Council for Professional Development (ECPD).

Since codes should be brief to be effective, they offer mostly general guidance. More specific directions may be given in supplementary statements or guidelines. These tell how to apply the code. Further specificity may also be attained by the interpretation of codes. This is done for engineers by the National Society of Professional Engineers. It has established a Board of Ethical Review which applies the Society's code to specific cases and publishes the results in *Professional Engineer* and in periodic volumes entitled *NSPE Opinions of the Board of Ethical Review*.

A number of companies (for example, Bechtel, Hughes Aircraft, McDonnell-Douglas) have instituted their own codes. These tend to concentrate on the moral issues encountered in dealing with vendors and clients, particularly the U.S. federal government.

Support Codes give positive support to those seeking to act ethically. A publicly proclaimed code allows an engineer who is under pressure to act unethically to say: "I am bound by the code of ethics of my profession, which states that. . . ." This by itself gives engineers some group backing in taking stands on moral issues. Moreover, codes can potentially serve as legal support in courts of law for engineers seeking to meet work-related moral obligations.

Deterrence and Discipline Codes can serve as the formal basis for investigating unethical conduct. Where such investigation is possible, a prudential motive for not acting immorally is provided as a deterrent. Such an investigation generally requires paralegal proceedings designed to get at the truth about a given charge without violating the personal rights of those being investigated. In the past, engineering professional societies have been reluctant to undertake such proceedings because they have lacked the appropriate sanctions needed for punishment of misconduct. Unlike the American Bar Association and some other professional groups, engineering societies cannot revoke the right to practice engineering in this country. Yet the American Society of Civil Engineers, for example, does currently suspend or expel members whose professional conduct has been proven unethical, and this alone can be a powerful sanction when combined with the loss of respect from colleagues and the local community that such action is bound to produce.

Education and Mutual Understanding Codes can be used in the classroom and elsewhere to prompt discussion and reflection on moral issues and to encourage a shared understanding among professionals, the public, and government organizations concerning the moral responsibilities of engineers. They can help do this because they are widely circulated and officially approved by professional societies.

Contributing to the Profession's Public Image Codes can present a positive image to the public of an ethically committed profession. Where the image is warranted, it can help engineers more effectively serve the public. It can also win greater powers of self-regulation for the profession itself, while lessening the demand for more government regulation. Where unwarranted, it reduces to a kind of window dressing that ultimately increases public cynicism about the profession.

Protecting the Status Quo Codes establish ethical conventions, which can help promote an agreed upon minimum level of ethical conduct. But it can also stifle dissent within the profession. On occasion this has positively discouraged moral conduct and caused serious harm to those seeking to serve the public. In 1932, for example, two engineers were expelled from the American Society of Civil Engineers for violating a section of its code forbidding public remarks critical of other engineers. Yet the actions of those engineers were essential in uncovering a major bribery scandal related to the construction of a dam for Los Angeles County.

Promoting Business Interests Codes can place "restraints of commerce" on business dealings with primary benefit to those within the profession. Basically self-serving items in codes can take on great undue influence. Obviously there is disagreement about which, if any, entries function in these ways. Some engineers believe that in the past the codes were justified in forbidding competitive bidding, while others agree with the decision of the Supreme Court in the case of the *National Society of Professional Engineers* v. *the United States* (April 25, 1978) that such a restriction is inappropriate.

CODES AND THE EXPERIMENTAL NATURE OF ENGINEERING

Given that codes may play all these roles, which functions are the most valuable and therefore should be emphasized and encouraged? This is an important question, if only because its answer can greatly influence the very wording of codes. For example, if the disciplinary function is to be emphasized, every effort would have to be made to ensure clear-cut and enforceable rules. This would also tend to make statements of minimal duty predominant, as with standards and laws, rather than statements concerned with higher ideals. By contrast, if the emphasis is to be on inspiration, then statements of high ideals might predominate. Nothing is less inspirational than arid, legalistic wordings, and nothing is less precise than highly emotional exhortations.

The perspective of engineering as social experimentation provides some help in deciding which functions should be primary in engineering codes. It clearly emphasizes those which best enable concerned engineers to express their views freely— especially about safety—to those affected by engineering projects. Only thus can clients and the public be educated adequately enough to make informed decisions about such projects. But as we have already noted and will discuss in more detail later, contemporary working conditions within large corporations do not always encourage this freedom of speech—conditions for which a code of ethics can provide an important counterbalance. Thus the supportive function seems to us of primary importance.

The guidance, inspirational, and educational functions of engineering codes are important also, as is their role in promoting mutual understanding among those affected by them. In seeking to create a common understanding, however, code writers must take every precaution to allow room for reasonable differences between individuals. Wordings in past codes, for example, sometimes used religious language not acceptable to many who did not share that orientation. Codes, we must bear in mind, seek to capture the essential substance of professional ethics; they can hardly be expected to express the full moral perspective of every individual.

The disciplinary function of engineering codes is in our view of secondary importance. There are scoundrels in engineering, as there are everywhere. But when exposed as such, they generally fall subject to the law. Developing elaborate paralegal procedures within professional societies runs the risk of needlessly and at considerable cost duplicating a function better left to the real legal system. At most, enforcement of professional ethics by professional societies should center upon areas that are not covered by law and that can be made explicit and clear-cut, preferably in separate code sections specifically devoted to those areas. In any case, the vast majority of engineers can be counted on to act responsibly in moral situations unless *discouraged* from doing so by outright threats and lack of support on the part of employers.

Probably the worst abuse of engineering codes in the past has been to restrict honest moral effort on the part of individual engineers in the name of preserving the profession's public image and protecting the status quo. Preoccupation with keeping a shiny public image may silence the healthy dialogue and lively criticism needed to ensure the public's right to an open expression. And an excessive interest in protecting the status quo may lead to a distrust of the engineering profession on the part of both government and the public. The best way to *increase* trust is by encouraging and aiding engineers to speak freely and responsibly about the public safety and good as they see it. And this includes a tolerance for criticisms of the codes themselves. Perhaps the worst thing that can happen is for codes to become "sacred documents" that have to be accepted uncritically.

LIMITATIONS OF CODES

Most codes are limited in several major ways. Those limitations restrict codes to providing only very general guidance, which in turn makes it essential for engineers to exercise a personal moral responsibility in their role as social experimenters rather than to expect codes to solve their moral problems by serving as simple algorithms. The limitations of codes are as follows.

First, as we have already mentioned, codes are restricted to general and vague wording. Because of this they are not straightforwardly applicable to all situations. After all, it is not humanly possible to foresee the full range of moral problems that can arise in a complex profession like engineering. New technical developments and shifting social and organizational structures combine to generate continually new and often unpredictable conditions. And even in the case of foreseeable situations it is not possible to word a code so that it will apply in every instance. Attempting to do so would yield something comparable to the intricate set of laws governing engineering rather than a manageable code.

A sense of responsibility is indispensable for the skillful and at times creative application of code guidelines to concrete situations. It is also the only way certain abuses of codes can be avoided—for example, abuses such as special interpretations being placed on general entries, or legalistic glosses on specific entries, to serve the private gain or convenience of specific individuals or groups.

Second, it is easy for different entries in codes to come into conflict with each other. Usually codes provide no guidance as to which entry should have priority in those cases, thereby creating moral dilemmas.

For example, take the following two former entries from the National Society of Professional Engineers (NSPE) code. Section 1: "The Engineer will be guided in all his professional relations by the highest standards of integrity, and will act in professional matters for each client or employer as a faithful agent or trustee." Section 2: "The Engineer will have proper regard for the safety, health, and welfare of the public in the performance of his professional duties."

Recent codes have attempted to address this important area of potential conflict. The NSPE code now states: "Engineers shall hold paramount the safety, health, and welfare of the public in the performance of their professional duties." The word "paramount" means "most important or superior in rank." But even so it is unclear that the provision means engineers should never, under any circumstances, follow a client's or company's directives because they believe those directives might not serve the best interests of the public. Here we emphasize again the need for responsible engineers who are able to make reasonable assessments of what "paramount" amounts to in cases where two professional obligations conflict.

A third limitation on codes is that they cannot serve as the final moral authority for professional conduct. To accept the current code of a professional society as the last moral word, however officially endorsed it may be, would be to lapse into a type of Ethical Conventionalism. It will be recalled that Ethical Conventionalism is the view that a particular set of conventions, customs, or laws is self-certifying and not to be questioned simply because it is the set in force at a given time or for a given place. Such a view, of course, rules out the possibility of criticizing that set of conventions from a wider moral framework.

Consider once again the following entry in the pre-1979 versions of the NSPE code: "He [the engineer] shall not solicit or submit engineering proposals on the basis of competitive bidding." This prohibition was felt by the NSPE to best protect the public safety by discouraging cheap engineering proposals which might slight safety costs in order to win a contract. Critics of the prohibition, however, contended that it mostly served the self-interest of engineering firms and actually hurt the public by "preventing" the lower prices that might result from greater competition. In a 1978 decision, *National Society of Professional Engineers* v. *United States*, the Supreme Court ruled that the ban on competitive bidding was unconstitutional and not appropriate in a code of ethics.

The point here is not who holds the correct moral view on this issue—that is a matter of ongoing debate and discussion. And indeed, it is precisely our point that no pronouncement by a code current at any given time should ever be taken as the final word silencing such healthy debates. Codes, after all, represent a compromise between differing judgments, sometimes developed amidst heated committee disagreements. As such, they have a great "signpost" value in suggesting paths through what can be a bewildering terrain of moral decision maker. But equally as such they should never be treated as "sacred canon."

The fourth limitation of codes results from their proliferation. Andrew Oldenquist (a philosopher) and Edward Slowter (an engineer and former NSPE president) point out how the existence of separate codes for different professional engineering societies can give members the feeling that ethical conduct is more "relative" than it is, and how it can convey to the public the view that none of the codes is "really right." But Oldenquist and Slowter have also demonstrated the substantial agreement to be found among the various engineering codes. These authors summarize the core concepts in each and arrange them in order of significance as having to do with (1) the public interest, (2) qualities of truth, honesty, and fairness, and (3) professional performance. They emphasize in their 1979 paper that the time has come for adoption of a unified code. The ABET and AAES codes are by no means perfect, but they are steps in the right direction.

▷ THE QUEST FOR A CODE OF PROFESSIONAL ETHICS: AN INTELLECTUAL AND MORAL CONFUSION

John Ladd

My role as a philosopher is to act as a gadfly. If this were Athens in the fifth century B.C. you would probably throw me in prison for what I shall say, and I would be promptly condemned to death for attacking your idols. But you can't do that in this day and age; you can't even ask for your money back, since I am not being paid. All that you can do is to throw eggs at me or simply walk out!

My theme is stated in the title: it is that the whole notion of an organized professional ethics is an absurdity—intellectual and moral. Furthermore, I shall argue that there are few positive benefits to be derived from having a code and the possibility of mischievous side effects of adopting a code is substantial. Unfortunately, in the time allotted to me I can only summarize what I have to say on this topic.

1. To begin with, ethics itself is basically an open-ended, reflective and critical intellectual activity. It is essentially problematic and controversial, both as far as its principles are concerned and in its application. Ethics consists of issues to be examined, explored, discussed, deliberated, and argued. Ethical principles can be established only as a result of deliberation and argumentation. These principles are not the kind of thing that can be settled by fiat, by agreement or by authority. To assume that they can be is to confuse ethics with law-making, rule-making, policy-making and other kinds of decision-making. It follows that, ethical principles, as such, cannot be established by associations, organizations, or by a consensus of their members. To speak of codifying ethics, therefore, makes no more sense than to speak of codifying medicine, anthropology or architecture.

2. Even if substantial agreement could be reached on ethical principles and they could be set out in a code, the attempt to impose such principles on others in the guise of ethics contradicts the notion of ethics itself, which presumes that persons are autonomous moral agents. In Kant's terms, such an attempt makes ethics heteronomous; it confuses ethics with some kind of externally imposed set of rules such as a code of law, which, indeed, is heteronomous. To put the point in more popular language: ethics must, by its very nature, be self-directed rather than other-directed.

3. Thus, in attaching disciplinary procedures, methods of adjudication and sanctions, formal and informal, to the principles that one calls "ethical" one automatically converts them into legal rules or some other kind of authoritative rules of conduct such as the bylaws of an organization, regulations promulgated by an official, club rules, rules of etiquette, or other sorts of social standards of conduct. To label such conventions, rules and standards "ethical" simply reflects an intellectual confusion about the status and function of these conventions, rules and standards. Historically, it should be noted that the term "ethical" was introduced merely to indicate that the code of the Royal College of Physicians was not to be construed as a criminal code (i.e., a legal code). Here "ethical" means simply non-legal.

4. That is not to say that ethics has no relevance for projects involving the creation, certification and enforcement of rules of conduct for members of certain groups. But logically it has the same kind of relevance that it has for the law. As with law, its role in connection with these projects is to appraise, criticize and perhaps even defend (or condemn) the projects themselves, the rules, regulations and procedures they prescribe, and the social and political goals and institutions they represent. But although ethics can be used to judge or evaluate a disciplinary code, penal code, code of honor or what goes by the name of a "code of ethics," it cannot be identified with any of these, for the reasons that have already been mentioned.

SOME GENERAL COMMENTS ON PROFESSIONALISM AND ETHICS

5. Being a professional does not automatically make a person an expert in ethics, even in the ethics of that person's own particular profession—unless of course we decide to call the "club rules" of a profession its ethics. The reason for this is that there are no experts in ethics in the sense of expert in which professionals have a special expertise that others do not share. As Plato pointed out long ago in the *Protagoras*, knowledge of virtue is not like the technical knowledge that is possessed by an architect or shipbuilder. In a sense, everyone is, or ought to be, a teacher of virtue; there are no professional qualifications that are necessary for doing ethics.

6. Moreover, there is no special ethics belonging to professionals. Professionals are not, simply because they are professionals, exempt from the common obligations, duties and responsibilities that are binding on ordinary people. They do not have a special moral status that allows them to do things that no one else can. Doctors have no special right to be rude, to deceive, or to order people around like children, etc. Likewise, lawyers do not have a special right to bend the law to help their clients, to bully witnesses, or to be cruel and brutal—simply because they think that it is in the interests of their client. Professional codes cannot, therefore, confer such rights and immunities; for there is no such thing as professional ethical immunity.

7. We might ask: do professionals, by virtue of their special professional status, have special duties and obligations over and above those they would have as ordi-

nary people? Before we can answer this question, we must first decide what is meant by the terms "profession" and "professional," which are very loose terms that are used as labels for a variety of different occupational categories. The distinctive element in professionalism is generally held to be that professionals have undergone advanced, specialized training and that they exercise control over the nature of their job and the services they provide. In addition, the older professions, lawyers, physicians, professors and ministers typically have clients to whom they provide services as individuals. (I use the term "client" generically so as to include patients, students, and parishioners.) When professionals have individual clients, new moral relationships are created that demand special types of trust and loyalty. Thus, in order to answer the question, we need to examine the context under which special duties and obligations of professionals might arise.

8. In discussing specific ethical issues relating to the professions, it is convenient to divide them into issues of *macro-ethics* and *micro-ethics*. The former comprise what might be called collective or social problems, that is, problems confronting members of a profession as a group in their relation to society; the latter, issues of micro-ethics, are concerned with moral aspects of personal relationships between individual professionals and other individuals who are their clients, their colleagues and their employers. Clearly the particulars in both kinds of ethics vary considerably from one profession to another. I shall make only two general comments.

9. Micro-ethical issues concern the personal relationships between individuals. Many of these issues simply involve the application of ordinary notions of honesty, decency, civility, humanity, considerateness, respect and responsibility. Therefore, it should not be necessary to devise a special code to tell professionals that they ought to refrain from cheating and lying, or to make them treat their clients (and patients) with respect, or to tell them that they ought to ask for informed consent for invasive actions. It is a common mistake to assume that *all* the extra-legal norms and conventions governing professional relationships have a moral status, for every profession has norms and conventions that have as little to do with morality as the ceremonial dress and titles that are customarily associated with the older professions.

10. The macro-ethical problems in professionalism are more problematic and controversial. What are the social responsibilities of professionals as a group? What can and should they do to influence social policy? Here, I submit, the issue is not one of professional roles, but of *professional power*. For professionals as a group have a great deal of power; and power begets responsibility. Physicians as a group can, for instance, exercise a great deal of influence on the quality and cost of health care; and lawyers can have a great deal of influence on how the law is made and administered, etc.

11. So-called "codes of professional ethics" have nothing to contribute either to micro-ethics or to macro-ethics as just outlined. It should also be obvious that they do not fit under either of these two categories. Any association, including a professional association, can, of course, adopt a code of conduct for its members and lay down disciplinary procedures and sanctions to enforce conformity with its rules. But to call such a disciplinary code a code of *ethics* is at once pretentious and sanctimonious. Even worse, it is to make a false and misleading claim, namely, that the profession in question has the authority or special competence to create an ethics, that it is able authoritatively to set forth what the principles of ethics are, and that it has its own brand of ethics that it can impose on its members and on society.

I have briefly stated the case against taking a code of professional ethics to be a serious ethical enterprise. It might be objected, however, that I have neglected to recognize some of the benefits that come from having professional codes of ethics. In order to discuss these possible benefits, I shall first examine what some of the objectives of codes of ethics might be, then I shall consider some possible benefits of having a code, and, finally, I shall point out some of the mischievous aspect of codes.

OBJECTIVES OF CODES OF PROFESSIONAL "ETHICS"

In order to be crystal clear about the purposes and objectives of a code, we must begin by asking: to whom is the code addressed? Although ostensibly codes of ethics are addressed to the members of the profession, their true purposes and objectives are sometimes easier to ascertain if we recognize that codes are in fact often directed at other addressees than members. Accordingly, the real addressees might be any of the following: (a) members of the profession, (b) clients or buyers of the professional services, (c) other agents dealing with professionals, such as government or private institutions like universities or hospitals, or (d) the public at large. With this in mind, let us examine some possible objectives.

First, the objective of a professional code might be "inspirational," that is, it might be used to inspire members to be more "ethical" in their conduct. The assumption on which this objective is premised is that professionals are somehow likely to be amoral or submoral, perhaps, as the result of becoming professionals, and so it is necessary to exhort them to be moral, e.g., to be honest. I suppose there is nothing objectionable to having a code for this reason; it would be something like the Boy Scout's Code of Honor, something to frame and hang in one's office. I have severe reservations, however, about whether a code is really needed for this purpose and whether it will do any good; for those to whom it is addressed and who need it the most will not adhere to it anyway, and the rest of the good people in the profession will not need it because they already know what they ought to do. For this reason, many respectable members of a profession regard its code as a joke and as something not to be taken seriously. (Incidentally, for much the same kind of reasons as those just given, there are no professional codes in the academic or clerical professions.)

A second objective might be to alert professionals to the moral aspects of their work that they might have overlooked. In jargon, it might serve to sensitize them or to raise their consciousness. This, of course, is a worthy goal—it is the goal of moral education. Morality, after all, is not just a matter of doing or not doing, but also a matter of feeling and thinking. But, here again, it is doubtful that it is possible to make people have the right feelings or think rightly through enacting a code. A code is hardly the best means for teaching morality.

Third, a code might, as it was traditionally, be a disciplinary code or a "penal" code used to enforce certain rules of the profession on its members in order to defend the integrity of the professional and to protect its professional standards. This kind of function is often referred to as "self-policing." It is unlikely, however, that the kind of disciplining that is in question here could be handled in a code of ethics, a code that would set forth in detail criteria for determining malpractice. On the contrary, the "ethical" code of a profession is usually used to discipline its members for other sorts of "unethical conduct," such as stealing a client away from a colleague, for making disparaging remarks about a colleague in public, or for departing from some other sort of norm of the profession. (In the original code of the Royal College of Physicians, members who failed to attend the funeral of a colleague were subject to a fine!) It is clear that when we talk of a disciplinary code, as distinguished from an exhortatory code, a lot of new questions arise that cannot be treated here; for a disciplinary code is quasi-legal in nature, it involves adjudicative organs and processes, and it is usually connected with complicated issues relating to such things as licensing.

A fourth objective of a code might be to offer advice in cases of moral perplexity about what to do: e.g., should one report a colleague for malfeasance? Should one let a severely defective newborn die? If such cases present genuine perplexities, then they cannot and should not be solved by reference to a code. To try to solve them through a code is like trying to do surgery with a carving knife! If it is not a genuine perplexity, then the code would be unnecessary.

A fifth objective of a professional code of ethics is to alert prospective clients and employers to what they may and may not expect by way of service from a member of the profession concerned. The official code of an association, say, of engineers, provides as authoritative statement of what is proper and what is improper conduct of the professional. Thus, a code serves to protect a professional from improper demands on the part of employer or client, e.g., that he lie about or cover up defective work that constitutes a public hazard. Codes may thus serve to protect "whistle-blowers." (The real addressee in this case is the employer or client.)

SECONDARY OBJECTIVES OF CODES— NOT ALWAYS SALUTARY

I now come to what I shall call "secondary objectives," that is, objectives that one might hesitate always to call "ethical," especially since they often provide an opportunity for abuse.

The first secondary objective is to enhance the image of the profession in the public eye. The code is supposed to communicate to the general public (the addressee) the idea that the members of the profession concerned are service oriented and that the interests of the client are always given first place over the interests of the professional himself. Because they have a code they may be expected to be trustworthy.

Another secondary objective of a code is to protect the monopoly of the profession in question. Historically, this appears to have been the principal objective of a so-called code of ethics, e.g., Percival's code of medical ethics. Its aim is to exclude from practice those who are outside the professional in-group and to regulate the conduct of the members of the profession so as to protect it from encroachment from outside. Sometimes this kind of professional monopoly is in the public interest and often it is not.

Another secondary objective of professional codes of ethics, mentioned in some of the literature, is that having a code serves as a status symbol; one of the credentials for an occupation to be considered a profession is that it have a code of ethics. If you want to make your occupation a profession, then you must frame a code of ethics for it: so there are codes for real estate agents, insurance agents, used-car dealers, electricians, barbers, etc., and these codes serve, at least in the eyes of some, to raise their members to the social status of lawyers and doctors.

MISCHIEVOUS SIDE-EFFECTS OF CODES OF ETHICS

I now want to call attention to some of the mischievous side-effects of adopting a code of ethics:

The first and most obvious bit of mischief, is that having a code will give a sense of complacency to professionals about their conduct. "We have a code of ethics," they will say, "so everything we do is ethical." Inasmuch as a code, of necessity, prescribes what is minimal, a professional may be encouraged by the code to deliver what is minimal rather than the best that he can do. "I did everything that the code requires. . . ."

Even more mischievous than complacency and the consequent self-congratulation, is the fact that a code of ethics can be used as a cover-up for what might be called basically "unethical" or "irresponsible" conduct.

Perhaps the most mischievous side-effect of codes of ethics is that they tend to divert attention from the macro-ethical problems of a profession to its micro-ethical problems. There is a lot of talk about whistle-blowing. But it concerns individuals almost exclusively. What is really needed is a thorough scrutiny of professions as collective bodies, of their role in society and their effect on the public interest. What role should the professions play in determining the use of technology, its development and expansion, and the distribution of the costs (e.g., disposition of toxic wastes) as well as the benefits of technology? What is the significance of professionalism from the moral point of view for democracy, social equality, liberty and justice? There are lots of ethical problems to be dealt with. To concentrate on codes of ethics as if they represented the real ethical problems connected with professionalism is to capitulate to *struthianism* (from the Greek word *struthos* = ostrich).

One final objection to codes that needs to be mentioned is that they inevitably represent what John Stuart Mill called the "tyranny of the majority" or, if not that, the "tyranny of the establishment." They serve to and are designed to discourage if not suppress the dissenter, the innovator, the critic.

By way of conclusion, let me say a few words about what an association of professionals can do about ethics. On theoretical grounds, I have argued that it cannot codify an ethics and it cannot authoritatively establish ethical principles or prescribed guidelines for the conduct of its members—as if it were *creating* an ethics! But there is still much that associations can do to promote further understanding of and sensitivity to ethical issues connected with professional activities. For example, they can fill a very useful educational function by encouraging their members to participate in extended discussions of issues of both micro-ethics and macro-ethics, e.g., questions about responsibility; for these issues obviously need to be examined and discussed much more extensively than they are at present—especially by those who are in a position to do something about them.

▷ **THINKING LIKE AN ENGINEER:**
THE PLACE OF A CODE OF ETHICS
IN THE PRACTICE OF A PROFESSION

Michael Davis

Most discussions of engineering ethics dismiss the idea of codes of ethics from the outset. Codes are described as self-serving, unrealistic, inconsistent, mere guides for novices, too vague, or unnecessary.[1] I will not do that here. Instead, I will argue that a code of professional ethics is central to advising individual engineers how to conduct themselves, to judging their conduct, and ultimately to understanding engineering as a profession. I will begin with a case now commonly discussed in engineering ethics, finding my general argument in a detailed analysis of a particular choice. While I believe the analysis to be applicable to all professions, I shall not argue that here.

THE CHALLENGER DISASTER[2]

On the night of 27 January 1986, Robert Lund was worried. The Space Center was counting down for a shuttle launch the next morning. Lund, vice-president for engineering at Morton Thiokol, had earlier presided over a meeting of engineers that unanimously recommended *against* the launch. He had concurred and informed his boss, Jerald Mason. Mason informed the Space Center. Lund had expected the flight to be postponed. The Center's safety record was good. It was good because the Center would not allow a launch unless the technical people approved.

Lund had not approved. He had not approved because the temperature at the launch site would be close to freezing at lift-off. The Space Center was worried about the ice already forming in places on the boosters, but Lund's worry was the "O-rings" sealing the boosters' segments. They had been a great idea, permitting Thiokol to build the huge rocket in Utah and ship it in pieces to the Space Center two thousand miles away. Building in Utah was so much more efficient than building on-site that Thiokol had been able to underbid the competition. The shuttle contract had earned Thiokol $150 million in profits.

But, as everyone now knows, the O-rings were not perfect. Data from previous flights indicated that the rings tended to erode in flight, with the worst erosion occurring on the coldest preceding lift-off. Experimental evidence was sketchy but ominous. Erosion seemed to increase as the rings lost their resiliency, and resiliency decreased with temperature. At a certain temperature, the rings could lose so much resiliency that one could fail to seal properly. If a ring failed in flight, the shuttle could explode.

Unfortunately, almost no testing had been done below 40°F. The engineers' scarce time had had to be devoted to other problems, forcing them to extrapolate from the little data they had. But, with the lives of seven astronauts at stake, the decision seemed clear enough: Safety first.

Or so it had seemed earlier that day. Now Lund was not so sure. The Space

Center had been "surprised," even "appalled," by the evidence on which the no-launch recommendation had been based. They wanted to launch. They did not say why, but they did not have to. The shuttle program was increasingly falling behind its ambitious launch schedule. Congress had been grumbling for some time. And, if the launch went as scheduled, the president would be able to announce the first teacher in space as part of his State of the Union message the following evening, very good publicity just when the shuttle program needed some.

The Space Center wanted to launch. But they would not launch without Thiokol's approval. They urged Mason to reconsider. He reexamined the evidence and decided the rings should hold at the expected temperature. Joseph Kilminster, Thiokol's vice-president for shuttle programs, was ready to sign a launch approval, but only if Lund approved. Lund was now all that stood in the way of launching.

Lund's first response was to repeat his objections. But then Mason said something that made him think again. Mason asked him to *think like a manager rather than an engineer*. (The exact words seem to have been, "Take off your engineering hat and put on your management hat.") Lund did and changed his mind. The next morning the shuttle exploded during lift-off, killing all aboard. An O-ring had failed.

Should Lund have reversed his decision and approved the launch? In retrospect, of course, the answer is obvious: No. But most problems concerning what we should do would hardly be problems at all if we could foresee all the consequences of what we do. Fairness to Lund requires us to ask whether he should have approved the launch given only the information available to him at the time. And since Lund seems to have reversed his decision and approved the launch because he began to think like a manager rather than an engineer, we need to consider whether Lund, an engineer, should have been thinking like a manager rather than an engineer. But, before we can consider that, we need to know what the difference is between thinking like a manager and thinking like an engineer.

One explanation of the difference stresses technical knowledge. Managers, it might be said, are trained to handle people; engineers, to handle things. To think like a manager rather than an engineer is to focus on people rather than on things. According to this explanation, Lund was asked to concern himself primarily with how best to handle his boss, the Space Center, and his own engineers. He was to draw upon his knowledge of engineering only as he might draw upon his knowledge of a foreign language, for example, to help him communicate with his engineers. He was to act much as he would have acted had he never earned a degree in engineering.

If that explanation of what Mason was asking of Lund seems implausible (as I think it does), what is the alternative? If Mason did not mean that Lund should make his knowledge of engineering peripheral (as it seems Mason, himself an engineer, did *not* when he personally reexamined the evidence), what was he asking Lund to do? What is it to think like an engineer if not simply to use one's technical knowledge of things? That is a question engineers have been asking for almost a century. Answers have often been expressed in a formal code of ethics.

That may seem odd. What business, it may be asked, do engineering societies have promulgating codes of ethics? What could they be thinking? Ethics is not a matter for majority vote but for private conscience, or, if not for private conscience, then for experts; and the experts in ethics are philosophers or clergy, not engineers. Such thoughts make any connection between engineering and ethics look dubious. So, before we can say more about what Lund should have done, we have to understand the connection.

THE POSSIBILITY OF ENGINEERING ETHICS

A code of (professional) ethics generally appears when an occupation organizes itself into a profession. Usually, the code is put in writing and formally adopted. Even when formalization is put off, however, the code may still be a subject of frequent reference, whether explicitly, as in "*our* code of ethics," or implicitly, as in, "That would not be proper for one of *us*."

Why this connection between codes of (professional) ethics and organized professions? Several explanations have been offered over the years.[3] But, for our purposes, the most helpful is that a code of ethics is primarily a *convention between professionals*.[4] According to this explanation, a profession is a group of persons who want to cooperate in serving the same ideal better than they could if they did not cooperate. Engineers, for example, might be thought to serve the ideal of efficient design, construction, and maintenance of safe and useful objects. A code of ethics would then prescribe how professionals are to pursue their common ideal so that each may do the best she can at minimal cost to herself and those she cares about (including the public, if looking after the public is part of what she cares about). The code is to protect each professional from certain pressures (for example, the pressure to cut corners to save money) by making it reasonably likely (and more likely than otherwise) that most other members of the profession will *not* take advantage of her good conduct. A code protects members of a profession from certain consequences of competition. A code is a solution to a coordination problem.

According to this explanation, an occupation does not need society's recognition in order to be a profession. It needs only a practice among its members of cooperating to serve a certain ideal. Once an occupation has become a profession, society has a reason to give it special privileges (for example, the sole right to do certain work) if, but only if, society wants to support serving the ideal in question in the way the profession has chosen to serve it. Otherwise, it may leave the profession unrecognized.

A profession, as such, is like a union in that it is organized to serve the interests of its members, and unlike a charity or government, which is organized to serve someone else's interests. But professions differ from unions in the interests they are organized to serve. Unions are, like businesses, primarily organizations of self-interest. They exist for the benefit of their members, just as businesses exist for the profit of their owners. A profession, in contrast, is organized to help members serve *others*—according to a certain ideal expressed in its code of ethics. In this sense, professions are organized for public service. That, I think, is true by definition. But it is not a mere semantic truth. When a group of individuals constitute themselves as a "profession," they explicitly invoke this way of understanding what they are up to. They invite examination according to the standards proper to such an undertaking. They give what they do a distinct context.

Understanding a code of (professional) ethics as a convention between professionals, we can explain why engineers cannot depend on mere private conscience when choosing how to practice their profession, no matter how good that private conscience, and why engineers should take into account what an organization of engineers has to say about what engineers should do.[5] What conscience would tell us to do *absent* a certain convention is not necessarily what conscience would tell us *given* that convention. Insofar as a code of professional ethics is a kind of (morally permissible) convention, it provides a guide to what engineers may reasonably expect of one another, what (more or less) "the rules of the game" are. Just as we must know the rules of baseball to know what to do with the ball, so we must know engineering ethics to know, for example, whether, *as engineers*, we should merely weigh safety against the wishes of our employer or instead give safety preference over those wishes.

A code of ethics should also provide a guide to what we may expect other members of our profession to help us do. If, for example, part of being an engineer is putting safety first, then Lund's engineers had a right to expect his support. When Lund's boss asked him to think like a manager rather than an engineer, he should, *as an engineer*, have responded, "Sorry, if you wanted a vice-president who would think like a manager *rather than* an engineer, you should not have hired an engineer."[6]

If Lund had so responded, he would, as we shall see, have responded as "the rules of the engineering game" require. But would he have done the right thing, not simply according to those rules but all things considered? This is not an empty question. Even games can be irrational or immoral. (Think, for example, of a game in which you score points by cutting off your fingers or by shooting people who happen to pass in the street below.) People are not merely members of this or that profession. They are also persons with responsibilities beyond their professions, moral agents who cannot escape conscience, criticism, blame, or punishment just by showing that they did what they did because their profession required it. While we have now explained why an engineer should, as an engineer, take account of his profession's code of ethics, we have not explained why anyone should be an engineer in this sense.

Let me put the point more dramatically. Suppose Lund's boss had responded to what we just imagined Lund to say to him: "Yes, we hired an engineer, but—we supposed—an engineer with common sense, one who understood just how much weight a rational person gives a code of ethics in decisions of this kind. Be reasonable. Your job and mine are on the line. The future of Thiokol is also on the line. Safety counts a lot. But other things do, too. If we block this launch, the Space Center will start looking for someone more agreeable to supply boosters."

If acting as one's professional code requires is really justified, we should be able to explain to Lund (and his boss) why, as a rational person, Lund should support his profession's code as a guide for all engineers and why, even in his trying circumstances, he cannot justify treating himself as an exception.

WHY OBEY ONE'S PROFESSIONAL CODE?

The question now is why, all things considered, an engineer should obey her profession's code. We should begin by dismissing two alternatives some people find plausible. One is that Lund should do as his profession requires because he "promised," for example, by joining an engineering society having a code of ethics. We must dismiss this answer because it is at least possible that Lund never did anything we could plausibly characterize as promising to follow a formal code. Lund could, for example, have refused to join any professional society having a code (as perhaps half of all U.S. engineers do). Yet, it seems such a refusal would not excuse him from conducting himself as an engineer should. The obligations of an engineer do not seem to rest on anything so contingent as a promise, oath, or vow. So, the "convention between professionals" (as I called it) is not a contract. It is more like what lawyers call a "quasicontract" or a "contract implied in law"; that is, an obligation resting not on an actual agreement (whether express or tacit) but on what it is fair to require of someone given what he has voluntarily done, such as accepted the benefits that go with claiming to be an engineer.

The other plausible alternative we can quickly dismiss is that Lund should do as his profession requires because "society" says he should. We may dismiss this answer in part because it is not clear that society does say that. One way society has of saying things is through law. No law binds all engineers to abide by their profession's code (as the law does bind all lawyers to abide by theirs).[7] Of course, society has ways of saying things other than by law, for example, by public opinion. But it seems doubtful that the public knows enough about engineering to have an opinion on most matters of engineering ethics. And even on the matter before us, can we honestly say that society wants engineers to do as their code requires (treat safety as paramount, as explained below) rather than (as most people would) treat safety as an important consideration to balance against others?

However that question is answered, it seems plain that neither public opinion nor law should decide what it is rational or moral to do. After all, there have been both irrational laws (for example, those requiring the use of outmoded techniques) and immoral laws (for example, those enforcing slavery). The public opinion supporting such laws could not have been much less irrational or immoral than the laws themselves.

The two answers we have now dismissed share one notable feature. Either would, if defensible, provide a reason to do as one's profession requires quite independently of what in particular the profession happens to require. The answers do not take account of the contents of the code of ethics. They are formal. The answer we shall now consider is *not* formal. It is that supporting a code of ethics with a certain content is rational because supporting any code with a content of that sort is rational.

Consider, for example, the code of ethics drafted by the Accreditation Board of Engineering and Technology (ABET) and adopted by all major American engineering societies except the National Society of Professional Engineers and the Institute of Electrical and Electronic Engineers. The code is divided into "fundamental principles," "fundamental canons," and (much more detailed) "guidelines." The fundamental principles simply describe in general terms an ideal of service. Engineers "uphold and advance the integrity, honor and dignity of the engineering profession by: I. using their knowledge and skill for the enhancement of human welfare, II. being honest and impartial, and serving with fidelity the public, their employers and clients [and so on]." What rational person could object to others' trying to achieve that ideal? Or at least, what rational person could object so long as their doing so did not interfere with what she was doing? Surely every engineer—indeed, every member of society—is likely to be better off overall if engineers uphold and advance the integrity, honor, and dignity of engineering in that way.

Below the fundamental principles are the fundamental canons. The canons lay down general duties. For example, engineers are required to "hold paramount the safety, health and welfare of the public," to "issue public statements only in an objective and truthful manner," to "act in professional matters for each employer or client as faithful agents and trustees," and to "avoid all conflicts of interest." Each engineer stands to benefit from these requirements both as ordinary person and as engineer. The benefits for an engineer as ordinary person are obvious: As an ordinary person, an engineer is likely to be safer, healthier, and otherwise better off if engineers *generally* hold paramount the public safety, only make truthful public statements, and so on. How engineers stand to benefit *as engineers* is less obvious. So, let us try a thought experiment.

Imagine what engineering would be like if engineers did not generally act as the canons require. If, for example, engineers did not generally hold paramount the safety, health, and welfare of the public, what would it be like to be an engineer? The day-to-day work would, of course, be much the same. But every now and then an engineer would be asked to do something that, though apparently profitable to his employer or client, would put other people at risk, some perhaps about whom he cared a great deal. Without a professional code, an engineer could not object *as an engineer*. An engineer could, of course, still object "personally" and refuse to do the job. But if he did, he would risk being replaced by an engineer who would not object. An employer or client might rightly treat an engineer's personal qualms as a disability, much like a tendency to make errors. The engineer would be under tremendous pressure to keep "personal opinions" to himself and get on with the job. His interests as an engineer would conflict with his interests as a person.

That, then, is why each engineer can generally expect to benefit from other engineers' acting as their common code requires. The benefits are, I think, clearly substantial enough to explain how an individual could rationally enter into a convention that would equally limit what he himself can do.

I have not, however, shown that every engineer *must* benefit *overall* from such a convention, or even that any engineer will consider these benefits sufficient to justify the burdens required to achieve them. Professions, like governments, are not always worth the trouble of maintaining them. Whether a particular profession is worth the trouble is an empirical question. Professions nonetheless differ from governments in at least one way relevant here. Professions are voluntary in a way that governments are not. No one is born into a profession. One must claim professional status to have it (by taking a degree, for example, or accepting a job for which professional status is required). We therefore have good reason to suppose that people are engineers because, on balance, they prefer to have the benefits of being an engineer, even given what is required of them in exchange.

If, as we shall now assume, the only way to obtain the benefits in question is to make it part of being an engineer that the public safety, health, and welfare come first, every engineer, including Lund, has good reason to want engineers *generally* to adhere to something like the ABET code. But why should an engineer adhere to it himself when, as in Lund's case, it seems he (or his employer or client) stands to benefit by departing from it?

If the question is one of justification, the answer is obvious. Lund would have to justify his departure from the code by appealing to such considerations as the welfare of Thiokol and his own self-interest. An appeal to such considerations is just what Lund could not incorporate into a code of ethics for engineers or generally allow other engineers to use in defense of what they did. Lund could not incorporate such an exception into a code because its incorporation would defeat the purpose of the code. A code of ethics is necessary in part because, without it, the self-interest of individual engineers, or even their selfless devotion to their employer, could lead them to harm everyone overall. Lund could not allow other engineers to defend what they did by appeal to their own interests or that of their employer for much the same reason. To allow such appeals would be to contribute to the breakdown of a practice Lund has good reason to support.

I take this argument to explain why, all things considered, Lund should have done as his profession's code requires, *not* why he should have done so in some pre-moral sense. I am answering the question "Why be ethical?" *not* "Why be moral?" I therefore have the luxury of falling back on ordinary moral principles to determine what is right, all things considered. The moral principle on which this argument primarily relies is the principle of fairness. Since Lund voluntarily accepts the benefits of being an engineer (by claiming to be an engineer), he is morally obliged to follow the (morally permissible) convention that helps to make those benefits possible.[8] What I have been at pains to show is how that convention helps to make those benefits possible, and why, even now, he has good reason to endorse the convention generally.

I have been assuming that engineers do in fact generally act in accordance with the ABET code, whether or not they know it exists. If that assumption were mistaken, Lund would have had no *professional* reason to do as the code requires. The code would be a dead letter, not a living practice. It would have much the same status as a "model statute" no government ever adopted, or the rules of a cooperative game no one plays. Lund would have had to rely on private judgment. But relying on private judgment is not necessary here. Lund's engineers seem to have recommended as they did because they thought the safety of the public, including astronauts, paramount. They did what, according to the code, engineers are supposed to do. Their recommendation is itself evidence that the code corresponds to a living practice.[9]

So, when Lund's boss asked him to think like a manager rather than an engineer, he was in effect asking Lund to think in a way that Lund must consider unjustified for engineers generally and for which Lund can give no morally defensible principle for making himself an exception. When Lund did as his boss asked (supposing he did), he in effect let down all those engineers who helped to establish the practice that today allows engineers to say "no" in such circumstances with the reasonable hope that the client or employer will defer to their professional judgment, and that other engineers will come to their aid if the client or employer does not defer.

Lund could, of course, still explain how his action served his own interests and those of Thiokol (or, rather, how they seemed to at the time).[10] He could also just thumb his nose at all talk of engineering ethics, though that would probably lead to the government's barring him from working on any project it funds, to fellow engineers' refusing to have anything to do with him, and to his employer's coming to view him as an embarrassment. What he cannot do is show that what he did was right, all things considered.

This conclusion assumes that I have not overlooked any relevant consideration. I certainly may have. But that is not important here. I have not examined Lund's decision in order to condemn him but in order to bring to light the place of a code of ethics in engineering. There is more to understand.

INTERPRETING A CODE OF ETHICS

So far we have assumed that Lund did as his boss asked, that is, that he thought like a manager rather than an engineer. Assuming that allowed us to give a relatively clear explanation of what was wrong with what Lund did: Lund acted like a manager when he was also an engineer and should have acted like one.

We must, however, now put that assumption aside and consider whether engineering ethics actually forbids Lund to do what it seemed he did, that is, weigh his own interests, his employer's, and his client's against the safety of the seven astronauts. Ordinary morality seems to allow such weighing. For example, no one would think you did something morally wrong if you drove your child to school, rather than letting him take the bus, even if your presence on the road increased somewhat the risk that someone would be killed in a traffic accident. Morality allows us to give special weight to the interests of those close to us.[11] If engineering ethics allows that too, then Lund—whatever he may have thought he was doing—would not actually have acted unprofessionally. Let us then imagine Lund's reading of the ABET code. What could he infer?

Of the code's seven fundamental canons, only two seem relevant: (1) "[holding] paramount the safety, health and welfare of the public" and (4) "[acting] in professional matters for each employer or client as faithful agents or trustees." What do these provisions tell Lund to do? The answer is not all that clear. Does "public" include the seven astronauts? They are, after all, employees of Thiokol's client, the Space Center, not part of the public as are, say, those ordinary citizens who watch launches from the beach opposite the Space Center. And what is it to be a "faithful agent or trustee" of one's client or employer? Is it to serve all the interests of a client or employer, or only the financial ones? And how is one to determine even those? Does the client or employer have the final word, or may an engineer make an independent assessment? After all, the actual result of Lund's decision was a disaster for both employer and client, though one both employer and client may have thought themselves justified in risking. And what is Lund to do if the public welfare requires what no faithful agent or trustee could do? Does "holding paramount" the public welfare include sometimes acting as a faithful agent or trustee would *not* act?

These questions are surprisingly easy to answer if we keep in mind the connection between professions and codes of ethics, remembering especially that a code is not a stone tablet inscribed with divine wisdom but the work of engineers, a set of rules that is supposed to win the support of engineers because the rules help engineers do what they want to do.

The language of any document, codes included, must be interpreted in light of what it is reasonable to suppose its authors intend.[12] For example, if "bachelor" appears undefined in a marriage statute, we interpret it as referring to single males, but if the same word appears in directions for a college's graduation ceremony, we instead interpret it as referring to all students getting their baccalaureate, whether male or female, single or married. That is the reasonable interpretation because we know that marriages usually involve single males (as well as single females) *rather than* people with baccalaureates while just the reverse is true of graduation ceremonies. So, once we figure out what it is reasonable to suppose engineers intend by declaring the "public" safety, health, and welfare "paramount," we should be able to decide whether interpreting "public" so that it includes "employees" is what engineers intend (or at least what, as rational persons, they should intend) and also whether they intend the paramountcy requirement to take precedence over the duty to act as a faithful agent or trustee.

The authors of a code of engineering ethics (whether those who originally drafted or approved it or those who now give it their support) are all more or less rational persons. They differ from most other rational persons only in knowing what engineers must know in order to be engineers and in performing duties they could not perform (or could not perform as well) but for that knowledge. It is therefore reasonable to suppose that their code of ethics would not require them to risk their own safety, health, or welfare, or that of anyone for whom they care, except for some substantial good (for example, high pay or service to some ideal to which they are committed). It also seems reasonable to suppose that no code they authored would include anything people generally consider immoral. Most engineers are probably morally decent people, unlikely to endorse an immoral rule.

But what if that were not true? What if most engineers were moral monsters or just self-serving opportunists? What then? Interpreting their code would certainly be different, and probably harder. We could not understand it as a *professional* code. We would have to switch to principles of interpretation we reserve for mere folkways, Nazi statutes, or the like. We would have to leave the presuppositions of ethics behind.

But, given those presuppositions, we can easily explain why a code of engineering ethics would make holding the public safety paramount a duty taking precedence over all others, including the duty to act as a faithful agent or trustee. Rational engineers would want to avoid situations in which only their private qualms stood between them and a use of professional knowledge they considered morally wrong or otherwise undesirable. Each would, as we saw, want to be reasonably sure that the knowledge of other engineers would serve the public, even when the interests of the public conflicted with those of employer or client. Given this purpose, what must "public" mean?

We *might* interpret "public" as equivalent to "everyone" (in the society, locale, or whatever). On this interpretation, the "public safety" would mean the safety of everyone more or less equally. A danger that struck only children, or only those with bad lungs, or the like, would not endanger "the public." This interpretation must be rejected. Since few dangers are likely to threaten everyone, interpreting "public" to mean "everyone" would yield a duty to the public too weak to protect most engineers from having to do things that would generally make life for themselves (and those they care about) far worse than it would otherwise be, even allowing for the occasional benefit they might obtain as individuals.

We might also interpret "public" as referring to "anyone" (in the society, local, or whatever). On this interpretation, public safety would be equivalent to the safety of some or all. Holding the public safety paramount would mean never putting anyone in danger. If our first interpretation of "public" made provisions protecting the public too weak, this second would make them too strong. For example, it is hard to imagine how we could have electric power stations, mountain tunnels, or chemical plants without some risk to someone. No rational engineer could endorse a code of ethics that made engineering virtually impossible.

We seem, then, to need an interpretation of "public" invoking some more relevant feature of people, rather than, as we have so far, just their number. I would suggest that what makes people a public is their relative innocence, helplessness, or passivity. On this interpretation, "public" would refer to those persons whose lack of information, technical knowledge, or time for deliberation renders them more or less vulnerable to the powers an engineer wields on behalf of his client or employer. An engineer should hold paramount the public safety, health, and welfare to assure that engineers will not be forced to give too little regard to the welfare of these "innocents."

On this third interpretation, someone might be part of the public in one respect but not in another. For example, the astronauts would be part of the public with respect to the O-rings because, not knowing of the danger, they were in no position to abort the launch to avoid the danger. The astronauts would, in contrast, *not* be part of the public with respect to the ice forming on the boosters because, having been fully informed of that danger, they were in a position to abort the launch if they were unwilling to take the risk the ice posed. This third interpretation of "public" thus seems to be free of the difficulties that discredited the preceding two. We now seem to have a sense of "holding the public safety paramount" that we may reasonably suppose rational engineers would endorse.

On this interpretation, the engineer's code of ethics would (all else equal) require Lund either to refuse to authorize the launch or to insist instead that the astronauts be briefed in order to get their informed consent to the risk. Refusing authorization would protect the public by holding the safety of the astronauts paramount. Insisting that the astronauts be briefed and decide for themselves would hold the safety of the public paramount by transferring the astronauts from the category of members of the public to that of informed participants in the decision. Either way, Lund would not, under the circumstances, have had to treat his own interests, those of his employer Thiokol, or those of his client the Space Center as comparable to those of the public (assuming, of course, what is not true, that we have considered all the public interests relevant here).

Is this the correct interpretation of "public"? It is if we have taken into account every relevant consideration. Have we? There is, of course, no way to know. But there is good reason to think we have. We can easily show that the only obvious alternative is wrong. That alternative is that "public" refers to all "innocents" *except* employees of the client or employer in question. Employees are to be excluded because, it might be said, they are paid to take the risks associated with their job. On this interpretation, Lund would not have to hold the safety of the astronauts paramount, since they would not be part of the public.

What is wrong with this fourth interpretation of "public"? Earlier, we understood "innocents" to include all persons whose lack of information, training, or time for deliberation renders them vulnerable to the powers an engineer wields on behalf of his client or employer. An employee who takes a job knowing the risks (and is otherwise able to avoid them) might be able to insist on being paid enough to compensate for them. She could then truly be said to be paid to take those risks. She would not be an "innocent." But she would, under our *third* interpretation, also not in that respect be part of the public to which an engineer owed a paramount duty. She would have given informed consent to the risk in question. So, the third and fourth interpretations would not differ concerning such an employee.

On the other hand, if the employee lacked the information to evaluate the risk, she would be in no position to insist on adequate compensation. She could not be said to be paid to take those risks. She would, in other words, be as innocent of, as vulnerable to, and as unpaid for the risks in question as anyone else in the public. Since nothing prevents an engineer, or someone for whom an engineer cares, from being the employee *unknowingly* at risk, engineers have as much reason to want to protect such employees as to protect the public in general. "Public" should be interpreted accordingly; that is, according to our third interpretation.

PROFESSIONAL RESPONSIBILITIES

Given the argument developed so far, engineers clearly are responsible for acting as their profession's code of ethics requires. Do their professional responsibilities go beyond the code? The answer, I think, is clearly yes. Engineers should not only do as their profession's code requires, but should also support it less directly by encouraging others to do as it requires and by criticizing, ostracizing, or otherwise calling to account those who do not. They should support their profession's code in these ways for at least four reasons: First, engineers should support their profession's code because supporting it will help protect them and those they care about from being injured by what other engineers do. Second, supporting the code will also help assure each engineer a working environment in which it will be easier than it would otherwise be to resist pressure to do much that the engineer would rather not do. Third, engineers should support their profession's code because supporting it helps make their profession a practice of which they need not feel morally justified embarrassment, shame, or guilt. And fourth, one has an obligation of fairness to do his part insofar as he claims to be an engineer and other engineers are doing their part in generating these benefits for all engineers.

NOTES

Early versions of this article were presented to the Society of Hispanic Professional Engineers, Chicago Chapter, 10 June 1987; and to the American Society of Civil Engineers, University of Illinois at Chicago, Student Chapter, 4 May 1988. I should like to thank those present, as well as my colleague Vivian Weil, for many helpful comments.

1. See, e.g., John Ladd, "The Quest for a Code of Professional Ethics: An Intellectual and Moral Confusion," in *AAAS Professional Ethics Project*, ed. Rosemary Chalk, Mark S. Frankel, and Sallie B. Chafer (Washington, D.C.: American Association for the Advancement of Science, 1980), pp. 154–59; Samuel Florman, "Moral Blueprints," *Harper's* 257 (1978): 30–33; John Kultgen, "The Ideological Use of Professional Codes," *Business and Professional Ethics Journal* 1 (1982): 53–69; and Heinz C. Luegenbiehl, "Codes of Ethics and the Moral Education of Engineers," *Business and Professional Ethics Journal* 2 (1983): 41–61. Note also how small a part codes have in a text on engineering ethics, such as Mike Martin and Roland Schinzinger, *Ethics in Engineering*, 2d ed. (New York: McGraw-Hill, 1989), esp. pp. 86–92, 103–4.

2. The following narrative is based on testimony contained in *The Presidential Commission on the Space Shuttle Challenger Disaster* (Washington, D.C.: U.S. Government Printing Office, 1986), esp. 1:82–103.

3. See, e.g., Robert M. Veatch, "Professional Ethics and Role-Specific Duties," *Journal of Medicine and Philosophy* 4 (1979): 1–19; Benjamin Freedman, "A Meta-Ethics for Professional Morality," *Ethics* 89 (1978): 1–19; and Lisa Newton, "The Origin of Professionalism: Sociological Conclusions and Ethical Implications," *Business and Professional Ethics Journal* 1 (1982): 33–43.

4. For more on this explanation, see my "The Moral Authority of a Professional Code," *NOMOS XXIX: Authority Revisited*, ed. J. Roland Pennock and John W. Chapman (New York: New York University Press, 1987), pp. 302–38; "The Use of Professions," *Business Economics* 22 (1987): 5–10; "Professionalism Means Putting Your Profession First," *Georgetown Journal of Legal Ethics* 2 (1988): 352–66; and "The Ethics Boom: What and Why," *Centennial Review* 34 (1990): 163–86.

5. Here, then, is an important contrast between my position and the "personal analysis" of professional duties one finds, for example, in Thomas Shaffer, "Advocacy as Moral Discourse," *North Carolina Law Review* 57 (1979): 647–70; or Charles Fried, "The Lawyer as Friend: The Moral Foundations of the Lawyer-Client Relation," *Yale Law Review* 85 (1976): 1060–89. Unlike these others, I do not treat professional activity as primarily involving a relation between one person with an important skill (the professional) and a series of others (the client, patient, or whatever). The appeal of the personal analysis probably comes from focusing too much on professions, like

law and medicine, that have a clearly defined client. One feature of engineering that should make it more interesting to students of professional ethics than it has been is the absence (or relative unimportance) of individual clients. In this respect, engineering may represent the future of law, and perhaps even of medicine.

6. Cf. my "The Special Role of Professionals in Business Ethics," *Business and Professional Ethics Journal* 7 (1988): 83–94.

7. Some engineers, so-called Professional Engineers (PEs), are bound by law in exactly the way lawyers, doctors, and other state-licensed professionals are. But most engineers in the United States—nearly 90 percent—are not so licensed. They practice engineering under the "manufacturer's exemption." They can practice engineering only through a company with a PE, who must ultimately "sign off" on their work.

8. I hope this appeal to fairness will raise no red flags, even though the principle of fairness has been under a cloud ever since the seemingly devastating criticism it received in Robert Nozick, *Anarchy, State, and Utopia* (New York: Basic Books, 1974). I have, it should be noted, limited my use to obligations generated by *voluntarily* claiming benefits of a cooperative practice that are otherwise not available. Most attacks on the principle of fairness have been on the "involuntary benefits" version. See, e.g., A. John Simmons, *Moral Principles and Political Obligations* (Princeton, N.J.: Princeton University Press, 1979), pp. 118–36. And even those attacks are hardly devastating. One can either refine the principle, as Richard Arneson has done in "The Principle of Fairness and Free-Rider Problems," *Ethics* 92 (1982): 616–33; or, as in my "Nozick's Argument *for* the Legitimacy of the Welfare State," *Ethics* 97 (1987): 576–94, show that Nozick's original criticism, and most subsequent criticism, depends on examples that, upon careful examination, fail to support the criticism.

9. I am not claiming that the engineers treated safety as paramount because they knew what the ABET code said. When you ask a lawyer about a professional code, she is likely to tell you she studied the ABA code in law school and, claiming to have a copy around, will produce it after only a few minutes of searching her desk or bookshelves. When you ask an engineer the same question, he is likely to tell you that his profession has a code while admitting both that he never studied it and that he has none around to refer to. Yet, anyone who has spent much time with working engineers knows they do not treat safety in the same way managers do (hence Mason's plea to "take off your engineering hat"). The engineers' code of ethics seems to be "hard-wired" into them. Interestingly, engineers are not the only professionals for whom the written code seems to play so small a part. For another example, see my "Vocational Teachers, Confidentiality, and Professional Ethics," *International Journal of Applied Philosophy* 4 (1988): 11–20.

10. I do not claim that he would explain his decision in this way. Indeed, I think his explanation would be quite different, though no less troubling. See my "Explaining Wrong-doing," *Journal of Social Philosophy* 20 (1989): 74–90.

11. Here, then, is why I reject the "universalistic" interpretation of engineering ethics in, e.g., Kenneth Alpern, "Moral Responsibility for Engineers," *Business and Professional Ethics Journal* 2 (1983): 39–48.

12. I am not here committing the "originalist fallacy" common a few years back in debates over how to interpret the U.S. Constitution. Though the first codes of ethics for American engineers were adopted early in this century, all have undergone radical revision within the last two decades. More importantly, as will be made plain below, I use "authors" to include all those who must currently support the code. My notion of interpretation is therefore much closer to that found in Ronald Dworkin, *Law's Empire* (Cambridge, Mass.: Harvard University Press, 1986).

▷ ACM CODE OF ETHICS AND PROFESSIONAL CONDUCT[1]

On October 16, 1992, ACM's Executive Council voted to adopt a revised Code of Ethics. The following imperatives and explanatory guidelines were proposed to supplement the Code as contained in the new ACM Bylaw 17.

Commitment to ethical professional conduct is expected of every voting, associate, and student member of ACM. This Code, consisting of 24 imperatives formulated as statements of personal responsibility, identifies the elements of such a commitment.

It contains many, but not all, issues professionals are likely to face. Section 1 outlines fundamental ethical considerations, while Section 2 addresses additional, more specific considerations of professional conduct. Statements in Section 3 pertain more specifically to individuals who have a leadership role, whether in the workplace or in a volunteer capacity, for example with organizations such as ACM. Principles involving compliance with this Code are given in Section 4.

The Code is supplemented by a set of Guidelines, which provide explanation to assist members in dealing with the various issues contained in the Code. It is expected that the Guidelines will be changed more frequently than the Code.

The Code and its supplemented Guidelines are intended to serve as a basis for ethical decision making in the conduct of professional work. Secondarily, they may serve as a basis for judging the merit of a formal complaint pertaining to violation of professional ethical standards.

It should be noted that although computing is not mentioned in the moral imperatives section, the Code is concerned with how these fundamental imperatives apply to one's conduct as a computing professional. These imperatives are expressed in a general form to emphasize that ethical principles which apply to computer ethics are derived from more general ethical principles.

It is understood that some words and phrases in a code of ethics are subject to varying interpretations, and that any ethical principle may conflict with other ethical principles in specific situations. Questions related to ethical conflicts can best be answered by thoughtful consideration of fundamental principles, rather than reliance on detailed regulations.

1. GENERAL MORAL IMPERATIVES

As an ACM member I will . . .

1.1 Contribute to Society and Human Well-Being

This principle concerning the quality of life of all people affirms an obligation to protect fundamental human rights and to respect the diversity of all cultures. An essential aim of computing professionals is to minimize negative consequences of computing systems, including threats to health and safety. When designing or implementing systems, computing professionals must attempt to ensure that the products of their efforts will be used in socially responsible ways, will meet social needs, and will avoid harmful effects to health and welfare.

In addition to a safe social environment, human well-being includes a safe natural environment. Therefore, computing professionals who design and develop systems must be alert to, and make others aware of, any potential damage to the local or global environment.

1.2 Avoid Harm to Others

"Harm" means injury or negative consequences, such as undesirable loss of information, loss of property, property damage, or unwanted environmental impacts. This principle prohibits use of computing technology in ways that result in harm to any of the following: users, the general public, employees, employers. Harmful actions include intentional destruction or modification of files and programs leading to serious loss of resources or unnecessary expenditure of human resources such as the time and effort required to purge systems of computer viruses.

Well-intended actions, including those that accomplish assigned duties, may lead to harm unexpectedly. In such an event the responsible person or persons are obligated to undo or mitigate the negative consequences as much as possible. One way to avoid unintentional harm is to carefully consider potential impacts on all those affected by decisions made during design and implementation.

To minimize the possibility of indirectly harming others, computing professionals must minimize malfunctions by following generally accepted standards for system design and testing. Furthermore, it is often necessary to assess the social consequences of systems to project the likelihood of any serious harm to others. If system features are misrepresented to users, co-workers, or supervisors, the individual computing professional is responsible for any resulting injury.

In the work environment the computing professional has the additional obligation to report any signs of system dangers that might result in serious personal or social damage. If one's superiors do not act to curtail or mitigate such dangers, it may be necessary to "blow the whistle" to help correct the problem or reduce the risk. However, capricious or misguided reporting of violations can, itself, be harmful. Before reporting violations, all relevant aspects of the incident must be thoroughly assessed. In particular, the assessment of risk and responsibility must be credible. It is suggested that advice be sought from other computing professionals. (See principle 2.5 regarding thorough evaluations.)

1.3 Be Honest and Trustworthy

Honesty is an essential component of trust. Without trust an organization cannot function effectively. The honest computing professional will not make deliberately false or deceptive claims about a system or system design, but will instead provide full disclosure of all pertinent system limitations and problems.

A computer professional has a duty to be honest about his or her own qualifications, and about any circumstances that might lead to conflicts of interest.

Membership in volunteer organizations such as ACM may at times place individuals in situations where their statements or actions could be interpreted as carrying the "weight" of a larger group of professionals. An ACM member will exercise care to not misrepresent ACM or positions and policies of ACM or any ACM units.

1.4 Be Fair and Take Action Not to Discriminate

The values of equality, tolerance, respect for others, and the principles of equal justice govern this imperative. Discrimination on the basis of race, sex, religion, age, disability, national origin, or other such factors is an explicit violation of ACM policy and will not be tolerated.

Inequities between different groups of people may result from the use or misuse of information and technology. In a fair society, all individuals would have equal opportunity to participate in, or benefit from, the use of computer resources regardless of race, sex, religion, age, disability, national origin or other such similar factors. However, these ideals do not justify unauthorized use of computer resources nor do they provide an adequate basis for violation of any other ethical imperatives of this code.

1.5 Honor Property Rights Including Copyrights and Patents

Violation of copyrights, patents, trade secrets and the terms of license agreements is prohibited by law in most circumstances. Even when software is not so protected, such violations are contrary to professional behavior. Copies of software should be made only with proper authorization. Unauthorized duplication of materials must not be condoned.

1.6 Give Proper Credit for Intellectual Property

Computing professionals are obligated to protect the integrity of intellectual property. Specifically, one must not take credit for other's ideas or work, even in cases where the work has not been explicitly protected, for example by copyright or patent.

1.7 Respect the Privacy of Others

Computing and communication technology enables the collection and exchange of personal information on a scale unprecedented in the history of civilization. Thus there is increased potential for violating the privacy of individuals and groups. It is the responsibility of professionals to maintain the privacy and integrity of data describing individuals. This includes taking precautions to ensure the accuracy of data, as well as protecting it from unauthorized access or accidental disclosure to inappropriate individuals. Furthermore, procedures must be established to allow individuals to review their records and correct inaccuracies.

This imperative implies that only the necessary amount of personal information be collected in a system, that retention and disposal periods for that information be clearly defined and enforced, and that personal information gathered for a specific purpose not be used for other purposes without consent of the individual(s). These principles apply to electronic communications, including electronic mail, and prohibit procedures that capture or monitor electronic user data, including messages, without the permission of users or *bona fide* authorization related to system operation and maintenance. User data observed during the normal duties of system operation and maintenance must be treated with strictest confidentiality, except in cases where it is evidence for the violation of law, organizational regulations, or this Code. In these cases, the nature or contents of that information must be disclosed only to proper authorities (See 1.9)

1.8 Honor Confidentiality

The principle of honesty extends to issues of confidentiality of information whenever one has made an explicit promise to honor confidentiality or, implicitly, when private information not directly related to the performance of one's duties becomes available. The ethical concern is to respect all obligations of confidentiality to employers, clients, and users unless discharged from such obligations by requirements of the law or other principles of this Code.

2. MORE SPECIFIC PROFESSIONAL RESPONSIBILITIES

As an ACM computing professional I will ...

2.1 Strive to Achieve the Highest Quality, Effectiveness and Dignity in Both the Process and Products of Professional Work

Excellence is perhaps the most important obligation of a professional. The computing professional must strive to achieve quality and to be cognizant of the serious negative consequences that may result from poor quality in a system.

2.2 Acquire and Maintain Professional Competence

Excellence depends on individuals who take responsibility for acquiring and maintaining professional competence. A professional must participate in setting standards for appropriate levels of competence, and strive to achieve those standards. Upgrading technical knowledge and competence can be achieved in several ways: doing independent study; attending seminars, conferences, or courses; and being involved in professional organizations.

2.3 Know and Respect Existing Laws Pertaining to Professional Work

ACM members must obey existing local, state, province, national, and international laws unless there is a compelling ethical basis not to do so. Policies and procedures of the organizations in which one participates must also be obeyed. But compliance must be balanced with the recognition that sometimes existing laws and rules may be immoral or inappropriate and, therefore, must be challenged.

Violation of a law or regulation may be ethical when that law or rule has inadequate moral basis or when it conflicts with another law judged to be more important. If one decides to violate a law or rule because it is viewed as unethical, or for any other reason, one must fully accept responsibility for one's actions and for the consequences.

2.4 Accept and Provide Appropriate Professional Review

Quality professional work, especially in the computing profession, depends on professional reviewing and critiquing. Whenever appropriate, individual members should seek and utilize peer review as well as provide critical review of the work of others.

2.5 Give Comprehensive and Thorough Evaluations of Computer Systems and Their Impacts, Including Analysis of Possible Risks

Computer professionals must strive to be perceptive, thorough, and objective when evaluating, recommending, and presenting system descriptions and alternatives. Computer professionals are in a position of special trust, and therefore have a special responsibility to provide objective, credible evaluations to employers, clients, users, and the public. When providing evaluations the professional must also identify any relevant conflicts of interest, as stated in imperative 1.3.

As noted in the discussion of principle 1.2 on avoiding harm, any signs of danger from systems must be reported to those who have opportunity and/or responsibility to resolve them. See the guidelines for imperative 1.2 for more details concerning harm, including the reporting of professional violations.

2.6 Honor Contracts, Agreements, and Assigned Responsibilities

Honoring one's commitments is a matter of integrity and honesty. For the computer professional this includes ensuring that system elements perform as intended. Also, when one contracts for work with another party, one has an obligation to keep that party properly informed about progress toward completing that work.

A computing professional has a responsibility to request a change in any assignment that he or she feels cannot be completed as defined. Only after serious consideration and with full disclosure of risks and concerns to the employer or client, should one accept the assignment. The major underlying principle here is the obligation to accept personal accountability for professional work. On some occasions other ethical principles may take greater priority.

A judgment that a specific assignment should not be performed may not be accepted. Having clearly identified one's concerns and reasons for that judgment, but failing to procure a change in that assignment, one may yet be obligated, by contract or by law, to proceed as directed. The computing professional's ethical judgment should be the final guide in deciding whether or not to proceed. Regardless of the decision, one must accept the responsibility for the consequences. However, performing assignments "against one's own judgment" does not relieve the professional of responsibility for any negative consequences.

2.7 Improve Public Understanding of Computing and Its Consequences

Computing professionals have a responsibility to share technical knowledge with the public by encouraging understanding of computing, including the impacts of computer systems and their limitations. This imperative implies an obligation to counter any false views related to computing.

2.8 Access Computing and Communication Resources Only When Authorized to Do So

Theft or destruction of tangible and electronic property is prohibited by imperative 1.2—"Avoid harm to others." Trespassing and unauthorized use of a computer or communication system is addressed by this imperative. Trespassing includes accessing communication networks and computer systems, or accounts and/or files associated with those systems, without explicit authorization to do so. Individuals and organizations have the right to restrict access to their systems so long as they do not violate the discrimination principle (see 1.4).

No one should enter or use another's computing system, software, or data files without permission. One must always have appropriate approval before using system resources, including .rm57 communication ports, file space, other system peripherals, and computer time.

3. ORGANIZATIONAL LEADERSHIP IMPERATIVES

As an ACM member and an organizational leader, I will . . .

3.1 Articulate Social Responsibilities of Members of an Organizational Unit and Encourage Full Acceptance of Those Responsibilities

Because organizations of all kinds have impacts on the public, they must accept responsibilities to society. Organizational procedures and attitudes oriented toward quality and the welfare of society will reduce harm to members of the public, thereby serving public interest and fulfilling social responsibility. Therefore, organizational leaders must encourage full participation in meeting social responsibilities as well as quality performance.

3.2 Manage Personnel and Resources to Design and Build Information Systems that Enhance the Quality of Working Life

Organizational leaders are responsible for ensuring that computer systems enhance, not degrade, the quality of working life. When implementing a computer system, organizations must consider the personal and professional development, physical safety, and human dignity of all workers. Appropriate human–computer ergonomic standards should be considered in system design and in the workplace.

3.3 Acknowledge and Support Proper and Authorized Uses of an Organization's Computing and Communications Resources

Because computer systems can become tools to harm as well as to benefit an organization, the leadership has the responsibility to clearly define appropriate and inappropriate uses of organizational computing resources. While the number and scope of such rules should be minimal, they should be fully enforced when established.

3.4 Ensure that Users and Those Who Will be Affected by a System Have Their Needs Clearly Articulated During the Assessment and Design of Requirements. Later the System Must Be Validated to Meet Requirements.

Current system users, potential users and other persons whose lives may be affected by a system must have their needs assessed and incorporated in the statement of requirements. System validation should ensure compliance with those requirements.

3.5 Articulate and Support Policies that Protect the Dignity of Users and Others Affected by a Computing System

Designing or implementing systems that deliberately or inadvertently demean individuals or groups is ethically unacceptable. Computer professionals who are in decision-making positions should verify that systems are designed and implemented to protect personal privacy and enhance personal dignity.

3.6 Create Opportunities for Members of the Organization to Learn the Principles and Limitations of Computer Systems

This complements the imperative on public understanding (2.7). Educational opportunities are essential to facilitate optimal participation of all organizational members. Opportunities must be available to all members to help them improve their knowledge and skills in computing, including courses that familiarize them with the consequences and limitations of particular types of systems. In particular, professionals must be made aware of the dangers of building systems around oversimplified models, the improbability of anticipating and designing for every possible operating condition, and other issues related to the complexity of this profession.

4. COMPLIANCE WITH THE CODE

As an ACM member I will . . .

4.1 Uphold and Promote the Principles of this Code

The future of the computing profession depends on both technical and ethical excellence. Not only is it important for ACM computing professionals to adhere to the principles expressed in this Code, each member should encourage and support adherence by other members.

4.2 Treat Violations of this Code as Inconsistent with Membership in the ACM

Adherence of professionals to a code of ethics is largely a voluntary matter. However, if a member does not follow this code by engaging in gross misconduct, membership in ACM may be terminated.

NOTES

1. This Code and the supplemental Guidelines were developed by the Task Force for the Revision of the ACM Code of Ethics and Professional Conduct: Ronald E. Anderson, chair, Gerald Engel, Donald Gotterbarn, Grace C. Hertlein, Alex Hoffman, Bruce Jawer, Deborah G. Johnson, Doris K. Lidtke, Joyce Currie Little, Dianne Martin, Donn B. Parker, Judith A. Perrolle, and Richard S. Rosenberg. The Task Force was organized by ACM/SIGCAS and funding was provided by the ACM SIG Discretionary Fund.

CHAPTER SEVEN

The Networked World

Up until a few years ago, most of the forecasts of the revolutionary impact of computers focused on the record keeping and number crunching capabilities of computers and, to some extent, on the promises of artificial intelligence and expert systems. More recently, the data lines connecting computers to one another have evolved into an enormously complex, massive, growing web of networks, and this web has come into focus as the harbinger of revolutionary change. In addition to on-line communication between individuals, data transmission from computer to computer, and a variety of on-line services including bulletin boards, news services, and shopping, plans are now in the making for a National Information Infrastructure (NII) that is likely to involve a coming together of mass media and entertainment industries, the software industry, and the telecommunications industry.

The movement in this direction has already been quite rapid as volume on the Internet continues to multiply and mergers between mass media conglomerates and software companies are announced. We frequently hear the development of the NII being paralleled to the development of our national system of highways. Data lines are, it is said, the new "superhighways of the future."

We begin this chapter with the case of Craig Neidorf. Neidorf was pursued by U.S. Secret Service agents and eventually indicted on six counts for wire fraud, computer fraud, and interstate transportation of stolen property. He was never convicted as the case was eventually dropped. The Neidorf case can be read as a supplement to the readings in Chapter Two for, on the face of it at least, Neidorf appears to be a hacker who has engaged in several of the behaviors that are generally considered troublesome; that is, he appears to have cracked into a BellSouth system and copied proprietary information. As well, he appears to have assisted others in committing similar crimes by publishing (electronically) information about how to crack. However, we have included the case here not so much to emphasize its criminal and cracking aspects, but to illustrate the issues that arise when individuals begin to exchange information and communicate electronically. The Neidorf case raised a stir in the computing community not so much because of Neidorf's alleged behavior but because of the activities of the Secret Service in their pursuit of Neidorf. With the Neidorf case, the computing community had its first taste of on-line law enforcement, and it seems to have tasted a bit like totalitarian control, implying the loss of civil liberties on-line.

As we probe the implications of a world closely connected electronically and increasingly dependent on these electronic connections, it is important that we not sit passively by, watching and predicting what it will all mean, rather than actively engaging in shaping it. We should be asking what form we want these electronic connections to take. Who should have control? What values should the system embody or promote? Who should have access? What social or personal interests should these connections serve?

A wide range of visions have been offered of the meaning of extensive on-line communication, and we have tried to include a variety of these here. One extremely important vision is that of Vice President Al Gore for he has been at the forefront of discussion and promotion of the NII, even before he ran for the vice presidency. The piece we have chosen to include here provides a brief glimpse of the promise that Gore sees in this new technology. Indeed, by the time of this speech, delivered to the International Telecommunications Union in Argentina in 1994, his vision of the NII has been incorporated into a vision of a "Global Information Infrastructure" (GII). Gore sees both the NII and the GII as bringing about extremely beneficial change. The GII, he thinks, will lead to "robust and sustainable economic progress, strong democracies, better solutions to global and local environmental challenges, improved health care, and—ultimately—a greater sense of shared stewardship of our small planet." The U.S., he clearly believes, will be at the forefront of this development and will benefit economically as well as in many other ways.

Gary Chapman and Marc Rotenberg are aware of the debates presently going on in Congress about the NII. They caution us about the issues that must be resolved as we go forward. There are many possibilities for the NII and we should be careful as we design it. Chapman and Rotenberg point to the forces that have given rise to the promotion of an NII, the competing interests and competing values that are at stake in developing a new system. Fearing that a commercial network will "cater to the lowest denominator" and will *not* insure universal access or social equity, they argue that the federal government ought to develop the system.

The next set of readings bring us back to issues raised by the Neidorf case. In "Civil Liberties in Cyberspace" Mitch Kapor argues that public "hysteria" about hackers has led to the perception that we will have to sacrifice civil liberties on-line in order to prevent computer crime. Resisting this, Kapor seeks an alternative vision of "cyberspace." By comparing communication on-line to other more traditional forms of communication and looking at the way we have regulated and not regulated the latter, he argues that we should not limit or regulate the content of bulletin boards and other forms of on-line communication and we should promote competition. The vision that he seems to be developing would make on-line communication similar to the world of books and magazines, in particular, in terms of offering a great variety from which individuals can chose.

The threats to our civil liberties posed in computer communication networks arise in several ways. First, civil liberties seem to be threatened when laws are passed that prohibit certain types of behavior on-line and government agencies are, thereby, empowered to interfere with on-line activities—so as to enforce the law. A second way that civil liberties may be threatened has to do with "hardwiring" the possibility of surveillance into the technology. Certain law enforcement agencies have now recognized that by using encryption technology, individuals now have the ability to transmit information electronically so that no one else can decode it. Law enforcement or security agencies fear what will happen when this technology is used by terrorists and criminals. In response they have proposed the adoption of the Clipper Chip which would insure that information could be decoded by law enforcement officials under controlled conditions. This has stirred a highly controversial debate which is explained by Steven Levy in the piece entitled "Battle of the Clipper Chip." Levy describes both sides of the debate. The outcome of this debate will fundamentally shape the future of electronic communication.

While the U.S. tradition of protecting free speech would seem to lead us to want to protect civil liberties on-line, the reality is that some on-line behavior is extremely dangerous. Moreover, civil liberties and the right to free speech are much more complex than many who advocate for freedom of speech on-line would have us believe. In order to understand these issues more deeply, we have included a philosophical piece on the rationale for freedom speech. Though he does not address computer technology, Greenawalt explores an array of consequentialist and nonconsequentialist reasons for free speech. In the end, he does not find a clear set of principles that help us determine when the government is unwarranted in interfering with freedom of speech. He concludes, rather, by thinking that the reasons he has described provide "a set of considerations, a set of standards . . . which help to identify which interferences with expression are most worrisome . . ."

In "An Electronic Soapbox" Eric Jensen brings the issues into clearer focus as he surveys current and proposed regulation of electronic bulletin boards focusing in particular on pornographic speech and computer crime. Jensen is quite concerned about the First Amendment and draws on the principles that have been used in regulating other forms of communication.

We conclude this chapter (and book) with a "cautionary tale." To insure that our readers think hard about some of the possible negative effects of creating worlds on-line, we offer a short story by E. M. Forster, *The Machine Stops*. This powerful tale is not about the information infrastructure, nor is it explicitly about computers, but it describes a dystopian world in which human beings have become almost wholly dependent on a characterless machine. The story cautions us about becoming overly dependent on technology to the extent that we lose touch with the natural world and lose touch with everything but our mental capacities.

CASE
THE UNITED STATES VS. CRAIG NEIDORF

A Debate on Electronic Publishing, Constitutional Rights and Hacking

Dorothy Denning

In 1983, the media publicized a series of computer break-ins by teenagers in Wisconsin nicknamed "414 hackers." At about the same time, the popular movie *Wargames* depicted a computer wizard gaining access to the North American Air Defense (NORAD) Command in Cheyenne Mountain, Colorado and almost triggering a nuclear war by accident. Since then, a stereotype of a *computer hacker*[1] has emerged based upon unscrupulous young people who use their computer skills to break into systems, steal information and computer and telecommunication resources, and disrupt operations without regard for the owners and users of the systems.

Well-publicized incidents, such as the Internet worm [6] and the German hackers who broke into unclassified defense systems and sold information to the KGB [7], have reinforced that stereotype and prompted policy makers and law enforcers to crack down on illegal hacking. In May 1990, 150 Secret Service agents executed 27 search warrants and seized 40 systems as part of Operation Sun Devil, a two-year investigation led by Arizona prosecutors into incidents estimated to have cost companies millions of dollars. Another investigation involving prosecutors in Atlanta and Chicago led to several indictments.

Reports on some of the seizures and indictments provoked an outcry from people in the computer industry who perceived the actions taken by law enforcers as a threat to constitutional rights. One case in particular that was cited as an example of threats against freedom of the electronic press was that of *Craig Neidorf*—a college student accused by the U.S. government of fraud and interstate transportation of stolen property regarding a document published in his electronic newsletter, *Phrack*. The trial began on July 23, 1990, and ended suddenly four days later when the government dropped the charges. I attended the trial as an expert witness for the defense.

OVERVIEW OF THE CASE

Craig Neidorf is a pre-law student at the University of Missouri. At the age of 13, he became interested in computers, an extension of an earlier intense interest in Atari 2600 and other video games. At 14, he adopted the handle Knight Lightning on computer networks and bulletin boards. At 16, he and a childhood friend started an electronic newsletter called *Phrack*. The name was composed from the words *phreak* and *hack*, which refer to telecommunications systems (phreaking) and computer systems (hacking). To *Phrack* readers and contributors, phreaking and hacking covered both legal and illegal activities, and some of the articles in *Phrack* provided information that could be useful for someone trying to gain access to a system or free use of telecommunications lines. To some law enforcers and computer security professionals, *Phrack* was seen as a possible breeding ground for computer criminals. They found issues of *Phrack* among the evidence of cases under investigation, and a hacker told them that *Phrack* had provided information that helped him get started.

Phrack published 30 issues from November 1985 through 1989. Neidorf's main role with the newsletter was editor of a column called "Phrack World News." In addition, he was the publisher of issue 14, and co-editor/publisher of issues 20–30. As publisher, he solicited articles from authors, assembled the articles he received into an issue, and distributed the issue to an electronic mailing list.

On January 18, 1990, Neidorf received a visit from an agent of the U.S. Secret Service and a representative of Southwestern Bell Security regarding a document about the Enhanced 911 (E911) emergency system. This document, which was in the form of a computer text file, had been published in Issue 24 of *Phrack*. During this visit, Neidorf, believing he had done nothing wrong, cooperated and turned over information. The next day, the visitors returned with a representative from the campus police and a search warrant. Neidorf was also asked to contact the U.S. Attorney's office in Chicago. He did, and on January 29 arrived at that office, accompanied by a lawyer, for further interrogation. Again, the young publisher turned over information and answered their questions. Neither he nor his attorney were informed that four days earlier evidence had been presented to a federal grand jury in Chicago for the purpose of indicting him. On February 1, the grand jury was given additional evidence and charged Craig Neidorf with six counts in an indictment for wire fraud, computer fraud, and interstate transportation of stolen property valued at $5,000 or more.

In June 1990, the grand jury met again and issued a new indictment that dropped the computer fraud charges, but added additional counts of wire fraud. Neidorf was now charged with 10 felony counts carrying a maximum penalty of 65 years in prison.

The indictment centered on the publication of the E911 text file in *Phrack*. The government claimed the E911 text file was a highly proprietary and sensitive document belonging to BellSouth and worth $23,900. They characterized the document as a road map to the 911 phone system, and claimed that its publication in *Phrack* allowed hackers to illegally manipulate the 911 computer systems in order to disrupt or halt 911 service. They further claimed that the document had been stolen from BellSouth by Robert Riggs, also known as The Prophet, and that the theft and publication of the document in *Phrack* was part of a fraudulent scheme devised by Neidorf and members of the hacking group Legion of Doom, of which Riggs was a member. The object of the scheme was to break into computer systems in order to obtain sensitive documents and then make the stolen documents available to computer hackers by publishing the documents in *Phrack*. The government claimed that as part of the fraudulent scheme, Neidorf solicited information on how to illegally access computers and telecommunication systems for publication in *Phrack* as "hacker tutorials." The term hacker was defined in the indictment as an individual "involved with the unauthorized access of computer systems by various means."

On May 21, 1990 Neidorf called me to request a copy of my paper about hackers, which I was preparing for the National Computer Security Conference [1]. Although I had not talked with him before that time, I knew who he was because I had been following his case in the *Computer Underground Digest*, an electronic newsletter, and in various Usenet bulletin boards. Based on what I had read, which included the E911 file as published in *Phrack*, I did not see how the E911 file could be used to break into the 911 system or, for that matter, any computer system. I was concerned that Neidorf may have been wrongly indicted. I was also concerned that a wrongful conviction—a distinct possibility in a highly technical trial—could have a negative impact on electronic publication.

In late June, I received a call from Neidorf's attorney, Sheldon Zenner of the firm Katten, Muchin & Zavis in Chicago. After several conversations with Neidorf and Zenner, I agreed to be an expert witness and provide assistance throughout the trial.

Zenner told me that John Nagle, an independent computer scientist in Menlo Park, California, had gathered articles, reports, and books on the E911 system from the Stanford University library and local bookstores, and by dialing a Bellcore 800 number. After Nagle showed me the published documents, I agreed with his conclusion that *Phrack* did not give away any secrets. Nagle was also planning to go to Chicago to help with the defense and possibly testify.

Meanwhile, I gathered articles, books, and programs that showed there are plenty of materials in the public domain that are at least as useful for breaking into systems as anything published in *Phrack*. (Some of these are referenced later.)

THE TRIAL

The trial began on July 23, 1990 in Chicago's District Court for the Northern District of Illinois. It was expected to last two weeks, with the government presenting its case during the first week. I helped prepare the cross examinations of the government's witnesses and expected to testify sometime during the second week.

After a day of jury selection, the trial began with Assistant U.S. Attorney William Cook making the opening remarks for the prosecution. Cook reviewed the government claims, weaving a tale of conspiracy between Neidorf, Riggs, and members of the Legion of Doom who had broken into BellSouth computers.

Zenner then presented his opening remarks for the defense. He reviewed Neidorf's history and involvement with *Phrack*, noting that the goal of the newsletter was the free exchange of information. He challenged the claims of the government and outlined the case for the defense. He noted how the government had indicted Neidorf despite his extensive cooperation with them. He said that Neidorf believed his actions were covered by the First Amendment, and that his beliefs were formed from college classes he took as a pre-law student on constitutional law and civil liberties.

The government's witnesses through Thursday afternoon included Riggs, the Secret Service agent, and employees of Bellcore and of BellSouth and its subsidiaries. The evidence brought out during the examination and cross-examination of these witnesses indicated the E911 text file was not the highly sensitive and secret document that BellSouth had claimed, that BellSouth had not treated the document as though it were, and that Neidorf had not conspired with Riggs. Although this seemed like cause for optimism, Zenner reminded us that the government loses very few cases.

On Friday morning, I arrived at the law offices to learn the government had been talking with Zenner about dropping the felony charges in exchange for a guilty plea to a misdemeanor. Neidorf, however, would not accept a charge for something he had not done. Meanwhile, Zenner was meeting with the U.S. attorneys. I went to the courtroom, where Zenner told me the government was now considering dropping all charges. Zenner was willing to lay out the case for the defense to the prosecution; he asked Nagle and me to go to the U.S. Attorney's office and answer all their questions. We went, and Cook went through the E911 file paragraph by paragraph asking us for evidence that the material was in the public domain. Nagle answered most of the questions, pointing Cook to the relevant public documents and demonstrating that the E911 *Phrack* file did not give away any secrets.

We then went to the courtroom to await the final decision. Shortly thereafter, the court resumed, and Judge Nicholas Bua announced the government's decision to drop charges, dismissed the jury, and declared a mistrial. Five of the jurors were asked to remain and were interviewed by Bua and both attorneys. At midday, the court adjourned.

Although Neidorf was freed of all criminal charges, he was not free of all costs. The trial cost of $100,000 was incurred by him and his family.

KEY DOCUMENTS

The government's case focused on several documents that were published in *Phrack* or were included in electronic mail between Neidorf and others. These included the following: the E911 text file and *Phrack* version of that file; the hacker tutorials published in *Phrack* Issue 22; a Trojan horse login program; an announcement of The Phoenix Project in *Phrack* Issue 19; and some email correspondence between Neidorf and Riggs. All these documents were introduced as evidence by the government during the presentation of its case.

The E911 Text File

Riggs testified that sometime during the summer of 1988, he accessed a BellSouth system called AIMSX and downloaded a file with a document issued by BellSouth Services titled "Control Office Administration of Enhanced 911 Services for Special Services and Major Account Centers," Section 660-225-104SV, Issue A, March 1988. The document, which contains administrative information related to E911 service, installation, and maintenance, bears the following notice on the first page: "Not for use or disclosure outside BellSouth or any of its subsidiaries except under written agreement." Sometime prior to September 1988, Riggs transferred the file to a public Unix™ system called Jolnet, where it remained until July 1989.

Riggs testified he sent the E911 text file to Neidorf via email from Jolnet in January 1989 for publication in *Phrack*. He said he asked Neidorf to edit the file so that it would not be recognizable by BellSouth, and to publish it under the handle "The Eavesdropper." Neidorf removed the nondisclosure notice and deleted names, locations, and telephone numbers, and published it in *Phrack* Issue 24 on February 24, 1989. The edited document was less than half the size of the original document, and was split into two *Phrack* files, the first (file 5) containing the main text and the second (file 6) containing the glossary of terms.

The government claimed that the E911 text file and *Phrack* version contained highly sensitive and proprietary information that provided a road map to the 911 system and could be used to gain access to the system and disrupt service. The claim was based on a statement made by an employee of Bellcore.

As noted earlier, Nagle had located articles and pamphlets that contained much more information about the E911 system than the *Phrack* file. During cross examination of the government's witness who was responsible for the practice described in the E911 document, Zenner showed the witness two of these pamphlets available from Bellcore via an 800 number for $13 and $21 respectively. The witness, who had not seen either report before and was generally unfamiliar with the public literature on E911, agreed that the reports also gave road maps to the E911 system and included more information than was in *Phrack*. The witness also testified that a nondisclosure stamp is routinely put on every BellSouth document when it is first written, thereby weakening any argument that the document contained particularly sensitive trade secrets.

The defense was prepared to argue that the E911 text file contained no information that was directly useful for breaking into the E911 system or any computer system. There were no dial-up numbers, no network addresses, no accounts, no passwords, and no mention of computer system vulnerabilities. The government claimed that the names, locations, organization phone numbers, and jargon in the E911 text file could be useful for *social engineering*—that is, deceiving employees to get information such as computer accounts and passwords. However, the *Phrack* version omitted the names, locations, and phone numbers, and the jargon was all described in the published literature. Thus, the E911 *Phrack* file seemed no more useful for social engineering than the related public documents.

The defense was also prepared to show that BellSouth had not treated the document as one would expect a document of such alleged sensitivity to be treated. Riggs testified that the account he had used to get into AIMSX had no password. AT&T security was notified in September 1988, that the E911 text file was publicly available in Riggs's directory on Jolnet, and Bellcore security was notified of this in October. This was two months before Riggs mailed the file to Neidorf for inclusion in *Phrack*, and about four months before its publication in *Phrack*. Still, no legal action was taken until July 1989, nine months from the time Bellcore was aware of the file's presence on Jolnet. At that point, Bellcore and BellSouth asserted to the government that a highly sensitive and dangerous document was stolen. They urged the U.S. Secret Service to act immediately because of the purported risk posed by the availability of this "dangerous" information. However, they did not tell the Secret Service that they had discovered all of this nine months earlier. The government responded immediately with a subpoena for Jolnet. The defense believed that BellSouth's delay in acting to protect the E911 document was inconsistent with its claim that the document contained sensitive information. To its credit, however, BellSouth did strengthen the security of its systems following the breakins.

The Hacker Tutorials

The government claimed that three files in *Phrack* Issue 22 were tutorials for breaking into systems and, as such, evidence of a fraudulent scheme to break into systems, steal documents, and publish them in *Phrack*. These files, which corresponded to one count of the indictment, were:

4. "A Novices Guide to Hacking—1989 Edition" by The Mentor.
5. "An Indepth Guide in Hacking Unix and The Concept of Basic Networking Utility" by Red Knight.
6. "Yet Another File on Hacking Unix" by Unknown User.

Files 4 and 5 of *Phrack* 22 briefly introduce the art of getting computer access through weak passwords and default accounts, while File 6 contains a password-cracking program. Most of file 5 is a description of basic commands in Unix, which can be found in any Unix manual. After examining these and other *Phrack* files, I concluded that *Phrack* contained no more information about breaking into systems than articles written by computer security specialists and published in journals such as the *Communications of the ACM, AT&T Bell Technical Journal, Information Age*, and *Unix/WORLD*, and in books. For example, Cliff Stoll's popular book *The Cuckoo's Egg* [7] has been characterized as a "primer on hacking." Information that could be valuable for breaking passwords is given in the 1979 paper on password vulnerabilities by Morris and Thompson of Bell Laboratories [4]. A recent article by Spafford gives details on the workings of the Internet worm [6].

Password-cracking programs are publicly available intentionally so that system managers can run them against their own password files in order to discover weak passwords. An example is the password cracker in COPS, a package that checks a Unix system for different types of vulnerabilities. The complete package can be obtained by anonymous FTP from ftp.uu.net. Like the password cracker published in *Phrack*, the COPS cracker checks whether any of the words in an on-line dictionary correspond to a password in the password file.

Another file that the prosecution brought into evidence during the trial was file 6 in *Phrack* Issue 26, "Basic Concepts of Translation," by The Dead Lord and The Chief Executive Officers. This file, which described translation in Electronic Switching System (ESS) switches, contained a phrase "Anyone want to throw the ESS switch into an endless loop????" in a section on indirect addressing in an index table. This remark can be interpreted as a joke, but even if it were not, the information in the article seems no worse than Ritchie's code for crashing a system, which is published in the Unix Programmer's Manual with the comment "Here is a particularly ghastly shell sequence guaranteed to stop the system: . . ." [5].

The government's claims that these files were part of a fraudulent scheme were disproved by Riggs's testimony and email (discussed later) showing that Neidorf and Riggs had not conspired to commit fraud by stealing property and publishing stolen documents.

By publishing articles that expose system vulnerabilities, *Phrack*, in one sense, is not unlike some professional publications such as those issued by the ACM. The Association encourages publishing such articles on the grounds that in the long term, the knowledge of vulnerabilities will lead to the design of systems that are resistant to attacks and failures. But, there is an important difference between the two publications.

ACM explicitly states that it does not condone unauthorized use or disruption of systems, it discourages authors of articles about vulnerabilities from writing in a way that makes attacks seem like a worthy activity, and it declines to publish articles that appear to endorse attacks of any kind. In addition, the ACM is willing to delay publication of an article for a short time if publishing the information could make existing systems subject to attack.

By comparison, *Phrack* appears to encourage people to explore system vulnerabilities. In "A Novice's Guide to Hacking," The Mentor gives 11 guidelines to hacking. The last says "Finally, you have to actually hack. . . . There's no thrill quite the same as getting into your first system . . ." Although the guidelines tell the reader "Do not intentionally damage *any* system," they also tell the reader to alter those system files "needed to ensure your escape from detection and your future access."[2] The wording can be interpreted as encouraging unauthorized but nonmalicious break-ins. Thus, whereas reading *Phrack* could lead one to the assessment that it promotes illegal break-ins, reading an ACM publication is likely to lead to the assessment that it discourages such acts and promotes protective actions.

The actual effect of either publication on illegal activities or computer security, however, is much more difficult to determine, especially since both publications are available to anyone. Computer security specialists who read *Phrack* may have found it useful to know what vulnerabilities intruders were likely to exploit, while hackers who read *Communications of the ACM* may have learned something new about breaking into systems or implanting viruses. The *Phrack* reports on people who were arrested may have discouraged some budding young hackers from performing illegal acts; they also may have reminded hackers to take greater measures to cover up their tracks and avoid being caught.

Even if *Phrack* promoted certain illegal actions, this does not make the publication itself illegal. The First Amendment protects such publication unless it poses an imminent danger to society. The threshold for this condition is sufficiently high that, although courts have discussed its theoretical existence, it has never been met.

The Trojan Horse Login Program

The government found a modified version of the AT&T System V 3.2 login program in Neidorf's files. The program, which was modified and sent to Neidorf by someone currently under indictment, was part of the AT&T Unix source code and had "copyright" and "proprietary" stamps scattered throughout. The modifications included a Trojan horse that captured accounts and passwords, saving them in a file that could later be retrieved. The government claimed that Neidorf's possession of this program demonstrated his intentions to promote illegal break-ins and the theft of proprietary information. To support its case, it brought into evidence email where Neidorf was relaying messages between two other parties. One party said he had other Unix sources, including 4.3 BSD Tahoe; the other asked for the Tahoe source so he could install the login program on some Internet sites.

The defense believed the government's allegations against Neidorf were weak on three grounds.

1st, as with any publisher, the mere receipt of a document is not proof of intent to perform illegal acts.

2nd, after observing that the source code contained notices that the code was copyrighted and proprietary, Neidorf asked someone at Bellcore security for advice on what to do. This action added credibility to his claim that he had no intent to perform illegal acts and that he did not know that publishing the E911 text could be illegal. Although the E911 file had a nondisclosure notice, the notice did not contain the words "copyright" or "proprietary."

3rd, how to write a Trojan horse login program is no secret. For example, such programs have been published in Stoll's book [7] and an article by Grampp and Morris [2]. Also, in his ACM Turning lecture, Ken Thompson, one of the Bell Labs coauthors of Unix, explained how to create a powerful Trojan horse that would allow its author to log onto any account with either the password assigned to the account or a password chosen by the author [8]. Thompson's Trojan horse had the additional property of being undetectable in the login source code. This was achieved by modifying the C-compiler so that it would compile the Trojan horse into the login program.

The Phoenix Project and Email Correspondence

Issue 19, File 7 of *Phrack* announced "The Phoenix Project," and portrayed it as a new beginning to the phreak/hack community where "Knowledge is the key to the future and it is FREE. The telecommunications and security industries can no longer withhold the right to learn, the right to explore, or the right to have knowledge." The new beginning was to take place at SummerCon '88 in St. Louis.

The government claimed this announcement was the beginning of the fraudulent scheme to solicit and publish information on how to access systems illegally, and its publication accounted for one of the counts in the indictment. Yet, the announcement explicitly says "The new age is here and with the use of every *LEGAL* means available, the youth of today will be able to teach the youth of tomorrow. . . . the practice of passing illegal information is not a part of this convention." Security consultants and law enforcers were invited to attend SummerCon.

Although Neidorf was not charged with any crimes in 1988, the Secret Service sent undercover agents to SummerCon '88 to observe the meeting. They secretly videotaped Neidorf and others through a two-way mirror during the conference for 15 hours. What did they record? A few minors drinking beer and eating pizza! Zenner asked to introduce these tapes as evidence for the defense, but the prosecution objected and Judge Bua sustained their objection.

Two counts of the indictment involved email messages from Neidorf to Riggs and "Scott C." These messages, which were also alleged to be part of the fraudulent scheme, were basically discussions of particular individuals, mainly members of the Legion of Doom. The messages contained no plots to defraud any organization and no solicitations for illegal information.

RIGHTS AND RESPONSIBILITIES

Neidorf's indictment came in the midst of a two-year investigation of illegal activity that involved the FBI, Secret Service, and other federal and local law enforcement agencies. As part of the investigation, the government seized over 40 systems and 23,000 disks. Several bulletin board systems were shut down in the process, including the Jolnet system on which Riggs stored the E911 document. In most cases, no charges have yet been made against the person owning the equipment, and equipment that seemed to have little bearing on any illegal activity, such as a phone answering machine, was sometimes included in the haul. The *Phrack* case and computer seizures raised concerns about freedom of the press, protection from unnecessary searches and seizures, and the liabilities and responsibilities of system operators and owners. In this section, I shall discuss these issues and give some of my own opinions about them.

Electronic Publications

Some observers interpreted Neidorf's indictment as a threat to freedom of the press in the electronic media. The practice of publishing materials obtained by questionable means is common in the news media, and publication of the E911 file in *Phrack* was compared with publication of the Pentagon Papers in the *New York Times* and *Washington Post*. The government had tried unsuccessfully to stop publication of the Pentagon Papers, arguing that publication would threaten national security. The Supreme Court held that such action would constitute a "prior restraint" on the press, prohibited by the First Amendment. It therefore surprises me that there is any doubt that electronic publications should be accorded the same protection as printed ones.

Shortly before the *Phrack* case came to trial, Mitchell Kapor and John Barlow founded the Electronic Frontier Foundation (EFF) in order to help raise public awareness about civil liberties issues and to support actions in the public interest to preserve and protect constitutional rights within the electronic media. The EFF hired the services of Terry Gross, attorney with the New York law firm Rabinowitz, Boudin, Krinsky & Lieberman, to provide legal advice for the *Phrack* case; Gross submitted two friend-of-the-court briefings seeking to have the indictment dismissed because it threatened constitutionally protected speech. The trial court judge denied EFF's motion, but as it turned out, the charges were dropped before the issue was seriously discussed during the *Neidorf* trial.

Although certain information may be published legally, authors and publishers should consider how such information might be interpreted and used. In the case of hacker publications, the majority of readers are impressionable young people who are the foundation of the future. Articles which encourage illegal break-ins or contain information obtained in this manner should not simply be dismissed as proper just because they are protected under First Amendment rights.

Searches and Seizures

The seizures of bulletin boards and other systems raised questions about the rights of the government to take property and retain it for an extended period of time when no charges have been made. At least one small business, Steve Jackson Games, claims to have suffered a serious loss as a result of having equipment confiscated for over three months. According to Jackson, the Secret Service raid cost his company $125,000, and he had to lay off almost half of his employees since all of the information about their next product, a game called GURPS CYBERPUNK, was on the confiscated systems. Some of the company's equipment was severely damaged, and data was lost. No charges have been made.

Seizing a person's computer system can be comparable to taking every document and piece of correspondence in that person's office and home. It can shut down a business. Moreover, by taking the system, the government has the capability of reading electronic mail and files unrelated to the investigation; such broad seizures of paper documents are generally not approved by judges issuing search warrants.

For these reasons, it has been suggested that the government not be allowed to take complete systems, but only the files related to the investigation. In most cases, this seems impractical. There may be megabytes or even gigabytes of information stored on disks, and it takes time to scan through that much information. In addition, the system may have nonstandard hardware or software, making it extremely difficult to transfer the data to another machine and process it. Similarly, if a computer is seized without its printer, it may be extremely difficult to print out files. Finally, originals are needed for evidence in court, and the evidence must be protected up to the time of trial. However, if the government can be reasonably confident that the owner of the system has not participated in or condoned the activities under investigation, then it may be practical for the government to issue a subpoena for certain files rather than seize the entire system.

When a complete system is seized, it seems reasonable that the government be required under court order to provide copies of files to the owner at the owner's request and expense within some time limit, say one week or one month.

If a system shared by multiple users is seized, the search should be restricted to mail and files belonging to the users under investigation.

Liabilities and Responsibilities of System Operators and Owners

The bulletin board seizures sent a chill through the legitimate network community, raising questions about the liabilities of an operator of a bulletin board or of any system. Operators of these boards asked if they needed to check all information passing through the system to make sure there is nothing that could be interpreted as a stolen, proprietary document or as part of a fraudulent scheme.

Computer bulletin boards have been referred to metaphorically as electronic meeting places where assembly of people is not constrained by time or distance. Public boards are also a form of electronic publication. It would seem, therefore, that they are protected by the constitution in the same way that public meeting places and non-electronic publications such as newspapers are protected. This, of course, does not necessarily mean they should be free of all controls, just as public meetings are not entirely free of control.

Bulletin board systems often provide private directories and electronic mail. Private mail and files should be given the same protections from surveillance and seizure as First Class Mail and private discussions that take place in homes or businesses. I believe the Electronic Communications Privacy Act provides this protection.

The E911 text file was obtained from a system with a null password. While this does not excuse the person who got into the system and copied the file, I believe that system owners should take greater measures to prevent break-ins and unauthorized use of their systems. There are known practices for protecting systems. While none of these are foolproof, they offer a high probability for keeping intruders out and detecting those that enter. Although the risks associated with insecure systems may not have been great until recently, thereby justifying weak security in favor of allocating more resources for other purposes, the risks are now sufficiently great that weak security is inexcusable for many environments. Moreover, system owners may be vulnerable to lawsuits if they do not have adequate protection for customer information or for life-critical operations such as patient monitoring or traffic control.

Our current laws allow a person to be convicted of a felony for simply entering a system through an account without a password. I recommend we consider adopting a policy where unauthorized entry into a system is at most a misdemeanor if certain standards have not been followed by the owner of the system and the damage to information on the system is not high. However, I recognize that it may be very difficult to set appropriate standards and to determine whether an organization has adhered to them.

I also recommend we consider establishing a range of offenses, possibly along the lines of those in the U. K. Computer Misuse Act, which became effective in August 1990:

- **Unauthorized access:** seeking to enter a computer system, knowing that the entry is unauthorized. Punishable by up to six months' imprisonment.
- **Unauthorized access in furtherance of a more serious crime:** Punishable by up to five years' imprisonment.
- **Unauthorized modification of computer material:** introducing viruses, Trojan horses, etc., or causing malicious damage to computer files. Punishable by up to five years' imprisonment.

CONCLUSIONS

Making a sound assessment of the claims made in the *Phrack* case requires expertise in the domains of computers, the Unix system, computer security, phone systems, and the public literature. Whereas Zenner brought in outside technical expertise to help with the defense, the prosecution relied on experts belonging to the victim, namely, employees of Bell. The indictment and costly trial may have been avoided if the government had consulted neutral experts before deciding whether to pursue the charges. The professional community represented by ACM may be a good source of such help.

In the context of the new milieu created by computers and networks, a new form of threat has emerged—the computer criminal capable of damaging or disrupting the electronic infrastructure, invading people's privacy, and performing industrial espionage. While the costs associated with these crimes may be small compared with computer crimes caused by company employees and former employees, the costs are growing and are becoming significant.

For many young computer enthusiasts, illegal break-ins and phreaking are a juvenile activity that they outgrow as they see the consequences of their actions in the world. However, a significant number of these hackers may go on to become serious computer criminals. To design an intervention that will discourage people from entering into criminal acts, we must first understand the hacker culture since it reveals the concerns of hackers that must be taken into account. We must also understand the concerns of companies and law enforcers. We must understand how all these perspectives interact.

The 1985 ACM Panel on Hacking [3] offered several suggestions for actions that could be taken to reduce illegal hacking, and my own investigation confirmed these while speculating about others [1]. Teaching computer ethics may help, and I applaud recent efforts on the part of computer professionals and educators to bring computer ethics not only into the classroom, but into their professional forums for discussion.

ACKNOWLEDGMENTS

Special thanks to Chuck Bushey, Peter Denning, Jef Gibson, Cynthia Hibbard, Steve Lipner, Craig Neidorf, Mike Schroeder, and Sheldon Zenner for many helpful suggestions; to Pete Mellor for information about the U. K. laws; and to my many friends and colleagues who patiently educate me in areas where I am vulnerable to my own blindness. The views here are my own and do not represent those of my employer.

NOTES

1. The term "hacker" originally meant anyone with a keen interest in learning about computer systems and using them in novel and clever ways. Many computer enthusiasts still call themselves hackers in this nonpejorative sense.
2. Most system managers regard any modification of system files as damage, because they must restore these files to a state that does not permit the intruder to re-enter the system.

REFERENCES

1. Denning, D. E. Concerning hackers who break into computer systems. In *Proceedings of the 13th National Computer Security Conference* (Oct. 1990).
2. Grampp, F. T., and Morris, R. H. UNIX operating system security. *AT&T Bell Lab. Tech. J., 63*, 8 (Oct. 1984).
3. Lee, J. A. N., Segal, G., and Stier, R. Positive alternatives: A report on an ACM panel on hacking, *Commun. ACM, 29*, 4 (Apr. 1986), 297–299; full report available from ACM Headquarters, New York.
4. Morris, R., and Thompson, K. Password security: A case history. *Commun. ACM 22*, 11 (Nov. 1979).
5. Ritchie, D. On the security of Unix. Unix programmer's manual, Section 2, AT&T Bell Laboratories.
6. Spafford, E. H. The Internet Worm: Crisis and aftermath. *Commun. ACM 32*, 6 (June 1989).
7. Stoll, C. *The Cuckoo's Egg*. Doubleday, N.Y. 1990.
8. Thompson, K. Reflections on trusting trust. Turing Award Lecture, *Commun. ACM 27*, 8, 761–763.

▷ GLOBAL INFORMATION INFRASTRUCTURE

Remarks As Delivered to the International Telecommunications Union—Monday, March 21, 1994

Vice President Al Gore

I have come here, 8,000 kilometers from my home, to ask you to help create a Global Information Infrastructure. To explain why, I want to begin by reading you something that I first read in high school, 30 years ago.

"By means of electricity, the world of matter has become a great nerve, vibrating thousands of miles in a breathless point of time. The round globe is a vast . . . brain, instinct with intelligence!"

This was not the observation of a physicist—or a neurologist. Instead, these visionary words were written in 1851 by Nathaniel Hawthorne, one of my country's greatest writers, who was inspired by the development of the telegraph. Much as Jules Verne foresaw submarines and moon landings, Hawthorne foresaw what we are now poised to bring into being.

The ITU was created only 14 years later, in major part for the purpose of fostering an internationally compatible system of telegraphy.

For almost 150 years, people have aspired to fulfill Hawthorne's vision—to wrap nerves of communications around the globe, linking all human knowledge.

In this decade, at this conference, we now have at hand the technological breakthroughs and economic means to bring all the communities of the world together. We now can at last create a planetary information network that transmits messages and images with the speed of light from the largest city to the smallest village on every continent.

I am very proud to have the opportunity to address the first development conference of the ITU because President Clinton and I believe that an essential prerequisite to sustainable development, for all members of the human family, is the creation of this network of networks. To accomplish this purpose, legislators, regulators, and businesspeople must do this: build and operate a Global Information Infrastructure. This GII will circle the globe with information superhighways on which all people can travel.

These highways—or, more accurately, networks of distributed intelligence—will allow us to share information, to connect, and to communicate as a global community. From these connections we will derive robust and sustainable economic progress, strong democracies, better solutions to global and local environmental challenges, improved health care, and—ultimately—a greater sense of shared stewardship of our small planet.

The Global Information Infrastructure will help educate our children and allow us to exchange ideas within a community and among nations. It will be a means by which families and friends will transcend the barriers of time and distance. It will make possible a global information marketplace, where consumers can buy or sell products.

I ask you, the delegates to this conference, to set an ambitious agenda that will help all governments, in their own sovereign nations and in international cooperation, to build this Global Information Infrastructure. For my country's part, I pledge our vigorous, continued participation in achieving this goal—in the development sector of the ITU, in other sectors and in plenipotentiary gatherings of the ITU, and in bilateral discussions held by our Departments of State and Commerce and our Federal Communications Commission.

The development of the GII must be a cooperative effort among governments and peoples. It cannot be dictated or built by a single country. It must be a democratic effort.

And the distributed intelligence of the GII will spread participatory democracy. To illustrate why, I'd like to use an example from computer science.

In the past, all computers were huge mainframes with a single central processing unit, solving problems in sequence, one by one, each bit of information sent back and forth between the CPU and the vast field of memory surrounding it. Now, we have massively parallel computers with hundreds—or thousands—of tiny self-contained processors distributed throughout the memory field, all interconnected, and together far more powerful and more versatile than even the most sophisticated single processor, because they each solve a tiny piece of the problem simultaneously and when all the pieces are assembled, the problem is solved.

Similarly, the GII will be an assemblage of local, national, and regional networks, that are not only like parallel computers but in their most advanced state will in fact be a distributed, parallel computer.

In a sense, the GII will be a metaphor for democracy itself. Representative democracy does not work with an all-powerful central government, arrogating all decisions to itself. That is why communism collapsed.

Instead, representative democracy relies on the assumption that the best way for a nation to make its political decisions is for each citizen—the human equivalent of the self-contained processor—to have the power to control his or her own life.

To do that, people must have available the information they need. And be allowed to express their conclusions in free speech and in votes that are combined with those of millions of others. That's what guides the system as a whole.

The GII will not only be a metaphor for a functioning democracy, it will in fact promote the functioning of democracy by greatly enhancing the participation of citizens in decision-making. And it will greatly promote the ability of nations to cooperate with each other. I see an new Athenian Age of democracy forged in the fora the GII will create.

The GII will be the key to economic growth for national and international economies. For us in the United States, the information infrastructure already is to the U.S. economy of the 1990s what transportation infrastructure was to the economy of the mid-20th century.

The integration of computing and information networks into the economy makes U.S. manufacturing companies more productive, more competitive, and more adaptive to changing conditions and it will do the same for the economies of other nations.

These same technologies are also enabling the service sectors of the U.S. economy to grow, to increase their scale and productivity and expand their range of product offerings and ability to respond to customer demands.

Approximately 60 percent of all U.S. workers are "knowledge workers"—people whose jobs depend on the information they generate and receive over our information infrastructure. As we create new jobs, 8 out of 10 are in information-intensive sectors of our economy. And these new jobs are well-paying jobs for financial analysts, computer programmers, and other educated workers.

The global economy also will be driven by the growth of the Information Age. Hundreds of billions of dollars can be added to world growth if we commit to the GII. I fervently hope this conference will take full advantage of this potential for economic growth, and not deny any country or community its right to participate in this growth.

As the GII spreads, more and more people realize that information is a treasure that must be shared to be valuable. When two people communicate, they each can be enriched—and unlike traditional resources, the more you share, the more you have. As Thomas Jefferson said, "He who receives an idea from me, receives instruction himself without lessening mine; as he who lights his taper at mine, receives light without darkening me."

Now we all realize that, even as we meet here, the Global Information Infrastructure is being built, although many countries have yet to see any benefits.

Digital telecommunications technology, fiber optics, and new high-capacity satellite systems are transforming telecommunications.

And all over the world, under the seas and along the roads, pipelines, and railroads, companies are laying fiber optic cable that carries thousands of telephone calls per second over a single strand of glass.

These developments are greatly reducing the cost of building the GII.

In the past, it could take years to build a network. Linking a single country's major cities might require laying thousands of kilometers of expensive wires. Today, a single satellite and a few dozen ground stations can be installed in a few months—at much lower cost.

The economics of networks have changed so radically that the operation of a competitive, private market can build much of the GII. This is dependent, however, upon sensible regulation.

Within the national boundaries of the U.S. we aspire to build our information highways according to a set of principles that I outlined in January in California. The National Information Infrastructure, as we call it, will be built and maintained by the private sector.

It will consist of hundreds of different networks, run by different companies and using different technologies, all connected together in a giant "network of networks," providing telephone and interactive digital video to almost every American.

Our plan is based on five principles:

First, encourage private investment;

Second, promote competition;

Third, create a flexible regulatory framework that can keep pace with rapid technological and market changes;

Fourth, provide open access to the network for all information providers; and

Fifth, ensure universal service;

Are these principles unique to the United States? Hardly. Many are accepted international principles endorsed by many of you. I believe these principles can inform and aid the development of the Global Information Infrastructure and urge this Conference to incorporate them, as appropriate, into the Buenos Aires Declaration, which will be drafted this week.

Let me elaborate briefly on these principles.

First, we propose that private investment and competition be the foundation for development of the GII. In the U.S., we are in the process of opening our communications markets to all domestic private participants.

In recent years, many countries, particularly here in Latin America, have opted to privatize their state-owned telephone companies in order to obtain the benefits and incentives that drive competitive private enterprises, including innovation, increased investment, efficiency and responsiveness to market needs.

Adopting policies that allow increased private sector participation in the telecommunications sector has provided an enormous spur to telecommunications development in dozens of countries, including Argentina, Venezuela, Chile, and Mexico. I urge you to follow their lead.

But privatization is not enough. Competition is needed as well. In the past, it did make sense to have telecommunications monopolies.

In many cases, the technology and the economies of scale meant it was inefficient to build more than one network. In other cases—Finland, Canada, and the U.S., for example—national networks were built in the early part of this century by hundreds of small, independent phone companies and cooperatives.

Today, there are many more technology options than in the past and it is not only possible, but desirable, to have different companies running competing—but interconnected—networks, because competition is the best way to make the telecommunications sector more efficient, more innovative—and more profitable as consumers make more calls and prices decline.

That is why allowing other companies to compete with AT&T, once the world's largest telephone monopoly, was so useful for the United States.

Over the last ten years, it has cut the cost of a long-distance telephone call in the U.S. more than 50 percent.

To promote competition and investment in global telecommunications, we need to adopt cost-based collection and accounting rates. Doing so will accelerate development of the GII.

International standards to ensure interconnection and interoperability are needed as well. National networks must connect effectively with each other to make real the simple vision of linking schools, hospitals, businesses, and homes to a Global Information Infrastructure.

Hand in hand with the need for private investment and competition is the necessity of appropriate and flexible regulations developed by an authoritative regulatory body.

In order for the private sector to invest and for initiatives opening a market to competition to be successful, it is necessary to create a regulatory environment that fosters and protects competition and private sector investments, while at the same time protecting consumers' interests.

Without the protection of an independent regulator, a potential private investor would be hesitant to provide service in competition with the incumbent provider for fear that the incumbent's market power would not be adequately controlled.

Decisions and the basis for making them must also be made public so that consumers and potential competitors are assured that their interests are being protected.

This is why in the U.S., we have delegated significant regulatory powers to an independent agency, the Federal Communications Commission. This expert body is well-equipped to make difficult technical decisions and to monitor, in conjunction with the National Telecommunications and Information Administration and the Department of Justice, changing market conditions.

We commend this approach to you.

We need a flexible, effective system for resolution of international issues, too—one that can keep up with the ever-accelerating pace of technological change.

I understand that the ITU has just gone through a major reorganization designed to increase its effectiveness. This will enable the ITU, under the able leadership of Mr. Tarjanne, to streamline its operations and redirect resources to where they are needed most. This will ensure that the ITU can adapt to future and unimaginable technologies.

Our fourth principle is open access. By this I mean that telephone and video network owners should charge non-discriminatory prices for access to their networks. This principle will guarantee every user of the GII can use thousands of different sources of information—video programming, electronic newspapers, computer bulletin boards—from every country, in every language.

With new technologies like direct broadcast satellites, a few networks will no longer be able to control your access to information—as long as government policies permit new entrants into the information marketplace.

Countries and companies will not be able to compete in the global economy if they cannot get access to up-to-date information, if they cannot communicate instantly with customers around the globe. Ready access to information is also essential for training the skilled workforce needed for high-tech industries.

The countries that flourish in the twenty-first century will be those that have telecommunications policies and copyright laws that provide their citizens access to a wide choice of information services.

Protecting intellectual property is absolutely essential.

The final and most important principle is to ensure universal service so that the Global Information Infrastructure is available to all members of our societies. Our goal is a kind of global conversation, in which everyone who wants can have his or her say.

We must ensure that whatever steps we take to expand our worldwide telecommunications infrastructure, we keep that goal in mind.

Although the details of universal service will vary from country to country and from service to service, several aspects of universal service apply everywhere. Access clearly includes making service available at affordable prices to persons at all income levels.

It also includes making high quality service available regardless of geographic location or other restrictions such as disability.

Constellations of hundreds of satellites in low earth orbit may soon provide telephone or data services to any point on the globe. Such systems could make universal service both practical and affordable.

An equally important part of universal access is teaching consumers how to use communications effectively. That means developing easy-to-use applications for a variety of contexts, and teaching people how to use them. The most sophisticated and cost-efficient networks will be completely useless if users are unable to understand how to access and take full advantage of their offerings.

Another dimension of universal service is the recognition that marketplace economics should not be the sole determinant of the reach of the information infrastructure.

The President and I have called for positive government action in the United States to extend the NII to every classroom, library, hospital, and clinic in the U.S. by the end of the century.

I want to urge that this conference include in its agenda for action the commitment to determine how every school and library in every country can be connected to the Internet, the world's largest computer network, in order to create a Global Digital Library. Each library could maintain a server containing books and journals in electronic form, along with indexes to help users find other materials. As more and more information is stored electronically, this global library would become more and more useful.

It would allow millions of students, scholars and businesspeople to find the information they need whether it be in Albania or Ecuador.

Private investment . . . competition . . . flexibility . . . open access . . . universal service.

In addition to urging the delegates of this conference to adopt these principles as part of the Buenos Aires Declaration, guiding the next four years of telecommunications development, I assure you that the U.S. will be discussing in many fora, inside and outside the ITU, whether these principles might be usefully adopted by all countries.

The commitment of all nations to enforcing regulatory regimes to build the GII is vital to world development and many global social goals.

But the power of the Global Information Infrastructure will be diminished if it cannot reach large segments of the world population.

We have heard together Dr. Tarjanne's eloquent speech setting forth the challenges we face. As he points out: the 24 countries of the OECD have only 16 percent of the world's population. But they account for 70 percent of global telephone mainlines and 90 percent of mobile phone subscribers.

There are those who say the lack of economic development causes poor telecommunications. I believe they have it exactly backwards. A primitive telecommunications systems causes poor economic development.

So we cannot be complacent about the disparity between the high and low income nations, whether in how many phones are available to people or in whether they have such new technologies as high speed computer networks or videoconferencing.

The United States delegation is devoted to working with each of you at this Conference to address the many problems that hinder development.

And there are many.

Financing is a problem in almost every country, even though telecommunications has proven itself to be an excellent investment.

Even where telecommunications has been identified as a top development priority, countries lack trained personnel and up-to-date information.

And in too many parts of the world, political unrest makes it difficult or impossible to maintain existing infrastructure, let alone lay new wire or deploy new capacity.

How can we work together to overcome these hurdles? Let me mention a few things industrialized countries can do to help.

First, we can use the Global Information Infrastructure for technical collaboration between industrialized nations and developing countries. All agencies of the U.S. government are potential sources of information and knowledge that can be shared with partners across the globe.

The Global Information Infrastructure can help development agencies link experts from every nation and enable them to solve common problems. For instance, the Pan American Health Organization has conducted hemisphere-wide teleconferences to present new methods to diagnose and prevent the spread of AIDS.

Second, multilateral institutions like the World Bank, can help nations finance the building of telecommunications infrastructure.

Third, the U.S. can help provide the technical know-how needed to deploy and use these new technologies. USAID and U.S. businesses have helped the U.S. Telecommunications Training Institute train more than 3500 telecommunications professionals from the developing world, including many in this room.

In the future, USTTI plans also to help businesspeople, bankers, farmers, and others from the developing world find ways that computer networking, wireless technology, satellites, video links, and other telecommunications technology could improve their effectiveness and efficiency.

I challenge other nations, the development banks, and the UN system to create similar training opportunities.

The head of our Peace Corps, Carol Bellamy, intends to use Peace Corps volunteers both to help deploy telecommunications and computer systems and to find innovative uses for them.

Here in Argentina, a Peace Corps volunteer is doing just that.

To join the GII to the effort to protect and preserve the global environment, our Administration will soon propose using satellite and personal communication technology to create a global network of environmental information.

We will propose using the schools and students of the world to gather and study environmental information on a daily basis and communicate that data to the world through television.

But regulatory reform must accompany this technical assistance and financial aid for it to work. This requires top-level leadership and commitment—commitment to foster investment in telecommunications and commitment to adopt policies that ensure the rapid deployment and widespread use of the information infrastructure.

I opened by quoting Nathaniel Hawthorne, inspired by Samuel Morse's invention of the telegraph.

Morse was also a famous portrait artist in the U.S.—his portrait of President James Monroe hangs today in the White House. While Morse was working on a portrait of General Lafayette in Washington, his wife, who lived about 500 kilometers away, grew ill and died. But it took seven days for the news to reach him.

In his grief and remorse, he began to wonder if it were possible to erase barriers of time and space, so that no one would be unable to reach a loved one in time of need. Pursuing this thought, he came to discover how to use electricity to convey messages, and so he invented the telegraph and, indirectly, the ITU.

The Global Information Infrastructure offers instant communication to the great human family.

It can provide us the information we need to dramatically improve the quality of their lives. By linking clinics and hospitals together, it will ensure that doctors treating patients have access to the best possible information on diseases and treatments. By providing early warning on natural disasters like volcanic eruptions, tsunamis, or typhoons, it can save the lives of thousands of people.

By linking villages and towns, it can help people organize and work together to solve local and regional problems ranging from improving water supplies to preventing deforestation.

To promote; to protect; to preserve freedom and democracy, we must make telecommunications development an integral part of every nation's development. Each link we create strengthens the bonds of liberty and democracy around the world. By opening markets to stimulate the development of the global information infrastructure, we open lines of communication.

By opening lines of communication, we open minds. This summer, from my country cameras will bring the World Cup Championship to well over one billion people.

To those of you from the 23 visiting countries whose teams are in the Finals, I wish you luck—although I'll be rooting for the home team.

The Global Information Infrastructure carries implications even more important than soccer.

It has brought us images of earthquakes in California, of Boris Yeltsin on a tank in Red Square, of the effects of mortar shells in Sarajevo and Somalia, of the fall of the Berlin Wall. It has brought us images of war and peace, and tragedy and joy, in which we all can share.

There's a Dutch relief worker, Wam Kat, who has been broadcasting an electronic diary from Zagreb for more than a year and a half on the Internet, sharing his observations of life in Croatia.

After reading Kat's Croatian diary, people around the world began to send money for relief efforts. The result: 25 houses have been rebuilt in a town destroyed by war.

Governments didn't do this. People did. But such events are the hope of the future.

When I began proposing the NII in the U.S., I said that my hope is that the United States, born in revolution, can lead the way to this new, peaceful revolution. However, I believe we will reach our goal faster and with greater certainty if we walk down that path together. As Antonio Machado, Spanish poet, once said, "Pathwalker, there is no path, we create the path as we walk."

Let us build a global community in which the people of neighboring countries view each other not as potential enemies, but as potential partners, as members of the same family in the vast, increasingly interconnected human family.

Let us seize this moment.

Let us work to link the people of the world.

Let us create this new path as we walk it together.

▷ THE NATIONAL INFORMATION INFRASTRUCTURE: A PUBLIC INTEREST OPPORTUNITY

Gary Chapman and Marc Rotenberg

Imagine a job search in the early 21st century. You go to your "home information appliance," which is your portal to the "national information infrastructure." You log on to a database of jobs available and the database interface walks you through a series of questions about what sort of job you're looking for, what your qualifications are, where you would like to work, and what sort of salary you expect. After a few moments, your screen displays a list of jobs that match your criteria. The data include the names and postal and e-mail addresses of the people to whom a resumé should be sent. You select all the names, and then call up an electronic copy of your resumé. The document is transferred instantly to the company representatives.

A couple of days later you get a message in your electronic mail to contact the personnel office of one of the companies that received your electronic resumé. You speak by voice with an automated appointment scheduler, which offers you an interview appointment at 1 p.m. The appointment will be by video, reports the scheduler. At 1 p.m. you are sitting in a comfortable chair in front of your home information appliance, having cleaned up the room a little beforehand. On your wall screen appears the interviewer, who thanks you for the resumé and opens the interview with some small talk. The interview is for a job creating multi-media products. Eventually, when the interviewer get down to talking about the job, she wants to see some of the work you've done. You open a secondary screen and start to display some of your best work—an interactive training film, perhaps, or part of an electronic book that sold reasonably well. As your work is playing you are describing the best parts to the interviewer in a running commentary, while the two of you exchange subtle looks over the video link. There's a part in the book that you have to warn her about, when the volume goes way up and there's a nearly subsonic "explosion"—sometimes it rattles things.

Eventually the interview is over and the interviewer asks if you have any questions. You ask if it's possible to find out more about the company, what the place looks like, who works there, and what sort of compensation and benefits package might be offered. The interviewer punches a few keys and a menu comes up on your screen offering you a selection of choices for finding out more about the company. The interviewer says thanks and good-bye, we'll contact you. She fades out and the menu stays on the screen.

You choose a short video on the company's history. When that's over you look at an interactive, hyper-video tour of the company's facilities. A little too slick, you think. Things are never as clean or as cheerful as they look in such packaged presentations. But the interviewer has offered you the chance to speak to some of the employees, people you might be working with. That's a good sign. You send a couple of them e-mail messages and their computers help find a time that you can speak to each other, over the video link of course. The appointments are automatically entered into your on-line datebook. Finally, the company sends you a package of material on compensation and benefits, which you print out on your color printer so that you can look at it later, maybe over some coffee. As you are picking up the high-resolution paper copies, you notice another company has responded to your resumé.

To some people this may sound like the way to find a job. Assuming that all of the communication described above is acceptably cheap, it would certainly streamline the process that most people go through now. The person in the scenario conducted a straightforward job search in the time it now takes to look at the "help wanted" ads. The process would appear to have some environmental benefit too, since it bypasses paper copies of resumés, cover letters, envelopes, and responses from the company, as well as travel to visit the facility for an interview (not to mention travel by post office personnel to deliver all the paper correspondence).

But it's precisely the fact that everyone gets to stay where they are, and "see" each other only through devices, that strikes other people as plainly Orwellian. In the case described above—a typical "advertisement" for new communications and computing technologies—what the interviewee learns about the company is completely managed by the company. The applicant misses the subtle, even indescribable cues that gives one an impression about a place or people when viewing them "in the flesh," a phrase that will definitely take on more meaning in the future. While the process in the above scenario is convenient, as well as technologically fascinating, it doesn't give the applicant a very robust impression of the workplace. What if the worker insists on seeing the workplace in a way that isn't perfectly packaged as a company video? Will that impose a disadvantage with respect to other applicants who might not be so curious or so wary?

And what happens to workers who can't afford, or who won't buy, a "home information appliance?"

The "national information infrastructure," which promises to make the job search described above technically feasible, has become a key component of President Clinton's technology policy, as well as a bandwagon for very powerful economic interests, including telephone and telecommunications companies, cable television operators, computer manufacturers, software developers, acolytes of an emerging "computer culture," and a wide variety of other people. Teachers and school administrators want the advantages of "remote learning" and access to sources of information. Librarians are both excited and concerned about how a national information infrastructure might change the character of a library. Entrepreneurs are enticed by the prospect of new businesses that can't even be imagined now. Business leaders are predicting that the "information economy" will lead the United States into a new era of prosperity: Apple Computer CEO John Sculley has projected a $5 trillion market for information services and appliances, a figure which is over 80% of the current U.S. Gross Domestic Product and nearly a third of the entire capital value of the nation. Vice President Al Gore, one of the leaders of the surge in interest in a national information infrastructure, has said, "Because of computer technology and related developments, the global civilization prematurely heralded many times in this century is now a palpable reality. And this global civilization provides the framework within which every problem, every challenge, and every opportunity must be defined."

In other words, for the soldiers of the digital revolution, virtually nothing will escape the transformation of society and the economy brought about by a new national information infrastructure.

The very word "infrastructure," which has been mocked by the press and by conservatives as a kind of "new age" term of Clinton era jargon, implies a sort of bedrock imperative, something essential to the function of society and the economy. Vice President Gore has popularized the phrase "digital highways," a metaphoric reference to the national highway system that his father helped develop when he was the Senator from Tennessee during the Eisenhower administration. The "highway" metaphor gives the national information infrastructure a concreteness—to employ a pun—that otherwise escapes many technologically unsophisticated listeners when they hear about a multi-billion dollar public investment in computer networks. No one can imagine American life without the superhighways that the nation was known for in the 1960s, and which today are viewed as a basic element—"infrastructure"— of the economy. The phrase "infrastructure" and the metaphor of a new national highway system are attached to new telecommunications technologies to impart a sense of inevitability, of national compulsion, to something that most citizens don't understand or are only dimly aware of. It also lends the luster of the public interest to a huge public investment that will handsomely reward very specific industries and which may tend to reinforce disparities in economic status. As Jerry Salvaggio has observed, "the information industry is investing billions of dollars into manufacturing an image as a guarantee that the information age is not a futuristic illusion."[1]

There is an obvious inevitability to the development of "information infrastructure," since there already exists a global telecommunications and data network that is growing and shaping world society and economic enterprise. Global data transmission has accelerated the spread of trans-national corporations, which are the most significant actors in the world economy today. Much of the crisis in "national economic competitiveness," the current mantra of policymakers, is actually the result of a globalization of production made possible by telecommunications. The reason that workers in Detroit or Massachusetts or California are competing not only against workers in North Carolina or Texas but in Taiwan and Mexico and perhaps Eastern Europe, can be traced to investments in computer networks that allow management and production to be geographically distant. Networks are layered on top of one another, from the local area network of a facility to the wide area network of a corporation to national or global networks facilitated by satellites in space. Vice President Gore has said that "Digitized information is now the lingua franca of the entire world. Those companies, those universities, and those nations best able to deal with information in that form turn out to be most successful." Computer networks have become the equivalent of trade routes or competitive advantage in sea power. With literally trillions of dollars riding on these networks (international currency networks are estimated to move around about a trillion dollars of value per day), it is to be expected that they will continue to grow in capacity, sophistication, and influence.

Although telecommunications networks have already altered the world picture dramatically, new technologies, government and corporate strategies, and international economic competition are all combining to catalyze a new public debate about the future of the "information age." The new technologies, such as high speed computers and high bandwidth fiber optic cabling, offer a significant expansion of a network's capacity for transmitting data. Systems built with such technologies can transmit moving video images, huge quantities of digitized data, voice, and high quality stereo sound all at once, and the fiber optic lines can carry thousands, even millions, of transmissions simultaneously. A fiber optic network mediated by high speed computers can transmit the equivalent of the thirty-odd volume Encyclopedia Brittanica every second, complete with pictures. Widespread deployment of such networks opens up an endless list of possibilities for transmitting information. There is even a cottage industry that comes up with new ways for such a network to be used if it is ever deployed, speculation similar to Apple Computer's much publicized "Knowledge Navigator" video.

The rough path to acceptance of national industrial policy as a strategy of economic development within industrialized nations has led to new government-industry partnerships in pursuit of competitive advantage in allegedly "critical technologies."[2] Japan and Germany have become the model for other nations, largely because of their success in forging productive partnerships between public sources of funding and private firms. The European Community's challenge to American dominance in commercial aircraft is also a frequently cited example of targeted technology investment. The U.S. lead in telecommunications technologies, computers, and software, has given U.S. policymakers, especially in the new Clinton administration, confidence that the United States can and should invest public money in these technologies in order to preserve the nation's comparative advantage and keep these industries internationally preeminent. Thus public investment in a national information infrastructure is viewed as a "demand pull" strategy for technological acceleration—if the government is a customer for state-of-the-art technologies, it supplies a guaranteed market for high tech firms. Guaranteed markets attract investors, and the resulting innovations will eventually find private markets, which will in turn build industries and create jobs, argue proponents of this strategy.

Economic competitiveness has climbed to the top of the stack of every policymaker's and legislator's agenda. The solution to a perceived problem of competitiveness in U.S. firms is productivity enhancement driven by technology. Data networks are widely viewed as a means for improving productivity and lowering costs. They can help speed up the distribution of information and data, and the capability for sending large amounts of data through a network rapidly and cheaply obviously avoids a lot of expenses. It has become commonplace to hear the argument of former White House Science Adviser George Keyworth, that the United States is "rapidly approaching the point where lack of [a fiber optic] network will become our competitive disadvantage."[3] Jonathan Aronson of the University of Southern California, however, points out that "It is unclear whether the provision of advanced communications and information technology results in productivity gains."[4] A number of studies have described the "productivity paradox" of huge investments in information technologies and stagnant or even negative rates of growth in productivity over the last fifteen years.[5]

The end of the Cold War and the collapse of the rationale for sustaining the "national security state," in which most of the nation's technological investments funded by public money went to the military, has given birth to a new concern for national economic status and enthusiasm for the futuristic promise of high tech. A powerful alliance of computer, telephone, cable television, software, and other industry executives, combined with scientists, engineers, and computer enthusiasts who are policymakers, activists, and legislators, has produced the rough outline of a "national vision," as Vice President Gore has described it. But there are many questions about this national vision that have yet to be answered. Oscar Gandy of the Annenberg School for Communications writes:

> Decisions to invest in telecommunications infrastructure, perhaps involving the creation of a privileged monopoly by means of special exceptions established for public purpose, may be seen by historians in the future as marking a critical event that led to either an uncharacteristically rapid expansion of individual freedoms and capacitations through the enhancement of access to information, or the beginning of a downward spiral toward the panoptic dystopia of constant surveillance and manufactured public opinion.[6]

The results of a sustained national commitment to "information infrastructure" may not be as black or as white as Gandy suggests, but his point that these two different extremes might each be plausible outcomes is important. The character of any future "information infrastructure" will inevitably reinforce a set of normative values, and probably at the expense of an alternative set of competing values. The present system of broadcast television, for example, not only reinforces a particular set of values, but in many cases introduces values to the nation and educates people perhaps more profoundly than any other source of instruction. The national information infrastructure could easily adopt the values of television, those of relentless acquisitiveness, conservative gender roles, widespread and common violence, stereotypes of racial and ethnic minorities, pious nationalism, etc. Or the national information infrastructure could be a considerably more open space for public debate, protecting and fostering diversity, democratic challenges to authority, and self-determined cultural, racial, ethnic, and gender identities. Current discussions about the national information infrastructure tend to focus on its technical character and strategies for its deployment, both tied to assumptions about the private market. What we have heard so far has tended to be the rumble from a "battle of the titans," the conflict between telephone companies, cable TV operators, newspaper publishers, and computer manufacturers. But the biggest debate of all, one in which the public should have a voice that matches or even surpasses all others, will be about how the structure of the proposed network will shape its content, its character, and its influence on society. This debate is only getting started.

At a meeting of the Board of Directors of Computer Professionals for Social Responsibility in March, held at Stanford University, the Board voted to take up the national information infrastructure as a new national "focus area" for the organization. CPSR's proven and highly regarded combination of technical expertise and sensitivity to the public interest will be an important asset in the public debate that should take center stage in the near future. For the benefit of CPSR members who might like to participate in the organization's work on this issue, this article will describe some of the background of the emerging national discussion about the national information infrastructure, or NII.

THE INTERNET

The NII, whatever its configuration, will build on experience with the Internet, the current computer network developed and supported with public funds and the largest computer network in the world. The Internet is actually a "network of networks." The Internet connects over 11,000 networks, in 102 countries, that conform to the Internet Protocol, a standardized way of linking computers. Data enclosed in an Internet Protocol "envelope" can pass from one Internet computer to another. The Transmission Control Protocol, or TCP, allows data to be broken into chunks to maximize the efficiency of the network. The combination of TCP/IP is now a universal standard for data transmission on the Internet. Other networks that don't use TCP/IP have established "gateways" for getting mail and other data through to the Internet. Many non-Internet networks are now capable of passing and receiving information to and from the Internet. In fact, the major private U.S.-based networks, such as CompuServe, MCI Mail, and America OnLine, all have Internet "gateways."[7]

The Internet has historical roots all the way back to the Arpanet, the first national network developed by the Advanced Research Projects Agency of the Department of Defense. Arpanet was first deployed in the late 1960s, and has been upgraded incrementally ever since. In the 1980s, the National Science Foundation received authorization from Congress to set up a network of supercomputer research centers.

Five such centers were introduced, all located on major university campuses. The network that was created to link these supercomputer sites together became NSFNet, now considered the core of the Internet. NSF contracted with the Michigan higher education network, Merit, to run NSFNet, and Merit subcontracts with a non-profit corporation called Advanced Network Services (ANS) for network services. There were two significant developments related to the ascendance of NSFNet. First, the National Science Foundation awarded funding to networking projects that distributed networking resources on college campuses—previously the network had been available only to a few elite researchers and institutions. This set a precedence of more equitable access to the Internet. Now nearly every four-year college and university in the United States is connected to the network, as well as over 1,000 high schools.

Second, the fact that Advanced Network Services was funded, as a nonprofit organization, by IBM and MCI opened the door to commercialization of some Internet components. In 1991 ANS created a for-profit subsidiary called CO+RE, Inc., to carry commercial traffic, previously prohibited on the Internet. Since many corporations had employees using both corporate networks and the Internet, and since managing two or more networks is expensive, private firms have become more attracted to the Internet as a commercial vehicle. Although regulations about the public nature of the Internet have limited commercial use, these rules are changing and more and more corporations are using the Internet as their primary telecommunications carrier.

These developments have contributed to the explosive growth of the Internet user community. Traffic on the Internet has been estimated to be expanding at the rate of 15% to 20% per month. Since 1985 the number of Internet hosts has grown from several dozen sites to over 2,000, and from about 2,000 hosts to over 400,000.[8] The user base is now roughly estimated at about ten to twelve million people in the United States, and perhaps as many as fifteen to twenty million worldwide. Users of commercial and private networks with gateways to the Internet probably add another three to five million people to the Internet-accessible population.

Innovative services offered on the Internet have also flourished. Not only does the Internet provide electronic mail (about 15% of traffic) and file transmission (about a third of all traffic), but now contains searchable databases, on-line access to government information, thousands of network discussion groups, downloadable software, hypertext, multi-user games and "virtual" domains, and even communication with the White House and some other offices of the federal government. The Internet will even start to deliver "radio" as a kind of electronic "magazine"—data sent over the Internet will be run through a local decompression and audio program for audio play of news, music, and talk. Internet "talk-radio" is not far away.

The history of the Internet and its antecedents is one of developing capacity, with that capacity then taxed by overuse, followed by the deployment of more capacity. This has been a constant process of incremental technical improvement being overtaken by growth in the number of users and what they want the network to do.

At this point, we are at a technical threshold for moving beyond the incremental improvement of the Internet to a new network paradigm. UCLA computer scientist Leonard Kleinrock believes that "It is clear that the data networks we inherited from the 1980s are inadequate to handle the applications and capabilities required by the 1990s." Kleinrock lists some of the problems with "packet switched" data networks: they are too slow, too costly, they have switching delays, high error rates, and they require too much processing, among other obstacles.[9] What is now at hand is a leap to broadband networks that will offer a new path of expanding capabilities. This move will be driven by the need to communicate forms of information too large for current networks, primarily image data, such as the terabytes of data that are passed from the Earth Imaging Satellite or Landsat, or the imagery that is increasingly a part of medical care. Consumer demand for High Definition Television (HDTV), as a replacement to the current television system which has remained essentially unchanged since the early 1960s, will also require high bandwidth networks. Broadband networks offer "order of magnitude" improvements in capacity and speed, as shown in Table 1.

A good portion of the hardware for a new broadband network in the United States is already available. Over a million miles of fiber optic cable is already underground in the United States, used mostly to carry long-distance telephone traffic. A lot of it is currently unused, so-called "dark fiber" waiting for a market. It is now cheaper to install fiber than to install copper wire in many facilities. Cable television networks are also a possibility for broadband services, since over half of the residences in the United States receive cable TV, and cable is in near 85% of U.S. homes.

The ultimate goal, however, is "fiber to the home." Various estimates have speculated on a cost of rewiring the entire U.S. telephone system with fiber of between $200 and $400 billion, within a time frame of twenty to thirty years.[10] Amortized over such a long period of time, the dollar figures are not as staggering as they might seem at first—the higher figure and the lowest time estimate is an investment of about $20 billion per year, or less than 10% of current annual defense budgets.

The problem is, of course, that the United States government is in a severe cash crunch. Private funders want to be assured of a return that will cover such a significant investment. And it's not clear either who the private investors might be, what kind of incentives they should be given to put up as much as $400 billion for a new national information infrastructure, or whether they should receive government help. It's not even completely clear whether there will be a market for services that will pay for the investment. But everyone is charging ahead with vigor anyway.

TABLE 1

	TODAY'S NETWORKS	BROADBAND NETWORKS
Packets per second	Thousands	Millions
Bandwidth	64 Kbps	155 Mbps to 2.5 Gbps
Bandwidth allocation	Fixed	Dynamic
Services	Voice, data	Voice, data, image
Switch delay	50–100 ms	2 ms
Error control	Link-to-link	End-to-end

Source: Leonard Kleinrock, "Technology Issues in the Design of the NREN," in Brian Kahin, ed., *Building Information Infrastructure* (Cambridge, MA: Harvard Business School Press, 1992) p. 185.

THE NREN

In late 1991, the United States Congress passed, and President Bush signed into law, the High Performance Computing and Communications Act. Chiefly sponsored by then Senator Al Gore, the HPCC program is designed to "ensure continued United States leadership in high-performance computing." For fiscal year 1992, the HPCC program was funded at $655 million, and for fiscal year 1993 it received $803 million, a 22% increase. The principal elements of HPCC include research and development on high-performance computing systems to improve the speed of computing by two or three orders of magnitude; research on advanced software technology in pursuit of several technical "grand challenges" in science and engineering; computer networking; human resources development; and basic research in computer science and technology relevant to high-performance computing.

The HPCC included funding for a new networking initiative called the National Research Education Network, or NREN. The NREN, like the rest of the HPCC, is an interagency program coordinated by the little-known Federal Coordinating Council on Science, Engineering, and Technology, or FCCSET (pronounced "Fixit"). The NREN is primarily run by the National Science Foundation and the Advanced Research Projects Agency (formerly DARPA—the word "defense" was dropped this year). The entire HPCC, however, is overseen by Dr. Donald A. Lindbergh, M.D., the director of the National Library of Medicine.

NREN is a program designed to increase the networking capabilities of leading scientific and technological research centers. The law says that the participating federal agencies will make available a network capable of transmitting information at speeds of one gigabit per second or greater by 1996. While the legislation describes a broad reach for the network—including "research institutions and educational institutions, government, and industry in every state"—as a practical matter the NREN is aimed at the community served by NSFNet. The NREN will not change the basic structure of the Internet, and it does not involve the deployment of any new fiber optic network.[11] What the NREN will do, by developing new tools for broadband communication, is to absorb some of the "high-end" use of the Internet—uses that involve the transmission of huge amounts of data and which tend to degrade performance for "low-end" Internet users. So the NREN is not a "new" network, although it introduces a new name to the Internet family of networks. It is a program that will add new capacities and new tools to the Internet. The NSF backbone is expected to upgrade to a gigabit per second capacity or greater, and most mid-level networks that make up the U.S. portion of the Internet should upgrade to 45 Mbps within the near future.[12] The NREN program will also fund software development to take advantage of these higher speeds. The HPCC as a whole will drive this development with research on several "grand challenges" in science and engineering.

However, the NREN has become more than just a program to speed up the Internet. It is increasingly a symbol of a new U.S. resolve to lead the world in the deployment of high speed, high bandwidth telecommunications services. A good deal of this inspiration is due to Vice President Al Gore's enthusiasm for the subject. When Gore started to get involved in computer networking issues an incremental upgrade to NSFNet was already in the works; the network had upgraded in 1990–91 and immediately started to make plans for the next step in order to keep pace with demand. The Bush administration, while not opposing the bill than contained funding for the NREN, insisted that special legislation wasn't necessary, since the administration had already budgeted and planned for the enhancement of NSFNet.

But Senator Gore mobilized his legislative colleagues to support the HPCC bill, and Gore himself began to give public speeches about the vision attached to the nation's information infrastructure. In large part due to the impetus provided by Gore, "the case and constituency for NREN," says Harvard's Brian Kahin, "has grown beyond academic 'research and education' to primary and secondary education, public libraries, and economic development writ large."[13] Now most of the people interested in promoting an integrated information infrastructure view NREN as the testbed for applications and technologies that will eventually be "ported" to broadband networks that serve the entire public. In fact, under pressure from constituencies outside the research community, Gore introduced a second bill, in 1992, called the Information Infrastructure and Technology Act, which will provide funding for the extension of networking resources to schools, libraries, state and local governments, and nonprofit institutions. (In some circles, the HPCC is known as "Gore I," and the Infrastructure Act as "Gore II.") The Congress has since proposed another new role for the network, as a support for planned "manufacturing technology extension centers," which are part of a package of legislation called the National Competitiveness Act of 1993, sponsored by Rep. George Brown in the House and Senator Hollings in the Senate.

For the reasons described earlier, national computer-based communication on high-speed networks has captured the public imagination, at least among business, policy and technical elites. By default, the NREN has become the vehicle for such enthusiasms, even though it was first proposed merely as a way to improve the "high-end" use of the Internet. The Clinton administration's manifesto on technology policy, introduced on February 22nd, states very clearly the objective of investing in a "national information infrastructure and establishment of a task force working with the private sector to design a national communications policy that will ensure rapid introduction of new communication technology."[14] The Clinton–Gore campaign announced the goal of a high speed, high bandwidth communications system to "every home, school, and business in the United States by the year 2015," although this hasn't been repeated since the election. Dr. Lindberg, director of the HPCC program, testified on March 25, 1993, that

> the HPCC program is developing computing, communications, and software technology the U.S. will need to meet its information and telecommunications needs. It will lay the foundation for an advanced national information infrastructure (NII) consisting of high-

speed communication links, high performance computers, and powerful, but user-friend-ly software that will give every American access to an unprecedented amount of infor-mation, as well as the tools needed to effectively process and use it. This infrastructure will spur gains in U.S. productivity and industrial competitiveness, improve our nation-al security, and improve the health and education of our citizens.[15]

Thus, since the Clinton administration took office, the High Performance Com-puting and Communications Program and its component, the National Research and Education Network, have been transformed from programs designed to improve the capabilities of U.S. computer science and computer networks to a general economic development strategy that will "spur gains in U.S. productivity and industrial com-petitiveness, improve our national security, and improve the health and education of our citizens." The Clinton administration has also introduced the concept of the NII as a natural follow-on to NREN and its associated results. But what this NII will actu-ally look like is not yet clear.

THE NATIONAL INFORMATION INFRASTRUCTURE

While the Internet and the NREN will continue to develop as models for advanced computer networking, they will also continue to fall short of a true national informa-tion infrastructure unless several key problems are solved. Marvin Sirbu of Carnegie Mellon University has summarized these problems well:

"Development of standardized methods for information finding: White Pages directories, Yellow Pages, information indexes.

"Development of widely standardized methods for retrieving information which may be scattered across hundreds of different hosts.

"Mechanisms for security and authentication.

"Development of billing and accounting systems which can track the transfer of intel-lectual property and provide a mechanism for compensating authors and maintainers.

"Development of standard document representation formats, which go beyond ASCII and allow sharing of graphics, images, voice annotation, animated sequences, and video."[16]

These are technical requirements for a robust information infrastructure, some of which must be supplemented by policy decisions and conventions of use. Sirbu might have added the requirement of a scalable interface for users, so that novice users will find the information network "intuitive" and easy to use, but expert users will be able to select a method of using the network that matches their skill.

The two problems that confront policymakers now are: who will decide how to solve these problems, and who will pay for the solutions?

System uniformity, architectural stability, economies of scale, universal access, and social equity would all seem to suggest that the best vehicle for implementing a national network is the federal government itself. This is the position of Vice President Gore, who argues that the government is the only guarantor of a system that will serve all Americans. This is the model of the NREN, in which academic and industry researchers are using government funds to expand the capacity of the Internet. Gore believes that the federal government should build a new national network and then turn it over to private contractors for systems management, the way that the Internet was developed and is now managed. John Markoff of The New York Times adds, "the whole project would be a key test for the industrial policy that Mr. Clinton and Mr. Gore view as a way to revive the economy."[17]

But opposing the Vice President and his allies are the large telecommunications corporations and opponents of President Clinton's industrial policy. Executives of AT&T, MCI, Sprint, and other long distance carriers maintain that their networks are well-poised to be transformed into a national information infrastructure, and that the government should stay out of the business of building a competing network. The commercial vendors of telecommunication services believe that they can offer an "upgrade path" of services that will be the most cost-effective. Competition will keep prices down, as demonstrated in the rate wars between long distance carriers. These players also argue that the government simply can't afford the massive investment required to develop a new network, especially in light of competing public demands such as universal and affordable health care.

Public interest organizations, libraries, educators, and other nonprofit service providers have tended to side with the government, fearing that a purely commercial network will undermine the nation's tradition of universal service and price out large constituencies who won't be able to afford new services. Jeff Chester of the Center for Media Education in Maryland warns that a national network developed and run by corporations will turn television into a "pay per view" system, compromising what little public character the current "over-the-air" free broadcast system has now. Librarians are concerned that the open and free model of libraries will be threatened by the commercialization of information resources. Overall, many people are worried that a purely commercial network simply will cater to the lowest common denominator of the market, meaning dozens of "home shopping" services, on-line computer games, "infomercials," and packaged, sensationalized news.

Unfortunately, as Jonathan Aronson notes, "the public is not well organized . . . [and] the 'public good,' broadly defined, usually is not reflected in the pressures on firms and policymakers regarding communications infrastructure."[18] While pronouncements about universal service and measures to attenuate the polarization of information "haves" and "have-nots" are routinely heard from business and government leaders, there is so far little evidence that such concerns are being incorporated into the policy debate. A first step will be the inclusion of public interest advocates on the government's recently announced National Information Infrastructure Council, an advisory body set up to chart the course of the NII.

The challenge that faces policymakers and network developers is how to incorporate public goods into an innovative system that will be driven primarily by market demand. In order for the information network to deserve the name "infrastructure," it must have a public character reflected in extra-market values such as equitable access, privacy, the inclusion of public space, freedom of expression, and some measure of democratic control. In some instances these values will conflict with the rationale of "economic competitiveness," which right now is the principal and nearly exclusive justification for the NII. The task of the public interest community is to make sure its values are part of the design, management, and use of the network.

PUBLIC INTEREST GOALS

How the public interest might best be defined is clearly not a simple task. The debate surrounding the future of the infrastructure combines aspects of traditional media and broadcasting policy with new questions about common carriage, connectivity, access and privacy. The important roles of the NSF and the university and research communities have added another layer of complexity to the policy analysis. Hybrids of technology have created hybrids of policy. Still the need to articulate public goals for the nation's infrastructure seems clear.

EDUCOM, an association of American colleges and universities, has recommended a number of principles for the development of the NII, including support for scientific and other forms of collaborative work, the opening of archives of federal technical, scientific and economic data, and the creation of a nationwide citizen network that provides access to educational programs, public information, and commercial information resources. These goals reflect the desire to accommodate private ventures while preserving the public character of the information infrastructure.[19]

Other initiatives focus on specific policy goals. The Benton Foundation in Washington, D.C., has launched a campaign to strengthen public interest advocacy on network issues, focusing specifically on the future of universal service. Karen Menichelli, associate director of the Benton Foundation, says that "universal service is one of the important measures of infrastructure success. Who will have access and on what terms are critical questions to examine." Universal service might include free or affordable access to basic services, such as news, public affairs, health, education, and electoral information. Locator and directory services might help users navigate network resources.

Miles Fidelman, director of the Center for Civic Networking, speaks of the need to encourage local networks that serve the interests of state agencies and community institutions. Such networks could invigorate civic participation and community life. Taylor Walsh, with the National Capital Area Public Access Network (CapAccess), expresses a similar sentiment when he says that "it seems appropriate, if not crucial, at this stage in the evolution of national networking policy to create parallel programs that help the infrastructure take shape at the local level." Many states are now exploring various ways to link civic groups and public sector organizations.

For example, information "kiosks" could allow citizens to locate state agencies, to schedule appointments, and to gather data on government programs. Such kiosks could be located in grocery stores, shopping centers, or even recreation centers. Iowa State Senator Richard Varn, who also chairs the State Information Policy Consortium, says that "The information age offers the opportunity for all levels of government to work together and to provide access to a broad range of government services through single access points."[20]

CPSR has also helped promote new local network initiatives. In 1992 CPSR organized a conference to explore Local Civic Networks. That meeting helped catalyze a number of local efforts to promote the development of community networks, including the Seattle Community Network now being pursued by members of CPSR/Seattle.

While these initiatives go forward, organizations and individuals are also setting out policy goals for the nation's infrastructure. The hope is that these principles will be incorporated into the design of network services and will be supported by legislative and regulatory decisions. Typically the public interest perspective on the national information infrastructure—what might be called in this world of acronyms the "NII PIP"—focuses on one or more underlying policy principles.

UNIVERSALITY

"Universal access" has a deep resonance in the history of U.S. communications policy. The country's commitment to public access to the phone network is a monumental achievement, considered by some to be the communications equivalent of Gutenberg's invention of the printing press. Broad public access to the telephone network literally wired together the nation and provided the opportunity for the rapid growth of new services and activities. Still, defining universal access in an era of "value-enhanced" services will not be an easy task. Not all users require "premium" channels, and market incentives are clearly necessary to encourage the growth of new commercial services. But neither can universal service simply mean an access point to the lowest service level, an "informational safety net" that may offer little more than yesterdays news, or last weeks employment listings.

Some weight must surely be given to infrastructure features that facilitate the delivery of other services. For example, if public support for the delivery of dialtone service to all subscribers in a region will lead to more efficient service delivery and encourage the development of new services, then both economists and consumers would agree that such subsidies are sound. Similarly if government agencies move toward interactive video services to provide public services, then there will be strong incentives to assure that all members of the target population have the technological capacity to utilize the services.

Universal service also encompasses the view that many groups are likely to be left behind as the information network develops if some action is not taken to ensure widespread public access. Lack of economic resources may certainly be one such factor, but geographical considerations, as well a lack of literacy and training, also act as barriers to access.

ACCESS

Building "on-ramps" to the Internet is also a part of the NII policy challenge Much of the technical debate focuses on the wires to the home—the telephone line, the cable line, fiber and ISDN—but the larger debate may be about who will be connected and on what terms. The NSF's commitment to support network access for universities and colleges during the 1980s certainly encouraged the spread of the network across the nation. Similar efforts are now underway in K–12 schools and public libraries.

Access to network services may be provided in a number of ways. Individuals and companies may purchase access through private network service providers. Public institutions may obtain access through federal and state grants.

Libraries remain an important access point for many network users. As Kitty Scoot of the Special Libraries Association said last year to the National Commission on Library and Information Science, "Librarians have traditionally been in the forefront of using electronic information services to support their customer base."

For many network users, libraries provide technical support, information resources, and oftentimes the first exposure to the full range of network activities.

As John H. Suzler of the Government Documents Roundtable of the American Library Association has said, "The primary NREN policy issue for libraries is developing a network that is based upon service of the 'public good,' the same as is in the development of public lands, the broadcasting spectrum, and the interstate highway system."

CONNECTIVITY

Connectivity encompasses a wide range of technical and policy issues. The Electronic Frontier Foundation has recommended the development of an "Open Platform" that might encourage the development of new commercial services, particularly through ISDN technology. Other policy initiatives focus on efforts to improve access to public information in government agencies.

For example, the Government Printing Office, which carries the responsibility for disseminating government publications across the nation could deliver services more effectively if connected to the Internet. Similarly, many federal agencies that have already computerized records and public documents might look to the network to make public information more widely available.

Says Jamie Love of Taxpayers Assets Project, "Putting the federal government on-line could save taxpayers billions of dollars."

Connectivity also has an important international dimension. As more countries adopt the TCP/IP protocols, it becomes possible to move information around the world and between locations as disparate as Bangkok and Budapest. The Internet Society, chaired by Vint Cerf, has encouraged the growth of international network communications. A recent INET report by Larry Landweber on international connectivity notes that "E-mail connections to Algeria, Angola, Gambia, Morocco, St. Lucia, and Vietnam have been reported."

Concerns about connectivity are only partly matters of technological configuration. Support for institutions, technical assistance, and government policy all factor into the growth of computer networks.

PRIVACY

One attribute that sets NII apart from other forms of infrastructure, such as road and bridges, is that this infrastructure is fundamentally about the transport of information, and as public safety is important on roadways, privacy is critical to the success of information networks.

Commercialization of the network is likely to increase pressure to collect and sell personal data. Much of the information moving through the digital network is transactional data, billing information. This information is particularly useful for marketing firms because it is easily compiled. It also falls through the cracks of most privacy restrictions.

There is an important if complex law in the United States that provides some privacy protection for network communications. That is the Electronic Communications Privacy Act, which built on the earlier federal wiretap law and provided protection for "in stream" computer communications and stored electronic mail.

However, it remains to be seen whether ECPA, passed in 1986, can handle the full range of emerging privacy concerns, including protection for wireless networks, controls on Caller ID, and electronic mail within the workplace. One new privacy issue that has attracted much concern in the network community is the use of cryptography and various government proposals to restrict or control new technologies that might promote privacy protection. One proposal from the FBI would require communication service providers to ensure that their networks were capable of wire surveillance. Another proposal from the NSA would require a key escrow arrangement for encrypted communications within the United States government.

Several organizations, recognizing the need to address these new privacy concerns, have included privacy protection as one of the policy tenants for network development. The Computer Systems Policy Project, a computer industry organization, includes privacy and confidentiality among its goals for the National Information Infrastructure. A Recent CSPP statement says that "consumers of NII services have a right to privacy in their use of the NII" and also that "NII users must be free to use effective, industry-developed encryption to ensure confidentiality of communications and data."

Similarly, CPSR recommended a number of privacy guidelines for the NREN at a 1992 hearing before the National Commission on Library and Information Sciences. These guidelines roughly follow from similar principles that have been developed by the European Community and Canada.

CPSR has also organized several conferences on cryptography policy and pursued litigation under the Freedom of Information Act to obtain government records about specific policy recommendations.

WHO DECIDES

At the federal level, a number of different Congressional Committees and agencies are likely to play a significant role in the development of network policy. Congress channels its work through committees and subcommittees that have specific responsibility for certain subject areas. At times, committees jurisdictions overlap. For example, Congressman Rick Boucher (D-VA), who heads the House Science, Space and Technology Subcommittee on Science, plays a critical role in all policy debate surrounding computer networking. At the same time, Congressman Ed Markey (D-MA), who heads the House Energy and Commerce Subcommittee on Telecommunications and Finance, is interested in infrastructure issues by virtue of his committee's responsibility for communications policy.

Moving to the executive branch of government, Vice President Gore will continue to play an important role in infrastructure debate. He will probably work closely with the new White House Science Advisor, Dr. Jack Gibbons, who previously served as head of the Congressional Office of Technology Assessment. Dr. Gibbons also heads the White House Office of Science and Technology Policy and he chairs the Federal Coordinating Council on Science, Engineering, and Technology.

The Federal Communications Commission may become more active in the infrastructure debate, though to date, most of the FCC activity has been directed to balancing the competing interests of the private communications firms in the broadcast, cable, and telecommunications industries. How far the telephone companies are permitted to go into the information delivery business remains one of the big telecommunications policy issues in Washington.

One area where the FCC could certainly lend some support to the NII debate would be the development of privacy policies. Agencies similar to the FCC in other countries, such as the Ministry of Post and Telecommunications in Japan, have played leading roles within their own governments in the formulation of privacy goals.

TIMING

The legislative clock in Washington, DC is a two-year cycle that marks the beginning and end of each Congress. For a proposal to become law, it must be introduced, discussed and debated, and acted upon within the two-year time frame. However, it is often the case that proposals are considered in one Congress and then enacted in a subsequent Congress.

So the failure to pass an initiative at first does not mean that it is doomed.

Federal agencies and the White House operate with somewhat more flexibility. Once implementing legislation is in place, commissions can be established, pilot projects funded, and rules developed. All of these decisions will generally be open to public comment, though through an agency process rather than a hearing on Capitol Hill. States operate with still more flexibility and may develop programs, initiate services, and support network activities as the opportunities arise.

Policy proposals tends to generate their own inertia, each recommendation accompanied by a call for "immediate action" before "the window of opportunity closes." In practice, the policy process is filled with twists and turns, and many opportunities to introduce new ideas and new directions. While some have characterized the current NII debate as the end of a process, more likely it is just the beginning.

NOTES

1. Jerry L. Salvaggio, "Projecting a Positive Image of the Information Society," in J. Slack and F. Fejes, eds., The Ideology of the Information Age (Norwood, NJ: Ablex Publishers, 1987) p. 154.

2. See Gary Chapman, "Defense Conversion and Technology Policy," The CPSR Newsletter (Palo Alto, CA: Computer Professionals for Social Responsibility, Fall 1992).

3. George A. Keyworth II and Bruce Abell, "Competitiveness and Telecommunications: America's Economic Future: House-to-House Digital Fiber Optic Network" (Indianapolis: The Hudson Institute, 1990) p. 8.

4. Jonathan Aronson, "Telecommunications Infrastructure and U.S. International Competitiveness," in Institute for Information Studies, A National Information Network: Changing Our Lives in the 21st Century (Nashville, Tennessee and Queenstown, Maryland: The Institute for Information Studies, 1992) pp. 58–59.

5. Erik Brynjolfson, "Information Technology and the 'Productivity Paradox': What We Know and What We Don't Know" (Cambridge, MA: MIT Sloan School of Management, November 1991).

6. Oscar H. Gandy, Jr., "Introduction," in Institute for Information Studies, A National Information Network: Changing Our Lives in the 21st Century, op. cit., p. xx.

7. For a detailed and readable description of the Internet, see Ed Krol, The Whole Internet Catalog and User's Guide (Sebastopol, CA: O'Reilly and Associates, 1992).

8. Larry Smarr and Charles E. Catlett, "Life After Internet: Making Room for New Applications," in Brian Kahin, ed., Building Information Infrastructure (Cambridge, MA: Harvard Business School Press, 1992) p. 145.

9. Leonard Kleinrock, "Technology Issues in the Design of the NREN," in Kahin, op. cit., 185.

10. Jonathan Aronson, op. cit., p. 80.

11. Brian Kahin, "Overview: Understanding the NREN," in Kahin, op. cit., p. 5.

12. Smarr and Catlett, op. cit., pp. 149–150.

13. Kahin, op. cit., p. 6.

14. U.S. Government, "Technology for America's Economic Growth: A New Direction to Build Economic Strength" (Washington, D.C.: White House Office of Communications, Executive Office of the President, February 22, 1993).

15. Dr. David A. B. Lindberg, M.D., testimony before the House Committee on Science, Space, and Technology, Subcommittee on Technology and Aviation, March 25, 1993.

16. Marvin Sirbu, "Telecommunications Technology and Infrastructure," in Institute for Information Studies, A National Information Network: Changing Our Lives in the 21st Century, op. cit., pp. 174–175.

17. John Markoff, "Building the Electronic Superhighway," The New York Times, January 24, 1993, p. 3–1.

18. Jonathan Aronson, op. cit., p. 77.

19. Computing Research Association, EDUCOM, and IEEE, Proceedings of the NREN Workshop (September 1992).

20. State Information Policy Consortium, National Information and Service Delivery System: A Vision for Restructuring Government in the Information Age (1992).

▷ CIVIL LIBERTIES IN CYBERSPACE

When does hacking turn from an exercise of civil liberties into crime?

Mitchell Kapor

On March 1, 1990, the U.S. Secret Service raided the offices of Steve Jackson, an entrepreneurial publisher in Austin, Tex. Carrying a search warrant, the authorities confiscated computer hardware and software, the drafts of his about-to-be-released book and many business records of his company, Steve Jackson Games. They also seized the electronic bulletin-board system used by the publisher to communicate with customers and writers, thereby seizing all the private electronic mail on the system.

The Secret Service held some of the equipment and material for months, refusing to discuss their reasons for the raid. The publisher was forced to reconstruct his book from old manuscripts, to delay filling orders for it and to lay off half his staff. When the warrant application was finally unsealed months later, it confirmed that the publisher was never suspected of any crime.

Steve Jackson's legal difficulties are symptomatic of a widespread problem. During the past several years, dozens of individuals have been the subject of similar searches and seizures. In any other context, this warrant might never have been issued. By many interpretations, it disregarded the First and Fourth Amendments to the U.S. Constitution, as well as several existing privacy laws. But the government proceeded as if civil liberties did not apply. In this case, the government was investigating a new kind of crime—computer crime.

The circumstances vary, but a disproportionate number of cases share a common thread: the serious misunderstanding of computer-based communication and its implications for civil liberties. We now face the task of adapting our legal institutions and societal expectations to the cultural phenomena that even now are springing up from communications technology.

Our society has made a commitment to openness and to free communication. But if our legal and social institutions fail to adapt to new technology, basic access to the global electronic media could be seen as a privilege, granted to those who play by the strictest rules, rather than as a right held by anyone who needs to communicate. To assure that these freedoms are not compromised, a group of computer experts, including myself, founded the Electronic Frontier Foundation (EFF) in 1990.

In many respects, it was odd that Steve Jackson Games got caught up in a computer crime investigation at all. The company publishes a popular, award-winning series of fantasy role-playing games, produced in the form of elaborate rule books. The raid took place only because law enforcement officials misunderstood the technologies—computer bulletin-board systems (BBSs) and on-line forums—and misread the cultural phenomena that those technologies engender.

Like a growing number of businesses, Steve Jackson Games operated an electronic bulletin board to facilitate contact between players of its games and their authors. Users of this bulletin-board system dialed in via modem from their personal computers to swap strategy tips, learn about game upgrades, exchange electronic mail and discuss games and other topics.

Law enforcement officers apparently became suspicious when a Steve Jackson Games employee—on his own time and on a BBS he ran from his house—made an innocuous comment about a public domain protocol for transferring computer files called Kermit. In addition, officials claimed that at one time the employee had had on an electronic bulletin board a copy of *Phrack*, a widely disseminated electronic publication, that included information they believed to have been stolen from a Bell-South computer.

The law enforcement officials interpreted these facts as unusual enough to justify not only a search and seizure at the employee's residence but also the search of Steve Jackson Games and the seizure of enough equipment to disrupt the business seriously. Among the items confiscated were all the hard copies and electronically stored copies of the manuscript of a rule book for a role-playing game called GURPS Cyberpunk, in which inhabitants of so-called cyberspace invade corporate and government computer systems and steal sensitive data. Law enforcement agents regarded the book, in the words of one, as "a handbook for computer crime."

A basic knowledge of the kinds of computer intrusion that are technically possible would have enabled the agents to see that GURPS Cyberpunk was nothing more than a science fiction creation and that Kermit was simply a legal, frequently used computer program. Unfortunately, the agents assigned to investigate computer crime did not know what—if anything—was evidence of criminal activity. Therefore, they intruded on a small business without a reasonable basis for believing that a crime had been committed and conducted a search and seizure without looking for "particular" evidence, in violation of the Fourth Amendment of the Constitution.

Searches and seizures of such computer systems affect the rights of not only their owners and operators but also the users of those systems. Although most BBS users have never been in the same room with the actual computer that carries their postings, they legitimately expect their electronic mail to be private and their lawful associations to be protected.

The community of bulletin-board users and computer networkers may be small, but precedents must be understood in a greater context. As forums for debate and information exchange, computer-based bulletin boards and conferencing systems support some of the most vigorous exercise of the First Amendment freedoms of expression and association that this country has ever seen. Moreover, they are evolving rapidly into large-scale public information and communications utilities.

These utilities will probably converge into a digital national public network that will connect nearly all homes and businesses in the U.S. This network will serve as a main conduit for commerce, learning, education and entertainment in our society, distributing images and video signals as well as text and voice. Much of the content of this network will be private messages serving as "virtual" town halls, village greens and coffeehouses, where people post their ideas in public or semipublic forums.

Yet there is a common perception that a defense of electronic civil liberties is somehow opposed to legitimate concerns about the prevention of computer crime. The conflict arises, in part, because the popular hysteria about the technically sophisticated youths known as hackers has drowned out reasonable discussion.

Perhaps inspired by the popular movie *WarGames*, the general public began in the 1980s to perceive computer hackers as threats to the safety of this country's vital computer systems. But the image of hackers as malevolent is purchased at the price of ignoring the underlying reality—the typical teenage hacker is simply tempted by the prospect of exploring forbidden territory. Some are among our best and brightest technological talents: hackers of the 1960s and 1970s, for example, were so driven by their desire to master, understand and produce new hardware and software that they went on to start companies called Apple, Microsoft and Lotus.

How do we resolve this conflict? One solution is ensure that our scheme of civil and criminal laws provides sanctions in proportion to the offenses. A system in which an exploratory hacker receives more time in jail than a defendant convicted of assault violates our sense of justice. Our legal tradition historically has shown itself capable of making subtle and not-so-subtle distinctions among criminal offenses.

There are, of course, real threats to network and system security. The qualities that make the ideal network valuable—its popularity, its uniform commands, its ability to handle financial transactions and its international access—also make it vulnerable to a variety of abuses and accidents. It is certainly proper to hold hackers accountable for their offenses, but that accountability should never entail denying defendants the safeguards of the Bill of Rights, including the rights to free expression and association and to freedom from unreasonable searches and seizures.

We need statutory schemes that address the acts of true computer criminals (such as those who have created the growing problem of toll and credit-card fraud) while distinguishing between those criminals and hackers whose acts are most analogous to noncriminal trespass. And we need educated law enforcement officials who will be able to recognize and focus their efforts on the real threats.

The question then arises: How do we help our institutions, and perceptions, adapt? The first step is to articulate the kinds of values we want to see protected in the electronic society we are now shaping and to make an agenda for preserving the civil liberties that are central to that society. Then we can draw on the appropriate legal traditions that guide other media. The late Ithiel de Sola Pool argued in his influential book *Technologies of Freedom* that the medium of digital communications is heir to several traditions of control: the press, the common carrier and the broadcast media.

The freedom of the press to print and distribute is explicitly guaranteed by the First Amendment. This freedom is somewhat limited, particularly by laws governing obscenity and defamation, but the thrust of First Amendment law, especially in this century, prevents the government from imposing "prior restraint" on publications.

Like the railroad networks, the telephone networks follow common-carrier principles—they do not impose content restrictions on the "cargo" they carry. It would be unthinkable for the telephone company to monitor our calls routinely or cut off conversations because the subject matter was deemed offensive.

Meanwhile the highly regulated broadcast media are grounded in the idea, arguably mistaken, that spectrum scarcity and the pervasiveness of the broadcast media warrant government allocation and control of access to broadcast frequencies (and some control of content). Access to this technology is open to any consumer who can purchase a radio or television set, but it is nowhere near as open for information producers.

Networks as they now operate contain elements of publishers, broadcasters, bookstores and telephones, but no one model fits. This hybrid demands new thinking or at least a new application of the old legal principles. As hybrids, computer networks also have some features that are unique among the communications media. For example, most conversations on bulletin boards, chat lines and conferencing systems are both public and private at once. The electronic communicator speaks to a group of individuals, only some of whom are known personally, in a discussion that may last for days or months.

But the dissemination is controlled, because the membership is limited to the handful of people who are in the virtual room, paying attention. Yet the result may also be "published"—an archival textual or voice record can be automatically preserved, and newcomers can read the backlog. Some people tend to equate on-line discussions with party (or party-line) conversations, whereas others compare them to newspapers and still others think of citizens band radio.

In this ambiguous context, free-speech controversies are likely to erupt. Last year an outcry went up against the popular Prodigy computer service, a joint venture of IBM and Sears, Roebuck and Co. The problem arose because Prodigy management regarded their service as essentially a "newspaper" or "magazine," for which a hierarchy of editorial control is appropriate. Some of Prodigy's customers, in contrast, regarded the service as more of a forum or meeting place.

When users of the system tried to protest Prodigy's policy, its editors responded by removing the discussion. When the protestors tried to use electronic mail as a substitute for electronic assembly, communicating through large mailing lists, Prodigy placed a limit on the number of messages each individual could send.

The Prodigy controversy illustrates an important principle that belongs on any civil liberties agenda for the future: freedom-of-speech issues will not disappear simply because a service provider has tried to impose a metaphor on its service. Subscribers sense, I believe, that freedom of speech on the networks is central for individuals to use electronic communications. Science fiction writer William Gibson once remarked that "the street finds its own uses for things." Network service providers will continue to discover that their customers will always find their own best uses for new media.

Freedom of speech on networks will be promoted by limiting content-based regulations and by promoting competition among providers of network services. The first is necessary because governments will be tempted to restrict the content of any information service they subsidize or regulate. The second is necessary because market competition is the most efficient means of ensuring that needs of network users will be met.

The underlying network should essentially be a "carrier"—it should operate under a content-neutral regime in which access is available to any entity that can pay for it. The information and forum services would be "nodes" on this network. (Prodigy, like GEnie and CompuServe, currently maintains its own proprietary infrastructure, but a future version of Prodigy might share the same network with services like CompuServe.)

Each service would have its own unique character and charge its own rates. If a Prodigy-like entity correctly perceives a need for an electronic "newspaper" with strong editorial control, it will draw an audience. Other, less hierarchical services will share the network with that "newspaper" yet find their own market niches, varying by format and content.

The prerequisite for this kind of competition is a carrier capable of high-bandwidth traffic that is accessible to individuals in every community. Like common carriers, these network carriers should be seen as conduits for the distribution of electronic transmissions. They should not be allowed to change the content of a message or to discriminate among messages.

This kind of restriction will require shielding the carriers from legal liabilities for libel, obscenity and plagiarism. Today the ambiguous state of liability law has tempted some computer network carriers to reduce their risk by imposing content restrictions. This could be avoided by appropriate legislation. Our agenda requires both that the law shield carriers from liability based on content and that carriers not be allowed to discriminate.

All electronic "publishers" should be allowed equal access to networks. Ultimately, there could be hundreds of thousands of these information providers, as there are hundreds of thousands of print publishers today. As "nodes," they will be considered the conveners of the environments within which on-line assembly takes place.

None of the old definitions will suffice for this role. For example, to safeguard the potential of free and open inquiry, it is desirable to preserve each electronic publisher's control over the general flow and direction of material under his or her imprimatur—in effect, to give the "sysop," or system operator, the prerogatives and protections of a publisher.

But it is unreasonable to expect the sysop of a node to review every message or to hold the sysop to a publisher's standard of libel. Message traffic on many individually owned services is already too great for the sysop to review. We can only expect the trend to grow. Nor is it appropriate to compare nodes to broadcasters (an analogy likely to lead to licensing and content-based regulation). Unlike the broadcast media, nodes do not dominate the shared resource of a public community, and they are not a pervasive medium. To take part in a controversial discussion, a user must actively seek entry into the appropriate node, usually with a subscription and a password.

Anyone who objects to the content of a node can find hundreds of other systems where they might articulate their ideas more freely. The danger is if choice is somehow restricted: if all computer networks in the country are restrained from allowing discussion on particular subjects or if a publicly sponsored computer network limits discussion.

This is not to say that freedom-of-speech principles ought to protect all electronic communications. Exceptional cases, such as the BBS used primarily to traffic in stolen long-distance access codes or credit-card numbers, will always arise and pose problems of civil and criminal liability. We know that electronic freedom of speech, whether in public or private systems, cannot be absolute. In face-to-face conversation and printed matter today, it is commonly agreed that freedom of speech does not cover the communications inherent in criminal conspiracy, fraud, libel, incitement to lawless action and copyright infringement.

If there are to be limits on electronic freedom of speech, what precisely should those limits be? One answer to this question is the U.S. Supreme Court's 1969 decision in *Brandenburg* v. *Ohio*. The court ruled that no speech should be subject to prior restraint or criminal prosecution unless it is intended to incite and is likely to cause imminent lawless action.

In general, little speech or publication falls outside of the protections of the Brandenburg case, since most people are able to reflect before acting on a written or spoken suggestion. As in traditional media, any on-line messages should not be the basis of criminal prosecution unless the Brandenburg standard is met.

Other helpful precedents include cases relating to defamation and copyright infringement. Free speech does not mean one can damage a reputation or appropriate a copyrighted work without being called to account for it. And it probably does not mean that one can release a virus across the network in order to "send a message" to network subscribers. Although the distinction is trickier than it may first appear, the release of a destructive program, such as a virus, may be better analyzed as an act rather than as speech.

Following freedom of speech on our action agenda is freedom from unreasonable searches and seizures. The Steve Jackson case was one of many cases in which computer equipment and disks were seized and held—sometimes for months—often without a specific charge being filed. Even when only a few files were relevant to an investigation, entire computer systems, including printers, have been removed with their hundreds of files intact.

Such nonspecific seizures and searches of computer data allow "rummaging," in which officials browse through private files in search of incriminating evidence. In addition to violating the Fourth Amendment requirement that searches and seizures be "particular," these searches often run afoul of the Electronic Communications Privacy Act of 1986. This act prohibits the government from seizing or intercepting electronic communications without proper authorization. They also contravene the Privacy Protection Act of 1980, which prohibits the government from searching the offices of publishers for documents, including materials that are electronically stored.

We can expect that law enforcement agencies and civil libertarians will agree over time about the need to establish procedures for searches and seizures of "particular" computer data and hardware. Law enforcement officials will have to adhere to guidelines in the above statutes to achieve Fourth Amendment "particularity" while maximizing the efficiency of their searches. They also will have to be trained to make use of software tools that allow searches for particular files or particular information within files on even the most capacious hard disk or optical storage device.

Still another part of the solution will be law enforcement's abandonment of the myth of the clever criminal hobbyist. Once law enforcement no longer assumes worst-case behavior but looks instead for real evidence of criminal activity, its agents will learn to search and seize only what they need.

Developing and implementing a civil liberties agenda for computer networks will require increasing participation by technically trained people. Fortunately, there are signs that this is beginning to happen. The Computers, Freedom and Privacy Conference, held last spring in San Francisco, along with electronic conferences on the WELL (Whole Earth 'Lectronic Link) and other computer networks, have brought law enforcement officials, supposed hackers and interested members of the computer community together in a spirit of free and frank discussion. Such gatherings are beginning to work out the civil liberties guidelines for a networked society.

There is general agreement, for example, that a policy on electronic crime should offer protection for security and privacy on both individual and institutional systems. Defining a measure of damages and setting proportional punishment will require further good-faith deliberations by the community involved with electronic freedoms, including the Federal Bureau of Investigation, the Secret Service, the bar associations, technology groups, telephone companies and civil libertarians. It will be especially important to represent the damage caused by electronic crime accurately and to leave room for the valuable side of the hacker spirit: the interest in increasing legitimate understanding through exploration.

We hope to see a similar emerging consensus on security issues. Network systems should be designed not only to provide technical solutions to security problems but also to allow system operators to use them without infringing unduly on the rights of users. A security system that depends on wholesale monitoring of traffic, for example, would create more problems than it would solve.

Those parts of a system where damage would do the greatest harm—financial records, electronic mail, military data—should be protected. This involves installing more effective computer security measures, but it also means redefining the legal interpretations of copyright, intellectual property, computer crime and privacy so that system users are protected against individual criminals and abuses by large institutions. These policies should balance the need for civil liberties against the need for a secure, orderly, protected electronic society.

As we pursue that balance, of course, confrontations will continue to take place. In May of this year, Steve Jackson Games, with the support of the EFF, filed suit against the Secret Service, two individual Secret Service agents, an assistant U.S. attorney and others.

The EFF is not seeking confrontation for its own sake. One of the realities of our legal system is that one often has to fight for a legal or constitutional right in the courts in order to get it recognized outside the courts. One goal of the lawsuit is to establish clear grounds under which search and seizure of electronic media is "unreasonable" and unjust. Another is to establish the clear applicability of First Amendment principles to the new medium.

But the EFF's agenda extends far beyond litigation. Our larger agenda includes sponsoring a range of educational initiatives aimed at the public's general lack of familiarity with the technology and its potential. That is why there is an urgent need for technologically knowledgeable people to take part in the public debate over communications policy and to help spread their understanding of these issues. Fortunately, the very technology at stake—electronic conferencing—makes it easier than ever before to get involved in the debate.

BATTLE OF THE CLIPPER CHIP

Steven Levy

On a sunny spring day in Mountain View, Calif., 50 angry activists are plotting against the United States Government. They may not look subversive sitting around a conference table dressed in T-shirts and jeans and eating burritos, but they are self-proclaimed saboteurs. They are the Cypherpunks, a loose confederation of computer hackers, hardware engineers and high-tech rabble-rousers.

The precise object of their rage is the Clipper chip, offically known as the MYK-78 and not much bigger than a tooth. Just another tiny square of plastic covering a silicon thicket. A computer chip, from the outside indistinguishable from thousands of others. It seems improbable that this black Chiclet is the focal point of a battle that may determine the degree to which our civil liberties survive in the next century. But that is the shared belief in this room.

The Clipper chip has prompted what might be considered the first holy war of the information highway. Two weeks ago, the war got bloodier, as a researcher circulated a report that the chip might have a serious technical flaw. But at its heart, the issue is political, not technical. The Cypherpunks consider the Clipper the lever that Big Brother is using to pry into the conversations, messages and transactions of the computer age. These high-tech Paul Reveres are trying to mobilize America against the evil portent of a "cyberspace police state," as one of their Internet jeremiads put it. Joining them in the battle is a formidable force, including almost all of the communications and computer industries, many members of Congress and political columnists of all stripes. The anti-Clipper aggregation is an equal-opportunity club, uniting the American Civil Liberties Union and Rush Limbaugh.

The Clipper's defenders, who are largely in the Government, believe it represents the last chance to protect personal safety and national security against a developing information anarchy that fosters criminals, terrorists and foreign foes. Its adherents pose it as the answer, or at least part of the answer, to a problem created by an increasingly sophisticated application of an age-old technology: cryptography, the use of secret codes.

For centuries, cryptography was the domain of armies and diplomatic corps. Now it has a second purpose: protecting personal and corporate privacy. Computer technology and advanced telecommunications equipment have drawn precious business information and intimate personal communications out into the open. This phenomenon is well known to the current Prince of Wales, whose intimate cellular phone conversations were intercepted, recorded and broadcast worldwide. And corporations realize that competitors can easily intercept their telephone conversations, electronic messages and faxes. High tech has created a huge privacy gap. But miraculously, a fix has emerged: cheap, easy-to-use, virtually unbreakable encryption. Cryptography is the silver bullet by which we can hope to reclaim our privacy.

The solution, however, has one drawback: cryptography shields the law abiding and the lawless equally. Law-enforcement and intelligence agencies contend that if strong codes are widely available, their efforts to protect the public would be paralyzed. So they have come up with a compromise, a way to neutralize such encryption. That's the Clipper chip and that compromise is what the war is about.

The idea is to give the Government means to override other people's codes, according to a concept called "key escrow." Employing normal cryptography, two parties can communicate in total privacy, with both of them using a digital "key" to encrypt and decipher the conversation or message. A potential eavesdropper has no key and therefore cannot understand the conversation or read the data transmission. But with Clipper, an additional key—created at the time the equipment is manufactured—is held by the Government in escrow. With a court-approved wiretap, an agency like the F.B.I. could listen in. By adding Clipper chips to telephones, we could have a system that assures communications will be private—from everybody but the Government.

And that's what rankles Clipper's many critics. Why, they ask, should people accused of no crime have to give Government the keys to their private communications? Why shouldn't the market rather than Government determine what sort of cryptosystem wins favor. And isn't it true that the use of key escrow will make our technology so unattractive to the international marketplace that the United States will lose its edge in the lucrative telecommunications and computer fields? Clipper might clip the entire economy.

Nonetheless, on Feb. 4 the White House announced its approval of the Clipper chip, which had been under study as a Government standard since last April, and the Crypto War broke out in full force. Within a month, one civil liberties group, Computer Professionals for Social Responsibility, received 47,000 electronic missives urging a stop to Clipper. "The war is upon us," wrote Tim May, co-founder of the Cypherpunks, in an urgent electronic dispatch soon after the announcement. "Clinton and Gore folks have shown themselves to be enthusiastic supporters of Big Brother."

And though the Clinton Administration's endorsement of Clipper as a Government standard required no Congressional approval, rumblings of discontent came from both sides of the Capitol. Senator Patrick J. Leahy, the Vermont Democrat whose subcomittee has held contentious hearings on the matter, has called the plan a "misstep," charging that "the Government should not be in the business of mandating particular technologies."

Two weeks ago, an AT&T Bell Laboratories researcher revealed that he had found a serious flaw in the Clipper technology itself, enabling techno-savvy lawbreakers to by-pass the security fuction of the chip in some applications. Besides being a bad idea, Clipper's foes now say, it doesn't even work properly.

Yet the defenders of Clipper have refused to back down, claiming that the scheme—which is, they often note, voluntary—is an essential means of stemming an increasing threat to public safety and security by strong encryption in everyday use. Even if Clipper itself has to go back to the drawing board, its Government designers will come up with something quite similar. The underlying issue remains unchanged: If something like Clipper is not implemented, writes Dorothy E. Denning, a Georgetown University computer scientist, "All communications on the information highway would be immune from lawful interception. In a world threatened by international organized crime, terrorism and rogue governments, this would be folly."

The claims from both sides sound wild, almost apocalyptic. The passion blurs the problem: Can we protect our privacy in an age of computers—without also protecting the dark forces in society?

The crypto war is the inevitable consequence of a remarkable discovery made almost 20 years ago, a breakthrough that combined with the microelectronics revolution to thrust the once-obscure field of cryptography into the mainstream of communications policy.

It began with Whitfield Diffie, a young computer scientist and cryptographer. He did not work for the Government, which was strange because in the 1960s almost all serious crypto in this country was done under Federal auspices, specifically at the Fort Meade, Md., headquarters of the supersecret National Security Agency. Though it became bigger than the C.I.A., the N.S.A. was for years unknown to Americans; the Washington Beltway joke was that the initials stood for "No Such Agency." Its working premise has always been that no information about its activities should ever be revealed. Its main mission involved cryptography, and the security agency so dominated the field that it had the power to rein in even those few experts in the field who were not on its payroll.

But Whitfield Diffie never got that message. He had been bitten by the cryptography bug at age 10 when his father, a professor, brought home the entire crypto shelf of the City College library in New York. Then he lost interest, until he arrived at M.I.T.'s Artifical Intelligence Laboratory in 1966. Two things rekindled his passion. Now trained as a mathematician, he had an affinity for the particular challenges of sophisticated crypto. Just as important, he says, "I was always concerned about individuals, an individual's privacy as opposed to Government secrecy."

Diffie, now 50, is still committed to those beliefs. When asked about his politics, he says, "I like to describe myself as an iconoclast." He is a computer security specialist for Sun Microsystems, a celebrated cryptographer and an experienced hand at Congressional testimony. But he looks like he stumbled out of a Tom Robbins novel—with blond hair that falls to his shoulders and a longish beard that seems a virtual trademark among code makers. At a Palo Alto, Calif., coffee-house one morning, he describes, in clipped, precise cadence, how he and Martin E. Hellman, an electrical engineering professor at Stanford University, created a crypto revolution.

Diffie was dissatisfied with the security on a new time-sharing computer system being developed by M.I.T. in the 1960s. Files would be protected by passwords, but he felt that was insufficient. The system had a generic flaw. A system manager had access to all passwords. "If a subpeona was served against the system managers, they would sell you out, because they had no interest in going to jail," Diffie says. A perfect system would eliminate the need for a trusted third party.

This led Diffie to think about a more general problem in cryptography: key management. Even before Julius Caesar devised a simple cipher to encode his military messages, cryptography worked by means of keys. That is, an original message (what is now called "plaintext") was encrypted by the sender into seeming gibberish (known as "ciphertext"). The receiver, using the same key, decrypted the message back into the original plaintext. For instance, the Caesar key was the simple replacement of each letter by the letter three places down in the alphabet. If you knew the key, you could encrypt the word *help* into the nonsense word *khos*; the recipient of the message would decrypt the message back to *help*.

The problem came with protecting the key. Since anyone who knew the Caesar key would be able to understand the encoded message, it behooved the Romans to change that key as often as possible. But if you change the key, how do you inform your spies behind enemy lines? (If you tell them using the old code, which may have already been cracked, your enemies will then learn the new code.) For centuries, generals and diplomats have faced that predicament. But a few years ago, it took on added urgency.

With computers and advanced telecommunications, customers outside Government were discovering a need for information security. Cryptography was the answer, but how could it be applied widely, considering the problem of keys? The best answer to date was something called a key-management repository, where two parties who wanted secrecy would go to a trusted third party who would generate a new key for the private session. But that required just what Diffie deplored—an unwanted third wheel.

"The virtue of cryptography should be that you don't have to trust anybody not directly involved with your communication," Diffie says. "Without conventional key distribution centers, which involved trusting third parties, I couldn't figure how you could build a system to secure, for instance, all the phones in the country."

When Diffie moved to Stanford University in 1969, he foresaw the rise of home computer terminals and began pondering the problem of how to use them to make transactions. "I got to thinking how you could possibly have electronic business, because signed letters of intent, contracts and all seemed so critical," he says. He devoured what literature he could find outside the National Security Agency. And in the mid-1970s, Diffie and Hellman achieved a stunning breakthrough that changed cryptography forever. They split the cryptographic key.

In their system, every user has two keys, a public one and a private one, that are unique to their owner. Whatever is scrambled by one key can be unscrambled by the other. It works like this: If I want to send a message to Whit Diffie, I first obtain his public key. (For complicated mathematical reasons, it is possible to distribute one's public key freely without compromising security; a potential enemy will have no advantage in code-cracking if he holds your public key alone.) Then I use that key to encode the message. Now it's gobbledygook and only one person in the world can decode it—Whit Diffie, who holds the other, private, key. If he wants to respond to me with a secret message, he uses my public key to encode his answer. And I decode it, using my private key.

It was an amazing solution, but even more remarkable was that this split-key system solved both of Diffie's problems, the desire to shield communications from eavesdroppers and also to provide a secure electronic identification for contracts and financial transactions done by computer. It provided the identification by the use of "digital signatures" that verify the sender much the same way that a real signature validates a check or contract.

Suddenly, the ancient limitations on cryptography had vanished. Now, perhaps before the millennium, strong cryptography could find its way to every telephone, computer and fax machine—if users wanted it. Subsequent variations on the Diffie-Hellman scheme focused on using crypto algorithms to insure the anonymity of transactions. Using these advances, it is now possible to think of replacing money with digital cash—while maintaining the comforting untraceability of bills and coins. The dark art of cryptography has become a tool of liberation.

From the moment Diffie and Hellman published their findings in 1976, the National Security Agency's crypto monopoly was effectively terminated. In short order, three M.I.T. mathematicians—Ronald L. Rivest, Adi Shamir and Leonard M. Adleman—developed a system with which to put the Diffie and Hellman findings into practice. It was known by their initials, RSA. It seemed capable of creating codes that even the N.S.A. could not break. They formed a company to sell their new system; it was only a matter of time before thousands and then millions of people began using strong encryption.

That was the National Security Agency's greatest nightmare. Every company, every citizen now had routine access to the sorts of cryptographic technology that not many years ago ranked alongside the atom bomb as a source of power. Every call, every computer message, every fax in the world could be harder to decipher than the famous German "Enigma" machine of World War II. Maybe even impossible to decipher!

The genie was out of the bottle. Next question: Could the genie be made to wear a leash and collar? Enter the Clipper chip.

When illustrating the government's need to control crypto, Jim Kallstrom, the agent in charge of the special operations division of the New York office of the F.B.I., quickly shifts the discussion to the personal: "Are you married? Do you have a child? O.K., someone kidnaps one of your kids and they are holding your kid in this fortress up in the Bronx. Now, we have probable cause that your child is inside this fortress. We have a search warrant. But for some reason, we cannot get in there. They made it out of some new metal, or something, right? Nothing'll cut it, right? And there are guys in there, *laughing* at us. That's what the basis of this issue really is—we've got a situation now where a technology has become so sophisticated that the whole notion of a legal process is at stake here!"

Kallstrom is a former head of the Bureau Tech Squad, involved in the bugging operation that brought John Gotti to justice. Some have described him as the F.B.I.'s answer to "Q," the gadget wizard of the James Bond tales.

"From the standpoint of law enforcement, there's a superbig threat out there— this guy is gonna build this domain in the Bronx now, because he's got a new steel door and none of the welding torches, none of the boomerangs, nothing we have is gonna blast our way in there. Sure, we want those new steel doors ourselves, to pro- tect our banks, to protect the American corporation trade secrets, patent rights, tech- nology. But people operating in legitimate business are not violating the laws—it becomes a different ball of wax when we have probable cause and we have to get into that domain. Do we want a digital superhighway where not only the commerce of the nation can take place but where major criminals can operate impervious to the legal process? If we don't want that, then we have to look at Clipper."

Wiretapping is among law enforcement's most cherished weapons. Only 919 Federal, state and local taps were authorized last year, but police agencies consider them essential to fighting crime. Obviously if criminals communicate using military- grade cryptosystems, wiretapping them becomes impossible.

For two years, the F.B.I. has been urging Congress to pass the proposed Digi- tal Telephony and Communications Privacy Act, which would in essence require that new communications technologies be designed to facilitate wiretapping. Even if the bill should somehow pass, overcoming the opposition of the communications indus- try and civil libertarians, the extra effort and expense will be wasted if the only thing the wiretappers can hear is the hissy white noise of encrypted phone conversations and faxes. If cryptography is not controlled, wiretapping could be rendered obsolete. Louis J. Freeh, the Director of the F.B.I., surely fears that prospect. He has told Con- gress that preserving the ability to intercept communications legally, in the face of these technological advances, is "the No. 1 law enforcement, public safety and national security issue facing us today."

Some people criticize Clipper on the basis that truly sophisticated criminals would never use it, preferring other easily obtained systems that use high-grade cryp- tography. Despite Clipper, kidnappers and drug kingpins may construct Kallstrom's virtual fort in the Bronx with impunity, laughing at potential wiretappers.

The Government understands the impossibility of eradicating strong crypto. Its objective is instead to prevent unbreakable encryption from becoming routine. If that happens, even the stupidest criminal would be liberated from the threat of surveil- lance. But by making Clipper the standard, the Government is betting that only a tiny percentage of users would use other encryption or try to defeat the Clipper.

At a rare public appearance in March at a conference on computers and privacy, Stewart A. Baker, then general counsel of the National Security Agency, tried to explain. "The concern is not so much what happens today when people go in and buy voice scramblers," said Baker, a dapper, mustached lawyer who worked as an Education Department lawyer in the Carter Administration. "It is the prospect that in 5 years or 10 years every phone you buy that costs $75 or more will have an encrypt button on it that will interoperate with every other phone in the country and suddenly we will discover that our entire communications network is being used in ways that are profoundly antisocial. That's the real concern, I think, that Clipper addresses. If we are going to have a standardized form of encryption that is going to change the world, we should think seriously about what we are going to do when it is misused."

Not all law-enforcement experts believe that cryptography will unleash a riot of lawlessness. William R. Spernow, a Sacramento, Calif., computer crime specialist who works on a grant from the Federal Bureau of Justice Assistance, has encountered a few cases in which criminals have encrypted information unbreakably, including one involving a pedophile who encrypted the identities of his young victims. Yet Spernow sees no reason to panic. "In cases where there's encryption, the officers have been able to make the case through other investigative means," he says. "If we hustle, we can still make our cases through other kinds of police work."

But crime is only part of the problem. What happens to national security if cryptography runs free? Those who know best, officials of the National Security Agency, won't say. When the agency's director, Vice Adm. John M. McConnell testified before a Senate subcommittee on May 3, he withheld comment on this question until the public hearing was terminated and a second, classified session convened in a secure room.

Still, the effect of strong crypto on N.S.A. operations is not difficult to imagine. The agency is charged with signals intelligence, and it is widely assumed that it monitors all the communications between borders and probably much of the traffic within foreign countries. (It is barred from intercepting domestic communications.) If the crypto revolution crippled N.S.A.'s ability to listen in on the world, the agency might miss out on something vital—for instance, portents of a major terrorist attack.

No compelling case has been made, however, that the key-escrow system would make it easier for authorities to learn of such an attack. The National Security Agency would take the legal steps to seek the telltale keys after it had first identified those potential terrorists and wiretapped their calls, then discovered the inpenetrable hiss of encryption. Even then, the keys would be useful only if the terrorists were encoding conversations with Clipper technology, the one kind the Government had the capability to decode instantly. What sort of nuclear terrorist would choose Clipper?

The Government response has been to say that potential terrorists might indeed use alternative crypto methods to converse among themselves. But if Clipper were the accepted standard, the terrorists would have to use it to communicate with outsiders—banks, suppliers and other contacts. The Government could listen in on those calls. However, the work of the Bell Labs researcher, Matthew Blaze, casts serious doubt on that contention. Blaze has uncovered a flaw in Clipper that would allow a user to bypass the security funtion of the chip. Anyone who tinkered with Clipper in this way could communicate in privacy with anyone else with a Clipper phone and Government wiretappers would be unable to locate the key to unscramble the conversations.

Nonetheless, it was the terrorist threat, along with national security concerns, that moved the Clinton Administration to support the key-escrow initiative. White

House high-tech policy makers share a recurrent fear: one day they might be sitting before an emergency Congressional investigation after the destruction of half of Manhattan by a stolen nuclear weapon planted in the World Trade towers and trying to explain that the Government had intercepted the communications of the terrorists but could not understand them because they used strong encryption. If Clipper were enacted, they could at least say, "We tried."

Obviously the government views the crypto revolution with alarm and wants to contain it. For years, much of its efforts have focused on the use of stringent export controls. While cryptography within the United States is unrestricted, the country's export laws treat any sort of encryption as munitions, like howitzers or nuclear triggers. The National Security Agency is the final arbiter and it will approve exports of cryptosystems in computer software and electronic hardware only if the protective codes are significantly weakened.

The N.S.A. stance is under attack from American businesses losing sales to foreign competitors. Listen to D. James Bidzos, the 39-year-old president of RSA Data Security, the Redwood City, Calif., company that controls the patents for public-key cryptography: "For almost 10 years, I've been going toe to toe with these people at Fort Meade. The success of this company is the worst thing that can happen to them. To them, we're the real enemy, we're the real target."

RSA is making a pitch to become the standard in encryption; its technology has been adopted by Apple, AT&T, Lotus, Microsoft, Novell and other major manufacturers. So imagine its unhappiness that its main rival is not another private company, but the National Security Agency, designer of the key-escrow cryptosystems. The agency is a powerful and dedicated competitor.

"We have the system that they're most afraid of," Bidzos says. "If the U.S. adopted RSA as a standard, you would have a truly international, interoperable, unbreakable, easy-to-use encryption technology. And all those things together are so synergistically theatening to the N.S.A.'s interests that it's driving them into a frenzy."

The export laws put shackles on Bidzos's company while his overseas competitors have no such restaints. Cryptographic algorithms that the N.S.A. bans for export are widely published and are literally being sold on the streets of Moscow. "We did a study on the problem and located 340 foreign cryptographic products sold by foreign countires," says Douglas R. Miller, government affairs manager of the Software Publishers Association. "The only effect of export controls is to cripple our ability to compete."

The real potential losses, though, come not in the stand-alone encryption category, but in broader applications. Companies like Microsoft, Apple and Lotus want to put strong encryption into their products but cannot get licenses to export them. Often, software companies wind up installing a weaker brand of crypto in all their products so that they can sell a single version worldwide. This seems to be the Government's intent—to encourage "crypto lite," strong enough to protect communications from casual intruders but not from Government itself.

In the long run, however, export regulation will not solve the National Security Agency's problem. The crypto business is exploding. People are becoming more aware of the vunerability of phone conversations, particularly wireless ones. Even the National Football League is adopting crypto technology; it will try out encrypted radio communication between coaches and quarterbacks, so rivals can't intercept last-minute audibles.

Anticipating such a boom, the N.S.A. devised a strategy for the 90's. It would concede the need for strong encryption but encourage a system with a key-escrow "back door" that provides access to communications for itself and law enforcement. The security agency had already developed a strong cryptosystem based on an algorithm called Skipjack, supposedly 16 million times stronger than the previous standard, D.E.S. (Data Encryption Standard). Now the agency's designers integrated Skipjack into a new system that uses a Law Enforcement Access Field (LEAF) that adds a signal to the message that directs a potential wiretapper to the appropriate key to decipher the message. These features were included in a chip called Capstone, which could handle not only telephone communications but computer data transfers and digital signatures.

Supposedly, this technology was designed for Government use, but in 1993 the National Security Agency had a sudden opportunity to thrust it into the marketplace. AT&T had come to the agency with a new, relatively low-cost secure-phone device called the Surity 3600 that was designed to use the nonexportable DES encryption algorithm. The N.S.A. suggested that perhaps AT&T could try something else: a stripped-down version of Capstone for telephone communications. This was the Clipper chip. As a result, AT&T got two things: an agreement that Uncle Sam would buy thousands of phones for its own use (the initial commitment was 9,000, from the F.B.I.) and the prospect that the phone would not suffer the unhappy fate of some other secure devices when considered for export. There was also the expectation that AT&T would sell a lot more phones, since private companies would need to buy Clipper-equipped devices to communicate with the Government's Clipper phones.

It was an ingenious plan for several reasons. By agreeing to buy thousands of phones, and holding out the promise that thousands, or even millions more might be sold, AT&T phones gained a price advantage that comes with volume. (The original price of the Surity 3600 was $1,195, considerably less than the previous generation of secure phones; Mykotronx, the company making the Clipper chip, says that each chip now costs $30, but in large orders could quickly go as low as $10.) That would give the phones a big push in the marketplace. But by saturating the market, Clipper had a chance to become the standard for encryption, depending on whether businesses and individuals would be willing to accept a device that had the compromise of a government controlled back door.

This compromise, of course, is the essence of Clipper. The Government recognizes the importance of keeping business secrets, intimate information and personal data hidden from most eyes and ears. But it also preserves a means of getting hold of that information after obtaining "legal authorization, normally a court order," according to a White House description.

The N.S.A. presented the idea to the Bush Administration, which took no action before the election. Then it had to convince a Democratic Administration to adopt the scheme, and started briefing the Clinton people during the transition. Many in the computer industry figured that with Vice President Al Gore's enthusiastic endorsement of the high-frontier virtues of the information highway, the Administration would never adopt any proposal so tilted in favor of law enforcement and away from his allies in the information industries. They figured wrong. A little more than two months after taking office, the Clinton Administration announced the existence of the Clipper chip and directed the National Institute of Standards and Technology to consider it as a Government standard.

Clipper was something the Administration—starting with the Vice President—felt compelled to adopt, and key escrow was considered an honorable attempt to balance two painfully contradictory interests, privacy and safety.

The reaction was instant, bitter and ceaseless. The most pervasive criticisms challenged the idea that a Clipper would be, as the standard said, "voluntary." The Government's stated intent is to manipulate the marketplace so that it will adopt an otherwise unpalatable scheme and make it the standard. Existing systems have to cope with export regulations and, now, incompatibility with the new Government Clipper standard. Is it fair to call a system voluntary if the Government puts all sorts of obstacles in the way of its competitors?

Others felt that it was only a matter of time before the National Security Agency pressured the Government to require key escrow of all cryptographic devices—that Clipper was only the first step in a master plan to give Uncle Sam a key to everyone's cyberspace back door.

"That's a real fear," says Stephen T. Walker, a former N.S.A. employee who is now president of Trusted Information Systems, a company specializing in computer security products. "I don't think the Government could pull it off—it would be like prohibition, only worse. But I think they might try it."

But mostly, people were unhappy with the essence of Clipper, that the Government would escrow their keys. As Diffie notes, key escrow reintroduces the vulnerability that led him to invent public key cryptography—any system that relies on trusted third parties is, by definition, weaker than one that does not. Almost no one outside the Government likes the key-escrow idea. "We published the standard for 60 days of public comments," says F. Lynn McNulty, associate director for computer security at the National Institute of Standards and Technology. "We received 320 comments, only 2 of which were supportive."

Many people thought that in the face of such opposition, the Administration would quietly drop the Clipper proposal. They were dismayed by the Feb. 4 announcement of the adoption of Clipper as a Government standard. Administration officials knew they were alienating their natural allies in the construction of the information superhighway but felt they had no alternative. "This," said Michael R. Nelson, a White House technology official, "is the Bosnia of telecommunications."

If Clipper is the administration's techno-bosnia, the crypto equivalent of snipers are everywhere—in industry, among privacy lobbyists and even among Christian Fundamentalists. But the most passionate foes are the Cypherpunks. They have been meeting on the second Saturday of every month at the offices of Cygnus, a Silicon Valley company, assessing new ways they might sabotage Clipper. The group was co-founded in September 1992 by Eric Hughes, a 29-year-old freelance cryptographer, and Tim May, a 42-year-old physicist who retired early and rich from the Intel company. Other Cypherpunk cells often meet simultaneously in six or seven locations around the world, but the main gathering place for Cypherpunks is the Internet, by means of an active mailing list in which members post as many as 100 electronic messages a day.

Cypherpunks share a few common premises. They assume that cryptography is a liberating tool, one that empowers individuals. They think that one of the most important uses of cryptography is to protect communications from the Government. Many of them believe that the Clipper is part of an overall initiative against cryptography that will culminate in Draconian control of the technology. And they consider it worth their time to fight, educating the general public and distributing cryptographic tools to obstruct such control.

Both Hughes and May have composed manifestos. Hughes's call to arms proclaims: "Cypherpunks write code. We know that someone has to write software to defend privacy, and since we can't get privacy unless we all do, we're going to write it."

May's document envisions a golden age in which strong cryptography belongs to all—an era of "crypto anarchism" that governments cannot contain. To May, cryptography is a tool that will not only bestow privacy on people but help rearrange the economic underpinnings of society.

"Combined with emerging information markets, cryptography will create a liquid market for any and all material that can be put into words and pictures," May's document says. "And just as a seemingly minor invention like barbed wire made possible the fencing-off of vast ranches and farms, thus altering forever the concepts of land and property rights in the frontier West, so too will the seemingly minor discovery out of an arcane branch of mathematics come to be the wire clippers which dismantle the barbed wire around intellectual property."

At a recent meeting, about 50 Cypherpunks packed into the Cygnus conference room, with dozens of others participating electronically from sites as distant as Cambridge, Mass., and San Diego. The meeting stretched for six hours, with discussions of hardware encryption schemes, methods to fight an electronic technique of identity forgery called "spoofing," the operation of "remailing" services, which allow people to post electronic messages anonymously—and various ways to fight Clipper.

While the Cypherpunks came up with possible anti-Clipper slogans for posters and buttons, a bearded crypto activist in wire-rim glasses named John Gilmore was outside the conference room, showing the latest sheaf of cryptography-related Freedom of Information documents he'd dragged out of Government files. Unearthing and circulating the hidden crypto treasures of the National Security Agency is a passion of Gilmore, an early employee of Sun Microsystems who left the company a multimillionaire. The Government once threatened to charge him with a felony for copying some unclassified-and-later-reclassified N.S.A. documents from a university library. After the story hit the newspapers, the Government once again declassified the documents.

"This country was founded as an open society, and we still have the remnants of that society," Gilmore says. "Will crypto tend to open it or close it? Our Government is building some of these tools for its own use, but they are unavailable—we have paid for cryptographic breakthroughs but they're classified. I wish I could hire 10 guys—cryptographers, librarians—to try to pry cryptography out of the dark ages."

Perhaps the most admired Cypherpunk is someone who says he is ineligible because he often wears a suit. He is Philip R. Zimmermann, a 40-year-old software engineer and cryptographic consultant from Boulder, Colo., who in 1991 cobbled together a cryptography program for computer data and electronic mail. "PGP," he called it, meaning Pretty Good Privacy, and he decided to give it away. Anticipating the Cypherpunk credo, Zimmermann hoped that the appearance of free cryptography would guarantee its continued use after a possible Government ban. One of the first people receiving the program placed it on a computer attached to the Internet and within days thousands of people had PGP. Now the program has been through several updates and is becoming sort of a people's standard for public key cryptography. So far, it appears that no one has been able to crack information encoded with PGP.

Like Diffie, Zimmermann developed a boyhood interest in crypto. "When I was a kid growing up in Miami, it was just kind of cool—secret messages and all," he says. Later, "computers made it possible to do ciphers in a practical manner." He was fascinated to hear of public key cryptography and during the mid-1980s he began experimenting with a system that would work on personal computers. With the help of some colleagues, he finally devised a strong system, albeit one that used some patented material from RSA Data Security. And then he heard about the Senate bill that proposed to limit a citizen's right to use strong encryption by requiring manufacturers to include back doors in their products. Zimmermann, formerly a nuclear freeze activist, felt that one of the most valuable potential uses of cryptography was to keep messages secret *from* the Government.

Zimmermann has put some political content into the documentation for his program: "If privacy is outlawed, only outlaws will have privacy. Intelligence agencies have access to good cryptographic technology. So do the big arms and drug traffickers. So do defense contractors, oil companies, and other corporate giants. But ordinary people and grassroots political organizations mostly have not had access to affordable 'military grade' public-key cryptographic technology. Until now."

He has been told that Burmese freedom fighters learn PGP in jungle training camps on portable computers, using it to keep documents hidden from their oppressive Government. But his favorite letter comes from a person in Latvia, who informed him that his program was a favorite among one-time refuseniks in that former Soviet republic. "Let it never be," wrote his correspondant, "but if dictatorship takes over Russia, your PGP is widespread from Baltic to Far East now and will help democratic people if necessary."

Early last year, Zimmermann received a visit from two United States Customs Service agents. They wanted to know how it was that the strong encryption program PGP had found its way overseas with no export license. In the fall, he learned from his lawyer that he was a target of a grand jury investigation in San Jose, Calif. But even if the Feds should try to prosecute, they are likely to face a tough legal issue: Can it be a crime, in the process of legally distributing information in this country, to place it on an Internet computer site that is incidentally accessible to network users in other countries? There may well be a First Amendment issue here: Americans prize the right to circulate ideas, including those on software disks.

John Gilmore has discovered that Government lawyers have their own doubts about these issues. In some documents he sued to get, there are mid-1980s warnings by the Justice Department that the export controls on cryptography presented "sensitive constitutional issues." In one letter, an assistant attorney general warns that "the regulatory scheme extends too broadly into an area of protected First Amendment speech."

Perhaps taking Phil Zimmermann to court would not be the Government's best method for keeping the genie in the bottle.

The Clipper program has already begun. About once a month, four couriers with security clearances travel from Washington to the Torrance, Calif., headquarters of Mykotronx, which holds the contract to make Clipper chips. They travel in pairs, two from each escrow agency: the NIST and the Treasury Department. The redundancy is a requirement of a protocol known as Two-Person Integrity, used in situations like nuclear missile launches, where the stakes are too high to rely on one person.

The couriers wait while a Sun work station performs the calculations to generate the digital cryptographic keys that will be imprinted in the Clipper chips. Then it splits the keys into two pieces, separate number chains, and writes them on two floppy disks, each holding lists of "key splits." To reconstruct the keys imprinted on the chip, and thereby decode private conversations, you would need both sets of disks.

After being backed up, the sets of disks are separated, each one going with a pair of couriers. When the couriers return to their respective agencies, each set of disks is placed in a double-walled safe. The backup copies are placed in similar safes.

There they wait, two stacks of floppy disks that grow each month, now holding about 20,000 key splits, the so-called back doors.

Will this number grow into the millions as the Government hopes? Ultimately the answer lies with the American public. Administration officials are confident that when the public contemplates scenarios like the Fortress in the Bronx or the Mushroom Cloud in Lower Manhattan, it will realize that allowing the Government to hold the keys is a relatively painless price to pay for safety and national security. They believe the public will eventually accept it in the same way it now views limited legal wiretapping. But so far the Administration hasn't recruited many prominent supporters. The main one is Dorothy Denning, a crypto expert who heads the computer science department at Georgetown University.

Since endorsing Clipper (and advocating passage of the Digital Telephony initiative) Denning has been savagely attacked on the computer nets. Some of the language would wither a professional wrestler. "I've seen horrible things written about me," Denning says with a nervous smile. "I try to actually now avoid looking at them, because that's not what's important to me. What's important is that we end up doing the right thing with this. It was an accumulation of factors that led me to agree with Clipper, and the two most important areas, to me, are organized crime and terrorism. I was exposed to cases where wiretaps had actually stopped crimes in the making, and I started thinking, 'If they didn't have this tool, some of these things might have happened.' You know, I hate to use the word responsibility, but I actually feel some sense of responsibility to at least state my position to the extent so that people will understand it."

The opponents of Clipper are confident that the marketplace will vote against it. "The idea that the Government holds the keys to all our locks, before anyone has even been accused of committing a crime, doesn't parse with the public," says Jerry Berman, executive director of the Electronic Frontier Foundation. "It's not America."

Senator Leahy hints that Congress might not stand for the Clinton Administration's attempt to construct the key-escrow system, at an estimated cost of $14 million dollars initially and $16 million annually. "If the Administration wants the money to set up and run the key-escrow facilities," he says, "it will need Congressional approval." Despite claims by the National Institute of Standards and Technology deputy director, Raymond G. Kammer, that some foreign governments have shown interest in the scheme, Leahy seems to agree with most American telecommunications and computer manufacturers that Clipper and subsequent escrow schemes will find no favor in the vast international marketplace, turning the United States into a cryptographic island and crippling important industries.

Leahy is also concerned about the Administration's haste. "The Administration is rushing to implement the Clipper chip program without thinking through crucial details," he says. Indeed, although the Government has been buying and using Clipper encryption devices, the process of actually getting the keys out of escrow and using them to decipher scrambled conversations has never been field tested. And there exists only a single uncompleted prototype of the device intended to do the deciphering.

Leahy is also among those who worry that, all policy issues aside, the Government's key-escrow scheme might fail solely on technical issues. The Clipper and Capstone chips, while powerful enough to use on today's equipment, have not been engineered for the high speeds of the coming information highway; updates will be required. Even more serious are the potential design flaws in the unproved key-escrow scheme. Matthew Blaze's discovery that wrong-doers could foil wiretappers may be only the first indication that Clipper is unable to do the job for which it was designed. In his paper revealing the glitch, he writes, "It is not clear that it is possible to construct EES (Escrow Encryption Standard) that is both completely invulnerable to all kinds of exploitation as well as generally useful."

At bottom, many opponents of Clipper do not trust the Government. They are unimpressed by the elaborate key-escrow security arrangements outlined for Clipper. Instead, they ask questions about the process by which the Clipper was devised—how is it that the N.S.A., an intelligence agency whose mission does not ordinarily include consumer electronics design, has suddenly seized a central role in creating a national information matrix? They also complain that the Skipjack cryptographic algorithm is a classified secret, one that cryptographic professionals cannot subject to the rigorous, extended testing that has previously been used to gain universal trust for such a standard.

"You don't want to buy a set of car keys from a guy who specializes in stealing cars," says Marc Rotenberg, director of the Electronic Privacy Information Center. "The N.S.A.'s specialty is the ability to break codes, and they are saying, 'Here, take our keys, we promise you they'll work.' "

At the March conference on computers and privacy, Stewart Baker responded to this sort of criticism. "This is the revenge of people who couldn't go to Woodstock because they had too much trig homework," he said, evoking some catcalls. "It's a kind of romanticism about privacy. The problem with it is that the beneficiaries of that sort of romanticism are going to be predators. PGP, they say, is out there to protect freedom fighters in Latvia. But the fact is, the only use that has come to the attention of law enforcement agencies is a guy who was using PGP so the police could not tell what little boys he had seduced over the net. Now that's what people will use this for—it's not the only thing people will use it for, but they will use it for that—and by insisting on having a claim to privacy that is beyond social regulation, we are creating a world in which people like that will flourish and be able to do more than they can do today."

Even if Clipper flops, the Crypto War will continue. The Administration remains committed to limiting the spread of strong cryptography unless there's a back door. Recently, it has taken to asking opponents for alternatives to Clipper. One suggestion it will not embrace is inaction. "Deciding that the genie is out of the bottle and throwing our arms up is not where we're at," says a White House official.

The National Security Agency will certainly not go away. "The agency is really worried about its screens going blank" due to unbreakable encryption, says Lance J. Hoffman, a professor of computer science at George Washington University. "When that happens, the N.S.A.—said to be the largest employer in Maryland—goes belly-up. A way to prevent this is to expand its mission and to become, effectively, the one-stop shop for encryption for Government and those that do business with the Government."

Sure enough, the security agency is cooking up an entire product line of new key-escrow chips. At Fort Meade, it has already created a high-speed version of the Skipjack algorithm that outperforms both Clipper and Capstone. There is also another, more powerful, encryption device in the works named Baton. As far as the agency is concerned, these developments are no more than common sense. "To say that N.S.A. shouldn't be involved in this issue is to say that Government should try to solve this difficult technical and social problem with both hands tied behind its back," Stewart Baker says.

But Phil Zimmermann and the Cypherpunks aren't going away, either. Zimmermann is, among other things, soliciting funds for a PGP phone that will allow users the same sort of voice encryption provided by the Clipper chip. The difference, of course, is that in his phone there is no key escrow, no back door. If the F.B.I. initiated a wiretap on someone using Zimmermann's proposed phone, all the investigators would hear is static that they could never restore to orderly language.

What if that static shielded the murderous plans of a terrorist or kidnapper? Phil Zimmermann would feel terrible. Ultimately he has no answer. "I am worried about what might happen if unlimited security communications come about," he admits. "But I also think there are tremendous benefits. Some bad things would happen, but the trade-off would be worth it. You have to look at the big picture."

▷ RATIONALES FOR FREEDOM OF SPEECH

Kent Greenawalt

This article explores the justifications for freedom of speech. If sound political philosophy supports something properly called a principle of free speech, there will be reasons why a government should be hesitant to punish verbal or written expression even when it has made a judgment that the expression is potentially harmful. The discussion in this article underlies the development of standards for determining which communications raise free speech problems and which may appropriately be suppressed, and it is also critical for the subsequent examination of constitutional issues.

. . . A principle of freedom of speech asserts some range of protection for speech. Given the uneven application of various reasons for free speech to different sorts of communications, there is some question whether one should speak of "a principle" or "principles" of free speech. For simplicity's sake, I adopt the singular form, but that form should not obscure the complexities of the subject.

BEYOND A MINIMAL PRINCIPLE OF LIBERTY

A political principle of free speech is warranted only if reasons to protect speech go beyond the reasons for what I shall call a *minimal principle of liberty*. According to a minimal principle of liberty, the government should not prohibit people from acting as they wish unless it has a positive reason to do so. The ordinary reason for prohibiting action is that the action is deemed harmful or potentially harmful in some respect; driving a car 100 miles per hour is forbidden because people are likely to get hurt. Although sometimes the government may compel behavior in order to generate benefits rather than prevent harms.[1] I shall disregard that subtlety and concentrate on harm. What legitimately counts as "harm" is an important and controversial aspect of political theory[2] but here I mean the term in an inclusive, nonrestrictive sense, including indirect harms, psychological harms, harms to the actor, and even harms to the natural order. Thus, as far as anything I say here is concerned, sexual intercourse between human beings and animals might be prohibited on the ground that it has deleterious indirect effects on family life, is psychologically bad for the people involved, or is intrinsically "unnatural.". . .

As far as speech is concerned, the minimal principle of liberty establishes that the government should not interfere with communication that has no potential for harm. To be significant, a principle of freedom of speech must go beyond this,[3] positing constraints on the regulation of speech which are more robust.

A principle of free speech could establish more stringent constraints than the minimal principle of liberty, either by barring certain possible reasons for prohibition or by establishing a special value for speech. The latter way is the easier to understand. If some human activities have special value, a good government will need stronger reasons to prohibit them than to prohibit other activities. If speech has more positive value than acts of physical aggression, for example, more powerful reasons will be needed to warrant its suppression. A related but more subtle point is that legislatures or other political actors may be prone in particular instances to undervalue certain kinds of acts; if that were true about speech, a principle of free speech might compensate for that tendency. In effect the principle would tell those involved in government that acts of speech should be assumed to have a higher value than they seem to have in the immediate context.

The second way in which a principle might give special protection to speech is by positing that the government is barred from employing certain reasons for prohibiting speech. Such a constraint might derive from a notion that particular reasons for prohibitions are at odds with how human beings should be regarded or with the proper role of government. Thus, it might be claimed that, because an aspect of the autonomy of human beings is that people should discover for themselves what is true, suppressing speech to prevent contamination by false ideas is impermissible. Or it might be said that the government cannot suppress political ideas that pose challenges to it, because one aspect of a legitimate government is that criticism of those presently in power may be entertained. The import of a "disqualifying" principle might be less extreme than total exclusion of a reason for prohibition. A reason might be viewed with great suspicion, but treated as a legitimate basis for prohibition if the case were sufficiently compelling.[4]

Using threads like these, a principle or theory of freedom of speech would claim that expression cannot be regulated on every basis that could surmount the minimal principle of liberty and satisfy ordinary prudential considerations regarding effective legislation.[5]

Some claims about the value of speech or about the inappropriateness of certain reasons for prohibition could be thought to be largely independent of wider assertions of political ideology, but many claims bear a distinctive relation to liberal political theory. A proponent of claims that involve a controverted liberal view of human autonomy and government might assert that the liberal view is fundamentally correct and should be embraced by all peoples or by all peoples at a certain stage of economic and social development; in that event, a complete defense of the claims about free speech would require argument for the superiority of the liberal perspective. Alternatively, one who advances liberal claims might assert that, since a particular society is grounded on liberal ideas, that society should act on their implications, at least in the absence of opposed premises for social life that are clearly preferable and attainable.

Because I aim to elucidate standards that could be endorsed by people who disagree about many fundamental matters, my account does not depend on a single systematic version of liberal political theory. But, doubting whether there is a better form of government for large developed countries and strongly believing that no other form is clearly preferable and attainable, I assume in this study that conclusions about freedom of speech that can be drawn from *basic premises* of liberal democracy are sound, without examining possible competing premises.[6] My reliance on basic premises does not mean that I accept without analysis every "liberal" idea; discrete arguments having to do with freedom of speech are scrutinized carefully. . . .

CONSEQUENTIALIST AND NONCONSEQUENTIALIST REASONS

There is no single correct way of presenting the justifications that matter for a principle of freedom of speech. One can distinguish, for example, between reasons that focus on individuals and those which focus on society at large, between reasons that relate to speakers and those which relate to listeners or a broader public, between reasons that relate to the form of government and those which do not, between reasons that reflect optimism about human capacities and those which reflect pessimism, between reasons that concentrate on the positive value of speech and those which emphasize the untrustworthiness of government. Because the reasons for free speech are based on complex and somewhat overlapping elements, no basic division or multiple categorization can be wholly satisfactory.

I have chosen to distinguish between consequentialist and nonconsequentialist reasons. This approach too has its drawbacks, requiring, among other things, somewhat strained divisions between arguments concerning individual autonomy and between arguments concerning democracy. Nonetheless, this familiar way of distinguishing reasons for action is useful here, because it differentiates claimed reasons that are to be viewed in light of factual evidence and claimed reasons that rest more purely on normative claims.[7]

A practice has value from a *consequentialist* point of view if it contributes to some desirable state of affairs. Thus, to say that free speech contributes to honest government is to advance a consequentialist reason for free speech. The force of a consequentialist reason is dependent on the factual connection between a practice and the supposed results of the practice. A *nonconsequentialist* reason claims that something about a particular practice is right or wrong without regard to the consequences. Notable among reasons of this sort are reasons cast in terms of present rights or claims of justice: "Suppressing Joan's ideas is wrong because it violates rights or is unjust."

CONSEQUENTIALIST JUSTIFICATIONS

During most of the twentieth century consequentialist arguments have dominated discussion of freedom of speech, although the last two decades have seen a resurgence of nonconsequentialist arguments cast in terms of basic human rights and dignity.[8] Consequentialist arguments reach public and private life; they reach governmental and nongovernmental matters; they reach speakers, listeners, and others who are indirectly affected.

"Truth" Discovery

The Basic Justification The most familiar argument for freedom of speech is that speech promotes the discovery of truth. Found in Milton's *Areopagitica*[9] and in eloquent opinions by Oliver Wendell Holmes[10] and by Louis Brandeis,[11] the argument is the core of John Stuart Mill's defense of freedom of speech in *On Liberty*.[12] Mill says that, if the government suppresses communications, it may suppress ideas that are true or partly true. Even if an idea is wholly false, its challenge to received understanding promotes reexamination which vitalizes truth. When Mill asserts that government suppression of ideas rests necessarily on a false assumption of infallibility, he overstates his case: suppression might reflect cynical skepticism about any truth, or a belief that, fallible as it is, the government is likely to judge more accurately than is a dissident minority; or a conviction that, true or not, some ideas are too destructive of a social order to be tolerated. But Mill's basic point that speech contributes greatly to the search for truth does not depend on whether suppression always represents a claim of infallibility. Mill's sense of truth is broad, covering correct judgments about issues of value as well as ordinary empirical facts and embracing knowledge conducive to a satisfactory personal life as well as facts of general social importance.

Although he does not assume that people will grasp the truth whenever it appears, Mill believes that, if voice is given to a wide variety of views over the long run, true views are more likely to emerge than if the government suppresses what it deems false. In this standard form, the truth-discovery justification combines a contained optimism that people have some ability *over time* to sort out true ideas from false ones with a realism that sees that governments, which reflect presently dominant assumptions and have narrow interests of their own to protect, will not exhibit exquisite sensitivity if they get into the business of settling what is true.

Often taken as an axiom in liberal societies, the truth-discovery justification is subject to a number of possible challenges: that objective "truth" does not exist; that, if truth does exist, human beings cannot identify it or cannot identify the conditions under which it is discovered; that, even if human beings can identify truth sometimes, free discussion does not evidently contribute to their capacity to do so; and that the way "free" discussion works in practice contravenes the open market of ideas that the truth-discovery justification assumes.[13] A searching answer to these doubts would require a systematic examination of notions of truth and evidences of truth and of human learning. . . .

Exposure and Deterrence of Abuses of Authority

Closely linked to truth discovery and interest accommodation is a consequentialist justification that warrants separate mention because of its historical significance and central importance: free speech as a check on abuse of authority, especially governmental authority. The idea, powerfully developed by Vincent Blasi in a well-known article,[14] is that, if those in power are subject to public exposure for their wrongs in the manner exemplified by journalists' accounts of the Watergate scandal, corrective action can be taken. And if public officials know they are subject to such scrutiny, they will be much less likely to yield to the inevitable temptation presented to those with power to act in corrupt and arbitrary ways.

In major part, the justification based on exposure and deterrence of government abuse can be seen as a subcategory of the truth-discovery justification. When truths about abuse of authority are revealed, citizens or other officials can take corrective action. But an extra dimension of truth discovery is important here. In areas of human life involving choice, what people do is partly dependent on what they think will become known. Most particularly, persons are less likely to perform acts which are widely regarded as wrong and which commonly trigger some sanction if they are not confident they can keep the acts secret. Thus the prospect of truth's being discovered influences what happens; public scrutiny deters. Viewed from the perspective of interest accommodation, a free press that exposes wrongs affects the balance of sensitivity in the direction of the interests of ordinary citizens as compared with the interests of the officials themselves and of those to whom they feel especially aligned by mutual advantage or common feeling. Perhaps the benefits of exposure and deterrence reach beyond anything neatly captured by truth discovery or interest accommodation. Apart from truths it actually reveals and even when what it claims turns out to be inaccurate, a critical press affects how officials and citizens regard the exercise of governmental power, subtly supporting the notion that government service is a responsibility, not an opportunity for personal advantage.

It is worth mentioning that the ways in which exposures of abuse contribute to healthy government are not limited to liberal democracies. Even in relatively authoritarian regimes where ordinary citizens have little to say about who makes up the government, the threat of exposure can restrain officials from personal abuses of office. In fact, in some countries, such as Yugoslavia, where selection for office remains largely the responsibility of a single party and proposals for complete change of that social system are beyond bounds, press criticism of official inadequacies can be quite sharp.

Autonomy: Independence of Judgment and Considerate Decision

By affording people an opportunity to hear and digest competing positions and to explore options in conversations with others, freedom of discussion is thought to promote independent judgment and considerate decision, what might be characterized as *autonomy*.[15] This is the consequentialist argument that connects free speech to autonomy.

This claim, as I mean to consider it here, is not true by definition. If freedom of speech failed to bring the range of relevant considerations before people as effectively as would a structure of discourse controlled by government or if, despite opportunities to converse and exposure to various relevant points of view, people in a regime of free speech passively followed the opinions of persons in authority or decided on the basis of irrational passions, then freedom of speech would not promote autonomy in this sense. The factual premises of the claim about autonomous decisions are that, when all ideas can be expressed, people will be less subject in their decisions to the dictates of others, and that they will be encouraged to exercise this independence in a considerate manner that reflects their fullest selves. The supposition is not that freedom of speech will actually produce fully autonomous persons or even that it will produce people who are by some measure more autonomous than not; the claim is only that people will be *more* autonomous under a regime of free speech than under a regime of substantial suppression.

I shall not attempt to establish the claimed factual links. Any attempt to do so convincingly faces severe difficulties. It is very hard to compare degrees of autonomy among citizens of different societies, and whether a country enjoys free speech is only one of many relevant cultural factors. Moreover, it is possible that a certain kind of freedom lulls people into a passive acceptance of things as they are, whereas stark suppression forces them to focus on their values. In support of the dangers of the "repressive tolerance" of freedom, it is sometimes remarked that political discussions at the dinner table in countries tending toward totalitarianism have a liveliness that is lacking in liberal democracies. On the other hand, lively conversation is sometimes an outlet for those incapable of making choices that influence events, and the liveliness of ordinary conversation under the most oppressive regimes, such as Nazi Germany, was certainly not great. Matters of degree are important here, and confidence in generalizations must be modest, but I think we are warranted in believing that government control of communication usually tends to induce unreflective reliance on authority and that, if one regards societies in history, comparative autonomy of individuals is linked to relative freedom of opinion.

If one grants that free speech contributes to autonomy, there is still the question of why independence of judgment and considerate decision are good. It may be believed that those who decide for themselves and in a rational manner are acting in a more distinctly human and intrinsically better way than those who passively submit to authority; these personal qualities will then be valued for their own sakes. The qualities may also be means of achieving other values. For example, despite the burden of anxiety that often accompanies serious personal choice, many people can work out for themselves a style of life that is more fulfilling than what they could achieve by simply conforming to standards set by others. Both the valuation of autonomy for its own sake and the belief that it contributes to other satisfactions are aspects of traditional liberal theory.

Emotional Outlet, Personal Development, and Sense of Dignity

The practice of free speech enhances in various other ways the lives of those who seek to communicate. For the speaker, communication is a crucial way to relate to others; it is also an indispensable outlet for emotion and a vital aspect of the development of one's personality and ideas.[16] The willingness of others to listen to what one has to say generates self-respect. Limits on what people can say curtail all these benefits. If the government declares out of bounds social opinions that a person firmly holds or wishes to explore, he is likely to suffer frustration and affront to his sense of dignity.

Because communication is so closely tied to our thoughts and feelings, suppression of communication is a more serious impingement on our personalities than many other restraints of liberty; but some noncommunicative restraints, for example, those relating to sexual involvements or drug use, may equally impair personal self-expression in a broad sense. An argument based on the value of liberty as an emotional outlet and means of personal development is not restricted to speech alone. Indeed, it may reach widely and strongly enough to some other matters so that alone it would not warrant anything properly identified as a distinctive principle of free speech. But if a principle of free speech is supportable on other grounds, this justification does provide an extra reason why speech should not be prohibited and, may help determine what the boundaries of protected speech should be.

Liberal Democracy

I turn now to arguments from democracy, which have been said in a comparative study to be the "most influential . . . in the development of twentieth-century free speech law."[17] Here, I consider the claim that free speech contributes importantly to the functioning of liberal democracy and to the values it serves.

This claim is largely reducible to reasons I have already discussed as those reasons apply to political discourse and decisions and to the participation of people in the political process. A liberal democracy rests ultimately on the choices of its citizens. Free speech can contribute to the possibility that they and their representatives can grasp truths that are significant for political life, it can enhance identification and accommodation of interests, and it can support wholesome attitudes about the relations between officials and citizens.[18] Government officials are especially to be distrusted in deciding what political messages may be heard, because of their interest in staying in office and in promoting the political ideas in which they believe. And government suppression of political messages is particularly dangerous because it can subvert the review of ordinary political processes which might serve as a check on other unwarranted suppression.[19] I have already mentioned the notion of unrestrained speech as a check on abuse of office; since citizens' votes are essential in a liberal democracy, the importance of their being informed of government misconduct is particularly great under that form of government. It has long been assumed, though it is perhaps hard to prove, that a better-informed citizenry will yield a better government and better political decisions.[20]

Whether participation in the political order is deemed uniquely important for people or one among many opportunities for realizing participatory values, that participation can be more autonomous if relevant information and arguments are available, and a regime of free speech may help develop the kinds of self-reliant, courageous citizens that Justice Brandeis holds up as an ideal in his opinion in *Whitney* v. *California*.[21] Finally, the healthy sense that one is participating as an equal citizen is enhanced if what one believes about politics can be communicated, and speech about injustice can help relieve frustration about an undesired course of political events.

Because a decent political process and informed decision-making by citizens are such critical aspects of a model of liberal democracy, and because government suppression of political ideas is so likely to be misguided, the application of a principle of freedom of speech to political affairs is centrally important. The sorts of underlying consequentialist reasons for freedom are not radically different for political speech from those for speech about nonpolitical facts and values, but these reasons take on extra weight when political matters are involved.

Promoting Tolerance

It has been suggested, in a thoughtful recent book by Lee Bollinger, that the main modern justification for a principle of free speech is its capacity to promote tolerance.[22] The basic idea is that if we are forced to acknowledge the right of detested groups to speak, we are taught the lesson that we should be tolerant of the opinions and behavior of those who are not like us. Almost certainly the core of Bollinger's claim is true; living in a regime of free speech helps teach tolerance of many differences, just as living in a regime of religious liberty helps teach tolerance of religious diversity. But it does not follow either that promoting tolerance is now the primary justification for free speech or that attention to tolerance should play the critical role in decisions whether to restrict speech.

If it is true that people in liberal societies have so internalized a norm of free speech that traditional justifications are no longer extensively argued and if the potential acts of suppression these justifications cover most strongly are not even attempted, that does not mean these justifications have somehow been supplanted by the aim of promoting toleration. And, even if Dean Bollinger is right that the tolerance justification has more force than any other for the extremist destructive speech of the Nazis, it is not the primary justification for many other forms of speech. Given the assumption that broad tolerance of how others live can be encouraged in different ways, it is doubtful that one would introduce and defend a principle of freedom of speech in the absence of other more basic justifications, and it is questionable whether a persuasive argument against particular suppression can be grounded mainly in the tolerance justification.[23]

NONCONSEQUENTIALIST JUSTIFICATIONS

Not all arguments for free expression rest on desirable consequences; some liberal conceptions of the relationship between state and citizen may suggest a liberty of citizens to express opinions which is independent of the likely consequences of prohibition. As the phrase "liberal conceptions" implies, these justifications draw more distinctly on characteristic value premises of liberal theory than do the consequentialist justifications, though embedded in many of the latter are common liberal assumptions about facts and values.

Social Contract Theory: Consent and the Private Domain

The Anglo-American tradition of liberal democracy has historically been linked to a theory of social contract, which grounds the legitimacy of the state in the consent of the governed and establishes significant limits on the authority of government. According to John Locke, whose views greatly influenced the revolutionary generation of Americans, the legitimate authority of government is based on consent and is limited to the protection of rights and interests that individuals could not adequately safeguard.[24] Individuals entering into a social contract consent to government power to secure their lives, liberty, and property, but they do not give the state authority to interfere in other domains. In his *Letter Concerning Toleration*, Locke employs this analysis to put control of religious beliefs and expressions outside the ambit of secular authority, but his conclusions have broader implications, reaching all states of mind and activities that do not threaten interference with the limited aims a government may permissibly have.

Locke apparently supposed that at some early age in history people actually entered into a social contract. That is implausible, but his theory can be interpreted in a hypothetical way, as indicating what form and purposes of government individuals leaving a state of nature would consent to. To be morally legitimate a government needs to take this form and pursue only the prescribed purposes. Even in this hypothetical version, the theory is now highly controversial, because it posits individuals outside of organized society with needs, desires, talents, and property. Such an approach pays insufficient regard to the extent to which human nature and human purposes are themselves determined by organized society, and it underestimates the positive contributions society and government can make to human flourishing. Still, the ideas that government should take a form to which people do or would consent and that it should do only those things which people need it to do (or which it is uniquely suited to accomplish) retain a powerful appeal in liberal societies. The implications of these ideas reach far beyond speech, but they have considerable relevance for speech as well.

I shall focus first on the conditions of consent. No doubt, valid consent to something can often be based on less than full information, but a problem arises when the authority that seeks consent also controls the available information. If someone asks my agreement to a course of action, then actively conceals much relevant information that would affect my judgment, my "consent" is of lessened or no effect. Under social contract theory, a government is legitimate only if it receives or warrants consent from the people under it. It may be debated exactly what conditions are required for valid actual consent or for the hypothetical consent of persons whose nature and social condition fit some model.[25] However, a claim of actual consent would certainly be undermined if information highly relevant to evaluation of the government was systematically suppressed; and rational actors in some idealized setting could not be expected to give valid consent in such circumstances and would be unlikely to approve in advance a regime that would conceal such information from actual citizens.[26] Thus, the idea that government should be of a kind that people would consent to and the idea that actual citizens should have the opportunity to consent to the legitimacy of their governments underlie a substantial argument against the suppression of political ideas and facts, even when a present majority approves that suppression.

I turn now to the notion of limited government. That notion most obviously constrains what can count as harms and as proper purposes for a liberal society. Suppressing expressions of belief simply to prevent mistakes about religion or aesthetics would not, for example, constitute a proper purpose. And the propriety of suppressing obscenity because it tends to make those who look at it unhappy would be doubtful, since liberal governments should not often be protecting individuals against themselves. Although I do not develop in this book any full theory about the limits of government, I do identify situations in which arguments about suppression of speech rest on contested claims about those limits.

Most claims in favor of prohibiting speech in modern Western societies do not rest on asserted harms that are controversial in this way, perhaps partly because critical assumptions about the limits of government are deeply entrenched. Usually the harm that is to be avoided by prohibiting speech is a harm that a liberal government undoubtedly can try to prevent. But questions about limits on governmental power may remain. These are more subtle questions about remoteness of cause and about the extent to which the government may interfere in a normally private realm to accomplish concededly valid objectives. To take an extreme case, imagine a proposal that, because the attitude of racial prejudice generates the social harm of racial discrimination,[27] the government should undertake compulsory psychological conditioning to erase that attitude from individuals who have it. Almost everyone would agree that such an interference with the private domain would be unacceptable, and many would say that the connection between private thought and harmful act is too remote or indirect to warrant social control[28] even though the government's ultimate objective is appropriate.[29] Similar concerns would be raised if, instead of trying to control thoughts themselves, the government forbade all expressions of racial prejudice. The communication of attitudes would be regarded as closer to the private domain of having the attitudes than to the public domain of acting upon the attitudes in a socially unacceptable way.

In summary, we can think of the traditional idea of limited government as operating at two levels in respect to free speech: as setting some constraints on appropriate governmental objectives and as requiring that the connection between prohibited speech and social harm be reasonably direct. Although social contract theory cannot plausibly be thought to yield the conclusion that all communication must be left untouched by government prohibition, the theory may illuminate some inhibitions on government interference with private individuals.

Recognition of Autonomy and Rationality

Respect for individual autonomy may curb interference with expression. In my treatment of consequentialist justifications, I have already suggested how speech can contribute to the development of autonomous individuals. Here I focus on two related nonconsequentialist arguments for the view that the government should treat people as it would treat autonomous persons. Of course, every governmental prohibition of action interferes with free choice and, therefore, with the *exercise* of autonomy. If autonomy is to undergird a principle of freedom of speech, a notion of autonomy is required which has some special relation to communication and which helps draw lines between permissible and impermissible regulation.

The most straightforward claim is that the government should always treat people as rational and autonomous by allowing them to have all the information and all the urging to action that might be helpful to a rational, autonomous person making a choice. This claim focuses on the autonomy of the recipient of communication. As Thomas Scanlon has put it, an "autonomous person cannot accept without independent consideration the judgment of others as to what he should believe or what he should do."[30] As we shall see in more detail later, a principle that the government should always treat its citizens as autonomous would not necessarily lead to freedom for every kind of communication—outright lies and subliminal manipulation may not contribute to autonomous choice and might be restricted. But a strong version of a principle that the government must always treat citizens as autonomous by maximizing opportunities for informed choice would be powerfully protective of many kinds of speech.

The difficulty with the principle in this strong form lies in its implausibility. The government must protect citizens from social harms, and many fellow citizens do not act in a rational and autonomous way. If some communications are especially likely to lead irrational people to do harmful things, why must the government permit them access to those communications as if they were rational and autonomous, rather than protect potential victims of their irrational actions? Few suppose that compulsory commitment of insane people who are demonstrably dangerous to others is a violation of liberal government; we cannot rule out in advance the possibility that the government may regulate communications in a manner that takes account of frequent deviations from an ideal of autonomy.

Further, a deep ambiguity lurks in the concept of rationality and autonomy. Does a rational and autonomous person always act with appropriate regard for the interests of others, or might such a person pursue his own interests unjustly at the expense of others? I do not want to explore here the complex question of whether rationality and autonomy imply acceptance of all valid moral claims. If it is supposed that the rational autonomous person always acts morally, then such a person can be trusted with as complete information and as much urging to action as is possible. In that event the only worry about treating actual people as rational and autonomous is how far people fall short of being rational and autonomous. Matters are more complicated if it is supposed, to the contrary, that rational, autonomous people may freely choose to pursue their own interests immorally. In that case, if rational, autonomous people were given, for example, full information about how to engage in undetectable cheating on their income taxes, many would take advantage of the information by cheating. A principle ensuring full freedom of speech might thus lead to social harms that could be avoided if some information were suppressed. Of course, one might contend that the government's treating people as autonomous is more important than preventing the social harms that would result from full information, but a defense of that position would then be needed.

In an article[31] whose major thesis he no longer defends,[32] Thomas Scanlon developed a somewhat more complex claim about autonomy and expression. He took as a standard for the limits of legitimate government "the powers of a state . . . that citizens could recognize while still regarding themselves as equal, autonomous, rational agents."[33] In this form the claim in favor of treating people as autonomous is grounded in a version of social contract theory that asks what rational autonomous people would agree to. This extra step actually eliminates assurance that the government should treat people as autonomous and rational on every occasion. For the reasons that have just been rehearsed, rational autonomous people deciding on the general limits of government interference would want to protect themselves from harms wrought by irrational people and by rational, immoral people (Scanlon is quite clear that his notion of autonomy and rationality does not guarantee moral action). To protect themselves from those harms, rational autonomous people *might* agree to constraints that would inhibit to some degree the extent to which all citizens, including themselves, would have available information and advocacy that would maximally serve rational and autonomous choice.

In brief, if one asks what limits on government rational autonomous people would set, they might well conclude that the government should not always allow people everything a rational autonomous person would want to have in making a particular choice. And if one simply asserts a principle that the government should never act to inhibit conditions for rational autonomous choice, it is hard to see how that principle could be supported.

What may remain is a less rigorous standard, namely, a premise of liberal democracy that human beings are largely rational and autonomous and should be treated as such.[34] That a proposed prohibition would not treat people in this manner counts against it, and prohibitions that do not respect autonomy may call for especially careful review of possible justifications.

Dignity and Equality

A justification for free speech which is closely related to the points just made but which focuses on the speaker more than on his or her listeners is the idea that the government should treat people with dignity and equality. As a matter of basic human respect we may owe it to each other to listen to what each of us has to say, or at least not to foreclose the opportunity to speak and to listen. Under this view, suppression represents a kind of contempt for citizens that is objectionable regardless of its consequences, and when suppression favors some points of view over others, it may be regarded as failing to treat citizens equally.

How to take this argument depends on whether any infringement of liberty impairs dignity and on whether any infringement that is significantly selective impairs equality. Many actions that people would like to engage in must be restricted, and some of these restrictions, e.g., denying the right to practice medicine to those not certified in a prescribed way, are bound to be "selective." The concerns about dignity and equality may seem not to be specially related to speech but to be arguments, perhaps rather weak ones, in favor of liberty generally.

There may, however, be a tighter connection between restrictions on communications and affronts to dignity and equality. Expressions of beliefs and feelings lie closer to the core of our persons than do most actions we perform; restrictions of expression may offend dignity to a greater degree than most other restrictions; and selective restrictions based on the content of our ideas may imply a specially significant inequality. So put, the notion of affront to dignity and equality bears a plausible relationship to free speech, though it also reaches other forms of liberty, such as liberty of sexual involvement and liberty of personal appearance, which lie close to how we conceive ourselves. . . .

THE IMPORT OF THE JUSTIFICATIONS

The nonconsequentialist justifications, like the consequentialist ones, fall short of setting clear principles that can be confidently applied to decide what practices of suppression are unwarranted. What all these perspectives do provide, however, is a set of considerations, a set of standards for the relation of government to citizens, which help to identify which interferences with expression are most worrisome and which operate as counters, sometimes powerful ones, in favor of freedom.

NOTES

1. This subject is complicated in ways that would demand examination were this not just a preface to a discussion of free speech. Parents may be directly compelled to confer benefits on their children. One argument for forbidding adultery is that it threatens families and the benefits children receive. Other acts might be compelled or forbidden in order that people develop regular habits of behavior that will lead overall to benefits for others. How far the last justification for control of adults is acceptable is something that may separate "liberal" societies from many others.
2. See generally J. Feinberg, *Harm to Others* (New York, Oxford University Press 1984).
3. See F. Schauer, *Free Speech: A Philosophical Enquiry* 5–12 (Cambridge, Cambridge University Press 1982).
4. One might say, to illustrate with an example not involving speech, that any governmental justification for enforced segregation based on violence that might flow from hostility between members of different racial groups should be viewed with extreme suspicion, but that temporary racial segregation in a prison might be warranted after an extensive race riot in which prisoners have been killed.

5. I add this phrase because the costs of administration and other considerations may make it unwise to forbid much behavior that could be forbidden under a minimal principle of liberty.

6. The discussion that follows suggests what I consider the basic premises of liberal democracy. My views on that subject are developed in *Religious Convictions and Political Choice*, especially at 14–29 (New York, Oxford University Press 1988). I do not think that the basic premises of liberal democracy include extreme rationalism, extreme individualism, neutrality among ideas of the good, or exclusive reliance for political choice on shared premises and publicly accessible grounds for determining truth.

7. It is likely that many nonconsequentialist claims rest on deep factual assumptions about human nature; so in this respect the distinction between consequentialist and nonconsequentialist reasons is less sharp than the text indicates. I address this problem in relation to a "natural duty" to obey the law in *Conflicts of Law and Morality* 159 86 (New York, Oxford University Press 1987).

8. For excellent modern discussions, see T. Emerson, "Towards a General Theory of the First Amendment," 72 *Yale Law Journal* 877 86 (1963); J. Feinberg, "Limits to the Free Expression of Opinion," in J. Feinberg and H. Gross, eds., *Philosophy of Law* 217–32 (3d ed., Belmont, Calif., Wadsworth Publishing Co. 1986); T. Scanlon, "Freedom of Expression and Categories of Expression," 40 *University of Pittsburgh Law Review* 519 (1979).

9. J. Milton, *Areopagitica* (London, for Hunter & Stevens 1819).

10. *Abrams* v. *United States*, 250 U.S. 616, 624, 630 (1919) (dissenting opinion).

11. *Whitney* v. *California*, 274 U.S. 357, 372, 377 (1927) (concurring opinion).

12. J. S. Mill, *On Liberty*, in *Three Essays* 22–68 (World Classics ed., London, Oxford University Press 1912) (1st ed. of *On Liberty* 1859).

13. See generally Baker, note 14 supra, at 965–81. See also B. DuVal, "Free Communication of Ideas and the Quest for Truth: Toward a Teleological Approach to First Amendment Adjudication," 41 *George Washington Law Review* 161, 191–94 (1972).

14. See V. Blasi, "The Checking Value in First Amendment Theory," 1977 *American Bar Foundation Research Journal* 521, providing both an account of this rationale for free speech and an argument about its implications.

15. See Richards, note 32 supra, at 167–69. The role of free speech in protecting those who "speak out against . . . existing institutions, habits, customs, and traditions" is stressed by Steven Shiffrin, *The First Amendment, Democracy, and Romance*, Ch. 2 (to be published).

16. See generally Baker, note 14 supra, at 966; Emerson, note 21 supra, at 879–80; Redish, note 12 supra, at 20–30. As these writings reflect, consequentialist arguments in respect to personality development and autonomy are not sharply distinct.

17. E. Barendt, *Freedom of Speech* 23 (Oxford, Clarendon Press 1985).

18. See generally A. Meiklejohn, *Political Freedom* (New York, Harper & Brothers 1960).

19. This, it seems to me, is the main reason why the fact of a majority vote to suppress is not sufficient. Even a majority should not be able to undermine the conditions for a fair political process. See, e.g., J. Ely, *Democracy and Distrust* 105–36 (Cambridge, Mass., Harvard University Press 1980).

20. This conclusion does not itself depend on a presumed equality of all citizens. Even if some citizens could not vote, as women in the past could not vote, or if citizens had weighted votes, there would still be strong reasons for each citizen to be as fully informed as possible.

21. See V. Blasi, "The First Amendment and the Ideal of Civic Courage: The Brandeis Opinion in *Whitney* v. *California*," 29 *William and Mary Law Review* 653 (1988).

22. L. Bollinger, *The Tolerant Society* (New York, Oxford University Press 1986). The book leaves some doubt about how far more traditional justifications that lie in the background still have force and how far the tolerance justification applies to matters other than dissenting and extremist speech. For a thorough and perceptive review of the book, see V. Blasi, 87 *Columbia Law Review* 387 (1987).

23. See P. Schlag, "Freedom of Speech as Therapy," 34 *University of California in Los Angeles Law Review*, 265, 281–82 (1986). One of the great strengths of Bollinger's book is its illuminating analysis of the dimensions of tolerance. Since too much tolerance, as Bollinger recognizes, presents social dangers of its own, the use of tolerance to decide whether to suppress is troublesome.

24. John Locke, [Second] *Treatise of Civil Government* and *A Letter Concerning Toleration*, ed. Charles L. Sherman (New York, D. Appleton-Century Co. 1937) (1st eds., London 1690 and 1689, respectively). Garry Wills, in *Inventing America* (Garden City, N.Y., Doubleday & Co. 1978), suggests that the influence of the less individualist Scottish "common sense" philosophy was greater than has been commonly realized.

25. As in the original-position analysis of John Rawls. See J. Rawls, *A Theory of Justice* (Cambridge, Mass., Harvard University Press 1971).

26. In considering possible hypothetical consent one needs to think of two stages of consent. The first involves the conditions under which the hypothetical actors consent, the second the conditions under which real people consent in an actual political order. For the first stage, it is hard to imagine any model that permits actively misleading hypothetical actors about actual facts (although they may be in *ignorance* of certain facts, especially relating to their own personal talents and position). But it is conceivable that actors deciding in hypothetical "presocial" conditions might knowingly consent to live in a political regime that would then engage in active suppression of important political ideas. They might do so, for example, if their judgment (as hypothetical rational beings) was that actual people are so irrational and destructive that necessary social solidarity can be achieved only by the government's rigidly controlling opinion. The sentence in the text assumes that their factual judgment would not lead the hypothetical actors to confer on the government such unbounded power over ideas.

27. I am assuming here (what not everyone accepts) that a liberal government can properly prevent "private" racial discrimination in housing and employment.

28. To be more precise, one would need to distinguish children from adults and educational from coercive efforts to influence thoughts. The government's latitude in respect to school children is greater in some respects than its latitude in respect to adults. Even for adults, education to influence thoughts may be warranted. What is objectionable is coercive effort to invade the "private domain."

29. Edwin Baker's "liberty model" for free speech, note 14 supra, at 964, might be regarded as in part an elaboration of an idea of limited government, although Baker does not subscribe to social contract theory.

30. T. Scanlon, "A Theory of Freedom of Expression," 1 *Philosophy & Public Affairs* 204, 215–16 (1972).

31. Id. The article and its claimed connection between freedom of speech and autonomy are perceptively criticized in R. Admur, "Scanlon on Freedom of Expression," 9 *Philosophy & Public Affairs* 287 (1980).

32. See Scanlon, note 21 supra.

33. Scanlon, note 64 supra, at 215.

34. Two writers who place great emphasis on respect for autonomy are David Richards, note 32 supra, at 85, 169, 183; and Edwin Baker, note 14 supra, at 991.

▷ AN ELECTRONIC SOAPBOX:
COMPUTER BULLETIN BOARDS
AND THE FIRST AMENDMENT

Eric Jensen

INTRODUCTION

Electronic bulletin-board systems are reminiscent of the message board at the grocery store. On a bulletin board, anyone with a computer and a modem may "post" messages, read those left by others, or hold direct conversations via computer. Due to the popularity of personal computers, the boards provide a significant new channel of communication.

Recent publicity involving bulletin boards focuses not on positive aspects, but on actual and potential abuse. Critics of these boards cite their use by extreme political groups, pedophiles, and "hackers" who conspire to steal computer data. Legislative response to this problem has been widespread, as states and the federal government have added provisions covering "computer crime" to their penal codes. To date, no legislature or court has specifically addressed the relationship of bulletin boards to other forms of communication or to the First Amendment.

This Comment first discusses the general nature of bulletin board services. It then summarizes current and proposed regulation which may affect the boards, focusing upon laws aimed at pornographic speech and computer crime. The final section of the Comment addresses the extent of First Amendment protection for messages left on bulletin boards. This involves balancing individual rights of free speech with governmental interests in preventing crime and protecting citizens from indecency. Assuming that a message may validly be prohibited, the Comment examines the proper standard of liability for the operator of the board. In this context the bulletin board is compared to other media and other "associations." Throughout, the Comment attempts to provide a coherent framework for First Amendment analysis of a unique communications medium.

BULLETIN BOARD SERVICES

Nature and Extent of Bulletin Boards

If one has a personal computer, gaining access to a computer bulletin board is as easy as dialing a phone number. The phone links your computer with that of someone with the software and hardware to enable his computer to act as a bulletin board. This "system operator" can place information on the board for users. In this way the bulletin board is similar to a database such as LEXIS or WESTLAW. Unlike these systems, however, the user can also leave information. In addition, the bulletin board allows instantaneous electronic conversations which, depending upon the sophistication of the system, can occur between two or two hundred people. This feature is similar to the services known as "electronic mail." Essentially, the bulletin board is a conduit for many different types of computer communication. The operator has ultimate, but not immediate, control over this conduit; he can turn the board on or off and delete messages, but cannot practically prescreen the messages.

The computer bulletin board market today is unregulated, as a result of a series of Federal Communications Commission (FCC) rulings which defined FCC authority under the Communications Act of 1934. The Act itself authorized the FCC to regulate interstate commerce by wire or radio. Title II of the Act regulated common carriers and Title III regulated broadcasters. The Act also regulated nonbroadcast users such as citizens band and ship radio.

In response to the increasing complexity and overlap of communications systems in the 1970s, the FCC redefined its authority in a series of rulings. The *Second Computer Inquiry*, initiated in 1976, established the current analytical framework. The *Second Computer Inquiry* distinguished between regulated, "basic" services, and unregulated, "enhanced" services. Basic service, which could only be offered by common carriers, was defined as the offering of "a pure transmission capability over a communications path that is virtually transparent in terms of its interaction with customer supplied information." Enhanced service "combined basic service with computer processing applications that act on the format, content, code, protocol or similar aspects of the subscriber's transmitted information, or provide the subscriber additional, different or restructured information, or involve subscriber interaction with stored information." The FCC specifically mentioned bulletin board-type services as one of the enhanced services resulting from new technology.

The unregulated nature of the bulletin board market allows anyone with approximately $2500 and some computer knowledge to start up a board. This low cost is one reason why there are between 3,500 and 4,500 active bulletin boards in the nation. The nature of these boards varies tremendously. Many of the boards are operated as a hobby and are open to anyone without charge. In contrast, to use a large commercial bulletin board such as CompuServe, one must be a subscriber. The subscriber pays a fee and is given an identification number and the password needed to access the system. These commercial boards are the most widely used; for example, in 1985 CompuServe had over 250,000 members. Finally, there are an increasing number of boards with very limited access. On these private boards the operator checks the background of each potential user before issuing a password. Unless one knows the operator, even the board's phone number is difficult to obtain. Some boards have both public and private attributes: Anyone can gain access to the open levels of the board, but only those known to the operator have the passwords needed for other portions of the board.

Computer bulletin boards cover a variety of topics. While computers are probably the most popular subject, there are boards for Fortune 500 executives, couples in search of a date or a racy conversation, extremists on the left, and right, devout Christians, U.F.O. enthusiasts, psychiatric patients, and even lawyers. The diversity of interests and the large number of boards indicate that the goal of a free market in the supply of communications has been better achieved with bulletin boards than in the newspaper or broadcasting industry. For very little, anyone with any message can reach the entire country and have the country reach him.

Despite the number and diversity, only a small minority of the people in the U.S. currently use computer bulletin boards. One important question, then, concerns potential demand for this new method of communication. In France, the government provides a service similar to bulletin boards, called "Teletel." The program began in 1983—when the government distributed the terminals necessary to use the service— and has been very popular. In December 1985 alone, over 22 million calls were logged. A widely used feature is the bulletin board "Le Kiosque," on which users can read news stories from the Paris papers, leave want ads and converse with friends. This success abroad, coupled with the conviction of U.S. companies that "videotex" has a huge market here, indicates that the computer bulletin board is a medium with much potential.

In summary, bulletin boards are more than just the newest high technology gimmick. A board has three unique characteristics: (1) the cost to start a system is much less than in other media, yet each bulletin board has a national reach; (2) it offers instant, multiple, interactive communication; and (3) the "conversation" it allows is written and anonymous.

The results from low cost are clear. One commentator has stated that "the technology brings back the era of the pamphleteer." The results of (2) and (3) are not as immediate. For some, the boards offer an opportunity to know and be known by a nationwide circle, a process called "networking." Written conversation favors the witty turn of phrase, not the loudest voice. The instant interaction allows board communication to avoid the fate of the well written, but slow moving letter. Finally, anonymity allows the timid to flower: identity, appearance, possibly even personality, become unimportant.

Bulletin Board Abuse

One issue raised by those concerned with the rise in the number of bulletin boards is their use for pornographic conversations. The Meese Commission Report on Pornography cites the example of one such service, known as "SEXTEX." This service allows users to conduct conference calls with unlimited parties, to shop for sexual material, and to leave personal ads for others. The Meese Commission also raised what it saw as a more serious problem: the 1984 ban on the selling of child pornography had created an underground "cottage industry" in the material. The Commission found that computer networks were becoming an increasingly significant part of this new industry.

Despite recent publicity concerning bulletin board pornography, the most prevalent abuse of bulletin boards involves "computer crime." This term can encompass such activities as the unauthorized copying of a computer program, theft of long distance access codes, and entry into government or private computers by teenage "hackers" or disgruntled employees. Whatever the particular type of crime, the overall problem is significant. An American Bar Association Task Force on Computer Crime recently estimated that the annual loss caused by computer crime was between $145 and $730 million. While bulletin boards are usually not directly involved in any of these crimes, they are used to receive and distribute information by the computer enthusiasts who commit the illegal acts.

CURRENT REGULATION OF BULLETIN BOARD ACTIVITIES

While the market for bulletin boards is unregulated, messages left on the boards are subject to restriction. Pornographic messages, while not yet limited by statutes aimed specifically at bulletin boards, can be limited under a number of existing regulations. Messages aiding in criminal activity have been more extensively addressed by legislatures; both the user and the operator of the board are subject to liability in different circumstances.

Regulation Aimed at Pornographic Conversations

In October 1986, Congress passed a law aimed at the use of children in pornography. It punished:

> Any person who . . . knowingly makes, prints, or publishes, or causes to be made, printed or published, any notice or advertisement seeking or offering—
> (A) to receive, exchange, buy, produce, display, distribute, or reproduce, any visual depiction, if the production of such depiction involves the use of a minor engaging in sexually explicit conduct . . .
> (B) participation in any act of sexually explicit conduct by or with any minor for the purpose of producing such a visual depiction of such conduct.

The legislative history mentions computer bulletin board users as one of the targets of the statute, but is unclear if the board operator could be held liable as well.

Another federal statute applicable to bulletin board conversations is Title 47, United States Code, § 223. This statute punishes anyone making an interstate phone call which is "obscene, lewd, lascivious, filthy, or indecent." The law was originally directed at punishing those making harassing phone calls, and therefore punishing aural communication. Yet the statutory language encompasses any use of the telephone and thus would appear to include even electronic computer communication. In addition to the federal law, many states have statutes prohibiting similar conduct.

In 1983, Section 223 was amended to cover "dial-a-porn" services. While not intended to apply to bulletin boards, the amended portions seem applicable to bulletin board operators whose boards are used by minors. It states:
Whoever knowingly—

> (A) . . . by means of a telephone, makes (directly or by recording device) any obscene or indecent communication for commercial purposes to any person under eighteen years of age . . . regardless of whether the maker of such communication placed the call; or
> (B) permits any telephone facility under such person's control to be used for an activity prohibited by subparagraph (A) shall be fined not more than $50,000 or imprisoned not more than six months, or both.

Finally, computer bulletin board messages might also be regulated under the federal and state provisions prohibiting distribution, transportation, and publishing of obscene materials. Application of these statutes would require a determination that electronic transmissions are "materials" and that posting on a bulletin board is the definition of distributing or publishing.

Despite the publicity concerning pornography and the number of statutes seemingly applicable to bulletin board conversations, as yet there have been no prosecutions for the posting of sexually-oriented messages. Thus, actual liability of board users and operators remains unsettled.

Regulations Aimed at Computer Crime

The threat of computer crime has been extensively addressed on both the federal and state level. Forty-five states have passed laws designed to punish the high technology criminal. These laws cover four areas: (1) unauthorized access or attempted access to computer systems; (2) theft or damage to data or to computer equipment; (3) use of the computer to defraud, specifically the use of telephone services without payment; and (4) unauthorized publishing of telephone credit card codes. The recently passed Computer Fraud and Abuse Act of 1986 significantly extends earlier federal jurisdiction over computer crime. It punishes any trespass with intent to defraud in a "federal interest computer," defined as: (1) any computer used exclusively by the federal government; or (2) by any financial institution; or (3) "which is one of two or more computers used in committing the offense, not all of which are located in the same state." The statute also contains a provision aimed specifically at bulletin boards, making it a misdemeanor to publish any computer password.

While the state statutes covering computer crime vary in form, their aims are similar. This Comment will use California law as an example, as it is among the most recent and comprehensive. California Penal Code § 502 clearly includes the users of computer bulletin boards. It punishes anyone "who intentionally accesses [a] computer network for the purposes of (1) devising or executing any scheme or crime to defraud or extort, or (2) obtaining money, property or services with false or fraudulent intent." As a method of communication, the bulletin board is an aid to conspiracy, both for computer-related and common crimes. In addition, under California law a board user who disseminates certain types of information can be punished for this act alone. Such material includes credit card numbers and codes, and copyrighted materials such as computer programs.

There have been several well publicized cases involving prosecutions for bulletin board related crime. In New Jersey, seven youths were arrested for conspiring to exchange credit card numbers, instructions for making explosives, and information that would allow the defendants to change the position of communication satellites. Four of the defendants were bulletin board operators, and the conspiracy consisted of information exchanged over the boards. There have been other cases involving bulletin boards used to harass or to extort money from other users. Since many of these cases involve juvenile defendants, the authorities have been reluctant to prosecute. This has delayed the development of case law in the area.

While it is clear that computer crime statutes can be used to punish bulletin board users, the liability of board operators has not been determined. California Penal Code, Section 502 would seem to apply to an operator only if he intentionally aids a crime. Section 502.7, which punishes the publishing of credit card numbers, also requires either intent to commit the crime or reason to believe that a crime will be committed. The arrest of a Mr. Tcimpidis in Los Angeles is the only known case involving an operator charged with a crime solely because of the information posted on his board. Mr. Tcimpidis denied knowledge of the stolen credit card number and charges were later dropped for lack of evidence.

The definition of "intent" in such circumstances is crucial. Even if an operator is not aware of a particular message, does his lack of monitoring in general create an implied consent to illegal postings? California cases do not supply a definitive answer, but it appears that a board operator cannot be found liable without some evidence that he was aware of or encouraged the crime.

While Mr. Tcimpidis was never tried, the case has had an impact on bulletin board activity. Many boards became private because operators feared liability for anything put on their boards. In addition, operators began to monitor the messages left by users.

Direct Regulation of Bulletin Boards

No statutes currently exist which directly regulate or license computer bulletin boards. Potential regulations would likely aim at eliminating the anonymous character of bulletin boards by requiring the operator to know the names of all users and to provide this list to authorities. Enforcing this proposal, or one aimed at licensing the bulletin board operators, would be frustrated by the characteristics of bulletin boards. Board software is inexpensive, and a bulletin board can be operated and accessed from any phone. If the operator limited users, detecting boards in violation of licensing or other regulations would be virtually impossible. In essence, licensing requirements would cause hobbyist boards to go underground. Only the few boards operated by companies with the resources to comply with regulations would remain public. Given the difficulties of enforcement, the government is unlikely to enact direct regulation.

Law Enforcement Monitoring of Bulletin Boards

One obvious response to the illegal use of bulletin boards is to monitor them. However, the tapping of boards by law enforcement authorities raises issues of privacy. An extensive discussion of these issues is beyond the scope of this Comment, but legislative or judicial determinations in this area do have an impact on the First Amendment status of bulletin boards.

Recently, Congress amended Title 3 of the 1968 Omnibus Crime Control and Safe Streets Act to specifically include "electronic communications" and "electronic communication systems." The law made it a felony to intercept the type of electronic signals used in communicating with bulletin boards. Court approval is now necessary before the government can gain access, and it is illegal for the board operator to divulge the content of messages other than to the person sending the message or the intended recipient. However, the law exempted from coverage communications "made through an electronic communication system that is configured so that such electronic communication is readily accessible to the general public." It is unclear how this will be applied to bulletin boards. For example, is a board which requires one to subscribe and pay a fee for the password "accessible to the general public?" While this statute indicates increased protection for computer communication, it is uncertain how it will affect bulletin boards which range in size from 25 to 250,000 users.

CONSTITUTIONAL FRAMEWORK

The First Amendment provides that: "Congress shall make no law respecting an establishment of religion, or prohibiting the free exercise thereof; or abridging the freedom of speech, or of the press; or the right of the people peacefully to assemble, and to petition the Government for a redress of grievances."

While certainly never envisioned by the writers of the First Amendment, speech on computer bulletin boards is entitled to protection under it. Analysis of the constitutional protection accorded bulletin board messages will focus upon two types of government regulation: rules aimed at obscene or pornographic messages, and those prohibiting bulletin board messages which aid criminal activity. Liability of both the message poster and the board operator will be considered. The context of bulletin board speech will also be closely examined, as it determines the governmental interest involved in regulation. Throughout this section, rights of privacy, press, and association are considered, as all can influence the degree of speech protection.

Punishing Posters for Their Speech

The Effect of a Right of Privacy In *Stanley* v. *Georgia*, the Supreme Court reversed a conviction for possession of obscenity where the material was discovered in the defendant's home. Although obscenity is not generally protected by the First Amendment, the Court found that there was a "fundamental . . . right to be free, except in very limited circumstances, from unwanted governmental intrusions into one's privacy." Material in the home did not present the danger that obscenity would be viewed by minors or an unwilling general public, as might occur with public distribution.

Later cases have limited the *Stanley* right of privacy to the "home area." In *United States* v. *Orito*, the Court considered a prosecution under Title 18, United States Code, § 1462 for interstate transportation of obscenity. The material was shipped for private use. The Court rejected the notion of First Amendment protection for private materials in general. It stated that "Congress may regulate on the basis of the natural tendency of material in the home being kept private and the contrary tendency once the material leaves that area, regardless of a transporter's professed intent."

In a strict physical sense, the users of a bulletin board are within the protected "home" zone of privacy. Although the messages themselves leave this zone, it is clear that for Fourth Amendment purposes they are considered "private" communications. Hence the right of privacy might arguably protect even obscene speech on a bulletin board. Yet the mailed material in *Orito* was also private for search and seizure purposes. Given *Orito* and other cases, speech on bulletin boards will likely be given no more First Amendment protection than any "public" speech.

Obscene and Pornographic Messages When the content of bulletin board speech is judged by the standards applicable to public speech, obscene messages clearly can be prohibited absolutely. The current test for obscenity was articulated in *Miller* v. *California*:

> (a) whether the 'average person applying contemporary community standards' would find that the work, taken as a whole, appeals to the prurient interest; (b) whether the work depicts or describes, in a patently offensive way, sexual conduct specifically

defined by the applicable state law; and (c) whether the work, taken as a whole, lacks serious literary, artistic, political, or scientific value.

While developed to regulate a "work" such as a book or movie, the *Miller* test has also been applied to "conversations" similar to that occurring on a bulletin board. Some of the statutes governing bulletin boards discussed in Part II, however, go beyond obscene speech. In regulating sex-related, but not obscene speech, the Supreme Court has emphasized the particular context of the material.

The context of child pornography has made it particularly appropriate for regulation. *New York* v. *Ferber* upheld a conviction for distribution of material depicting children engaging in sexual conduct. The statute in *Ferber* regulated child pornography which would not be classified as obscene under the *Miller* standard. However, the Court upheld the statute, ruling that in the case of child pornography, a showing of obscenity was not required. It stated that the state's compelling interest in protecting children used in such pornography would not be achieved by prohibiting only obscene speech.

The Court's focus on the welfare of the child led to a limited holding in *Ferber*: "We note that distribution of descriptions of other depictions of sexual conduct, not otherwise obscene, which do not involve live performance or photographic or other visual reproduction of live performances, retains First Amendment protection." This explicit language permits written discussions occurring on bulletin boards. It is unclear if the child pornography law discussed in Part II is in conformity with *Ferber*, as it applies to written advertisements for the "visual depiction" of sex acts.

However, pornographic material, even if not obscene, is not always accorded full protection under the First Amendment. In a leading case concerning indecent speech and the electronic media, *FCC* v. *Pacifica Foundation*, the Court held that an offensive radio monologue could properly be the subject of sanction by the FCC. Two government interests were articulated: (1) protection of the individual's privacy in his home, which was infringed by the pervasiveness of broadcasting; and (2) protection of young people, as the nature of broadcasting allowed it to be "uniquely accessible to children, even those too young to read." The majority found that this context, coupled with the vulgar and shocking nature of the speech, allowed regulation. However, the language used by the Court to emphasize the narrowness of its holding is particularly applicable to bulletin boards: "this case does not involve a two-way radio conversation between a cab driver and a dispatcher."

In cases following *Pacifica*, the courts have declined to extend its rationale to media other than broadcasting. Both cable television and mail-order advertisements have been held entitled to full First Amendment protection. Computer bulletin boards are also a form of communication in which the *Pacifica* concerns do not weigh heavily. First, although bulletin board messages do come into the home, it takes a conscious decision and a substantial investment on the part of an individual in order for this to occur. Second, given that messages are typed and received on a computer screen, they are not particularly accessible to very young children. Indeed, unless an adult possesses computer expertise, they are inaccessible even to him. While the specialized nature of bulletin boards may change, it cannot at present be characterized as a medium that intrudes, unwanted, into the privacy of the home.

Therefore, a statute punishing bulletin board users for pornographic converations would seemingly infringe on protected speech. This same argument has been raised concerning federal and state statutes that regulate indecent and harassing phone calls. In *Walker* v. *Dillard*, the Fourth Circuit struck down a Virginia statute making it a misdemeanor to "curse or abuse anyone, or use vulgar, profane, threatening or indecent language over any telephone. . . ." It found that the statute was constitutionally overbroad because it punished protected speech. In *Gormley* v. *Director, Connecticut State Dept. of Probation*, the court upheld a similar but more narrowly directed Connecticut statute. The court held that since the statute punished only those who harassed, and intended to harass, others, the statute prohibited conduct, not speech. The statute could be violated without speech occuring at all, and given the "compelling interest in the protection of innocent individuals from fear, abuse or annoyance," any incidental infringement on speech that might occur was permissible. *Walker* and *Gormley* indicate that regulations directed at consensual bulletin board conversations would be invalid.

Recent regulation of "dial-a-porn" activities provides an analogous situation to that of bulletin boards. "Dial-a-porn" involves recorded pornographic messages which callers can listen to for a fee. In determining the scope of regulation, the FCC recognized that the harmful effect of such services on children could not constitutionally justify a complete ban. It cited *Butler* v. *Michigan*, in which the Supreme Court had refused to reduce the adult population to reading only what was fit for children. Thus, the FCC proposed time and manner restrictions to prevent use of the service by minors. In *Carlin Communications, Inc.* v. *FCC*, even these limited restrictions were set aside as not the least intrusive means of achieving the governmental interest. Given *Carlin's* "exacting scrutiny" of the FCC's limited regulation of pornographic speech over the phone, a broader regulation aimed at bulletin board conversation would appear to fatally infringe upon First Amendment rights.

Messages Aiding in Criminal Activity The other governmental regulation aimed specifically at computer bulletin boards involves the prohibition of the posting of credit card numbers and computer passwords. A statute of this type is clearly aimed at the content of the speech, or as Tribe labels it, a "track one" regulation. The "message" that a credit card number provides is the means by which the reader can defraud. The Court has upheld "track one" regulation in some situations. If the speech falls into a definitionally unprotected area such as libel or obscenity, it can be restricted. If not "unprotected," the speech may still be regulated if the statute survives "strict scrutiny."

Advocacy of illegal action is one type of speech found to be unprotected by the First Amendment. *Brandenburg* v. *Ohio* articulates the constitutional test for this type of speech, holding that the state could not punish "except where such advocacy is directed to inciting or producing imminent lawless action and is likely to incite or produce such action."

If this standard is applied to the posting of computer passwords, it is clear that not every posting is directed towards illegal action. Someone may post their password for a friend to use. The federal statute avoids this constitutional problem by requiring a showing of intent to defraud by the person posting the code. However, California punishes posting "with knowledge or reason to believe" that the number will be used illegally. This language is identical to that which was found overbroad by the Washington Court of Appeals in *State* v. *Northwest Passage, Inc.* That case addressed the conviction of a newspaper for its explanation of the coding system used for telephone credit cards. The court found prosecution under this statute akin to punishing a mystery writer if the murder method in his book was used for an actual crime.

Northwest Passage did not focus on the "likelihood" part of the *Brandenburg* test. It appears the court recognized that when credit card numbers are known, the temptation towards their use is such that fraud is highly likely.

Northwest Passage was reversed on appeal to the Washington Supreme Court. The higher court did not analyze the case under an incitement standard, but applied a "strict scrutiny" balancing test similar to that applied in *Widmar* v. *Vincent* to content-based regulation. *Widmar* required that the state prove the regulation was "necessary to serve a compelling state interest and . . . narrowly drawn to achieve that end." In *Northwest Passage* the high court found a compelling state interest in preventing telephone fraud. It held that the statute was limited to achieve that end, as it prohibited neither political speech nor speech of lesser value, only the card numbers themselves. Finally, it found that the state was not required to rely only upon the statute punishing illegal use of credit card numbers since, while less restrictive, it was completely ineffective once the card number had been published.

While the Supreme Court has not considered a case similar to *Northwest Passage*, it appears that its analysis would resemble that of the Washington high court. Once limited to dissemination for the purposes of fraud, it is difficult to justify First Amendment protection for the posting of numbers whose only message is the means by which to steal.

Punishing the Board Operator for Speech by Posters

Distinction Between Press and Other Disseminators An issue equally as important as the protection of the messages of users is the vicarious liability of the operator for those messages. The operator's ultimate control over the contents of the bulletin board has led commentators to compare bulletin boards to other media in order to determine the proper standard of liability. This approach, however, presupposes that a bulletin board can be considered "press." In *Legi-Tech, Inc.* v. *Keiper*, a computerized legislative information retrieval service was denied access to a state-owned computer database containing legislative material. The court treated Legi-Tech as a form of the press, indicating that it was deserving of the same right of access to the state database as any member of the press: "Should New York decide to deny access to [its database] to newspapers and the broadcast media as well as Legi-Tech, that decision would surely face a most hostile scrutiny under the First Amendment." This holding indicates that bulletin boards which provide computerized information to subscribers, as did Legi-Tech, could also be classified as press.

Labeling a computer bulletin board an organ of the press, similar to Legi-Tech, would in some cases give it greater constitutional protection than a nonmedia organization. However, in a recent decision, a majority of the Supreme Court agreed that at least in the context of defamation law, the rights of "the institutional media are no greater and no less than those enjoyed by other individuals or organizations engaged in the same activities." *Dun & Bradstreet, Inc.* v. *Greenmoss Builders, Inc.* involved an erroneous report of bankruptcy sent to the subscribers of a credit reporting agency. The Court agreed that the speech of the agency was not to be judged under the rigorous defamation standard of *New York Times* v. *Sullivan*. The majority based this result on the distinction between speech concerning public and private matters, not a media/nonmedia distinction. The rejection of such a distinction indicates both that a bulletin board need not be classified as "press" in order to warrant First Amendment protection, and that whether or not it is "press," if a board's content concerns private matters, it receives no special treatment.

Operator Liability Compared to That of Other Media   Even if *Dun & Bradstreet* is seen as eliminating the legal distinction between media and private information providers, it is still useful to compare bulletin boards with different types of press. Liability for a publisher, republisher, and common carrier, for the same statement, varies according to the unique characteristics of each medium. As computer bulletin boards have attributes in common with all three, the rationale for a particular standard must be considered in light of this new medium. Therefore, while this section will discuss differing standards of media liability for defamatory or obscene speech, its emphasis is on the attributes of the press, and not particular standards for defamatory or obscene bulletin board statements.

Liability of Publishers

The extent of newspapers' liability for defamatory advertisements was determined in *New York Times* v. *Sullivan*. The Times had been sued by an Alabama police commissioner over an advertisement placed by a civil rights group concerning the response of authorities to protests. The lower courts applied the common law rule that a publication was "libelous per se" if the words tended to injure a person's reputation. If injury was proven, the publisher's only defense was to prove the statements were true. The Supreme Court found that newspapers were entitled to greater protection under the First Amendment, even though, in this case, the advertisement was inaccurate. The constitutional protection accorded speech involving official conduct of public officials required that the plaintiff prove "actual malice," i.e., that the statement was made with knowledge of its falsehood or with reckless disregard for its truth.

While *New York Times* involved an advertisement, in later defamation cases, this fact was not emphasized. By implication, the courts have reasoned that a newspaper has as much control and ability to verify an advertisement as an article. Later cases have applied the *New York Times* standard only to certain types of speech, following the common law rule in many circumstances. However, the Court in these cases clearly has viewed newspapers as having full control over whatever is published. It has applied *New York Times* not to benefit the publisher, but to encourage valued political speech.

In comparison to a newspaper, the operator of a bulletin board has much less control over information "published." The nature of bulletin boards prevents the operator from considering the nature of a message before it is published. An operator's only recourse to the posting of a defamatory message is to remove it. In the context of a newspaper, such a "retraction" would not serve as a defense to a defamation suit. Yet since a board operator lacks prior control, a strong argument can be made that such a retraction standard should not apply.

In summary, the board operator cannot act in the same manner as a publisher. Since the content-based *New York Times* standard requires "malice," it appears equitable to apply it to appropriate bulletin board speech. The stricter common law rule, however, seems inappropriate.

Where the speech itself is not considered harmful, courts have not held newspapers to a strict standard of liability. For example, in *Yuhas* v. *Mudge* a magazine publisher was sued for injuries sustained from fireworks which it advertised. The court found no liability, as the magazine had not guaranteed or endorsed the product. It also cited the New Jersey statute prohibiting unconscionable advertising, which required that the publisher have knowledge of the intent of the advertiser.

The court in *Yuhas* was primarily concerned with the economic effect of making the newspaper an insurer for the actions of advertisers. It found that imposing such a duty "would have a staggering adverse effect on the commercial world and our economic system." Whatever the validity of such an argument in the context of magazines and newspapers, the hobbyist nature of bulletin boards would make such an insurer role impossible. The social benefits from bulletin board speech indicate that a board operator should not pay for all injuries related to the board.

Liability of Republishers

Publishers can be divided into two classes. The first is the original publisher, such as a newspaper or magazine, who is held liable as described above. This category also includes the reporter, editor, and owner of the publication. The second category is the republisher, those persons indirectly involved in the publishing process. This section will focus on the liability of a particular type of republisher, the disseminator. The disseminator circulates, sells, or otherwise deals in the physical embodiment of the published material. He provides a useful analogy since, like a board operator, he has some control over the material that is published, but is not necessarily aware of its content.

In *Smith* v. *California*, the Supreme Court considered a statute imposing absolute liability on a bookseller for his possession of material judged to be obscene. The court invalidated the regulation, reasoning that if the statute was allowed:

> Every bookseller would be placed under an obligation to make himself aware of the contents of every book in his shop. It would be altogether unreasonable to demand so near an approach to omniscience.... The bookseller's limitation in the amount of reading material with which he could familiarize himself, and his timidity in the face of his absolute criminal liability ... would tend to restrict the public's access to forms of the printed word which the state could not constitutionally suppress directly. The bookseller's self-censorship, compelled by the State, would be a censorship affecting the whole public, hardly less virulent for being privately administered.

The Court's approach in *Smith* is a practical one, concerned with the problems of a small bookshop trying to protect itself from suit. Given the generally small-scale nature of bulletin boards, this approach best indicates the actual impact of different standards of liability on the board operators. Just like the bookseller in *Smith*, a bulletin board operator cannot completely prevent illegal speech. The most he can do is monitor the board completely and often. Even this measure may not provide adequate protection. The actions of operators after the publicized *Tcimpidis* case reveal the "chilling" of speech resulting from the threat of strict liability. Many boards became private in order to protect the operator from untrustworthy users and government monitoring.

While *Smith* articulated the problems with a strict liability standard, it specifically refrained from creating a new standard. As interpreted by the lower courts, *Smith* directs that liability for possession of obscenity include some finding of "scienter." Eyewitness proof of the defendant's knowledge has not been found necessary. *Gold* v. *United States* upheld a conviction for transportation of obscenity, holding that circumstances indicated the defendant was aware of the obscene contents of a package when he accepted it from the airline. This type of constructive intent requirement is equally applicable to the operator of a computer bulletin board. While the operator should not be found liable for occasional acts of users, proof that a board is consistently used for illegal activities should be sufficient to impose liability. Although this standard may present problems in application, it strikes a better balance between speech and societal interests than a "scienter" definition requiring that the operator have specific knowledge of the posted message.

Liability of Common Carriers

Traditionally, telephone and telegraph operators, as common carriers, have functioned under a lesser standard of liability for the statements of third persons than have publishers or disseminators. Restatement (Second) of Torts, § 621 states in part:

(1) One who provides a means of publication of defamatory matter published by another is privileged to do so if . . .
(2) A public utility under a duty to transmit messages is privileged to do so, even though it knows the message to be false and defamatory, unless
   (a) the sender of the message is not privileged to send it, and
   (b) the agent who transmits the message knows or has reason to know that the sender is not privileged to publish it.
   [Comment g elaborates:]
   Since it is the user of the telephone rather than the telephone company who is treated as transmitting a telephone message . . . the company is not subject to liability for a defamatory statement communicated by a customer.

Although the courts have expressed various reasons for this common carrier standard, there appear to be three essential policy interests. The first is protecting the right of the people to quick and continued public communication service. This right would be endangered if the utility restricted messages for the fear of liability. The second is enabling the public utility to perform its statutory duty to provide communications to all. This rationale implicitly recognizes the high cost per user if the company monitored and controlled calls to protect itself. Finally, there is the practical recognition that, especially in the case of a telephone transmission, the utility does not control or endorse a message, but merely provides a conduit. It is only when this third rationale is violated, and the utility becomes an intentional transmitter of libelous material, that the courts have imposed liability.

Bulletin boards appear to possess some of the characteristics of a common carrier. The board also provides a conduit for the conversations of others. The conversation may take place over the lines of the phone company, but nonetheless it is the board operator who has allowed the multiple computer interaction that takes place.

It is unlikely, however, that the operator will be accorded the same privilege as a common carrier. Bulletin boards are not viewed as an essential mode of communication as is the phone system. Nor is the operator under a duty to open his board to all, and thus cannot expect the same public privilege. Finally, although bulletin boards may be a conduit for computer messages, the messages remain written on the bulletin board for an indefinite period of time. While an operator may not be able to prescreen a message, he does have an opportunity to delete it. This opportunity allows a greater inference of knowledge on the part of the operator than can be made of the phone company.

In summary, bulletin boards have some of the attributes of publishers, disseminators, and common carriers. The operator of a computer bulletin board may post a message as would an electronic newspaper, but the service he provides is essentially a conduit for the words of others. Yet, the operator does have some control over the conduit. The appropriate constitutional standard should be that applied to those who disseminate material, but do not themselves create it. As applied by such cases as *Gold* v. *United States*, it involves determining in each case whether the facts indicate the operator must have known of the illegal message. Such a constructive intent requirement best serves speech and societal interests.

The Bulletin Board as an Association

The characterization of bulletin boards that is least intuitive, and which requires ignoring the bulletin board metaphor itself, is the designation of a board as an association. People from all across the country gather electronically and exchange views, recipes, or epithets, just as would the local Jaycees. As an association engaged in speech, a bulletin board is entitled to constitutional protection. This right was expressed in *NAACP* v. *Alabama*:

> [I]t is beyond debate that freedom to engage in association for the advancement of beliefs and ideas is an inseparable aspect of the "liberty" assured by the Due Process Clause of the Fourteenth Amendment, which embraces freedom of speech. Of course, it is immaterial whether the beliefs sought to be advanced by association pertain to political, economic, religious or cultural matters, and state action which may have the effect of curtailing the freedom to associate is subject to the closest scrutiny.

The Posters' Rights as Members of an Association In order to enforce the criminal sanctions against illegal speech on a board it is necessary to identify the individual responsible. This is a two step process. First, the bulletin board operator must install a system which "tags" every message with the name of the person leaving it. Second, the bulletin board operator must be required to divulge the names of his users to the authorities. Both of these identification requirements arguably infringe on protected rights of association and speech.

Initially, the board user's right not to use his real name and instead to use "Conan the Librarian," can be labeled a right of anonymity. In *Talley* v. *California*, the Court indicated support for this right, striking down an ordinance which banned any handbill unless it contained the name of the person who wrote, prepared, or manufactured it. The Court did not rule on an ordinance more narrowly aimed at preventing fraud or other conduct, but held that the statute before them would reach speakers whose right not to be identified was protected by the First Amendment.

Gibson v. *Florida Legislative Committee* considered an association's right to refuse to disclose names of its members. A legislative committee had ordered the president of the Miami NAACP to divulge contents of membership and contributor lists in connection with an investigation of Communists in that organization. The Court found that the privacy the NAACP sought to protect was in many cases indispensible to the right of association protected by the Constitution. Therefore the state was required to show "a substantial relation between the information sought and a subject of overriding and compelling state interest" in order to inquire into membership of any legitimate organization. The Court concluded that since there was no proof of a connection between the NAACP and subversive activities, the state could not examine the lists.

Buckley v. *Valeo* illustrates a recent application of the *Gibson* standard. Appellants had challenged disclosure requirements of the Federal Election Campaign Act. The Court found that the requirements served "substantial" government interests in preventing corruption and informing the electorate. This interest was balanced against the deterring effect disclosure might have on political contribution, and found to outweigh any infringement of the First Amendment right to associate politically. In refusing to presume harm to individual rights, the Court required a showing of a "reasonable probability" of chilling speech or of harassment before allowing an exemption from the statute.

The standards of *Gibson* and *Buckley* must be considered in light of the particular traits of computer bulletin boards. The state interest in identifying users is that of preventing the boards from being used for criminal activities. The government could validly argue that no other means would allow detection of those responsible. In assessing the infringement on associational rights, the particulars of the statute are critical. If it required all boards to divulge all users, it would seem to run afoul of the requirement in *Gibson* of a nexus between the organization and illegal activity. Absent clear evidence that an entire board is involved in illegal activity, such a requirement would seem to "chill" speech without closely serving a government interest. A requirement that the board operator divulge the true name of one accused of posting illegal messages, however, would probably be permissible. In weighing the First Amendment infringement, the reach of *Buckley* is critical. If it is extended to areas beyond political contributions, the board users would be required to make a showing of probable harm from disclosure in order to protect membership lists. If such extension does not occur, then the burden is on the state to establish compelling reasons why the names of board members should be made public.

Liability of the Board Operator as Moderator   Treatment of a bulletin board as an association giving users some right to anonymity indicates that the board operator also has rights as the "moderator" of the group. It can be argued that these rights determine the proper standard of operator liability for the messages of his associates.

The Supreme Court has examined vicarious liability of a group's leaders in the context of an economic boycott in Mississippi. In *NAACP* v. *Claiborne Hardware Co.*, it considered a state court holding that the groups involved in the boycott were liable for over one million dollars in losses which were sustained by the merchants. The Supreme Court reversed, finding that peaceful boycotting was protected, and that only liability for damages caused by unlawful acts could be recovered. The Court refused to hold groups such as the NAACP strictly liable for acts by their members:

> Civil liability may not be imposed merely because an individual belonged to a group, some members of which committed acts of violence. For liability to be imposed by reason of association alone, it is necessary to establish that the group itself possessed unlawful goals and that the individual held a specific intent to further those illegal aims.

The Court specifically commented upon the liability of Charles Evers, the NAACP representative involved in the boycott. Evers had made emotional speeches in favor of the boycott, and was unquestionably its primary leader. The Court refused to impute the violence to Evers without a showing that he authorized, directed, or ratified it.

In *Sawyer* v. *Sandstrom*, the Fifth Circuit considered a similar case in which the defendant was held liable for having "the wrong kinds of friends." The defendant was arrested at a pool hall where his associates had openly conducted drug deals. Since there was no showing of participation in a criminal act, the court found that the defendant was being punished for engaging in association. It held that even in such a criminal context, the association was constitutionally protected and the loitering statute at issue overbroad.

If liability of a computer bulletin board operator is determined in accordance with *Claiborne* and *Sawyer*, the operator would rarely be liable for posted messages. The specific intent to further criminal action could not be imputed to the operator merely because he was the operator, or because illegal messages had been posted before. The board operator would "ratify" such individual action only if it was clear that he had knowledge of the illegal message and had not acted to remove it. If evidence was shown of widespread illegal activity on the board, however, then the association could be said to have criminal aims, and as the leader, the operator would be presumed to have the intent to aid such activity.

The association analogy is concededly imperfect. Unlike a group such as the NAACP, computer bulletin board members communicate only through the board. This gives the board operator much more control over an individual's speech than Evers had over the actions of boycotting NAACP members in *Claiborne*. Nonetheless, this focus on speech and other rights in the group context provides a perspective that more closely reflects the role of a bulletin board operator than do traditional press models.

CONCLUSION

Today, computer bulletin boards are associated with juvenile "hackers," who with mischievous intent cause serious problems. Soon, bulletin boards may also be linked with underground rings of pedophiles and pornographers. While it is true that bulletin boards can be misused, the bulletin board itself is a powerful new tool for speaking, listening, and relating. Whatever its future, it is entitled to First Amendment protection appropriate for the speech involved.

Obscene and child-related pornography are valid subjects of regulation. Yet the characteristics of bulletin boards indicate that other sexually related conversations do not create problems that will constitutionally permit regulation. Computer crime is a serious problem, and to the extent that computer bulletin boards are involved, users must be punished to deter such acts. The remedy of holding the operator liable for all messages, however, is neither consistent with the treatment of media in other areas, nor with the standard used to determine the liability of an association's leader. Only an operator who clearly allows or aids in illegal activity on his board should be found at fault. Finally, the board as an "electronic gathering" best describes its psychological and practical function and provides a framework for analysis which respects the First Amendment and the interests of society.

▷ THE MACHINE STOPS

E. M. Forster

PART I

THE AIRSHIP

Imagine, if you can, a small room hexagonal in shape like the cell of a bee. It is lighted neither by window nor by lamp, yet it is filled with a soft radiance. There are no apertures for ventilation, yet the air is fresh. There are no musical instruments, and yet, at the moment that my meditation opens, this room is throbbing with melodious sounds. An armchair is in the center, by its side a reading desk—that is all the furniture. And in the armchair there sits a swaddled lump of flesh—a woman, about five feet high, with a face as white as a fungus. It is to her that the little room belongs.

An electric bell rang.

The woman touched a switch and the music was silent.

"I suppose I must see who it is," she thought, and set her chair in motion. The chair, like the music, was worked by machinery, and it rolled her to the other side of the room, where the bell still rang importunately.

"Who is it?" she called. Her voice was irritable, for she had been interrupted often since the music began. She knew several thousand people; in certain directions human intercourse had advanced enormously.

But when she listened into the receiver, her white face wrinkled into smiles, and she said:

"Very well. Let us talk, I will isolate myself. I do not expect anything important will happen for the next five minutes—for I can give you fully five minutes, Kuno. Then I must deliver my lecture on 'Music during the Australian Period.' "

She touched the isolation knob, so that no one else could speak to her. Then she touched the lighting apparatus, and the little room was plunged into darkness.

"Be quick!" she called, her irritation returning. "Be quick, Kuno; here I am in the dark wasting my time."

But it was fully fifteen seconds before the round plate that she held in her hands began to glow. A faint blue light shot across it, darkening to purple, and presently she could see the image of her son, who lived on the other side of the earth, and he could see her.

"Kuno, how slow you are."

He smiled gravely.

"I really believe you enjoy dawdling."

"I have called you before, Mother, but you were always busy or isolated. I have something particular to say."

"What is it, dearest boy? Be quick. Why could you not send it by pneumatic post?"

"Because I prefer saying such a thing. I want—"

"Well?"

"I want you to come and see me."

Vashti watched his face in the blue plate.

"But I can see you!" she exclaimed. "What more do you want?"

"I want to see you not through the Machine," said Kuno. "I want to speak to you not through the wearisome Machine."

"Oh, hush!" said his mother, vaguely shocked. "You mustn't say anything against the Machine."

"Why not?"

"One mustn't."

"You talk as if a god had made the Machine," cried the other. "I believe that you pray to it when you are unhappy. Men made it, do not forget that. Great men, but men. The Machine is much, but it is not everything. I see something like you in this plate, but I do not see you. I hear something like you through this telephone, but I do not hear you. That is why I want you to come. Come and stop with me. Pay me a visit, so that we can meet face to face, and talk about the hopes that are in my mind."

She replied that she could scarcely spare the time for a visit.

"The airship barely takes two days to fly between me and you."

"I dislike airships."

"Why?"

"I dislike seeing the horrible brown earth, and the sea, and the stars when it is dark. I get no ideas in an airship."

"I do not get them anywhere else."

"What kind of ideas can the air give you?"

He paused for an instant.

"Do you not know four big stars that form an oblong, and three stars close together in the middle of the oblong, and hanging from these stars, three other stars?"

"No, I do not. I dislike the stars. But did they give you an idea? How interesting; tell me."

"I had an idea that they were like a man."

"I do not understand."

"The four big stars are the man's shoulders and his knees. The three stars in the middle are like the belts that men wore once, and the three stars hanging are like a sword."

"A sword?"

"Men carried swords about with them, to kill animals and other men."

"It does not strike me as a very good idea, but it is certainly original. When did it come to you first?"

"In the airship—" He broke off, and she fancied that he looked sad. She could not be sure, for the Machine did not transmit *nuances* of expression. It gave only a general idea of people—an idea that was good enough for all practical purposes, Vashti thought. The imponderable bloom, declared by a discredited philosophy to be the actual essence of intercourse, was rightly ignored by the Machine, just as the imponderable bloom of the grape was ignored by the manufacturers of artificial fruit. Something "good enough" had long since been accepted by our race.

"The truth is," he continued, "that I want to see these stars again. They are curious stars. I want to see them not from the airship, but from the surface of the earth, as our ancestors did, thousands of years ago. I want to visit the surface of the earth."

She was shocked again.

"Mother, you must come, if only to explain to me what is the harm of visiting the surface of the earth."

"No harm," she replied, controlling herself. "But no advantage. The surface of the earth is only dust and mud; no life remains on it, and you would need a respirator, or the cold of the outer air would kill you. One dies immediately in the outer air."

"I know; of course I shall take all precautions."

"And besides—"

"Well?"

She considered, and chose her words with care. Her son had a queer temper, and she wished to dissuade him from the expedition.

"It is contrary to the spirit of the age," she asserted.

"Do you mean by that, contrary to the Machine?"

"In a sense, but—"

His image in the blue plate faded.

"Kuno!"

He had isolated himself.

For a moment Vashti felt lonely.

Then she generated the light, and the sight of her room, flooded with radiance and studded with electric buttons, revived her. There were buttons and switches everywhere—buttons to call for food, for music, for clothing. There was the hot-bath button, by pressure of which a basin of (imitation) marble rose out of the floor, filled to the brim with a warm deodorized liquid. There was the cold-bath button. There was the button that produced literature. And there were of course the buttons by which she communicated with her friends. The room, though it contained nothing, was in touch with all that she cared for in the world.

Vashti's next move was to turn off the isolation switch, and all the accumulations of the last three minutes burst upon her. The room was filled with the noise of bells, and speaking tubes. What was the new food like? Could she recommend it? Had she had any ideas lately? Might one tell her one's own ideas? Would she make an engagement to visit the public nurseries at an early date?—say this day month.

To most of these questions she replied with irritation—a growing quality in that accelerated age. She said that the new food was horrible. That she could not visit the public nurseries through press of engagements. That she had no ideas of her own but had just been told of one—that four stars and three in the middle were like a man: she doubted there was much in it. Then she switched off her correspondents, for it was time to deliver her lecture on Australian music.

The clumsy system of public gatherings had been long since abandoned; neither Vashti nor her audience stirred from their rooms. Seated in her armchair she spoke, while they in their armchairs heard her, fairly well, and saw her, fairly well. She opened with a humorous account of music in the pre-Mongolian epoch, and went on to describe the great outburst of song that followed the Chinese conquest. Remote and primeval as were the methods of I-San-So and the Brisbane school, she yet felt (she said) that study of them might repay the musician of today: they had freshness; they had, above all, ideas.

Her lecture, which lasted ten minutes, was well received, and at its conclusion she and many of her audience listened to a lecture on the sea; there were ideas to be got from the sea; the speaker had donned a respirator and visited it lately. Then she fed, talked to many friends, had a bath, talked again, and summoned her bed.

The bed was not to her liking. It was too large, and she had a feeling for a small bed. Complaint was useless, for beds were of the same dimension all over the world, and to have had an alternative size would have involved vast alterations in the Machine. Vashti isolated herself—it was necessary, for neither day nor night existed under the ground—and reviewed all that had happened since she had summoned the bed last. Ideas? Scarcely any. Events—was Kuno's invitation an event?

By her side, on the little reading desk, was a survival from the ages of litter—one book. This was the Book of the Machine. In it were instructions against every possible contingency. If she was hot or cold or dyspeptic or at a loss for a word, she went to the book, and it told her which button to press. The Central Committee published it. In accordance with a growing habit, it was richly bound.

Sitting up in the bed, she took it reverently in her hands. She glanced round the glowing room as if someone might be watching her. Then, half ashamed, half joyful, she murmured "O Machine! O Machine!" and raised the volume to her lips. Thrice she kissed it, thrice inclined her head, thrice she felt the delirium of acquiescence. Her ritual performed, she turned to page 1367, which gave the times of the departure of the airships from the island in the Southern Hemisphere, under whose soil she lived, to the island in the Northern Hemisphere, whereunder lived her son.

She thought, "I have not the time."

She made the room dark and slept; she woke and made the room light; she ate and exchanged ideas with her friends, and listened to music and attended lectures; she made the room dark and slept. Above her, beneath her, and around her, the Machine hummed eternally; she did not notice the noise, for she had been born with it in her ears. The earth, carrying her, hummed as it sped through silence, turning her now to the invisible sun, now to the invisible stars. She awoke and made the room light.

"Kuno!"

"I will not talk to you," he answered, "until you come."

"Have you been on the surface of the earth since we spoke last?"

His image faded.

Again she consulted the book. She became very nervous and lay back in her chair palpitating. Think of her as without teeth or hair. Presently she directed the chair to the wall, and pressed an unfamiliar button. The wall swung apart slowly. Through the opening she saw a tunnel that curved slightly, so that its goal was not visible. Should she go to see her son, here was the beginning of the journey.

Of course, she knew all about the communication system. There was nothing mysterious in it. She would summon a car and it would fly with her down the tunnel until it reached the lift that communicated with the airship station: the system had been in use for many, many years, long before the universal establishment of the Machine. And of course she had studied the civilization that had immediately preceded her own—the civilization that had mistaken the functions of the system, and had used it for bringing people to things, instead of for bringing things to people. Those funny old days, when men went for change of air instead of changing the air in their rooms! And yet—she was frightened of the tunnel: she had not seen it since her last child was born. It curved—but not quite as she remembered; it was brilliant—but not quite as brilliant as a lecturer had suggested. Vashti was seized with the terrors of direct experience. She shrank back into the room, and the wall closed up again.

"Kuno," she said, "I cannot come to see you. I am not well."

Immediately an enormous apparatus fell onto her out of the ceiling, a thermometer was automatically inserted between her lips, a stethoscope was automatically laid upon her heart. She lay powerless. Cool pads soothed her forehead. Kuno had telegraphed to her doctor.

So the human passions still blundered up and down in the Machine. Vashti drank the medicine that the doctor projected into her mouth, and the machinery retired into the ceiling. The voice of Kuno was heard asking how she felt.

"Better." Then, with irritation: "But why do you not come to me instead?"

"Because I cannot leave this place."

"Why?"

"Because, any moment, something tremendous may happen."

"Have you been on the surface of the earth yet?"

"Not yet."

"Then what is it?"

"I will not tell you through the machine."

She resumed her life.

But she thought of Kuno as a baby, his birth, his removal to the public nurseries, her one visit to him there, his visits to her—visits which stopped when the Machine had assigned him a room on the other side of the earth. "Parents, duties of," said the book of the Machine, "cease at the moment of birth. P. 422327483." True, but there was something special about Kuno—indeed there had been something special about all her children—and, after all, she must brave the journey if he desired it. And "something tremendous might happen." What did that mean? The nonsense of a youthful man, no doubt, but she must go. Again she pressed the unfamiliar button, again the wall swung back, and she saw the tunnel that curved out of sight. Clasping the Book, she rose, tottered onto the platform, and summoned the car. Her room closed behind her: the journey to the Northern Hemisphere had begun.

Of course, it was perfectly easy. The car approached and in it she found armchairs exactly like her own. When she signaled, it stopped, and she tottered into the lift, One other passenger was in the lift, the first fellow creature she had seen face to face for months. Few traveled in these days, for, thanks to the advance of science, the earth was exactly alike all over. Rapid intercourse, from which the previous civilization had hoped so much, had ended by defeating itself. What was the good of going to Peking when it was just like Shrewsbury? Why return to Shrewsbury when it would be just like Peking? Men seldom moved their bodies; all unrest was concentrated in the soul.

The airship service was a relic from the former age. It was kept up because it was easier to keep it up than to stop it or to diminish it, but it now far exceeded the wants of the population. Vessel after vessel would rise from the vomitories of Rye or of Christchurch (I use the antique names), would sail into the crowded sky, and would draw up at the wharves of the south—empty. So nicely adjusted was the system, so independent of meteorology, that the sky, whether calm or cloudy, resembled a vast kaleidoscope whereon the same patterns periodically recurred. The ship on which Vashti sailed started now at sunset, now at dawn. But always, as it passed above Rheims, it would neighbor the ship that served between Helsingfors and the Brazils, and, every third time it surmounted the Alps, the fleet of Palermo would cross its track behind. Night and day, wind and storm, tide and earthquake impeded man no longer. He had harnessed Leviathan. All the old literature, with its praise of Nature and its fear of Nature, rang false as the prattle of a child.

Yet as Vashti saw the vast flank of the ship, stained with exposure to the outer air, her horror of direct experience returned. It was not quite like the airship in the cinematophote. For one thing it smelled—not strongly or unpleasantly, but it did smell, and with her eyes shut she should have known that a new thing was close to her. Then she had to walk to it from the lift, had to submit to glances from the other passengers. The man in front dropped his Book—no great matter, but it disquieted them all. In the rooms, if the Book was dropped, the floor raised it mechanically, but the gangway to the airship was not so prepared, and the sacred volume lay motionless. They stopped—the thing was unforeseen—and the man, instead of picking up his property, felt the muscles of his arm to see how they had failed him. Then someone actually said with direct utterance: "We shall be late"—and they trooped on board, Vashti treading on the pages as she did so.

Inside, her anxiety increased. The arrangements were old-fashioned and rough. There was even a female attendant, to whom she would have to announce her wants during the voyage. Of course, a revolving platform ran the length of the boat, but she was expected to walk from it to her cabin. Some cabins were better than others, and she did not get the best. She thought the attendant had been unfair, and spasms of rage shook her. The glass valves had closed; she could not go back. She saw, at the end of the vestibule, the lift in which she had ascended going quietly up and down, empty. Beneath those corridors of shining tiles were rooms, tier below tier, reaching far into the earth, and in each room there sat a human being, eating, or sleeping, or producing ideas. And buried deep in the hive was her own room. Vashti was afraid.

"O Machine! O Machine!" she murmured, and caressed her Book, and was comforted.

Then the sides of the vestibule seemed to melt together, as do the passages that we see in dreams; the lift vanished, the Book that had been dropped slid to the left and vanished, polished tiles rushed by like a stream of water, there was a slight jar, and the airship, issuing from its tunnel, soared above the waters of a tropical ocean.

It was night. For a moment she saw the coast of Sumatra edged by the phosphorescence of waves, and crowned by lighthouses, still sending forth their disregarded beams. These also vanished, and only the stars distracted her. They were not motionless, but swayed to and fro above her head, thronging out of one skylight into another, as if the universe and not the airship was careening. And, as often happens on clear nights, they seemed now to be in perspective, now on a plane; now piled tier beyond tier into the infinite heavens, now concealing infinity, a roof limiting for ever the visions of men. In either case they seemed intolerable. "Are we to travel in the dark?" called the passengers angrily, and the attendant, who had been careless, generated the light and pulled down the blinds of pliable metal. When the airships had been built, the desire to look direct at things still lingered in the world. Hence the extraordinary number of skylights and windows, and the proportionate discomfort to those who were civilized and refined. Even in Vashti's cabin one star peeped through a flaw in the blind, and after a few hours' uneasy slumber, she was disturbed by an unfamiliar glow, which was the dawn.

Quick as the ship had sped westward, the earth had rolled eastward quicker still, and had dragged back Vashti and her companions toward the sun. Science could prolong the night, but only for a little, and those high hopes of neutralizing the earth's diurnal revolution had passed, together with hopes that were possibly higher. To "keep pace with the sun," or even to outstrip it, had been the aim of the civilization preceding this. Racing airplanes had been built for the purpose, capable of enormous speed, and steered by the greatest intellects of the epoch. Round the globe went eastward quicker still, horrible accidents occurred, and the Committee of the Machine, at the time rising into prominence, declared the pursuit illegal, unmechanical, and punishable by Homelessness.

Of Homelessness more will be said later.

Doubtless the Committee was right. Yet the attempt to "defeat the sun" aroused the last common interest that our race experienced about the heavenly bodies, or indeed about anything. It was the last time that men were compacted by thinking of a power outside the world. The sun had conquered, yet it was the end of his spiritual dominion. Dawn, midday, twilight, the zodiacal path, touched neither men's lives nor their hearts, and science retreated into the ground, to concentrate herself upon problems that she was certain of solving.

So when Vashti found her cabin invaded by a rosy finger of light, she was annoyed and tried to adjust the blind. But the blind flew up altogether, and she saw through the skylight small pink clouds, swaying against a background of blue, and as the sun crept higher, its radiance entered direct, brimming down the wall, like a golden sea. It rose and fell with the airship's motion, just as waves rise and fall, but it advanced steadily, as the tide advances. Unless she was careful, it would strike her face. A spasm of horror shook her, and she rang for the attendant. The attendant too was horrified, but she could do nothing; it was not her place to mend the blind. She could only suggest that the lady should change her cabin, which she accordingly prepared to do.

People were almost exactly alike all over the world, but the attendant of the airship, perhaps owing to her exceptional duties, had grown a little out of the common. She had often to address passengers with direct speech, and this had given her a certain roughness and originality of manner. When Vashti swerved away from the sunbeams with a cry, she behaved barbarically—she put out her hand to steady her.

"How dare you!" exclaimed the passenger. "You forget yourself!"

The woman was confused, and apologized for not having let her fall. People never touched one another. The custom had become obsolete, owing to the Machine.

"Where are we now?" asked Vashti haughtily.

"We are over Asia," said the attendant, anxious to be polite.

"Asia?"

"You must excuse my common way of speaking. I have got into the habit of calling places over which I pass by their unmechanical names."

"Oh, I remember Asia. The Mongols came from it."

"Beneath us, in the open air, stood a city that was once called Simla."

"Have you ever heard of the Mongols and of the Brisbane school?"

"No."

"Brisbane also stood in the open air."

"Those mountains to the right—let me show you them." She pushed back a metal blind. The main chain of the Himalayas was revealed. "They were once called the Roof of the World, those mountains."

"What a foolish name!"

"You must remember that, before the dawn of civilization, they seemed to be an impenetrable wall that touched the stars. It was supposed that no one but the gods could exist above their summits. How we have advanced, thanks to the Machine!"

"How we have advanced, thanks to the Machine!" said Vashti.

"How we have advanced, thanks to the Machine!" echoed the passenger who had dropped his Book the night before and who was standing in the passage.

"And that white stuff in the cracks?—what is it?"

"I have forgotten its name."

"Cover the window, please. These mountains give me no ideas."

The northern aspect of the Himalayas was in deep shadow: on the Indian slope the sun had just prevailed. The forest had been destroyed during the literature epoch for the purpose of making newspaper pulp, but the snows were awakening to their morning glory, and clouds still hung on the breasts of Kinchinjunga. In the plain were seen the ruins of cities, with diminished rivers creeping by their walls, and by the sides of these were sometimes the signs of vomitories, marking the cities of today. Over the whole prospect airships rushed, crossing and intercrossing with incredible aplomb, and rising nonchalantly when they desired to escape the perturbations of the lower atmosphere and to traverse the Roof of the World.

"We have indeed advanced, thanks to the Machine," repeated the attendant, and hid the Himalayas behind a metal blind.

The day dragged wearily forward. The passengers sat each in his cabin, avoiding one another with an almost physical repulsion and longing to be once more under the surface of the earth. There were eight or ten of them, mostly young males, sent out from the public nurseries to inhabit the rooms of those who had died in various parts of the earth. The man who had dropped his Book was on the homeward journey. He had been sent to Sumatra for the purpose of propagating the race. Vashti alone was traveling by her private will.

At midday she took a second glance at the earth. The airship was crossing another range of mountains, but she could see little, owing to clouds. Masses of black rock hovered below her and merged indistinctly into gray. Their shapes were fantastic; one of them resembled a prostrate man.

"No ideas here," murmured Vashti, and hid the Caucasus behind a metal blind.

In the evening she looked again. They were crossing a golden sea, in which lay many small islands and one peninsula.

She repeated, "No ideas here," and hid Greece behind a metal blind.

PART II

THE MENDING APPARATUS

By a vestibule, by a lift, by a tubular railway, by a platform, by a sliding door—by reversing all the steps of her departure did Vashti arrive at her son's room, which exactly resembled her own. She might well declare that the visit was superfluous. The buttons, the knobs, the reading desk with the Book, the temperature, the atmosphere, the illumination—all were exactly the same. And if Kuno himself, flesh of her flesh, stood close beside her at last, what profit was there in that? She was too well bred to shake him by the hand.

Averting her eyes, she spoke as follows:

"Here I am. I have had the most terrible journey and greatly retarded the development of my soul. It is not worth it, Kuno; it is not worth it. My time is too precious. The sunlight almost touched me, and I have met with the rudest people. I can stop only a few minutes. Say what you want to say, and then I must return."

"I have been threatened with Homelessness," said Kuno.

She looked at him now.

"I have been threatened with Homelessness, and I could not tell you such a thing through the Machine."

Homelessness means death. The victim is exposed to the air, which kills him.

"I have been outside since I spoke to you last. The tremendous thing had happened, and they have discovered me."

"But why shouldn't you go outside?" she exclaimed. "It is perfectly legal, perfectly mechanical, to visit the surface of the earth. I have lately been to a lecture on the sea; there is no objections to that; one simply summons a respirator and gets an Egression permit. It is not the kind of thing that spiritually minded people do, and I begged you not to do it, but there is no legal objection to it."

"I did not get an Egression permit."

"Then how did you get out?"

"I found out a way of my own."

The phrase conveyed no meaning to her, and he had to repeat it.

"A way of your own?" she whispered. "But that would be wrong."

"Why?"

The question shocked her beyond measure.

"You are beginning to worship the Machine," he said coldly. "You think it irreligious of me to have found out a way of my own. It was just what the Committee thought, when they threatened me with Homelessness."

At this she grew angry. "I worship nothing!" she cried. "I am most advanced. I don't think you irreligious, for there is no such thing as religion left. All the fear and the superstition that existed once have been destroyed by the Machine. I only meant that to find out a way of your own was—Besides there is no new way out."

"So it is always supposed."

"Except through the vomitories, for which one must have an Egression permit, it is impossible to get out. The Book says so."

"Well, the Book's wrong, for I have been out on my feet."

For Kuno was possessed of a certain physical strength.

By these days it was a demerit to be muscular. Each infant was examined at birth, and all who promised undue strength were destroyed. Humanitarians may protest, but it would have been no true kindness to let an athlete live; he would never have been happy in that state of life to which the Machine had called him; he would have yearned for trees to climb, rivers to bathe in, meadows and hills against which he might measure his body. Man must be adapted to his surroundings, must he not? In the dawn of the world our weakly must be exposed on Mount Taygetus; in its twilight our strong will suffer euthanasia, that the Machine may progress, that the Machine may progress, that the Machine may progress eternally.

"You know that we have lost the sense of space. We say space is 'annihilated,' but we have annihilated not space but the sense thereof. We have lost a part of ourselves. I determined to recover it, and I began by walking up and down the platform of the railway outside my room. Up and down, until I was tired, and so did recapture the meaning of 'Near' and 'Far.' 'Near' is a place to which I can get quickly *on my feet*, not a place to which the train or the airship will take me quickly. 'Far' is a place to which I cannot get quickly on my feet; the vomitory is 'far,' though I could be there in thirty-eight seconds by summoning the train. Man is the measure. That was my first lesson. Man's feet are the measure for distance, his hands are the measure for ownership, his body is the measure for all that is lovable and desirable and strong. Then I went further: it was then that I called to you for the first time, and you would not come.

"This city, as you know, is built deep beneath the surface of the earth, with only the vomitories protruding. Having paced the platform outside my own room, I took the lift to the next platform and paced that also, and so with each in turn, until I came to the topmost, above which begins the earth. All the platforms were exactly alike, and all that I gained by visiting them was to develop my sense of space and my muscles. I think I should have been content with this—it is not a little thing—but as I walked and brooded, it occurred to me that our cities had been built in the days when men still breathed the outer air, and that there had been ventilation shafts for the workmen. I could think of nothing but these ventilation shafts. Had they been destroyed by all the foodtubes and medicine tubes and music tubes that the Machine has evolved lately? Or did traces of them remain? One thing was certain. If I came upon them anywhere, it would be in the railway tunnels of the topmost story. Everywhere else, all space was accounted for.

"I am telling my story quickly, but don't think that I was not a coward or that your answers never depressed me. It is not the proper thing, it is not mechanical, it is not decent to walk along a railway tunnel. I did not fear that I might tread upon a live rail and be killed. I feared something far more intangible—doing what was not contemplated by the Machine. Then I said to myself, 'Man is the measure,' and I went, and after many visits I found an opening.

"The tunnels, of course, were lighted. Everything is light, artificial light; darkness is the exception. So when I saw a black gap in the tiles, I knew that it was an exception, and rejoiced. I put in my arm—I could put in no more at first—and waved it round and round in ecstasy. I loosened another tile, and put in my head, and shouted into the darkness: 'I am coming, I shall do it yet,' and my voice reverberated down endless passages. I seemed to hear the spirits of those dead workmen who had returned each evening to the starlight and to their wives, and all the generations who had lived in the open air called back to me, 'You will do it yet, you are coming.' "

He paused, and, absurd as he was, his last words moved her. For Kuno had lately asked to be a father, and his request had been refused by the Committee. His was not a type that the Machine desired to hand on.

"Then a train passed. It brushed by me, but I thrust my head and arms into the hole. I had done enough for one day, so I crawled back to the platform, went down in the lift, and summoned my bed. Ah, what dreams! And again I called you, and again you refused."

She shook her head and said:

"Don't. Don't talk of these terrible things. You make me miserable. You are throwing civilization away."

"But I had got back the sense of space, and a man cannot rest then. I determined to get in at the hole and climb the shaft. And so I exercised my arms. Day after day I went through ridiculous movements, until my flesh ached, and I could hang by my hands and hold the pillow of my bed outstretched for many minutes. Then I summoned a respirator, and started.

"It was easy at first. The mortar had somehow rotted, and I soon pushed some more tiles in, and clambered after them into the darkness, and the spirits of the dead comforted me. I don't know what I mean by that. I just say what I felt. I felt, for the first time, that a protest had been lodged against corruption, and that even as the dead were comforting me, so I was comforting the unborn. I felt that humanity existed, and that it existed without clothes. How can I possibly explain this? It was naked, humanity seemed naked, and all these tubes and buttons and machineries neither came into the world with us, nor will they follow us out, nor do they matter supremely while we are here. Had I been strong, I would have torn off every garment I had, and gone out into the outer air unswaddled. But this is not for me, nor perhaps for my generation. I climbed with my respirator and my hygienic clothes and my dietetic tabloids! Better thus than not at all.

"There was a ladder, made of some primeval metal. The light from the railway fell upon its lowest rungs, and I saw that it led straight upward out of the rubble at the bottom of the shaft. Perhaps our ancestors ran up and down it a dozen times daily, in their building. As I climbed, the rough edges cut through my gloves so that my hands bled. The light helped me for a little, and then came darkness and, worse still, silence which pierced my ears like a sword. The Machine hums! Did you know that? Its hum penetrates our blood, and may even guide our thoughts. Who knows! I was getting beyond its power. Then I thought: 'This silence means that I am doing wrong.' But I heard voices in the silence, and again they strengthened me." He laughed. "I had need of them. The next moment I cracked my head against something."

She sighed.

"I had reached one of those pneumatic stoppers that defend us from the outer air. You may have noticed them on the airship. Pitch dark, my feet on the rungs of an invisible ladder, my hands cut; I cannot explain how I lived through this part, but the voices still comforted me, and I felt for fastenings. The stopper, I suppose, was about eight feet across. I passed my hand over it as far as I could reach. It was perfectly smooth. I felt it almost to the center. Not quite to the center, for my arm was too short. Then the voice said: 'Jump. It is worth it. There may be a handle in the center, and you may catch hold of it and so come to us your own way. And if there is no handle, so that you may fall and are dashed to pieces—it is still worth it: you will still come to us your own way.' So I jumped. There was a handle, and—"

He paused. Tears gathered in his mother's eyes. She knew that he was fated. If he did not die today he would die tomorrow. There was not room for such a person in the world. And with her pity disgust mingled. She was ashamed at having borne such a son, she who had always been so respectable and so full of ideas. Was he really the little boy to whom she had taught the use of his stops and buttons, and to whom she had given his first lessons in the Book? The very hair that disfigured his lip showed that he was reverting to some savage type. On atavism the Machine can have no mercy.

"There was a handle, and I did catch it. I hung tranced over the darkness and heard the hum of these workings as the last whisper in a dying dream. All the things I had cared about and all the people I had spoken to through tubes appeared infinitely little. Meanwhile the handle revolved. My weight had set something in motion and I spun slowly, and then—.

"I cannot describe it. I was lying with my face to the sunshine. Blood poured from my nose and ears and I heard a tremendous roaring. The stopper, with me clinging to it, had simply been blown out of the earth, and the air that we make down here was escaping through the vent into the air above. It burst up like a fountain. I crawled back to it—for the upper air hurts—and, as it were, I took great sips from the edge. My respirator had flown goodness knows where, my clothes were torn. I just lay with my lips close to the hole, and I sipped until the bleeding stopped. You can imagine nothing so curious. This hollow in the grass—I will speak of it in a minute—the sun shining into it, not brilliantly but through marbled clouds—the peace, the nonchalance, the sense of space, and, brushing my cheek, the roaring fountain of our artificial air! Soon I spied my respirator, bobbing up and down in the current high above my head, and higher still were many airships. But no one ever looks out of airships, and in any case they could not have picked me up. There I was, stranded. The sun shone a little way down the shaft, and revealed the topmost rung of the ladder, but it was hopeless trying to reach it. I should either have been tossed up again by the escape, or else have fallen in, and died. I could only lie on the grass, sipping and sipping, and from time to time glancing around me.

"I knew that I was in Wessex, for I had taken care to go to a lecture on the subject before starting. Wessex lies above the room in which we are talking now. It was once an important state. Its kings held all the southern coast from the Andredswald to Cornwall, while the Wansdyke protected them on the north, running over the high ground. The lecturer was concerned only with the rise of Wessex, so I do not know how long it remained an international power, nor would the knowledge have assisted me. To tell the truth, I could do nothing but laugh during this part. There was I, with a pneumatic stopper by my side and a respirator bobbing over my head, imprisoned, all three of us, in a grass-grown hollow that was edged with fern."

Then he grew grave again.

"Lucky for me that it was a hollow. For the air began to fall back into it and to fill it as water fills a bowl. I could crawl about. Presently I stood. I breathed a mixture, in which the air that hurts predominated whenever I tried to climb the sides. This was not so bad. I had not lost my tabloids and remained ridiculously cheerful, and as for the Machine, I forgot about it altogether. My one aim now was to get to the top, where the ferns were, and to view whatever objects lay beyond.

"I rushed the slope. The new air was still too bitter for me and I came rolling back, after a momentary vision of something gray. The sun grew very feeble, and I remembered that he was in Scorpio—I had been to a lecture on that too. If the sun is in Scorpio and you are in Wessex, it means that you must be as quick as you can or it will get too dark. (This is the first bit of useful information I have ever got from a lecture, and I expect it will be the last.) It made me try frantically to breathe the new air, and to advance as far as I dared out of my pond. The hollow filled so slowly. At times I thought that the fountain played with less vigor. My respirator seemed to dance nearer the earth; the roar was decreasing."

He broke off.

"I don't think this is interesting you. The rest will interest you even less. There are no ideas in it, and I wish that I had not troubled you to come. We are too different, Mother."

She told him to continue.

"It was evening before I climbed the bank. The sun had very nearly slipped out of the sky by this time, and I could not get a good view. You, who have just crossed the Roof of the World, will not want to hear an account of the little hills that I saw— low colorless hills. But to me they were living and the turf that covered them was skin, under which their muscles rippled, and I felt that those hills had called with incalculable force to men in the past, and that men had loved them. Now they sleep— perhaps for ever. They commune with humanity in dreams. Happy the man, happy the woman, who awakes the hills of Wessex. For though they sleep, they will never die."

His voice rose passionately.

"Cannot you see, cannot all you lecturers see, that it is we that are dying, and that down here the only thing that really lives is the Machine? We created the Machine, to do our will, but we cannot make it do our will now. It has robbed us of the sense of space and of the sense of touch; it has blurred every human relation and narrowed down love to a carnal act, it has paralyzed our bodies and our wills, and now it compels us to worship it. The Machine develops—but not on our lines. The Machine proceeds—but not to our goal. We exist only as the blood corpuscles that course through its arteries, and if it could work without us, it would let us die. Oh, I have no remedy—or, at least, only one—to tell men again and again that I have seen the hills of Wessex as Aelfrid saw them when he overthrew the Danes.

"So the sun set. I forgot to mention that a belt of mist lay between my hill and other hills, and that it was the color of pearl."

He broke off for the second time.

"Go on," said his mother wearily.

He shook his head.

"Go on. Nothing that you say can distress me now. I am hardened."

"I had meant to tell you the rest, but I cannot: I know that I cannot: good-bye."

Vashti stood irresolute. All her nerves were tingling with his blasphemies. But she was also inquisitive.

"This is unfair," she complained. "You have called me across the world to hear your story, and hear it I will. Tell me—as briefly as possible, for this is a disastrous waste of time—tell me how you returned to civilization."

"Oh—that!" he said, starting. "You would like to hear about civilization. Certainly. Had I got to where my respirator fell down?"

"No—but I understand everything now. You put on your respirator, and managed to walk along the surface of the earth to a vomitory, and there your conduct was reported to the Central Committee."

"By no means."

He passed his hand over his forehead, as if dispelling some strong impression. Then, resuming his narrative, he warmed to it again.

"My respirator fell about sunset. I had mentioned that the fountain seemed feebler, had I not?"

"Yes."

"About sunset, it let the respirator fall. As I said, I had entirely forgotten about the Machine, and I paid no great attention at the time, being occupied with other things. I had my pool of air, into which I could dip when the outer keenness became intolerable, and which would possibly remain for days, provided that no wind sprang up to disperse it. Not until it was too late did I realize what the stoppage of the escape implied. You see—the gap in the tunnel had been mended; the Mending Apparatus; the Mending Apparatus, was after me.

"One other warning I had, but I neglected it. The sky at night was clearer than it had been in the day, and the moon, which was about half the sky behind the sun, shone into the dell at moments quite brightly. I was in my usual place—on the boundary between the two atmospheres—when I thought I saw something dark move across the bottom of the dell, and vanish into the shaft. In my folly, I ran down. I bent over and listened, and I thought I heard a faint scraping noise in the depths.

"At this—but it was too late—I took alarm. I determined to put on my respirator and to walk right out of the dell. But my respirator had gone. I knew exactly where it had fallen—between the stopper and the aperture—and I could even feel the mark that it had made in the turf. It had gone, and I realized that something evil was at work, and I had better escape to the other air, and, if I must die, die running toward the cloud that had been the color of a pearl. I never started. Out of the shaft—it is too horrible. A worm, a long white worm, had crawled out of the shaft and was gliding over the moonlit grass.

"I screamed. I did everything that I should not have done; I stamped upon the creature instead of flying from it, and it at once curled round the ankle. Then we fought. The worm let me run all over the dell, but edged up my leg as I ran. 'Help!' I cried. (That part is too awful. It belongs to the part that you will never know.) 'Help!' I cried. (Why cannot we suffer in silence?) 'Help!' I cried. Then my feet were wound together. I fell, I was dragged away from the dear ferns and the living hills, and past the great metal stopper (I can tell you this part), and I thought it might save me again if I caught hold of the handle. It also was enwrapped, it also. Oh, the whole dell was full of the things. They were searching it in all directions; they were denuding it, and the white snouts of others peeped out of the hole, ready if needed. Everything that could be moved they brought—brushwood, bundles of fern, everything, and down we all went intertwined into hell. The last things that I saw, ere the stopper closed after us, were certain stars, and I felt that a man of my sort lived in the sky. For I did fight, I fought till the very end, and it was only my head hitting against the ladder that quieted me. I woke up in this room. The worms had vanished; I was surrounded by artificial air, artificial light, artificial peace, and my friends were calling to me down speaking-tubes to know whether I had come across any new ideas lately."

Here his story ended. Discussion of it was impossible, and Vashti turned to go.

"It will end in Homelessness," she said quietly.

"I wish it would," retorted Kuno.

"The Machine has been most merciful."

"I prefer the mercy of God."

"By that superstitious phrase, do you mean that you could live in the outer air?"

"Yes."

"Have you ever seen, round the vomitories, the bones of those who were extruded after the Great Rebellion?"

"Yes."

"They were left where they perished for our edification. A few crawled away, but they perished, too—who can doubt it? And so with the Homeless of our own day. The surface of the earth supports life no longer."

"Indeed."

"Ferns and a little grass may survive, but all higher forms have perished. Has any airship detected them?"

"No."

"Has any lecturer dealt with them?"

"No."

"Then why this obstinacy?"

"Because I have seen them," he exploded.

"Seen *what*?"

"Because I have seen her in the twilight—because she came to my help when I called—because she, too, was entangled by the worms, and, luckier than I, was killed by one of them piercing her throat."

He was mad. Vashti departed, nor, in the troubles that followed, did she ever see his face again.

PART III

THE HOMELESS

During the years that followed Kuno's escapade, two important developments took place in the Machine. On the surface they were revolutionary, but in either case men's minds had been prepared beforehand, and they did but express tendencies that were latent already.

The first of these was the abolition of respirators.

Advanced thinkers, like Vashti, had always held it foolish to visit the surface of the earth. Airships might be necessary, but what was the good of going out for mere curiosity and crawling along for a mile or two in a terrestrial motor? The habit was vulgar and perhaps faintly improper: it was unproductive of ideas, and had no connection with the habits that really mattered. So respirators were abolished, and with them, of course, the terrestrial motors, and except for a few lecturers, who complained that they were debarred access to their subject matter, the development was accepted quietly. Those who still wanted to know what the earth was like had after all only to listen to some gramophone or to look into some cinematophote. And even the lecturers acquiesced when they found that a lecture on the sea was none the less stimulating when compiled out of other lectures that had already been delivered on the same subject. "Beware of first-hand ideas!" exclaimed one of the most advanced of them. "Firsthand ideas do not really exist. They are but the physical impressions produced by love and fear, and on this gross foundation who could erect a philosophy? Let your ideas be secondhand, and if possible tenthhand, for then they will be far removed from that disturbing element—direct observation. Do not learn anything about this subject of mine—the French Revolution. Learn instead what I think that Enich-armon thought Urizen thought Gutch thought Ho-Yung thought Chi-Bo-Sing thought Lafcadio Hearn thought Carlyle thought Mirabeau said about the French Revolution. Through the medium of these ten great minds the blood that was shed at Paris and the windows that were broken at Versailles will be clarified to an idea which you may employ most profitably in your daily lives. But be sure that the intermediates are many and varied, for in history one authority exists to counteract another. Urizen must counteract the skepticism of Ho-Young and Enicharmon, I must myself counteract the impetuosity of Gutch. You who listen to me are in a better position to judge about the French Revolution than I am. Your descendants will be even in a better position than you, for they will learn what you think. I think, and yet another intermediate will be added to the chain. And in time"—his voice rose—"there will come a generation that has got beyond facts, beyond impressions, a generation absolutely colorless, a generation

seraphically free
From taint of personality,

which will see the French Revolution not as it happened, nor as they would like it to have happened, but as it would have happened had it taken place in the days of the Machine."

Tremendous applause greeted this lecture, which did but voice a feeling already latent in the minds of men—a feeling that terrestrial facts must be ignored, and that the abolition of respirators was a positive gain. It was even suggested that airships should be abolished too. This was not done, because airships had somehow worked themselves into the Machine's system. But year by year they were used less, and mentioned less by thoughtful men.

The second great development was the reestablishment of religion.

This, too, had been voiced in the celebrated lecture. No one could mistake the reverent tone in which the peroration had concluded, and it awakened a responsive echo in the heart of each. Those who had long worshipped silently now began to talk. They described the strange feeling of peace that came over them when they handled the Book of the Machine, the pleasure that it was to repeat certain numerals out of it, however little meaning those numerals conveyed to the outward ear, the ecstasy of touching a button however unimportant, or of ringing an electric bell however superfluously.

"The Machine," they exclaimed, "feeds us and clothes us and houses us; through it we speak to one another, through it we see one another, in it we have our being. The Machine is the friend of ideas and the enemy of superstition: the Machine is omnipotent, eternal; blessed is the Machine." And before long this allocution was printed on the first page of the Book, and in subsequent editions the ritual swelled into a complicated system of praise and prayer. The word "religion" was sedulously avoided, and in theory the Machine was still the creation and the implement of man. But in practice all, save a few retrogrades, worshiped it as divine. Nor was it worshiped in unity. One believer would be chiefly impressed by the blue optic plates, through which he saw other believers; another by the Mending Apparatus, which sinful Kuno had compared to worms; another by the lifts, another by the Book. And each would pray to this or to that, and ask it to intercede for him with the Machine as a whole. Persecution—that also was present. It did not break out, for reasons that will be set forward shortly. But it was latent, and all who did not accept the minimum known as "undenominational Mechanism" lived in danger of Homelessness, which means death, as we know.

To attribute these two great developments to the Central Committee is to take a very narrow view of civilization. The Central Committee announced the developments, it is true, but they were no more the cause of them than were the kings of the imperialistic period the cause of war. Rather did they yield to some invincible pressure, which came no one knew whither, and which, when gratified, was succeeded by some new pressure equally invincible. To such a state of affairs it is convenient to give the name of progress. No one confessed the Machine was out of hand. Year by year it was served with increased efficiency and decreased intelligence. The better a man knew his own duties upon it, the less he understood the duties of his neighbor, and in all the world there was not one who understood the monster as a whole. Those master brains had perished. They had left full directions, it is true, and their successors had each of them mastered a portion of those directions. But Humanity, in its desire for comfort, had overreached itself. It had exploited the riches of nature too far. Quietly and complacently, it was sinking into decadence, and progress had come to mean the progress of the Machine.

As for Vashti, her life went peacefully forward until the final disaster. She made her room dark and slept; she awoke and made the room light. She lectured and attended lectures. She exchanged ideas with her innumerable friends and believed she was growing more spiritual. At times a friend was granted Euthanasia, and left his or her room for the homelessness that is beyond all human conception. Vashti did not much mind. After an unsuccessful lecture, she would sometimes ask for Euthanasia herself. But the death rate was not permitted to exceed the birth rate, and the Machine had hitherto refused it to her.

The troubles began quietly, long before she was conscious of them.

One day she was astonished at receiving a message from her son. They never communicated, having nothing in common, and she had only heard indirectly that he was still alive, and had been transferred from the Northern Hemisphere, where he had behaved so mischievously, to the Southern—indeed, to a room not far from her own.

"Does he want me to visit him?" she thought. "Never again, never. And I have not the time."

No, it was madness of another kind.

He refused to visualize his face upon the blue plate, and speaking out of the darkness with solemnity said:

"The Machine stops."

"What do you say?"

"The Machine is stopping, I know it; I know the sign."

She burst into a peal of laughter. He heard her and was angry, and they spoke no more.

"Can you imagine anything more absurd?" she cried to a friend. "A man who was my son believes that the Machine is stopping. It would be impious if it was not mad."

"The Machine is stopping?" her friend replied. "What does that mean? The phrase conveys nothing to me."

"Nor to me."

"He does not refer, I suppose, to the trouble there has been lately with the music?"

"Oh, no, of course not. Let us talk about music."

"Have you complained to the authorities?"

"Yes, and they say it wants mending, and referred me to the Committee of the Mending Apparatus. I complained of those curious gasping sighs that disfigure the symphonies of the Brisbane school. They sound like someone in pain. The Committee of the Mending Apparatus say that it shall be remedied shortly."

Obscurely worried, she resumed her life. For one thing, the defect in the music irritated her. For another thing, she could not forget Kuno's speech. If he had known that the music was out of repair—he could not know it, for he detested music—if he had known that it was wrong, "the Machine stops" was exactly the venomous sort of remark he would have made. Of course, he had made it at a venture, but the coincidence annoyed her, and she spoke with some petulance to the Committee of the Mending Apparatus.

They replied, as before, that the defect would be set right shortly.

"Shortly! At once!" she retorted. "Why should I be worried by imperfect music? Things are always put right at once. If you do not mend it at once, I shall complain to the Central Committee."

"No personal complaints are received by the Central Committee," the Committee of the Mending Apparatus replied.

"Through whom am I to make my complaint, then?"

"Through us."

"I complain then."

"Your complaint shall be forwarded in its turn."

"Have others complained?"

This question was unmechanical, and the Committee of the Mending Apparatus refused to answer it.

"It is too bad!" she exclaimed to another of her friends. "There never was such an unfortunate woman as myself. I can never be sure of my music now. It gets worse and worse each time I summon it."

"I too have my troubles," the friend replied. "Sometimes my ideas are interrupted by a slight jarring noise."

"What is it?"

"I do not know whether it is inside my head or inside the wall."

"Complain in either case."

"I have complained, and my complaint will be forwarded in its turn to the Central Committee."

Time passed, and they resented the defects no longer. The defects had not been remedied, but the human tissues in that latter day had become so subservient that they readily adapted themselves to every caprice of the Machine. The sigh at the crisis of the Brisbane symphony no longer irritated Vashti; she accepted it as part of the